·4· m

THE INSTITUTES OF GAIUS

AND

RULES OF ULPIAN

PRINTED BY THE ABERDEEN UNIVERSITY PRESS LIMITED

FOR

T. & T. CLARK, LAW PUBLISHERS, EDINBURGH

GLASGOW . . . . . J. SMITH AND SON
LONDON . . . . . STEVENS AND SONS
   ,, ... STEVENS AND HAYNES

THE

INSTITUTES OF GAIUS

AND

RULES OF ULPIAN

THE FORMER FROM STUDEMUND'S APOGRAPH
OF THE VERONA CODEX

WITH

TRANSLATION AND NOTES, CRITICAL AND EXPLANATORY
AND COPIOUS ALPHABETICAL DIGEST

BY

JAMES MUIRHEAD
LATE PROFESSOR OF THE CIVIL LAW IN THE UNIVERSITY OF EDINBURGH

EDINBURGH
T. & T. CLARK, Law Publishers
1904

115585

(Reprint of the 1880 Edition)

PREFACE.

—o—

SOME apology may be thought necessary for a new edition of the Institutional Commentaries of Gaius, with Translation and Notes, in presence of the two excellent ones we already possess from the pens of Mr. Poste and Messrs. Abdy and Walker. It is that neither of these incorporates the results of Studemund's revision of the Verona Codex.

I began this book with no other intention than that of correcting from his Apograph my own copy of the text previously in use. I soon found that the margins were insufficient to contain the amendments his fac-simile revealed, and that every here and there an interleaved note was required. Before long I was so impressed with the value of the corrections and additions that it became a matter of regret to me that they were not accessible to students. So I set myself, in the hours I could spare from other duties, to prepare an edition for college use; and, to make it more serviceable, I eventually resolved to add to it a translation and notes.

Had the recent editions of Krueger, Huschke, and Polenaar, which all embody Studemund's amendments, been published earlier, my task probably would never have been undertaken; they are the work of much more competent hands than mine, directed by profound knowledge of their subject, and by great critical and palæographical experience. But that of Krueger, edited in conjunction with Studemund himself, did not appear until the end of 1877; Huschke's appeared last year; and the last part of Polenaar's only in the beginning of the present one. Their successive publication has contributed to the delay in the appearance of the present volume; for they occasioned three revisions of my text after its completion, that I might have the opportunity of introducing any readings of theirs that seemed to me preferable to my own. It was with agreeable surprise I found how little those I had adopted varied from those of Krueger and Huschke; frequently when I differed from them I accepted their interpretations

v

without hesitation; sometimes, notwithstanding my unbounded respect for the authority of two such masters, I have unfortunately felt constrained to adhere to my own humble opinion, and mention its divergence in the footnotes.

To affirm that the Institutes of Gaius are worthy of being submitted to the student in as complete and perfect a form as it is possible to give them, is happily at the present day superfluous; they are everywhere regarded and studied as the necessary complement of those of Justinian. In the one we have the outlines of the nearly completed fabric of Roman jurisprudence, when its law and equity had almost ceased to be distinguishable; in the other we have before us the separate fabrics of the *jus civile* and the *jus honorarium*, and can see the portals of the latter opening to those who have been repulsed from the former. In other words, we can trace step by step in the pages of Gaius the process whereby Rome's natural law was developed alongside her civil law, and the way prepared for that matured jurisprudence which the compilations of Justinian have preserved.

In the short Introduction that follows will be found all that it seems essential for the student to know of Gaius and his Institutes, of the Verona Codex and Studemund's Apograph. I have particularly to request his attention to the explanations he will find there of the peculiarities of typography it has been considered expedient to employ in the text and translation.

To the Institutes of Gaius I have appended what are commonly known as Ulpian's Fragments,—a portion, and unfortunately all we possess, of an abridgment by an unknown hand, made probably in the early part of the fourth century, of his Book of Rules. In regard to them and their author I have also said a few words in the Introduction.

To both I have added a copious Alphabetical Digest. I well remember the difficulties I experienced in my student-days from the want of such a *conspectus;* and I cherish the hope that it may prove of service to some who are only commencing their study of the law of Rome. To others also it may possibly be found useful, who have no intention of devoting themselves to jurisprudence, yet are occasionally puzzled by allusions they find to its rules and institutions in the pages of the classical writers.

Some *corrigenda* are noted on p. 435.

EDINBURGH, *November*, 1879.

INTRODUCTION.

—o—

I.—GAIUS.

1. *Gaius' Period and Place in Jurisprudence.*—Of the history of Gaius we unfortunately know little; for though he was *Gaius Noster*, as Justinian calls him, with the Byzantines of the fifth and sixth centuries,—'the Gaius whom we all know so well,' —he is unmentioned by any of his contemporaries or successors of the classical period. That before the death of Hadrian he was old enough to take note of passing events we gather from an observation of his own in a passage from his pen preserved in the Digest; and internal evidence testifies that his works were written in the reigns of Antoninus Pius and Verus and Marcus Aurelius. Whether he was a Roman or a provincial jurist is a matter of controversy. The latter view is espoused by Mommsen, who has assigned his reasons for entertaining it in an elaborate paper in the *Jahrbuecher des gemeinen deutschen Rechts*, vol. iii, p. 1; but Huschke, whose opinion on any question of Ante-Justinianian law or its history must always be received with the utmost respect, seems inclined to arrive at a different result. Whether or not he possessed the *jus respondendi*, which he himself describes in § 7 of the First Book of his Institutes, is also disputed: some, relying on the fact that Justinian's instructions to his Digest Commissioners were to make use only of those authors who had the imperial licence, and that Gaius is one whom they utilised to a large extent, maintain the affirmative; while others think that in his case, and because of his repute in the schools, those instructions were disregarded.

It is quite certain that we have no record of any of his Responses; and there is good reason to think that he was not so much a practitioner as a teacher and a literary jurist. He himself refers in his Institutes to three or four earlier works: one on the writings of Q. Mucius Scaevola, one on the Edict, one on *Bonorum Possessio*, and another on the Rights of Patrons. On the Edict, both urban and provincial, he wrote voluminously; and amongst other treatises of his from which passages are preserved in the Digest the more important are his Commentary on the Twelve Tables and his *Libri Rerum Cottidianarum*,—his *Aurea* or Golden Sayings, as they came to be called at a later period. To the last Justinian specially refers in his preface to his Institutes. From the remains of them which we possess it is impossible to judge of their purpose; they are written more carefully and elaborately than one would expect to be the case with daily jottings, as some regard them, and rather give the impression of being materials for a more ambitious work, which its author did not live to complete.

2. *His Institutes.*—The *Institutionum Commentarii Quattuor*, reproduced in the following pages, seem to have been written partly in the reign of Antoninus Pius, partly in that of Marcus Aurelius. It has been suggested that they are not directly the work of Gaius, but rather notes of his lectures made by an auditor. There are no doubt turns of expression in them that afford grounds for such a surmise; but taking them as a whole they do not convey the idea of the record of a spoken discourse; they are much more of the nature of a text, requiring exposition and illustration by a speaker. Had they not been a genuine work of Gaius, they could hardly have enjoyed the reputation which caused them to be used as the elementary text-book from the time of the establishment of the Constantinople law-school in 425 down to that of Justinian's reforms in 533, to be drawn upon so largely as authoritative statements of Roman law in the *Collatio Legum Romanarum et Mosaicarum* in the beginning of the fifth century, and to be epitomised by Alaric's commissioners for his *Lex Romana Visigothorum* in 506.

That Justinian, in the Institutes that bear his name, had borrowed largely from the earlier ones of Gaius, was a fact well known; but it was not until the Verona MS. was deciphered that the extent of his obligations to them was disclosed. It was impossible to discover it from the West Gothic Epitome, in two books, of the matter contained in the first three of the genuine Commentaries; and comparison of the Justinianian Institutes with passages in the Digest that bear to be excerpted from those of Gaius showed no more than this,—that in several places the later work was a literal transcript of the earlier. But now we know, that although other books dating from the Antoninian period were brought into requisition by the authors of the Justinianian compilation, and that a good deal of new matter was clumsily introduced to adapt it to the existing state of the law, not only was Gaius taken as their model in plan and construction, but his text was really made the basis of theirs.

3. *The Verona Codex.*—In 1732, and again in 1742, Scipio Maffei, in describing some of the manuscripts in the Chapter Library at Verona, referred to and printed a stray leaf, which he supposed had been cut either out of a copy of the Pandects or out of some compendium of Justinian's Institutes, and of which the greater part dealt with the subject of interdicts. Somehow this escaped the notice of the jurists until 1816, when Haubold lighted upon it, and at once came to the conclusion it was a leaf from the long-lost Gaius. Almost at the same moment, by a curious coincidence, Niebuhr was passing through Verona, visited the library, came upon the same leaf, and arrived at the same conclusion. But simultaneously he made a much more important discovery; for, underneath what had previously passed for no more than a copy of the Epistles of St. Jerome, he detected the very copy of the Institutes of Gaius from which the leaf in question had been extracted.

Niebuhr's discovery was promptly communicated to Savigny; and in the following year, at his suggestion, Goeschen and Bekker were deputed by the Prussian Academy of Sciences to proceed to Verona to make a transcript. Bekker having soon afterwards been prevented by other duties from going on with the undertaking, Bethmann-Hollweg became Goeschen's associate. Their task was no easy one; for not only had the MS. of St. Jerome to be removed, but on some leaves an intermediate writing; and the difficulty of reviving the original characters was increased by the fact that in many places they had been erased with pumice-stone, and the parchment thus rendered susceptible of serious injury from the use of even the mildest chemicals. They succeeded so far, however, as to be able to give to the world in the end of 1820 the first edition of the complete *Institutiones* or Institutional Commentaries of Gaius.

Two years later Blume was in Verona, and seized the opportunity to revise those pages of the MS. that had yielded Goeschen his least fruitful results. It appears from a communication of Blume's to one of the German law journals in 1864, that, through loss in transit by post of a communication to Hugo, the world never got the full benefit of his readings. This is the more to be deplored, as it is to his somewhat reckless use of chemicals, far more powerful than those Goeschen had ventured to employ, that some pages of the MS. have been reduced to a condition which leaves even the most sanguine little ground for expectation that they will ever be deciphered.

4. *Studemund's Apograph.*—Although Boecking, in 1866, published what he called an Apograph of the Verona Codex, yet it was in reality produced not from the original, but from the copies made by Goeschen, Hollweg, and Blume, preserved in the Royal Library at Berlin. Leaving out of account as of little value what was done by Tedeschi in 1856, the only conscientious revision of the MS. that has been accomplished since Goeschen and Hollweg's is that of Studemund, commissioned, as they had been, by the Prussian Academy. He began his labours in 1866, and in 1867 and 1868 had the benefit occasionally of the advice and assistance of Mommsen and Krueger. Interruptions from various causes, and the deplorable condition of some of the leaves, made the revision a work of years; but when completed the results were considered so valuable, that the same learned body at whose instigation the task had been commenced resolved that jurisprudence should have the benefit of them in a reproduction approaching as nearly as possible to a fac-simile. Types truthfully representing the letters of the MS., with its abbreviations and other marks, were cast for the purpose from a photographic reproduction of one of the sheets; and the Apographum was eventually published in a magnificent quarto volume in the beginning of 1874.

The MS., it must be admitted, displays many imperfections. It seems to have been written, as the best judges are at one in thinking, in the earlier half of the sixth century, and probably, as the absence of the Greek quotations suggests, in Italy. Of the 258 pages, each of 24 lines, which it originally embraced, six, *i.e.* three leaves, have disappeared, viz. those between pages 80 and 81, 126 and 127, and 194 and 195, as now numbered. Of those that remain there are but two—those on the leaf published by Maffei— that are not palimpsest; and of those of them that have been three times written on very little is decipherable. Throughout they abound in contractions and conventional abbreviations; of these one cannot well complain, for they are in accordance with the practice of the period. But the execution is slovenly,—the work apparently of a scribe more than usually careless, who seems to have frequently fallen half asleep over his task, here omitting not words merely but lines or even sentences, there repeating them not once only but sometimes twice. He has often incorporated in his text what in that he was reproducing were merely marginal or inter-linear glosses, due not to Gaius but an annotator; and his own transcript has here and there been subjected to correction, or what was intended as such, by a later hand.

Studemund has most properly refrained from any attempt to remedy those defects, and as far as possible reproduced the text of the MS. exactly as it stands. But he carefully distinguishes those parts of it whose reading is so clear as to be past question, and those which he believes he has accurately deciphered but in which he may be mistaken; the former he reproduces in dark characters, the latter in faint ones. Where letters can be counted, yet not deciphered, they are indicated by asterisks; where no more can be said than that writing had once existed, a line —— or lines are introduced to represent the illegible text; while here and there, following the MS., a space of a line or two is left entirely blank, indicating the transition from one subject to another. There are no numerals to indicate paragraphs; these were the device of Goeschen, and are occasionally found to be inconvenient as our knowledge of the text is increased.

5. *The Present Edition.*—The method of treatment that was alone legitimate in the reproduction of the Codex would be very inappropriate in an edition designed for the use of students and intended to represent the text of Gaius as completely as can be done with confidence. The blanks in the MS. must be filled wher-ever that can be done from other reliable sources, such as the

Collatio and the Digest and Institutes of Justinian; contractions and conventional signs must be interpreted and rendered in the words they seem to have been intended to represent; obvious clerical errors must be corrected; and manifest glosses, though they ought rarely to be deleted, should yet be carefully indicated. The editors and critics of the half century before 1874, operating on material less perfect than that which, thanks to Studemund, we now possess, have made this in many parts of the text comparatively easy; and not without considerable diffidence and hesitation can one venture anywhere to call in question the conclusions of such masters as Goeschen and Boecking, Huschke and Krueger, unless there be something revealed by the Apograph that throws a doubt on their accuracy. There are some passages, however, in which I have ventured to differ from them, alike in interpreting contractions, correcting clerical errors, and noting explanatory glosses. Illustrations of what seem to me legitimate amendments in each of those varieties of editorial duty will be found in II, § 112, II, § 118, and IV, § 16 respectively; and others will hardly fail to catch the eye of the careful reader.

6. *Typographical Explanations.*—Impressed with the importance of keeping the text as pure as possible, and of guarding against any suggestion of the absolute certainty of a reading which there is any room to question, I have had recourse to varieties of type, and to braces [ ] and marks of parenthesis ( ); and to the following explanations of them I ask the reader's particular attention:—

(1) As much of the text as, according to the testimony of the Apograph, may be regarded as absolutely certain, is printed in ordinary roman type.

(2) Trifling errors, omissions, and surplusages in the MS., if obviously clerical, are corrected, supplied, and deleted as of course, and without indication of them by peculiarity of type or otherwise.

(3) What appear to be glosses, and not part of the original, are put within braces [ ], but without peculiarity of type.

(4) What to Studemund is the apparent reading, but not absolutely certain, is printed in *italics;* but if verified from other sources it is in roman type.

(5) What is illegible in the MS., but either obvious from the context or supplied from other reliable sources, is in *italics*, within marks of parenthesis ( ).

(6) What there is no trace of in the MS., but is required to complete the sense, and is either supplied from other reliable sources or manifestly justified by the context, is in *italics*, within braces [ ].

(7) Passages that are illegible in the MS., and pages that have disappeared, if incapable of being supplied, without drawing purely on conjecture, are indicated by dashes, thus — — —; where there is material for it, the reconstructions that have been proposed are referred to in the footnotes.

7. *The Translation and Notes.*—In the translation I have aimed at accuracy rather than grace. I have abstained, as far as practicable, from the use of modern technical words; where they are unavoidable, and those of Scots and English law are different, I have naturally given the preference to the former; they have the advantage in most cases of coming nearer the Roman ones. The following are explanations of the peculiarities of type that occur in it:—

(1) Words that are interpolated to elucidate the meaning are put within braces, thus [ ], but printed in roman type.

(2) Passages that are illegible, or only partially legible in the text, but as to whose meaning there can be no reasonable doubt, are printed simply in *italics*.

(3) What is supplied conjecturally as representing the probable general import of an illegible or imperfect passage is put in *italics* within braces [ ].

In the notes there is reference throughout to the corresponding passages, if any, in the Institutes of Justinian; and the rubrics of his titles are printed in capital letters in their proper places. The words 'tit. I. afd.,' which are of constant recurrence, mean the last preceding title of the Institutes whose rubric is so printed. In dates of enactments, etc., where a double number is given, the first refers to the year of Rome, the second to that before or after Christ, as the case may be. The authorities referred to by abbreviations are tabulated immediately after the Introduction.

II.—ULPIAN.

8. His Place in Jurisprudence.
9. His 'Book of Rules.'
10. The Present Edition.

8. *His Place in Jurisprudence.*—Domitius Ulpianus was a Phœnician, born probably about the year 170. While officiating

as an assessor to one of the praetors in Rome, he attracted the notice of Papinian, then praetorian prefect under Septimius Severus, and was by him promoted to his council. He is not said to have held office or taken any active part in public life under Caracalla ; his greater works were written in the reign of that emperor, from which we may infer that he was holding aloof from politics, and devoting himself to jurisprudential literature. Although one of the historians speaks of him as praetorian prefect under Heliogabalus, this is hardly credible ; for it was his efforts, when acting as the adviser of Alexander, to undo the mischievous policy of that prince, that brought upon him the enmity of the praetorian guard and induced his assassination.

The relations of Ulpian with Alexander Severus, and latterly with his mother Mammaea, were of the most friendly and confidential character. It has been frequently charged to his memory that he encouraged the persecution of the Christians ; but the accusation rests on the most slender basis, and is contradicted by the whole life and conduct of the young prince whose guardian he was, and whose character he had a large part in forming. The general testimony of history affirms not merely his wisdom but his humanity ; and supports the verdict of Lampridius that, if the reign of Alexander was a beneficent one, it was chiefly because he was guided by the advice of Ulpian,—*quia Ulpiani consiliis praecipue rempublicam rexit.*

The greatest of Ulpian's literary works are his commentary on the *jus civile*, under the title of *Ad Sabinum libri LI*, and his commentary on the edict under the title of *Ad Edictum libri LXXXIII*. In addition to these there is a commentary on the Julian and Papia-Poppaean law in twenty books, one on the office of the proconsul in ten, six books on testamentary trusts, a variety of monographs, some books of Responses, Opinions, Disputations, etc., and an institutional treatise in two books,—*Institutionum libri II*. But, with exception of a very few fragments elsewhere, these are known to us only through the extracts which Justinian has preserved in the Digest, and which are so numerous that they constitute about one-third of the whole collection.

9. *His ' Book of Rules.'*—Ulpian was the author of two sets of Rules, one in seven books, the other in a single book,—*Liber singularis Regularum,* of which we have a few extracts in the

Collatio and the Digest. An abridgment of this *Liber singularis* seems to have been made by an unknown hand soon after the year 320; the design of the epitomist, apparently, having been to exclude what had become obsolete or was simply of historical interest, and to retain only so much as gave expression to still current law.

Of this epitome a manuscript of the tenth century came into the possession of Jean Du Tillet, who published it in 1549, under the name of '*Tituli ex corpore Ulpiani*'; it is now in the Vatican, and is the only one known to exist. But it is incomplete. Ulpian, as we know from the sources already referred to, dealt with both obligations and actions; and, so far as can be judged, followed much the same lines as Gaius. But the manuscript of the epitome finishes abruptly with the law of succession, and is besides defective in its opening passages. It is nevertheless a precious monument of the classical jurisprudence. It is the remains, not of an institutional book, but of a handbook for the practitioner; a *vade mecum*, as modern law-writers would call it, of which every line almost embodies a doctrine. *Ulpiani Regulae*, says Mommsen most truly, *ea brevitate perspicuitate, proprietate conscriptae sunt, quam adhuc secuti sumus, omnes, assecutus est nemo.*

10. *The Present Edition.*—A book of which there exists but one Codex, and that has passed during three centuries through such hands as those of Cujas, Le Caron (Charondas), Schulting, Meerman, Cannegieter, Hugo, Boecking, Mommsen, Vahlen, Huschke, and Krueger, can need but little editing. My task therefore has been comparatively easy,—a holding of the balance between divergent readings in those places in which the manuscript is defective, indistinct, or manifestly corrupt; it is only very rarely that I have thought it necessary to suggest a reading of my own. I have abstained from following the attempts of some editors to indicate the places where passages have been omitted by the abridger; for the book is not Ulpian's, but only an epitome of Ulpian's; and it is enough to rectify the clerical errors and omissions of the transcriber of the manuscript, without vainly trying to reproduce the original *Liber Regularum* as it came from the pen of its author.

As regards the typography of the text, words in *italics* represent those that in the Codex are uncertain or corrupt, and words in *italics* within braces [ ] represent those omitted *per incuriam* in the Codex, and supplied by the editors. In the translation words in *italics* within braces [ ] represent the probable general import of defective passages in the text, which in most cases it has not been attempted to reconstruct; words in roman type within braces [ ] have been interpolated for the sake of greater lucidity.

TABLE OF AUTHORITIES.

—o—

(The following Authorities are referred to in the Notes by the abbreviations prefixed to them. Those used to indicate the works of the ordinary classical writers are too familiar to require mention.)

Apogr. = *Gaii Institutionum . . . Codicis Veronensis Apographum . . . edidit Guilelmus Studemund, Lipsiae*, 1874.

Archiv. Giurid. = *Archivio Giuridico*, Pisa, Bologna, 1868-79; 23d volume now current.

Ascon. = *Asconii Pediani in Ciceronis Orationes Commentarii.* They were written about A.D. 60, and are to be found in various editions of Cicero.

Bas. = *Basilicorum Libri LX.* The latest and best edition is that of W. E. Heimbach, 6 vols., Leipzig, 1833-70.

Bekker, Akt. = *Die Aktionen des roemischen Privatrechts*, by Ernst Immanuel Bekker, Prof. in Greifswald, 2 vols., Berlin, 1871, 1873.

Bethmann-Hollweg, R. CP. = *Der roemische Civilprosess*, by M. A. von Bethmann-Hollweg (died 1878), 3 vols., Bonn, 1864-66, forming the first part of his *Civilprosess des gemeinen Rechts in geschichtlicher Entwicklung.*

Bk. (in notes to Gaius) = Boecking's (Eduard) 5th edition of Gaius, Leipzig, 1866. Boecking died 1870.

Bk. (in notes to Ulp.) = Boecking's 4th edition of Ulpian's Fragments, Leipzig, 1855.

Bl. = Blume's Collation of the Verona ms., utilised by Goeschen in his second edition of Gaius, and by Lachmann in his edition of 1842.

Boeth. = *Boethii Comment. in Ciceronis Topica.* They are in various editions of Cicero. Boethius died A.D. 524.

Bruns, Fontes = *Fontes Juris Romani Antiqui*, by Carl Geo. Bruns, Prof. in Berlin; 3d ed., Tuebingen, 1876.

C. = Justinian's *Codex repetitae praelectionis*, in all editions of the *Corpus Juris*, and re-edited from the best mss. by Krueger, Leipzig, 1873-77.

C. Greg. = The Gregorian Code in the *Codicis Gregoriani et Codicis Hermogeniani Fragmenta.* The former was published about A.D. 295, the latter about 365. The last edition is that of Haenel, Bonn, 1837. Krueger proposes to reprint them in the third part of his, Mommsen's, and Studemund's *Collectio Librorum Juris Antejustiniani.*

C. Th. = *Codex Theodosianus.* It was published in 438. The last edition is that of Haenel, Bonn, 1842.

ii · · · xvii

CANN. = *Dom. Ulpiani Fragmenta . . . quibus notas adjecit Joannes Cannegieter, Lugd. Bat.* 1874.

COLLAT. = *Lex Dei, sive Mosaicarum et Romanarum Legum Collatio,* of the third or fourth decade of the 5th century. Last separate edition by Blume, Bonn, 1833. Also in Huschke's *Jurisprudentia Antejustiniana* and other collections of ante-Justinianian law. A new edition by Mommsen promised for that of Krueger, etc.

CONSULT. = *Consultatio veteris cujusdam Jurisconsulti,* of the first half of the 5th century. Last separate edition by Pugge, Bonn, 1834. Also in Huschke's and other collections of ante-Justinianian law; and a new edition promised by Krueger.

CUJ. = Cujas's editions of Ulpian of 1566 and 1586, the latter reproduced in his *Opera Omnia,* 2d Naples edition (1757), vol. i, col. 301.

CUJ. NOTAE = Cujas's Notes on Ulpian, in the same volume.

CUJ. OBSERV. = *Cujacii Observationum et Emendationum, libri XXVIII,* in same edition of his works, vol. lii, col. 1.

DANZ; DANZ, R. R.; or DANZ, GESCH. D. R. R. = *Lehrbuch der Geschichte des roemischen Rechts,* by Dr. H. A. A. Danz, Professor in Jena, 2d ed., 2 vols., Leipzig, 1871.

DANZ, SACRALE SCHUTZ = *Der sacrale Schutz im roemischen Rechtsverkehr,* by the same author, Jena, 1857.

D'ARNAUD = *Georgii D'Arnaud Variarum Conjecturarum libri duo, Leowardiae,* 1744. D'Arnaud died 1740.

D. or DIG. = Justinian's Digest or Pandects, in all editions of the *Corpus Juris Civilis.* The most trustworthy version is that of Mommsen, 2 vols., Berlin, 1872. The text of it is reprinted in his and Krueger's edition of the *Corpus Juris,* not yet completed.

DIRKS. MANUALE = *Manuale Latinitatis Fontium Juris Civilis . . . auct. Henr. Ed. Dirksen, Berolini,* 1837. Dirksen died 1868.

DU TILLET = The *editio princeps* of Ulpian, *cura Jo. Tilius, Parisiis,* 1549. I have not been able to consult this edition, but have used the still rarer one published *Patavii,* 1554, which I understand is a literal reproduction.

EPHEM. EPIGRAPH. = *Ephemeris Epigraphica,* a periodical supplement to the Berlin *Corpus Inscriptionum Latinarum,* published by the Archæological Institute in Rome, vols. i-iv, 1872-79.

EPIT. = The Epitome of Gaius, sometimes called the West Gothic Gaius, preserved in the *Breviarium Alaricianum* of 506. It has been often published separately; and is to be found in several of the Gothofredan editions of the *Corpus Juris,* and in Schulting's, Hugo's, and other collections of ante-Justinianian law.

FEST. = *Sexti Pomp. Festi de Verborum Significatione quae supersunt, cum Pauli epitome.* The best edition is Mueller's, Leipzig, 1839; but there is a good selection of passages illustrative of legal antiquities in Bruns, *Fontes* etc.

FR. DE JURE FISCI = *Fragmentum de jure fisci,* of the end of the second or beginning of the third century, discovered by Niebuhr at Verona at the same time as the MS. of Gaius. It will be found in Huschke's, Krueger's, and other ante-Justinianian collections.

FR. DOS. = *Fragmentum Regularum incerti auctoris, Cervidii Scaevola ut videtur, a Dositheo servatum,* in Huschke's, Krueger's, and other collections.

FRONT. DE CONTROV. = *Julii Frontini de controversiis agrorum libri II.* Frontinus flourished about 80 or 90 A.D. I have used the edition in *Die Schriften der roem. Feldmesser*, by Blume, Lachmann, and Rudorff, 2 vols., Berlin, 1848, 1852.

FR. VAT. = the so-called Vatican Fragments, dating from about 430, published by Cardinal Mai in 1823, from a MS. in the Vatican library. There is a fac-simile, with notes, by Mommsen, in the Transactions of the Royal Academy of Berlin for 1859. The text is in Huschke's and other collections of ante-Justinianian law; and Mommsen promises a new edition for that of Krueger, etc.

G. or GOESCH. = Goeschen's editions of Gaius, 1820 and 1824. He died in 1837, and his papers were used by Lachmann for the edition of 1842.

GOU. = *Kritische Aanteekeningen op Gajus*, critical notes on Studemund's revision, by J. E. Goudsmit, Professor in Leyden. Leyden, 1875.

HAENEL, CORP. LEG. = *Corpus Legum ab Imperatoribus Romanis ante Justinianum latarum, quae extra Constitutionum Codices supersunt . . . . Instruxit Gustavus Haenel, Lipsiae*, 1857.

HE. = Heffter's (A. G.) edition of the Fourth Book of Gaius, Berlin, 1827.

HEIMBACH, CREDITUM = *Die Lehre von dem Creditum*, by Gustav Ernst Heimbach, Leipzig, 1849.

HEINECC. AD L. JUL. = *Jo. Gottl. Heineccii ad legem Juliam et Papiam Poppaeam Commentarii*. I have used the edition of Amsterdam, 1731. Heineck died in 1741.

HOLLWEG: see BETHMANN-HOLLWEG.

HU. (in notes to Gai.) = Huschke's (Phil. Eduard) editions of Gaius, and particularly his *editio separata tertia*, revised after Studemund's Apograph, Leipzig, 1878.

HU. (in notes to Ulpian) = Huschke's edition of Ulpian in his *Jurisprudentia Antejustiniana*.

HU. BEITR. = Huschke's *Gaius: Beitraege zur Kritik und zum Verstaendnisse seiner Institutionen*, Leipzig, 1855.

HU. J. A. = Huschke's *Jurisprudentiae Antejustinianae quae supersunt*, 4th edition, Leipzig, 1879.

HU. MULTA = Huschke's *Die Multa und das Sacramentum in ihren verschiedenen Anwendungen*, Leipzig, 1874.

HU. NEXUM = Huschke *Ueber das Recht des Nexum und das alte roemische Schuldrecht*, Leipzig, 1846.

HU. STUDIEN = Huschke's *Studien des roemischen Rechts*, Breslau, 1830.

HUGO (in notes to Ulp.) = Hugo's (Gustav) editions of Ulpian, particularly that of Berlin, 1834. Hugo died 1844.

HUGO, J. C. A. = *Jus Civile Antejustinianeum . . . a societate jurisconsultorum curatum, edente Gustavo Hugo*, in 2 vols., Berlin, 1815.

I. or INST. = The Institutes of Justinian; best editions those of Krueger and Huschke.

IHERING, G. D. R. R. = *Geist des roemischen Rechts auf den verschiedenen Stufen seiner Entwicklung*, by Rudolph von Ihering, Prof. in Vienna, 3d edition, 4 vols., Leipzig, 1873. There is a French translation by Meulenaere, under the title of *L'Esprit du Droit Romain*, 4 vols., Paris, 1878.

INST. GLOSS. TAUR. = The Turin Gloss of Justinian's Institutes, in Savigny's *Geschichte*, ii, 428, and (by Krueger) in *Z. f. RG.* vii, 44.

JAHRB. D. G. R. = *Jahrbuch des gemeinen deutschen Rechts*, by Bekker, etc., 6 vols., Leipzig, 1857-68.

K. (or KR., in notes to Gai.) = Krueger's notes in his and Studemund's edition of Gaius; see K. U. S.

K. (or KR., in notes to Ulp.) = Krueger's notes to his edition of Ulpian in his *Coll. libr. jur. Antej.*; see KR. J. A.

K. U. S. = Krueger and Studemund's edition of Gaius after the latter's Apograph, with an *epistula critica* by Mommsen, Berlin, 1877.

KARLOWA, R. CP. = *Der roemische Civilprozess zur Zeit der Legisactionen*, by O. Karlowa, Prof. in Heidelberg, Berlin, 1872.

KELLER, LITISCONTESTATION = *Litiscontestation und Urtheil nach classischem roemischem Recht*, by Fried. Ludw. von Keller, Zurich, 1827. Keller died 1860.

KELLER, R. CP. = *Der roemische Civilprocess und die Actionen*, by F. L. von Keller, 5th edition, by Adolf Wach, Leipzig, 1877.

KR. J. A. = Krueger's *Collectio librorum Juris Antejustiniani*, now in course of publication, in co-operation with Mommsen and Studemund.

KRUEGER, KRIT. VERS. = Krueger's *Kritische Versuche im Gebiete des roemischen Rechts*, Berlin, 1870.

KUNTZE R.R. = *Institutionen und Geschichte des roemischen Rechts*, by Joh. Emil Kuntze, Prof. in Leipzig, 2 vols., Leipzig, 1869.

L. (in notes to Gai.) = Lachmann (Karl), in his edition of 1842.

L. (in notes to Ulp.) = Lachmann's *Kritischer Beitrag zu Ulpians Fragmenten*, in *Z. f. g. RW.*, ix, 174.

LANGE, ROEM. ALT. = Lange's (Ludwig) *Roemische Alterthuemer*, 2d ed., 3 vols., Berlin, 1863-71.

LEX BURGUND. = *Lex Romana Burgundionum*, *circa* 520; last edition by Aug. Fried. Barkow, Greifswald, 1826.

M. (in notes to Gai.) = Mommsen's observations in his introductory *epistula critica* and in the footnotes to Krueger's edition of 1877.

M. (in notes to Ulp.) = Mommsen's observations in Boecking's edition of 1855.

M. U. M. ROEM. ALT. = *Handbuch der Roemischen Alterthuemer*, by Joachim Marquardt and Theodor Mommsen, Berlin, 1871-78. Volumes 1-3, dealing with the *Staatsrecht* (the 3d not yet published), are by Mommsen; vols. 4-6, dealing with the *Staatsverwaltung*, by Marquardt. A 7th vol., also by Marquardt, will deal with the *Privatleben*.

MEERM. THES. = Meerman's (G.) *Novus Thesaurus Juris Civilis et Canonici*, in 7 vols., published at the Hague in 1751-58; and a supplemental volume by his son, J. L. B. Meerman, in 1780.

MOMMS. ROEM. FORSCH. = Mommsen's *Roemische Forschungen*, 2 vols., Berlin, 1864, 1879.

MOMMS. STADTR. VON SALPENSA, ETC. = *Die Stadtrechte der lateinischen Gemeinden von Salpensa und Malaga*, edited by Mommsen in the Transactions of the Royal Society of Sciences of Saxony, Philologico-Historical Series, vol. ii, (1857).

NOV. = Justinian's Novels (*Novellae Constitutiones*), in most editions of the *Corpus Juris*.

ORELL. AND HENZ. = *Inscriptionum Latinarum Collectio*, the first two vols. by Jo. Caspar Orelli, Zurich, 1828, the third by Henzen, Zurich, 1856.

OTTON. THESAUR. = Otto's (Everard) *Thesaurus Juris Romani*, 5 vols., Utrecht 1733-35.

P. = *Gai Institutiones Jur. Civ. secundum Guilelmi Studemund collationem . . . . appositis Justiniani Institutionibus . . . edidit B. J. Polenaar, Lugd. Bat.* 1876-79.

PAUL. = *Julii Pauli Sententiarum ad filium libri V.* Paulus was a contemporary of Ulpian's; his Sentences will be found in Huschke's, Krueger's, and other collections of ante-Justinianian law.

PAUL. DIAC.: see **FEST.** above.

PAUL. EX FESTO: see **FEST.** above.

PERNICE = *Marcus Antistius Labeo: das Roemische Privatrecht im ersten Jahrhunderte der Kaiserzeit,* by Dr. Alfred Pernice, Professor in Halle, 1st and 2d vols., Halle, 1873, 1878.

PETRA, TAVOLETTE = *Le Tavolette cerate di Pompei,*—a series of wax-tablets recording the business transactions of an auctioneer, discovered in Pompeii in 1875, published in 1877 by Prof. Giulio in Petra, Director of the Museum at Naples.

REV. DE LEGISLAT. = *Revue de Législation ancienne et moderne,* by Laboulaye, De Roziere, etc., 6 vols., Paris, 1870-76.

ROEDER = *Versuche der Berichtigung von Ulpiani Fragmenta,* by Karl Dav. Aug. Roeder, Goettingen, 1856.

RUDORFF, EDICT. = *Edicti Perpetui quae reliqua sunt, constituit adnotavit, edidit Adolfus Frid. Rudorff, Lipsiae,* 1869.

RUDORFF, R. RG. = *Roemische Rechtsgeschichte,* by A. F. Rudorff, 2 vols., Leipzig, 1857. Rudorff died in 1873.

SAV. G. D. R. R. = *Geschichte des Roemischen Rechts im Mittelalter,* by Fried. Carl von Savigny, 2d edition, 7 vols., Heidelberg, 1834-51. The illustrious author died in 1861.

SAV. OBL. = *Das Obligationenrecht als Theil des heutigen roemischen Rechts,* by the same author, 2 vols., 1851, 1853. This is in continuation of his *System,* but is unfortunately incomplete.

SAV. SYST. = *System des heutigen roemischen Rechts,* by the same author, 8 vols., Berlin, 1840-49. This is the first part of his contemplated *System,* and contains the general doctrines.

SAV. VERM. SCHR. = *Vermischte Schriften,* by the same author, 5 vols., Berlin, 1850.

SCHEURL, BEITR. = *Beitraege zur Bearbeitung des roemischen Rechts,* by Ch. G. Adolf von Scheurl, Professor in Erlangen, Erlang. 1853.

SCHILL. ANIMADV. = *Animadversiones criticae ad Ulpiani Fragmenta,* by Fried. Ad. Schilling, 4 parts, Leipzig, 1830, 1831. Schilling died 1865.

SCHILL. BEMERK. = *Bemerkungen ueber roemische Rechtsgeschichte,* by the same author, Leipzig, 1829.

SCHOELL, TAB. = *Legis Duodecim Tabularum reliquiae,* by Rudolf Schoell, Leipzig, 1866. It has been followed by Bruns in the version of the Twelve Tables given by him in his *Fontes.*

SCHMIDT, INTERD. = *Das Interdiktenverfahren der Roemer,* by Karl Adolf Schmidt, Leipzig, 1853.

SCHULT. = Schulting's (Anton.) edition of Ulpian in his *Jurisprudentia vetus Ante-justinianea, Lugd. Bat.* 1717. Schulting died 1734.

SERV. IN VIRGIL. = *Commentarii in Virgilium Mauri Servii Honorati.* Servius flourished about 420. I have used the edition by Lion, 2 vols., Goettingen, 1826.

TH. (or THEOPH. PAR.) = Theophilus' Greek Paraphrase of Justinian's Institutes, almost contemporary with them. The best edition is that by Reitz, published at the Hague in 1751.

ULP. = *Ulpiani Fragmenta* or *Excerpta ex Ulpiani Libro singulari Regularum*.
ULP. INST. = Fragments from Ulpian's Institutions in Huschke's, Krueger's, and other collections of ante-Justinianian law.

VAHLEN = his edition of Ulpian, Bonn, 1856.
VALER. PROB. = *M. Valerii Probi de juris civilis notarum significatione commentarius.* Probus flourished in the reign of Nero. The authoritative edition is that of Mommsen in Keil's collection of the latin grammarians, (vol. iv, p. 971, Leipz. 1864). The *Notae* will also be found in Huschke's, Krueger's, and other collections of ante-Justinianian law.
VANG. LAT. JUN. = *Ueber die Latini Juniani*, by Carl Adolph von Vangerow, Marburg, 1833. Vangerow died 1870.
VOIGT, JUS NAT. = *Das Jus Naturale, Aequum et bonum, und Jus gentium der Roemer*, by Moritz Voigt, 4 vols., Leipzig, 1856-75.
VOIGT, BEDEUTUNGSWECHSEL = *Ueber den Bedeutungswechsel gewisser die Zurechnung . . . bezeichnender lateinischer Ausdruecke*, by the same author, in the Trans. Roy. Society of Sciences of Saxony, Phil.-Hist. Series, vol. vi, (1872).

Z. F. G. RW. = *Zeitschrift fuer geschichtliche Rechtswissenschaft*, by Savigny, Goeschen, Rudorff, etc., 15 vols., Berlin, 1815-50.
Z. F. RG. = *Zeitschrift fuer Rechtsgeschichte*, by Rudorff, Bruns, etc., 13 vols., Weimar, 1861-78.

GAII

INSTITUTIONUM JURIS CIVILIS

COMMENTARII IV

EDITIO AD STUDEMUNDI APOGRAPHUM

CURATA.

GAII INSTITVTIONVM IVRIS CIVILIS
COMMENTARII QVATTVOR.

—◦—

1 (*Omnes populi, qui legibus et moribus reguntur, partim suo
(proprio, partim communi omnium hominum iure utuntur : nam
(quod*) quisque populus ipse sibi ius constituit, id ipsius proprium est uocaturque ius ciuile, quasi ius proprium ciuitatis;
quod uero naturalis ratio inter omnes homines constituit, id
apud omnes populos peraeque custoditur uocaturque ius gentium, quasi quo iure omnes gentes utuntur. populus itaque
Romanus partim suo proprio, partim communi omnium hominum iure utitur. quae singula *qualia*[1] sint, suis locis proponemus.

---

1 *All peoples that are under the government of laws and customs
use in part their own law, in part what is common to mankind :
for what each* people has established on its own account is
peculiar to itself, and is called its civil law, in the sense of
being the proper law of the particular state or *ciuitas;* whereas
what its natural reasonableness has caused to be received by
mankind generally is observed by all peoples alike, and is
called the law of nations,—that, as it were, which all nations
make use of. The Roman people, therefore, employs a body
of law which is partly its own, partly common to all men.
What each branch includes will be explained in due course.

§§ 1-8. Comp. tit. I. *DE IVRE NATVRALI,
GENTIVM, ET CIVILI* (i, 2). In the
ms. before § 1, is the rubric—*I. De
iure ciuili et naturali,* in a later
hand.

§ 1   § 1, tit. I. afd. First three lines

of par. illegible; supplied from Gai.
(*lib. i. Inst.*) in fr. 9, D. *de. I. et I.*
(i, 1).
[1] Stud. thinks *qualia* erroneous;
P. has *quaenam.*

1

2   Constant autem iura [1] populi Romani ex legibus, plebiscitis,
senatusconsultis, constitutionibus principum, edictis eorum
3 qui ius edicendi habent, responsis prudentium.   Lex est
quod populus iubet atque constituit.   Plebiscitum est quod
plebs iubet atque constituit.   plebs autem a populo eo distat,
quod populi appellatione uniuersi ciues significantur, connu-
meratis etiam patriciis; plebis autem appellatione sine patriciis
ceteri ciues significantur; unde olim patricii dicebant plebiscitis se non teneri, *quia* [1] sine auctoritate eorum facta essent;
sed postea lex Hortensia [2] lata est, qua cautum est ut plebiscita
uniuersum populum tenerent : itaque eo modo legibus exae-

---

2   The laws of the Roman people are the product of *leges*
[*i.e.* comitial enactments], plebiscits, senatusconsults, imperial
constitutions, edicts of those enjoying the *ius edicendi*, and
3 responses of the jurisprudents.   A *lex* is a law enacted and
established by the whole body of the people; a plebiscit, one
enacted and established by its plebeian members.   The difference between *plebs* and *populus* is this,—that the latter denotes
the whole mass of the citizens, patricians included, whereas the
former denotes only the citizens who are not patricians.   It
was because of this distinction that of old the patricians
maintained that plebiscits were not binding upon them,
because enacted without their authorisation.   But in course
of time the Hortensian law was passed, declaring that plebiscits should be of force universally; and thus they were put

§ 2.   Comp. § 3, tit. I. afd.
[1] *Constant autem iura* in the
MS.; Hu. prefers *constat autem ius
ciuile.*
§ 3.   Comp. § 4, tit. I. afd.
[1] Instead of *quia* P. prefers *quae ;*
the MS. has *q'*, which does not appear to occur elsewhere as a contraction of either word.
[2] The *lex Hortensia* was enacted
467 | 287; comp. Plin. *H. N.* xvi,
10; Gell. xv, 27, § 4. On the *L. Vale-
ria Horatia*, 305 | 449, (Liv. iii, 55,)
and *L. Publilia Philonis*, 415 | 339,
(Liv. viii, 12,) which at first sight
appear to have long before introduced the same change as the *L.
Hortensia*, see Mommsen, *Roem.
Forsch.*, vol. I, pp. 163-6, 200-1,
215-17.   He distinguishes between
the *comitia tributa* and the *concilium plebis*, holding that the enact-

ments of the former were always
called *leges*, and only those of the
latter called *plebiscita*.   According
to his view, the *L. Val. Horatia*
created the *comitia tributa*, while
the *L. Publilia* endowed it with
the capacity to legislate under the
presidency and on the proposal of the
praetor; the *L. Hortensia*, on the
other hand, referred to the *concilium
plebis*, and declared that its enactments should for the future be binding on the citizens generally, without
the necessity of approval by the
patres.   (For he argues that exceptionally, and with that approval,
as in the case of the *lex Canuleia*,
309 | 445, a plebiscit sometimes did
have the effect of a *lex* even before
the *L. Hortensia ;* a view which so
far justifies Polenaar's reading *quae*
above referred to.)

4 quata sunt.   Senatusconsultum est quod senatus iubet atque
  constituit, idque legis uicem optinet, quamuis fuerit quaesitum.
5 Constitutio principis est quod imperator decreto [1] uel edicto [1]
  uel epistula [1] constituit.   nec umquam dubitatum est quin id
  legis uicem optineat, cum ipse imperator per legem [2] imperium
6 accipiat.   Ius autem edicendi habent magistratus populi
  Romani.   sed amplissimum ius est in edictis duorum praeto-
  rum, urbani [1] et peregrini,[2] quorum in prouinciis iurisdictionem
  praesides earum habent; item in edictis aedilium curulium,[3]

---

4 on a par with *leges*.   A senatusconsult is a law enacted and
  established by the senate, and, although at one time doubted,
5 has all the force of statute.   An imperial constitution is
  what the emperor has established by decree, edict, or letter. It
  has never been disputed that such a constitution has the full
  force of a *lex*; for it is by a *lex* that the emperor is invested
6 with the *imperium*.   The *ius edicendi* [or right to publish
  edicts] is an attribute of the magistrates of the Roman people.
  Nowhere has it a more ample exponent than in the edicts of
  the two praetors, the urban and the peregrin, whose jurisdiction is exercised in the provinces by the provincial governors;
  as also in that of the curule aediles, whose jurisdiction is

§ 4.   Comp. § 5, tit. I. afd.
§ 5.   Comp. § 6, tit. I. afd.
       [1] *Decretum* was a decision given by the emperor on a question brought before him judicially; *edictum*, a law formally promulgated; *epistula*, a declaratory statement of the law in answer to an application either from an official or a private party, usually called a *rescriptum*.
       [2] See the *Lex de imperio Vespasiani*, in Bruns' *Fontes*, p. 118; Tac. *Hist.* iv, 3.
§ 6.   Comp. § 7, tit. I. afd. One would have expected here a definition of the *edicta magistratuum*, and possibly it has been accidentally omitted by the transcriber; Hu. interpolates—*Edicta sunt praecepta eorum qui ius edicendi habent.*
       [1] The urban praetorship was created as an immediate consequence of the *leges Liciniae* of 387 | 367 (opening the consulate to the plebeians,) and with the view of keeping the administration of the law in the hands of the patricians. See Liv. vi, 42; Pompon. in fr. 2, § 27, D. *de O. I.* (i, 2). This magistrate is referred to in various old laws as *praetor qui inter ciues ius dicit.*
       [2] The peregrin praetorship was created in or about the year 507 | 247; the duty of the new magistrate being to administer justice between foreigners resident in Rome, or between foreigners and citizens. See Liv. Epit. xix; fr. 2, § 28, D. *de O. I.* (i, 2).
       [3] The curule aediles were first created at the same time as the urban praetor. Amongst their various functions they had the oversight and regulation of the slave and cattle markets, with jurisdiction in questions arising out of market transactions. See Liv. vi, 42; Mommsen, in M. u. M. *Roem. Alt.* ii, 470.

quorum iurisdictionem in prouinciis populi Romani[4] quaestores
habent; nam in prouincias Caesaris[4] omnino quaestores non
mittuntur, et ob id hoc edictum in his prouinciis non pro-
7 ponitur.   Responsa prudentium sunt sententiae et opiniones
eorum quibus permissum est iura condere. quorum omnium
si in unum sententiae concurrunt, id quod ita sentiunt legis
uicem optinet; si uero dissentiunt, iudici licet quam uelit
sententiam sequi ; idque rescripto diui Hadriani significatur.

8   Omne autem ius quo utimur [1] uel ad personas pertinet, uel
ad res, uel ad actiones. sed [2] prius uideamus de personis.
9   Et quidem summa diuisio de iure personarum haec est, quod
10 omnes homines aut liberi sunt aut serui.   Rursus liberorum
11 hominum alii ingenui sunt, alii libertini.   Ingenui sunt qui

---

exercised in the popular provinces by the quaestors : (there
are no quaestors sent to the imperial provinces, where, con-
7 sequently, the aedilitian edict is not propounded).   The
responses of the jurisconsults are the decisions and opinions
of individuals licensed to lay down the law. If those consulted be unanimous, their decision or opinion has the force
of statute ; but if they differ, the judge may adopt any of
their opinions he pleases ; so it is declared in a rescript of our
late emperor Hadrian's.

8   The whole body of law in use amongst us relates either
to persons, things, or actions. Let us first turn our attention
to persons.
9   The primary division of the law of persons is this,—that all
10 men are either free or slaves.   Of freemen again some are
11 *ingenui* and others *libertini*.   *Ingenui* are those that have

---

[4] Comp. ii, 21. The division of
the provinces into popular and imperial was due to Augustus; after the
third century they were all imperial.
§ 7.   Comp. § 8, tit. I. afd.; Th. i, 2, § 8.
§ 8.   This par. is preceded in the MS.
by the rubric, in a later hand,—*II.
De iuris diuisione.* Gai. in fr. 1, D.
de stat. hom. (i, 5) ; § 12, tit. I. afd.
[1] It is a question how the phrase
omne ius quo utimur is to be understood : it may be rendered either as
above, or as ʻ Every right exercised
by us.ʼ

[2] The MS. has *sed*; K. u. S. and
Hu. read *et*.
§§ 9-12. Preceded in the MS. by marginal
rubric, in a later hand,—*III. De condicione hominum.*
§§ 9-10.   Comp. tit. I. *DE IVRE PER-
SONARVM* (i, 3).
§ 9.   Gai. in fr. 3, D. *de stat. hom.* (i, 5) ;
pr. tit. I. afd.
§ 10.   Comp. § 5, tit. I. afd.
§§ 11-35.   Comp. tit. I. *DE INGENVIS*
(i, 4) and *DE LIBERTINIS* (i, 5).
§ 11.   Comp. pr. I. *de ingen.* and pr.
de libert.

liberi nati sunt ; libertini, qui ex iusta servitute manumissi
12 sunt.   Rursus libertinorum [*tria sunt genera : nam aut ciues
[Romani aut latini aut dediticiorum*] numero sunt.   de quibus
singulis dispiciamus ; ac prius de dediticiis.
13   Lege itaque Aelia Sentia[1] cauetur, ut qui serui a dominis
poenae nomine uincti sint, quibusue stigmata inscripta sint,
deue quibus ob noxam quaestio tormentis habita sit et in
ea noxa fuisse conuicti sint, quiue ut ferro aut cum bestiis
depugnarent traditi sint, inue ludum custodiamue coniecti
fuerint, et postea uel ab *eodem*[2] domino uel ab alio manumissi,
eiusdem condicionis liberi fiant cuius condicionis sunt per-
14 egrini dediticii.   Vocantur autem [*peregrini dediticii*][1] hi
qui quondam aduersus populum Romanum armis suscep-
15 tis pugnauerunt, deindi uicti se dediderunt.   Huius ergo

---

been born free ; *libertini* those manumitted from lawful slavery.
12 Again, of *libertini* or freedmen *there are three classes ; for they
may be either Roman citizens, or latins, or classed with the dediticians.* Let us deal with these separately, beginning with the last.
13   By the Aelia-Sentian law it is provided in regard to slaves
who have been put in chains or branded by their masters by
way of punishment, or who have been put to the torture on
account of some offence of which they have eventually been
convicted, or who have been given up to fight in the arena
either with men or beasts, or who have been committed either
to a gladiatorial training school or to prison, that if afterwards
they be manumitted either by the owner who has thus dealt
with them or by a later one, they shall as freemen be of the
14 same condition as the *peregrini dediticii*.   Those are called
peregrini dediticii who, having taken up arms and made war
against the Roman people and been vanquished, have after-
15 wards unconditionally surrendered.   Slaves disgraced in any

---

§ 12. Comp. Vlp. i, 5 ; Fr. Dos. §§ 4 f.
The words in ital. are supplied by
G. from the Epit., and adopted by
all eds.
§ 13. A rubric interlineated—*IIII. De
dediticiis uel lege Aelia Sentia.*
Comp. Sueton. *Aug.* 40 ; Dio
Cass. lv, 13 ; Vlp. i, 11 ; Paul. iv,
12, §§ 3, 5-8 ; Th. i, 5, § 3.
[1] The *lex Aelia Sentia*, enacted
757 | 4, contained a body of regula-
tions on the subject of enfranchisements, and was intended to restrain

that immoderate resort to them
from motives of ostentation that had
been flooding the state with citizens
of slave origin.
[2] So G. and most eds. ; the ms.
has *eo.*
§ 14.   Rubric interlineated—*V. De peregrinis dediticiis.* Comp. Liv. i, 38
Th. i, 5, § 3.
[1] These words are on the margin
of the ms., in a later hand.
§ 15.   Comp. i, 26.

turpitudinis seruos quocumque modo et cuiuscumque aetatis manumissos, etsi pleno iure[1] dominorum fuerint, numquam aut ciues Romanos aut latinos fieri dicemus, sed omni modo

16 dediticiorum numero constitui intellegemus.   Si uero in nulla tali turpitudine sit seruus, manumissum modo ciuem Ro-

17 manum, modo latinum fieri dicemus.   nam in cuius persona tria haec concurrunt, ut maior sit annorum triginta, et ex iure Quiritium domini, et iusta ac legitima manumissione[1] libere- tur, id est uindicta[2] aut censu[3] aut testamento,[4] is ciuis Romanus fit; sin uero aliquid eorum deerit, latinus erit.

18   Quod autem de aetate serui requiritur lege Aelia Sentia introductum est.   nam ea lex minores XXX annorum seruos non aliter uoluit manumissos ciues Romanos fieri, quam si uindicta, apud consilium, iusta causa manumissionis adpro-

19 bata, liberati fuerint.   Iusta autem causa manumissionis

---

of the ways described, no matter how or at what age they may have been manumitted, and even though their manumitter may have held them in full ownership [*i.e.* both bonitarian and quiritarian], can never become either Roman citizens or latins, but must ever be classed as dediticians.

16   If, however, no such disgrace attach to a slave, he becomes on manumission sometimes a Roman citizen, sometimes a

17 latin.   He becomes a Roman citizen in whose person these three requisites concur,—that he is above thirty years old, that he is held by his owner on quiritarian title, and that he is freed by a legally recognised mode of manumission, *i.e.* by *vindicta*, census, or testament; if any of these requisites fail he will be a latin.

18   The requirement as to the age of the slave was introduced by the Aelia-Sentian law, which declared that slaves manu- mitted under the age of thirty should not become Roman citizens unless their manumission were *vindicta*, and upon

19 adequate cause approved by the council.   There is such

---

[1] *Pleno iure* means both *in bonis* and *ex iure Quiritium;* comp. i, 54; ii, §§ 40, 41. The difference between these two terms is explained in ii, 40, note, and Vlp. i, 16.

§ 17.   Comp. Vlp. i, §§ 6-10, 12, 16; Th. i, 5, § 4.

    [1] Comp. Fr. Dos. § 5; also note to § 41.

    [2] Comp. Boeth. *in Cic. Top.* i, 2, § 10 (Bruns, p. 294); Th. as above.

[3] Comp. Boeth. and Th. as in note 1.

    [4] Comp. ii, §§ 224, 267; Vlp. i, 23; ii, 7; Th. as in note 1.

§ 18.   Interlineation in MS.—*VI. De manumissione uel causae probatione.* Comp. Vlp. i, 12; Vlp. in fr. 16, pr. D. *de manum. uind.* (xl, 4); Fr. Dos. § 13.

§ 19.   Comp. i, 39; § 5, I. *qui quib. ex caus.* (i, 6); Th. i, 6, § 5.

est ueluti si quis filium filiamue aut fratrem sororemue naturalem,[1] aut alumnum, aut paedagogum,[2] aut seruum procuratoris habendi gratia, aut ancillam matrimonii causa apud
20 consilium manumittat.   Consilium[1] autem adhibetur in urbe Roma quidem quinque senatorum et quinque equitum Romanorum puberum; in prouinciis autem uiginti recuperatorum ciuium Romanorum.   idque fit ultimo die conuentus;[2] sed Romae certis diebus apud consilium manumittuntur. maiores uero triginta annorum serui semper manumitti solent,[3] adeo ut uel in transitu manumittantur, ueluti cum praetor aut proconsul[4] in balneum uel in theatrum eat.
21   Praeterea minor triginta annorum seruus manumissus potest

---

adequate cause when, for instance, in presence of the council, a man manumits his natural child, brother, or sister, or his foster-child, his children's instructor, a slave that he means to make his procurator, or a woman-slave whom he means to
20 marry.   The council consists in Rome of five senators and five Roman knights of the age of puberty; in the provinces of twenty recuperators, Roman citizens. It is held in the provinces on the last day of the assize; but in Rome there are certain fixed days for council manumissions. But slaves above thirty may be manumitted at any time, even *en route*, as when the praetor or a proconsul is on his way to the bath or the theatre.
21   A slave under thirty at manumission may become a Roman

---

[1] The phrase *filius naturalis* is used in the texts to indicate sometimes a child by birth as distinguished from adoption, sometimes a child by a mistress or a slave, as distinguished from a lawful wife.
[2] This word is used in different senses here and in § 39; in the one place, as by Vlp. in fr. 13, D. *de manum uind.* (xl, 4), it may mean the manumitter's own teacher; in the other, as by the same Vlp. in fr. 35, D. *de fideic. lib.* (xl, 5), his children's.
§ 20. Interlineated rubric—*VII. De concilio adhibendo.*
[1] Comp. Vlp. i, 13; Th. i, 6, § 4.
[2] The provinces in the time of Gaius were divided into districts (*iuridici conuentus iurisdictiones*); and in winter the governor made his circuit, holding an assize at the principal town of each. This assize also got the name of *conuentus*, and the same word was used as a collective appellation for the individuals —Roman citizens settled in the province—who were qualified to act as jurymen, and required to attend (*conuentus ciuium Romanorum*). See Th. as in note 1.
[3] Comp. § 2, I. *de libertin.* (i, 5).
[4] The MS. and most eds. have *pro consule;* but see iv, 189.
§ 21. Comp. ii, 154; Vlp. i, 14; § 1, I. *qui quib. ex caus.* (i, 6). The last line of p. 4 of the MS. is legible, but not very comprehensible; p. 5, with exception of a few isolated words, is undecipherable. Momms. (K. u. S. footnote) suggests as the completion of the sentence begun on p. 4— *alius heres nullus excludit; idque eadem lege Aelia Sentia cautum est.* This does not correspond with the few letters decipherable in the MS., but

ciuis Romanus fieri, si ab eo domino qui soluendo non erat
testamento eum liberum et *heredem relictum* — — — —
21*b* — — — —.   [21*b*] — — — — — — —.

---

citizen if his insolvent owner have by testament both
given him his freedom and instituted him as heir, [*provided
[no similar institution of another slave precede his, and no
[other person voluntarily accept the inheritance under the
[will; so it was enacted by the same Aelia-Sentian law. Out
[of a regard for freedom the rule will apply, according to
[Proculus, even though the slave thus instituted heir have no*
21*a* [*express grant of liberty. In conformity with the declaration
[of the Aelia-Sentian law that it is only the slave first thus
[instituted in a testament that is to be free, it has been ruled that
[if a man institute as his heirs with freedom all his bastard
[children by a certain slave-woman of his, none of them will be
[free; for neither is it possible in such a case to say which of
[them is instituted first, nor ought the deceaseds creditors to be
[defrauded by the withdrawal of so many slaves from his insolvent
[estate; and a senatusconsult, passed to amend the Fufia-Can-
[inian law, declares null and void any device resorted to by a*
21*b* [*testator to defeat the provisions of the statute.*]   [21*b*] — —

22   [*Under the Aelia-Sentian law a slave under thirty, manu-
[mitted either by testament or, on cause shown, among friends,
[becomes a latin (although it can hardly be said that it is to that
[law that his name of latin is due); so does a slave over thirty,
[if manumitted by an owner, who had him only in* bonis (*even
[though the manumission may have been in solemn form*); *or if*

no doubt accurately expresses the
idea. Hu. (footnote) suggests—
*seruus similiter cum libertate heres
scriptus testamento non praecedat, et
nemo alius ex eo testamento heres
sit; idque eadem lege Aelia Sentia
cautum est. idem fauore libertatis
de eo seruo Proculus existimat, qui
sine libertate heres scriptus sit.*

§§ 21*a*, 21*b*. The same ed. conjectures that
the continuation of p. 5 may have
run as follows (the words legible in
the MS. being in Roman type):—21*a*.
*Cum uero lege Aelia Sentia testa-
mento primus scriptus solus ciuis
Romanus fiat, placuit, si quis forte
ex ancilla sua natos* spurios *liberos
et heredes scripserit, omnes seruos
manere, quia quis primus sit ex ea
oratione non intelligitur, nec in
fraudem* creditorum *plures* ex

*patrimonio debent decedere; denique
senatusconsulto ad legem. Fufiam
Caniniam facto prouisum est, ne in
potestate debitoris esset eius* legis
auctoritatem *per hanc artem euer-
tere.* 21*b. Ex iure Quiritium fit
seruus noster non per hoc solum
quod pecunia nostra conparatur, sed
ulterius requiritur iusta serui ac-
quisitio propterea quod quaedam
etiam non iustae sunt acquisitiones;
nam ea,* quae traditione alienantur,
quamuis mancipi sint, nec uel mancipatione uel in iure cessione uel usucapione acquiruntur, tantum in bonis
fiunt.* As authority for § 21*a*, Hu.
refers to the Epit. i, 2, § 2; and for
21*b*, to Gai. i, 35; ii, §§ 41, 204;
Vlp. i, 16; Fr. Dos. § 9.

§ 22. The commencement of this par.
is on p. 5. Hu., founding on iii, 56;

22 — — — — — homines latini Iuniani appellantur;
latini ideo quia adsimulati sunt latinis *coloniariis*;[1] Iuniani
ideo, quia per legem Iuniam[2] libertatem acceperunt, cum olim
23 serui uiderentur esse.   Non tamen illis permittit lex Iunia

---

[*manumitted amongst friends without cause shown, provided in
either case there be no other impediment. All these were formerly maintained in what had the semblance of freedom; the
praetor giving them protection as freemen, though according to
quiritarian law they were still slaves. But now persons thus
manumitted*] are called Junian latins: latins, because they are
assimilated to the colonial latins; Junian, because they owe
their freedom to the Junian law, having been previously
23 regarded as slaves.   This law does not allow them either

Epit. i, 2, § 2; Vlp. i, §§ 10, 12;
Fr. Dos. §§ 5, 6, reconstructs as
follows:—*Latinus fit ex lege Aelia
Sentia seruus minor* XXX *annorum
qui testamento uel inter amicos causa
probata liberatur, quanquam latinum ipsa lex Aelia Sentia nondum
fecit; item qui ea aetate maior a
domino, cuius est in bonis, quamuis
iusta manumissione manumittitur,
uel qui inter amicos liberatur, si
modo alia causa libertatem non im-
pediat. Hi omnes tamen olim quidem in forma libertatis seruabantur,
cum praetor eos, licet serui ex iure
Quiritium essent, in libertate tuere-
tur. nunc uero hi homines*, etc.
[1] Comp. i, 181; iii, 56. On the
nature of colonial latinity see
Savigny, *Verm. Schr.* iii, 279; Marquardt in M. u. M. *Roem. Alt.* iv,
47-57; Voigt, *Ius. Nat.* ii, pp.
714-26, 738-45; Mommsen and
Huebner on the *lex Coloniae Iul.
Genetiuae*,—the charter or act of
incorporation of a Latin colony,
founded by Julius Cæsar at Urso,
not far from Seville, and partially
discovered on bronze tablets in the
years 1871 and 1875,—in the *Ephem.
Epigraph.* vol. ii, pp. 105-51, 221-
82, vol. iii, pp. 91-112; Giraud on
same law, under title of *Les Bronses
d'Osuna*, Par. 1874, *Les Bronses
d'Osuna, Remarques nouvelles*, Par.
1875, and *Les nouveaux Bronses
d'Osuna*, Par. 1877. (The first
published portion of the law is reprinted by Bruns, under the title of
Lex Vrsonitana, in his *Fontes*, p. 106.)

There is a good deal on the same
subject in the writings of Berlanga,
Mommsen, Huebner, Giraud, Van
Swinderen, Van Lier, and others on
the *Leges Malacitana et Salpensana*,
—charters granted by Domitian to
the *municipia* of Malaga and Salpensa, considerable portions of
which, engraved on bronze, were
found near Malaga in the year 1851.
They are included by Bruns in his
Fontes, pp. 120, 124.
There is an interesting controversy
on the question whether those *municipia* were *municipia latina* or *mun.
ciuium Romanorum;* the former
view is taken by most of the authors
above named; the latter by Zumpt
in his *Studia Romana* (Berol. 1859),
pp. 269 f., and by Houdoy, *Le droit
municipal chez les Romains* (Paris,
1876), pp. 76 f.
[2] Gai. always mentions this law
simply as the *L. Iunia*, and so does
Justinian in tit. C. *de lat. lib. toll.*
(vii, 6); but in § 3, I. *de libertin.*
(i, 5), and Th. i, 5, § 3, it is called
lex Iunia Norbana. M. Junius
Silanus and L. Norbanus Balbus
were consuls in the year 772 | 19;
and this date is usually assigned to
the enactment. Mommsen, however (*Jahrb. d. g. R.* ii, 833), and
others, argue against both name and
date, on the ground that comitial
legislation had by that time
ceased.
§ 23. Comp. ii, §§ 110, 275; Vlp. xx,
§§ 14, 15; xxii, 8; Fr. Vat. §
172.

uel ipsis testamentum facere, uel ex testamento alieno capere,
24 uel tutores testamento dari.   Quod autem diximus ex testamento eos capere non posse ita intellegemus, *ne quid inde*
directo[1] hereditatis legatorumue nomine eos posse capere
dicamus; alioquin per fideicommissum capere possunt.
25   Hi uero qui dediticiorum numero sunt nullo modo ex testamento capere possunt, non magis quam quilibet peregrinus;
quin nec ipsi testamentum facere possunt secundum id quod
26 *magis* placuit.   Pessima itaque libertas eorum est qui dediticiorum numero sunt; nec ulla lege aut senatusconsulto aut
constitutione principali aditus illis ad ciuitatem Romanam
27 datur.   Quin et in urbe Roma uel intra centesimum urbis
Romae miliarium morari prohibentur; et si *contra* fecerint,
ipsi bonaque eorum publice uenire iubentur ea condicione, ut
ne in urbe Roma uel intra centesimum urbis Romae miliarium
seruiant, neue umquam manumittantur; et si manumissi
fuerint, serui populi Romani esse iubentur. et haec ita lege
Aelia Sentia conprehensa sunt.

------

themselves to make a testament, or to take under that of
another person, or to be appointed testamentary tutors.
24 Our statement, however, that they cannot take under a testament, is to be understood as meaning that they cannot take
directly under it, either by way of inheritance or legacy; for
they may take by trust bequest.
25   Those, on the other hand, that are classed amongst the
dediticians, cannot, any more than any other peregrin, take in
any way under a testament; nor, according to the prevailing
26 doctrine, can they themselves make one.   Their freedom,
therefore, is of the most miserable sort; nor can they ever,
either by law, senatusconsult, or imperial enactment, be
27 admitted to the privileges of Roman citizenship.   Nay
more, they are forbidden to live in Rome or within the
hundredth milestone from the city.   On contravention, they
themselves and their effects are ordered to be put up to public
sale for the benefit of the exchequer, and that under the condition that they shall not be employed in Rome or within the
hundredth milestone, nor ever again be manumitted; if this
last condition be disregarded they become slaves of the
Roman people. All this was provided by the Aelia-Sentian law.

------

§ 24. Comp. ii, 275; Vlp. xxv, 7.

[1] *Inde directo* is an emendation of
Goudsmit's; the ms. reads *indirecto,*

which K. u. S. and Hu. change into
directo.

§ 25. Comp. iii, 75; Vlp. xx, §§ 14,
15; xxii, 2.

28   Latini uero multis modis ad ciuitatem Romanam perueniunt.
29   Statim enim ex lege Aelia Sentia cautum est ut [1] minores triginta
       annorum [2] manumissi et latini facti, si uxores duxerint uel
       ciues Romanas uel latinas coloniarias uel eiusdem condicionis
       cuius et ipsi essent, idque testati fuerint adhibitis non minus
       quam septem testibus ciuibus Romanis puberibus, et filium
       procreauerint,[3] cum is filius anniculus [4] esse coeperit, datur eis
       potestas per eam legem [1] adire praetorem, uel in prouinciis
       praesidem prouinciae, et adprobare se ex lege Aelia Sentia
       uxorem duxisse et ex ea filium anniculum habere: et si is
       apud quem causa probata est id ita esse pronuntiauerit, tunc
       et ipse latinus [5] et uxor eius, si et ipsa eiusdem [*condicionis*
       [*sit, et ipsorum filius si et ipse eiusdem*] [6] condicionis sit, ciues

---

28   Latins may attain to Roman citizenship in many ways.
29   Thus, by the Aelia-Sentian law it was provided that a slave
       who had been manumitted before attaining the age of thirty,
       and had thus become a latin, and who afterwards married a
       woman that was either a Roman citizen, or a colonial latin,
       or even of the same condition as himself, and had the fact
       attested by not fewer than seven witnesses, Roman citizens
       above puberty, called together for the purpose, and had a son
       born to him of the marriage, might, on said son's completing
       his first year, go before the praetor, or in a province before
       the governor, and prove that, in terms of the Aelia-Sentian
       law, he had married a wife and had by her a year-old son
       and if the magistrate before whom cause had thus been shown
       pronounced accordingly, then the latin himself, his wife if she
       were of the same condition, *and their child if he also were of*

---

§§ 28-35. The matter of these pars. is
introduced by a rubric, in a later
hand, on a vacant line at foot of p.
6—*latini ad ciuitatem Romanam
perueniant.* Probably it began with
Quibus modis, but those words are
no longer visible.

§ 29. Comp. Vlp. iii, 3. Gai. here and
elsewhere attributes the provision
referred to in this par. to the Aelia-
Sentian law; as Vlp. explains, and
as is probable from context, it was
introduced by the Junian law. In
§ 80 Gai. speaks of the *lex Aelia
Sentia et Iunia* as if the Junian law
were an amended version of the
earlier enactment.

[1] P., K. u. S., and Hu. omit the
words *cautum est ut* as a gloss; as
does P. the *per eam legem* in the
middle of the par.

[2] Comp. § 31.

[3] A daughter answered the purpose as well as a son; comp. §§ 32a,
72, and Vlp. iii, 3.

[4] See fr. 134, D. *de verb. sign.*
(1, 16).

[5] After *latinus* what seems to be
Iunianus is interlined; but only
the termination (*anus*) is certain.

[6] The words in italics are not in
the ms., but suggested by Goesch.,
and accepted by most editors as
essential; see next par.

30 Romani esse iubentur.   Ideo autem *in persona filii*[1]
adiecimus 'si et ipse eiusdem condicionis sit,' quia si uxor
latini ciuis Romana est, qui ex ea nascitur, ex nouo senatus-
consultoquod auctore diuo Hadriano factum est, ciuis Romanus
31 nascitur.   Hoc tamen ius adipiscendae ciuitatis Romanae
etiamsi *soli*[1] minores triginta annorum manumissi et latini
facti ex lege Aelia Sentia habuerunt, tamen postea, senatusconsulto quod Pegaso et Pusione consulibus factum est, et
maioribus triginta annorum manumissis latinis factis con-
32 cessum est.   Ceterum etiamsi ante decesserit latinus quam
anniculi filii causam probauerit, potest mater eius causam probare, et sic et ipsa fiet ciuis Romana — — — — — —.

30 *the same condition*, were declared to be Roman citizens. The
reason why in reference to the son we add ' if he also be of
the same condition,' is this,—that if the wife of a latin happen
to be a Roman citizen, then, by a recent senatusconsult, of
which our late emperor Hadrian was the author, any child
born of the marriage will be a Roman citizen in right of birth.

31 Although by the Aelia-Sentian law it was only slaves manumitted and made latins under the age of thirty that were able
to acquire Roman citizenship in the way described, yet afterwards, by a senatusconsult passed at the instance of the
consuls Pegasus and Pusio, the same privilege was extended
to those manumitted and made latins after attaining that age.

32 If a latin have died before proving his claim to citizenship on
the strength of a year-old son, the mother may establish it,
and so both herself become a Roman citizen [*and acquire that*

§ 30. Comp. § 80; Vlp. iii, 3. The
senatusconsult here referred to
seems to have been a very comprehensive one regulating birth-status;
see § 67, note.
 [1] So P.; Hu. and previous eds.
have *in ipsorum filio*; K. u. S. *in
huius persona;* the ms. is indistinct.
§ 81. Comp. § 29. Pegasus and Pusio
were consuls in the reign of Vespasian (a. 70-79), but year unknown;
see § 5, I. *de fideicom. hered.* (ii,
23).
 [1] So Hu. and K. u. S.; the ms.
has *socii*, but with a dot—equivalent
to deletion—over some if not all of
the letters.
§ 82. Comp. iii, 5; Paul. in *Collat.*
xvi, 3, § 15. The last two words
in the text, *ciuis Romana*, are the
two first and only quite certain

words in the first line of p. 8 of
ms.; lines 2-5 are more or less
illegible. M. (K. u. S. p. xviii)
proposes—et sic et ipsa fiet ciuis
Romana *et filius, scilicet si latina sit.
Si mater ante patrem decesserit uel
post eum causa non probata, et
spatium supersit, rem peraget per
tutores* ipse filius, ciuisque *Romanus
fiet; scilicet ita* debet causam probare ut *supra expositum est.* Hu.
proposes—et sic et ipsa fiet ciuis
Romana, *si latina est, et filius, isque
tamquam iustis nuptiis procreatus,
quasi suus postumus heres patris
bona apiscitur. si uero et pater et
mater decesserint,* ipse filius, *cuius
interest cum ciuitate Romana bona
consequi quae ab eis relicta sunt,*
debet causam probare, ut *tamen
pupilli tutor causam agat.*

32a *Quae* supra diximus de filio anniculo, dicta intellegemus *(etiam
(de filia annicula).*

32b — — — — — id est fiunt ciues Romani, si Romae
inter uigiles sex annis *militauerint.* Postea dicitur factum
esse senatusconsultum, quo data est illis ciuitas Romana *si*

32c *triennium militiae expleuerint.* Item edicto *Claudii latini
ius* Quiritium *consecuntur,*[1] si nauem marinam *aedificauerint,*
quae non minus quam decem milia modiorum[2] *(frumenti)*[3]
capiat, eaque nauis, uel quae in eius locum substituta

33 *(sit sex)*[3] annis *frumentum Romam portauerit.* Praeterea
— — — — — ut, si Latinus qui patrimonium *sestertium*

[*status for her child, that is to say if she herself be a latin. If she*
[*have predeceased her husband, or died after him but before cause*
[*has been shown, the son will proceed himself through his tutor,*
[*and thus acquire citizenship; that is to say, he will show cause*

32a [*on his own account in the manner above described.*] What
has been said in regard to a year-old son is to be understood
as *equally applicable to a year-old daughter.*

32b [*Further, by the Visellian law, those, whether under or over*
[*thirty years of age, who on manumission have become latins,*
[*acquire the* ius quiritium], that is to say, become Roman
citizens, when they have served six years in Rome in the
night watch. It is said that by a senatusconsult of later date
citizenship was conceded to them after three years' service.

32c Then, by an edict of Claudius', a latin acquires quiritarian
rights by building a vessel large enough to hold 10,000 pecks
of grain, and continuing for *six* years to import corn to Rome

33 either in it or in another vessel equally large. Further [*by*
[*an enactment of the time of Nero*], if a latin worth 200,000

---

§ 32a. See § 29, note 3.

§ 32b. Comp. Vlp. iii, 5. Lines 7 and 8
of p. 8 are entirely illegible. On
authority of Vlp., Hu. thus reconstructs them:—*Praeterea ex lege
Visellia tam maiores quam minores
xxx annorum manumissi et latini
facti ius Quiritium adipiscuntur,* etc.

The Visellian law, referred to in
connection with other provisions in
tit. C. *ad leg. Visell.* (ix, 21), and
tit. C. *quando ciu. actio crim.
praeiud.* (ix, 31), has been attributed
to the year 777 | 24, when Ser.
Cornel. Cethegus and L. Visellius
Varro were consuls; but Momms.
(*Jahrb. d. g. R.* ii, 885) claims for
it an earlier date, on the ground

referred to in note 2 to § 22, and on
the strength of an inscription.

§ 32c. Comp. Suet. *Claud.* 18; Vlp.
iii, 5.

[1] The ms. has *secuntur.*

[2] The *modius* equalled 1·896 imp.
gall., or ·948 of an imp. peck.

[3] Those words, illegible in the ms.,
are supplied on the authority of Vlp.

§ 33. Comp. Vlp. i, 5. A lacuna of
about half a line, in which the only
letters legible are *ne . s.* On the
strength of Tac. *Ann.* xv, 43, Hu.
suggests—*a Nerone constitutum est
edicto;* P.—*Nerone auctore* (for which
word the letter *a* would be a sufficient
contraction) *senatus permisit;* and
K. u. S.—*a Nerone constitutum est.*

cc milium plurisue habebit, in urbe Roma domum aedificauerit,
in quam non minus quam partem dimidiam patrimonii sui
34 inpenderit, ius Quiritium consequatur.   Denique Traianus
constituit ut si (*latinus*) in *urbe* triennio *pistrinum exer-
cuerit, (in quo in)* dies singulos non minus quam centenos
(*modios*) frumenti *pinseret*, ad ius Quiritium perueniret.
34a — — — — — —.   [35]   — — — — — —

---

sesterces or more spend not less than half that sum in building a house in Rome, he will thereby acquire quiritarian
34 rights.   Still later Trajan enacted that a latin who had
worked a mill in Rome for three years, grinding in it daily
not less than a hundred *pecks* of corn, should thereby attain
34a to the same distinction.   [*A latin may also become a citizen
[by direct grant of citizenship from the emperor, or, in the case of
35 [a woman, by giving birth to three children.   Finally, those
[who are latins because they have been manumitted informally*

§ 34. Comp. Vlp. iii, 1.
§ 34a. The first three lines of p. 9 are
entirely illegible, but probably contained a reference either to acquisition of citizenship *beneficio principali*, as mentioned by Vlp. iii, 2,
or to the privilege of the *latina ter
enixa* mentioned by him in § 1.
§ 35. Lines 4-14 of p. 9 are to a great
extent illegible, but most probably
dealt with acquisition of citizenship
iteratione, referred to in Vlp. iii, 4;
Fr. Dos. § 14; Fr. Vat. § 221; Gai.
Epit. i, 1, § 4. K. in his *Krit.
Versuche*, p. 116, proposed a reconstruction, which in K. u. S. he has
amended as follows:—*Minores* XXX
annorum manumissi, si *latini facti
sunt quia causa manumissionis apud*
consilium *adprobata non fuerit;
item maiores* XXX *annorum qui uel
inter amicos uel ab eo manumissi
sunt cuius in bonis non ex iure
Quiritium fuerunt, fient ciues
Romani si is cuius ex iure Quiritium sunt iuste manumissionem*
iterauerit. ergo si seruus *tuis quidem
in bonis, ex iure Quiritium autem
meus est, latinus quidem* a te solo
fieri potest, *nec tamen a me iterum
manumissus ullo modo ciuis Romanus libertus fit; sed si tu postea ius
Quiritium consecutus manumissionem iteraueris ciuis, Romanus
fit. Patronatus sane ius tibi in*

eo conseruatur quocunque modo,
etc.
Hu. proposes:—*Item minores*
XXX *annorum* manumissi, si *latini
facti sunt quod inter amicos causa
apud* consilium *probata est, postea
uero maiores* XXX *annorum facti,
item maiores* XXX *annorum ideo
latini facti quod uel inter amicos
uel quocunque modo ab eo, cuius tantum in bonis erant, manumissi sunt,
iteratione ius Quiritium consequi
possunt, id est fiunt ciues Romani,
si is, cuius ex iure Quiritium sunt,
iuste manumissionem* iterauerit.
ergo si seruus *tuis quidem in bonis,
ex iure Quiritium autem meus est,
latinus quidem* a te solo fieri potest,
*nec pariter tamen iuste postea siue
a te siue a me iterum manumissus,
ciuis Romanus* libertus fit. *sed si
postea ius* Quiritium consecutus *in
manumisso fuerit is a quo latinus
factus est, iterando eum ad ius
Quiritium perducere potest, idque ius
ei datur* quocunque modo, etc.
Neither of those reconstructions
adapts itself very well to the words
decipherable in the MS.; and Krueger's reference to the *patronatus* is
entirely unsupported. They differ
on the two important questions—
(1) what latins could by iteration become citizens? and (2) from whom
could the iteration proceed?

35 datur, quocunque modo ius Quiritium fuerit consectus. *(cuius*
   (autem et) in bonis [1] et ex iure Quiritium sit manumissus, ab
   eodem scilicet et latinus fieri potest et ius Quiritium consequi.
36 *(Non tamen cuicumque uolenti manumittere licet.   nam*
37 *(is qui)* in fraudem creditorum uel in fraudem patroni [1] manumittit nihil agit, quia lex Aelia Sentia inpedit libertatem.
38 Item eadem lege minori xx annorum domino non aliter manumittere permittitur, quam si uindicta apud consilium iusta
39 causa manumissionis adprobata fuerit.[1]   Iustae autem
   causae manumissionis sunt ueluti si quis patrem aut matrem
   aut paedagogum aut conlactaneum manumittat.   sed et illae

---

[*when under the age of thirty, may become citizens by iteration*
[*or renewal of the manumission, and that immediately if it be*
[*renewed in solemn form,—after they have reached thirty if*
[*renewed informally ; while those whose latinity is attributable*
[*to the fact that they have been manumitted by an owner who*
[*held them only* in bonis, *may acquire citizenship on iteration*
[*either by him who was their quiritarian owner at the time of*
[*the first manumission, or by the original manumitter*] on his
subsequently acquiring quiritary right over them, no matter
how.   A slave, therefore, who is manumitted by an owner
holding him at once on bonitarian and quiritarian title, may
from him acquire first the position of a latin and then that of
a Roman citizen.

36 *It is not every man who pleases that can manumit.*   Thus
37 the act of one who does so in fraud of his creditors or of his
   patron is void ; the Aelia-Sentian law is here an obstacle to
38 liberty.   By the same law an owner under twenty years
   old cannot manumit otherwise than *vindicta*, upon adequate
39 cause established before the council.   That the slave being
   manumitted is the manumitter's father or mother, or his
   teacher, or his foster-brother, is regarded as such an adequate

---

[1] On the difference between ownership *ex iure Quiritium* and *in bonis*,
and the effect of manumission by a
person having only the latter, see
i, 54, ii, 40, note, and Vlp. i, 16 ;
on manumission *inter amicos*, see
note to § 41.
§§ 36-41. Comp. tit. I. *QVI QVIBVS EX
CAVSIS MANVMITTERE NON POSSVNT*
(i, 6).
§ 36. Lines 19 and 20, p. 9, are vacant
in the ms., and Stud. finds no trace
of writing. The words in ital. are
from pr. tit. I. afd.

§ 37. Comp. Vlp. i, 15.
   [1] This assumes manumission by a
   freedman ; the enfranchisement of
   his slave destroyed his patron's
   reversionary interest in the latter.
§ 38. § 4, tit. I. afd. Comp. §§ 20, 41 ;
   Vlp. i, 13 ; Fr. Dos. § 13 ; *Lex
   Salpensana*, c. 28 (Bruns, p. 123).
   [1] So the ms. ; Hu. substitutes
   manumiserit.
§ 39. § 5, tit. I. afd. Comp. § 19.
   Several words in this par. are
   omitted by P. as glosses.

causae quas superius in seruo minore XXX annorum exposuimus, ad hunc quoque casum de quo loquimur adferri possunt.
item ex diuerso hae causae quas in minore XX annorum
domino rettulimus, porrigi possunt et ad seruum minorem
40 XXX annorum. Cum ergo certus modus manumittendi
minoribus XX annorum dominis per legem Aeliam Sentiam
constitutus sit, euenit ut qui XIIII annos aetatis expleuerit,
licet testamentum facere possit et in eo heredem sibi instituere legataque relinquere, tamen si adhuc minor sit annorum
41 XX, libertatem seruo dare non possit. Et quamuis latinum
facere uelit minor XX annorum dominus, tamen nihilo minus
debet apud consilium causam probare, et ita postea inter
amicos manumittere.
42 Praeterea lege Fufia Caninia certus modus constitutus est

---

cause ; to which may be added those causes already enumerated in speaking of the manumission of a slave under thirty ;
(while, contrariwise, those just specified may be added to
those mentioned when speaking of slaves under thirty as
40 equally applicable to their case.) A certain limitation
being thus imposed by the Aelia-Sentian law upon the power
of an owner under twenty to make manumissions, it results that
although when he has completed his fourteenth year he may
make a testament, and thereby institute an heir and bequeath
legacies, yet if he be still under twenty he cannot enfranchise
41 one of his slaves. Although an owner under twenty may
intend nothing more than to make his slave a latin, he is none
the less required to establish the cause of manumission before
the council, and then he may manumit informally.
42 The Fufia-Caninian law also has imposed a limitation upon

§ 40. § 7, tit. I. afd.
§ 41. Comp. §§ 20, 38; Fr. Dos. §§ 6,
  7, 13. There were various informal
  modes of manumission, of which the
  principal were—(1) *inter amicos*, by
  verbal declaration in presence of
  friends; (2) *per epistulam*, by letter,
  used when slave from home ; and
  (3) *per mensam*, by an invitation to
  the slave to sit at table with his
  owner; see Th. i, 5, § 4. Gai. is in
  the habit of including all those
  informal modes of manumission
  under the specific *man. inter amicos*.
  Their effect was to make the *manumissus* only a latin, § 17.

§§ 42-46. Comp. tit. I. *DE LEGE
  FVFIA CANINIA SVBLATA* (i, 7).
  Before § 42 is a vacant line, intended
  probably for a rubric.
§ 42. Pr. tit. I. afd. Comp. ii, 228 ;
  Paul. iv, 14. The *L. Fufia Caninia*
  has hitherto been usually known
  under the name *L. Furia Caninia*,
  and attributed to the year 761 | 8,
  apparently for no other reason than
  that M. Furius Camillus was one of
  the consuls of that year. It seems
  to be referred to, along with the
  Aelia-Sentian law, in Sueton. *Aug.*
  40.

43 in seruis testamento manumittendis.   nam ei qui plures
quam duos neque plures quam decem seruos habebit, usque
ad partem dimidiam eius numeri manumittere permittitur;
ei uero qui plures quam x neque plures[1] quam xxx seruos
habebit, usque ad tertiam partem eius numeri manumittere
permittitur.   at ei qui plures quam xxx neque plures
quam centum habebit, usque ad partem quartam potestas
manumittendi datur.   nouissime ei qui plures quam c habebit nec plures quam D,[2] non plures manumittere permittitur
quam quintam partem.   *neque plures numerantur;*[3] sed
praescribit lex ne cui plures manumittere liceat quam c
contra, si[4] quis unum seruum omnino aut duos habet, ad
hanc legem[5] *non pertinet*, et ideo liberam habet potestatem
44 manumittendi.   Ac ne ad eos quidem omnino haec lex
pertinet qui sine testamento manumittunt.   itaque licet iis
qui uindicta aut censu aut inter amicos manumittunt, totam
familiam liberare, scilicet si alia causa non inpediat libertatem.
45 *Sed quod* de numero seruorum testamento manumittendorum

---

43 testamentary manumission.   It allows the owner of from
two to ten slaves to manumit to the extent of one-half of the
actual number; him who has more than ten but not over
thirty to manumit a third of them; and him who has over
thirty but not more than a hundred to manumit a fourth.
Lastly, he who has more than a hundred but not more than
five hundred is not allowed to manumit more than a fifth of
the number.   *The enumeration proceeds no further;* but the
enactment forbids any one to manumit more than a hundred
of his slaves in all.   On the other hand, it does not affect him
who has only one slave or at most two; his power of manu--
44 mitting is unrestricted.   Nor does the enactment apply in
any way to manumissions otherwise than by testament.
Accordingly, by *vindicta*, or by the census, or informally, a
man may if he pleases manumit his whole slave establish-
45 ment, provided always there be no other impediment.   As
regards the number that may be manumitted by testament, it

§ 43. Comp. Vlp. i, 24 ; Paul. iv, 14, § 4.
  [1] The words *quam x neque plures*
are a marginal amendment.
  [2] The words *nec plures quam* D
are an interlinear addition, which
P. omits.
  [3] So Gou. ; the MS. has only *atur*,
without any space between those
letters and the antecedent *plures* ;

after *neque plures* Hu. supplies—
quam D *habentis ratio habetur, ut ex
eo numero pars definiatur.*
  [4] The *contra si* is from P. ; the
MS. has *cqsi* ; K. u. S. and Hu.
quod si.
  [5] *Ad hanc legem* is the reading of
the MS. ; P. suggests *ad hunc lex.*
§ 45. Comp. Vlp. I, 24.

diximus ita intellegemus, *ne umquam ex eo* numero ex quo
dimidia aut tertia aut quarta aut quinta pars liberari potest,
— — — —[1] liceat quam ex antecedenti numero licuit.
et hoc ipsa (*ratione*)[2] *prouisum* est : erat enim sane absurdum,
ut x seruorum domino quinque liberare liceret, quia usque
ad dimidiam partem eius numeri manumittere ei conceditur,
alteri autem[3] xii seruos habenti non plures liceret manumittere
quam iiii ; at eis qui plures quam x neque — — —
45a — — —.[4]　　[45a] — — — — — —　　[46] Nam

---

is to be understood that a man entitled to enfranchise the
half, or a third, fourth, or fifth part of his whole establishment *is in no case to be limited to a smaller number than* he
might have liberated had such establishment been reckoned
on the immediately preceding [*i.e.* the next lowest] scale.
This interpretation of the statute *is dictated by common sense ;*
for verily it would be absurd that, while the owner of ten
slaves might enfranchise five of them, because the statute
empowers him to manumit to the extent of a half, another
owning twelve should not be allowed to enfranchise more
than four ; and so he who has more than ten, but not [*more*
[*than fourteen, may enfranchise five, though this number is*
45a [*greater than a third of his whole establishment.*　　*If any one*
[*have intended to manumit by testament a greater number than*
[*aforesaid, the order in which he has named them is to be scrupu-*

[1] P. fills the lacuna with *pauciores
manumitti ;* K. u. S. and Hu. *pauciores manumittere.*

[2] So P. ; Hu. and K. u. S. have
ipsa lege. Both are objectionable, so
that Gou. suggests *speciali senatusconsulto.* The *ipsa* in the ms., however, is quite distinct, although the
next word is illegible.

[3] Hu. reads *ulterius autem,* P.
simply *ut,* K. u. S. *domino uero.*
The letters in the ms. are interlined,
and the reading in the text seems
best to correspond to both.

[4] The par. ends on p. 12, which
is almost quite illegible. Hu. conjectures—neque *plures quam* xxx
*habent, eadem ratione utique etiam
quinque, quot* x *habenti licuit,
manumittere licet.* I prefer something like this—neque *plures quam*
xiv *habent, quinque manumittere
permittitur, licet amplior sit numerus
quam tertia pars.*

§ 45a. P. 12 of the ms. is illegible. But

in the Epit. i, 2, § 2, immediately
preceding the words standing in the
text as part of § 46, we read :—*Si
aliquis ex testamento plures manumittere uoluerit quam continet
numerus supra scriptus, ordo ser-
uandus est : ut illis tantum libertas
ualeat qui prius manumissi sunt,
usque ad illum numerum quem ex-
planatio continet superius compre-
hensa : qui uero postea supra constitutum numerum manumissi leguntur, integre in seruitute eos certum
est permanere.　Quod si non nominatim serui uel ancillae in testamento
manumittantur, sed confuse omnes
seruos suos uel ancillas is qui testamentum facit liberos facere uoluerit,
nulli penitus firma esse iubetur hoc
ordine data libertas, sed omnes in
seruili condicione, qui hoc ordine
manumissi sunt,　permanebunt.*
Comp. ii, 239 ; Vlp. i, 25.

§ 46.　Comp. 21a ; 45a, note ; Epit. i, 2,
§ 2 ; ii, 239.

46 et si testamento scriptis in orbem seruis libertas data sit,
quia nullus ordo manumissionis inuenitur, nulli liberi erunt;
quia lex Fufia Caninia quae in fraudem eius facta sint
rescindit. sunt etiam specialia senatusconsulta quibus rescissa sunt ea quae in fraudem eius legis excogitata sunt.

47   In summa sciendum est, [cum] lege Aelia Sentia cautum
sit ut creditorum fraudandorum causa manumissi *liberi* non
fiant, etiam hoc ad peregrinos pertinere,—senatus ita censuit
ex auctoritate Hadriani : cetera uero iura eius legis ad peregrinos non pertinere.

48   Sequitur de iure personarum alia diuisio. nam quaedam
personae sui iuris sunt, quaedam alieno iuri subiectae sunt.

49 Sed rursus earum personarum quae alieno iuri subiectae sunt,

---

[*lously observed ; the gift of freedom will avail those only who
[*are first manumitted and within the lawful number, as explained
[*above, while those mentioned afterwards and beyond that num-
[*ber unquestionably remain in slavery. If the slaves be not
[*manumitted each by name, but the testator has attempted to
[*enfranchise them in mass, the freedom thus conferred will be of
[*no avail to any of them ; on the contrary, all who have been
[*thus manumitted will still continue in their old condition as
46 [*slaves.]   And so, if the names of the slaves to be enfranchised be written in the testament in a circle, as there is
thus no order or sequence that can be followed, none of them
will be free; for the Fufia-Caninian law nullifies anything
done in fraud of it. There are besides some special senatusconsults rescinding acts devised to defeat the statute.

47   Finally, it is to be noted that the provision of the Aelia-Sentian law negativing the freedom of slaves manumitted in fraud
of creditors applies even to peregrins,—so it was declared by
the senate at the instance of Hadrian ; the other provisions
of the statute, however, have not been extended to them.

48   Now comes another division of the law of persons; for some
are *sui iuris* [or their own masters], others *alieni iuris* [or
49 domestically dependent].   Further, of those who are *alieni*

§ 47. Comp. § 37.
§§ 48-54. Comp. tit. I. *DE HIS QVI SVI
    VEL ALIENI IVRIS SVNT* (i, 8). In
    the ms. there is a vacant line before
    § 48, probably for a rubric.
§§ 48-51. Pr. tit. I. afd., which of course
    omits mention of *manus* and *man-
    cipium.*

§ 49. Comp. Fr. Vat. §§ 298, 300; *L.
    Salpensana,* c. 22 (Bruns, p. 121).
    Persons *in potestate* are dealt with
    in §§ 52-107, 125-186; those *in
    manu* in §§ 108-115, 137 ; and
    those *in mancipio* in §§ 116-123,
    138-141.

aliae in potestate, aliae in manu, aliae in mancipio sunt.
50 Videamus nunc de iis quae alieno iuri subiectae sint: si cog-
nouerimus quae istae personae sint, simul intellegemus quae
51 sui iuris sint.   Ac prius dispiciamus de iis qui in aliena
potestate sunt.
52   In potestate itaque sunt serui dominorum,—quae quidem
potestas iuris gentium [1] est : nam apud omnes peraeque gentes
animaduertere possumus dominis in seruos uitae necisque
potestatem esse,[2]—et quodcumque per seruum adquiritur,
53 id domino adquiritur.[3]   sed hoc tempore neque ciuibus
Romanis, nec ullis aliis hominibus qui sub imperio populi
Romani sunt, licet supra modum et sine causa in seruos suos
saeuire : nam, ex constitutione imperatoris Antonini, qui sine
causa seruum suum occiderit non minus teneri iubetur
quam qui alienum seruum occiderit. sed et maior quoque
asperitas dominorum per eiusdem principis constitutionem
coercetur: nam, consultus a quibusdam praesidibus prouinciarum de his seruis qui ad fana deorum uel ad statuas
principium confugiunt, praecepit, ut si intolerabilis uideatur

---

iuris, some are *in potestate*, others *in manu*, others *in mancipio*.
50 Let us see first who are *alieni iuris* ; if we know who they
51 are, from that we can gather who are *sui iuris*.   And let us
begin with those who are in another person's *potestas*.
52   Slaves, then, are in the *potestas* of their owners,—and this
potestas is *iuris gentium ;* for we find that amongst all nations
alike owners have the power of life and death over their
slaves,—and whatever is acquired by a slave is acquired for
53 his owner.   But at the present day neither Roman citizens
nor any other persons subject to the sway of Rome are allowed
to inflict excessive or causeless cruelties upon their slaves;
for, by a constitution of our emperor Antonine's, any one
causelessly killing his slave is as much amenable to justice as
if he had killed a slave of a third party.   Even great severity
on the part of owners is restrained by a constitution of our
same sovereign's; for, being consulted by some provincial
governors as to what was to be done with slaves seeking an
asylum in temples or at imperial statues, he replied that if
the harshness of their owners seemed really to be intolerable,

§ 52.   § 1, tit. I. afd.   [2] Comp. ii, §§ 86, 88; iii, §§ 163,
         [1] Comp. Vlp. in fr. 4, D. *de I.*   166.
et I. (i, i).   § 53.   § 2, tit. I. afd.; Vlp. in *Collat.*
         [3] Comp. Senec. *de benef.* iii, 23, § 8.   iii, 3, §§ 1-3.

dominorum saeuitia, cogantur seruos suos uendere.   et
utrumque recte fit : [1] male enim nostro iure uti non debemus ;
qua ratione et prodigis interdicitur bonorum suorum adminis-
54 tratio.[2]   Ceterum cum apud ciues Romanos duplex sit
dominium,—nam uel in bonis uel ex iure Quiritium uel ex
utroque iure cuiusque seruus esse intellegitur,—ita demum
seruum in potestate domini esse dicemus si in bonis eius sit,
etiamsi simul ex iure Quiritium eiusdem non sit : nam qui
nudum ius Quiritium in seruo habet, is potestatem habere
non intellegitur.

55   Item in potestate nostra sunt liberi nostri quos iustis
nuptiis [1] procreauimus.   quod ius proprium ciuium Romanorum est : [2] fere enim nulli alii sunt homines qui talem in filios

---

these last should be compelled to sell the slaves in question.
And in both cases he resolved justly ; for one ought not to
misuse his right,—a principle we acknowledge in interdicting
54 the administration of his estate to a spendthrift.   But as
amongst Roman citizens there is a double ownership,—for a
slave may belong to a man either on a bonitarian or a quiritarian title, or on both at once,—a slave is in the *potestas* of
the owner who has him *in bonis* [or in bonitarian right],
although not at the same time holding the quiritarian title ;
for he who has the bare quiritarian right over a slave is not
regarded as having him *in potestate*.

55   Likewise in our *potestas* are those of our children begotten
in a marriage approved by the *ius ciuile*.   This right is one
peculiar to Roman citizens : there are scarcely any other men

[1] After *fit* the ms. has *regula ;*
the word has evidently been a
marginal note on the original, but
stupidly transferred by the transcriber to the text. See the same
mistake in iii, §§ 113, 126.
    [2] Comp. Vlp. xx, 13 ; Paul. iii,
4a, § 7.
§ 54. Comp. § 35 ; ii, 40, and note ; ii,
88 ; iii, 166 ; Vlp. i, 16 ; Th. i, 5,
§ 4. It is from the δεσπότης βονιτάριος of the latter that the phrase
' bonitarian ownership ' is borrowed,
as a convenient rendering of *in
bonis.*
§ 55. Comp. tit. I. *DE PATRIA POTE-
STATE* (i, 9) ; also Vlp. v, 1.
    [1] *Iustae nuptiae* would not be

adequately rendered by ' lawful
wedlock.' There were many *iniusta*
or *illegitima matrimonia* that were
quite lawful, though only as *iuris
gentium* alliances, unproductive of
the pure civil law consequences
of Roman marriage ; see § 77, last
clause ; ii, 241.
    [2] That the colonial latins had a
patria potestas of their own, as also
a *manus* and *mancipium,* is said to
be established by chaps. 21 and 22
of the *lex Salpensana,* referred to in
note to § 22. It is evident that the
burgesses of Salpensa, and probably
also of Malaga, enjoyed those rights ;
but this may possibly have been due
to some special concession to those

suos habent potestatem qualem nos habemus; idque diui
Hadriani edicto, quod proposuit de his qui sibi liberisque
suis ab eo ciuitatem Romanam petebant, significatur.³ (nec
me praeterit Galatarum gentem credere in potestate parentum
liberos esse.)

56 [Iustas autem nuptias ciues Romani contraxisse intelleguntur]
si ciues Romanas uxores duxerint, uel etiam latinas pere-
grinasue cum quibus conubium habeant : cum enim conubium
id efficiat¹ ut liberi patris condicionem sequantur, euenit ut
non [solum]² ciues Romani fiant sed et in potestate patris sint.

57 Unde causa cognita¹ ueteranis quibusdam concedi solet
principalibus constitutionibus conubium cum his latinis

---

who have over their sons such a power as we have;—a fact
noticed by our late emperor Hadrian in an edict of his in
reference to persons applying for a grant of citizenship for
themselves and their children. (It does not escape me, however, that the Galatians maintain that their children are *in
potestate* of their parents.)

56 *Roman citizens are held to have contracted a marriage approved
by the* ius ciuile *if they have taken Roman citizens for their
wives, or even latins or peregrins with whom they have*
conubium [or right of intermarriage]. For as it is a consequence
of this right of intermarriage that the children follow the
condition [or status] of their fathers, it thus comes to pass not
only that they become Roman citizens, but that they are in

57 their father's *potestas*.   Further, after investigation of the
circumstances, imperial constitutions have occasionally conceded to veterans the right of intermarriage with such latin

municipia, which appear to have
been exceptionally favoured. See
Houdoy, *Le droit municipal chez les
Romains* (Par. 1876), pp. 32 f. See
also the passage in the *L. Salpensana*, in Bruns, p. 121.

³ After *significatur* P. interpolates
sic, so as to impute the words *nec
me praeterit*, etc., to Hadrian; and
Hu. gives effect to the same idea by
introducing *ait* after *praeterit*. But
it is difficult to suppose that the
emperor, in granting a favour to
a suppliant, would have sought thus
to depreciate his gift; besides, *nec
me praeterit* is a locution of which
Gaius was fond, as see i, 73; iii, 76;
iv, 24.

§§ 56-96.   Comp. tit. I. *DE NVPTIIS*
(i, 10).

§ 56. Lines 5 and 6 of p. 15 are blank,
and, according to Stud., have never
been written on. The first may
probably have been for a rubric, and
the second for such words as printed
above in ital.; they are from pr.
tit. I. afd. Comp. Vlp. v, §§ 2, 3,
4, 8.

¹ Comp. § 80.

² The sense requires the interpolation of *solum, modo*, or some
equivalent.

§ 57. There exist numerous *tabulae
honestae missionis* containing such
concessions, some of them found in
Britain; see examples in Bruns,
pp. 177-79.

¹ So P. interprets the *cc* of the
ms.; K. u. S., Hu., and other eds.,
convert them into *et*.

peregrinisue quas primas post missionem uxores duxerint; et qui ex eo matrimonio nascuntur et ciues Romani et in potestate parentum fiunt.

58 [*Non omnes ciues Romanas nobis uxores ducere licet*]: nam a
59 quarundam nuptiis abstinere debemus.   Inter eas enim personas quae parentum liberorumue locum inter se optinent, nuptiae contrahi non possunt, nec inter eas conubium est, ueluti inter patrem et filiam uel matrem et filium uel auum et neptem; et si tales personae inter se coierint, nefarias et incestas nuptias contraxisse dicuntur.   et haec adeo ita sunt, ut quamuis per adoptionem parentum liberorumue loco sibi esse coeperint, non possint inter se matrimonio coniungi, in tantum ut etiam dissoluta adoptione idem iuris maneat. itaque eam quae mihi adoptione filiae seu neptis loco esse coeperit, non potero uxorem ducere, quamuis eam emanci-
60 pauerim.[1]   Inter eas quoque personas quae ex transuerso

---

or peregrin women as they should take for their first wives after their discharge; the issue of such marriages are Roman citizens and in the *potestas* of their parents.

58 *It is not every woman who is a Roman citizen that we may lawfully take to wife :* from some marriages we are bound to
59 abstain.   Marriage cannot be contracted, nor is there any *conubium*, between those who stand to each other in the relation of ascendants and descendants, for example, father and daughter, mother and son, grandfather and granddaughter; if such persons have formed a union, they are said to have contracted a nefarious and incestuous marriage.   So far is this the case, that, though the relationship of parent and child may have been created only by adoption, they cannot be united in marriage,—no, not even when the bond of adoption has been dissolved.   Therefore, I cannot take her to wife who by adoption has once become my daughter or granddaughter, even though I may subsequently have emancipated her.
60 The same observation applies to the case of persons related

---

§ 58. Again two vacant lines in the **ms.** Hu. suggests—*Cum seruilibus uero personis ne nuptiae quidem sunt. Sed nec liberas omnes nobis uxores ducere licet.* But probably the first line was meant for a rubric, and the next one intended to run somewhat as printed above in ital. The words are from § 1, tit. I. afd.; *ciues Romanas* being interpolated to adapt them to the state of matters in the time of Gai.

§ 59. § 1, tit. I. afd. Comp. Vlp. v, 6; Paul. in *Collat.* vi, 3, §§ 1, 2.
[1] Although the artificial relationship was dissolved (§ 158), yet it was repugnant to one's sense of propriety to allow those who had once been related as parent and child to afterwards become husband and wife.

§§ 60, 61. § 2, tit. I. afd. Comp. Vlp. and Paul. as in last note.

gradu cognatione iunguntur, est quaedam similis obseruatio,
61 sed non tanta.   sane inter fratrem et sororem prohibitae
sunt nuptiae, siue eodem patre eademque matre nati fuerint
siue alterutro eorum.   sed si qua per adoptionem soror mihi
esse coeperit, quamdiu quidem constat adoptio, sane inter me
et eam nuptiae non possunt consistere; cum uero per eman-
cipationem adoptio dissoluta sit, potero eam uxorem ducere;
sic etiam si ego emancipatus fuero nihil impedimento erit
62 nuptiis.   Fratris filiam uxorem ducere licet : idque primum
in usum uenit cum diuus Claudius Agrippinam fratris sui
filiam uxorem duxisset;[1] sororis uero filiam uxorem ducere
non licet.[2]   et haec ita principalibus constitutionibus signifi-
63 cantur.   Item amitam et materteram uxorem ducere non
licet; item eam, quae mihi quondam socrus aut nurus aut
priuigna aut nouerca fuit.   ideo autem diximus 'quondam,'
quia si adhuc constant eae nuptiae, per quas talis adfinitas
quaesita est, alia ratione mihi nupta esse non potest; quia

---

61 collaterally, though not quite to the same extent.   As a
matter of course marriage is prohibited between brother and
sister, whether so related through both parents or only through
one.   If a woman have become my sister by adoption, then
assuredly, so long as the bond exists, we cannot marry; but
if the adoption be put an end to by her emancipation I may
take her to wife; and the impediment will equally be removed
62 by my emancipation.   A man may lawfully marry his
brother's daughter, the practice having been introduced by
the emperor Claudius, who took to wife his brother's daughter
Agrippina; but he is not allowed to marry his sister's
daughter.   The distinction is recognised in various imperial
63 constitutions.   It is also unlawful to marry a father's or
mother's sister.   Neither can I marry her who has aforetime
been my mother-in-law or step-mother, or daughter-in-law or
step-daughter.   I say 'aforetime;' for if the marriage which
has created the affinity still subsist, I cannot take her to wife

---

§ 62.   Comp. Vlp. v, 6 ; §§ 3, 5, tit. I. afd.
  [1] Comp. Tac. *Ann.* xii, 5-7 ; Suet.
Claud. § 26. Domitian, following
the example of Claudius, married
the daughter of his brother Titus ;
Suet. *Dom.* 22. Nerva is said to have
repealed the Claudian enactment ;
but the rule it established seems to
have revived.

[2] Marriage with the daughter of
either a brother or sister was forbidden by Constantius in 339; l. 1, C.
Th. *de incest. nupt.* (iii, 12).

§ 63.   Comp. Vlp. v, 6 ; Paul. in *Collat.*
vi, 3, § 3 ; §§ 6, 7, tit. I. afd. Most
eds. throw *item amitam . . . licet*
into § 62, and begin § 63 with *item
eam.*

neque eadem duobus nupta esse potest, neque idem duas
uxores habere.

64   Ergo si quis nefarias atque incestas nuptias contraxerit,
neque uxorem habere uidetur neque liberos. itaque hi qui
ex eo coitu nascuntur matrem quidem habere uidentur,
patrem uero non utique,[1] nec ob id in potestate eius sunt,
[*sed tales sunt*[2]] quales sunt hi quos mater uulgo[3] concepit:
nam et hi patrem habere non intelleguntur, cum *is etiam*
incertus sit; unde solent spurii filii appellari, uel a Graeca
uoce quasi σποράδην concepti, uel quasi sine patre filii.[4]

65   [*Aliquando autem euenit, ut liberi qui statim ut nati*] sunt
parentum in potestate non fiant, postea tamen redigantur in
66   potestatem.   (*Nam si latinus*)[1] ex lege Aelia Sentia uxore
ducta filium procreauerit, aut latinum ex latina, aut ciuem Ro-

---

for this other reason,—that neither can the same woman have
two husbands, nor can the same man have two wives.

64   He who contracts a nefarious and incestuous marriage is
held to have neither wife nor children; therefore the issue of
the connection, while indeed they are held to have a mother,
yet are not held to have a father, and so are not in his *potestas*.
They are in much the same position as those whom a woman
has conceived in promiscuous intercourse; for these are not
regarded as having any father, his identity being uncertain.
Whence it is that they are called spurious children, either
(from a Greek word) as being, as it were conceived here and
there, σποράδην, or as being children without a father.

65   *It sometimes happens that children who* are not in the
potestas of their parents *at birth* are yet subjected to it after-
66   wards.   *For instance, if a latin* who has married in terms of
the Aelia-Sentian law have begotten a son,—whether a latin of
a latin wife, or a Roman citizen of a Roman wife,—he will not

---

§ 64. § 12, tit. I. afd. Comp. Vlp. iv, 2;
   v, 7.
      [1] P. transposes thus—*non uero
   patrem, nec ob id in potestate eius
   sunt; quales utique sunt hi,* etc.
      [2] The words *sed tales sunt* are sup-
   plied by K. u. S. after the lead of the
   Inst.; Hu. reads *sed sunt quales
   ii,* etc.
      [3] *Vulgo* would not be properly
   translated by 'out of wedlock,' for
   the children of a concubine were not

spurii but *liberi naturales;* comp.
§ 19, note 1.
      [4] Such a child often had the letters
   S. P. (*sine patre*) appended to his
   name.
§ 65. Two lines vacant, the first pro-
      bably for a rubric. The second is
      supplied from § 13, tit. I. afd.
§ 66. Comp. §§ 29, 80; Vlp. vii, 4.
      [1] The words *nam si latinus* are
   illegible, but obvious from context.

manum ex ciue Romana, non habebit eum in potestate ; — —
— — —² simul ergo eum in potestate sua habere incipit.
67 Item si ciuis Romanus latinam aut peregrinam uxorem duxerit
per ignorantiam, cum eam ciuem Romanam esse crederet, et
filium procreauerit, hic non est in potestate eius, quia ne
quidem ciuis Romanus est, sed aut latinus aut peregrinus, id
est eius condicionis cuius et mater fuerit; quia non aliter
quisquam ad patris condicionem accedit quam si inter patrem
et matrem eius conubium sit.   sed ex senatusconsulto¹
permittitur ei causam erroris probare, et ita uxor quoque
et filius ad ciuitatem Romanam perueniunt, et ex eo tempore incipit filius in potestate patris esse.   idem iuris est
si eam per ignorantiam uxorem duxerit quae dediticiorum
numero est, nisi quod uxor non fit ciuis Romana.
68 Item si ciuis Romana per errorem nupta sit peregrino
. tamquam ciui Romano, permittitur ei causam erroris probare,

---

have that son in his *potestas ;* [*but if afterwards, on cause shown*
[*under the statute, the father become a Roman citizen,*] he
67 thereupon at once begins to have him *in potestate.*   So, if a
Roman citizen have in ignorance taken to wife a latin or a
peregrin, believing her to be a Roman citizen, and have
begotten a son, the latter is not in his father's *potestas,* because
he is not a Roman citizen, but either a latin or a peregrin,
that is, of the same condition as his mother ; for no one can
follow his father's [status or] condition unless there has been
conubium between his father and mother.   But by the senatusconsult he is allowed to prove cause of error, whereby both
his wife and son attain to citizenship ; and from that moment
his son begins to be in his *potestas.*   And the same rule holds
if through ignorance he has married a woman from amongst
those who are accounted dediticians, except that she does not
68 become a Roman citizen.   So also if a woman who is a
Roman citizen has by mistake married a peregrin as if he

---

² About a line almost entirely illegible.   Bk. suggests—*sed si postea
causa probata ciuitatem Romanam
consecutus est pater,* which suits the
sense, and, with the usual contractions, suits the space.   The suggestions of K. u. S. and Hu. are
substantially the same.
§§ 67, 68.   Comp. §§ 26, 80 ; ii, 142 ;
iii, §§ 5, 73 ; Vlp. vii, 41.
¹ There is reason for thinking that
this Sct. is the same as referred to in

§§ 30, 80, 81, 92, and Vlp. iii, 3,
and in all of them attributed to
Hadrian—a comprehensive enactment regulating the birth-status of
children, and *inter alia* introducing
erroris causae probatio as a means
of improving it.   The fact that both
Hadrian and Antoninus Pius found
it necessary to explain it by rescripts (§§ 73, 74) argues for its then
recent enactment.

et ita filius quoque eius et maritus ad ciuitatem Romanam
perueniunt, et aeque simul incipit filius in potestate patris
esse.   idem iuris est si peregrino tamquam latino ex lege
Aelia Sentia nupta sit; nam et de hoc specialiter senatusconsulto cauetur.   idem iuris est aliquatenus si ei qui
dediticiorum numero est tamquam ciui Romano aut latino e
lege Aelia Sentia nupta sit, nisi quod scilicet qui dediticiorum
numero est in sua condicione permanet, et ideo filius, quamuis
fiat ciuis Romanus, in potestatem patris non redigitur.

69 Item si latina peregrino, cum eum latinum esse crederet,
nupserit, potest ex senatusconsulto *filio nato* causam erroris
probare, (*et ita*) omnes fiunt ciues Romani, et filius in potestate
70 patris esse incipit.   Idem constitutum est si latinus per
errorem peregrinam quasi latinam aut ciuem Romanam e lege
71 Aelia Sentia uxorem duxerit.   Praeterea si ciuis Romanus,
qui se credidisset latinum esse, ob id latinam [*duxerit*], permit-

---

also were a citizen, she is permitted to prove cause of error,
whereby both her son and her husband acquire the status of
citizens, the former beginning at the same time to be *in
potestate* of the latter.   The same is the case if she have
married a peregrin under the belief she was marrying a latin
in terms of the Aelia-Sentian law; this is a contingency
specially provided for in the senatusconsult.   And the same
is also to some extent the case if she have married a man
from the ranks of those reckoned as dediticians, believing him
to be either a Roman citizen or a latin privileged by the
Aelia-Sentian law; only here the quasi-deditician husband
retains his status, and his son, though becoming a Roman
69 citizen, does not pass into his *potestas*.   So likewise if a
latin woman have married a peregrin whom she believed to
be a latin, she may, under the senatusconsult, on the birth of
a son, prove cause of error, whereby all of them become
Roman citizens, and the son passes into the *potestas* of his
70 father.   Exactly the same is the rule where a latin has by
mistake married a peregrin woman, in the manner enjoined by
the Aelia-Sentian law, under the impression she was a latin
71 or a Roman citizen.   Further, if a Roman citizen, believing
himself to be a latin, have on that account married a latin

---

§ 71.   The statement in the first part of
the par. is unsatisfactory; for it was
not cause of error, but cause of
marriage that was shown by a latin
married in terms of the Aelia-

Sentian law.   It is this probably
that has led Hu. to make a transposition, and to read—*ob id latinam
tamquam e lege Aelia Sentia uxorem
duxerit, permittitur*, etc.

titur ei filio nato erroris causam probare, tamquam [*si*] e lege
Aelia Sentia uxorem duxisset. Item *his* qui, cum ciues
Romani essent, peregrinos se esse credidissent et peregrinas
uxores duxissent, permittitur ex senatusconsulto filio nato
causam erroris probare: quo facto *fiet* peregrina uxor ciuis
Romana et filius — —[1] non solum *ad ciuitatem Romanam*
72 peruenit sed etiam in potestatem patris redigitur. Quaecumque de filio esse diximus, eadem et de filia dicta intellege-
73 mus. Et quantum ad erroris causam probandam attinet,
nihil interest cuius aetatis filius sit *filiaue*, — — — —
— — —,[1] si minor anniculo sit filius filiaue, causa probari
non potest. nec me praeterit, in aliquo rescripto diui Hadriani
ita esse constitutum, tamquam quod ad erroris *quoque causam*
74 *probandam* — — — — — — —.[2] Si peregrinus ciuem
Romanam uxorem *duxerit an et is causam probare (possit)*

---

woman, he is allowed on the birth of a son to prove cause of
error, just as if he had married in terms of the Aelia-Sentian
law. He also who, being really a Roman citizen, but believing himself to be a peregrin, has married a peregrin woman,
is allowed by the senatusconsult, on the birth of a son, to
prove his cause of error; whereupon the peregrin wife becomes
a Roman citizen, and the son *born of the marriage* not only
attains to citizenship but passes into the *potestas* of his father.
72 Whatever has here been said of a son applies equally to a
73 daughter. As regards proving cause of error, it is immaterial what be the age of the child, [*the senatusconsult saying*
[*nothing on the subject; unless, indeed, the Aelia-Sentian law be*
[*founded on, and then*] proof of the marriage will not be allowed
if the son or daughter be less than a year old. I do not over-
look that, as if in reference to this matter of proving cause of
error, it is laid down in a rescript of Hadrian that — —
74 — — — — — —. *It is a question whether* a peregrin,
if he have married a woman that is a Roman citizen, *can
prove cause of error* — — — — — — — — —.

---

[1] Gou. fills the lacuna with *qui ex
ea natus est*, P. with *quoque statim*,
Hu. with *quoque ex ea*.
§ 72. Comp. § 29, note 3; Vlp. iii, 3.
§ 73. Comp. § 29.
   [1] Hu. fills the lacuna (two lines)
with—*cum senatusconsulto nihil de
ea re caueatur: nisi forte latinus
uel latina proponatur, quia etiam*

ex ipsa lege Aelia Sentia latini, si
minor, etc.
   [2] The same ed. fills this lacuna (last
three lines of p. 19) thus: *anniculum
filium factum necesse sit; sed non
semper uideri debet generale ius in-
ductum, cum* imperator *epistulam ad
quendam dedit.*
§ 74. Comp. § 68.

quaeritur. — — — — — — —[1] *hoc ei* specialiter concessum est. sed cum peregrinus ciuem Romanam uxorem
duxisset, et filio nato alias[2] ciuitatem Romanam consecutus esset, deinde cum quaereretur an causam probare
posset, rescripsit imperator Antoninus proinde posse eum
causam probare, 'atque si peregrinus mansisset.' ex quo
75 colligimus etiam peregrinum causam probare posse.   *Ex
iis* quae diximus apparet, siue ciuis Romanus peregrinam,
siue peregrinus ciuem Romanam uxorem duxerit, eum qui
nascitur peregrinum *esse.* sed *si* quidem per errorem *tale*
matrimonium contractum fuerit, emendari uitium eius [*licet*],
secundum ea[1] quae superius diximus; si uero nullus error
interuenerit, [*sed*] scientes condicionem suam ita coierint,
nullo casu emendatur *uitium eius matrimonii.*

76   *Loquimur* autem de his *scilicit* [*inter*] *quos conubium non*
sit.   Nam alioquin si ciuis Romanus peregrinam cum qua

But in the case of a peregrin who had taken a Roman citizen
to wife, and, after the birth of a son, had himself otherwise
become a citizen, when the question was raised whether he
could prove cause, our emperor Antonine decided by rescript
that he might, 'just as if he had continued to be a peregrin.'
From which latter observation we gather that even a peregrin
75 may prove cause.   From what has been said it is apparent
that, whether it be a Roman citizen that has taken a peregrin
wife, or a peregrin that has taken a Roman wife, the issue
will be a peregrin; but if such a marriage have been entered
into through mistake, the flaw in it may be removed in the
way that has been described. If, however, there have been
no error, but the parties have entered into the relationship in
knowledge of each other's condition, then in no case can the
defect of the marriage be remedied.
76   We have been speaking, of course, of persons between
whom *conubium* does not exist.   When, on the other hand, a

---

[1] Between two and three lines (p.
20) illegible. What Gai. seems to
have said is, that he was unable to
point to any enactment enabling a
peregrinus, the husband of a citizen
wife, himself to acquire citizenship
by showing error; but that, judging
from an expression of Antoninus
Pius' in one of his rescripts, it must
be held that such procedure was
competent. The only error, how-

ever, that he could plead was error
as to his own condition.
[2] Say by gift of citizenship from
the emperor; for this did not confer
the *potestas* unless expressly coupled
with the *ciuitas,* § 93; ii,185a; iii,20.
§ 75.   Comp. § 68.
[1] For *secundum ea* the ms. has *ex
clea*; K. u. S., *ex senatusconsulto
licet secundum ea.*
§ 76.   Comp. § 56.

ei conubium est uxorem duxerit, sicut supra quoque diximus,
iustum matrimonium contrahit, et tunc ex iis qui nascitur
77 ciuis Romanus est et in potestate patris erit.   *Item* si ciuis
Romana peregrino cum quo ei conubium *est nupserit*, peregrinus sane *procreatur, et is iustus patris* filius est[1] tamquam
si ex peregrina eum procreasset. (hoc tamen tempore, e
senatusconsulto quod auctore diuo Hadriano factum est,
etiam si non fuerit conubium inter ciuem Romanam et pere-
78 grinum, qui nascitur iustus patris filius est.)   Quod autem
diximus inter ciuem Romanam peregrinumque — — —

Roman citizen has married a peregrin woman with whom he
has *conubium*, it is, as we have already explained, a lawful
Roman marriage that is contracted, and the issue of it will be
77 a Roman citizen and in his father's *potestas*.   And so, if a
woman who is a Roman citizen has given herself in marriage
to a peregrin with whom she has *conubium*, the issue will be
a peregrin and the lawful child of his father, just as if his
mother had been a peregrin. (At the present day, however, in
virtue of a senatusconsult which we owe to the late emperor
Hadrian, the issue of a marriage between a Roman citizen
woman and a peregrin is held to be a lawful child of his
father even though there may not have been *conubium*
78 between the parents.)   Our statement that [*where a mar-
[riage has been contracted*] between a Roman citizen and a

§ 77. The latter half of this par. speaks
of the legality and validity of a marriage that was not *iustum matrimonium*; see references in notes to §§
55, 56.
    [1] It would appear that prior to the
passing of the senatusconsult there
was doubt as to the actual position
of a child in such a case as here put;
its purpose was to declare that if a
marriage had actually taken place
between hiscitizenmother and peregrin father, he was to be recognized
as hisfather'slawful son,the absence
of *conubium* notwithstanding.
§ 78. Comp. Vlp. v, 8. This par.,
which is in explanation of the opening statement in § 75, is to a considerable extent illegible; and there
is some reason to believe that the
transcriber has accidentally omitted
a few words. The first lacuna in the
text represents four lines of the MS.
(5-8 of p. 21), and the second, one

line (the 11th); but in both there
are several words perfectly distinct.
The reconstructions proposed severally by K. (K. u. S. footnote), M.
(K. u. S. p. xviii), and Hu. differ
very considerably, and none is altogether satisfactory; but probablythe
rendering in the translation pretty
accurately expresses the meaning of
the passage. Vlpian's words are—
*lex Minicia ex alterutro peregrino
natum deterioris parentis condicionem sequi iubet.*
    Prior to Studemund's recension
of the Verona MS. the *L. Minicia* here
referred to had always been spoken
of as *lex Mensia*; it is so called in
the Vatican MS. of Vlp. Its date is
unknown; but from next par. it
must have been of some antiquity,
and at all events anterior to the *leges
de ciuitate* of the years 664 | 90 and
665 | 89.

— — — — — peregrinus ex eo coitu nascatur. sed hoc
maxime casu necessaria *lex Minicia* [*fuit*]; *nam remota ea lege,*
— — — — — conubium, qui nascitur iure gentium matris
condicioni accedit. qua parte autem iubet lex ex ciue Romano
et peregrina peregrinum nasci, superuacua uidetur; nam et
79 remota ea lege *hoc utique* iure gentium futurum erat.   Adeo
autem hoc ita est ut — — — — — —[1] solum exterae
nationes *et gentes*, sed etiam qui Latini nominantur; sed ad
alios Latinos pertinet,[2] qui proprios populos propriasque ciui-
80 tates habebant et erant peregrinorum numero.   Eadem *ratione*

---

peregrin, the issue will be a peregrin, [*is made on the authority
[of the Minician law, according to which the child born of an
[unequal marriage*] follows the condition of the parent [*of lower
[status. For*] by that enactment [*it was provided that if, without
[*conubium, a Roman citizen took a peregrin to wife, or if a
[peregrin took to wife a Roman citizen,*] the issue of the marriage
should be accounted a peregrin. It was mainly to meet the
latter case that the Minician law was necessary; for in the
absence of such an enactment [*the child would have followed
[the condition of its mother; such is the rule of the ius* gentium
[*where there is marriage without* conubium]. That part of
the enactment, however, which declares that the child of a
Roman citizen and a peregrin woman shall be born a peregrin
seems superfluous; for this would be the case under the law
79 of nations irrespective altogether of the statute.   So far
does this go, that [*it is simply on the strength of the rule of the
[ius* gentium *that the child born of a marriage between a Roman
[citizen and a woman that is a Junian latin follows the condition
[of its mother. No doubt the word 'peregrin' in the Minician
[law has been held to include*] not only strictly foreign nations
and peoples, but also those who pass by the name of Latins;
but the allusion is to Latins of a different sort, who had their
own separate communities and separate states, and were
80 really included among the peregrins.   Conversely, and

---

§ 79. Comp. § 80; Vlp. v, §§ 8, 9.
[1] More than two lines totally illegible. The following probably expresses the sense of what is lost :—
Adeo autem hoc ita est, ut *etiam ex
ciue Romano et latina Iuniana qui
nascitur, ex solo iuris gentium regula,
matris condicioni accedat. Sane
'peregrinorum' appellatione in lege
Minicia conprehendi intellegebantur
non* solum exterae nationes, etc.
[2] The allusion is to the distinction

between the Junian latins, irregularly enfranchised freedmen, dwell-
ing alongside and under the patronage of Roman citizens, and the old
Latins of Italy and members of the
Latin colonies, who both formed
communities apart, and were members of their own *ciuitates.* See
upon this Vangerow, *die Latini
Iuniani,* p. 91; Voigt, *Ius. Nat.,*
etc., ii, p. 721; Gai. i, 131.
§ 80. Comp. § 30; Vlp. iii, 3.

ex contrario ex latino et ciue Romana, siue *ex lege Aelia Sentia*
siue *aliter contractum* fuerit matrimonium, ciuis Romanus
nascitur.   fuerunt tamen qui putauerunt ex lege Aelia Sentia
contracto matrimonio latinum nasci, quia uidetur eo casu
per legem Aeliam Sentiam et Iuniam conubium inter eos
dari, et semper conubium efficit[1] ut qui nascitur patris condicioni accedat; aliter uero contracto matrimonio, eum qui
nascitur iure gentium matris condicionem sequi, et ob id esse
ciuem Romanum.   sed hoc iure utimur, ex senatusconsulto[2]
quo auctore diuo Hadriano significatur, ut *quoquo modo*[3] ex

81 latino et ciue Romana natus, ciuis Romanus nascatur.   His
conuenienter et illud senatusconsultum, diuo Hadriano auctore,
significauit ut ex latino et peregrina, item contra ex peregrino
et latina [*qui*] nascitur, is matris condicionem sequatur.

82 Illud quoque his consequens est, quod ex ancilla et libero
iure gentium seruus nascitur, et contra ex libera et seruo

---

upon the same principle, the child of a [Junian] latin father
and Roman citizen mother is a Roman citizen, and that
whether the parents have married in accordance with the
Aelia-Sentian law or not.   Some, indeed, have thought that,
if the marriage had been contracted as enjoined by that enactment, the issue would be a latin, the Aelia-Sentian and
Junian laws apparently conceding right of intermarriage in
such a case to the parents, and the rule being that, where
there is *conubium*, the issue follows the condition of the
father; but that if the marriage had not been contracted
under the statute, the issue, according to the rule of the *ius
gentium*, would follow the condition of the mother, and thus
be a Roman citizen.   But we follow the rule laid down in
Hadrian's senatusconsult,—that, in whatever way their marriage may have been contracted, the issue of a latin husband

81 and a Roman citizen wife shall be a Roman citizen.   In
entire conformity with all that has been said above, this also
is laid down in the same senatusconsult,—that the child born
of a latin father and peregrin mother, or *vice versa*, follows the
condition of its mother.

82 Further, it follows from the rules we have been explaining
that, by the *ius gentium*, the issue of a slave mother and a
freeman is born a slave, while conversely the issue of a free

---

[1] Comp. § 56.
[2] See §§ 30, 67, 68, note 1; Vlp.
iii, 3.

[3] The ms. has merely *qm*; K. u. S.
have *omni modo*.
§ 82.   Comp. § 88; Vlp. v, 9.

83 liber nascitur.   Animaduertere tamen debemus ne iuris gentium regulam uel lex aliqua uel quod legis uicem optinet
84 aliquo casu commutauerit.   ecce enim ex senatusconsulto Claudiano poterat ciuis Romana, quae alieno seruo uolente domino eius coiit, ipsa ex pactione libera permanere sed seruum procreare; nam quod inter eam et dominum istius serui conuenerit eo senatusconsulto ratum esse iubetur.   sed postea diuus Hadrianus, iniquitate rei et inelegantia iuris motus, restituit iuris gentium regulam, ut cum ipsa mulier libera
85 permaneat, liberum pariat.   [*Item*] ex ancilla et libero poterant liberi nasci; nam ea lege cauetur, ut si quis cum aliena

---

83 woman and a slave is born free.   But we must be careful to see whether in any case this rule of the *ius gentium* may not have been altered by statute,—by some *lex* or other
84 enactment of equal effect.   Take the Claudian senatus-consult: under its provisions a Roman citizen woman cohabiting with another person's slave with the owner's consent, might, in virtue of agreement with the latter, herself retain her freedom, and yet give birth to a slave; for the senatusconsult declared that any such agreement between her and her slave-paramour's owner should be sustained as valid. But afterwards Hadrian, moved by the want of equity in the matter and the incongruity of the rule, re-established the priniciple of the *ius gentium*,—that if the woman herself remain free it will be to a freeman that she will give birth.
85 So also there might be free children born of a slave mother and a free father; for by the same enactment it was provided

§ 83.   Comp. Vlp. in fr. 24, D. *de statu hom.* (i, 5).

§ 84.   As regards the *S. C. Claudianum* generally, see §§ 91, 160; Tac. *Ann.* xiii, 53; Paul. ii, 21; tit. Th. C. *ad S. C. Claudian.* (iv, 11); tit. C. *de S. C. Claud. toll.* (vii, 24); tit. I. *de success. sublat.* (iii, 12).

§§ 85, 86.   Before the opening words of § 85, P. has *Ex contrario per legem* . . . , K. u. S. *Item per legem* . . . , and Hu. *Item e lege latina;* their idea being that the allusions in these two pars. are to some other enactmen, than the Claudian Sct.   I see no good reason for this view.   There is nothing very unusual in speaking of a Sct. as a *lex;* the Claudian law on the tutory of women, for example, was in fact a Sct., yet is always spoken of as *lex Claudia;* see § 157, note.   The conventional arrangement referred to in § 85 may quite well have been one of the provisions of the Claudian Sct., though not mentioned elsewhere; and the rule in the first part of § 86, which Gai. calls *pars eiusdem legis*, seems to be the same as is alluded to by Paul. ii, 21, § 14, and by him attributed to the Claudian Sct. The *apud quos talis lex non est* does not refer to the absence of local statute, but to the non-applicability of the particular provision of the Sct. immediately before alluded to, —slavery of the issue when the free mother *was aware of* the condition of the slave father.   Comp. § 89.

3

ancilla quam credebat liberam esse coierit, siquidem masculi
nascantur, liberi sint, si uero feminae, ad eum pertineant cuius
mater ancilla fuerit.   sed et in hac specie diuus Vespasianus,
inelegantia iuris motus, restituit iuris gentium regulam, ut
omni modo, etiamsi masculi nascantur, serui sint eius cuius
86 et mater fuerit.   Sed illa pars eiusdem legis salua est, ut.
ex libera et seruo alieno, quem sciebat seruum esse, serui
nascantur.   itaque apud quos talis lex non est, qui nascitur
iure gentium matris condicionem sequitur et ob id liber est.
87   Quibus autem casibus matris et non patris condicionem
sequitur qui nascitur, isdem casibus in potestate eum patris,
etiamsi is ciuis Romanus sit, non esse plus quam manifestum est; et ideo superius rettulimus quibusdam casibus
per errorem non iusto contracto matrimonio senatum interuenire et emendare uitium matrimonii, eoque modo plerumque
efficere ut in potestatem patris filius redigatur.
88   Sed si ancilla ex ciue Romano conceperit, deinde manu-

---

that if a freeman had cohabited with another person's slave,
believing her to be free, the male issue should be free, while
the female issue should belong to the owner of the slave
mother.   But here, again, Vespasian, struck by the absurdity
of the provision, interfered, and re-established the *iuris
gentium* rule, that, even if the issue of the connection were
males, they should be slaves of him to whom the mother
86 belonged.   This part of the enactment, however, is still in
force,—that the issue of a free woman and another person's
slave, of whose condition she was well aware, will be slave.
But in the case of parents to whom it does not apply, [*i.e.*
when the free mother is ignorant of the condition of the slave
father,] the issue, according to the *ius gentium*, follows the
condition of the mother and consequently is free.
87 It is abundantly manifest that, when a child follows not
his father's but his mother's condition, he cannot be in the
potestas of his father, even though the latter be a Roman
citizen; and therefore it is that we have above explained how,
in certain cases of marriage that through mistake has not been
contracted according to law, the senate has interfered to
remedy the defect, and thus almost always brought about the
result of putting the child born of it in his father's *potestas*.
88 But if a slave woman, who has conceived by a Roman

§ 87.   Comp. §§ 67 f.
§ 88.   Comp. §§ 55, 89 ; Vlp. in fr. 46, D. *de adopt.* (i, 7).

missa ciuis Romana facta sit, et tunc pariat, licet ciuis
Romanus sit qui nascitur, sicut pater eius, non tamen in
potestate patris est, quia neque ex iusto coitu conceptus est
neque ex ullo senatusconsulto talis coitus quasi iustus consti-
89 tuitur.   Quod autem placuit, si ancilla ex ciue Romano
conceperit, deinde manumissa pepererit, qui nascitur liberum
nasci, naturali ratione fit: nam hi qui illegitime concipiuntur
statum sumunt ex eo tempore quo nascuntur; itaque si ex
libera nascuntur, liberi fiunt, nec interest ex quo mater eos
conceperit cum ancilla fuerit: at hi qui legitime concipi-
90 untur ex conceptionis tempore statum sumunt.   itaque
si cui mulieri *ciui Romanae praegnati* aqua et igni interdictum fuerit,[1] eoque modo peregrina *facta* tunc pariat,
conplures distinguunt et putant, siquidem ex iustis nuptiis
conceperit ciuem Romanum ex ea nasci, si uero uulgo
91 conceperit peregrinum ex ea nasci.   Item si qua mulier
ciuis Romana praegnas ex senatusconsulto Claudiano ancilla

---

citizen, on subsequent manumission herself become a Roman
citizen, and then give birth to her child, although it will be
a citizen as its father is, yet it will not be in his *potestas*, for
it was not conceived in lawful intercourse, nor is there any
senatusconsult that deals with such intercourse as if it had
89 been lawful.   The rule that, if a slave woman conceive by
a Roman citizen but do not give birth to her child until after
manumission, the child will be free born, rests upon considerations of natural reason.   For children illegitimately conceived
take their status from the moment of birth, so that if born of
a free woman they are free, it being quite immaterial by
whom their mother conceived them in her slavery; but
children legitimately conceived date their status from the
90 moment of conception.   Therefore if a pregnant woman who
is a Roman citizen be interdicted fire and water, and, after thus
becoming a peregrin, give birth to a child, many draw a distinction, and hold that if she have conceived in lawful Roman
wedlock the child will be a Roman citizen, but that if she have
conceived in casual intercourse it will be born a peregrin.
91 So if a pregnant woman who is a Roman citizen become a
slave under the Claudian senatusconsult, because she has been

---

§ 89. Comp. Vlp. v, 10; Vlp. in fr. 24,
   D. *de statu hom.* (i, 5).
§ 90. Comp. § 161; Vlp. in fr. 18, D.
   de statu hom. (i, 5).

[1] See § 128, note 2.
§ 91. Comp. §§ 64, 160, and note to §
   84; Vlp. xi, 11; Paul. ii, 24, § 2;
   pr. tit. I. *de ingen.* (i, 4).

facta sit, ob id quod alieno seruo, inuito et denuntiante
domino eius, [*coierit*], *conplures distinguunt* et existimant,
si quidem ex iustis nuptiis conceptus sit, ciuem Romanum ex
ea nasci, si uero uulgo conceptus sit, *seruum* nasci eius cuius
92 mater facta *esset ancilla.*   Peregrina quoque si uulgo conceperit, deinde ciuis Romana *facta tunc pariat,* ciuem Romanum parit ; si uero ex peregrino secundum leges moresque
peregrinorum conceperit, ita uidetur ex senatusconsulto quod
auctore diuo Hadriano factum est ciuem Romanum parere,
si et patri eius ciuitas Romana donetur.

93   Si peregrinus sibi liberisque suis ciuitatem Romanam
petierit, *non aliter filii* in potestate eius fient quam si *imperator eos in potestatem* redegerit: quod ita demum is facit
si causa cognita aestimauerit hoc filiis expedire. diligentius
autem exactiusque causam cognoscit de inpuberibus absenti-
busque : et haec ita edicto diui Hadriani significantur.

94 Item si quis cum uxore praegnate ciuitate Romana donatus

---

cohabiting with another person's slave against the will and in
spite of the remonstrances of the slave's owner, many again
draw a distinction, and think that if she had conceived in
lawful Roman wedlock her child will be born a Roman citizen,
but that if she had conceived in illicit intercourse it will on
birth be the slave of him who has become the mother's owner.

92 If a peregrin woman who has conceived in illicit intercourse
afterwards become a Roman citizen, and then give birth to
her child, it will be of a Roman citizen that she is delivered ;
if, however, she have conceived by a peregrin according to the
laws and customs of peregrins, it appears from Hadrian's
senatusconsult that she will give birth to a Roman citizen
then only when the father also of the child has had a gift of
citizenship.

93   If a peregrin have petitioned for a grant of citizenship for
himself and his children, these will not be in his *potestas*
unless the emperor has expressly subjected them to it. This
he does only when, having investigated the whole circumstances, he considers it for their advantage ; and, as enjoined
in an edict of Hadrian's, the inquiry is to be all the more
careful and minute if the children be under puberty or absent
94 at the time.   Further, if a peregrin have obtained a gift of

§ 92. Comp. §§ 77, 94 ; also note to   § 93. Comp. § 55 ; ii, 135a ; iii, 20 ;
    §§ 67, 68.   Plin. *Paneg.* 37.
                                      § 94. Comp. §§ 92, 93.

sit, quamuis is qui nascitur, ut supra dixi, *ciuis* Romanus
sit, tamen in potestate patris non fit: idque subscriptione
diui Hadriani significatur.   qua de causa, qui intellegit
uxorem suam esse praegnatem, dum ciuitatem sibi et uxori
ab imperatore petit, simul ab eodem petere debet ut
95 eum qui natus erit in potestate sua habeat.   Alia causa
est eorum qui Latii iure cum liberis suis ad ciuitatem
Romanam perueniunt; nam horum in potestate fiunt liberi.
96 quod ius quibusdam peregrinis ciuitatibus datum est uel a
populo Romano uel a senatu uel a Caesare, — — — —

---

citizenship for himself and his pregnant wife, while, as already
said, the child when born will be a Roman citizen, yet he will
not be in his father's *potestas ;* so it is declared in a rescript
of our late emperor Hadrian's.   Consequently, in seeking from
the emperor a gift of citizenship for himself and his wife,he
should, if he knows her to be pregnant, at the same time ask
that he may have the child who may be born of her in his
95 *potestas.*   The case is different with those who by right of
latinity attain citizenship along with their children ; for their
96 children do become subject to their *potestas.*   This latinity
has been granted to some peregrin states either by the Roman
people, the senate, or the emperor, [*and is called the greater*

---

§§ 95, 96. One of the ways in which a
colonial or municipal latin might
acquire Roman citizenship was by
filling a municipal office for a certain
time ; it is to this that Pliny alludes
in the formula, *per Latium uenire
in ciuitatem (Paneg.* 37).

Studemund's revision of the
Verona ms. has established the fact,
which many had doubted, that of
this *Latium* or *ius Latii* there were
two varieties, a greater and a lesser.
But the distinction is not yet absolutely certain.

Filling up the lacuna as proposed
by K. u. S.—*Huius autem iuris
duae species sunt: nam,* etc.—the
difference in favour of the *maius
Latium,* so far as can be gathered
from the text, was that, in municipalities which enjoyed it, not only
the magistracy but also the de-
curionate was a stepping-stone to
citizenship. If this had really been
the distinction, there would have
been no occasion for Gai. to allude
to it; he is speaking not so much

of acquisition of citizenship as of
acquisition of the *patria potestas ;*
and it seems sufficiently obvious
that what he meant to point out
was, that sometimes, *but not always,*
this was a result of the *ius Latii.*

There is reason to believe that
sometimes not only did the magistrate or decurion himself become a
Roman citizen on termination of his
period of office, but his wife and
children became citizens along with
him, while in other cases he was
the sole beneficiary ; this depended
on the terms of the municipal
charter.   The first, in all probability, was technically *maius
Latium,*—what seems to have been
enjoyed by the municipality of Salpensa (see the *L. Salpensana,* c. 21,
Bruns, p. 120) ; the second technically *minus Latium.*

The lacuna in the text represents
about half a line of the ms.   P. suggests—*maiusque Latium adpellatur.
Nam* aut, etc. The same critic—
whose view is that the Verona ms.

aut maius est Latium aut minus : *maius est Latium cum et hi
qui* decuriones *leguntur, et ei* qui honorem aliquem aut magistratum gerunt, ciuitatem Romanam consecuntur; minus
Latium est cum hi tantum uel qui[1] magistratum uel honorem
gerunt ad ciuitatem Romanam perueniunt.   idque conpluribus epistulis principum significatur.

97   [*Non solum tamen naturales liberi, secundum ea quae*] diximus, in potestate nostra sunt, uerum et hi quos adoptamus.
98 Adoptio autem duobus modis fit, aut populi auctoritate, aut
99 imperio magistratus, ueluti praetoris.   Populi auctoritate
adoptamus eos qui sui iuris sunt : quae species adoptionis

[*latinity.   For*] latinity is either the greater or the lesser.
There is the greater latinity when those who are elected to
the office of decurions, or who fill some high office or magistracy, acquire Roman citizenship [*along with their parents,
[wives, and children*]; the lesser, when those who [*are appointed
[decurions, or*] hold a magisterial or other high office, themselves
alone attain to citizenship.   So it is stated in many imperial
epistles.

97   *It is not only our children by birth, however,* that are in our
potestas in the manner we have described, but those also whom
98 we adopt.   Adoption is effected in two ways,—either by
authority of the people, or by the *imperium* of a magistrate,
99 such as the praetor.   By authority of the people we adopt
those who are *sui iuris.*   This species of adoption is called

was copied from an older one written
in double columns, and consequently
in much shorter lines—is of opinion
that the copyist has accidentally
omitted two of those lines, and that
the text should read thus :— *Maius
est Latium cum et hi qui decuriones
leguntur, et ei qui honorem aliquem
aut magistratum gerunt, ciuitatem
Romanam [cum parentibus uxoribusque ac liberis] consecuntur; minus
Latium est cum hi tantum [ipsi qui
decuriones fiunt], uel qui magistratum uel honorem,* etc.

As the text stands there is no
appreciable difference between the
maius and *minus Latium.*   Polenaar's amended definition of the
former consists with cap. 21 of the
lex municipalis Salpensana (except
that this reads *coniugibusque* instead of *uxoribusque*), and corresponds exactly with the opinion
arrived at by Rudorff and Mommsen

before the Verona text had been
deciphered by Stud. as above.   See
Rudorff, *Disp. crit. de maiore ac
minore Latio* (Berol. 1860) ; Mommsen, *die Stadtrechte von Salpensa,*
etc., p. 405; Voigt, *Ius. Nat.* ii, 724.

[1] It is in favour of Polenaar's
conjecture, just referred to, that we
have in the MS. *cum hi tantum uel
qui magistratum,* etc., which Hu.
and K. u. S. think necessary to
amend, the former by transposing
the *uel qui,* the latter by deleting
the *uel* altogether.

§§ 97-107.   Comp. tit. I. *DE ADOPTIONI-
BVS* (i, 11).

§ 97.   Two lines blank in the MS.; on
the first (line 6, p. 26) are faint
traces of a rubric.   The passage in
ital. is supplied from pr. tit. I. afd.
Comp. Vlp. viii, 1.

§§ 98, 99.   § 1, tit. I. afd. Comp. Cic.
pro domo, xiii, 34; xxix, 77; Gell.
v, 19; Vlp. viii, §§ 2, 3.

dicitur adrogatio, quia et is qui adoptat rogatur, id est interrogatur, an uelit eum quem adoptaturus sit iustum sibi filium
esse ; et is qui adoptatur rogatur an id fieri patiatur ; et
populus rogatur an id fieri iubeat. imperio magistratus
adoptamus eos qui in potestate parentum sunt, siue primum
gradum liberorum optineant, qualis est filius et filia, siue
100 inferiorem, qualis est nepos neptis, pronepos proneptis.   Et
quidem illa adoptio quae per populum fit nusquam nisi Romae
fit ; at haec etiam in prouinciis apud praesides earum fieri
101 solet.   Item per populum feminae non adoptantur, nam id
magis placuit ; apud praetorem uero, uel in prouinciis apud
proconsulem legatumue,[1] etiam feminae solent adoptari.
102 Item inpuberem apud populum adoptari aliquando prohibitum est, aliquando permissum : nunc ex epistula optimi
imperatoris Antonini[1] quam scripsit pontificibus, si iusta
causa adoptionis esse uidebitur, cum quibusdam condicioni-
bus permissum est.   apud praetorem uero et in prouinciis

---

adrogation ; because both he who is adopting is asked, *rogatur*,
whether he will have as his lawful son him he is about to adopt,
and he who is being adopted is asked whether he submits, and
the people is asked whether it ordains that so it shall be.
By the *imperium* of a magistrate we adopt those who are in
the *potestas* of parents, whether they be to take the position of
descendants of the first degree, as son or daughter, or of a
more remote one, such as grandson or granddaughter, great-
100 grandson or great-granddaughter.   Note that that sort of
adoption which is effected by the vote of the people can proceed only in Rome ; but the latter may be effected even in
101 the provinces before the provincial governors.   Further,
women are never adopted by popular vote,—the general
opinion was against it ; but it is not uncommon for them to
be adopted before the praetor, or in the provinces before the
102 proconsul or legate.   Still further, adoption of a pupil
before the people has sometimes been forbidden, sometimes
allowed,—at present, according to a letter of our most excellent emperor Antonine, addressed to the pontiffs, if an adequate
cause be shown for it, it will be allowed on certain conditions ;

§ 100. Comp. Vlp. viii, 4.
§ 101. Comp. Gai. in fr. 21, D. *de
adopt.* (i, 7), where he says that
women might be adopted by imperial rescript.
    [1] The proconsuls were governors
of the popular or senatorial provinces, the legates, governors of the
imperial ones.
§ 102. Comp. Vlp. viii, 5 ; § 3, tit. I. afd.
    [1] Antoninus Pius, in whose reign
Gai. was writing this first book.

apud proconsulem legatumue cuiuscumque aetatis [*personas*] [2]
103 adoptare possumus.   Illud uero utriusque adoptionis commune est, quod et hi qui generare non possunt, quales
104 sunt spadones, adoptare possunt.   feminae uero nullo
modo adoptare possunt, quia ne quidem naturales liberos in
105 potestate habent.   Item siue quis per populum siue apud
praetorem uel apud praesidem prouinciae adoptauerit, potest
106 eundem alii in adoptionem dare.   Sed et illa quaestio, an
minor natu maiorem natu adoptare possit, utriusque adop-
107 tionis communis est.   Illud proprium est eius adoptionis
quae per populum fit, quod is qui liberos in potestate habet,
si se adrogandum dederit, non solum ipse potestati adrogatoris
subicitur, sed etiam liberi eius in eiusdem fiunt potestate
tamquam nepotes.

108   [*Nunc de his personis uideamus quae in manu nostra sunt.*

---

but we may adopt a person of any age before the praetor, or
103 in the provinces before the proconsul or legate.   On the
other hand, it is common to both species that those who are
unable to procreate of their bodies, such as eunuchs, may yet
104 adopt ;   but women cannot in either way, for they have not
105 their natural children in their *potestas*.   Further, whether
the adoption have proceeded before the people, or before the
praetor or a provincial governor, the adopter may give his
106 adopted child in adoption to a third party.   The question,
too, whether the younger in years can adopt the elder, is
107 common to both sorts of adoption.   But this result is
peculiar to that which proceeds before the people,—that if a
man who himself has children in his *potestas* give himself in
adrogation, not only does he himself become subject to the
potestas of the adrogator, but his children do so too in the
character of grandchildren.

108   *Let us now turn our attention to persons that are in our*

---

[2] Added by K. u. S.

§ 103.   § 9, tit. I. afd., where a distinction is made between natural and
artificial disability.   Comp. Vlp.
viii, 6.
§ 104.   Comp. Vlp. viii, 8a ; § 10, tit. I.
afd.
§ 105.   Comp. § 8, tit. I. afd.
§ 106.   The answer was in the negative.

See Cic. *pro domo*, xiii, 34 ; § 4,
tit. I. afd.
§ 107. § 11, tit. I. afd.' Comp. Vlp. viii, 8.
§ 108.   Two vacant lines (1 and 2 of p.
28) in the MS.; the first intended
probably for a rubric, and the
second to contain words such as
those in ital., suggested by Goesch.
and approved by all editors.

109 [*quod*] et ipsum ius proprium ciuium Romanorum est.   Sed
in potestate quidem et masculi et feminae esse solent; in
110 manum autem feminae tantum conueniunt.   Olim itaque
tribus modis in manum conueniebant, usu, farreo, coemptione.
111 Usu in manum conueniebat, quae anno continuo nupta
perseuerabat;[1] *nam uelut*[2] annua possessione usucapiebatur,[3]
in familiam uiri transibat, filiaeque locum optinebat.   itaque
lege duodecim tabularum cautum *est ut* si qua nollet eo modo
in manum mariti conuenire, *ea quotannis* trinoctio abesset atque
eo modo cuiusque anni [*usum*] interrumperet.   sed hoc totum
ius partim legibus sublatum est,[4] partim ipsa desuetudine
112 oblitteratum est.   Farreo in manum conueniunt per
quoddam genus sacrificii quod Ioui Farreo fit, in quo farreus
panis adhibetur: unde etiam confarreatio dicitur.   conplura
praeterea huius iuris ordinandi gratia cum certis et sollem-

---

manus, (*which* also is a right peculiar to Roman citizens).
109 Both males and females may be *in potestate*, but it is only
110 females that can be *in manu*.   Of old they used to pass
into this relationship either by use, confarreation, or co-
111 emption.   A woman passed *in manum* by use who, after
marriage, cohabited with her husband for a year continuously;
for she was usucapted, as it were, by a year's possession, and
so passed into her husband's family, and acquired in it the
position of a daughter.   Therefore it was provided by the law
of the Twelve Tables, that if a wife was unwilling in this way
to pass into the *manus* of her husband, she should every year
absent herself for three nights, and thus interrupt the currency
of each year's *use*.   But all the law in reference to this matter
is obsolete, being in part repealed by statute, in part obliterated
112 by disuse.   *Manus* is created *farreo* by a certain kind of
sacrifice offered to Jupiter Farreus, in which a spelt cake,
panis farreus, is employed; hence the word *confarreatio*.
Various other formalities are observed in the course of the

---

§ 110. Comp. Serv. *in Vergil. Georg.* i,
31 (Bruns, p. 299); Boeth. *in Cic.
Top.* ii, 3, § 14 (Bruns, p. 294).
§ 111. Comp. Cic. *pro Flacco*, xxxiv,
84; Gell. iii, 2, §§ 12, 13; Serv. as
in last note.
  [1] The ms. has *perseuerabant;* Pol.
perseuerantur [*in domo mariti com-
morabatur*].
  [2] The ms. has *nūn;* Husch. *quia
enim uelut;* K. u. S. *quae enim ueluti.*

[3] For the description of usucap-
tion, the cure of a defective right of
property by possession for a certain
period, see ii, §§ 41-44.
[4] Comp. Tac. *Ann.* iv, 16.
§ 112. Comp. § 136; Vlp. tit. ix;
Dion. Hal. ii, 25, 27, 30-32; Plin.
H. N. xviii, 3, § 10; Tac. *Ann.*
iv, 16, 53; Serv. *in Aen.* iv, 103,
374 (Bruns, p. 297); *in Georg.* i,
31 (Bruns, p. 299).

nibus uerbis, praesentibus decem testibus, aguntur et fiunt.
quod ius etiam nostris temporibus in usu est: nam flamines
maiores, id est Diales Martiales Quirinales, item *reges* sacrorum
nisi *ex* farreatis *nati non leguntur, ac ne* ipsi quidem *sine*
113 confarreatione *sacerdotium* habere possunt.   Coemptione
uero in manum conueniunt per mancipationem, *id est* per
quandam imaginariam uenditionem ; nam adhibitis non minus
quam v testibus ciuibus Romanis puberibus, item libripende,[1]
114 — — — —[2] cuius in manum conuenit.   Potest autem

ceremony, accompanied by certain solemn words of style, and
all in the presence of at least ten witnesses. The rite is
observed even to this day; for no person is elected to the
office of one of the greater flamens, *i.e.* a flamen of Jupiter,
Mars, or Quirinus, nor yet to be a *rex sacrorum*, unless born
of farreate parents; nor can any such person fill any such
priestly office unless he himself have been married by con-
113 farreation.   By coemption a woman passes into a man's
manus by means of a mancipation, *i.e.* a sort of imaginary
sale; for, in the presence of five Roman citizens of the age of
puberty, brought together as witnesses, as also of a balance-
holder, [*the man purchases*] with an *as* [*the woman he is receiving*
[in manum, *and reciprocally*] the woman purchases him whose
114 *manus* she is entering.   She can perform this coemption,

§ 113. Comp. § 123; Non. Marcell.
  xii, 50 (Bruns, p. 287); Serv. *in*
  Aen. iv, 103, 214 (Bruns, p. 297);
  Boeth. *in Cic. Top.* ii, 3, § 14
  (Bruns, p. 294); Isidor. *Orig.* v,
  24, § 26 (Bruns, p. 301).
  [1] On the function of the *libripens*
  or balance-holder, see below, § 119.
  [2] In what is here marked as a
  lacuna, the MS. has *a emit eum
  mulierem.* Gou. accepts it, rendering the initial *a* by *asse;* K. u. S.
  read simply *emit is mulierem.*
  Neither of these readings can well
  be accepted. They, as well as
  others that have been proposed,
  proceed on the assumption that the
  man was the party fictitiously purchasing the woman. But it is clear
  that they were both active agents in
  the matter; for while Gai. speaks
  of the man as *coemptionator* (§ 118),
  he refers to the woman as *quae facit
  coemptionem* (§§ 114, 115). Servius,
  Boethius, and Isidore, all speak of
  the *coemptio* as a reciprocal purchase, Non. Marcellus referring only
  to the purchase by the woman.

There is reason, therefore, to believe—as seems to be the opinion
of P., though he does not suggest
a reconstruction—that the copyist
has omitted some words describing
the transaction as a mutual one, and
that the original text may have been
to this effect—*asse emit uir mulierem
quam in manum recipit* (see ii, § 98),
et inuicem emit eum mulier cuius in
manum conuenit. This, so far, is
the view now adopted by Hu., who
in his last edition reads—asse emit
eum *mulier* et is *mulierem* cuius, etc.
  It is not to be lost sight of in
regard to the solemnities of coemp-
tions and mancipations generally,
that in early latin *emere* did not
mean to purchase for a money price,
but simply to take, receive, or acquire; see Fest. v. *Redemptores*
(Bruns, p. 259), Paul. ex Festo,
vv. *Abemito* and *Emere* (Bruns, pp.
236, 241).
§ 114. Comp. § 136 ; ii, §§ 139, 159. The
  transcriber has here been so careless
  that some parts of the par. are introduced no fewer than three times.

coemptionem facere mulier non solum cum marito suo sed
etiam cum extraneo; scilicet aut matrimonii causa facta coemptio dicitur, aut fiduciae causa : quae enim cum marito suo facit
coemptionem, [*ut*] apud eum filiae loco sit, dicitur matrimonii
causa fecisse coemptionem ; quae uero alterius rei causa facit
coemptionem aut cum uiro suo aut cum extraneo, ueluti tutelae
euitandae causa,[1] dicitur fiduciae causa fecisse coemptionem.

115 quod est tale : si qua uelit quos habet tutores deponere[1] et
alium nancisci, illis tutoribus [*auctoribus*][2] coemptionem
facit; deinde a coemptionatore remancipata ei cui ipsa uelit,
et ab eo uindicta manumissa, incipit eum habere *tutorem a quo
manumissa est;* qui tutor fiduciarius dicitur, *sicut* [*ex*] *inferi-*
115a *oribus*[3] *apparebit.*   Olim etiam *testamenti faciendi gratia*
fiduciaria fiebat coemptio ; tunc enim non aliter feminae testa-
menti faciendi ius habebant, exceptis quibusdam personis,
quam si coemptionem fecissent remancipataeque et manumissae fuissent.   sed hanc necessitatem coemptionis faciendae

---

however, not only with her husband, but even with a stranger,
—in other words, it may be performed either matrimonially or
fiduciarily : for she who performs it with her husband that
she may stand to him in the position of a daughter, is said to
do so for the sake of marriage ; whereas she who performs it,
whether with her husband or with a stranger, with some other
object in view, as, for instance, getting rid of a tutory, is said

115 to have done so for a fiduciary purpose.   It is managed
thus : if she wants to set aside her existing tutors and obtain
another in their stead, she performs coemption with *auctoritas*
of the former ; being then remancipated by her coemptionator
to a person of her own selection, and afterwards by this last
manumitted *vindicta.* she begins to have as her tutor him who
has manumitted her, and who, as we shall see hereafter, is

115a called her fiduciary tutor.   Fiduciary coemption was also
had recourse to of old to enable a woman to make a will ; for
then women, with a few exceptions, had not the right to
execute a testament unless they had performed coemption,
afterwards being remancipated, and finally manumitted.   But
the necessity for this coemption was abolished by the senate

---

[1] See § 115. As regards fiduciary coemption *testamenti faciendi gratia,*
see § 115a, and that *interimendorum
sacrorum causa* (not mentioned by
Gai.), Cic. *pro Mur.* xii, 27.
§ 115. Comp. §§ 118, 166, 195a; Fest.
v. *Remancipatam* (Bruns, p. 160).

[1] So K. u. S. and Hu.; the MS.
has *reponere.*
[2] K. u. S. change *tutoribus,* which
is in the MS., into *auctoribus.*
[3] So the MS.; K. u. S. substitute
inferius.
§ 115a. Comp. Liv. xxxix, 9.

ex auctoritate diui Hadriani senatus remisit;[1] — — — —.[2]

115b— — — — — —, nihilo minus filiae loco incipit esse : nam si omnino qualibet ex causa uxor in manu uiri sit, placuit eam filiae iura nancisci.

116   Superest ut exponamus quae personae in mancipio sint.
117   Omnes igitur liberorum personae, siue masculini siue feminini sexus, quae in potestate parentis sunt, mancipari ab hoc eodem modo possunt quo etiam serui mancipari possunt.
118   Idem iuris est in earum personis quae in manu sunt : nam feminae a coemptionatoribus eodem modo possunt — — — — — — — — apud coemptionatorem filiae loco sit — — nupta sit, tamen nihilo minus etiam quae ei nupta non sit, nec
118aob id filiae loco sit, ab eo mancipari possit.   [Sed] plerumque[1]

---

on the authority of our late emperor Hadrian; [and women [are now held to have ipso iure as much right in this matter
115b[as if they had gone through the old form.   But, observe, [that though a woman's coemption with her husband may be [intended to be only fiduciary], she nevertheless begins to stand to him in the position of a daughter ; for, no matter what the cause of a wife's being in the manus of her husband, it is held that she thereby acquires a daughter's rights.

116   We have yet to explain what persons are in mancipio.
117   Well, then, all children, whether male or female, that are in the potestas of a parent may be mancipated by him exactly
118   in the same way as slaves.   And so with persons in manu ; for women may be mancipated by their coemptioners in the same way [as are children by their parents ; and though she [alone] stands to her coemptionator in the position of a daughter who is married to him, yet none the less may one who is not married to him, and therefore not related to him
118aas a daughter, be mancipated by him.   But for the most

---

[1] Comp. ii, § 112.
[2] Hu. thus conjecturally fills up the lacuna :—censentur enim ipso iure feminae capite deminutae.
§ 115b. Hu. conjecturally fills up the lacuna as follows:—Si tamen mulier fiduciae causa cum uiro suo fecerit coemptionem, etc., K. u. S. agreeing as to all but the first three words. Comp. §§ 114, 118, 136 ; iii, 14.
§ 116. A vacant line in the MS. before this par.
§ 117. Comp. § 132.

§ 118. About a line and a half partially illegible ; and reason to believe that some words have been omitted per incuriam. Bk., followed almost literally by Hu., renders the passage thus—eodem modo possunt mancipari quo liberi a parente mancipantur ; adeo quidem ut quamuis ea sola apud coemptionatorem filiae loco sit quae ei nupta sit, etc. Comp. §§ 114, 115, 123, 127.
§ 118a. Comp. § 132.
[1] So Hu. and P. ; G. and K. u. S. prefer Plerumque uero tunc.

[*tum*] solum et a parentibus et a coemptionatoribus mancipantur, cum uelint parentes coemptionatoresque e suo iure eas
personas dimittere, sicut inferius euidentius apparebit.

119   Est autem mancipatio, ut supra quoque diximus, imaginaria
quaedam uenditio : quod et ipsum ius proprium ciuium
Romanorum est.   eaque res ita agitur : adhibitis non minus
quam quinque testibus ciuibus Romanis puberibus, et praeterea alio eiusdem condicionis qui libram aeneam teneat, qui
appellatur libripens, is qui mancipio accipit [1] rem [2] tenens ita
dicit : HVNC EGO HOMINEM EX IVRE QVIRITIVM MEVM ESSE AIO,
ISQVE MIHI EMPTVS [3] ESTO HOC AERE AENEAQVE LIBRA ; deinde
aere percutit libram, idque aes dat ei a quo mancipio accipit,[1]

120   quasi pretii loco.   Eo modo et seruiles et liberae personae
mancipantur ; animalia quoque quae mancipi sunt,[1] quo in

---

part parents and coemptionators proceed to mancipation only
when they wish to release from their right those who are
subject to it, as will appear more clearly in the sequel.

119   Now, mancipation, as already observed, is a sort of imaginary
sale ; and the right to make use of it is peculiar to Roman
citizens.   It is gone about thus : in the presence of not fewer
than five Roman citizens of the age of puberty, called together
as witnesses, and of another person of the same condition
holding a pair of copper scales, who is called a *libripens*, the
mancipee or party taking *mancipio*, having hold of the thing
that is being transferred, says,—' I say that this slave is mine
in quiritary right, and be he my purchase with this *as* and
these copper scales ; ' and thereupon he strikes the scales
with the coin, which he then gives to the mancipant or party
from whom the slave is being received, as if by way of price.

120   In this manner both slave and free persons are mancipated ;
as also such animals as are *mancipi*, among which are reckoned

§ 119.   Comp. § 113 ; Vlp. xix, §§ 3,
4 ; Th. i, 12, § 6 ; Boeth. *in Cic. Top.*
v, 28 (ed. Baiter, p. 322) ; Isidor.
Orig. v, 25, § 31 (Bruns, p. 302).
   [1] As regards the use in the translation of the words mancipee and
mancipant, as renderings respectively of *is qui mancipio accipit* and
ei a quo mancipium accipitur, it is
to be observed that it was usual to
say of the transferor *seruum mancipat*, and of the transferee *ei mancipatur ;* see § 132.
   [2] Bk., K. u. S., and Hu. read *aes
tenens*, and P. *stipem tenens.* The
reading *aes* is that given by Boeth-

ius, but the *rem* in the MS. is quite
distinct, and justified by Gai. i, 121,
Vlp. xix, 6, and Isidore as above.
The same phrase, *rem tenens*,
occurs in the formula of *in iure cessio*
in Gai. ii, 24, where again it is a
question of transfer of a slave.
   [3] On the early meaning of the word
emptus, see § 113, note 2.
§ 120.   Comp. ii, §§ 15, 17, 29, 31 ; Vlp.
xix, 1.
   [1] For a *resumé* of the various explanations that have been suggested
of the famous distinction between
res mancipi and *nec mancipi*, see
Danz, *Gesch. d. R. R.*, § 119.

numero habentur boues equi muli asini; item praedia tam
urbana quam rustica quae et ipsa mancipi sunt, qualia sunt
121 italica,[2] eodem modo solent mancipari.   In eo solo praediorum mancipatio a ceterorum mancipatione differt, quod personae seruiles et liberae, item animalia quae mancipi sunt,
nisi in praesentia [1] sint mancipari non possunt; adeo quidem
ut eum qui mancipio accipit adprehendere id ipsum quod
ei mancipio datur necesse sit; (unde etiam mancipatio
dicitur quia manu res capitur):[2] praedia uero absentia[3]
122 solent mancipari.   Ideo autem aes et libra adhibetur quia
olim aereis tantum nummis utebantur, et erant asses dupundii
semisses et quadrantes,[1] nec ullus aureus uel argenteus
nummus in usu erat, sicut ex lege XII tabularum intellegere

---

oxen, horses, mules, and asses.   Such immoveables likewise,
whether houses or lands, as are *mancipi*—and those are so
that are of italic right—are mancipated in the same way.
121 Mancipation of immoveables differs from other mancipations
in this respect only, that slave and free persons, as also
animals that are *mancipi*, cannot be mancipated unless they
be on the spot, it being necessary that the mancipee should
lay hold of the very thing which is being transferred to him
as a *mancipium*,—the ceremony gets the name of *mancipatio*
because the thing in question is taken with the hand,—
whereas immoveables are very often mancipated elsewhere.
122 The copper and scales are employed because formerly only
copper money was in use, the *as* namely, and the double, half,
and quarter *as*, no gold or silver coin being current; this we
gather from the law of the Twelve Tables.   The efficacy of

---

[2] *Praedia italica* were provincial
lands enjoying the same privileges
as lands in Italy (*ius italicum*) in
particular, that were capable of
being held in property on a perfect
Roman title (*ex iure Quiritium*), and
of being transferred by the forms of
conveyance of the *ius ciuile*. See
Savigny, *Z. f. g. RW.* v, 242, and
vi, 356; also *Verm. Schr.* i, 73.
§ 121.   Comp. Vlp. xix, 6; Isidor. *Orig.*
v, 25, § 31 (Bruns, p. 302).
[1] Comp. § 119; iv, 16.
[2] Comp. ii, 22; Varro *de L. L.*
vi, § 85.
[3] Comp. iv, 17.
§ 122.   The two first blanks are variously
supplied.   The sentence containing

them, according to K. u. S., may
have run thus—sed in pondere
posita; nam et asses librales erant,
et dupundii *bilibres;* unde, etc. Hu.
has—sed in pondere; *namque ueluti*
asses librales erant, et dupundii *dua-*
rum librarum; unde, etc. In the
third blank, which represents rather
more than half a line of the MS.,
Bk. reads—*item qui dabat olim;* but
Stud. says this is not justified by
what is still legible. Hu. suggests
—*tunc igitur et* qui dabat *alicui,* etc.
Comp. Varro *de L. L.* v, §§ 169,
170; Plin. *H. N.* xxxiii, 3, § 13.
[1] The words *et erant asses . . .*
quadrantes are dropped by P. as a
gloss.

possumus: eorumque nummorum uis et potestas non in numero erat sed in pondere — — — asses librales erant, et dupundii — — —; unde etiam dupundius dictus *est quasi* duo pondo, quod nomen adhuc in usu retinetur. semisses quoque et quadrantes pro rata scilicet portione ad pondus examinati erant.— — — *pecuniam, non* adnumerabat eam, sed appendebat; unde serui quibus permittitur administratio pecuniae, dispensatores appellati sunt et *adhuc uocantur.*

123   — — — — — — — — mancipati mancipataeue seruorum loco constituuntur, adeo quidem, ut ab eo cuius in mancipio sunt, neque hereditatem neque legata aliter capere possint quam si simul eodem testamento liberi esse iubeantur, sicut iuris est in persona seruorum. sed differentiae ratio manifesta est, cum a parentibus et a coemptionatoribus iisdem uerbis mancipio accipiantur quibus serui; quod non similiter fit in coemptione.

---

such copper money depended not on number but on weight. The *asses* weighed each a pound, and the double *as* [*two* [*pounds*]—the word *dupundius*, which is still in use, means *duo pondo;* while the half and quarter *as* were of a weight carefully proportioned to the pound. [*In those times those who* [*had to pay*] money did not count but weigh it; whence those slaves who had charge of their owner's money were, and still are, called dispensers.

123   [*If it be asked wherein consists the difference between a woman* [*who has performed coemption and persons mancipated by parents* [*or coemptionators, our answer is that whereas the former retains* [*her freedom*], the latter are really in the position of slaves; so much so that, like these last, they cannot take either an inheritance or a legacy from him who holds them *in mancipio*, unless by the same testament he has given them their freedom. The reason of the difference is manifest: persons mancipated by parents and coemptionators are appropriated by the mancipee with the very same words with which he would appropriate a slave; but the words are different in coemption.

§ 123. Four lines of the MS. (19-22, p. 32) in great part illegible. Stud. declares his inability to trace several words and letters which appeared decipherable to G. and Bl.; and none of the many readings suggested can be accepted. It is evident, however, that it was the purpose of the par. to indicate the difference in effect of the mancipation involved in *coemptio* and the mancipation by a parent or *coemptionator;* the former placed the woman so emancipated in the position of a daughter, while the latter put her in the position of a slave. Comp. ii, §§ 159, 160.

124   Videamus nunc quo modo hi qui alieno iuri subiecti sunt eo iure liberentur.

125   Ac prius de his dispiciamus qui in potestate sunt.   Et
126   quidem serui quemadmodum potestate liberentur, *ex his intellegere* possumus quae de seruis manumittendis superius
127   exposuimus.   Hi uero qui (*in potestate*) *parentis sunt,* (*mortuo (eo sui iuris fiunt. sed hoc*) distinctionem recipit; nam (*mortuo (patre sane*) omni modo filii filiaeue sui iuris efficiuntur; mortuo uero auo (*non omni modo nepotes neptesque sui iuris (fiunt, sed ita si post mortem aui*) in patris sui potestatem recasuri non (*sunt. itaque*) si *moriente auo* (*pater eorum et (uiuat et in potestate*) patris [*sui*] fuerit, *tunc post* (*obitum aui in (patris*) sui potestate *fiunt ; si uero is, quo tempore auus* moritur, aut iam (*mortuus est aut*) *exiit de potestate* [*patris, tunc hi, quia [in potestatem*][1] eius cadere non possunt, sui iuris fiunt.
128   Cum autem is cui ob aliquod maleficium ex lege, [*uelut ex*

---

124   Let us see now how those who are subject to another person's right may be released from it.

125   And let us deal first with those that are *in potestate.*   How
126   slaves are freed from the *potestas* [of owners] may be understood from what has already been said on the subject of their
127   manumission.   As for those who are in the *potestas* of a parent, *they become their own masters, sui iuris, on his death.* But there is this distinction,—that while, *by the death of their father,* sons and daughters invariably become *sui iuris, grandchildren,* on the death of their grandfather, *do not in every case become so, but only when by that event* they do not fall under the *potestas* of their father.   Accordingly, if on the death of their grandfather *their father be alive, and have been till that moment in the* potestas of his father, the grandchildren, after *the death of the latter,* are in the *potestas* of their father; but if, at the time of their grandfather's death, their father either be already *dead* or have passed out of the *potestas* of *his father, the grandchildren, because they cannot pass into the* potestas *of*
128   *their father,* become *sui iuris.*   Then again, as a person who, on account of crime and in terms of [*some such enact-*

---

§§ 124-135. Comp. tit. I. QVIBVS MODIS IVS POTESTATIS SOLVITVR (i, 12).
§ 124.   Pr. tit. I. afd.
§ 126.   Comp. §§ 13-47.
§ 127.   Pr. tit. I. afd., from which most of the words in italics within paren-
theses, illegible in the text, are borrowed.   Comp. Vlp. x, 2.
   [1] Words omitted in the MS. and supplied from the Inst.
§ 128.   Comp. Vlp. x, 3; § 1, tit. I. afd.

[*lege*]¹ Cornelia, aqua et igni interdicitur² ciuitatem Romanam amittat, sequitur ut quia eo modo ex numero ciuium Romanorum tollitur, proinde ac mortuo eo desinant liberi in potestate eius esse : nec enim ratio patitur ut peregrinae condicionis homo ciuem Romanum in potestate habeat. pari ratione et si ei qui in potestate parentis sit aqua et igni interdictum fuerit, desinit in potestate parentis esse, quia aeque ratio non patitur ut peregrinae condicionis homo in potestate sit ciuis Romani parentis.

129   Quodsi ab hostibus captus fuerit parens, quamuis seruus hostium fiat, tamen pendet ius liberorum propter ius postliminii, *quo* hi qui ab hostibus capti sunt, si reuersi fuerint, omnia pristina iura recipiunt; itaque reuersus habebit liberos in potestate: si uero illic mortuus sit, erunt quidem liberi sui iuris; sed utrum ex hoc tempore quo mortuus est apud hostes parens, an ex illo quo ab hostibus captus est, dubitari potest. ipse quoque filius neposue si ab

---

[*ment as*] the Cornelian law, has been interdicted fire and water, forfeits his civic privileges, it follows that, as he is thus removed from the ranks of the citizens of Rome, his children cease to be in his *potestas* exactly as if he were dead ; for it would be contrary to all principle to admit that a man of peregrin condition can have a Roman citizen in his *potestas*. In like manner, if a person who is in the *potestas* of a parent be interdicted fire and water, he ceases to be *in potestate ;* for it is equally against principle that a man of peregrin condition should be in the *potestas* of a parent who is a Roman citizen.

129   But if a parent be taken captive by an enemy, although for the time he becomes a slave in the enemy's hands, yet his right over his children is merely suspended, and that on account of the *ius postliminii*, whereby those captured by an enemy resume all their old rights on recrossing the frontier ; on his return he will again have his children in his *potestas*. If, however, he die in captivity, his children will be *sui iuris ;* but whether as from the time of his death in captivity, or as from that of his capture, may be a matter of doubt. In like manner, if a son or grandson be taken captive,

---

¹ The words *uelut ex lege* interjected by Hn. ; for there were several Cornelian laws, as well as other penal statutes, that imposed the penalty of interdiction of fire and water. The particular one referred to may have been the *L. Cornelia de sicariis*.

² This was originally done by a

popular decree excommunicating and forbidding shelter to an individual who had voluntarily become an exile in order to avoid punishment, Cic. *pro domo*, xxx, 78 ; but in course of time it was a sentence judicially pronounced upon a criminal, depriving him of his status as a citizen.

§ 129. § 5, tit. I. afd. Comp. Vlp. x, 4.

4

hostibus captus fuerit, similiter dicemus propter ius post-
130 liminii potestatem quoque parentis in suspenso esse.   Praeterea exeunt liberi uirilis sexus de parentis potestate si
flamines Diales inaugurentur, et feminini sexus si uirgines
131 Vestales capiantur.   Olim quoque quo tempore populus
Romanus in Latinas regiones colonias deducebat, qui iussu
parentis in *coloniam Latinam* nomen dedissent, (*desinebant in
(potestate*)[1] parentis esse, quia efficerentur alterius ciuitatis ciues.
132   (*Praeterea*) emancipatione desinunt liberi in potestate
parentium esse.   sed filius quidem tribus mancipationibus,
ceteri uero liberi, siue masculini sexus siue feminini, una
mancipatione exeunt de parentum potestate : lex enim XII
tabularum tantum in persona filii de tribus mancipationibus
loquitur his uerbis : ' si pater filium [*ter*] uenumduit, a patre
filius liber esto.' (*eaque*) res ita agitur : mancipat pater

the *potestas* of his parent will be suspended by reason of the
130 same *ius postliminii*.   Further, children of the male sex
pass out of the *potestas* of a parent on inauguration as flamens
of Jupiter, and those of the female sex on their being taken
131 as Vestal virgins.   Formerly also, in the days when Rome
was in the habit of despatching bands of colonists into latin
districts, a child who with his parent's authority enrolled his
name in such a band, *ceased to be in that parent's* potestas,
because he had become a citizen of another state.
132   There is yet another way in which children cease to be in
the *potestas* of parents, namely, by emancipation. A son indeed
does so only after three mancipations; but as for other
children, whether males or females, their exit from the *potestas*
is accomplished by one : for the law in the Twelve Tables—
' if a father have *thrice* sold his son, then be the son free from
his father '—speaks of three mancipations only in the case of a
son.   It is managed thus : the father mancipates his son to a

§ 130.   Comp. § 145; iii, 114; Vlp. x, 5.
§ 131.   Comp. iii, 56; Cic. *pro Caec.*
xxxiii, 98; *pro domo*, xxx, 78;
Boeth. *in Top.* ii, 4, § 18 (ed. Bait.
p. 302).
  [1] These words are illegible, but
self-evident.
§ 132. A vacant line in the MS. before
this par., and the initial word (borrowed from the Inst.) unwritten.
Comp. § 135; ii, 141; iv, 79; Epit.
i, 6, § 3; Vlp. x, 1; § 6, tit. I. afd.;
Th. i, 12, § 6. The last few lines of
the par. are thus completed by Hu.

—isque eum postea similiter *uindicta manumittit, quo facto, eum rursus
in potestatem patris fuerit reuersus,*
tertio pater eum mancipat uel eidem
uel alii—sed hoc in usu est, ut eidem mancipetur—*eaque mancipatione desinit in potestate patris esse,
ac si nondum manumissus sit, sed
adhuc in causa mancipii apud eum
cui mancipatus est.   a quo si rursus
manumittatur, sui iuris fit.* Restitutions by other eds. are to much the
same effect. See the form of mancipation in § 119.

filium alicui ; is eum uindicta manumittit ; eo facto reuertitur
in potestatem patris ; is eum iterum mancipat uel eidem uel
alii, (sed in usu est eidem mancipari,) isque *eum* postea
similiter -- — — — in potestatem — — — —
tertio pater eum mancipat uel eidem uel alii, (sed hoc in usu
est ut eidem mancipetur,) — — — — ac si nondum manumissus sit, sed adhuc in causa mancipii. — — — — —

133 — — — — — —.   [133 *a*] — — — — — —.

third party ; the latter manumits him *vindicta ;* thereupon he
falls again into his father's *potestas ;* the father again mancipates him either to the same person as before or to a different
one,—it is the usual practice to mancipate to the same,—who
again in like manner *manumits him* vindicta, *whereupon he
once more returns* into the *potestas* of his father ; then a third
time his father mancipates him either to the same person or
to another,—but our practice is again to mancipate to the
same,—*and by this last mancipation he ceases to be in the
potestas of his father,* though not yet manumitted, but still
in the position of a *mancipium [in the hands of the individual
[to whom he has been mancipated ; but if he be once again
133 [manumitted by the latter, he then becomes* sui iuris. *There-
[fore, when the son has been mancipated the third time, his father
[ought to take· care that the mancipee remancipates to him,* i.e.
[the father, that so he may become the manumitter, and thus, in
[the event of his son's death, be entitled, rather than the mancipee,
133a[to his succession.   Females and grandsons by a son pass out
[of the* potestas *of their father or grandfather, and become* sui
[iuris, *by one mancipation.   But though this be the case, yet
[unless they have been remancipated by the mancipee to their
[father or grandfather, and by him manumitted, he, the father
[or grandfather, will not be entitled to succeed to them ; if, how-
[ever, he be their manumitter after remancipation, he will be
133b[entitled to their succession.]   We must keep in mind that it*

§§ 133, 133a. Of page 36 of the ms. not
more than three or four words are
legible.   It probably contained at
greater length what we find thus
stated in the Epit. i, 6, § 3—*Tamen
cum tertio mancipatus fuerit filius a
patre naturali fiduciario patri, hoc
agere debet naturalis pater, ut ei a
fiduciario patre remancipetur et a
naturali patre manumittatur, ut si
filius ille mortuus fuerit, ei in hereditate naturalis pater, non fiduciarius, succedat.   Feminae uel nepotes
masculi ex filio una emancipatione de
patris uel aui exeunt potestate et sui
iuris efficiuntur.   Et hi ipsi, quam-
libet una mancipatione de patris uel
aui potestate exeant, nisi a patre
fiduciario remancipati fuerint et a
naturali patre manumissi, succedere
eis naturalis pater non potest, nisi
fiduciarius a quo manumissi sunt.
Nam si remancipatum eum sibi naturalis pater uel auus manumiserit,
ipse eis in hereditate succedit.* Comp.
last sentence of § 6, tit. I. afd.
§ 133b.   None of what is borrowed from
the Inst. and printed under this

133*b*(*Admonendi autem sumus liberum arbitrium esse ei qui filium*
(*et ex eo nepotem in potestate habebit, filium quidem potestate*
(*dimittere, nepotem uero in potestate retinere : uel ex diuerso*
(*filium quidem in potestate retinere, nepotem uero manumittere,*
(*uel omnes sui iuris efficere.   eadem et de pronepote dicta esse*
(*intellegemus.*)

134   — — — — — — — et duae intercedentes manumissiones proinde fiunt, ac fieri solent cum ita eum pater
de potestate dimittit ut sui iuris efficiatur.   deinde aut patri
remancipatur, et ab eo is qui adoptat uindicat apud praetorem [1]
filium suum esse, et illo contra non uindicante a praetore
uindicanti filius addicitur; aut non remancipatur patri, *sed
ab eo uindicat is qui adoptat* (*apud quem in tertia*) [2] mancipatione est : sed sane commodius est patri remancipari.   in
ceteris uero liberorum personis, seu masculini seu feminini

---

*is in the option of a man who has at the same time a son and a
grandson by that son in his* potestas, *to release the son from it
but retain the grandson ; or he may retain his son in it, releasing
his grandson ; or he may make both* sui iuris. *And the same
observation applies to the case of a great-grandson.*

134   [*Then again, parents cease to have in their* potestas *those of
[their children whom they have given in adoption.   In the case
[of a son who is being given in adoption, three mancipations*] and
two intermediate manumissions are carried through, just as
when he is being dismissed from his father's *potestas* in order
that he may become *sui iuris.*   Then either he is remancipated
to his father, and from him vindicated by the adopter before
the praetor, who adjudges him to the adopter in the event of
the father asserting no counter-vindication; or else, without
any remancipation to his father, he is vindicated by the
adopter directly from the party *in whose* ius *he is in virtue of
the third* mancipation : but it is certainly more convenient
that he be remancipated to his father.   As regards other
descendants than sons, no matter whether male or female, one

---

number, is legible in the MS.   But,
from fr. 28, D. *de adopt.* (i, 7),
we know it to have been taken
from the first book of Gai., and,
judging from the Epit., this seems
its proper place.   Comp. Epit. i, 6,
§ 3 ; § 7, tit. I. afd.
§ 134.   The commencement of this par.
is on p. 36, and illegible.   Goesch.
and Husch. supply it as follows :—

*Praeterea parentes etiam liberos in
adoptionem datos in potestate habere
desinunt.   et in filio quidem, si in
adoptionem datur, tres mancipationes* et duae, etc.   As regards the
par. generally, comp. § 8, tit. I. afd.
[1] The *uindicatio* referred to is the
procedure by *in iure cessio,* described
below, ii, 24.
[2] So rendered by all recent eds.

sexus, una scilicet mancipatio sufficit, et aut remancipantur parenti aut non remancipantur. Eadem et in prouinciis apud
135 praesidem prouinciae solent fieri. Qui et filio semel iterumue mancipato conceptus est, licet post tertiam mancipationem patris sui nascatur, tamen in aui potestate est, et ideo ab eo et emancipari et in adoptionem dari potest. at is qui ex eo filio conceptus est qui in tertia mancipatione est, non nascitur in aui potestate : sed eum Labeo[1] quidem existimat in eiusdem mancipio esse cuius et pater sit : utimur autem hoc iure, ut quamdiu pater eius in mancipio sit, pendeat ius eius ; et si quidem pater eius ex mancipatione manumissus erit, cadat in eius potestatem ; si uero is dum in mancipio sit decesserit,
135a sui iuris fiat. Eadem scilicet — — — — — — —;
nam, ut supra diximus, quod in filio faciunt tres mancipationes,
136 hoc facit una mancipatio in nepote. [136] — — — — —

---

mancipation is sufficient, which may or may not be followed by remancipation to the parent. The same process is gone
135 through in the provinces before the governor. A child begotten by a son after his first or second mancipation, even though he be not born till after the third, is nevertheless in the *potestas* of his grandfather, by whom consequently he may be emancipated or given in adoption. But one begotten after the son's third mancipation is not born in his grandfather's *potestas*. According to Labeo, he is *in mancipio* of the person to whom his father has been mancipated : but our rule is that so long as his father continues *in mancipio* the child's status is in suspense ; if the former be manumitted from *mancipium*, the latter will fall under his *potestas*, but if he die *in mancipio*
135a the child will be *sui iuris*. [*The same rule applies to the case* [*of a great-grandson by a grandson, though the latter has been* [*mancipated only once ;*] for, as already said, the same results that follow three mancipations of a son follow one mancipa-
136 tion of a grandson. [*The fact that a woman has passed* in [manum *does not as a matter of course release her from her* [*father's* potestas, *unless she have performed coemption ; for by a* [*senatusconsult in reference to the wife of the flamen of Jupiter,*

§ 135. Comp. §§ 89, 182; § 9, tit. I. afd.
[1] See § 196, note 1.
§ 135a. More than a line and a half (p. 38, ll. 2, 3) illegible. The text may have run to this effect—Eadem scilicet *intellegerc debemus de pronepote ex nepote nato, licet nepos*

semel tantum mancipatus fuerit ; nam, etc.
§ 136. In the outset nearly three lines (p. 38, ll. 6-8) are illegible; in the middle rather more than a line (l. 12). To fill the first blank Hu. suggests —*Mulier eo quod in manum conuenit, nisi coemptionem* fecerit, *pa-*

Maximi et Tuberonis *cautum est, ut haec quod ad* sacra
tantum uideatur in manu esse, quod uero ad ceteras *causas*
proinde habeatur atque si in manum non *conuenisset.* — —
— — — — — — potestate parentis liberantur ; nec interest an in uiri sui manu sint an extranei, quamuis hae solae
loco filiarum habeantur quae in uiri manu sunt.

137   — — — — — —.   [137a] (*Sed et remancipatione*)

[*passed at the instance of*] Maximus and Tubero, it was enacted
that she should be regarded as *in manu* only as concerned the
sacra, but that to all other intents she should be held as if
she had not passed *in manum* at all.   [*Those, however, who pass*
[in manum *by coemption are thereby*] freed from their parent's
potestas ; nor does it matter whether they be in the *manus* of
husbands or strangers, (although she only is in the position of
a daughter who is *in manu* of her husband).

137   [*Women* in manu *are liberated therefrom in the same ways*
[*as a daughter is freed from the* potestas, *namely, by the death*
[*of those in whose* manus *they are, or by their being interdicted*
137a[*fire and water.*]   *By remancipation also they cease to be in*

*rentis potestate hodie liberatur ; nam
de flaminica Diali lege Asinia Antistia ex auctoritate Cornelii* Maximi, etc.

To justify this reading Hu. relies
chiefly on Tac. *Ann.* iv, 16. Tac.
relates that Tiberius, having experienced difficulty in filling up the
office of *flamen Dialis,* through a
paucity of persons qualified by farreate birth (see Gai. i, 112), induced
the senate, in the year 776 | 28, to
pass a law to the intent set forth
above. To this enactment, which,
judging from the language of Tac.,
must have been a senatusconsult,
Hu., at his own hand, gives the
name of *L. Asinia Antistia,* from
the two consuls of the year; adding
(to make his conjecture correspond
with the mention of Maximus and
Tubero in the ms.) that it had originally been recommended by Cornelius
Maximus and (Q. Aelius) Tubero,
two celebrated jurists of the end of
the republic, but hardly contemporaries.

But Augustus had previously dealt
with the matter; so Tac. himself
mentions in the passage above referred to. The occasion was the re-
establishment of the office of *flamen
Dialis,* long in abeyance. This was

in the year 743 | 11; see Dio Cass.
liv, 27, Suet. *Aug.* 31. The consuls
of that year were Q. Ael. Tubero and
Paulus Fabius Maximus. We are
therefore fairly entitled to assume
that as Augustus did in fact do
something to (as Tac. puts it) adapt
the old confarreation to modern
ideas,—that as he certainly was
dealing with the position of the
flamen Dialis in the year 743, and
that as the consuls of that year were
a Maximus and a Tubero,—the reference in Gai. is to them; see Karlowa, *die Roem. Ehe* (Bonn, 1868),
p. 42.   Hence I prefer something
like this—*nam senatusconsulto de
flaminica Diali* (Gai. i, 112, last
clause) *facto, ex auctoritate* Maximi,
etc.

The second lacuna Hu. supplies
with the words—*eae uero mulieres,
quae in manum conueniunt per coemptionem,* potestate, etc. This probably represents accurately the
meaning of the words that are
awanting.

§§ 137, 137a. Here apparently was introduced an account of the ways of
ending the *manus.* The first three
and a quarter lines (p. 12, ll. 16-19)
of the passage are illegible, and so
are three and a half (with exception

137*a* desinunt in manu esse; et si ex ea mancipatione manumissae
fuerint, sui iuris efficiuntur. — — — — — —
nihilo magis potest cogere, quam et filia patrem. sed filia
quidem nullo modo patrem potest cogere, etiam si adoptiua
sit: haec autem [*uirum*] repudio misso proinde compellere
potest atque si ei nunquam nupta fuisset.

138   Ii qui in causa mancipii sunt, quia seruorum loco habentur,
139 uindicta, censu, testamento manumissi sui iuris fiunt.   Nec
tamen in hoc casu lex Aelia Sentia locum habet: itaque
nihil requirimus cuius aetatis sit is qui manumittit et qui
manumittitur; ac ne illud quidem an patronum creditoremue
manumissor habeat. ac ne numerus quidem legis Fufiae
140 Caniniae finitus in his personis locum habet.   Quin etiam

---

manu; and on manumission after remancipation become *sui
iuris.* [*But between the woman who has performed coemption
[with a stranger and her who has performed it with her
[husband there is this difference,—that the former may compel
[her coemptionator to remancipate her to any one she pleases,
[whereas the latter] can no more compel her husband to do so
than can a daughter compel her father to emancipate her.   A
daughter can never do this, even though she be only an adoptive one; but a wife, who has had a writing of divorce sent to
her, may compel her husband to free her from the *manus,* as
if she had never been married to him.

138   Those in the position of *mancipia,* being regarded as if they
were slaves, become *sui iuris* on their manumission either
uindicta, or through the medium of the census, or by testa-
139 ment.   But in their case the Aelia-Sentian law does not
apply; therefore it is unnecessary to inquire as to the age
either of the manumitter or the manumitted, or whether the
.   manumitter has a patron or creditors; and such persons are
not affected by the limitations of the Fufia-Caninian law as
to the number [of persons an individual may manumit].
140 Moreover, they may obtain their freedom by means of the

---

of the words *cogere coemptionatorem*)
in the middle of it (ll. 21-24). To
supply the first blank, Hu. suggests
—*Feminae quae in manu sunt similiter eo iure liberantur atque filiae
quae in potestate sunt, uelut morte
eius cuius in manu sunt, siue ei aqua
et igni interdictum fuerit. Sed et
remancipatione,* etc. To supply the
second, K. u. S. suggest—*Inter eam
uero quae cum extraneo, et eam
quae cum uiro suo coemptionem*

*fecerit, hoc interest, quod illa quidem
cogere coemptionatorem potest ut se
remancipat cui ipsa uelit, haec autem uirum suum* nihilo magis, etc.
Both those restitutions probably
fairly represent the import of the
illegible lines. Comp. § 118.

§ 138. Comp. §§ 17 (notes), 123; ii, 160;
iii, 114.
§ 189. Comp. §§ 18, 37, 38, 42-47.
§ 140. Comp. iv, §§ 75, 79; Papin. in
Collat. ii, 3; § 7, I. *de nox. act.* (iv, 8).

inuito quoque eo cuius in mancipio sunt censu libertatem
consequi possunt, excepto eo quem pater ea lege mancipio
dedit ut sibi remancipetur; nam quodammodo tunc pater
potestatem propriam reseruare sibi uidetur eo ipso quod
mancipio recipit. ac ne is quidem dicitur inuito eo cuius in
mancipio est censu libertatem consequi, quem pater ex noxali
causa [mancipio dedit],[1] ueluti quod furti eius nomine damnatus est, [et eum][1] mancipio actori[2] dedit: nam hunc actor
141 pro pecunia habet.   In summa admonendi sumus aduersus
eos quos in mancipio habemus nihil nobis contumeliose facere
licere; alioquin iniuriarum[1] tenebimur. ac ne diu quidem in
eo iure detinentur homines; sed plerumque hoc fit dicis gratia
modo[2] uno momento, nisi scilicet ex noxali causa manci-
parentur.[3]

142   Transeamus nunc ad aliam diuisionem.   nam ex his

---

census even against the will of him who has them *in mancipio*,
except when he holds under condition of remancipation to the
father from whom he has received them; in such case the
father is held to have in a manner reserved his power over his
child by his bargain that he is to have him back again as a
mancipium. Nor can he who has been given by his father
as a noxal *mancipium*,—as when his father, having on his
account been condemned in an *actio furti*, has surrendered
him to the pursuer,—obtain his freedom by means of the census
against the will of the party to whom he has been surrendered;
for the latter holds him instead of pecuniary compensation.
141 And be it observed, finally, that we must not treat with indignity those we hold *in mancipio*, otherwise we shall be liable
to them in an *actio iniuriarum*. It is not for any long time
that persons are detained in this condition, but usually as a
mere matter of form and only for a moment, unless they have
been mancipated noxally.

142   Let us pass now to another division [of the law of persons]:

---

[1] Rejected by M. (K. u. S. footnote) as glosses.
   [2] The noxal surrender was not
necessarily to the owner of the
stolen property, but to the party entitled to the *actio furti*; see iv, 203.
§ 141. Comp. § 118a, and references in
note to last par.

[1] Comp. iii, §§ 220, f.
[2] So Hu.; the ms. has *m*.
[3] So the ms.; P. reads by way of
emendation—*mancipati sint a parente*.
§§ 142-154. Comp. tit. I. DE TVTELIS
(i, 13).
§§ 142, 143. Pr. tit. I. afd.

personis quae neque in potestate neque in manu neque
in mancipio sunt, quaedam uel in tutela sunt uel in curatione, quaedam neutro iure tenentur. uideamus igitur quae
in tutela, quae in curatione sint : ita enim intellegemus
143 ceteras personas quae neutro iure tenentur.   Ac prius dispiciamus de his quae in tutela sunt.
144   Permissum est itaque parentibus liberis quos in potestate
sua habent testamento tutores dare : masculini quidem sexus
inpuberibus, [*feminini etiam puberibus, et tum quo*] que [1] cum
nuptae sint. ueteres [2] enim uoluerunt feminas, etiamsi perfectae aetatis sint, propter animi leuitatem [3] in tutela esse.
145 Itaque si quis filio filiaeque testamento tutorem dederit, et
ambo ad pubertatem peruenerint, filius quidem desinit habere
tutorem, filia uero nihilo minus in tutela permanet : tantum
enim ex lege Iulia et Papia Poppaea [1] iure liberorum tutela

for of those who are neither in *potestas, manus,* nor *mancipium,*
some are under tutory or curatory, and others under neither
of those guardianships. Let us see, therefore, who are under
tutory, and who under curatory ; for thus we shall understand
143 who they are that are in neither.   And let us begin with
those who are in tutelage.
144   It is permitted, then, to parents to appoint tutors by testament to those of their children who are *in potestate,*—to males
if under puberty, [*to females even if above it, and even*] though
they be married. For the old jurists thought it right that
women, although of full age, should continue under tutory
145 because of their fickleness of judgment.   Therefore, if a
man have by testament appointed a tutor to his son and
daughter, and these both arrive at the age of puberty, the
former thereupon ceases to have a tutor, but the latter still
continues to be in tutelage ; for it is only in respect of the
privilege they enjoy under the Julian and Papia-Poppaean

§ 144. Comp. Vlp. xi, §§ 1, 14, 15;
§ 3, tit. I. afd.
    [1] The words in ital. are not in the
MS.; they are supplied as manifestly
omitted *per incuriam,* and necessary
to complete the sense. K. u. S.
interpolate—*feminini autem sexus
cuiuscumque aetatis sint, et tum quoque,* etc. ; Hu.—*feminini uero inpuberibus puberibusque,* etc.
    [2] A technical word with the classi-
cal jurists, designative of their pre-
decessors of the republican period.

[3] Comp. § 190 and notes; Vlp.
xi, 1.
§ 145. Comp. § 194; iii, 44; Vlp. xi,
28a.
    [1] A 'matrimonial code,' carried by
Augustus in the year 762 | 9, as a
revision and amendment of the
L. *Iulia de maritandis ordinibus*
(passed 757 | 4, after having been
twenty-one years before the legislative bodies) : see Tac. *Ann.* iii, §§ 25,
28 ; Dio Cass. lvi, 10. It was regarded as one of the most important

liberantur feminae. loquimur autem exceptis uirginibus
Vestalibus, quas etiam ueteres in honorem sacerdotii liberas
esse uoluerunt :[2] itaque etiam lege XII tabularum cautum est.

146 Nepotibus autem neptibusque ita demum possumus testamento tutores dare, si post mortem nostram in patris sui
potestatem iure recasuri non sint. itaque si filius meus mortis
meae tempore in potestate mea sit, nepotes quos ex eo [habeo]
non poterunt ex testamento meo habere tutorem, quamuis in
potestate mea fuerint; scilicet quia mortuo me in patris sui

147 potestate futuri sunt.   Cum tamen in conpluribus aliis
causis postumi pro iam natis habeantur, et in hac causa
placuit non minus postumis quam iam natis testamento tutores
dari posse, si modo in ea causa sint ut, si uiuis nobis nascan-

---

law as mothers of children, that women are freed from tutory.
We must except, however, the Vestal virgins, whom even the
ancients, out of respect for their priestly office, held to be free :
so in fact it was provided by the law of the Twelve Tables.

146 To our grandsons and granddaughters we can appoint tutors
by will then only when they are not on our death to pass by
operation of law into the *potestas* of their father. Accordingly,
if my son be in my *potestas* at the time of my death, my
grandchildren by him cannot have a tutor under my testament, notwithstanding that they may be in my *potestas ;* for

147 on my death they will be in that of their father.   As in
other cases posthumous children are regarded as already born,
so in this ; for it is held that we may by testament appoint
tutors to our children to be born as well as to those already
in life, provided, as regards the former, that if they be born

---

pieces of Roman statute law, and
formed the subject of innumerable
commentaries.

 The purpose of the *lex de mari-
tand. ordinib.* seems to have been
to prevent misalliances, encourage
equal marriages, and regulate divorce; the Papia-Poppaean additions went farther, endeavouring
not only to multiply marriages, but
to insure their fruitfulness. This
was attempted by a system of re-
wards and penalties, Amongst the re-
wards were — for men, a gradation of
honours according to the number of
their lawful children alive or killed
in battle, and admission to office in
the state in the case of a parent at
an earlier age than in the case of an

individual who was childless; for
women, relief from tutory, and right
more or less restricted, of independent testamentary disposition, if
they were the mothers of a certain
number of children. Of the penalties of celibacy and unfruitful marriage, the chief was incapacity in
many cases to take a testamentary
succession or bequest. Many testamentary gifts thus lapsed or became
technically *caduca.* For their disposal the statute contained elaborate provisions : hence the name of
Lex Caducaria so often applied to it.
 [2] See Plut. *Numa*, 10 ; Schoell,
Tab. v, 1.
§ 146. § 3, tit. I. afd.   Comp. § 127.
§ 147. § 4, tit. I. afd.

tur, in potestate nostra fiant: hos [*enim*] [1] etiam heredes instituere possumus, [2] cum extraneos postumos heredes instituere

148   permissum non sit. [3]   [*Vxori*] quae in manu est, proinde
ac filiae, item nurui quae in filii manu est, proinde ac nepti,
tutor dari potest.

149   Rectissime autem tutor sic dari potest: LVCIVM TITIVM
LIBERIS MEIS TVTOREM DO; LVCIVM [*TITIVM VXORI MEAE*]
TVTOREM DO.   sed et si ita scriptum sit: LIBERIS MEIS uel

150   VXORI MEAE TITIVS TVTOR ESTO, recte datus intellegitur.   In
persona tamen uxoris quae in manu est recepta est etiam
tutoris optio, id est ut liceat ei permittere quem uelit ipsa
tutorem sibi optare, hoc modo: TITIAE VXORI MEAE TVTORIS

---

in our lifetime they will be in our *potestas*. For we may
institute such posthumous children as our heirs; although
we cannot so institute the after-born children of a stranger.

148   A tutor may be appointed to a wife, *in manu* as if she were
a daughter, and to a daughter-in-law in the *manus* of a son as
if she were a granddaughter.

149   The most regular way of appointing a testamentary tutor
is by words such as these: ' I appoint Lucius Titius as tutor
to my children;' ' I appoint Lucius [*Titius*] as tutor [*to my
[wife]*.'   But if it be in these terms: ' Be Titius tutor to my
children,' or ' to my wife,' the appointment will equally be

150   sustained as regular.   In the case of a wife *in manu*, however, an option may be conferred upon her; that is to say, a
husband may permit his wife to choose whom she will as her
tutor, in this way: ' To my wife Titia I give the choice of

---

[1] Added by Hu. and adopted by
K. u. S.
[2] Comp. ii, 180.
[3] Comp. ii, 242.
§ 148. Comp. ii, 159; Boeth. *in Cic.
Top.* ii, 4, § 18 (ed. Baiter, p. 302).
§ 149. Comp. ii, 289; Paul. in Fr. Vat.,
§ 229. In the MS. we have *ltitiu
mliberismeistutdolic. tutdo*, which
Bk. and Hu. (in previous editions)
render—' *L. Titium liberis meis tutorem do lego* ' aut ' *do*.' Gou., pointing out that we have no example
of *lego* being employed in the testamentary appointment of a tutor,
renders the *lic. tutdo* of the MS. by
Lucium tutorem do, as a second and
simpler style. This is adopted by
P. in his text; but in a footnote he
suggests that the second style pos-

sibly applied to the appointment of
a tutor to a wife, and that the copyist
may have omitted the appropriate
words. This view, I think, may be
accepted for two reasons—(1) that
though we often have *Titius* standing alone, we nowhere in the text
find *Lucius;* (2) that the second
branch of the par. seems to refer to
an antecedent form of appointing a
tutor to a wife, in which the word
do has been used. Hu., in his last
edition, adopts a similar reading;
but K. u. S. drop the *lic.tutdo*
altogether.
§§ 150-153. Comp. Liv. xxxix, 19; *L.
Salpensana*, c. 22 (Bruns, p. 121).
The words *tutorem optare* in § 150
are not in the MS., but manifestly
have been omitted *per incuriam*.

OPTIONEM DO; quo casu licet uxori [*tutorem optare*] uel in
151 omnes res uel in unam forte aut duas.   Ceterum aut plena
152 optio datur aut angusta.   Plena ita dari solet ut proxime
supra diximus.   angusta ita dari solet: TITIAE VXORI MEAE
TVTORIS OPTIONEM DVMTAXAT[1] SEMEL DO, aut DVMTAXAT BIS DO.
153 Quae optiones plurimum inter se differunt. nam quae plenam
optionem habet, potest semel et bis et ter et saepius tutorem
optare: quae uero angustam habet optionem, si dumtaxat
semel data est optio, amplius quam semel optare non potest;
si tantum bis, amplius quam bis optandi facultatem non
154 habebit.   Vocantur autèm hi qui nominatim testamento
tutores dantur, datiui, qui ex optione sumuntur, optiui.
155   Quibus testamento quidem tutor datus non sit, iis ex lege
XII [*tabularum*] agnati sunt tutores, qui uocantur legitimi.
156 Sunt autem agnati per uirilis sexus personas cognatione iuncti,
quasi a patre cognati, ueluti frater eodem patre natus, fratris
filius neposue ex eo, item patruus et patrui filius et nepos ex

---

her tutor.' When this is done she is free to choose either a
tutor who is to act with her in all her affairs, or one who is to
151 act for her in one or two matters only.   Her option may be
152 either limited or unlimited.   It is unlimited when conferred in such terms as above; limited when conceived in this
way: 'I give my wife Titia the choice of her tutor, but only
153 once,' or 'only twice.'   There is a great difference between
these two options; for she who has unlimited option may
choose a tutor once, twice, thrice, or oftener if she likes;
whereas she whose option is limited by 'once' cannot choose
oftener than once, while if limited by 'twice' she has no
154 right to choose oftener than twice.   Tutors appointed in a
testament by express nomination are called tutors dative;
those selected in virtue of a power of option, tutors optive.
155   Those to whom no tutor has been appointed by testament,
by the law of the Twelve Tables have their agnates as tutors,
156 —hence called tutors-at-law.   And by agnates are to be
understood persons who are of kin through males,—cognate,
as it were, through the father; as, for instance, a brother by
the same father, such a brother's son or a grandson through
the latter, a father's brother, a father's brother's son, or a
father's brother's grandson through the last. Those who are

---

§ 152. [1]In MS. *dumtaxat tut. optionem.* § 155. Pr. tit. I. afd. Comp. Schoell,
§ 154. Comp. Vlp. xi, 14.   Tab. v, 6; Vlp. xi, 8.
§§ 155-158. Comp. tit. I. DE LEGITIMA § 156. § 1, tit. I. afd. Comp. iii, 10;
AGNATORVM TVTELA (i, 15).   Vlp. xi, 4.

eo. at hi qui per feminini sexus personas cognatione con-
iunguntur non sunt agnati, sed alias naturali iure cognati.
itaque inter auunculum et sororis filium non agnatio est, sed
cognatio. item amitae, materterae filius non est mihi agnatus,
sed cognatus, et inuicem scilicet sic ego illi eodem iure
coniungor; quia qui nascuntur, patris, non matris familiam
157 secuntur.   Sed olim quidem, quantum ad legem xii tabularum attinet, etiam feminae agnatos habebant tutores. sed
postea lex Claudia [1] lata est, quae, quod ad feminas attinet,
[*agnatorum*] tutelas sustulit: itaque masculus quidem inpubes
fratrem puberem aut patruum habet tutorem; femina uero [2]
158 talem habere tutorem non potest [*cogi*].[3]   Sed agnationis
quidem ius capitis deminutione perimitur, cognationis uero
ius eo modo non commutatur; quia ciuilis ratio ciuilia quidem
iura corrumpere potest, naturalia uero non potest.

---

of kin through females are not agnates, but merely by natural
law cognates. Therefore there is no agnation between a
mother's brother and her son,—only cognation. The son of
my father's or mother's sister is not my agnate, but my
cognate, and I of course stand to him in the same relationship;
for children follow the family of their father, not that of their
157 mother.   Of old, and under the law of the Twelve Tables,
women also had their agnates for their tutors. But afterwards,
by the Claudian law, this tutory was abolished in so far as
women were concerned; so that now, while a male under the
age of puberty has as his tutor his own or his father's brother,
a woman cannot be compelled to have such a person as her
158 tutor.   The right of agnation is put an end to by *capitis
deminutio.* This, however, makes no alteration in the right
of cognation; for, though purely civil considerations may
destroy civil rights, they cannot have that effect on natural
ones.

§ 157. Comp. § 171; Vlp. xi, 8; l, 3,
C. *de leg. tut.* (v, 80).
    [1] We have no precise information
as to the enactment of the Claudian
law here referred to; though called a
lex it was probably a senatusconsult
passed on the proposal of Claudius,
as Lange (*Roem. Alt.*) thinks, in
the year 800 | 47; comp. note to §§
173, 174.
    [2] That is to say, women above
puberty; for it does not appear that

female any more than male pupils
were ever exempted from the tutory-
at-law of their agnates.
    [3] So Gou. The ms. has only *pote*,
with a blank space following it sufficient for five or six letters. K. u. S.
and Hu. have simply *potest;* but this
seems too absolute; there could be
nothing to prevent a woman *select-
ing* her brother or uncle as her tutor.
§ 158. § 3, tit. I. afd. Comp. iii,
    §§ 21, 27; Vlp. xi, 9.

159   Est autem capitis deminutio prioris capitis permutatio.[1]
      eaque tribus modis accidit: nam aut maxima est capitis
      deminutio, aut minor, quam quidam mediam uocant, aut
160   minima.   Maxima est capitis deminutio cum aliquis simul
      et ciuitatem et libertatem amittit; quae accidit incensis [1] *qui*
      ex forma censuali uenire iubentur.   quod ius — — — —
      — — — — *ex lege* — — — — — — —,[2] *qui contra eam*
      legem in urbe Roma *domicilium* habuerint: item feminae [3]
      quae ex senatusconsulto Claudiano ancillae fiunt eorum
      dominorum, quibus inuitis et denuntiantibus nihilo minus [4]
161   cum seruis *eorum* coierint.   Minor siue *media* est capitis

------

159   By *capitis deminutio* is meant the changing of one's former
      caput.   And it occurs in three ways; for every *capitis
      deminutio* is either of the highest degree, of the lesser (which
160   some call intermediate), or of the lowest.   It is of the
      highest degree when a man loses at once both citizenship and
      freedom; as happens to persons who have wilfully evaded
      inscription in the censorial register, and consequently, by the
      rules of the census-taking, are ordered to be sold as slaves.
      It occurs also — — — — — — who, in contravention
      of the statute, have taken up their abode within the burgh-
      limits of Rome.   A woman, too, according to the Claudian
      senatusconsult, becomes the slave of him with whose male
      slave she has been carrying on an improper intimacy, against
      the will and in spite of the formal warnings of his owner.
161   There is lesser or intermediate *capitis deminutio* when citizen-

§§ 159-164. Comp. tit. I. *DE CAPITIS
MINVTIONE* (i, 16).
§ 159.   Pr. tit. I. afd.   Comp. Vlp. xi,
10; Boeth. *in Cic. Top.* ii, 4, § 18
(ed. Baiter, p. 302); Paul. *ex Festo*,
v. *Deminutus capite* (Bruns, p. 240).
   [1] Gai. (*ad ed. prov.*) in fr. 1, D.
de cap. min. (iv, 5), has *status permutatio;* and this is substituted by
K. u. S. and Hu. for the *cap. perm.*
of the MS.
   By *caput* is to be understood the
family position of a citizen.   It is
sometimes defined as a man's position in regard to freedom, citizenship, and family rights; but the
two first came under consideration
only as affecting the last.
§ 160.   Comp. Vlp. xi, 11; § 1, tit. I.
afd.; Boeth. as in note to last par.
   [1] Comp. Cic. *pro Caec.* xxxiv, 99;
Dion. Hal. iv, 15; Vlp. xi, 11.

   [2] Nearly two lines (p. 44, ll. 1-3),
with exception of *ex lege*, are illegible in the MS.   It has been suggested—and M. (K. u. S. p. xix)
and Hu. adhere to the view—that
the allusion may have been to the
provision in the Aelia-Sentian law
that deditician-freedmen should not
reside in Rome under penalty of
being again reduced to slavery; see
§ 27.   The difficulty, as Gou. properly observes, is that it could not
be said of such a freedman—*simul
ciuitatem et libertatem amittit;* for
he was not a citizen.
   [3] Comp. § 91; Vlp. xi, 11; § 1, I.
de success. sublat. (iii, 12).
   [4] So Hu.; the MS. has *dominis*,
omitted by P. and K. u. S. as a gloss.
§ 161.   § 2, tit. I. afd.   Comp. § 128,
note 2; Vlp. xi, 12; Boeth. as in
note to § 159.

deminutio cum ciuitas amittitur, libertas retinetur; quod
162 accidit ei cui aqua et igni interdictum fuerit.   Minima est
capitis deminutio cum et ciuitas et libertas retinetur, sed
status hominis commutatur; quod accidit in his qui adoptantur, item in his quae coemptionem faciunt, et in his qui
mancipio dantur quique ex mancipatione manumittuntur;
adeo quidem ut quotiens quisque mancipetur ut [1] manumit-
163 tatur, totiens capite deminuatur.   Nec solum maioribus
deminutionibus ius agnationis corrumpitur, sed etiam minima;
et ideo si ex duobus liberis alterum pater emancipauerit, post
obitum eius neuter alteri agnationis iure *tutor esse* poterit.
164   Cum autem ad agnatos tutela pertineat, non simul ad
omnes pertinet, sed ad eos tantum qui proximo gradu sunt.
164a— — — — — — —.

---

ship is lost but liberty retained; which happens to him who is
162 interdicted fire and water.   There is *capitis deminutio* of the
lowest degree when both citizenship and liberty are retained, and
only the status or condition of the individual [in private life]
is changed; it happens in the case of persons who are adopted,
of women who perform coemption, and of individuals who are
given *in mancipium* and manumitted therefrom; for as often
as there is mancipation with a view to manumission, so often
163 is there a *capitis deminutio.*   It is not by the greater *capitis
deminutiones* alone that the right of agnation is destroyed, but
even by that of the lowest degree; consequently, if a father
emancipate one of two children, neither of them can be the
other's tutor by right of agnation after the father's death.
164   Although it is true that the right of tutory belongs to a
pupil's agnates, yet it does not belong to all of them, but only
164a to those who are nearest of degree.   [*Failing agnates, it
[passed by the law of the Twelve Tables to the* gens; *but the
[rights of the* gens *in this respect have long ago gone into disuse.*]

§ 162. Comp. Vlp. xi, 13; § 3, tit.
I. afd.; Boeth. as in note to §
159.
[1] So P.; the ms. and K. u. S. have
aut : Hu. [*aut ut remancipatur*] *aut
ut manumittatur.*
§ 163. Comp. Vlp. xi, 13; § 3, I. *de leg.
agn. tut.* (i, 15).
§ 164. § 7, tit. I. afd.
§ 164a. The first 17 lines of p. 45 of
the ms. are almost entirely illegible.
There is reason to believe they contained a reference to the tutory
exercised by the *gens* on failure of
agnates; see iii, 17. That by the

Twelve Tables the tutory-at-law of a
pupil passed on that event to his
gens is nowhere expressly stated.
But we know (iii, 17) that failing
agnates a man's succession devolved
on his *gens;* and it was a general
principle that, except when an inheritance fell to a woman, the rights
of succession and tutory went together (§ 165).   Besides, we have to
guide us the analogy of the curatory
of a lunatic, which went to his
agnates, and failing them to his
gens; see Cic. *de Inv. II,* l, 148; fr.
53, pr. D. *de V. S.* (l, 16).

165   Ex eadem lege duodecim tabularum libertarum et inpuberum libertorum *tutela ad* patronos liberosque eorum
pertinet; *quae et ipsa* tutela legitima uocatur, non (*quia nomi-*
(*natim*) ea lege de hac tutela (*cauetur, sed*) *quia* proinde accepta
est per interpretationem atque si uerbis legis *introducta*[1]
esset: eo enim ipso (*quod hereditates*) libertorum libertarum-
que, si intestati decessissent, iusserat lex ad patronos liberosue
eorum pertinere, crediderunt ueteres[2] uoluisse legem etiam
tutelas ad eos pertinere, quia et agnatos, quos ad hereditatem
uocauit, eosdem et tutores esse iusserat.

166   Exemplo patronorum receptae sunt et aliae tutelae quae
fiduciariae uocantur, id est, quae ideo nobis competunt quia
liberum caput mancipatum nobis uel a parente uel a coemp-

---

165   By the same law of the Twelve Tables the tutory of freedwomen and of freedmen under puberty belongs to their patrons
and their patrons' children. This tutory likewise is spoken
of as a tutory-at-law. Not, however, *because it is expressly
mentioned* in the Tables, but because it has been recognised
by interpretation as fully as if it had been so mentioned; for
inasmuch as it was declared by the Tables *that the inheritances*
of freedmen and freedwomen dying intestate should belong to
their patrons and patrons' children, the old jurists concluded
that it must be the intent of the statute that the tutory of
such freedmen and freedwomen should go in the same direction, seeing that, when it calls agnates to a succession, it at
the same time confers upon them the right of tutory.

166   On the analogy of that of patrons, certain other tutories
have been recognised which are called fiduciary, *i.e.* which are
competent to us as manumitters of a free person mancipated

---

§ 165. Comp. tit. I. *DE LEGITIMA
PATRONORVM TVTELA* (i, 17), from
which the words in ital., illegible in
the MS., are supplied; Vlp. xi, 8.
    [1] So Hu. and K. u. S.; the MS.
has *accepta*; P. *praecepta*.
    [2] See § 144, note 2.

§§ 166-184. Comp. tits. I. *DE LEGITIMA
PARENTVM TVTELA* and *DE FIDVCI-
ARIA TVTELA* (i, 18, 19). In the
MS., immediately after *exemplo patronorum* in beginning of § 166, we
have the words *de fiduciaria*, probably an unfinished rubric.
§ 166. Comp. §§ 115, 172, 175, 195a;
Vlp. xi, 5; tits. I. afd. K. u. S., on
the authority of Inst. i, 19, and § 172,

below, make an interpolation, and
render the par. thus:—Exemplo
patronorum receptae *sunt et aliae
tutelae, quae et ipsae legitimae uocantur. nam si quis filium aut filiam,
nepotem aut neptem ex filio, et deinceps alteri ea lege mancipio dedit ut
sibi remanciparetur, deinde remancipatum remancipatamue manumisit,
legitimus eorum tutor erit.* Sunt
et aliae tutelae quae fiduciariae,
etc. Hu. (in his last edition) adopts
this addition; and makes the *sunt
et aliae* the commencement of a
separate par. (§ 166a). But, looking
at the language of § 175, it is doubtful whether this be justified.

167 tionatore manumiserimus. Sed latinarum et latinorum
inpuberum *tutela non omni modo ad manumissores libertinorum* [1]
pertinet, sed ad eos quorum ante manumissionem ex iure
Quiritium [*fuerunt: unde si ancilla ex iure Quiritium*] [2] tua
sit, in bonis mea, a me quidem solo, non etiam a te manumissa
latina fieri potest, et bona eius ad me pertinent; sed eius
tutela tibi conpetit: nam ita lege Iunia cauetur. itaque si
ab eo cuius et in bonis et ex iure Quiritium ancilla fuerit
facta sit latina, ad eundem et bona et tutela pertinent.

168 Agnatis et patronis et liberorum capitum manumissoribus
permissum est feminarum tutelam alii in iure cedere; [1] pupillorum autem tutelam non est permissum cedere, quia non

169 uidetur onerosa, cum tempore pubertatis finiatur. [2] Is

170 autem cui ceditur tutela cessicius uocatur. quo mortuo
aut capite deminuto reuertitur ad eum tutorem tutela qui
cessit; ipse quoque qui *cessit* si mortuus aut capite deminutus

---

167 to us either by a parent or a coemptionator. But the
tutory of Junian latin freedwomen, and of latin freedmen
under puberty, does not in all cases belong to their manumitters, but rather to those who before their manumission
were their quiritarian owners. *Therefore, if a woman-slave be
yours in quiritarian* and mine in bonitarian right, it is I alone,
not you, that can by manumission make her a latin, and her
estate will be mine; but her tutory will belong to you: for so
it is provided by the Junian law. Accordingly, if a woman
have been made a latin by a person who held her both in
bonitarian and quiritarian ownership, her estate [on her death]
and her tutory [during her life] will both be his.

168 Agnates, patrons, and manumitters of free persons are
permitted to transfer the tutory of females to another person
by cession in court; but that of male pupils cannot be ceded,
for, as it terminates with the arrival of puberty, it cannot be

169 regarded as burdensome. He to whom a tutory is thus

170 ceded gets the name of *tutor cessicius.* On his death or
capitis deminutio it reverts to him by whom it had been
ceded; while if it be the latter that dies or is *capite deminutus*,

---

§ 167. Comp. § 35; iii, 56; Vlp. xi, 19.
  [1] The ms. has *libertineorum;* P.
omits the word; K. u. S. make it
eorum; Hu. *libertorum eorum.*
  [2] These words are the suggestion
of Goesch., approved by most eds.;

they have obviously been omitted
per incuriam.
§ 168. Comp. Vlp. xi, §§ 6, 8, 17.
  [1] Comp. ii, 24.
  [2] Comp. § 196.
§§ 169, 170. Comp. Vlp. xi, 7.

sit, a cessicio tutela discedit et reuertitur ad eum qui post
eum qui cesserat secundum gradum in ea tutela habuerit.
171 Sed quantum ad agnatos pertinet nihil hoc tempore de
cessicia tutela quaeritur, cum agnatorum tutelae in feminis
172 lege Claudia[1] sublatae sint.   Sed fiduciarios quoque quidam
putauerunt cedendae tutelae ius non habere, cum ipsi se oneri
subiecerint. quod etsi placeat, in parente tamen qui filiam
neptemue aut proneptem alteri ea lege mancipio dedit ut sibi
remanciparetur, remanc ipatamque manumisit, idem dici non
debet, cum is et legitimus tutor habeatur, et non minus huic
quam patronis honor praestandus sit.
173   Praeterea senatusconsulto mulieribus permissum est in
absentis tutoris locum alium petere; quo petito prior desinit;
174 nec interest quam longe absit is tutor.   sed excipitur ne
in absentis patroni locum liceat libertae tutorem petere.

---

it passes from the *cessicius* and reverts to him who is entitled
171 to it as next of degree after the cedent.   So far, however,
as agnates are concerned, there can nowadays never be any
question about this *cessicia tutela*, seeing that the agnatic
tutory of women has been abolished by the Claudian law.
172 Some jurists have been of opinion that fiduciary tutors have
no power of ceding their office, since they have subjected
themselves to the burden by their own act. Even if this
opinion be correct, the rule will not apply to a parent who
has given his daughter or granddaughter or great-granddaughter to a third party *in mancipium*, on the express condition of remancipation to himself, and who has manumitted
her on such remancipation; for he is regarded as also a tutor-
at-law, and is entitled to no less consideration than a patron.
173   Moreover, by the senatusconsult, women are allowed to
apply for the appointment of a new tutor in room of one who
is absent; the latter's tutory comes to an end by the new
appointment, apart from any consideration of how far away
174 he is.   There is an exception, however, in the case of a
freedwoman; for she cannot thus obtain the supercession of

§ 171. Comp. § 157; Vlp. xi, 8.
  [1] See § 157, note.
§ 172. Comp. §§ 132, 166, 175, 192; tit.
  I. *de leg. parent. tut.* (i, 18).
§§ 173, 174. Comp. Vlp. xi, 22. The
author and date of the Sct. referred
to cannot be determined with certainty. It seems, judging from §§

173-182, and Vlp. xi, §§ 20-23, to
have dealt pretty comprehensively
with the subject of the tutory of
women, and may possibly have been
the same enactment that is elsewhere referred to under the name
of *lex Claudia;* comp. § 157,
note 1.

175 Patroni *autem* loco habemus *etiam* parentem, qui *ex eo quod ipsi sibi* remancipatam filiam neptemue aut proneptem manumisit, legitimam tutelam nanctus est.   huius quidem liberi fiduciarii tutoris loco numerantur; patroni autem liberi eandem tutelam adipiscuntur quam et pater eorum habuit.
176 *Sed aliquando* etiam in patroni absentis locum *permittitur* tuto-
177 rem petere, ueluti ad hereditatem adeundam.   *Idem* senatus
178 censuit et in persona pupilli patroni *filii*.   *Item* [1] lege Iulia de maritandis ordinibus ei quae in legitima tutela pupilli sit permittitur dotis constituendae gratia a praetore urbano tutorem
179 petere;   sane [*enim*] [1] patroni filius, etiamsi inpubes sit, libertae *efficietur* tutor, *quamquam* in nulla re auctor fieri potest, cum ipsi nihil permissum sit sine tutoris auctoritate agere.
180 Item si qua in tutela legitima furiosi aut muti sit, permittitur ei senatusconsulto dotis constituendae gratia tutorem petere.

---

175 her absent patron.   And under the word patron we here include a parent who, by the mere fact of manumission of a daughter, granddaughter, or great-granddaughter who has been remancipated to him, has thereby become her tutor-at-law.   The children of such a parent are accounted fiduciary tutors; but the children of a patron succeed to a tutory of the
176 same character as their father's.   Yet sometimes a woman is allowed to apply for the appointment of a tutor to herself in place even of an absent patron; for instance, when she desires
177 to enter upon an inheritance.   The senate has granted the same relief in such circumstances to a woman in the tutory
178 of her patron's son, himself a pupil.   Further, by the Julian law regulating the marriages of the orders, a woman in the tutory-at-law of a pupil may petition the urban praetor to appoint her an [interim] tutor for the purpose of making a
179 dotal provision;   (for there is no question that a patron's son, even though under puberty, becomes tutor of his father's freedwoman, notwithstanding that, as he cannot act in any matter without his own tutor's *auctoritas*, he cannot be *auctor*
180 in any of her affairs.)   A woman likewise who is in the tutory of a lunatic or a mute is allowed by the senatusconsult to apply for a tutor for the purpose of making a dotal

§ 175. Comp. §§ 166, 172; tit. I. de fiduc. tut. (i, 19).
§§ 176, 177. Comp. Vlp. xi, 22.
§ 178. Comp. Vlp. xi, 20.
  [1] So P.; the ms. seems to have nam e lege Julia; K. u. S. and Hu. nam et lege Julia. As regards this Julian law see § 145, note 1.
§ 179.   Comp. § 18, I. de excus. tut. (i, 25).
  [1] This word is interpolated because the par. seems to be a parenthetical explanation.
§ 180. Comp. Vlp. xi, 21.

181 Quibus casibus saluam manere tutelam patrono patronique
182 filio manifestum est.   Praeterea senatus censuit ut si tutor
pupilli pupillaeue suspectus a tutela remotus sit, siue ex iusta
causa fuerit excusatus, in locum eius alius tutor detur, quo
183 facto prior tutor amittit tutelam.   Haec omnia similiter et
Romae et in prouinciis obseruantur; *scilicet* [*ut Romae a prae-*
[*tore*] [1] *et in* prouinciis a praeside prouinciae tutor (*peti debeat*).[2]
184   Olim cum legis actiones [1] in usu erant, etiam ex illa causa
tutor dabatur, si inter tutorem et mulierem pupillumue lege
agendum erat. *nam quia ipse tutor* in re sua auctor esse non
poterat, alius dabatur, quo auctore legis actio perageretur : qui
dicebatur praetorius *tutor*, quia a praetore urbano *dabatur.*
sed post sublatas legis actiones quidam putant hanc speciem
dandi *tutoris in usu esse desiisse ; (aliis uero)* [2] *placet adhuc in
usu esse* si legitimo judicio [3] agatur.

---

181 settlement.   But in all such cases, as is manifest, the [per-
manent] tutory of the patron or his son remains undisturbed.
182 Further, the senate has ordained that if the tutor of a male or
female pupil be removed from office as suspect, or be excused
on some good ground from undertaking it, another shall be
appointed in his place, on whose appointment the original
183 tutor loses his tutory.   Upon all these matters the rules are
the same in the provinces as in Rome; *in the latter* the
application for appointment of a tutor must *be made to the
praetor*, in the former to the governor.
184   In the olden time, when the actions-of-the-law were in use,
it was the practice to appoint an [interim] tutor when a
process was instituted between an [ordinary] tutor and his
female or pupil ward: as the [ordinary] tutor could not be
auctor in a matter in which he himself was concerned, another
was appointed, with whose *auctoritas* the action-of-the-law
might be carried through all its stages, and who was called
a praetorian tutor, because his nomination proceeded from
the urban praetor. But, after the actions-of-the-law were
abolished, the practice of appointing a tutor in this way, according to some authorities, went altogether into disuse, *while
according to others* it is still competent in a *legitimum iudicium.*

---

§ 182. Comp. Vlp. xi, 23.
§ 183. Comp. Vlp. xi, 20.
   [1] So K. u. S. P. has—[*nisi*] *scilicet* [*quod Romae a praetore urbano
uel peregrino praetore*] *et*, etc.
   [2] These words are illegible, with
exception of the *pe* of *peti;* but
their propriety is obvious.

§ 184. Comp. Vlp. xi, 24; § 3, I. *de
auct. tut.* (i, 21); pr. I. *de his p.
quos agere poss.* (iv, 10).
   [1] Comp. iv, §§ 11, 12.
   [2] The first three letters of *aliis* are
quite legible. K. u. S. and Hu.
have *aliis autem.*
   [3] Comp. iv, 104.

185   Si cui nullus omnino tutor sit, ei datur in urbe Roma ex
lege Atilia [1] a praetore urbano et maiore parte tribunorum
plebis, qui Atilianus tutor uocatur; in prouinciis uero a prae-
186 sidibus prouinciarum ex lege Iulia et Titia.[2]   Et ideo si
cui testamento tutor sub condicione aut ex die certo datus sit
quamdiu condicio aut dies pendet tutor dari potest; item si
pure datus fuerit, quamdiu nemo heres existat, tamdiu ex his
legibus tutor petendus est; qui desinit tutor esse posteaquam
187 aliquis ex testamento tutor esse coeperit.   Ab hostibus
quoque tutore capto ex his legibus tutor peti debet, qui desinit
tutor esse si is qui captus est in ciuitatem reuersus fuerit:
nam reuersus recipit tutelam iure postliminii.
188   Ex his apparet quot sint species tutelarum. si uero

---

185   If a pupil have no tutor at all, then in Rome, in terms of
the Atilian law, one is given him by the urban praetor and a
majority of the plebeian tribunes, who is called an Atilian
tutor; while in the provinces one is appointed to him by the
186 governor, in terms of the Julian and Titian law.   If therefore any one have a tutor appointed to him by testament, but
only conditionally or as from a certain date, a tutor may be
given him by the magistrate until the condition is fulfilled or
the time has arrived.   So also, although the testamentary
appointment have been unconditional, so long as no heir has
come forward a tutor may be applied for under those statutes.
But [in all these cases] the magisterially appointed tutor
ceases to hold that position the moment there is one qualified
187 under the testament.   Further, if a tutor be taken captive
by an enemy, application should be made under those statutes
for the appointment of another, who will cease to hold office
when the former has recrossed the frontier; for on his return
he recovers his tutory *iure postliminii.*
188   From what has been said it is clear how many species there
are of tutories.   But if we proceed to inquire in what number

§§ 185-187. Comp. tit. I. *DE ATILIANO
TVTORE* (i, 20).
§ 185.   Pr. tit. I. afd. Comp. Vlp.
xi, 18.
   [1] The date is unknown, but before
568 | 186; see Liv. xxxix, 19.
   [2] Th. (i, 20, pr.) says these were
two separate laws. Hu. (*Beitraege,*
pp. 31, 32) thinks a *lex Iulia* was
enacted in the first instance by
Augustus (Octavian) in 722 | 32,
applying the Atilian law to the imperial provinces; and that it was

immediately thereafter extended by
M. Titius, *cos. suff.* to the popular
ones. In some at least of the semi-
independent *municipia* the appointment seems to have been by the
municipal authorities, as prescribed
by the charter; see *lex Salpens.*
c. 29 (Bruns, p. 123), and note 2 to
§ 55, above.
§ 186.   § 1, tit. I. afd.
§ 187.   § 2, tit. I. afd.
§ 188.   Comp. Vlp. xi, 2; Paul. fr. 7,
pr. D. *de cap. min.* (iv, 5).

quaeramus in quot genera hae species deducantur, longa erit disputatio : nam de ea re ualde ueteres[1] dubitauerunt, nosque[2] diligentius hunc tractatum executi sumus et in edicti interpretatione et in his libris quos ex Quinto Mucio fecimus hoc tantisper[3] sufficit admonuisse, quod quidam quinque genera esse dixerunt, ut Q. Mucius;[4] alii tria, ut Serv. Sulpicius;[5] alii duo, ut Labeo;[6] alii tot genera esse crediderunt quot etiam species essent.

189   Sed inpuberes quidem in tutela esse omnium ciuitatium iure contingit; quia id naturali rationi conueniens est, ut is qui perfectae aetatis non sit alterius tutela regatur; nec fere ulla ciuitas est in qua non licet parentibus liberis suis inpuberibus *testamento tutorem*[1] dare; quamuis, ut supra diximus,[2] soli ciues Romani uideantur liberos[3] suos in potestate

---

of genera those species can be ranged, we get into a fertile field of dispute, the matter being one about which the old jurists seem to have had much hesitation, and which we have discussed very fully in our treatise on the Edict and our commentary on Quintus Mucius. It is sufficient here to observe that some, as for instance Quintus Mucius, hold that there are five such genera ; that others, like Servius Sulpicius, limit the number to three, and others again, like Labeo, to two ; while some hold the number of genera to be equal that of the species.

189   That persons under the age of puberty should be in tutelage is the law everywhere; for it is in accordance with natural reason that he who is not of perfect age should be controlled by the tutory of another. Indeed, there is scarcely any country that does not recognise the right of a parent to appoint a *testamentary tutor* to his children under puberty; although, as already said, it is only citizens of Rome that have their

---

[1] See § 144, note 2.
[2] So K. u. S.; the MS. and P. have *nos qui;* Hu. *nos quia.*
[3] The MS. reads *hoc totum tantisper ;* for *totum* Hu. proposes *solum ;* and P. *tantum ;* none of the three words seems appropriate. Mommsen's suggestion of *loco* (K. u. S. footnote) is more probable.
[4] Quintus Mucius Scaevola, the younger, consul in 659 | 95, according to Cicero the greatest jurist of his day.
[5] Servius Sulpicius Rufus, consul

in 708 | 51, and according to Cicero not much behind Q. Mucius in the practice of his profession, while excelling him as a scientific jurist.
[6] About Labeo, see § 196, note 1.
§ 189.   Comp. § 6, tit. I. afd.
[1] The MS. has *co.st.tut.*, which P. thinks may be a corruption of *cust. u. tut.*, i.e. *custodes uel tutores.*
[2] See § 55.
[3] The MS. and Hu. have *tantum* before this word.

190 habere.   Feminas uero perfectae aetatis in tutela esse fere nulla pretiosa ratio suasisse uidetur : nam quae uulgo creditur, quia leuitate animi plerumque decipiuntur et aequum erat eas tutorum auctoritate regi, magis speciosa uidetur quam uera; mulieres enim [1] quae perfectae aetatis sunt ipsae sibi negotia tractant, et in quibusdam causis dicis gratia tutor interponit auctoritatem suam ; saepe etiam inuitus auctor fieri a praetore

191 cogitur.   Unde cum tutore nullum ex *tutela* iudicium mulieri datur : at ubi pupillorum pupillarumue negotia tutores tractant, eis post pubertatem tutelae iudicio rationem reddunt.

192 Sane patronorum et parentum legitimae tutelae uim aliquam habere intelleguntur eo quod hi neque ad testamentum facien-dum,[1] neque ad res mancipi alienandas,[2] neque ad obligationes suscipiendas [3] auctores fieri coguntur, praeterquam si magna causa alienandarum rerum mancipi obligationisque suscipiendae interueniat. eaque omnia ipsorum causa constituta

---

190 children in their *potestas*.   But it is difficult to discover any good reason why women of full age should be in tutelage ; that commonly assigned—that owing to their weakness of judgment they are easily imposed upon, and therefore ought, in common fairness to them, to be guided by the *auctoritas* of a tutor—is more specious than true.   For women of perfect age manage their business affairs for themselves; the inter-position of tutorial *auctoritas* in some cases is merely for form's sake ; for not unfrequently their tutor is compelled by

191 the praetor to be *auctor* whether he will or not.   It is for this reason that a woman has no *tutelae iudicium* against her tutor; whereas when tutors administer the affairs of pupils, whether male or female, they must, on their attaining puberty,

192 render them an account in an action of that sort.   The tutories-at-law of patrons and parents, on the other hand, derive such efficacy as they possess from the fact that such persons cannot be compelled to grant their *auctoritas* either to the execution of a testament by their female wards, or the alienation by them of *res mancipi*, or the undertaking by them of obligations, unless, as regards alienation or obligement, there be a weighty reason to justify it.   And all this is in the

§ 190. Comp. § 144; Vlp. xi, 1; Cato apud Liv. xxxiv, 2; Cic. *pro Mur.* xii, 27; Isidor. *Orig.* ix, 7, § 30.
    [1] Comp. ii, 122; Vlp. xi, §§ 25, 27.
§ 191. Comp. § 7, tit. I. afd.
§ 192. Comp. Vlp. xi, 27; Cic. *pro Flacco*, xxxiv, 84.

[1] Comp. ii, §§ 112, 118, 122; iii, 43; Vlp. xx, 16; xxix, 28.
[2] Comp. ii, §§ 47, 80; Paul. in Fr. Vat. §§ 1, 45.
[3] Comp. iii, §§ 108, 176; Cic. *pro Flacco*, xxxv, 86; *pro Caec.* xxv, 72.

sunt, ut, quia ad eos intestatarum mortuarum hereditates
pertinent, neque per testamentum excludantur ab hereditate,
neque alienatis pretiosioribus rebus susceptoque aere alieno
193 minus locuples ad eos hereditas perueniat.   Apud peregrinos non similiter ut apud nos in tutela sunt feminae; sed
tamen plerumque quasi in tutela sunt : ut ecce lex Bithynorum,[1] si quid mulier *contrahat, maritum auctorem esse iubet*[2]
aut filium eius puberem.
194   Tutela autem liberantur ingenuae quidem trium [*liberorum*
[*iure,*[1] *libertinae uero quattuor, si in patroni*] liberorumue eius
legitima tutela sint; nam [et ceterae] quae alterius generis
tutores habent, [uelut Atilianos aut fiduciarios], trium libero-
195 rum iure tutela liberantur.   Potest autem pluribus modis
libertina alterius generis [*tutorem*] habere, ueluti si a femina
manumissa sit; tunc enim e lege Atilia petere debet tutorem,

interest of the patrons and parents themselves; in order that,
as they are entitled to the succession of their female wards
dying intestate, they may neither be excluded from it by will,
nor find it diminished in value by the alienation of the more
precious articles belonging to it or the burdening of it with
193 debt.   Amongst peregrins women are not in tutelage exactly
as with us, although very often in a sort of quasi-tutelage; a
law of the Bithynians, for instance, requires that, if a woman
enter into a contract, her husband or a son above puberty
shall be *auctor.*
194   Women of free birth are released from tutory in right of
their having three children. [*Freedwomen in the tutory-at-*
[*law of their patrons or patrons' children are released from it in*
[*right of four;*] but if they have any other sort of tutors,
Atilian, for instance, or fiduciary, they also are released in right
195 of three.   For there are various ways in which a freedwoman may have another sort of tutor than her patron; for
example, if it be by a woman that she has been manumitted she
must have a tutor appointed under the Atilian law, or in the

§ 193. Comp. Cic. *pro Flacco,* xxx, § 74.
[1] Bithynia was originally one of the popular provinces, but by Hadrian eventually made an imperial one.
[2] Reading doubtful, the MS. running—*siquitmul. hat. marit. auteē. iuuet.*
§ 194. Comp. § 145; iii, 44; Vlp. xxix, 3. The words in ital. are due to

Hollweg, and have been adopted substantially by all subsequent eds. The *et ceterae* and *uelut Atil. aut fiduc.* are omitted by P. as glosses.
[1] The concession of privileges to those who were mothers of a certain number of children was one of the means provided, in the Papia-Poppaean law for encouraging marriage; see § 145, note 1.
§ 195. Comp. § 185.

uel in prouinciis e [*lege Iulia et*] Titia: *nam* in patronae
195a *tutela*[1] *esse non potest.*　Item *si* a masculo manumissa
[*fuerit*] et auctore eo coemptionem fecerit, deinde remancipata
et manumissa sit, patronum quidem habere tutorem desinit,
incipit autem habere eum tutorem a quo manumissa est, qui
195b fiduciarius dicitur.　Item si patronus (*eiusue filius*)[1] in
adoptionem se dedit, debet *liberta* (*e lege Atilia uel Iulia et*)[2]
195c Titia tutorem petere.　Similiter ex iisdem legibus petere
debet tutorem *liberta* si patronus decesserit, *nec ullum* uirilis
sexus liberorum in familia *reliquerit.*

196　Masculi (*autem cum*) puberes esse coeperint tutela liberantur.　(*puberem autem*) Sabinus[1] quidem et Cassius[1] *ceterique nostri praeceptores*[1] eum esse putant qui habitu corporis

---

provinces under the Julian and Titian, seeing she cannot be
195a in the tutory of her patroness.　Again, if she have been
manumitted by a male, and with his *auctoritas* have performed
coemption, and have thereafter been remancipated and manumitted, she ceases to have her patron as tutor, and begins to
have in that capacity him by whom she was latterly manu-
195b mitted, and who is called her fiduciary tutor.　So if a
patron *or his son* have given himself in adoption, the freedwoman must have a tutor appointed *under either the Atilian*
195c *or Julian and Titian* law.　In like manner she must apply
for a tutor under these same laws if her patron be dead, no
male member of his family surviving him.

196　Males are freed from tutelage on attaining puberty,
Sabinus, Cassius, and the other leaders of our school hold *him
to have arrived at puberty* who manifests it by his bodily

---

[1] Comp. Vlp. in fr. 2, pr. D. *de
R. I.* (1, 17).
§ 195a.　Comp. §§ 115, 166.
§ 195b.　Comp. Vlp. xi, 9; § 4, I. *quib.
mod. tut. fin.* (i, 22).
　[1] Suggested by Stud. as corresponding fairly to the traces visible
in the ms.
　[2] Stud., in a footnote, observes
that the ms. has faint traces of something like *elegtitiaet.*
§ 195c.　Comp. § 179.
§ 196.　Comp. tit. I. *QVIBVS MODIS
TVTELA FINITVR* (i, 22); Vlp. xi, 28.
　[1] The reference in the words *nostri
praeceptores* and *diuersae scholae
auctores*—and it is of frequent
recurrence—is to the two rival
schools or sects of the Sabinians or

Cassians and the Proculians; comp.
Pompon. in fr. 2, § 47, D. *de O. I.*
(i, 2).
　They both arose in the time of
Augustus; the founder of the first
being Ateius Capito, and his immediate successors Massurius Sabinus
and Caius Cassius Longinus; that of
the second being Antistius Labeo,
and his successors Nerva the elder
and Proculus.　Pomponius says that
Capito and his followers were con-
servative in their doctrine, Labeo
and his school of a more critical
spirit, and readier to innovate; the
former were inclined to bow to
authority, the latter to inquire for
themselves.　It can hardly be said,
however, that this is always mani-

pubertatem ostendit, *id est eum* qui generare potest; sed in
his qui pubescere non possunt, quales sunt spadones, eam
aetatem esse spectandam cuius aetatis puberes fiunt; sed
diuersae scholae auctores[1] annis putant pubertatem aesti-
mandam, id est eum puberem esse existimant — — — —.[2]

197   — — — — — — aetatem peruenerit in qua res suas
tueri possit, sicuti apud peregrinas gentes custodiri superius

---

development, in other words, who can procreate; but that in
those who can never do so, eunuchs for example, that age
is to be regarded as definitive at which persons usually
reach puberty.   The authorities of the other school think
that puberty ought always to be dealt with as a matter of
years, and hold him to have reached it [*who has attained the age*
[*of fourteen*].   — — — — —.

197   — — — — — —.   [*By the Plaetorian law it is pro-*
[*vided that in certain cases a minor who has passed the years*
[*of pupillarity shall have the assistance of a curator appointed*
[*by the praetor; but his office lasts only until he has fulfilled*
[*the duty for which he has been appointed, and not until the*
[*minor has*] reached the age at which he can take care of his
own affairs.   This practice, as already said, prevails also in

---

fest in the records of their controversies.

Gai. professed himself a Sabinian,
but was not an indiscriminate adherent of the school.

Of the many treatises on the subject the best modern one is that of
Dirksen (*die Schulen der Roem.
Juristen*) in his *Beitraege zur Kunde
des Roem. Rechts*, Leipz. 1825.

[2] The conclusion of the par. is on
p. 53, the whole of which is illegible,
but *qui xIIII annos expleuit* is the
likely reading; comp. § 168, Vlp. xi,
28.   It is possible that on the same
page Gai. may have mentioned some
of the other modes of extinction of
a tutory which we find enumerated
in tit. I. afd.

§§ 197, 198.   Comp. tit. I. *DE CVRATO-*
RIBVS (i, 23).   Part of the illegible
p. 53 seems to have been devoted to
the subject of curatory. In the Epit.
i, 8, we have—*Peractis pupillaribus
annis, quibus tutores absoluuntur, ad
curatores ratio minorum incipit pertinere.   Sub curatore sunt minores
aetate, maiores euersores, insani.
Hi qui minores sunt usque ad ui-*

*ginti et quinque annos impletos sub
curatore sunt.   Qui uero euersores
aut insani sunt, omni tempore uitae
suae sub curatore esse iubentur, quia
substantiam suam rationabiliter gu-
bernare non possunt.* For the reason
stated in next note, however, this
cannot be a correct representation of
what was contained in the pages of
Gaius. Comp. Vlp. tit. xii; Paul.
iii, 4*a*, § 7.

§ 197.   In the absence of the context the
meaning of this par. is by no means
clear.   There is no previous allusion
to curatory of minors above puberty
among foreigners; § 189 refers to
pupils, *i.e.* minors under puberty.
In Rome the curatory of minors was
introduced *in certain cases* by a *lex
Plaetoria* of the sixth century *u. c.*
(Cic. *de Offic.* iii, 15, § 61; Vlp. xii, 4),
on which see Savigny, *Z. f. g. RW.*
x, 232, and *Verm. Schr.* ii, 321; also
Hu. *Z. f. RG.* xiii, 311.   Marc.
Aurelius made the hitherto exceptional practice a universal rule,—
'*statuit ut omnes adulti curatores
accipiunt, non redditis causis*' (Capitolin. *in Marc.* c. 10).

198 indicauimus.   Ex isdem causis et in prouinciis a praesidibus earum curatores dari *solent*.[1]

199   Ne tamen et pupillorum et eorum qui in curatione sunt negotia a tutoribus curatoribusue consumantur aut deminuantur,
curat praetor ut et tutores et curatores eo nomine satisdent.

200 sed hoc non est perpetuum ; nam et tutores testamento dati
satisdare non coguntur, quia fides eorum et diligentia ab ipso
testatore probata est ; et curatores ad quos non e lege curatio
pertinet, sed uel a consule uel a praetore uel a praeside
prouinciae *dantur*, plerumque non coguntur satisdare, scilicet
quia satis *honesti* (*electi sunt*).

---

198 foreign countries.   In the same cases curators are appointed
in the provinces by the governors.

199   To prevent the destruction or dilapidation of the estates of
pupils and persons in curatory by their tutors or curators,
the praetor requires them to give their personal undertaking,
backed by that of sureties, that nothing of the sort shall

200 happen.   But not universally; for not only are testamentary
tutors not compelled to do so, because their integrity and
diligence have been approved by the testator himself, but
curators who do not hold their office by mere devolution of
law, but have been appointed by a consul, praetor, or provincial governor, are generally relieved from the necessity of
giving such an undertaking, having in fact been selected
because of their sufficient trustworthiness.

§ 198. The words *ex iisdem causis*
doubtless refer to the cases enumerated in the Plaetorian law; for Gai.
was writing this first book before
the enactment of Marc. Aurel. referred to in last note.
 [1] The ms. and previous eds. (except K. u. S.) have *uolunt* or *uoluit*,
evidently a mistake.
§§ 199, 200. Comp. tit. I. *DE SATIS-
DATIONE TVTORVM VEL CVRATORVM*
(i, 24), from which the final words,
electi sunt, are borrowed.
 The words *satisdare* and *satis-*

datio are of constant recurrence in
the texts. Very exceptionally the
simple undertaking of the party
himself, technically *repromissio*,
was held to amount to *satisdatio* (fr.
61, D. *de V. S.*, 1, 16) ; but usually
sureties were required in addition
(fr. 1, D. *qui satisdare cogantur*,
ii, 8) ; and this was invariably the
case where the security was required
by the praetor,—a pledge or hypothec could not be accepted instead (fr. 7, D. *de stipulat. praetor.*
xlvi, 5).

[*COMMENTARIVS SECVNDVS.*]

1   [*Superiore commentario de iure personarum*] exposuimus ;
    modo uideamus de rebus : quae uel in nostro patrimonio sunt,
    uel extra nostrum patrimonium habentur.
2   Summa itaque rerum diuisio in duos articulos diducitur :
3   nam aliae sunt diuini iuris, aliae humani.   Diuini iuris
4   sunt ueluti res sacrae et religiosae.   sacrae sunt, quae
    diis superis consecratae sunt ; religiosae, quae diis Manibus
5   relictae sunt.   Sed sacrum quidem hoc solum existimatur
    quod ex auctoritate populi Romani *consecratum est*, ueluti lege
6   de ea re lata aut senatusconsulto facto.   religiosum uero
    nostra uoluntate facimus mortuum inferentes in locum no-
7   strum, si modo eius mortui funus ad nos pertineat.   sed

---

1   In the preceding Commentary we have explained the law
    concerning persons.   Let us now turn our attention to things.
    And these are either in our patrimony or beyond it, [*i.e.*
    either capable or incapable of being subjected to a private
    person's rights.]
2   The first division then of things is into two classes ; for some
3   are of divine and others of human right.   Of divine right are
4   those that are sacred and religious.   Sacred are those con-
    secrated to the gods above ; religious those devoted to the gods
5   below.   That alone is esteemed sacred which has been con-
    secrated by authority of the state, say by a comitial enactment
6   or a senatusconsult passed for the purpose.   But we can at
    our own hand make ground belonging to us religious by burying
    a corpse in it, provided we be the persons charged with the
7   funeral obsequies.   It is generally held that ground in the

---

§§ 1-11. Comp. pr. §§ 1-10, tit. I. *DE*
    RERVM DIVISIONE (ii, 1).
§ 1. The first line of p. 55 of the MS.
    is blank. Comp. pr. tit. I. afd.,
    from which the missing words are
    supplied.
§§ 2, 3.   Gai. in fr. 1, pr. D. *de diu. rer.*
    (i, 8). Comp. iii, 97.

§ 4. Comp. § 8, tit. I. afd.
§ 5. Comp. Fest. v. *Sacer* (Bruns,
    p. 261) ; § 8, tit. I. afd.
§ 6. Comp. Gell. iv, 9, § 8 ; § 9, tit. I.
    afd.
§ 7.   Comp. i, 6 ; Front. *de controu.*
    agr. (ed. Lachm. p. 36) ; Th. ii, 1,
    40.

in prouinciali solo placet plerisque solum religiosum non
fieri, quia in eo solo dominium populi Romani est uel Caesaris,
nos autem possessionem tantum uel usumfructum habere
uidemur: utique tamen etiamsi non sit religiosum pro religioso habetur.   item quod [in prouinciis][1] non ex auctoritate populi Romani consecratum est, proprie sacrum non est,
8 tamen pro sacro habetur.   Sanctae quoque res, ueluti muri
9 et portae, quodammodo diuini iuris sunt.   Quod autem
diuini iuris est, id nullius in bonis est: id uero quod humani
(*iuris est plerumque alicuius in bonis est ; potest autem et
(nullius in bonis esse : nam res hereditariae antequam aliquis*
9a (*heres existat nullius in bonis sunt.*)   [9a] — — — — — —
10 — domino.   Hae autem quae humani iuris sunt aut publi-
11 cae sunt aut priuatae.   Quae publicae sunt nullius *uidentur*
in bonis esse; ipsius enim uniuersitatis esse creduntur.
priuatae sunt quae singulorum sunt.

---

provinces cannot thus be made religious, as the ownership of it
belongs either to the Roman people or to the emperor, private
persons having only the possession or usufruct of it; but
though it may not strictly be religious, it is at any rate
regarded as quasi-religious.   In the same way what is consecrated without the authority of the state [*i.e.* at a private party's
own hand], is not properly speaking sacred, but is dealt with as
8 quasi-sacred.   Holy places, such as a city's walls and gates,
9 are also in a manner of divine right.   What is of divine
right cannot be amongst any [private] person's belongings.
But what is of human right *ordinarily does belong to some
one ; though it may belong to no one, as is the case with the
items of an inheritance, which, until an heir has come forward,*
9a *are not in any person's estate.*   [9a] — — — — — —
10 — —.   Things of human right are either public or private.
11 Those that are public are not regarded as belonging to individuals ; they are held to belong to the corporate body itself.
Those are private that belong to individuals.

---

[1] These words, according to M.
(K. u. S. footnote), should be expunged as a gloss.
§ 8.   Gai. (*lib. ii. Inst.*) in fr. 1, pr. D.
de diu. rer. (i, 8); § 10, tit. I. afd.
§ 9.   Gai. in fr. 1, pr. D. *de diu. rer.*
(i, 8); comp. § 7, tit. I. afd. The

first eleven lines of p. 56 are entirely
illegible; the words in ital., which
are from the Dig. as quoted, may
have occupied the first three or
four.
§§ 10, 11.   Gai. in fr. 1, pr. D. *de diu.
rer.* (i, 8).

12   Quaedam praeterea res corporales sunt,quaedam incorporales.
13   [*Corporales*] hae sunt quae tangi possunt, uelut fundus, homo,
      uestis, aurum, argentum et denique aliae res innumerabiles.
14   Incorporales sunt quae tangi non possunt, qualia sunt ea
      quae in iure consistunt, sicut hereditas, ususfructus, obliga-
      tiones quoquo modo contractae.   nec ad rem pertinet [*quod in*
      [*hereditate res corporales continentur; nam*] et fructus qui ex
      fundo percipiuntur corporales sunt, et id quod ex aliqua
      obligatione nobis debetur plerumque corporale (*est, ueluti*)
      fundus homo pecunia: nam ipsum ius successionis et ipsum
      ius utendi fruendi et ipsum ius obligationis incorporale est.
      eodem numero sunt et iura praediorum urbanorum et rusti-
14a corum, (*quae etiam seruitutes uocantur.*)   [14a] — — —
      altius tollendi — — — *luminibus uicini aedium, aut* non

---

12   Further, some things are corporeal, some incorporeal.
13   Corporeal are those that are tangible, such as land, a slave, a
14   garment, gold, silver, and other things innumerable.   In-
      corporeal are those that are intangible,—things that have a
      mere jural existence, such as an inheritance, a usufruct, obliga-
      tions, in whatsoever way contracted.   Nor does it affect our
      definition *that there are corporeals included in an inheritance;*
      for the fruits gathered from the soil [by a usufructuary] are
      also corporeal, and what is due to us under an obligation is
      generally corporeal, as, for example, land, a slave, money : it is
      the right of succession, the right of usufructing, and the right
      under the obligation that is incorporeal.   To the same class
      belong those rights over urban and rural estates *which go by*
14a *the name of servitudes.   Urban servitudes are such as these :*
      the right of building higher *and thus obstructing* a neighbour's

---

§§ 12-14. Comp. tit. I. DE REBVS IN-
   CORPORALIBVS (ii, 2), from which
   the words supplied in § 14 are derived. See also Gai. fr. 1, § 1, D.
   de diu. rer. (i, 8). Comp. Cic. *Top.*
   v, §§ 26, 27.
§§ 14a-15a. These pars. are on p. 57 of
   the ᴍs., the greater part of which is
   illegible.
§ 14a. Comp. pr. §§ 1, 2, tit. I. DE
   SERVITVTIBVS (ii, 3). The beginning of the par. may have run thus :
   Urbanorum praediorum iura sunt
   altius tollendi *et eo modo officiendi*
   luminibus uicini aedium, aut non,
   etc. ; see Gai. in fr. 2, 6, D. *de seruit.*
   praed. urb. (viii, 2). The next five

lines give us nothing decipherable,
except the words *ius aquae ducendae;*
whence it may be concluded that
they contained a partial enumeration of the rural as well as the
urban *seruitutes praediorum.* The
Epit. ii, 2, § 3, enumerates them
thus : *Praediorum urbanorum iura
sunt stillicidia, fenestrae, cloacae,
altius erigendae domus aut non erigendae, et luminum,·ut ita quis fabri-
cet ut uicinae domui lumen non
tollat. Praediorum uero rusticorum
iura sunt uia uel iter, per quod
pecus aut animalia debeant ambu-
lare uel ad aquam duci, et aquaeductus.*

extollendi ne luminibus *uicini officiatur :* item fluminum et
stillicidiorum ius, — — — — — — —.

15   Res — — — — *nec mancipi. mancipi sunt* — — —
— — —; item aedes *in italico solo*[1]— — — — — —
— — praediorum *urbanorum* nec mancipi (*habentur*). item
15a stipendiaria praedia et tributaria nec mancipi sunt.   Sed
quod diximus — — — — *mancipi esse* — — — — —
statim ut nata sunt mancipi esse putant; Nerua uero et
Proculus et ceteri diuersae scholae auctores[1] non aliter ea
mancipi esse putant quam si domita sunt; et si propter
nimiam feritatem domari non possunt, tunc uideri mancipi
esse incipere *cum ad eam aetatem peruenerint qua* domari

---

lights, and his right to prevent us building higher lest thereby
his light should be obstructed; the rights of roof-gutter and
rain-drop, [*and others. Among rural servitudes are rights of*
[*way and passage for men or animals, and right of aqueduct.*]
15   Further, things *are either* mancipi *or* nec mancipi. *Mancipi*
are *lands* and houses in places of italic right, [*slaves and*
[*animals domesticated by yoke or saddle. Rural praedial servi-*
[*tudes likewise are* mancipi *but those over*] urban estates are
regarded as *nec mancipi.*   Stipendiary and tributary pro-
15a vincial lands are also *nec mancipi.*   The statement that
[*animals we are wont to tame are* mancipi *is variously under-*
[*stood ; for while the authorities of our school are of opinion*
[*that such animals—oxen, mules, horses, and asses*]—are *res*
mancipi from the moment of birth, Nerva and Proculus, and
the leaders of the other school, hold that they become so only
when tamed, or, if this be impossible because of their unusual
ferocity, when they attain the age at which such animals are

§ 15. The next seven or eight lines, for
the most part undecipherable, seem
to have contained a reference to the
distinction between *res mancipi* and
nec mancipi (i, 120, note 1), and an
enumeration of the former. It might
be reconstructed thus: Res *autem*
uel mancipi sunt uel nec mancipi.
Mancipi sunt *praedia rustica in*
italico solo ; item aedes in italico
solo; *item serui, et animalia man-*
sueta quae collo dorsoue domantur.
seruitutes quoque praediorum rusti-
corum mancipi sunt; sed seruitutes
praediorum urbanorum nec mancipi *habentur.* item stipendiaria
praedia et tributaria nec mancipi
sunt. Comp. i, §§ 120, 121; ii,
§§ 17, 21, 29 ; Vlp. xix, §§ 1, f.
    [1] As regards *praedia in italico*
solo, see i, 120, note 2.
§ 15a. The last three lines of p. 57 are
almost illegible. They must have
run to the following effect: Sed
quod diximus *ea animalia quae*
domari solent mancipi esse *uarie*
accipitur. Nostri quidem praecep-
tores haec animalia, qualia sunt
boues muli equi asini, statim, etc.
Comp. Isidor. *Orig.* ix, 4, § 45
(Bruns, p. 303).
    [1] See i, 196, note 1.

16 solent.   (*Sed*) ferae bestiae nec mancipi sunt, uelut ursi leones; item ea animalia quae fere bestiarum numero sunt, uelut elephanti et cameli; et ideo ad rem non pertinet quod haec animalia etiam collo dorsoue domari *solent; nam nec* [*notitia*][1] quidem eorum animalium illo tempore fuit quo *constituebatur* quasdam res mancipi esse, quasdam non

17 mancipi.   Item fere omnia quae incorporalia sunt nec mancipi sunt, exceptis seruitutibus praediorum rusticorum; nam eas mancipi esse constat, quamuis sint ex numero rerum incorporalium.

18 Magna autem differentia est inter mancipi res et nec
19 mancipi.   nam res nec mancipi ipsa traditione pleno iure alterius fiunt, si modo corporales sunt et ob id recipiunt
20 traditionem.   itaque si tibi uestem uel aurum uel argentum tradidero, siue ex uenditionis causa siue ex donationis siue quauis alia ex causa, statim tua fit ea res, si modo *ego eius*
21 *dominus sim iure ciuili.*[1]   *In eadem* causa sunt prouincialia praedia, quorum alia stipendiaria alia tributaria uocamus.

---

16 generally broken in.   But wild beasts, such as bears and lions, are *nec mancipi;* so are such semi-wild beasts as elephants and camels.   Nor does it matter that those last are often broken in as draught or carrying animals; for none of them were even known at the time when it was settled what things
17 should be *mancipi* and what *nec mancipi.*   Almost all incorporeals are *nec mancipi,* except rural praedial servitudes; for these are held to be *res mancipi,* though incorporeal.
18 There is an important difference between *res mancipi* and
19 *res nec mancipi.*   For what are *nec mancipi* pass to another in full ownership by simple delivery, provided they are corporeal and thus deliverable.   Therefore, if I have delivered to you a garment, or gold, or silver, whether in pursuance of a sale, or as a donation, or upon any other sufficient cause, it straightway becomes yours, provided always that I who
21 deliver it am in law its owner.   In exactly the same position are provincial lands, some of which we call stipendiary,

§ 16. Comp. Vlp. xix, 1.
   [1] So Hu.; K. u. S. have *nam [ne] nomen quidem eorum animalium illo tempore [notum] fuit.*
§ 17. Comp. i, 120, and notes; ii, §§ 15, 29; Vlp. xix, 1.
§§ 18-20. Comp. Vlp. xix, 6; Fr. Vat. § 313; Boeth. *in Cic. Top.* v, 5,
§ 28 (ed. Bait. p. 321); Th. ii, 1, § 40.
§ 19. See § 40, note.
§ 20. [1] So P. renders the *io* or *ic* of MS., disregarded by K. u. S., and placed by Hu. at the beginning of next par.
§ 21. Comp. i, 7; ii, 6; § 40, I. *de rer. diu.,* ii, 1; Th. ii, 1, § 40.

stipendiaria sunt ea quae in his prouinciis sunt quae propriae
populi Romani esse intelleguntur; tributaria sunt ea quae
in his prouinciis sunt quae propriae Caesaris esse creduntur.
22 Mancipi uero res sunt quae per mancipationem ad alium
transferuntur; unde etiam mancipi res sunt dictae. quod
23 autem ualet mancipatio [*idem ualet et in iure cessio.   Et man-*
[*cipatio*] quidem quemadmodum fiat superiore commentario
24 tradidimus.   In iure cessio autem hoc modo fit: apud magistratum populi Romani, ueluti praetorem, [uel apud praesidem
prouinciae],[1] is cui res in iure ceditur rem tenens ita dicit:
HVNC EGO HOMINEM [2] EX IVRE QVIRITIVM MEVM ESSE AIO;
deinde, postquam hic uindicauerit, (*praetor interrogat*)[3] eum qui
cedit an contra uindicet; quo negante aut tacente tunc ei
qui uindicauerit eam rem addicit; idque legis actio uocatur.
hoc fieri potest etiam in prouinciis apud praesides earum.

---

and others tributary.   Stipendiary lands are those situated in
provinces regarded as specially belonging to the Roman
people; tributary those lying in provinces held to belong
22 specially to the emperor.   But those things are *res mancipi*
that are transferred by mancipation; hence their name.
[*Equally effectual with it is* in iure cessio, i.e. *cession in court.*]
23 How mancipation is effected has been explained in the pre-
24 ceding Commentary.   Cession in court proceeds thus: in
the presence of one of the Roman magistrates, a praetor say,
he to whom the thing in question is being ceded, having hold
of it, says—' I say that this slave is mine in quiritarian right;'
when he has thus vindicated, the praetor asks the cedent
whether he makes any counter-vindication; on the latter
replying in the negative or remaining silent, the praetor
adjudges the thing to the vindicant.   The procedure is spoken
of as a *legis actio;* and it may be employed even in a province,

§§ 22, 23. The words in ital. in these pars., suggested by G., are adopted by most eds. P. proposes : *quae priuatim fieri potest, idem ualet utique in iure cessio.*
§ 22. Comp. i, 121; Vlp. xix, 3; Varro *de R. R.* ii, 10, § 4 (Bruns, p. 283); Boeth. *in Cic. Top.* v, 5, § 28 (ed. Bait. 322).
§ 23. Comp. i, 119.
§ 24. Comp. i, 134; ii, 96; iv, 16; Vlp. xix, §§ 9, 10; Boeth. *in Cic. Top.* v, 5, § 28 (ed. Bait. p. 322);

Isidor. *Orig.* v, 25, § 32 (Bruns, p. 302).
[1] These words are manifestly a gloss, as the statement occurs more directly in the end of the paragraph.
[2] In illustrative styles or *formulae* of transactions referring to moveables, a slave is usually made the object.
[3] The words *praetor interrogat* are from Boeth., who is professedly quoting from Gai.

25 *Plerumque tamen* et fere semper mancipationibus utimur:
quod enim ipsi per nos praesentibus amicis agere possumus,
hoc non est necesse cum maiore difficultate apud praetorem
26 aut apud praesidem prouinciae *agere.*   *Quod si* neque
mancipata neque in iure cessa sit res mancipi, — — — —
27 — —.   [27]   — — — — — — — —.
28 (*Res*) incorporales traditionem non recipere manifestum est.
29 Sed iura praediorum urbanorum in iure cedi possunt; rusticorum uero etiam mancipari possunt.
30 Vsusfructus in iure cessionem tantum recipit: nam dominus
proprietatis alii usumfructum in iure cedere potest, ut ille
usumfructum habeat et ipse nudam proprietatem (*retineat*).
ipse usufructuarius in iure cedendo domino proprietatis usum-

---

25 before the governor.   Usually, however, indeed almost
always, we make use of mancipation; for as we can carry out
the latter ourselves in the presence of a few friends, it is unnecessary to have recourse to the more troublesome procedure
26 before a praetor or provincial governor.   If a *res mancipi*
have been neither mancipated nor ceded in court, — — —
27 — — —.   [27] — — — — — — — —.
28 It is manifest that incorporeals are incapable of transfer by
29 delivery.   But urban praedial rights may be ceded in court,
and rural ones may also be mancipated.
30 A usufruct can be transferred only by *cessio in iure;* for an
owner can cede the usufruct of what belongs to him to another,
so that the cessionary shall have the usufructuary right, he
himself retaining the bare property.   The effect of cession of
the right of usufruct by the usufructuary to the owner of the
property is that it thereby passes from the cedent and merges

---

§ 26. The initial words of this par. are
on the last line of p. 59; of p. 60
not above a dozen words are decipherable. The par. possibly contained a statement of the consequences of neglect of mancipation
or cession in court in conveyance
of a *res mancipi;* although this
matter is afterwards referred to in
§ 41.

§ 27. This par. is assumed to have included the latter half of p. 60 and first
twelve lines of p. 61. These last are
partially legible, though no line completely so. It is not improbable
that they contained some explana-

tion of the *ius commercii*, as in Vlp.
xix, §§ 4, 5; and the words extant
on p. 61 show that it also included
some reference to the qualities of
land in the provinces, according as
it did or did not enjoy the privileges
of the *ius italicum* (upon which see
i, 120, note 2).

§ 28. Comp. § 19; Gai. in fr. 43, § 1,
D. *de adq. rer. dom.* (xli, 1).

§ 29. Comp. § 17.

§§ 30-33. Comp. tit. I. *DE VSVFRVCTV*
(ii, 4).

§ 30. Comp. § 33; Vlp. xix, 11; Paul.
iii, 6, § 32; Fr. Vat. § 45; § 3, tit.
I. afd.

fructum *efficit ut a* se discedat et conuertatur in proprietatem :
alii uero in iure cedendo nihilo minus ius suum retinet ;
31 creditur enim ea cessione nihil agi. Sed haec scilicet in
italicis praediis[1] ita sunt, quia et ipsa praedia mancipationem
et in iure cessionem recipiunt. alioquin in prouincialibus
praediis, siue quis usumfructum siue ius eundi agendi aquamue
ducendi, uel altius tollendi aedes aut non tollendi ne luminibus
uicini officiatur,[2] ceteraque similia iura constituere uelit, pac-
tionibus et stipulationibus[3] id efficere potest ; quia ne ipsa
quidem praedia mancipationem aut in iure cessionem recipiunt.
32 *Sed* cum ususfructus et hominum et ceterorum animalium
constitui possit, intellegere debemus horum usumfructum
etiam in prouinciis per in iure cessionem constitui posse.
33 Quod autem diximus usumfructum in iure cessionem tantum
recipere non est temere dictum, quamuis etiam per mancipa-

---

again in the property; by cession in court to a third party,
however, the usufructuary still retains his right,—the cession
31 is held in that case to be resultless. But this applies only
to a usufruct of lands that have italic privilege ; for they are
susceptible both of mancipation and cession in court. In the
case of [unprivileged] provincial lands, if a man desire to
constitute a usufruct, or a right of footpath or cattle road, of
aqueduct, of higher-building or preventing higher-building
lest a neighbour's lights should be interfered with, or any
similar description of servitude, he must carry out his object
by means of pacts and stipulations ; for lands such as these
are not themselves susceptible of mancipation or cession in
32 court. But there may be usufruct both of slaves and
animals ; and it should be understood that such a servitude
may be constituted by *in iure cessio* even in the provinces.
33 Our statement that a usufruct can be transferred only by
cession in court is not made inconsiderately ; for although it
is true that it may be constituted by mancipation in this

§ 31. Comp. Gai. in fr. 3, pr. D. *de
usufr.* (vii, 1) ; § 1, tit. I. afd. ; § 4,
I. *de seruitut.* (ii, 3).
  [1] See i, 120, note 2.
  [2] There is here, as in § 14*a*, a little
confusion of the easement and the
burden. *Seruitus* was used to express either ; but properly it was
the burden, *ius seruitutis* being the
easement.

[3] The *pactio* was the agreement to
constitute ; the *stipulatio* a subsequent engagement (under a penalty)
by the owner of the servient tene-
ment not to interfere with the exercise of the right by the owner of the
dominant one. See fr. 2, § 5, fr. 4,
§ 1, fr. 38, §§ 10, f., D. *de V. O.*
(xlv, 1).
§ 33. Comp. § 30 ; Fr. Vat. §§ 47, 50.

tionem constitui possit eo quod in mancipanda proprietate
detrahi potest; non enim ipse ususfructus mancipatur, sed
cum in mancipanda proprietate deducatur, eo fit ut apud alium
ususfructus apud alium proprietas sit.

34 Hereditas quoque in iure cessionem tantum recipit.

35 Nam si is ad quem ab intestato legitimo iure pertinet
hereditas, in iure eam alii ante aditionem cedat, id est antequam heres extiterit, proinde fit heres is cui in iure cesserit,
ac si ipse per legem ad hereditatem uocatus esset; post obligationem uero si cesserit nihilo minus ipse heres permanet
et ob id creditoribus tenebitur, debita uero pereunt eoque
modo debitores hereditarii lucrum faciunt; corpora uero eius
hereditatis perinde transeunt ad eum cui cessa est hereditas,

36 ac si ei singula in iure cessa fuissent.   Testamento autem
scriptus heres ante aditam quidem hereditatem in iure cedendo
eam alii nihil agit; postea uero quam adierit si cedat, ea
accidunt quae proxime diximus de eo ad quem ab intestato
legitimo iure pertinet hereditas, si post obligationem in iure

---

sense—that an owner reserves it in mancipating his property,
here it is not the usufruct that is mancipated, but in the
mancipation of the property the usufruct is reserved, and thus
it comes to pass that the usufruct is in one person while the
property is in another.

34 An inheritance also is not otherwise transferable than by
35 cession in court.   For if he who on intestacy is entitled to
an inheritance as *heir-at-law* cede it in court to another
person before entry, that is, before he has assumed the position
of heir, the cessionary becomes heir just as if the inheritance
had devolved upon him by operation of law. If, however, the
cession be after the heir-at-law has accepted the responsibilities of his position, he nevertheless still remains heir and
responsible to the deceased's creditors, while debts due to the
inheritance are extinguished, and the deceased's debtors by so
much the gainers; but the corporeal items of the inheritance
pass to the cessionary just as if they had each been ceded to
36 him separately.   Cession of an inheritance by the *testamentary* heir before entry is of no avail; if, however, he cede
after entry, the same results follow that we have described in
speaking of cession by an heir-at-law *ab intestato* after assump-

§ 34. Before this par. a line and a half   §§ 35, 36.   Comp. iii, §§ 85, 86; Vlp.
vacant in the ms. Comp. Vlp. xix, 11.   xix, §§ 12-15.

37 cedat.   Idem et de necessariis heredibus diuersae scholae
auctores[1] existimant, quod nihil uidetur interesse utrum
[*aliquis*] adeundo hereditatem[2] fiat heres an inuitus existat;
quod quale sit suo loco[3] apparebit : sed nostri praeceptores
putant nihil agere necessarium heredem cum in iure cedat
hereditatem.

38   Obligationes quoquo modo contractae nihil eorum recipiunt :
nam quod mihi ab aliquo debetur, id si uelim tibi deberi,
nullo eorum modo quibus res corporales ad alium transferuntur
id efficere possum : sed opus est ut iubente me tu ab eo
stipuleris; quae res efficit ut a me liberetur et incipiat tibi

39 teneri.   quae dicitur nouatio obligationis.   sine hac uero
nouatione non poteris tuo nomine agere, sed debes ex persona
mea quasi cognitor aut procurator meus experiri.

40   Sequitur ut admoneamus apud peregrinos quidem unum esse

---

37 tion of the heir's responsibilities.   The authorities of the
other school think that cession by a necessary heir also pro-
duces those same results, it being in their opinion immaterial
whether a man becomes heir by his own act of entry or has
that character imposed upon him against his will,—the distinction will be explained in the proper place; our school, on
the other hand, holds that cession of an inheritance by a
necessary heir is altogether inoperative.

38   There is nothing of this sort in obligations, howsoever contracted; for by none of those modes whereby corporeals are
transferred can I bring it about that what a man owes me, he
shall in future, if I wish it, owe to you.   What must be done
is this: you must yourself, on my instruction, take from him
a stipulatory engagement [for the same debt]; thereby he is
discharged so far as I am concerned, but begins to be bound

39 to you.   This is called novation of an obligation.   Without
such novation you cannot proceed against him in your own
name, but must sue in mine as my cognitor or procurator.

40   We have next to observe that among peregrins there is but

---

§ 87. Comp. iii, 87.
   [1] See i, 196, note 1.
   [2] The ms. has *hereditatemstatem*;
which has led P. to interject *statim*,
not, however, before *fiat*, but before
existat.
   [3] See §§ 152, f.
§ 38. Comp. iii, 176.
§ 89. Comp. iv, §§ 82, 86.
§§ 40-61. Comp. tit. I. *DE VSVCAPIONI-*

BVS ET LONGI TEMPORIS POSSESSIO-
NIBVS (ii, 6).
§ 40. Comp. i, §§ 54 (and note), 167;
ii, 88; iii, 166; Tb. i, 5, § 4. The
latter passage runs (vers. Reitz.):
Est igitur, ut dixi, naturale domi-
nium (φυσιχὴ δεσποτεία) *et legitimum*
dominium (ἔννομος δεσποτεία). *Ac*
naturale dicitur in bonis, et dominus
bonitarius : legitimum dicitur iure

dominium : nam aut dominus quisque est aut dominus non
intellegitur. Quo iure etiam populus Romanus olim utebatur.
aut enim ex iure Quiritium unusquisque dominus erat, aut
non intellegebatur dominus. sed postea diuisionem accepit
dominium, ut alius possit esse ex iure Quiritium dominus,
41 alius in bonis habere.   nam si tibi rem mancipi neque
mancipauero neque in iure cessero sed tantum tradidero, in
bonis quidem tuis ea res efficitur, ex iure Quiritium uero mea
permanebit donec tu eam possidendo usucapias : semel enim
inpleta usucapione proinde pleno iure incipit, id est et in
bonis et ex iure Quiritium,[1] tua res esse, ac si ea mancipata
42 uel in iure cessa [*esset*.   *Vsucapio autem*] mobilium quidem
rerum anno conpletur, fundi uero et aedium biennio ; et ita
lege XII tabularum cautum est.

---

one sort of ownership; for a man either is owner or is not.
And so it was of old time with the people of Rome ; a man
was either owner according to the law of the Quiritians, or he
was not held to be owner at all. But afterwards property
underwent this distinction,—that while one man may be
owner of a thing in quiritary right, another may have it *in*
41 *bonis.*   Thus, suppose I have neither mancipated a *res
mancipi,* nor conveyed it to you by cession in court, but have
simply delivered it, while you will thereby have it *in bonis,*
it will still remain mine in quiritary right until you have
usucapted it by possession ; for the moment your usucapion
of it is completed it forthwith begins to be yours in plenary
ownership, *i.e.* both in bonitarian and in quiritarian right,
exactly as if it had been mancipated to you or ceded to you
42 in court.   The usucapion of moveables is completed in one
year, that of lands and houses in two ; so it is provided in the
Twelve Tables.

*Quiritium, id est Romanorum. . . . .
. . Sed si quis utrumque habebat
dominium, dicebatur pleno iure
(τελείῳ δικαίῳ) dominus, utpote ambo
habens, legitimum et naturale.* The
distinction was abolished by Just., l.
un. C. *de nudo iure Quir. toll.* (v, 25).

§ 41. Comp. § 204 ; iii, 80 ; Vlp. i, 16 ;
Boeth. *in Cic. Top.* iii, 5, § 28 (ed.
Bait. p. 322).   .
  [1] The words *id est . . . . Quiritium* are omitted by P. as a gloss.

§ 42. The initial words, supplied by L.,
are accepted by most eds. Comp.
Cic. *Top.* iv, 23 ; *pro Caec.* xix, 54 ;

Schoell, *Tab.* vi, 3 ; Gai. ii, 204 ;
Vlp. xix, 8 ; pr. tit. I. afd. ; Th. ii,
6, pr. P. altogether rejects the par.,
as not only a gloss, but an erroneous
one ; seeing it contradicts the repeated statement of Cic. that houses
were not mentioned in the provision
of the XII Tab. as to usucapion, but
the rule as to lands analogically extended to them by the early jurists,
or rather by the pontiffs, in whose
hands (Pomp. in fr. 2, § 6, D. *de
O. I.* i, 2) was the interpretation
(*interpretandi scientia*) of the XII
Tables.

43   Ceterum etiam earum rerum usucapio nobis conpetit quae non a domino nobis traditae fuerint, siue mancipi sint eae res siue nec ,mancipi, si modo eas bona fide acceperimus, cum

44   crederemus eum qui traderet dominum esse.   quod ideo receptum uidetur ne rerum dominia diutius in incerto essent, cum sufficeret domino ad inquirendam rem suam anni aut bienii spatium, quod tempus ad usucapionem possessori tributum est.

45   Sed aliquando etiamsi maxime quis bona fide alienam rem possideat, non tamen illi usucapio procedit, uelut si quis rem furtiuam aut ui possessam possideat; nam furtiuam lex XII tabularum[1] usucapi prohibet, ui possessam lex Iulia et Plautia.[2]

46   Item prouincialia praedia usucapionem non recipiunt.

47   [*Item olim*][1] mulieris quae in agnatorum tutela erat res

---

43   We may also acquire by usucapion things, whether *mancipi* or *nec mancipi*, that have been conveyed to us by one not their owner, provided we have accepted them in good faith, believing that the party conveying them was in truth their

44   owner.   This rule seems to have been received in order to prevent a too prolonged uncertainty as to a question of ownership; one or two years—the time allowed to a possessor for usucapion—being thought ample for an owner making inquiries after a thing belonging to him.

45   But sometimes, even though a man possess in the best of faith, there can be no usucapion in his favour, as when what he possesses has been stolen or acquired by a previous holder by force; for the Twelve Tables prohibit the usucapion of stolen goods, and the Julian and Plautian law that of things

46   violently taken possession of.   Further, provincial lands

47   are not susceptible of usucapion.   *Formerly also* the *res mancipi* of a woman in tutelage of her agnates could not be

§§ 43-64. These pars. postponed by P. —as appears to me without any justification--to §§ 65-79.

§§ 43, 44.   Comp. Gai. in fr. 1, D. *de usurp.* (xli, 3); Vlp. xix, 8; pr. tit. I. afd.

§ 45.   Comp. §§ 1, 2, tit. I. afd.
[1] See Schoell, *Tab.* viii, 17. A similar provision as to *res furtiuae* was contained in a *lex Atinia* of 557 | 197 (?); comp. Gell. xvii, 7, § 1; § 2, tit. I. afd.
[2] From Th. ii, 6, § 2, it appears that these were two distinct laws; probably the *lex Plautia de ui*, men-

tioned by Cic. *pro Mil.* xiii, 35, and the *lex Iulia de ui*, which forms the subject of tit. D. xlviii, 7, but whose history is somewhat obscure.

§ 46.   Comp. §§ 7, 21; pr. tit. I. afd.; l. un. C. *de usucap. transf.* (vii, 31).

§ 47.   Comp. i, 192; Cic. *ad Att.* i, 5, § 6; Schoell, *Tab.* v, 2.
[1] G. and most eds. interject these two words; but this necessitates the rejection of *res*, which stands before *mulieris* in the MS. P. manages to retain it by thus supplying the deficiency in the text: [*item ante legem* [*Claudiam, si erant*] *res mulieris*, etc.

mancipi usucapi non poterant, praeterquam si ab ipsa *auctore*
tutore traditae essent: id ita lege XII tabularum *manifestatur.*[2]
48 Item liberos homines et res sacras et religiosas usucapi non
49 posse manifestum est.   Quod ergo uulgo dicitur furtiuarum
rerum et ui possessarum usucapionem per legem XII tabularum prohibitam esse, non eo pertinet ut (*ne ipse*) fur (*quiue*
(*per*) uim (*possidet*) usucapere possit, (nam huic alia ratione
usucapio non conpetit, quia scilicet mala fide possidet); sed
nec ullus alius, quamquam ab eo bona fide emerit, usucapi-
50 endi ius habeat.   Vnde in rebus mobilibus non facile
(*procedit ut bonae fidei possessori usucapio*) conpetat, quia qui
alienam rem uendidit et tradidit furtum committit; idemque
accidit etiam si ex alia causa tradatur. sed tamen hoc
aliquando aliter se habet; nam si heres rem defuncto com-
modatam aut locatam uel apud eum depositam, existimans
eam esse hereditariam, uendiderit aut donauerit, furtum non
committit;[1] item si is ad quem ancillae ususfructus pertinet,

---

usucapted unless they had been delivered with her tutor's
48 *auctoritas;* this is clearly shown in the Twelve Tables.   And
it is also manifest that free persons and things sacred and
49 religious cannot be usucapted.   The common saying that
by the law of the Twelve Tables usucapion is prohibited of
things stolen or forcibly taken possession of does not mean
that the actual thief, or person taking possession by force,
cannot usucapt,—his usucapion is impossible for a different
reason, namely, that he possesses in bad faith,—but that no
other person has the right of usucapting them, even though
he may have purchased them in good faith from the *malae*
50 *fidei* possessor.   As regards moveables, therefore, *usucapion
is hardly possible for a* bonae fidei *possessor*, seeing that he who
sells and delivers what belongs to another commits a theft;
and so it is if the delivery be on some other ground.   Sometimes, however, it is otherwise; for if an heir sell or make a
present of a thing that has been lent or located to or deposited
with the deceased, under the impression that it belongs to
the inheritance, he does not steal it; neither does the usufructuary of a slave woman who sells or makes a gift of a

---

partum etiam suum esse credens uendiderit aut donauerit, furtum non committit; furtum enim sine adfectu furandi non committitur.[2] aliis quoque modis accidere potest ut quis sine uitio furti rem alienam ad aliquem transferat et efficiat ut a
51 possessore usucapiatur.[3]   Fundi quoque alieni potest aliquis *sine ui* possessionem nancisci, quae uel ex negligentia domini uacet uel quia dominus sine successore decesserit uel longo tempore afuerit: quam si ad alium bona fide accipientem transtulerit, poterit usucapere possessor; et quamuis ipse qui uacantem possessionem nactus est intellegat alienum esse fundum, — — — — —[1] ad usucapionem nocetur, [cum] inprobata sit eorum sententia qui putauerint *furtiuum* fundum [2] fieri posse.
52   Rursus ex contrario accidit ut qui sciat alienam rem se possidere usucapiat, ueluti si rem hereditariam cuius posses-

---

child to which she has given birth, under the belief that it is his; for there can be no theft without intent to steal. And there are yet other ways in which it may happen that a man transfers to another, without any taint of theft, what belongs to a third party, and thus puts the possessor in a position to
51 usucapt it.   It is quite possible also for a man to take possession without any violence of land that is not his, if it be unoccupied either through the negligence of the owner, or because he has died leaving no successor, or has for a long time been absent; and if the party who has thus obtained possession transfer it to another who takes it in good faith, the latter may usucapt; for the knowledge of the appropriator of the vacant possession that the land in question belongs to a third party [*will not impede the usucapion of the* bonae fidei [*possessor*], the opinion of those who used to think that land may bear the taint of theft being now universally condemned.
52   On the other hand, it [sometimes] happens that a person may usucapt who takes possession of what he well knows to

[2] § 5, tit. I. afd. Comp. Gai. in fr. 36, § 1, fr. 37, pr. D. *de usurp.* (xli, 3).
[3] § 6, tit. I. afd.
§ 51. Comp. Gai. in fr. 37, § 1, fr. 38, D. *de usurp.* (xli, 3); § 7, tit. I. afd.
[1] Nearly a line illegible, with exception of *nihilomm.* Gou. proposes: *tamen* nihilo *magis bonae fidei possessori*, etc.; while for *nihilo*

magis K. u. S. and Hu. read *nihil hoc.*
[2] Comp. Gell. xi, 18, §§ 12, 13.
§ 52. Comp. iii, 201. There seems good reason for believing that *bona fides* was not originally a condition of usucapion; consequently the usucapions mentioned in §§ 52-61 were merely varieties in which, for special reasons, the original doctrine was not departed from.

sionem heres nondum nactus est aliquis possederit; nam ei
concessum [est usu]capere, si modo ea res est quae recipit
usucapionem : quae species possessionis et usucapionis pro
53 herede uocatur.   Et in tantum haec usucapio concessa est
54 ut et res quae solo continentur anno usucapiantur.   quare
autem hoc casu[1] etiam soli rerum annua constituta sit usucapio illa ratio est, quod olim rerum hereditariarum possessione[2] ipsae hereditates usucapi credebantur, [scilicet anno]:[3]
lex enim XII tabularum soli quidem res biennio usucapi iussit,
ceteras uero anno;[4] ergo hereditas in ceteris rebus uidebatur
esse, quia soli non est quia neque corporalis est: et quamuis
postea creditum sit ipsas hereditates usucapi non posse, tamen
in omnibus rebus hereditariis, etiam quae solo tenentur, annua
55 usucapio remansit.   Quare autem omnino tam inproba

---

belong to another, as for instance when he appropriates something belonging to an inheritance, but which the heir has not
yet reduced into possession; in such a case he is allowed to
usucapt, provided the thing in question be susceptible of
usucapion.   This variety of possession and usucapion is said
53 to be *pro herede*, [i.e. in the character of heir.]   And to
such an extent has this usucapion been conceded, that even
54 immoveables may thus be usucapted in a year.   The reason
why in this case a one year's usucapion of immoveables was
introduced is this—that formerly by possession of the con-
stituent items of an inheritance the inheritance itself was believed to be usucapted, and that in a year.   (For the provision
of the Twelve Tables was that immoveables were to be usucapted in two years, but other things in one; and an inheritance seemed to be included amongst the 'other things,' for
it is not immoveable, because not even corporeal.)   And,
although afterwards it came to be admitted that an inheritance
as such was not susceptible of usucapion, still the one year's
usucapion continued to be applied to every item of the
55 hereditary estate, even though immoveable.   That such an
iniquitous possession and usucapion should ever have been

---

§§ 53, 54.   Comp. Cic. *ad Att.* i, 5, § 6;
Sen. *de benef.* vi, 5.
§ 54.   [1] The MS. has *etiam hoc casu.*
[2] For *possessiones ut*, which stands
in the MS., G., Bk., Hu., and K. u. S.
read *possessione uelut;* P. *possessione,*
[*eae*], *sicut.   Possessiones usucapi* is
certainly an unusual phrase, though
there is something very like it in the

possessionem usurecipi of § 61.   I
am disposed, however, to delete both
the final *s* and the *ut*, and to read
this simply *possessione.*
[3] These words seem to be a gloss.
[4] See § 42.
§ 55.   Comp. Cic. *de legib.* ii, 19, §§ 48,
49; 20, §§ 50, 51; Fest. v. *Sine
sacris hereditas* (Bruns, p. 267).

possessio et usucapio concessa sit illa ratio est, quod uoluerunt
ueteres maturius hereditates adiri, ut essent qui sacra facerent,
quorum illis temporibus summa obseruatio fuit, et ut credi-
56 tores haberent a quo suum consequerentur.   Haec autem
species possessionis et usucapionis etiam lucratiua uocatur :
57 nam sciens quisque rem alienam lucrifacit.   sed hoc tempore iam non est lucratiua : nam ex auctoritate Hadriani
senatusconsultum factum est ut tales usucapiones reuocaren-
tur ; et ideo potest heres ab eo qui rem usucepit hereditatem
petendo perinde eam rem consequi atque si usucapta non
58 esset.   necessario tamen herede [1] extante nihil ipso iure
pro herede usucapi potest.
59   Adhuc etiam ex aliis causis sciens quisque rem alienam

---

recognized may be accounted for by the anxiety of our
ancestors to accelerate entry to an inheritance, in order that
there might be some one to attend to the sacred rites [of the
family], on which great store was set in those days, and that
the creditors [of the deceased] might have some one from
56 whom they could recover what was due to them.   This sort
of possession and usucapion is also sometimes called *usucapio
lucrativa ;* because the possessor knowingly enriches himself
57 with what belongs to another.   But at the present day it
is no longer lucrative ; for, by a senatusconsult enacted by
authority of the emperor Hadrian, such usucapions may be
revoked, and the heir recover from the usucaptor by *hereditatis
58 petitio* as if there never had been any usucapion.   If a
necessary heir exist, however, nothing can be *ipso iure* usucapted *pro herede.*
59   There are yet other cases in which a man may usucapt

---

§ 56. Comp. fr. 71, D. *de furt.* (xlvii, 2) ;
fr. 33, § 1, D. *de usurp.* (xli, 3).
§ 57. By Marc. Aurel. it was made an
offence, under the name of *crimen
expilatae hereditatis,* for a person,
not pretending a title, to take possession of an inheritance either before
or after the heir's entry ; see tit. D.
expil. hered. (xlvii, 19).
§ 58. Comp. iii, 201. It is remarkable
that, prior to Studemund's revision of
the text, all eds. made both these two
pars. affirm the reverse of the truth.
    [1] See the meaning of *necessarius
heres* in § 153. Hu. reads [*suo*] *et
necessario tamen herede ;* on the
ground that the ms. has *et* before

necessario, and that it can be explained only on the supposition that
suo has been omitted. (Who were
sui et necessarii, see described in
§ 156. The difference in position of
the two classes is well explained by
Vlp. xxii, 24.) But as, in iii, 201,
Gai. again uses simply the word
necessarii, I do not think Huschke's
emendation can be accepted.
§ 59. Comp. iii, 201. The thing conveyed *fiduciae causa* was itself
spoken of as a *fiducia ;* as such, even
though it might be a *res soli,* it
came under the category of 'other
things' (§ 54), and so could be usucapted in a year.

usucapit: nam qui rem alicui fiduciae causa mancipio dederit
uel in iure cesserit, si eandem ipse possederit, potest usucapere, anno scilicet, [*etiam*] soli si sit. quae species usucapionis dicitur usureceptio, quia id quod aliquando habuimus
60 recipimus per usucapionem.   Sed cum fiducia contrahitur
aut cum creditore pignoris iure, aut cum amico quo tutius
nostrae res apud eum essent, si quidem cum amico contracta
sit fiducia sane omni modo conpetit usureceptio; si uero cum
creditore, soluta quidem pecunia omni modo conpetit, nondum uero soluta ita demum conpetit si neque conduxerit eam
rem a creditore debitor, neque precario rogauerit ut eam rem
possidere liceret; quo casu lucratiua usucapio conpetit.
61 Item si rem obligatam sibi populus uendiderit, eamque
dominus possederit, concessa est usureceptio: sed hoc casu
praedium biennio usurecipitur: et hoc est quod uulgo dicitur

---

what he knows to belong to another. Thus, if an individual
have taken possession of a thing which he had previously
mancipated or ceded in court to another for a fiduciary purpose, he may usucapt in a year, even though the thing in
question be immoveable. This sort of usucapion is called
usureception; because we recover by usucapion what was
60 once our own.   Such a fiduciary conveyance may be either
to a creditor by way of real security, or to a friend in whose
hands we think our property will be safer than in our own.
In the latter case usureception on our part is competent under
any circumstances. In the former it is always competent
after we have paid our debt; but before payment it is competent only if we have neither taken the thing from our
creditor in location, nor on our own request obtained possession of it from him during his pleasure; in the absence of
either of those obstacles there may be a lucrative usucapion.
61 Then again, if a man have taken possession of lands of his
that have been mortgaged to the state, and that have been
sold by its officials, usureception is competent, but only in

---

§ 60. Comp. Boeth. *in Cic. Top.* iv, 10,
§ 41 (Bruns, p. 295); Isidor. *Orig.*
v, 25, § 23 (Bruns, p. 302). The
fiduciary nature of the transaction,
when in the form of a mancipation,
was expressed in the *uerba nuncupata*, as to which see § 104, note 7.
A bronze tablet, with the record of a
mancipatio fiduciae causa engraved
thereon, supposed to be of the first
or second century, was found near
Seville in 1867; the inscription is
in Bruns, p. 180.

§ 61. Comp. Liv. xxii, 60; Varro *de
L. L.* v, 40; Schol. Bob. *in or. pro
Flacco* (ed. Bait. p. 244); Mommsen
on *cautiones praedibus praediisque*,
in his *Stadtrechte von Salpensa*, etc.,
pp. 466, f.

ex praediatura possessionem usurecipi : nam qui mercatur a populo praediator appellatur.

62   Accidit aliquando ut qui dominus sit alienandae rei potestatem non habeat, et qui dominus non sit alienare possit.
63   Nam dotale praedium maritus inuita muliere per legem Iuliam [1] prohibetur alienare, quamuis ipsius sit uel mancipatum ei dotis causa uel in iure cessum uel usucaptum. quod quidem ius utrum ad italica [2] tantum praedia, an etiam ad
64   prouincialia [3] pertineat, dubitatur.   Ex diuerso agnatus furiosi curator rem furiosi alienare potest ex lege XII tabularum ; [1] item procurator — — — — —; [2] item creditor

---

two years; this is the meaning of the common saying that possession is usurecapted *ex praediatura*, a purchaser from the state being called *praediator*.

62   It sometimes happens that he who is owner cannot alienate,
63   and that one who is not owner can.   For by the Julian law a husband is forbidden to alienate dotal lands against the will of his wife, although they may have been mancipated to him or ceded to him in court or usucapted by him as a dotal provision.   But it is a matter of doubt whether this prohibition is confined to immoveables of italic right or applies also to
64   provincial lands.   Contrariwise the agnatic curator of a lunatic is empowered by the Twelve Tables to alienate his ward's property ; a procurator [*may alienate perishables belonging to his [principal*], and a creditor by agreement may alienate a pledge

§§ 62-64. Comp. pr. § 1, tit. I. *QVIBVS ALIENARE LICET VEL NON* (ii, 8). Adopting a suggestion of Heimbach's most eds. place those pars. between §§ 79 and 80; and unquestionably there is some reason for so doing, as §§ 80-88 deal with the same subject-matter. But there does not seem to be sufficient to justify the transposition; which is the view taken by M. (K. u. S. p. xix).
§ 62. Pr. tit. I. afd.
§ 63. Comp. Paul. ii, 21*b*, § 2; pr. tit. I. afd.
  [1] The enactment referred to is the *L. Iulia de adulteriis*, of the year 736 | 18.
  [2] See i, 120, note 2.
  [3] Comp. §§ 7, 21.
§ 64. [1] Comp. Cic. *de inu.* ii, 50, § 148;

ad Herenn. i, 13, § 33; Vlp. xii, 2; Schoell, *Tab.* v, 7.
  [2] The first half of line 8, p. 69, is illegible in the MS. Bk. suggests— *id cuius libera administratio ei data est;* Gou.—*cui pecuniae administratio data est;* K. u. S. —*rem absentis, cuius negotiorum libera administratio ei permissa est;* M. (K. u. S. p. xx)—*si quid ne corrumpatur distrahendum est;* Hu.—*iure ciuili, cuius persona officio muneris eadem est.* None of these readings seems to correspond with the traces of individual letters made out by Stud.; but Mommsen's seems preferable in point of doctrine, a procurator not being entitled to sell anything but perishables without special mandate, fr. 63, D. *de proc.* (iii, 3).

pignus ex pactione, quamuis eius ea res non sit.[3] sed hoc forsitan ideo uideatur fieri quod uoluntate debitoris intellegitur pignus alienari, qui olim pactus est ut liceret creditori pignus uendere si pecunia non soluatur.

65   Ergo ex his quae diximus apparet quaedam naturali iure alienari, qualia sunt ea quae traditione alienantur, quaedam ciuili; nam mancipationis [1] et in iure cessionis [2] et usucapionis [3] ius proprium est ciuium Romanorum.

66   Nec tamen ea tantum quae traditione nostra fiunt naturali nobis ratione adquiruntur, sed etiam *quae* occupando ideo — — —[1] *quia* antea nullius essent, qualia sunt omnia quae

67 terra mari coelo capiuntur.   Itaque si feram bestiam aut uolucrem aut piscem — — — — — —,[1] *eo usque* nostrum

---

held by him, although it is not his. (But it may perhaps be held in the last case that the pledge is to be understood as alienated by consent of the debtor, who agreed in the outset that his creditor might sell it if the debt were not paid.)

65   It appears, therefore, from what has been said, that some things are alienated according to natural law,—those, for example, that are transferred by delivery,—and others according to the civil law; for mancipation, cession in court, and usucapion, are peculiar to Roman citizens.

66   But it is not only those things that become ours by delivery that we acquire on a natural title, but also what we *appropriate* by occupancy as previously unowned; such are all things that are captured either on land, in the sea, or in

67 the air.   Therefore if we capture a wild beast, or a bird, or a fish, [*it becomes ours the moment it is caught,*] and is held to

[3] Comp. § 1, tit. I. afd.

§§ 65-79. Comp. §§ 11-34, tit. I. *DE RERVM DIVISIONE* (ii, 1).

§ 65. Comp. Gai. in fr. 1, pr. D. *de A. R. D.* (xli, 1); § 11, tit. I. afd.
    [1] Comp. i, 119.
    [2] Comp. § 24.
    [3] Comp. § 41.

§ 66. Comp. Gai. in fr. 1, § 1, D. *de A. R. D.* (xli, 1); § 12, tit. I. afd.
    [1] There are about fourteen letters on line 20, p. 69, more or less illegible in the MS., of which various reconstructions have been proposed. The *nostra fecerimus* of Bk. doubtless expresses the meaning, though

it, like the other conjectural renderings, does not quadrate with the traces discernible.

§ 67. Comp. Gai. in fr. 3, § 2, fr. 5, pr. D. *de A. R. D.* (xli, 1); § 12, tit. I. afd.
    [1] About a line and a half (lines 23, 24, p. 69) illegible, with exception of word *captum.* Bk. proposes— *ceperimus, quidquid ita* captum *fuerit, continuo nostrum fit, et eo* usque, etc.; Hu.—*ceperimus, simul atque* captum *hoc animal est, statim nostrum fit, et* eo usque, etc.; K. u. S. —*ceperimus quidquid ita* captum *fuerit, statim nostrum fit, et* eo usque, etc.

esse intellegitur donec nostra custodia coerceatur; cum
uero custodiam nostram euaserit et in naturalem libertatem
se receperit, rursus occupantis fit, quia nostrum esse *desinit*.
naturalem autem libertatem recipere uidetur cum aut oculos
nostros euaserit, aut licet in conspectu sit nostro difficilis
68 tamen *eius* [2] persecutio sit.   In his autem animalibus quae
ex consuetudine abire et redire solent, ueluti columbis et
apibus, item ceruis qui in siluas ire et redire solent, talem
habemus regulam traditam ut si reuertendi animum habere
desierint etiam nostra esse desinant et fiant occupantium :
reuertendi autem animum uidentur desinere habere cum
69 reuertendi consuetudinem deseruerint.   Ea quoque quae ex
hostibus capiuntur naturali ratione nostra fiunt.
70   Sed et id quod per adluuionem nobis adicitur eodem iure
nostrum fit : per adluuionem autem id uidetur adici quod ita
paulatim flumen agro nostro adicit ut aestimare non possimus
quantum quoquo momento temporis adiciatur : hoc est quod
uulgo dicitur per adluuionem id adici uideri quod ita paulatim

---

continue ours so long as it is under the restraint of our
keeping; but the moment it evades our custody and regains
its natural liberty it becomes the property of the next captor,
having ceased to be ours. And it is regarded as having
regained its natural liberty when we can no longer see it, or
68 when, though still visible, its pursuit is difficult.   As regards,
however, such animals as are in the habit of going and coming,
—pigeons, for instance, and bees, and deer, which are wont
to go to the woods and come back again,—the rule is traditional that they cease to be ours and fall to the next captor
when they no longer have the *animus revertendi ;* and that is
held to have occurred when they have discontinued their
69 habit of returning.   Things captured from an enemy also
become ours by natural law.
70   By the same law that becomes ours which is brought to
us by alluvion. That is held to be thus brought to us which
a river adds to our land so gradually that we cannot appreciate
how much is being added at any particular moment,—which,
as the saying goes, is added so gradually as to elude our

[2] Instead of *eius*, which we have
in the Dig. and Inst., the ms. reads
inrei. M. (K. u. S. p. xx) suggests
inde rei ; Hu. *in re eius.*
§ 68. Comp. Gai. in fr. 5, § 5, D. *de A.
R. D.* (xli, 1); §§ 14, 15, tit. I. afd.

§ 69. Comp. Gai. in fr. 5, § 7, D. *de
A. R. D.* (xli, 1); § 17, tit. I.
afd.
§ 70. Comp. Gai. in fr. 7, § 1, D. *de
A. R. D.* (xli, 1); § 20, tit. I.
afd.

71 adicitur ut oculos nostros fallat.   Itaque si flumen partem
aliquam ex tuo praedio resciderit, et ad meum praedium
72 attulerit, haec pars tua manet.   At si in medio flumine
insula nata sit, haec eorum omnium communis est qui ab
utraque parte fluminis prope ripam praedia possident; si uero
non sit in medio flumine, ad eos pertinet qui ab ea parte quae
73 proxima est iuxta ripam praedia habent.   Praeterea id
quod in solo nostro ab aliquo aedificatum est, quamuis ille
suo nomine aedificauerit, iure naturali nostrum fit, quia
74 superficies solo cedit.   Multoque magis id accidit et in
planta quam quis in solo nostro posuerit, si modo radicibus
75 terram conplexa fuerit.   Idem contingit et in frumento
76 quod in solo nostro ab aliquo satum fuerit.   Sed si ab eo
petamus *fundum*[1] uel aedificium, et inpensas in aedificium
uel in seminaria uel in sementem factas ei soluere nolimus,
poterit nos per exceptionem[2] doli mali[3] repellere, utique si

---

71 vision.   If, therefore, the [force of the] stream have torn
away a part of your ground and swept it over to mine, the
72 part so detached still remains yours.   An island rising in
the middle of a river is the common property of the riparian
proprietors; but if it be not in the middle of the stream it will
73 belong to the riparian owners on the nearer side.   Further,
what one has built on our ground, although he may have
built it on his own account, by natural law becomes ours,
74 because the superstructure follows the *solum*.   All the
more is this the case with a plant which some person has
planted in our ground, provided it have laid hold of the earth
75 with its roots.   And the same happens with corn which
76 another person has sown in our ground.   But if we claim
from him the land or the house, yet decline to repay him his
outlay in building, planting, or sowing, he can defeat us with
an exception of fraud, at least if he have been a *bonae fidei*

---

§ 71. Comp. Gai. in fr. 7, § 2, D. *de
A. R. D.* (xli, 1); § 21, tit. I. afd.
§ 72. Comp. Gai. in fr. 7, § 3, D. *de
A. R. D.* (xli, 1); § 22, tit. I. afd.
§ 73. Comp. Gai. in fr. 7, § 12, D. *de
A. R. D.* (xli, 1); §§ 29, 30, tit. I.
afd.
§ 74. Comp. Gai. in fr. 6, § 13, D. *de
A. R. D.* (xli, 1); § 31, tit. I. afd.
§ 75. Comp. Gai. in fr. 9, pr. D. *de
A. R. D.* (xli, 1); § 32, tit. I. afd.
§ 76. Comp. Gai. in fr. 9, pr. D. *de
A. R. D.* (xli, 1); §§ 30, 32, tit. I. afd.

[1] So Bk., Hu., and K. u. S.; the
ms. has *fructum*.
[2] *Per exceptionem;* comp. iv, 116.
[3] *Exceptio doli mali* was the generic name for a plea by the defender, which, while admitting the
pursuer's claim to be well-founded
in strict law, yet disputed it in
equity as involving fraud (iv, 119).
But in many of its applications it
was known by a more specific name,
such as *ex. rei uenditae et traditae,
ex. pacti conuenti,* etc.

77 bonae fidei possessor fuerit. Eadem ratione probatum est quod in chartulis siue membranis meis aliquis scripserit, licet aureis litteris, meum esse, quia litterae chartulis siue membranis cedunt: *at aeque*[1] si ego eos libros easue membranas petam, nec inpensam scripturae soluam, per exceptionem doli

78 mali summoueri potero. sed si in tabula mea aliquis pinxerit ueluti imaginem, contra probatur: magis enim dicitur tabulam picturae cedere; cuius diuersitatis uix idonea ratio redditur: certe secundum hanc regulam si me possidente petas imaginem tuam esse, nec soluas pretium tabulae, poteris per exceptionem doli mali summoueri; at si tu possideas, consequens est ut utilis mihi actio[1] aduersum te dari debeat;

---

77 possessor.   Upon the same principle it is admitted that what one has written, even in letters of gold, on my paper or parchment, is mine, because the writing cedes to the paper or parchment; but here, in like manner, if I sue for the books or parchments, yet refuse to pay the cost of the writing, my

78 action may be defeated by an exception of fraud.   If, however, some one has painted a portrait say on my pannel, the rule is reversed, and the pannel said to cede to the picture,—an anomaly for which no satisfactory reason can be assigned. According to this rule, if you raise an action against me who am in possession, and maintain that the portrait is yours, but fail to pay me the value of the pannel, you may be defeated by an exception of fraud. If, however, you are in possession, it results that I am entitled to an *utilis actio*·

§ 77. Comp. Gai. in fr. 9, § 1, D. *de A. R. D.* (xli, 1); § 33, tit. I. afd.
 [1] So Hu. in his earlier editions; the ms. has *itaque.*

§ 78. Comp. Gai. in fr. 9, § 2, D. *de A. R. D.* (xli, 1); § 34, tit. I. afd.
 [1] It often happened that a man was unable to obtain the benefit of some judicial remedy introduced either by the common law, statutory enactment, or the praetor's edict, because, although his case was within the spirit of the provision upon which he was founding, it yet was not within the letter of it.
 The remedy might have been promised to or against a particular class of individuals, but he or the party in relation to whom he desired relief might not belong to that class; or it might have been promised in certain specified circum-stances, but those that had arisen, though generically the same, might yet specifically be different. In such a case the praetor was in the practice of intervening, and of introducing some modification—and there were various ways in which he did so—into the formula or style of the ordinary action, exception, or interdict (*actio directa* or *uulgaris, ex. dir.,* etc.), whereby such action was adapted to and made serviceable (*utilis*) in the special circumstances that had emerged. This is the meaning of *utilis actio* in its usual acceptation; and the phrases *utilis exceptio, utile interdictum,* were used in the same sense.
 Sometimes the new remedy was one of such extensive applicability and great importance as to deserve a special name, as in the case of the

7

quo casu, nisi soluam impensam picturae, poteris me per exceptionem doli mali repellere, utique si bonae fidei possessor fueris. illud palam est, quod siue tu subripuisses tabulam siue alius, competit mihi furti actio.[2]

79   In aliis quoque speciebus naturalis ratio requiritur: proinde si ex uuis (*aut oliuis aut spicis*)[1] meis uinum aut oleum aut frumentum feceris, quaeritur utrum meum sit id uinum aut oleum aut frumentum, an tuum. item si ex auro aut argento meo uas aliquod feceris, uel ex tabulis meis nauem aut armarium aut subsellium fabricaueris; item si ex lana mea uestimentum feceris, uel si ex uino et melle meo mulsum feceris, siue ex medicamentis meis emplastrum aut collyrium feceris, [*quaeritur utrum tuum sit id quod ex meo* [*effeceris*][2] an meum. quidam materiam et substantiam spec-

---

against you; but then, if I decline to pay the cost of the picture, you can defeat me with an exception of fraud, at least if you are a *bonae fidei* possessor. It is clear that if either you yourself or another person obtained the pannel surreptitiously, I have an *actio furti*.

79   On a change of species also the question of ownership depends on natural considerations. Thus, if you have made wine, oil, or wheat out of my grapes, *olives, or ears of corn*, the question arises whether the wine, oil, or grain is mine or yours ; just as, when you have made a vase of some sort out of my gold or silver, or have constructed a boat, or a chest, or a chair out of my planks, or have manufactured clothing out of my wool, or have converted my wine and honey into mead, or my drugs into a plaster or eye-salve, [*it becomes a question* [*whether what you have made out of my materials is yours*] or mine. Some are of opinion that the raw material,—the sub-

---

actio Publiciana, which, by means of an interpolated fiction, was just an adaptation of the *rei uindicatio* to circumstances in which it was not strictly competent (iv, 36); but more frequently the ordinary name of the action, etc., whose range of usefulness was being thus extended, was retained, and the word *utilis* ad-. jected, as *utile iudicium familiae erciscundae, utile interdictum ne quid in loco publico, utilis actio de pecunia constituta*, etc.

In Gai. iii, 219, may be seen very distinctly the difference between the

actio and the *utilis actio ex lege Aquilia;* and from § 16, I. *de leg. Aq.* (iv, 3), it will be observed that even the *utilis actio*, under the name of *actio in factum ex lege Aquilia*, might be adapted to circumstances somewhat different from those to which it was usually applied.

[2] Comp. iii, 203.

§ 79.   Comp. Gai. in fr. 7, § 7, D. de *A. R. D.* (xli, 1); § 25, tit. I. afd.

[1] Supplied from Inst.

[2] Supplied by L., and adopted by most eds.

tandam esse putant, id est ut cuius materia sit illius et res
quae facta sit uideatur esse, idque maxime placuit Sabino et
Cassio;[3] alii uero *eius rem* esse putant qui fecerit, idque
maxime diuersae scholae auctoribus[3] uisum est: sed eum
quoque cuius materia et substantia fuerit furti aduersus eum
qui subripuerit habere actionem; nec minus aduersus eundem
condictionem[4] ei competere, quia extinctæ res, licet uindicari[5] non possint, condici tamen furibus et quibusdam aliis
possessoribus possunt.

80   Nunc admonendi sumus neque feminam neque pupillum
sine tutoris auctoritate rem mancipi alienare posse; nec
mancipi uero feminam quidem posse, pupillum non posse.
81 ideoque si quando mulier mutuam pecuniam alicui sine
tutoris auctoritate dederit, quia facit eam accipientis, cum
scilicet pecunia res nec mancipi sit, contrahit obligationem.
82 at si pupillus idem fecerit, quia [*pecuniam*] non (*facit accipi-*

---

stantial element, is to be looked at, that is to say, that the
owner of the material is to be held the owner of the manufactured article; this is the view that commended itself to
Sabinus and Cassius.   Others are of opinion that the thing
manufactured belongs to the maker of it,—the view preferred
by the authorities of the other school; but that he to whom
the material, the substance, belonged has not only an *actio
furti* but also a *condictio* against him who has surreptitiously
appropriated it; because, though things no longer extant
cannot be vindicated, they may yet be claimed by condiction
from thieves and certain other possessors.

80   We have next to be reminded that neither women nor pupils
can alienate their *res mancipi* without the *auctoritas* of their
tutors; a woman, however, may herself alienate her *res nec*
81 *mancipi*, though a pupil cannot.   Therefore if at any time
a woman lend money without the authorisation of her tutor,
it is a valid obligation that she thereby contracts; for, as the
money lent is a *res nec mancipi*, she effectually makes it the
82 property of the borrower.   But if a pupil do the same he

[3] See i, 196, note 1.
[4] Comp. iv, §§ 4, 5.
[5] Comp. iv, §§ 3, 5.
§§ 80-85. Comp. § 2, tit. I. QVIBVS
ALIENARE LICET VEL NON (ii, 8),
and see note to §§ 62-64. In the
ms. §§ 80-85 are introduced with
the rubric—R. V. De pupillis an ali-

quid a se alienare possunt, partly in
the original, partly in a later hand.
§ 80. Comp. i, 192; ii, 47; Gai. in fr.
9, D. *de auct. tut.* (xxvi, 8); Vlp.
xi, 27; Fr. Vat. § 1; § 2, tit. I. afd.
§ 81. Comp. iii, 90.
§ 82. Comp. § 2, tit. I. afd.; Th. ii, 8,
§ 2.

(entis)[1] *sine tutoris auctoritate,*[2] *nullam* contrahit obligationem : unde pupillus uindicare quidem nummos suos potest sicubi extent, id est *eos petere suos ex iure Quiritium esse,*[3] — — — — — — —. unde de pupillo quidem quaeritur *an nummos quos* mutuos dedit ab eo qui accepit — — — — *actione* eos

83 persequi possit, *quoniam* — — — — *potest.*[4]   *At ex contra- rio omnes res tam mancipi quam* nec mancipi mulieribus et

---

contracts no obligation, *for he cannot pass the property of the money he is advancing* without his tutor's *auctoritas ;* therefore the pupil may vindicate his coins as far as still extant, that is, *may claim them as his in quiritary right,* [*it being incom- [petent for him to claim them in an action presupposing the [validity of the loan.*] It is a question, however, whether, when the money advanced as a loan [*has been consumed*] by the receiver, the pupil may not then recover it by a [*personal*] action, seeing that he can [*without his tutor's* auctoritas *acquire

83 [*a claim founded on the consumption*].   *But, on the other hand, both* res mancipi *and* res nec mancipi *may be paid to*

---

[1] These words, with exception of the last syllable (*tis*), are illegible in the ms., and borrowed from § 2, tit. I, afd.

[2] Those three words not in the Inst.; but suggested by *s* in the ms. after the *tis* of *accipientis*, and in themselves almost necessary.

[3] K. u. S. and Hu. concur in the reading here given, though it is difficult to discern in the ms.

[4] The latter part of the par. (lines 18-23, p. 73, of ms.) is to a great extent illegible. K. u. S. suggest— *mulier uero minime hoc modo* repe- tere potest, *sed ita : DARI SIBI OPOR- TERE.* Vnde de pupillo quidem quae- ritur, an, si nummi, quos mutuos dedit, ab eo qui accepit *bona fide consumpti fuerint, ex mutuo* actione eos persequi possit, quoniam *obliga- tionem etiam sine tutoris auctoritate adquirere sibi* potest. M. (K. u. S. p. xx) suggests—*neque tamen stricto iure petere potest sibi eos dari opor- tere.* Vnde de pupillo quidem quae- ritur an nummis quos mutuos dedit, ab eo qui accepit *consumptis, ciuili* actione eos persequi possit, quoniam *dari eos sibi oportere intendere non* potest. Hu. has—*mulier uero per mutui actionem a reo pecuniam re-* petere potest, *sed non suum esse petere.* Vnde de pupillo quidem quaeritur, an nummis [*iis*] quos mutuos dedit, ab eo qui accepit *con- sumptis, aliqua* actione eos persequi possit, quoniam *nisi a possidente uindicari non* potest. None of these reconstructions is quite satisfac- tory.

The view given effect to in the translation is simply this : the pupil lending without *auctoritas* had no *actio ex mutuo,* for there was no valid *mutuum ;* but, if the money was still extant in the hands of the borrower, he might recover it by a *uindicatio* as still his own ; while if it had been consumed by the bor- rower, and so was no longer extant, he might claim the amount of it in a *condictio sine causa,* on the ground expressed by Pompon. in fr. 206, D. *de R. I.* (l, 16)—*iure naturae aequum est neminem cum alterius detrimento et iniuria fieri locupletiorem.* See fr. 19, § 1, D. *de reb. cred.* (xii, 1).

§ 83.   Comp. § 2, tit. I. afd.; pr. I. *de auct. tut.* (i, 21). The rendering of the illegible half line (l. 24, p. 73) in the ms. seems obvious from the context, and is that adopted by both K. u. S. and Hu.

pupillis sine tutoris auctoritate solui possunt, quoniam meliorem condicionem suam facere eis etiam sine tutoris auctori-
84 tate concessum est.   itaque si debitor pecuniam pupillo
soluat, facit quidem pecuniam pupilli; sed ipse non liberatur,
quia nullum obligationem pupillus sine tutoris auctoritate
dissoluere potest, quia nullius rei alienatio ei [1] sine tutoris
auctoritate concessa est; sed tamen si ex ea pecunia locupletior factus sit et adhuc petat, per exceptionem doli mali [2]
85 summoueri potest.   Mulieri uero etiam sine tutoris auctoritate recte solui potest, nam qui soluit liberatur obligatione;
quia res nec mancipi, ut proxime diximus,[1] a se dimittere
mulier etiam sine tutoris auctoritate potest: quamquam hoc
ita est si accipiat pecuniam; at si non accipiat, sed habere se
dicat et per acceptilationem [2] uelit debitorem sine tutoris
auctoritate liberare, non potest.
86   Adquiritur autem nobis non solum per nosmet ipsos sed
etiam per eos quos in potestate manu mancipioue habemus;

women and pupils without their tutors' *auctoritas*, seeing that
even without it they are free to better their condition.
84 Therefore if a debtor pay money to a pupil he makes that
money the pupil's: but he is not himself discharged; for a
pupil, inasmuch as he is unable to alienate anything without
his tutor's *auctoritas*, cannot without it extinguish any claim
he has under an obligation.   But if he be the richer for that
money, and nevertheless sue for it, his action may be defeated
85 by an exception of fraud.   To a woman, however, payment
may be made quite effectually even without her tutor's
auctoritas; the debtor paying is freed from his obligation,
because, as has just been explained, a woman does not need
tutorial *auctoritas* in divesting herself of a *res nec mancipi*.
At least this is the case if she have really received the money;
if she have not received it, though she may say she has, and
may mean to discharge her debtor by acceptilation without
her tutor's authority, she cannot do so.
86   Acquisitions are made for us not only through our own
instrumentality but also through that of persons in our

§ 84. Comp. § 2, tit. I. afd.; Th. ii, 8,
   § 2.
     [1] So quite distinctly in the MS.;
but Hu. substitutes—*cui nec ullius
rei alienatio sine*, etc.
     [2] See § 76, note 3.
§ 85. Comp. iii, 171.

[1] See § 80.
[2] Acceptilation described, iii, 169.
§§ 86-100. Comp. tit. I. *PER QVAS PER-
   SONAS NOBIS ADQVIRITVR* (ii, 9).
§ 86. Gai. in fr. 10, pr. D. *de A. R. D.*
   (xli, 1); pr. tit. I. afd. Comp. Vlp.
   xix, §§ 18-21.

item per eos seruos in quibus usumfructum habemus; item
per homines liberos et seruos alienos quos bona fide posside-
87 mus: de quibus singulis diligenter dispiciamus.   Igitur
[*quod*] liberi nostri quos in potestate habemus, item quod
serui mancipio accipiunt uel ex traditione nanciscuntur, siue
quid stipulentur uel ex aliqualibet causa adquirant, id nobis
adquiritur: ipse enim qui in potestate nostra est nihil suum
habere potest; et ideo si heres institutus sit nisi nostro iussu
hereditatem adire non potest; et si iubentibus nobis adierit,
hereditas nobis adquiritur proinde atque si nos ipsi heredes
instituti essemus; et conuenienter scilicet legatum per eos
88 nobis adquiritur: dum tamen sciamus, si alterius in bonis
sit seruus, alterius ex iure Quiritium, ex omnibus causis ei
89 soli per eum adquiri cuius in bonis est.   Non solum autem
proprietas per eos quos in potestate habemus adquiritur nobis,
sed etiam possessio; cuius enim rei possessionem adepti
fuerint, id nos possidere uidemur; unde etiam per eos usu-
90 capio procedit.   Per eas uero personas quas in manu man-

---

potestas, manus, or *mancipium,* of slaves we are usufructing,
and of freemen and other people's slaves possessed by us in
good faith.   We shall deal with each of those classes separately.
87 Whatever then our children *in potestate* or our slaves receive
in mancipation or acquire by delivery, whatever claim they
obtain either by stipulation or on any other ground, is acquired
for us; for he who is *in potestate* can have nothing of his own.
Therefore if he be instituted heir under a testament he cannot
enter to the inheritance except on our instructions; and if we
have ordered him to enter, the inheritance is acquired for us,
just as if we ourselves had been instituted heirs.   In like
88 manner a legacy to them is acquired for us.   But let it be
borne in mind that if a slave be *in bonis* of one person and in
the quiritarian ownership of another, it is in every case for
89 his bonitarian proprietor alone that he acquires.   It is not
only property that is acquired for us by those in our *potestas,*
but also possession: we are held to possess what they have
acquired possession of; consequently through them we can
90 complete a usucapion.   Through the instrumentality of

§ 87. Gai. in fr. 10, § 1, D. *de A. R. D.*
(xli, 1).   Comp. § 189; §§ 1, 2,
tit. I. afd.; Vlp. xix, §§ 18, 19.
§ 88. Comp. §§ 40, 41; Vlp. xix,
20.
§ 89. Gai. in fr. 10, § 2, D. *de A. R. D.*
(xli, 1); § 2, tit. I. afd.

§ 90. Nowhere does the reason appear
why persons *in manu mancipioue*
should be less in the possession of
the *paterfamilias* than his children
in potestate.   Comp. § 94; iii, 199;
Modest. in fr. 54, § 4, D. *de A. R. D.*
(xli, 1).

cipioue habemus proprietas quidem adquiritur nobis ex omnibus causis, sicut per eos qui in potestate nostra sunt; an
autem possessio adquiratur quaeri solet, quia ipsas non possi-
91 demus.   De his autem seruis in quibus tantum usumfructum
habemus ita placuit, ut quidquid ex re nostra uel ex operis
suis adquirant id nobis adquiratur; quod uero extra eas
causas, id ad dominum proprietatis pertineat: itaque si iste
seruus heres institutus sit, legatumue *quid* ei [*aut*] *donatum*
92 fuerit,[1] non mihi sed domino proprietatis adquiritur.   Idem
placet de eo qui a nobis bona fide possidetur, siue liber sit siue
alienus seruus; quod enim placuit de usufructuario, idem
probatur etiam de bonae fidei possessore: itaque quod extra
duas istas causas adquiritur, id uel ad ipsum pertinet si liber
93 est, uel ad dominum si seruus est.   Sed bonae fidei possessor cum usuceperit seruum, quia eo modo dominus fit, ex
omni causa per eum sibi adquirere potest. usufructuarius

---

persons whom we hold *in manu* or *in mancipio* property is
acquired for us on any title, just as it is through that of
persons in our *potestas;* but it is a question whether we can
acquire possession through their means, seeing they them-
91 selves are not possessed by us.   As regards a slave of
whom we have only a usufruct, the rule is that whatever he
acquires by his own labour, or by means of funds with which
we have provided him, is acquired for us, but that acquisitions from any other source belong to his owner; therefore if
he be instituted heir or have something bequeathed or gifted
to him, the acquisition enures not to me but to his pro-
92 prietor.   The same is the rule as regards a person *bona
fide* possessed by us, whether he be a freeman or a slave
belonging to a third party: the doctrine applicable to a
usufructuary is equally applicable to a possessor in good faith;
whatever therefore is acquired by a person so possessed from
any other source than the two referred to, belongs to himself
93 if he be free, to his owner if he be a slave.   When, however, the *bonae fidei* possessor usucapts the slave, as he thus
becomes his owner, he may in future acquire by his means
from any source.   But a usufructuary cannot usucapt; firstly,

---

§§ 91-93. Gai. in fr. 10, §§ 3-5, D. *de
A. R. D.* (xli, 1); §§ 4, 5, tit. I. afd.
Comp. iii, §§ 164, 165; Vlp. xix, 21.
§ 91. [1] The ms. has *legatumue quod* (or
quid, the contraction, *q*, applying to
either) *ei datum fuerit*, which K. u. S.

and Hu. retain. The correction in
the text is from the Inst. *Legatum
dare* is a phrase not unknown to the
law, and is used frequently by Vlp.;
but it does not occur elsewhere in
Gai.

uero usucapere non potest; primum quia non possidet sed
habet ius utendi fruendi; deinde quia scit alienum seruum
94 esse.   De illo quaeritur, an per eum seruum in quo usumfructum habemus possidere aliquam rem et usucapere possimus, quia ipsum non possidemus. per eum uero quem bona
fide possidemus sine dubio et possidere et usucapere possumus. loquimur autem in utriusque persona secundum
definitionem quam proxime exposuimus, id est si quid ex re
95 nostra uel ex operis suis adquirant.   Ex his apparet per
liberos homines quos neque iuri nostro subiectos habemus
neque bona fide possidemus, item per alienos seruos in quibus
neque usumfructum habemus neque iustam possessionem,
nulla ex causa nobis adquiri posse.   et hoc est quod uulgo dicitur per extraneam personam nobis adquiri *non posse*. *tantum
de* possessione quaeritur an per (*procuratorem*) [1] nobis adquira-
96 tur.   In summa sciendum est his qui in potestate manu
mancipioue sunt nihil in iure cedi posse ; cum enim istarum

---

because he does not possess, but has only the right of using
and taking fruits and profits; secondly, because he knows
94 that the slave belongs to another.   It is a question whether
we can possess and usucapt through a usufructed slave, for he
is not in our possession; but there is no doubt that we can
possess and usucapt through a person whom we possess in
good faith. (In both cases of course we are speaking under
reference to the limitation already mentioned, namely, if
their acquisitions be due to means we have furnished, or to
95 their own labour.)   From what has been said it is apparent
that we cannot on any ground acquire through the instrumentality of freemen who are neither subject to our *potestas*
nor possessed by us in good faith, nor yet by that of other
people's slaves whom we do not hold either in usufruct or in
lawful possession. This is the meaning of the adage that we
cannot acquire through a stranger; the only doubt being
about possession,—whether we cannot acquire it through the
96 instrumentality of *a procurator*.   Finally, it is to be observed
that there can be no cession in court to those who are in our
potestas, manus, or *mancipium ;* for, as none of them can have

§ 94. Comp. § 4, tit. I. afd.
§ 95. Comp. Paul. v, 2, § 2; § 5, tit. I.
afd.
   [1] Only the first letter of *procuratorem* is legible in the ms. Hu.
makes it *per personam liberam*, so as

to include a tutor or curator. But
persona libera never occurs in Gai.;
it is always *libera persona*. The
Inst. have *per liberam personam,
ueluti per procuratorem*.
§ 96. Comp. §§ 24, 87.

personarum nihil suum esse possit, conueniens est scilicet ut nihil suum esse¹ in iure uindicare possint.

97   [*Hactenus*] tantisper admonuisse sufficit quemadmodum singulae res nobis adquirantur: nam legatorum ius, quo et ipso singulas res adquirimus, opportunius alio loco referemus. uideamus itaque nunc quibus modis per uniuersitatem res

98 nobis adquirantur.   Si cui heredes facti sumus,¹ siue cuius bonorum possessionem petierimus,² siue cuius bona emerimus,³ siue quem adoptauerimus,⁴ siue quam in manum ut uxorem

99 receperimus,⁵ eius res ad nos transeunt.   Ac prius de hereditatibus dispiciamus, quarum duplex condicio est : nam

100 uel ex testamento uel ab intestato ad nos pertinent.   Et

---

anything of their own, it follows that they cannot appear before a magistrate and vindicate a thing as theirs.

97   Thus far we have said enough for the present about the [modes of] acquiring things singly; the matter of legacies, whereby also things are thus acquired, will be referred to more conveniently elsewhere.   Let us now see how things are

98 acquired *per universitatem*, [*i.e.* on a universal title.]   If we have become heirs of any one, or have applied for possession of a deceased person's estate, or have bought the estate of an insolvent, or have adopted any one [by adrogation], or have received a woman into our *manus* as our wife, his or her

99 effects become ours.   We shall deal first with inheritances ; which are of two sorts,—those that come to us by testament,

100 and those that belong to us on intestacy.   To begin with, let us see what falls to us by testament.

---

¹ The second *suum esse*, according to M., should be deleted as a gloss.

§§ 97-100. See § 6, tit. I. afd., from which the initial word of § 97, unwritten in the MS., is borrowed. The MS. has a vacant line before § 97, probably for a rubric.

§ 97. The law of legacies is introduced in § 191.

§ 98. This par. contains an enumeration of the principal varieties of universal acquisition (*adquisitio per universitatem*).

  ¹ The succession of the *ius ciuile*, either under a testament (ii, §§ 104-190), or *ab intestato* (iii, §§ 1-52).

  ² Succession under the praetorian rules modifying those of the *ius*

ciuile ; the explanations of them are dispersed through the passages referred to in last note.

  ³ *Bonorum emptio* was purchase in gross of the estate of an insolvent; see iii, §§ 77-81.

  ⁴ When a man adopted a *paterfamilias* by adrogation, the estate of the latter (so far as not annihilated by the *capitis deminutio*) *ipso iure* passed to the adrogator; iii, §§ 83, 84, compared with i, § 99.

  ⁵ There was a similar *ipso iure* passage of a woman's estate to the man whose *manus* she entered, whether as his wife or merely *fiduciae causa ;* iii, §§ 83, 84, compared with i, §§ 108-115.

prius est ut de his dispiciamus quae nobis ex testamento obueniunt.

101   Testamentorum autem genera initio duo fuerunt : nam aut calatis comitiis testamentum faciebant, quae comitia bis in anno testamentis faciendis destinata erant, aut in procinctu, id est cum belli causa arma sumebant; procinctus est enim expeditus et armatus exercitus. alterum itaque in pace et
102 in otio faciebant, alterum in proelium exituri.   Accessit deinde tertium genus testamenti quod per *aes* et libram agitur : qui [*enim*] neque calatis comitiis neque in procinctu testamentum fecerat, is, si subita morte urguebatur, amico familiam suam, id est patrimonium suum, mancipio dabat, eumque rogabat quid cuique post mortem suam dari uellet. quod testamentum dicitur per aes et libram, scilicet quia per
103 mancipationem peragitur.   Sed illa quidem duo genera testamentorum in desuetudinem abierunt; hoc uero solum quod per aes et libram fit in usu retentum est. sane nunc aliter ordinatur quam olim solebat; namque olim familiae emptor, id est qui a testatore familiam accipiebat mancipio,

---

101   Originally testaments were of two sorts; for they were made either *in calatis comitiis*—comitia that were convened twice a year for the purpose, or *in procinctu*, when the people were arming for battle; for *procinctus* means an army equipped and armed.   The one sort therefore was made in time of peace and leisure, the other when the testator was going
102 forth on a campaign.   Afterwards came a third sort,—that executed by the copper and the scales : he who had not made his testament either in the comitia or on the eve of battle, if urged by the imminent approach of death, conveyed his *familia, i.e.* his patrimony, by mancipation to a friend, whom he instructed what he wished to have given to each of his beneficiaries after his death.   This is called a testament by the copper and the scales because it is executed by mancipa-
103 tion.   The two earlier varieties are out of date; that by the copper and the scales is the only one now in use.   But it is very true that it is not now ordered as it was of old. Formerly the *familiae emptor*, that is to say the person who received the estate by mancipation from the testator, held the

---

§§ 101-108.   Comp. tit. I. *DE TESTA- MENTIS ORDINANDIS* (ii, 10).
§§ 101-103.   Comp. Vlp. xx, 2; § 1, tit. I. afd.; Th. ii, 10, § 1; Gell.

xv, 27, §§ 1, 2 ; Paul. ex Festo, vv. *Endo procinctu* and *Procincta classis* (Bruns, pp. 241, 257).

heredis locum obtinebat, et ob id ei mandabat testator quid cuique post mortem suam dari uellet; nunc uero alius heres testamento instituitur a quo etiam legata relinquuntur, alius dicis gratia propter uteris iuris imitationem familiae
104 emptor adhibetur.   Eaque res ita agitur : qui facit [*testamen-* *[tum]*, adhibitis, sicut in ceteris mancipationibus,[1] v testibus ciuibus Romanis [2] puberibus et libripende, postquam tabulas testamenti scripserit, mancipat alicui dicis gratia familiam suam ; in qua re his uerbis familiae emptor utitur : FAMILIA [3] PECVNIAQVE [4] TVA ENDO MANDATELAM TVAM CVSTODELAMQVE

---

position of heir, and therefore it was that the testator gave him instructions what he wished to be given to any particular individual after his death.   But now one person is instituted heir in the testament, and on him the legacies are charged; while another is introduced merely for form's sake, in imita-
104 tion of the *familiae emptor* of the old law.   The procedure is as follows: the testator having (as in all 'other manci- pations) obtained the attendance of five witnesses, Roman citizens above puberty, and a balance-holder, after he has written the tablets of his testament, as a matter of form mancipates his estate to some one.   This person, the *familiae emptor*, makes use of these words : ' Your estate and belong-

---

104. Comp. Vlp. xx, §§ 2, 9.

[1] Comp. i, § 119. It is to be observed that while *mancipatio* is spoken of there as *imaginaria uen- ditio*, the *test. per aes et libram* as here described was only *imaginaria mancipatio* (Vlp. xx, 2).

[2] Citizens or Junian latins, Vlp. xx, 8.

[3] The first part of the formula stands in the text as follows : *FAM- ILIAM PECVNIAMQVE TVAM ENDO MANDATELA TVAM CVSTODELAQVE MEA, QVO TV IVRE TESTAMENTVM FACERE POSSIS . . . ESTO MIHI EMPTA*. The *m* at the end of the initial words has induced many eds., including Hu., to interpolate before the *QVO TV* the words *ex iure Quiritium esse aio, eaque*. But this subverts the idea of the proceeding. Studemund's revision has also shown the unwarrantableness of the *endo mandatela*, *TVTELA*, *custodelaque mea* of previous eds., strangely enough still retained by Hu.; it quite destroyed the force of the

formula,—' I take into my charge, but subject to your instructions.'

[4] Gai., § 102, defines *familia* as *patrimonium;* that makes it synony- mous with *pecunia*, as defined by Paul. in fr. 5, D. *de V. S.* (l, 16). But the early jurists were not given to useless tautologies; and originally there must have been a distinction. Kuntze (*R. R.* ii, pp. 88, 89) is of opinion that *familia*, or *res fami- liaris*, included the family estate proper,—the *res mancipi* attached to the family, and not easily alienable by the *paterfamilias; pecunia* the *res nec mancipi*, the lesser articles that made up the *bona* held by the *paterfamilias* as *dominus*, and more fully at his disposal.   Lange (*Roem. Alt.* i, pp. 129, 136) holds that in prehistoric Rome the *familia* could not be alienated by the *pater- familias* either *inter uiuos* or *mortis causa*, but that the *bona* (*duona*) were alienable from the first. I am inclined to think that the distinc- tion between the *familia* and *pecunia*

MEAM, QVO TV IVRE TESTAMENTVM FACERE POSSIS SECVNDVM
LEGEM PVBLICAM,[5] HOC AERE (et ut quidam adiciunt AENEAQVE
LIBRA) ESTO MIHI EMPTA ;[6] deinde aere percutit libram, idque
aes dat testatori uelut pretii loco.   deinde testator tabulas
testamenti tenens ita dicit : HAEC ITA VT IN HIS TABVLIS
CERISQVE SCRIPTA SVNT, ITA DO, ITA LEGO, ITA TESTOR, ITAQVE
VOS QVIRITES TESTIMONIVM MIHI PERHIBETOTE ;[7] et hoc dicitur
nuncupatio :[8] nuncupare est enim palam nominare, et sane

---

ings, be they mine by purchase, with this bit of copper (and,'
as some add, ' these copper scales), subject to your instructions,
but in my keeping, that so you may lawfully make your
testament according to the statute ;' then he strikes the scales
with the coin, and gives the latter to the testator as if by
way of price.   The testator, holding his testamentary writings
in his hand, then says: ' As is written in these tablets, so do
I give, so do I legate, so do I declare my will; therefore,
Quirites, grant me your testimony.'   This last act is called
the nuncupation, *nuncupare* meaning to declare publicly;
whatever the testator has written in detail in his testa-

---

corresponded pretty nearly to that
between estate by descent and purchase in England, or heritage and
conquest in Scotland.

[5] The phrase *SECVNDVM LEGEM
PVBLICAM*, which recurs in the formula of the *nexi liberatio*, in iii,
174, refers in all probability to some
provision of the Twelve Tables,—
either the general one recited by
Gai. § 224, ' *uti legassit suae rei,
ita ius esto*,' or one not preserved to
us that dealt specifically with this
particular mode of testament-
making.

[6] *Empta*, as already observed, (i,
113, note 2,) did not originally and of
necessity mean acquired in property
for a money price; says Paul. ex
Festo, v. *Emere* (Bruns, p. 241)
—'*Emere, quod nunc est mercari,
antiqui accipiebant pro sumere*.'

[7] On the import of the phrase
testimonium perhibere see Danz, *R.
R.* ii, pp. 15-17, and authorities
there quoted. It appears from Paul.
iii, 4a, § 4, that the witnesses were
not silent onlookers, but actual
parties to the transaction; their
part, according to Danz, being to
affirm the regularity of the solemnity, — that the testament was

iustum, *i.e.* made according to
law.

[8] Huschke(*Nexum*)has shown that
part of the value of every *negotium
per aes et libram*, whether employed
in execution of a conveyance of property *inter uiuos*, a bond, or a testamentary disposition, was its pub-
licity,—its sanction and attestation
by the five witnesses who were the
representatives of the five Servian
classes, and therefore of the nation.
The *negotium per aes et libram*,
latterly at least, was in all those
cases a purely formal act; its import
was defined by the *nuncupatio* that
accompanied it, and which constituted the *lex mancipii* (Gai. i, §§
140, 172), *nexi*, or *testamenti* (fr. 14,
D. *qui test. fac. poss.* xxviii, 1), as
the case might be, and in reference to
which we have in the Twelve Tables
the provision (Fest. v. *Nuncupata*,
ed. Muell., p. 173)—*cum nexum faciet mancipiumque, uti lingua nun-
cupassit ita ius esto*.   The declared
terms of any jural transaction constituted its *lex*, — the law that
governed it; and it is not improbable
that it is to this *lex* that we owe the
word *legare*,—'*uti legassit suae rei,
ita ius esto*.'

quae testator specialiter in tabulis testamenti scripserit ea
105 uidetur generali sermone nominare atque confirmare.   In
testibus autem non debet is esse qui in potestate est aut
familiae emptoris aut ipsius testatoris, quia, propter ueteris
iuris imitationem, totum hoc negotium quod agitur testamenti
ordinandi gratia creditur inter familiae emptorem agi et testatorem; quippe olim, ut proxime diximus, is qui familiam
testatoris mancipio accipiebat heredis loco erat; itaque
106 reprobatum est in ea re domesticum testimonium.   unde
et si is qui in potestate patris est familiae emptor adhibitus
sit, pater eius testis esse non potest; ac ne is quidem qui in
eadem potestate est, uelut frater eius.   sed et si filiusfamilias
ex castrensi peculio [1] post missionem faciat testamentum, nec
pater eius recte testis adhibetur nec is qui in potestate patris
107 est.   De libripende eadem quae et de testibus dicta esse
108 intellegemus: nam et is testium numero est.   Is uero qui
in potestate heredis aut legatarii est, cuiusue heres ipse aut

---

mentary tablets he is regarded as declaring and confirming
105 by this general statement.   No one ought to figure among
the witnesses who is in the *potestas* either of the *familiae
emptor* or of the testator, seeing that, in imitation of the old
law, the whole business of ordering the testament is held to be
between those two parties; for, as already said, in old time
he who received the estate by mancipation from the testator
occupied the position of heir.   It is for this reason that, in a
matter of this sort, the testimony of members of the same
106 household has been rejected.   Accordingly if the person
acting as *familiae emptor* happen to be *in potestate*, his father
cannot be a witness; neither can anyone in the same *potestas*
as he,—for instance, his brother.   And even in the case of a
filiusfamilias making a testament disposing of his *peculium
castrense* after his discharge from the army, neither his father
nor any person in his father's *potestas* can officiate as a
107 witness.   What has been said about witnesses applies
equally to the balance-holder; for he also is reckoned of their
108 number.   But a man who is in the *potestas* of an heir or
legatee, or to whose *potestas* either of these is subject, or who

§ 105. Comp. Vlp. **xx**, §§ 3-5; § 9, tit.
 I. afd.
§ 106. See references in last note.
 [1] *Castrense peculium* was the
separate estate amassed by a *filiusfamilias* while on military service,

and which he dealt with as *de
facto* his own; see Vlp. **xx**, 10;
Paul. iii, 4*a*, § 3; pr. I. *quib. non
est permiss.* (ii, 12).
§ 107. Comp. Vlp. **xx**, 3.
§ 108. Comp. §§ 10, 11, tit. I. afd.

legatarius in potestate est, quique in eiusdem potestate est,
adeo testis et libripens adhiberi potest, ut ipse quoque heres
aut legatarius iure adhibeantur.   sed tamen quod ad heredem
pertinet quique in eius potestate est cuiusue is in potestate
est, minime hoc iure uti debemus.

109   Sed haec diligens obseruatio in ordinandis testamentis militibus propter nimiam inperitiam constitutionibus principum
remissa est : nam quamuis neque legitimum numerum testium
adhibuerint neque uendiderint familiam neque nuncupauerint

110 testamentum, recte nihilo minus testantur.   Praeterea permissum est iis et peregrinos et latinos instituere heredes uel
iis legare ; cum alioquin peregrini quidem ratione ciuili pro-
hibeantur capere hereditatem legataque, latini uero per legem

111 Iuniam.   Caelibes[1] quoque, qui lege Iulia[2] hereditatem
legataque capere uetantur, item orbi,[3] id est qui liberos non
habent, quos lex — — — — — — — —.[4]

---

is *in potestate* of the same person as either of them, may be
employed as a witness or balance-holder ; nay, even an heir
or legatee himself may lawfully so officiate.   So far, however,
as regards an heir, as well as those in his *potestas* and the
person to whose *potestas* he is subject, we ought to take
advantage of this right as seldom as possible.

109   But such strict observance of the formalities in ordering of
testaments is dispensed with by imperial enactments in the
case of soldiers, on account of their great inexperience in
business matters; for although they may neither have provided the number of witnesses required by law, nor mancipated their *familia*, nor nuncupated their will, they do not

110 the less test validly.   Further, they are allowed to institute
latins and peregrins as their heirs, or to bequeath them
legacies; whereas in the ordinary case peregrins are prohibited by the civil law from taking an inheritance or a
legacy, and latins similarly prohibited by the Junian law.

111 Unmarried persons, though forbidden by the Junian law to
take an inheritance or a legacy, and *orbi* or childless persons,

---

§§ 109-111. Comp. tit. I. *DE MILITARI
TESTAMENTO* (ii, 11). Those three
pars. are preceded by the rubric *de
testamentis militum*, apparently in
the same hand.
§ 109. Comp. § 114; Vlp. xxiii, 10;
pr. tit. I. afd.
§ 110. Comp. i, 23; ii, §§ 218, 275;
Vlp. xxii, §§ 2, 3.

§ 111. The conclusion of what Gai. said
on the subject of soldiers' testaments fails us, a leaf of the MS. (pp.
80* and 80**) being lost.
[1] Comp. §§ 144, 286 ; Vlp. xxii, 3.
[2] See i, 145, note 1.
[3] Comp. § 286a.
[4] Hu. completes the par. thus :
quos lex *Papia plus quam dimidias*

112   — — — — — — — — ex *auctoritate* diui Hadriani
senatusconsultum factum est quo permissum *est (sui iuris)*[1]
feminis etiam sine coemptione testamentum facere, si modo
non minores essent annorum XII, *tutoribus auctoribus ;*[2]

whom [*the Papian law does not allow to take more than a half*
[*of an inheritance or bequest that has been left to them, may take*
[*in full under a soldier's testament.*]

112   [*It is not every one that can make a testament. Those can-*
[*not do so who are not* sui *but* alieni iuris,—*our children, that*
[*is to say, whether they be so by birth or by adoption. Neither*
[*can persons* sui iuris, *who are under the age of puberty,* i.e.
[*males under fourteen and females under twelve. Neither can*
[*persons who are insane, except during their lucid intervals.*
[*At one time neither could women of full age, if their tutors*
[*dissented, without going through the formality of coemption,*
[*and thus replacing their old tutors with others of their*
[*own selection, whose* auctoritas *they could command. But*
[*eventually*] a senatusconsult was passed, on the proposition
of the emperor Hadrian, allowing women who were *sui iuris*
to make a testament without coemption, provided they were
not under the age of twelve, with the *auctoritas* of their tutors.

partes hereditatis legatorumque
capere uetat, ex militis testamento
solidum capiunt. See §§ 286, 286a.
§§ 112,113. Comp. tit. I. *QVIBVS NON EST*
PERMISSVM TESTAMENTA FACERE
(ii, 12). It is probable that on the
missing leaf, and on page 81, of
which all but the last three lines
are illegible, Gai. spoke of the testamentary incapacity of persons *alieni*
iuris, lunatics, and pupils. In the
Epit. ii, 2, we have as follows :
§ 1. *Id quoque statutum est, quod*
non omnibus |liceat facere testa-
mentum : sicut sunt hi qui sui iuris
non sunt sed alieno iuri subiecti, hoc
est filii tum ex nobis nati quam
adoptiui. § 2. *Item testamenta*
facere non possunt inpuberes, id est
minores quattuordecim annorum,
aut puellae duodecim. § 3. *Item et hi*
qui furiosi,id est mente insani fuerint,
non possunt facere testamenta. sed
hi qui insani sunt, per interualla
quibus sani sunt possunt facere testa-
menta. Comp. Vlp. xx, §§ 10-16.
§ 112. Comp. i, 115a ; Paul. iii, 4a,
§ 1. The probable import of the
commencement of the par. is indicated in the translation.

[1] Stud. notes that there is room
for *puberibus ;* but the context excludes the possibility of such a word
having been used. Hu. suggests
capite non minutis, as less 'insipid'
than *sui iuris.*
[2] For *tutoribus auctoribus* the MS.
has simply *tab.* Most eds. have
treated those letters as introduced
per incuriam, under the idea that
XII *tab.* (meaning the Twelve
Tables) came so often from the
scribe's pen, that the *tab.* naturally
followed the XII when this was used
in a different collocation. But we
have *tutore auctore* represented con-
stantly by *ta.* (as in the very next
par.); consequently there seems little
difficulty in rendering *tab.* by
tutoribus auctoribus. No doubt the
phrase is unusual ; but we have it
in i, § 115, and to all appearance it
occurs again in ii, § 118, which see.
Omitting those two words, Hu.
introduces *tutore auctore* between
testamentum and *facere*. It would
rather appear from the terms of §
122, that after the senatusconsult
this *auctoritas* could rarely, if ever,
be withheld.

[scilicet ut quae tutela liberatae[3] non essent ita[4] testari
113 deberent.][5]   Videntur ergo melioris condicionis esse feminae quam masculi; nam masculus minor annorum XIIII
testamentum facere non potest, etiamsi tutore auctore testamentum facere uelit; femina uero *post*[1] XII *annum* testamenti faciendi ius nanciscitur.[2]
114   Igitur si quaeramus an ualeat testamentum, inprimis
aduertere debemus an is qui id fecerit habuerit testamenti
factionem :[1] deinde, si habuerit, requiremus an secundum iuris
ciuilis regulam testatus sit, exceptis militibus, quibus propter
nimiam *inperitiam*, ut diximus,[2] quomodo uelint uel *quomodo
possint* permittitur testamentum facere.

(This requirement, of course, applied only to those who had
113 not been released from tutelage.)   Women, therefore, seem
to be in a better position than men; for a male under
fourteen cannot make a testament, even though he may wish
to do so *tutore auctore*, whereas a female acquires the right of
testament-making on reaching twelve.
114   In considering whether or not a testament is valid we must
inquire, firstly, whether the maker had *testamenti factio ;*
secondly, whether he has made it according to the rules of
the civil law, (unless he be a soldier, who, as already said, on
account of his inexperience, is allowed to make a testament
in any way he will or can.)

[3] Comp. i, 194; Vlp. xxix, 8.
[4] So the ms.; but most cds. substitute *tutore auctore*. This is unnecessary with *tut. auctoribus* in the
preceding clause.
[5] The words *scilicet . . . deberent*
look like a gloss.
§ 113. Comp. Vlp. xx, §§ 12, 15; pr.
tit. I. afd.
[1] The ms. has *potest;* hence Hu.
is induced to read—*femina uero
potest; [nam si est] XII annorum,
testamenti faciundi [tutore auctore]
ius nanciscitur*.
[2] There is a vacant line in the
ms. between this and the next
par.
§ 114. Comp. Gai. in fr. 4, D. *qui test.
fac. poss.* (xxviii, 1).
[1] It is very usual to say that
testamenti factio was of three sorts—
(1) capacity to make a testament,
(2) capacity to be instituted heir
or made a legatee in it, and (3)

capacity to act as a witness to it.
There seems to be no sufficient
warrant for the third.   All that
Vlp. says (xx, 2) is that the witnesses must be persons with whom
the testator has *test. factio*, i.e. whom
he may lawfully make his heirs or
legatees.   No doubt Vlp. also observes (xx, 8) that a Junian latin
might witness a will, *quoniam cum
eo test. factio est ;* and it is assumed
that this must have been *test. factio*
of the third sort, because he had not
the first.   But then he had the
second; he might be instituted heir,
(Vlp. xxii, 3,) although he could
not take the inheritance unless he
became a citizen within a certain
limited period.   *Test. factio* of the
first sort is called by the civilians
actiua, that of the second *passiua*.
Comp. § 4, I. *de qual. et diff. her.*
(ii, 19).
[2] See § 109.

115   Non tamen ut iure ciuili *ualeat* testamentum sufficit ea
obseruatio quam supra exposuimus de familiae uenditione et
116 de testibus et de nuncupationibus:¹   ante omnia requiren-
dum est an institutio heredis sollemni more facta sit; nam
aliter facta institutione, nihil proficit familiam testatoris ita
uenire testesque ita adhibere et nuncupare ita testamentum ut
117 supra diximus.   Sollemnis autem institutio haec est : TITIVS
HERES ESTO ; sed et illa iam conprobata uidetur : TITIVM
HEREDEM ESSE IVBEO ; at illa non est conprobata : TITIVM
HEREDEM ESSE VOLO ; sed et illae a plerisque inprobatae sunt :
TITIVM HEREDEM INSTITVO, item : HEREDEM FACIO.
118   Obseruandum praeterea est, ut si mulier quae in tutela est
faciat testamentum, *tutoribus auctoribus id* facere debeat :¹
119 alioquin inutiliter iure ciuili testabitur.   Praetor tamen si
septem signis testium signatum sit testamentum, scriptis here-

---

115   It is not enough, however, to render a testament valid
according to the *ius ciuile* that all the rules we have above
explained about sale of the *familia*, witnesses, and nun-
116 cupations have been observed.   Above all things we must
see whether the institution of the heir has been made with
the customary solemnity ; if it has been made otherwise, then
it avails nothing that the testator's *familia* has been sold, the
witnesses adhibited, and the testament nuncupated in the
117 way previously described.   Here is a solemn institution :
' Be Titius my heir ; ' and this one, ' I order that Titius shall
be my heir,' seems also to be approved ; but, ' I wish Titius to
be heir,' is not approved, nor by most persons are these, ' I
institute Titius as heir,' and ' I make Titius my heir.'
118   It is further to be observed that if a woman who is in
tutelage make a testament, she must do so with *auctoritas* of
her tutors ; otherwise, according to the civil law, her testa-
119 ment will be useless.   If, however, it be sealed with the
seals of seven witnesses, the praetor will grant possession of

---

§§ 115-187. Comp. tit. I. *DE EXHEREDA-*
TIONE LIBERORVM (ii, 13).
§ 115.   Comp. pr. tit. I. afd.
    ¹ See § 104.
§ 116. Comp. § 229; Vlp. xxiv, 15;
    § 84, I. *de legat.* (ii, 20).
§ 117.   Comp. Vlp. xxi. All this ' *in-*
anis obseruatio ' abolished by Constantius, I. 15, C. *de test.* (vi, 23).
§ 118. Comp. i, 192; ii, 112; iii, 43;
    Vlp. xx, 16.

¹ The MS. has *tutores habet facere*
debeat. K. u. S. and Hu., like
previous eds., read *tutore auctore*
fac. deb. I prefer the reading given
above ; the original probably was
tut. ab. (or *tab.*) *id facere debeat,*
which has been wrongly apprehended by the copyist in transcribing.
See § 112, note 2.

§ 119. Comp. § 147; Cic. *II. Verr.* i, 45,
    § 117; Vlp. xxiii, 6; xxviii, 6.

dibus secundum tabulas testamenti *bonorum possessionem* [1] pollicetur,[2] [*et*] si nemo sit ad quem ab intestato iure legitimo
pertineat hereditas, uelut frater eodem patre natus aut patruus
aut fratris filius, ita poterunt scripti heredes retinere hereditatem : nam idem iuris est et si alia ex *causa* testamentum
non ualeat, uelut quod familia non uenierit aut nuncupationis

the defunct's estate to the testamentary heirs in terms of the
will. If in such a case there be no one on whom the estate
devolves by law as heir *ab intestato*, say a brother by the
same father, or a father's brother, or a brother's son, the heirs
nominated in the testament will be in a position to retain the
inheritance; for the rule is the same here as if the testament were invalid on some other ground, as, for instance,
failure on the part of a testator to mancipate his *familia* or

[1] *Bonorum possessio* was one of
the most important institutions of
praetorian equity, often spoken of as
praetorian succession, in contradistinction to the *hereditas* or succession
of the *ius ciuile*,—the right of beneficial enjoyment of a deceased person's
estate, and that *tuitione praetoris*,
even though the legal title of heir
might for some reason be awanting.

It was of three varieties—(1)
b. p. secundum tabulas, (2) *b. p. contra tabulas*, and (3) *b. p. intestati*.

The first—that referred to in this
par., and again in § 147—was
granted when the wishes of a testator
were in danger of being frustrated
because of some informality of his
testament which rendered it in law
invalid; the testamentary heir in
such a case often obtained a grant
of *bonor. possessio* according to the
tenor of the will, which prevented
the succession passing to the heir *ab
intestato*.

The second was granted in cases
where the testament was in point
of form unchallengeable, yet in its
provisions inequitable, as when an
emancipated child of the testator's
was passed over (§ 135); the testament was not upset, because *iure
ciuili* it was quite valid, but the
praeteritus was allowed to participate to a greater or smaller extent
in the benefits of the succession by
bon. pos. contra tabulas, i.e. against
the tenor of the will.

The third was granted on intestacy

to those who were not heirs *ab intestato* according to the rules of the
ius ciuile, but preferred to such
persons by the more equitable provisions of the praetor's edict ; see
examples in iii, §§ 26-31.

As Gai. points out in iii, 32, the
grantee of any of those *bonor. possessiones* did not thereby become
heir, *nam praetor heredes facere non
potest*. He was therefore unable to
make use of the legal remedies
available to heirs for the realisation
and protection of their rights; so
that it became necessary for the
praetor to devise new remedies on
his behalf.

These were in some respects more
efficient than those competent to
heirs. Whence this result,—that a
man, whose position as heir under
the civil law was unchallenged and
unchallengeable, often deemed it
advisable to fortify it with a grant of
bon. possessio, that so he might have
the advantage of the remedies competent to a *bonor. possessor* (iii, 34).

The subject of *bonor. possessio* is
dealt with in tit. I. iii, 9.

[2] *Bon. pos. polliceri, in integrum
restitutionem polliceri*, and such
like, are technical expressions for
the praetor's declaration in his
Edict that in such or such cases he
would grant such or such a remedy.
To say that he 'promises' it, might
lead to misunderstanding; therefore
'grants' or 'will grant' is preferred in the translation.

120 uerba testator locutus non sit.   Sed uideamus an [1] etiamsi
frater aut patruus extent potiores scriptis heredibus habeantur:
rescripto enim imperatoris Antonini [2] significatur eos qui secundum tabulas testamenti non iure factas bonorum possessionem
petierint, posse aduersus eos qui ab intestato uindicant here-
121 ditatem defendere se per exceptionem doli mali.[3]   quod sane
quidem ad masculorum testamenta pertinere certum est ; item
ad feminarum quae ideo *non* utiliter testatae sunt quod uerbi
gratia familiam non uendiderint aut nuncupationis uerba
locutae non sint: an autem et ad ea testamenta feminarum
quae sine tutoris auctoritate fecerint haec constitutio pertineat
122 uidebimus.[1]   Loquimur autem de his scilicet feminis quae
non in legitima parentium aut patronorum tutela sunt, sed de
his quae alterius generis tutores habent, qui etiam inuiti
coguntur auctores fieri :[1] alioquin parentem et patronum sine
auctoritate eius facto testamento non summoueri palam est.

---

120 pronounce the words of nuncupation.   But is it the case
that a brother or a father's brother, supposing them to exist,
are really preferred to the heirs named in the testament?
[Hardly]; for by a rescript of our emperor Antonine's it is
declared that persons who have applied for possession of a
defunct's estate in terms of a testament not executed according to law, can defend themselves with an exception of fraud
121 against those claiming the inheritance *ab intestato*.   That
this rescript applies to testaments of men is certain ; and it is
equally certain that it applies to any made by women that
are invalid because they have omitted to mancipate their
familia or to recite the words of nuncupation : but whether
it applies to such testaments of theirs as have been made
without tutorial *auctoritas* is a matter for consideration.
122 We are referring, of course, to women who are not under the
tutory-at-law of parents or patrons, but have tutors of some
other sort,—tutors who may be compelled to grant their
auctoritas whether they will or not : that a parent or patron
is not to be displaced by a testament made without his
auctoritas is quite clear.

§ 120. Comp. § 149, and notes.
[1] Hu. and several other eds. interpolate *non* after *an*, entirely
subverting the meaning of the
par.
[2] Doubtful whether it be Antoninus Pius or Marcus Aurelius that
is here referred to: probably the
latter, as the former is referred to
in § 195 as *diuus Pius*.
[3] See § 76, note 3.
§ 121. Comp. §§ 104, 115, 118.
[1] The question is answered indirectly in next par.
§ 122. Comp. i, §§ 190, 192.
[1] Comp. § 115.

123   Item qui filium in potestate habet curare debet ut eum uel
heredem instituat uel nominatim [1] exheredet ; alioquin si eum
silentio praeterierit inutiliter testabitur : adeo quidem ut
nostri praeceptores [2] existiment, etiamsi uiuo patre filius defunctus sit, neminem heredem ex eo testamento existere posse,
quia scilicet statim ab initio non constitérit institutio ; sed
diuersae scholae auctores,[2] si quidem filius mortis patris
tempore uiuat, sane inpedimento eum esse scriptis heredibus
[et illum ab intestato heredem fieri] [3] confitentur ; si uero
ante mortem patris interceptus sit, posse ex testamento
hereditatem adiri putant, nullo iam filio inpedimento ; quia
scilicet existimant [non] [4] statim ab initio inutiliter fieri testa-
124 mentum filio praeterito.   Ceteras uero liberorum personas
si praeterierit testator ualet testamentum.   [sed] praeteritae
istae personae scriptis heredibus in partem adcrescunt,[1] si sui

123   Moreover, a testator who has a son *in potestate* must take
care either to institute him as heir or by name to disinherit
him ; if he pass him over in silence his testament will be
useless. So far do the 'authorities of our school carry this
doctrine that, even though the son predecease his father, they
hold there can be no heir under the testament, the institution
having been void from the first. Those of the other school,
however, while they admit that, if the son survive his father,
the heirs nominated in the testament will be cut out by him
and he take *ab intestato*, yet are of opinion that, if he predecease his father, the inheritance may be taken up under the
testament, the son being no longer an obstacle ; for their view
is that a testament is not *ab initio* invalid because a son of
124 the testator's has been passed over.   If, however, it be not
a son but other descendants [*in potestate*] that have been
passed over, the testament is valid ; but those passed over
come in for a share by accretion along with the heirs nomi-

§ 123. Pr. tit. I. afd. Comp. Vlp. xxii,
16. From these it appears that the
Sabinian doctrine, approved by Gai.,
was still adhered to as the true one.
The *sui heredes* were joint-owners
with the *paterfamilias* during his
lifetime (§ 157), but without administration ; and on his death
they simply continued their ownership (Paul. in fr. II, D. *de lib. et
post.* xxviii, 2), unless, by testamentary disherison, he had effectually deprived them of their right.
So it was at least in the case of sons.

[1] This did not mean 'by name'
in the strictest sense of the words,
§ 127 ; and probably it was enough
that there was a distinct indication
who was intended. See Gai. in fr.
24, D. *de man. uind.* (xl, 4).
[2] See i, 196, note 1.
[3] With P., I am disposed to regard
the words within brackets as a gloss.
[4] This *non* is approved by all eds.
§ 124. Comp. Vlp. xxii, 17 ; pr. tit. I.
afd.
[1] There was accretion to the heirs,
—their number was increased.

heredes[2] sint in *uirilem*, si extranei in dimidiam: id est, si quis tres uerbi gratia filios heredes instituerit et filiam praeterierit, filia adcrescendo pro quarta parte fit heres, et ea ratione id consequitur quod ab intestato patre *mortuo* habitura esset; at si extraneos ille heredes instituerit et filiam praeterierit, filia adcrescendo ex dimidia parte fit heres. quae de filia diximus eadem et de nepote deque omnibus liberorum personis *seu* masculini seu feminini sexus dicta intellegemus.

125 Quid ergo est? licet eae, secundum ea quae diximus, scriptis heredibus dimidiam partem *modo* detrahant, tamen praetor eis contra tabulas bonorum possessionem promittit qua ratione extranei heredes a tota hereditate repelluntur *et*

126 *efficiuntur* sine re heredes.[1]   et hoc iure *utebamur, quasi*[1] nihil inter feminas et masculos interesset: sed nuper imperator Antoninus[2] significauit rescripto *suas*[3] non plus nancisci feminas per bonorum possessionem quam quod iure adcrescendi

---

nated in the will,—an equal share if these be *sui heredes*, a half of the whole inheritance if they be strangers. In other words, if a man have instituted say his three sons as his heirs, but have passed over his daughter, she by accretion becomes heir to the extent of a fourth of the inheritance, and by this means obtains exactly what she would have been entitled to on her father's death had he died intestate; but if a testator have instituted strangers as his heirs, and passed over his daughter, she by accretion becomes heir for a half. And as with a daughter, so with a grandson or any other descen-

125 dant, whether male or female, [except a son.]   But what of that? Although, according to this statement of the law, they cut the heirs nominated in the testament out of only a moiety of the inheritance, yet the praetor promises them possession of the defunct's estate contrary to the tenor of the will, so that the stranger-heirs are really excluded from the whole inheritance, and become heirs in name only, *heredes sine re.*

126 This was the law we used to act upon, as if there were no difference between males and females; but recently our emperor Antonine has intimated, by a rescript of his, that in future women shall obtain no more by grant of possession of

[2] See §§ 156, 157.
§ 125.   Comp. § 129; Vlp. xxviii, §§ 2, 3.
    [1] Comp. § 148; Vlp. xxviii, 13.
§ 126.   Comp. Iust. in l. 4, C. *de lib. praet.* (vi, 28).
    [1] So Stud.; only the final *i* is visible in the ms.

[2] See § 120, note.
[3] The ms. and K. u. S. have *suo,* referring to *rescripto;* P. and Hu. *suas,* referring to *feminas,* and thus distinguishing them from the *emancipatae* in next line.

consequerentur. quod in emancipatarum quoque personis
obseruandum est : (nam quod praeteritae)[4] adcrescendi iure
habiturae essent si in potestatae fuissent, id ipsum etiam per
127 bonorum possessionem habeant.   *Sed si quidem* filius a
patre exheredetur, nominatim[1] exheredari *debet, alioquin* non
prodest eum[2] exheredari.   nominatim autem exheredari uidetur
sine ita exheredetur: TITIVS FILIVS MEVS EXHERES (ESTO, siue
(*ita:* FILIVS MEVS)[3] EXHERES ESTO, non adiecto proprio nomine.
128 *Ceterae uero* liberorum personae, uel feminini sexus uel masculini, *satis* inter ceteros exheredantur, *id est his uerbis :*
(CETERI)[1] OMNES EXHEREDES SVNTO : *quae uerba (semper post)*[2]
129 institutionem heredum adici solent.   Sed *hoc ita (est iure
(ciuili)* ;[1] nam praetor omnes uirilis sexus (*liberos, tam filios
(quam ceteros),*[2] id est nepotes quoque et pronepotes, — — —
— — — — —.[3]

---

the defunct's estate than they are entitled to by accretion.
And this rule applies also to women who have been emancipated; for, *if they be passed over,* they are to take no more
by *bonorum possessio* than they would have got by accretion
127 had they been still *in potestate.*   If a son be disinherited
by his father it must be by name,—disherison in any other
way does no good; and he is held to be nominately disinherited either thus : 'Be my son Titius disinherited,' or thus:
' Be my son disinherited,' without the addition of any proper
128 name.   But other descendants, whether male or female, are
sufficiently disinherited *inter ceteros,* that is by such words as,
' Be all the others disinherited,' which are usually inserted
129 after the institution of the heirs.   Such is *the rule of the
civil law.*   But the praetor requires that all descendants of
the male sex—*not sons only,* but others also, such as grandsons and great-grandsons—[*shall be disinherited by name ; but*

[4] So P.; K. u. S. suggest *ut hae
quoque quod ;* Hu. *ut nimirum hae
quoque quod.*
§ 127.   Comp. Vlp. xxii, 20; § 1, tit. I. afd.
   [1] See § 123, note.
   [2] So. P., on the strength of §§ 140,
141; the ms. has *psiet;* K. u. S.
uidetur.
   [3] The words in parenthesis, illegible in the ms., are supplied from
the Inst.
§ 128.   Comp. Vlp. xxii, 20; pr. §1, tit.
I. afd.; Iust. in l. 4, C. *de lib.
praet.* (vi, 28).
   [1] *Ceteri* seems the obvious read-

ing, although the space is rather too
great for it.
   [2] Illegible, but obvious enou.h.
A nominate disherison, according to
a rescript of Trajan's, might either
precede or follow the institution ;
see Vlp. in fr. 1, pr. D. *de her. inst.*
(xxviii, 5).
§ 129.   Comp. § 185.
   [1] The context naturally suggests
this reading.
   [2] So K. u. S.; P. and Hu. have
liberorum personas; only the initial *lib.* is legible in the ms.
   [3] Hu. suggests as completion of

130   Postumi quoque liberi (*uel heredes*) institui debent uel ex-
131   heredari.   Et in eo par omnium condicio (*est, quod et in*) filio
        (*postumo et in quolibet ex ceteris*) liberis, siue (*feminini sexus siue*)
        masculini, praeterito, ualet (*quidem testamentum, sed postea*
        (*agnatione postumi*) siue postumae rumpitur, et ea ratione
        (*totum*) infirmatur.   (*ideoque*) si mulier ex qua (*postumus aut*
        (*postuma*) sperabatur abortum (*fecerit, nihil inpedimento est*
132   (*scriptis heredibus ad hereditatem adeundam.   Sed feminini*)
        quidem sexus personae (*uel nominatim uel*) inter ceteros (*exhere-*
        (*dari solent, dum tamen si inter ceteros exheredentur aliquid eis*
        (*legetur, ne uideantur per obliuionem*) praeteritae (*esse : masculini*
        (*uero sexus personas*) placuit non aliter recte (*exheredari nisi*
        (*nominatim exheredentur, hoc scilicet modo : QVICVMQVE MIHI*

[*allows females, daughters, that is to say, and granddaughters*
[*and great-granddaughters, to be disinherited either by name or*
[*in the* ceteri *clause.*]
130   Descendants that may possibly be born after the making
        of a testament must also be either instituted or disinherited.
131   They are all on the same footing in this respect,—*that,*
        whether it be a son or any other male or female descendant to be
        born after the making of the testament that is unmentioned in
        it, it is nevertheless valid; *but on the agnation* of any such
        after-born, it is broken and thereby rendered altogether void.
        Therefore if a woman from whom a child is expected mis-
        carry [after the execution of a testament], *there is nothing to*
        prevent the heirs named in it entering upon the inheritance.
132   *Females may be disinherited either by name or amongst ' the*
        others,' the precaution being taken, when they are disinherited
        by the latter mode, of leaving them a legacy to show that they
        have not been passed over through forgetfulness ; but, as regards
        after-born males, it has been held that they cannot validly be
        disinherited otherwise than by name, *thus : ' Any son that*

the par. — *nominatim exheredari*
iubet, feminini uero sexus liberos,
id est filias et nepotes et proneptes,
exheredari aut nominatim aut inter
ceteros satis habet. This will about
fill the vacant two lines and a quarter (lines 8-10, p. 86).

§§ 130-134. Pp. 86 and 87 of the MS.
are for the most part illegible; but
those pars. are reproduced in the
Inst.—the two last also in an ex-
tract from Gai. in the Dig.,—and

from them completed. Between lines
2 and 11 of p. 87 there seems to have
been some matter which Justinian
has not reproduced; it is indicated as
§ 132a. In the MS. § 130 runs— *Pos-*
tumi quoque liberi nominatim, etc. ;
the *nominatim* has been excluded as
an inaccurate gloss. The word *pos-*
tumi can be adequately rendered in
the translation only by a periphrasis.

§§ 130-132. § 1, tit. I. afd. Comp. Vlp.
xxii, §§ 15, 18-21 ; xxiii, 2.

132*a* (*FILIVS GENITVS FVERIT, EXHERES ESTO*).   [132*a*] — — —

133 — — — — —.   (*Postumorum autem loco sunt et hi qui in*
(*sui heredis locum succedendo quasi agnascendo fiunt parenti-*
(*bus*) sui heredes : ut ecce si filium et (*ex eo nepotem*) neptemue
(*in potestate habeam, quia filius gradu praecedit, is solus iura*
(*sui heredis habet, quamuis nepos*) quoque et neptis ex (*eo in*
(*eadem potestate sint ; sed si filius meus me uiuo moriatur, aut*
(*qualibet ratione exeat de potestate mea, incipit nepos neptisue in*
(*eius locum succedere, et*) eo modo iura suorum (*heredum quasi*

134 (*agnatione*) nanciscuntur.   Ne ergo eo modo rumpatur
mihi testamentum, (*sicut ipsum filium uel heredem*) instituere
uel exheredare debeo ne (*non iure faciam testamentum, ita et*)
nepotem neptemue ex eo necesse est mihi (*uel heredem instituere*
(*uel exheredare, ne forte, me uiuo filio mortuo, succedendo in*
(*locum eius nepos neptisue*) quasi agnatione rumpat testamentum: idque lege Iunia Vellaea[1] prouisum est—in qua
simul exheredationis modus notatur—ut uirilis sexus [*postumi*]

132*a* *may be born to me hereafter is hereby disinherited.*'   [132*a*] —

133 — — — — — — —.   *In the same position as after-born*
descendants are those who, on coming in place of a suus heres,
by quasi-agnation become sui heredes *of their parents.   For*
example, if I have in my potestas *a son and a grandchild,*
male or female, by that son, the latter, being of the nearer degree,
alone has the rights of a suus heres, *notwithstanding that my*
grandchild by him is also in my potestas; *but if my son die in*
my lifetime, or for any reason cease to be in my potestas, *my*
grandchild steps into his place, and thus by quasi-agnation

134 acquires the privileges of a *suus heres*.   Now, just as I
must either institute or disinherit *my son in order to make my*
testament legally valid ab initio, so must I, in order to prevent
its being broken, *either institute or disinherit* my grandchild
by that son, *lest possibly the latter should die during my life-*
time, and my grandchild, succeeding in his father's place,
should break my testament by quasi-agnation.   And it was
expressly enacted by the Junia-Vellaean law—in which the
form of disinheriting is at the same time described—that

---

§ 133. Gai. in fr. 13, D. *de iniusto rupto*
(xxviii, 3); § 2, tit. I. afd.; Vlp.
xxiii, 3.
§ 134. See refs. in last note.
    [1] So the law is named in the MS.,
though usually called Junia Velleia.
It is generally supposed to have been

enacted probably in the year 799 |
46, and consulate of M. Junius
Silanus and Velleus Tutor; see fr.
2, pr. D. *ad SC. Velleian.* (xvi, 1).
But as senatusconsults had by that
time taken the place of *leges*, it
probably was of earlier date.

nominatim, feminini uel nominatim uel inter ceteros exhere-
tur, dum tamen iis qui inter ceteros exheredantur aliquid legetur.
135   Emancipatos liberos iure ciuili neque heredes instituere
neque exheredare necesse est, quia non sunt sui heredes: sed
praetor omnes, tam feminini quam masculini sexus, si heredes
non instituantur exheredari iubet, uirilis sexus nominatim,
feminini uel nominatim uel inter ceteros: quodsi neque
heredes instituti fuerint neque ita ut supra diximus exheredati,
praetor promittit eis contra tabulas bonorum possessionem.[1]
135a In potestate patris non sunt qui cum eo ciuitate Romana
donati sunt, nec in accipienda ciuitate Romana *pater petiit*[1] *a
principe*[2] ut eos in potestate haberet, *aut si* petiit non impetra-
uit; nam qui *in potestatem* patris ab imperatore rediguntur
136 nihil differunt — —.[3]   Adoptiui filii, quamdiu manent

---

males must be disinherited by name, while females may be
disinherited either by name or *inter ceteros*, provided in the
latter case some legacy be left them.
135   By the civil law it is unnecessary either to institute or disinherit emancipated children, because they are not *sui heredes.*
But the praetor requires that, if they be not instituted, they
shall all, both males and females, be disinherited,—the former
by name, the latter either by name or amongst 'the others.' If
they be neither instituted heirs nor disinherited in the manner
aforesaid, the praetor will grant them *bonorum possessio contra
tabulas*, [*i.e.* possession of the defunct's estate contrary to the
135a tenor of his testament.]   Those children are not in their
father's *potestas* who have obtained along with him a gift of
citizenship, if either the *potestas* had not been specially
applied for from the sovereign, or, being applied for, had not
been granted; but those who have been subjected by the
emperor to their father's *potestas* differ in no respect from
136 [*children born in it*].   Further, adoptive sons, so long as

---

§ 135. § 8, tit. I. afd. Comp. Vlp. xxii,
28; xxviii, 4. But it was under
condition of collation with the un-
emancipated *sui heredes*, at least in
the time of Vlp.
 [1] Comp. § 119, note 1.
§ 135a. Comp. i, §§ 93, 94; iii, 20;
Vlp. in *Collat.* xvi, 7, § 2. Some
words in the ms. are indistinct, and
one or two illegible.
 [1] The indistinct letters in the ms.
do not resemble *petiit*,—there is too
much space for it. The sense, how-

ever, suggests it; and Hu., to pro-
long it, adds *statim.*
 [2] So I think may be rendered
the *ap* of the ms., which K. u.
S. ignore, and Hu. renders *aut
post.*
 [3] The ms. appears to have something like *athisunit.* P. suggests
ab suis heredibus, and Hu. *a sic
natis;* as K. u. S. observe, one
might expect *ab his qui in potestate
patris nati sunt.*
§ 136. Comp. § 4, tit. I. afd.

in adoptione, naturalium loco sunt; emancipati uero a patre adoptiuo, neque iure ciuili neque quod ad edictum praetoris
137 pertinet inter liberos numerantur.   Qua ratione accidit ut ex diuerso, quod ad naturalem parentem pertinet, quamdiu quidem sint in adoptiua familia extraneorum numero habeantur; si uero emancipati fuerint ab adoptiuo patre, tunc incipiant in ea causa esse qua futuri essent si ab ipso naturali patre [*emancipati*] fuissent.
138 Si quis post factum testamentum adoptauerit sibi filium, aut per populum eum qui sui iuris est, aut per praetorem eum qui in potestate parentis fuerit, omni modo testamentum
139 eius rumpitur quasi agnatione sui heredis.   Idem iuris est si cui post factum testamentum uxor in manum conueniat, uel quae in manu fuit nubat: nam eo modo filiae loco esse incipit
140 et quasi sua.[1]   nec prodest siue haec siue ille qui adoptatus est in eo testamento sit institutus institutaue: nam de exheredatione eius superuacuum uidetur quaerere, cum testamenti

---

they remain in the adoptive family, are in the same position as natural children; on emancipation, however, by their adoptive parent they are no longer included amongst his descendants, either by the civil law or by the praetor's edict.
137 And thus it comes to pass, conversely, that, so long as they are in the adoptive family, they are reckoned as strangers in relation to their natural parent; if, however, they be emancipated by their adoptive parent, they then begin to be in the same position they would have occupied had they been emancipated by their natural parent.
138 If a man after making his testament adopt a son,—either a person who is *sui iuris* by vote of the people, or a *filiusfamilias* by magisterial authority,—his testament is invariably broken
139 by this quasi-agnation of a *suus heres*.   The result is the same if after making his testament he take a wife *in manum*, or if a woman already in his *manus* become his wife; in either way she begins to hold the position of a daughter and be-
140 comes *quasi sua heres*.   Nor does it prevent such result that either the wife or the adopted child has been instituted heir in the testament;—it is unnecessary to say anything of their

---

§ 137. § 4, tit. I. afd., from which the penultimate *emancipati* is supplied.
§§ 138-151. Comp. tit. I. QVIBVS MODIS TESTAMENTA INFIRMANTVR (ii, 17).
§ 138. § 1, tit. I. afd. Comp. i, §§ 98 f.; Vlp. xxiii, §§ 2, 3.

§ 139. Comp. i, § 114; Vlp. xxiii, 3.
[1] After *sua* the MS. has an *i*, which Hu. converts into [*heres*] *fit*.
§ 140. Comp. fr. 18, D. *de iniusto rupto* (xxviii, 3).

faciendi tempore suorum heredum numero non fuerit

141 Filius quoque qui ex prima secundaue mancipatione manumittitur, quia reuertitur in potestatem patriam, rumpit ante factum testamentum; nec prodest [si] in eo testamento heres

142 institutus uel exheredatus fuerit.   Simile ius olim fuit in eius persona cuius nomine ex senatusconsulto erroris causa probatur, quia forte ex peregrina uel latina, quae per errorem quasi ciuis Romana uxor ducta esset, natus esset: nam siue heres institutus esset a parente siue exheredatus, siue uiuo patre causa probata siue post mortem eius, omni modo

143 quasi agnatione rumpebat testamentum.   Nunc uero ex nouo senatusconsulto quod auctore diuo Hadriano factum est, si quidem uiuo patre causa probatur, aeque ut olim omni modo rumpit testamentum; si uero post mortem patris, praeteritus quidem rumpit testamentum; si uero heres in eo scriptus est uel exheredatus, non rumpit testamentum, ne scilicet diligenter facta testamenta rescinderentur eo tempore

144 quo renouari non possent.   Posteriore quoque testamento

---

disherison, for at the time the testament was made they were

141 not of the testator's *sui heredes*.   A son also, who is manumitted after a first or second mancipation, breaks a previous testament of his father's by reverting into his *potestas;* nor does it matter though in said testament he may have been

142 either instituted or disinherited.   Formerly the rule was the same in the case of a person on whose account cause of error had been established under the senatusconsult, say because he had been born of a peregrin or latin woman whom his father had married by mistake, believing her to be a citizen; for, whether he had been instituted or disinherited by his parent, and whether the cause of error had been established before or after his father's death, in any case the testa-

143 ment was broken by his quasi-agnation.   But now, by a later senatusconsult, due to the late emperor Hadrian, if the cause of error have been established in the father's lifetime the testament is invariably broken just as it used to be; but if cause be not shown till after the father's death, while it will still be broken if the son have been passed over, that will not happen if he has been either instituted in it or disinherited, lest otherwise a carefully executed testament be set aside when

144 it is no longer possible to re-make it.   An earlier testa-

§ 141. Comp. i, § 132; Vlp. xxiii, 3.   § 144. § 2, tit. I. afd. Comp. Vlp.
§ 142. Comp. i, §§ 67-74.   xxiii, 2.

quod iure factum est superius rumpitur; nec interest an
extiterit aliquis ex eo heres an non extiterit: hoc enim
solum spectatur an existere potuerit. ideoque si quis ex
posteriore testamento quod iure factum est aut noluerit heres
esse, aut uiuo testatore aut post mortem eius antequam hereditatem adiret decesserit, aut per cretionem exclusus fuerit,[1]
aut condicione sub qua heres institutus est defectus sit, aut
propter caelibatum ex lege Iulia summotus fuerit ab hereditate:[2] quibus casibus paterfamilias intestatus moritur: nam
et prius testamentum non ualet, ruptum a posteriore, et pos-
terius aeque nullas uires habet, cum ex eo nemo heres exti-
145 terit.   Alio quoque modo testamenta iure facta infirmantur,
uelut [*cum*] is qui fecerit testamentum capite deminutus sit;
quod quibus modis accidat primo commentario[1] relatum est.
146 hoc autem casu inrita fieri testamenta dicemus, cum alioquin
et quae rumpuntur inrita fiant, [*et quae statim ab initio non iure*
[*fiunt inrita sint; sed et ea quae iure facta sunt et postea propter*

---

ment is also broken by a later one duly executed. And it
is immaterial whether any one has become heir under the
second one or not; the sole question is, could there have
been an heir under it? Therefore if the heir under a later
testament, made according to the requirements of law, either
has declined the inheritance, or has predeceased the testator,
or, having survived him, has died before entry, or has been
excluded by cretion or through failure of a condition upon
which his institution depended, or has been debarred by the
Julian law on account of celibacy,—in any of those cases
the party dies intestate ; for his earlier testament is invalid,
having been broken by the later one, and this is equally of no
145 avail since no one becomes heir in terms of it.   There is
yet another way in which a testament duly executed may be
annulled, namely by the testator's *capitis deminutio;* and
how this may occur has been explained in our first Com-
146 mentary.   But in this case we say it is irritated, [*i.e.* becomes untenable.] No doubt those which are broken become
untenable, as *are those also that at the first were not exe-*
cuted according to law; while, on the other hand, those that
were originally made in due form, but have subsequently been

---

[1] Comp. §§ 166 f.   [1] Comp. i, §§ 159-162.
        [2] Comp. §§ 111, 286; Vlp. xxii, 4.   § 146.   § 5, tit. I. afd., from which the
§ 145.   § 4, tit. I. afd.   Comp. Vlp.   words in italics, omitted in the MS.,
    xxiii, 4.   are borrowed.

[*capitis deminutionem inrita fiunt,*] possunt nihilominus rupta dici : sed quia sane commodius erat singulas causas singulis appellationibus distingui, ideo quaedam non iure fieri dicuntur, quaedam iure facta rumpi uel inrita fieri.

147   Non tamen per omnia inutilia sunt ea testamenta quae uel ab initio non iure facta sunt uel iure facta postea inrita facta aut rupta sunt : nam si septem testium signis signata sint testamenta, potest scriptus heres secundum tabulas bonorum possessionem petere, si modo defunctus testator et ciuis Romanus et suae potestatis mortis tempore fuerit : nam si ideo inritum factum sit testamentum quod puta ciuitatem uel etiam libertatem testator amisit, aut quod is in adoptionem se dedit et mortis tempore in adoptiui patris potestate fuit, non potest scriptus heres secundum tabulas bonorum possessionem

148   petere.   [*Qui igitur*][1] secundum tabulas testamenti quae aut statim ab initio non iure factae sunt, aut iure factae postea ruptae uel inritae [*factae*][2] erunt, bonorum posses-

---

rendered untenable by capitis deminutio, may none the less be said to be broken.   But as it is obviously more convenient to distinguish particular cases by particular names, we say of some testaments that they have not been executed according to law, and of others that have been duly executed that they are either broken or irritated.

147   Those testaments, however, are not altogether useless that either have not at first been executed according to law, or, having been so executed, have afterwards been irritated or broken.   For if a testament be sealed with the seals of seven witnesses, the heir named in it may apply for possession of the defunct's estate in terms of the writing, provided the testator was a citizen and *sui iuris* at the moment of his death ; but such application is incompetent if the testament have been irritated say by the testator's loss of citizenship or liberty, or by his having given himself in adoption and having continued till his death in the *potestas* of his adoptive

148   father.   Those who have a grant of possession of a defunct's estate in terms of a testament that was either from the first not executed according to law, or that, having been duly executed, has afterwards been broken or irritated, will have

§ 147. § 6, tit. I. afd. Comp. § 119, and note 1 ; Vlp. xxiii, 6 ; xxviii, §§ 5, 6.
§ 148. Comp. iii, §§ 35-38 ; Vlp. xxiii, 6 ; xxviii, 13.

[1] Supplied by K. u. S. ; P. supplies *sed si qui*, and Hu. *si qui*.
[2] So P. ; K. u. S., following the MS., have simply *erunt* ; Hu. [*factae*] *sunt*.

sionem accipiunt, si modo possunt hereditatem obtinere,
habebunt bonorum possessionem cum re: si uero ab iis auo-
cari hereditas potest, habebunt bonorum possessionem sine
149 re.   Nam si quis heres iure ciuili institutus sit,[1] uel ab
intestato iure legitimo heres sit, is potest ab iis hereditatem
auocare; si uero nemo sit alius iure ciuili heres, ipsi retinere
hereditatem possunt; *nec ullum* ius aduersus eos habent — —
— *legitimo iure deficiuntur.*   — — — — — *quoque notauimus,*
etiam legitimis quoque (*heredibus*) potiores scripti habentur,
— — — — factum sit testamentum quod familia non
uenierit aut nuncupationis uerba testator locutus non sit;
cum enim agnati petant hereditatem, — — — — — — —.[2]

---

bonorum possessio cum re [real and effectual possession], if only
they can retain the inheritance; but if it can be taken past
them, their grant of possession will be *sine re* [without real
149 effect].   For if an individual have been instituted heir [in
an earlier testament executed] according to the requirements
of the civil law, or be heir-at-law *ab intestato*, he is in a position to deprive them of the inheritance; but if there be no
other person that is heir by the civil law, they can retain it;
for [*cognates and other persons*] not enjoying the character of
heirs under the civil law have no right in preference to them.
[*Sometimes, however, as*] we have already observed, the heirs
instituted in the invalid testament are preferred even to the
heirs-at-law, [*as when the objection to the regularity of its exe-
[cution is merely] that the testator had not duly mancipated
his *familia* or expressed the words of nuncupation; if in such
a case the agnates claim the inheritance, [*they may, according
[to a constitution of our emperor Antonine's, be defeated by ex-*

---

§§ 149-151. P. 92 of the ms., which contains the greater part of these pars.,
is to a considerable extent illegible;
while of much that Stud. has reproduced he does not profess himself
certain.

§ 149.   Comp. §§ 119-121.
     [1] After *sit* the ms. has *uel ex
primo uel ex posteriore testamento :*
these words I have expunged as an
inaccurate gloss ; for if there were a
valid later testament there could not
well be any claim under an earlier
invalid one, § 144.
     [2] The par. may, I think, be com-
pleted as follows: nec ullum ius
aduersus eos habent *cognati quiue*

legitimo iure deficiuntur. *Aliquando
tamen, ut supra* quoque notauimus,
etiam legitimis quoque *heredibus*
potiores scripti habentur, *ueluti si
ideo non iure* factum sit testamentum quod familia non uenierit aut
nuncupationis uerba testator locutus non sit; cum enim agnati petant
hereditatem *per exceptionem doli
mali ex constitutione imperatoris
Antonini* (§ 120) *summoueri possunt.*
     The meaning I take to be this: a
grant of *bonor. possessio* to a person
instituted in an invalid will was,
under the limitations mentioned in
§ 147, effectual (*cum re*) as against a
cognate or other merely praetorian

150 — — — — — — lege bona caduca fiunt et ad populum
deferri iubentur si defuncto nemo — — - —.

151 Potest ut iure facta testamenta *contraria* (*uoluntate*)
infirmentur. Apparet [*autem*] non posse (*ex eo solo infirmari*)
testamentum (*quod postea*) testator (*id noluerit*) ualere, usque
adeo ut si linum eius inciderit nihilo minus iure ciuili ualeat.
quin *etiam si deleuerit quoque aut obleuerit* tabulas testamenti,
non ideo protinus[1] *desinent ualere quae fuerant scripta, licet
eorum* probatio *difficilis* sit. quid *ergo est* si quis ab intestato
bonorum possessionem petierit, *et is qui* ex eo testamento

---

150 [*ception of fraud.   Nor does the Julian law take away the
[*inheritance from those named in the invalid testament if they
[*have obtained* bonorum possessio *under the edict; for by
[*that*] enactment the estate of a person deceased becomes
caduciary and falls to the state only [*when he has no heir
[either civil or praetorian*].

151   It is possible even for a duly executed testament to be
invalidated by a contrary manifestation of will. It appears,
however, that it is not enough to invalidate it that the testator has afterwards meant it to be of no effect; so little is this
the case that even if he have cut the strings that secured it,
still it is valid by the civil law; nay, even if he have deleted
some part of it, what was there written does not *straightway*
cease to be valid, although the proof of it may be troublesome.
But what if some one claim *bonorum possessio* as by right of
intestacy, and he who under the testament is entitled to the

successor claiming *ab intestato*. As
against persons claiming under an
earlier and valid testament, or *ab
intestato* as heirs of the *ius ciuile*
(*sui*, agnates, and patrons), it was,
as a rule, ineffectual (*sine re*);
but, as against agnates at least, it
was effectual if the ground of in-
validity was nothing more serious
than omission of the *mancipatio* or
uerba nuncupationis.
   The reconstructions of K. u. S.
and Hu. proceed on a somewhat
different track, and seem to me
hardly reconcilable with the doctrine of § 120.
§ 150. The only legible words, besides those in the text, are *Iulia* on
line 10, and *possessores* on line 11.
K. ingeniously conjectures: *Sane
lege* Iulia *scriptis non aufertur hereditas si bonorum* possessores *ex

edicto constituti sint. nam ita demum ea* lege bona caduca fiunt et
ad populum deferri iubentur, si defuncto nemo *heres uel bonorum possessor existat*. Comp. Vlp. xxviii, 7,
last clause. The Julian law referred
to is the L. Iulia et Papia Poppaea
(i, § 145, note 1), whose caduciary
provisions were often spoken of
under the name of *Lex caducaria*.
Comp. generally on subject of *caduca*, Vlp. xvii, §§ 1-3.
§ 151. This par. occupies the last ten
lines of p. 92, to a considerable extent illegible, and the first two of
p. 93. Comp. § 7, tit. I. afd., from
which the words in ital. in the second
and third lines are supplied.
[1] So P.; the ms. seems to have
non ideo minus, for which Hu. substitutes *non ideo magis*, and K. u. S.
nihilo minus non.

heres est petat hereditatem ? — — — — — — — — perueniat hereditas :[2] et hoc ita rescripto imperatoris Antonini
significatur.

152 Heredes autem aut necessarii dicuntur aut sui et necessarii
153 aut extranei.   Necessarius heres est seruus cum libertate
heres institutus ; ideo sic appellatus quia siue uelit siue nolit
omni modo post mortem testatoris protinus liber et heres est.
154 Vnde qui facultates suas suspectas habet, solet seruum suum
primo aut secundo uel etiam ulteriore gradu[1] liberum et
heredem instituere, ut si creditoribus satis non fiat potius
huius heredis quam ipsius testatorius bona ueneant,[2] id est ut
ignominia quae accidit ex uenditione bonorum hunc potius

---

inheritance raise his *hereditatis petitio ?* [*The latter may in
[that case be displaced by exception of fraud, and the inherit-
[ance thus be prevented from falling to one whom, according to
[the last manifestation of his will, the testator did not mean
[to be his heir*]; such is the rule laid down by our emperor
Antonine in one of his rescripts.
152 Heirs are called either *necessarii*, or *sui et necessarii*, or
153 *extranei*.   A necessary heir is the slave instituted with gift
of freedom ; so called because in every case, whether he will
or not, he straightway on the testator's death becomes free and
154 heir.   Accordingly it is not unusual for a man who has
doubts about his solvency to institute one of his slaves as
free and heir in the first or second place, or even in a lower
one ; so that, if the creditors cannot be paid in full, the deceased's estate may be sold rather as that of the heir thus
instituted than of the testator himself, and the consequent

---

[2] Hu., who, like K. u. S., makes
the question begin and end with
quid ergo est, reconstructs thus :
*Potest eum per exceptionem doli
mali repellere, si modo ea mens testatoris fuisse probetur, ut ad eos
qui ab intestato uocantur perueniat
hereditas.* K. (in K. u. S., and
modifying somewhat his previous
reconstruction in his *Krit. Vers.*, p.
12) proposes : *Per exceptionem doli
mali repelletur ; si uero nemo ab
intestato bonorum possessionem petierit, fiscus scripto heredi quasi in-
digno auferat hereditatem, ne ullo
modo ad eum quem testator heredem
habere noluit* perueniat hereditas.
There does not seem room for all

this on the two lines (23 and 24)
appropriate to it. I prefer : *Potest
scriptus heres per exceptionem doli
mali repelli, ne ad illum qui non
habet uoluntatem defuncti* perueniat
hereditas. As authority see ii, 198;
Vlp. in fr. 1, § 8, D. *si tab. test. null.
ex tab.* (xxxviii, 6), and in fr. 4, § 10,
D. *de dol. mal. exc.* (xliv, 4).
§§ 152-173. Comp. tit. I. *DE HEREDVM
QVALITATE ET DIFFERENTIA* (ii,
19). A vacant line in the MS., probably for a rubric, before § 152.
§ 152. Pr. tit. I. afd.
§ 153. § 1, tit. I. afd.
§ 154. § 1, tit. I. afd. Comp. i, 21.
  [1] See § 174.
  [2] Comp. iii, 79.

heredem quam ipsum testatorem contingat; quamquam apud
Fufidium[3] Sabino[4] placeat eximendum eum esse ignominia,[5]
quia non suo uitio sed necessitate iuris bonorum uenditionem
155 pateretur; sed alio iure utimur.   Pro hoc tamen incommodo illud ei commodum praestatur, ut ea quae post mortem
patroni sibi adquisierit, siue ante bonorum uenditionem siue
postea, ipsi reseruentur; et quamuis *pro portione*[1] bona
uenierint iterum ex hereditaria causa bona eius non uenient,
nisi si quid ei ex hereditaria causa fuerit adquisitum, uelut si
latinum adquisierit[2] [*et*] locupletior factus sit; cum ceterorum
hominum quorum bona uenierint pro portione, si quid postea
156 adquirant, etiam saepius eorum bona uenire solent.[3]   Sui
autem et necessarii heredes sunt uelut filius filiaue, nepos

---

disgrace attach to the former rather than to the latter.
Sabinus, according to Fufidius, was of opinion that the slave
should be exempt from ignominy, since he had to submit
to the sale not from any fault of his own but as a legal neces-
155 sity; but the law is otherwise.   In return, however, for
that drawback he enjoys this advantage,—that he is entitled
to retain what he himself has acquired after the death of his
patron, whether before or after the sale; and although the
sale of the estate may have yielded the creditors only a percentage on their claims, yet his goods will not be sold a second
time on account of hereditary debts, unless it be things
acquired by him from a hereditary source, such as the estate
of a deceased latin [freedman of the testator's] that has fallen in
to him and left him a profit; whereas when the goods of other
insolvents are brought to sale and yield only a percentage,
their subsequent acquisitions may be sold again and again
156 [until the creditors have been paid in full].   Heirs *sui et
necessarii* are such as a son or daughter, a grandson or grand-

---

[3] A jurist of whom little is known,
but mentioned by Africanus (fr. 5,
D. *de auro*, xxxiv, 2) as the author
of some books of 'Questions.'
[4] See i, § 196, note 1.
[5] Comp. Cic. *p. Quint.* xv, §§ 49,
50; *lex Iulia municip.* cap. 25
(Bruns, p. 97); l. 3, C. Th. *de inoff.
test.* (ii, 19). Comp. also pr. I. *de
succ. sublat.* (iii, 12); Th. iii, 21, pr.
§ 155.   Comp. § 1, tit. I. afd.
[1] The MS. has *propter contrac-
tione*; Heise's emendation is unanimously accepted.
[2] The MS. runs—*si latinus ad-*
9

quisierit locupletior factus sit. Various emendations have been proposed; that in the text is due to
Gou., and justified by Gai., ii, 195.
As Gou. observes, *latinum adquirere*
is the same thing as *latini liberti
mortui bona adquirere.* Comp. iii,
58; Plin. Ep. x, 105, (*ius latinorum
suorum mihi reliquit.*)
[3] Cp. fr. 7, D. *de cess. bon.* (xlii, 3).
§§ 156-158. § 2, tit. I. afd., from
which the words in italics are borrowed. Comp. § 128, note; iii, §§
2 f.; Paul. in fr. 11, D. *de lib. et
post.* (xxviii, 2); Vlp. xxii, 24.

neptisue ex filio, [*et*] deinceps *ceteri* qui modo in potestate
morientis fuerunt : sed uti nepos neptisue suus heres sit non
sufficit eum in potestate aui mortis tempore fuisse, sed opus
est ut pater quoque eius uiuo patre suo desierit suus heres
esse, aut morte interceptus aut qualibet ratione liberatus
potestate; tum enim nepos neptisue in locum sui patris
157 succedunt.   Sed sui quidem heredes ideo appellantur quia
domestici heredes sunt et uiuo quoque parente quodammodo
domini existimantur ; unde etiam si quis intestatus mortuus
sit, prima causa est in successione liberorum.   necessarii uero
ideo dicuntur quia omni modo, [*siue*] uelint [*si*]ue [*nolint*,
158 [*tam*] ab intestato quam ex testamento heredes fiunt.   sed
his praetor permittit abstinere se ab hereditate, ut potius
159 parentis bona ueneant.   idem iuris est et in uxoris persona quae in manu est, quia filiae loco est, et in nuru quae in
160 manu filii est, quia neptis loco est.   quin etiam similiter
abstinendi potestatem facit praetor etiam ei qui in causa
mancipii est [1] [*si*] cum libertate heres institutus sit, *quam-*

---

daughter by a son, and so on, who were in potestate of the
deceased when dying.   But to make a grandchild a *suus heres*
it is not enough that he was in the *potestas* of his grandfather
at the time of his death,—it is also necessary that his father
should have ceased to be *suus* in the grandfather's lifetime,
having either been cut off by death or for some reason released
from the *potestas ;* for then the grandson or granddaughter
157 steps into the place of their father.   They are called *sui*
heredes because they are heirs of the house, and even in their
parent's lifetime are regarded as in a manner owners [of the
[family estate] ; wherefore, if any one die intestate, the first
place in the succession belongs to his children.   And they are
called *necessarii,* because in every case, as well on intestacy
as under a testament, they become heirs *whether they will or*
158 *not.*   But the praetor allows them to abstain from the inheritance, that so the estate [if insolvent] may rather be sold
159 in name of their [deceased] parent.   The rule is the same as
regards a wife *in manu,* for she is in the position of a daughter,
and of a daughter-in-law *in manu* of a son, for she is in the
160 position of a granddaughter.   Nay, the same power of abstaining is conceded by the praetor even to a person *in causa*
mancipii who has been instituted heir with freedom ; and this

---

§ 159.   Comp. iii, 3; i, 111; ii, 139.   [1] The MS. adds *id est mancipato :*
§ 160.   Comp. i, §§ 123, 138; iii, 114.   omitted as obviously a gloss.

uis[2] necessarius, non etiam suus heres sit, tamquam seruus.
161 Ceteri qui testatoris iuri subiecti non sunt extranei heredes
appellantur: itaque liberi quoque nostri qui in potestate
nostra non sunt heredes a nobis instituti [sicut][1] extranei
uidentur; qua de causa et qui a matre heredes instituuntur
eodem numero sunt, quia feminae liberos in potestate non
habent.[2] serui quoque qui cum libertate heredes instituti
sunt et postea a domino manumissi[3] eodem numero habentur.
162 Extraneis autem heredibus deliberandi potestas data est de
163 adeunda hereditate uel non adeunda.   Sed siue is cui
abstinendi potestas est inmiscuerit se bonis hereditariis, siue
is cui de adeunda [*hereditate*] deliberare licet adierit, postea
relinquendae hereditatis facultatem non habet nisi si minor
sit annorum xxv: nam huius aetatis hominibus, sicut in
ceteris omnibus causis deceptis, ita etiam si temere damnosam
hereditatem susceperint praetor succurrit.   scio quidem diuum
Hadrianum etiam maiori xxv annorum ueniam dedisse, cum

---

although he is only a necessary heir, like a slave, and not a
161 *suus*.   Other heirs, who are not subject to the testator's right,
are called *extranei*, stranger-heirs.   Those of our children,
therefore, who are not in our *potestas*, if we institute them, are
regarded as strangers ; and for the same reason so are those instituted heirs by their mother, seeing women do not have their
children *in potestate*.   Slaves also, who have been instituted
heirs with liberty, but afterwards manumitted by their owner,
162 belong to the same class.   To such stranger-heirs there is
given a power of deliberating whether or not they will enter
163 upon an inheritance.   But if an heir who has the right
of abstaining have once intromitted with hereditary effects, or
one who is entitled to deliberate as to entering have once
entered, he has not the power of afterwards relinquishing the
inheritance, unless he be under twenty-five years of age; for,
as the praetor grants relief to men of this age in every other
case in which they have been taken advantage of, so does he
when they have accepted a detrimental inheritance.   I am
aware, however, that the late emperor Hadrian once granted
the same relief to an individual above twenty-five, on his dis-

[2] So K. u. S. and Hu., correcting
the MS., which has *cum*.
§ 161. § 3, tit. I. afd. Comp. Vlp. xxii, 25.
[1] According to M., a gloss.

[2] Comp. i, 104 ; Vlp. xxvi, 7.
[3] Comp. § 188.
§§ 162, 163. § 5, tit. I. afd. Comp.
Paul. iii, 4b, § 11.

post aditam hereditatem grande aes alienum, quod aditae
hereditatis tempore latebat, apparuisset.

164   Extraneis heredibus solet cretio dari, id est finis deliberandi, ut intra certum tempus uel adeant hereditatem, uel si
non adeant temporis fine summoueantur: ideo autem cretio
appellata est quia cernere est quasi decernere et constituere.

165 Cum ergo ita scriptum sit: HERES TITIVS ESTO, adicere
debemus: CERNITOQVE IN CENTVM DIEBVS PROXIMIS QVIBVS
SCIES POTERISQVE. QVODNI ITA CREVERIS, EXHERES ESTO.

166 Et qui ita heres institutus est, si uelit heres esse, debebit
intra diem cretionis cernere, id est haec uerba dicere: QVOD
ME PVBLIVS *MEVIVS* TESTAMENTO SVO HEREDEM INSTITVIT, EAM
HEREDITATEM ADEO CERNOQVE; quodsi ita non creuerit, finito
tempore cretionis excluditur: nec quicquam proficit si pro
herede gerat, id est si rebus hereditariis tamquam heres

167 utatur.   At is qui sine cretione heres institutus est, aut

---

covery after entry of the existence of a debt of large amount
which was latent when that step was taken.

164   To stranger-heirs it is the practice to prescribe cretion, that
is, a term for deliberating, so that they must either enter within
the time fixed, or, on its expiry without their having entered,
be displaced; it is so called because *cernere* means to decide and

165 determine.   When therefore we have written, 'Titius be my
heir,' we ought to add these words : ' and cern within the next
hundred days in which you know and can; in default, be dis-

166 inherited.'   If the individual so instituted desire to be heir,
he must cern within the time for cretion, that is, announce
his resolution in these words: 'Whereas Publius Mevius has
instituted me heir in his testament, I enter upon and cern to
his inheritance.' If he have not cerned in this way, he is
debarred when the cretionary term is ended; nor does it
avail him anything that he is behaving as heir, that is, dealing with the items of the inheritance as if he were heir.

167 But he who is instituted heir without cretion, or called to the

---

§ 164. Comp. Vlp. xxii, 27; Varro *de*
    L. L. vii, 98 (Bruns, p. 281). The
    cretio here described was no longer
    used in the Justinianian law.
§ 165. Comp. §§ 171, 177; Vlp. xxii,
    27. The cretion was perfect or im-
    perfect according as it was or was
    not under pain of disherison; Vlp.
    xxii, 34.

§ 166. Comp. Vlp. xxii, §§ 25, 26, 28;
    § 7, tit. I. afd. It would appear
    that the cerniture was declared in
    the presence of witnesses convoked
    for the purpose. Comp. Cic. *ad*
    Att. xiii, 46, § 2, and Varro *de*
    L. L. vi, 81 (Bruns, p. 278).
§ 167. Comp. iii, 87; Vlp. xxii, 25; §
    7, tit. I. afd.

qui ab intestato legitimo iure ad hereditatem uocatur, potest
aut cernendo aut pro herede gerendo uel etiam nuda uoluntate suscipiendae hereditatis heres fieri : eique liberum est
quocumque tempore uoluerit adire hereditatem ; sed solet
praetor postulantibus hereditariis creditoribus tempus constituere intra quod si uelit adeat hereditatem, si minus, ut
168 liceat creditoribus bona defuncti uendere.   *Sicut* autem
[*qui*] cum cretione heres institutus est nisi creuerit hereditatem non fit heres, ita non aliter excluditur quam si non
creuerit intra id tempus quo cretio finita sit ; itaque licet ante
diem cretionis constituerit hereditatem non adire, tamen
paenitentia actus superante die cretionis cernendo heres esse
169 potest.   At is qui sine cretione heres institutus est, quiue
ab intestato per legem uocatur, sicut uoluntate nuda heres fit,
ita et contraria destinatione statim ab hereditate repellitur.
170 Omnis autem cretio certo tempore constringitur. in quam
rem tolerabile tempus uisum est centum dierum : potest
tamen nihilo minus iure ciuili aut longius aut breuius tempus

---

inheritance *ab intestato* by devolution of law, may become
heir either by cerning or by behaving as heir, or even by an
informal expression of his intention to take up the inheritance, and it is free to him to enter to it at any time he
chooses ; but it is the practice for the praetor, on the petition of the creditors of the deceased, to fix a time within
which the heir must enter, if such be his pleasure, or the
creditors be entitled, if he do not, to sell the deceased's estate.
168 But just as an heir instituted with cretion does not become
heir unless he has cerned, so he is not otherwise excluded
than by failure to cern before the cretionary term has expired ;
therefore though, before the last day of cretion, he may have
resolved not to enter upon the inheritance, yet, repenting of
his resolution, he may still become heir by cerniture while
169 any part of the term remains.   He, on the other hand, who
is instituted heir without cretion, or who is called by law on
intestacy, as he becomes heir by any informal declaration of
will, is likewise at once excluded from the inheritance by any
170 declaration to the contrary.   Every cretion is limited to a
certain time. A hundred days have been considered a reasonable allowance, although by the civil law either a longer or a

§ 168. Comp. Vlp. xxii, 30.   § 170. Comp. Cic. *ad Att.* xiii, 46, § 2 ;
§ 169. Comp. Vlp. xxii, 29 ; § 7, tit.   *Testamentum Dasumii, p.* C. 109,
    I. afd.   (Bruns, p. 202).

171 dari ; longius tamen interdum praetor coartat.   Et quamuis
omnis cretio certis diebus constringatur, tamen alia cretio
uulgaris uocatur, alia certorum dierum : uulgaris illa quam
supra exposuimus, id est in qua adiciuntur haec uerba : QVIBVS
SCIET POTERITQVE : certorum dierum, in qua detractis his uerbis
172 cetera scribuntur.   Quarum cretionum magna differentia est:
nam uulgari cretione data nulli dies conputantur nisi quibus
scierit quisque se heredem esse institutum et possit cernere ;
certorum uero dierum cretione data, etiam nescienti se heredem institutum esse numerantur dies continui ; item ei quoque
qui aliqua ex causa cernere prohibetur, et eo amplius ei qui
sub condicione heres institutus est, tempus numeratur ; unde
173 melius et aptius est uulgari cretione uti.   [Continua haec
cretio uocatur quia continui dies numerantur ; sed quia *tam*[1]
dura est haec cretio altera *magis in usu*[2] habetur ; unde etiam
uulgaris dicta est.]

----

shorter period may be granted ; but a longer one is some-
171 times abridged by the praetor.   And although every cretion
is under a certain limitation of time, yet one variety is called
ordinary cretion, and another determinate ; the first is that
we have been describing, and in which there are contained
in the cretion-clause the words, ' in which he knows and can ; '
the second occurs when we have the cretion-clause without
172 those words.   There is a great difference between the two ;
for where ordinary cretion is enjoined, no days are counted
but those during which the party knows that he has been
instituted heir, and is in a position to cern ; whereas where
the cretion is determinate, the days are reckoned continuously,
even against a party who is not aware that he has been instituted heir, against him who from any cause is prevented
cerning, and against him who is instituted only conditionally.
It is better and fitter therefore to employ the ordinary cre-
173 tion.   The determinate cretion is [also] called continuous,
because the days are reckoned continuously ; but, as it is so
strict, the other is more frequently employed, and therefore
called ordinary.

§§ 171, 172. Comp. Cic. *ad Att.* xi, 12,
§ 41 ; *de orat.* i, 22, § 101 ; Vlp.
xxii, §§ 31, 32.

§ 173. This par. looks like a gloss ;
it is little more than an amplifi-
cation, somewhat clumsy, of the
final words of the preceding one.

[1] The MS. has *tm*, which usually
stands for *tamen* ; K. u. S. so print
it, while P. has *tam*, and Hu. omits
the word altogether.

[2] The MS. has *minus* ; intended
possibly, as G. suggests, for *mgin-
usu*.

174   Interdum duos pluresue gradus heredum facimus, hoc modo :
LVCIVS TITIVS HERES ESTO, CERNITOQVE IN DIEBVS [CENTVM]
PROXIMIS QVIBVS SCIES POTERISQVE.   QVODNI ITA CREVERIS,
EXHERES ESTO.   TVM MEVIVS HERES ESTO, CERNITOQUE IN
DIEBVS CENTUM et reliqua ; et deinceps in quantum uelimus
175 substituere possumus.   Et licet nobis uel unum in unius
locum substituere pluresue, et contra in plurium locum uel
176 unum uel plures substituere.   Primo itaque gradu scriptus
heres hereditatem cernendo fit heres et substitutus excluditur ;
non cernendo summouetur, etiamsi pro herede gerat, et in
locum eius substitutus succedit ; et deinceps si plures gradus
177 sint in singulis simili ratione idem contingit.   Sed si cretio
sine exheredatione sit data, id est in haec uerba : SI NON
CREVERIS TVM PVBLIVS MEVIVS HERES ESTO, illud diuersum
inuenitur, quod si prior omissa cretione pro herede gerat, substitutum in partem admittit, et fiunt ambo aequis partibus
heredes ; quodsi neque cernat neque pro herede gerat, tum sane

---

174   Sometimes we make two or more degrees of heirs, thus :
' Lucius Titius be my heir, and cern within the next hundred
days in which you know and can ; if you have not cerned,
be disinherited : in that case Mevius be my heir, and cern
within a hundred days,' and so on ; and we may substitute
175 successively to any extent we like.   And we may substitute either one person or several in the place of one ; or, on
the other hand, either one or several in the place of several.
176 The party, therefore, who is named heir in the first degree,
becomes heir by cerniture, and the substitute is excluded ; by
not cerning, the former is displaced, even though he behave as
heir, and the substitute succeeds in his stead ; and if there be
several degrees the same rules apply to each of them in suc-
177 cession.   But if cretion be enjoined without disherison,
that is to say in such words as ' if you do not cern, then
Publius Mevius be heir,' the rule is different ; because if
the institute-heir has neglected to cern, yet has behaved as
heir, the substitute is admitted *pro parte*, and both become
heirs for a moiety.   If, however, the institute neither cern nor

§§ 174-178. Comp. tit. I. *DE VVLGARI*
SVBSTITVTIONE (ii, 15). In the ms.
those pars. are introduced with the
rubric *de substitutionibus*, apparently by the original hand.
§ 174.   Comp. Vlp. xxii, 33 ; pr. tit. I. afd.
§ 175.   Comp. § 1, tit. I. afd.

§ 176. Comp. § 166.
§§ 177, 178. Comp. Vlp. xxii, 34, from
which it appears that the rule was
modified by Marc. Aurelius, and
gestio pro herede by the institute
held sufficient to altogether exclude
the substitute.

in uniuerso summouetur et substitutus in totam hereditatem
178 succedit.   Sed Sabino quidem placuit, quamdiu cernere et
eo modo heres fieri possit prior, etiamsi pro herede gesserit,
non tamen admitti substitutum ; cum uero cretio finita sit,
tum pro herede gerente *admitti substitutum :* [1] *aliis* [2] uero
placuit etiam superante cretione eum [3] pro herede gerendo
in partem substitutum admittere et amplius ad cretionem
reuerti non posse.

179   Liberis nostris inpuberibus quos in potestate habemus non
solum ita ut supra diximus substituere possumus, id est ut si
heredes non extiterint alius nobis heres sit; sed eo amplius
ut etiamsi heredes nobis extiterint et adhuc inpuberes mortui
fuerint, *sit iis* aliquis heres, uelut hoc modo : TITIVS FILIVS
MEVS MIHI HERES ESTO.   SI FILIVS MEVS MIHI (*HERES NON ERIT*,
(*SIVE HERES*) ERIT ET *PRIVS* MORIATVR QVAM IN SVAM TVTE-

---

behave as heir, then undoubtedly he is altogether displaced,
178 and the substitute succeeds to the whole inheritance.   It
was the opinion of Sabinus that, so long as the institute had
it in his power to cern and thus become heir, there was no
room for the substitute, even though he, the institute, might
have been behaving as heir; and that it was only after the
period of cretion had expired that, notwithstanding the institute's *gestio pro herede,* the substitute was admitted.   But it
was held by the lawyers of the other school that if the institute, while his time for cretion was still running, chose to act
as heir, he thereby let in the substitute for a share, and could
not afterwards fall back on his cretion.

179   To our impuberate descendants *in potestate* we may not only
make a substitution in the manner already described, that is
to say by providing that, if they do not become heirs, another
person shall be our heir instead of them,—but we may also
appoint some one to be their heir in the event of their having
become our heirs, but died in pupillarity; as, for example,
thus : ' Be my son Titius my heir; if he do not become my
heir, or if, having done so, he die before passing into his own

---

[1] This appears to be the reading
of the MS., and is approved by P.
and K. u. S.; Hu. renders it—*tum
pro herede gerentem admittere substitutum.*
    [2] See i, 196, note 1.
    [3] Before this word the MS. has
posse, deleted as suggested by K.
(K. u. S. footnote).
§§ 179-184. Comp. tit. I. *DE PVPIL-
LARI SVBSTITVTIONE* (ii, 16).
§ 179. Pr. tit. I. afd., from which the
words in ital. are borrowed. Comp.
Vlp. xxiii, 7.

180 LAM VENERIT, *TVNC* SEIVS HERES ESTO.   quo casu si quidem
non extiterit heres filius, substitutus patri fit heres; (*si*
(*uero*)[1] heres extiterit filius et ante pubertatem decesserit,
ipsi filio fit heres substitutus. quam ob rem duo quodammodo sunt testamenta, aliud patris aliud filii, tamquam
si ipse filius sibi heredem instituisset; aut certe unum
181 est testamentum duarum hereditatum.   Ceterum ne post
obitum parentis periculo insidiarum subiectus uideatur
pupillus, in usu est uulgarem quidem substitutionem palam
facere, id est eo loco quo pupillum heredem instituimus.
uulgaris substitutio ita uocat ad hereditatem substitutum si
omnino pupillus heres non extiterit; quod accidit cum uiuo
parente moritur, quo casu nullum substituti maleficium sus-
picari possumus, cum scilicet uiuo testatore omnia quae in
testamento scripta sint ignorentur : illam autem substitutionem per quam, *etiamsi* heres extiterit pupillus et intra
pubertatem decesserit, substitutum uocamus, separatim in
inferioribus tabulis scribimus, easque tabulas proprio lino pro-
priaque cera consignamus, et in prioribus tabulis cauemus ne

---

180 tutelage, then be Seius my heir.'   In this case, if the son
has not become his father's heir, the substitute takes that position ; if, however, the son have become heir, but died in pupillarity, the substitute becomes the son's heir, [not the father's.]
There are thus in a manner two testaments,—one the father's,
the other the son's, just as if the latter had instituted an heir
for himself; or at any rate there is one testament disposing
181 of two inheritances.   But lest the pupil after his parent's
death should be exposed to the risk of foul play, it is usual to
make the ordinary substitution openly, *i.e.* in that part of the
testament which contains the institution of the pupil as heir.
By the ordinary substitution the substitute is called to the
inheritance only in the event of the pupil not having become
heir at all; this happens when he predeceases his parent;
and until then we cannot suspect any misconduct on the part
of the substitute, seeing that so long as the testator lives the
contents of his testament are unknown.   But the substitution
whereby we appoint a substitute in the event of the pupil
having become heir but died before reaching puberty we insert
by itself in the later tablets, which we tie up and seal with

§ 180. Pr. § 2, tit. I. afd.   the MS.
   [1] From the Inst., but hardly suf-   § 181. Comp. Epit. ii, 4, § 2; § 3, tit.
ficient to fill the illegible space in   I. afd.; Th. ii, 16, 3.

inferiores tabulae uiuo filio et adhuc inpubere aperiantur.   sed
longe tutius est utrumque genus substitutionis [separatim][1] in
inferioribus tabulis consignari ; quod, si ita [consignatae uel][1]
separatae fuerint substitutiones ut diximus, ex priore potest
182 intelligi in altera quoque[2] idem esse substitutus.   Non
solum autem heredibus institutis inpuberibus liberis ita substituere possumus, ut si ante pubertatem mortui fuerint sit is
heres quem nos uoluerimus, sed etiam exheredatis : itaque eo
casu si quid pupillo ex hereditatibus legatisue aut donationi-
bus propinquorum adquisitum fuerit, id omne ad substitutum
183 pertinet.   Quaecumque diximus de substitutione inpuberum liberorum, uel heredum institutorum uel exheredato-
184 rum, eadem etiam de postumis[1] intellegemus.   Extraneo
uero heredi[1] instituto ita substituere non possumus ut si heres
extiterit et intra aliquod tempus decesserit alius ei heres sit ;
sed hoc solum nobis permissum est, ut eum per fideicommis-

---

cord and seals of their own ; and in the earlier ones we give
instructions that the others are not to be opened so long as
our son is alive and still a pupil. It is much safer, however,
to seal up both the substitutions in the final tablets ; because,
if they have been sealed up or separated in the manner above
described, it may readily be conjectured from the one that the
182 same person is also substituted in the other.   It is not only
to those of our children under puberty whom we have instituted heirs that we can make a substitution to the effect that,
if they die in pupillarity, the person whom we have chosen
shall be their heir,—we may do so also for children we have
disinherited ; and in such a case if the pupil have acquired
anything in the shape of inheritances, bequests, or donations
183 from kinsmen, it will all belong to the substitute.   All that
has been said about substitution for impuberate children,
whether instituted or disinherited, applies equally to those
184 that may be after-born.   But we cannot substitute to a
stranger-institute on the footing that, if he become heir but
die within a certain period, another person shall be his heir ;
all that we can do is, by creation of a trust, to lay him under

---

[1] According to M. and K. u. S.,
the words *separatim* and *consignatae
uel* are glosses, and the first obviously inaccurate.

[2] Between *altera* and *quoque* the
MS. has *alter*, obviously *per incuriam*.

§ 182. § 4, tit. I. afd. Comp. Vlp.
xxiii, 8.

§ 183. § 4, tit. I. afd.
[1] See §§ 180 f.

§ 184. § 9, tit. I. afd.
[1] Before *heredi*, P., following the
Inst., interjects *uel puberi filio*.

sum obligemus ut hereditatem nostram uel totam uel [*pro*] parte restituat; quod ius quale sit suo loco[2] trademus.

185   Sicut autem liberi homines, ita et serui, tam nostri quam
186 alieni, heredes scribi possunt.   Sed noster seruus simul et liber et heres esse iuberi debet, id est hoc modo: STICHVS SERVVS MEVS LIBER HERESQVE ESTO, uel HERES LIBERQVE ESTO :
187 nam si sine libertate heres institutus sit, etiamsi postea manumissus fuerit a domino, heres esse non potest, quia institutio in persona eius non constitit; ideoque licet alienatus sit non
188 potest iussu domini noui cernere hereditatem.   Cum libertate uero heres institutus, si quidem in *eadem* causa durauerit, fit ex testamento liber *et inde* necessarius heres : si uero ab ipso testatore manumissus fuerit, suo arbitrio hereditatem adire potest; quodsi alienatus sit, iussu noui domini adire hereditatem debet, qua ratione per eum dominus fit heres : nam *ipse neque* heres neque liber esse potest.[1]

---

obligation to convey the inheritance wholly or partially to another: how this is done we shall explain in its proper place.

185   Slaves, whether our own or belonging to another person,
186 may be instituted heirs quite as well as freemen.   But a slave of our own must be manumitted and appointed heir simultaneously, thus : 'Let Stichus my slave be free and heir,'
187 or 'my heir and free.'   For, if he have been instituted heir without grant of freedom, he cannot be heir, even though he may in the meanwhile have been manumitted by his owner, the institution having been invalid from the point of view of his *persona* at the time; and, for the same reason, if he have been alienated in the meanwhile he cannot cern on the in-
188 structions of his new owner.   A slave instituted with gift of liberty, if he have till the last remained in the ownership of the testator, becomes free under the testament and hence a necessary heir; if, however, he have been manumitted by the testator, it is in his own discretion to enter upon the inheritance; if he have been alienated, he can enter only on the order of his new owner, who thus becomes heir through the slave,—for the latter can now neither be heir nor

---

[2] §§ 246 f., 277.
§§ 185-190. Comp. tit. I. *DE HEREDI-
BVS INSTITVENDIS* (ii, 14).
§§ 185, 186. Comp. Vlp. xxii, 7; Paul.
iii, 4*b*, § 7; pr. tit. I. afd.
§ 187. Comp. Vlp. xxii, § 11.

§ 188. Comp. §§ 87, 153; Vlp. xxii,
§§ 11, 12; § 1, tit. I. afd.
[1] P., borrowing from the Inst.,
adds—*etsi cum libertate heres institutus fuerit ; destitisse enim a libertatis datione uidetur dominus.*

189 Alienus quoque seruus heres institutus, si in eadem causa
durauerit, *iussu* domini hereditatem adire debet; si uero
alienatus ab eo fuerit, *aut uiuo* testatore aut post mortem
eius, antequam cernat, debet iussu noui domini *cernere*: si
uero manumissus est suo arbitrio adire hereditatem potest.

190 Si autem seruus alienus heres institutus est uulgari cretione
data, ita intellegitur dies cretionis cedere si ipse seruus
scierit se heredem institutum esse, nec ullum inpedimentum
sit quominus certiorem dominum faceret ut illius iussu
cernere possit.

191   Post haec uideamus de legatis.   quae pars iuris extra propositam quidem materiam uidetur: nam loquimur de his iuris
figuris quibus per uniuersitatem res nobis adquiruntur: sed
cum omni modo de testamentis deque heredibus qui testamento instituuntur locuti sumus, non sine causa sequenti
loco poterit haec iuris materia tractari.

---

189 free.   If another man's slave instituted as heir continue
in the same ownership, he enters upon the inheritance
or not as his owner may direct; if he have been alienated,
either during the testator's lifetime or after his death, but
before cretion, he must cern on the order of his new owner;
but if he have been manumitted, he may use his own discre-
190 tion as to entering upon the inheritance.   If he have been
instituted under ordinary cretion, the cretionary period is held
to begin to run only when the slave himself has become
aware of his institution, and there is nothing to prevent him
informing his owner of the fact, and so being in a position
to cern on his command.

191   After all this let us turn our attention to legacies. It is a
branch of the law not exactly within our present subject-
matter; for we are dealing with the modes known to the law
of acquiring things on a universal title.   But as we have
discussed from every point of view the law of testaments and
testamentary heirs, this matter of legacies may, not without
reason, be treated of in the next place.

---

§ 189. Comp. § 87; Vlp. xxii, 13; § 1,
    tit. I. afd.
§ 190. Comp. § 172.
§§ 191-228. Comp. tit. I. DE LEGATIS
    (ii, 20). The rubric *de legatis* is in-

troduced in the MS., in a later hand,
on a vacant line between §§ 191 and
192.
§ 191. Pr. tit. I. afd. Comp. above,
    § 97.

192   Legatorum itaque genera sunt quattuor: aut enim per
uindicationem legamus, aut per damnationem, aut sinendi
modo, aut per praeceptionem.
193   Per uindicationem hoc modo legamus: TITIO uerbi gratia.
HOMINEM STICHVM DO LEGO; sed [*et*] si *alterutrum*[1] uerbum
positum sit, ueluti DO aut LEGO, aeque per uindicationem
legatum est: *item, ut magis uisum est, si* ita legatum fuerit:
SVMITO, uel *ita : SIBI HABETO, uel* ita: CAPITO, aeque per
194 uindicationem *legatum est.*   *Ideo autem* per uindicationem
legatum appellatur quia post *aditam* hereditatem statim ex
iure Quiritium res legatarii fit; et si eam rem legatarius uel
ab herede uel ab alio quocumque qui eam possidet petat,
uindicare[1] debet, id est intendere *suam rem* ex iure Quiritium
195 esse.   In eo solo dissentiunt prudentes, *quod Sabinus* quidem
et Cassius ceterique nostri praeceptores[1] quod ita legatum sit
statim post aditam hereditatem putant fieri legatarii, etiamsi

192   There are then four kinds of legacies; for we legate either
by vindication, by damnation, by permission, or by preception.
193   By vindication we legate thus: 'To Titius I give and legate,'
for example, 'the slave Stichus.' If one or other only of
the words be used, as 'I give,' or 'I legate,' the bequest is
equally one by vindication. And so it is, according to the
prevailing opinion, if the words employed be—'Titius is to
194 take,' (*sumito* or *capito*,) or 'is to have for himself.'   A
legacy by vindication is so called because the thing bequeathed
becomes the property of the legatee in quiritarian right the
moment the inheritance has been entered upon; and, if the
legatee have on account of it to sue either the heir or any
third party in possession, he must do so by vindication, *i.e.*
he must plead that the thing is his in quiritarian right.
195 On this point alone the jurists disagree,—that Sabinus, Cassius,
and the rest of our school, are of opinion that the thing legated
at once becomes the property of the legatee when the inheritance
has been entered on, even though he be ignorant of the bequest,
but that if he have [*declined it*] after hearing of it, it is as if it
had not been bequeathed; whereas Nerva and Proculus, and
the other leaders of their school, hold that the bequest does
not become the property of the legatee unless such be his

§ 192. Comp. Vlp. xxiv, 2; § 2, tit. I. afd.   § 194.   Comp. Th. ii, 20, § 2.
§ 193. Comp. Vlp. xxiv, 3.   [1]Comp. iv, 41.
     [1]The ms. apparently has *alterum*;   § 195.   Comp. Paul. iii, 6, § 7.
so has Hu.; G., Bk., F., and K. u. S.,   [1]See i, 196, note 1.
alterutrum.

ignoret sibi legatum esse [dimissum],[2] *sed*[3] posteaquam scierit
et — —[4] legatum, perinde esse atque si legatum non esset;
Nerua uero et Proculus ceterique illius scholae auctores[1] non
aliter putant rem legatarii fieri quam si uoluerit eam ad se
pertinere. sed hodie ex diui Pii Antonini constitutione hoc
magis iure uti uidemur quod Proculo placuit; nam cum
legatus fuisset latinus[5] per uindicationem coloniae, ' Deliberent,'
inquit, 'decuriones, an ad se uelint pertinere, proinde ac si
196 uni legatus esset.'   Eae autem solae res per uindicationem
legantur recte quae ex iure Quiritium ipsius testatoris sunt;
sed eas quidem res quae pondere numero mensura constant,
placuit sufficere si mortis tempore sint ex iure Quiritium
testatoris, ueluti uinum oleum frumentum pecuniam nume-
ratam; ceteras res uero placuit utroque tempore testatoris ex
iure Quiritium esse debere, id est et quo faceret testamentum

---

pleasure.   At the present day, as appears from a constitution
of our late emperor Antoninus Pius, we seem rather to follow
the rule laid down by Proculus; for, when a latin had been
legated by vindication to a colony, he wrote: 'The decurions
must deliberate whether they wish to have him, just as if he
196 had been legated to an individual.'   Those things alone can
competently be legated by vindication which belong to the
testator himself in quiritarian right. As regards those that
pass by weight, number, or measure, such as wine, oil, corn,
and current coin, it is held to be sufficient that they belonged
to the testator in quiritarian right at the time of his death;
but as regards other things it is held that they must have
been his in quiritarian right at both times, *i.e.* both when he
made his testament and at the time he died, otherwise the

---

[2] Hu. and K. u. S. regard this
word as a gloss, the former on the
ground that although *dimittere legatum* occurs in the West Gothic
Gaius, in the sense of *leg. relinquere*, it is not to be found in any
of the Roman texts. M. (K. u. S.
p. xxi) makes it *demissum*. P.
retains it, but in a different acceptation. As *admittere legatum* (§ 200)
means to accept a legacy, so, according to him, does *dimittere*
mean to reject it. He accordingly
severs *dimissum* from the preceding words, and, filling up the lacuna
with *etiam spretum*, reads—*dimissum, et posteaquam scierit etiam
spretum legatum perinde esse*, etc.,

i.e. a legacy that the legatee has
expressly repudiated (or put away
from him), or even one that, knowing of its bequest, he has simply
disregarded, etc.
[3] The ms. has *et*.
[4] The letters in the ms. look like
ceerit, but are very indistinct. G.
(on suggestion of Niebuhr), Bk., and
now Hu., think *spreuerit* a likely
reading; it finds its justification in
iii, 62, and § 8, tit. I. afd. P., as
mentioned in last note, proposes
etiam spretum; M. suggests *omiserit; K. u. S., repudiauerit.
[5] Comp. § 155, note 2; iii, §§
56-58.
§ 196. Comp. Vlp. xxiv, 7.

197 et quo moreretur, alioquin inutile est legatum.   Sed sane
    hoc ita est iure ciuili : postea uero auctore Nerone Caesare
    senatusconsultum factum est, quo cautum est ut si eam rem
    quisque legauerit quae eius numquam fuerit, proinde utile sit
    legatum atque si optimo iure relictum esset : optimum autem
    ius est per damnationem legati; quo genere etiam aliena res
198 legari potest, sicut inferius[1] apparebit.   Sed si quis rem
    suam legauerit, deinde post testamentum factum eam aliena-
    uerit, plerique putant non solum iure ciuili inutile esse lega-
    tum sed nec ex senatusconsulto confirmari.   quod ideo dictum
    est, quia et si per damnationem aliquis rem suam legauerit
    eamque postea alienauerit, plerique putant, licet ipso iure de-
    beatur legatum, tamen legatarium petentem posse per excep-
    tionem doli mali[1] repelli, quasi contra uoluntatem defuncti
199 petat.   Illud constat, si duobus pluribusue per uindicationem
    eadem res legata sit, siue coniunctim siue disiunctim,[1] partes
    ad singulos pertinere et deficientis portionem collegatario ad-

---

197 legacy will be useless.   Such at least was the rule of the civil
    law.   But afterwards, on the suggestion of the emperor Nero,
    a senatusconsult was enacted, wherein it was provided that if
    a man legated a thing that had never been his, the legacy
    should be as valid as if it had been bequeathed in the most
    favourable form : and the most favourable form of legacy is
    by damnation; for in that way, as will appear presently, one
198 may bequeath even what belongs to a third party.   If a
    man have legated something of his own, but have alienated it
    after making his testament, most jurists hold that the legacy
    is not only invalid by the civil law, but is not even validated
    by the senatusconsult. The ground of this opinion is that
    when a man has bequeathed something of his own by damna-
    tion and afterwards alienated it, while, according to most
    authorities, the legacy is due *ipso iure*, nevertheless, the
    legatee, if he sue for it, may be defeated by an exception of
    fraud, as making a claim inconsistent with the real intent of
199 the deceased.   It is a well-established rule that if the same
    thing be legated by vindication to two or more persons,
    whether conjointly or disjointly, they take each a share, while

§ 197.   Comp. Vlp. xxiv, 11a.
    [1] See § 202.
§ 198.   Comp. § 12, tit. I. afd.
    [1] See § 76, note 3.
§ 199.   Comp. § 206; Vlp. xxiv, 12;
    Paul. iii, 6, § 26; § 8, tit. I. afd.

[1] After *disiunctim* the MS. has *et
omnes ueniant ad legatum;* but this
is so inconsistent with the immediately following *deficientis portio*
that the words must be rejected as
a gloss.

crescere.   coniunctim autem ita legatur : TITIO ET SEIO HOMI-
NEM STICHVM DO LEGO ; disiunctim ita : LVCIO TITIO HOMINEM
200 STICHVM DO LEGO.   SEIO EVNDEM HOMINEM DO LEGO.   Illud
quaeritur, quod sub condicione per uindicationem legatum est,
pendente condicione cuius esset : nostri praeceptores[1] heredis
esse putant exemplo statuliberi,[2] id est eius serui qui testamento sub aliqua condicione liber esse iussus est, quem constat
interea heredis seruum esse ; sed diuersae scholae auctores[1]
putant nullius interim eam rem esse ; quod multo magis
dicunt[3] de eo quod [sine condicione][4] pure legatum est, antequam legatarius admittat legatum.

201   Per damnationem hoc modo legamus : HERES MEVS STICHVM
SERVVM MEVM DARE DAMNAS[1] ESTO ; sed et si DATO scriptum

the share of any one who fails accresces to his co-legatee.   A
thing is legated conjointly thus : ' To Titius and Seius I give
and legate the slave Stichus ; ' and disjointly thus : ' To Lucius
Titius I give and legate the slave Stichus : I give and legate
200 the same slave to Seius.'   When a thing is conditionally
legated by vindication, it is a question whose it is while the
condition is unfulfilled.   Our authorities hold it belongs to
the heir, on the analogy of a *statuliber, i.e.* a slave who has by
testament a conditional grant of freedom, and who, as is
admitted, belongs in the meanwhile to the heir.   But the
authorities of the other school think that in the meantime the
thing belongs to no one ; and *a fortiori* they maintain the same
doctrine in reference to an unconditional legacy not yet
accepted by the legatee.

201   By damnation we legate in this way : ' Be my heir bound
to give my slave Stichus ; ' but though the words be simply—
' Let my heir give,' the legacy is still one by damnation.

§ 200. Comp. Gai. in fr. 29, § 1, D.
qui et a quib. man. (xl, 9) ; Vlp. in
fr. 12, § 2, D. *fam. ercisc.* (x, 2).
  [1] See i, 196, note 1.
  [2] Comp. Vlp. ii, §§ 1, 2.
  [3] Comp. § 195.
  [4] As the text stands, either *sine
condicione* or *pure* must be regarded
as a gloss. Van der Hoeven (*Z. f.
RG.* vii, p. 258) suggests *sine condicione per uindicationem ;* his theory
being that the two last words were
represented by the contraction *pu*,
which the transcriber has trans-
formed into *pure*.
§ 201. Comp. Vlp. xxiv, 4 ; Th. ii, 20,
  § 2.

[1] *Damnas* is a word for which it
is not easy to give a precise English
equivalent   It is thus explained by
Serv. (*in Aen.* xii, 727)—*In iure cum
dicitur,* ' *Damnas esto,*' *hoc est damnatus es ut des, hoc est damno te ut
des neque alias libereris.* The phrase
damnas esto was employed where a
penalty or liability was imposed by
a law, whether a public statute, such
as the *lex Mamilia, lex Iulia Municipalis, lex Aquilia,* etc., or a law
established by a private individual
by a public act (§ 104, note 8) as in
the *uerba nuncupata* of a *nexum*
or a testament, or in the dedication
of a monument whose safety the

202 fuerit, per damnationem legatum est.   Eoque genere legati
etiam aliena res legari potest, ita ut heres [*rem*] redimere et
203 praestare aut aestimationem eius dare debeat.   Ea quoque
res quae in rerum natura non est, si modo futura est, per
damnationem legari potest, uelut 'fructus qui in illo fundo
204 nati erunt,' aut 'quod ex illa ancilla natum erit.'   Quod
autem ita legatum est, post aditam hereditatem, etiamsi pure
legatum est, non, ut per uindicationem legatum,[1] continuo
legatario adquiritur, sed nihilo minus heredis est; et ideo
legatarius in personam agere debet, id est intendere heredem
sibi dare oportere,[2] et tum heres [*rem*], si mancipi sit, mancipio dare[3] aut in iure cedere[4] possessionemque tradere debet;
si nec mancipi sit, sufficit si tradiderit:[5] nam si mancipi rem
tantum tradiderit nec mancipauerit, usucapione pleno iure fit
legatarii:[6] conpletur autem usucapio, sicut alio *quoque loco*

---

202 By this form of legacy even what belongs to another may be
bequeathed; and then the heir is bound either to purchase
203 and convey it or else to pay its value.   What has no natural
existence can also be legated by damnation, provided it may
be expected to come into existence later; as, for instance, the
crop to be produced from particular lands, or the child to be
204 born of a particular woman-slave.   A thing thus legated,
even unconditionally or without limitation of time, does not
straightway become the property of the legatee when the
inheritance is entered upon, like a legacy by vindication, but
none the less still belongs to the heir.   Therefore the legatee
must sue for it by a personal action, *i.e.* must plead that the
heir is bound to give him it; the heir, if the thing be *res
mancipi*, must then mancipate it or cede it in court, and give
up the possession; but if it be *nec mancipi*, it is enough that
he deliver it.   If, being a *res mancipi*, he has merely delivered
it without mancipation, it becomes the legatee's in plenary
right by usucapion; and, as explained elsewhere, that usu-

founder was protecting by a penalty.
A party contravening the prohibition, or failing to perform the duty
thus imposed, was said to be *damnas*
or *damnatus* (iii, 175); and there is
reason to believe that, in early times,
when proceedings against him became necessary, and the liability
was for a definite sum of money,
they were taken not by action but
by *manus iniectio* (iv, 21).
  The meaning of the phrase *damnas*
10

esto is very fully discussed by
Brini, *Archivio Giuridico*, xxi, pp.
225 f.
§ 202. Comp. § 197; Vlp. xxiv, 8; § 4,
   tit. I. afd.
§ 203.   § 7, tit. I. afd.
§ 204. [1]Comp. § 194.
      [2]Comp. § 213; iv, 41.
      [3]Comp. i, 119.
      [4]Comp. § 24.
      [5]Comp. § 19.
      [6]Comp. § 41.

diximus, mobilium quidem rerum anno, earum uero quae solo
205 tenentur biennio.⁷   Est et illa differentia *huius et* per uindicationem legati, quod si eadem res duobus pluribusue per
damnationem legata sit, siquidem coniunctim, plane singulis
partes debentur, *sicut in illo [quod per]* uindicationem legatum *est*,¹ *si uero* disiunctim, singulis solida res debetur; *ita fit*
ut scilicet heres alteri rem alteri aestimationem eius praestare
debeat; et in coniunctis deficientis portio non ad collegata-
rium pertinet sed in hereditate remanet.

206   Quod autem diximus deficientis portionem *in* per damnationem quidem legato in hereditate retineri, in per uindicationem uero collegatario adcrescere, admonendi sumus ante
legem Papiam¹ iure ciuili ita fuisse; post legem uero Papiam
deficientis portio caduca² fit, et ad eos pertinet qui in eo testa-
207 mento liberos habent.   et quamuis prima causa sit in
caducis uindicandis² heredum liberos habentium, deinde, si
heredes liberos non habeant, legatariorum liberos habentium,

capion is completed in the case of moveables in one year, and
205 in that of things connected with the soil in two.   There is
this further difference between a legacy of this sort and one
by vindication,—that if the same thing be legated by damnation to two or more persons, and that conjointly, a share of it
is due to each of them, as in a legacy bequeathed by vindication; but if it be legated to them disjointly, the whole legacy
is due to each, so that the heir must give the thing itself to
one, and its value to the other.   In a conjoint legacy of this
sort the share of one who fails to take does not fall to his
co-legatee, but remains in the inheritance.
206   But in saying that the share of a legatee failing to take
remains in the inheritance in the case of a legacy by damnation, but goes by accretion to his co-legatee in that of one by
vindication, we must bear in mind that so it was by the civil
law before the Papian enactment; since the Papian law the
lapsed share becomes caducous, and falls to those persons
named in the testament who happen to have children.
207 Although the right to claim caduciary bequests belongs in the
first place to the heirs who have children, and next, if there
be none such, to the legatees who have children, yet it is

⁷Comp. § 42.
§ 205. Comp. § 199; Vlp. xxiv, 13.
¹Passage indistinct in the MS.;
the rendering adopted is that of
K. u. S.

§§ 206-208. Comp. §§ 150, note, and
199, 205; Vlp. i, 21; xxiv, §§ 12, 13.
¹Comp. § 150, note; i, 145,
note 1.
²Comp. §§ 286, 286a.

tamen ipsa lege Papia significatur ut collegatarius coniunctus,
si liberos habeat, potior sit heredibus, etiamsi liberos habebunt.

208 sed plerisque placuit, quantum ad hoc ius quod lege Papia coniunctis constituitur, nihil interesse utrum per uindicationem
an per damnationem legatum sit.

209   Sinendi modo ita legamus: HERES MEVS DAMNAS[1] ESTO
SINERE LVCIVM TITIVM HOMINEM STICHVM SVMERE SIBIQVE

210 HABERE.   Quod genus legati plus quidem habet [*quam*] per
uindicationem legatum, minus autem quam per damnationem :
nam eo modo non solum suam rem testator utiliter legare
potest sed etiam heredis sui, cum alioquin per uindicationem
nisi suam rem legare non potest, per damnationem autem

211 cuiuslibet extranei rem legare potest.   Sed si quidem mortis
testatoris tempore res uel ipsius testatoris sit uel heredis,
plane utile legatum est, etiamsi testamenti faciendi tempore

212 neutrius fuerit.   quodsi post mortem testatoris ea res heredis esse coeperit, quaeritur an utile sit legatum : et plerique
putant inutile esse. quid ergo est ? licet aliquis eam rem

-----

expressly provided by the Papian law that a conjoint co-legatee
who has children shall be preferred even to the heirs that

208 have children.   And it is generally held, as regards the right
thus conferred by the Papian law upon conjoint legatees, that
it is immaterial whether the legacy be by vindication or by
damnation.

209   By permission, *sinendi modo*, we legate thus : ' Be my heir
bound to allow Lucius Titius to take and have for himself the

210 slave Stichus.'   There is more in a legacy of this sort than
in one by vindication, but less than in one by damnation.
For in this form a testator may effectually legate not only
what is his own but also what is his heir's ; whereas by vindication a man can legate only what belongs to himself, while
by damnation he may legate the property of any third party.

211 If, at the time of the testator's death, the thing legated belong
either to him or his heir, then clearly the legacy is valid,
although at the time of executing the testament it may have

212 belonged to neither.   If however it have not become the
property of the heir until after the testator's death, it is a
question whether the legacy be of any use ; the general
opinion is that it is not. But what of that ? Although a man

§ 209. Comp. Vlp. xxiv, 5 ; Th. ii, 20, § 20.   § 210. Comp. Vlp. xxiv, 10 ; Paul. iii,
    [1] The MS. has *DARE DAMNAS*   6, § 11.
ESTO, obviously *per incuriam*. See § 212. Comp. § 197.
§ 201, note 1.

legauerit quae neque eius umquam fuerit neque postea heredis eius umquam esse coeperit, ex senatusconsulto Neroniano pro-
213 inde uidetur[1] ac si per damnationem relicta esset.   sicut autem per damnationem legata res non statim post aditam hereditatem legatarii efficitur, sed manet heredis eo usque donec is[1] tradendo uel mancipando uel in iure cedendo lega- tarii eam fecerit, ita et in sinendi modo legato iuris est; et ideo huius quoque legati nomine in personam actio est QVID-
214 QVID HEREDEM EX TESTAMENTO DARE FACERE OPORTET.[2]   sunt tamen qui putant ex hoc legato non uideri obligatum heredem ut mancipet aut in iure cedat aut tradat, sed sufficere ut legatarium rem sumere patiatur; quia nihil ultra ei testator imperauit quam ut sinat, id est patiatur, legatarium rem sibi
215 habere.   Maior illa dissensio in hoc legato interuenit: si eandem rem duobus pluribusue disiunctim legasti,[1] quidam putant utrisque solidam deberi, sicut per *damnationem;*[2] non-

---

have legated [by permission] a thing that was never his, and has never subsequently become his heir's, yet by the Neronian senatusconsult it is regarded as if bequeathed by damnation.
213 Just as a thing legated by damnation does not at once become the property of the legatee when the inheritance is entered upon, but continues to belong to the heir until the latter has made it the legatee's by tradition, mancipation, or cession in court, so is it when the legacy is bequeathed *sinendi modo;* consequently the action for a legacy of this sort is also a per- sonal one, the claim being for 'whatever the heir ought to
214 give or do under the testament.'   There are some jurists, however, who think that in this kind of legacy the heir is under no obligation to mancipate, cede in court, or deliver the thing bequeathed, but that it is enough that he suffer the legatee to take it; because the testator has laid no further command upon him than that he shall permit or suffer the
215 legatee to appropriate the thing.   There is this more im- portant difference of opinion in reference to a legacy of this sort: if you have legated the same thing to two or more

---

[1] K. (K. u. S. footnote) thinks *utile* should be interpolated before *uidetur.*
§ 213.   Comp. § 204; Th. ii, 20, § 2.
[1] The MS. interjects *heres* between *is* and *tradendo.*
[2] Comp. iv, §§ 41, 47.
§ 214.   Comp. Alfen. in fr. 29, D. *locati,* (xix, 2).

§ 215.   Comp. Cels. in fr. 14, D. *de usu et usufr. leg.* (xxxiii, 2); Iust. in l. un. § 11, C. *de. caduc. toll.* (vi, 51).
[1] So the MS.; Hu. reads *legata sit,* changing *rem* into *res.*
[2] The MS. has *uindicationem;* the reason for preferring *damnationem* is obvious.   P. and K. u. S. regard the three words as a gloss.

nulli occupantis esse meliorem condicionem aestimant, quia
cum eo genere legati damnetur heres patientiam praestare ut
legatarius rem habeat, sequitur ut si priori patientiam prae-
stiterit et is rem sumpserit, securus sit aduersus eum qui
postea legatum petierit, quia neque habet rem ut patiatur
eam ab eo sumi, neque dolo malo fecit quominus eam haberet.

216 Per praeceptionem hoc modo legamus : LVCIVS TITIVS HOMI-
217 NEM STICHVM PRAECIPITO.   Sed nostri quidem praeceptores [1]
nulli alii eo modo legari posse putant nisi ei qui aliqua ex
parte heres scriptus esset : praecipere enim esse praecipuum
sumere ; quod tantum in eius persona procedit qui aliqua ex
parte heres institutus est, quod is extra portionem hereditatis
218 praecipuum legatum habiturus sit.   ideoque si extraneo legatum fuerit, inutile est legatum, adeo ut Sabinus existimauerit
ne quidem ex *senatusconsulto* Neroniano [1] posse conualescere :
'nam eo,' inquit, 'senatusconsulto ea tantum confirmantur
quae uerborum uitio iure ciuili non ualent, non quae propter

---

persons disjointly, some hold that the whole of it is due to
each, as in the case of a legacy by damnation ; but others
think that he who first appropriates it is in the better position,
because, as all that the heir is bound to prestate in such a case
as this is sufferance, it follows that if he have accorded this
sufferance to the first comer, and the latter have taken the
thing away, the heir is safe against any subsequent claim for
the legacy, seeing he neither has the thing, so as to be in a
position to suffer it to be taken from him, nor has he done
anything fraudulent to prevent the legatee appropriating it.

216 By preception we legate in this fashion : ' Let Lucius Titius
217 first take the slave Stichus.'   Our authorities are of opinion
that no one can have a legacy bequeathed to him in this form
who is not instituted heir to a part of the inheritance ; for
praecipere is to take a *praecipuum*, [*i.e.* something separated
from the rest of the estate before any distribution] ; and that
can be done only by one who is instituted heir for a part,
because he is to have what is legated to him by preception
218 over and above his share of the inheritance.   Therefore if
the legacy be to one who is not an heir, it is useless, so much
so that Sabinus held it incapable of convalescence under the
Neronian senatusconsult ; ' for,' says he, ' those legacies alone
are validated by that senatusconsult which are invalid by the

§ 216.   Comp. Vlp. xxiv, 6 ; Th. ii, 20, § 2.   § 218.   Comp. Vlp. xxiv, 11*a*.
§ 217.   [1] See i, 196, note 1.   [1] Comp. § 197.

ipsam personam legatarii non debentur.' sed Iuliano et Sexto [2]
placuit etiam hoc casu ex senatusconsulto confirmari legatum;
nam ex uerbis etiam hoc casu accidere ut iure ciuili inutile sit
legatum inde manifestum esse, quod eidem aliis uerbis recte
legetur, ueluti per uindicationem, per damnationem, sinendi
modo; tunc autem uitio personae legatum non ualere cum ei
legatum sit cui nullo modo legari possit, uelut peregrino [3] cum
quo testamenti factio [4] non sit; quo plane casu senatusconsulto
219 locus non est.   Item nostri praeceptores quod ita legatum
est nulla actione [1] putant posse consequi eum cui ita fuerit
legatum quam iudicio familiae erciscundae,[2] quod inter heredes
de hereditate erciscunda, id est diuidunda, accipi solet: officio
enim iudicis id contineri ut ei quod per praeceptionem legatum
220 est adiudicetur.   Vnde intellegimus nihil aliud secundum

civil law because of some defect of language,—not such as are
not due because of some disability in the legatee.' But Julian
and Sextus held that even here the legacy was validated by
the senatusconsult; that in this case also it is through erroneous wording that the legacy is by the civil law invalid, is
manifest, [say they], from the consideration that it would
have been valid if bequeathed in another form of words,
namely by vindication, damnation, or permission; and a
legacy is only then invalid through disability of the individual
when it is in favour of a person to whom a legacy cannot be
bequeathed in any way, as, for instance, a peregrin with whom
there is no testamenti factio.   In such a case there is obviously
219 no room for the senatusconsult.   Our authorities are also of
opinion that the only process whereby a legatee can recover a
legacy bequeathed to him in this form is a iudicium familiae
erciscundae,—the action resorted to amongst heirs for 'hercis-
cating' an inheritance, i.e. dividing it; for it is part of the
official duty of the judge to adjudicate a legacy by preception
220 [to the heir entitled to it].   Hence we gather that, accord-

[2] The original words in the MS.
were Iuliano ex Sexto, not et; the
latter is an interlinear alteration.
It is impossible to say which is right.
The Iulianus here referred to is
Salvius Iulianus, the consolidator of
the praetorian edict in the reign of
Hadrian. The Sextus has generally
been supposed to refer to Pomponius;
Mommsen (Z. f. RG. vii, 479) thinks
it may be Sextus Caecilius Africanus;
the first was a contemporary of
Julian's, the latter one of his scholars.

[3] Comp. § 285; Vlp. xxii, 2.
[4] See § 114, note 1.
§ 219. Comp. Paul. iii, 6, § 1; Th. ii,
    20, § 2.
   [1] Previous eds. read [alia]ratione;
but the MS. gives quite distinctly
the contracted form of actione, only
interpolating an accidental r before
it.
   [2] Comp. iv, 42; Vlp. xix, 16;
§§ 4, 7, I. de offic. iud. (iv, 17).
§ 220. Comp. Vlp. xxiv, 11; Paul. iii,
    6, § 8.

nostrorum praeceptorum opinionem per praeceptionem legari
posse nisi quod testatoris sit : nulla enim alia res quam hereditaria deducitur in hoc iudicium. itaque si non suam rem eo
modo testator legauerit, iure quidem ciuili inutile erit legatum ;
sed ex senatusconsulto confirmabitur. aliquo tamen casu
etiam alienam rem per praeceptionem legari posse fatentur,
ueluti si quis eam rem legauerit quam creditori fiduciae causa [1]
mancipio dederit ; nam officio iudicis coheredes cogi posse existimant soluta pecunia *luere* [2] eam rem, ut possit praecipere is
221 cui ita legatum sit. [3]   sed diuersae scholae auctores putant
etiam extraneo per praeceptionem legari posse, proinde ac si
ita scribatur : TITIVS HOMINEM STICHVM CAPITO, superuacuo ad-
iecta PRAE syllaba ; ideoque per *uindicationem eam rem* legatam
uideri : quae sententia dicitur diui Hadriani constitutione con-
222 firmata esse.   Secundum hanc igitur opinionem si ea res ex
iure Quiritium [1] defuncti fuerit *potest* [2] a legatario uindicari, siue

---

ing to the opinion of our school, nothing can be legated by
preception that is not the property of the testator ; for nothing
that does not belong to the inheritance is included in this
action.   Therefore if a testator have legated in this way something that is not his, the legacy will be invalid by the civil
law ; but it will be validated by the senatusconsult.   There is
a case, however, in which they admit that what belongs to a
third party may be legated by preception, namely when a
man has legated a thing which he has fiduciarily mancipated
to a creditor ; for they hold it to be within the powers of the
judge to require the co-heirs, by payment of the debt, to
release the thing in question, that so he to whom it has been
221 legated may take it by preception.   The authorities of the
other school think that a legacy may be left by preception
even to a stranger, as if the words ran—' Titius is to take the
slave Stichus ;' holding that the addition of the syllable *prae*
[*i.e.* before distribution] is superfluous, and the thing therefore
to be regarded as legated by vindication.   This opinion is said
to have been confirmed by a constitution of the late emperor
222 Hadrian's.   According to this view, therefore, if the thing
legated belonged to the deceased in quiritarian right, it may
be vindicated by the legatee, whether he be one of the heirs

[1] Comp. § 60.
[2] So L. and most subsequent eds. ;
the MS. has *soluere.*
[3] Comp. Gai. in fr. 26, fr. 28, D.
fam. ercisc. (x, 2).

§ 222. Comp. §§ 40, 196, 197.
[1] See i, 54, and note ; ii, 40, and
note.
[2] So G. and most eds. ; the MS.
has *posse ;* P. suggests *paret posse.*

is unus ex heredibus sit siue extraneus; si³ in bonis tantum
testatoris fuerit, extraneo quidem ex senatusconsulto utile erit
legatum, heredi uero familiae herciscundae iudicis officio prae-
stabitur; quodsi nullo iure fuerit testatoris, tam heredi quam
223 extraneo ex senatusconsulto utile erit.   Si¹ tamen heredibus secundum nostrorum opinionem, siue etiam extraneis
secundum illorum opinionem, duobus pluribusue eadem res
coniunctim aut disiunctim legata fuerit, singuli partes habere
debent.

224   Sed olim quidem licebat totum patrimonium legatis atque
libertatibus erogare, nec quicquam heredi relinquere praeterquam inane nomen heredis; idque lex XII tabularum permittere uidebatur, qua cauetur ut quod quisque de re sua testatus
esset id ratum haberetur, his uerbis: 'uti legassit suae rei, ita
iusesto:'¹ quare² qui scripti heredeserant ab hereditate se³ ab-

---

or a stranger; if it was only *in bonis* of the testator, the legacy
will be effectual to a stranger by the senatusconsult, while to
an heir it will be made available by the judge in an *actio
familiae erciscundae*; if it did not belong to the testator either
in quiritarian or bonitarian right, it will be effectual under
223 the senatusconsult either to an heir or to a stranger.   If the
same thing be legated [by preception] to two or more persons,
either conjointly or disjointly,—whether they be heirs, according to our opinion, or strangers, according to that of the other
school,—each is entitled to a share of it.
224   In olden times it was lawful to exhaust the whole patrimony in legacies and gifts of freedom, and leave nothing for
the heir but the empty name. And this seemed to be permitted by the law of the Twelve Tables, which, in the words
—'As a man has legated in regard to his belongings, so be it

---

³ The MS. seems originally to have
had *quod si*, with interlinear emendation *et si*; P. and K. u. S. retain
the former, Hu. the latter.
§ 223. Comp. Iust. in l. un. § 11, C.
de caduc. toll. (vi, 51).
  ¹ So M. (K. u. S. p. xxi); the
MS. and all eds. have *siue*.
§§ 224-228. Comp. tit. I. *DE LEGE FAL-
CIDIA* (ii, 22). In the MS., before
§ 224, there is a vacant line, on
which is the rubric *ad legem Falci-
diam* in a later hand.
§ 224. Comp. pr. tit. I. afd.; Th. ii,
22, pr.
  ¹ The MS. has *uti legasset suae res*,

ita, etc. P., in an excursus appended to Book III. of his *Syntag-
ma*, argues that the provision ran
—*uti legassit suae res* (for *rei*) *ius,
esto*, i.e. 'as a man may have testamentarily disposed of his family
patrimonial rights (*ius suae rei*), so
be it.' Comp. Schoell, *Tab.* v, 3;
Cic. *de inuent.* ii, 50, § 148; *Auctor ad Herenn.* i, 13, § 23; Vlp. xi,
14; Pomp. in fr. 120, D. *de V. S.*
(l, 16); Nov. xxii, c. 2. See also
above § 104 and notes.
  ² So K. u. S. and Hu.; the MS. has
que, which P. interprets *qua aetate.*
  ³ So the MS.; P. reads *saepe.*

225 stinebant, et idcirco plerique intestati moriebantur.   Itaque
lata est lex Furia, qua, exceptis personis quibusdam,[1] ceteris
plus mille assibus legatorum nomine mortisue causa capere [2]
permissum non est.   sed et haec lex non perfecit quod uoluit:
qui enim uerbi gratia quinque milium aeris patrimonium
habebat, poterat quinque hominibus singulis millenos asses
226 legando totum patrimonium erogare.   Ideo postea lata est
lex Voconia, qua cautum est ne cui plus legatorum nomine
mortisue causa capere liceret quam heredes caperent: ex qua
lege plane quidem aliquid utique heredes habere uidebantur;
sed tamen uitium simile nascebatur: nam in multas legatariorum personas distributo patrimonio poterat [testator] adeo
heredi minimum relinquere, ut non expediret heredi huius

law,' provided that whatever testamentary disposition a man
might make of his estate should be sustained; *whence it came
about that* those who were instituted heirs often abstained
from the inheritance, and many persons thus died intestate.
225 For this reason the Furian law was enacted, whereby all but
certain excepted persons were forbidden to take more than a
thousand *asses* by way of legacy or otherwise by reason of
death.   But this enactment did not accomplish what it intended; for a testator who had say five thousand *asses* of patrimony could still give away the whole of it by legating to five
226 different people a thousand *asses* each.   So, after a while,
the Voconian law was passed, providing that it should not be
lawful for any one to take more in name of legacy or otherwise by reason of death than remained to the heirs.   Thanks
to it, it seemed very clear that the heirs must at all events get
something: yet here too a defect soon showed itself almost of
the same sort as before; for, by distributing his estate amongst
a multitude of legatees, a testator was able to leave so little to
his heir as to make it not worth the latter's while, for the sake
of this small gain, to undertake the burdens of the whole in-

§ 225.   The *lex Furia testamentaria* was
a plebiscit passed in 571 | 183 (?).
Comp. Cic. *pro Balbo*, viii, § 21;
Vlp. i, 2; xxviii, 7; Fr. Vat. § 301;
Th. ii, 22, pr.
[1] The excepted persons were kinsmen up to the sixth degree, including the *sobrino natus;* Fr. Vat.
§ 301.
[2] According to Ihering (*G. d. R.
R.* vol. iii, part 1, p. 114, note) the
mortis causa capio referred to may
have been the result of an institution of A. as heir on condition of his
paying say 10,000 *asses* to B.   This
was not in form a legacy to B.; but
if he accepted it, it was on his part
mortis causa capio.   For other forms
of it see fr. 8 pr., fr. 31, pr. § 2, fr.
38, D. *de mort. c. donat.* (xxxix, 6).
§ 226.   The *lex Voconia*, a plebiscit of
585 | 169, introduced by Q. Voco-
nius Saxa at the instance of the
elder Cato, was one of the most
famous of the Roman sumptuary
laws.   In its first chapter it pro-

227 lucri gratia totius hereditatis onera sustinere.   Lata est
itaque lex Falcidia, qua cautum est ne plus ei legare liceat
quam dodrantem : itaque necesse est ut heres quartam partem
228 hereditatis habeat : et hoc *nunc* iure utimur.   In libertatibus quoque dandis nimiam licentiam conpescuit lex Fufia
Caninia, sicut in primo commentario rettulimus.
229   Ante heredis institutionem [*in*]utiliter legatur, scilicet quia
testamenta uim ex institutione heredis accipiunt, et ob id
uelut caput et fundamentum intellegitur totius testamenti
230 heredis institutio.   Pari ratione nec libertas ante heredis
231 institutionem dari potest.   Nostri praeceptores[1] nec tutorem
eo loco dari posse existimant : sed Labeo et Proculus[1] tutorem

227 heritance.   Therefore the Falcidian law was enacted, which
provides that it shall not be lawful for a testator to dispose of
more than three-fourths of his estate in legacies; thus the
heir must necessarily have a fourth of the inheritance.   This
228 is the law now in observance.   The Fufia-Caninian law
likewise, as stated in our first Commentary, has placed some
restriction on extravagance in [testamentary] gifts of freedom.
229   Until an heir has been instituted it is useless to bequeath a
legacy; for it is from the institution of an heir that testaments
derive their efficacy,—in fact, the institution is regarded as the
230 starting-point and foundation of the whole deed.   For the
same reason a gift of freedom cannot precede the heir's institu-
231 tion.   Neither, according to our school, can the appointment
of a tutor; but Labeo and Proculus think that, as a tutor's

hibited a citizen, whose fortune
was estimated in the censorial register at 100,000 *asses* or more, from
instituting a woman, even his
daughter or sister, as his heir ; Cic.
II. Verr. i, 41, 42, §§ 107, 108 ;
below, § 274 ; Aug. *de ciu. Dei*,
iii, 21.   In its second, however, it
allowed such a citizen to leave to
women legacies of a greater amount
than was sanctioned by the Furian
law, provided these did not in the
aggregate exceed one-half of the
testator's estate ; Quintil. *Declam.*
246.   The third, that referred to in
the text, forbade any one to take
more as a legacy or otherwise through
death under the testament of such a
citizen than remained to the heir or
heirs ; Cic. *II. Verr.* i, 43, § 110 ;
Th. ii, 22, pr.
§ 227.   The Falcidian law, also a ple-

biscit, and enacted in 714 | 40, re-
pealed the restrictions of the Furian
and Voconian laws in the matter of
bequest, substituting the provision
in the text.   It apparently did not
contain any reference to other *mortis
causa capio* than that resulting from
a legacy.   Comp. Dio. Cass. xlviii,
33 ; Vlp. xxiv, 32 ; Paul. iii, 8, § 1 ;
Paul. in fr. 1, pr. D. *ad l. Falcid.*
(xxxv, 2) ; pr. tit. I. afd.
§ 228.   Comp. i, 42.
§§ 229-237.   Comp. §§ 34-36, tit. I. *DE
LEGATIS* (ii, 20).   In the ms., on a
vacant line before § 229, we have
the rubric *de inutiliter relictis
legatis*.
§§ 229, 230.   Comp. Vlp. i, 20 ; xxiv,
15 ; § 34, tit. I. afd.
§ 231.   Comp. § 3, I. *qui dari tut. poss.*
(i, 14).
[1] See i, 196, note 1.

posse dari, quod nihil ex hereditate erogatur tutoris datione.

232 Post mortem quoque heredis inutiliter legatur, id est hoc modo: CVM HERES MEVS MORTVVS ERIT DO LEGO,[1] aut DATO.[2] ita autem recte legatur: CVM HERES MORIETVR, quia non post mortem heredis relinquitur, sed ultimo uitae eius tempore. rursum ita non potest legari: PRIDIE QVAM HERES MEVS MORIE-

233 TVR; quod non pretiosa ratione receptum uidetur.   Eadem

234 et de libertatibus dicta intellegemus.   Tutor uero an post mortem heredis dari possit quaerentibus eadem forsitan poterit esse quaestio *quae*[1] de [*eo*] agitatur qui ante heredum institutionem datur.

235   Poenae quoque nomine inutiliter legatur.   poenae autem nomine legari uidetur quod coercendi heredis causa relinquitur, quo magis heres aliquid faciat aut non faciat, ueluti quod ita legatur: SI HERES MEVS FILIAM SVAM TITIO IN MATRIMONIVM CONLOCAVERIT, X [*MILIA*] SEIO DATO, uel ita: SI FILIAM TITIO IN

---

appointment takes nothing out of the inheritance, he may be

232 nominated [even before an heir has been instituted].   It is useless also to legate as after the heir's death, thus: 'On my heir's death I give and legate,' or—'let him give.'   But a legacy 'when my heir is dying' is quite regular; for it is not left after the heir's death but in his last moments.   On the other hand one cannot legate thus: 'The day before my heir dies;' a rule which seems to have been adopted without any

233 adequate reason.   The same remarks are to be understood

234 as applying to gifts of freedom.   Whether a tutor can be appointed after the death of the heir is a question that probably depends on the same consideration as that previously mooted, namely, whether he can be appointed before an heir has been instituted.

235   A legacy by way of penalty is also useless.   And that is held to be legated by way of penalty which is bequeathed for the purpose of coercing the heir to do or forbear from something; as, for instance, a legacy in these terms: 'If my heir bestow his daughter in marriage on Titius, then let him give ten thousand sesterces to Seius;' or in these: 'If my heir do

§ 232.   Comp. iii, 100; Vlp. xxiv, 16; Paul. iii, 6, §§ 5, 6; iv, 1, § 11; § 35, tit. I. afd.
  [1] Comp. § 193.
  [2] Comp. § 201.
§ 233.   Comp. Vlp. i, 20.
§ 234.   Comp. § 231; Paul. in fr. 7, D. *de test. tut.* (xxvi, 2).

[1] The MS. has *quam*, and omits the *eo*. At the best the sentence is clumsy.
§ 235.   On a vacant line before this par. the MS. has the rubric *de poenae causa relictis legatis* in the original hand.   Comp. Vlp. xxiv, 17; xxv, 13; § 36, tit. I. afd.

MATRIMONIVM NON CONLOCAVERIS, X MILIA TITIO DATO; sed et
si *heredem*, [*si*] uerbi gratia intra biennium monumentum sibi
non fecerit, X [milia] Titio dare iusserit, poenae nomine legatum *est*. *et denique* ex ipsa definitione multas similes species
236 *circumspicere*[1] possumus.   Nec libertas quidem poenae
237 nomine dari potest, quamuis de ea re fuerit quaesitum.   De
tutore uero nihil possumus quaerere, quia non potest datione
tutoris heres conpelli quidquam facere aut non facere: ideo,
quando etiam[1] poenae *nomine* tutor datus fuerit, magis sub
condicione quam poenae nomine datus uidebitur.

238   Incertae personae legatum inutiliter relinquitur. incerta
autem uidetur persona quam per incertam opinionem animo
suo testator subicit, *uelut cum* ita legatum sit : QVI PRIMVS AD
FVNVS MEVM VENERIT, (*EI HERES*) MEVS X [*MILIA*] DATO ; idem

---

not bestow his daughter in marriage on Titius, then let him
give Titius ten thousand sesterces.' Further, if he have
ordered his heir to give ten thousand sesterces to Titius in
the event say of his, the heir's, failure to erect a monument
within two years to him, the testator, the legacy is again by
way of penalty.   And, briefly, from the mere definition, we
can conceive for ourselves many other instances of the same
236 sort of thing.   Not even freedom can be given by way
of penalty, (although on this point there has been doubt.)
237 As regards a tutor the question cannot arise.   An heir cannot
be compelled to do or forbear from anything merely by the
fact that a tutor is appointed in the will; if therefore any
such appointment seem on the face of it to have been made by
way of penalty, it must be held conditional rather than penal.
238   A legacy to an uncertain person is also useless.   And that
person is regarded as uncertain of whose individuality the
testator has formed no definite idea in his own mind, as
when he legates thus : 'To the person who comes first to my
funeral my heir shall give ten thousand sesterces.' The law
is the same if the testator have legated to all and sundry in

---

[1] P. and K. u. S. both admit that
this seems to be the reading of the
MS., but doubt its propriety; Hu.
adopts it.

§ 236.   Comp. § 36, tit. I. afd.

§ 237.   Comp. Marcian. in fr. 2, D. *de
poen. causa relict.* (xxxiv, 6).

[1] So P. ; the MS. has *quae datur*,
which he thinks must have been an
inaccurate rendering by the transcriber of the *qdo ēt* of the original.

Hu. reads *facere ideo quod datur.*
[*Si igitur*] *poenae nomine*, etc. M.
(K. u. S. footnote), *ideoque* [*etsi
secundum mentem testatoris is qui
tutor*] *datus est poenae nomine*, etc.

§§ 238-245.   Comp. §§ 25-33, tit. I. DE
LEGATIS (ii, 20).

§ 238.   Comp. Vlp. xxiv, 18; Paul. iii,
6, § 13; § 25, tit. I. afd., from
which, except *milia*, the words in
italics are borrowed.

iuris est si generaliter omnibus legauerit: QVICVMQVE AD FVNVS MEVM VENERIT. in eadem causa est quod ita relinqui- tur: QVICVMQVE FILIO MEO IN MATRIMONIVM FILIAM SVAM CON- LOCAVERIT, EI HERES MEVS X MILIA DATO; illud quoque[1] quod ita relinquitur: QVI POST TESTAMENTVM (*SCRIPTVM PRIMI*) CONSVLES DESIGNATI ERVNT, aeque incertis personis legari uidetur; et denique aliae multae huiusmodi species sunt. Sub certa uero demonstratione incertae personae recte lega- tur, ueluti: EX COGNATIS MEIS QVI NVNC SVNT QVI PRIMVS AD
239 FVNVS MEVM VENERIT, EI X MILIA HERES MEVS DATO.   Libertas quoque non uidetur incertae personae dari posse, quia lex
240 Fufia Caninia iubet nominatim seruos liberari.   Tutor quo-
241 que certus dari debet.   Postumo quoque alieno inutiliter legatur. *est autem* alienus postumus qui natus inter suos heredes testatori futurus non est: ideoque ex emancipato quoque filio conceptus nepos extraneus *postumus est; item qui in* utero est eius quae iure ciuili[1] non intellegitur uxor,[2]

---

such words as—' Whoever shall come to my funeral.' Of the same character is a legacy in these terms : ' To any man that bestows his daughter in marriage on my son my heir shall give ten thousand sesterces.' A legacy bequeathed thus ' Whoever shall be the next consuls designate after the execu- tion of my testament,' is equally regarded as in favour of uncertain persons; and there are many other varieties of it. One may competently legate, however, to an uncertain person who is indicated by a definite description; as, for example: ' To that one of my kinsman now alive who comes first to my
239 funeral my heir shall give ten thousand sesterces.'   It is also·held impossible to make a testamentary gift of freedom to an uncertain person; for the Fufia-Caninian law ordains
240 that slaves shall be enfranchised by name.   Further, it is
241 only a definite person that can be appointed as tutor.   A legacy to a stranger after-born is also invalid. By a stranger after-born we mean a person who will not on birth be one of the *sui heredes* of the testator; therefore the grandchild be- gotten of an emancipated son will be a stranger after-born; and a child *in utero* of a woman whom the *ius ciuile* does not recognise as a wife is held to be a stranger after-born

---

[1] After *illud quoque* the MS. has *in eadem causa est;* but these words are deleted as an unnecessary gloss.
§ 239. Comp. i, §§ 42, 45a; § 25, tit. I. afd.

§ 240. Comp. § 289; § 27, tit. I. afd.
§ 241. § 25, tit. I. afd.   Comp. § 287.
[1] In contradistinction to *iure gen- tium.*
[2] A marriage without *conubium*

242 extraneus postumus patri intellegitur.   Ac ne heres
    quidem potest institui postumus alienus: est enim incerta
243 persona.   Cetera uero quae supra diximus ad legata proprie
    pertinent quamquam non inmerito quibusdam placeat poenae
    nomine heredem institui non posse : nihil enim interest utrum
    legatum dare iubeatur heres si fecerit aliquid aut non fecerit,
    an coheres ei adiciatur; quia tam coheredis adiectione quam
    legati datione conpellitur ut aliquid contra propositum suum
    faciat aut non faciat.

244   An ei qui in potestate sit eius quem heredem instituimus
    recte legemus quaeritur.   Seruius[1] recte legari probat, sed
    euanescere legatum si quo tempore dies legatorum cedere
    solet[2] adhuc in potestate sit; ideoque siue pure legatum sit
    et uiuo testatore in potestate heredis esse desierit, siue sub
    condicione et ante condicionem id acciderit, deberi legatum.

---

242 even in relation to his father.   Nor can a stranger after-
243 born be instituted heir ; for he is an uncertain person.   The
    foregoing observations apply more especially to legacies.   But
    some hold, and not without reason, that an heir cannot be
    instituted by way of penalty ; for it is a matter of indiffer-
    ence whether an heir be ordered to pay a legacy in the event
    of his doing or not doing something, or [in that event] have
    a co-heir conjoined with him ; because alike by the addition
    of a co-heir and by the giving of a legacy he is compelled to
    do or forbear contrary to his own inclination.

244   It is a question whether we can lawfully legate to one who
    is in the *potestas* of the instituted heir.   Servius holds that
    we can, but that the legacy evanishes if at the time it vests
    the legatee be still *in potestate;* consequently that, if the
    legacy be unconditional and the legatee have ceased to be *in
    potestate* during the testator's lifetime, or if it be conditional
    and he become *sui iuris* before the condition is fulfilled, it
    must be paid.   Sabinus and Cassius think that a conditional

was not *matrimonium iuris ciuilis*
(i, 56; Vlp. v, 2); its issue were
not *in potestate* of their father (i,
§§ 67, 80) ; therefore they could not
be his *sui heredes* if born in his lifetime (ii, 156); and the text is only
consequent in declaring that they
must be *postumi alieni* (or *extranei*)
if born after his death (or, rather,
after the execution of his testament).
§ 242. Comp. i, 147; ii, 287; § 28, tit.
I. afd. Justinian there states the
law inaccurately; it was he himself

who first declared that a *postumus
alienus* might be instituted heir; see
pr. I. *de bon. poss.* (iii, 9).
§ 243. Comp. §§ 229, 232, 235; § 36,
tit. I. afd.
§ 244. Comp. Vlp. xxiv, 23; § 32, tit.
I. afd.
  [1] Servius Sulpicius Rufus; see i,
188, note 5.
  [2] Comp. Vlp. xxiv, 31. For the
meaning of the technical phrases
dies cedit and *dies uenit* see fr. 213,
D. *de V. S.* (l, 16).

Sabinus et Cassius[3] sub condicione recte legari, pure non
recte, putant; licet enim uiuo testatore possit desinere in
potestate heredis esse, ideo tamen inutile legatum intellegi
oportere, quia quod nullas uires habiturum foret si statim
post testamentum factum decessisset testator, hoc ideo ualere
quia uitam longius traxerit absurdum esset;[4] *sed* diuersae
scholae auctores[3] nec sub condicione recte legari, quia quos
in potestate habemus eis non magis sub condicione quam
245 pure debere possumus.   Ex diuerso constat ab eo qui in
potestate [*tua*] est herede instituto, recte tibi legari; sed si
tu per eum heres extiteris euanescere legatum, quia ipse tibi
legatum debere non possis; si uero filius emancipatus aut
seruus manumissus erit uel in alium translatus, et ipse heres
extiterit aut alium fecerit, deberi legatum.

246 *Nunc* transeamus ad fideicommissa.   [247] Et prius de
247 hereditatibus uideamus. ·

---

legacy to him is valid, but not a pure one; that even though
it be possible for him to cease to be in the heir's *potestas*
during the testator's lifetime, still the legacy must be regarded as useless, because it would be absurd that what would
have been of no effect had the testator died the moment after
making his testament should become valid for no other reason
than that his life has been prolonged. The authorities of the
other school are of opinion that we cannot legate to such a
person even conditionally; because we can no more be conditionally indebted to persons in our *potestas* than we can be
245 unconditionally.   On the other hand it is admitted that
you may competently have bequeathed to you a legacy that is
to form a charge upon a person in your *potestas* who has been
instituted heir; but if through his instrumentality you have
become heir the legacy evanishes, because you cannot owe a
legacy to yourself. If however your son be emancipated, or
your slave either manumitted or alienated, and either he or
another person through his means have become heir, then
your legacy will be due.

246 Now let us pass to *mortis causa* trusts, *fideicommissa*
247 And let us begin with [fideicommissary] inheritances.

---

[3] See i, 196, note 1.
[4] This is the so-called *regula
Catoniana;* on which see tit. D. *de
reg. Cat.* (xxxiv, 7).
§ 245. Comp. Vlp. xxiv, 24; § 33, tit. I. afd.

§§ 246-259. Comp. tit. I. *DE FIDEI-
COMMISSARIIS HEREDITATIBVS* (ii,
23).
§§ 246, 247. Pr. tit. I. afd. The ms. has
Hinc transeamus, etc.

248   Inprimis igitur sciendum est opus esse ut aliquis heres
       recto iure instituatur, eiusque fidei committatur ut eam heredi-
       tatem alii restituat; alioquin inutile est testamentum in quo
249   nemo recto iure heres instituitur.[1]   Verba autem [utilia][1]
       fideicommissorum haec [recte][1] maxime in usu esse uidentur
       —PETO, ROGO, VOLO, FIDEICOMMITTO, quae proinde firma singula
250   sunt atque si omnia in unum congesta sint.   Cum igitur
       scripserimus: [LVCIVS] TITIVS HERES ESTO, possumus adicere:
       ROGO TE, LVCI TITI, PETOQVE A TE, VT CVM PRIMVM POSSIS HERE-
       DIDATEM MEAM ADIRE, CAIO SEIO REDDAS RESTITVAS.   possumus
       autem et de parte restituenda rogare; et liberum est uel sub
       condicione uel pure relinquere fideicommissa, uel ex die certa.
251   Restituta autem hereditate is qui restituit nihilo minus heres
       permanet; is uero qui recipit hereditatem aliquando heredis
252   loco est aliquando legatarii.   Olim autem nec heredis loco
       erat nec legatarii sed potius emptoris: tunc enim in usu erat
       ei cui restituebatur hereditas nummo uno eam hereditatem

---

248   The first thing to be noted is that it is necessary that some
       one be regularly instituted heir according to law, and that it
       be committed to his honour to restore the inheritance to a
       third party; for a testament is useless in which there is no
249   one in due form instituted heir.   Of the words suitable for
       fideicommissary disposition these seem most in use,—*peto,
       rogo, uolo, fideicommitto;* and each by itself is as effective as
250   if all were used together.   When therefore we have written
       in our testament—'Lucius Titius be heir,' we may add: 'I
       ask you, Lucius Titius, and desire of you, that as soon as you
       have been able to enter upon the inheritance, you give it up
       and restore it to Caius Seius.'   But we may limit our request
       to restitution of a part of the inheritance; and it is in our
       power to bequeath the trust-gift either conditionally or uncon-
251   ditionally, or as from a certain date.   On restitution of the
       inheritance he who has restored it nevertheless still remains
       heir; he who has received it is sometimes in the position of
252   heir, sometimes in that of a legatee.   But formerly he was
       in the place neither of heir nor of legatee, but rather of a
       purchaser.   For it was then the practice that the inheritance

§ 248. § 2, tit. I. afd.
        [1] Comp. § 229.
§ 249. § 3, I. *de sing. reb. p. fid. rel.*
        (ii, 24). Comp. Vlp. xxv, §§ 1, 2;
        Paul. iv, 1, §§ 5, 6
        [1] Apparently glosses.

§ 250. § 2, tit. I. afd.
§ 251. § 3, tit. I. afd. Comp. § 255.
§ 252. The *pro forma* sale was to pave
        the way for the interchange of the
        stipulations. Comp. Th. ii, 23,
        § 3.

dicis causa uenire; et quae stipulationes inter [*uenditorem* [*hereditatis et emptorem interponi solent, eaedem interponebantur* [*inter*][1] heredem et eum cui restituebatur hereditas, id est hoc modo : heres quidem stipulabatur ab eo cui restituebatur hereditas, ut quicquid hereditario nomine condemnatus *soluisset*,[2] siue quid alias bona fide dedisset, eo nomine *indemnis esset*,[3] et omnino si quis cum eo hereditario nomine ageret ut recte defenderetur; ille uero qui recipiebat hereditatem inuicem stipulabatur ut si quid ex hereditate ad heredem peruenisset id sibi restitueretur, ut etiam pateretur eum hereditarias actiones procuratorio aut cognitorio nomine [4] exequi.

253 Sed posterioribus temporibus [1] Trebellio Maximo et Annaeo Seneca consulibus senatusconsultum factum est,[2] quo cautum

---

should, for form's sake, be sold for a single coin to the person to whom it was to be restored, and the same stipulations that *were usually interchanged between the vendor and purchaser of an inheritance were interchanged between* the heir and the person to whom the inheritance was restored, in this way : the heir took a promise from him to whom he was restoring the inheritance that he, the heir, should be kept scathless in respect of any payment made in pursuance of any judgment given against him on account of the inheritance, or of anything given otherwise in good faith, and that he should in every case be duly defended when sued in his character of heir; while he, in turn, who received the inheritance, took a promise from the heir that the latter would restore anything belonging to it that might come into his hands, and that he would allow the stipulant to prosecute all actions competent in respect of the inheritance as his, the heir's, procurator or

253 *cognitur*.   But at a later period, in the consulate of Trebellius Maximus and Annaeus Seneca, it was provided by a

---

[1] These words interpolated by G. and justified by context.

[2] So K. u. S.; the ms. and most eds. have *fuisset*; P. reads *ut quidquid hereditario nomine* [*dedisset, siue cuius rei nomine*] *condemnatus fuisset*, etc.

[3] Savigny's reading, universally accepted; the ms. has *indenisset*.

[4] Comp. iv, §§ 82-87.

§ 253. § 4, tit. I. afd.   Comp. Vlp. xxv, 14; Paul iv, 2.

[1] So the ms., K. u. S., and Hu.;

P. reads *postea Neronis temporibus*.

[2] It appears from one of the numerous wax tablets recording the business transactions of an *argentarius* (banker and auctioneer), discovered at Pompeii in 1875, that Trebellius Pollio and L. Annaeus Seneca were consuls in the latter half of the year 56, (Petra, *Tavolette*, p. 21); this fixes a date hitherto uncertain. The Sct. is reproduced by Vlp. in fr. 1, § 1, D. *ad SC. Trebell.* (xxxvi, 1).

11

est ut si cui hereditas ex fideicommissi causa restituta sit,
actiones quae iure ciuili heredi et in heredem conpeterent ei
et in eum darentur cui ex fideicommisso restituta esset hereditas; per quod senatusconsultum desierunt illae cautiones in
usu haberi : praetor enim utiles actiones³ ei et in eum qui
recepit hereditatem, quasi heredi et in heredem, dare coepit,
254 eaeque in edicto proponuntur.   Sed rursus quia heredes
scripti, cum aut totam hereditatem aut paene totam plerumque
restituere rogabantur, adire hereditatem ob nullum aut minimum lucrum recusabant, atque ob id extinguebantur fideicommissa, *postea* Pegaso et Pusione [*consulibus*]¹ senatus
censuit, ut ei qui rogatus esset hereditatem restituere perinde
liceret quartam partem retinere atque e lege Falcidia in legatis
retinendis² conceditur; (ex singulis quoque rebus, quae per
fideicommissum relinquuntur, eadem retentio permissa est;)
per quod senatusconsultum ipse onera hereditaria sustinet;
ille autem qui ex fideicommisso reliquam partem hereditatis

---

senatusconsult that, when an inheritance was restored to any
person on the ground of a trust, the actions competent by the
civil law to or against the heir should be given to or against
the party to whom the inheritance was restored *ex fideicommisso*.   In consequence of this senatusconsult the stipulations
of which we have been speaking went out of use; for the
praetor began to grant *utiles actiones* to and against the recipient of the inheritance, as if to or against an heir; and
254 these are set forth in the edict.   Still later, and because the
instituted heirs, when asked to restore the whole or nearly the
whole of the inheritance, often refused to enter upon what
was to yield them little or no profit, and thus caused the
extinction of the fideicommissary gifts, the senate, in the consulate of Pegasus and Pusio, decreed that an heir who was
asked to restore an inheritance should be entitled to retain a
fourth part of it, just as by the Falcidian law he is entitled to
do in respect of legacies; (and the same retention is allowed
in the case of single things bequeathed by trust-gift.)   By
this senatusconsult it is the heir himself that has to bear the
burdens of the inheritance, while he who receives the rest of
it in terms of the trust is in the position of a partiary legatee,

---

³ See § 78, note 1.
§ 254. § 5, tit. I. afd. Comp. Vlp.
xxv, §§ 14, 15; Paul. iv, 3.
¹ Pegasus and Pusio were consuls in the reign of Vespasian,
sometime between the years 70
and 80.
² So the MS.; M. regards the
word as a gloss; K. u. S. substitute *retinere*, Hu. *retinendi ius.*

rec ipit legatarii partiarii loco est, id est eius legatarii cui pars
bonorum legatur; quae species legati partitio[3] uocatur, quia
cum herede legatarius partitur hereditatem : unde effectum
est ut quae solent stipulationes inter heredem et partiarium
legatarium interponi, eaedem interponantur inter eum qui ex
fideicommissi causa recipit hereditatem et heredem, id est ut
et lucrum et damnum hereditarium pro rata parte inter eos
255 commune sit.   Ergo siquidem non plus quam dodrantem[1]
hereditatis scriptus heres rogatus sit restituere, tum ex Trebelliano senatusconsulto restituitur hereditas, et in utrumque
actiones hereditariae pro rata parte dantur, in heredem quidem
iure ciuili, in eum uero qui recipit hereditatem ex senatusconsulto Trebelliano ; quamquam heres etiam pro ea parte
quam restituit heres permanet, eique et in eum solidae
actiones conpetunt; sed non ulterius oneratur nec ulterius
illi dantur actiones quam apud eum commodum hereditatis
256 remanet.   at si quis plus quam dodrantem uel etiam totam
hereditatem restituere rogatus sit, locus est Pegasiano senatus-

---

i.e. a legatee to whom a share of the estate is legated. (A
legacy of this sort is called *partitio*, because the legatee shares,
partitur, the inheritance with the heir.) The result is that
the same stipulations that are wont to pass between an heir
and a partiary legatee are exchanged between the fideicommissary recipient of the inheritance and the heir, namely, that
the profit and loss of the succession shall be common to both
255 in proportion to their respective interests.   If therefore the
instituted heir be asked to restore no more than three-fourths
of the inheritance, he does so under the Trebellian senatusconsult, and actions affecting the inheritance are granted
against both parties according to their respective interests,—
against the heir, by the civil law, against the individual to
whom the inheritance is restored, under the Trebellian senatusconsult. For although the heir remains heir even as regards
the part he has restored, and [according to the civil law] action
is competent to or against him *in solidum*, yet [under the sena-
tusconsult] he is not held responsible, nor are actions granted
to him, beyond the beneficial interest in the inheritance that
256 he still retains.   But if the heir be asked to restore more
than three-fourths, perhaps the whole, of the inheritance, the

[3] Comp. Vlp. xxiv, 25; Th. ii, 23, § 5.
§§ 255, 256. § 6, tit. I. afd. Comp.
Vlp. xxv, 14.

[1] Comp. § 5, tit. I. *de hered. inst.*
(ii, 14).

257 consulto.   Sed is qui semel adierit hereditatem, si modo
sua uoluntate adierit, siue retinuerit quartam partem siue
noluerit retinere, ipse uniuersa onera hereditaria sustinet:
sed quarta quidem retenta quasi partis et pro parte [1] stipulationes interponi debent, tamquam inter partiarium legatarium et heredem; si uero totam hereditatem restituerit, ad
exemplum emptae et uenditae hereditatis stipulationes [2]
258 interponendae sunt.   Sed si recuset scriptus heres adire
hereditatem ob id quod dicat eam sibi suspectam esse quasi
damnosam, cauetur Pegasiano senatusconsulto ut, desiderante
eo cui restituere rogatus est, iussu praetoris adeat et restituat,
proindeque ei et in eum qui receperit actiones dentur ac iuris
est ex senatusconsulto Trebelliano: quo casu nullis stipulationibus opus est, quia simul et huic qui restituit securitas
datur, et actiones hereditariae ei et in eum transferuntur qui
259 receperit hereditatem.   Nihil autem interest utrum aliquis

---

257 Pegasian senatusconsult comes into play.   If he have once
entered, provided always he has done so voluntarily, then,
whether he have retained his fourth or have not cared to do
so, he is liable for the whole burdens of the succession: if he
have retained his fourth, stipulations similar to those between
an heir and a partiary legatee must be interchanged for his
share and in proportion thereto, *partis et pro parte;* but if
he have restored the whole inheritance, then stipulations are
to be interchanged after the model of those employed when
258 an inheritance has been bought and sold.   But if he refuse
to enter, alleging that he has reason to suspect the inheritance may be a source of loss to him, it is provided by the
Pegasian senatusconsult that, on the application of the party
to whom he is asked to make restitution, he may be required
to enter and restore by order of the praetor, and that actions
shall be granted to and against the recipient as would be done
under the Trebellian senatusconsult.   In this case there is no
need of any stipulations, for at the same time security is
afforded to him who has restored the inheritance, and the
actions affecting it are transferred to and against him who
259 has got it back.   It is of no moment whether an heir

---

§ 257. § 6, tit. I. afd. Comp. Vlp.   of the charges.
    xxv, 15; Paul. iv, 3, § 2.   [2] Comp. § 252.
        [1] *Partis, i.e.* that each shall have   § 258. § 6, tit. I. afd. Comp. Vlp.
his share of the assets; *pro parte,*   xxv, 16; Paul. iv, 4.
that each shall bear his own share   § 259. § 8, tit. I. afd.

ex asse[1] heres *institutus*[2] aut totam hereditatem aut pro
parte restituere rogetur, an ex parte heres institutus aut totam
eam partem aut partis partem restituere rogetur : nam et hoc
casu de quarta parte eius partis ratio ex Pegasiano senatusconsulto haberi solet.

260   Potest autem quisque etiam res singulas per fideicommissum
relinquere,uelut fundum hominem uestem argentum pecuniam,
et uel ipsum heredem rogare ut alicui restituat uel legata-
261 rium, quamuis a legatario legari non possit.[1]   Item potest
non solum propria testatoris res per fideicommissum relinqui,
sed etiam heredis aut legatarii aut cuiuslibet alterius : itaque
et legatarius non solum de ea re rogari potest ut eam alicui
restituat quae ei legata sit, sed etiam de alia, siue ipsius legatarii siue aliena sit. hoc solum obseruandum est, ne plus
quisquam rogetur alicui restituere quam ipse ex testamento
262 ceperit ; nam quod amplius est inutiliter relinquitur.   Cum

---

instituted to the whole inheritance be asked to restore the
whole or a part of it, or an heir instituted only to a share
be asked to restore the whole or a part of that share ; for even
in the latter case account will be taken under the Pegasian
senatusconsult of a fourth of the share [to which he has been
instituted.]

260   It is also competent for a testator to bequeath single things
by fideicommissary gift,—land, for example, or a slave, a garment, plate, money ; and either to ask the heir himself to
restore it to some third party, or—though it is impossible to
make a legacy a charge upon him—to ask the legatee to do
261 so.   It is not only what belongs to the testator himself that
may be bequeathed by trust, but also what belongs to the
heir, a legatee, or even an utter stranger ; and therefore a
legatee may be requested to give up to another person not
only what is legated to him, but even something else, whether
belonging to himself or to a third party.   There is this only
to remark,—that no man can be asked to give up more than
he himself has got under the testament : a fideicommissary
262 bequest beyond that is useless.   When something belong-

---

[1] Comp. § 5, tit. I. *de hered. inst.*
(ii, 14).
[2] The ms. has *instituatur.*
§§ 260-267. Comp. tit. I. *DE SINGVLIS
REBVS PER FIDEICOMMISSVM RE-
LICTIS* (ii, 22).

§ 260. Pr. tit. I. afd.
[1] Comp. § 271 ; Vlp. xxiv, 20.
§ 261. § 1, tit. I. afd. Comp. Vlp.
xxv, 5 ; Paul. iv, 1, §§ 7, 8.
§ 262. § 1, tit. I. afd. Comp. Vlp. and
Paul. as in last note.

autem aliena res per fideicommissum relinquitur, necesse est
ei qui rogatus est aut ipsam redimere et praestare aut aestimationem eius soluere, *sicut iuris est si*[1] per damnationem
aliena res legata sit : sunt tamen qui putant si rem per fideicommissum relictam dominus non uendat extingui fideicommissum ; *sed aliam esse causam* per damnationem legati.

263   Libertas quoque seruo per fideicommissum dari potest, ut
264 uel heres rogetur manumittere uel legatarius.   (*nec interest,*
(*utrum de suo proprio*) seruo testator roget, an de eo qui ipsius
265 heredis aut legatarii uel etiam extranei sit.   Itaque et
alienus seruus redimi et manumitti debet : quodsi dominus
eum non uendat, sane extinguitur fideicommissaria libertas,
266 *quia hoc* (*casu*)[1] *pretii* conputatio nulla interuenit.   Qui
autem ex fideicommisso manumittitur non testatoris fit libertus, etiamsi testatoris seruus (*fuerit*), sed eius qui manumittit.
267 at qui directo testamento liber esse iubetur, uelut hoc modo :

———————

ing to a third party is bequeathed by trust-gift, he who is
asked to give it up must either purchase and convey it or pay
its value instead, *as in the case of* a legacy by damnation of
what belongs to another.   There are some, however, who
think that, if the owner of a thing bequeathed by trust-gift
will not sell it, the bequest is extinguished ; but that the rule
is different as regards a legacy by damnation.

263   Further, there may be a grant of freedom to a slave by
means of a trust, either the heir or a legatee being desired to
264 manumit him.   Nor does it matter whether the request be
to enfranchise a slave of the testator's, or one belonging to
265 the heir, a legatee, or even a stranger.   If the slave be
another person's, he must be purchased and manumitted ;
but if his owner will not sell him, the fideicommissary gift
of freedom becomes void ; for in this case there is no room
266 for an alternative money value.   A slave who is manumitted in pursuance of a trust does not become a freedman
of the testator's, even though he may have belonged to him
267 but is a freedman of the manumitter's.   But he who has a

———————

[1] So G. and most eds. ; see Labeo
in fr. 30, § 6, D. *de leg. III.* (xxxii).
The ms. seems to have s . . . *miri*
. . . *es.*
§§ 263, 264.   § 2, tit. I. afd., from which
the words in ital. in § 264 are borrowed. Comp. § 272 ; Vlp. ii, §§ 7,
10 ; xxv, 18 ; Paul. iv, 12, § 4 ; iv, 13.
§ 265.   Comp. §2, tit. I. afd.

[1] *Casu* illegible in the ms. Comp.
Vlp. ii, 11 ; Vlp. in fr. 9, § 3, D.
de statulib. (xl, 7)—*libertas pecunia
lui non potest.*
§§ 266, 267.   § 2, tit. I. afd., from
which the words in brackets in §
267 (with exception of *Quiritium*)
are borrowed. Comp. Vlp. ii, §§
7, 8 ; Th. i, 14, § 1.

STICHVS SERVVS MEVS LIBER ESTO, uel hoc : STICHVM SERVVM
MEVM LIBERVM ESSE IVBEO, is (ipsius testatoris) fit libertus.
nec alius ullus directo ex testamento libertatem habere potest
quam qui utroque tempore testatoris ex iure (*Quiritium*
(*fuerit, et quo faceret*) testamentum et quo moreretur.

268 Multum autem (*differunt ea*) quae per fideicommissum *relin-*
269 *quuntur* ab his quae directo iure legantur.   nam ecce per
      fideicommissum — — heredis relinqui potest : cum alioquin
270 legatum — — — inutile sit.   Item intestatus moriturus
      potest ab eo ad quem bona eius pertinent fideicommissum alicui
270a relinquere, cum alioquin ab eo legari non possit.   (*Item*
      (*legatum codicillis*) relictum non aliter ualet quam si a testatore
      confirmati fuerint, id est, nisi in testamento cauerit testator
      ut quidquid in codicillis scripserit id ratum sit; fideicom-
      missum uero etiam non confirmatis codicillis relinqui potest.

---

direct grant of freedom by testament in such words as these :
'My slave Stichus is to be free,' or, 'I order that my slave
Stichus shall be free,' is a freedman of the testator himself.
No one, however, can have a grant of freedom directly under
a testament who did not belong to the testator in quiritarian
right both at the time of the latter's testament-making and at
the time of his death.

268 Trust bequests differ in many respects from direct legacies.
269 — — — — — — — —.   [270] Further, an individual
270 about to die intestate may burden his successor with a trust
      in favour of a third party; but he cannot so burden him with
270a a legacy.   *Further, a legacy bequeathed by a codicil* is not
      valid unless the latter have been confirmed by the testator,
      i.e. unless he have provided in his testament that any dispo-
      sition made by him by codicil shall be given effect to; but a
      trust-gift may be bequeathed by a codicil not thus confirmed.

§ 268. Before this par. there are two vacant lines (p. 123, lines 1, 2), with faint traces of a rubric. The first four letters of *differunt* were legible to Bl.; but he has so greatly injured the page with his chemicals that some of what he could read must now be taken on trust. Part of it seems to have dealt with the same matter as tit. I. *DE CODICILLIS* (ii, 25).

§ 269. To complete this is hopeless; any reconstruction is pure guess-work, and may be put in half-a-dozen ways.

§ 270. Comp. Vlp. xxv, 4; § 1, tit. I. afd.

§ 270a. The first three words, though illegible in the MS., seem warranted by the context. Comp. Vlp. xxv, 8; Paul. iv, 1, § 10; § 1, tit. I. afd.

271 Item a legatario legari non potest; sed fideicommissum relinqui
    potest. quin etiam ab eo quoque cui per fideicommissum
    relinquimus rursus alii per fideicommissum relinquere possu-
272 mus.   Item seruo alieno directo libertas dari non potest, sed
273 per fideicommissum potest.   Item codicillis nemo heres
    institui potest neque exheredari, quamuis testamento confir-
    mati sint; at is qui testamento heres institutus est potest
    codicillis rogari ut eam hereditatem alii totam uel ex parte
    restituat, quamuis testamento codicilli confirmati non sint.
274 Item mulier, quae ab eo qui centum milia aeris census est per
    legem Voconiam heres institui non potest, tamen fideicom-
275 misso relictam sibi hereditatem capere potest.   Latini quo-
    que, qui hereditates legataque directo iure lege Iunia capere
276 prohibentur, ex fideicommisso capere possunt.   Item cum

---

271 Further, a legacy cannot be charged upon a legatee, but a
    trust-gift may; nay, we may even burden an individual to
    whom we leave a trust-gift with a trust in favour of a third
272 party.   Further, while freedom cannot be bequeathed directly
    to another man's slave, it may be given by trust deed.
273 Further, no one can either be instituted or disinherited by a
    codicil, even though it be confirmed by testament; but the
    heir instituted in the testament may be required by codicil to
    make over the inheritance, in whole or in part, to a third
    party, notwithstanding the codicil may not have been con-
274 firmed by the testament.   Further, although by the Voco-
    nian law a woman cannot be instituted heir by a man whose
    estate is valued in the censorial register at not less than a
    hundred thousand *asses*, yet she may nevertheless take an
    inheritance he has bequeathed to her by means of a trust.
275 Latins also, though prohibited by the Junian law from taking
    inheritances or legacies left to them directly, may yet take
276 under a *fideicommissum*.   Further, although a man is for-

---

§ 271. Comp. §§ 260, 261; Vlp. xxiv,
  20; pr. § 1, I. *de sing. reb.* (ii,
  24).
§ 272. Comp. §§ 264, 267; § 2, I. *de
  sing. reb.* (ii, 24).
§ 273. Comp. Vlp. xxv, 11; § 10, I.
  de fideicom. hered. (ii, 23); § 2, tit.
  I. afd.
§ 274. See § 226, note.
§ 275. Comp. i, §§ 23, 24; Vlp. xxii,
  8; xxv, 7.
§ 276. It is generally assumed that the
  allusion here to a senatusconsult is

erroneous, and that the provision
referred to was one of those introduced by the *lex Aelia Sentia*, and
mentioned above, i, 18.
  From this view I differ. A testamentary gift merely of freedom
made the slave under thirty a latin
the moment the testament became
operative by the succession of a
suus or entry of a stranger (i, 22;
Vlp. i, 11); and as a latin he might
competently be instituted heir in
another testament, though unable

senatusconsulto prohibitum sit proprium seruum minorem annis XXX liberum et heredem instituere, plerisque placet posse nos iubere liberum esse cum annorum XXX erit, et rogare
277 ut tunc illi restituatur hereditas.   Item quamuis non [pos-[simus] post mortem eius qui nobis heres extiterit alium in locum eius heredem instituere, tamen possumus eum rogare ut cum morietur alii eam hereditatem totam uel ex parte restituat; et quia post mortem quoque heredis fideicommissum dari potest, idem efficere possumus et si ita scripserimus: CVM TITIVS HERES MEVS MORTVVS ERIT, VOLO HEREDITATEM MEAM AD PVBLIVM MEVIVM PERTINERE : utroque autem modo, tam hoc quam illo, Titius heredem suum obligatum relinquit de
278 fideicommisso restituendo.   Praeterea legata [per] formu-

---

bidden by senatusconsult to institute his slave under thirty as free and heir, yet it is the general opinion that he may declare that he shall be free on attaining that age, and desire
277 that the inheritance be then given up to him.   Further, although we cannot institute a person to be our heir after the death and in the place of him who has actually become our heir, yet we may request the latter to make over the inheritance to another, either wholly or in part, when he is dying; and, as we can leave a trust-gift to be given after the death of the heir, we can effect the same result by expressing ourselves thus : ' When Titius, my heir, is dead, I wish my inheritance to go to Publius Mevius;' in either way, either the former or the latter, Titius leaves his heir bound to restore
278 the trust-gift.   Moreover, we sue for legacies by *formula ;*

to enter unless he had converted his latinity into citisenship within the cretionary period (Vlp. xxii, 8). In the case in the text, however, the enfranchisement and institution proceeded from one and the same act, and had to take effect simultaneously or else both be useless. But the grant of freedom could not make the slave more than a latin (i, 18; Vlp. i, 12); as a latin he could not enter to the inheritance; and until he had entered he could not be free.

The case, so far as appears from the text, was not one directly met by the Aelia-Sentian law, which, however, expressly authorised such enfranchisement and manumission by an *insolvent* testator (i, 21; Vlp.

i, 14). It may have been for the purpose of authoritatively negativing the idea that a *solvent* testator might follow the same course that a senatusconsult was considered necessary.

Exactly the same rule as is here laid down was applied where a slave instituted heir with freedom was only *in bonis* of the testator (Vlp. xxii, 8); and the reason given is the same as is here suggested— *quia latinitatem consequitur, quod non proficit ad hereditatem capiendam.*

§ 277. Comp. § 184.
§ 278. Comp. Vlp. xxv, 12. What is meant is this,—that while in actions for legacies the magistrate, according to the usual procedure,

lam[1] petimus: fideicommissa uero Romae quidem apud consulem
uel apud eum praetorem qui praecipue de fideicommissis ius
dicit[2] persequimur; in prouinciis uero apud praesidem prouinciae.
279 Item de fideicommissis semper in urbe ius dicitur; de legatis
280 uero cum res aguntur.   Fideicommissorum usurae et fructus
debentur, si modo moram solutionis fecerit qui fideicommissum debebit; legatorum uero usurae non debentur: idque
rescripto diui Hadriani significatur. scio tamen Iuliano[1]
placuisse in eo legato quod sinendi modo relinquitur[2] idem
iuris esse quod in fideicommissis; quam sententiam et his
281 temporibus magis optinere uideo.   Item legata Graece
282 scripta non ualent; fideicommissa uero ualent.   Item si
legatum per damnationem[1] relictum heres infitietur, in duplum

---

but in Rome we sue for trust-gifts before the consul or the
praetor who is specially charged with jurisdiction in matter
279 of trusts, and in the provinces before the governor.   Further,
in Rome itself judicial proceedings regarding trusts may go
on at any time; but those regarding legacies can go on only
280 during term.   Interest and fruits and profits are due upon
a trust-gift if the debtor be *in mora* in paying it, but interest
is not due upon legacies; so it is stated in a rescript of our
late emperor Hadrian's.   I am aware, however, that Julian
thought the rule to be the same in the case of a legacy bequeathed *sinendi modo* as in that of a trust-gift; and I observe
281 that his opinion is now generally adopted.   Further,
legacies bequeathed in Greek words are not valid, but trust-
282 gifts are.   Further, if an heir deny that a legacy has been
left by damnation, the action against him is for double the

---

sent an issue (*formula*) to a judge
(*iudex*) for trial, in those for trust-
gifts the procedure was from first to
last before the consul, fideicommissary praetor, or provincial governor,
without any remit to a *iudex*.
  [1] See iv, §§ 30, 39, f.
  [2] Comp. § 1, I. *de fid. hered.* (ii,
23); Pomp. in fr. 2, § 32, *de O. I.*
(i, 2).
§ 279. Augustus fixed two law terms,
a summer and winter one; Claudius
is said to have combined them,
leaving December and January entirely free, and giving frequent
holidays, especially at the seasons
of harvest and vintage; Galba

amended his scheme; and later the
matter was regulated by an Oration
cf Marc. Aurelius', which prolonged
the year's sittings to 230 days and
rearranged the vacations (Capitolin.
Marc. 10).
§ 280. Paul. held that interest was due
on legacies as well as trust-bequests,
iii, 8, § 4; so did Vlp. in fr. 34, D.
de usur. (xxii, 1).
  [1] See § 218, note 2.
  [2] See § 209.
§ 281. Comp. Vlp. xxv, 9.
§ 282. Comp. iv, §§ 9, 171; Paul. i,
19, § 1; § 7, I. *de obl. quae q. ex
contr.* (iii, 27).
  [1] See § 201.

cum eo agitur; fideicommissi uero nomine semper in sim-
283 plum persecutio est.   Item quod quisque ex fideicommisso
plus debito per errorem soluerit repetere potest, at id quod ex
causa falsa per damnationem legati plus debito solutum sit
repeti non potest.   idem scilicet iuris est de eo legato quod
non debitum uel ex hac uel ex illa causa per errorem solutum
fuerit.

284   Erant etiam aliae differentiae quae nunc non sunt:
285 ut ecce peregrini poterant *fideicommissa capere, et fere*[1] haec
fuit origo fideicommissorum : sed postea id prohibitum est ; et
nunc ex oratione diui Hadriani senatusconsultum factum est
286 ut ea fideicommissa fisco uindicarentur.   Caelibes quoque
qui per legem Iuliam[1] hereditates[2] legataque capere prohi-
286a bentur, olim fideicommissa uidebantur capere posse.   Item
orbi, qui per legem Papiam[1] [ob id quod liberos non habe-
bant][2] dimidias partes hereditatum legatorumque perdunt,

---

amount of it ; but for a trust-gift action is always *in simplum.*
283 Further, there may be repetition of anything paid by mistake
beyond what was due under a trust ; but what has been paid
upon some erroneous ground in excess of what is due under a
legacy by damnation cannot be recovered.   The rule is the
same in regard to a legacy which, though not due at all, has,
from some cause or other, been paid by mistake.
284   There used to be other differences, which do not now exist.
285 For instance, peregrins used to be able to take trust-gifts,—
in fact, this may almost be said to have been the origin of
them ; but afterwards this was prohibited ; and now, by a
senatusconsult passed at the instance of our late emperor
Hadrian, such *fideicommissa* are to be claimed for the fisc.
286 Celibates, too, who were forbidden by the Julian law to take
inheritances or legacies, were yet in former times regarded
286a as qualified to take trust-gifts.   Further, childless persons,
who by the Papian law, and because they have no children,
forfeit one-half of their inheritances and legacies, were for-

---

§ 283.   Comp. Vlp. xxiv, 33; Paul. iii,
    6, § 9⊥; § 7, I. *de obl. quae q. ex
    contr.* (iii, 27).
§ 284.   Comp. § 268.
§ 285.   Comp. i, 25 ; ii, §§ 110, 118;
    Vlp. xx, §§ 14, 15; xxii, 2; Th. ii,
    23, § 1.
    [1] The ms. has *fidem commissam
    facere et ferre,* etc.
§ 286.   Comp. §§ 111, 144; Vlp. xvii,
    1; xxii, 3; Constantin. in. I. un. C.

Th. *de infirm. poen. caelib. et orb.*
    (viii, 16).
    [1] See i, 145, note 1.
    [2] After *Iuliam* the ms. has appa-
    rently *nas ;* Hu. thinks this should
    be *ttas,* and accordingly interpolates
    testamentarias before *hereditates.*
§ 286a.   See refs. in last note.
    [1] See i, 145, note 1.
    [2] P. deletes these words as a gloss,
    which K. u. S. also esteem them.

olim solida fideicommissa uidebantur capere posse. sed postea
senatusconsulto Pegasiano³ proinde fideicommissa quoque ac
legata hereditatesque capere *pro semisse*⁴ prohibiti sunt; eaque
translata sunt ad eos qui [*in eo*]⁵ testamento liberos habent,
aut si nullus liberos habebit ad populum, sicuti iuris est in
legatis et in hereditatibus quae eadem aut simili ex causa
287 [*caduca fiunt*].⁶   Item olim incertae personae uel postumo
alieno per fideicommissum relinqui poterat, quamuis neque
heres institui neque legari ei posset; sed senatusconsulto
quod auctore diuo Hadriano factum est idem in fideicommissis
288 quod in legatis hereditatibusque constitutum est.   Item
poenae nomine iam non dubitatur nec per fideicommissum
quidem relinqui posse.
289   Sed quamuis in multis iuris partibus longe latior causa sit
fideicommissorum quam eorum quae directo relinquuntur, in

---

merly considered qualified to take trust-gifts in full. But
latterly, by the Pegasian senatusconsult, they are as much
forbidden to take trust-gifts beyond a half as inheritances and
legacies; the lapsed portion is now transferred to those persons named in the testament who have children, or, if there
be none such, to the state, as is the rule in regard to legacies
and inheritances which for that or any similar reason *become*
287 *caducous*.   Further, it was formerly possible to bequeath
by trust to an uncertain person or a stranger after-born,
although it was impossible either to institute him heir or leave
him a legacy; but, by a senatusconsult passed at the instance
of our late emperor Hadrian, the rule has been made the same
288 for trust-gifts as for legacies and inheritances.   Further,
there is now no doubt that even a trust-gift cannot be
bequeathed by way of penalty.
289   But although in many of their jural characteristics trust-
gifts are not so circumscribed as direct bequests, while in

³ Comp. § 254. It is possible that
Pegasiano is a mistake for *Planci-
ano*, see Vlp. xxv, 17, n. 3, and that
it is the same Sct. as referred to in
§ 285.
  ⁴ So P.; the MS. has *p'sem*, which
most eds. render *posse*.
  ⁵ *In eo* added by P.
  ⁶ *Caduca fiunt* added by P. Previous eds. (as does Hu. still) made
§ 286a end with *hereditatibus*, and

the next one begin—[*cum*]*que eadem
aut simili ex causa item olim*, etc.
§ 287. Comp. §§ 238, 241; Vlp. xxii,
4; xxv, 13; § 12, I. *de hered. inst.*
(ii, 14).
§ 288. Comp. §§ 235 f., 243; Vlp. xxv,
13.
§ 289. Comp. i, 149; Vlp. in fr. 3, § 1;
Paul. in fr. 7, D. *de test. tutela*
(xxvi, 2).

quibusdam tantumdem ualeant, tamen tutor non aliter testa-
mento dari potest quam directo, ueluti hoc modo: LIBERIS
MEIS TITIVS TVTOR ESTO, uel ita : LIBERIS MEIS TITIVM TVTOREM
DO; per fideicommissum uero dari non potest.

---

other respects the two are equally effectual, yet a tutor cannot
be appointed by testament otherwise than directly, for example thus; 'Be Titius tutor to my children,' or, 'I make
Titius tutor to my children;' he cannot be appointed fideicommissarily.

[*COMMENTARIVS TERTIVS.*]

1   [*Intestatorum hereditates ex lege XII tabularum*[1] *primum ad*
2 [*suos heredes*[2] *pertinent.   Sui autem heredes existimantur*
[*liberi qui in potestate morientis fuerunt, ueluti filius filiaue,*
[*nepos neptisue ex filio, pronepos proneptisue ex nepote filio nato*
[*prognatus prognataue: nec interest naturales sint liberi an*
[*adoptiui: ita demum tamen nepos neptisue et pronepos pro-*
[*neptisue suorum heredum numero sunt si praecedens persona*
[*desierit in potestate parentis esse, siue morte id acciderit siue*
[*alia ratione, ueluti emancipatione;*[1] *nam si per id tempus*

---

1   *The inheritances of intestates, by the law of the Twelve Tables,*
2 *belongs in the first place to* sui heredes.   *Those are held to*
be sui heredes *who were in the* potestas *of the deceased at his
death,—a son or daughter for instance, a grandson or granddaughter, or a great-grandson or great-granddaughter by a
grandson who was the issue of a son; and it is quite immaterial
whether they be children by birth or by adoption. As regards
grandson and granddaughter, great-grandson and great-granddaughter, however, they are reckoned* sui heredes *then only when
the person next before them has ceased to be in the* potestas *of the
common parent, whether this have happened by death or otherwise, say by emancipation; for if, at the moment of a man's*

---

§§ 1-8. Comp. tit. I. *DE HEREDITATI-
BVS QVAE AB INTESTATO DEFERVN-
TVR* (iii, 1).
§§ 1-5. A sheet of the ms. is lost, cut
out, as is supposed, by the scribe
who overlaid the parchment with
Jerome's Epistles. The first side
probably was blank; the contents
of the second, down to the middle
of § 5, are supplied from the *Collat.*
xvi, 2, §§ 1-5, which bear expressly
to be from the Inst. of Gai. It is
not improbable that they were preceded by a par. corresponding to the
pr. of tit. I. afd., introducing the
subject of intestacy.

§ 1. § 1, tit. I. afd. Comp. Vlp. xxvi,
1; Paul. in *Collat.* xvi, 3, § 3.
[1] '*Si intestatus moritur, cui suus
heres nec escit, agnatus proximus
familiam habeto,*' Schoell, *Tab.* v, 4.
[2] For the reason why the *sui
heredes* were so called, see ii, 157.
Poste calls them self-heirs; but this
phrase, though with terseness and
accuracy describing their position,
is not sufficiently self-explanatory
for general use.
§ 2. §§ 2, 2b, tit. I. afd. Comp. Vlp.
xxvi, 1; Paul. in *Collat.* xvi, 3,
§§ 4, 8.
[1] Comp. i, 132.

[*quo quis moritur filius in potestate eius sit, nepos ex eo suus*
[*heres esse non potest. idem et in ceteris deinceps liberorum*
3 [*personis dictum intellegemus.   Vxor quoque quae in manu*
[*morientis est sua heres est, quia filiae loco est; item nurus*
[*quae in filii manu est, nam et haec neptis loco est: sed ita*
[*demum erit sua heres si filius, cuius in manu fuerit, cum pater*
[*moritur in potestate eius non sit. idemque dicemus et de ea*
[*quae in nepotis manu matrimonii causa*[1] *sit, quia proneptis*
4 [*loco est.   Postumi quoque qui, si uiuo parente nati essent, in*
5 [*potestate eius futuri forent, sui heredes sunt.   Idem iuris est*
[*de his quorum nomine ex lege Aelia Sentia uel ex senatuscon-*
[*sulto post*] mortem patris causa probatur: nam et hi uiuo
6 patre causa probata in potestate eius futuri essent.   Quod
etiam de eo filio qui ex prima secundaue mancipatione post
mortem patris manumittitur intellegemus.

7   Igitur cum filius filiaue et ex altero filio nepotes neptesue

---

death, his son be in his potestas, a grandson by that son cannot
be his suus heres. The same remark applies to the rest of a man's
3 descendants in their order.   The wife, too, that is in his manus
when he dies, is a sua heres, because she is in the position of a
daughter. So is his daughter-in-law in his son's manus, for
she stands to him in place of a granddaughter; she will be sua
heres, however, only if the son, in whose manus she has been, was
not in potestate of his father at the moment of the latter's death.
The same may be said of her who is matrimonially in manu of
a grandson; for she stands in the position of a great-grand-
4 daughter.   Posthumous children also who, had they been born
in the lifetime of the parent [whose succession is in question],
5 would have been in his potestas, are sui heredes.   Those
are in the same position on whose account cause has been proved
under the Aelia-Sentian law or under the senatusconsult after
their father's death; for, had it been proved during the
6 latter's lifetime, they would have been in his potestas.   And
a son who, .after a first or second mancipation, has been
manumitted after his father's death, is also to be regarded as
in the same position.
7   When therefore a man leaves a son or daughter, and

§ 3. Comp. i, 136; ii, §§ 139, 159; Vlp.
xxii, 14; Gell. xviii, 6, § 9.
     [1] Comp. i, §§ 114, 118.
§ 4. § 2b, tit. I. afd. Comp. ii, 130;
Vlp. xxii, 15.
§ 5. Comp. i, §§ 29, 31, 32; ii, 142; Vlp.
vii, 4; Paul. in Collat. xvi, 3, § 7.

§ 6. Gai. in Collat. xvi, 2, § 6. Comp.
i, 132; ii, 141; Vlp. xxiii, 3; Paul.
in Collat. xvi, 3, § 7. Manumission
after a third mancipation would not
have had the same effect.
§§ 7, 8. Gai. in Collat. xvi, 2, §§ 7, 8;
§ 6, tit. I. afd. Comp. Vlp. xxvi, 2.

extant, pariter ad hereditatem uocantur; nec qui gradu
proximior est ulteriorem excludit: aequum enim uidebatur
nepotes neptesue in patris sui locum portionemque succedere.
pari ratione et si nepos neptisue sit ex filio, et ex nepote pronepos pronepotisue, simul omnes uocantur ad hereditatem.

8 Et quia placebat nepotes neptesue, item pronepotes pronep-
tesue in parentis sui locum succedere, conueniens esse uisum
est non in capita sed in stirpes hereditatem diuidi, ita ut
filius partem dimidiam hereditatis ferat, et ex altero filio duo
pluresue nepotes alteram dimidiam; item si ex duobus filiis
nepotes extent, et ex altero filio unus forte uel duo, ex altero
tres aut quattuor, ad unum aut ad duos dimidia pars pertineat,
et ad tres aut quattuor altera dimidia.

9   Si nullus sit suorum heredum, tunc hereditas pertinet ex
10 eadem lege XII tabularum[1] ad agnatos. *Vocantur autem*
agnati qui legitima cognatione iuncti sunt: legitima autem

---

grandsons or granddaughters by another son, they are called
simultaneously to the inheritance; the nearer in degree does
not exclude the more distant; for it seemed but fair that the
grandsons and granddaughters should succeed in their father's
place and to his share.   Upon the same principle, if there be
a grandson or granddaughter by a son, and a great-grandson or
great-granddaughter by a grandson, they are all called simul-
8 taneously.   And as it was thought right that grandsons
and granddaughters, great-grandsons and great-granddaughters, should succeed in the place of their parents, it seemed to
accord with this view that the inheritance should be divided
in stirpes rather than *in capita*, [*i.e.* by reckoning branches
rather than individuals,] so that a son should have one half of
the inheritance, and the grandsons by another son, whether
two or more, should have the other half.   So, if there be
grandsons, issue of two sons,—one or perhaps two by one of
them, three or four by the other, one half belongs to the one
or two, and the other half to the three or four.

9   If there be no *suus heres*, then, by the same law of the
Twelve Tables, the inheritance belongs to the agnates.
10 Those are called agnates who are allied by *legitima cognatio*,

§§ 9-17. Comp. tit. I. *DE LEGITIMA*   § 10.   Gai. in *Collat.* xvi, 2, § 10, from
AGNATORVM SVCCESSIONE (iii, 2).   which the few words illegible in the
§ 9.   Gai. in *Collat.* xvi, 2, § 9.   Comp.   MS. are supplied; § 1, tit. I. afd.
Vlp. xxvi, 1; Paul. in *Collat.* xvi,   Comp. Vlp. xxvi, 1; Paul. in *Collat.*
3, § 13; pr. tit. I. afd.   xvi, 3, §§ 13, 15; Vlp. in *Collat.*
   [1] See note 1 to § 1.   xvi, 6, § 1.

cognatio est ea quae per uirilis sexus personas (*coniungitur :*
(*itaque eodem*) patre nati fratres agnati (*sibi sunt, qui etiam*
(*consanguinei*) uocantur, nec requiritur an etiam matrem
eandem habuerint; item patruus fratris filio et inuicem is illi
agnatus est; eodem numero sunt fratres patrueles inter se, id
est qui ex duobus fratribus progenerati sunt, quos plerique
etiam consobrinos[1] uocant: qua ratione *scilicet etiam ad*
plures gradus agnationis peruenire poterimus.

11   Non tamen omnibus simul agnatis dat lex xii tabularum
hereditatem, sed his *qui tunc*[1] cum certum est aliquem in-
12 testato decessisse proximo gradu sunt.   Nec in eo iure
successio est: ideoque si agnatus proximus hereditatem omiserit, *uel antequam adierit* decesserit, sequentibus nihil iuris
13 ex lege conpetit.   Ideo autem non mortis tempore quis
(*proximus*) *fuerit requirimus, sed eo* tempore quo certum

[*i.e.* the kinship of the *ius ciuile ;*] and that is *legitima cognatio*
in which the alliance is through persons of the male sex.
Therefore brothers born of the same father, *often called
brothers consanguinean*, are each other's agnates, without reference to the consideration whether or not they have the
same mother; an uncle on the father's side is an agnate of his
brother's son, and the latter in turn an agnate of his uncle;
agnates also, each of the other, are *fratres patrueles, i.e.* the
children of two brothers, by most people called *consobrini.*
It is plain that in this way we may arrive at many degrees
of agnation.

11   It is not, however, to all a man's agnates at once that the
Twelve Tables give his inheritance, but only to those who
are nearest in degree at the time it has been ascertained that
12 he has died intestate.   Nor is there any succession in this
right of the nearest agnate; consequently if he have not
taken up the inheritance, or have died before entry, those
13 next in degree have no claim to it under the statute.   The
reason why we seek for the nearest agnate, not as at the time
of a man's death, but as at the time when it has been ascer-

---

[1] *Consobrini* originally meant children of sisters, but was extended so
as to mean first cousins without
distinction.

§ 11.   Gai. in *Collat.* xvi, 2, § 11; § 1,
tit. I. afd.   Comp. § 18; Paul. in
Collat. xvi, 8, § 17; § 6, tit. I.
afd.

[1] The ms. seems to have *quibus*

tum; corrected from *Collat.* and
Inst.

§ 12.   Gai. in *Collat.* xvi, 2, § 12. Comp.
§ 22; Vlp. xxvi, 5; Paul. iv, 8,
§§ 23, 26 ; § 7, tit. I. afd.

§ 13.   Gai. in *Collat.* xvi, 2, § 18 from
which the few words illegible in the
ms. have been supplied. Comp.
§ 11; § 6, tit. I. afd.

12

fuerit aliquem intestatum decessisse, quia si quis (*testamento*) facto decesserit, melius esse uisum est tunc *eius*[1] requiri proximum cum certum esse coeperit neminem ex eo testamento fore heredem.

14 Quod ad feminas tamen attinet, in hoc iure aliud in ipsarum hereditatibus capiendis placuit, aliud in ceterorum bonis[1] ab his capiendis: nam feminarum *hereditates* proinde ad nos agnationis iure redeunt atque masculorum nostrae uero hereditates ad feminas ultra consanguineorum gradum non pertinent; itaque soror fratri sororiue legitima heres est, amita uero et fratris filia legitima heres esse [*non* [*potest; sororis autem nobis loco est*] etiam mater aut nouerca quae per in manum conuentionem apud patrem nostrum iura filiae *nacta*[2] est.

15 Si ei qui defunctus erit sit frater et alterius fratris filius, sicut ex superioribus[1] intellegitur, frater prior[2] est, quia

tained that he has died intestate, is this,—that, if he died leaving a testament, the proper course seemed to be to look for the agnate nearest to him at the moment it became certain that no one was to be heir under that testament.

14 As regards women, one rule has been received in this branch of the law as to taking an inheritance from them, but quite a different one as to taking by them; for, while the inheritances of females devolve on us by right of agnation just as do those of males, our inheritances do not belong to females beyond the consanguinean degree. Therefore, while a sister is heir-at-law of her brother or sister, a father's sister or a brother's daughter *cannot be* heir-at-law [of her nephew or uncle]. A mother or stepmother, however, who by passing *in manum* of our father has acquired the rights of a daughter of his, *stands to us in the position of a sister.*

15 If a person deceased be survived by a brother and the son of another brother, the brother, as may be gathered from

[1] So P.; the MS. appears to have *etiis*, which Hu. renders *ex iis*, and K. u. S. omit.

§ 14. Gai. in *Collat.* xvi, 2, § 14, from which the words [*non . . . loco est*], omitted in the MS. are supplied. Comp. Vlp. xxvi, 6; Paul. in *Collat.* xvi, 3, §§ 16, 20; Vlp. in *Collat.* xvi, 7, § 1; §§ 3, 8a, 8b, tit. I. afd.
[1] This word omitted by many eds. as a gloss, on the ground that it would hardly be applied by a classical jurist to a *legitima hereditas*;

but we find Gai. frequently—as in §§ 36 f.—using *hereditas* for *bonorum possessio*, which in strictness is equally inaccurate.
[2] The MS. has *nancta*; Hu., following the *Collat.*, substitutes *consecuta*.

§ 15. Gai. in *Collat.* xvi, 2, § 15. Comp. Paul. in *Collat.* xvi, 3, § 18; § 5, tit. I. afd.
[1] See § 11.
[2] So the MS.; the *Collat.* and Inst. have *potior*, which K. u. S. adopt.

gradu praecedit : sed alia facta est iuris interpretatio inter
16 suos heredes.[3]   Quodsi defuncti nullus frater extet, [sed]
sint liberi fratrum, ad omnes quidem hereditas pertinet ; sed
quaesitum est, si dispari forte numero sint nati, ut ex uno
unus uel duo, ex altero tres uel quattuor, utrum in stirpes
diuidenda sit hereditas, sicut inter suos heredes iuris est,
an potius in capita : iam dudum tamen placuit in capita
diuidendam esse hereditatem ; itaque quotquot erunt ab
utraque parte personae, in tot portiones hereditas diuidetur,
ita ut singuli singulas portiones ferant.

17   Si nullus agnatus sit, eadem lex XII tabularum [1] gentiles [2]
ad hereditatem uocat.   qui sint autem gentiles primo commentario [3] rettulimus ; et cum illic admonuerimus totum
gentilicium ius in desuetudinem abisse, superuacuum est hoc
quoque loco de eadem re curiosius [4] tractare.

---

what has been said, is preferred, for he is nearer of degree;
but a different interpretation is put upon the law in the case
16 of *sui heredes*.   If he leave no brother, but is survived by
children of brothers predeceased, the inheritance belongs to
all of them.   It used to be a question, when the families
were of unequal number,—one brother having one or two
children say, another three or four,—whether the inheritance
should be divided *in stirpes*, as is the rule with *sui heredes*,
or *in capita*.   It has long been settled, however, that the
division must be *in capita ;* therefore, whatever be the number
of individuals in the two families collectively, the inheritance
must be divided into the same number of shares, so that each
individual may have one.

17   On failure of agnates, the gentiles, by the same law of
the Twelve Tables, are called to the inheritance.   Who the
gentiles are we have explained in our First Commentary ; it
would be superfluous again to go into the details of the
matter, seeing, as there already observed, that the whole law
affecting them has become obsolete.

---

[3] Comp. § 8.
§ 16.   Gai. in *Collat.* xvi, 2, § 16. Comp.
Vlp. xxvi, 4 ; Paul. in *Collat.* xvi,
8, §§ 17, 19 ; § 4, tit. I. afd.
§ 17.   Comp. Vlp. in *Collat.* xvi, 4,
§ 2.
[1] ' *Si agnatus nec escit, gentiles
familiam habento,*' Schoell, *Tab.*
v, 5.

[2] Comp. Liv. x, 8 ; Cic. *Top.* vi,
29 ; Paul. *ex Festo,* v. *Gentilis*
(Bruns, p. 242).
[3] See i, 164a, note.
[4] Between *re* and *curiosius* the
MS. has *tin,* with a dot over the *n*,
usually a mark of deletion. Hu.
and many earlier eds. read *iterum ;*
Gou. and P. *et*.

18   Hactenus lege XII tabularum finitae sunt intestatorum¹
     hereditates : quod ius quemadmodum strictum fuerit palam
19   est intellegere.   Statim enim emancipati liberi nullum ius
     in hereditatem parentis ex ea lege habent, cum desierint sui
20   heredes esse.   Idem iuris est si ideo liberi non sint in
     potestate patris quia sint cum eo ciuitate Romana donati nec
21   ab imperatore in potestatem redacti fuerint.   Item agnati
     capite deminuti non admittuntur ex ea lege ad hereditatem,
22   quia nomen agnationis capitis deminutione perimitur.   Item
     proximo agnato non adeunte hereditatem, nihilo magis sequens
23   iure legitimo admittitur.   Item feminae agnatae quaecum-
     que consanguineorum gradum excedunt nihil iuris ex lege
24   habent.   Similiter non admittuntur cognati qui per femi-
     nini sexus personas necessitudine iunguntur, adeo quidem
     ut nec inter matrem et filium filiamue ultro citroque here-
     ditatis capiendae ius conpetat, praeterquam si per in

18   Here, according to the Twelve Tables, there was an end of
     the inheritances of intestates ; and how strict the law was in
19   regard to them is very evident.   Thus children the moment
     they are emancipated have no longer any right under the
     statute in the inheritance of their ancestor, for they have
20   ceased to be *sui heredes*.   The rule is the same where
     children happen not to be *in potestate* of their father for the
     reason that, though they have received with him a gift of
     citizenship, the emperor has not declared them subject to his
21   *potestas*.   Further, agnates who have undergone *capitis
     deminutio* are by the statute excluded from the inheritance,
     because agnation is thereby in every sense destroyed.
22   Further, if the nearest agnate fail to enter, the next in degree
     is none the more on that account entitled to admission under
23   the statute.   Further, female agnates beyond the consan-
24   guinean degree of relationship have no right under it.   In
     like manner those kinsmen are not admitted that are related
     merely through females.   So far does this go that, as between
     a mother and her son or daughter, there is not on either
     side any right to take an inheritance, except when consan-

§ 18. Comp. pr. I. *de SC. Tertull.*   § 21. Comp. i, 158; iii, 27; Vlp.
(iii, 3).   xxvii, 5; § 1, I. *de succ. cognator.*
    ¹ After this word Hu. interpolates   (iii, 5).
ingenuorum.   § 22. Comp. §§ 12, 28.
§ 19. Comp. § 9, I. *de hered. q. ab. int.* § 23. Comp. § 14.
(iii, 1).   § 24. Comp. Vlp. xxvi, §§ 7, 8; pr. I.
§ 20. Comp. i, §§ 93, 94 ; ii, 135a.   *de SC. Tertull.* (iii, 3).

manum conuentionem consanguinitatis iura[1] inter eos con-
stiterint.

25   Sed hae iuris iniquitates edicto praetoris emendatae sunt
26 Nam eos omnes[1] qui legitimo iure deficiuntur uocat ad hereditatem[2] proinde ac si in potestate parentum mortis tempore
fuissent, siue soli sint, siue etiam sui heredes, id est qui in
27 potestate patris fuerunt, concurrant.   Agnatos autem capite
deminutos non secundo gradu[1] post suos heredes uocat, id
est non eo gradu uocat quo per legem uocarentur si capite
minuti non essent, sed tertio, proximitatis nomine; (licet
enim capitis deminutione ius legitimum perdiderint, certe
cognationis iura retinent):[2] itaque si quis alius sit qui integrum ius agnationis habebit, is potior erit, etiamsi longiore

---

guinity has been established between them by *in manum
conuentio.*

25   But those inequalities of the *ius ciuile* have been corrected
26 by the praetor's edict.   For he calls to the inheritance all
descendants who have no statutory title, just as if they had
been in the *potestas* of their ancestor at the time of his death;
and that whether they stand alone, or whether *sui heredes*—
persons, that is to say, who were actually *in potestate* of the
27 deceased parent—claim along with them.   As for agnates
who have undergone *capitis deminutio*, he does not call them
in the second class immediately after the *sui heredes,*—he does
not call them, that is to say, in that class in which they
would have been called by the statute had they not been
capite minuti, but in the third class, on the ground of propinquity; (for although by their *capitis deminutio* they have
lost their statutory title, they still retain the rights of kinship).
If, therefore, there be any other person whose right as an
agnate remains unimpaired, he will be preferred to them, even

[1] The rights arising from the relationship of brother and sister or of
sisters; comp. § 14.

§ 25.   A vacant line in the MS. before
this par. Comp. pr. § 2, I. *de
bonor. poss.* (iii, 9).

§§ 26-31.   Comp. tit. I. *DE SVCCESSIONE
COGNATORVM* (iii, 5).

§ 26.   Comp. §§ 19, 20; Vlp. xxviii, 8;
Vlp. in *Collat.* xvi, 7, § 2; § 9, I. *de
hered. q. ab. int.* (iii, 1); pr. tit. I. afd.
    [1] So the MS. For *eos* G. and all

subsequent eds., except P., substitute *liberos;* but unnecessarily, as
the context sufficiently limits the
pronoun.
    [2] Comp. § 32.

§ 27.   Comp. § 21; Vlp. xxviii, 9; § 1,
tit. I. afd.
    [1] Here and in subsequent pars.
there is a confusion between *gradus*
and *ordo; sui, agnati, cognati,* were
ordines rather than *gradus.*
    [2] Comp. i, 158.

28 gradu fuerit.[3]   Idem iuris est, ut quidam putant, in eius
    agnati persona qui proximo agnato omittente hereditatem
    nihilo magis iure legitimo admittitur; sed sunt qui putant
    hunc eodem gradu a praetore uocari quo etiam per legem
29 agnatis hereditas datur.   Feminae certe agnatae quae
    consanguineorum gradum excedunt tertio gradu uocantur, id
30 est si neque suus heres neque agnatus ullus erit.   Eodem
    gradu uocantur etiam eae personae quae per feminini sexus
31 personas copulatae sunt.   Liberi quoque qui in adoptiua
    familia sunt ad naturalium parentum hereditatem hoc eodem
    gradu uocantur.
32   Quos autem praetor uocat ad hereditatem, hi heredes ipso
    quidem iure non fiunt: nam praetor heredes facere non
    (*potest; per legem enim tantum uel similem iuris constitu-*

---

28 though he be of a more distant degree.   The rule is the
    same, as some think, in the case of the remoter agnate who,
    on the declinature of the inheritance by him who is nearest
    of degree, nevertheless is not on that account admitted by
    statutory right.   There are others, however, who think that
    such a man is called by the praetor in the same class in
    which the inheritance goes by statute to the agnates.
29 Female agnates beyond the consanguinean degree are un-
    doubtedly called in the third class; in the absence, that is
30 to say, of both *sui* and agnates.   In the same class are
    called also such persons as are related through females.
31 Children, too, who are in an adoptive family, are called in
    this same class to the inheritance of their natural parents.
32   Those, however, whom the praetor calls to an inheritance
    do not become heirs *ipso iure;* the praetor cannot make
    men heirs,—*it requires a comitial enactment or some similar*

---

[3] For ex., a deceased brother's
son, who was an agnate, would be
preferred to a brother who, by
cap. deminutio, had become only a
cognate.

§ 28. Comp. §§ 12, 22; § 7, I. *de leg.
agn. succ.* (iii, 2).   According to
the first view here suggested,—and
which as appears from § 7, I., referred to, eventually prevailed,—he
would take only as a cognate, in
concurrence with other cognates of
the same degree, and might himself
be excluded by cognates of nearer
degree; according to the second, he

would take as an agnate, to the entire
exclusion of cognates.
§ 29. Comp. § 23; Paul. iv, 8, § 22a;
§ 3, I. *de leg. agn. succ.* (iii, 2).
§ 30. Comp. § 24; Vlp. xxviii, 9; § 2,
tit. I. afd.
§ 31. § 3, tit. I. afd.
§ 32. § 2, I. *de bonor. poss.* (iii, 9),
from which the words in ital., mostly
illegible in the MS., are supplied;
for the ordinary contraction, however, of *praetor dat bonorum possessionem* (*prdatbp*), the MS. appears
to Stud. to have *propter.* Comp. ii,
119, note 1; iii, § 80; Vlp. xxviii, 12.

(*tionem heredes fiunt*), ueluti per senatusconsultum et constitutionem principalem : sed *cum eis praetor dat bonorum
possessionem*, loco heredum constituuntur.

33   (*Adhuc autem etiam*) alios conplures gradus (*fecit praetor
(in bonorum possessionibus dandis, dum id agebat ne quis sine
(successore moreretur*). de quibus in his commentariis consulto (*non agimus, quia*) hoc ius totum propriis commentariis
33a *executi sumus*.   (*Hoc*) solum admonuisse sufficit — — —
— — — — — in *manum conuentionem* iura consanguinitatis nacta — — — — — — — —.

33b   — — — — — — — —.   [34] (*Aliquando tamen neque*

---

statutory provision, such as a senatusconsult or imperial constitution, to do that.   But *as the praetor gives such persons
possession of the deceased's estate*, they are [practically] put in
the position of heirs.

33   *Various other classes of* bonorum possessores *have been created
by the praetor in his anxiety to prevent persons dying without
successors*, which we purposely refrain from dealing with in
these pages, seeing we have explained the whole of this
33a branch of the law elsewhere in a special treatise.   It is
enough to observe — — — — — — — —.

33b   [Bonorum possessio *was introduced by the praetor for the
[purpose of amending the old law.   And it was not only in the
[case of the inheritances of intestates that he amended the old
[law in this way, as has been above described, but also in the
[case of those of persons who have left a testament.   For, if a*

---

§ 33. The illegible words in the first
sentence of this par. (p. 132, lines 6,
7 of the ms.) are supplied from § 2,
I. *de bonor. poss.* (iii, 9). Those illegible in the second sentence are
naturally suggested by the context.

§ 33a. This par. begins on line 10 of
p. 132 of the ms. Of the fourteen
lines that follow there is very little
decipherable, while on p. 133 only a
few letters can be made out. It is
generally supposed that the first of
these pages contained an account of
the provisions of the Tertullian
senatusconsult ; in regard to which
see tit. I. *de SC. Tertull.* (iii, 8), and
Vlp. xxvi, 8. The Orphitian senatusconsult (I. iii, 4), though enacted
during the lifetime of Gai., was probably posterior to his Institutes.

§ 33b. Assuming that § 34 stood in Gai.
as printed in the text, *i.e.* as it

stands in § 1, I. *DE BONORVM POS-
SESSIONIBVS* (iii, 9), Huschke's conjecture seems more than probable
that it may have been preceded by
what we now have in the pr. of that
title ; indeed the initial *aliquando
tamen* of § 34 necessitates it. The
words of the pr. are : *Ius bonorum
possessionis introductum est a praetore emendandi ueteris iuris gratia.
Nec solum in intestatorum hereditatibus uetus ius eo modo praetor emen-
dauit, sicut supra dictum est, sed in
eorum quoque qui testamento facto
decesserint. Nam si alienus postumus heres fuerit institutus, quamuis
hereditatem iure ciuili adire non
poterat, cum institutio non ualebat,
honorario tamen iure bonorum possessor efficiebatur, uidelicet cum a
praetore adiuuabatur.* Comp. §§
25 f.; ii, §§ 242, 287.

34 *(emendandi neque impugnandi ueteris iuris, sed magis confir-*
(mandi gratia pollicetur bonorum possessionem. nam illis
(quoque), qui *recte (facto testamento heredes instituti sunt, dat*
*(secundum tabulas bonorum possessionem: item ab in)*testato
heredes suos et agnatos ad bonorum possessionem uocat.
quibus casibus beneficium eius in eo solo uidetur aliquam
utilitatem habere, ut is qui ita bonorum possessionem petit
interdicto cuius principium est QVORVM BONORVM[1] uti possit:
cuius interdicti quae sit utilitas suo loco proponemus: alioquin remota quoque bonorum possessione ad eos hereditas
pertinet iure ciuili.

35   Ceterum saepe quibusdam ita datur bonorum possessio ut
is cui data sit [*non tamen ideo*][1] optineat hereditatem; quae

36 bonorum possessio dicitur sine re.   nam si uerbi gratia iure

---

[*man have instituted a stranger after-born as his heir, the latter*
[*cannot enter to the inheritance according to the* ius ciuile, *the*
[*institution being invalid; but by the* ius honorarium *he*
[*becomes* bonorum possessor, *the praetor coming to his aid.*]

34 *Sometimes, however, it is for the purpose neither of amending
nor of impugning, but rather of confirming the old law, that
the praetor promises possession of a deceased person's estate; for
he grants it in terms of the deed to those who have been instituted heirs under a regularly executed testament; while in the
event of* intestacy he calls both *sui heredes* and agnates.
In such cases his grant seems to be useful only in this respect,—that he who thus petitions for possession of the
estate can employ the interdict which begins with the
words '*Quorum bonorum,*' whose advantages we shall explain
in the proper place; but in any case, even were the *bonorum
possessio* put out of view, the inheritance belongs to such
persons by the *ius ciuile.*

35   It frequently happens that *bonorum possessio* is given under
circumstances which prevent the grantee therewith obtaining
the [beneficial interest in the] inheritance; a possession of
this sort is said to be only nominal, *bonorum possessio sine re.*

36 Suppose, for example, that the heir instituted under a duly

§ 34. Ever since first suggested by G.
there has been a general consensus
of opinion that this par., begun on
p. 133 and ended on p. 134, was, in
the first half of it, the same as § 1,
tit. I. afd.; and I have given effect
to this view by introducing the passage in the text as reasonably certain.
Comp. Paul. in *Collat.* xvi, 8, § 5.

[1] Comp. iv, 144.
§ 35. Comp. ii, 148; Vlp. xxiii, 6;
xxviii, 13.
[1] So P., and preferable to the
simple *non* of other eds. The introduction of a negative is absolutely
necessary.
§ 36. Comp. Vlp. xxviii, 13.

facto testamento heres institutus creuerit [1] hereditatem, sed
bonorum possessionem secundum tabulas testamenti petere
noluerit, contentus eo quod iure ciuili heres sit, nihilo minus
ii, qui nullo facto testamento ad intestati bona uocantur,
possunt petere bonorum possessionem; sed sine re ad eos
hereditas [2] pertinet, cum testamento scriptus heres euincere
37 hereditatem possit.   Idem iuris est si intestato aliquo
mortuo suus heres *noluerit petere bonorum possessionem, con-
(tentus legitimo iure :* [1] nam*) et agnato conpetit quidem bonorum possessio, sed sine re, quia euinci hereditas a suo herede
potest. et *conuenienter,* [2] si ad agnatum iure ciuili pertinet
hereditas, et is adierit hereditatem sed bonorum possessionem
petere noluerit, si quis [3] ex proximis cognatis petierit, sine re
habebit bonorum possessionem propter eandem rationem.
38 Sunt et alii quidam similes casus, quorum aliquos superiore
commentario tradidimus.

---

executed testament has declared his acceptance of the inheritance, but, content with his legal title of heir, has refrained
from petitioning for possession of the estate in terms of the
deed, those who are called *ab intestato* in the absence of a
testament are entitled to demand *bonorum possessio;* but it
will be theirs *sine re,* [*i.e.* without beneficial result,] seeing
37 the testamentary heir can evict.   The law is the same
when, on a man's death intestate, his *suus heres* has refrained from demanding *bonorum possessio,* content *with his
right under the statute;* here again an agnate-heir may have
bonorum possessio, but *sine re,* for the inheritance may be
evicted by the *suus heres.*   In the same way, if the inheritance belong by the *ius ciuile* to an agnate, and he have
entered, but refrained from demanding *bonorum possessio,*—if
this be claimed by one of the nearest cognates, the latter will
38 get it only *sine re,* for the same reason as before.   There
are other cases of the same sort, some of which have been
mentioned in the immediately preceding Commentary.

[1] Comp. ii, §§ 164 f.
[2] *Hereditas* in this and subsequent
pars. is occasionally used as meaning the deceased's estate,—the *bona*
of which possession had been granted. See § 14, note 1.
§ 37. [1] The words *legitimo iure,* illegible except the initial *l,* are supplied
by Hollweg, and justified by the
context.

[2] The ms. has *illud conuenientur;*
for which P. suggests *illud conueni-
en[ter inueni]tur;* K. (K. u. S. footnote), *illud conueni[ens inueni]tur;*
and Hu., *illud conuenien[ter dice]tur.*
[3] The ms. has *et si quis;* most
eds. retain the *et,* Hu. reading *et sic
quis.*
§ 38.   Comp. ii, §§ 119, 148, 149.

39   Nunc de libertorum bonis uideamus.   [40] Olim itaque
40 licebat liberto patronum suum inpune testamento praeterire :
nam ita demum lex XII tabularum ad hereditatem liberti
uocabat patronum, si intestatus mortuus esset libertus nullo
suo herede relicto : itaque intestato quoque mortuo liberto, si
is suum heredem reliquerat, nihil in bonis eius patrono iuris
erat ; et siquidem ex naturalibus liberis aliquem suum heredem reliquisset, nulla uidebatur esse querella ; si uero uel
adoptiuus filius filiaue, uel uxor quae in manu esset, [suus uel]
   sua heres esset, aperte iniquum erat nihil iuris patrono super-
41 esse.   Qua de causa postea praetoris edicto haec iuris ini-
quitas emendata est : siue enim faciat testamentum libertus,
iubetur ita testari ut patrono suo partem dimidiam bonorum
suorum relinquat, et si aut nihil aut minus quam partem dimidiam reliquerit, datur patrono contra tabulas testamenti partis
dimidiae bonorum possessio ; [1] si uero intestatus moriatur, suo

---

39   Let us see now about the estates of freedmen.   [40] For-
40 merly a freedman might pass over his patron in his testament
with perfect impunity ; for the law of the Twelve Tables
called a patron to the inheritance of his freedman then only
when the latter had died intestate leaving no *suus heres*.
Accordingly if a freedman dying intestate did leave a *suus
heres*, his patron had no right in his estate, and if that *suus
heres* was one of the freedman's natural children there was no
cause for complaint ; if, however, it was either an adoptive
son or daughter, or his wife *in manu*, that was his *suus heres*,
then it was obviously unfair that no right should remain to
41 the patron.   Accordingly this want of equity in the law
was afterward corrected by the praetor's edict. A freedman,
if he make a testament, is thereby required to do it in such a
way as to leave to his patron one-half of his estate ; if he
have left him nothing, or less than a half, the patron may
obtain *bonorum possessio* of one-half of it contrary to the
terms of the testament. If the freedman die intestate, leav-

---

§§ 39-76. Comp. tit. I. *DE SVCCESSIONE
LIBERTORVM* (iii, 7). Before § 39 a
line vacant in the MS., probably for
a rubric.
§§ 39, 40.   Pr. tit. I. afd.   Comp.
i, 165 ;   Vlp. xxvii, 1 ;   xxix,
1.
§ 41.   § 1, tit. I. afd., from which the
words in italics, illegible in the

MS., are supplied.   Comp. Vlp.
xxix, 1.
   [1] This is not to be taken absolutely ; for, as appears from the end
of the par., a testament made in
favour of his children by birth by a
freedman who was not a *centenarius*
(§ 42), was free from challenge by
his patron.

herede relicto adoptiuo filio, uel uxore quae in manu ipsius
esset, uel nuru quae in manu filii eius fuerit, datur aeque
patrono aduersus hos suos heredes partis dimidiae bonorum
possessio. prosunt autem liberto ad excludendum patronum
naturales liberi, non solum quos in potestate mortis tempore
habet sed etiam emancipati et in adoptionem dati, si modo
aliqua ex parte heredes scripti (*sint, aut praeteriti contra*)
tabulas testamenti bonorum possessionem ex edicto petierint:
42 nam exheredati nullo modo repellunt patronum.   Postea
lege Papia [1] aucta sunt iura patronorum quod ad locupletiores
libertos pertinet: cautum est enim ea lege, ut ex bonis eius
qui sestertiorum (*centum milium plurisue*) [2] patrimonium
reliquerit, et pauciores quam tres liberos habebit, siue is testamento facto siue intestato mortuus erit, uirilis pars patrono
debeatur; itaque cum unum filium unamue filiam heredem
reliquerit libertus, perinde pars dimidia patrono debetur ac
si sine ullo filio filiaue moreretur; cum uero duos duasue here-

---

ing as his *suus heres* either an adoptive son, or the wife who
had been in his *manus*, or a daughter-in-law who had been *in
manu* of his son, the patron is equally entitled to possession of
a half of the estate in opposition to those *sui heredes*. Not
only, however, will those of his children by birth avail the
freedman to exclude his patron who were in his *potestas* at
his death, but also those he had emancipated or given in
adoption, provided they have either been instituted to a share
of his inheritance, or, *having been passed over*, have petitioned
under the edict for *bonorum possessio* contrary to the tenor of
the will; but those who have been disinherited by no means
42 exclude the patron.   The rights of patrons having very
wealthy freedmen were afterwards enlarged by the Papian
law.   By that enactment it was provided that, of the estate of
a freedman who left a fortune of or over a hundred thousand
sesterces and fewer than three children, and whether he died
testate or intestate, one equal share should go to the patron.
Accordingly if a freedman have left one son or one daughter
as his heir, a half of his estate is due to his patron, just as if
he had died without any child; but if he have left two sons

---

§ 42.   § 2, tit. I. afd.
[1] See i, 145, note.
[2] Of those three words only the
letters *mili* are distinct in the ms.,
with room for about twenty more.
Centum milium are from the Inst.,
and *plurisue* will about fill the remaining space.

des reliquerit tertia pars debetur, si tres relinquat repellitur patronus.

43   In bonis libertinarum nullam iniuriam antiquo iure patiebantur patroni : cum enim hae in patronorum legitima tutela essent, non aliter scilicet testamentum facere poterant quam patrono auctore. itaque *si ei*[1] auctor ad testamentum faciendum factus erat, — — — — — — — —[2] factus erat, *sequebatur* hereditas ; si uero auctor ei *factus* non erat, et *intestata liberta moriebatur*, ad — — — — — — posset
44 patronum a bonis *libertae* — — repellere.[3]   Sed postea

---

or daughters as his heirs, only a third part is due; while if he have left three the patron is altogether excluded.

43   As regards the estates of their freedwomen, patrons suffered no injury by the old law; for as the former were under the tutory-at-law of the latter, they could not otherwise make a testament than *patrono auctore.* Therefore if a patron had interponed his authority to a testament made by his freedwoman, [*either he had himself to blame if he had not therein [been named heir, or, if he had been so named*], he took the inheritance under the will; if, on the other hand, he had not interponed his *auctoritas*, or she had died intestate, [*the in-[heritance belonged to him as patron, a woman having no* sui [heredes ; *so that it is impossible to conceive a case*] in which a patron could be kept out of the succession of his freedwoman
44 *against his will.*   But afterwards the Papian law, in liber-

§43. Before this par. a vacant line. Comp. i, 192; Vlp. xxix, 2.
[1] The ms. and all eds. have *siue* instead of *si ei.*
[2] The first 2 lines of p. 187 mostly illegible. Krueger's reconstruction (*Krit. Vers.* p. 182) has been generally approved; it runs—*aut de se queri debebat quod heres ab ea relictus non erat, aut ipsum ex testamento, si heres* factus erat, etc.
[3] The greater part of lines 5-7 are illegible. Krueger (*Krit. Vers.* p. 132) reconstructs thus : *quia suos heredes femina habere non potest, ad patronum* pertinebat, nec *cogitari* ullus *casus poterat quo quis* posset patronum a bonis libertae *inuitum* repellere. Hu. proposes: ad *eundem, quia suos heredes femina habere non potest, hereditas* pertinebat : nec *cogitari* ullus *heres poterat, qui iure ciuili* posset patronum a bonis li-

bertae *inuitum* repellere. Krueger's seems the preferable reading, with this emendation,—that *ad patronum* should go before *quia*, etc., the *ad* appearing in the ms. after *moriebatur.*

§ 44. Comp. i, 145, note; i, 194; iii, 47; Vlp. xxix, §§ 2, 3. The par., which is on lines 8-17 of p. 187, is to a considerable extent illegible. The first lacuna in the text may very well be filled with *condere testamentum, prospexit,* and the second with *quos liberta mortis tempore*, both as proposed by K. (*Krit. Vers.* p. 183), and justified by Vlp. xxix, 3. The third K. fills thus, Hu. substantially adopting his reading: eique *ex bonis eius quae c milium sestertiorum plurisue reliquerit patrimonium, si testamentum fecerit, dimidia pars debeatur ; si uero intestata liberta decessit, tota* hereditas ad

lex Papia, cum quattuor liberorum iure libertinas tutela patronorum liberaret, et eo modo concederet *eis* etiam sine tutoris
auctoritate — — — — ut pro numero liberorum — — — —
habuerit, uirilis pars patrono debeatur, *eique* ex bonis eius,
quae — — — — — — — hereditas ad patronum
pertinet.

45   Quae diximus de patrono eadem intellegemus et de filio

...ating freedwomen enjoying the privilege of four children
from the tutelage of their patrons, and thus conceding to
them the power of *executing a testament* without their tutor's
authority, [*provided that a share of a freedwoman's inheritance,*
[*varying according to the number of children by whom she was*
[*survived, should still be due to her patron.* — — — — — —.
[*If, however, she die intestate, the whole*] inheritance belongs to
the patron.

45   What has been said of a patron applies equally to his son,

patronum pertinet. M. (K. u. S.
p. xxi) proposes: *scilicet* ex bonis
eius quae *centum milium sestertium
plurisue substantiam habeat. nam
si minoris ea fuerit, non nisi ab intestato* hereditas ad patronum pertinet.
But neither of those conjectural
readings seems to be justified by the
letters Stud. has deciphered; for the
c milium sestertiorum plurisue,
Stud. has *omnia...dorideoiuris,* and
for the other words letters equally
inappropriate.

I find no warrant for the assumption that the Papian law applied
any special rule to the case of a
freedwoman who had a fortune of
100,000 sesterces or more. A patron
was entitled to a share of the estate
of a *libertus centenarius,*—a *freedman*
who left a fortune of that amount,
whether he died testate or intestate,
provided he left *no more than two*
children (§ 42). But if a *freedwoman,* whatever her fortune, died
intestate, her patron was her heir-
at-law, however numerous her children; while it was not unless she
had *four* children at least that she
could at her own hand make a testament and thereby prejudice her
patron's right.

The position of matters under the
Papian amendment seems to have
been this: If a freedwoman had

fewer than four children she continued incapable of making a testament without her patron's *auctoritas;* but the moment her fourth
child was born she was freed from
tutelage, and might at any time
thereafter, and even though her
children had all died in the interval,
make a testament entirely at her
own hand. If she died intestate,
her patron took everything as heir-
at-law; for, even if she had children, they were not *sui heredes,* and
so could not exclude him. If she
left a will, she could not thereby
defeat her patron's right to a share
at least of her estate as *portio legitima;* for, whatever the nature of
her testamentary arrangements,—
whether she left her fortune to her
children or to strangers,—he was entitled to a share which, if not left to
him directly, he might obtain by a
grant of *bonor. possessio.* And this
share varied according to the number of children, whether instituted
or not, by whom she was survived;
if three, say, he was entitled to a
fourth, if only one, to a half; while
if all her children had predeceased
her, he was entitled to her whole
succession, thus altogether defeating
her testamentary disposition.

§ 45.   Comp. § 58; Vlp. xxix, 4; pr. I.
de adsign. lib. (iii, 8).

patroni ; *item de nepote ex filio*, pronepote *ex nepote filio nato*
46 *prognato*.   Filia uero patroni, et *neptis ex filio et proneptis
ex* nepote filio *nato prognata, olim quidem eo iure* [*utebantur*]
quod [1] lege XII tabularum patrono datum est, — — — —[2]
sexus patronorum liberos — — — —[3] testamenti liberti
[*aut*] ab intestato contra filium adoptiuum, uel uxorem nurumue quae in manu fuerit, bonorum possessionem petat, trium
liberorum iure lege Papia consequitur; aliter hoc ius non
47 habet.   Sed ut ex bonis libertae testatae quattuor liberos
habentis [1] uirilis pars ei debeatur, ne liberorum quidem iure
consequitur, ut quidam putant, sed *tantum* [2] intestata liberta
mortua uerba legis Papiae faciunt ut ei uirilis pars debeatur.
si uero testamento facto mortua sit liberta, tale ius ei datur
quale datum est contra tabulas testamenti liberti, id est quale

---

to his grandson by a son, and to his great-grandson by a
46 grandson who is the issue of a son.   As for his daughter,
his granddaughter by a son, and his great-granddaughter by a
grandson, the issue of a son, they had in old times the same
right as was conferred by the Twelve Tables on the patron
himself.   [*The praetor, however, calls only*] the male descendants
of patrons.   [*If a daughter demand possession of the estate of
[a freedman, contrary to the tenor of his*] testament, or claim it
on intestacy as against an adoptive son or a wife or daughter-
in-law who had been *in manu*, it is under the Papian law
that she does so, and in virtue of her privilege of three
47 children ; otherwise she has no such right.   Some think
that this privilege of maternity does not entitle a patron's
daughter to a proportionate share of the estate of a freedwoman with four children who has executed a testament,—
that, according to the letter of the Papian law, it is only in the
event of the freedwoman dying intestate that a child's share
is due to her.   But if the freedwoman have left a testament,
the patron's daughter has really the same rights as against
the will that she would have were it that of a freedman,—that
is to say, the same rights that male descendants of a patron

---

§ 46. Comp. Vlp. xxix, 5.
    [1] *Olim . . . quod* is the reading of
K. (K. u. S. footnote); the MS. is
very indistinct.
    [2] K. fills this blank with
praetor autem non nisi uirilis sexus,
etc.
    [3] The same ed. fills the second
blank with liberos *uocat ; filia*

uero ut contra tabulas testamenti,
etc.
§ 47. Comp. Vlp. xxix, 5.
    [1] The fact that she was mother of
four children freed a *liberta* from
tutelage, and enabled her to make a
will at her own hand; see § 44.
    [2] So P.; the MS. and other eds.
have *tamen*.

et uirilis sexus patronorum liberis contra tabulas testamenti
liberti habent :[3] quamuis parum diligenter ea pars legis scripta
48 sit.   Ex his apparet extraneos heredes patronorum longe
remotos esse ab omni eo iure quod *uel in* intestatorum bonis
uel *contra* tabulas testamenti patrono conpetit.
49   Patronae olim ante legem Papiam hoc solum ius habebant
in bonis libertorum quod etiam patronis ex lege XII tabularum
datum est.   nec enim ut contra tabulas testamenti ingrati
liberti, uel ab intestato contra filium adoptiuum uel uxorem
nurumue bonorum possessionem partis dimidiae peterent, prae-
50 tor similiter ut de patrono liberisque eius curabat.   Sed lex
Papia duobus liberis honoratae ingenuae patronae, libertinae
tribus, eadem fere iura dedit quae ex edicto praetoris patroni
habent ;[1] trium uero liberorum iure honoratae ingenuae patro-

---

have as against the testamentary writings of a freedman ;
[such is the true meaning of the enactment], although in this
48 part of it it is not very carefully worded.   From what has
been said it is clear that stranger-heirs of a patron have no
participation in the rights competent to him either in regard
to the estates of his intestate freedmen, or, by procedure
contra tabulas, in regard to those who have died testate.
49   Formerly, and before the Papian law, patronesses had no
greater right in the estates of their freedmen than had been
accorded to patrons by the law of the Twelve Tables; the
praetor did not concede to them, as he did to a patron and his
children, the right to claim either possession of the estate of
an ungrateful freedman contrary to the tenor of his testament,
or possession of half the estate of a freedman dying intestate
as against his adoptive son or his wife or daughter-in-law.
50 The Papian law, however, gave a patroness of free birth who
had the honour of being the mother of two children, and to a
freedwoman-patroness who was the mother of three, almost
the same rights as are enjoyed by patrons under the edict.
Further, it gave to a free-born patroness with three children

---

[3] On the death intestate of a freedwoman her patron's daughter, if she
enjoyed the *ius trium liberorum,* took
an equal share with the children by
whom the freedwoman was survived;
if the latter died testate, leaving
her succession to her children, the
patron's daughter had no claim; but
if the testatrix left her estate to
strangers, there was a claim *contra
tabulas* for *bonor. possessio dimidiae
partis,* so that a patron's daughter

was thus in much the same position
as a *patrona* (§ 52). At least this
seems to be the meaning of the par.
§ 48. Comp. §§ 53, 64.
§ 49. Comp. §§ 40, 41; Vlp. xxvii, 1;
xxix, 6.
§ 50. Comp. §§ 41, 42; Vlp. xxix, §§
6, 7.
[1] *I.e.* the right to *bonor. possessio
dimidiae partis* where the succession
was testamentarily left to others
than the freedman's *sui* by birth.

nae ea iura dedit quae per eandem legem patrono data sunt;[2]
51 libertinae autem patronae non idem iuris praestitit.   Quod
autem ad libertinarum bona pertinet, si quidem intestatae
decesserint, nihil noui patronae liberis honoratae lex Papia
praestat: itaque si neque ipsa patrona neque liberta *capite
deminuta* sit, ex lege XII tabularum ad eam hereditas pertinet
et excluduntur libertae liberi; quod iuris est etiam si liberis
honorata non sit patrona: numquam enim, sicut supra diximus,[1] feminae suum heredem habere possunt: si uero uel
huius uel illius capitis deminutio interueniat, rursus liberi
libertae excludunt patronam, quia, legitimo iure capitis
deminutione perempto, euenit ut liberi libertae cognationis
52 iure potiores habeantur.   Cum autem testamento facto
moritur liberta, ea quidem patrona quae liberis honorata
non est nihil iuris habet contra libertae testamentum;
ei uero quae liberis honorata sit hoc ius tribuitur per

---

the same rights it had itself conferred upon a patron; but
51 these were not extended to a freedwoman-patroness.   As
regards the estates of freedwomen who had died intestate, the
Papian law conceded nothing new to a patroness privileged
by reason of her children; so that if neither the patroness
herself nor her freedwoman be *capite deminuta*, the inheritance
belongs to the former according to the law of the Twelve
Tables, and the freedwoman's children are excluded.   The
rule is the same even if the patroness be not privileged as
the mother of children; for, as already observed, a woman
can never have a *suus heres*.   If, however, there have been
capitis deminutio either of the patroness or of her freedwoman,
the latter's children then exclude the patroness; for, on the
extinction of her statutory right by *capitis deminutio*, the
children of her freedwoman are preferred in right of kinship.
52 When the deceased freedwoman has left a testament, a
patroness who has no privilege by reason of children has no
right in opposition to it; on her, however, who is the mother
of children, the Papian law confers the same right that a

---

[2] *I.e.* right to a *uirilis portio* of
the estate of a *centenarius* leaving
not more than two children.
§ 51. Comp. i, 158; Vlp. xxvii, 5.
[1] Comp. ii, 161; iii, 43.
§ 52. Comp. §§ 41, 47; Vlp. xxix, 7.
A *liberta* who had not a patron but

a patroness could make a will, even
though she had not the *ius liberorum*, and was still in tutelage; for
she was under the tutory not of her
patroness but of an Atilian tutor,
who could not withhold his *auctoritas* (ii, 122).

legem Papiam quod habet ex edicto patronus contra tabulas
liberti.

53   Eadem lex patronae filio liberis honorato — —[1] *patroni*[2]
iura dedit; sed in huius persona etiam unius filii filiaeue ius
sufficit.

54   Hactenus omnia [*in bona civium Romanorum libertinorum*]
iura quasi per indicem tetigisse satis est.   alioquin diligentior
55   interpretatio propriis commentariis exposita est.   Sequitur
56   ut de bonis latinorum libertinorum dispiciamus.   Quae
pars iuris ut manifestior fiat, admonendi sumus id quod alio
loco diximus, eos qui nunc latini Iuniani dicuntur olim ex

---

patron enjoys under the edict in opposition to the testament
of his freedman.

53   The same enactment has conferred on the son of a patroness,
himself honoured on account of children, almost the same
right it gives to a patron (?); but in his case one son or
daughter suffices.

54   It is enough to have thus touched in a sort of outline upon
all those rights [*of patrons in the estates of those of their*
[*freedmen who are Roman citizens*]; a more minute exposition
55   of them is given elsewhere in a special treatise.   We have
now to deal with the estates of freedmen who are latins.

56   To render this branch of our subject more intelligible, let us
bear in mind what was said in another place,—that those who
are now called Junian latins were formerly by quiritarian

§ 53. Comp. Paul. fr. 18, Pap. fr. 42,
pr. D. *de bon. libertor.* (xxxviii, 2).
[1] In the blank the ms. has *cre.*
M. (K. u. S. footnote) suggests *ciui
Romano*; K. (*Krit. Vers.* p. 127),
fere; P., *omnia fere*; Hu., *prope.*
[2] The ms. and most eds. have
patroni, Gou. and P., *patronae.*
A patron had greater rights than a
patroness; but it seems unreason-
able to suppose that a son could
have greater rights than the mother
he represented.

§ 54. It is generally supposed that
there is something omitted in the
ms.; the words interpolated seem to
express what is meant. The treatise
to which Gai refers was possibly his
commentary on the *lex Iulia et
Papia.*

§ 55. Preceded in the ms. by a vacant
line, probably for a rubric. The
following sentences may serve as an
introduction to the next six or seven

13

pars.:—'The capacity of the Junian
latin to execute a testament was.
denied by the law. The law, therefore, and not his will, could alone
decide to whom his estate should
fall. There was no room, however,
to speak of any real *successio ab intestato*, for a latin had no agnates.
Even his patron could not succeed
ab intestato; for the patronal right
of succession was based on a fictitious agnation; and such a fiction
could not possibly be entertained
where the capacity to be a party in
an agnatic relationship was absolutely denied.   Accordingly no one,
not even his patron, would have
had a right to the estate of a deceased latin, had not the Junian law
made express provision for its disposal.'   (Vang. *Lat. Iun.* p. 129).
§ 56.   Comp. i, §§ 22, 181; Vlp. i, 10;
Fr. Dos. §§ 5, 6; § 4, tit. I. afd.;
l. un. pr. C. *de lat. lib. toll.* (vii, 6).

iure Quiritium seruos fuisse, sed auxilio praetoris in libertatis
forma seruari solitos; unde etiam res eorum peculii iure ad
patronos pertinere solita est: postea uero per legem Iuniam [1]
eos omnes quos praetor in libertate tuebatur liberos esse
coepisse et appellatos esse latinos Iunianos; latinos ideo, quia
lex eos liberos perinde esse uoluit atque si essent ciues
Romani ingenui [2] qui ex urbe Roma in latinas colonias
deducti latini coloniarii esse ceoperunt; Iunianos ideo, quia
per legem Iuniam liberi facti sunt, etiamsi non essent ciues
Romani. [2] legis itaque Iuniae lator, cum intellegeret futurum ut ea fictione res latinorum defunctorum ad patronos
pertinere desinerent, *quia (scilicet)* [3] *neque ut* serui decederent
ut possent iure peculii res eorum ad patronos pertinere, neque
liberti latini *Iuniani* [4] bona possent manumissionis iure ad
patronos pertinere,[5] necessarium *existimauit*, ne beneficium
istis datum in iniuriam patronorum conuerteretur, cauere [6] ut

---

law slaves, although, by help of the praetor, they used to have
assured to them a semblance of freedom; consequently that
their effects used to belong to their patrons as in law no
more than *peculium;* but that afterwards, by the Junian law,
all those whom the praetor protected in [the enjoyment of
de facto] freedom, began really to be freemen, and to be called
Junian latins,—latins, because it was the intention of the
statute that they should be in the position of those freeborn
Roman citizens who, having been despatched from the City
to latin colonies, became colonial latins; Junian, because by
the Junian law they became free, although they were not
Roman citizens. And so the author of the Junian law, fore-
seeing that by this fiction the estates of deceased latins would
cease to belong to their patrons,—for, as they were not to die
slaves, their effects could not belong to their patrons in virtue
of an owner's *ius peculii*, neither could the estate of a Junian
freedman belong to his patron in right of manumission,—
thought it necessary, in order to prevent the boon conferred

[1] The *lex Iunia Norbana;* see i, 22, note 2.

[2] The passages *atque . . . ingenui,* and *etiamsi . . . Romani,* according to M. (K. u. S. footnote), are glosses.

[3] Illegible in the ms.; suggested by Stud., and adopted by P. and all later eds.

[4] The ms. has *liberti latini hominis,* which is evidently a mistake, though accepted by most eds. If *liberti* be deleted as a gloss, as suggested by K. u. S., *hominis* may stand; but I prefer to retain the former, and replace the latter with *Iuniani.*

[5] The patron's right was a *successio legitima,* sanctioned by the Twelve Tables (i, 165), which knew only citizen freedmen, and nothing of Junian latins.

[6] The ms. has *cauere uoluit;* Hu. reads the latter word *uoluitque.*

bona eorum proinde ad manumissores pertinerent ac si lex
lata non esset : itaque iure quodammodo peculii bona latino-
57 rum ad manumissores ea lege pertinent.   *Vnde accidit ut
longe* differant ea iura quae in bonis latinorum ex lege Iunia
constituta sunt ab his quae in hereditate ciuium Romanorum
58 libertorum obseruantur.   Nam ciuis Romani liberti hereditas ad extraneos heredes patroni nullo modo pertinet; ad
filium autem patroni nepotesque ex filio et pronepotes ex
nepote [*filio nato*][1] *prognatos* omnimodo pertinet, etiamsi a
parente fuerint exheredati; latinorum autem bona tamquam
peculia seruorum etiam ad extraneos heredes pertinent, et ad
59 liberos manumissoris exheredatos non pertinent.   Item ciuis
Romani *liberti* hereditas ad duos pluresue patronos aequaliter
pertinet, licet dispar in eo seruo dominium habuerint; bona
uero latinorum pro ea parte pertinent pro qua parte quisque
60 eorum dominus fuerit.   Item in hereditate ciuis Romani
liberti patronus alterius patroni filium excludit, et filius

---

upon the freedmen becoming an injury to their patrons,
to provide that their estates should belong to their manumitters just as if the enactment had not been passed; accordingly, in virtue of the enactment, the estates of [deceased]
latins belong to their enfranchisers in a manner *iure peculii.*
57 Hence it happens that the rights created in the estates of
latins by the Junian law differ very much from those that are
recognised in reference to the inheritance of a freedman who
58 is a Roman citizen.   For, first, the inheritance of a citizen
freedman in no case belongs to the stranger-heirs of his
patron,—on the contrary it belongs in all cases to the patron's
son, his grandsons by a son, or great-grandsons by a grandson
who is the issue of a son, and that even though they may
have been disinherited by their parent; whereas the estates
of latins, just as if they were the *peculia* of slaves, pass
even to stranger-heirs, and do not belong to the disinherited
59 children of the manumitter.   Further, the inheritance of a
citizen freedman belongs to two or more patrons equally, even
though they may have owned him in unequal shares when
a slave; whereas they succeed to the estates of their latin
freedmen in shares corresponding to those they each had as
60 owners.   Further, in the inheritance of a citizen freedman
one patron excludes the son of another, and the son of one

§ 58. Comp. §§ 45-48.   § 60. Comp. Vlp. xxvii, §§ 2, 3; Paul.
    [1] These words introduced by L.,   iii, 2, § 1; § 3, tit. I. afd.
and adopted by all eds.

patroni alterius patroni nepotem repellit: bona autem latinorum et ad ipsum patronum et ad alterius patroni heredem
simul pertinent, pro qua parte ad ipsum manumissorem per-
61 tinerent.   Item si unius patroni tres forte liberi sunt et
alterius unus, hereditas ciuis Romani liberti in capita diuiditur,
id est tres fratres tres portiones ferunt et unus quartam ; bona
uero latinorum pro ea parte ad successores pertinent pro qua
62 parte ad ipsum manumissorem pertinerent.   Item si alter
ex his patronis suam partem in hereditate ciuis Romani
liberti spernat, uel ante moriatur quam cernat, tota hereditas
ad alterum pertinet ; bona autem latini pro parte *deficientis* [1]
patroni caduca [2] fiunt et ad populum pertinent.

63   Postea, Lupo et Largo consulibus, senatus censuit ut bona
latinorum primum ad eum pertinerent qui eos liberasset;
deinde ad liberos [1] eorum non nominatim exheredatos, uti

---

patron excludes the grandson of another; but the estate of a
latin belongs at the same time to his [surviving] patron and
his [deceased] patron's heir, [and to the latter] to the extent to
61 which it belonged to the [deceased] manumitter.   Further,
if there be three children say of one patron and one child of
another, the inheritance of a citizen freedman is divided *in
capita, i.e.* the three brothers take three shares, and the single
child gets the fourth ; the estate of a latin, however, belongs
to successors in the same proportions in which it belonged
62 to the manumitters themselves.   Further, if one of two
patrons decline his share of the inheritance of a citizen freedman, or die before declaring his acceptance of it, the whole
inheritance belongs to the other ; but the estate of a latin, as
regards the share of a patron failing to take, becomes caducous
and falls to the state.
63   Afterwards, during the consulate of Lupus and Largus, the
senate decreed that the estates of [deceased] latins should
belong in the first place to those who had manumitted them ;
in the next place to the latter's descendants not nominately disinherited, according to proximity ; [failing such descendants,]

---

§ 61. Comp. Vlp. xxvii, § 4; Paul. iii,
2, § 3 ; § 3, tit. I. afd.
§ 62. Comp. Paul. iii, 2, § 2.
   [1] So G. and most eds.; the MS.
   has *decedentis.*
   [2] See Vlp. tit. xvii.
§ 63. Comp. § 4, tit. I. afd., where the
SC. referred to is called *Sctum Lar-*

gianum. There was a Largus consul *p. C.* 42.
   [1] *Liberi* is to be understood here
in the sense in which the word is
used by the praetor in his edict ; as
meaning, not descendants generally,
but children whom a testator was
required to disinherit,—*sui* and
quasi sui ; see § 71.

quisque proximus esset; tunc antiquo iure ad heredes eorum
64 qui liberassent pertinerent.   Quo senatusconsulto quidam
[*id*][1] actum esse putant, ut in bonis latinorum eodem iure
utamur quo utimur in hereditate ciuium Romanorum libertinorum; *idque*[2] maxime Pegaso[3] placuit.   quae sententia aperte
falsa est: nam ciuis Romani liberti hereditas numquam ad
extraneos patroni heredes pertinet; bona autem latinorum
etiam[4] ex hoc ipso senatusconsulto non obstantibus liberis
manumissoris etiam ad extraneos heredes pertinent; item in
hereditate ciuis Romani liberti liberis manumissoris nulla
exheredatio nocet, in bonis latinorum nocere nominatim
factam exheredationem ipso senatusconsulto significatur.
uerius est ergo hoc solum eo senatusconsulto actum esse, ut
manumissoris liberi qui nominatim exheredati non sint prae-
65 ferantur extraneis heredibus.   Itaque emancipatus filius
patroni praeteritus, quamuis contra tabulas testamenti parentis
sui bonorum possessionem non petierit, tamen extraneis here-

---

then to the heirs of the manumitters in accordance with the
64 old law.   It is a result of this senatusconsult, as some
jurists maintain, that we must follow the same rule in reference to the estates of latins that we do in reference to the
inheritance of citizen freedmen,—a view that commended
itself notably to Pegasus.   But their opinion is manifestly
erroneous.   For the inheritance of a citizen freedman never
belongs to stranger-heirs of the patron; whereas, by the very
terms of the senatusconsult, the estates of latins do belong to
stranger-heirs of the manumitter, failing his children.   Further,
in the inheritance of a citizen freedman, the children of the
manumitter are not prejudiced by any disherison; whereas it
is expressly declared in the senatusconsult that nominate
disherison does prejudice them as regards the estates of latins.
The more correct view therefore is that all that was done by
this senatusconsult was to declare that children of the manumitter, not individually disinherited, should be preferred to
65 stranger-heirs.   An emancipated son of a patron, consequently, who has been passed over in his testament, although
he may not have petitioned for possession of the estate of his
parent contrary to the tenor of the will, is yet preferred to
stranger-heirs in the estates of latins [manumitted by his

§ 64.   Comp. §§ 48, 58.

[1] G. and all eds.

[2] So G. and all eds.; the ms. has *idemque*.

[3] See ii, 254, note 1.

[4] K. u. S. think this word has crept in *per incuriam*, and should be deleted.

66 dibus in bonis latinorum potior habetur.   Item filia ceterique
sui heredes, licet iure ciuili inter ceteros exheredati sint, et
ab omni hereditate patris sui summoueantur, tamen in bonis
latinorum, nisi nominatim a parente fuerint exheredati, poti-
67 ores erunt extraneis heredibus.   Item ad liberos qui ab
hereditate parentis se abstinuerunt,[1] *nihilo minus bona* latinorum pertinent; (*nam hi quoque* exheredati nullo modo dici possunt, non magis quam qui testamento silentio praeteriti sunt).
68   Ex his omnibus satis illud apparet, si is qui latinum *fecerit,*
69 — — — — — — — — —.   Item *illud quoque* constare
uidetur, si solos liberos ex disparibus partibus *patronus* — —
— — — — tant ad eos pertinere, quia nullo interueniente
70 extraneo herede senatusconsulto locus non est.   *Sed* si cum

---

66 parent].   A daughter, too, and other *sui heredes,* although
they may have been disinherited in a *ceteri* clause according
to the requirements of the *ius ciuile,* and thus excluded from
any participation in their father's inheritance, are nevertheless preferred to his stranger-heirs in the estates of latins of
his, unless they have been nominately disinherited by him.
67 Further, the estates of latins belong to children notwithstanding they may have held aloof from their parent's inheritance;
for such children can no more be said to have been individually disinherited than can those who have been passed
over by a testator in silence.
68   From all this it is sufficiently evident that he who has
made his slave a latin — — — — — — — — —.
69 Further, *this also seems to be the general opinion,—that if a
patron have left his children his sole heirs, but instituted them
to unequal shares, [the sounder view is that of those who think
[that the estate of a deceased latin will belong to them in
[proportion to their shares of the inheritance];* for, as there
is now no question of the intervention of a stranger-heir,
70 the senatusconsult does not apply.   But if, along with his

---

§ 67. A few letters in the MS. are altogether illegible, and others uncertain. The reading given above is
that of K. u. S.; there have been
others proposed, but all are substantially to the same effect.
    [1] Comp. ii, 158.
§ 68. With exception of the first word
(*fecerit*), the last line of p. 143 of the
MS. is illegible; so, with the exception of a word here and there, are
the first twenty-one lines of p. 144.
§ 69. Last line and a half of p. 144 ille-

gible. P. suggests—patronus *heredes reliquerit, rectius existimare
qui latinum pro hereditariis partibus* putant ad eos, etc. K. u. S.
propose—patronus *heredes instituerit, ex eisdem partibus bona latini,
si patri heredes existant,* ad eos,
etc. Hu. proposes—patronus *heredes reliquerit, quod pro hereditariis
partibus, non pro uirilibus, bona
latina* putant ad eos, etc.
§ 70. Caelius (spelt *Selius* in the MS.)
Sabinus flourished in the reign of

liberis suis etiam extraneum heredem patronus reliquerit,
Caelius Sabinus ait tota bona pro uirilibus partibus ad liberos
defuncti pertinere, quia cum extraneus heres interuenit non
habet lex Iunia locum, sed senatusconsultum; Iauolenus
autem ait tantum eam partem ex senatusconsulto liberos
patroni pro uirilibus partibus habituros esse quam extranei
heredes ante senatusconsultum lege Iunia habituri essent,
reliquas uero partes pro hereditariis partibus ad eos pertinere.
71 Item quaeritur an hoc senatusconsultum ad eos patroni liberos
pertineat qui ex filia nepteue procreantur, id est ut nepos
meus ex filia potior sit in bonis latini mei quam extraneus
heres; item [an] ad maternos latinos hoc senatusconsultum
pertineat quaeritur, id est ut in bonis latini materni potior sit
patronae filius quam heres extraneus matris. Cassio placuit
utroque casu locum esse senatusconsulto; sed huius sententiam plerique inprobant, quia senatus de his liberis patrono-

---

children, the patron have also left a stranger-heir, Caelius
Sabinus maintains that the whole estate [of the deceased
latin] will belong to the patron's children in equal shares,
since, owing to the intervention of a stranger-heir, it is not
the Junian law but the senatusconsult that comes into play;
Javolenus, however, holds that under the senatusconsult the
patron's children will take in equal shares so much only of
the [latin's] estate as, before the senatusconsult and under
the Junian law, the stranger-heir would have been entitled to,
and that the remainder will belong to them in proportion to
71 their shares in their father's inheritance.   Then it is asked
whether this senatusconsult applies to those descendants of a
patron who are the issue of a daughter or granddaughter,—
that is, whether my grandson by my daughter is to be preferred to a stranger-heir in the estate of a latin of mine? It
is also asked whether the senatusconsult applies to a mother's
latins,—that is, whether the son of a patroness has a better
right to the estate of a latin of hers than her stranger-heirs?
Cassius held that in both cases there was room for the
senatusconsult. But this opinion of his is disapproved by
most jurists, on the ground that the senatusconsult does not
have in view those descendants of a patron who really are

Vespasian (fr. 2, § 47, D. *de orig. iur.* i,
2), and probably was a son of Masurius Sabinus referred to in i, 196, note
1. Iauolenus Priscus was his successor as chief of the Sabinian school.

§ 71. The Cassius here mentioned—C.
Cassius Longinus—was leader of the
Sabinian School immediately before
Caelius Sabinus; from him they got
their occasional name of Cassians.

rum¹ nihil sentiat qui aliam familiam sequerentur; idque ex
eo adparet quod nominatim exheredatos summouet; nam
uidetur de his sentire qui exheredari a parente solent si
heredes non instituantur; neque autem matri filium filiamue,
neque auo materno nepotem neptemue, si eum eamue heredem
non instituat, exheredare necesse est, siue de iure ciuili quaeramus, siue de edicto praetoris quo praeteritis liberis contra
tabulas testamenti bonorum possessio promittitur.

72   Aliquando tamen ciuis Romanus libertus tamquam latinus
moritur, uelut si latinus saluo iure patroni ab imperatore ius
Quiritium consecutus fuerit; *item*¹ si latinus inuito uel ignorante patrono ius Quiritium ab imperatore consecutus sit;
quibus casibus ut diuus Traianus constituit,¹ dum uiuit iste
libertus, ceteris ciuibus Romanis libertis similis est et iustos
liberos procreat, moritur autem latini iure, nec ei liberi eius
heredes esse possunt; et in hoc tantum habet testamenti

-----

members of a different family.   And this is evident from the
fact that it excludes children individually disinherited, and
thus seems to have in view only such children as it is the
custom for a parent to disinherit if he is not instituting them
heirs.   But it is not necessary for a mother to disinherit her
son or daughter if she is not instituting him or her as her
heir, nor for a maternal grandfather to disinherit his grandson
or granddaughter: it is unnecessary whether we look to the
ius ciuile or to the edict of the praetor promising possession
of an estate contrary to the tenor of a testament to children
passed over in it.

72   Sometimes a freedman that is a Roman citizen dies as if he
were a latin, as, for instance, when a latin has obtained from
the emperor a grant of citizenship under reservation of patronal
rights; as also when a latin has obtained the *ius Quiritium*
from the emperor against his patron's will or without his
knowledge.   In those cases, as was enacted by the late
emperor Trajan, so long as such a freedman lives he is in like
position with all other citizen freedmen, and the children he
begets are lawful children; yet he dies as a latin, and his
children cannot be his heirs; his testamentary capacity is

-----

¹ The MS. has *patronarum*; in
either form the word is probably a
gloss, in the latter an inaccurate
one.
§ 72.   Comp. § 4, tit. I. sfd.
¹ After *fuerit* the MS. has *nam ut*
diuus Traianus constituit, a text that
makes *quibus casibus* unmeaning.
Hu., altering the *nam* into *item*,
transposes the other four words, and
by placing them after *quibus casibus*
restores these their value.

factionem, ut patronum heredem instituat eique si heres esse
73 noluerit alium substituere possit.   Et quia hac constitutione uidebatur effectum ut ne umquam isti homines tamquam
ciues Romani morerentur, quamuis eo iure postea *usi* essent
quo uel ex lege *Aelia Sentia* uel ex senatusconsulto ciues
Romani essent, diuus Hadrianus, iniquitate rei motus, auctor
fuit senatusconsulti faciendi, ut qui ignorante uel recusante
patrono ab imperatore ius Quiritium consecuti essent, si eo
iure postea usi essent quo ex lege Aelia Sentia uel ex senatusconsulto, si latini *mansissent*,[1] ciuitatem Romanam consequerentur, proinde ipsi haberentur ac si lege Aelia Sentia uel
senatusconsulto ad ciuitatem Romanam peruenissent.
74   Eorum autem quos lex Aelia Sentia dediticiorum numero
facit, bona modo quasi *ciuium* libertorum, modo quasi latino-
75 rum ad patronos pertinent.   Nam eorum bona qui, si in
aliquo uitio non essent, manumissi ciues Romani futuri essent,
quasi ciuium Romanorum patronis eadem lege tribuuntur.

---

limited to this,—that he may institute his patron as his heir,
and substitute some third party in his place in the event of
73 his declining the inheritance.   As it seemed to be the effect
of this constitution [of Trajan's] that such freedmen could
never die as Roman citizens, even although they afterwards
took advantage of the procedure for becoming citizens either
under the Aelia-Sentian law or under the senatusconsult, the
late emperor Hadrian, moved thereto by the unfairness of the
case, induced the senate to decree that if those who had
obtained the *ius Quiritium* from the emperor, without the
knowledge or notwithstanding the objections of their patrons,
afterwards made use of the procedure whereby, had they
remained latins, they would have acquired Roman citizenship
either under the Aelia-Sentian law or under the senatusconsult, they were to be regarded as if they had in fact
attained citizenship under one or other of these enactments.
74   The estates of those whom the Aelia-Sentian law ranks
as dediticians belong to their patrons, sometimes after the
manner of the estates of citizen freedmen, sometimes after the
75 manner of those of latins.   The estates of those who, had
there been no blemish on their characters, would, on manumission, have been citizens, are by that statute given to their
patrons, just as if they were the estates of citizens.   For

---

§ 73. Comp. i, §§ 29, 66-71.   § 74. Comp. i, 13.
   [1] So G. and all eds.; the ms. has   § 75. Comp. i, §§ 25, 26; Vlp. xx, §§
manumissi essent.   14, 15.

non tamen *hi* habent etiam testamenti factionem : nam id
plerisque placuit, nec inmerito : nam incredibile uidebatur
pessimae condicionis hominibus uoluisse legis latorem testa-
76 menti faciendi ius concedere.   Eorum uero bona qui, si non
in aliquo uitio essent, manumissi futuri latini essent, proinde
tribuuntur patronis ac si latini decessissent : nec me praeterit
non satis in ea re legis latorem uoluntatem suam uerbis
expressisse.

77   Videamus autem et de ea successione quae nobis ex
78 emptione bonorum conpetit.   Bona autem ueneunt aut
uiuorum aut mortuorum : uiuorum, ueluti eorum qui frauda-
tionis causa latitant nec absentes defenduntur ;[1] item eorum
qui ex lege Iulia bonis cedunt ;[2] item iudicatorum post

---

dediticians have no testamentary capacity,—so most have
held, and not without reason ; for it seemed incredible that
the legislature could have meant to concede the right of
76 making a testament to men of the basest condition.   The
estates of those again who, had they been of unblemished
character, would, when manumitted, have been latins, are
given to their patrons just as if they had died latins.   It does
not escape me, however, that on this point the author of the
enactment has not expressed his meaning quite satisfactorily.

77   Let us consider now the succession that devolves on us by
78 *emptio bonorum.*   It is the estates of insolvent debtors,
whether living or dead, that are thus brought to sale.   There
is sale of the estates of living debtors in the case of those who
fraudulently keep out of the way of their creditors and are
not defended in their absence ; of those who have ceded their
effects under the Julian law ; and of judgment-debtors after

§§ 77-81. Comp. tit. I. *DE SVCCESSIO-*
NIBVS SVBLATIS (iii, 12).

§ 77. Comp. pr. tit. I. afd. *Emptio*
bonorum was purchase of the estate
of an insolvent, the purchaser becoming his universal successor.
Gai. (iv, 35) attributes its introduction to Publ. Rutilius, generally
understood to be P. Rutilius Rufus,
the celebrated orator, jurist, and
statesman, who became consul in
649 | 104.

§ 78. [1] Comp. Cic. *pro. Quint.* xix, 60,
xxiii, 74 ; Vlp. in fr. 7, D. *quib. ex*

causa in poss. eatur (xlii, 4) ; Th.
iii, 12, pr.

[2] Comp. tit. D. *de cess. bonor.*
(xlii, 3) ; tit. C. *qui bonis cedere*
possunt (vii, 71).   It is doubtful
whether the *lex Iulia* here referred
to was the work of Julius Caesar or
of Augustus ; more probably it was
the latter, as the *lex Coloniae Iuliae*
Genetiuae (i, 22, note 1), due to the
former, preserves unmodified the
rigorous system of personal execution previously in use.

tempus · quod eis partim lege XII tabularum partim edicto
praetoris ad expediendam pecuniam tribuitur.³ mortuorum
bona ueneunt ueluti eorum quibus certum est neque heredes
neque bonorum possessores neque ullum alium iustum succes-
79 sorem existere.⁴   Si quidem uiui bona ueneant, iubet ea
praetor per dies continuos XXX *possideri et* ¹ proscribi, si uero
mortui, *per* dies XV ; postea iubet conuenire creditores et ex
eorum numero ² magistrum creari, id est eum per quem bona
ueneant: *idque*, si uiui bona ueneant, in diebus *X fieri* iubet,³
si mortui, in dimidio.⁴   *diebus itaque uiui* bona *XXXX*,⁵ mortui
uero XX,⁶ emptori addici iubet.⁷ quare autem tardius uiuen-

---

expiry of the period which, partly under the law of the
Twelve Tables and partly under the praetor's edict, is allowed
them for procuring the money.   There is sale of the estates
of deceased debtors in the case, for example, of persons to
whom it is certain that there will be neither heir, nor *bonorum*
79 *possessor*, nor any other lawful successor.   If it be the estate
of a living debtor that is being sold, the praetor orders it to
be taken and held possession of, and publicly advertised, for
thirty continuous days; or if it be the estate of a deceased
debtor, for fifteen days.   He then orders the creditors to meet,
and one of their number to be appointed *magister*, the party,
that is to say, by whom the estate is to be sold; and the sale
itself he orders to be carried through in *ten* days if the estate
be that of a living debtor, and in half that time if it be that
of one who is dead.   He thus orders that the estate of a
living debtor shall be adjudged to the purchaser in *forty* days,

---

³ The allusion is to the praetorian
amendment of the old procedure-in-
execution of the XII Tables, upon
which we get a little light from the
lex Rubria, chaps. 21, 22 (Bruns,
pp. 86-91).

⁴ Comp. ii, §§ 154, 158.

§ 79. Comp. Cic. *pro Quint.* viii, 30;
Th. iii, 12, pr.

¹ The MS. has *possederit;* a reading which P. retains, and justifies by
introducing certain words, making
the passage run—*iubet ea praetor,
[postquam ea aliquis ex edicto] per
dies continuos XXX possederit, proscribi.*

² The MS. has *ex eo numero.*

³ This is Mommsen's reading (in
K. u. S. footnote). The MS. has—
itaque, si uiui bona ueneant, in die-
bus V fieri iubet. K. (*Krit. Versuche*,
p. 137), reading the V as a contraction of *uenditionem*, proposes—*itaque, si uiui bona ueneant, in diebus
[X bonorum] uenditionem fieri iubet.*
Hu. has—*itaque . . . in diebus [X
legem bonorum] uendendorum fieri
iubet.*

⁴ So the MS.; Hu., dropping the
dimidio, utilizing the next word, and
interjecting v, makes it *in diebus V*.

⁵ The MS. has XXX, an obvious
error.

⁶ Hu. has—*[die] tandem uiui bona
XX, mortui uero X*, etc.

⁷ The *addictio* was the act of the
magister. The same word was used
to express the knocking-down of a
lot by an auctioneer to the highest
bidder at a sale (Cic. *pro Caec.* vi, 16).

tium bonorum uenditio conpleri iubetur illa ratio est, quia
de uiuis curandum erat ne facile bonorum uenditiones
paterentur.[8]

80   Neque autem bonorum *possessorum* neque *bonorum empto-
rum res* pleno iure *fiunt*, sed in bonis efficiuntur ; *ex iure
Quiritium* autem ita demum adquiruntur si usuceperunt.
interdum quidem bonorum emptoribus *ne usus* quidem *capio
contingit, ueluti si per eos* — — — — — — — — —.[1]

81   *Item quae debita* — — — — aut ipse debuit, neque bonorum
possessor *neque* bonorum emptor ipso iure debet — — — —

---

and that of a deceased debtor in twenty. The reason why the
sale of the estates of living debtors is ordered to be completed
more slowly is, that care ought to be taken, where living
persons are concerned, that they have not to submit to sale
of their estates unnecessarily.

80   Neither in *bonorum possessio* nor in *bonorum uenditio* do the
things thereby acquired belong to the possessors or purchasers
in full ownership,—they are theirs only *in bonis ;* but they
acquire them eventually in quiritarian right by usucapion.
In the case of *bonorum emptores*, however, usucapion is sometimes impossible, as for instance when — — — — — — —.

81   [*What was due to him to whom the estate formerly belonged*], or
due by him, is neither due *ipso iure* to the *bonorum possessor*
or *bonorum emptor* [*nor due by him ; consequently it is neces-*

---

[8] The proper reading of this par.
(from *idque* down to *addici iubet*)
is much controverted. Th., in his
account of *bonor. emptio*, specifies
three acts of the *magistrate* in reference to the insolvent's estate, viz.
(1) grant of *bonorum possessio*, (2)
order upon the creditors to elect a
trustee and advertise the bankruptcy, and (3) approval of the
price and the conditions of sale ;
between each of those acts, he says,
there was an interval of days, which
he leaves undefined ; and then, after
a third interval, came (4) the *addictio*. As against this we have in
the *notae* of Valer. Probus—B. E. E.
P. P. V. Q. I. (*bona ex edicto possideri
proscribi uenireque iubebo*), and the
bona possiderei proscreibei ueneire of
the *L. Rubria de Gallia Cisalpina*,
c. 22 (Bruns, p. 91), which both
point to three orders by the prae-

tor (though not the same as are
mentioned by Th.), viz. to take possession, to advertise, and to sell ;
and these orders imply only two
intervals, which may correspond to
those of Gaius, viz. 30 + 10 = 40,
and 15 + 5 = 20. See also Cic.
ad Att. vi, 1.

§ 80. Comp. Paul. in fr. 2, § 19, D.
pro emptore (xli, 4) ; Th. iii, 12, pr.
[1] Two lines illegible, with exception of the words *bonorum emptor*.
See Vlp. in fr. 7, § 3, D. *quib. ex
caus. in poss. eatur* (xlii, 4).

§ 81. Comp. iv, §§ 33, 145 ; Th. iii, 12,
pr. These indicate the drift of the
passage, viz. that in regard to what
was due to or by a *bonor. possessor*
or a *bonor. emptor*, neither held the
position of creditor or debtor in
strict law, yet nevertheless might
sue or be sued by means of *utiles
actiones ;* (see ii, 78, note 1).

de omnibus rebus — — — — *in sequenti commentario* proponemus.

82   Sunt autem etiam alterius generis successiones quae neque
lege XII tabularum neque praetoris edicto, sed eo iure [*quod*]
83 consensu receptum est introductae sunt.   *Ecce* enim [1] cum
paterfamilias se in adoptionem dedit, mulierue in manum
conuenit,[2] omnes eius res incorporales et corporales, quaeque
ei debitae sunt, patri adoptiuo coemptionatoriue adquiruntur,
exceptis his quae per capitis deminutionem pereunt, quales
sunt *ususfructus*,[3] operarum obligatio (*libertinorum*) quae per
iusiurandum contracta est,[4] et (*lites quae aguntur*)[5] legitimo
84 iudicio.[6]   Ex diuerso quod is debuit (*qui se in*) adoptionem
dedit *quaeue* in *manum conuenit*, (*non*) *transit ad* coemptionatorem aut ad patrem adoptiuum, *nisi si* hereditarium aes
alienum (*fuerit. tunc*) *enim, quia* ipse pater adoptiuus aut
coemptionator heres fit, directo tenetur iure ; (*is uero*) qui se

---

[*sary that he sue or be sued by means of* utiles actiones, *which*]
we shall give an account of in our next Commentary.
82   There are besides successions of another sort, which owe
their introduction neither to the Twelve Tables nor to the
praetor's edict, but to those rules that have been received by
83 general consent.   Thus when a *paterfamilias* has given
himself in adoption, or a woman has passed *in manum*, all their
belongings, corporeal and incorporeal, and everything that is
due to them, become acquisitions of the adoptive father or
the *coemptionator*, except those that come to an end by *capitis
deminutio*, such as a right of usufruct, undertakings of service
on the part of freedmen contracted by oath, and suits pro-
84 ceeding in a *iudicium legitimum*.   Contrariwise, [liability
for] what was due by him who has given himself in adoption,
or her who has passed *in manum*, does not pass to the *coemptionator* or adoptive father, unless the debt be a hereditary
one ; in that case, as the adoptive father or the *coemptionator* himself becomes heir, he becomes directly liable, he

---

§§ 82-84.   Comp. tit. I. *DE ADQVISI-*
TIONE PER ADROGATIONEM (iii, 10).
§ 82.   Pr. tit. I. afd.
§ 83.   Comp. §§ 1, 2, tit. I. afd.
    [1] So the Inst.; the MS. has *etenim*.
    [2] Comp. Cic. *Top.* iv, 23.
    [3] P., following the Inst., reads—
quales sunt [*ius agnationis, usus,*]
ususfructus.
    [4] Comp. Vlp. in fr. 7, D. *de oper.
lib.* (xxxviii, 1).

[5] Studemund's suggestion, as ac-
cordant with the traces visible in
the MS.   K. u. S. and Hu., following Rudorff and Gou., and on
the authority of fr. 58, D. *de
O. et A.* (xliv, 7), read *lites con-
testatae.*
    [6] Comp. iv, 104.
§ 84.   Comp. iv, §§ 88, 80; Vlp. in fr.
2, pr. § 1, D. *de cap. min.;* § 3, tit.
I. afd.

adoptandum dedit, quaeue in manum conuenit, desinit esse
heres. De eo uero quod *proprio nomine* eae personae debue-
rint, licet neque pater adoptiuus teneatur neque coemptionator, (*et ne*) ipse quidem qui se in adoptionem *dedit* (*uel*)
quae in manum conuenit maneat obligatus obligataue, *quia
scilicet* [1] per capitis deminutionem *liberetur*, tamen in eum
eamue utilis actio datur,[2] *rescissa* capitis deminutione, et si
aduersus hanc actionem non defendantur, quae bona eorum
futura fuissent si se alieno iuri non subiecissent uniuersa
uendere creditoribus praetor permittit.

85   [*Si quis*] legitimam *hereditatem* (*ei delatam, antequam cer*)-
nat aut pro herede gerat, alii in iure cedat, pleno iure fit ille

---

who has given himself in adoption, or she who has passed
in manum, ceasing to be heir. As regards, however, debts
due by such persons on their own account, although neither
the adopted father nor *coemptionator* is liable, and neither the
man who has given himself in adoption nor the woman who
has passed *in manum* continues bound by the obligation,
seeing they have been relieved from it by their *capitis
deminutio*, an *utilis actio* is nevertheless given against him or
her, the *capitis deminutio* being held rescinded; and if no
defence be entered for them against this action, the praetor
will allow their creditors to sell the whole goods and effects
which would have been theirs had they not subjected themselves to another person's right.

85   *If an individual, before he has formally declared his acceptance of an inheritance that has devolved upon him by law, or*

---

[1] The MS. has *si* after this word.
[2] See ii, 78, note.
§§ 85-87. Comp. ii, §§ 34-37, of which
these are substantially a repetition.
P. considers them spurious, and
an interpolation by some scholar of
Gaius'; and consequently relegates
them to an appendix. But his
argument against their authenticity
—that neither *cernere* nor *pro
herede gerere* can be used with propriety in regard to a *legitima hereditas*—is very inconclusive; for in
ii, § 167, we find Gaius saying—*is
qui ... ab intestato legitimo iure ad
hereditatem uocatur, potest aut cer-*

*nendo aut pro herede gerendo ...
heres fieri.*
§§ 85, 86. Comp. §§ 34, 36; Vlp. xix,
§§ 12-15. Stud. observes that lines
5, 6, and 8 of p. 150 of the MS.
seem to have been written in ver-
milion. The fifth is entirely illegible; of the sixth only the words
legitimam h. are decipherable; of
the eighth only the first half is
legible. The meaning, however, is
so obvious that no difficulty is experienced in supplying deficiencies.
The readings of K. u. S. and Hu.
are substantially the same as that
given above.

heres cui cessa est hereditas, (*proinde ac si ipse per*) legem ad
hereditatem uocaretur; quodsi posteaquam heres extiterit
cesserit, adhuc heres manet, et ob id creditoribus ipse tenebitur; sed res corporales transferet proinde ac si singulas in
iure cessisset, debita uero pereunt, eoque modo debitores
86 hereditarii lucrum faciunt.   Idem iuris est si testamento
scriptus heres, posteaquam heres extiterit, in iure cesserit
hereditatem; ante aditam uero hereditatem cedendo nihil agit.
87 Suus autem et necessarius heres an aliquid agant in iure
cedendo quaeritur: nostri praeceptores nihil eos agere existimant; diuersae scholae auctores idem eos agere putant quod
ceteri post aditam hereditatem; nihil enim interest utrum
aliquis cernendo aut pro herede gerendo heres fiat, an iuris
necessitate hereditati adstringatur.

88   (*Nunc transeamus*) ad obligationes, quarum summa diuisio

---

before he has behaved as heir, transfer it to a third party by
in iure cessio, he to whom the inheritance is thus ceded
becomes heir, with all the rights of heir, *just as if he himself*
had been called to the inheritance as heir-at-law.   If, however,
it is not until after he has assumed the character of heir that
he has ceded the inheritance, he still remains heir, and it is
he consequently that will be liable to the deceased's creditors;
the corporeals he must hand over, as if they had been ceded
individually; but claims are extinguished, and the debtors of
86 the deceased thus become gainers.   The law is the same if
a testamentary heir transfer the inheritance by *in iure cessio*
after he has taken the position of heir; by ceding before he
87 has entered, however, he really does nothing.   Whether the
suus or the necessary heir does anything effectual by ceding
an inheritance in court is a matter of controversy.   Our
authorities think that they do not.   Those of the other school
think that their act has the same effect as that of other heirs
ceding the inheritance after entry; it being of no moment
whether a man become heir by formal acceptance or by
behaviour as heir, or be astricted to the inheritance by necessity of law.

88   *Now let us pass* to obligations.   Their primary division is

§ 87. Comp. ii, 87.
§§ 88, 89.   Comp. tit. I. DE OBLIGA-
TIONIBVS (iii, 13).

§ 88.   The first two words, unwritten in
the MS., are supplied from pr. tit.
I. afd.

in duas species diducitur: omnis enim obligatio uel ex contractu nascitur uel ex delicto.

89   Et prius uideamus de his quae ex contractu nascuntur. harum autem quattuor genera sunt: aut enim re[1] contrahitur obligatio aut uerbis aut litteris aut consensu.

90   Re contrahitur obligatio uelut mutui datione: [*mutui autem*

---

into two classes; for every obligation originates either in contract or in delict.

89   First let us consider those that arise from contract. Of these there are four genera; for an obligation is contracted either by thing done, by [spoken] words, by writing, or by consent.

90   An obligation is contracted by thing done by giving a

§ 89.   Comp. § 2, tit. I. afd. The verbal and literal contracts are often spoken of by the civilians as formal contracts, in contradistinction to the real and consensual ones, which they call material. In the verbal and literal contracts the obligation was created by words of style, written or spoken, no matter whether or not any substantial *causa obligandi* underlay them. The absence of such substantial *causa* might possibly afford an equitable defence to any action upon the contract; but *ipso iure* it was valid and effectual simply on the strength of the formal words made use of by the parties.

Earlier than any of those four classes were the *nexum* and the *iusiurandum*,—one a civil, the other a religious contract (or form of contracting), and both formal. The *nexum* is referred to by Gai. only in connection with the discharge of an obligation thereby created (iii, 173); the *iusiurandum* he refers to in § 84, in connection with the special case in which it was still employed; but practically both were long out of date. The *nexum* has been the subject of many disquisitions, and opinions about it are conflicting; the more notable theories are summarised, and the references to it in the ancient writers collected, by Danz, *R. R.* ii, pp. 18 f. Danz himself (*Sacrale Schutz*), and Voigt in his *Ius Naturale, etc.*, are the leading writers on the *iusiurandum;* see a *resumé* of Danz's views, and

references to his authorities, ancient and modern, in his *R. R.* ii, pp. 32 f. See further, note to § 92, last paragraph.

[1] To translate *res* as 'the thing' (Sandars) or 'the thing itself' (Abdy and Walker) is too narrow, while 'performance' (Poste) is ambiguous. It is really equivalent to *factum*, and appropriately rendered by 'act' (Hunter, p. 281). It is in this sense Gai. says that obligations *ex delicto* are all of one and the same genus (§ 182); they all arise *re*,—by thing done; see Gai. in fr. 4 D. *de O. et A.* (xliv, 7). It is in the same sense that the so-called innominate contracts are spoken of as real, whether falling under the category *do ut des, do ut facias, facio ut des*, or *facio ut facias;* see fr. 5, § 1, D. *de praescr.* *uerb.* (xix, 5). There were other obligations that were said to be created *re*,—by facts and circumstances, such as those arising from vicinage, from joint ownership, from jettison at sea, from *negotiorum gestio*, etc., some of which are dealt with in tit. I. *de obl. q. ex contr.* (iii, 27).

§§ 90, 91.   Comp. tit. I. *QVIBVS MODIS RE CONTRAHITVR OBLIGATIO* (iii, 14).   Just. enumerates four real contracts—*mutuum, commodatum, depositum, pignus;* Gai. mentions only the first.   Commodate, deposit, and pledge were, long before his time, all well known as transactions of daily life, and are frequently referred to in his pages.   But their contractual

[datio] proprie in his [fere] rebus contingit quae pondere numero mensura constant, qualis est pecunia numerata uinum oleum frumentum aes argentum aurum; quas res aut numerando aut metiendo aut pendendo in hoc damus, ut accipientium fiant et quandoque nobis non eaedem sed aliae eiusdem naturae reddantur : unde etiam mutuum appellatum est, quia quod ita tibi a me datum est ex meo tuum fit.   Is quoque qui non debitum accepit ab eo qui per errorem soluit re obligatur ; nam proinde ei condici potest SI PARET EVM DARE OPORTERE,[1] ac si mutuum accepisset. unde quidam putant pupillum aut mulierem, cui sine tutoris auctoritate non debitum per errorem datum est, non teneri condictione non magis quam mutui datione.[2] sed haec species obligationis non uidetur ex con-

---

loan for consumption. This occurs for the most part only in the case of things that are weighed, counted, or measured, such as money, wine, oil, corn, bronze, silver, gold. In transferring such things by number, measure, or weight, we do so with the intent that they shall become the property of the receiver, and that not the identical articles, but others of the same sort, shall some time or other be returned to us. Hence the word *mutuum;* for what is thus given by me to you, from mine becomes thine.   He also is laid under obligation. by thing done who has taken payment of what is not really due to him from a party paying it in mistake ; for on this ground a condition will lie against him, with an intention 'if it appear that he ought to give,' in the same way as if he had received the money in loan. Accordingly some are of opinion that a pupil or a woman, to either of whom, without tutorial *auctoritas,* something has been paid in error that was not really due, is no more liable in a *condictio indebiti* than [on an action] for money lent. But this sort of obligation is not to be regarded as arising from contract ; for he who gives a thing by way of payment means rather to distract than

characteristics were not yet well settled ; commodate and pledge were still often dealt with as varieties of *creditum* (Vlp. in fr. 1, fr. 4, § 1, D. *de reb. cred.* xii, 1), giving rise to a *certi condictio* in the same way as *mutuum;* while deposit had not yet been altogether freed from the impress of the rule of the xii Tables (Paul. in *Collat.* x, 7, § 11), which regarded failure of duty on the part

14

of a depositary as a delict rather than a breach of contract.
§ 90. Gai. in fr. 1, 2, D. *de O. et A.* (xliv, 7), from which the interpolated words in ital. are supplied ; pr. tit. I. afd. *Fere* seems to be a gloss.
§ 91. § 1, tit. 1. afd. Comp. § 6, I. *de obl. q. quasi ex contr.* (iii, 27).
[1] Comp. iv, §§ 5, 41.
[2] Comp. ii, §§ 80-84.

tractu consistere, quia is qui soluendi animo dat magis dis-
trahere uult negotium quam contrahere.

92   Verbis obligatio fit ex interrogatione et responsione, ueluti DARI SPONDES? SPONDEO, DABIS? DABO, PROMITTIS? PRO-
MITTO, FIDEPROMITTIS? FIDEPROMITTO, FIDEIVBES? FIDEIVBEO,

---

to contract, [*i.e.* rather to dissolve a contract than to enter
into one.]

92   A verbal obligation is created by question and answer thus:
'Do you religiously engage that such or such a thing shall be
given?' 'I religiously engage [*spondeo*];' 'Will you give?' 'I
will give;' 'Do you promise?' 'I promise;' 'Do you promise
on your plighted faith?' 'I promise on my plighted faith [*fide-
[promitto*];' 'Do you authorize on your plighted faith?' 'I
authorize on my plighted faith [*fideiubeo*];' 'Will you do?'

§§ 92-96. Comp. tit. I. *DE VERBORVM
OBLIGATIONE* (iii, 15).
§ 92. Comp. pr. § 1, tit. I. afd.; Paul.
ii, 3.

It is difficult in translation to
convey an idea of the differences
between those formulae. *Spondes ?
spondeo*, was the oldest of them all,
and even in the time of Gai. still
affected by peculiarities (see §§ 93,
120) that testified to its antiquity
and its origin in the *iusiurandum*.
It might be employed either between
the creditor and the principal debtor,
or between the creditor and a surety
(§§ 115, 116).

Promittis ? promitto, became the
usual words of style in stipulation,
unless when coupled with *dare;* so
that the debtor in it ordinarily got
the name of *promissor* (§ 100, etc.).
But there is some reason to believe
that originally they amounted to a
minor form of oath, *promittere manum* (Serv. *ad Aen.* iv, 103), *por-
rigere dextram* (Plin. *H. N.* xi,
45, § 250), being to appeal to Fides,
whose seat was in the right hand
(Liv. i, 21; xxiii, 9; Serv. *ad Aen.*
iii, 607).

The simplicity of *dabis? dabo,
facies? faciam,* shows them to be of
later introduction than the two
former. *Dare* meant to give in
property (§ 99; iv, 4); *facere* applied
to any other act, positive or negative, including giving otherwise
than in property (see iv, 2, note 2;
fr. 175, fr. 189, fr. 218, D. *de V. S.*
1, 16).

*Fidepromitto (i.e. idem fide mea
promitto), fideiubeo (i.e. fide mea
iubeo),* were styles used only by
sureties, the former when the undertaking of the principal debtor arose
from verbal contract, the latter no
matter how the principal debtor had
contracted (§ 119). The force of
them lay in the *tua* and *mea:
idem fide TVA promittis, iubes?*
(§§ 112, 116); *fide MEA promitto,
iubeo.*

The phrase 'plighted faith' in
the translation seems justified by the
fidem obligare, fidem dare of the
lay writers; see Cic. *Phil.* v, 18,
§ 51; *Cato maj.* xx, 75; *de off.* xiii,
39; Plaut. *Persa*, v, 242. This *fides,*
which Cic. calls *fundamentum iusti-
tiae,* and which he defines as *dicto-
rum conuentorumque constantia et
ueritas,* truthfulness in and adherence to one's assurances and agreements (*de off.* i, 7, § 21), was reckoned
by the Romans of the Republic
the highest of the virtues. To rely
upon it was *credere,* a derivative
from the Sansc. *crat,* trust or belief,
and *dhá,* Gr. θε, to place (A. W.
Schlegel, as quoted by Pernice, i,
409, n. 8). To break it, *fidem fallere,* might not entitle the injured
creditor to relief by action if it had
been plighted informally, but the
defaulter incurred the risk of infamy
with all its serious consequences;
and thus it was that Rome progressed
so long with an imperfect system of
contracts. See § 89, note; § 119a,
note 1.

93 FACIES? FACIAM.   Sed haec quidem uerborum obligatio
DARI SPONDES? SPONDEO propria ciuium Romanorum est;
ceterae uero iuris gentium sunt, itaque inter omnes homines,
siue ciues Romanos siue peregrinos, ualent; et quamuis ad
Graecam uocem expressae fuerint, uelut hoc modo : [Δώσεις;
[Δώσω· Ὁμολογεῖς; Ὁμολογῶ· Πίστει κελεύεις; Πίστει κελεύω·
[Ποιήσεις; Ποιήσω], [etiam haec] tamen inter ciues Romanos
ualent, si modo Graeci sermonis intellectum habeant; et e
contrario quamuis Latine enuntientur, tamen etiam inter
peregrinos ualent si modo Latini sermonis intellectum habeant.
at illa uerborum obligatio DARI SPONDES? SPONDEO adeo
propria ciuium Romanorum est, ut ne quidem in Graecum
sermonem per interpretationem proprie transferri possit,
94 quamuis dicatur a Graeca uoce figurata esse.[1]   Vnde dicitur
uno casu hoc uerbo peregrinum quoque obligari posse, uelut
si imperator noster principem alicuius peregrini populi de
pace ita interroget: PACEM FVTVRAM SPONDES? uel ipse
eodem modo interrogetur : quod nimium subtiliter dictum est,
quia si quid aduersus pactionem fiat, non ex stipulatu agitur,

---

93 ' I will do.'   The verbal obligation by the words *dari spondes?
spondeo* is peculiar to Roman citizens; the others are *iuris
gentium*, and valid between any persons, whether citizens or
peregrins. Even when expressed in Greek thus—δώσεις; δώσω·
ὁμολογεῖς; ὁμολογῶ· πίστει κελεύεις; πίστει κελεύω· ποιήσεις;
ποιήσω, they are valid between Roman citizens, provided they
understand that language; just as when conceived in Latin
they will be binding as between peregrins who understand
the Latin language.   But the verbal obligation ' *dari spondes ?
spondeo*' is so peculiarly Roman that it cannot adequately be
rendered in Greek, notwithstanding that the word *spondeo* is
94 said to be derived from that language.   There is one case,
however, in which it is held that this word *spondeo* will impose
an obligation even upon a foreigner, namely, when the emperor thus interrogates, or is interrogated by, the sovereign of
a foreign state in regard to a treaty of peace : ' Do you religiously engage, *spondes*, to be at peace with us in future ?'   But
this is too ingeniously put; for if there be a violation of the
treaty, redress is had by the arbitrament of war and not by

§ 93. Comp. §§ 119, 179; § 1, tit. I.
afd.; Th. iii, 15, § 1, from which
the Greek words, wanting as usual
in the ms., are supplied.
[1]Cp. Fest. v. *Sponders* (Bruns, p.

268). The Latin *spondeo, sponsio*,
were said to be derived from the Greek
σπένδω,σπονδαί,which speaks for their
original religious significance.
§ 94. Comp. Liv. ix, §§ 5, 41.

95 sed iure belli res uindicatur.   Illud dubitari potest, si quis
— — — — —.

96   Sunt et aliae obligationes — — — — — — — —.

96a — — — — — — — — iureiurando homines obligantur,

---

95 an *actio ex stipulatu.*   It may be doubted whether, if a man
[*were interrogated* promittis ? *and were to answer* ὁμολογῶ, *there*
[*would be any valid obligation.*]

96   There are other verbal obligations [*that may be contracted*
[*without any antecedent interrogatory, as when a woman—*
[*whether simply affianced and addressing the man she is to*
[*marry, or already married and addressing her husband—con-*
[*stitutes a dowry by* dotis dictio. *She may include in it either*
[*moveables or immoveables. And it is not only the woman her-*
[*self that may be thus laid under obligation ; so may her father ;*
[*and any debtor of hers may also, by* dotis dictio *addressed to*
[*her future husband, give the money he owes her the character of*
[*dowry. But these are the only three persons that, without*
[*any antecedent interrogatory, can lawfully be bound by* dotis
[dictio. *Any other person promising a dowry for a woman can*
[*become liable only according to the provisions of the common*
[*law ;* i.e. *he must answer to a question, and let his* promissio
96a [*follow a* stipulatio.   *There is another case in which a verbal*

---

§§ 95, 96. Only a few words are legible on p. 153.

§ 95. K. u. S., relying probably on fr. 1, §§ 2, 6, D. *de uerb. obl.* (xlv, 1), and Th. iii, 15, § 1, think the par. may have run either—Illud dubitari potest, si quis *interroganti 'dare spondes?' respondeat 'promitto' uel 'dabo,' an recte obligetur,* or—si quis *interroganti 'promittis?' respondeat* Ὁμολογῶ, *an recte obligetur.*

§ 96. Gai. seems in this and the next par. to have passed to the description of some other verbal contracts than those created by question and answer ; and, from one or two words distinguishable on p. 153, it would appear that he alluded in the first place to *dotis dictio.* Regarding this contract, which had become obsolete before the time of Justinian, we have the following in the Epit. ii, 9, § 3 :—'*Sunt et aliae obligationes quae nulla praecedente interrogatione contrahi possunt, id est ut si mulier, siue sponso uxor futura siue iam marito, dotem dicat. Quod tam de mobilibus rebus quam de fundis fieri*

potest. *Et non solum in hac obliga-tione ipsa mulier obligatur, sed et pater eius et debitor ipsius mulieris, si pecuniam quam illi debebat sponso creditricis ipse debitor in dotem dix-erit. Hae tantum tres personae nulla interrogatione praecedente pos-sunt dictione dotis legitime obligari. Aliae uero personae si pro muliere dotem uiro promiserint, communi iure obligari debent, id est ut et in-terrogata respondeant et stipulata promittant.'* Comp. Ter. *Andr.* v, 4, vv. 48, 49, and thereon Donat.; Vlp. vi, §§ 1, 2; Vlp. in fr. 19, § 2, D. *de aedil. ed.* (xxi, 1); Fr. Vat. §§ 99, 100; l. 4, Th. C. *de dot.* (iii, 13) ; l. 6, C. *de dotis prom.* (v, 2).

§ 96a. In the first and undecipherable part of this par., Gai. seems to have referred to the *iurata promissio ope-rarum liberti,* and in the second to have expressed the opinion that, as regards citizens at least, that was the only undertaking that was obli-gatory simply because fortified with an oath. Says the Epit. ii, 9, § 4: —'*Item et alio casu, uno loquente et*

utique cum quaeritur de iure Romanorum. nam apud peregrinos quid iuris sit, singularum ciuitatium iura requirentes
aliud *intellegere poterimus.*[1]

97   Si id quod dari stipulamur tale sit ut dari non possit,
inutilis est stipulatio, uelut si quis hominem liberum quem
seruum esse credebat, aut mortuum quem uiuum esse credebat,
aut locum sacrum uel religiosum quem putabat humani iuris
97a esse, dari stipuletur.   [*Item si quis rem quae in rerum*
[natura esse non potest, uelut hippocentaurum, stipuletur,] aeque
98 inutilis est stipulatio.   Item si quis sub ea condicione
stipuletur quae existere non potest, ueluti 'si digito caelum
tetigerit,' inutilis est stipulatio.   sed legatum sub inpossibili

---

[*obligation is contracted by the promise of one of the parties as*
[*sole speaker, and not in answer to a question, namely when a*
[*freedman gives his oath to his patron that he will make him*
[*some present or perform for him certain duties or services,—an*
[*obligation, however, that derives its efficacy not so much from the*
[*formality of the words used as from the sanctity of the oath*
[*that accompanies them. But it is very doubtful whether an*
[*oath be obligatory in any other case*], at least so far as the law
of Rome is concerned. As regards peregrins, if we were to
look into the laws of their particular states, we might possibly
find a different rule prevailing.

97   If what we have stipulated shall be given to us be such that
it cannot be given, the stipulation is useless; as when one
stipulates for a freeman whom he believes to be a slave, or
for a slave deceased whom he believes to be alive, or for
ground sacred or religious which he believes to be of human
97a right.   *If one stipulate for something that can have no exist-*
ence, such as a hippocentaur, the stipulation is equally useless.
98 So is one subject to a condition that can never be fulfilled, as
'if he touch the sky with his finger.' The leaders of our

---

sine interrogatione alii promittente,
contrahitur obligatio, id est si libertus
patrono aut donum aut munus aut
operas se daturum esse iurauit: in
qua re supradicti liberti non tam
uerborum solennitate quam iuris-
iurandi religione retinentur.   Sed
nulla altera persona hoc ordine obli-
gari potest.' Comp. § 88; Paul. ii,
32; tit. D. *de oper. libertor.* (xxxviii,
1); tit. C. *de op. lib.* (vi, 3).
[1] Stud. thinks there are traces of
a few additional letters at the end of

the par.; possibly *in aliis ualere.*
Comp. § 120.
§§ 97-109. Comp. tit. I, *DE INVTILIBVS*
STIPVLATIONIBVS (iii, 19). A vacant
line before § 97.
§ 97. Comp. Gai. in fr. 1, § 9, D. *de O.*
et A. (xliv, 7); §§ 1, 2, tit. I. afd.
§ 97a. The emendation, suggested by
L. and approved by most eds., is
made on the authority of § 1, tit. I.
afd.
§ 98. Comp. § 11, tit. I. afd.; § 10, I.
de hered. inst. (ii, 14).

condicione relictum nostri praeceptores[1] proinde deberi putant ac si sine condicione relictum esset ; diuersae scholae
auctores[1] non minus legatum inutile existimant quam stipulationem : et sane uix idonea diuersitatis ratio reddi potest.
99 Praeterea inutilis est stipulatio si quis, ignorans rem suam
esse, dari sibi eam stipuletur: *quippe quod alicuius est*, id ei
100 dari non potest.   Denique inutilis est talis stipulatio, si
quis ita dari stipuletur: POST MORTEM MEAM DARI SPONDES?
uel ita : [*POST MORTEM TVAM DARI SPONDES! ualet autem si*
[*quis ita dari stipuletur : CVM MORIAR, DARI SPONDES! uel ita :*]
CVM MORIERIS DARI SPONDES? id est ut in nouissimum uitae
tempus stipulatoris aut promissoris obligatio conferatur : nam
inelegans esse uisum est ab heredis persona incipere obligationem. rursus ita stipulari non possumus : PRIDIE QVAM
MORIAR, aut PRIDIE QVAM MORIERIS, DARI SPONDES? quia non
potest aliter intellegi 'pridie quam aliquis morietur' quam si
mors secuta sit; rursus morte secuta in praeteritum redduci-

---

school hold that a legacy bequeathed under an impossible
condition is as much due as if it had been left unconditionally ;
those of the other school think the legacy quite as much a
nullity as the stipulation; and certainly it is difficult to
99 justify the distinction.   Further, that stipulation is null
in which a man stipulates that something shall be given
him, not knowing that it is already his; for what already
100 belongs to him cannot be given to him in property.   Finally,
a stipulation is void that is conceived thus : ' Do you engage
that such a thing shall be given me after my death ?' or '*after
your death ?*' *It is valid, however, if in such words as :* ' *Do you
engage to give when I am dying ?*' or 'when you are dying ?'
i.e. if the obligation be made coincident with the last breath
of the stipulant or promiser ; for it has been reckoned inconsistent with principle that an obligation should begin in the
person of the heir.   Again, we cannot stipulate thus : ' Do you
engage that it shall be given the day before I die ?' or 'the
day before you die ?' for 'the day before' can be known only
after death ; but after death the stipulation refers to the past,

---

[1] See i, 196, note 1.

§ 99.   Comp. Gai. in fr. 1, § 10, D. *de
O. et A.* (xliv, 7); iv, 4 ; §§ 2, 22,
tit. I. afd.

§ 100.   Comp. §§ 13, 15, tit. I. afd. The
emendation here was suggested by
Hu. in his *Studien*, p. 279, and has

been approved by all subsequent
eds. His principal authorities for
it are Gai. ii, 232 ; fr. 45, §§ 1, 3,
fr. 121, § 2, D. *de uerb. obl.* (xlv, 1);
Fr. Vat. § 98 ; l. 15, § 1, C. *de con-
trah. et commit. stip.* (viii, 38) ; Th.
iii, 19, § 14.

tur stipulatio et quodammodo talis est: HEREDI MEO DARI
101 SPONDES? quae sane inutilis est.   Quaecumque de morte
diximus, eadem et de capitis deminutione dicta intellegemus.
102   Adhuc inutilis est stipulatio si quis ad id quod interro-
gatus erit non responderit, ueluti si sestertia X a te dari
stipuler et tu sestertia V promittas, aut si ego pure stipuler,
103 tu sub condicione promittas.   Praeterea inutilis est stipulatio si ei dari stipulemur cuius iuri subiecti non sumus:
unde illud quaesitum est, si quis sibi et ei cuius iuri subiectus
non est dari stipuletur, in quantum ualeat stipulatio: nostri
praeceptores[1] putant in uniuersum ualere, et proinde ei soli
qui stipulatus sit solidum deberi, atque si extranei nomen non

---

and is equivalent to this: 'Do you engage that it shall be
101 given to my heir?' which undoubtedly is invalid.   These
observations about death apply equally to *capitis deminutio.*
102   A stipulation is likewise void if the answer do not correspond to the question; for instance, if, when I stipulate for
ten *sestertia,* you promise five, or if, when I stipulate purely,
103 you promise conditionally.   Again, a stipulation is null in
which we stipulate that a thing shall be given to a person to
whose right we are not subject.   Hence the question,—suppose a man stipulates for something to be given to himself
and another person to whom he is not subject, how far is the
stipulation valid?   Our authorities think that it is good to
the full, and that the debt is due *in solidum* to the stipulant,

---

§ 101.   Comp. § 153.
§ 102.   Comp. Epit. ii, 9, §§ 8-10; § 5,
tit. *I.* afd.   The MS. reads—*ettunce-
stertiau,'miliapmittas,* which is generally rendered as above, the *n* after
tu and the *milia* being deleted as
accidental interpolations.

Thus rendered, however, the doctrine—supported by the Epit. and
Just. Inst.—is in disaccord with the
statements of Vlp. in fr. 1, § 4, and
Paul. in fr. 88, § 8, D. *de uerb. obl.*
(xlv, 1), where it is laid down that
a promise for five in response to a
stipulation for ten was effectual for
the smaller sum.

Hu. (*Beitraege,* p. 62) maintains
that if the *n* and the *milia* of the
MS. be retained, the *sestertia* changed
into *sestertium,* and the passage read
et tu nummum sestertium V *milia
promittas,* the contrariety between
Gai. on the one hand, and Paul. and

Vlp. on the other, will disappear.
For then, he argues, there would be a
difference not as to the quantity but
as to the *thing* the parties were bar-
gaining about; a *sestertium,* though
of the value of a thousand *nummi
sestertii,* being not money at all, but
a certain weight (2½ pounds) of silver.

Had the contrariety between the
X and the V of the text not existed,
there might have been more to say
for this ingenious suggestion.   But
there can be no doubt that in ordinary language *sestertia decem* and
nummum sestertium decem milia
were s) nonymous; and whether the
reading of Hu. or that given above
be adopted, the statement of Gai. is
still the same.   As to how it may be
reconciled with those of Paul. and
Vlp., see note to § 5, tit. I. afd.
§ 103.   Comp. § 4, tit. I. afd.
   [1] See i, 196, note 1.

adiecisset : sed diuersae scholae auctores[1] *dimidium ei* debere
existimant, pro altera *uero parte inutilem esse* stipulationem.
Alia causa est — — — — — dari spondes — — — — —
solidum deberi, *et me* — — — — — etiam *Titio* — —
104 — —.[2]   (*Item*) inutilis est stipulatio si ab eo stipuler qui
iuri meo subiectus est, item si is a me stipuletur. [*sed*] seruus
quidem, et qui in mancipio est, et (*filiafamilias*), et quae in
manu est, non solum ipsi *cuius iuri subiecti subiectaeue* sunt
105 obligari non possunt, sed ne alii quidem ulli.   Mutum
neque stipulari neque promittere posse palam est. idem etiam
in surdo receptum est; quia et is *qui stipulatur* uerba pro-
mittentis, et qui *promittit uerba stipulantis* exaudire debet.
106 Furiosus nullum negotium *gerere* potest, quia non intellegit
107 quid agat.   Pupillus omne negotium recte gerit, ut tamen,[1]

---

just as if the stranger's name had not been added; those of
the other school hold that one half is due to the stipulant, but
the stipulation void as to the other half.   The case is different
where you engage to give ['*to me or Titius ;*' *for then*] the
whole is due to me, [*and I alone can sue upon the stipulation*,
[*although by payment*] to Titius [*you will be effectually dis-*
104 [*charged*].   Further, a stipulation is useless in which I take
a promise from one who is subject to my right, or he takes
a promise from me ; indeed, slaves, persons *in mancipio, filiaefamilias*, and women *in manu*, are not only incapable of becoming obliged to him to whose right they are subject, but
105 cannot be obliged to any other person.   That mutes can
neither stipulate nor promise is quite plain.   The same is the
rule as regards a person who is deaf ; for the stipulant must
hear the words of the promiser, and the promiser those of the
106 stipulant.   A madman cannot be a party to any business-
matter, because he does not understand what he is about.
107 But all sorts of business affairs may be legally transacted by a

---

[2] Three lines and a half to a great
extent illegible. Hu. conjectures—
Alia causa est, *si ueluti*, '*seruo uel
filiofamilias meo et mihi* dari spondes?' *stipulatus sim. tunc enim constat* solidum deberi, et me *solidum a
promissore petere posse* : quod etiam
fit *cum tantum uelut* '*filiofamilias*'
stipulor. K. u. S. suggest—Alia
causa est, *si ita stipulatus sim* :
'*mihi aut Titio* dari spondes?' *quo
casu constat mihi* solidum deberi, et
me *solum ex ea stipulatione agere*

posse, quamquam etiam Titio *soluendo liberaris.*
§ 104. Comp. § 6, tit. I. afd., from
    which it will be seen that a *filius-
    familias* might.
§ 105. Comp. Gai. in fr. 1, §§ 14, 15, D.
    de O. et A. (xliv, 7) ; § 7, tit. I. afd.
§ 106. § 8, tit. I. afd. Comp. Gai. in
    fr. 1, § 12, D. *de O. et A.* (xliv, 7).
§ 107. § 9, tit. I. afd. Comp. ii, 83 ;
    iii, §§ 119, 176.
    [1] Hu., following L., reads *ita
    tamen ut tutor.*

sicubi tutoris auctoritas necessaria sit, adhibeatur, ueluti si ipse obligetur; nam alium sibi obligare etiam sine tutoris
108 auctoritate potest.   Idem iuris est in feminis quae in tutela
109 sunt.   Sed quod diximus de pupillo, utique de eo uerum est qui iam aliquem intellectum habet; nam infans et qui infanti proximus est non multum a *furioso* differt, quia huius aetatis pupilli nullum intellectum habent: sed in his pupillis propter utilitatem benignior iuris interpretatio facta est.
110   Possumus tamen ad id quod stipulamur alium adhibere qui idem stipuletur, quem uulgo adstipulatorem uocamus.
111 Huic proinde actio conpetit proindeque ei recte soluitur ac nobis; sed quidquid consecutus erit mandati iudicio nobis
112 restituere cogetur.   Ceterum potest etiam aliis uerbis uti adstipulator quam quibus nos usi sumus: itaque si uerbi gratia ego ita stipulatus sim: DARI SPONDES? ille sic adstipulari potest: IDEM FIDE TVA PROMITTIS? uel IDEM FIDEIVBES?

---

pupil, provided that, where tutorial authorisation is required, his tutor has intervened, as when he is undertaking an obligation; for he may take another person bound to him without
108 his tutor's *auctoritas.*   The law is the same in the case of
109 women in tutelage.   But what has been said about a pupil applies only to one who has some intelligence; for an infant, or a child approximating to infancy, is little different from a lunatic, pupils of such age having no understanding; yet even in their case, for utility's sake, the law is favourably interpreted.
110   It is in our power, in entering into a stipulation, to conjoin with us a third party, who stipulates in the same terms as we have done; such a person is commonly called an
111 *adstipulator.*   Action is competent to him on the stipulation, and payment of what is stipulated for may as effectually be made to him as to us; but whatever he has recovered he may be compelled to make over to us by means of an *actio*
112 *mandati.*   The adstipulator need not use the very same words that we have used; for example, if a stipulant have employed the formula *spondes?* he may use *fide tua promittis?*

§ 108. Comp. i, 192; iii, §§ 119, 176.
§ 109. § 10, tit. I. afd. Comp. Gai. in fr. 1, § 13, D. *de O. et A.* (xliv, 7). A vacant line intervenes in the MS. between this and the next par.
§§ 110-114. These pars. deal with *adstipulatio,* whose ordinary purpose

is explained in § 117. They have no counterpart in the Inst., Just. having rendered the device unnecessary by tit. C. *ut act. ab heredib. et contra hered. incipiant* (iv, 11).
§ 111. Comp. §§ 117, 155, 215.

113 uel contra.   Item *minus*[1] adstipulari potest, [plus non
    potest:][2] itaque si ego sestertia x stipulatus sum, ille sestertia
    v stipulari potest; contra uero plus non potest.   item si ego
    pure stipulatus sim, ille sub condicione stipulari potest;
    contra uero non potest.   non solum autem in quantitate sed
    etiam in tempore minus et plus intellegitur; plus est enim
114 statim aliquid dare, minus est post tempus *dare.*[3]   In hoc
    autem iure quaedam singulari iure obseruantur: nam adsti-
    pulatoris heres non habet actionem.[1]   item seruus adstipulando
    nihil agit, *quamuis*[2] ex ceteris omnibus causis stipulatione
    domino adquirat.[3]   idem de eo qui in mancipio est magis
    placuit; nam et is serui loco est: is autem qui in potestate
    patris est agit aliquid, sed parenti non adquirit, quamuis ex
    omnibus ceteris causis stipulando ei adquirat; ac ne ipsi
    quidem aliter actio conpetit quam si sine capitis deminutione
    exierit de potestate parentis,[4] ueluti morte eius aut quod ipse

---

113 or *fideiubes?* and *vice versa.*   He may stipulate for less,
    but not for more.   Therefore if I have stipulated for ten
    sestertia, he may limit his stipulation to five; but he cannot
    go beyond the ten.   So, if I have stipulated purely, he may
    stipulate conditionally; but not contrariwise.   And more or
    less may depend upon time as well as quantity: to give a
    thing at once is to give more; to give it after a while is to
114 give less.   In this branch of the law there are some pecu-
    liarities.   Thus, an adstipulator's heir cannot sue upon the
    contract.   Adstipulation by a slave is of no avail, although
    in all other cases of stipulation he thereby acquires for his
    owner.   The same rule holds in regard to a person *in man-
    cipio;* for he is in the position of a slave.   A son, however,
    who is in the power of his father, may effectually adstipulate,
    yet does not thereby acquire anything for his father, although
    he does so in every other case of stipulation; and no action
    on the adstipulation is competent to such a *filiusfamilias*
    until he has passed out of his parent's *potestas* without *capitis
    deminutio*, as, for instance, by his father's death or his own

---

§ 113. [1] The ms. has *mrginus*.   The
copyist has introduced into the
middle of the word the letters *rg*
— *regula*, which he had found
noted on the margin of the archetype.   See the same error in i, 58,
and iii, 126.
    [2] These words seem to be a gloss.

[4] Comp. iv, 53; § 5, tit. I. *de
fideiuss.* (iii, 20).
§ 114. [1] Comp. iv, 18.
    [2] So G. and K. u. S.; the ms. has
quia.
    [3] Comp. ii, 87; iii, 163; § 1, I.
de stip. seru. (iii, 17).
    [4] Comp. i, §§ 127, 130.

flamen Dialis inauguratus est.   eadem de filiafamilias et quae
in manu est dicta intellegemus.

115   Pro eo quoque qui promittit solent alii obligari, quorum
alios sponsores, alios fidepromissores, alios fideiussores appel-
116 lamus.   Sponsor ita interrogatur: IDEM DARI SPONDES?
fidepromissor [*ita*]: IDEM FIDEPROMITTIS? fideiussor ita: IDEM
FIDE TVA ESSE IVBES? uidebimus[1] [de his][2] autem[3] quo
nomine possint proprie appellari qui ita interrogantur: IDEM
117 DABIS? IDEM PROMITTIS? IDEM FACIES?   Sponsores quidem
et fidepromissores et fideiussores saepe solemus accipere dum
curamus ut diligentius nobis cautum sit; adstipulatorem uero
fere tunc solum adhibemus cum ita stipulamur ut aliquid
post mortem nostram detur.[1]   [*ita*][2] stipulando nihil agimus;[3]
adhibetur autem adstipulator ut is post mortem nostram

---

inauguration as a flamen of Jupiter.   And the same rules are
to be understood as applying to a *filiafamilias* and a woman
in manu.

115   For him who promises other persons frequently become
bound, of whom some are called sponsors, others fidepromis-
116 sors, others fidejussors.   A sponsor is interrogated thus:
'Do you religiously engage that the same thing shall be
given?' a fidepromissor: 'Do you promise the same on
your plighted faith?' a fidejussor: 'Do you authorise the
same thing on your plighted faith?'   How those are called
who are interrogated thus: 'Will you give the same?' 'Do
you promise the same?'   'Will you do the same?' we shall
117 see bye and bye.   We often take sponsors, fidepromissors,
or fidejussors when we are anxious to have an undertaking to
us better secured; but we hardly ever associate with us an
adstipulator except when we are stipulating for something to
be given after our death.   So stipulating our act is useless;
therefore we conjoin with us an adstipulator that he may sue

§§ 115-127. Comp. tit. I. DE FIDEIVS-
    SORIBVS (iii, 20).
§ 115. A vacant line before this par.
    Comp. Paul. i, 9, § 5; pr. tit. I. afd.
§ 116. Comp. § 92, note; Epit. ii, 9,
    § 2; § 7, tit. I. afd.
    [1] Gai. does not recur to the sub-
    ject; but such persons went by the
    generic name of *adpromissores.*

[2] Apparently a gloss.
[3] Hu. has *an aliquo.*
§ 117. Comp. Gai. in fr. 1, § 8, D. *de
    O. et A.* (xliv, 7); pr. tit. I. afd.
    [1] Comp. §§ 110-114.
    [2] Instead of *ita* Hu. introduces
    the words *quia enim ut ita nobis
    detur.*
    [3] Comp. § 100.

agat : qui si quid fuerit consecutus, de (*restituendo*) eo mandati iudicio heredi *meo* tenetur.[4]

118   Sponsoris uero et fidepromissoris similis condicio est, fide-
119 iussoris ualde dissimilis.   Nam illi quidem nullis obligationibus accedere possunt nisi uerborum, quamuis interdum ipse qui promiserit non fuerit obligatus, uelut si (*mulier*) aut pupillus sine tutoris auctoritate,[1] aut quilibet post mortem suam,[2] dari promiserit; (at illud quaeritur, si seruus aut peregrinus spoponderit,[3] an pro eo sponsor aut fidepromissor
119a obligetur.)   Fideiussor uero omnibus obligationibus, id est siue re siue uerbis siue litteris siue consensu contractae fuerint obligationes, *adici* potest.   ac ne illud quidem interest utrum ciuilis an naturalis obligatio [1] sit cui adiciatur; adeo

---

after our death, who is bound by an *actio mandati* to make over to our heir whatever he may have recovered.

118   The positions of sponsor and fidepromissor are much the
119 same, but that of a fidejussor is materially different.   The former cannot become accessory to any but a verbal obligation. [And they are bound even] although, as sometimes happens, the original promiser is not,—a woman, for instance, or a pupil, promising without tutorial *auctoritas*, or any person whatever promising that something shall be given after his death.   But if a slave or a peregrin have promised by the formula *spondeo*, it is questionable whether a sponsor
119a or fidepromissor can become bound for him.   A fidejussor, on the other hand, may be superadded to an obligation of any sort, whether contracted by thing done, by spoken words, by writing, or by consent.   And it is immaterial whether the obligation to which he accedes be civil or natural; he may

[4] Comp. §§ 215, 216.
§ 119.   Comp. § 1, tit. I. afd.
    [1] Comp. §§ 107, 108.
    [2] Comp. §§ 100, 117.
    [3] The *sponsio* of a peregrin or a slave was an absolute nullity, engagement in that form being competent only to citizens, § 93.
§ 119a.   Comp. § 1, tit. I. afd.
    [1] A civil obligation was enforcible directly by action at the instance of the creditor in it; a natural obligation was one that, by reason of absence of formalities, defect in the capacity of the individual, or other *ciuilis ratio*, was not enforcible by action, though recognised as a *uinculum aequitatis* (Papin. in

fr. 95, § 4, D. *de solut.* xlvi, 3), and held consequently to be a sufficient foundation for an accessory undertaking by a *fideiussor* (as above), or for a real security (fr. 5, pr. D. *de pign.* xx, 1); as a sufficient answer to a *condictio indebiti* (fr. 16, § 4, D. *de fidej.* xlvi, 1); as pleadable in compensation (fr. 6, D. *de comp.* xvi, 2); as a good basis for a *constitutum* (fr. 1, § 7, D. *de pec. const.* xiii, 5), or a novation (fr. 1, § 1, D. *de nou.* xlvi, 2); and as in many cases affording an effectual equitable exception to an action by the other party (fr. 7, § 7, D. *de pact.* ii, 14).

quidem ut pro seruo quoque obligetur, siue extraneus sit qui
a seruo fideiussorem accipiat, siue ipse dominus in id quod sibi
120 debeatur.[2]   Praeterea sponsoris et fidepromissoris heres
non tenetur, nisi si de peregrino fidepromissore quaeramus et
alio iure ciuitas eius utatur;[1] fideiussoris autem etiam heres
121 tenetur.[2]   Item sponsor et fidepromissor lege Furia biennio
liberantur, et quotquot erunt numero eo tempore quo pecunia
peti potest, in tot partes diducitur inter eos obligatio, et
singuli uiriles partes *dare iubentur;*[1] fideiussores uero[2] per-

---

become bound even for a slave, whether it be a stranger that
is taking him as fidejussor, or the owner of the slave in re-
120 spect of what the latter owes him.   Besides, the heir of a
sponsor or fidepromissor is not bound, unless in the case of a
peregrin fidepromissor in whose country a different rule is
followed; but a fidejussor's heir is as much bound as himself.
121 Further, sponsors and fidepromissors are freed from liability
after two years, in terms of the Furian law; and, whatever
be their number when the debt is sued for, the obligation is
divided into just so many parts, and each has to pay an
equal share.   But fidejussors are bound for ever, and, what-

---

[2] Comp. Gai. in fr. 70, § 3, D. *de
fideiuss.* (xlvi, 1).
§ 120.   Comp. iv, 118.
  [1] Comp. § 96.
  [2] Comp. § 2, tit. I. afd.
§ 121.   The *L. Furia de sponsu* (iv, 22)
is assigned by Rudorff (*R. RG.* i,
p. 51) to the year 409 | 345; by
Hu. to the beginning of the fifth
century of the city; by Voigt (*Ius
Nat., etc.,* iv, p. 424) to 536 | 218;
by Bruns (*Z. f. RG.* xii, 134) to
the second half of the sixth century; and by Appleton (*Étude sur
les sponsores, etc., Rev. de Légis-
lat.,* 1876, p. 558) to 654 | 100 or
655 | 99.
  Huschke's reason (*Beitraege,* p.
83) for assigning it so early a date
is that both it and the *L. Publilia*
(§ 127) authorized a *legis actio per
manus iniectionem pro iudicato* (iv,
22); and therefore they must have
been earlier than the *L. Valeria* of
413 | 341, which declared that every
manus iniectio, except in the cases
of *iudicatum* and *depensum,* should
be *pura* (iv, 25).
  It now appears, however, from

Studemund's *Apographum,* that it
was not a *lex Valeria* but a *lex
Vallia* that made this change, and
of its authorship and precise date
we are ignorant; all we know (iv,
§§ 24, 25) is that it was subsequent
to the *L. Furia.*
  But Bruns draws attention to the
fact that in an inscription edited by
Mommsen (*Ephem. Epigraph.* ii,
198), and which he attributes to the
first half of the sixth century of the
city, *man. iniectio pro iudicato* is
authorised as the means of recovering certain penalties thereby imposed; whence he argues that the
L. Vallia must have been later.
  As regards the *L. Furia* in particular, Bruns concludes from internal evidence that it must have been
later than the *L. Cincia,* which dates
from 550 | 204.
  [1] So Hu.; the ms. has *hocabentur.*
K. u. S., interpolating *in* before
uiriles, make it *obligantur,*—a reading against which Hu. protested by
anticipation in his *Beitraege,* p.
88.
  [2] Comp. § 4, tit. I. afd.

petuo tenentur, et quotquot erunt numero singuli in solidum
obligantur: *itaque* liberum *est creditori a quo* (*uelit*) solidum
petere: sed *nunc ex epistula* diui Hadriani (*conpellitur*) creditor
a singulis qui modo soluendo *sint partes petere.* eo igitur
distat haec epistula a lege Furia, quod si quis ex sponsoribus
aut fidepromissoribus soluendo non sit, hoc onus ad [*ceteros
[non pertinet; sed ex fideiussoribus etsi unus tantum soluendo*
121a[*sit, ad eum onus*][3] ceterorum quoque pertinet.   Sed cum
lex Furia tantum in Italia locum habeat, euenit *ut in ceteris
prouinciis* sponsores quoque et fidepromissores proinde ac
fideiussores in perpetuum teneantur et singuli in solidum
obligentur, nisi ex epistula diui Hadriani hi quoque *adiuuen-*
122 *tur* in parte.   Praeterea inter sponsores et fidepromissores
lex *Apuleia* quandam societatem introduxit: nam si quis
horum plus sua portione soluerit, de eo quod amplius dederit
aduersus ceteros *actiones* constituit. quae lex ante legem
Furiam lata est, quo tempore in solidum obligabantur. unde

---

ever be their number, are liable each for the whole; so that
it is free to the creditor to sue any one he pleases for the
whole amount. Now however, by a letter of our late emperor Hadrian's, a creditor is compelled to limit his demand
against each of them who is solvent to a proportionate share
of the whole. The provision in this letter differs from that
of the Furian law to this extent,—that if any of several
sponsors or fidepromissors be insolvent, the burden *upon the
others is not thereby increased, whereas, should only one of
several fidejussors be solvent, he has to bear the burden of those*
121a *that are insolvent.*   But as the Furian law is in force only
in Italy, it follows that in the provinces sponsors and fidepromissors, in the same way as fidejussors, are liable for ever,
and each for the whole; unless it be held that these last also
122 have partial relief under the letter of Hadrian.   Moreover,
the Apuleian law introduced a kind of partnership between
sponsors and fidepromissors; for if any one of them had paid
more than his share, it allowed him action against the others
for the excess. But this law was enacted before the Furian,
and at a time when the liability was *in solidum.* It is
therefore a question whether the boon conferred by the

---

[3] This addition is Mommsen's in
K. u. S.; Hu. reads—*hoc onus [ad
ceteros non pertinet, si uero ex fideius-
soribus], ad ceteros quoque pertinet.*

§ 122. Comp. § 4, tit. I. afd. Rudorff
and Hu. attributes the *lex Apuleia*
to 364 | 390; Voigt to 524 | 230;
and Appleton to 652 | 102.

quaeritur an post legem Furiam adhuc legis Apuleiae beneficium supersit: et utique extra Italiam superest; nam lex
quidem Furia tantum in *Italia* ualet, Apuleia uero etiam in
ceteris prouinciis: *sed an et in Italia*[1] beneficium legis
Apuleiae supersit ualde quaeitur. (*Ad fideiussores autem
(lex) Apuleia* non pertinet: itaque si creditor ab uno totum
consectus fuerit, huius solius detrimentum *erit*, scilicet si is
pro quo fideiussit soluendo non sit: (*sed ut ex*) supra dictis
apparet, is a quo creditor totum petit poterit ex epistula diui
123 Hadriani desiderare ut pro parte in se detur actio.   Praeterea lege Cicereia cautum est, ut is qui sponsores aut fidepromissores accipiat, praedicat palam et declaret et de qua re
satis accipiat, et quot sponsores aut fidepromissores in eam
obligationem accepturus sit; et nisi praedixerit, permittitur
sponsoribus et fidepromissoribus intra diem XXX praeiudicium[1]
postulare, quo quaeratur an ex ea lege praedictum sit; et si
iudicatum fuerit praedictum non esse, liberantur. qua lege

Apuleian law has survived the Furian. Certainly it survives out of Italy; for while the Furian law applies only in
Italy, the Apuleian extends to the provinces generally; but
whether or not it survives in Italy is extremely doubtful.
The enactment does not apply, however, to fidejussors; consequently, if a creditor have obtained payment of the whole
debt from one of several fidejussors, that one, if the party for
whom he has become surety be insolvent, has to bear the whole
loss. But then, as is manifest from what has been already
said, a surety from whom a creditor seeks payment of the
whole debt may require that action against him be limited to
123 his share, in accordance with Hadrian's letter.   Then again
it is provided by the Cicereian law that any one accepting
sponsors or fidepromissors shall first openly state and declare
what is the matter in respect of which he is taking security,
and how many sponsors or fidepromissors he proposes to
have; if he fail in this, the sponsors and fidepromissors may
at any time within thirty days demand a praejudiciary inquiry as to whether or not the provisions of the enactment
have been complied with; and if the judgment be that no
such declaration had been made, they are discharged of lia-

---

[1] The ms. has *set an etiam alis.*
§ 123. The only Cicereius we read of was
praetor in 681 | 173. The name of

this law appears for the first time in
Stud. *Apograph.*
[1] Comp. iv, 44.

fideiussorum mentio nulla fit: sed in usu est, etiam si fideiussores accipiamus, praedicere.

124   Sed beneficium legis Corneliae omnibus commune est: qua
lege idem pro eodem apud eundem eodem anno uetatur in
ampliorem summam obligari creditae pecuniae quam in x̄x̄
milia; et quamuis sponsor uel fidei promissor [1] in *ampliorem* [2]
pecuniam, ueluti si sestertium C milium [*se obligauerit, tamen
*[*duntaxat XX damnatur*]; [3] pecuniam autem creditam [4] dicimus
non solum eam quam credendi causa damus, sed omnem quam
tum cum contrahitur obligatio certum est debitum iri, id est
[*quae*] sine ulla condicione deducitur in obligationem; itaque
et ea pecunia quam in diem certum dari stipulamur eodem
numero est, quia certum est eam debitum iri, licet post tempus
petatur. appellatione autem pecuniae [5] omnes res in ea lege
significantur; itaque si uinum uel frumentum, etiam si fundum
125 uel hominem stipulemur, haec lex obseruanda est.   Ex

---

bility.   In this enactment no mention is made of fidejussors;
but it is the practice to make a declaration even in their case.
124   The relief conferred by the Cornelian law, however, is
common to all classes of sureties. By this law the same
person is forbidden to become bound for the same debtor, to
the same creditor, and in the same year for more than
20,000 sesterces of *credita pecunia ;* and although a sponsor,
fidepromissor, *or fidejussor,* may have bound himself for more,
say for 100,000, *yet judgment against him will be limited to
20,000.* By *pecunia credita* we mean not only money advanced
in loan, but all that, at the time of contracting the obligation,
we are certain will become a debt, *i.e.* all that is unconditionally
made matter of obligation; and there is thus included in it
money which we stipulate is to be paid at a time fixed,
because it is certain that such money will fall due, although
it can be sued for only when the time of payment has arrived.
And by *pecunia*, in the sense of the Cornelian law, we are to
understand every sort of thing; therefore, even if we are
stipulating for wine or corn, for land or for a slave, the rule of
125 the statute is to be obeyed.   In some cases, however, it allows

---

§ 124. The *lex Cornelia* (*de sponsoribus*)
Hu. thinks may have been enacted
in 673 | 81; but Voigt attributes
it to 427 | 327.

    [1] So the ms.; Hu. reads *uel pro-
missores* [*uel fideiussores*].

    [2] Instead of *ampliorem* the ms.
has *amplam.*

    [3] The addition is Huschke's,
adopted substantially by K. u. S.

    [4] Comp. Isidor. *Orig.* v, 25, § 14
(Bruns, p. 302); fr. 37-39, D. *de
reb. cred.* (xii, 1).

    [5] Comp. fr. 178, pr., fr. 222, D.
de V. S. (l, 16).

§ 125. The *lex Iulia de vicesima here-*

quibusdam tamen causis permittit ea lex in infinitum satis
accipere, ueluti si dotis nomine, uel eius quod ex testamento
tibi debeatur, aut iussu iudicis satis accipiatur. et adhuc lege
uicesima hereditatium cauetur, ut ad eas satisdationes quae
126 ex ea lege proponuntur lex Cornelia non pertineat.   In eo
quoque iure par condicio est omnium, sponsorum, fidepro-
missorum, fideiussorum, quod ita obligari non possunt ut
plus debeant[1] quam debet is pro quo obligantur: at ex
diuerso ut minus debeant obligari possunt, sicut in adstipulatoris persona diximus; nam ut adstipulatoris ita et horum
obligatio accessio est principalis obligationis, nec plus in
127 accessione esse potest quam in principali re.   In eo quoque
par omnium causa est, quod si quid pro *reo* soluerint, eius
recuperandi causa habent cum eo mandati iudicium;[1] et hoc
amplius sponsores ex lege Publilia[2] propriam habent actionem
in duplum, quae appellatur depensi.[3]

---

security to be taken to any extent, as when it is given on
account of a dotal provision, or of a debt due under a testament, or when it is required by order of a judge. Further,
the law imposing a five per cent. succession duty exempts the
suretyships it calls into play from the operation of the Corne-
126 lian law.   In this respect also all are on a par, whether
sponsors, fidepromissors, or fidejussors,—that they cannot be
bound for more than is due by him for whom they are sureties ;
but, on the other hand, they may be bound for less, as explained in reference to an adstipulator; for, like the obligation
of an adstipulator, that of a surety is accessory to the principal
one, and there cannot be more in the accessory than in the
127 principal.   Finally, they all stand on the same footing in
this respect,—that if they have paid anything for the principal
debtor, they have an action of mandate against him for its
recovery; and sponsors, by the Publilian law, have over and
above an action peculiar to themselves for double the amount,
which goes by the name of *actio depensi.*

ditatum, enacted 759 | 6, imposed a
duty of 5 per cent. on testamentary successions and bequests;
Dio Cass. lv, 25, lvi, 28; Plin.
Paneg. 37.
§ 126. Comp. 113; § 5, tit. I. afd.
  [1] The MS. again has *ut rg plus
debeant,* the scribe having intro-
15

duced a marginal *rg,* = *regula,* into
his text. See § 113, note.
§ 127. Comp. § 6, tit. I. afd.
  [1] Comp. § 111.
  [2] This law was enacted possibly
in 355 | 399, or more probably in
371 | 383.
  [3] Comp. iv, 22.

128 Litteris obligatio fit ueluti nominibus transscripticiis. fit
autem nomen transscripticium duplici modo, uel a re in
129 personam uel a persona in personam.   [*A re in personam*
*[trans]*scriptio fit, ueluti si id quod ex emptionis causa aut
conductionis aut societatis mihi debeas, *inde* [1] expensum tibi
130 tulero.   A persona in personam transscriptio fit, ueluti si
id quod mihi Titius debet tibi *inde* [1] expensum tulero, id est
131 si Titius te [2] delegauerit [3] mihi.   Alia causa est eorum
nominum quae arcaria uocantur: in his enim rei, non litterarum obligatio consistit, quippe non aliter ualent quam si

---

128 A literal obligation is created by transcribed entries; and
these are made in two ways,—either from thing to person, or
129 from person to person. *There is transcription from thing to*
person when, for example, I enter to your debit a sum you
already owe me by reason of a purchase, a conduction, or a
130 partnership.   There is transcription from person to person
when, for example, I enter to your debit what is due me by
Titius, provided always he has delegated you to me in his
131 stead.   The case is different with those [direct] entries [of
cash payments] which go by the name of *nomina arcaria*.
In these the obligation is really one created by thing delivered
rather than by writing, seeing it has no effect unless the

§§ 128-134. Comp. tit. I. *DE LITTERA-*
RVM OBLIGATIONE (iii, 21). That
title refers to a different sort of
literal obligation from any of those
explained by Gai. in these pars., all
of which had gone out of use before
the time of Justinian. Th., however, alludes to them, and gives
some details of interest in reference
to that mentioned in § 129.

§ 128. The *transscriptio* here referred to
took place in the *codex expensi et*
accepti, which, so long as the periodical census was regularly observed,
every citizen was required to keep;
see Ps. Ascon. *in II. Verr.* i, 23, § 60
(Bruns, p. 292). Danz (*R.R.* ii,
pp. 43-61) gives a *resumé* of the
principal theories broached in reference to the Roman house-books,
and the *nomina* they contained.

§ 129. The words in italics are omitted
in the MS., but self-evident. In
reference to the par. generally,
comp. §§ 137, 138; Cio. *de off.* iii,
14, §§ 58-60; *pro Q. Rosc. com.*

i-iii; Sen. *de benef.* ii, 23, iii, 15;
Th. iii, 21. Heimbach (*Creditum*,
p. 329), criticising Reitz's text of
Theoph., draws attention to the
fact that, in his account of the *lit.*
obligatio as contained in the most
authoritative MSS., there are preserved—not in a Greek dress, but
in the original Latin—two formulae
which are said to have been both
spoken and written by the parties;
by the creditor—*centum aureos quos*
mihi ex causa locationis debes expen-
sos tibi tuli? and by the debtor—
expensos mihi tulisti.
  [1] So Hu.; the MS. has *id.*

§ 130. See references in note to § 128.
  [1] So Hu.; the MS. has *id.*
  [2] The MS. has *te se*; Hu. *te*
[pro] se.
  [3] Comp. Vlp. in fr. 11, pr. D. *de*
nouat. (xlvi, 2).

§ 131. A loan *ex arca*, paid in cash out
of the household money-chest, became a *nomen arcarium* when booked in the lender's *codex*.

numerata sit pecunia; numeratio autem pecuniae rei facit
obligationem: qua de causa recte dicemus arcaria nomina
nullam facere obligationem, sed obligationis factae testi-
132 monium praebere.   Vnde proprie dicitur arcariis nominibus
etiam peregrinos obligari, quia non ipso nomine sed numera-
tione pecuniae obligantur, quod genus obligationis iuris
133 gentium est.   transscripticiis uero nominibus an obligentur
peregrini merito quaeritur, quia quodammodo iuris ciuilis est
talis obligatio: quod Neruae[1] placuit: Sabino[1] autem et
Cassio[1] uisum est, si a re in personam fiat nomen transscripticium, etiam peregrinos obligari; si uero a persona in
134 personam, non obligari.   Praeterea litterarum obligatio

---

money has actually been told; but the paying down of money
is creative of a real obligation; therefore it may be said with
perfect accuracy that an entry of a cash payment does not
make an obligation, but only affords evidence of one already
132 created.   Hence it may be said quite properly even that
peregrins are bound by *arcaria nomina;* for they are bound
not by the entry, but by the paying down of the money,—
133 a cause of obligation which is *iuris gentium.*   Whether
they can be bound by transcribed entries has very reasonably
been questioned; for an obligation so created is in a manner
an invention of the *ius ciuile.* Nerva was of opinion that
they could not; but Sabinus and Cassius hold that they may
be bound by transcription from thing to person, though not
134 by that from person to person.   Further, a *litterarum obli-*

---

§ 132. P. places *etiam* after *unde* instead of after *nominibus.* Hu.
(*Beitraege,* p. 94), followed by Bk.
and K. u. S., interjects *non* before
proprie, on the ground that if an
arcarium nomen did not create any
obligation at all (§ 131), it could not
be obligatory on a peregrin. But
Gai. says in the same sentence—*in
arcariis nominibus rei . . obligatio
consistit.* Consequently I prefer to
keep the text as it is, believing that
Gaius meant here to distinguish
between the recognised liability of
a peregrin upon a *nomen arcarium*
as a real and *iuris gentium* contract,
and the doubtfulness of his liability
upon a *nomen transscripticium* as a
literal and *iuris ciuilis* one.

§ 133. The new obligation arising from
transscriptio a persona in personam

had no foundation except in the *ius
ciuile;* where the *transscriptio* was *a
re in personam* the foundation of the
prior *iuris gentium* obligation, thus
novated, still remained.

  [1] See i, 196, note 1.

§ 134. Comp. Cic. *ad Att.* v, 21, vi, 2;
Ps. Ascon. *in II. Verr.* i, 36, § 91
(Bruns, p. 293). The *chirographum*
of the Greek provinces was a written
acknowledgment of debt under the
hand of the debtor, and was obligatory upon him, if a peregrin, for the
simple reason that amongst peregrins a *nudum pactum* was creative
of action; if, however, he was a
citizen, it was obligatory in the
first instance only if it embodied a
stipulation, and therefore as a *uerborum obligatio,* though capable of
becoming in time a *litterarum obli-*

fieri uidetur chirographis et syngraphis, id est si quis debere
se aut daturum se scribat, ita scilicet si eo nomine stipulatio
non fiat : quod genus obligationis proprium peregrinorum est.

135   Consensu fiunt obligationes in emptionibus et uenditioni-
bus, locationibus conductionibus, societatibus, mandatis.
136 Ideo autem istis modis consensu dicimus obligationes contrahi, quia neque uerborum neque scripturae ulla proprietas
desideratur, sed sufficit eos qui negotium gerunt consensisse :
unde inter absentes quoque talia negotia contrahuntur, ueluti
per epistulam aut per internuntium, cum alioquin uerborum
137 obligatio inter absentes fieri non possit.[1]   Item in his con-

---

gatio is held to arise out of chirographa and syngraphae,—
documents whereby a man either acknowledges himself indebted, or engages to give something without employing the
formula of stipulation ; this sort of obligation is peculiar to
peregrins.

135   Obligations arise from consent in purchases and sales,
136 locations and conductions, partnerships, mandates.   We say
that in these forms obligations are contracted by consent,
because no formality either of words or writing is required,
it being enough that the parties to the business have arrived
at a common understanding ; accordingly such contracts may,
through the intervention of a letter or a messenger, be entered
into even between those who are not in each other's presence,
which is impossible in the case of an obligation by spoken
137 words.   Further, in the consensual contracts the parties are

gatio, as explained in tit. I. afd.
The peculiarity of the *syngrapha*—
which also contained an acknowledgment of debt and informal
promise to pay—seems to have been
either that it was executed in dupli-
cate, and one of the documents retained by each of the parties, or
that, after execution, like the more
modern indenture or *charte-partie*,
it was cut in two, and a part taken
by each for preservation and as a
precaution against fraud.
§§ 135-138. Comp. tit. I. DE CON-
SENSV OBLIGATIONE (iii, 22).
§ 135. Gai. in fr. 2, pr. D. *de O. et A.*
(xliv, 7) ; pr. tit. I. afd.
§ 136. Gai. in fr. 1, 2, D. *de O. et A.*
(xliv, 7) ; §§ 1, 2, tit. I. afd.

[1] Comp. § 12, I. *de inut. stip.* (iii,
19).   The inconvenience resulting
from the rule that there could be no
stipulation *inter absentes* was obviated in this way : If a man had no
slave of his own in or near the place
where he desired to obtain a debtor's
promise, he employed one resident
there ; that slave, pretending that
for the time he was the property of
and represented the absent creditor,
acted as stipulant, and took a promise on his behalf ; and a minute
of the transaction, in which the
absentee was described as owner of
the stipulating slave, was usually
written out and signed by the parties.
This seems at least to be a legitimate
inference from Justinian's words in

tractibus alter alteri obligatur de eo quod alterum alteri ex
bono et aequo praestare oportet, cum alioquin in uerborum
obligationibus alius stipuletur, alius prommittat,[1] et in nomini-
138 bus alius expensum ferendo obliget, alius obligetur.[2]   Sed
absenti expensum ferri potest, etsi uerbis obligatio cum
absente contrahi non possit.[1]

139   (*Emptio et uenditio contrahitur*) cum de pretio conuenerit,
quamuis nondum pretium numeratum sit, ac ne arra quidem
data fuerit: nam quod arrae nomine datur argumentum est
140 emptionis et uenditionis contratae.   Pretium autem certum
esse debet: nam alioquin si ita inter nos conuenerit ut quanti

---

reciprocally liable for what each ought in fairness and equity
to do for the other; whereas in verbal obligations, while one
stipulates, only the other promises; and in *nomina*, while one,
by making an entry to the other's debit, lays him under
138 obligation, it is only the latter that is obliged.   But an
entry to a man's debit may be made in his absence, although
a verbal contract with one who is not present is impossible.

139   Purchase and sale is contracted the moment parties have
agreed about the price, although it have not been paid, nor
any earnest given; for what is given in name of earnest is
only evidence that a purchase and sale has been contracted.
140 But the price must be definite: if the agreement between us
be that a thing is bought for such a price as may be put upon

l. 14, pr. § 1, C. *de contr. stip.*
(viii, 38).
 Relying on the statement of Gai.
i, § 54—that in iii, 166, is more to
the point—that it was for his bonitarian and not his quiritarian owner
that a slave acquired a claim of
stipulation, Ubbelohde (*Z. f. RG.*
xiii, pp. 488 f.) surmises that the
practice must have been for the
absentee to get a friend in the place
of contract to take delivery of a
slave on his account; that would
place the slave *in bonis* of the absentee, and entitle him to act for
the latter; after the stipulation he
would be redelivered to his old
owner, who had still retained the
quiritarian right. This acquisition
of the slave, however, as he thinks,
must have become a mere form, and
have often been neglected; otherwise
Justinian would not have said in his
preamble that stipulations had often
been challenged on the ground that

the stipulating slave was not really
the property of the party for whom
the minute bore that he was acting.
The emperor's declaration was that
an averment of ownership in such a
minute was not afterwards to be disputed, however false in point of fact.
§ 137. Gai. in fr. 8, D. *de O. et A.*
(xliv, 7); § 3, tit. I. afd.
  [1] Comp. § 92.
  [2] Comp. §§ 129, 130.
§ 138. This par. seems to be a gloss,
suggested, doubtless, by the reference
to *nomina* in § 137. Most eds. introduce it after § 136; but even there
it looks like an annotation.
  [1] Comp. § 136; § 12, I. *de inut.
stip.* (iii, 19).
§§ 139-141. Comp. tit. I. *DE EMPTIONE
ET VENDITIONE* (iii, 23). These
pars. are preceded by a rubric, probably *de emptione et uenditione*, of
which only the first four letters
are legible.
§ 140. Pr. tit. I. afd.

Titius rem aestimauerit tanti sit empta, Labeo [1] negauit ullam
uim hoc negotium habere ; cuius opinionem Cassius [1] probat :
Ofilius [2] et eam emptionem et uenditionem [*esse putauit*];
141 cuius opinionem Proculus [1] secutus est.   Item pretium in
numerata pecunia consistere debet : nam in ceteris rebus an
pretium esse possit, ueluti *homo* [1] aut toga aut fundus alterius
rei [*pretium*],[2] ualde quaeritur. nostri praeceptores [3] putant
etiam in alia re posse consistere pretium ; unde illud est, quod
uulgo putant, per permutationem rerum emptionem et *uenditionem* contrahi, eamque speciem emptionis uenditionisque
uetustissimam esse ; argumentoque utuntur Graeco poeta Ho-
mero, qui aliqua parte sic ait :

[ἔνθεν ἄρ᾽ οἰνίζοντο καρηκομόωντες Ἀχαιοί,
ἄλλοι μὲν χαλκῷ, ἄλλοι δ᾽ αἴθωνι σιδήρῳ,
ἄλλοι δὲ ῥινοῖς, ἄλλοι δ᾽ αὐτῇσι βόεσσιν,
ἄλλοι δ᾽ ἀνδραπόδεσσιν.] [4]

diuersae scholae auctores [3] dissentiunt, aliudque esse existi-

---

it, say by Titius, then, according to Labeo, in whose opinion
Cassius concurs, the transaction can have no effect, while
Ofilius, and with him Proculus, holds that it amounts to pur-
141 chase and sale.   Further, the price must be fixed in current
money.   Whether the price of a thing can consist of something else, such as a slave, a toga, or a bit of land, has, not
without reason, been a matter of controversy.   Our authorities
think that it may ; hence the common notion amongst them,
that barter is just a contract of purchase and sale, and the
very earliest form of it ; for which, by way of argument, they
quote the Greek poet Homer, who says somewhere : ' *The long-
haired Achaeans bought wine, some for brass, some for glistening
steel, some for hides, some for cattle, some for slaves.*' The
authorities of the other school do not take this view, but hold

---

[1] Comp. i, 196, note 1.
[2] Aulus Ofilius did not belong to
either of the schools, but was a distinguished jurist in the time of
Julius Caesar (fr. ii, § 44, D. *de
orig. iuris*, i, 2), and supposed to
have been his adviser and assistant
in the digest of the law he did not
live to complete (Suet. *Iul.* c. 44).
Ofilius was also a teacher of repute,
and had among his pupils both
Capito and Labeo (fr. 2, § 47, D. as
above).The text furnishes an instance
of divergence of opinion between
Labeo and Proculus, showing that it

was not an indiscriminate adherence
that the latter accorded his master.
§ 141.   Comp. § 2, tit. I. afd.
[1] The MS. has *hoc modo*, which is
corrected from the Inst.
[2] This word seems necessary to
complete the sense. The Inst. have
pretium esse possit, and so have
most eds. ; but the two latter words
can be spared.
[3] See i, 196, note 1.
[4] Hom. *Il.* vii, 472-475.   The
quotation, as usual, is not in the
MS., *et reliqua* being all that stands
for it ; it is supplied from the Inst.

mant permutationem rerum, aliud emptionem et uenditionem; alioquin (*non posse*)[5] rem expediri permutatis rebus, quae uideatur res uenisse, et quae pretii nomine data esse, sed rursus utramque rem uideri et uenisse et utramque pretii nomine datam esse absurdum uideri.   sed ait Caelius Sabinus,[6] si rem tibi uenalem habenti, ueluti fundum, [acceperim, et][7] pretii nomine hominem forte dederim, fundum quidem uideri uenisse, hominem autem pretii nomine datum esse, ut fundus acciperetur.

142   Locatio autem et conductio similibus regulis constituitur: nisi enim merces certa statuta sit, non uidetur locatio et
143   conductio contrahi.   unde si alieno arbitrio merces permissa sit, uelut quanti Titius aestimauerit, quaeritur an locatio et conductio contrahatur: qua de causa si fulloni polienda curandaue, sarcinatori sarcienda uestimenta dederim, nulla statim mercede constituta, postea tantum daturus quanti inter nos conuenerit, quaeritur an locatio et conductio con-

---

barter to be one thing, purchase and sale another and different one; otherwise it would be impossible to determine, as between two things given in exchange, which was the article sold, and which given in name of price; while to hold that each was at the same time both ware and price would be absurd.   But, says Caelius Sabinus, if I come to you who have something for sale, say a plot of ground, and give you for it a slave in name of price, the ground will be considered sold, and the slave given as price, that so I may have the land.

142   Location and conduction are subject to much the same rules [as purchase and sale]; for unless a definite remuneration be agreed upon, location and conduction cannot be said to have
143   been contracted.   Hence, if the remuneration be left to the determination of a third party,—say 'whatever sum Titius may fix,'—it is a question whether there be here a contract of location and conduction.   And the same question arises when I give clothes to a fuller to be pressed or scoured, or to a tailor to be mended, no sum being fixed at the time as remuneration, but it being understood that, after the job is finished, I am to give so much as may then be agreed upon

---

[5] These two words, illegible in the MS., supplied from the Inst.
[6] See § 70, note.
[7] These two words, according to K. u. S., are a gloss.
§§ 142-147. Comp. tit. I. *DE LOCA-TIONE ET CONDVCTIONE* (iii, 23).

A vacant line precedes these pars. in the MS., probably for a rubric.
§ 142. Comp. Gai. in fr. 2, pr. D. *loc.* (xix, 2); pr. tit. I. afd.
§ 143. Comp. Gai. in fr. 25, pr. D. *loc.* (xix, 2); Gai. in fr. 22, D. *de praescr. uerb.* (xix, 5); § 1, tit. I. afd.

144 trahatur.   *Item*[1] si rem tibi utendam dederim et inuicem
aliam rem utendam acceperim, quaeritur an locatio et con-
145 ductio contrahatur.   Adeo autem emptio et uenditio et
locatio et conductio familiaritatem aliquam inter se habere
uidentur, ut in quibusdam causis quaeri soleat utrum emptio
et uenditio contrahatur an locatio et conductio: ueluti si qua
res in perpetuum locata sit, quod euenit in praediis municipum,
quae ea lege locantur ut quamdiu uectigal[1] praestetur neque
ipsi conductori neque heredi eius praedium auferatur; sed
146 magis placuit locationem conductionemque esse.   Item si[1]
gladiatores ea lege tibi tradiderim ut in singulos qui integri
exierint pro sudore denarii xx mihi darentur, in eos uero
singulos qui occisi aut debilitati fuerint denarii mille, quaeritur utrum emptio et uenditio an locatio et conductio
contrahatur: et magis placuit eorum qui integri exierint
locationem et conductionem contractam uideri, at eorum qui
occisi aut debilitati sunt emptionem et uenditionem esse;

144 between us.   It is also doubtful if there be location and
conduction when I have given you the use of a thing, receiv-
145 ing from you the use of something else in return.   So much
do purchase and sale and location and conduction seem to
have in common, that in some cases there is room for question
whether it is the one or the other that has been contracted;
as, for example, when a thing is located in perpetuity, as
happens in the case of lands belonging to a municipality
granted by it in lease under a provision that, so long as the
rent charged upon them is duly paid, they shall not be withdrawn either from the lessee or from his heir.   The prevailing
opinion is that this is a contract of location and conduction.
146 Again, if I have furnished you with a band of gladiators, on
an agreement that for each of them that shall come scathless
out of the combat I am to have twenty *denarii* in payment
of his exertions, and a thousand for each that is killed or
disabled, it is disputed whether the contract be one of purchase and sale or of location and conduction. It has been
held that as regards those who are unhurt it is one of location
and conduction, but one of purchase and sale as regards those
who have been killed or disabled.   Therefore, what the con-

§ 144.   Comp. § 2, tit. I. afd.
  [1] So P., K. u. S., and Hu.; the
MS. has *uel*.
§ 145.   Comp. § 3, tit. I. afd.
  [1] Between *quamdiu* and *uectigal*

the MS. has *id*, for which Hu. substitutes *inde*.
§ 146.   [1] Before *si* the MS. has *quaeritur*;
obviously unnecessary.

idque ex accidentibus apparet, tamquam sub condicione facta cuiusque uenditione an locatione :[2] (iam enim non dubitatur
147 quin sub condicione res ueniri aut locari possint.)[3]   Item quaeritur, si cum aurifice mihi conuenerit ut is ex auro suo certi ponderis certaeque formae anulos mihi faceret, et acciperet uerbi gratia denarios CC, utrum emptio et uenditio an locatio et conductio contrahatur : Cassius[1] ait materiae quidem emptionem uenditionem contrahi, operarum autem locationem et conductionem ; sed plerisque placuit emptionem et uenditionem contrahi. atqui si meum aurum ei dedero, mercede pro opera constituta, conuenit locationem conductionem contrahi.
148 Societatem coire solemus aut totorum bonorum aut unius alicuius negotii, ueluti mancipiorum emendorum aut uenden-
149 dorum.   Magna autem quaestio fuit an ita coiri possit

tract is will appear from the chapter of accidents, just as if there had been both a conditional sale and a conditional location of each individual gladiator ; (for that things may be
147 sold and located under a condition is undoubted.)   And again, if I have agreed with a goldsmith that he shall make me with his own gold some rings of a certain weight and pattern, and get say two hundred *denarii* for them, it is a point of controversy whether this be purchase and sale or location and conduction. Cassius thinks there is purchase and sale of the material, location and conduction of the labour expended upon it ; but the general opinion is that the contract is one of purchase and sale. But if I provide the gold, agreeing to give the goldsmith so much for his labour, the contract is admittedly one of location and conduction.
148 We may enter into a partnership either as regards our whole means and estate, or as regards some particular business,
149 such as the buying and selling of slaves.   It was once a

[2] The passage *idque . . . locatione* is not very intelligible. It would be better thus : *ideoque ex accidentibus apparet, tanquam sub condicione facta cuiusque et uenditione et locatione*, [*utrum emptio et uenditio contracta sit an locatio et conductio*]. Two conditional contracts were entered into as regards each of the gladiators, one of sa e, the other of location ; the event was to determine which became operative.

[3] Comp. Vlp. in fr. 20, pr. D. *loc.* (xix, 2).
§ 147.   § 4, tit. I. afd. Comp. Gai. in fr. 2, § 1, D. *loc.* (xix, 2).
[1] See iii, 71, note.
§§ 148-154. A vacant line precedes. Comp. tit. I. DE SOCIETATE (iii, 25).
§ 148. Pr. tit. I. afd.
§ 149. Comp. § 2, tit. I. afd., from which G., followed by all eds., has supplied the words in italics.

societas ut quis maiorem partem lucretur, minorem damni
praestet: quod Quintus Mucius [1] [*contra naturam societatis
[esse censuit; sed Seruius Sulpicius,*[1] *cuius*] etiam praeualuit
sententia, adeo ita coiri posse societatem existimauit, ut
dixerit illo quoque modo coiri posse ut quis nihil omnino
damni praestet sed lucri partem capiat, si modo opera eius
tam pretiosa uideatur ut aequum sit eum cum hac pactione
in societatem admitti: nam et ita posse coiri societatem
constat ut unus pecuniam conferat, alter non conferat, et
tamen lucrum inter eos commune sit; saepe enim opera ali-
150 cuius pro pecunia ualet.   Et illud certum est, si de partibus
lucri et damni nihil inter eos conuenerit, aequis ex partibus
commodum et incommodum inter eos commune esse; sed si
in altero partes expressae fuerint, uelut in lucro, in altero
uero omissae, in eo quoque quod omissum est similes partes
151 erunt.   Manet autem societas eo usque donec in eodem
sensu perseuerant; at cum aliquis renuntiauerit societati,

---

great question whether partnership could exist on the understanding that one of the parties was to have a larger share of
the profit than he was to bear of the loss. Quintus Mucius
*held such an arrangement inconsistent with the nature of
partnership; but Servius Sulpicius*, whose opinion prevailed,
saw nothing to prevent it, and went so far as to maintain
that it might even be contracted on the footing that one of
the partners should bear none of the loss at all, yet take a
share of the profits, if only his services were esteemed so
valuable as to render it fair that he should be admitted to the
partnership on such terms. That there may be partnership
where one of the partners contributes money capital, while
the other does not, is allowed on all hands; for a man's
150 services are often as much worth as his money.   It is clear
that if nothing have been agreed between the partners as to
their respective shares of profit and loss, they will equally
benefit by the one and suffer from the other; but if the agreement be express as to one of the incidents of the contract,
the share say of the profit which each is to take, and no
mention be made of the loss, a corresponding share in it will be
151 held implied.   A copartnery continues as long as the partners
are of the same mind; if one of them renounce, it is dissolved.

---

[1] See i, 188, note 4.
§ 150. Comp. §§ 1, 3, tit. I. afd. Between *conuenerit* and *aequis* the MS.

interjects *tamen*; P. substitutes
totum.
§ 151. § 4, tit. I. afd.

societas soluitur: sed plane si quis in hoc renunciauerit
societati ut obueniens aliquod lucrum solus habeat, ueluti
si mihi totorum bonorum socius, cum ab aliquo heres esset
relictus, in hoc renuntiauerit societati ut hereditatem solus
lucri faciat, cogetur hoc lucrum communicare; si quid uero
aliud lucri fecerit quod non captauerit, ad ipsum solum
pertinet : mihi uero quidquid omnino post renuntiatam
152 societatem adquiritur soli conceditur.   Soluitur adhuc
societas etiam morte socii, quia qui societatem contrahit
153 certam personam sibi eligit.   Dicitur etiam capitis deminutione solui societatem, quia ciuili ratione capitis deminutio
morti *coaequatur*; [1] sed *utique* si adhuc consentiant in socie-
154 tatem noua uidetur incipere societas.   Item si cuius ex
sociis bona publice aut priuatim uenierint, soluitur societas.
154*a* Sed *haec quoque* societas de qua *loquimur* —. — consensu

---

But clearly if he have renounced in order to have all to
himself some profit that is close at hand,—as when one who
is my partner in a partnership of our whole means and effects,
being left heir by some third party, renounces, on purpose
that he may enjoy alone the whole gain of the succession,—
he will be compelled to communicate a share.   Any gains
coming to him otherwise, however, and which he had not in
view in renouncing, fall entirely to him; while, of course,
whatever I acquire after the renunciation falls to me alone.
152 Partnership is also dissolved by death; for he who has contracted a partnership has chosen a particular person for his
153 partner.   It is also held to be dissolved by *capitis deminutio*,
which, according to the theory of our civil law, is equivalent
to death; but if the partners consent to remain as before, a
154 new partnership is held to be thereby commenced.   Further
if the estate of any one of the partners have been confiscated,
or sold by his creditors on his bankruptcy, the partnership is
154*a* dissolved.   But the partnership of which we are speaking

---

§ 152. § 5, tit. I. afd.
§ 153. Comp. fr. 4, § 1, fr. 58, § 2, fr.
63, § 10, fr. 65, § 11, D. *pro socio*
(xvii, 2).
[1] Comp. iii, §§ 100, 101.
§ 154. Comp. §§ 7, 8, tit. I. afd.
§ 154*a*. The lacuna after *loquimur* represents four letters, of which the
second seems to be *o*, and the fourth
q; and instead of *iurisque gentium*
the ꟺs. has *iuris cogentium*. The
par. is generally supposed to be

corrupt; but of the many attempts
to reconstruct it none is quite satisfactory. It is possible that Gai. had
in view the distinction alluded to by
Pompon. in fr. 59, pr. D. *pro soc.*
(xvii, 2), between *societates priuatae*
and *societates uectigalium*, which
latter were governed in some respects by rules of their own; and
that he meant to limit his preceding observations to partnerships of
the former class,—*societates uolun-*

contrahitur nudo *iurisque gentium est; itaque inter* omnes
homines naturali ratione *consistit.*

155   *Mandatum* consistit siue nostra gratia mandemus siue aliena.
itaque siue ut mea negotia geras, siue ut alterius, mandauerim,
contrahitur mandati obligatio, et inuicem alter alteri tenebimur[1] in id quod uel *me tibi uel* te mihi bona fide praestare
156 *oportet.*[2]   nam si tua gratia tibi mandem superuacuum est
mandatum; quod enim tu tua gratia facturus sis, id de tua
sententia, non ex meo mandatu facere *debes;* itaque si otiosam
pecuniam domi *te* habentem hortatus fuerim ut eam faenerares, *quamuis eam* ei mutuam dederis a quo seruare non
potueris, non tamen habebis mecum *mandati* actionem: *item*
si hortatus sim *ut rem* aliquam emeres, quamuis non ex-
pedierit tibi eam emisse, non tamen tibi mandati tenebor.[1]
et adeo haec ita sunt ut quaeratur an mandati teneatur qui

---

is that which is contracted by bare consent, and which is *iuris
gentium;* consequently its existence depends everywhere on
considerations of natural law.

155   There is mandate whether the commission given by us be
on our own account or on that of another person.   Accordingly, whether I instruct you to transact some business for
myself, or to do so for some other person, an obligation of
mandate is contracted, and we are reciprocally responsible for
156 what each ought in good faith to do for the other.   A
mandate to you to act on your own behalf is superfluous; if
you do act for yourself, you ought to do so according to your
own judgment, and not upon my instructions.   Therefore if,
knowing you to have money lying idly at home, I advise you
to put it out at interest, and you lend it to a person from
whom you are unable to recover it, you will have no action
of mandate against me; neither will I be responsible if I have
advised you to employ it in making a purchase which has
turned out disadvantageous.   It has even been questioned
whether a man would be responsible to you in an action of

---

tariae, as Vlp. calls them in fr. 63,
§ 8, tit. D. afd. If so, all that is
necessary is to fill the blank with
the words *ea est quae (eaeq).* The
force of the remark lies in the *naturali ratione;* if the *socii* persisted in
consenting to be partners, their consent, which was the *naturalis ratio*
of the contract, was not to be defeated by such *ciuiles rationes* as
cap. deminutio or bankruptcy.

§§ 155-162. Comp. tit. I. DE MAN-
DATO (iii, 26).
§ 155. Comp. Gai. in fr. 2, pr. D.
mand. (xvii, 1); pr. tit. I. afd.
[1] Comp. Gai. in fr. 5, pr. D. *de
Q. et A.* (xliv, 7).
[2] The MS. has *oportere.*
§ 156. Comp. Gai. in fr. 2, pr. §§ 5, 6, D.
mand. (xvii, 1); pr. §§ 5, 6, tit. I. afd.
[1] So G. and most eds.; the MS.
has *teneri;* P. *teneri* [*potero*].

mandauit tibi ut *Titio* pecuniam faenerares.   Seruius[2] negauit;
nec magis hoc *casu obligationem* consistere putauit quam si
generaliter alicui mandetur uti pecuniam suam faeneraret:
sequimur [*autem*] Sabini[3] opinionem *contra sentientis*,[4] quia
non aliter Titio credidisses quam si tibi mandatum esset.

157 Illud *constat, si quis de ea re* mandet quae contra bonos mores
est, non contrahi obligationem, ueluti si tibi mandem ut Titio

158 furtum aut iniuriam facias.   Item si quis post[1] mortem
meam faciendum [*mihi*] mandet, inutile mandatum est, quia
generaliter placuit ab heredis persona obligationem incipere

159 non posse.   Sed recte quoque *contractum*[1] mandatum, si
dum adhuc integra res sit reuocatum fuerit, euanescit.

160 Item si adhuc integro mandato mors alterutrius alicuius
interueniat, id est uel eius qui mandauerit uel eius qui
mandatum susceperit, soluitur mandatum; sed utilitatis
causa receptum est, ut si mortuo eo qui mihi mandauerit,

mandate who commissioned you to lend your money say to
Titius.   Servius denied that he would, holding that in such a
case the mandant was no more obliged than he who in general
terms advised another to lend out his money at interest; but
we adopt the opinion of Sabinus, who took the opposite view,
holding that here you would not have lent your money to
157 Titius but for the mandate you had received.   There is no
doubt of this, that if a man commission another to do something that is immoral, no obligation is contracted, as, for
example, when I commission you to steal from Titius or
158 assault him.   If a man give me a mandate to do something
after my death, it is useless, according to the general rule that
an obligation cannot commence in the person of an heir.
159 A mandate, however regularly granted, evanishes if revoked
160 before anything has been done in pursuance of it.   It is
dissolved likewise by the supervening death of either mandant
or mandatory, no step having been taken towards its execution; but, in order not to diminish the utility of such contracts, the law allows that, if after, but in ignorance of, the

[2] See i, 188, note 5.
[3] See i, 196, note 1.
[4] So all the later eds.; the MS. and previous eds. have *consentientis*.
§ 157. § 7, tit. I. afd.
§ 158. Comp. § 100.
[1] After *post* K. u. S. interpolate *mortem suam uel post*.

§ 159. § 9, tit. I. afd.
[1] Instead of *contractum* (as in Inst.) the MS. has *consummatur*, usually rendered *consummatum*. But, as P. observes, this means 'carried out,' which is inconsistent with the idea of *res integra*.
§ 160. § 10, tit. I. afd.

ignorans eum decessisse executus fuero mandatum, posse me
agere mandati actione; alioquin iusta et probabilis ignorantia
damnum mihi adferret. et huic simile est quod plerisque
placuit, si debitor meus manumisso dispensatori meo per
ignorantiam soluerit, liberari eum, cum alioquin stricta iuris
ratione non posset liberari eo quod alii soluisset quam cui
161 soluere deberet.   Cum autem is cui recte mandauerim
egressus fuerit mandatum, ego quidem eatenus cum eo habeo
mandati actionem quatenus mea interest inplesse eum mandatum, si modo inplere potuerit; at ille mecum agere non
potest. itaque si mandauerim tibi ut uerbi gratia fundum
mihi sestertiis C emeres, tu sestertiis CL emeris, non habebis
mecum mandati actionem, etiamsi tanti uelis mihi dare
fundum quanti emendum tibi mandassem; idque maxime
Sabino et Cassio[1] placuit : quodsi minoris emeris, habebis
mecum scilicet actionem, quia qui mandat ut C milibus
emeretur, is utique mandare intellegitur uti minoris si posset

---

death of my mandant, I have executed his commission, I may
still have my action of mandate; otherwise my very excusable
error might be to me a source of loss. On similar grounds
most are of opinion that if my debtor pay to a former slave of
mine who acted as my steward, in ignorance of the latter's
manumission, he is discharged of liability; although, according to the strict rule of law, a man is not discharged by payment to another than the person to whom such payment
161 ought to have been made.   If he to whom I have given a
mandate in proper form exceed the limits of his commission,
I may claim against him, in an *actio mandati*, damages for the
loss I have sustained by his failure to fulfil his contract,
provided fulfilment were possible; but he has no action
against me. Accordingly, if I have commissioned you say to
buy for me certain land for a hundred thousand sesterces, and
you buy it for a hundred and fifty thousand, you will not have
any action against me, even though you be willing to give me
the ground at my own price,—such, at least, is the opinion of
Sabinus and Cassius; but if you buy it for less money than I
named, you will have action of mandate against me, seeing
that one who authorises a purchase at the price of a hundred
thousand, is held to authorise such purchase at a lower price

§ 161. Comp. Paul. in fr. 3, § 2, and Gai. fr. 4, D. *mand.* (xvii, 1); § 8, tit. I. afd.
[1] See i, 196, note 1.

162 emeretur.   In summa sciendum [*est, quotiens faciendum*] aliquid gratis dederim, quo nomine si mercedem statuissem locatio et conductio contraheretur, mandati esse actionem, ueluti si fulloni polienda curandaue uestimenta [*dederim*] aut sarcinatori sarcienda.

163   Expositis generibus obligationum quae ex contractu nascuntur, admonendi sumus adquiri nobis non solum per nosmet ipsos, sed etiam per eas personas quae in nostra potestate manu

164 mancipioue sunt.   Per liberos quoque homines et alienos seruos quos bona fide possidemus adquiritur nobis; sed tantum ex duabus causis, id est si quid ex operis suis uel ex re nostra

165 adquirant.   Per eum quoque seruum in quo usumfructum habemus similiter ex duabus istis causis nobis adquiritur.

166 Sed qui nudum ius Quiritium in seruo habet, licet dominus sit, minus tamen iuris in ea re[1] habere intellegitur quam usufructuarius et bonae fidei possessor: nam placet ex nulla

---

162 if possible.   Finally, let it be understood that if I have given a thing to be done for me gratuitously, the giving of which, had it been to be done for reward, would have amounted to a contract of location and conduction, an action of mandate will lie; as when I have given clothes to a fuller to be pressed or scoured, or to a tailor to be repaired.

163   Now that the various sorts of obligations arising from contract have been explained, we must call attention to this,— that they may be acquired for us not only by our own instrumentality, but also by those who are in our *potestas, manus,* or

164 *mancipium.*   They are also acquired for us by freemen and by slaves belonging to other people whom we possess in good faith; but only in two cases, namely, when the acquisition is

165 due either to their labour or to our funds.   In the same two cases we acquire an obligation through a slave of whom we

166 have the usufruct.   But he who has only the bare quiritarian title to a slave is held to have even less right in this respect, though he be owner, than a usufructuary or a possessor in good faith; it is held that in no case can there be acquisition

---

§ 162. Comp. § 13, tit. I. afd.   The
    words in ital. supplied by G.
§§ 163-167.   Comp. tit. I. *PER QVAS
    PERSONAS NOBIS OBLIGATIO ADQVI-
    RITVR* (iii, 28).
§ 163. Comp. ii, 86 ; pr. tit. I. afd.

§§ 164, 165. §§ 1, 2, tit. I. afd. Comp.
    ii, §§ 86, 91, 92.
§ 166. Comp. ii, 88.
    [1] So the MS.; Hu. amends thus—
    [*adquisita ab*] *eo re.*

causa² ei adquiri posse; adeo ut etsi nominatim ei dari stipulatus fuerit seruus, mancipioue nomine eius acceperit, quidam
167 existiment nihil ei adquiri.   Communem seruum pro
dominica parte dominis adquirere certum est, excepto eo
quod uni nominatim stipulando aut¹ mancipio accipiendo²
illi soli adquirit, uelut cum ita stipuletur : TITIO DOMINO MEO
DARI SPONDES ? aut cum ita mancipio accipiat : HANC REM EX
IVRE QVIRITIVM L. TITII DOMINI MEI ESSE AIO, EAQVE EI EMPTA
167a ESTO HOC AERE AENEAQVE LIBRA.   Illud quaeritur [an] tamquam domini nomen adiectum domini efficit,¹ idem faciat
unius ex dominis iussum intercedens. nostri praeceptores²
perinde ei qui iusserit soli adquiri existimant, atque si nominatim ei soli stipulatus esset seruus mancipioue accepisset;
diuersae scholae auctores² proinde utrisque adquiri putant,
ac si nullius iussum interuenisset.

---

for him [by direct operation of law]; and some go so far as to
think that he acquires nothing even when a slave has stipulated
expressly in his name, or has taken in his name a conveyance
167 by mancipation.   There is no doubt that a slave owned in
common acquires for his owners according to their respective
proprietary interests in him, except when he expressly stipulates or takes by mancipatory conveyance in the name of one
of them in particular; then he acquires for that one alone, as
when he stipulates thus : 'Do you engage to give to my
master Titius ?' or when he takes a conveyance in these
terms : 'I say that this thing belongs to my master Lucius
Titius in quiritarian right, and be it his by purchase with
167a this bit of copper and these copper scales.'   It is disputed
whether or not the previous instructions of one in particular
of the owners will make the acquisition his as effectually as
the mention of his name. The leaders of our school think
that he alone acquires who gave authority to the slave, just as
if the slave had stipulated for or taken a conveyance to him
nominatim ; those of the other school maintain that in such a
case all the owners share in the acquisition, as if there had
been no instruction from any of them.

² The MS. adds *alia*, obviously *per
incuriam*.
§ 167. Comp. § 3, tit. I. afd.; § 3, I.
de stip. seru. (iii, 17).
¹ Before *aut* the MS. has *uel mancipando*, again an obvious mistake.
² Comp. i, 119.

§ 167a. Comp. ii, 87 ; § 3, tit. I. afd.;
§ 3, I. *de stip. seru.* (iii, 17).
¹ This seems to me the reading of
the MS. K. u. S., however, following G., have *quod domini nomen
adiectum efficit ;* Hu.—*quod nomen
adiectum unius domini efficit.*
² Comp. i, 196, note 1.

168   Tollitur autem obligatio praecipue solutione eius quod
debetur : unde quaeritur, si quis consentiente creditore aliud
pro alio soluerit, utrum ipso iure liberetur, quod nostris prae-
ceptoribus [1] placet, an ipso iure maneat obligatus, sed aduersus
petentem exceptione doli mali defendi debeat, quod diuersae
scholae auctoribus [1] uisum est.

169   *Item* per acceptilationem tollitur obligatio. acceptilatio
autem est ueluti imaginaria solutio : quod enim ex uerborum
obligatione tibi debeam, id si uelis mihi remittere poterit sic
fieri, ut patiaris haec uerba me dicere : QVOD EGO TIBI PROMISI,

170   HABESNE ACCEPTVM? et tu respondeas: HABEO.   Quo genere,
ut diximus, [*tantum eae obligationes soluuntur quae ex uerbis*
[*consistunt*,] non etiam ceterae ; consentaneum enim uisum est
uerbis factam obligationem posse aliis uerbis dissolui : sed et
id quod ex alia causa debeatur potest in stipulationem deduci

171   et per acceptilationem [*dissolui.   Quamuis uero dixerimus*
[*perfici acceptilationem*] imaginaria solutione, tamen *mulier*

---

168   An obligation is extinguished first and foremost by payment of what is due.   Hence it is a question whether a debtor
who, with consent of his creditor, has paid something that is
not due in place of that which is, is thereby freed by direct
operation of law, as our authorities maintain, or is not still
bound according to the letter of the law, as held by the
authorities of the other school, and obliged to meet any action
against him with an exception of dole.

169   An obligation is also extinguished by acceptilation, which
is as it were an imaginary payment.   For if you wish to release me what I owe you on a verbal obligation, it may be
done by your letting me say : 'That which I promised you
have you received?' and by your answering : 'I have.'

170   By this process, as already said, *only obligations by verbal contract can be extinguished*, not other kinds ; for it seems according to reason that an obligation contracted by spoken words
should be dissoluble by other words.   But what is due upon
some other ground may be embodied in a stipulation and then

171   extinguished by acceptilation.   *Although we have said that
acceptilation is effected* by imaginary payment, yet a woman

---

§§ 168-181. Comp. tit. I. *QVIBVS
MODIS OBLIGATIO TOLLITVR* (iii, 29).
§ 168. Comp. pr. tit. I. afd.
    [1] Comp. i, 196, note 1.
§§ 169, 170.   § 1, tit. I. afd., from

which the words in ital. are borrowed.
§ 171. Comp. ii, 85.   The words in
ital. are supplied by Hu.; instead of
perfici, K. u. S. suggest *contineri*.

sine tutoris auctoritate acceptum facere non potest, cum alio-
172 quin solui ei sine tutoris auctoritate possit.   Item quod
debetur, pro parte *recte soluitur;* an autem in partem acceptum
fieri possit *quaesitum [est].*
173   Est etiam alia species imaginariae solutionis per aes et
libram; quod et ipsum genus certis in causis receptum est,
ueluti si quid eo nomine debeatur quod per aes et libram
174 gestum *sit,* siue quid ex iudicati causa deb[*eatur. eaque*
[*res ita ag*]itur: *adhibentur* non minus quamquinque testes
et libripens; deinde is qui liberatur ita oportet loquatur: QVOD
EGO TIBI TOT MILIBVS *CONDEMNATVS (SVM), ME EO NOMINE
A TE* SOLVO LIBEROQVE HOC AERE AENEAQVE LIBRA : HANC TIBI
LIBRAM PRIMAM POSTREMAMQVE *EXPENDO* [*SECVNDVM*] LEGEM
PVBLICAM.   deinde asse percutit libram, eumque *dat ei* a quo

---

cannot acceptilate without her tutor's *auctoritas,* notwithstanding that without it payment may effectually be made to
172 her.   Again, while a debt may quite well be paid in part,
it is a question whether partial acceptilation be competent.
173   Another sort of imaginary payment is that by the copper
and the scales; a procedure employed only in certain cases,
as when the debt has been formally created *per aes et libram,*
174 or is due upon a judgment.   *It is gone about thus:* in the
presence of at least five witnesses and a scale-bearer, he
who is being freed from his obligation must speak as follows : ' Whereas I have been condemned to you in so many
thousand sesterces, *in respect thereof I now release and free
myself from you* with this copper and these copper scales ; *I
weigh out* to you this the first and last pound, *according to the
statute.'*   Then he strikes the scales with the *as,* and gives it

---

§ 172. Comp. § 1, tit. I. afd. The MS.
has *quod debet pro parte debet recte
solui recte soluit a. āt in partem,*
etc.

§ 173. Comp. Fest. v. *Nexum* (Bruns,
p. 248); Varro *de L. L.* vii, § 105
(Bruns, p. 281).

§ 174. The words introduced in the
beginning of the par. are the suggestion of K. u. S. The formula,
which is not found elsewhere, is
indistinct in the MS. It is thus
deciphered by Stud.,—letters not
absolutely certain being in italics,
and those that are illegible represented by dots:—qegotibitotmilib-
condemnat .... *megonmen. cte*soluo-
liueroqh' aereaeneaqlibrahanctibili-
bramprimamp'tremanqe*xpendo*elege-
mpublic*am.* The rendering adopted in the text is that of Karlowa
(*R. CP.* p. 151) ; it is approved by
K. u. S.; Goudsm'. and Pol. read *recte*
instead of *a te;* Hu. interpolates
dum between *libra* and *hanc. Expendo* has its explanation in the account Gai. gives of the origin of the
negotium per aes et libram in i, 174.
The *secundum* in the end of the
formula is introduced on the authority of Gai. ii, 104. On the *negotium per aes et libram* in other
applications, see (in addition to the
authorities referred to in last note)
Gai. i, 119; ii, 104 (and note 8);
iii, 89, note ; iii, 167.

175 liberatur ueluti soluendi causa. Similiter legatarius heredem eodem modo liberat de legato quod per damnationem[1]
relictum est, ut tamen *scilicet, sicuti* iudicatus *condemnatum*
se esse significat, ita heres (*testamento*)[2] se dare *damnas*[3] esse
dicat. de eo tamen tantum potest heres eo modo liberari quod
pondere numero constet,[4] et ita si certum sit: quidam et de
eo quod mensura constat *idem*[5] existimant.

176 Praeterea nouatione tollitur obligatio, ueluti si quod tu
mihi debeas a Titio dari stipulatus sim; nam interuentu nouae
personae noua nascitur obligatio et prima tollitur translata
in posteriorem, adeo ut interdum, licet posterior stipulatio
inutilis sit, tamen prima nouationis iure tollatur, ueluti si
quod mihi debes a Titio post mortem eius, uel a muliere
pupilloue sine tutoris auctoritate, stipulatus fuero; quo casu
rem amitto, nam et prior debitor liberatur et posterior obli-

---

to him from whom he is being released, as if in payment.
175 In the same way a legatee releases the heir from obligation
for a legacy which has been bequeathed *per damnationem;*
but, while the judgment debtor recites that he is *condemnatus,*
the heir declares himself *testamento damnas* to pay the legacy.
But an heir can be freed in this way only in respect of what
can be weighed or counted, and is of definite amount; some
include what may be measured.

176 Further, an obligation is extinguished by novation, as when
I stipulate with Titius that he shall pay me what you owe me;
for, by the intervention of a new party, a fresh obligation is
created, and the original one is put an end to, being translated
into the new. So far does this go, that sometimes the original obligation is extinguished on the principle of novation
even though the new one be invalid, as when I stipulate that
what you owe me shall be paid by Titius after his death, or
by a woman or a pupil acting without tutorial *auctoritas;* in
such a case I lose everything, for, while the original debtor is

---

§ 175. Comp. ii, 201.
[1] See ii, §§ 201 f.
[2] So Karlowa, followed by P.,
K. u. S., and Hu.
[3] The ms. has *damnat*, but Stud.
does not think the last letter absolutely certain. The eds. all read
damnatum; but as every formula
had to adopt the words of the formal
act to which it referred (iv, 23, Vlp.
xxiv, 29, and note), and as *damnas*

esto was the phrase employed to
impose the burden on the heir,
damnas sum must have been recited
by him in operating his discharge.
[4] Such things alone could be
covered by the word *expendo.*
[5] So G. and all eds.; the ms. has
inde.
§ 176. § 3, tit. I. afd. Comp. Gai. ii,
38; iii, §§ 100, 107, 108, 119; Fr.
Vat. § 263.

gatio nulla est.   non *idem* iuris est si a seruo stipulatus fuero ;
nam tunc [*prior*][1] proinde adhuc obligatus tenetur, ac si postea
177 a nullo stipulatus fuissem.   Sed si eadem persona sit a qua
postea stipuler, ita demum nouatio fit si quid in posteriore
stipulatione noui sit, forte si condicio *uel dies uel sponsor*[1]
178 adiciatur aut detrahatur.   Sed quod de sponsore diximus,
non constat : nam diuersae scholae auctoribus[1] placuit nihil
ad nouationem proficere sponsoris adiectionem aut detrac-
179 tionem.   Quod autem diximus si condicio adiciatur nouationem fieri sic intellegi *oportet*, ut ita dicamus factam
nouationem si condicio extiterit; alioquin si defecerit durat
prior obligatio : sed uideamus num is qui eo nomine agat doli
mali aut pacti conuenti exceptione possit summoueri, quia
uidetur inter eos id actum, ut ita ea res peteretur si posteri-
oris stipulationis extiterit condicio.   Seruius tamen Sulpicius[1]

---

discharged, the second obligation is null.   But the rule is
different if my [novatory] stipulation be with a slave ; in this
case the original debtor still remains bound as fully as if there
177 had been no subsequent stipulation at all.   A subsequent
stipulation with the same person as the first will operate a
novation then only when there is in it something new ; for
instance when a condition, or a specification of time, or a
178 sponsor, is either introduced or excluded.   This, however, is
not universally admitted so far as a sponsor is concerned ; for
the authorities of the other school hold that his introduction
179 or exclusion does not produce novation.   In saying that
there is novation when a condition is introduced, we are to be
understood as meaning that there will be novation when the
condition is fulfilled ; if it fail, the original obligation still
subsists.   But it may be a question whether the creditor suing
in such a case upon the original obligation may not be defeated by an exception of dole or of covenant, seeing that
apparently it was the true intention of parties that action for
the debt should be competent only on fulfilment of the condition annexed to the second stipulation.   Servius Sulpicius

---

[1] Supplied from Inst.
§ 177.   § 3, tit. I. afd.
    [1] The MS. has—*condicio uel spon-*
sor ā dies adiciatur. P. regards
the *ā dies* as a mistake of the transcriber, whose eye had carelessly
caught the first few letters of *adici-*
atur. But as the Inst. have *si con-*

dicio aut dies aut fideiussor adici-
atur, it would seem that the *dies*
has only been transposed.
§ 178.   [1] See i, 196, note 1.
§ 179.   Comp. Gai. fr. 80, §§ 1, 2,
D. *de pact.* (ii, 14) ; § 3, tit. I.
afd.
    [1] See i, 188, note 5.

existimauit statim et pendente condicione nouationem fieri,
et si defecerit condicio ex neutra causa agi posse [*et*] eo modo
rem perire ; qui consequenter et illud respondit, si quis id quod
sibi Lucius Titius deberet a seruo fuerit stipulatus, nouationem
fieri et rem perire, quia cum seruo agi non potest : [*sed*] in
utroque casu alio iure utimur : nec magis his casibus nouatio
fit, quam si id quod tu mihi debeas a peregrino, cum quo
sponsus[2] communio non est, SPONDES uerbo stipulatus sim.[3]

180   Tollitur adhuc obligatio litis contestatione,[1] si modo legitimo

---

held that there was novation at once, and while the condition
was still open ; and that on its failure neither obligation could
be sued upon, so that the claim of the creditor was altogether
extinguished. Upon the same principle he gave an opinion
upon a case put to him, that, if a man stipulated with a slave
for something due him, say by Lucius Titius, he operated a
novation, and thereby extinguished the claim, action against
the slave being impossible. But in both cases we follow a
different rule ; there is no novation in either of them, any
more than when, using the formula *spondes ?* I stipulate with a
peregrin, whom the law does not hold qualified to act as sponsor.

180   Finally, an obligation is extinguished by litiscontestation or

---

[2] So Bk., K. u. S., and Hu. The ms. has *sponsio*; G. *sponsionis*; Savigny and P. *sponsi*.
[3] Comp. §§ 93, 119, 176.

§§ 180, 181. Comp. § 10, I. *de except.* (iv, 13).

These two pars. deal with what has been called necessary or processual novation, in contradistinction to the voluntary or conventional novation described in those immediately preceding. And it amounted to this,—that in certain cases of action upon a debt the joinder of issue extinguished the original contention of the creditor that his debtor was bound to pay the debt, substituting for it this new one,—that the debtor ought to be condemned; consequently, if the action was for any reason not carried to a conclusion, the creditor could not *ipso iure* raise a new one, his original claim having ceased to exist.

Under the early system of procedure by *legis actio* (described by Gai. iv, §§ 11-29), if a man had once raised an action, no matter what the nature or form of it, but

failed to bring it to a conclusion, he had no power to begin anew ; he had exhausted his remedy (iv, 108). But under the formular system (iv, §§ 30-52), in use in the classical period, this *ipso iure* exhaustion of his judicial remedy (*consumptio actionis*) on joinder of issue was limited to *iudicia legitima in personam*, with an *intentio in ius concepta* (iv, 107) ; if it was desired to put a stop to an action *in rem*, or to any other sort of *actio in personam*, upon the ground that the parties had previously joined issue on the same question, it was necessary to state an exception of *res in iudicium deducta*, the fresh action being *ipso iure* quite competent (iv, 106).

Gai., in §§ 180, 181, above, does not expressly affirm that the novation resulting from litiscontestation was limited to actions *in personam* with an *intentio in ius concepta* (see iv, §§ 45-47); but the illustration in § 181 shows this to have been his meaning (Keller, *Litiscontestation*, p. 85).

§ 180. [1] *Litiscontestatio* was marked in

iudicio[2] fuerit actum nam tunc obligatio quidem principalis
dissoluitur, incipit autem teneri reus litis contestatione ; sed
si condemnatus sit, sublata litis contestatione incipit ex causa
iudicati teneri.   et hoc [est] quod apud ueteres[3] *scriptum* est,
ante litem contestatam dare debitorem oportere, post litem
contestatam condemnari oportere, post condemnationem iudi-
181 catum facere oportere.   Vnde fit, ut si legitimo iudicio
debitum petiero, postea de eo ipso iure[1] agere non possim,
quia inutiliter intendo DARI MIHI OPORTERE,[2] quia litis contestatione dari oportere desiit: aliter atque si imperio continenti iudicio[3] egerim ; tunc enim nihilo minus obligatio
durat, et ideo ipso iure postea agere possum, sed debeo per

---

joinder of issue, provided it be in a *legitimum iudicium ;* for
thereby the primary obligation is extinguished, and the defender begins to be bound by the litiscontestation ; and if he
be condemned, the litiscontestation falls aside, and he begins
to be obliged by the judgment.   Hence the saying of the old
jurists that, before joinder of issue, the creditor's contention is that his debtor ought to pay ; after joinder, that he
ought to be condemned ; after condemnation, that he ought
181 to satisfy the judgment.   Accordingly, if I have proceeded
against my debtor in a *legitimum iudicium,* I cannot afterwards, as a matter of abstract right, sue him again for the
same debt, because I can no longer validly maintain that
he ought to pay, the 'ought to pay' having been put an
end to by the litiscontestation.   It is different if I have been
proceeding in a *iudicium imperio continens ;* then the original
obligation nevertheless continues ; consequently I am by law
entitled to raise a fresh action ; but if I do, I must be defeated

---

the early procedure by the calling of
witnesses to hear the magistrate
settle the issue to be determined by
the court or judge to whom it was
remitted for trial ; Paul. *ex Fest.* v.
Contestari (Bruns, p. 239).   In the
classical procedure it was marked by
the praetor's delivery to the pursuer
of the written formula, which contained the issue.

    [2] This phrase seems almost un-
translatable.   Neither ' statutable
action ' (Abdy and Walker), nor
' statutory action ' (Poste), is an
adequate rendering ; for, as Gai.
observes (iv, 109), an action might
have been introduced by statute,

yet not be *legit. iud.,* while contrariwise it might be *legit. iud.* though
introduced not by statute but by
praetorian equity.   See iv, §§ 103 f.
    [3] See i, 144, note 2.
§ 181.   [1] The words *ipso iure* are important ; for there were cases in
which fresh action might be allowed
on grounds of equity by *restitutio
in integrum* or otherwise ; see fr.
25, fr. 46, § 5, D. *de admin. et
peric. tut.* (xxvi, 7) ; l. 2, C. *de iudiciis*
(iii, 1).
    [2] Comp. iv, 41.
    [3] Equally untranslatable with *legi-
timum iudicium ;* see description in
iv, 105.

exceptionem rei iudicatae uel in iudicium deductae summoueri.[4]
quae autem legitima iudicia et quae imperio *continentia*
sequenti commentario referemus.[5]

182   Transeamus nunc ad obligationes quae ex delicto *nascuntur,*
uelnti si quis furtum fecerit, bona rapuerit, damnum dederit,
iniuriam commiserit: quarum omnium rerum uno genere
consistit obligatio,[1] cum ex contractu obligationes in IIII genera
diducantur, sicut supra exposuimus.[2]

183   Furtorum autem genera Seruius Sulpicius[1] et Masurius
Sabinus[2] IIII esse dixerunt, manifestum et nec manifestum
conceptum et oblatum : Labeo[3] duo, manifestum et nec manifestum; nam conceptum et oblatum species potius actionis
esse furto cohaerentes quam genera furtorum ; quod sane

184 uerius uidetur, sicut inferius apparebit.   *Manifestum*[1]
furtum quidam id esse dixerunt quod dum fit deprehenditur :

---

182   Let us pass now to those obligations that originate in delict,
as when theft has been committed, robbery, wrongful damage
to property, or [personal] injury. The obligation in all of these
is of the same sort ; whereas, as we have seen, contractual
obligations are of four sorts.

183   According to Servius Sulpicius and Masurius Sabinus,
theft is of four varieties,—manifest and non-manifest theft,
discovery of stolen goods, and introduction of them into the
premises of a third party. But Labeo recognised only two
varieties, the manifest and non-manifest; discovery of stolen
goods, and introduction of them into the premises of a third
party, he regards rather as grounds of action presupposing
theft than varieties of it; and this seems the more correct

184 view, as will appear presently.   A theft, according to some,
is to be regarded as manifest then only when it is detected

if an exception be pleaded of judgment recovered or of previous joinder of issue on the same question. What are *legitima
iudicia* and what *iudicia imperio continentia* will be explained
in our next Commentary.

[4] Comp. iv, 106.
[5] See iv, §§ 104, 105.
§§ 182-208. Comp. tit. I. *DE OBLI-
GATIONIBVS QVAE EX DELICTO
NASCVNTVR* (iv, 1).
§ 182. Comp. Gai. in fr. 4, D. *de O. et
A.* (xliv, 7) ; pr. tit. I. afd.
[1] All created *re*, that is by thing
done.

[2] See § 89.
§ 183. Comp. Gai. in fr. 2, D. *de furt.*
(xlvii, 2) ; Gell. xi, 18 ; Paul. ii, 81,
§ 2; § 3, tit. I. afd.
[1] See i, 188, note 5.
[2] See i, 196, note 1.
§§ 184, 185. Comp. Gell., Paul., Inst.,
as in last par.
[1] The MS. has *metum fructum.*

alii uero ulterius, quod eo loco deprehenditur ubi fit, ueluti
si in oliueto oliuarum, in uineto uinarum, furtum factum est,
quamdiu in eo oliueto aut uineto *fur sit*,[2] aut si in domo
furtum factum sit, quamdiu in ea domo fur sit : alii adhuc ulterius, eousque — —[3] manifestum furtum esse dixerunt donec
perferret eo quo perferre fur destinasset : alii adhuc ulterius,
quandoque eam rem fur tenens uisus fuerit ; quae sententia
non optinuit : sed et illorum sententia qui existimauerunt,
donec perferretur eo quo fur destinasset, deprehensum *furtum
manifestum* esse, ideo non *uidetur* probari quod *magnam
recipit* dubitationem *utrum unius diei an* etiam plurium
dierum spatio id terminandum sit ; quod eo pertinet, quia
saepe in aliis ciuitatibus subreptas res in alias ciuitates uel
in alias prouincias destinant fures perferre : ex duabus itaque
superioribus opinionibus alterutra adprobatur ; magis tamen
185 plerique posteriorem probant.   *Nec* manifestum furtum
quid sit ex iis quae diximus intellegitur : nam quod mani-
186 festum non est, id nec manifestum est.   Conceptum furtum

---

while being committed ; others extend the definition to theft
detected while the thief is still in the place of its commission,
—while he is still in the olive-garden, say, from which he has
been stealing olives, or the vineyard in which he has been
stealing grapes, or, if the theft have been committed in a
house, before he has left it ; others go further, and hold a
theft to be manifest until the thief has reached his destination
with the stolen property ; while others go further still, and
reckon the theft manifest if at any time the thief be discovered with the goods in his hands.   This last opinion has
not met with favour ; nor does that which regards a theft as
manifest until the thief has reached his destination seem to
be approved, there being great dubiety as to the time, whether
one day or several, within which that must occur,—for a thief
often means to carry the things he has stolen in one city into
another city or province.   One or other of the first and second
opinions, therefore, is adopted, and more generally the second.
185 What is non-manifest theft may be gathered from what has
been already said ; whatever is not manifest is non-manifest.
186 There is said to be *furtum conceptum* when stolen goods are
sought for and discovered on a man's premises in the presence

---

[2] The MS. has *fuerit*.   inserts *cuiusque rei*.
[3] P. conjectures that the illegible   § 186. § 4, tit. I. afd. Comp. §§ 191,
word may have been *scilicet;* Hu.   192; Paul. ii, 31, §§ 3, 5.

dicitur cum apud aliquem testibus praesentibus furtiua res
quaesita et inuenta est : nam in eum propria actio constituta
187 est, quamuis fur non sit, quae appellatur concepti.   Oblatum
furtum dicitur cum res furtiua tibi ab aliquo oblata sit, eaque
apud te concepta sit; *utique*[1] si ea mente data tibi fuerit ut
apud te potius quam apud eum qui dederit conciperetur :
nam tibi, apud quem concepta est, propria aduersus eum qui
optulit, quamuis fur non sit, constituta est actio [*quae*]
188 appellatur oblati.   Est etiam prohibiti furti [*actio*] aduersus
eum qui furtum quaerere uolentem prohibuerit.
189   Poena manifesti furti ex lege XII tabularum capitalis[1] erat :
nam liber uerberatus addicebatur ei cui furtum fecerat ; utrum
autem seruus efficeretur ex addictione an adiudicati loco con-
stitueretur ueteres quaerebant :[2] — — — — —.[3] *sed* postea

---

of witnesses; it gives rise to a special action against him,
even though he be not the thief, which goes by the name of
187 *actio furti concepti.*   *Furtum oblatum* occurs when stolen
property has been brought to you by some one and discovered
on your premises, at least if it have been given to you with
the intent that it should be found in your house rather than
his; you, on whose premises the discovery has been made,
are entitled to an action against the individual who introduced the stolen goods, even though he be not the thief, which
188 is called an *actio furti oblati.*   The *actio furti prohibiti* is
that made use of against a man who prevents search being
made [on his premises] for stolen property.
189   The punishment of manifest theft, according to the Twelve

§ 187. § 4, tit. I. afd. Comp. § 191;
Paul. ii, 31, §§ 3, 5.
[1] The MS. has *uelutique.*
§ 188. § 4, tit. I. afd. Comp. § 192.
§§ 189, 190. Comp. Cic. *pro Tullio*, v,
47; Gell. xi, 18, xx, 1; Serv. *ad
Aen.* viii, 205; Macrob. *Sat.* i, 4,
§ 19; § 5, tit. I. afd.
[1] A capital punishment was one
that affected the *caput* of the individual by depriving him of life,
liberty, or citizenship.
[2] Gai. seems to be pointing to
the distinction between an individual who by judicial sentence
became in the fullest sense the
slave of the party to whom he was
awarded, and an *adiudicatus*, *i.e.*
an insolvent debtor handed over to
his creditor to work off his debt,

and who was only *de facto* in the
position of a slave, *de iure* a freeman. That the convicted manifest
thief could not have been in the
position of a mere *adiudicatus* (who
forfeited neither freedom nor citizenship) seems clear; if he had been,
his punishment could not have
been described as capital. Gell.
(xi, 18, § 8) says that if the theft
was by night, or the thief armed,
the punishment was death; but that,
in the absence of either of those
aggravations, *decemuiri . . . liberos
uerberari addicique iusserunt ei*, etc.
This may be ambiguous; but in xx,
1, § 7, he says distinctly—*furem
manifestum ei cui furtum factum est
in seruitutem tradit.*
[3] The illegible passage (two-thirds

inprobata est asperitas poenae, et tam ex serui persona quam
190 ex liberi quadrupli actio praetoris edicto constituta est.   Nec
manifesti furti poena per legem [XII] tabularum dupli inro-
191 gatur, eamque etiam praetor conseruat.   Concepti et oblati
poena ex lege XII tabularum tripli est, *eaque* similiter a prae-
192 tore seruatur.   Prohibiti actio quadrupli est, ex edicto
praetoris introducta : lex autem eo nomine nullam poenam
constituit ; hoc solum praecipit, ut qui quaerere uelit nudus
quaerat, linteo[1] cinctus, lancem habens ; qui si quid inuenerit,[2]

Tables, was capital.   If the thief was a freeman, he was
scourged and given up by magisterial decree to him whose
goods he had stolen ; but whether this addiction made him a
slave, or only put him in the condition of an insolvent judgment debtor, was a point of controversy with the old lawyers.
[*If a slave, he was first scourged and then thrown from the*
[*Tarpeian rock.*] But afterwards these punishments were
disapproved on account of their severity ; and an action for
fourfold the value of the thing stolen, applicable alike to freemen and slaves, was substituted by the praetorian edict.
190 Non-manifest theft was punished by the Twelve Tables with
a twofold penalty, and this the praetor has left untouched.
191 The punishment for stolen goods discovered or introduced,
according to the Tables, was of threefold the value of the
stolen property ; and this too the praetor has retained.
192 The *actio furti prohibiti* for fourfold the value was introduced
by the edict.   The Twelve Tables had not provided any
punishment for this offence ; all they required was that he
who proposed to search another's premises for stolen pro-

of a line) was thus supplied by Hu.
in his third edition—*in seruum
aeque uerberatum animaduertebatur*, and this conjecture has been
adopted by K. u. S. Hu. in his
last edition, however, proposes—*in
eum autem, qui* [*seruus erat aeque*] *uerberatum animaduertebatur.*
Neither reading is satisfactory ; and
we can hardly suppose that Gai.
would content himself with so feeble
a word as *animaduertere*, when he
was in the same breath denouncing
the *asperitas poenae*. Gell. (§ 8)
says—*iusserunt . . . seruos . . . uer-
beribus adfici et e saxo praecipitari.*
Hence Schoell (*Leg. XII Tab. rel.*
p. 146) suggests—*seruus aeque uerberatus e saxo deiciebatur.*

§ 191. Comp. iv, 173 ; Gell. xi, 18 ;
    Paul. ii, 31, § 14 ; § 4, tit. I. afd.
§ 192. Comp. Plato *de leg.* xii, 7 ;
    Schol. Aristoph. *Nub.* 499 ; Paul.
    ex Festo, v. *Lance et licio* (Bruns, p.
    244) ; Gell. xi, 18, xvi, 10 (where
    he says that the practice of search
    lance et licio was abolished by the
    lex Aebutia, as to which see below,
    iv, 30, note 1) ; *Lex Burgund.* tit.
    12 ; § 4, tit. I. afd. ; Inst. Gloss.
    Taurin. iv, 1, § 4 (*Z. f. RG.* vii, 78).
        [1] So the MS. ;   many editors,
    following Gellius, etc., substitute
    licio ; Hu., both here and in sub-
    sequent pars., retains the *linteo* and
    adds *licio*.
        [2] So those four words in the MS.
    But there is good reason to doubt

193 iubet id lex furtum manifestum esse.   Quid sit autem
linteum quaesitum est : sed uerius *est eum* consuti genus esse,
quo necessariae partes tegerentur.   *quae res* tota [1] ridicula est ;
nam qui uestitum quaerere probibet, is et nudum quaerere
prohibiturus est, eo magis quod ita quaesita re inuenta maiori
poenae subiciatur.   deinde quod lancem siue ideo haberi
iubeatur ut manibus *occupatis* [2] nihil subiciat, siue · ideo ut

---

perty should do so naked, wearing nothing but a *linteum*
and carrying a platter ; and if he found anything, then,
according to the Tables, the case was to be dealt with as
193 one of manifest theft.   What this *linteum* was has been
doubted, but it seems to have been some sort of cloth or
towel worn round the loins for decency's sake.   But the
whole thing is ridiculous ; for he who would prevent a man
wearing his ordinary dress from making a search, would
equally prevent him when naked, especially as the discovery
of a thing when sought for would subject the prohibiter to a
heavier penalty.   And as regards the platter, whether it be
said that its use was enjoined in order that, the hands of

their accuracy, and to warrant the
surmise that Gai. had formed an
erroneous notion of the distinction
between *furtum conceptum* and *furtum prohibitum.*   That he was
puzzled is evident from what he
says in the next par.   The view
that occurs to me, and that seems
to obviate the difficulty he there
expresses, is this : that in the earlier
law search required in every case to
be made *lance et licio,* and at a later
period (§ 186 ; § 4, tit. I. afd.) in
the presence of witnesses ; that if
the search was permitted, and the
stolen property discovered, there
was *furtum conceptum* with a threefold penalty ; but that if it were
prevented there was under the
Twelve Tables a constructive *furtum manifestum,* and under the
edict an offence called *furtum
prohibitum,* punished with the
same fourfold penalty as manifest
theft.
   If this be the correct view, *quod
si prohibitus fuerit* ought to be substituted for *qui si quid inuenerit ;*
for the *actio furti prohibiti* appears
to have been based, not on the discovery of the stolen goods in spite

of prohibition,—indeed it is extremely doubtful whether under
such circumstances search was possible, for to enter a man's house
against his will was an offence (Gai.
in fr. 18, D. *de in ius uoc.* ii, 4),—
but on the prohibition itself (§ 188).
If there had been an *actio furti prohibiti* only when the stolen property
had been discovered, what shadow
of reason could there have been for
the contention of some of the jurists
(§ 194) that *furtum prohibitum* was
theft only by fiction of law, *lege,
non natura ?*
   § 193. See references and remarks in
notes to last par.
   [1] The ms. has *qrlextota ;* but the
lex seems to be a gloss,—some annotator's explanation of what he
understood by the *res.* Hu. reads
quare lex tota.
   [2] The ms. has *occupantis ;* the
correction is Vangerow's in his dis-
sertation *de furto concepto ex lege
XII Tab.* (Heidelb. 1845),—a mono-
graph very amusing in its exposure
of the vagaries of the civilians on
this subject, but which itself rests
content with the explanation of Gai.
as in all respects satisfactory.

quod inuenerit ibi inponat, neutrum eorum procedit si id
quod quaeratur eius magnitudinis aut naturae sit ut neque
subici neque ibi inponi possit.   certe non dubitatur cuius-
194 cumque materiae sit ea lanx satis legi fieri.   Propter hoc
tamen quod lex ex ea causa manifestum furtum esse iubet,
sunt qui scribunt furtum manifestum aut lege [*intellegi*]¹ aut
natura; lege id ipsum de quo loquimur, natura illud de quo
superius exposuimus: sed uerius est natura tantum manifestum furtum intellegi; neque enim lex facere potest ut qui
manifestus fur non sit, manifestus sit, non magis quam qui
omnino fur non sit, fur sit, et qui adulter aut homicida non
sit, adulter uel homicida sit; at illud sane lex facere potest,
ut proinde aliquis poena teneatur atque si furtum uel adul-
terium uel homicidium admisisset, quamuis nihil eorum
admiserit.

195   Furtum autem fit non solum cum quis intercipiendi causa
rem alienam amouet, sed generaliter cum quis rem alienam

---

the holder being occupied in carrying it, he could not surreptitiously take anything into the premises, or in order that
he might place upon it anything found by him, neither reason
could be satisfactory when the article sought for was of such
a size or nature that it could neither be smuggled into the
premises nor put upon the platter.   There is no doubt that the
law was complied with if a platter was there, no matter of
194 what material it might be.   On the strength of the declaration of the Tables that the discovery of stolen articles in this
way is to be treated as manifest theft, some maintain that a
theft may be] manifest either by force of law or in point of
fact; by force of law in the case we have just been dealing
with, in point of fact in that previously explained.   But it is
more accurate to say that theft can be manifest only when it
is so in point of fact; the law can no more make a man a
thief who is not so, than it can make that person an adulterer
or a homicide who is innocent of adultery or manslaughter;
but it may do this,—it may declare a man liable to punishment as if he had committed theft, adultery, or manslaughter,
although he be not actually guilty of any of them.
195   There is theft not only when a man removes another's property with the intention to deprive him of it, but generally
when one meddles with what belongs to another against the

---

§ 194. Comp. Gai. in fr. 2, § 1, D. *de*   ¹ Huschke's addition.
usufr. ear. rer. (vii, 5).   § 195. § 6, tit. I. afd. Cp. Paul. ii, 31, § 1.

196 inuito domino contrectat.   Itaque si quis re quae apud eum
     deposita sit utatur, furtum committit; et si quis utendam rem
     acceperit, eamque in alium usum transtulerit, furti obligatur,
     ueluti si quis argentum utendum acceperit, [*quod*]¹ quasi
     amicos ad *cenam inuitaturus* rogauerit,² et id peregre secum
     tulerit, aut si quis equum gestandi gratia commodatum
     longius *secum* ³ aliquo duxerit, quod ueteres scripserunt de eo
197 qui in aciem ⁴ perduxisset.   Placuit tamen eos qui rebus
     commodatis aliter uterentur quam utendas accepissent ita
     furtum committere, *si intellegant* id se inuito domino facere,
     eumque si intellexisset non permissurum; at si permissurum
     credant, extra furti crimen uideri : optima sane distinctione,
198 quia furtum sine dolo malo non committitur.¹   Sed et si

---

196 owner's will.   Accordingly, if a man take the use of a thing
     deposited with him, he commits a theft. So does he who,
     having received a thing to be used in a particular way, takes
     the use of it in another way; as, for instance, when a man on
     his own request, and on the representation that he is about to
     entertain his friends, has received the use of certain silver
     plate, which he carries away with him into the country : or
     when one takes with him to a distance—to use an illustration
     of the old jurists, when he takes into battle—a horse bor-
197 rowed by him merely for a ride.   But the statement that a
     borrower commits theft by using what he has borrowed for
     another purpose than that for which it was lent, must be
     taken with this qualification,—if he know that the owner
     does not consent, and that the latter, if he were aware of
     what was being done, would not allow it. If the borrower
     believe that it would be allowed, the idea of theft is excluded ;
     and the distinction is a very proper one, seeing that there can
198 be no theft without wrongful intent.   Even when a man

§ 196. § 6, tit. I. afd. Comp. Gell. vi,
15; Valer. Max. viii, 2, § 4 ; Paul.
ii, 31, § 29.
     ¹ Inserted by all eds. except Hu.,
P., and K. u. S. who drop the subsequent *rogauerit*, and so find *quod*
unnecessary.
     ² This word in the ms., but
deleted by the eds. just mentioned.
     ³ The ms. has *longius cum aliquo ;
secum* is Goeschen's amendment,
approved by most eds.; K. u. S.
drop the word altogether; Hu. re-

forms the sentence,—*longius [quam
quo rogauerit] aliquo*, etc.
     ⁴ The ms. has *in aciem* quite dis-
tinctly ; but Hu. in his last edition
has substituted *uls Ariciam*, under
the belief that the reference is to
the story told by Valer. Max. of a
man who was condemned for theft
because, having borrowed a horse
to ride to Aricia, he took it a little
further.
§ 197. § 7, tit. I. afd.
     ¹ Comp. ii, 50 ; Paul. ii, 31, § 1.
§ 198. § 8, tit. I. afd.

credat aliquis inuito domino se rem contrectare, domino autem
uolente id fiat, dicitur furtum non fieri. unde,[1] cum Titius
seruum meum *sollicitauerit*[2] ut quasdam res mihi subriperet
et ad eum perferret, [*et seruus*][3] id ad me pertulerit, ego, dum
uolo Titium in ipso delicto deprehendere, *permiserim seruo*
quasdam res ad eum perferre, quaesitum est utrum furti an
serui corrupti iudicio[4] teneatur Titius mihi, an neutro ?
responsum neutro eum teneri ; furti ideo quod non inuito
me res contrectauerit, serui corrupti ideo quod deterior seruus
199 factus non sit.   Interdum autem etiam liberorum hominum
furtum fit, ueluti si quis liberorum nostrorum qui in potestate
nostra sunt, siue etiam uxor quae in manu nostra sit,[1] siue
etiam adiudicatus[2] uel auctoratus[3] meus subreptus *fuerit*.
200 Aliquando etiam suae rei quisque furtum committit, ueluti si
debitor rem quam creditori pignori dedit subtraxerit, uel si

---

believes that he is dealing with a thing against the will of
its owner, yet if in fact the owner consents, it is held that no
theft is committed.   Hence, when Titius was importuning
a slave of mine to carry away things belonging to me and
give them to him, (of which my slave informed me,) and I,
desiring that Titius should be taken in the act, allowed my
slave to take some articles to him, this question arose,—Was
Titius liable to me in an action for theft, or in an action
for corrupting my slave ? or was he liable in neither? The
answer was that he was liable in neither; that he was not
liable for theft, because there had been no meddling with my
property against my will, nor for corrupting my slave, because
the latter was not a whit the worse for what had happened.
199 Sometimes there may be theft even of free persons ; as when
any of my children in my *potestas* is stealthily carried off, or
my wife *in manu,* or even my judgment debtor, or one of my
200 sworn gladiators.   Sometimes, too, a man may steal what is
his own, as when a debtor surreptitiously takes away some-

---

[1] After *unde* the MS. has *illud
quaesitum et probatum est,* which
have been expunged as a gloss.
[2] So the Inst.; the MS. has *colligi-
taret.*
[3] Supplied from the Inst.
[4] Comp. § 23, I. *de act.* (iv, 6).
§ 199.   Comp. § 9, tit. I. afd.
[1] Comp. ii, 90 (*ipsas non possidemus*).
[2] See § 189, note 2; iv, 21, note
6. The MS. and most eds. have

iudicatus; the amendment is due to
Hu., who rightly observes that the
iudicatus or judgment debtor was
not in any sense in the possession
of his creditor until *adiudicatio,*—
a step in execution rendered necessary by his having no effects.
[3] See *Collat.* iv, 8, § 2, ix, 2,
§ 2 ; *L. Iulia Municipalis,* cap. 25
(Bruns, p. 79).
§ 200. Comp. § 204; Paul. ii, 31, §§
21, 36 ; § 10, tit. I. afd.

bonae fidei possessori rem meam possidenti subripuerim : unde
placuit eum qui seruum suum, quem alius bona fide posside-
201 bat, ad se reuersum celauerit, furtum committere.   Rursus
ex diuerso interdum alienas res occupare et usucapere concessum est, nec creditur furtum fieri, ueluti res hereditarias
quarum heres *non est* nactus possessionem, nisi necessarius
heres *esset ;* [1] nam necessario herede extante placuit nihil pro
herede usucapi posse.   *Item debitor rem* quam fiduciae causa
creditori mancipauerit aut in iure cesserit, *secundum* ea [2]
quae in superiore commentario rettulimus, sine furto possidere
202 et usucapere potest.   Interdum furti tenetur *qui* ipse furtum
non fecerit, qualis est cuius ope consilio furtum factum est :
in quo numero est qui nummos tibi excussit ut eos alius subriperet, uel obstitit tibi ut alius subriperet, aut oues aut boues
tuas fugauit ut alius eas exciperet : et hoc ueteres [1] scripserunt

---

thing he has given to his creditor as a pledge, or when I
stealthily take away something of mine from a party possessing it in good faith ; and accordingly it has been ruled that he
who conceals his own slave, who has run away from a third
201 party possessing him in good faith, is guilty of theft.   On
the other hand we are sometimes allowed to possess ourselves
of another's property, and acquire a title to it by usucapion,
without any theft being held to have been committed ; as
[when we take possession of] things belonging to an inheritance
before the heir has entered, provided always he is not a necessary heir ; for it is held that if there be a necessary heir there
can be no usucapion *pro herede.*   A debtor, also, may, without
any imputation of theft, possess and reacquire by usucapion a
thing he has fiduciarily conveyed to his creditor by mancipation or cession before a magistrate, as explained in the preced-
202 ing Commentary.   Occasionally a man may be chargeable
with theft although he may not have been the actual thief
namely, when it has been committed with his aid or counsel.
He belongs to this class who has knocked money out of your
hand that another might make off with it, or has impeded
your movements that another might take something from you,
or has scattered your sheep or cattle—as, in an old case in the
books, by the use of a red flag—that another might get them
away from you.   But if any of such things have been done in

§ 201. Comp. ii, §§ 52, 56-60; Paul. ii,
31, § 11.
  [1] So the ms.; K. u. S. and Hu.
have *extet ;* I fail to see why.

[2] The ms. has *dum ea.*
§ 202. § 11, tit. I. afd. Comp. iv, 37;
  Paul. ii, 31, § 10; §§ 12, 18, tit. I. afd.
  [1] See i, 144, note 2.

de eo qui panno rubro fugauit armentum. sed si quid per
lasciuiam et non data opera ut furtum committeretur factum
sit, uidebimus an utilis² *actio dari*³ debeat, cum per legem
Aquiliam⁴ quae de damno lata [*est*] etiam culpa puniatur.

203   Furti autem actio ei conpetit cuius interest rem saluam esse,
licet dominus non sit: itaque nec domino aliter conpetit quam
204 si eius intersit rem non perire.   Vnde constat creditorem de
pignore subrepto furti agere posse; adeo quidem ut quamuis
ipse dominus, id est ipse debitor, eam rem subripuerit, nihilo
205 minus creditori conpetat actio furti.   Item si fullo polienda
curandaue aut sarcinator sarcienda uestimenta mercede certa
acceperit, eaque furto amiserit, ipse furti habet actionem, non
dominus; quia domini nihil *interest*¹ ea non periisse, cum
iudicio locati a fullone aut sarcinatore suum *consequi* possit, si
modo is fullo aut sarcinator *rei* praestandae² sufficiat; nam si
soluendo non est, tunc quia ab eo dominus suum consequi non

---

pure wantonness, and not of set purpose to facilitate a theft,
it will be for consideration whether an *utilis* [Aquilian] *actio*
ought not to be allowed, since, by the Aquilian law concerning
wrongful damage to property, even *culpa* is punishable.

203   The *actio furti* is competent to him whose interest it is that
the thing should be safe, even though not its owner; therefore the owner can raise it then only when it is his interest
204 that the thing should not be lost.   Hence it is acknowledged that a creditor may raise it in respect of theft of what
has been pledged to him, and that even when it is the owner,
205 that is to say his debtor, that has taken it from him.   So, if
clothes have been given to a fuller to be pressed or scoured,
or to a tailor to be repaired, and that for a fixed recompense,
if he has lost them by theft it is he that has the *actio furti*,
and not the owner; for it matters not to the latter whether
they be lost or not, seeing he can recover damages from the
fuller or tailor, if he be solvent, by an action of location.   If,
however, he be insolvent, then, as the owner cannot recover

---

²See ii, 78, note 1.
³The ᴍs. has *atque deari;* the
Inst. *actio dari;* but for *atque* one
might perhaps read *Aquilia.*
⁴Comp. § 211.
§ 203.   § 13, tit. I. afd. Comp. Paul.
ii, 31, § 4.   Ou the *condictio furtiua*
see iv, 4.
§ 204.   Comp. Paul. ii, 31, § 19; § 14,
tit. I. afd.

§ 205.   Comp. Paul. ii, 31, § 29; § 15,
tit. I. afd.; § 5, I. *de locat. et cond.*
(iii, 24).
¹So the Inst.; the ᴍs. has *id
est.*
²The ᴍs. has *rempstandepic;*
P. reads *representandae pecuniae;*
Hu. *rei praestandae plene;* K. u. S.
as above.

potest, ipsi furti actio conpetit, quia hoc casu ipsius interest
206 rem saluam esse.   *Quae de* [1] fullone aut sarcinatore diximus,
eadem transferemus et ad eum cui rem commodauimus : nam
ut illi mercedem capiendo custodiam praestant, ita hic quoque
utendi commodum percipiendo similiter necesse habet cus-
207 todiam praestare.   Sed is apud quem res deposita est custodiam non praestat, tantumque in eo obnoxius est si quid ipse
dolo [*malo*] [1] fecerit ; qua de *causa* [*si*] *res* [2] ei subrepta fuerit
quae restituenda est,[3] eius nomine actione depositi non tenetur,
nec ob id eius interest rem saluam esse ; furti itaque agere non
potest, sed ea actio domino conpetit.
208   In summa sciendum est quaesitum esse an inpubes rem
alienam amouendo furtum faciat. plerisque placet, quia
furtum ex *adfectu* consistit,[1] ita demum obligari eo crimine

---

from him what he is entitled to, he, the owner, may sue the
actio furti, because in this case he has an interest in the
206 safety of his property.   What has been said of a fuller
or tailor applies equally to him to whom we have lent some
specific article ; for as the former, in consideration of the payment they are to receive, are responsible for the safe custody
of the thing entrusted to them, so of necessity is the latter,
for the simple reason that he is enjoying the advantage of
207 using it.   A depositary, however, is not responsible for the
safe-keeping of what has been deposited with him, being liable
only in so far as he himself has done something doleful ; consequently if it be taken from him surreptitiously, as he cannot
on that account be convened in an action of deposit, and has
really no interest in the safety of the thing, it is not he but
the owner that is entitled to the *actio furti.*
208   Finally, it is a question whether a child below the age of
puberty commits theft by taking away what belongs to
another. Most agree that, as theft depends upon intent,
such a child can only oblige himself in respect of it when he

§ 206.   § 16, tit. I. afd. Comp. *Collat.*
x, 2, §§ 1, 6 ; § 2, I. *quib. mod. re
contr. obl.* (iii, 14).
     [1] The ms. has *deque.*
§ 207.   § 17, tit. I. afd. Comp. § 3,
I. *quib. mod. re contr. obl.* (iii,
14).
     [1] *Malo* from Inst., omitted in
the ms.
     [2] For *qua de causa* [*si*] *res*, the
ms. has *quadegreis.*
     17

[3] So the ms., quite distinctly and
intelligibly. Hu. and K. u. S., preferring apparently the version of
the Inst., read *quia restituendae
eius,* and drop the subsequent
itaque ; P. does the same, except
that he reads *qui* instead of *quae* or
quia.
§ 208.   § 18, tit. I. afd. Comp. Gai. in
fr. 111, pr. D. *de R. I.* (l, 17).
     [1] Comp. § 197.

inpuberem si proximus pubertati ² sit et ob id intellegat se
delinquere.

209   Qui res alienas rapit, tenetur etiam furti : quis enim magis
alienam rem inuito domino contrectat quam qui rapit ? ¹
itaque *recte dictum* est eum inprobum furem esse : sed propriam actionem eius delicti nomine praetor introduxit quae
appellatur ui bonorum raptorum, et est intra annum quadrupli,² post annum simpli : quae actio utilis est etsi quis unam
rem, licet minimam, rapuerit.

210   Damni iniuriae actio constituitur per legem Aquiliam,

---

is close upon puberty and therefore understands that he is
committing an offence.

209   He also who takes anything belonging to another by
robbery, is held guilty of theft ; for who can with more truth
be said to meddle with another man's property without its
owner's consent than he who takes it away by force ? He
is therefore rightly spoken of as an atrocious thief. The
praetor, however, has introduced an action appropriate to this
particular offence under the name of *actio ui bonorum raptorum*,
for fourfold the value of the thing stolen if raised within the
year, and for the single value afterwards ; and it is competent
even though but a single thing, however trifling, has been
carried off.

210   The *actio damni iniuriae* was introduced by the Aquilian

---

² Comp. § 109.

§ 209. Comp. tit. I. *VI BONORVM RAP-
TORVM* (iv, 2), and particularly the
principium.

¹ The Inst. have *quam qui ui
rapit*, and most eds. introduce the
ui into the text of Gai. But if it
were a necessary adjunct one would
have equally to correct the initial
and final words, and read *qui res
alienas ui rapit*, and *ui rapuerit*.

² The MS. has *quadrupli actio*,
but the latter word has been expunged as a gloss.

§§ 210-219. Comp. tit. I. *DE LEGE
AQVILIA* (iv, 3). This law, according to Th. (iv, 3, § 15) and a
scholiast of the Bas. (lx, 3, l. 1),
was a plebiscit enacted at the instance of a tribune of the name of
Aquilius, at a crisis in the feud
between the senate and the people ;

a date which historians are inclined
to identify with the third secession
in 467 | 287, and probably immedi-
ately after the passing of the *lex
Hortensia*, which gave plebiscits the
force of *leges*.

In a passage in Cicero (*Brut.*
xxxiv, 131) it is called the *L.
Aquilia de iustitia ;* for the two
latter words Orelli substitutes *damni
iniuriae ;* Hu. (*Beitr.* p. 106) is of
opinion they should be *de rupitia*.
We know from Festus, under the
words *Rupitias* and *Sarcito* (Bruns,
pp. 261, 264), that the XII Tables
contained a law (or laws) in which
those words occurred ; and many
civilians are of opinion that they
constituted or formed part of a provision such as *rupitias sarcito, rupitias qui faxit sarcito, qui rupitias
dederit sarcito*, or the like,—'let

cuius primo capite cautum est [*ut*] si quis hominem alienum,
alienamue quadrupedem quae pecudum numero sit, iniuria
occiderit, quanti ea res in eo anno plurimi fuerit,[1] tantum[2]
211 domino dare damnetur.   iniuria autem occidere intellegitur
cuius dolo aut culpa id acciderit, nec ulla alia lege damnum
quod sine iniuria datur reprehenditur; itaque inpunitus est
qui sine culpa et dolo malo casu quodam damnum committit.[1]
212 Nec solum corpus in actione huius legis aestimatur; sed sane
si[1] seruo occiso plus dominus capiat damni quam pretium
serui sit, id quoque aestimatur, ueluti si seruus meus ab
aliquo heres institutus, antequam iussu meo hereditatem cer-
neret,[2] occisus fuerit: non enim tantum ipsius pretium aestimatur, sed et hereditatis amissae quantitas. item si ex

law; whose first chapter provides that he who wrongfully
kills another man's slave, or a quadruped of his cattle, shall
be condemned to pay the owner a sum equal to the highest
211 value it could have fetched during the year.   He is held
to have killed wrongfully to whose dole or fault death is
attributable, there being no law that imputes blame for loss
occasioned without wrong-doing; therefore a man goes un-
punished who, by some accident, and without fault or dole,
212 does some damage to another's property.   It is not the mere
corpus that is considered in measuring damages under this
enactment; for there is no question that if a slave be killed,
and the consequent loss to his owner be greater than his
intrinsic value, that also will be taken into account.   For
example, if a slave of mine, who has been instituted heir by
some one, be killed before he has by my authority declared
his acceptance of the inheritance, not only his individual
value will fall within the assessment, but also the amount
of the inheritance that has thus gone past me.   So too if one

him who has destroyed property replace it.' (See the literature on
the subject in Sell, *die Actio de
rupitiis sarciendis der* XII *Tafeln*,
Bonn, 1877). It was to amend this
very vague and general provision,
together with all subsequent legislation on the subject of *damnum
iniuria* not of a special character,
that the Aquilian law was enacted
(fr. 1, pr. D. *ad leg. Aquil.* ix, 2);
hence, if Hu. be right, its name of
L. Aquilia de rupitia.

§ 210. Pr. tit. I. afd. The words of
cap. i. are given by Gai. in fr. 2, pr.
D. *ad leg. Aquil.* (ix, 2).

[1] For meaning of *quanti ea res
fuerit* see fr. 179, fr. 193, D. *de
V. S.* (l, 16).
[2] The words of the enactment
were *tantum aes dare domino damnas esto* (see ii, § 201, note 2),
which has induced Hu. to interpolate *aes* after *tantum.*

§ 211. Comp. Vlp. in *Collat.* vii, 3, §§
1, 4; §§ 2, 3, 14, tit. I. afd.
[1] *Casus* . . . *a nullo praestantur*,
fr. 28, D. *de R. I.* (l, 17).

§ 212. Comp. § 10, tit. I. afd.
[1] The MS. has *sanei ;* Hu. changes
it into *si ueluti.*
[2] Comp. ii, 87; Vlp. xix, 19.

gemellis uel ex comoedis uel ex symphoniacis unus occisus
fuerit, non solum occisi fit aestimatio, sed eo amplius [id]³
quoque conputatur quod ceteri qui supersunt depretiati sunt.
idem iuris est etiam si ex pari mularum unam uel etiam ex
213 quadrigis equorum unum occiderit.   Cuius autem seruus
occisus est, is liberum arbitrium habet uel capitali crimine
reum facere eum qui occiderit, uel hac lege damnum persequi.
214 Quod autem adiectum est in hac lege : QVANTI IN EO ANNO
PLVRIMI EA RES FVERIT, illud efficit, si clodum puta aut luscum
seruum occiderit qui in eo anno integer fuerit, [ut non quanti
[clodus aut luscus, sed quanti integer fuerit]¹ aestimatio fiat;
quo fit ut quis plus interdum consequatur quam ei damnum
datum est.
215   Capite secundo [aduersus] adstipulatorem¹ qui pecuniam
in fraudem stipulatoris acceptam fecerit,² quanti ea res est,³
216 tanti actio constituitur.   qua et ipsa parte legis damni

---

of twins, or one of a company of actors or musicians be killed,
not only his separate value will be taken account of, but also
the depreciated value of those that remain.   And so also if
one of a pair of mules be killed, or even one of a team of four
213 chariot horses.   A man whose slave has been killed has it
in his option either to proceed against the delinquent by prosecution for a capital crime, or to sue him for damages under
214 this enactment.   The introduction in the enactment of the
words, ' Whatever within the year was the highest value of
the thing,' has this effect,—that if it is a lame or one-eyed
slave that has been killed, but who has been sound during
the year, the measure of damages will be *not his value as lame
or one-eyed, but his value as sound and whole ;* so that it may
sometimes happen that an owner will recover more than
covers the loss he has sustained.
215   By the second chapter of the same Aquilian law an action
for the value involved is allowed against an adstipulator who,
in fraud of the stipulant, has granted the debtor a discharge
216 by acceptilation.   It is plain as regards this part also of

---

³ Supplied from Inst.
§ 213.   Comp. § 11, tit. I. afd.
§ 214.   Comp. § 9, tit. I. afd.
    ¹ The words in ital. are Huschke's;
Bk., K. u. S., and other eds., interpolate to the same effect ; P. is content with *ita.*
§ 215.   Comp. § 12, tit. I. afd.
    ¹ Comp. §§ 110, 117.

² Comp. § 169.
³ See § 210, note 1.
§ 216.   An adstipulator acceptilating in
fraud of the stipulant destroyed and
deprived him of an incorporeal
item of his estate (ii, 14), viz. his
claim against his debtor; there
was therefore *damnum iniuria
datum.*

nomine actionem introduci manifestum est : sed id caueri non
fuit necessarium, cum actio mandati ad eam rem sufficeret ; [1]
nisi quod ea lege aduersus infitiantem in duplum agitur.[2]

217   Capite tertio de omni cetero damno cauetur. itaque si quis
seruum uel eam quadrupedem quae pecudum [*numero est
[uulnerauerit, siue eam quadrupedem quae pecudum*] numero
non est, ueluti canem, aut feram bestiam, ueluti ursum, leonem
uulnerauerit uel occiderit, hoc capite actio constituitur : in
ceteris quoque animalibus, item in omnibus rebus quae anima
carent, damnum iniuria datum hac parte uindicatur ; si quid
enim ustum aut ruptum aut fractum [*fuerit*], actio hoc capite
constituitur, quamquam potuerit sola rupti appellatio in omnes
istas causas sufficere : ruptum [*enim intellegitur quod quoquo
[modo corruptum*] est ; unde non solum usta [aut rupta][1] aut
fracta, sed etiam scissa et conlisa et effusa et quoquo modo
uitiata aut [2] perempta atque deteriora facta hoc uerbo continen-

the enactment, that it was because of damage done that the
action was introduced. The provision, however, would hardly
have been necessary, and an action of mandate would have
been sufficient to meet the case but for this,—that in the
action under the statute the condemnation of a defender
denying his liability is in double damages.

217   In the third chapter provision is made for all other cases of
damage to property. Therefore, if any one *have wounded* a
slave, or a quadruped of a man's cattle, or have wounded
or killed *a quadruped* that is *not of his cattle*, such as a dog,
or a wild beast, such as a bear or a lion, a remedy is provided
by this clause. In the case of other animals, as well as of
inanimate things generally, if wrongful damage be done to
them, redress is given by this same part of the enactment,
which confers a right of action wherever anything has been
burned, destroyed, or broken. This enumeration is almost
unnecessary, seeing that the single word *ruptum*, destroyed,
includes all three—*ruptum* in fact *being equivalent to* corruptum, *spoiled, no matter in what way ;* therefore not only things
burned, destroyed, or broken, but also things cut, bruised,
emptied out, or in any way vitiated, demolished, or deteriorated,

[1] Comp. § 111. Notwithstanding
what Gai. says there and here, it is
extremely doubtful whether an *actio
mandati* was known to the law at
the time of the enactment of the *L.
Aquilia.*
[2] Comp. iv, §§ 9, 171.
§ 217. § 13, tit. I. afd., from which the
words in ital., omitted in the MS.,
are supplied. Comp. Vlp. in *Collat.*
ii, 4 ; xii, 7.
[1] Not in Inst. ; apparently a
gloss.
[2] These two words also omitted
from the Inst. Hu. reads—*uitiata
itaque perempta aut deteriora.*

218 tur.   Hoc tamen capite non quanti in eo anno, sed quanti
in diebus xxx proximis ea res fuerit, damnatur is qui
damnum dederit; ac ne 'plurimi' quidem uerbum adicitur:
et ideo quidam putauerunt liberum esse *iudici*[1] ad id tempus ex diebus xxx aestimationem redigere quo plurimi
res fuerit, uel ad id *quo* minoris fuerit: sed Sabino placuit
proinde habendum ac si etiam hac parte 'plurimi' uerbum
adiectum esset; nam legis latorem contentum fuisse, [*quod*
219 [*prima parte eo uerbo usus esset.*][2]   *Ceterum* placuit ita
demum ex ista lege actionem esse si quis corpore suo damnum dederit; *ideoque*[1] alio modo damno dato utiles actiones[2]
dantur, ueluti si quis alienum hominem aut pecudem incluserit
et fame necauerit, aut iumentum tam uehementer egerit ut
rumperetur; item si quis alieno seruo persuaserit ut in arborem
ascenderet uel in puteum descenderet, et is ascendendo aut
descendendo ceciderit [*et*] aut mortuus fuerit aut aliqua parte
corporis laesus sit; item[3] si quis alienum seruum de ponte *aut*

---

218 are covered by this one word.   Under this clause, however,
he who has done the damage is condemned, not in the value
the thing has borne during the year, but in its value during the
thirty days immediately preceding.   As the word 'highest'
is not added, some have thought that it was in the discretion
of the judge to put upon the thing either its highest value
during the thirty days, or any lower value it possessed during
that period; but according to Sabinus the clause is to be read
as if it contained the word 'highest,' the author of the law
having contented himself *with mentioning it in the first clause.*
219 It has been held that the statute confers a right of action
then only when a man has caused damage with his body, [*i.e.*
by his own direct act.]   *Vtiles actiones*, however, are granted
when it has been done in any other way; as, for example,
when a man has shut up another's slave or beast, and caused
it to die of starvation, or driven another's horse so hard as to
cause it to founder; likewise if he have persuaded another
man's slave to mount a tree or descend a well, and the slave
falls in mounting or descending, and is either killed, or hurt
in some part of his body; so also if he have pushed another

§ 218. Comp. §§ 14, 15, tit. I. afd.
[1] The ms. has *iudicium.*
[2] Omitted in the ms.; supplied
from Inst.
§ 219. Comp. § 16, tit. I. afd.
[1] This word is taken from the
Inst.; the ms. has *quo.*

[2] See ii, 78, note 1.
[3] For *item* K. u. S., following the
Inst., substitute *sed*, Hu. substituting *at enim uero*; the *quamquam
hic* is omitted by K. u. S., and by
Hu. changed into *hunc quoque.*
The object of both is to make the

ripa in flumen proiecerit et is suffocatus fuerit, quamquam hic[3] corpore suo damnum dedisse eo quod proiecerit non difficiliter intellegi potest.

220   Iniuria autem committitur non solum cum quis pugno puta aut fuste percussus uel etiam *uerberatus* erit, sed et si cui con- uicium factum fuerit, siue quis bona alicuius quasi debitoris sciens eum nihil sibi debere proscripserit,[1] siue quis ad in- famiam alicuius libellum aut carmen scripserit, siue quis matremfamilias aut praetextatum adsectatus fuerit, et denique

221 aliis pluribus modis.   Pati autem iniuriam uidemur non solum per nosmet ipsos, sed etiam per liberos nostros quos in potestate habemus, item per uxores nostras cum in manu nostra sint;[1] itaque si *Titiae*, filiae meae,[2] quae Titio nupta est,

---

man's slave off a bridge or river bank into the water whereby he is drowned, (although here it can easily be seen that, by the push given to the slave, the delinquent did the mis- chief by his direct act.)

220   [Personal] injury is committed not only when one is struck say with the fist or with a stick, or when he is flogged, but also when he is opprobriously addressed in public; when a man announces the sale, as if in bankruptcy, of the goods of one who he pretends is his debtor, but who, as he well knows, is not indebted to him at all; when one writes defamatory matter about another either in prose or verse; when one per- sistently follows an honest woman or a young lad; and in

221 many other ways besides.   We may suffer injury not only in our own persons, but also in those of our children *in*

statement of Gaius not only agree with that of Justinian, but be con- sistent in itself. Just. denies that an *utilis actio* was required, the direct one being competent, as the damage was *corpore datum*; Gai. admits that the damage was so caused, yet declares an *utilis actio* to be the proper remedy. But there was room for argument that the *damnum* was not *corpore datum*, —that it was due not to the push from the bridge, but to the subse- quent suffocation, which might not have happened had the slave been able to swim. This view,—that the death was only indirectly due to the push,—may have been the prevail- ing one in the time of Gai. though disapproved by him and departed from by Just.; therefore I prefer,

with P., to let the text stand as in the MS.

§§ 220-225. Comp. tit. I. *DE INIVRIIS* (iv, 4).

§ 220. Comp. § 1, tit. I. afd.; Paul. v, 4, §§ 1, 3, 4, 14 f.
    [1] See § 78.

§ 221. Cp. § 2, tit. I. afd.; Paul. v, 4, § 3.
    [1] K. u. S. and Hu., following L., read *quamuis in manu* [*non*] *sint*; Gou., M. (K. u. S. p. xxii), and P. approve the reading of the MS. There is really no more reason for changing the statement about the wife than for making the reference to children run *quamuis eos in potestate non habemus.*
    [2] The MS. has *ueltiae filiae*; P. reads *Gaiae Titiae filiae meae*; K. u. S. simply *filiae meae*; Hu. *ueluti filiaefamiliae meae,*—admis-

iniuriam feceris, non solum filiae nomine tecum agi iniuriarum
222 potest, uerum etiam meo quoque et Titii nomine.   Seruo
autem ipsi quidem nulla iniuria intellegitur fieri, sed domino
per eum fieri uidetur: non tamen isdem modis quibus etiam
per liberos nostros uel uxores iniuriam pati uidemur, sed ita
cum quid atrocius commissum fuerit quod aperte in con-
tumeliam domini fieri uidetur, ueluti si quis alienum seruum
uerberauerit; et in hunc casum formula proponitur; at si quis
seruo conuicium fecerit uel pugno eum percusserit, non proponitur ulla formula, nec temere petenti datur.

223   Poena autem iniuriarum ex lege xii tabularum propter
membrum quidem ruptum talio erat: propter os uero fractum
aut conlisum trecentorum assium poena erat, ueluti si libero
os fractum erat; at si seruo, CL: propter ceteras uero iniurias
xxv assium poena erat constituta.   et uidebantur illis temporibus in magna paupertate satis idoneae istae *pecuniariae*
224 *poenae*.[1]   Sed nunc alio iure utimur: permittitur enim

---

potestate and our wives *in manu;* therefore if you have done
injury to my daughter who is married to Titius, action will
lie against you on account of it not only in name of my
222 daughter but also in mine and in that of Titius.   A slave
cannot himself be held to have suffered injury; but it may
be done to his owner through him.   Through him, however,
we do not suffer it in the same ways as through our children
or wives, but only when something very atrocious has been
done to him, which is obviously intended as an insult to us,
as when some one has flogged him; for such a case there is a
formula in the edict; but there is no formula there to meet
the case of opprobrious language addressed to him, or a blow
given him with the fist, nor, if one were asked for, would it
be granted without mature consideration.

223   By the Twelve Tables the penalties of [personal] injury
were,—for destruction of any of the members, talion; for a
bone broken or dislocated, three hundred *asses* if the sufferer
was a freeman, a hundred and fifty if a slave; for any other
injury, twenty-five *asses*.   In those times of great poverty
224 these money penalties were deemed sufficient.   But now the

---

sible only on his theory that *manus*
was immaterial as regarded the husband's right to sue.
§ 222. § 3, tit. I. afd.
§ 223. § 7, tit. I. afd. Comp. Schoell,
Tab. viii, cap. 2, 3, 4; Fest. v.
Talionis (Bruns, p. 269); Gell. xx,

1, §§ 12-18; Paul. v, 4, §§ 6, 7;
Paul. in *Collat.* ii, 5, § 5.
    [1] So K. u. S., following G. and
Bk.; the ms. has *pecuniae poenae;*
Hu. adds *esse.*
§ 224. Comp. Paul. v, 4, § 7; Paul. in
Collat. ii, 6; § 7, tit. I. afd.

nobis a praetore *ipsis* iniuriam aestimare, et iudex uel tanti
condemnat quanti nos aestimauerimus, uel minoris, *prout ei*
uisum fuerit; sed cum atrocem iniuriam praetor aestimare
soleat, si simul constituerit quantae pecuniae nomine fieri
debeat uadimonium,[1] hac ipsa quantitate taxamus formulam,[2]
et iudex, *quamuis* possit uel minoris damnare, plerumque
tamen propter ipsius praetoris auctoritatem non audet minuere
condemnationem.[3]   Atrox autem iniuria aestimatur uel ex
facto, ueluti si quis ab aliquo uulneratus aut uerberatus fusti-
busue caesus fuerit; uel ex loco, ueluti si cui in theatro aut in
foro iniuria facta sit; uel ex persona, ueluti si magistratus
iniuriam passus fuerit, uel senatoribus ab humili persona facta
sit iniuria.

---

law is different; we are now allowed by the praetor to put
our own estimate on the injury done us, and the judge may
condemn in the full amount of it or in a smaller sum as he
thinks fit.   But as it is the practice of the praetor himself to
put an estimate on injury of atrocious character, if he have
once fixed what shall be the amount of the security to be
found by the defender for his appearance at the trial, we then
tax our formula at the same figure; and although it is in the
power of the judge to give less, yet in deference to the praetor's
authority he seldom ventures to limit the condemnation.
An injury is esteemed atrocious either by reason of the nature
of it, as when a man is wounded, or flogged, or beaten with
sticks; or by reason of the place, as when an injury is done
to a man in a theatre or in the forum; or by reason of the
person, as when injury has been suffered by a magistrate, or
when it is done to a senator by a man of the lower orders.

[1] See iv, §§ 184-186.
[2] Comp. iv, 51.
[3] See iv, 52.
  § 9, tit. I. afd.   Comp. Paul. v,
§ 10; Paul. in *Collat.* ii, 2. The

par. finishes on line 11, p. 187; and
a little lower, in another hand, we
have—Lib. III. Explic. The next
page (188) is blank.

[*COMMENTARIVS QVARTVS.*]

1 [*Superest ut de actionibus loquamur. Quod si quaeratur*]
quot genera actionum sint, uerius uidetur duo esse, in rem et
in personam : nam qui IIII esse dixerunt et sponsionum
generibus, non animaduerterunt quasdam species actionum
2 inter genera se rettulisse.¹   In personam actio est qua agimus
cum aliquo ¹ qui nobis uel ex contractu uel ex delicto obligatus
est, id est cum intendimus ² dare, facere, praestare oportere.³

---

1 *There remains for consideration the subject of actions. If it
be asked* how many genera of them there are, the more correct
answer seems to be that there are two,—actions *in rem* and
actions *in personam ;* those who, taking into account the
different sorts of *actio per sponsionem*, have maintained that
there are four, have not observed that they were confounding
2 genus and species.   That action is *in personam* whereby we
proceed against some person who is under obligation to us by
reason either of contract or delict; that is to say, when we
contend that he ought to give us something, or do something

§§ 1-10. Comp. tit. I. *DE ACTIONIBVS*
(iv, 6).
§ 1.   Comp. pr. § 1, tit. I. afd.; Vlp. in
fr. 25, pr. D. *de O. et A.* (xliv, 7).
The first five words in ital. are from
pr. tit. I. afd., the last three conjectural, but more than probable.
Those words represent the contents
of the first line of p. 189 of the MS.,
which is vacant.
  ¹ The four here alluded to according to Hu., founding on §§ 4,
91, 95, were—(1) *personalis actio ;*
(2) *petitoria formula ;* (3) *in rem
actio per sponsionem cuius summa
per formulam petitur ;* (4) *per sponsionem cuius summa sacramenti
actione petitur,*—the last three being
varieties of the *actio in rem.*
§ 2.   References as in § 1.
  ¹ The MS. has *qua agimus quotiens
cum aliquo.* Hu. transposes *quo-*

tiens, and, instead of *cum intendimus* (as in the MS.) reads *quotiens
eum intendimus.*
  ² Comp. § 41.
  ³ For the meanings of *dare* and
facere, as descriptive of the matter
of an obligation, see iii, 92, note.
The formula (§ 30) *dare oportere*
was employed when the pursuer's
claim was for something definite,
which he averred the defender was
bound to give him in property
(*certi condictio*) ; *dare facere oportere*
—for *facere oportere* never stood
alone — was employed where the
pursuer, after stating in a *demonstratio* (§ 40) the ground of his
action, asked a judgment as to what
in the circumstances the defender
should give (in the technical sense)
or do (*incerti condictio*).
  There is more difficulty about

3 In rem actio est cum aut corporalem rem intendimus
nostram esse, *aut* ius aliquod nobis conpetere, uelut utendi
aut utendi fruendi, *eundi*, agendi, aquamue ducendi uel
altius tollendi prospiciendiue: actio[1] ex diuerso aduersario
4 est *negatiua.*   Sic itaque discretis actionibus certum est
non posse nos rem nostram ab alio ita petere: SI PARET EVM
DARE OPORTERE; nec enim quod nostrum est nobis dari potest,
cum scilicet id dari nobis intellegatur quod [*ita datur ut*]
nostrum fiat; nec res quae nostra [*iam est, nostra*] amplius
fieri potest.[1]   plane odio furum, quo magis pluribus actionibus
teneantur, receptum[2] est ut extra poenam dupli aut quadrupli

---

3 for us, or make us some other prestation.   It is *in rem*
either when we contend that some corporeal is ours, or that
we are entitled to some right, such as one of usufruct, of foot
or carriage way, of drawing water, of building higher, or of
having a prospect.   The action competent to our adversary,
4 on the other hand, is negative of those rights.   [Real and
personal] actions being thus differentiated, it is clear that in
claiming from another what is ours we cannot do so in the
form, 'Should it appear that he ought to give;' for what is
our own cannot be given to us, seeing that to give us a thing
means to so give it that it shall become ours; but what is
already ours cannot be made more ours than it is already.
Nevertheless, in detestation of thieves, and to make them
responsible in a greater number of actions, it has been received as law that, over and above the double and quadruple

praestare. There is no instance of
praestare oportere in a formula,
either alone or in conjunction with
other words.   Some have held it
intended to cover the *damnum
decidere,* and such like phrases employed in actions *ex delicto* (§ 37);
others that it refers to the possible
secondary claims arising out of
bonae fidei obligations, such as responsibility for *culpa,* eviction,
mora, etc.; others again that it
was meant to apply to the claim in
an action with a formula *in factum
concepta* (§ 46), *dare* and *dare
facere oportere* being confined to
formulae *in ius conceptae* (§ 45).
The probability is that, as being,
like *praestatio,* a word of very
general meaning, it was intended
to include every personal claim not
covered by *dare* or *dare facere.*

§ 3. Comp. §§ 41, 87; §§ 1, 2, tit. I.
afd.; fr. 25, pr. D. *de O. et A.*
(xliv, 7).
[1] Before *actio* K. u. S., on the suggestion of M., interpolate *quibus
casibus,* Hu. *item.* P. reads—*actio
ex diuerso aduersario [contraria
nihilo minus etiam actio est in rem,
quamquam]* est negatiua. The reference is to what was technically
called *actio negatoria,*—that whereby a proprietor sought to have it
judicially declared that his property
was free from some pretended servitude or other burden; see fr. 5, § 6,
D. *si ususfr. pet.* (vii, 6).
§ 4. § 14, tit. I. afd., from which the
passages in ital. are supplied.
[1] Comp. iii, 99.
[2] Hu., following Inst., substitutes
effectum.

rei recipiendae nomine [3] fures *etiam* [4] hac actione teneantur: SI
PARET EOS DARE OPORTERE,[5] quamuis sit etiam aduersus eos
5 haec actio qua rem nostram esse petimus.   Appellantur
autem in rem quidem actiones uindicationes, in personam
uero actiones quibus dari fieriue oportere intendimus, con-
dictiones.

6   Agimus autem interdum ut rem [1] tantum consequamur, in-
7 terdum ut poenam tantum, alias ut rem et poenam.   Rem
tantum persequimur uelut actionibus [*quibus*] [1] ex contractu
8 agimus.   Poenam tantum *persequimur* [1] uelut actione furti
et iniuriarum, et secundum quorundam opinionem actione ui
bonorum raptorum: nam ipsius rei et uindicatio et condictio
9 nobis conpetit.   Rem uero et poenam persequimur uelut ex
his causis ex quibus aduersus infitiantem in duplum agimus:
quod accidit per actionem iudicati,[1] depensi,[1] damni *iniuriae*

---

penalties to which they are subject, they are also liable to an
action [for the value of stolen goods] in the form, 'should
it appear that they ought to give;' although there also lies
against them the action whereby we claim a thing as ours.
5 Actions *in rem* are called vindications; while those *in
personam* in which we contend that something ought to be
given to or done for us are called condictions.
6   Sometimes we proceed in an action solely to obtain a thing,
sometimes solely to obtain a penalty, sometimes for both
7 purposes at once.   In actions upon contract, for example,
8 we sue only for a thing.   We sue only for a penalty in the
actions of theft and personal injury; to which some add
robbery, seeing that for the thing taken from us we have a
9 vindication or condiction.   We sue for both thing and
penalty in those cases in which we claim double the value on
the defender's denial; which happens in the action upon a
judgment, the *actio depensi*, the action upon the Aquilian law

---

[3] See iii, §§ 189, 190.
[4] So the Inst.; the ᴍs. has *ex.*
[5] Comp. ii, 79, last clause.
§ 5.   Comp. § 15, tit. I. afd.   It should
be noticed that Gai. limits the *condictio* to personal actions proceeding
on a *dare* or *dare facere*; see § 2,
note 8.
§ 6.   Comp. § 16, tit. I. afd.
[1] *Res* here includes *factum prae-
standum,*—what we ask shall be
done for us, as well as what we ask
shall be given us.

§ 7.   Comp. § 17, tit. I. afd.
[1] Added by L., and adopted by
most eds.; Hu. does without it by
dropping the final *agimus.*
§ 8.   Comp. §§ 18, 19, tit. I. afd.; Just.
differs as to the character of the *a.
ui bonor. raptor.*
[1] The ᴍs. has *consequimur.*
§ 9.   Comp. § 171; Paul. i, 19, § 1;
§ 19, tit. I. afd.
[1] See Cic. *pro Flacco,* xxi, 49.
[2] Comp. iii, 127; below, § 22.

legis Aquiliae,[3] *aut* legatorum nomine quae per damnationem certa relicta sunt.[4]

10   Quaedam praeterea sunt actiones quae ad legis actionem exprimuntur, quaedam sua ui ac potestate constant: quod ut manifestum fiat, opus est ut prius de legis actionibus loquamur.

11   Actiones quas in usu ueteres habuerunt legis actiones appellabantur, uel ideo quod legibus proditae erant, (quippe tunc edicta praetoris, quibus conplures actiones introductae sunt, nondum in usu habebantur,) uel ideo quia ipsarum legum uerbis accommodatae erant et ideo inmutabiles proinde atque leges obseruabantur: unde *cum quis*[1] de uitibus succisis ita egisset ut in actione 'uites' nominaret, responsum [*est*] eum rem perdidisse, quia debuisset 'arbores' nominare eo quod lex

---

on account of wrongful damage, and the action to recover a legacy of definite amount bequeathed by damnation.

10   Further, there are some actions that are expressly founded on some *legis actio,* others that are effectual on their own inherent merits. To make this distinction clear, we must first explain the nature of the *legis actiones.*

11   The actions employed by our ancestors were called *legis actiones* either because they had been introduced by *leges,* legislative enactments, (the edicts of the praetor, which were subsequently a fertile source of actions, not being then in use), or because the very words of the laws to which they were due were imported into them, so that in style they became as immutable as those laws themselves. Hence, when a man who was proceeding against another for cutting down his vines used the word 'vines' in his action, it was ruled that he had lost his case,—that he ought to have employed the word 'trees,' seeing that the law of the Twelve Tables,

[3] Comp. iii, §§ 210, 216.
[4] Comp. ii, §§ 201, 282; iii, 175.
§ 10.   Comp. §§ 31a, 32, 33.
§ 11.   Comp. Pompon. in fr. 2. §§ 6, 12, 38, D. *de O. I.* (i, 2). See also Varro, *de L. L.* vi, 30 (Bruns, p. 277).

The phrase *legis actiones* is used by Gai. in two different senses. In one, as in the *sacramenti actio* of § 13, it means the *modus agendi,* the form of procedure; and of these there were five, which are enumerated in § 12. In the other it means the particular action made use of, as

the *actio arborum furtim caesarum* alluded to in this par.; these were very numerous,—there probably was one for every law that was contravenable,—but (most of them explicated by sacramental procedure. It is to be borne in mind that certain non-contentious proceedings, whose form was prescribed by statute, were also called *legis actiones,* as, for example, *in iure cessio* (ii, 24).

[1] The MS. has *eum qui,* retained by K. u. S.; but this necessitates the deletion of *eum* after *responsum est.*

XII tabularum, ex qua de uitibus succisis actio conpeteret,
12 generaliter de arboribus succisis loqueretur.[2]   Lege autem
agebatur modis quinque, sacramento, per iudicis postulationem, per condictionem, per manus iniectionem, per pignoris
capionem.

13   Sacramenti actio generalis erat: de quibus enim rebus ut
aliter ageretur lege cautum non erat, de his sacramento
agebatur.[1] eaque actio perinde periculosa erat falsi — —,[2]

---

under which an action for vines cut down was competent
12 spoke in general terms of the cutting down of 'trees.'   The
procedure in those *legis actiones* was in one or other of five
modes,—by sacrament, by petition for a judge, by condiction,
by personal arrest, or by distress.

13   The sacramental procedure was general in its application;
for wherever no other mode was prescribed by statute, this
was followed.   It was a perilous procedure for the [*false*

---

[2]Comp. fr. 1, fr. 2, fr. 3, pr. D. *arb. furt. caes.* (xlvii, 7). That an action should be thrown out on such a technicality seems on the first blush very shocking. Yet it is no more than an anticipation of a rule of modern practice,—that in a statutory prosecution any variance from the words of the statute will be fatal to the charge, as, for example, saying that an act was done 'wickedly and feloniously,' instead of 'wilfully, maliciously, and unlawfully' (case of *Affleck*, 1 Br. 354).

§ 12. *Sacramento*, §§ 13-17 ; *per condictionem*, §§ 18-20; *per manus iniectionem*, §§ 21-25 ; *per pignoris capionem*, §§ 26-29. The description of the procedure *per iudicis postulationem* is lost. On all these see Karlowa, *R. CP.*

§ 13. Gaius' account of the *actio sacramento* is unfortunately very incomplete. It begins on p. 191 of the MS., but p. 192 is undecipherable, and the final sentences were on a leaf between pp. 194 and 195, that seems to have been cut out by the writer of the superimposed St. Jerome. We are thus left to a great extent in the dark as to the true nature of the procedure.

The difference between two definitions of *sacramentum* given by Festus (Bruns, p. 262),—in one of which it is spoken of as an oath of

verity, and in the other (agreeing with the statement of Varro, *de L. L.* v, 180) as a sum of money staked by each of the parties, to abide the issue of the suit and to be forfeited by the loser,—has led to a host of more or less conjectural explanations. A classification of them is given by Danz, *Z. f. RG.* vi, 339 ; and amongst subsequent publications illustrative of the subject may be mentioned Karlowa, as in last note ; Huschke, *Multa ;* and Muenderloh, *ueber Schein und Wirklichkeit an der legis actio sacramenti in rem, Z. f. RG.* xiii, 445.

[1] It was the general mode of procedure both in real and personal actions, and in the latter whether the claim arose *ex contractu* or *ex delicto.* Comp. § 20.

[2]Eight letters illegible, — the more remarkable that the line in which they occur and the two that follow, *i.e.* from *falsi* to *uictus erat*, are accidentally repeated in the MS. He. proposes falsis *sacramentis ;* Rudorff falsi*dicis ;* Danz, falsi *sacramenti causa ;* M. (K. u. S. p. xxii), falsi *damnatis* or falsi *conuictis ;* Hu., falsi*loquo propter iusiurandum* (*falsiloq pp ī̄ī̄*). This last recommends itself as in harmony with the immediately following *reo propter sponsionem* and *actori propter restipulationem ;* but its acceptance

atque hoc tempore periculosa est actio certae creditae pecuniae propter sponsionem qua periclitatur reus si temere neget,[3] [et] restipulationem qua periclitatur actor si non debitum petat:[4] nam qui uictus erat summam sacramenti praestabat poenae nomine,[5] *eaque in publicum cedebat praedesque* eo nomine praetori dabantur,[6] non ut nunc sponsionis et resti-
14 pulationis poena lucro cedit *aduersario qui uicerit.*   Poena autem sacramenti aut quingenaria erat aut quinquagenaria: nam de rebus mille aeris plurisue quingentis assibus, de minoris uero quinquaginta assibus sacramento contende-batur; nam ita lege XII tabularum cautum erat. [at] si de libertate hominis controuersia erat, etsi pretiosissimus homo esset, tamen ut L assibus sacramento contenderetur

---

[*swearer*]; in the same way as at the present day the action for a definite sum of money due is perilous for a defender rashly denying his liability, on account of his sponsion, and for a pursuer claiming what is not due to him, on account of his restipulation.   For he who was defeated forfeited the amount of his sacrament by way of penalty; it fell to the state, and sureties were given for it to the praetor, instead of its becoming so much gain to the successful adversary, as does the amount of the sponsion or restipulation under the present
14 system.   The sacramental penalty was either five hundred or fifty *asses,*—five hundred when the object of litigation was valued at or over a thousand, fifty when less than that; so it was provided by the law of the Twelve Tables.   If, however, the dispute was as to the freedom of an alleged slave, then, although he might be ever so valuable, the same law provided that the parties should contend by sacrament with fifty *asses,*

depends upon the prior considera-tion whether Hu. is right in regard-ing the *sacramentum* as an oath of verity, which the phrase *poena sacra-menti,* § 14, tends to confirm.
    [3] Comp. § 171.   [4] Comp. § 180.
    [5] Comp. Varro, *de L. L.* v, 180. The question, so far as the *sacra-mentum* was concerned, was, whose was just, whose unjust,—*utrius sac-ramentum iustum, utrius iniustum sit;* see Cic. *pro. Caec.* xxxiii, § 97; *pro. Mil,* xxvii, § 74; *pro domo,* xxix, § 78.   He whose *sacramentum* was pronounced just recovered his deposit, while the other party forfeited his.
    [6] The giving of sureties for the

money was the later practice; in the earlier, according to Varro (as in last note), it was actually de-posited *ad pontem,* and probably in the hand of the pontiffs, who he says (v, 83) had constructed the bridge *ut in eo sacra et uls et cis Tiberim non mediocri ritu fiant.* Ihering, (in *G. d. R. R.* i, p. 298,) founding on Pomp. in fr. 2, § 6, D. *de O. I.* (i, 2), thinks that origin-ally the whole procedure was before one of the pontiffs, and that the forfeited deposit was a payment to the college for its judicial services, *i.e.* that it was court dues.
    § 14. Comp. Fest. v. *Sacramentum* (Bruns, p. 262); Varro, *de L. L.* v, 180.

eadem lege cautum est, fauore scilicet libertatis,[1] ne onera-
14*a* rentur adsertores.[2]　　[14*a*] — — — — — —.　　[15] —
15 — — — — — ad iudicem accipiendum uenirent ; postea
uero reuersis dabatur.　*ut* autem [*die*] xxx. *iudex daretur*[1]
per legem Pinariam[2] factum est; ante eam autem *legem*

---

and that out of favour for freedom, and that those acting on
the pretended slave's behalf should not be unduly burdened.
14*a* — — — — — —.　　[15] — — — — — — — should
15 appear to receive a judge ; and the appointment was made on
their return.　That he should be appointed on the thirtieth
day was a provision of the Pinarian law ; prior to its enact-

---

[1] Liv. iii, 44 f.

[2] P. has *ne morarentur adserta-
tores.* No one who was claimed as a
slave could maintain his defence in
person ; he had to be represented by
an *adsertor libertatis.*

§ 14*a*. On p. 192 of the ms. the only
letters legible are *sin* on l. 5, *iidq. s*
on l. 6, *staeomnesaones* on l. 12,
onecassae on l. 17, *ecaptus* on l. 18,
and *ad iudicem accipund* at the end
of l. 24 (the last on the page).

Hu. thinks that lines 1 to middle
of 11 may have run to the following effect : — *E diuerso, si inter
populum et priuatum controuersia
erat uel ad centumuiros ibatur, siue
res mille aeris plurisue siue minoris
esset, sacramenti poena ex lege
Hateria Tarpeia a praetore aesti-
mabatur, modo ne minor quingentis
neque maior III milibus aeris statueretur. praeterea lege Iulia Papiria
cautum est, ne pluris quam ipsa res
esset sacramentum statueretur. si
uero magistratus pro populo agebat,
etiam priuatus tantum sacramento
interrogabatur. idque semper fiebat,
cum ex lege aliqua eum, qui contra
legem fecisset, in sacrum iudicare
licebat, id est ut a magistratu sacramento interrogaretur, se contra legem
non fecisse.* As authorities he refers
to § 95; *lex Silia de pond.* as in
Fest. v. *Publ. pondera* (Bruns, p.
40); *Lex. de infer.* v, 6 (C. I. L.,
I, 1409, p. 263); Cic. *de Rep.* ii, 85,
§ 60; Fest. v. *Sacramentum Sacramento* (Bruns, p. 262).

§ 15. Hu. supposes that the par. began
on l. 11, and proposes the following
reconstruction : *Ceterum cum etiam
istae omnes actiones, quibus sacra-*

*mento agebatur, aut in rem aut in
personam essent, si in personam
agebatur, cum uterque in ius uenis-
set, actor id, quod sibi ab altero
dari fieriue oporteret, apprehendens
eum intendebat, uelut hoc modo :*
AIO TE MIHI HS. X MILIA DARE
OPORTERE. *aduersarius* negabat.
deinde actor dicebat : QVANDO
NEGAS, SACRAMENTO QVINGENARIO
TE PROVOCO. *aduersarius quoque*
dicebat : QVANDO AIS EGOOVE ABS
TE EA RE CAPTVS SVM, SIMILITER
EGO TE SACRAMENTO QVINGENA-
RIO PROVOCO. *Itaque uterque*
alterum sacramento (*in fano Iouis
uel Dii Fidii*) adigebat, die tamen
demum XXX. iudicem accipiebant et
litem contestabantur, id est uterque
nominata causa litis dicebat : STLI-
TEM MIHI TECVM ESSE EFFOR,
TESTES ESTOTE ! *quam ob rem in
eum diem inuicem sibi denuntiabant
ut in ius* ad iudicem, etc. Huschke's
principal authorities are — for the
first part of his reconstruction,
Valer. Prob. ; and for the second
Paul. ex Festo, v. *Contestari* (Bruns,
p. 239), and Diomed. *Ars. gramm.*
i, p. 878, ed. Keil.

[1] Comp. Ps.-Ascon. *in II. Verr.* i,
26 (Bruns, p. 292).

[2] Mommsen, Rudorff, and Hu.
identify this law with one referred
to by Macrob. *Sat.* i, 13, § 21, as
dealing with the matter of intercala-
tion, and which he says was enacted
in the consulate of L. Pinarius and
P. Furius, *i.e.* in 282 | 472 (Liv. ii,
56). With Voigt (*Ius. Nat.* ii, p. 187),
I am inclined to think that the enactment to which Gai refers must
have been later, not earlier, than

statim[3] dabatur iudex. illud ex superioribus intellegimus, si de re minoris quam [*M*] aeris agebatur, quinquagenario sacramento, non quingenario eos contendere solitos fuisse. Postea tamen quam iudex datus esset conperendinum diem ut ad iudicem uenirent denuntiabant;[4] deinde cum ad iudicem uenerant, antequam apud eum *causam* perorarent, solebant breuiter ei et quasi per indicem rem exponere: quae dicebatur causae *coniectio*,[5] quasi causae suae in breue coactio.

16   Si in rem agebatur, mobilia quidem et mouentia, quae modo in ius adferri adduciue possent, in iure uindicabantur ad hunc modum: qui uindicabat[1] festucam tenebat; deinde ipsam rem adprehendebat, ueluti hominem, et ita dicebat: HVNC EGO HOMINEM EX IVRE QVIRITIVM MEVM ESSE AIO SECVNDVM SVAM

---

ment the judge was named at once. As we have seen already, it was with a sacrament of fifty *asses*, and not five hundred, that the parties contended where the object in dispute was of less value than a thousand. On the judge being appointed they cited each other to attend him on the third day thereafter. When they had come before him, and before entering upon the merits of his case, each explained shortly and in outline the leading points of it; this was called the *causae coniectio*,—an epitome of the whole cause.

16   When the proceedings were *in rem*, moveable and self-moving things that could be carried or brought into court were vindicated in this way: the vindicant held in his hand a rod; then he took hold of the thing in dispute, say a slave, and made his averment thus: ' I say that this man is mine in quiritarian right, on the title I have already explained; behold, I have laid my *uindicta* upon him;' and at the same moment

the XII Tables. He suggests the year 322 | 432, when L. Pinarius Mamercinus Rufus and L. Furius Medullimus Fusus were two of the military tribunes; and thinks Varro, whom Macrob. cites as his authority, may have made the mistake of confounding the military tribunes with the earlier consuls of the same name.

[3] Before Studemund's revision of the Verona Codex most eds. were in the habit of reading *nondum* instead of *statim*; thus inferring that it was the L. *Pinaria* that first authorized remit to a single judge instead of to the centumviral court.

[4] Comp. Cic. *pro Mur.* xii, 27; Ps.-Ascon. as in note 1; Paul. ex Festo, v. *Res comperendinata* (Bruns, p. 260); Gell. x, 24, § 9.
[5] The MS. has *collectio*. But see Ps.-Ascon. as in note 1; fr. 1, D. *de R. I.* (l, 17).
§ 16. Comp. ii, 24, containing the formula of *in iure cessio*, which was nothing else than a *rei uindicatio* arrested in its first stage, because of no opposition on the part of the nominal respondent.
[1] 'Id est, qui uindex erat. Vt autem *iudex* est is qui iudicat ubi et quid sit *ius*, sic *uindex* ubi et quae sit *uis* demonstrat,' Polenaar.

18

CAVSAM,² SICVT DIXI ; ECCE TIBI, VINDICTAM INPOSVI,³ et simul homini festucam inponebat. aduersarius eadem similiter dicebat et faciebat.⁴ cum uterque uindicasset praetor dicebat: MITTITE AMBO HOMINEM. illi mittebant. qui prior uindica[uerat ita alterum interroga]bat:⁵ POSTVLO ANNE DICAS QVA EX CAVSA VINDICAVERIS? ille respondebat: IVS

---

he touched him with the rod. Thereupon the other party spoke and acted in like manner. Each having thus vindicated, the praetor said : 'Both of you let the man alone.' They did so. He who had made the first vindication then interrogated the other thus : 'I ask you, will you state upon what title you have vindicated?' to which the other party

² There is some difference of opinion as to the meaning of the words *sec. suam causam*, and their relation to the immediately following *sicut dixi*. Hu. holds that the words *sec. suam causam* were intended as an affirmation that the pursuer was claiming the slave as already his on a sufficient title, and not now claiming him for the first time as in an *in iure cessio*; further, that the *sicut dixi* has no particular reference to the *sec. suam causam*, but is the connecting link between the two parts of the *uindicatio*,— 'as I have asserted my ownership by word of mouth, so do I now by my act.' K. u. S. also disconnect *sicut dixi* from what goes before, from which it may perhaps be inferred that they put the same meaning as Hu. upon *sec. suam causam*.

I am disposed, however, to hold by the older idea—still maintained by several of the later civilians of eminence, for instance Ihering (*G. d. R. R.* iii, p. 88)—that the *sec. suam causam, sicut dixi* refer to a previous informal statement by the first vindicant of the title upon which he maintained his ownership; without it he could hardly in fairness ask his adversary what was *his* title. But, although this may account for the introduction of the words into the ritual of the *uindicatio*, it is not to be supposed that they would be used *only* when a preliminary statement of his title had actually been made by the first

vindicant; they became words of style, spoken as of course.

³ P. thinks *inposui* a gloss, (1) as unwarranted by the *S.S.C.S.D.E.T.V.* of Valer. Prob., and (2) as inconsistent with the immediately following *simul inponebat*.

⁴ That the respondent (*aduersarius*) contravindicated, or at least made a counter averment of ownership in the same terms as the first vindicant, and accompanied by the same ceremonial, is denied by some jurists, on the ground that the result might be a judicial finding that neither party was owner; and they impute to Gai. an inaccuracy, due they think to his unfamiliarity with a procedure that had become a mere matter of history. But we have other authority for it in Plaut. *Rud.* iv, 3, l. 84; Cio. *pro Mur.* xii, 26 (*fundus Sabinus meus est: immo meus*); and Gai. himself in his description of *in iure cessio* (ii, 24). The action was in fact originally a *duplex iudicium;* which may account for Gai. not calling the parties *actor* and *reus* (pursuer and defender), but *qui uindicabat* or *qui prior uindicabat* in the one case, and *aduersarius* in the other.

⁵ Added by G., and adopted by most eds. Hu. has *qui prior uindica[uerat ita aduersarium, et rursus post is alterum interroga]bat.* This interrogatory is probably the earliest specimen of the *interrogatio in iure* that played an important part in judicial procedure at a later period; see tit. D. *de interrog. in iure* (xi, 1).

FECI SICVT VINDICTAM INPOSVI. deinde qui prior uindica-
uerat dicebat: QVANDO TV INIVRIA VINDICAVISTI, D AERIS SACRA-
MENTO TE PROVOCO; aduersarius quoque dicebat similiter: [6] ET
EGO TE; [scilicet L asses sacramenti nominabant.][7] deinde
eadem sequebantur quae cum in personam ageretur.[8] postea
praetor secundum alterum eorum uindicias dicebat,[9] id est
interim aliquem possessorem constituebat, eumque iubebat
praedes[10] aduersario dare litis et uindiciarum, id est rei et
fructuum:[11] alios autem praedes ipse praetor ab utroque accipiebat sacramenti, quod id in publicum cedebat. festuca
autem utebantur quasi hastae loco, signo quodam iusti
dominii, [*quod*] *maxime*[12] sua esse credebant quae ex hostibus

---

replied: 'I have done what I had a right to do in lay-
ing my *uindicta* upon him.' Then again the first: 'Since
you have vindicated without right, I challenge you with a
sacrament of fifty *asses*;' to which the other answered in like
manner: 'And I you.' Then followed the same procedure as
in the *actio in personam*. When it was completed the praetor
granted the *uindiciae* or interim possession to one or other
of them, requiring him to give sureties to his adversary *litis
et uindiciarum*, i.e. for the thing itself and its profits; and he
further required each of them to furnish sureties for his
sacrament, because that was to fall to the state. The rod
spoken of was used in place of a spear, the symbol of lawful
ownership, men esteeming those above all things to be theirs
which they had taken from an enemy; wherefore it is that a

[6] Other eds. put this word *similiter*
into the mouth of the respondent as
part of his challenge.
[7] The MS. has *scil. l asses*, etc.
K. u. S. interpolate, and read *scilicet
[si de re maioris quam M aeris agebatur, D, si de minoris,] L asses*,
etc.; Hu.—*scilicet [si de re minoris
quam M aeris agebatur,] L asses*, etc.
Gou. regards *scil.* and the three
words that follow as a gloss, and
the second *l* as merely a mis-spelling.
I also read them as a gloss, but one
which in the second *l* makes a very
proper correction. The illustration
Gai. is employing is a vindication of
a slave, and he consequently errs
(§ 14) in speaking of challenge with
a sacrament of five hundred *asses*;
says the glossarist—'it was fifty.'
In the translation I have made the

correction in the first instance and
omitted the gloss.
[8] Comp. § 15.
[9] Comp. Fest. v. *Vindiciae* (Bruns,
p. 272). Most authors are of opinion
that the *uindiciae* were granted as
a matter of course to the *de facto*
possessor at the moment. Ihering
(*G. d. R. R.* iii, p. 102, note 129c)
combats this view, holding that
the matter was one entirely in the
discretion of the magistrate, who
acted on his first impression of the
justice of the case.
[10] Comp. Paul. ex Festo, v. *Praes*
(Bruns, p. 256); Varro, *de L. L.* vi,
74 (Bruns, p. 278).
[11] Comp. § 94; Ps.-Ascon. *in II.
Verr.* i, 115 (Bruns, p. 298).
[12] The MS. has *dominio XXI.
me.*

cepissent; unde in centumuiralibus iudiciis [13] hasta prae-
17 ponitur.[14]   Si qua res talis erat ut sine incommodo non
posset in ius adferri uel adduci, ueluti si columna [1] aut grex
alicuius pecoris esset, pars aliqua inde sumebatur, deinde in
eam partem quasi in totam rem praesentem fiebat uindicatio;
itaque ex grege uel una ouis aut capra in ius adducebatur, uel
etiam pilus inde sumebatur et in ius adferebatur; ex naue
uero et columna aliqua pars defringebatur. similiter si de
fundo uel de aedibus siue de hereditate controuersia erat, pars
aliqua inde sumebatur et in ius adferebatur, et in eam partem
perinde atque in totam rem praesentem fiebat uindicatio, ueluti
ex fundo gleba sumebatur et ex aedibus tegula, et si de hereditate controuersia erat aeque — — — —.[2]

17*a* — — — — — — — —.

─────────

17 spear is set up in front of the centumviral bench.   If the
thing in question was such as could not conveniently be carried
or brought into court, a pillar, for example, or a flock or herd
of animals, a part was taken and the vindication made upon
it as if the whole had been there; a single sheep or goat of a
herd was driven into court, or perhaps only a little of the
wool or hair of one of them taken into it; while from a ship
or a pillar a small portion was broken off.   In like manner if
the dispute was about land or houses, or about an inheritance, some small part was taken into court, and the vindication made upon it as if the whole had been there; for
example, a turf was taken from the land or a tile from the
house; and if the thing in controversy was an inheritance,
then too — — — —.

17*a* — — — — — — — —.

[13] Comp. Cic. *de Orat.* i, 28, § 173;
Paul. ex Festo, v. *Centumuiralia*
(Bruns, p. 238); Quintil. *I. O.* v, 2,
§ 1. According to Cic. the centumviral court seems to have been a
competent forum in a great range
of cases; but in the time of Gai.,
according to the prevalent opinion,
it sat only for the trial of some
questions of inheritance. See below,
§ 31.
[14] Comp. Suet. *Aug.* 86; Quintil.
as in last note.
§ 17. See Cic. *pro Mur.* xii, 26, where
he narrates with much ridicule the
procedure followed when lands were
in dispute; see further the ingenious
explanation of its origin and import
by Muenderloh, as quoted in § 13,
note; also Gell. xx, 10.
[1] P. interpolates *aut nauis.*
[2] The par. probably concluded with
res aliqua inde sumebatur, or words
to the same effect; they are wanting
in the ms., as explained in next note.
§ 17*a*. Between what are numbered
pp. 194 and 195 of the ms. a leaf is
amissing, cut out, as Stud. thinks,
by the writer of St. Jerome's
Epistles. We thus lose 48 lines of
the text, which contained the conclusion of the account of the *legis
actio sacramento,* the whole account
of that *per iudicis postulationem,*
and part of the account of that *per
condictionem.*

17b — — — — — — ad iudicem capiendum *praesto esse de-*
berent.[1]   condicere autem denuntiare est prisca lingua.[2]
18 Itaque haec quidem actio proprie condictio uocabatur : nam
actor aduersario denuntiabat ut ad iudicem capiendum die
xxx. adesset ; nunc uero non proprie condictionem dicimus
actionem in personam [*esse qua*][1] intendimus *dari*[2] nobis
oportere : nulla enim hoc tempore eo nomine denuntiatio fit.
19 Haec autem legis actio constituta est per legem Siliam et
Calpurniam ; lege quidem Silia certae pecuniae, lege uero
20 Calpurnia de omni certa re.   Quare autem haec actio desi-

---

17b — — — — — —, when they should be bound to attend to
have a judge appointed. For *condicere* in early Latin meant
18 the same as *denuntiare*, to give formal notice. This procedure therefore was quite properly called *condictio* ; for the
pursuer gave notice to his opponent to appear on the thirtieth
day for the appointment of a judge. In now giving the name
of condiction to the personal action in which we maintain
that something ought to be given to us, our language is not so
appropriate ; for at the present day there is no notice given
19 such as we have been speaking of.   This *legis actio* was
established by the Silian and Calpurnian laws ; the Silian law
introducing it in the case of money due of definite amount,
the Calpurnian extending it to every other thing that was
20 definite and certain.   But it may well be asked what was

§ 17b. See last note. The first line and
a half of p. 195 is illegible.
  Hu. conjecturally supplies the first
part of the par. thus : *Per condictio-*
nem tantum agebatur de his rebus
quas nobis dari oportet, quam actio-
nem etiam nunc condictionem uoca-
mus. Et perinde hoc modo agebant,
detracto tamen ipso sacramento, ac si
sacramento in personam ageretur.
The line and a half at top of p. 195
he thus reconstructs : *obseruabant*
enim eundem diem et aequalem mo-
dum capiendi iudicis *condicendique*
diem quo ad iudicem, etc.
  [1] Of *deberent* (Hu.) only the first
two letters are legible ; K. u. S.
and P. prefer *debebant*.
  [2] Comp. Paul. ex Festo, v. *Condi-*
cere (Bruns, p. 239) ; § 15, I. *de act.*
(iv, 6).
§ 18. Comp. §§ 5, 33 ; § 15, I. *de act.*
(iv, 6).
  [1] These two words supplied from
the Inst.

[2] The ms. has *id.*
§ 19. There is no means of fixing the
dates of those two enactments with
anything like certainty. While
Voigt (*Iust. Nat.* iv, 401) puts the *L.*
Silia between 311 | 443 and 329 |
425, and Ihering (*G. d. R. R.* ii, p.
390) attributes it to the first half of
the fifth century (*u. c.*), Hu. (*Multa,*
p. 492) thinks it cannot have been
earlier than the first half of the sixth
century, and possibly the same year
(510 | 244) as the *L. Silia* regulating
weights and measures. But this
brings it too near, and even post-
pones it to, the introduction of the
formular system sanctioned by the
lex Aebutia, if 507 | 247 be the
proper date of that law. See § 30,
note 1.
§ 20. Comp. § 13. The *condictio* had
this very obvious advantage,—that
it did not necessitate the appearance
of the parties in court until they
met for the appointment of a *iudex*.

derata sit, cum de eo quod nobis dari oportet potuerimus sacramento aut per iudicis postulationem agere, ualde quaeritur.

21   Per manus iniectionem aeque [*de*] his rebus agebatur de
quibus ut ita ageretur lege *aliqua*[1] cautum est, uelut iudicati
lege XII tabularum:[2] quae actio talis erat.   qui agebat sic dicebat: QVOD TV MIHI IVDICATVS (siue DAMNATVS)[3] ES SESTER-
TIVM X MILIA, QVANDOC[4] NON SOLVISTI, OB EAM REM EGO TIBI
SESTERTIVM X MILIVM IVDICATI MANVM INICIO, et simul aliquam
partem corporis eius prendebat ; nec licebat iudicato manum
sibi depellere et pro se lege agere, sed uindicem[5] dabat qui
pro se causam agere solebat : qui uindicem non dabat domum

---

the need for it, seeing that where it was alleged that something ' ought to be given,' action was already competent either
by sacrament or by petition for a judge.

21   *Manus iniectio* was employed in those cases in which it was
expressly prescribed by statute, as, under the provisions of the
Twelve Tables, in proceedings upon a judgment.   The procedure was as follows :—the pursuer addressed the other party
thus : ' Whereas by judgment ' (or ' by damnation ') ' you are
indebted to me in the sum of ten thousand sesterces, inasmuch as you have not paid them, in respect thereof I now lay
hands upon you for ten thousand sesterces of judgment debt;'
and at the same time he laid hold of some part of the body of
his debtor.   The latter was not allowed to resist the arrest or
defend himself in person, but had to provide a [substitute,
called a] *uindex*, who acted on his behalf ; if he failed to provide one, he was carried home by the arrester and put in

---

Further, the court was one presided
over by the praetor ; and if Ihering
(see above, § 13, note 6) be right in
thinking that the sacramental procedure took place before a pontiff,
this was in itself a mighty change,
—the substitution of a civil for an
ecclesiastical tribunal.

§ 21. Comp. the *lex Coloniae Iuliae
Genetiuae* (see above, i, 22, note 1),
c. 61, in *Ephem. Epigraph.* iii, 91;
Serv. *ad Aen.* x, 419 (Bruns, p. 298).

[1] So G. and most eds. ; the MS. has
Aquilia.

[2] Comp. Gell. xx, 1, § 45 ; Schoell,
Tab. iii, 1-4.

[3] Keller (*R. CP.* § 19) proposes
to add *siue CONFESSVS. Damnatus*
refers to the *damnas esto* of a *nexum*-
testament, or penal statute ; see ii,
201, note 1.

[4] So the MS., and approved by
Karlowa (*R. CP.* p. 157) and by
K. u. S.; Festus (ed. Mueller, p. 258)
says that so *quando* was spelt in
the XII Tables. G., whose reading
was followed for some time, had
quae dolo malo. Hu. in his second
edition, on the authority of M.,
substituted *quae ad hoc;* in his
two later editions he has [*eaque*]
quando oportet. P. has *quando
causam.*

[5] Comp. Fest. v. *Vindex* (Bruns,
p. 272); Gell. xvi, 10, § 5. The
creditor's right over his debtor's person being in question, the latter
could not act for himself ; the *uindex*
took his place much in the same way
as did an *adsertor libertatis* (§ 14,
note 2) in a *uindicatio in seruitutem.*
See § 16, note 1.

22 ducebatur ab actore et uinciebatur.⁶   Postea quaedam leges
ex aliis quibusdam causis pro iudicato manus iniectionem in
quosdam dederunt, sicut lex Publilia in eum pro quo sponsor dependisset, *si* in sex mensibus proximis quam pro eo
depensum esset non soluisset sponsori pecuniam ; item lex
Furia de sponsu aduersus eum qui a sponsore plus quam
uirilem partem exegisset, et denique conplures aliae leges in
23 multis causis talem actionem dederunt.   Sed aliae leges
ex quibusdam [*causis*] constituerunt¹ [*in*] *quosdam*² actiones
per manus iniectionem, sed puram, id est non pro iudicato,
uelut *lex* [*Furia*] testamentaria³ aduersus eum qui legatorum
nomine mortisue causa plus *M*⁴ assibus cepisset, cum ea lege
non esset exceptus ut ei plus capere liceret ; item lex Marcia⁵

---

22 **chains.**   Some subsequent laws allowed *manus iniectio pro
iudicato*, as upon a judgment, in certain other cases.   It was
allowed, for example, by the Publilian law against a debtor
who had failed within six months to refund to a sponsor
who had paid his debt for him ; the Furian law respecting
suretyship allowed it against a creditor who had exacted from
one of several sponsors more than his proportion of the debt ;
and·by numerous other statutes it was sanctioned in a variety
23 of other cases.   A different set of enactments authorised
in certain cases what was called *manus iniectio pura*, that is,
not proceeding upon the footing of a judgment ; the Furian
testamentary law, for instance, allowed it against a man who
had taken more than a thousand asses in name of legacy
or other singular *mortis causa* gift, he not being one of the
excepted individuals who, under its provisions, might take a
greater sum : and the Marcian law against usury provided

---

⁶ Comp. *L. Col. Iul. Genetiuae*, as
above ; Gell. xx, 1, § 45.   The *lex
Poetilia* of 429 | 325 or 441 | 313—
see Liv. viii, 28 ; Varro, *de L. L.* vii,
105 (ed. Muell. p. 162, in preference
to Bruns, p.281)—has generally been
supposed to have abolished the imprisonment, and chains, and slavery
or death that often followed the
manus iniectio ; but the words of the
L. Col. Iul. Genetiuae, probably of
the year 710 | 44, are—*ni uindicem
dabit iudicatumue faciet, secum du-
cito ; iure ciuili uinctum habeto*. See
also the statement of Gai. in § 25.
This imprisonment, however, was
meant simply to secure the person of

the debtor ; the creditor's real satis-
faction could only come out of his
estate.

§ 22.   Comp. iii, § 121 (*L. Furia*), § 127
(*L. Publilia*).

§ 23.   ¹ The MS. has—*Sed aliae leges in
multis causis ex quibusdam si con-
stituerunt* ; the reading above is that
of Gou., followed by K. u. S.
² *In quosdam* due to Hu., following § 22 ; the MS. has *quasdam*
without *in* ; P. substitutes *quidem*.
³ See ii, 225.   Instead of *lex Furia*
the MS. has *lege*.
⁴ The MS. has *c*.
⁵ Enacted   402 | 352 (Liv. vii,
21).

aduersus faeneratores, ut si usuras exegissent, de his reddendis
24 per manus iniectionem cum eis ageretur.   Ex quibus legibus et si quae aliae similes essent cum agebatur, manum sibi
depellere et pro se lege agere [*reo licebat*]: nam et actor in
ipsa legis actione non adiciebat hoc uerbum PRO IVDICATO,
sed nominata causa ex qua agebat ita dicebat : OB EAM REM
EGO TIBI MANVM INICIO; cum hi quibus pro iudicato actio
data erat, nominata causa ex qua agebant, ita inferebant: OB
EAM REM EGO TIBI PRO IVDICATO MANVM INICIO: nec me
praeterit in forma legis Furiae testamentariae PRO IVDICATO
uerbum inseri, cum in ipsa lege non sit; quod uidetur nulla
25 ratione factum.   Sed postea lege Vallia, excepto iudicato
et eo pro quo depensum est, ceteris omnibus cum quibus per
manus iniectionem agebatur permissum est sibi manum depellere et pro se agere : itaque iudicatus et is pro quo depensum est etiam post hanc legem uindicem dare debebant, et
nisi darent domum ducebantur.[1]   *istaque*[2] quamdiu legis

---

that if a lender exacted interest upon his loan, *manus iniectio*
24 might be used upon him to compel its restitution.   In the
case of arrest under these enactments, and any similar ones
(if there were such), it was lawful for the arrested party to
resist and defend himself in person.   For here the pursuer, in
reciting the words of style, did not make use of the phrase ' as
upon a judgment,' but, specifying the ground of his action,
said simply, ' in respect thereof I lay hands upon you.'   Those
on the other hand to whom the action as if upon a judgment
was allowed, after specifying the ground of it, used the words,
' in respect thereof I lay hands upon you as upon a judgment.'
I am aware that in the formula employed in proceedings
under the Furian testamentary law the words ' as upon a
judgment' are inserted, though they are not in the law itself ;
25 but this appears to me unwarranted.   Subsequently, by the
Vallian law, all against whom proceedings might be taken by
manus iniectio, except judgment debtors and principals for
whom a sponsor had made payment, were permitted to resist
the arrest and defend in person.   The judgment debtor, however, and the principal indebted to his sponsor, had still, notwithstanding this enactment, to find a substitute ; on failure
they were carried home by their creditors.   And so it always

---

§ 24. The words *reo licebat* are Huschke's;
previous eds. have only *licebat*.
§ 25. On the *lex Vallia*, see iii, 121,
note.

[1] See *L. Col. Iul. Genetiuae*, as in
§ 21, note.
[2] The MS. has *itaque*, K. u. S.
and P., following L., *idque*.

actiones in usu erant semper ita obseruabantur; unde nostris
temporibus is cum quo iudicati depensiue agitur iudicatum
solui satisdare cogitur.[3]

26   Per pignoris capionem lege agebatur de quibusdam rebus
27 moribus, [de quibusdam][1] lege.   Introducta est moribus rei
militaris : nam et propter stipendium licebat militi ab eo qui
distribuebat,[1] nisi daret, pignus capere; dicebatur autem ea
pecunia quae stipendii nomine dabatur aes militare.[2] item
propter eam pecuniam licebat pignus capere ex qua equus[3]
emendus erat, quae pecunia dicebatur. aes equestre :[4] item
propter eam pecuniam ex qua hordeum equis erat conpa-
28 randum, quae pecunia dicebatur aes hordiarium.[5]   Lege
autem introducta est pignoris capio, ueluti lege XII tabularum
aduersus eum qui hostiam emisset nec pretium redderet;[1]

---

was while the legis actiones continued in use; wherefore it is
that even now, in an action upon a judgment, and in an actio
depensi, the defender must give security for payment of the
sum in which he may eventually be condemned.

26   The legis actio by pignoris capio or distress was introduced
27 in some cases by custom, in others by statute.   It was introduced by custom in some matters affecting the army : for a
soldier could distrain upon the paymaster if his pay or aes
militare was in arrear; and a knight could distrain for the
aes equestre or sum to which he was entitled for the purchase
of a horse, and for his aes hordiarium or forage money.
28 The Twelve Tables authorized it against him who had purchased a victim for sacrifice but failed to pay the price; as

---

[3] Comp. § 102.

§ 26. Gell. (vi, 10) says that the proper
spelling is capio, not captio; the
latter form, however, occurs once or
twice in the Verona MS.
  [1] Added by G., and substantially adopted by all subsequent
eds.

§ 27. Comp. Fest. v. Vectigal (Bruns,
p. 271).
  [1] The MS. has distruebat; Hu. has
qui id iis tribu[ere deb]ebat; K. u. S.
and P. qui [id] distribuebat. The
paymaster, against whom the capio
was competent, was the tribunus
aerarius; Paul. ex Festo, v. Aerarii
tribuni.
  [2] The army first began to receive
pay in 349 | 405, Liv. iv, 59. Comp.
Varro, de L. L. v, §§ 181, 182

(Bruns, p. 275); Cato apud Gell. vi,
10, § 2.
  [3] So Savigny and most eds.; the
MS. has eciuis; Hu. equus iis.
  [4] Comp. Paul. ex Festo, v. Equestre aes (Bruns, p. 241); this capio
was also against the tribunus aerarius, the purchase-money coming
from the public; Liv. i, 43.
  [5] Comp. Paul. ex Festo, v. Hordiarium aes (Bruns, p. 243). As the
maintenance of the cavalry horses
was a burden upon widows, it was
they possibly who were proceeded
against; see Liv. i, 43; Cic. de Re-
publ. ii, 20, § 36.

§ 28. [1] Competent, according to Goettling
(Roem. Staatsverfassung, p. 185), to
the colleges of priests, who kept and
sold animals fit for sacrifice.

item aduersus eum qui mercedem non redderet pro eo iumento
quod quis ideo locasset ut inde pecuniam acceptam in *dapem*,
id est in sacrificium, inpenderet;[2] item lege censoria[3] data est
pignoris capio publicanis[4] uectigalium publicorum populi
Romani aduersus eos qui aliqua lege *uectigalia* deberent.[5]

29 Ex omnibus autem istis causis certis uerbis pignus capiebatur
et ob id plerisque placebat hanc quoque actionem legis actionem esse; quibusdam *aliter*[1] placebat, primum quod pignoris
capio extra ius peragebatur, id est non apud praetorem,
plerumque etiam absente aduersario, cum alioquin ceteris
actionibus non aliter uti possent quam apud praetorem prae-
sente aduersario; praeterea quod nefasto quoque die, id est
quo non licebat lege agere,[2] pignus capi poterat.

---

also against the person who failed to pay for a beast which
another had let him on hire in order to raise money for an
offering to Jupiter Dapalis; and by the censorial law the same
remedy was allowed to the farmers of the public revenue
29 against those whose taxes were unpaid.   In all these cases
the *pignoris capio* was accompanied with a set form of words,
and hence it also has generally been accounted a *legis actio*.
Some however think that it should not be so regarded, firstly,
because it took place *extra ius*, that is, not before the praetor,
and often in the absence of the adversary, whereas the other
legis actiones were competent only before the praetor and in
the presence of the adversary; and, secondly, because it might
take place on a *dies nefastus* or day upon which procedure by
legis actio was unlawful.

[2] Twice a year, at the spring and
autumn seed-time, it was the custom
for the husbandman to offer a feast
(*daps*) to *Iupiter dapalis* in implor-
ing rain for his fields and cattle;
Cato, *de R. R.* §§ 131, 132; Paul. ex
Festo, v. *Daps* (ed. Mueller, p. 68).
If, to obtain the wherewithal to
make this offering, he had to let out
his draught cattle for hire, and this
was not paid, then he had *pign. capio*
against the hirer.

[3] The *leges censoriae* were the conditions and stipulations contained in
the contracts entered into by the
censors with the farmers of the revenue and others on behalf of the
public; comp. Cic. *de nat. deor.* iii,
19, § 49; *II. Verr.* i, 55, § 143;
Varro, *de R. R.* ii, 1, § 16 (Bruns,
p. 282).

[4] P. interpolates *id est conduc-
toribus*.

[5] Comp. Cic. *II. Verr.* iii, 11, §
27; 47, §§ 112, 113.

§ 29.   Gai. lays stress on the fact that
pignoris capio began extrajudicially;
but so did the *actio sacramenti* (for
the *in ius uocatio* was a private act);
and so did the *condictio* and the
manus iniectio.   In this respect,
therefore, it was not peculiar.

[1] *Aliter* suggested by Gou.; the
MS. has *at.*, with a line over the
letters.   K. u. S. read *autem*, and
interpolate *contra*; Hu., following G., also reads *autem*, and interpolate *legis actionem non esse*;
P. reads *haud*.

[2] Comp. Varro, *de L. L.* vi, 30
(Bruns, p. 277); Ovid. *Fast.* i, 47;
Macrob. *Sat.* i, 16.

30   Sed istae omnes legis actiones paulatim in odium uenerunt;
      namque ex nimia subtilitate ueterum qui tunc iura condide-
      runt eo res perducta est ut uel qui minimum errasset litem
      perderet; itaque per legem Aebutiam [1] et duas Iulias [2] sub-
      latae sunt istae legis actiones, effectumque est ut per concepta
31   uerba, id est per formulas, litigaremus.   Tantum ex duabus
      causis permissum est lege agere, damni infecti et si centum-
      uirale iudicium *futurum est.* *sane quidem* [1] cum ad cen-
      tumuiros *itur*, ante lege agitur sacramento apud praetorem
      urbanum uel peregrinum; [2] damni uero infecti nemo uult
      lege agere, [3] sed potius stipulatione quae in edicto proposita

------

30   But all those *legis actiones* gradually fell into discredit;
      for, owing to the extreme subtility of the jurists of the re-
      public, whose province it then was to declare the law, it came
      about that a litigant making even the slightest mistake lost
      his cause; therefore, by the Aebutian and two of the Julian
      laws, the *legis actiones* were abolished, and litigation by certain
      set forms of words, *i.e. per formulas*, put in place of them.
31   Only in two cases is it still competent to proceed by *legis
      actio*, namely, in that of *damnum infectum*, and when the
      action is one to be referred to the centumviral court. When
      this latter course is in view there must first be a *legis actio* by
      sacrament before the urban or peregrine praetor; but in the
      case of *damnum infectum* no one thinks of proceeding by *legis
      actio*, but rather takes his adversary bound to him by the

§ 30. Comp. §§ 11, 39 f.; Gell. xvi, 10, § 8.

[1] There is great difference of opinion as to the date of this enactment, those suggested ranging from the middle of the fifth to the middle of the seventh century of the city; but the preponderance of surmise attributes it to about the same date as the institution of the peregrin praetorship in 507 | 247. It did not abolish the *legis actiones*, for Cicero speaks of them ten times for once that he mentions the *formulae;* but it probably authorized the praetor to introduce such new judicial remedies as he thought proper alongside of them,—*adiuuandi uel supplendi uel corrigendi iuris ciuilis gratia, propter utilitatem publicam* (Papin. fr. 7, § 1, D. *de I. et I.* i, 1).

[2] Comp. § 104. 'The two *leges Iuliae* (presumably the *iudiciariae*

of Augustus) still further restricted the employment of the *legis actiones*. Details are uncertain; but probably they *inter alia* abolished the court of the *decemuiri* as an independent one, and diminished the number of the *centumuirales causae* ' (Keller, *R. CP.* § 28). See next par.

§ 31. As regards centumviral causes see § 16, note 10. It is the opinion of Bethman-Hollweg (*R. CP.* i, p. 204, note 13) and Karlowa (*R. CP.* p. 216), that *pignoris capio* was the appropriate action of the law for *damnum infectum;* and this view has been given effect to in the text.

[1] So K. u. S.; the ᴍꜱ. has *saneq;* Hu. *saneque.*

[2] After *peregrinum* the ᴍꜱ. has *pr.*, which I take to mean *praetorem*, and have omitted as a gloss.

[3] *Damnum infectum* was damage cr danger apprehended from the

est⁴ obligat aduersarium *suum ; itaque et⁵* commodius *ius et plenius est [quam]*⁶ per pignoris [*capionem*].

31*a* — — — — — — — apparet.   [32] *Item* ¹ in ea for-
32 mula² quae publicano proponitur talis fictio est, ut quanta pecunia olim, si pignus captum esset, id pignus is a quo captum erat luere deberet, tantam pecuniam condemnetur.
33 Nulla autem formula ad condictionis fictionem exprimitur : siue enim pecuniam siue rem aliquam certam debitam nobis petamus, eam ipsam dari nobis oportere intendimus, nec ullam adiungimus condictionis fictionem ; itaque simul intellegimus

---

stipulation set forth in the edict, and thus acquires a remedy at once more convenient and more effectual than that by *pignoris capio.*

31*a* — — — — — — — —.   [32] So in the formula settled
32 to meet the case of a publican [or farmer of the revenue] there is a fiction of this sort,—that whatever sum, had there in former times been a distress, the debtor would have had to pay for redeeming what had been distrained, in that he shall
33 be condemned.   But no formula contains any reference to a feigned *legis actio per condictionem.* When we claim as due to us either a definite sum of money or any other thing definite and certain, we simply contend that that sum or thing ought to be given to us, and say nothing as to what our right would have been under the older procedure ; from which it is to be understood that those formulae in which our contention

---

ruinous or neglected condition of a neighbour's property. Probably if the owner, on formal warning, failed to make the necessary repairs, the complainer was entitled to resort to *pignoris capio*, take possession, and make them himself. But preference was usually given to the procedure authorized by the edict,— *cautio damni infecti*, followed if necessary by *missio in possessionem ;* see § 2, I. *de diu. stip.* (iii, 18).

⁴Comp. *lex Rubria de Gallia cisalpina*, c. 20 (Bruns, p. 88) ; § 2, I. *de diu. stip.* (iii, 18).

⁵So the ᴍꜱ., *ei* being interlined as a correction of *et ;* K. u. S., Hu., and P. *idque et.*

⁶Interpolated to give effect to the view stated above. K. u. S., Hu., and P. make *est* the end of the par., and *per pignoris* the beginning of a

new one, continued on p. 199 (now entirely illegible).

§ 31*a*. K. u. S. and Hu., following earlier eds., suppose Gai. on p. 199 to have given some further explanation of the *legis actio per pign. capionem ;* but this idea is a result of their separation of the words *per pignoris*, at the foot of p. 198, from those immediately preceding them. Gai. seems rather to have dealt with those actions *quae ad legis actionem, exprimuntur* (§ 10), by the introduction into the formulae of a reference to the *legis actiones* they had displaced.

§ 32.   Comp. § 28.
¹This word doubtful ; G. makes it *uelet*, Hu. and P. *contra ;* the proper reading depends on what preceded it, and that is unknown.
²The ᴍꜱ. has *forma*.
§ 33.   Comp. §§ 18, 19.

eas formulas quibus pecuniam aut rem aliquam nobis dari[1] oportere intendimus sua ui ac potestate ualere. eiusdem naturae sunt actiones commodati, fiduciae, negotiorum gestorum et aliae innumerabiles.

34　　Habemus adhuc alterius generis fictiones in quibusdam formulis, ueluti cum is qui ex edicto bonorum possessionem petiit ficto se herede agit: cum enim praetorio iure *is*, non legitimo, succedat in locum defuncti, non habet directas actiones, et neque id quod defuncti fuit potest intendere suum esse, (*neque id quod ei*)[1] *debebatur* potest intendere [*dari*] sibi oportere; itaque ficto se herede intendit ueluti hoc modo: IVDEX ESTO.　SI AVLVS AGERIVS,[2] id est si ipse actor, *LVCIO TITIO HERES ESSET, TVM SI*[3] *FVNDVM DE QVO AGITVR EX IVRE QVIRITIVM EIVS ESSE PARERET;*[4] — — — —,[5] praeposita *simi-*

---

is that a sum of money or some other thing ought to be given us, depend for their efficacy on their own inherent strength. And the same may be said of the actions of commodate, fiduciary covenant upon a conveyance, unauthorized management of another person's affairs, and others innumerable.

34　　We have a different sort of fiction in some formulae, as when a man who, in terms of the edict, has sought possession of the estate of an individual deceased, sues under the pretence that he is heir. Coming in place of the defunct, as he does, by praetorian and not by legal right, he has no direct actions, and can neither maintain that what belonged to his predecessor is his, nor that what was due to the latter ought to be paid to

[1] The MS. has *dare*; but this occurs very frequently in passages in which the eds. have felt themselves constrained to substitute *dari*.

§ 34. Comp. iii, §§ 82, 81.

[1] Hollweg and most eds.

[2] Aulus Agerius and Numerius Negidius are the typical names given by Gai. to the pursuer and defender respectively in his illustrations of the *formulae.*

[3] The words printed above as *Lucio Titio heres esset tum si* are very much abbreviated in the MS., and anything but distinct.

[4] K. u. S. read '*tum si [eum] fundum de quo agitur ex iure Quir. eius esse oporteret*,' and Hu. and other editors in substantially the same way. All that can be said of the MS. is that for the last three words it has ten almost undecipherable letters; for while Bl. in his recension thought he could make out *fuisse . . . t*, Stud. cannot vouch for them. But Gai. says of this action (§ 111)—*imitatur ius legitimum;* what it imitated was the '*si paret hominem ex iure Quir. A. Agerii esse*' of the formular *rei uindicatio* (§ 41); and '*si eius esse pareret*' is a much closer imitation than '*si eius esse oporteret*.' Probably the preference of the editors for the latter locution is due to the fact that it seems employed by Gai. in the formula of the Publician. But it is very questionable whether, for the reason suggested in note 1 to § 86, it can even there be accepted.

[5] K. u. S. (footnote) suggest *et si . . debeatur pecunia;* M. (K. u. S.

liter[6] *fictione illa,*[7] ita subicitur : TVM SI *PARERET*[8] NVMERIVM
NEGIDIVM²[*AVLO*] AGERIO SESTERTIVM X MILIA DARE OPORTERE.

35 Similiter et bonorum emptor ficto se herede agii. sed interdum et alio modo agere solet: nam ex persona eius
cuius bona emerit sumpta intentione, conuertit condemnationem in suam personam, id est ut quod illius esset uel illi
dari oporteret, eo nomine aduersarius huic condemnetur :
quae species actionis appellatur Rutiliana, quia a praetore
Publio Rutilio,¹ qui et bonorum uenditionem introduxisse
dicitur, conparata est. superior autem species actionis qua
ficto se herede bonorum emptor *agit* Seruiana² [*uocatur.*

36 [*Eiusdem generis est quae Publiciana*]¹ uocatur : datur autem

---

him. Accordingly, pretending to be heir, he frames his *intentio* thus : ' So and so be judge. Supposing Aulus Agerius,'
i.e. the actual pursuer, ' to be the heir of Lucius Titius ; if in
that case it would appear that the land in question is his in
quiritarian right.' [*If the action be for something that was*
[*owing to Lucius Titius*], the same fiction is prefixed, and the
formula proceeds : ' if in that case *it would appear* that Numerius Negidius ought to give Aulus Agerius ten thousand
35 sesterces.'   In like manner the purchaser of a bankrupt's
estate may sue on the pretence that he is heir.   But sometimes he sues in another way ; for, allowing the *intentio* to run
in the name of the bankrupt whose estate he has purchased,
he formulates the clause of condemnation in his own name,
that is to say, [he claims] that his adversary shall be condemned to him in respect of what belonged or was due to the
bankrupt.   This last action is called the Rutilian, having been
devised by the praetor Publius Rutilius, the inventor of the
procedure by sale of the bankrupt's estate.   The other, in
which the purchaser proceeds upon a fiction of heirship, is
36 called Servian.   *The action known as the Publician is of the*

---

p. xxii) *et sic de debito cum ;* Hu. *si
uero de debito agatur ;* P. *et si illi
debebatur aeque.*
    ⁶ So Scheurl (*Beitraege,* p. 132) ;
K. u. S., Hu., and P. have *simili ;*
the letters that follow in the MS. are
uncertain.
    ⁷ So Bl. in his recension of the
MS. ; K. u. S. and M. have *heredis ;*
Hu. *intentio.*
    ⁸ So K. u. S. on the suggestion of
M. ; the MS. had *paret.* But the
emendation had previously been suggested by Scheurl,(*Beitraege,*p.133).

§ 35. Comp. iii, §§ 77-81.
    ¹ See iii, 77, note.
    ² Not to be confounded with the
a. *Seruiana de rebus coloni,* § 31, I.
de act. (iv, 6).
§ 36. Comp. §§ 3, 4, I. *de act.* (iv, 6) ;
fr. 1, pr. D. *de Publ. in rem act.*
(vi, 2).   The date of the introduction of this action is uncertain.
The general opinion is that its
author was Q. Publicius, praetor in
685 | 69, the assumption being that
it must have been of later date than
the ordinary *petitoria in rem for-*

haec actio ei qui ex iusta causa traditam sibi rem nondum usucepit, eamque amissa possessione petit; nam quia non potest eam ex iure Quiritium suam esse intendere, fingitur rem usucepisse, et ita quasi ex iure Quiritium dominus factus esset, intendit ueluti hoc modo : IVDEX ESTO.   SI QVEM HOMI-NEM AVLVS AGERIVS EMIT [*ET*] IS EI TRADITVS EST, ANNO POSSEDISSET, TVM SI EVM HOMINEM DE QVO AGITVR EX IVRE 37 QVIRITIVM EIVS ESSE *PARERET*[2] et reliqua.   Item ciuitas Romana peregrino fingitur si eo nomine agat aut cum eo agatur, quo nomine nostris legibus actio constituta est, si modo iustum sit eam actionem etiam ad peregrinum extendi, uelut si [1] furti nomine agat peregrinus aut cum eo [*agatur;*

---

same sort. It is granted to a person who, before completing his usucapion, has lost the possession of a thing that has been delivered to him on a good title, and who now claims it. As he is not in a position to aver that it is his in quiritarian right, a fiction of usucapion is introduced, and, as if he had really become quiritarian proprietor, he formulates an *intentio* in these terms: 'So and so be judge. Suppose such or such a slave, whom Aulus Agerius bought, and who was delivered to him, to have been possessed by him for a year ; if it would appear in such case that said slave is his in quiri-37 tarian right,' etc.   Roman citizenship is also fictitiously attributed to a peregrin who is either suing or being sued in an action upon some law of our own, if it be reasonable that it should be extended to peregrins, as, for example, if he sue [*or be sued*] in an *actio furti.* [*If he be sued*] the formula runs

mula (§ 41), which, from the way it is mentioned by Cic. *II. Verr.* ii, 12, § 31 (*anno* 684 | 70), is thought not to have been then very long in use. Voigt however, (*Ius. Nat.* iv, p. 505,) attributes it to M. Publicius Malleolus, praetor 516 | 238 ; holding that originally its formula was not petitory, but *per sponsionem mere praeiudicialem*, like the ordinary *rei uindicatio* (§ 93), without any fiction of completed usucapion.

[1] So most eds. ; K. u. S. have *item usucapio fingitur in ea actione quae Publiciana*, etc.

[2] The MS. has *öret*, which most editors render *oporteret* ; Scheurl (*Beitraege*, p. 133) and Kuntze (*R.R.* ii, p. 296) have *pareret*. *Oportere* is a word of style appropriate to

an *actio in personam*, and altogether out of place in one *in rem*. 'It is the technical expression for the *necessitas alicuius soluendae rei* that creates the *uinculum iuris* of an obligation' (Scheurl). But the contention of the pursuer in the Publician, like that of the *bonorum possessor* (§ 34), was that the object of dispute *was already* his, not that it *ought to be* his.

§ 37. Comp. Cic. *de nat. deor.* iii, 30, § 74 ; *II. Verr.* ii, 12, § 31.

[1] After *si* Hu. interpolates *furti uel ope consilio facti*. But they are unnecessary ; the accomplice was in law as much a thief as the actual agent (iii, 202) ; the action competent in either case went by the name of *actio furti.*

[*nam si cum eo*]² agatur formula ita concipitur: IVDEX ESTO.
SI PARET [*A DIONE HERMAEI FILIO (aut SI PARET OPE*]³ CON-
SILIOVE DIONIS HERMAEI FILII)⁴ FVRTVM FACTVM ESSE⁵ PATERAE
AVREAE, QVAM OB REM EVM, SI CIVIS ROMANVS ESSET, PRO FVRE
DAMNVM DECIDERE⁶ OPORTERET et reliqua; item si peregrinus
furti agat, ciuitas et Romana fingitur. similiter si ex lege
Aquilia peregrinus damni iniuriae agat aut cum eo agatur,
38 ficta ciuitate Romana iudicium datur.   Praeterea aliquando
fingimus aduersarium nostrum capite deminutum non esse:
nam si ex contractu nobis obligatus obligataue sit et capite
deminutus deminutaue fuerit, uelut mulier per coemptionem,

---

thus: 'So and so be judge: should it appear that [*Dio, son of
[Hermaeus, has stolen,*' or that '*with the aid*] or counsel of Dio,
son of Hermaeus, there has been stolen a golden cup, by reason
whereof, were he a Roman citizen, he would have to make
amends as a thief,' etc. In the same way a peregrin feigns
citizenship when he is pursuer in the same action; and there
is the same fiction if he be either pursuer or defender in an
action on the Aquilian law for wrongful damage to property.
38 Further, we sometimes proceed upon a fiction that our opponent has not been *capite deminutus*. For if one who is indebted
to us on a contract undergo *capitis deminutio*, a female say by
coemption, or a male by adrogation, he ceases by the civil law

---

² Added by K. u. S.

³ The addition is suggested by Gou. and adopted by K. u. S., though by both expressed in a greater number of words.

⁴ The MS. has *er. meiftlio.*

⁵ Most eds. interpolate *Lucio Titio.* Of course there must have been a name in the formula, though Gai. has not thought it necessary to express it.

⁶ Comp. Cic. *de nat. deor.* iii, 30, § 74; Fest. v. *Vindiciae* (Bruns, p. 273). Hu. (*Beitr.* p. 121), Ritschl (*Rhein. Mus. f. Phil.* 1861, p. 384), and Voigt (*Bedeutungswechsel*, p. 151), all point out that *damnum* in the XII Tables did not mean damage—*noxia* was the technical word for that, but the amends or pecuniary reparation a man was bound to make for wrong done.

Voigt is of opinion that the words *pro fure damnum decidere* mean 'to make amends as if he were the thief,' and that they are appropriate only to the case of a counselling accomplice; in other words, that they cannot have been used in the ordinary formula of the *actio furti* against the actual offender. But there is no authority for this idea. The phrase, in all probability, was used originally in sacramental procedure against a thief,—*aio te pro fure damnum decidere oportere.* The penalty of *furtum manifestum*, according to the old law, was slavery; to avoid this the thief was allowed to compound (Vlp. in fr. 7, § 14, D. *de pact.* ii, 14); hence the action requiring him to pay the amount of his composition; and the phrase employed in it was retained by the praetors under the formular system.

§ 38.   Comp. i, 162; ii, 98; iii, 84; iv, 80; Vlp. in fr. 2, § 1, D. *de cap. min.* (iv, 5); § 3, I. *de adquis. per adrog.* (iii, 10).

masculus per adrogationem, desinit iure ciuili debere nobis nec directo intendi potest dare eum eamue oportere; sed ne in potestate eius sit ius nostrum corrumpere, introducta est contra eum eamue actio utilis [1] rescissa capitis deminutione, id est in qua fingitur capite deminutus deminutaue non esse.

39 Partes autem formularum hae sunt: demonstratio, intentio,
40 adiudicatio, condemnatio. Demonstratio est ea pars formulae quae — — —[1] ut demonstretur res de qua agitur, uelut haec pars formulae: QVOD AVLVS AGERIVS NVMERIO NEGIDIO HOMINEM VENDIDIT, item haec: QVOD AVLVS AGERIVS
41 [APVD] NVMERIVM NEGIDIVM HOMINEM DEPOSVIT. Intentio est ea pars formulae qua actor desiderium suum concludit, uelut haec pars formulae: SI PARET NVMERIVM NEGIDIVM AVLO AGERIO SESTERTIVM X MILIA DARE OPORTERE; item haec: QVID-QVID PARET NVMERIVM NEGIDIVM AVLO AGERIO DARE FACERE [OPORTERE];[1] item haec: SI PARET HOMINEM [2] EX IVRE QVIRI-

---

to be our debtor, nor can we contend directly that he is bound to give us what he owed; but, to prevent it being in his power thus to defeat our right, we may have against him an *utilis actio*, the *capitis deminutio* being rescinded,—in other words an action embodying the fiction that he has not been *capite deminutus*.

39 The clauses of a formula are these,—the demonstration, the
40 intention, the adjudication, and the condemnation. The demonstration is that part of the formula which [*is inserted* [*at the outset*] on purpose to show what is the matter in dispute; for example, thus: 'Whereas Aulus Agerius sold a slave to Numerius Negidius;' or thus: 'Whereas Aulus Agerius
41 deposited a slave with Numerius Negidius.' The intention is the clause in which the pursuer embodies his demand; for example, thus: 'Should it appear that Numerius Negidius ought to give ten thousand sesterces to Aulus Agerius;' or, 'Whatever it shall appear that Numerius Negidius ought to give to or do for Aulus Agerius;' or, 'Should it appear that the slave so and so belongs to Aulus Agerius in quiritarian

[1] See ii, 78, note 1.
§ 40. Comp. Paul. in *Collat.* ii, 6, §§ 1, 4, 5.
 [1] The MS. has p'cipuediunserit', but the eighth, ninth, eleventh, and twelfth letters uncertain; M. (K. u. S. p. xxii) suggests *praecipit id quod geritur*; K. u. S. (footnote) *principio ideo ponitur*; Hu. and P. *ideo*
19

inseritur, the other letters, in the form of *praecipuae*, being introduced by them in § 39, after *formularum*.
§ 41. Comp. Cic. *pro Rosc. com.* iv, 11; *II. Verr.* ii, 12, § 31; *L. Rubria*, c. 20 (Bruns, p. 88).
 [1] Added by all eds.
 [2] After *hominem* Hu. interpolates

42 TIVM AVLI AGERII ESSE.   Adiudicatio est ea pars formulae qua permittitur iudici rem alicui ex litigatoribus adiudicare, uelut si inter coheredes familiae erciscundae agatur, aut inter socios communi diuidundo, aut inter uicinos finium regundorum : *nam illic ita est :* QVANTVM[1] ADIVDICARI OPORTET,

43 IVDEX TITIO[2] ADIVDICATO.   Condemnatio est ea pars formulae qua iudici condemnandi absoluendiue potestas permittitur, uelut haec pars formulae : IVDEX NVMERIVM NEGIDIVM AVLO AGERIO SESTERTIVM X MILIA CONDEMNA. SI NON PARET, ABSOLVE ; item haec : IVDEX NVMERIVM NEGIDIVM AVLO AGERIO DVMTAXAT [*X MILIA*] CONDEMNA. SI NON PARET, ABSOLVITO ; item haec : IVDEX NVMERIVM NEGIDIVM AVLO AGERIO CONDEMNATO et reliqua, ut non adiciatur DVMTAXAT [*X MILIA*].

44 Non tamen istae omnes partes simul[1] inueniuntur, sed[2]

---

42 right.'   The adjudication is the clause whereby the judge is authorized to adjudicate a thing to one in particular of the litigants, as when co-heirs are suing for partition of an inheritance, or partners for division of their estate, or conterminous proprietors for settlement of boundaries ; it runs thus : ' So much as ought to be adjudicated, do you, judge, adjudicate

43 to Titius.'   The condemnation is the clause whereby the judge is empowered to condemn or absolve ; as, for example : ' Do you, judge, condemn Numerius Negidius to Aulus Agerius in ten thousand sesterces ; should it not so appear, absolve him ;' or, ' Do you, judge, condemn Numerius Negidius to Aulus Agerius, but not beyond ten thousand sesterces ; should it not so appear, absolve him ;' or ' Do you, judge, condemn Numerius Negidius to Aulus Agerius,' etc., without the

44 addition of ' but not beyond ten thousand sesterces.'   Those

---

Stichum. But this seems unnecessary. Of course the thing vindicated had to be named, whether a slave or lands, Paul. *ad. Ed.* in fr. 6, D. *de R. V.* (vi, 1) ; but Gai. here, as elsewhere, contents himself with a skeleton style.

§ 42. Comp. Vlp. xix, 16 ; § 20, I. *de act.* (iv, 6) ; §§ 4-6, I. *de off. iud.* (iv, 17).
   [1] So most eds. ; the MS. has *qtam.*
   [2] So the MS.; but Hu. reads *cui oportet* (*cuiō*), which certainly seems more consistent with the nature of the action. P., assuming that *Titio* is an erroneous rendering by the copyist of the abbreviation *tt* of the original, substitutes *tantum.*

§ 43. Comp. §§ 47-52, 57, 68, 78 ; *lex Rubria*, c. 20 (Bruns, p. 88). The writer of the MS. seems to have become confused by the repetition of X *milia ;* he omits the words twice where they should be, and inserts them once—after *condemnato,* deleted above—where they should not.

§ 44. This par. has been subjected to much interpolation at the hands of the eds., and, as it seems to me, more than necessary. Gai. says that the four parts of a formula were never found together ; the eds., with exception of He., Hu., and perhaps K. u. S., dispute this, and hold that

quaedam[2] inueniuntur, quaedam non inueniuntur. certe intentio aliquando sola inuenitur, sicut in praeiudicalibus formulis, qualis est qua quaeritur aliquis libertus sit, uel quanta dos sit, et aliae conplures :[3] demonstratio autem et adiudicatio et condemnatio numquam solae inueniuntur, nihil enim omnino [*demonstratio*][4] sine intentione uel condemnatione ualet; item condemnatio sine demonstratione uel intentione, uel adiudica[*tio sine demonstratione et inten*]tione[5] nullas uires habet; ob id numquam solae inueniuntur.

---

clauses, however, are not all found together in a formula; some are present, others not. Sometimes, indeed, the intention alone is found : this occurs in praejudiciary formulae such as that for determining whether an individual is or is not a freedman, what is the amount of a marriage portion, and various other questions. The demonstration, adjudication, and condemnation, however, never stand alone : for [*a demon-[stration]* is utterly useless apart from an intention or condemnation ; a condemnation is equally inoperative apart from a demonstration or intention ; and an adjudication [*is useless [without a demonstration and intention]*. This is why they [*i.e.* the demonstration, adjudication, and condemnation] are never found by themselves.

the three divisory actions contained them all. I am inclined to think they contained only demonstration, intention, and adjudication.

Rudorff (*Edict.* p. 86) conjecturally constructs the formula of the *actio communi diuidundo* thus : *Iudex esto. Quod ille fundus illi et illi communis est, quam ob rem ille illum communi diuidundo provocauit, quantum ob eam rem alteri ab altero aut Titio adiudicari oportet, id iudex alteri aut Titio adiudicato, quodque alterum alteri ob eam rem dare facere praestare oportet ex fide bona, eius iudex alterum alteri condemna; si non paret absolue.* Here are (1) demonstration, (2) intention, (3) adjudication, (4) a second intention, and (5) condemnation; but it is because there are two actions conjoined in one formula,—a *iudicium diuisorium* and an *incerti condictio*, to which latter alone the second intention and the condemnation belong. The *condictio* was not a necessary adjunct of the divisory formula; if introduced at all, it was only where simple division would not be equitable without some payment or concession on one side or other.

But I much doubt that it ever was so introduced ; it appears to me pretty clear from the language of §§ 4-6, I. *de off. iud.* (iv, 17), that it was of the office of the judge, without being moved thereto by anything on the face of the pleadings, and simply as incident to the adjudication, to pronounce such order or condemnation, over and above his adjudication, as was necessary to do justice between the parties.

[1] After *simul* Hu. and P. interpolate *in omnibus formulis.*

[2] After *sed* Hu. interpolates *solae* ; and after *quaedam* he adds *tantum.* K. u. S. leave a blank after *sed*, and (footnote) on the authority of M., propose to fill it with *abesse potest una aliaue ; item solae.*

[3] Comp. iii, 128; Paul. v, 9, § 1.

[4] So K. u. S., Hu., and most eds.

[5] Bk. and K. u. S. have *sine demonstratione uel intentione* ; P. *sine demonstratione et intentione et con-*

45   Sed eas quidem formulas in quibus de iure quaeritur in ius
conceptas uocamus, quales sunt quibus intendimus nostrum
esse aliquid ex iure Quiritium, aut nobis dari oportere, aut
pro fure damnum [*decidi oportere; in*]¹ quibus iuris ciuilis
46 intentio est.   ceteras uero in factum conceptas uocamus,
id est in quibus nulla talis intentionis conceptio est, [*sed*]
initio formulae nominato eo quod factum est, adiciuntur ea
uerba per quae iudici damnandi absoluendiue potestas datur;
qualis est formula qua utitur patronus contra libertum qui
eum contra edictum praetoris in ius uocauit :¹ nam in ea ita
est : RECVPERATORES ² SVNTO.   SI PARET ILLVM PATRONVM AB
ILLO [*ILLIVS*] PATRONI ³ LIBERTO CONTRA EDICTVM PRAETORIS ⁴
IN IVS VOCATVM ESSE, RECVPERATORES ILLVM LIBERTVM ILLI
PATRONO SESTERTIVM X MILIA CONDEMNATE.   SI NON PARET,
ABSOLVITE.   ceterae quoque formulae quae sub titulo DE IN

---

45   We say of those formulae which raise a question of civil
right that they are conceived *in ius ;* such are those in which
we contend that something is ours on quiritarian title, or that
something ought to be given us, or that some one ought to
make amends as a thief ; in them our intention is founded
46 upon a rule of the *ius ciuile.*   On the other hand we call
those *in factum conceptae* which contain no such intention,
but in which, after reference in the outset to what has
occurred, words are introduced empowering the judge to condemn or absolve.   The formula employed by a patron against
a freedman who has summoned him in contravention of the
edict is of this description, and is in these terms : ' So and so
be recuperators.   Should it appear that so and so, a patron,
was summoned by so and so, a freedman of said patron, in
contravention of the praetor's edict, do you, recuperators,
condemn said freedman to said patron in ten thousand sesterces ; should it not so appear, absolve him.'   The other
formulae set forth in the title of the edict ' *de in ius uocando*

---

demnatione. Hu. interpolates only
sine intentione ; but it is difficult to
see how a demonstration could be
dispensed with in a divisory action.
§ 45.   Comp. §§ 41, 60.
    ¹ So all eds. Comp. § 37 and
thereto note 6.
§ 46.   Comp. § 60 ; § 12, I. *de act.*
(iv, 6).
    ¹ Comp. §§ 183, 187 ; § 3, I. *de
poena tem. lit.* (iv, 16).

² See § 105, note.
³ The ms. has *patrono ;* the *illius*
is due to Hollweg, and adopted by
Hu.
⁴ The ms. has *illius praetoris ;* but
it was not the practice to name the
author of any particular provision
of the edict ; and probably the *illius*
here is the one that ought to have
stood before *patroni*, as mentioned
in last note.

IVS VOCANDO[5] propositae sunt in factum conceptae sunt, uelut
aduersus eum qui in ius uocatus neque uenerit neque uindicem
dederit ; item contra eum qui ui exemerit eum qui in ius
uocatur ; et denique innumerabiles eius modi aliae formulae
47 in albo proponuntur.   Sed ex quibusdam causis praetor et
in ius et in factum conceptas formulas proponit, uelut depositi
et commodati. illa enim formula quae ita concepta est :
IVDEX ESTO. QVOD AVLVS AGERIVS APVD NVMERIVM NEGIDIVM
MENSAM ARGENTEAM DEPOSVIT, QVA DE RE AGITVR, QVIDQVID
OB EAM REM NVMERIVM NEGIDIVM AVLO AGERIO DARE FACERE
OPORTET EX FIDE BONA, EIVS[1] IVDEX NVMERIVM NEGIDIVM AVLO
AGERIO CONDEMNATO N. R.[2] SI NON PARET, ABSOLVITO, in ius

---

are also *in factum conceptae* ; for example that against a person
who, having been duly summoned, has neither appeared nor
found a *uindex*, that against a person who has forcibly carried
off another duly summoned in an action, and many others
47 that are set forth in the album.   To meet certain cases the
praetor has provided in the edict formulae both *in ius* and *in
factum conceptae*, as in deposit and commodate.   The formula
conceived as follows is *in ius* : 'So and so be judge.   Whereas
Aulus Agerius deposited with Numerius Negidius the silver
table in question, whatever it appears that on that account
Numerius Negidius ought in good faith to give to or do for
Aulus Agerius, in that, judge, condemn Numerius Negidius
to Aulus Agerius, — — ; should it not so appear, absolve

[5] Comp. tits. D. *si q. in ius uoc.*
etc. (ii, 5, 6, and 8) ; tit. C. *de in ius
uoc.* (ii, 2).

§ 47. Comp. § 60. Many attempts have
been made, but all unsuccessfully, to
explain the reason of the double
formula described in this par.   The
solution of the difficulty might be
easier if we knew for certain what
were the *quaedam causae* to which
Gai. refers,—whether his *uelut* is to
be taken as enumerative (which it
sometimes is) or as merely indicative.
    The par. is useful, however, as
clearly displaying the distinction
between an *intentio in ius concepta*
and one in *factum concepta.*   In the
former the question for the *iudex* to
determine was one of law, though of
course involving inquiry into facts,
—'is or is not the defender indebted to the pursuer under a con-

tract of deposit ? and if so, in how
much ? '   In the latter the question
was purely one of fact,—' was the
thing deposited, and has the depositary dolefully failed to restore it ?
If so, condemn him in its value.'
    [1] The MS. has *eius id iudex ;* and
some eds. so read the passage, referring *eius* to the preceding *ex fide
bona.*   The syntax, however, is *eius*
(i.e. *nomine*) *condemna*, and *id* must
be deleted.
    [2] Hu. (*Studien*, p. 316) interprets
these letters as *nisi restituat*, on the
strength of a passage of Vlpian's (fr.
1, § 21, D. *depositi*, xvi, 3), where he
says that, in the particular case he
is referring to, the defender in an
a. depositi would be condemned if
he did not give up the thing deposited,—*nisi restituat.*   But this affords no proof that the words were
inserted in the *formula ;* acquittal

concepta est; at illa formula quae ita concepta est: IVDEX
ESTO.   SI PARET AVLVM AGERIVM ₁APVD NVMERIVM NEGIDIVM
MENSAM ARGENTEAM DEPOSVISSE, EAMQVE DOLO MALO NVMERII
NEGIDII AVLO AGERIO REDDITAM NON ESSE, QVANTI EA RES ERIT,²
TANTAM PECVNIAM IVDEX NVMERIVM NEGIDIVM AVLO AGERIO
CONDEMNATO.   SI NON PARET, ABSOLVITO, in factum concepta
est.   similes etiam commodati formulae sunt.

48   Omnium autem formularum quae condemnationem habent ad
pecuniariam aestimationem condemnatio *nunc* ¹ concepta est:
itaque et si corpus aliquod petamus, ueluti fundum hominem
uestem [*aurum*] argentum,² iudex non ipsam rem condemnat
eum cum quo actum est, sicut olim fieri solebat,³ [*sed*] aestimata
49 re pecuniam eum condemnat.   Condemnatio autem uel
50 certae pecuniae in formula proponitur uel incertae.   cer-

---

him.' When framed in the following terms the formula is *in
factum*: 'So and so be judge. Should it appear that Aulus
Agerius deposited with Numerius Negidius a silver table,
and that, through dole on the part of Numerius Negidius, it
has not been returned to Aulus Agerius, then, judge, whatever be the value of the table, in that sum condemn Numerius
Negidius to Aulus Agerius; should it not so appear, absolve
him.' The formulae in commodate are in similar terms.

48   In formulae containing a condemnatory clause the actual
condemnation is always in a money estimate; and even if our
claim be for some *corpus*,—land, a slave, a garment, *gold*,
silver, the judge does not condemn the defender in the
thing itself, as used to be done under the older system, but,
49 having put a value upon it, condemns him in money.   The
clause of condemnation may either fix a certain sum of money
50 or leave it uncertain.   A certain sum is named when the

---

in the event of restitution must
have been implied in the *bona fides*
of the *iudicium*, and was enjoined
directly by the rule *omnia iudicia
absolutoria sunt* (§ 114).
    ³Comp. fr. 179, fr. 198, D. *de
V. S.* (l, 16). While in the *actio
in factum* the condemnation was to
be in the actual value (or in some
cases twice the value, fr. 1, § 1, D.
depositi) of the thing not returned,
in that *in ius* it was to be in the
interresse,—the damage sustained by
the depositor.
§§ 48-60. Comp. §§ 32-85, tit. I. DE
ACTIONIBVS (iv, 6).

§ 48. Comp. § 32, tit. I. afd.
    ¹ So P. renders the *n* of the MS.
overlooked by other eds.
    ² The MS. has *argumentum*; but
the enumeration we have here is so
frequent (comp. ii, §§ 18, 20) as to
leave no doubt as to its meaning, or
as to the propriety of interpolating
aurum.
    ³ Under the procedure *sacra-
mento*; it had to be followed by
an *arbitrium litis aestimandae*, for
converting the condemnation into
money.
§§ 49-51. Comp. § 43.

tae pecuniae *uelut* in ea formula qua certam pecuniam petimus; nam illic ima parte formulae ita est: IVDEX NVMERIVM NEGIDIVM AVLO AGERIO SESTERTIVM X MILIA CON-
51 DEMNA. SI NON PARET, ABSOLVE.   incertae uero condem-
natio pecuniae duplicem significationem habet: est enim una *quidem cum* [1] aliqua praefinitione, quae uulgo dicitur cum taxatione, uelut si incertum aliquid petamus; *nam illic ima parte* formulae ita est: IVDEX NVMERIVM NEGIDIVM AVLO AGERIO DVMTAXAT SESTERTIVM X MILIA CONDEMNA.   SI NON PARET, ABSOLVE: uel incerta est et *infinita condemnatio*,[2] *uelut* si rem aliquam a possidente nostram esse petamus, id est si in rem agamus uel ad exhibendum; nam illic ita est: QVANTI *EA RES ERIT*, TANTAM PECVNIAM, IVDEX, NVMERIVM NEGIDIVM [*AVLO AGERIO*] CONDEMNA.   SI NON PARET, AB-
52 SOLVITO.   *Quid ergo est?*[1] iudex, si condemnet, certam pecuniam condemnare debet, etsi certa pecunia in condem-natione posita non sit.   Debet autem iudex attendere, *ut*

---

formula is one in which a definite sum is claimed; in such a case the final clause runs thus: 'Do you, judge, condemn Numerius Negidius to Aulus Agerius in ten thousand ses-
51 terces; should it not so appear, absolve him.'   A clause of condemnation in an uncertain amount may mean either of two things.   It may mean one in which there is a sort of anticipatory limitation, commonly called taxation, following on an illiquid claim: and then the final clause of the formula is as follows: 'Do you, judge, condemn Numerius Negidius to Aulus Agerius in not more than ten thousand sesterces; should it not so appear, absolve him.'   Or it may mean one altogether uncertain and unlimited, as when we claim a thing from the party in possession of it on the averment that it is ours, in other words, when our action is *in rem* or *ad exhibendum;* then it runs: 'Whatever be the value of the thing, do you, judge, condemn Numerius Negidius to Aulus Agerius in that amount; should it not so appear, absolve him.'
52 *What does all this come to?*   That a judge, if he condemn, must do so in a definite sum of money, even though no definite sum be mentioned in the clause of condemnation.

---

[1] So Bk.; the MS. has *quae*, but with an interlinear substitution of *c* for the final *e*. K. u. S. and Hu. have simply *una cum*; P. *una qua cum.*

[2] So I interpret the letter *c* in MS.

§ 52.   Comp. § 32, tit. I. afd.
[1] So K. u. S. and Hu., but very doubtful.   The reading proposed by Hu. in his earlier editions,—*Qui de re uero est iudex*, comes quite as close to the MS.

cum certae pecuniae condemnatio posita sit, neque maioris
neque minoris summa posita condemnet, alioquin litem suam
facit ;² item si taxatio posita *sit*, ne pluris condemnet quam
texatum sit, alias enim similiter litem suam facit :² minoris
autem damnare ei permissum est.   at si etiam —— —— —— ——.
52a —— —— —— —— —— ——.
53   Si quis intentione plus conplexus fuerit (*causa cadit*),¹ id
est rem perdit, nec a praetore in integrum restituitur, praeterquam quibusdam casibus in quibus —— —— —— —— —— ——.²
(*Plus autem quattuor*) modis petitur : re, tempore, loco, causa.
(*re, ueluti si quis pro X*) milibus quae ei debentur xx milia

---

But he must take care that, when a definite sum is mentioned in it, he does not condemn in either a larger or smaller
sum, otherwise he makes the cause his own ; if the condemnation be taxed, and he condemn in more than the maximum,
he runs the same risk ; but he may lawfully condemn in less.
52a —— —— —— —— ——.   [52a] —— —— —— —— —— ——.
53   If a pursuer have claimed in his intention more than he is
entitled to, he fails in his suit, that is to say, he loses his claim
altogether, nor can he be reinstated by the praetor except in
those few cases in which —— —— —— ——.   *Too much may
be claimed in four ways,—in respect of amount, time, place,
or circumstances. There is over-claim in respect of amount*

---

²Comp. pr. I. *de obl. q. quasi ex
del.* (iv, 5). 'A judgment that did
not correspond to the formula had
none of that efficacy which the
praetor guaranteed to one that was
within its terms.   According to
the Roman system of procedure the
pursuer was in such a case destitute
of any remedy against the defender ; for, after judgment had
been pronounced, it was impossible
for the judge to rectify it, and a
fresh action against the defender
was inadmissible. Under these circumstances the judge himself, instead of the defender, was declared
responsible to the pursuer, who had
thus been deprived of his remedy,'
Ihering, *G. d. R. R.* ii, p. 75, note.
§ 52a. P. 206 of the ms. is to a great
extent illegible.   The first seven
lines are thus conjecturally rendered
by Hu.—at si etiam *taxatio posita
non sit, quanti uelit condemnare
potest.* [52a] *Vnde, quia quod petit,
qui formulam accipit* intendere de-

bet, nec *amplius iudex quam* certa
condemnatione constringitur, *sed
nec iterum eandem formulam accipit
qui egit, et in condemnatione certam
pecuniam quam petit ponere debet ;
ne consequatur minus quam uelit.*
§ 53.   Comp. Paul. i, 10, § 1 (and in
Consult. v, 4) ; § 33, tit. I. afd., from
which the words in ital., illegible in
the ms., are supplied.
   ¹ *Causa cadere, lite cadere, formula cadere, formula excidere,*
though sometimes used more generally, yet in strictness meant to fail
through some mistake of form or
procedure, rather than on the merits;
see Cic. *de Inu.* ii, 19, § 57; Quintil.
Inst. Or. iii, 6, § 69.
   ² Three lines illegible, with the
single exception of the word *patitur.*
Hu. proposes—*in quibus omnes ac-
tores praetor non* patitur *ob errorem
suum damno affici ; nam minoribus
xxv annorum semper ut in aliis
causis et hic succurrit.* Comp. § 33,
tit. I. afd.

petierit, aut si (*is cuius*) ex parte res est totam eam aut maiore
ex parte (*suam*) esse intenderit. (*tempore, ueluti si quis ante
(diem uel*) ante (*condicionem petierit. loco, ueluti si quod
(certo loco*) dari promissum est, id (*alio loco sine commemora-
(tio)*ne eius loci petatur, ueluti si (*quis ita stipulatus fuerit :
(EPHESI*) DARE SPONDES ? *deinde* Romae pure (*intendat dari
(sibi oportere*). — — — — — — — [3] petere, id est non
adiecto loco. causa plus petitur uelut si quis in intentione
tollat electionem debitoris quam is [4] habet obligationis iure,
uelut si quis ita stipulatus sit: SESTERTIVM X MILIA AVT
HOMINEM STICHVM DARE SPONDES ? deinde alterutrum [5] ex his
petat; nam quamuis petat quod minus est, plus tamen petere
uidetur, quia potest aduersarius interdum facilius id praestare
quod non petitur. similiter si quis genus stipulatus sit, deinde

---

when, instead of ten thousand sesterces which are due to him,
a man claims twenty thousand; or when, owing an equal
share of a thing, he avers that the whole or the greater part
is his. *There is over-claim in point of time when he sues
before the day of payment or the fulfilment of a condition.
There is over-claim in respect of place when* what it has been
promised shall be paid *at a certain place* is sued for *elsewhere
without mention* of that place; as when *a person who has
stipulated thus :* 'Do you engage to pay *at Ephesus ?*' afterwards sues in Rome, *contending*, without any qualification,
that the money ought to be paid to him. — — — —
— —. There is over-claim in respect of circumstances
when a pursuer in his intention deprives his debtor of an
election to which he is entitled by the terms of the obligation.
Suppose a man has acquired a claim under a stipulation
conceived in such terms as: 'Do you engage to give me ten
thousand sesterces or the slave Stichus?' if he thereupon sue
for one in particular of these alternatives, although it be that
of least value, still he is claiming more than he is entitled to;
for it may be that it would be easier for the defender to give
that which is not sued for. So if a man who has stipulated
generically sues specifically, as when, having stipulated in

[3] Four lines illegible, with the
exception of *dare mihi oportere*
(consecutively). To utilise them
Hu. alters the reading given above
(from the Inst.) in this way—uelut
si *a te stipulatus sim :* ' x *milia sestertium* dare spondes?' and proceeds
—deinde *uero* Romae pure *hoc
modo intendam : si paret te sester-*

tium x milia ex stipulatu dare mihi
oportere; *plus enim petere ideo in-
tellegor, quia utilitatem promissori
adimo, 'quam si Ephesi daret habiturus esset. Ephesi tamen etiam pure
potero* petere, id est, etc.
[4] The MS. has *quamuis.*
[5] So the Inst. ; the MS. has *alterutrum eorum*; Hu. *alterutrum solum.*

speciem petat, uelut si quis purpuram stipulatus sit generaliter,
deinde Tyriam specialiter petat; quin etiam licet uilissimam
petat, idem iuris est propter eam rationem quam proxime
diximus. idem iuris est si quis generaliter hominem stipulatus sit, deinde nominatim aliquem petat uelut Stichum,
quamuis uilissimum. itaque sicut ipsa stipulatio concepta est,
54 ita et intentio formulae concipi debet.   Illud satis apparet
in incertis formulis plus peti non posse, quia cum certa
quantitas non petatur, sed QVIDQVID aduersarium DARE FACERE
OPORTERET intendatur, nemo potest plus intendere. idem
iuris est et si in rem incertae partis actio data sit, uelut
talis: QVANTAM PARTEM PARET IN EO FVNDO, QVO DE AGITVR,
actoris ESSE: quod genus actionis in paucissimis causis dari
55 solet.   Item palam est si quis aliud pro alio intenderit nihil
eum periclitari, eumque ex integro agere posse, quia *nihil ante
uidetur egisse ; ueluti si* is qui hominem Stichum petere deberet
Erotem petierit, aut si quis ex testamento dari sibi oportere

---

general terms for purple, he specifically claims that of Tyre;
nay, even although he were to claim specifically the poorest
of purples, still, for the reason already stated, he would be
demanding too much.   And the same is the case when a man,
having stipulated generally for a slave, sues for one in particular by name, say Stichus, no matter how worthless he
may be.   The intention therefore of the formula must be conceived in exactly the same terms as the stipulation that is
54 sued upon.   In uncertain formulae, as is clear enough,
there can be no excess of claim; for as no definite sum
is sued for, but simply 'whatever' his adversary 'ought
to give or do,' no pursuer can possibly frame his intention
beyond that.   The same observation applies to the case of an
actio in rem in reference to an uncertain share; for example,
'whatever share of the land in question appears to belong'
to the pursuer; but an action of this sort is very seldom
55 granted.   It is equally clear that a man who in his intention has named one thing instead of another, runs no risk,
and may proceed anew, being regarded as if he had not yet
sued at all; as when he who ought to have claimed the slave
Stichus has actually sued for Eros, or when one whose claim
is really upon a stipulation has averred in his intention that

---

§ 54. In the first *intentio* in this par.
Hu. substitutes *oportere pareat* for
oportet ; but that the latter was
quite regular appears from the *for-*
mula in ius recited in § 47, and its
repetition in § 60.
§ 55. Comp. § 35, tit. I. afd.; Th. iv,
6, § 35.

intenderit cui ex stipulatu debebatur, aut si cognitor aut procu-
56 rator[1] intenderit sibi dari oportere.   Sed plus quidem intendere sicut supra diximus periculosum est; minus autem intendere licet; sed de reliquo intra eiusdem praeturam agere non
permittitur: nam qui ita agit per exceptionem excluditur, quae
57 exceptio appellatur litis diuiduae.[1]   At si in condemnatione
plus petitum sit quam oportet, actoris quidem   periculum
nullum est; sed [reus, cum][2] iniquam formulam acceperit, in
integrum restituitur ut minuatur condemnatio: si uero minus
positum fuerit quam oportet, hoc solum [actor][2] consequitur
quod posuit; nam tota quidem res in iudicium deducitur,
constringitur autem condemnationis fine, quam iudex egredi
non potest. nec ex ea parte praetor in integrum restituit:
facilius enim reis praetor succurrit quam actoribus: loquimur
autem exceptis minoribus xxv annorum; nam huius aetatis
58 hominibus in omnibus rebus lapsis praetor succurrit.   Si

---

the defender ought to give him something due under a testament, or when one who is only a cognitor or procurator has
contended that the defender was bound to pay [not to his
56 principal but] to him.   To claim too much in the intention,
as already observed, is hazardous; but it is quite allowable
to claim too little.   Action for the remainder, however, is not
permitted within the same praetorship; if raised sooner, it
will be barred by an exception of *lis diuidua*, divided suit.
57 If a greater sum than ought to be is named in the clause of
condemnation, the pursuer does not thereby incur any risk;
but the defender, on account of the unfairness of the formula,
will be reinstated by the praetor in order to have the condemnation reduced.   If, on the other hand, a smaller sum be
mentioned in this clause than ought to have been, the pursuer
can get no more than is so mentioned; his whole claim has
been submitted to the arbitrament of the judge, but the
formula is controlled by the last clause of it, beyond which
the judge is not allowed to travel.   Nor is there here any
room for his reinstatement by the praetor, who is always
much readier to lend assistance to a defender than to a pursuer: unless indeed the latter be under twenty-five years of
age; for the praetor will always interfere in aid of a minor,
58 in any case in which he may have been prejudiced.   If too

---

[1] Comp. § 86.
§ 56.   Comp. § 34, tit. I. afd.
[1] Comp. § 122; § 34, tit. I. afd.
§ 57.   Comp. § 43.

[1] So G. and all eds.; ms. has *ga*.
[2] Added by G. and adopted by
most eds.
§ 58.   Comp. § 40.

in demonstratione plus aut minus positum sit, nihil in
iudicium deducitur, et ideo res in integro manet : et hoc est
59 quod dicitur falsa demonstratione rem non perimi.   Sed sunt
qui putant minus recte comprehendi, ut qui forte Stichum et
Erotem emerit recte uideatur ita demonstrare : QVOD EGO DE
TE HOMINEM EROTEM EMI, et si uelit de Sticho alia formula [1]
agat, quia uerum est eum qui duos emerit singulos quoque
emisse : idque ita maxime *Labeoni* [2] uisum est : sed si is qui
unum emerit de duobus egerit, falsum demonstrat.   idem et
60 in aliis actionibus set, uelut commodati et depositi.   Sed
nos apud quosdam scriptum inuenimus, in actione depositi,
et denique in ceteris omnibus ex quibus damnatus unusquisque ignominia notatur,[1] eum qui plus quam oporteret
demonstrauerit litem perdere, ueluti si quis una re deposita
duas pluresue [*se de*]posuisse demonstrauerit, aut si is cui
pugno mala percussa est, in actione iniuriarum etiam aliam

---

much or too little be condescended on in the demonstration,
there is nothing really submitted to the judge, and the pursuer's claim remains intact; this is what is meant by the
saying that a claim is not extinguished by an erroneous
59 demonstration.   Some lawyers, among whom Labeo is pre-
eminent, think that to found in it on less than is due is quite
regular,—that if, for example, a man has purchased Stichus
and Eros, he may quite correctly say in his demonstration,
'Whereas I bought from you the slave Eros,' and may, if he
likes, have a separate formula applicable to Stichus, the fact
being indisputable that he who has bought two slaves has
bought each of them; but that if a man who has bought only
one, mention two in his action, he demonstrates falsely.   And
they apply the same principles to other actions, such as those
60 of commodate and deposit.   But we have read in the pages
of some of the jurists, in reference to the action of deposit
and those actions generally in which condemnation entails
infamy, that he who in his demonstration has condescended
on more than he ought to have done, loses his claim; as when
a man who has deposited only one thing states in his demonstration that he has deposited two or more, or when one who
has had a blow from the fist on his face, avers in an *actio*

§ 59. Comp. Vlp. in fr. 38, D. *de act.*   [2] The ᴍs. has *laticoni.* See i,
empt. (xix, 1).   196, note 1.
    [1] After this word the ᴍs. has *id,*   § 60.   [1] An enumeration of those actions
which Hu. renders *iterum,* and P.,   in § 182.
omitting *alia formula, idem.*

partem corporis percussam sibi demonstrauerit : [2] quod an debeamus credere uerius esse, diligentius requiremus. certe cum duae sint depositi formulae, alia in ius concepta, alia in factum, sicut supra quoque notauimus,[3] et in ea quidem formula quae in ius concepta est initio res de qua agitur demonstratorio modo [4] designetur, deinde inferatur iuris contentio his uerbis : QVIDQVID OB EAM REM ILLVM ILLI DARE FACERE OPORTET ; in ea uero quae in factum concepta est, *statim initio intentionis* alio modo res de qua agitur designetur his uerbis : SI PARET ILLVM APVD [*ILLVM REM*] [5] ILLAM DEPOSVISSE, dubitare non debemus quin si quis in formula quae in factum conposita est plures res designauerit quam deposuerit, litem perdat, quia in intentione plus *posuisse (uidetur).* [6]

60a — — — — — — — —.   [61] — — — — — —

---

iniuriarum that he has been struck on some other part of his body. Let us examine the matter to see whether this be the true view of it. As we have already observed, there are two formulae applicable to the case of deposit,—one *in ius*, and the other *in factum concepta*. In that which is *in ius concepta* the matter of dispute is first set forth in a demonstratory manner, and then the pursuer's contention in point of law is inferentially stated in the words, ' whatever in respect thereof so and so ought to give to or do for so and so ;' in that *in factum concepta*, on the other hand, the matter of dispute is described *in the first part of the intention* in a different way, in these words : ' Should it appear that so and so deposited such and such a thing with so and so.' There is no room to doubt that if a person using this formula *in factum concepta* has described in it more things than he actually deposited, he loses his action, because he has put too much in his intention.

60a — — — — — — — —.   [61] — — — — — — that,

[2] The offence was more or less aggravated according to the part struck, etc. ; see iii, 225, and § 9, I. *de iniur.* (iv, 4).

[3] See § 47.

[4] So the ms., quite distinctly ; Hu. substitutes *demonstretur, id est modo.*

[5] Added by Hu., and generally accepted.

[6] The last word is supplied conjecturally by G. Whether the par. should end here is extremely doubtful : pp. 210, 211 of the ms. are entirely illegible, therefore we have no means of knowing.

§§ 60a-68. Comp. §§ 36-40, I. DE ACTIONIBVS (iv, 6).

§ 60a. It is generally assumed that on pp. 210, 211, Gai. dealt with the same matters as are referred to in §§ 36-39, tit. I. afd.

61 continetur ut habita ratione eius quod inuicem actorem ex
eadem causa praestare oporteret, in reliquum eum cum quo
62 actum est condemnare.   Sunt autem bonae fidei iudicia
haec: ex empto uendito, locato conducto, negotiorum gestorum,
mandati, depositi, fiduciae, pro socio, tutelae, [*rei uxoriae*,
[*commodati*, *pigneraticium*, *familiae erciscundae*, *communi*
63 [*diuidundo*,] *praescriptis uerbis.*   (*In his*)[1] tamen iudici nullam omnino inuicem compensationis rationem habere — —[2]
formulae uerbis praecipitur; sed quia id bonae fidei iudicio
conueniens uidetur, *ideo*[3] officio eius contineri creditur.
64 Alia causa est illius actionis qua argentarius experitur: nam
is cogitur cum conpensatione agere, *et ea* conpensatio uerbis
formulae exprimitur, *adeo quidem ut itaque*[1] ab initio conpensatione facta minus intendat sibi dari oportere: ecce enim si

61 account being taken of anything which the pursuer is bound
to pay on his side in respect of the same matter, the defender
62 is to be condemned only in the balance.   The *bonae fidei*
actions are those arising out of purchase and sale, location
and conduction, unauthorized management of another's affairs,
mandate, deposit, fiduciary covenant upon a conveyance, partnership, tutory, *a woman's dowry, commodate, and the contract
of pledge; together with those for partitioning an inheritance
amongst the heirs and for dividing common property,* and that
63 *praescriptis uerbis.*   There is nothing in the wording of the
formula in those actions that enjoins the judge thus to set off
claims between the parties; but as such a course is consonant
with the notion of a *bonae fidei iudicium,* it is held to be within
64 the scope of the judge's office.   The rule is different in the
case of the action made use of by a banker.   He is required
to set off his customer's counter-claim, and this is stated in
the formula in so many words, so that here, from the very
first, the averment in the intention is that the defender is
bound to pay less than the nominal amount of his debt; for

§ 61. Comp. § 89, tit. I. afd., to the latter half of which the legible portion of this par. (on p. 212) corresponds. Comp. also Paul. ii, 5, § 8.

§ 62. Comp. § 28, tit. I. afd., from which the words in ital. are supplied (the *a rei uxoriae* being introduced on the suggestion of § 29). Comp. also Cic. *Top.* xvii, 66.

§ 63. K. u. S. think this par. corrupt, and that it should run—*In his tamen iudici nulla omnino parte*

inuicem conpensationis rationem, etc.

[1] So K. u. S.; Hu. proposes *uerum.* But there is no space in the MS. between *uerbis* in last par. and *tamen* in this.

[2] The letters in the MS. seem to be *ntrartae,* which K. u. S. read *diserte.*

[3] The MS. has *id.*

§ 64. Comp. § 68.
[1] K. u. S. delete *itaque;* Hu. and P. substitute *statim.*

sestertium x milia debeat Titio, atque ei xx debeantur, sic
intendit : SI PARET TITIVM SIBI X MILIA DARE OPORTERE AMPLIVS
65 QVAM IPSE TITIO DEBET.   Item bonorum emptor cum deductione agere iubetur, *id est ut* in hoc solum aduersarius eius
condemnetur quod superest, deducto eo quod inuicem ei
66 bonorum emptor defraudatoris nomine debet.   Inter conpensationem autem quae argentario opponitur, et deductionem
quae obicitur bonorum emptori, illa differentia est, quod in
conpensationem hoc solum uocatur quod eiusdem generis et
naturae est ; ueluti pecunia cum pecunia conpensatur, triticum
cum tritico, uinum cum uino, adeo ut quibusdam placeat non
omni modo uinum cum uino aut triticum cum tritico con-
pensandum, sed ita si eiusdem naturae qualitatisque sit ; in
deductionem autem uocatur et quod non est eiusdem generis ;
itaque si[1] pecuniam petat bonorum emptor et inuicem frumentum aut uinum is debeat, deducto[2] quanti id erit, in reli-

example, if the banker be due Titius ten thousand sesterces,
and the latter be due the banker twenty thousand, he words
his intention thus : ' If it appear that Titius ought to pay him
ten thousand sesterces more than he himself is due to Titius.'
65 The purchaser too of a bankrupt's estate, when proceeding
against one of its debtors, is required to sue *cum deductione ;*
in other words, the defender is to be condemned only in so
much as still remains due after deducting anything owing to
66 him by the pursuer as representing the bankrupt.   There
is this difference, however, between the compensation pleadable against a banker and the deduction required of the
purchaser of a bankrupt's estate, that only things of the same
sort can be set off one against the other,—money against
money, wheat against wheat, wine against wine, some even
going so far as to hold that wine cannot in every case be com-
pensated with wine, or wheat with wheat, but only when of the
same variety and quality ; but that may be made a matter of
deduction which is not of the same sort, so that if the purchaser of a bankrupt's estate claim money, and he on his side
be due corn or wine, the value of the latter is deducted, and

§ 65. Comp. iii, 81.
§ 66. Comp. Paul. ii, 5, § 3.
[1] After *si* is *u*, with a small *o*
superscribed,—the ordinary contraction of *uero*. This leads K. u. S.
(footnote) to surmise that something
like the following has been omitted :
itaque *si frumentum aut uinum
petat bonorum emptor et inuicem*

*defraudatoris nomine pecuniam is
debeat, quanto amplius ea pecunia
id frumentum aut uinum erit, in
condemnatione ponitur ;* si uero,
etc.

[2] After *deducto* the ms. has something like *fore*, which induces Hu.
to read *deducta ea re*, and P. *deducto
a bonorum emptore.*

67 quum experitur.   Item uocatur in deductionem et id quod
in diem debetur; conpensatur autem hoc solum quod prae-
68 senti debetur.   Praeterea conpensationis quidem ratio in
intentione ponitur; quo fit ut si facta conpensatione plus
nummo uno intendat argentarius, causa cadat[1] et ob id rem
perdat: deductio uero ad condemnationem ponitur, quo loco
plus petenti periculum non interuenit; utique bonorum emptore agente, qui licet de certa pecunia agat, incerti tamen
condemnationem concipit.

69   Quia tamen superius[1] mentionem habuimus de actione
qua in peculium filiorumfamilias seruorumque *agitur*, opus
est ut de hac actione, et de ceteris quae eorumdem nomine
in parentes dominosue dari solent, diligentius admoneamus.

70 Inprimis itaque si iussu patris dominiue negotium gestum
erit, in solidum praetor actionem in patrem dominumue
conparauit: et recte, quia qui ita negotium gerit, magis patris

---

67 he obtains only the balance.   Further, while a debt with a
postponed term of payment may be a matter of deduction
there can be set-off only of what is payable on the instant.
68 Besides, the amount of a set-off is stated in the intention, so
that if a banker, after allowing compensation, condescends on
a single sesterce too much, he fails in his suit, and thereby
loses his claim; [matter of] deduction, however, is stated in
the clause of condemnation, and the mention there of too
large a sum does no harm, at least in the case of action by
the purchaser of a bankrupt's estate, whose formula, though
founding on a claim of definite amount, is yet framed with an
indefinite condemnation.
69   Allusion has been made in a previous page to the action
directed against the *peculium* of *filiifamilias* and slaves; we
must now explain it more minutely, as well as those other
actions that are granted against parents and owners on their
70 account.   In the first place then, if any transaction have
been entered into on the order of father or owner, an action
of praetorian introduction lies against such father or owner
for the full amount of the debt incurred: and very properly,
because the other party to such a transaction relies in it
rather on the credit of the father or owner than on that of

§ 67. Comp. fr. 7, pr. D. *de conpens.*
(xvi, 2).
§ 68. Comp. §§ 53, 57.
[1] Comp. § 53, note 1.
§§ 69-74. Comp. tit. I. *QVOD CVM EO
QVI IN ALIENA POTESTATE EST*

NEGOTIVM GESTVM ESSE DICITVR
(iv, 7).
§ 69. Comp. pr. tit. I. afd.
[1] In § 60a, *i.e.* in the course of the
illegible pages 210 or 211 of the MS.
§ 70. Comp. § 1, tit. I. afd.

71 dominiue quam filii seruiue fidem sequitur.   Eadem ratione
conparauit duas alias actiones, exercitoriam et institoriam: [1]
tunc autem exercitoria locum habet cum pater dominusue
filium seruumue magistrum naui praeposuerit, et quid cum eo
eius rei gratia cui praepositus fuit [negotium] [2] gestum erit;
cum enim ea quoque res ex uoluntate patris dominiue contrahi
uideatur, aequissimum esse uisum est in solidum actionem
dari: quin etiam, licet naui extraneum quisque magistrum
praeposuerit, siue seruum siue liberum, tamen ea praetoria
actio in eum redditur: ideo autem exercitoria actio appellatur,
quia exercitor uocatur is ad quem cottidianus nauis quaestus
peruenit.   institoria uero formula tum locum habet cum quis
tabernae aut cuilibet negotiationi filium seruumue aut quemlibet extraneum, siue seruum siue liberum, praeposuerit, et
quid cum eo eius rei gratia cui praepositus est contractum
fuerit: ideo autem institoria uocatur, quia qui tabernae prae-
ponitur institor appellatur: quae et ipsa formula in solidum
72 est.   Praeterea tributoria *quoque actio* in patrem domi-

---

71 the son or slave.   On the same principle the praetor has
devised two other actions, the exercitorian and institorian.
The exercitorian comes into play when a father or owner has
placed his son or slave in command of a vessel, and the latter
has entered into some undertaking on the ship's account; as
his contract in such a case is virtually authorized by his father
or owner, it seemed in the highest degree equitable to grant
[the other party] an action for the full amount. And what is
more, even if it be a stranger, whether a freeman or a slave,
that has been put in command of the vessel, this praetorian
action will be allowed against the person who placed him
there. It is called exercitorian, because *exercitor* is the name
given to the individual who is drawing the daily profits of the
ship. The institorian action is employed when a person has
committed the management of a shop or business of any kind
to his son or slave, or to some stranger, whether free or not,
and some contract has been entered into by the latter on
account of the shop or business entrusted to him; it is called
institorian, because the individual placed in charge of a shop
is spoken of as its *institor*. This action likewise is *in solidum*.
72 Besides these there is the tributorian action against a father

§ 71. Comp. § 2, tit. I. afd.; Paul. ii,
tits. 6, 8.
   [1] The MS. has throughout *insti-
tutor* and *institutoria*, which K. u. S.
   20

(footnote) remark is also the reading
of the best MSS. of the Inst.
   [2] Seems to be a gloss.
§ 72. Comp. § 3, tit. I. afd. The end

numue constituta est cum filius seruusue *in peculiari* — —[1]
merce sciente patre dominoue negotietur; nam si quid eius
rei gratia cum eo contractum fuerit, ita praetor ius dicit, ut
73 quidquid in his mercibus — — — — — —.   [73] —

_____

or owner, whose son or slave has with his father's or owner's
knowledge invested his *peculium* in merchandise; if in the
course of his trade he have entered into any contract, the rule
laid down by the praetor is, [*that all the goods acquired by him*
[*in course of business, and all the money made in it, shall be*
[*divided between his father or owner and the other creditors, in*
[*proportion to their respective claims. And as the father or*
[*owner himself is allowed to make the distribution, if any of the*
[*creditors complain that less than he was entitled to has been*
[*apportioned to him,* tributum, *the praetor will accord him the*
73 [*action that goes by the name of tributorian.   There has also*
[*been introduced the* actio de peculio et de in rem verso, *i.e.*
[*in respect of a* peculium *and of what has been turned by a*
[filiusfamilias *or a slave to his father's or owner's profit; in*
[*order that, although the child or slave may have contracted*
[*without his father's or owner's consent, yet the latter shall*
[*be made to pay in full for anything turned to his profit,*
[*or, if there be nothing of that sort, that he shall be compelled*
[*to pay to the extent of the child's or slave's* peculium.
[*Everything is held to be turned to the father's or owner's profit*
[*that has been necessarily expended by his son or slave on his*
[*account; as when the latter has borrowed money and therewith*
[*paid his father's or owner's creditors, or repaired buildings of*
[*his which were becoming ruinous, or bought wheat for his*
[*establishment, or even purchased for him land or any other*
[*necessary. Accordingly, if, of say a thousand sesterces which*
[*your son or slave has borrowed from Titius, he has paid five*
[*hundred to a creditor of yours, but has spent the other five*
[*hundred in some other way, you will be condemned for the first*
[*five hundred in full, but as regards the rest only for so much*
[*as is included in the* peculium; *whence it is apparent that, if*
[*the whole thousand sesterces have been expended to your profit,*
[*the whole thousand may be recovered from you by Titius.   For*
[*though it is in one and the same action that a claim is made*
[*both against the* peculium *and in respect of expenditure for the*

of the par. is on p. 215, and quite
illegible; but it probably corresponded very closely to the reading
of the Inst. (which see).
[1] The MS. seems to have *quoptio*;
Hu. reads *cuiusuis pretii*; Gou.

suggests *forte*.
§ 73. Comp. §§ 4-4c, tit. I. afd.; Paul.
ii, 9. What is said about the latter
part of § 72 in the note thereto
applies equally to the first part of
this one.

— — — — — — deducitur quod patri dominoue quique in eius potestate sit a filio seruoue debetur, et quod superest hoc solum peculium esse intellegitur; aliquando tamen id quod ei debet filius seruusue qui in potestate patris dominiue sit non deducitur ex peculio, uelut si is cui debet in huius 74 ipsius peculio sit.[1]   Ceterum dubium non est quin et is qui iussu patris dominiue contraxerit, cuique exercitoria uel institoria formula conpetit, de peculio aut de in rem uerso agere possit; sed nemo tam stultus erit, ut qui aliqua illarum actionum sine dubio solidum consequi possit, uel in difficultatem se deducat probandi habere peculium eum cum quo contraxerit exque eo peculio posse sibi satisfieri, uel id quod prosequi- 74a tur in rem patris dominiue uersum esse.   Is quoque cui tributoria actio conpetit de peculio uel de in rem uerso agere potest; sed huic sane plerumque expedit hac potius actione

---

[*father's or owner's benefit, yet it embraces two distinct condem-* [*nations; and accordingly the judge before whom it is tried* [*ought first to see whether anything has been turned to the* [*father's or owner's profit, and not proceed to consider the* [*amount of* peculium *unless nothing, or at least something* [*less than the whole, has been so expended. In proceeding to* [*estimate the amount of the* peculium, *anything that may be*] due by the son or slave to his father or owner, or any one in the *potestas* of these last, is first deducted, and only what remains is regarded as *peculium*. Sometimes, however, what is due by the son or slave to an individual in the *potestas* of his father or owner is not deducted; for instance, when such 74 individual is a slave belonging to the *peculium*.   There is no doubt that he who has entered into a contract on the order of father or owner, as well as he to whom an exercitorian or institorian formula is competent, may sue by the *actio de peculio uel de in rem uerso;* but no one who could recover in full by one of the three first named actions would be so foolish as to encumber himself with the burden of proving that either the person with whom he had contracted possessed a *peculium*, and that there was enough in it to satisfy his claim, or that the outcome of the contract had been turned to the advan- 74a tage of the father or owner.   He also to whom the tributorian is competent may sue *de peculio uel de in rem uerso*, and indeed it is more for his advantage to do so. For

[1] Usually called a *seruus uicarius*, § 74. Comp. § 5, tit. I. afd.
§ 17, I. *de legat.* (ii, 20).   § 74a. Comp. § 5, tit. I. afd.

uti quam tributoria; nam in tributoria eius solius peculii
ratio habetur quod in his mercibus est in quibus negotiatur
filius seruusue quodque inde receptum erit, at in actione
peculii, totius : et potest quisque tertia forte aut quarta uel
etiam minore parte peculii negotiari, maximam uero partem
peculii in aliis rebus habere; longe magis, si potest adprobari
id quod [*dederit qui*]¹ contraxit in rem patris dominiue uersum esse, ad hanc actionem transire debet; nam, ut supra
diximus,² eadem formula et de peculio et de in rem uerso
agitur.

75   Ex maleficio filiorumfamilias seruorumque, ueluti si furtum
fecerint aut iniuriam commiserint, noxales actiones proditae
sunt, uti liceret patri dominoue aut litis aestimationem
sufferre aut noxae¹ dedere: erat enim iniquum nequitiam
eorum ultra ipsorum corpora parentibus dominisue damnosam
76 esse.   Constitutae sunt autem noxales actiones aut legibus

---

in the tributorian account is taken only of so much of the
peculium as has been converted into merchandise by the son
or slave, with the profits thereof, while in that *de peculio* the
whole of it is reckoned ; and it may happen that only a third
or a fourth or even a smaller part of the *peculium* has been
expended on mercantile wares, the greater portion having
been otherwise invested.   Still more is it for the creditor's
advantage to employ the action *de peculio* if he is in a position
to prove that what *he gave his debtor under the contract* was
converted to the uses of the latter's father or owner ; for, as
already said, it is by one and the same formula that a party
sues *de peculio* and *de in rem uerso.*

75   In respect of the wrong-doing of *filiifamilias* and slaves, as
when they have committed theft say, or personal injury,
noxal actions have been provided, whereby the father or
owner has the option either of submitting to pecuniary
damages, or of surrendering the wrong-doer in reparation ;
for it was held unfair that parents or owners should be losers
on account of the wickedness of those subject to them in
76 more than the bodies of these last.   Those noxal actions
have been established either by enactment or by the praetorian

---

¹ Added by Hu.; K. u. S. interpolate *dederit is qui cum filio ser-*
uoue.
² In § 73 ; comp. § 4, tit. I. afd.
§§ 75-78. Comp. tit. I. DE NOXALIBVS

ACTIONIBVS (iv, 8).
§ 75. Pr. § 2, tit. I. afd. Comp. i, 140 ;
Paul. ii, 31, § 7.
    ¹ See § 1, tit. I. afd. and note.
§ 76. § 4, tit. I. afd.

aut edicto praetoris: legibus, uelut furti lege xii tabularum,[1]
damni iniuriae *item*[2] lege Aquilia;[3] edicto praetoris, uelut
77 iniuriarum[4] et ui bonorum raptorum.[5]   Omnes autem noxales actiones capita[1] sequuntur: nam si filius tuus seruusue
noxam commiserit, quamdiu in tua potestate est tecum est
actio; si in alterius potestatem peruenerit, cum illo incipit
actio esse; si sui iuris coeperit esse, directa actio cum ipso
est et noxae deditio extinguitur. ex diuerso quoque directa
actio noxalis esse incipit: nam si paterfamilias noxam commiserit, et is se in adrogationem tibi dederit aut seruus tuus
esse coeperit, [*quod*] quibusdam casibus accidere primo commentario[2] tradidimus incipit tecum noxalis actio esse quae
78 ante directa fuit.   Sed si filius patri aut seruus domino
noxam commiserit, nulla actio nascitur: nulla enim omnino
inter me et eum qui in potestate mea est obligatio nasci potest;
ideoque et si in alienam potestatem peruenerit aut sui iuris

---

edict: by enactment, as in the case of theft, in accordance
with the law of the Twelve Tables, and of wrongful damage
to property, in accordance with the Aquilian law; by the
edict of the praetor, as in personal injury and violent away-
77 taking of another's goods.   Noxal actions invariably follow
the wrong-doer. Therefore if your son or slave have committed an offence, action lies against you so long as he remains
in your *potestas*; if he pass into that of another person, action
begins to lie against the latter; if he become *sui iuris*, direct
action begins to lie against himself, and noxal surrender is no
longer demandable. Conversely an action which is in the
first instance direct, may afterwards become noxal; for if a
paterfamilias has committed a delict, and subsequently gives
himself to you in arrogation or becomes your slave,—and this,
as we have explained in our First Commentary, might happen
occasionally,—the action which was originally direct begins
78 to be a noxal one against you.   But if a child or slave have
committed a delict against his father or owner, there is no
action, obligation between me and an individual subject
to my *potestas* being an impossibility; consequently, even
though he pass into the *potestas* of a third party or become

[1] Comp. iii, §§ 189 f.
[2] The ms. has *ā*.
[3] Comp. iii, 210.
[4] Comp. iii, 224.
[5] Comp. iii, 209.

§ 77. § 5, tit. I. afd.
[1] So the ms.; most eds. make it *caput*.
[2] See i, 160.

§ 78. Comp. § 6, tit. I. afd.

esse coeperit, neque cum ipso neque cum eo cuius nunc in potestate est agi potest. unde quaeritur, si alienus seruus filiusue noxam commiserit mihi, et is postea in mea esse coeperit potestate, utrum intercidat actio an quiescat : nostri praeceptores[1] intercidere putant, quia in eum casum deducta sit in quo *actio*[2] consistere non potuerit, ideoque licet exierit de mea potestate agere me non posse; diuersae scholae auctores[1] quamdiu in mea potestate sit quiescere actionem putant, quia ipse mecum agere non possim, cum uero exierit 79 de mea potestate tunc eam resuscitari.   Cum autem filius-familias ex noxali causa mancipio datur, diuersae scholae auctores[1] putant ter eum mancipio dari debere, quia lege XII tabularum cautum sit [*ne aliter filius de potestate patris*][2] exeat quam si ter fuerit mancipatus : Sabinus et Cassius ceterique nostrae scholae auctores[1] sufficere unam mancipationem credi-derunt, *et illam*[3] 'tres' legis XII tabularum ad uoluntarias mancipationes pertinere.

---

sui iuris, I cannot proceed either against him or against the third party to whom he has become subject. Hence the question,—suppose another man's slave or son has committed a delict against me, and has afterwards become subject to my *potestas*, is my right of action extinguished or merely suspended ? The leaders of our school think that it is extin-guished, matters having been brought into a position in which an action could not have arisen, and that therefore I cannot sue even though he should eventually pass out of my *potestas ;* those of the other school are of opinion that my action is only suspended while the child or slave is in my *potestas,* because I cannot proceed against myself, but that it revives on the 79 potestal relationship coming to an end.   The jurists of the other school are further of opinion that when a *filiusfamilias* is noxally mancipated there must be three mancipations, in consequence of the provision in the Twelve Tables that a son is not released from his father's *potestas* unless mancipated three times; but Sabinus and Cassius, and the other teachers of our school, hold one mancipation sufficient, being of opinion that the word 'three' in the Twelve Tables refers only to such mancipations as are voluntary.

[1] See i, 196, note 1.
[2] According to Bl. the ms. has the usual contraction for *actio*; Stud. has doubts; K. u. S. omit the word; Hu. substitutes *initio*; P. *omnino.*

§ 79. Comp. i, §§ 132, 140, 141; also § 7, tit. I. afd.
[1] See i, 196, note 1.
[2] Added by G., and generally adopted.
[3] So the ms., *uocem* being under-

80   Haec ita de his personis quae in potestate [*sunt*], siue ex
contractu siue *ex maleficio* earum *nomine actio sit*.[1] quod
uero ad eas personas quae in manu mancipioue sunt ita ius
dicitur, ut cum *ex aliquo actu*[2] earum[3] agatur, nisi ab eo cuius
iuri subiectae sint *in solidum* defendantur, bona quae earum
futura forent si *eius iuri* subiectae non essent *ueneant :* sed
cum rescissa *capitis deminutione cum*[4] iis imperio continenti
iudicio[5] agitur,[6] — — — — — —.

80a   — — — — — — —.   [81] — — — — — —

81   diximus, *quamquam* non permissum fuerit et mortuos homines

---

80   These rules apply in the case of individuals *in potestate*,
whether the action [against those to whom they are subject]
be in respect of a contract of theirs or of a delict. As regards
those *in manu* or *in mancipio* the rule is that, if action be
raised upon *any act* of theirs, unless they be defended *in
solidum* by him to whom they are subject, the estate which
would have been theirs but for their subjection will be put
up to sale. If, however, they be proceeded against in a
iudicium imperio continens, the *capitis deminutio* having been
rescinded, — — — — — —.

80a   — — — — — — — —.   [81] — — — — — —,

81   although it is not allowed to make a noxal surrender of dead

---

stood. K. u. S. read *et illas ;* Hu.
etenim, the *legis* being changed into
lege.

§ 80. Comp. iii, 84; iv, 88. The par.
is incomplete; p. 219 being illegible, with exception of the first
word, *agitur.*

[1] The MS. has *inomisiaēēt.* K. u.
S. leave the letters uninterpreted ;
Gou. suggests *in alios actio esset ;*
Hu., following Bk., *controuersia sit*
(for *esset*) ; P. has *instituta actio est.*
The nearest interpretation seems
that I have given above, *sit* being
substituted for *esset,* just as is
agatur for the *ageretur* of the MS.
two lines lower.

[2] The letters in the MS. are uncertain, but seem to be *exoliiactu.*
K. u. S. and Hu. read *ex contractu.*
The traces seem to me nearer *ex
aliq actu,* which includes both contract and delict, and is used in the
words of the edict, fr. 2, § 1, D. *de
cap. min.* (iv, 5); see fr. 2, § 5, D.
de reb. cred. (xii, 1), fr. 225, D. *de
V. S.* (l, 16). On the consequences
of delict by *capite minuti* see fr. 2,
§ 3, D. *de cap. min.* (iv, 5).

[3] Probably the words *legitimo
iudicio* ought to be interpolated
after *earum.*

[4] These three words not recognis-
able in the apparent *ipmp* of the MS.;
but justified on reference to iii, 84.

[5] Comp. §§ 104, 105.

[6] Hu., referring to Vlp. xi, 27,
thus completes the par.—*si aduersus eam actionem non defendantur,
etiam cum ipsa muliere dum in
manu est agi potest, quia tum tutoris
auctoritas necessaria non est.* But
this takes no account of persons *in
mancipio,* though equally within
the scope of Gaius' explanation.

§ 80a. The illegible page 219 is supposed to have contained an exposition of a man's liability for mischief
done by an animal belonging to
him, corresponding to tit. I. *SI
QVADRVPES PAVPERIEM FECISSE
DICITVR* (iv, 9); he had either to
pay damages or noxally surrender
it.

§ 81. More than half of the first line of
p. 220 is uncertain, and as deciphered incomprehensible. One of
the rules in regard to noxal actions

dedere, tamen etsi quis eum dederit qui fato suo uita exces-
serit aeque liberatur.

82   Nunc admonendi sumus agere nos aut nostro nomine aut
alieno, ueluti cognitorio, procuratorio, tutorio, curatorio ; cum
olim, quo tempore legis actiones in usu fuissent, alieno nomine
83 agere non liceret[1] *praeterquam*[2] ex certis causis.[3]   Cognitor
autem certis uerbis in litem coram aduersario substituitur :
nam actor ita cognitorem dat : QVOD EGO A TE uerbi gratia
FVNDVM PETO, IN EAM REM LVCIVM TITIVM TIBI COGNITOREM DO;
aduersarius ita : QVIA TV A ME FVNDVM PETIS, IN EAM [*REM*]
TIBI PVBLIVM MEVIVM COGNITOREM DO.   potest ut actor ita

---

men, yet if a defender have surrendered a slave that has
succumbed to the common fate of humanity [*i.e.* has died a
natural death], he is equally freed from his liability.

82   The next matter of observation is, that we may sue either
in our own name or through an agent, such as a cognitor,
procurator, tutor, or curator; whereas formerly, when the
legis actiones were in use, it was unlawful, except in certain
83 cases, to sue in another person's name.   A cognitor is made
our substitute in a cause by certain formal words spoken in
presence of the adversary ; by the pursuer thus : 'Whereas
I am claiming from you,' for example, 'such and such lands,
I give you Lucius Titius as my cognitor in the matter;' and
by the defender thus : 'As you are claiming from me such
and such lands, I give you Publius Mevius as my cognitor in
the matter.' Or the pursuer may say : 'Whereas I mean to

---

was, that if the offending slave or
animal died before litiscontestation,
the owner was no longer liable, fr.
39, § 4, D. *de nox. act.* (ix, 4), fr.
1, § 18, D. *si quadrup. paup.* (ix,
1); and this may have been stated
in the text. But what if the death
were after litiscontestation? Was
it sufficient for the owner to give up
the dead body? That question
seems to have been answered in the
negative; as Vlp. says in fr. 1, § 14,
D. *si quadr. paup.* (ix, 1),—*noxae dedere est tradere uiuum.* And rightly,
if either the owner or a third party
had culpably caused his death;
in either of those cases the owner
was still liable,—in the former because by his own act he had deprived himself of his *facultas
dedendi*, in the latter because he
was entitled to damages from the

third party in fault. It might be,
however, that after litiscontestation
the slave or animal had died a
natural death; what then? This
not improbably was the question to
which an answer is given in what
of the text remains.

§§ 82-87. Comp. tit. I. *DE HIS PER
QVOS AGERE POSSVMVS* (iv, 10);
also Fr. Vat. §§ 317-341.

§ 82. Comp. Cic. *pro Rosc. com.* xviii,
53; Ps.-Ascon. *in Cic. Div.* § 11
(Bruns, p. 291); pr. tit. I. afd.
   [1] Comp. fr. 123, pr. D. *de R. I.*
(I, 17).
   [2] The ms. has *propequam*; P.
proprie quam.
   [3] *Pro populo, pro libertate, pro
tutela,* pr. tit. I. afd.

§ 83. Comp. § 97; Paul. ex Festo, v.
Cognitor (Bruns, p. 238); Fr. Vat.
§§ 318 f.; Isodor. *Differ.* 123.

—

dicat: QVOD EGO TECVM AGERE VOLO, IN EAM REM COGNITOREM
DO ; aduersarius ita : QVIA TV MECVM AGERE VIS, IN EAM REM
COGNITOREM DO : nec interest praesens an absens cognitor
detur; sed si absens datus fuerit, cognitor ita erit si cognouerit
84 et susceperit officium cognitoris.   Procurator uero nullis
certis uerbis in litem substituitur, sed ex solo mandato, et
absente et ignorante aduersario, constituitur : quin etiam sunt
qui putant eum quoque procuratorem uideri cui non sit
mandatum, si modo bona fide accedat ad negotium et caueat
ratam rem dominum habiturum : quamquam et ille cui mandatum [est] plerumque satisdare debet,[1] quia saepe mandatum
initio litis in obscuro est et postea apud iudicem ostenditur.
85 Tutores autem et curatores quemadmodum constituantur
86 primo commentario rettulimus.   Qui autem alieno nomine
agit, intentionem quidem ex persona domini sumit, condemnationem autem in suam personam conuertit : nam si uerbi
gratia Lucius Titius [pro] Publio Meuio agat, ita formula con-

---

raise an action against you, I give you so and so as my
cognitor in it;' and the defender: 'As you propose to raise
an action against me, I give you in it so and so as my
cognitor.' And it is immaterial whether the party thus
accredited as cognitor be present or absent; but if he have
been nominated in absence, he will not actually be cognitor
until he has heard of his appointment and accepted office.
84 No words of style are used in appointing a procurator as substitute in a litigation ; a mandate to him is sufficient, though
granted in the absence and without the knowledge of the
adversary. Some jurists go so far even as to hold that a man
may be regarded as a procurator who has no mandate, provided he intervene in good faith and give security that his
principal will ratify his actings ; although he who has a
mandate is also in most cases bound to give the same caution,
the existence of the mandate being often not quite clear in
the first stage of a process, though afterwards proved before
85 the judge.   How tutors and curators are appointed has
86 been explained in our First Commentary.   A person suing
on another's account frames his intention in name of his principal, but formulates the condemnation in his own favour.
Suppose Lucius Titius to be suing as agent of Publius Mevius,

§ 84. Comp. Paul. ex Festo as in last   [1] Comp. §§ 90, 98. .
  note; Paul. i, 3; Fr. Vat. §§ 112,   § 85.   § 2, tit. I. afd. Comp. i, §§ 144 f.
  333 ; § 1, tit. I. afd.   § 86.   Comp. § 55; Th. iv, 10, § 2.

cipitur : SI PARET NVMERIVM NEGIDIVM PVBLIO MEVIO SESTER-
TIVM X MILIA DARE OPORTERE, IVDEX NVMERIVM NEGIDIVM LVCIO
TITIO SESTERTIVM X MILIA CONDEMNA. SI NON PARET, ABSOLVE ;
in rem quoque si agat intendit PVBLII MEVII REM ESSE EX IVRE
QVIRITIVM, et condemnationem in suam personam conuertit.

87 Ab aduersarii quoque parte si interueniat aliquis cum quo
actio constituitur, intenditur dominum dare oportere, condemnatio autem in eius personam conuertitur qui iudicium accepit; sed cum in rem agitur, nihil in intentione facit eius persona
cum quo agitur, siue suo nomine siue alieno aliquis iudicio
interueniat : tantum enim intenditur rem actoris esse.[1]

88   Videamus nunc quibus ex causis is cum quo agitur, uel hic
89 qui a[git co]gatur[1] satisdare.   Igitur si uerbi gratia in rem
tecum agam, satis mihi dare debes : aequum enim uisum est
[te i]deo[1] quod interea tibi rem, quae an ad te pertineat dubium est, possidere conceditur, cum satisdatione mihi cauere

---

the formula will run thus : 'If it appear that Numerius
Negidius ought to pay Publius Mevius ten thousand sesterces,
then, judge, condemn Numerius Negidius to Lucius Titius in
ten thousand sesterces ; if otherwise, acquit him ;' while if
the action be in rem he will maintain in his intention that
the thing in question belongs to Publius Mevius in quiritarian
right, and make the condemnation run in his own favour.

87 If it be on the side of the defender that an agent is intervening, it is averred in the intention that the principal is
indebted, but the condemnation is directed against the agent,
—the person who has really joined issue in the action. If,
however, the proceedings be in rem, there is no mention of
the defender in the intention, whether he be defending on his
own account or as agent for another ; all that is said in it is
that the thing belongs to the pursuer.

88   Let us see now in what cases the defender or pursuer is
89 required to give security.   If then I am proceeding against
you in rem, you must find caution ; as the possession of what
probably does not belong to you is conceded to you in the
meantime, it is but equitable that you should give me the
security of sureties, so that if, in the event of your being

§ 87. Comp. Fr. Vat. § 340 (1) ; Th. iv,
10, § 2.
[1] Comp. §§ 3, 41.
§§ 88-102. Comp. tit. I. DE SATISDA-
TIONIBVS (iv, 11).
§ 88. See i, 199, note.

[1] So G., K. u. S., and Hu. ; the
MS. has qui agat' satisdare ; Bk. reads
qui agit, satisdare [debeat].
§ 89. Cp. pr. tit. I. afd. ; Paul. i, 11, § 1.
[1] So Hu. and K. u. S. ; the MS.
has de eo ; G. [te] de eo.

ut si uictus sis, *nec rem*[2] ipsam restituas nec litis aestimationem sufferas, sit mihi potestas aut tecum agendi aut cum
90 sponsoribus tuis.   Multoque magis debes satisdare mihi si
91 alieno nomine iudicium accipias.   Ceterum cum in rem
actio duplex sit,—aut enim per formulam petitoriam agitur
aut per sponsionem,—siquidem per formulam petitoriam agitur, illa stipulatio locum habet quae appellatur ' iudicatum
solui,'[1] si uero per sponsionem, illa quae appellatur ' pro-
92 praede litis et uindiciarum.'[2]   Petitoria autem formula
93 haec est qua actor intendit rem suam esse.   Per sponsionem
uero hoc modo agimus : prouocamus aduersarium tali sponsione : SI HOMO, QVO DE AGITVR, EX IVRE QVIRITIVM MEVS EST,
SESTERTIOS XXV NVMMOS DARE SPONDES ?   deinde formulam
edimus qua intendimus sponsionis summam nobis dari oportere ; qua formula ita demum uincimus si probauerimus rem
94 nostram esse.   Non tamen haec summa sponsionis exigitur :
nec enim poenalis est sed praeiudicialis, et propter hoc solum

---

defeated, you fail either to restore the thing in dispute or pay
me the value of the cause, [*i.e.* the amount of your *condemnatio,*] I may have the power of suing either you or them.
90 All the more ought you to give me security when you join
91 issue for a third party.   But as an action *in rem* is twofold,
—for it may be either by petitory formula or by sponsion,—if
you sue by petitory formula there is room for what is called
the *stipulatio iudicatum solui,* [*i.e.* that the judgment will be
satisfied] ; while if you sue by sponsion there is room for
that known as the *stipulatio pro praede litis et uindiciarum.*
92 The petitory formula is that in which the pursuer asserts
93 that the thing in dispute is his.   By sponsion we proceed
as follows : we challenge our adversary with such a sponsion
as : ' If the slave in question is mine in quiritarian right, do
you engage to give me twenty-five sesterces ? ' then we draw
up a formula in which we contend that the amount of the
sponsion is due to us ; and our success in it depends on our
94 proving that the slave is ours.   The amount of the sponsion,
however, is not exacted ; for it is not penal but prejudicial,
and entered into solely that by means of it a judgment may

---

[2] The ms. has *remn'.*
§ 90.   Comp. pr. tit. I. afd.; Fr. Vat.
    § 317.
§ 91.   Comp. Fr. Vat. § 336.
    [1] Comp. pr. tit. I. afd.

[2] Comp. §§ 16, 94.
§ 92.   Comp. § 41.
§ 93.   Comp. Cic. *II. Verr.* i, 45, §
    115.
§ 94.   Comp. § 18, § 16, and notes 7-9.

fit ut per eam de re iudicetur; unde etiam is cum quo agitur
non restipulatur; ideo autem appellata est 'pro praede litis
uindiciarum' stipulatio, quia in locum praedium successit;
quia¹ olim, cum lege agebatur, pro lite et uindiciis, id est
pro re et fructibus, a possessore petitori dabantur praedes.²
95 Ceterum si apud centumuiros agitur summam sponsionis non
per formulam petimus sed per legis actionem; sacramento
enim *reus prouocatur* :¹ eaque sponsio sestertium CXXV num-
96 mum² *fieri solet*³ propter legem *Creperiam*.⁴   Ipse autem
97 qui in rem agit, si suo nomine agat, satis non dat.   Ac nec
si per cognitorem quidem agatur ulla satisdatio uel ab ipso
uel a domino desideratur: cum enim certis et quasi sollemni-

---

be arrived at on the question of property; and for the same
reason the defender does not restipulate. The stipulation is
called *pro praede litis et uindiciarum* because it has come in
place of *praedes* ; for formerly, under the system of the *legis
actiones praedes*, sureties were given by the possessor to the
pursuer *pro lite et uindiciis*, that is, for the thing in dispute
95 and its fruits and profits.   If, however, we are proceeding in
the centumviral court we claim the amount of the sponsion
by a *legis actio* and not by a formula, for the defender is
challenged with a sacrament; and the sponsion in this case
is one of a hundred and twenty-five sesterces, in consequence
96 of the Creperian law.   The pursuer of an *actio in rem*, suing
97 on his own account, does not give security.   Nor if the
action be by a cognitor is any security required either from
him or his principal; for as a cognitor is substituted for his

---

¹ So the ms.; K. u. S. and Hu.
read *qui* ; P. *quod*.
² So the ms., but deleted by
K. u. S. and Hu. See Paul. ex
Festo, v. *Praes* (Bruns, p. 256).
§ 95. Comp. § 31; also § 16, note
10.
¹ K. u. S. read *reum prouocamus* ;
Hu. *sacramento [quingenario] modo
reo prouocato;* P. *sacramento maiore prouocato.*
² The old sacramental 500 *asses*
(§ 14) ; the sesterce having been declared equivalent to 4 *asses* (instead
of 2½ as formerly) at the time of the
second Punic war; see Plin. *H. N.*
xxxiii, 13, § 45.
³ Indistinct in the ms.; K. u. S.
substitute *fit scilicet;* but Stud.

(*Apogr.* footnote) rejects *scil.*, and
thinks *fieri solet* possible.
⁴ Name not quite distinct, but so
Stud. deciphers it. Mommsen (M.
u. M. *Roem. Alt.* ii, part 2, p. 209,
footnote) supposes it to have been
the enactment reducing the value of
the sesterce, and perhaps conferring
on the centumviral court its jurisdiction in questions of inheritance.
Hu. thinks the reference must be to
the *lex Iulia Papiria* of 324 | 430,
converting cattle - penalties into
money-penalties (100 *asses* for an
ox, 10 for a sheep) ; but the relation
of this enactment to the subject in
hand is far from apparent.
§ 96. Comp. pr. tit. I. afd.
§ 97. Comp. § 83; Fr. Vat. § 317.

bus uerbis in locum domini substituatur cognitor, merito
98 domini loco habetur.   Procurator uero si agat satisdare
iubetur ratam rem dominum habiturum: periculum enim est
ne iterum dominus de eadem re experiatur; quod periculum
[*non*] interuenit si per cognitorem actum fuerit, quia de qua
re quisque per cognitorem egerit de ea non magis amplius
99 actionem habet quam si ipse egerit.   Tutores et curatores
eo modo quo et procuratores satisdare debere uerba edicti
100 faciunt; sed aliquando illis satisdatio remittitur.   Haec ita
si in rem agitur; si uero in personam, ab actoris quidem
parte quando satisdari debeat quaerentes, eadem repetemus
101 quae diximus in actione qua in rem agitur.   ab eius uero
parte cum quo agitur, siquidem alieno nomine aliquis interueniat, omni modo satisdari debet, quia nemo alienae rei sine
satisdatione defensor idoneus intellegitur: sed siquidem cum
cognitore agatur, dominus satisdare iubetur; si uero cum pro-
curatore, ipse procurator.   idem et de tutore et de curatore
102 iuris est.   Quodsi proprio nomine aliquis iudicium accipiat
in personam, certis ex causis [1] satisdari solet, quas ipse praetor

---

principal by certain quasi-solemn words, he is rightly enough
98 regarded as in the same position as his principal.   A procurator, however, if he is suing, must give security that his
principal will ratify his actings; for there is some risk that
the principal may subsequently proceed anew in the very
same matter.   But there is no such risk where it is a
cognitor that is suing; for a man suing by a cognitor has no
more power to raise a new action about the same matter than
99 he would have were he suing in person.   By the terms of
the edict tutors and curators are required to give the same
security as procurators; but it is sometimes dispensed with.
100 These observations apply to the case of an action *in rem*.
Where it is *in personam* the rules are the same so far as the
101 pursuer is concerned.   As regards the defender, if a third
party appear for him, security must be given in any circumstances; for no one is esteemed an adequate defender in
another person's cause without it.   If the defence be conducted by a cognitor, it is the principal that must give
security; if by a procurator, it is the agent that gives it.
102 The rule is the same in the case of a tutor or curator.   In
certain cases mentioned by the praetor the defender in an

§§ 98-101. Comp. pr. § 1, tit. I. afd.   [1] After *causis* Hu. interpolates
§ 102. Cp. § 1, tit. I. afd.; Fr. Vat. § 336.   *iudicatum solui.*

significat: quarum satisdationum duplex causa est, nam aut
propter genus actionis satisdatur, aut propter personam quia
suspecta sit: propter genus actionis, ueluti iudicati² depensiue,³
aut cum de moribus mulieris agetur;⁴ propter personam,
ueluti si cum eo agitur qui decoxerit,⁵ cuiusue bona a creditoribus possessa proscriptaue sunt,⁶ siue cum eo herede agatur
quem praetor suspectum aestimauerit.⁷

103   Omnia autem iudicia¹ aut legitimo iure consistunt aut
104 imperio *continentur*.² Legitima sunt iudicia quae in
urbe Roma uel intra primum urbis Romae miliarium inter
omnes ciues Romanos sub uno iudice accipiuntur; eaque e
lege Iulia iudiciaria nisi in anno et sex mensibus iudicata

---

action *in personam* must give security even when conducting
his own defence. And this security may be required either
because of the nature of the action, or because of some sus-
picion attaching to the defender personally: on account of the
nature of the action in the *actio iudicati*, the *actio depensi*,
and the *actio rei uxoriae* when the wife's conduct is called in
question; on account of the person, as when the action is
against an embezzler or a bankrupt, or against an heir whom
the praetor regards as suspect.

103   All proceedings before *iudices* are either *iudicia legitima* or
104 *iudicia imperio continentia*. Those are *iudicia legitima* which
are carried on in Rome or within the first milestone from the
city, between parties who are all citizens, and before a single
judge. According to one of the Julian judiciary laws they

² Comp. §§ 21, 171.
³ Comp. iii, 27; iv, §§ 22, 171.
⁴ Comp. Vlp. vi, §§ 9, 12; 1, 1, C. Th. *de dot.* (iii, 13); 1, 11, § 2, C. *de repud.* (v, 17).
⁵ It is difficult to give a precise meaning to this word. See Cic. *Philipp.* ii, 18, § 44; Sen. *Ep.* 36, § 5; Spartian. *Hadr.* 18; 1, 12, C. *de susceptor.* (x, 70).
⁶ Comp. iii, 79; Cic. *pro Quint.* viii, 80.
⁷ Comp. Vlp. in fr. 31, D. *de reb. auct. iud. poss.* (xlii, 5).
§ 103.   Comp. i, 184; iii, §§ 83, 181; iv, 80.
¹ *Iudicium* is sometimes employed loosely as synonymous with *actio*. Properly it was the name given to a process after the magistrate had

sent it to a court for trial; either to a single *iudex* (then *iudicium* in the narrowest sense), or to an arbiter (then sometimes called *arbitrium*), or to recuperators (*iudicium recuperatorium*).
² So G. and all eds.; the ms. has *continunt*.
§ 104.   The law here referred to is the *lex Iulia Iudiciaria (iudiciorum priuatorum)*, mentioned above, § 30. It is probable that it was this enactment that settled, by enumeration of their conditions, what *iudicia* should be dealt with as *legitima* and what as *imperio continentia*; otherwise one would have expected to have found included amongst the latter, contrary to what appears in § 109, all those that arose out of actions due solely to praetorian agency.

fuerint expirant:[1] et hoc est quod uulgo dicitur e lege Iulia
105 litem anno et sex mensibus mori.   Imperio uero continentur recuperatoria et quae sub uno iudice accipiuntur
interueniente peregrini persona iudicis aut litigatoris; in
eadem[1] causa sunt quaecumque extra primum urbis Romae
miliarium tam inter ciues Romanos quam inter peregrinos
accipiuntur: ideo autem imperio contineri iudicia dicuntur,
quia tamdiu ualent quamdiu is qui ea praecepit impe-
106 rium habebit.[2]   Et siquidem imperio continenti iudicio

---

come to an end in a year and a half if judgment have not
been pronounced by that time; and this is what is meant
by the vulgar saying that by the Julian law an action dies
105 in eighteen months.   Those *iudicia* are *imperio continentia*
that proceed before recuperators, as also those before a single
judge, in which either he or any of the litigants is a peregrin,
and those carried on, whether by citizens or peregrins, at a
greater distance than a mile from Rome; they are so called
because they last only so long as the *imperium* of the magis-
106 trate who granted them.   Now, suppose a man sues in a

---

[1] It is said that prior to this enactment all such actions were perpetual,
i.e. might be in dependence for an
indefinite period (Hu., note to this
par.). That might be so with a
iudicium formulated upon an action
based upon the *ius ciuile*; but that
it should have been the case with
one that had no foundation except
in the *ius honorarium*, and that
could in no sense be called statutory
before Julian's consolidated edict
(temp. Hadr. l, 2, § 18, C. *de uet.
iur. enucl.* i, 17), had been approved
by a senatusconsult, is inconsistent
with all one's ideas of the *tuitio
praetoris*, and not easily reconciled
with what Gai. states in §§ 110, 111.
It seems more probable that while
the *lex Iulia* limited the duration
of *iudicia* founded on the *ius ciuile*,
it extended that of such as were
founded solely on the edict, provided
always the three conditions above
mentioned were concurrent. In fact
it augmented the number of the *legitima iudicia* by giving to the term
a new and more artificial meaning.

§ 105. Reference to recuperators, instead
of to a *iudex*, was practised originally
in causes to which foreigners were
parties, and in virtue of provisions

for recuperation in the treatise between Rome and friendly states,
Fest. v. *Reciperatio* (Bruns, p. 259).
In course of time, thanks probably
to its expedition, it came to be
adopted in certain cases even where
none but citizens were concerned.
This happened, for example, in all
litigations of private right, fiscal or
otherwise, raised by the state against
citizens; in the *actio iniuriarum* and
a. ui bonor. raptorum; in actions
for penalties incurred through contravention of magisterial edicts for
regulating procedure (see §§ 46, 185),
etc. In many cases it was free to
the magistrate to remit either to a
iudex or to recuperators, the latter
being preferred where a speedy
judgment was desirable. Reference
to recuperators was the ordinary
practice in the provinces; for peregrins could act in that character,
though incompetent as *iudices*.

[1] So G. and all eds.; the ms. has
simply *ea*.

[2] Comp. Vlp. in fr. 13, § 1, D. *de
iurisd.* (ii, 1).

§ 106. Comp. iii, §§ 180, 181, and note;
iv, § 121. The reason why here
fresh proceedings might be commenced *ipso iure* was that the earlier

actum[1] fuerit, siue in rem siue in personam, siue ea formula quae in factum concepta est, siue ea quae in ius habet intentionem postea nihilo minus ipso iure de eadem re agi potest; et ideo necessaria est exceptio rei iudicatae uel in iudicium deductae.

107 *si* uero[1] legitimo iudicio in personam actum sit ea formula quae iuris ciuilis habet intentionem, postea ipso iure de eadem re agi non potest,[2] et ob id exceptio superuacua est; si uero uel in rem uel in factum actum fuerit, ipso iure nihilo minus postea agi potest,[3] et ob id exceptio necessaria est rei

108 iudicatae uel in iudicium deductae.   Alia causa fuit olim legis actionum : nam qua de re actum semel erat, de ea postea

---

iudicium of this latter sort, and no matter whether his action be *in rem* or *in personam*, or his formula *in ius* or *in factum*, he is nevertheless entitled, in strict law, to sue again on the same premises: to prevent this an exception is necessary either of judgment recovered or of previous submission of the

107 matter to the arbitrament of a judge.   But if he sue in a *legitimum iudicium*, by an action *in personam* with a formula containing an *intentio iuris ciuilis*, further action by him on the same premises is *ipso iure* incompetent, and an exception is consequently superfluous; but if his action have been *in rem* or [his formula] *in factum*, he is *ipso iure* entitled to sue afresh, so that here also an exception becomes necessary

108 either of judgment recovered or matter put in issue.   It was different formerly with the *legis actiones* : [under that system], if there had once been an action about any par-

ones were *ipso iure* of no effect,—they were effectual only in virtue of the *imperium*.

[1] The MS. has *pactum*, i.e. *peractum* ; but *actum* is more appropriate, and the word employed in next par.

§ 107. References as in note to § 106.

[1] The MS. has *at* (or *ai*) *u* (with superscribed *o*); Hu. reads *at si;* P. *at ubi.*

[2] Because of the novation involved in the litiscontestation, iii, §§ 180, 181.

[3] There could be no novation in an *actio in rem*, or in one *in personam* with a *formula in factum concepta ;* in the former because no obligation was involved, in the latter because none was averred.

§ 108. This is not to be understood as a statement that under the system of the *legis actiones* no account could

be taken of any plea in defence that under the formular system became matter of exception. It may be that pleas arising from statute, such as those founded on the *leges Furiae, lex Cincia, lex Plaetoria,* etc., were presented in what Ihering (*G. d. R. R.* iii, p. 49) calls an after-suit; but the probability is that *res iudicata* or *res in iudicium deducta* was pleaded in the form of a prescription (§ 133), which, if proved, was a bar to the entertaining of the action (Keller, *R. CP.* § 43; Bath. Hollweg, *R. CP.* ii, p. 401). This view receives some countenance from the fact that the *exceptio rei iudicatae* is occasionally spoken of as a *praescriptio, e.g.* in fr. 42, D. *de lib. causa* (xl, 12), fr. 63, D. *de re iud.* (xlii, 1), etc.

ipso iure agi non poterat; nec omnino ita ut nunc usus erat
109 illis temporibus exceptionum.   *Ceterum* potest ex lege quidem esse iudicium sed legitimum non esse; et contra ex lege
non esse, sed legitimum esse; nam si uerbi gratia ex lege
Aquilia uel Ollinia uel Furia in prouinciis agatur, imperio
continebitur iudicium; idemque iuris est et si Romae apud
recuperatores agamus, uel apud unum iudicem interueniente
peregrini persona; et ex diuerso si ex ea causa ex qua nobis
edicto praetoris datur actio, Romae sub uno iudice inter omnes
ciues Romanos accipiatur iudicium, legitimum est.
110   Quo loco admonendi sumus eas quidem actiones quae ex
lege senatusue consultis proficiscuntur, perpetuo solere praetorem accommodare, eas uero quae ex propria ipsius iurisdic-
111 tione pendent, plerumque intra annum dare.   Aliquando
tamen (*et perpetuo eas dat, uelut quibus*)[1] *imitatur* ius legiti-

---

ticular thing, it was *ipso iure* impossible to sue again; nor
were there in those days any exceptions in use such as
109 we have now.   A *iudicium* may quite well be based on
a *lex* [or statute] and yet not be a *iudicium legitimum*,
and conversely may be *legitimum* though not founded
on statute.   For if proceedings be taken in a province
on the Aquilian law say, or the Ollinian or Furian, the
iudicium will be *imperio continens;* and so it will though
the proceedings be in Rome, if they be before recuperators,
or even before a single judge when he or either of the parties
happens to be a peregrin.   On the other hand, if the proceedings
be in Rome, at the instance of parties who are all citizens,
and before a single judge who also is a citizen, the *iudicium*
will be *legitimum* even though the action be one introduced
by the praetor's edict.
110   It may here be observed that actions attributable to a law
or senatusconsult may be granted by the praetor at any distance of time, but those that depend on his proper jurisdiction
are granted by him for the most part only within a year [of
111 the occurrence to which they relate].   Sometimes, however,
he grants actions of this sort even in perpetuity,—such

---

§ 109. Of the *L. Ollinia* mentioned in
this par. nothing is known. It is
probable that the copyist has made
a mistake in the name, as Gai. would
likely take as his illustration some
statute with which every one was
familiar.   But the error, if it be one,
does not affect the argument.

§§ 110-114.   Comp. tit. I. *DE PER-
PETVIS ET TEMPORALIBVS ACTIONI-
BVS, ET QVAE AD HEREDES VEL IN
HEREDES TRANSEVNT* (iv, 12).
§ 110. Comp. pr. tit. I. afd.
§ 111. Comp. pr. tit. I. afd.
[1] So Hu.; the words are illegible
in the ms. K. u. S., P., and M. (K.

21

mum : quales sunt eae quas bonorum possessoribus ceterisque
qui heredis loco sunt *eoue efficiuntur dare solet*.[2] furti quoque
manifesti actio, quamuis ex ipsius praetoris iurisdictione
proficiscatur,[3] perpetuo datur; et merita, cum[4] pro capitali
poena pecuniaria constituta sit.

112   Non[1] omnes actiones quae in aliquem aut ipso iure conpetunt aut a praetore dantur etiam in heredem aeque conpetunt aut dari solent: est enim certissima iuris regula ex
maleficiis poenales actiones in heredem nec conpetere nec
dari solere, uelut furti, ui bonorum raptorum, iniuriarum,
damni iniuriae : sed *heredibus quidem* [uidelicet actoris][2]
huiusmodi actiones conpetunt nec denegantur, excepta iniuriarum actione et si qua alia similis inueniatur actio.

113 Aliquando tamen [*etiam*] ex contractu actio neque heredi ne-

namely, as are modelled upon the common law ; as, for example, those he is in the practice of giving to *bonorum
possessores* and other persons in the position of or by him
treated as heirs. The *actio furti manifesti*, too, though it is
a creature of the praetor's jurisdiction, is perpetual ; and very
properly, seeing the pecuniary penalty in it is merely a
substitute for the [original] capital punishment.

112   Not every action that is competent against a man at common law, or that will be granted against him by the praetor,
is equally competent or will equally be granted against his
heir; for it is one of the best settled rules of law that penal
actions resulting from delict, such as those consequent on
theft, robbery, wrongful damage to property, or personal
injury, neither are competent nor will be granted against the
heir of the delinquent. Such actions, however, are competent
and will not be denied to the heirs [of the party wronged],
with the exception of the *actio iniuriarum* and others, if there
113 be such, of the same class.   Sometimes even an action

u. S. footnote) substantially agree
with Hu. Gou. prefers *praetor
quibusdam actionibus dandis.*
   [2] For the last four words I am
indebted partly to Gou. and partly
to Hu. K. u. S. and P. use instead
the one word *accommodat*, as in the
Inst. ; but not only is the space
in the MS. much too great for it,—
the *quueejjci...iiias* of the *Apogr.*
come very near *eoueefficiunt'ds.* A
bonorum emptor may be taken as
an example of a person *qui heredis
loco praetore efficitur* (§ 35).
   [3] Comp. iii, 189.

[4] So the MS.; Hu. has *cum tantum.*
§ 112. Comp. Gai. in fr. 111, § 1, D.
de R. I. (1, 17); § 1, tit. I. afd.
   [1] Hu. reads *contra non.*
   [2] The words *uid. actoris* seem to
be a gloss. There are four letters
illegible after *hdi*, which I assume
to have been *bqui ;* hence the reading *heredibus quidem.* Hu. reads
heredi defuncti uidelicet actoris ; K.
u. S. read *heredibus,* and omit the
next three words ; P. *heredibus quidem,* omitting the other two.
§ 113. Comp. § 1, tit. I. afd., from
which *etiam* is borrowed.

que in heredem conpetit : nam adstipulatoris heres non habet actionem,[1] *et* sponsoris et fidepromissoris heres non tenetur.[2]

114   Superest ut dispiciamus, si ante rem iudicatam is cum quo agitur post acceptum iudicium satisfaciat actori, quid officio iudicis conueniat, utrum absoluere, an ideo potius damnare quia iudicii accipiendi tempore in ea causa fuerit ut damnari debeat :[1] nostri praeceptores[2] absoluere eum debere existimant; nec interesse[3] cuius generis sit iudicium : et hoc est quod uulgo dicitur Sabino et Cassio[2] placere omnia iudicia *absolutoria esse.* — — — —[4] *de bonae fidei* iudiciis *autem* idem sentiunt, quia in eiusmodi iudiciis liberum est officium iudicis.[5] tantumdem et de in rem actionibus putant, *quia*[6] — — — — — — — — sunt etiam in personam tales

---

upon contract is not competent to or against an heir ; for the heir of an *adstipulator* cannot sue, and the heir of a *sponsor* or *fideipromissor* cannot be sued.

114   Now let us see what is the duty of the judge if, before judgment, but after issue joined, the defender has satisfied the pursuer's demand ; is he to acquit, or is he bound to condemn, on the ground that, at the moment when the cause was remitted to him, the defender's position was such as to warrant condemnation ?   Our authorities think that he ought to pronounce judgment of acquittal, and that no matter what the nature of the action; this is the meaning of the common saying that according to Sabinus and Cassius all *iudicia* are absolvitory.   *The leaders of the other school* — — — —. As regards *bonae fidei iudicia,* however, they are of the same opinion, because in them the judicial office has free scope.   And they extend the same rule to actions *in rem ;* because — — — — — — — —.   There are even some

---

[1] Comp. iii, 114.
[2] Comp. iii, 120.

§ 114.   Comp. § 2, tit. I. afd. P. 227 is for the most part illegible, the 1st, 4th, and 24th lines being the only ones that are complete.   There is reason to believe that in lines 6-22 Gai. proceeded to refer to the *actiones arbitrariae*, both *in rem* and *in personam*, in which the judge was authorized, if he found the case proved, to make such order on the defender as he considered would meet the justice of the case, and, if it were complied with, to acquit him ; see § 31, tit. I. *de act.* (iv, 6).

[1] Comp. iii, 180.
[2] Comp. i, 196, note 1.
[3] So G. and most eds.; the MS. and P. have *interest.*
[4] The suggestion of K. u. S. (footnote) commends itself,—that Gai. here affirmed of the Proculians that they held a different opinion in so far as *stricti iuris* actions were concerned; the only objection is that there is not room for it in the lacuna of half a line.
[5] Comp. § 30, tit. I. *de act.* (iv, 6).
[6] The next few words, according to K. u. S., are *quia formulae uerbis id ipsum exprimatur.*

actiones in quibus[7] — — — — — — — actum
fuit.

115   Sequitur ut de exceptionibus dispiciamus.   [116] Con-
116 paratae sunt autem exceptiones defendendorum eorum gratia
cum quibus agitur : saepe enim accidit ut quis iure ciuili
teneatur, sed iniquum sit eum iudicio condemnari : ueluti si
stipulatus sim a te pecuniam tamquam credendi causa nume-
raturus, nec numerauerim ; nam eam pecuniam a te peti posse
certum est ; dare enim te oportet, cum ex stipulatu teneris ;
sed quia iniquum est te eo nomine condemnari, placet per
116a exceptionem doli mali te defendi debere.   item si pactus
fuero tecum ne id quod mihi debeas a te petam, nihilo minus
id ipsum[1] a te petere possum dari mihi oportere, quia obligatio
pacto conuento non tollitur ; sed placet debere me petentem

---

actions *in personam* of this class, in which — — — —
— — — —.

115   We must next turn our attention to exceptions. [116] They
116 have been devised for the sake of defenders ; for it often
happens that a man may be liable according to strict law, and
yet that it would be contrary to equity to condemn him.
Suppose that, under the expectation that I was about to
advance you in loan a certain sum of money, you have given
me a stipulatory engagement for that amount, and that after
all I have not made the advance : there is no doubt that I am
entitled to sue you for the money, for you are bound to pay
it, being obliged by the stipulation ; but as it would be inequitable in such circumstances that you should be condemned,
you are allowed in defence to plead an exception of dole.
116a Again, suppose I have agreed not to take proceedings against
you for what you owe me, I am nevertheless entitled to sue,
and to maintain that you are bound to pay me the very thing
I had agreed not to claim, because an obligation cannot be
extinguished by [bare] agreement ; but it is held that if you
plead an *exceptio pacti conuenti* in answer to my claim, I will

---

[7] This may have been the commencement of a reference to some
of the *actiones arbitrariae in personam.* Huschke's reconstruction
is too conjectural to be reproduced.
§§ 115-125. Comp. tit. I. DE EXCEP-
TIONIBVS (iv, 13).
§ 115. Pr. tit. I. afd.

§ 116. Comp. pr. § 2, tit. I. afd.
§ 116a. Comp. § 3, tit. I. afd.
    [1] K. u. S. regard *id ipsum* as a
gloss ; Hu. substitutes *id ipso iure.*
But, as Gou. points out, the words
are appropriate, as indicating the
very *id* which it had been agreed
should not be sued for.

117 per exceptionem pacti conuenti repelli.   In his quoque
actionibus quae [non]¹ in personam sunt exceptiones locum
habent, ueluti si metu me coegeris aut dolo induxeris ut tibi
rem aliquam mancipio *darem ; nam si*² eam rem a me petas,
datur mihi exceptio per quam, si metus causa te fecisse uel
117a dolo malo arguero, repelleris.   item si fundum litigiosum
sciens a non possidente emeris eumque a possidente petas,
opponitur tibi exceptio per quam omni modo summoueris.
118 Exceptiones autem alias in edicto praetor habet propositas,
alias causa cognita accommodat. quae omnes uel ex legibus
uel ex his quae legis uicem optinent substantiam capiunt, uel
119 ex iurisdictione praetoris proditae sunt.   Omnes autem
exceptiones in contrarium concipiuntur, *quia*¹ adfirmat is cum
quo agitur : nam et uerbi gratia reus dolo malo aliquid actorem

---

117 be defeated.   There is room for exceptions even in actions
that are not *in personam*, as when you have constrained me
by threats, or induced me by doleful representations, to convey something to you by mancipation ; for if you raise an
action against me to obtain possession of it, I am entitled to
an exception, whereby, if I prove that there was intimidation or
117a dole on your part, your action will be defeated.   So also if
you have knowingly purchased, from one not in possession of
them, lands then forming the subject-matter of a litigation, and
you raise action for them against the possessor, he will be
entitled to state an exception which will effectually displace
118 your claim.   Some exceptions are published by the praetor
in the edict, others are granted on cause shown.   And all are
either founded on statute or some enactment that has the
force thereof, or have been devised by the praetor in the exer-
119 cise of his jurisdiction.   All exceptions are formulated
negatively ; for the affirmative proceeds from the pursuer.
For example, if the defender avers that there has been dole on

§ 117.   Comp. § 4, tit. I. afd.
    ¹ Added by G.
    ² The ᴍs. has *deminansin.* P.
reads *rem aliquam mancipi d[ar]em
man[cipio] ; si enim,* etc., which is
ingenious.
§ 117a.   Comp. Fr. de Iure Fisci, § 8 ; fr.
1, § 1, fr. 2, D. *de litig.* (xliv, 6).
§ 118.   Comp. § 7, tit. I. afd.
§ 119.   Comp. Paul. in fr. 22, pr. D.
de except. (xliv, 1).
    ¹ So Gou.; the ᴍs. has *qui;* K. u. S.,
Hu., and most eds. *quam.* Although

there were one or two actions in
which the pursuer maintained a
negative, *e.g.* in denial of the existence of a servitude over his property, yet the rule was that he
maintained an affirmative ; and in
his exception the defender by implication admitted that, on sub-
stantiating his averment, the pursuer
would be entitled to judgment if
something had *not* happened—that,
namely, which was averred by the
defender—to exclude it.

facere dicat, qui forte pecuniam petit quam non numerauit,
sic exceptio concipitur: SI IN EA RE NIHIL DOLO MALO AVLI
AGERII FACTVM SIT NEQVE FIAT; item si dicat contra pactionem
pecunia peti, ita concipitur exceptio: SI INTER AVLVM AGERIVM
ET NVMERIVM NEGIDIVM NON CONVENIT NE EA PECVNIA PETE-
RETVR; et denique in ceteris causis similiter concipi solet:
ideo scilicet quia omnis exceptio obicitur quidem a reo, sed ita
formulae inseritur ut condicionalem faciat condemnationem,
id est ne aliter iudex eum cum quo agitur condemnet, quam
si nihil in ea re qua de agitur dolo actoris factum sit; item ne
aliter iudex eum condemnet quam si nullum pactum con-
uentum *de* non petenda pecunia factum *fuerit*.

120   Dicuntur autem exceptiones aut peremptoriae aut dila-
121 toriae.   Peremptoriae sunt quae perpetuo ualent nec euitari
possunt, ueluti quod metus causa,[1] aut dolo malo,[1] aut quod
contra legem senatusue consultum factum est,[2] aut quod res
iudicata est,[3] uel in iudicium deducta est,[3] item pacti conuenti

---

the part of the pursuer, who perhaps is claiming repayment of
money which he has never advanced, the exception will be in
such terms as these : ' if there neither has been nor is any dole
in the matter on the part of Aulus Agerius;' if his averment be that the pursuer is claiming payment notwithstanding
an agreement to the contrary, it will run thus: ' if there has
been no agreement between Aulus Agerius and Numerius
Negidius that the money should not be sued for;' and in
other cases it will be framed in like manner.   It is always
the defender that states the exception, but it is so engrafted
on the formula as in effect to render the clause of condemnation conditional: in other words, it instructs the judge, in the
one case, that he is not to condemn the defender unless there
have been no dole in the matter on the part of the pursuer;
in the other, that he is not to condemn unless there has been
no agreement between the parties that action would not be
taken upon the debt.

120   Exceptions are said to be either peremptory or dilatory.
121 Those are peremptory that remain available always, and
cannot be excluded ; such are the exceptions of constraint or
dole, of contravention of a law or senatusconsult, of judgment
recovered, of submission of a cause to the arbitrament of a judge,

§ 120.   Comp. § 8, tit. I. afd.   [2] Comp. § 118.
§ 121.   Comp. § 9, tit. I. afd.   [3] Comp. iii, 181 ; iv, 106.
    [1] Comp. § 117.

122 quod factum est ne omnino pecunia peteretur.[4]   Dilatoriae
sunt exceptiones quae ad tempus ualent, ueluti illius pacti
conuenti quod factum est uerbi gratia ne intra quinquennium
peteretur; finito enim eo tempore non habet locum exceptio.
cui similis exceptio est litis diuiduae [1] et rei residuae : [2] nam
si quis partem rei petierit et intra eiusdem praeturam reliquam
partem petat, hac exceptione summouetur quae appellatur
litis diuiduae ; [1] item si is qui cum eodem plures lites habebat,
de quibusdam egerit, de quibusdam distulerit ut ad alios
iudices eant,[3] si intra eiusdem praeturam de his quas ita
distulerit agat, per hanc exceptionem quae appellatur rei
123 residuae [2] summouetur.   Obseruandum est autem ei cui
dilatoria obicitur exceptio, ut differat actionem ; alioquin si
obiecta exceptione egerit, rem perdit ; nec enim, post illud
tempus quo integra re [eam] [1] euitare poterat, adhuc ei potestas
agendi superest, re in iudicium deducta et per exceptionem
124 perempta.   Non solum autem ex tempore sed etiam ex

---

122 and of absolute agreement not to sue.   Those are dilatory
that are available only for a time, such as that of an agreement not to sue say for five years ; on their expiry there is no
longer any room for the exception.   To the same class belong
the *exceptio litis diuiduae* and *exceptio rei residuae :* for if an
individual have raised action for part only of that to which he
is entitled, and afterwards, and within the same praetorship,
sues for the remainder, he may be barred by an exception of
divided suit ; and if a man who has several causes of action
against the same party, and has proceeded in some of them,
but held over others in order to bring them before other
judges, have begun to sue upon these last within the same
praetorship, he may be met with an exception of claim held
123 over.   When a dilatory exception is pleaded the pursuer
should be careful to postpone his action ; if he go on in face
of it, he will lose his case ; and, if this have been once submitted to a judge and thrown out on the strength of the
exception, he will be unable to proceed afresh even after the
time when, had matters been entire, the exception might have
124 been elided.   Dilatory exceptions may be founded not

[4] Comp. §§ 119, 126.
§ 122.   Comp. § 10, tit. I. afd.
[1] Comp. §§ 56, 131.
[2] Comp. l. 10, C. *de iud.* (iii,
1).
[3] The ms. has *egant*. Hu. reads
agantur ; but, as Gou. observes,

though *apud iudicem agere* is frequent enough, *ad iudicem agere* is a
phrase unknown.
§ 123.   Comp. § 10, tit. I. afd.
[1] Added by Hu., and generally
adopted.
§ 124.   Comp. § 11, tit. I. afd.

persona dilatoriae exceptiones intelleguntur, quales sunt
cognitoriae,[1] uelut si is qui per edictum cognitorem dare non
potest per cognitorem agat, uel dandi quidem cognitoris ius
habeat, sed eum det cui non licet cognituram suscipere: nam
si obiciatur exceptio cognitoria, si ipse talis erit ut ei non
liceat cognitorem dare, ipse agere potest; si uero cognitori
non liceat cognituram suscipere, per alium cognitorem aut per
semet ipsum liberam habet agendi potestatem, et tam hoc
quam illo modo euitare [*potest*][2] exceptionem: quodsi dissi-
125 mulauerit *eam et*[3] per cognitorem egerit, rem perdit.   Sed
peremptoria quidem exceptione *si reus per errorem* non fuerit
usus, in integrum restituitur *adiciendae* exceptionis gratia:
dilatoria uero si non fuerit *usus*, an in integrum restituatur,
quaeritur.
126   Interdum euenit ut exceptio quae prima facie iusta uidea-

---

only on some objection to the time of suing, but also on some
objection to the person of the pursuer, as in the *exceptiones
cognitoriae.* Suppose, for example, that a man is suing by a
cognitor who is not by the edict entitled to do so, or that he
has accredited as his cognitor a person who cannot act in that
capacity: if an *exceptio cognitoria* be stated, the principal who
is not entitled to appoint such an agent may sue in person,
while, if the objection be to the qualification of the party
nominated as cognitor, he may appoint another instead of him
or sue in person, and in either way elide the exception; but
if [in either case] he disregard it, and allow the action to
proceed in the name of the cognitor [originally nominated],
125 he loses his cause.   If a defender have by inadvertence
omitted to avail himself of a peremptory exception competent
to him, he will be reinstated by the praetor in order that it
may be added [to the formula]; but it is disputed whether
there can be such reinstatement when it is only a dilatory
exception that has been overlooked.
126   It sometimes happens that an exception, which *prima facie*

---

[1] Comp. § 83; Paul. i, 2, §§ 1, 2;
Fr. Vat. §§ 322 f.; Quintil. *Inst.
Or.* vii, 1, §§ 19 f.
   [2] Added by G., and adopted by
all eds.
   [3] So Hu., following Hollweg, and
justified by Th. iv, 18, § 11. The
ms. has *cum ei* or *cum et*, the two
last letters being indistinct. K. u.

S. read [*et*] *cum ei* [*per cognitorem
agere non liceret, nihilo minus*] *per
cognitorem*; M. (K. u. S. p. xxii)
proposes *tum et per cognitorem.*
§ 125. Comp. §§ 53, 57, 123; l. 2, C.
sent. rescind. non posse (vii, 50).
§§ 126-129. Comp. tit. I. *DE REPLICA-
TIONIBVS* (iv, 14).
§ 126. Pr. tit. I. afd.

—

tur inique noceat actori: quod cum accidit alia adiectione
opus est adiuuandi actoris gratia: quae adiectio replicatio
uocatur, quia per eam replicatur atque resoluitur uis exceptionis: nam si uerbi gratia pactus sum tecum ne pecuniam
quam mihi debes a te peterem, deinde postea in contrarium
pacti sumus, id est ut petere mihi liceat, et, si agam tecum,
excipias tu ut ita demum mihi condemneris si non conuenerit
ne eam pecuniam peterem, nocet mihi exceptio pacti conuenti;
namque nihilo minus hoc uerum manet etiam si postea in
contrarium pacti sumus; sed quia iniquum est me excludi
exceptione, replicatio mihi datur ex posteriore pacto hoc
modo: SI NON POSTEA CONVENERIT VT MIHI EAM PECVNIAM
126*a* PETERE LICERET.   Item si argentarius pretium rei quae
in auctionem uenierit persequatur, obicitur ei exceptio ut ita
demum emptor damnetur si ei res quam emerit tradita *est* ;
et est iusta exceptio: sed si in auctione praedictum est ne ante
emptori traderetur quam si pretium soluerit, replicatione tali

---

seems just enough, will yet bear inequitably upon the pursuer.
When this occurs it becomes necessary to introduce yet
another clause into the formula for the pursuer's benefit, which
is called a replication, because thereby the force of the exception is replicated and destroyed.   Suppose, for example, that I
have agreed not to proceed against you for money you owe me,
and that subsequently we enter into a counter-agreement that
I may sue if I please; if I do sue, you may except that you
are to be condemned to me only if there have been no agreement not to sue.   That exception forms a bar to my action;
for there was such an agreement between us, although followed by one contradicting it.   But, as it would be inconsistent with equity that my claim should thus be defeated, I
am allowed a replication upon the subsequent agreement in
these terms: 'if there have been no later agreement giving
126*a* me leave to sue.'   Or suppose an auctioneer sues for the
price of a thing he has sold by auction, and that the exception
is taken that the defender ought not to be condemned unless
the thing he has purchased has been delivered to him, the
exception is good; but if it was one of the conditions of sale
that there should be no delivery until payment of the price, the

§ 126*a*.   A great mass of accounts and
other documents (on wax tablets)
relating to the auction business of
an *argentarius* in the years 53-62

p. C. were discovered at Pompeii
in 1875, and have since been published; see Petra, *Tavolette*, etc.

argentarius adiuuatur : AVT SI PRAEDICTVM EST NE ALITER
EMPTORI *RES* TRADERETVR QVAM SI PRETIVM EMPTOR[1] SOLVERIT.

127 Interdum autem euenit ut rursus replicatio, quae prima facie
iusta sit, inique reo noceat ; quod cum accidit adiectione opus

128 est adiuuandi rei gratia, quae duplicatio uocatur.   Et si
rursus ea prima facie iusta uideatur, sed propter aliquam
causam inique actori noceat, rursus ex [*contrario alia*][1] adiectione opus est qua actor adiuuetur, quae dicitur triplicatio.

129 Quarum omnium adiectionum usum interdum etiam ulterius
quam diximus uarietas negotiorum introduxit.

130   Videamus etiam de praescriptionibus quae receptae sunt

131 pro actore.   Saepe enim ex una eademque obligatione
aliquid iam praestari oportet, aliquid in futura praestatione
est, ueluti cum in singulos annos uel menses certam pecuniam
stipulati fuerimus : nam finitis quibusdam annis aut mensibus,
huius quidem temporis pecuniam praestari oportet, futurorum
autem annorum sane quidem obligatio contracta intellegitur,

---

auctioneer may have this replication : 'or if it was announced
previous to the sale that the thing would not be delivered

127 to the purchaser until he had paid the price.'   But it sometimes happens that a replication, though it in turn may *prima
facie* seem just, yet operates inequitably against the defender ;
in that case an additional clause is added on his account,

128 which gets the name of duplication.   If this again appear
prima facie to be just, but for any reason be really inequitable to the pursuer, still another clause is necessary on the

129 other side for his relief, which is called a triplication.   And
the employment of such interjected clauses may go even
further than we have indicated, if the circumstances of the
case require it.

130   Let us also consider the nature of the prescriptions employed

131 for the sake of pursuers.   It often happens that out of one
and the same obligation there arises both an immediate and a
future claim, as when we have stipulated for a certain sum
yearly or monthly ; at the end of the first year or month the
payment in respect of it then becomes due, but there is not
yet any claim for the payments applicable to future years,

---

[1] For *emptor*, as in the MS., Hu.
substitutes *emptae rei*.
§ 127.   § 1, tit. I. afd.
§ 128.   § 2, tit. I. afd.
   [1] The MS. has merely *ex* ; K. u.
S. delete it ; Hu reads *ex* [*ea*], and

in former editions *contra*.   *Alia* is
from the Inst.
§ 129.   Comp. § 3, tit. I. afd.
§ 130.   Comp. Cic. *de fin.* i, 1, § 3.
§ 131.   Comp. Cic. *de orat.* i, 37, §
   168.

praestatio uero adhuc nulla est; si ergo uelimus id quidem
quod praestari oportet petere et in iudicium deducere, futuram
uero obligationis praestationem in integro relinquere, necesse
est ut cum hac praescriptione agamus : EA RES AGATVR CVIVS
REI DIES FVIT; alioquin si sine hac praescriptione egerimus
ea scilicet formula qua incertum petimus, cuius intentio his
uerbis concepta est : QVIDQVID PARET NVMERIVM NEGIDIVM
AVLO AGERIO DARE FACERE OPORTERE,[1] totam obligationem, id
est etiam futuram, in hoc iudicium deducimus, et *quae* ante
131a tempus obligatio — — — — — — —.[2]   Item si uerbi
gratia ex empto agamus *ut* nobis fundus mancipio detur
debemus *hoc modo*[1] *praescribere :* EA RES AGATVR DE FVNDO
MANCIPANDO, ut postea, si uelimus uacuam possessionem nobis

---

although an obligation for them is held to have been contracted. If therefore we desire to sue for what is now
payable, and submit our claim in respect of it to judicial
decision, and at the same time to reserve entire our future
claims under the same obligation, we must have a prescription
in these terms : ' The matter of action is what is now payable ;'
if this prescription be omitted, and our formula be an indefinite one, with an *intentio* in these terms : ' whatever it
appears that in respect thereof Numerius Negidius ought to
give to or do for Aulus Agerius,' the whole obligation, even
as it affects the future, is submitted to the judge, and so much
of it as is sued for prematurely [*can neither be included in the
condemnation nor sued for afresh when the term of payment
131a has arrived*].   In like manner if, for example, we are suing
by an *actio ex empto* for mancipatory conveyance to us of
lands we have bought, we ought to have a prescription in this
way : ' The matter of action is the mancipation of the lands in
question,' so that, if we afterwards desire delivery of vacant

[1] Comparing this with the formula in the next par., it would appear that the *intentio* of an *incerti condictio* might be either in the form *quidquid paret d. f. oportere*, or in that of *quidquid d. f. oportet.*
[2] About a line and a half (p. 283, ll. 4, 5) illegible. Gou. proposes—et *quae* ante tempus obligatio *in iudicium fuit deducta consumpta est, quo fit ut postea permissum non sit de eadem re denuo agere.* Hu. has—et *quod* ante tempus obligationis emensum petitio nullo modo fieri ex ea potest nec est permissa, reliquum*

perdimus. K. u. S. (footnote) sug-gest—et *quae* ante tempus obliga-tionis *in iudicium deducuntur, ea neque in condemnationem ueniunt neque postea rursus de iis agere potest.* M. (K. u. S. p. xxii)—et *quae* ante tempus obligatio *in iudicium deducitur*, etc., substituting *uenit* and *ea* for the *ueniunt* and *iis* of K. u. S.
§ 131a. Comp. fr. 48, § 7, D. *de aedil. ed.* (xxi, 1).
[1] K. u. S. have *ita ;* but, accord-ing to Stud., there are four illegible letters in the MS. (*hocm*).

tradi, — — — — — —² sumus, totius illius iuris obligatio
illa *incerta* actione : QVIDQVID OB EAM REM NVMERIVM NEGI-
DIVM AVLO AGERIO DARE FACERE OPORTET, *propter*³ *intentionem*
consumitur, ut postea nobis agere uolentibus de uacua posses-
132 sione tradenda nulla supersit actio.   *Praescriptiones sic*
appellatas esse ab eo quod ante formulas praescribuntur plus
quam manifestum est.

133   Sed his quidem temporibus, sicut supra¹ quoque notauimus,
omnes praescriptiones ab actore proficiscuntur : olim autem
quaedam et pro reo opponebantur : qualis illa erat praescriptio : EA RES AGATVR *SI IN EA*² PRAEIVDICIVM HEREDITATI
NON FIAT, quae nunc in speciem exceptionis deducta est,³ et
locum habet cum petitor hereditatis alio genere iudicii prae-

----

possession [*we may sue afresh for it by a new action; if we
neglect to have such a prescription*], all that we can claim under
the obligation is exhausted by [joinder of issue upon] the
indefinite formula—' whatever in respect thereof Numerius
Negidius is bound to give to or do for Aulus Agerius ;' and,
should we afterwards want delivery of vacant possession, no
132 action remains to us for obtaining it.   That prescriptions
are so called because they are prefixed to the formulae is more
than manifest.
133   At the present day, as already observed, all prescriptions
originate with the pursuer.   But at one time there were some
prefixed for the benefit of the defender.   Of this sort was the
prescription : ' This action may proceed provided the question
of inheritance be not thereby prejudged.'   But now it is converted into a sort of exception, employed when there is danger
that the claimant of an inheritance, suing [not by *hereditatis
petitio* but] by some other action, say for some specific article,
may get a decision on the question of succession ; for it would
be unfair [*that a judgment in reference to some trifle should*

----

²Rather more than a line illegible.
Gou. suggests—*contra uenditorem
agere possimus eadem actione ;
alioquin si non praescribimus,
totius*, etc. K. u. S. suggest—*uel
tradita ea de euictione nobis caueri,
iterum ex empto agere possimus.
nam si praescribere* [*obliti*] sumus,
etc. Hu. supplies—*eius tradendae
causa ex stipulatu uel ex empto agere
supersit ;* [*nam si*] *obliti sic praescribere* sumus, etc.

³So Bekker (*Akt.* i, p. 343), and
preferable to the *per* of K. u. S. and
Hu. Some eds. read *per litis con-
testationem.* See iii, §§ 180, 181,
and note.
§ 133.   Comp. § 108, note.
¹See § 130.
²K. u. S. *si in ea re ;* Hu. *si ea
re.*
³See an example of this sort of
exception in fr. 1, § 1, D. *fam. erc.*
(x, 1).

iudicium hereditati faciat, ueluti cum singulas res *petat*; esset enim iniquum — — — — — — — —.[4]

34   — — — — — — — —[1] intentione formulae (*de iure (quaeritur)*,[2] id est cui dari oportet; et sane domino dari

---

[*prejudge the general question of inheritance*]. — — — — — —.

34   — — — — — — — — in the intention of the formula *the question that is raised is one of right*, namely, who it is

[4] P. 234 of the MS. is entirely illegible. Bl. thought he could make out as the last words of p. 233, *per unius rei*; and, utilizing these, K. u. S. suggest as the completion of the par.—*est enim iniquum per unius rei petitionem hereditati praeiudicium fieri.* Hu. suggests—*est enim iniquum per unius rei forte minimae rei petitionem, de qua apud unum iudicem agitur, de tota hereditate iudicari, cuius lis ad centumuiros defertur* (comp. l. 12, pr. C. *de her. pet.* iii, 31). *Et olim quidem, quamdiu ex hac causa praescribebatur, iudex principaliter de hoc cognoscebat, an hereditati praeiudicium fieret; quod si pronunciauerat, iudicium de singulis rebus petitis nullum erat, ideoque finita de hereditate quaestione, actor qui uicerat denuo eas petere poterat. Nunc uero cum in speciem exceptionis haec praescriptio deducta sit, nisi actor obiecta ea actionem differat, rem perdit, quia reus, si praeiudicium fieri probauerit, absoluitur, et iterum petenti actori nocet exceptio rei iudicatae.*

134. See note 4 to last par. It is possible that Gai. proceeded to give one or two other illustrations of prescriptions that had formerly been prefixed for the benefit of defenders (see § 108, note). It is clear at all events that he passed to prescriptions that may be said to have been in the interest of both parties, and intended to give notice of some point in the pursuer's case which the structure of the formula would otherwise have left undisclosed.

Pages 235 and 236 of the MS. are not palimpsest. They constitute the leaf that was published by Scipio Maffei in 1732.

[1] From what is extant of the par.

Hu. surmises that if a stipulation unusual in its character, say for one or other of two things of which the stipulant had the choice, had been contracted by a slave,—and such a stipulation, like every other, made his owner creditor, and entitled him to sue in his own name,—it was necessary to set forth the fact of the slave's agency in a *praescriptio*, there being no room for it in the *intentio*. Borrowing an illustration from fr. 141, pr. D. *de V. O.* (xlv, 1), he supposes a slave to have stipulated for 'this or that, which I please;' and proceeds to suggest that when the owner came to sue it would be necessary for him to have a formula with a prescription in terms like these : '*Ea res agatur, quod Stichus Auli Agerii seruus de Numerio Negidio stipulatus est. si paret Numerium Negidium Aulo Agerio decem milia dare oportere*;' and he thinks that Gai., having given some such illustration, proceeded thus : *itaque in* intentione formulae, etc.

But it is by no means clear that it was only when there was something unusual in a slave's stipulation that a *praescriptio* was required; there could not logically be any more need of it when his choice was founded on, than when the action was in virtue of a stipulation by him in the simplest of forms. It is possible therefore that there was a prescription in every case in which the stipulation sued upon had been by a slave or other party subject to the *ius* of the individual who thereby became creditor in the contract (iii, 168); and this seems to be the opinion of K. u. S.

[2] So Hu.; and the reading, judged by the context, is reasonable: ac-

oportet quod seruus stipulatur; at in praescriptione de *facto*[3]
quaeritur, quod secundum naturalem significationem uerum
135 esse debet.   Quaecumque autem diximus de seruis, eadem
de ceteris quoque personis quae nostro iuri subiectae sunt
dicta intellegemus.
136   Item admonendi sumus, si cum ipso agamus qui incertum
promiserit, ita nobis formulam esse propositam ut praescriptio
inserta sit formulae loco demonstrationis, hoc modo: IVDEX
ESTO. QVOD AVLVS AGERIVS DE NVMERIO NEGIDIO *INCERTVM
STIPVLATVS EST*, CVIVS REI DIES FVIT, QVIDQVID OB EAM REM
NVMERIVM NEGIDIVM AVLO AGERIO DARE FACERE OPORTET et
137 reliqua.   Si[1] cum sponsore aut fideiussore agatur, praescribi
solet in persona quidem sponsoris hoc modo : EA RES AGATVR
QVOD AVLVS AGERIVS DE LVCIO TITIO INCERTVM STIPVLATVS EST,
QVO NOMINE NVMERIVS NEGIDIVS SPONSOR EST, CVIVS REI DIES

---

that is entitled to payment; and undoubtedly it is the
owner that is entitled to payment in virtue of his slave's
stipulation : but in the prescription the question is as to facts,
which ought to be stated according to their natural [rather
135 than their jural] meaning.   What has been said of slaves
applies equally to other persons subject to our *potestas*.
136   We must further keep in mind that if we are proceeding
against an individual who himself by stipulatory promise
has engaged to us indefinitely, we can have our formula so
worded as to put the prescription in place of the demonstration, thus : 'So and so be judge. Whereas Aulus Agerius
stipulated with Numerius Negidius for something indefinite,
whose term of payment is past, whatever in respect thereof
Numerius Negidius ought to give to or do for Aulus
137 Agerius,' and so on.   But if the proceedings be against
a *sponsor* or *fideiussor*, there is in the case of the former a
prescription in these terms: 'This is the matter of action,
—that Aulus Agerius stipulated with Lucius Titius for something indefinite, on account whereof Numerius Negidius became sponsor, and whose term of payment is past;' and

cording to the natural meaning of
the words, it was the slave that
stipulated ; according to the legal
one, it was his owner.
   [3] So Savigny and all subsequent
eds. ; the MS. has *pacto*.
§ 136. For *incertum stipulatus est* the
MS. has *icertestipem;* the reading is
that of G., followed by all eds.

except Hu., who converts the final
m into *modo*.
§ 187. The prescriptions in this par.
served a twofold purpose; they
indicated the origin of the claim,
and limited it to what had fallen
due.
   [1] So the MS.; Hu. *quod si*; P.
at si.

FVIT; in persona uero fideiussoris: EA RES AGATVR QVOD
NVMERIVS NEGIDIVS PRO LVCIO TITIO INCERTVM FIDE SVA ESSE
IVSSIT, CVIVS *REI DIES* FVIT; deinde formula subicitur.

138   Superest ut de interdictis dispiciamus.
139   Certis igitur ex causis praetor aut proconsul principaliter [1]
auctoritatem suam finiendis controuersiis inter*ponit;*[2] quod
tum maxime facit cum de possessione aut quasi possessione
inter aliquos contenditur; et in summa aut iubet aliquid
fieri aut fieri prohibet: formulae autem *et uerborum*[3] *concep-
tiones* quibus in ea re utitur interdicta *decretaque*[4] [*uocantur*].[5]
140 Vocantur autem decreta cum fieri aliquid iubet, ueluti cum
praecipit ut aliquid exhibeatur aut restituatur; interdicta
uero cum prohibet fieri, uelut cum praecipit ne sine *uitio*
possidenti uis fiat,[1] neue in loco sacro aliquid fiat:[2] unde

in the case of a *fideiussor* it will be thus worded: 'The matter
of action is this,—that Numerius Negidius gave his fidejus-
sionary undertaking for Lucius Titius for something indefinite,
whose term of payment is past;' and then will come the
formula.

138   The next matter for consideration is that of interdicts.
139   There are certain cases in which the praetor or proconsul
peremptorily interpones his authority with a view to bring
disputes to an end, but most frequently when these are about
possession or quasi-possession. To state the matter shortly,
he either orders or prohibits something to be done; and the
formulae and styles he makes use of for the purpose are called
140 interdicts and decrees. They are called decrees when he
orders something to be done, as when he commands that
something shall be produced or restored; interdicts, when he
prohibits something to be done, as when he commands that
violence shall not be used towards an individual in non-
vitious possession, or that a sacred place shall not be dese-

§§ 138-170. Comp. tit. I. *DE INTER-
DICTIS* (iv, 15).
§ 139. Comp. pr. tit. I. afd.
    [1] The MS. has *principialiter;*
there are different opinions about
its meaning.
    [2] So all the later eds.; the MS.
has *proponit.*
    [3] So Hu. and most recent eds.;
the MS. has *uerborum et.*
    [4] Only the first three letters

legible in the MS., with just sufficient space for the remainder.
    [5] K. u. S. are of opinion that
something more has dropped out of
the text than the *uocantur*, and that
it probably ran: *interdicta[uocantur,
uel accuratius interdicta]decretaque.*
§ 140. Comp. § 1, tit. I. afd.
    [1] Comp. § 148.
    [2] Comp. tit. D. *ne quid in loco
sacro fiat* (xliii, 6).

omnia interdicta aut restitutoria aut exhibitoria aut prohibi-
141 toria uocantur.[3]   Nec tamen cum quid iusserit fieri aut fieri
prohibuerit statim peractum est negotium, sed ad iudicem
recuperatoresue *itur*, et ibi editis formulis quaeritur an aliquid
aduersus praetoris edictum factum sit, uel an factum non sit
quod is fieri iusserit. et modo cum poena agitur, modo sine
poena : cum poena, ueluti cum per sponsionem agitur, sine
poena, ueluti cum arbiter petitur ; et quidem ex prohibitoriis
interdictis semper per sponsionem agi solet, ex restitutoriis
uero uel exhibitoriis modo per sponsionem, modo per formulam agitur quae arbitraria uocatur.
142   Principalis igitur diuisio in eo est quod aut prohibitoria
143 sunt interdicta aut restitutoria aut exhibitoria.   Sequens in
eo est diuisio quod uel adipiscendae possessionis causa conparata sunt uel retinendae [1] uel reciperandae.
144   Adipiscendae possessionis causa interdictum accommodatur
bonorum possessori,[1] cuius principium est QVORVM BONORVM ;
eiusque uis et potestas haec est, ut quod quisque ex his bonis

---

crated.   Hence every interdict is said to be either restitutory,
141 or exhibitory, or prohibitory.   But the matter is not at
once at an end when he has pronounced his order or prohibition ; it then goes to a judge or to recuperators, and, formulae
having been adjusted, the question is tried whether or not
anything has been done in contravention of his prohibition, or
whether or not there has been failure to do what he has
ordered to be done.   And this subsequent procedure is sometimes penal, sometimes not : penal, when the proceedings are
by sponsion ; non-penal, when an arbiter is demanded.   The
procedure following upon a prohibitory interdict is always by
sponsion ; that following on a restitutory or exhibitory one
may be either by sponsion or by an arbitrary formula.
142   The principal division then of interdicts is this,—that they
143 are either prohibitory, restitutory, or exhibitory.   The next
division is that they are provided as a means either of acquiring possession, or of retaining it, or of recovering it.
144   There is an interdict for acquiring possession, beginning
with the words *quorum bonorum*, provided for a *bonorum
possessor :* its force and effect is that anything belonging to

[3] Comp. § 142.
§ 141.   Comp. §§ 162-170; Vlp. v, §§
1, 2.
§ 142.   Comp. § 140; § 1, tit. I. afd.
§ 143.   Comp. § 2, tit. I. afd.

[1] After *retinendae* the MS. has
possessionis causa interdictum.
§ 144.   § 3, tit. I. afd.
[1] Comp. iii, 34.

quorum possessio alicui data est, si[2] pro herede aut pro
possessore[3] possideat, id ei cui bonorum possessio data est
restituatur.   pro herede autem possidere uidetur tam is qui
heres est quam is qui putat se heredem esse; pro possessore
is possidet qui sine causa aliquam rem hereditariam, uel
etiam totam hereditatem, sciens ad se non pertinere, possidet.
ideo autem adipiscendae possessionis uocatur quia ei tantum
utile est qui nunc primum conatur adipisci rei possessionem ;
itaque si quis adeptus possessionem amiserit, desinit ei id
145 interdictum utile esse.   Bonorum quoque emptori similiter
proponitur interdictum, quod quidam possessorium uocant.
146 Item ei qui publica bona emerit eiusdem condicionis interdictum proponitur, quod appellatur sectorium, quod sectores
147 uocantur qui publice bona mercantur.   Interdictum quoque quod appellatur Saluianum adipiscendae possessionis
[causa] conparatum est, eoque utitur dominus fundi de

---

the deceased's estate that may at the moment be in the possession of another either *pro herede* or *pro possessore* must be
restored to him to whom the possession has been granted.
He is regarded as possessing *pro herede* not only who is heir
but also who [erroneously] believes himself to be so ; he
possesses *pro possessore* who, without any title, is in possession
of the whole or part of an inheritance, knowing that it does
not belong to him. And the interdict in question is said to
be for acquiring possession, because it is of use only to a
person endeavouring to obtain possession for the first time ;
for if he have lost it after once obtaining it, such an interdict
145 ceases to be of any service to him.   A similar interdict is
provided for the purchaser of a bankrupt's estate, which by
146 some is termed *interdictum possessorium*.   One of the same
sort, under the name of *interdictum sectorium*, is propounded
for the purchaser of a confiscated estate at public sale ; so
called because *sector* is the name given to a person trafficking
147 in that way.   What is known as the Salvian interdict is also
one for acquiring possession ; it is employed by a landlord for

[2] K. u. S. and Hu. delete *si*.
[3] On the strength of fr. 1, D.
quor. bonor. (xliii, 2), which recites the words of the edict, Hu.
interpolates *possidet, doloue fecit
quo minus*, substituting *possideret*
for the *possideat* of the ms.
§ 145. Comp. iii, §§ 77-80.

§ 146. Comp. Ps.-Ascon. *in II. Verr.*
i, 52 (Bruns, p. 292). The sale *sub
hasta* of the forfeited estate of a
condemned criminal, of an inheritance that had fallen to the fisc, etc.,
was called *sectio*.
§ 147. § 3, tit. I. afd.

22

rebus coloni quas is pro mercedibus fundi pignori futuras
pepigisset.

148   Retinendae possessionis causa solet interdictum reddi cum
ab utraque parte de proprietate alicuius rei controuersia est,
et ante quaeritur uter ex litigatoribus possidere et uter petere
debeat ; cuius rei gratia conparata sunt VTI POSSIDETIS et
149 VTRVBI.   Et quidem VTI POSSIDETIS interdictum de fundi
uel aedium possessione redditur, VTRVBI uero de rerum mobi-
150 lium possessione.   Et si quidem de fundo uel aedibus interdicitur, eum potiorem esse praetor iubet qui eo tempore
quo interdictum redditur nec ui nec clam nec precario ab
aduersario possideat ; si uero de re mobili, eum potiorem esse
iubet qui maiore parte eius anni [1] nec ui nec clam nec precario
ab aduersario possederit ; idque satis ipsis uerbis interdic-
151 torum significatur.   Sed in VTRVBI interdicto non *solum sua
cuique* [1] possessio *prodest*, sed etiam alterius quam iustum est

---

obtaining possession of effects of his farm-tenant which he has
bargained shall stand hypothecated for the rent.
148   An interdict for retaining possession is granted when there
are two parties disputing about the property of a thing, and
there is a prior question which of them ought to be regarded
as in possession of it, and which ought to stand pursuer in the
action for its recovery ; for deciding this matter the interdicts
149 *uti possidetis* and *utrubi* have been devised.   The first is
employed when the question is about the possession of land
or of a house ; the second when it is about the possession of
150 moveables.   When the controversy is about land or about a
house the praetor gives the preference to him who is in possession at the moment of the interdict, and that, so far as his
opponent is concerned, neither violently, clandestinely, nor on
sufferance ; but if it be about a moveable, he is preferred who
has been in possession of it for the greater part of the year, and
that neither by violent, clandestine, nor precarious exclusion
of his adversary, all as indicated sufficiently in the words of
151 the respective interdicts.   But in the interdict *utrubi* it is
not merely a man's own possession that counts to him, but also
any other person's that can rightly be regarded as accessory ;
as, for example, that of an individual to whom he has succeeded

---

§§ 148, 149. Comp. § 160; Paul. v, 6,
  § 1 ; §§ 4, 4a, tit. I. afd. ; Th. iv, 15,
  § 3.
§ 150.   Comp. § 160 ; § 4, tit. I. afd.
  [1] Comp. fr. 156, D. *de V. S.* (l, 16).

§ 151. Comp. fr. 14-16, De *de diu.
  temp. pr.* (xliv, 3) ; fr. 13, §§ 12,
  13, D. *de adq. u. am. poss.* (xli, 2).
  [1] The contraction in the MS. is
  qq.

ei accedere, uelut eius cui heres extiterit, eiusque a quo
emerit uel ex donatione aut dotis nomine acceperit: itaque
si nostrae possessioni iuncta alterius iusta possessio exuperat
aduersarii possessionem, nos eo interdicto uincimus.   nullam
autem propriam possessionem habenti accessio temporis nec
datur nec dari potest: nam ei quod nullum est nihil accedere
potest: sed et si uitiosam habeat possessionem, id est aut ui aut
clam aut precario ab aduersario adquisitam, *non datur accessio ;*
152 *nam ei* [*possessio*] sua nihil prodest.   Annus autem retrorsus
numeratur: itaque si tu uerbi gratia VIII mensibus possederis
prioribus et ego VII posterioribus, ego potior ero, quod *trium
priorum* [1] mensium possessio nihil tibi in hoc interdicto prodest,
153 quia alterius anni possessio est.   Possidere autem uidemur
non solum si ipsi possideamus sed etiam si nostro nomine
aliquis in possessione sit, licet is nostro iuri subiectus non sit,
qualis est colonus et inquilinus: per eos quoque apud quos
deposuerimus, aut quibus commodauerimus, aut quibus *gra-*

---

as heir, or from whom he has purchased a thing, or received it
as a gift or by way of dowry: consequently if the rightful possession of another, taken along with our own, have exceeded
that of our opponent, we are successful in this interdict.
But no accession of time is or can be given to a person who
has no possession of his own; for there can be no accession
to a nullity.   Nor can there be any accession in favour of a
party whose own possession is vitious, *i.e.* acquired from his
opponent violently, clandestinely, or in defiance of the recal
of a grant during pleasure; for his own possession [in such
152 a case] is of no avail to him.   The year is reckoned back-
wards: therefore if you have been in possession say for eight
months before me, and I have possessed for the last seven, I
must prevail; for the three first months of your possession
do not count to you so far as this interdict is concerned, seeing
153 the possession during them was in a different year.   We
are regarded as possessing not only when we do so ourselves,
but when any person is in possession in our name, even
though he be not subject to our *potestas*, but merely a tenant
say, either of a farm or of a house.   We are also regarded as
possessing by those with whom we have deposited a thing or
to whom we have lent it, as also by those to whom we have

§ 152. Comp. Paul. v, 6, § 1; Th. iv,   § 153.   § 5, tit. I. afd.   Comp. Gai. in
15, § 4.   fr. 9, D. *de adq. vel amitt. poss.*
   [1] The ms. has *trumporum.*   (xli, 2).

tuitam habitationem *praestiterimus* [1] ipsi possidere *uidemur :*
et hoc est quod uulgo dicitur retineri possessionem posse per
quemlibet qui nostro nomine sit in possessione. quin etiam
plerique putant animo quoque (*retineri*) *possessionem*, [*id est*
[*ut quamuis neque ipsi simus in*] [2] possessione neque nostro
nomine alius, tamen si non *relinquendae possessionis* animo, sed
postea reuersuri *inde discesserimus*, retinere possessionem uide-
amur. Apisci uero possessionem per quos possimus secundo
commentario rettulimus; [3] nec ulla dubitatio est quin animo
possessionem apisci non possimus. [4]

154 Reciperandae possessionis causa solet interdictum dari si
quis ex possessione [*fundi uel aedium*] [1] *ui* deiectus sit : nam
ei proponitur interdictum cuius principium est:VNDE TV ILLVM
VI DEIECISTI, per quod is qui deiecit cogitur ei restituere rei
possessionem, si modo is qui deiectus est nec ui nec clam nec

---

granted a [*usufruct, or a right of use or*] gratuitous habita-
tion ; and this is what is meant by the common saying that
possession may be retained through any person that is in possession in our name. Nay, most jurists go so far as to think
that it may be retained by a mere effort of will, *i.e. that
although neither we ourselves are in possession* nor yet any other
person on our account, still, if we have left a place without
any intention of relinquishing the possession of it, but really
meaning to return, we are to be regarded as retaining possession. In our Second Commentary we have explained who they
are through whom we may acquire possession ; there has never
been any doubt that for such acquisition a mere effort of will
is ineffectual.

154 An interdict is granted for recovering possession when a
man has been forcibly ejected [*from his land or house*]; to meet
his case there is one published beginning with the words
unde tu illum ui deiecisti, whereby the ejector is compelled to
restore the possession, provided the party ejected was not [at
the time] possessing as the result of violent, clandestine, or
precarious taking from the ejector himself ; for he who has

---

[1] So Bk. and K. u. S. The ms.
has *rtituerimus*, and then a repetition of *aut quibus gratuitam habitationem.* This induces Hu. to read
praestiterimus, aut quibus [*usumfructum uel usum con*]*stituerimus.*

[2] Borrowed from the Inst., with
the necessary grammatical altera-
tions.

[3] Comp. ii, §§ 89-95.
[4] Comp. Paul. v, 2, § 1.
§ 154. Comp. Cic. *pro Caec.* xi, §§ 31,
32 ; *pro Tull.* §§ 44, 45 ; Paul. v, 6,
§§ 4-8 ; fr. 1, pr. D. *de ui* (xliii,
16) ; § 6, tit. I. afd.
[1] These three words are from the
Inst.

precario *possederit* (*ab altero*), cum qui a me ui aut clam aut
155 precario possidet inpune *deici potest*.[2]   Interdum tamen *etsi*
eum ui deiecerim qui a me ui aut clam aut precario possederit, cogor ei restituere possessionem, ueluti si armis eum ui
deiecerim : nam propter atrocitatem delicti in tantum patior
animaduersionem [1] *ut* omni modo *debeam ei restituere posses-*
sionem. armorum autem appellatione non solum scuta et gla-
dios et galeas significari intellegemus, sed et fustes et lapides.
156   Tertia diuisio interdictorum in hoc est, quod aut simplicia
157 sunt aut duplicia.   *Simplicia sunt ueluti in* quibus alter
actor alter reus est, qualia sunt omnia restitutoria . aut
exhibitoria : nam actor est qui desiderat aut exhiberi aut
restitui, reus is est a quo desideratur ut exhibeat aut resti-
158 tuat.   Prohibitoriorum autem interdictororum alia duplicia,
159 alia simplicia sunt.   Simplicia sunt ueluti quibus prohibet

---

taken possession from me by violence or clandestinity, or in
defiance of my recal of a grant during pleasure, may be ejected
155 by me with impunity.   Yet sometimes, if I have forcibly
ejected a party who had taken possession from me violently,
clandestinely, or precariously, I will be compelled to restore
the possession to him,—then, namely, when I have ejected
him by force of arms ; on account of the gravity of the offence
I have to suffer punishment at least to this extent, that I
must in any case reinstate him in possession.   And under the
word ' arms ' we are to understand not only shields, swords, and
helmets, but also sticks and stones.
156   A third division of interdicts is due to the consideration
157 that they are either single or double.   Those are single in
which one party is pursuer, the other defender, as is the case
in all the restitutory and exhibitory interdicts ; he is pursuer
who desires exhibition or restitution, and he defender at whose
158 hands exhibition or restitution is required.   Of the prohi-
159 bitory interdicts some are double, some single.   Those, for
example, are single in which the praetor forbids the defender

[2] So K. u. S. Hu. reads—*nec pre-*
cario [*ab eo*] *possideret ; enimuero*
eum qui . . . inpune deicio. The
final letter is illegible in the MS., and
may have been either *t'*, which would
make the reading *deicitur*, or *o*, as
assumed by Hu., or *p* (contraction
for *potest*), as assumed by K. u. S.
§ 155. Comp. refs. in note to last par. ;
also fr. 3, §§ 2-12, D. *de ui* (xliii, 16).

[1] The MS. has *aonem ;* K. u. S.
and P. read *patior actionem ;* to this
Hu. objects, and substitutes *ratio*
facti habetur ; but the *patior* of the
MS. is quite distinct, though *aonem*
is not perfectly certain. See *anim-*
aduersio employed in this sense
in fr. 131, § 1, D. *de V. S.* (l,
16).

§§ 156-159. Comp. § 7, tit. I. afd.

praetor in loco sacro aut in flumine publico ripaue eius aliquid facere reum : nam actor est qui desiderat ne quid fiat,

160 reus is qui aliquid facere conatur.   Duplicia sunt uelut VTI POSSIDETIS interdictum et VTRVBI : ideo autem duplicia uocantur quia *par* utriusque litigatoris in his condicio est, nec quisquam praecipue reus uel actor intellegitur, sed unusquisque tam rei quam actoris partes sustinet; quippe praetor pari sermone cum *utroque* loquitur : nam summa conceptio eorum interdictorum haec est :[1] VTI *NVNO* POSSIDETIS, QVOMINVS ITA POSSIDEATIS, VIM FIERI VETO ; item alterius :[2] VTRVBI HIC HOMO DE QVO AGITVR[3] MAIORE PARTE HVIVS ANNI FVIT, QVOMINVS IS EVM DVCAT, VIM FIERI VETO.

161   Expositis generibus interdictorum sequitur ut de ordine et de exitu eorum dispiciamus; et incipiamus a simplicibus.

162 [*Si*] igitur restitutorium uel exhibitorium interdictum redditur, ueluti ut restituatur ei possessio qui ui deiectus est, aut

---

to go on with any operation in a sacred place, or in a public river, or on its bank; he is pursuer who wishes to prevent it,

160 and he defender by whom it is attempted.   Double are such interdicts as the *uti possidetis* and *utrubi*.   They are so called because in them the litigants stand on the same footing, neither being regarded as peculiarly pursuer or peculiarly defender, but each holding both characters, inasmuch as the praetor addresses both in exactly the same terms.   For, putting them in the briefest possible shape, those interdicts run thus : the first—'I forbid any violence being done to prevent you two continuing to possess as you do now ;' the second—'I forbid any violence being done to prevent that one of you with whom the slave in question has been for the greater part of this year from taking said slave away with him.'

161   The various sorts of interdicts having been described, we have next to consider the procedure in them, and its issue.

162 We shall begin with the single ones.   If then a restitutory or exhibitory interdict be granted, ordaining for example that possession be restored to a party who has been forcibly

---

§ 160. Comp. § 149, and note.
[1] Comp. Fest. v. *Possessio* (Bruns, p. 254); fr. 1, pr. D. *uti possid.* (xliii, 17).
[2] Comp. tit. D. *utrubi* (xliii, 31).
[3] Before *maiore* the ᴍs. has *apud quem.* These words are not in the

formula of the interdict in the Dig. (see last note); I have therefore expunged them as a gloss, which K. u. S., M., and P. also regard them.

§ 161. Comp. § 8, tit. I. afd.
§ 162. Comp. §§ 141, 157.

exhibeatur libertus cui patronus operas indicere uellet,[1] modo
sine periculo res ad exitum perducitur, modo cum periculo.

163 Namque si arbitrum postulauerit is cum quo agitur, accipit
formulam quae appellatur arbitraria, et iudicis arbitrio, si quid
restitui uel exhiberi debeat, id sine periculo exhibet aut
restituit et ita absoluitur; quodsi nec restituat neque exhibeat, quanti ea res est[1] condemnatur. sed et actor sine poena
experitur cum eo *quem* neque exhibere neque restituere
quicquam *oportet*, praeterquam si calumniae iudicium[2] ei
oppositum fuerit decimae partis: *quamquam Proculo*[3] *placuit
non esse permittendum* calumniae iudicio [*uti*] *ei*[4] qui arbitrum
postulauerit, quasi hoc ipso confessus uideatur restituere se
uel exhibere debere: sed alio iure utimur; et recte; *potius*

―――――――

ejected, or that a freedman be produced upon whom his patron
wishes to impose certain duties of service, the matter is
brought to an issue sometimes with and sometimes without

163 any risk being incurred.   For, if the defender have demanded a reference to an arbiter, he obtains what is called an
arbitrary formula; and if, on the discretionary order of the
judge, he restores or exhibits that which he is held to be in
law bound to restore or exhibit, he does so without incurring
any penalty, and is at once absolved; while if he fail to
restore or exhibit, he is simply condemned in what the pursuer can show himself entitled to as damages. The pursuer
also litigates without any risk with a party who is not bound
to exhibit or restore anything, unless a *iudicium calumniae*,
concluding for a tenth part of the value of the cause, be raised
against him. Proculus, indeed, was of opinion that a defender
who had demanded an arbiter could not be allowed a *calumniae
iudicium*, as his application for an arbiter involved an admission that he was bound to restore or exhibit; but we follow
a different practice, and rightly; for his application for an

―――――――

[1] Comp. fr. 2, § 1, *de interd.*
(xliii, 1); fr. 13, § 2, D. *de oper. lib.*
(xxxviii, 1).
§ 163.   Comp. Vlp. Inst. fr. 5.
   [1] Comp. fr. 2, § 2, D. *quod leg.*
(xliii, 3); fr. 8, § 11, D. *de tab.
exhib.* (xliii, 5); fr. 6, fr. 15, D. *de
ui* (xliii, 16). *Quanti res est* often
means the market value of the thing
in dispute (fr. 179, fr. 193, D. *de
V. S.* l, 16); but here, to judge
by the passages referred to, it means

what is commonly expressed by *id
quod interest*—damages, the amount
of the pursuer's loss imputable to
the defender.
   [2] Comp. §§ 175, 181.
   [3] Comp. i, 196, note 1.
   [4] So Gou.; K. u. S. have *placuit
denegandum calumniae iudicium ei;*
Hu. *placuisse dicitur prohibendum
calumniae iudicio esse eum;* P. follows Gou.

enim ut modestiore uia litiget[5] arbitrum quisque petit quam
164 quia *confitetur.*[6]   [*ceterum*] obseruare debet is qui uult arbitrum petere ut statim petat antequam ex iure exeat, id est
antequam a praetore *discedat :* sero enim petentibus non indul-
165 getur.   Quod si arbitrum non petierit, sed tacitus de iure
exierit, cum periculo res ad exitum perducitur : nam actor
prouocat aduersarium sponsione ni contra edictum praetoris
non exhibuerit aut non restituerit ; ille autem aduersus
sponsionem aduersarii restipulatur ; deinde actor quidem
sponsionis *formulam edit* aduersario, ille huic inuicem restipulationis : sed actor sponsionis — — —[1] et aliud iudicium
de re restituenda uel exhibenda, ut si sponsione *uicerit,* nisi
ei res exhibeatur aut restituatur.[2] — — — — — — — —.

---

arbiter should be imputed not so much to any admission on
his part, as to his desire to litigate by the less pretentious
164 procedure.   A defender who desires to have an arbiter
appointed must take care to apply for him at once, and before
withdrawing from the presence of the praetor *in iure ;* if the
demand be not made until a later stage it will not be granted.
165 If he have not made any such application, but have left the
court without speaking, the matter proceeds to its issue at his
risk ; for the pursuer challenges him with a sponsion upon
the question whether it is not in defiance of the praetor's
interdict that he has failed to exhibit or restore, and the
defender restipulates as against this sponsion.   The parties
then have formulae adjusted upon their respective sponsion
and restipulation, the pursuer *getting words added to his for-*
mula containing a remit to the judge upon the main question
of restitution or exhibition ; so that, if he is successful on his
sponsion, and exhibition or restitution is still refused, [*the*
[*judge has power to condemn the defender not only in the amount*
[*of the sponsion but also in damages*]. — — — — — —
— —.

---

[5] So K. u. S. and Hu. ; Gou. has
potius enim ut per modestiorem
actionem litiget. The word *mode-*
stius is used in this sense by Pap. in
fr. 25, § 1, D. *de pec. con.* (xiii, 5).
    [6] So Gou. and K. u. S. ; Hu. has
quia causae non fidit ; P. *quia con-*
uictus sit.
    § 164.   *Ceterum* added by Hu. and
adopted by P. ; K. u. S. have *ob-*
seruare [*autem*].
    § 165.   Cp. Cic. *pro Caec.* viii, 23, xxxi,

91 ; *pro Tull.* § 53 ; Gai. iv, 141.
    [1] In this lacuna Bk., K. u. S.,
and Hu. insert *formulae subicit ;*
but these words do not correspond
to the traces visible in the ms.
    [2] P. 241 of the ms. ends with
restituatur ; p. 242 is entirely illegible ; and on p. 243 not half a
dozen words are decipherable. The
words in ital. in the translation
probably represent generally the
sense of the final words of this par.

166   — — — — — — — — fructus licitando,[1] *is tantisper in
possessione constituitur,* si modo aduersario suo fructuaria
stipulatione (*cauerit*), cuius uis et potestas *haec est, ut si contra
eum de possessione pronuntiatum fuerit, eam summam* aduersario *soluat.*   Haec autem licendi contentio fructus licitatio
uocatur scilicet quia — — — — — — —.[2] *postea alter
alterum sponsione* prouocat quod[3] aduersus edictum praetoris

166   — — — — — — — — —.   [*Interdict having been pro-
[nounced, and the parties having made pretence of violence towards
[each other, then, in order to prevent any real and serious contest
[about the interim enjoyment of the land or house in question
[while the proceedings are in dependence, the praetor requires
[them to bid for it ; and he who is successful*] in the bidding is
awarded the interim possession, provided he has given security
to his opponent by a *fructuaria stipulatio,* whose effect is that
he must pay to the latter the sum promised in the event of
judgment being against him, the promiser, on the main question of possession.   This bidding and counter-bidding is called
fructus licitatio, bidding for the fruits, because [*neither of the
[bidders gets the thing itself, but only the right to possess it and
[draw the fruits and profits of it in the meantime*].   Afterwards
each challenges the other with a sponsion, on the suggestion

§ 166. It is presumable that, in the remainder of pp. 242, 243, Gai., having finished his observations on the
procedure in the single interdicts,
must have commenced to explain
that followed in the double ones,—
the matter dealt with in pp. 244-
246. The illegibility of pp. 242,
243 is particularly to be regretted;
if they could be deciphered they
would probably throw some light on
the *uis ex conuentu uis moribus facta*
(Cic. *pro Caec.* i, 2, viii, 22) that
followed the interdict *uti possidetis,*
and that is incidentally mentioned
in § 170. For, notwithstanding the
final words of that interdict, *uim
fieri ueto,* the very first thing the
parties did, and were expected to do,
was to offer (or pretend to offer)
violence to each other in regard to
the possession. It was only thus
that a question could be raised for
the judge,—' both parties have done
violence; which of them is it that has
done it in defiance of the interdict,
—that has done it in disturbance of
the possession previously existing?'
   [1] The first word or two on p. 244

are illegible. Krueg. (*Krit. Vers.* p.
92) suggests *et uter eorum uicerit*
fructus licitando, etc.; but these
words do not correspond to the letters in the *Apographum.* The beginning of the sentence may have
been something like this, suggested
by Hu., footnote: *Reddito uero interdicto, si ab alterutro alteri uis
facta sit, statim de ea sponsiones et
restipulationes fiunt. ne tamen in-
ciuili et propria ui possessionem
obtinere conentur, praetor fructus
licitationem inter eos instituit, et uter
eorum uicerit* fructus licitando, etc.
   [2] Gou. proposes—*neuter eorum qui
licentur ipsam rem, sed tantisper
possidendi et fruendi re adquirit
facultatem;* K. (K. u. S. footnote)
—*de eo inter se certant uter eorum
fructus interim percipiat;* Hu.—
*dum uolunt uterque frui tantisper
re, proprie quod eis praetor uendit,
est, ut id interea liceat.* None of
these reconstructions much re-
sembles what is visible in the ms.;
which, however, is greatly injured at
this place by Bluhme's chemicals.
   [3] P. substitutes *ni.*

possidenti sibi uis facta est, et inuicem ambo restipulantur
aduersus sponsionem : uel — — — — — — — —.[4]
166a— — — — — iudex apud quem de ea re agitur illud scilicet
requirit [quod] praetor interdicto conplexus est, id est uter
eorum eum fundum easue aedes per id tempus quo interdictum redditur nec ui nec clam nec precario possideret.
cum iudex id explorauerit, et forte secundum me iudicatum
sit, aduersarium mihi et sponsionis et restipulationis summas
quas cum eo feci condemnat, et conuenienter me sponsionis
et restipulationis quae mecum factae sunt absoluit; et hoc
amplius, si apud aduersarium meum possessio est, quia is
fructus licitatione uicit, nisi restituat mihi possessionem,
167 Cascelliano siue secutorio iudicio condemnatur.[1]   Ergo is
qui fructus licitatione uicit, si non probat ad se pertinere
possessionem, sponsionis et restipulationis et fructus licitationis summam poenae nomine soluere et praeterea posses-

---

that, contrary to the praetor's interdict, violence has been done
to him while possessing, and both reciprocally restipulate in
166a answer to the sponsion ; — — — — — — —.   [For-
[mulae having thereafter been adjusted upon all those sponsions
[and restipulations], the judge to whom the matter is remitted
proceeds to consider the question dealt with by the praetor in
his interdict, namely, which of the parties possessed the land or
house in question, and that neither violently, clandestinely, nor
on sufferance, at the time when the interdict was pronounced.
Having done so, and given judgment (let us suppose) in my
favour, he finds my opponent liable to me in the amounts of
the sponsion and restipulation I entered into with him, and
conformably acquits me in respect of the sponsion and restipulation in which I was promiser; whilst my opponent, if the
possession be with him, because he had over-bid me in the
fructus licitatio, is over and above condemned in the Cascel-
167 lian or after-process, if he do not restore it.   He therefore
who has been successful in the fructus licitatio, if he fail to
establish that he is entitled to possession, has to pay as a
penalty the sums severally covered by his sponsion, restipu-

---

[4] Schmidt (Interd. p. 288) suggests—uel si unus tantum sponsione
prouocauit alterum, una inter eos
sponsio et una tantum restipulatio
aduersus eam fit; Hu.—uel stipulationibus iunctis duabus una inter eos
sponsio itemque restipulatio una
alterius aduersus eam fit. quod et
commodius ideoque magis in usu est.
§ 166a. Hu. suggests as the commencement of the par.: Deinde ab utroque
editis formulis omnium stipulationum et restipulationum quas fieri
placuit, iudex, etc.
[1] Comp. § 169; fr. 3, § 11, D.
uti poss. (xliii, 17).

sionem restituere iubetur, et hoc amplius fructus quos interea
percepit reddit; summa enim fructus licitationis non pretium
est fructuum, sed poenae nomine soluitur, quod quis alienam
possessionem per hoc tempus retinere et facultatem fruendi
168 nancisci conatus est.   Ille autem qui fructus licitatione
uictus est, si non probauerit ad se pertinere possessionem,
tantum sponsionis et restipulationis summam poenae nomine
169 debet.   Admonendi tamen sumus liberum esse ei qui
fructus licitatione victus erit, omissa fructuaria stipulatione,
sicut Cascelliano siue secutorio iudicio de *possessione recipe-*
randa experitur, ita (similiter) [1] *de* fructus licitatione *agere :* in
quam *rem* proprium iudicium conparatum est quod appellatur
fructuarium, quo nomine actor iudicatum solui [2] satis accipit :
dicitur autem et hoc iudicium secutorium, quod sequitur
sponsionis uictoriam ; sed non aeque Cascellianum uocatur.
170   Sed quia nonnulli interdicto reddito cetera ex interdicto

---

lation, and *licitatio*, and is required besides to restore possession and return the fruits he has drawn in the meanwhile ;
for the amount of the *fructus licitatio* is not the purchase-
price of the fruits, but paid by way of penalty, in consideration that the party has attempted for the time to retain a
possession that belonged to another, and the power of taking
168 the fruits and profits.   He, on the other hand, who has
been unsuccessful in the *fructus licitatio*, if he fail to prove
that the possession is his, owes no more than the amount of
his sponsion and restipulation, and that by way of penalty.
169 It must not, however, be overlooked that it is in the power of
the unsuccessful party in the *fructus licitatio* to disregard the
fructuary stipulation, and take separate proceedings upon the
licitatio, just as he does in the Cascellian or after-process for
recovery of the possession ; and for this purpose a separate
procedure, called a *iudicium fructuarium*, has been devised, in
respect whereof the pursuer is entitled to have security from
the defender for payment of whatever the judge may find to
be due.   This *iudicium fructuarium* is also spoken of as an
after-process, because it is a sequel to success in the sponsion ;
it does not, however, get the name of Cascellian.
170   But as some persons, after interdict had been pronounced,

§ 169. Comp. § 166.
 [1] Gou., K. u. S., and Hu. are all
agreed upon this word, although no
more than the initial *s* is legible.

[2] Comp. § 91.
§ 170. It is from Studemund's revision
of the Verona MS. that we first become acquainted with the secondary

facere nolebant, atque ob id non poterat res expediri, praetor *in eam rem prospexit et* conparauit interdicta quae secundaria appellamus, quod secundo loco *redduntur : quorum (uis et (potestas haec est, ut qui)* [1] *cetera ex interdicto non faciat, ueluti qui uim non faciat aut fructus non liceatur, aut qui* fructus licitationis *satis* non det, aut si [2] *sponsiones* [3] *non faciat sponsionumue* [4] *iudicia non accipiat, siue possideat, restituat* [5] *aduersario* possessionem, *(siue non possideat, uim)* [6] illi possidenti ne faciat. Itaque etsi alias *potuerit interdicto* VTI POSSIDETIS *uincere si cetera ex* interdicto — — — — [7] tamen 170*a* per interdictum secundarium — — — —. [8]   [170*a*] — —
— — — — —.

---

occasionally refused to take the necessary steps under it, and so put a stop to further procedure, the praetor turned his attention to the matter and introduced interdicts of another sort, which we call secondary, because they are had recourse to only in the second instance. Their *purpose and effect is this,*—that he who fails to do what is incumbent upon him [with a view to further procedure] under the interdict,—who, for example, will not offer [conventional] violence [to his adversary], or will not bid for the fruits, or will not give security for the *fructus licitatio,* or will not be a party to the sponsions, or will not defend the *iudicia* founded upon them, —must, if he possess, restore the possession to the other party, or, *if he do not possess,* must abstain from offering violence to the possessor.   And thus, although he might very possibly have been successful in the interdict *uti possidetis, had he been ready to do* what was necessary on his part [to further the procedure], *the possession* is nevertheless, by this 170*a* secondary interdict, *transferred to his adversary.*   [170*a*] —
— — — — —.

---

interdict described in this par., and get an enumeration of the various steps of procedure in the *int. uti possidetis.* Although a considerable portion of the par. is printed in ital. as not absolutely certain, yet as a whole it may be taken as accurate. Comp. Front. *de contr. agr.* p. 44.

[1] So K. (*Krit. Vers.* p. 84), K. u. S., Hu., and P.

[2] Hu. proposes to delete *si.*

[3] The ᴍꜱ. has *sponsionibus.*

[4] Hu. reads [*ex*] *sponsionibusue.*

[5] Before *restituat* Hu. interpolates *cum fructibus.*

[6] So K. u. S., Hu., and P.

[7] K. (*Krit. Vers.* p. 102) proposes *paratus sit facere ;* Hu. *fecisset, si non fecit ;* P. *facere uoluisset.*

[8] K. (*Krit. Vers.* p. 102) proposes *possessio in aduersarium transfertur ;* Hu. *uincitur.* K. u. S. (footnote) suggests the transposition of *tamen,* making the sentence run thus : *Itaque etsi alias potuerit interdicto uti possidetis uincere, tamen si cetera ex interdicto facere uoluerit, per interdictum secundarium possessio in aduersarium transfertur.*

§ 170*a.* Lines 11-24 of p. 246 of the

171   — — — — — — — (*modo*) pecuniaria poena, modo iurisiurandi *religione* — — — : eaque praetor — — — — — —[1]
aduersus (*infitiantem ex quibusdam*) *causis* dupli actio constituitur, *ueluti si iudicati*[2] *aut depensi*[3] aut damni iniuriae[4]
aut legatorum per *damnationem* relictorum[5] nomine agitur :
ex quibusdam causis sponsionem facere permittitur, uelut de
pecunia certa credita[6] et pecunia constituta ;[7] sed certae
quidem creditae pecuniae tertiae partis, constitutae uero
172 pecuniae partis dimidiae.   Quodsi neque sponsionis neque
dupli actionis periculum ei cum quo agitur iniungatur,[1] ac ne
statim quidem ab initio pluris quam simpli sit actio, permittit

---

171   [*We have to observe in the next place that, in the old law,*
[*endeavour was made to restrain rash and precipitate litigation*],
sometimes by pecuniary penalties, sometimes by the religious
compulsitor of an oath ; and these [*devices are still made use
[of by*] the praetor. [*As regards in the first place a defender*]
denying his liability, action is granted against him in certain
cases for double the amount of his debt, as in the case of
the *actio iudicati*, the *actio depensi*, the action upon the
Aquilian law, and the action for a legacy bequeathed by
damnation. In certain other cases a [penal] sponsion is
allowed, as in the actions *de pecunia certa credita* and *de
pecunia constituta ;* in the former the sponsion is for a third
172 part more, in the latter for a half.   Where the risk neither
of a sponsion nor of an action for double the amount of his
debt is laid upon the defender, and the action is not one that
from the first is for more than the simple sum claimed, the

MS. are almost entirely illegible.
But we have *secundarium* on l. 13,
quamuis hanc opinionem on l. 14,
and *Sabinus et Cassius secuti fuerint*
on l. 15. We may conclude therefore that Gai. went here into some
further explanation of the *interdictum secundarium.*

§§ 171-183. Comp. tit. I. *DE POENA
TEMERE LITIGANTIVM* (iv, 16). All
but the last three lines of p. 247,
and two or three letters on ll. 8, 9,
are illegible ; even the last three
lines are only partially legible.

§ 171. Comp. §§ 9, 13 ; pr. tit. I.
afd.
    [1] Hu., borrowing from the Inst.,
thus completes the par.: *Nunc admonendi sumus, ne facile homines
ad litigandum procederent, iam an-*

*tiquo iure placuisse temeritatem liti-
gandi uariis incommodis, modo pecuniaria poena, modo iurisiurandi
religione, coercendam esse :* eaque
praetor *quoque tuetur. ideo ex
parte eius cum quo agitur* aduersus,
etc.

[2] Comp. § 9.
[3] Comp. iii, 127.
[4] Comp. iii, §§ 210 f. ; iv, 9.
[5] Comp. iii, §§ 201-204.
[6] Comp. Cic. *pro Rosc. com.* iv,
10, v, 14 ; Gai. iii, 124 ; iv, 13.
[7] Comp. Paul. ii, 2, § 9 ; § 9, I.
de act. (iv, 6) ; tit. D. *de const. pec.*
(xiii, 5).

§ 172. Comp. § 1, tit. I. afd. ; fr. 44,
§ 4, D. *fam. ercisc.* (x, 2).
    [1] So L. and all eds. ; the MS. has
coniungatur.

praetor iusiurandum exigere 'non calumniae causa infitias
ire :'[2] unde *quamuis*[3] heredes uel qui heredum loco habentur
simplotenus[4] obligati sint, item feminis pupillisque *eximatur*
173 *periculum* sponsionis, iubet tamen eos iurare.   Statim
autem ab initio pluris quam simpli actio est ueluti furti
manifesti quadrupli, nec manifesti dupli, concepti et oblati
tripli : nam ex his causis et aliis quibusdam, siue quis neget
siue fateatur, pluris quam simpli est actio.

174   Actoris quoque calumnia [1] coercetur modo calumniae iudicio
175 modo contrario, modo iureiurando, modo restipulatione.   Et
quidem calumniae iudicium aduersus omnes actiones locum
habet, et est decimae partis *rei*,[1] *sed*[2] aduersus adsertorem

---

praetor allows an oath to be exacted from him 'that he is
not vexatiously denying his liability.'   Accordingly, although
heirs and those in the position of heirs are not held liable for
more than single payment, and women and pupils are exempt
from the risk of a sponsion, still the praetor requires all of
173 them to give their oath [of calumny].   Of actions that
from the first are for more than single payment, we have the
action of manifest theft for fourfold, that of non-manifest
theft for twofold, and those for receipt of stolen property and
introduction of it into another person's premises, which are
for threefold ; in these and in some other cases the action is
for more than single payment, no matter whether the defender
deny his liability or admit it.

174   Vexatious conduct on the part of a pursuer is likewise
repressed, sometimes by a *iudicium calumniae*, sometimes by
a *iudicium contrarium*, sometimes by his oath, sometimes by
175 restipulation.   There is room for a *calumniae iudicium* [*i.e.*
an instruction to the judge, in the event of the defender's
acquittal, to inquire whether the proceedings of the pursuer
were groundless and vexatious] in all actions ; it justifies
condemnation in a sum equal to one-tenth of the value of the
cause of action, but as against an *adsertor libertatis* one-third.

---

[2] Comp. Paul. i, 5, § 1.
[3] The ms. has *qu* ; Hu. *quia*.
[4] So Stud. ; Bk. suggests *iure
ciuili non amplius;* K. u. S. (footnote), *nisi ex suo facto;* Hu. *aliis
quoque poenis obligati [non] sunt.*
§ 173.   § 1, tit. I. afd. Comp. Gai. iii,
§§ 189-191.
§ 174.   Comp. § 1, tit. I. afd. Gai. deals

with the *calumniae iudicium* in §§
175-179 ; the *contrarium iudicium*
in §§ 177-179 ; the restipulation in
§ 180.
[1] See Paul. i, 5, § 1.
§ 175.   [1] Comp. § 163.
[2] K. u. S. read *praeterquam quod*,
adding *est* after *partis;* Hu. has *tantum*, with same addition.

176 tertiae partis.[3]   Liberum est autem ei cum quo agitur aut
    calumniae iudicium opponere aut iusiurandum exigere non
177 calumniae causa agere.   Contrarium autem iudicium ex
    certis causis constituitur, ueluti si iniuriarum agatur,[1] et si
    cum muliere eo nomine agatur quod dicatur uentris nomine
    in possessionem missa dolo malo ad alium possessionem
    transtulisse,[2] et si quis eo nomine agat quod dicat se a prae-
    tore in possessionem missum ab *aliquo*[3] admissum non esse :[4]
    sed aduersus iniuriarum quidem actionem decimae partis
178 datur, aduersus uero duas istas quintae.   Seuerior autem
    coercitio est per contrarium iudicium : nam calumniae iudicio
    x. partis nemo damnatur nisi qui intellegit non recte se agere,
    sed uexandi aduersarii gratia actionem instituit, potiusque ex
    iudicis errore uel iniquitate uictoriam sperat quam ex causa
    ueritatis ; calumnia enim in adfectu est, sicut furti crimen :
    contrario uero iudicio omni modo damnatur actor si causam

---

176 It is for the defender to elect whether he will have this
    calumniae iudicium superinduced upon the action, or insist
    upon the pursuer's oath that he is not litigating vexatiously.
177 The *contrarium iudicium* [or cross-action] is competent only
    in certain cases, as when the action is an *actio iniuriarum*, or
    an action against a woman on the allegation that, having been
    put into possession of an estate to preserve it for an infant *in
    utero*, she fraudulently transferred it to another, or an action
    by any one on the allegation that, having obtained from the
    praetor a grant of possession, the defender opposed his entry :
    when it is in response to an *actio iniuriarum* it is for a tenth
    part [of the claim made therein], but when in answer to either
178 of the other two, it is for a fifth part.   The *contrarium
    iudicium* is more coercive than the *calumniae iudicium :* for
    in this last a man is never condemned in the tenth unless he
    really knew that his proceedings were unjustifiable, and was
    in fact litigating for the purpose of annoying his opponent,
    basing any hopes of success rather on the possible mistakes
    or unfairness of the judge than on the goodness of his cause ;
    for *calumnia*, vexatious litigation, like theft, depends on in-
    tention.   In the *contrarium iudicium*, on the other hand, the

---

[3] Comp. Paul. v, 33, § 7; tit. C.
Th. *de lib. causa* (iv, 18); tit. C. *de
adsert. toll.* (vii, 17).
§ 176. Comp. Paul. ii, 1, § 2.
§ 177. [1] Comp. Paul. v, 4, § 11; fr. 43,
D. *de iniur.* (xlvii, 10).

[2] Cp. tit. D. *si uentr. nom.* (xxv, 5).
[3] The ms., K. u. S., Hu., and P.
have *alio quo*.
[4] Comp. tit. D. *ne uis fiat ei q. in
poss.* (xliii, 4).
§ 178. Comp. iii, 197.

non tenuerit, licet *falsa* [1] opinione inductus crediderit se recte

179 agere.   Vtique autem ex quibus causis contrario iudicio agi
potest, etiam calumniae iudicium locum habet; sed alterutro
tantum iudicio agere permittitur: qua ratione si iusiurandum de calumnia exactum fuerit, quemadmodum calumniae
iudicium non datur, ita et contrarium dari non [1] debet.

180 Restipulationis quoque poena ex certis causis fieri solet; et
quemadmodum contrario iudicio omni modo condemnatur
actor si causam non tenuerit, nec requiritur an scierit non
recte se agere, ita etiam restipulationis poena omni modo

181 damnatur actor.[1]   — — — — restipulationis poena petitur,
ei neque calumniae iudicium opponitur neque iurisiurandi
religio iniungitur; nam contrarium iudicium in his causis
locum non habere palam est.

182   Quibusdam iudiciis damnati ignominiosi fiunt, ueluti furti,

---

pursuer, if he have failed in his suit, is invariably condemned,
even though, labouring under some misapprehension, he may

179 have believed that his proceedings were well-founded.   Of
course, in those cases in which the *contrarium iudicium* is
competent, there is room also for the *iudicium calumniae;* but
we can employ only one or other of these remedies.   Upon
the same principle, just as a *iudicium calumniae* is disallowed
where the defender has required an oath of calumny from the
pursuer, so must the *contrarium iudicium* be excluded in the

180 same circumstances.   A restipulatory penalty is also imposed in certain cases; and just as in the *contrarium iudicium*
the pursuer who has failed in proving his averments is invariably condemned, without any inquiry whether or not he knew
that he was suing improperly, so is he [when unsuccessful]
invariably mulcted in the amount of his penal restipulation.

181 *When a man sues under a restipulatory penalty,* neither can
a *iudicium calumniae* be imposed upon him, nor can he be
fettered by the sanctity of an oath : that in such a case there
can be no *iudicium contrarium* is quite clear.

182   In some actions a defender who is condemned therein is

---

[1] So M. (K. u. S. footnote) and
P.; the ms. has *alia;* G., K. u. S.,
and Hu. *aliqua.*
§ 179.   Comp. § 176.
    [1] The ms. has *non dari.*
§ 180.   Comp. §§ 13, 171.
    [1] Hu. assumes this to be the end
of the par.; K. (K. u. S. footnote)
supposes some of the words in the

illegible half line at the commencement of p. 250 of the ms. to have
belonged to it,—possibly *si sponsione
uictus est.*
§ 181.   For the illegible initial words K.
(K. u. S. footnote) suggests *a quo
autem;* Hu. supplies *sed cum ab
actore cum.*
§ 182.   Comp. § 2, tit. I. afd. The

ui bonorum raptorum, iniuriarum : item pro socio, fiduciae, tutelae, mandati, depositi : sed furti aut ui [*bonorum*] raptorum aut iniuriarum *non solum* damnati notantur ignominia sed etiam pacti, *ut in* edicto praetoris scriptum est; et recte: plurimum enim interest utrum ex delicto aliquis an ex contractu debitor sit.[1] *Item* illa parte edicti id ipsum nominatim *exprimitur* — — — — — — — nomine iudicio interuenire; *interest enim* — — —.[2]

183   In summa sciendum est eum qui — — — —[1] et eum qui uocatus est — — — — — — —.[2] *quasdam (tamen personas)*

branded with infamy; this happens, for example, in the actions for theft, robbery, or personal injury; as also in those arising out of partnership, fiduciary agreement, tutory, mandate, and deposit. In the three first, according to the praetor's edict, it is not only a defender who has actually been condemned that becomes infamous, but also one who has compromised; and very properly; for it makes a great difference whether a man's indebtedness arises from delict or from contract. In the same chapter of the edict it is expressly declared [*that a person who is infamous is in most cases dis-* [*qualified for addressing a court of law on another person's* [*behalf, for appointing a cognitor or procurator, and for him-* [*self acting in either capacity*] in judicial matters; for it is of importance [*that litigation should be conducted honourably*].

183   Finally be it observed that he [*who is moving in a litigation* [*must formally summon his adversary ; if the latter do not obey*

words of the edict referred to in the legible part of the par. are in fr. 1, D. *de his qui not. infam.* (iii, 2); from which it will be observed that infamy resulted only when the party was defending *proprio nomine.*
[1] Infamy was avoided by compromise when the debt was *ex contractu,* but not when *ex delicto.*
[2] K. u. S. suggest the following reconstruction (legible words and letters being in roman type)—*exprimitur pactum quoque ignominiosum fieri qua* prohibe*tur pro aliis* postulare, *uel procurator* dari [*uel*] procuratorem adhibere *cognitoremue, uel cognito*rio nomine iudicio interuenire. The statement here is incorrect; the reference to the infamatory result of compromise of a claim *ex delicto* is in the edict *de infamia* (fr. 1, D. *de his q. not. inf.* iii, 2); that forbidding infamous persons to

act as procurators, etc., is in the edict *de postulando* (fr. 1, § 8, D. *de post.* iii, 1). Hu. proposes—*exprimitur ut qui ignominiosus sit plerumque* prohibe*atur pro aliis* postulare, *item cognit*orem dare, procuratorem adhibere, *uel cognito*rio *aut procurat*orio nomine iudicio interuenire ; interest enim *cum honestis litigare.* This is a very reasonable reconstruction. Comp. Paul. i, 2, § 1 ; Fr. Vat. § 324; fr. 1, § 8, D. *de post.* (iii, 1).
§ 183.   Comp. §§ 46, 187; fr. 1-4, fr. 23-25, D. *de in ius uoc.* (ii, 4).
[1] Hu. proposes *experitur, in ius uocare opor*tere. K. u. S. agree as to the idea, but are unable to suggest probable words for the illegible half line.
[2] Here Hu. proposes *si non sequitur, sine auctoritate* praetoris *posse secum ducere.*

23

sine perm issu praetoris in ius uocare non licet, *ueluti parentes patronos* patronasque, liberos et parentes *patroni patronaeue ;*
184 et in eum qui aduersus ea egerit poena constituitur.   Cum autem in ius uocatus fuerit aduersarius, neque eo die *finiri potuerit* negotium, uadimonium ei faciendum *est, id est ut*
185 promittat se certo die sisti.   Fiunt autem uadimonia quibusdam ex causis pura, id est sine satisdatione, quibusdam cum satisdatione, quibusdam iureiurando, quibusdam recuperatoribus suppositis, id est ut qui non steterit is protinus a recuperatoribus in summam uadimonii condemnetur : eaque
186 singula diligenter praetoris edicto significantur.   Et siquidem iudicati depensiue agetur, tanti fit uadimonium quanti ea res erit ; si uero ex ceteris causis, quanti actor iurauerit non calumniae causa postulare sibi uadimonium promitti : nec tamen [*pluris quam partis dimidiae, nec*] pluribus quam sestertium c milibus fit uadimonium : itaque si centum milium res erit, nec iudicati depensiue agetur, non plus quam

---

[*the summons, the pursuer may bring him into court*]. There are certain persons, however, whom it is unlawful to summon without the praetor's permission, such as parents, patrons, and the children or parents of patrons ; any one contravening in
184 this respect is liable to a penalty.   When the defender has been summoned into court, but the case cannot be concluded the same day, he must give his *uadimonium, i.e.* his stipula-
185 tory undertaking to appear again on a day fixed.   In some cases *uadimonia* are pure, *i.e.* without sureties, in some sureties are necessary, in some they are coupled with an oath, while in others there is a reference to recuperators, *i.e.* the defender consents that if he fail to appear he may at once be condemned by them in the amount of his *uadimonium ;* all
186 these are carefully distinguished in the edict.   In the case of an *actio iudicati* or an *actio depensi* the *uadimonium* is of the same amount as is sued for.   In other cases it is fixed at such an amount as may be named by the pursuer, under an oath that he is not naming it vexatiously, so long as it does not [*relatively exceed one-half of the sum at stake*] nor [absolutely] a hundred thousand sesterces ; so that if the matter of dispute be worth a hundred thousand sesterces, and the action neither

---

§ 184. Comp. iii, 224 ; Varro, *de L. L.* vi, 74 (Bruns, p. 278).

§ 185. Comp. tit. D. *qui satisdare cog., uel iurato promittunt, uel suae promissioni committantur* (ii, 8).

§ 186. The words in ital. are added by Hu., and adopted by K. u. S. and P., and from the context absolutely necessary.

187 sestertium quinquaginta milium fit uadimonium.   Quas
autem personas sine permissu praetoris inpune in ius uocare
non possumus, easdem nec uadimonio inuitas obligare
possumus, praeterquam si praetor aditus permittat.

---

an *actio iudicati* nor an *actio depensi*, the *uadimonium* cannot
187 exceed fifty thousand.   But we cannot require those persons
whom we cannot summon with impunity without the praetor's
permission to become bound to us in a *uadimonium* against
their will, unless the praetor allow it on special application.

§ 187.   Comp. § 183; fr. 1-8, D. *in ius uocati* (ii, 6).

DOMITII VLPIANI

QVAE VOCANT

F R A G M E N T A

SIVE EXCERPTA EX

VLPIANI LIBRO SINGVLARI REGVLARVM.

EXCERPTA EX

DOMITII VLPIANI

LIBRO SINGVLARI REGVLARVM.

—o—

1   — — — — — — — — prohibet, exceptis quibusdam

---

1   [*A statute is either perfect, or imperfect, or short of perfect.*
[*It is perfect when it forbids something to be done, and if done*
[*rescinds it; the Aelia-Sentian law is a statute of this sort.*
[*That is imperfect which forbids a thing, yet if it be done*
[*neither rescinds it nor imposes a penalty on the contravener;*
[*such is the Cincian law, which*] prohibits [*donations beyond a*
[*specified amount*], except to certain kinsmen, yet does not

RUBRIC. In place of this rubric the MS.
has the words *INCIPIVNT TITVLI
EX CORPORE VLPIANI*, followed by
a list of the titles into which the
treatise is divided. As those titles,
however, are generally admitted not
to be Ulpian's, nor even the work
of the epitomist to whom we owe
these 'Excerpts' (see Introduction),
I have thought it expedient to
reproduce the list.

   Owing probably to a displacement
of pages in the copy of the archetype
used by the transcriber, the text of
the MS. begins with what is here
numbered as § 4, *Mores sunt tacitus
consensus populi longa consuetudine
inueteratus;* then comes the list of
titles just referred to; next §§ 5-9;
next §§ 1-3; and after them §§ 10 f.
This order was preserved in the
earliest editions, the sentence *Mores
sunt*, etc., being printed as a sort of
motto. The mistake is obvious.
It is evident that Ulpian, before
proceeding to deal with persons,
devoted a few pars. to law in general and its sources; but the commencement of what he said on the
subject is lost, and probably was

not contained in the copy from
which the Vatican MS. was transcribed. We know, however, from
fr. 10, D. *de I. et I.* (i, 1) that what
stands as the pr. and §§ 1 and 3 of the
first title of the first book of the Inst.
were from this treatise of Ulpian's.

§ 1. All eds. are agreed that the par.
must have commenced with such
words as these: *Lex aut perfecta
est aut imperfecta aut minus quam
perfecta. Perfecta lex est quae uetat
aliquid fieri, et si factum sit rescindit,
qualis est lex — — —. Imperfecta
lex est quae uetat aliquid fieri, et si
factum sit nec rescindit nec poenam
iniungit ei qui contra legem fecit,
qualis est lex Cincia, quae supra
certum modum donari* prohibet, etc.

   As Ulpian's probable illustration
of a *lex perfecta*, Cuj. suggests the
L. Aelia Sentia.

   Macrob. (in *Somn. Scip.* ii, 17)
defines a *lex imperfecta* as one *in
qua nulla deuiantibus poena sanci-
tur.* On the *L. Cincia* (of 550 | 204)
see Cic. *ad. Att.* i, 20, § 7; Tac.
Ann. xi, 5; Fr. Vat. §§ 298-313.
Another illustration of an imperfect
law is the *L. Valeria* (Liv. x, 9).

2 cognatis,[1] et si plus donatum sit non rescindit.   Minus quam perfecta lex est quae uetat aliquid fieri, et si factum sit non rescindit, sed poenam iniungit ei qui contra legem fecit; qualis est lex Furia testamentaria, quae plus quam mille assium legatum mortisue causa [1] prohibet capere, praeter exceptas personas,[2] et aduersus eum qui plus ceperit quadrupli poenam constituit.

3   Lex aut rogatur, id est fertur; aut abrogatur, id est prior lex tollitur; aut derogatur, id est pars *primae* [*legis*][1] tollitur; aut subrogatur, id est adicitur aliquid primae legi; aut obrogatur, id est mutatur aliquid ex prima lege.

4   Mores sunt tacitus consensus populi longa consuetudine inueteratus.

[*I. DE LIBERTIS.*]

5   Libertorum genera sunt tria, ciues Romani, latini Iuniani, dediticiorum numero.

---

2 nullify what is given in excess.   Short of perfect is that which forbids a thing, and if it be done does not rescind it, but imposes a penalty upon the contravener; of this class is the Furian testamentary law, which forbids all but certain excepted persons to take more than a thousand *asses* as a legacy or otherwise by reason of death, and imposes a fourfold penalty upon him who has taken a larger sum.

3   We say of a law '*rogatur*' when it is passed; '*abrogatur*,' when it is repealed; '*derogatur*,' when part of it is repealed; '*subrogatur*,' when something is added to it; '*obrogatur*,' when some of its provisions are altered.

4   By '*mores*' we mean the tacit consent of a people, become inveterate by long observance.

[*I. OF FREEDMEN.*]

5   There are three classes of freedmen,—Roman citizens, Junian latins, and those numbered among the dediticians.

---

[1] Hu. proposes as an amendment *exceptis* [*personis*] *quibusdam* [*uelut*] *cognatis*, on the ground that the exception was not confined to cognates.

§ 2. On the *L. Furia*, see xxviii, 7; Gai. ii, 225; iv, 23.
  [1] See Gai. ii, 225, note 2.
  [2] See Gai. ii, 225, note 1.

§ 3. Comp. Fest. and Paul. Diac. vv. *Rogatio, Abrogare, Derogare, Obrogare, Exrogare* (Bruns, pp. 261, 240, 250, 241); Modest. in fr. 102, D. *de V. S.* (l, 16).
  [1] So Cuj. and most eds.; the ms. has *pars prima*.

§ 4. Comp. § 9, I. *de iure naturali* (i, 2).
§ 5. Comp. Gai. i, 12.

6   Ciues Romani sunt liberti, qui legitime [*manumissi sunt,*
    [*id est aut uindicta aut*] [1] censu aut testamento, nullo iure
7   inpediente. [2]   Vindicta manumittuntur apud magistratum
    populi Romani, [1] *uelut consulem proconsulem praetoremue.* [2]
8   Censu manumittebantur olim qui lustrali censu Romae iussu
9   dominorum inter ciues Romanos censum profitebantur.   Vt
    testamento manumissi liberi sint lex duodecim tabularum
    facit, quae confirmat — ¯ — —. [1]
10 — — — — — — [1] hodie autem ipso iure liberi sunt ex
    lege Iunia, qua lege latini sunt nominati [2] inter amicos [3]
    manumissi.

---

6   Those freedmen are Roman citizens that have been manu-
    mitted formally, *i.e.* by *uindicta*, census, or testament, in the
7   absence of any legal impediment.   Manumission *uindicta*
    takes place before a magistrate of the Roman people, such
8   as a consul, proconsul, or praetor.   Those used formerly to
    be manumitted *censu* who, at the lustral census in Rome, by
    order of their owners, gave in their names for enrolment as
9   Roman citizens.   That those manumitted by testament are
    free results from the provisions of the Twelve Tables declar-
    ing the validity of *testaments.*
10 [*Latins are freedmen* de facto *in possession of freedom simply*
    [*by the pleasure of their owners.   Formerly their enjoyment of it*
    [*depended on their protection in it by the praetor*]; but now
    they are *ipso iure* free by the Junian law, wherein slaves
    manumitted *inter amicos* are spoken of as latins.

§ 6.   Comp. Gai. i, §§ 17, 44.
    [1] This addition substantially the
same with all eds.
    [2] Such as the restrictions of the
Aelia-Sentian law, referred to below,
§§ 11-15, or Fufia-Caninian law, § 24.
§ 7.   See refs. in Gai. i, 17, note 2;
also tit. D. *de man. uind.* (xl, 2);
l. 4, C. *de uind.* (vii, 1).
    [1] Here, as in xx, 16, the MS. has
praetoriani for *populi Romani.*
    [2] So Momms. (*Stadr. v. Salpensa,*
note 131); the MS. has *apud magistratum praetoremue, uelut consulem,
proconsulem.*
§ 8.   See refs. in Gai. i, 17, note 3.
§ 9.   See refs. in Gai. i, 17, note 4; also
below, §§ 20-25.
    [1] M. thinks *testamenta* sufficient;
Cuj. suggested *testamento datas
libertates;* to which Hu., following
L., adds *his uerbis 'uti legassit
suae rei, ita ius esto.'*

§ 10.   Comp. Gai. i, 22, and note; iii,
56.
    [1] Cuj. (*Observ.* xix, 30) proposed
to fill the blank thus : *Inter amicos
manumissi olim non erant ipso iure
liberi, sed uoluntate domini in libertate morabantur, et eos seruire non
permittebatur praetor.* Hu. has :
*Latini sunt liberti qui non legitime,
uelut inter amicos, nullo iure inpediente, manumissi sunt, quos olim
praetor tantum tuebatur in forma
libertatis; nam ipso iure serui mane-
bant.* M. proposes more simply :
*Latini sunt liberti qui uoluntate
domini in libertate morantur. quos
olim praetor tuebatur in possessione
libertatis,* etc.
    [2] So the MS. and the earliest eds.
L. and Bk. have *latini sunt nominatim;* Hu. *latini Iuniani nominati
sunt;* K. *latini fiunt nominatim.*
    [3] See Gai. i, 41, note.

11 Dediticiorum numero sunt qui poenae causa uincti sunt a
    domino, *quibusue stigmata*[1] scripta fuerunt, qui[*ue*] propter
    noxam torti nocentesque inuenti sunt, quiue traditi sunt ut
    ferro aut cum bestiis depugnarent, [*inue ludum*][2] uel custo-
    diam coniecti fuerunt, deinde quoquo modo manumissi sunt :
    idque lex *Aelia Sentia*[3] facit.

12 Eadem lege cautum est ut minor triginta annorum seruus
    uindicta manumissus ciuis Romanus non fiat nisi apud con-
    silium causa probata fuerit ; *ideo*[1] sine consilio manumissum
    Cassius[2] seruum manere putat. testamento uero manumissum
    perinde haberi iubet atque si domini uoluntate in libertate
13 esset ;[3] ideoque latinus fit.   Eadem lex eum dominum qui
    minor uiginti annorum est prohibet seruum manumittere

---

11 Those [freedmen] are ranked as dediticians who have been
    put in chains by their owners as a punishment, or branded, or
    put to the torture because of some offence and thereof found
    guilty, or given up to fight either with the sword or with wild
    beasts, or cast into a gladiatorial training-school or into prison,
    and have afterwards been manumitted, no matter how. All
    this is in terms of the Aelia-Sentian law.

12 By the same law it is provided that a slave under thirty
    manumitted *uindicta* shall not become a citizen unless cause
    has been proved before the council ; hence *Cassius* (?) is of
    opinion that if manumitted without the [approval of] the
    council he remains a slave. It ordains, however, that if he
    have been manumitted by testament he shall be regarded as
    in possession of freedom by the pleasure of his owner ; conse-
13 quently he becomes a latin.   The same enactment forbids
    an owner under twenty to manumit his slave without proving

§ 11. Comp. Gai. i, 13, and refs.
  [1] So Cuj., after Gai. ; the ms. has
quib. uestigia. Branding seems to
have been resorted to when the slave
was a deserter (*fugitiuus*) ; see Quintil. *Inst. Orat.* vii, 4, § 14.
  [2] Added from Gai.
  [3] The ms. here as elsewhere has
L. Ascia. See Gai. i, 13, note 1.
§ 12. Comp. Gai. i, §§ 13, 22.
  [1] So the ms. ; Bk. and Vahl., following L., have *id est* ; Hu. *proinde*
(*pinde*).
  [2] The ms. has *Caesaris.* Hence
various suggestions,—*censuue, lex
Aelia Sentia, Cassius, Caelius Sabinus, eius cetatis,* etc. Bk. and
Vahl. prefer *L. Aelia Sentia,* and K.

Caesaris. The phrase *lex putat* is
certainly very unusual, although
Non. Marcell. (v. *Iurgium,* Bruns,
p. 286) attributes it to Cicero.
Caesaris seruum manere is hardly
justifiable when the question is of
manumissicn of a slave belonging
not to the emperor but to a private
party. Therefore I have given the
preference to the Cassius of Puchta ;
although Hollweg's *Caelius Sabinus*
(*Cael. Sabis.*) is not improbable.
The *L. Aelia Sentia* was passed in
757 | 4 (Gai. i, 13, note 1), and
Cassius (Gai. iii, 71, note) was con-
sul in 783 | 30.
  [3] Comp. above, § 10.
§ 13. Comp. Gai. i, §§ 38, 41.

13a praeterquam si causam apud consilium probauerit.   In
consilio autem adhibentur Romae[1] quinque senatores et quinque equites Romani, in prouinciis uiginti reciperatores ciues
14 Romani.   Ab eo domino qui soluendo non est seruus testamento liber esse iussus et heres institutus, et si minor sit
triginta annis uel in ea causa sit ut dediticius fieri debeat,
ciuis Romanus et heres fit; si tamen alius ex eo testamento
nemo heres sit. quod si duo pluresue liberi heredesque esse
iussi sint, primo loco scriptus liber et heres fit; quod et ipsum
15 lex *Aelia Sentia* facit.   Eadem lex in fraudem creditoris et
patroni manumittere prohibet.
16   Qui tantum in bonis, non etiam ex iure[1] Quiritium seruum
habet, manumittendo latinum facit.   in bonis tantum alicuius
seruus est uelut hoc modo, si ciuis Romanus a ciue Romano[2]
seruum emerit, isque traditus ei sit, neque tamen mancipatus
ei neque in iure cessus neque ab ipso anno possessus sit : nam

---

13a cause before the council.   This council consists in Rome of
five senators and as many knights, and in the provinces of
14 twenty recuperators, Roman citizens.   A slave ordered to
be free and instituted heir in the testament of his insolvent owner becomes a Roman citizen and heir under the will,
even though he be under thirty or so circumstanced that
he ought [otherwise] to be a deditician, provided always that
there is no other testamentary heir.   If two or more be
ordered to be free and heirs, the one first mentioned becomes
15 free and heir ; this too the Aelia-Sentian law enacts.   The
same statute prohibits manumission in fraud of a creditor or
patron.
16   He who holds a slave in bonitarian ownership only, and not
also in quiritarian right, by manumitting him makes him a
latin.   And a slave is *in bonis* only when, for example, a Roman
citizen buys him from another citizen, and delivery follows,
but the slave is neither mancipated, nor ceded in court, nor
possessed by the purchaser for a year ; for until one or other

---

§ 13a. Comp. Gai. i, 20.
    [1] The ms. has *Romani*.
§ 14. Comp. Gai. i, 21, and note; ii,
    154.
§ 15. Comp. Gai. i, §§ 37, 47.
§ 16. Comp. Gai. i, §§ 17, 35. Also
    below, xix, §§ 4, 7, 20; Gai. ii, §§
    41, 204 ; iii, 80.
    [1] Here, as in many other places,

the ms. has *ex ius* instead of *ex iure*.
    [2] If the acquisition was from a
peregrin, then, even though the
thing was *res mancipi* by the *ius
ciuile*, yet in his hands it was *res
nec mancipi*, and the full property
passed by tradition according to the
rules of the *ius gentium*; comp. Fr.
Vat. § 47.

quamdiu horum quid fiat,³ is seruus in bonis quidem empto-
17 ris est, ex iure¹ Quiritium autem uenditoris est.   Mulier
quae in tutela est, item pupillus et pupilla, manumittere non
18 possunt.   Communem seruum unus ex dominis manumittendo partem suam amittit, eaque adcrescit socio; maxime si
eo modo manumiserit quo, si proprium haberet, ciuem Romanum facturus esset.   nam si inter amicos eum manumiserit,
19 plerisque placet eum nihil egisse.   Seruus in quo alterius
est ususfructus, alterius proprietas, a proprietatis domino
manumissus liber non fit, sed seruus sine domino est.
20   Post mortem heredis aut ante institutionem heredis testamento libertas dari non potest, excepto testamento militis.
21 Inter medias heredum institutiones libertas data utrisque
adeuntibus non ualet : solo autem priore adeunte iure
antiquo ualet.   sed post legem Papiam Poppaeam,¹ quae

---

of these takes place, the slave, though *in bonis* of the purchaser, is still in the quiritarian ownership of the seller.
17 A woman who is in tutelage cannot manumit [without her
tutor's *auctoritas*]; neither can a pupil, whether male or
18 female.   One of two joint-owners manumitting a common
slave loses his share, which accrues to his partner.   This is
so, at any rate, if the manumission have been in a form
which, had he been sole owner, would have made the slave a
citizen : for if it have been only *inter amicos*, the general
19 opinion is that it is of no effect.   Manumission by the
owner of a slave usufructed by a third party does not make
him free; he becomes a slave without an owner.
20   Freedom cannot be given by testament, unless it be that of
a soldier, [when it is] either [to take effect] after the heir's
21 death or [given] prior to his institution.   Nor is such a gift
valid if introduced between two institutions, and both the heirs
enter; but it was, according to the old rule, if the sole intrant
was the heir first instituted.   Since the Papia-Poppaean law,

---

³ Before *fiat* many eds. insert *non.*
But *quamdiu* in the sense of *donec*
is by no means unusual with Ulpian;
see fr. 15, D. *quib. mod. ususfr.
amitt.* (vii, 4), fr. 1, D. *de penu.
leg.* (xxxiii, 9).

§ 17. Comp. Gai. i, §§ 40, 192; below,
xi, 27. M. thinks the words *nisi
tutore auctore (ntā)* should be added
after *possunt.*

§ 18. Comp. Paul. iv, 12, §§ 1, 5; § 4,
I. *de donat.* (ii, 7).

§ 19. Comp. Fr. Dos. § 13; Vlp. in
fr. 9, § 20, D. *de her. inst.* (xxviii,
5); Iustin. in l. 1, pr. C. *commun.
de man.* (vii, 15). M. suggests the
addition of such words as *donec
manet ususfructus, quo finito latinus
efficitur.*

§ 20. Comp. xxiv, §§ 15, 16; Gai. ii,
§§ 230, 233; §§ 34, 35, I. *de legat.*
(ii, 20).

§ 21. Comp. Gai. ii, §§ 206-208, 286.
¹ See Gai. i, 145, note 1.

partem non adeuntis caducam facit, si quidem primus heres
uel [*ius liberorum uel*]² ius antiquum³ habeat, ualere eam
posse placuit; quod si non habeat, non ualere constat, quod
loco non adeuntis legatarii patres heredes fiunt.⁴ sunt tamen
22 qui et hoc casu ualere eam⁵ posse dicunt.⁶   Qui testamento
liber esse iussus est, mox *quam uel*¹ unus ex heredibus adierit
23 hereditatem liber fit.   Iusta libertas testamento potest dari
his seruis qui testamenti faciendi et mortis tempore ex iure
Quiritium testatoris fuerunt.
24   Lex Fufia Caninia iubet testamento ex tribus seruis non
plures quam duos manumitti, et usque ad decem dimidiam
partem manumittere concedit ; a decem usque ad triginta
tertiam partem, ut tamen adhuc quinque manumittere liceat

---

which makes the share of an heir who does not enter caducous,
it is held that the gift of freedom will still be valid if the heir
first instituted [be the intrant and] have *either the privilege
of children* or the old right of accretion ; if he have not, it is
held to be invalid, for the legatees who are fathers come in
place of the non-entering heir. There are some, however, who
maintain that even in this case the gift of freedom will be
22 valid.   A slave whom a testament orders to be free becomes
free the moment that an heir, though only one of several, has
23 entered.   Freedom such as the *ius ciuile* recognises can be
given by testament [only] to those slaves who belonged to the
testator on quiritarian title both at the date of his testament
and the time of his death.
24   The Fufia-Caninian law ordains that of three slaves no more
than two shall be enfranchised by testament, and up to ten
allows manumission of half the actual number ; from ten to
thirty a third, but so that at least five may be manumitted as

² So L., Bk., Hu., and K. ; Schult. has *liberos uel ;* M. proposes *ius patris uel*, which is adopted by Vahl.
³ The *ius antiquum* was the right of accretion (*ius adcrescendi*) that existed before the Papia-Poppaean caduciary legislation, and which was allowed to continue in favour of certain near kinsmen of the testator ; see below, tit. xviii, and notes.
⁴ Comp. Gai. ii, 207.
⁵ So Hu. and K. The ms. has *eius eā ;* hence Hugo *iure eam ;* L., Bk., and Vahl., *eius causam ;* and M. *e testamento eam.*

⁶ Comp. xvii, 8.
§ 22. Comp. fr. 23, § 1, fr. 25, D. *de manum. test.* (xl, 4). The assumption is that the enfranchisement stood in the testament posterior to all the institutions.
¹ The ms. has *quamuis*, which Bk. and Vahl. retain ; *quam uel* is the suggestion of Marezoll, adopted by Hu. and K.
§ 23. Comp. Gai. ii, 267. If the slave was only *in bonis* of the testator, he became a latin ; see xxii, 8.
§ 24. Comp. Gai. i, §§ 42-45. In the ms. the law is called *L. Fusia Caninia.*

aeque ut ex priori numero; a triginta usque ad centum quartam partem, aeque ut decem ex superiori numero liberari
possint; a centum usque ad quingentos partem quintam,
similiter ut ex antecedenti numero uiginti quinque possint
fieri liberi. et denique praecipit ne plures omnino quam
25 centum ex cuiusquam testamento liberi fiant.   Eadem lex
cauet ut libertates seruis testamento nominatim dentur.

[II. DE STATV LIBERO VEL STATV LIBERIS.]

1 Qui sub condicione testamento liber esse iussus est statu
2 liber appellatur.   Statu liber quamdiu pendet condicio
3 seruus heredis [est].   Statu liber seu alienetur ab herede
siue *usu capiatur*[1] ab aliquo, libertatis condicionem secum
4 trahit.   Sub hac condicione liber esse iussus : SI DECEM
MILIA HEREDI DEDERIT, etsi ab herede abalienatus sit, emptori
dando pecuniam ad libertatem peruveniet; idque lex duodecim
5 tabularum iubet.   Si per heredem factum sit quominus

---

in the previous case; from thirty to a hundred a fourth, but so
that at least ten may be freed as under a lower number; from
a hundred to five hundred a fifth, it being in any case competent to enfranchise the twenty-five enfranchisable within
the lower numbers. And it adds finally that not more than a
hundred shall under any circumstances become free under a
25 testament.   The same enactment requires that testamentary
gifts of freedom shall be conferred on slaves by name.

[II. OF STATV LIBERI.]

1 He goes by the name of *statu liber* who in a testament is
2 ordered to be free under some condition.   So long as
the condition is pendent he remains a slave of the heir's.
3 Whether he be alienated by the heir or usucapted by a third
4 party, he still carries with him his conditional liberty.   A
slave ordered to be free on condition of his paying ten thousand sesterces to the heir, if he be alienated by the latter,
acquires his liberty on paying the money to his purchaser; so
5 it is ordained by the law of the Twelve Tables.   If by any

---

§ 25. Comp. Gai. i, 45a; ii, 239.

TIT. II, §§ 1, 2. Comp. Fest. v. *Statu*
    liber (Bruns, p. 268); Gai. ii, 200;
    fr. 1, pr., fr. 3, pr. D. *de statulib.*
    (xl, 7).
§ 3. Cp. fr. 2, pr. D. *de statulib.* (xl, 7).

[1] So Cuj. and all eds. ; the MS.
    has *suscipiatur*.
§ 4. Cp. fr. 6, §§ 3, 7, D. *de statu.* (xl, 7).
§ 5. Comp. Fest. as in note to §§ 1, 2;
    fr. 3, §§ 1, 11, D. *de statulib.* (xl, 7);
    fr. 24, D. *de cond. et dem.* (xxxv,
    1); fr. 161, D. *de R. I.* (l, 17).

statu liber condicioni pareat, proinde fit liber atque si condicio
6 expleta fuisset.   Extraneo pecuniam dare iussus et liber
esse, si paratus sit dare, et is cui iussus est dare aut nolit
accipere aut antequam acceperit moriatur, proinde fit liber ac
si pecuniam dedisset.
7   Libertas et directo potest dari hoc modo : LIBER ESTO, LIBER
SIT, LIBERVM ESSE IVBEO, et per fideicommissum, ut puta :
ROGO, FIDEI COMMITTO HEREDIS MEI, VT STICHVM [1] SERVVM
8 MANVMITTAT.   Is qui directo liber esse iussus est, orcinus
fit libertus ; is autem cui per fideicommissum data est libertas,
9 non testatoris sed manumissoris fit libertus.   Cuius fidei
committi potest ad rem aliquam praestandam, eiusdem etiam
10 libertas fidei committi potest.   Per fideicommissum libertas
dari potest tam proprio seruo testatoris quam heredis aut
11 legatarii uel cuiuslibet extranei seruo.   Alieno seruo per
fideicommissum data libertate, si dominus eum iusto pretio
non uendat, extinguitur libertas, quoniam nec pretii conpu-

---

act of the heir's a *statu liber* is prevented complying with the
condition, he becomes free, just as if it had been fulfilled.
6 If a slave ordered to pay money to a stranger as the condition of his freedom be ready to pay it, but the person to whom
he is desired to pay it either refuse to accept it or die before
doing so, he thereupon becomes free, exactly as if he had
paid.
7   Freedom may be given [by testament] either directly thus :
'Be free,' 'Let him be free,' or 'I order him to be free ;' or
by *fideicommissum* thus : 'I request,' 'I entrust to my heir's
8 good faith that he manumit the slave Stichus.'   A slave
who has a direct gift of freedom becomes a *libertus orcinus*
[*i.e.* whose patron is in the nether world] ; but he to whom
freedom is given fideicommissarily is a freedman not of the
9 testator's but of the manumitter's.   Any person to whose
good faith it can be committed to prestate a thing may also
have it committed to his good faith to confer freedom.
10 Liberty can be given by *fideicommissum* either to the testator's
own slave, to one belonging to the heir or a legatee, or to one
11 belonging to any third party.   When given to the slave of
a third party, if the latter will not sell him for a fair price, the
gift of liberty is extinguished, because it is impossible to fix

---

§ 6. Comp. fr. 3, § 10, fr. 20, § 3, fr.
   28, pr. D. *de statulib.* (xl, 7).
§§ 7, 8.   Comp. xxv, §§ 2, 18 ; Gai. ii,
   §§ 263, 266, 267.

[1] The MS. has *iste cum.*
§§ 10, 11. Comp. Gai. ii, §§ 264, 265,
   272.

12 tatio pro libertate fieri potest.   Libertas sicut dari ita et
adimi tam testamento quam codicillis testamento confirmatis
potest; ut tamen eodem modo adimatur quo et data est.

[III. DE LATINIS.]

1   Latini ius Quiritium consequuntur his modis : beneficio
principali, liberis, iteratione, militia, naue, aedificio, pistrino;
praeterea ex senatusconsulto *ingenua* quae sit ter enixa.
2 Beneficio principali latinus ciuitatem Romanam accipit si ab
3 imperatore ius Quiritium impetrauerit.   Liberis ius Quiritium consequitur latinus qui minor triginta annorum manumissionis tempore fuit. nam lege Iunia cautum est ut si

---

12 a money equivalent in lieu of freedom.   As freedom can be
conferred, so also can it be adeemed either by testament or
by codicil confirmed by testament; only it must be adeemed
in the same way in which it was given.

[III. OF LATINS.]

1   Latins acquire the *ius Quiritium* in these ways; by imperial grant, by children, by iteration, by service in the night
watch, by ship-trading, by house-building, by flour-milling: so
also, under the senatusconsult, does a *free-born latin* woman
2 who has thrice given birth to children.   A latin acquires
Roman citizenship by imperial grant if he have obtained the
3 *ius Quiritium* from the emperor on his own petition.   By
children a latin who was under thirty years old at the
time of his manumission acquires the *ius Quiritium*.   For it is

---

§ 12. Comp. **xxiv**, 29, and note 1; fr.
  50, D. *de fideic. lib.* (xl, 5); fr. 14,
  pr. D. *de legat. II.* (xxxi).

TIT. III, § 1. Comp. Gai. i, §§ 28-35.
  Acquisition of citizenship *aedificio*
  and *pistrino*, not further referred to
  by Vlp., are explained by Gai. in §§
  33, 34. As regards a woman *ter
  enixa*, the MS. has *uulgo quae sit ter
  enixa*. Most eds. retain the *uulgo*;
  one or two substitute *mulier*; and
  Sav. suggested *Volusiano*, a name
  he devised for the Sct. immediately
  before alluded to. Nowhere is there
  any corroboration of the *uulgo*; and
  it is almost incredible that the law
  could thus have rewarded prostitu-

tion. In Paul. iv, 9, § 8, we read—
*Latina ingenua, ius Quiritium con-
secuta si ter peperit, ad legitimam
filii hereditatem admittitur; non est
enim manumissa.* Not a hint of
such a thing as illegitimacy; the
whole stress is on the *ingenua*; according to him it was a woman that
was a latin by birth, not by manumission, that became a citizen on
her third accouchement,—for a
triple birth at one confinement did
not answer the purpose (Paul. iv, 9,
§ 2). Therefore for the *uulgo* of
the MS. I have substituted *ingenua*
§ 2. Comp. Gai. i, 34a; iii, 72.
§ 3. Comp. Gai. i, §§ 29-32.

ciuem Romanam uel latinam uxorem duxerit, testatione in-
terposita quod liberorum quaerendorum causa uxorem duxerit,
postea filio filiaue nato nataue et anniculo facto, possit apud
praetorem uel praesidem prouinciae causam probare et fieri
ciuis Romanus, tam ipse quam filius filiaue eius et uxor,
scilicet si et ipsa latina sit; nam si uxor ciuis Romana sit,
partus quoque ciuis Romanus est ex senatusconsulto quod
4 auctore *diuo Hadriano* factum est.   Iteratione fit ciuis
Romanus qui, post latinitatem quam acceperat maior triginta
annorum, iterum iuste manumissus est ab eo cuius ex iure
Quiritium seruus fuit. sed huic concessum est ex senatus-
5 consulto etiam liberis ius Quiritium consequi.[1]   Militia ius
Quiritium accipit latinus [*si*] inter uigiles Romae sex annis
militauerit, ex lege Visellia. praeterea ex senatusconsulto
concessum est ei ut si triennio inter uigiles militauerit ius
6 Quiritium consequatur.   Naue latinus ciuitatem Romanam
accipit si non minorem quam decem milium modiorum nauem
fabricauerit et Romam sex annis frumentum portauerit, ex
edicto diui Claudi.

---

provided by the Junian law that if he have taken to wife
either a Roman citizen or a latin, declaring before witnesses
that he was marrying in order that he might get children,
he may, after the birth of a son or daughter, and when it
has completed its first year, show cause before the praetor or
provincial governor, and thus not only himself become a
Roman citizen, but also his child and his wife,—these, of
course, only if the wife too be a latin; for if she be a Roman
citizen, then, in terms of Hadrian's senatusconsult, her
4 child is born a citizen.   By iteration he becomes a Roman
citizen who, having been made a latin after he had passed
the age of thirty, is anew formally manumitted by the person
who had the quiritarian right in him when a slave.   But by
senatusconsult it is allowed even to such a latin to acquire
5 citizenship by children.   A latin acquires the *ius Quiritium*
by military service, under the Visellian law, when he has
done duty in Rome for six years in the night watch.   A later
senatusconsult concedes it to him on three years' service.
6 By an edict of the late emperor Claudius', a latin acquires
citizenship *naue* who has built a ship capable of carrying not
less than 10,000 pecks, and has imported corn in it to Rome
for six years.

§ 4.   Comp. Gai. i, 35.   § 5.   Comp. Gai. i, 32*b*.
      [1] This Sct. referred to by Gai. i, 31.   § 6.   Comp. Gai. i, 32*c*.
24

[IIII. DE HIS QVI SVI IVRIS SVNT.]

1 Sui iuris sunt familiarum suarum principes, id est pater familiae itemque mater familiae.

2 Qui matre quidem [certa],[1] patre autem incerto nati sunt, spurii appellantur.

[V. DE HIS QVI IN POTESTATE SVNT.]

1 In potestate sunt liberi parentum ex iusto matrimonio nati.

2 Iustum matrimonium est si inter eos qui nuptias contrahunt conubium sit, et tam masculus pubes quam femina potens sit, et utrique consentiant si sui iuris sunt, aut etiam parentes

3 eorum si in potestate sunt.   Conubium est uxoris iure

[IV. OF PERSONS SVI IVRIS.]

1 Those are *sui iuris* who are the heads of their own families, —the *paterfamilias* that is to say, and the *materfamilias*.

2 Children of a known mother but unknown father are called spurious.

[V. OF PERSONS IN POTESTATE.]

1 Children who are the issue of a marriage approved by the *ius ciuile* are in the *potestas* of their parents.

2 A marriage is *iustum* [*i.e.* approved by the *ius ciuile*] when there is *conubium* between the contracting parties, when the man has reached puberty and the woman become marriageable, and when both of them if *sui iuris*, or their parents if

3 they be *in potestate*, give their consent.   *Conubium* is capa-

TIT. IV, § 1.   Comp. Vlp. in fr. 195, § 2, D. *de V. S.* (l, 16).   *Paterfamilias* did not necessarily involve the idea of paternity; *materfamilias*, as used in the text, never involved that of maternity.   That man was *paterfamilias* who was not subject to any ascendant, either because none survived or because he had been emancipated; he needed not to have wife or children, and might himself be a mere infant.   So with a woman; she did not require to be a wife, nor yet the mother of children; she might be wife and mother, and yet herself be *filiafamilias*; if married, but not *in manu*, she was not a member of her husband's family, and her children were never members of hers; if independent, she was *familiae suae et caput et finis.*

§ 2.   Comp. v, 7, and refs.
  [1] Added by all eds.

TIT. V, § 1.   Comp. Gai. i, 55, and note 1.
§ 2.   Comp. Gai. i, §§ 56 f.
§ 3.   Comp. Serv. *in Aen.* i, 73.   The definition in the text is unsatisfactory, for it confines the idea to the man.   Like *commercium* (xix, 5, note), the word might be employed either abstractly, concretely, or relatively.   Abstractly, a person was said to have *conubium* who was qualified to enter into a *matrimonium iuris ciuilis* in the absence of other impediments; in this sense every Roman citizen had it, although he might not have it in the concrete, as, for example, when he was a child of tender years and too

4 ducendae facultas.   Conubium habent ciues Romani cum
  cuibus Romanis; cum latinis autem et peregrinis ita si con-
5 cessum sit.   Cum seruis nullum est conubium.   [6] Inter
6 parentes et liberos infinite[1] cuiuscumque gradus [*sint*] conubium non est. inter cognatos autem ex transuerso gradu
  olim quidem usque ad quartum gradum[2] matrimonia contrahi
  non poterant : nunc autem etiam ex tertio gradu[2] licet uxorem ducere, sed tantum fratris filiam, non etiam sororis filiam
  aut amitam uel materteram, quamuis eodem gradu sint. *eam*
  quae[3] nouerca uel priuigna uel nurus uel socrus nostra fuit,
7 [*uxorem*][4] ducere non possumus.   Si quis eam quam non

---

4 city for marrying a wife according to law.   Roman citizens
  have it with Roman citizens; with latins and peregrins only
5 when these have had it specially conceded to them.   With
6 slaves there is no *conubium.*   Nor is there *conubium* between ascendants and descendants, however distant the degree
  of relationship.   Formerly marriage could not be contracted
  between persons related collaterally as far as the fourth degree.
  Now, however, a man may take as his wife a woman related
  to him even in the third degree; but only his brother's
  daughter,—not his sister's nor yet his father's or mother's
  sister, although they are in the same degree.   Nor can we
  marry her who has been our step-mother, step-daughter,
7 daughter-in-law, or mother-in-law.   If a man marry a woman

young to marry. But though a citizen had *conubium* in the abstract, yet as a rule he had it not relatively with a Junian latin, say, or a peregrin (§ 4), for these last did not possess it in the abstract. And even though both parties had it in the abstract, they might not have it relatively and *inter se ;* as when marriage between them was excluded on account of propinquity or affinity (§ 6). In the sense therefore in which the word is used in the text it would have been better defined as right of intermarriage.

§ 4.   Comp. Gai. i, 56.

§ 5.   Hu. in his edition of Gai. introduces a similar statement in a par. which he numbers i, 57a. Comp. Paul. ii, 19, § 6.

§ 6.   Reproduced in the *Collat.* vi, 2, §§ 1-3, where they are attributed to ' *Vlpianus, libro regularum singulari, sub titulo de nuptiis.*' Comp. Gai. i, §§ 59-63.

[1] Bk. regards this word as a gloss.

[2] The degree of relationship between two individuals was determined by counting upwards from the first to the common ancestor and down again to the second, each generation each way marking a degree. Thus first cousins were related in the fourth degree, each being removed two generations or degrees from their grandfather as common ancestor. By the same mode of calculation uncle and niece were related in the third degree. See pr. § 7, I. *de grad. cogn.* (iii, 6).

[3] This is the reading of the *Collat.* ; the ms. has *eademque uxore.*

[4] From the *Collat.* ; omitted in the ms., or erroneously imported into the preceding line, as mentioned in last note.

§ 7.   Comp. iv, 2; *Collat.* vi, 2, § 4; Gai. i, 64.

licet uxorem duxerit, incestum matrimonium contrahit :
ideoque liberi in potestate eius non fiunt, sed quasi uulgo[1]
concepti spurii sunt.

8 Conubio interueniente liberi semper patrem sequuntur :
non interueniente conubio matris condicioni accedunt, excepto eo qui ex peregrino et ciue Romana peregrinus nascitur,[1]
quoniam lex Minicia[2] ex alterutro peregrino natum dete-

9 rioris parentis condicionem sequi iubet. Ex ciue Romano
et latina latinus nascitur, et ex libero et ancilla seruus ;
quoniam, cum his casibus conubia non sint, partus sequitur

10 matrem. In his qui iure contracto matrimonio nascuntur
conceptionis *tempus spectatur* :[1] in his autem qui non legitime
concipiuntur, editionis. ueluti si ancilla conceperit, deinde
manumissa pariat, liberum parit ; nam quoniam non legitime
concepit, cum editionis tempore libera sit, partus quoque liber
est.

----

whom it is not lawful for him to marry, his marriage is incestuous ; his children therefore are not in his *potestas*, but are
spurious, as if conceived in promiscuous intercourse.

8 If there be *conubium* between the parents, the children
always follow the father. In the absence of *conubium* they
follow the condition of the mother, except that the issue of a
peregrin father and Roman citizen mother is by birth a peregrin ; for the Minician law ordains that a child born of
parents of whom either is a peregrin shall take his status

9 from the inferior one. The child of a Roman citizen father
and a latin mother is a latin, and the child of a free man and
a slave woman is a slave ; for, as in these cases there is no
conubium between the parents, the child follows its mother's

10 condition. In the case of the issue of a marriage contracted according to law, it is the date of conception that is
referred to [in determining their status], but when they have
been conceived illegitimately it is the time of their birth.
Consequently if a slave have conceived, but be manumitted
before her confinement, it is to a freeman that she gives birth ;
for although she conceived illegitimately, yet as she was free
at the time of her delivery, her child also is free.

----

[1] See Gai. i, 64, note 2.

§ 8. Comp. Gai. i §§ 78, 67.
  [1] As regards the issue of a latin
father and Roman mother, see
above, iii, 3.
  [2] *Mensia* in the MS.; see Gai. i,
78, note.

§ 9. Comp. Gai. i, §§ 79, 82.
§ 10. Comp. Gai. i, §§ 89-92.
  [1] So most eds.; the MS. has *tempore expectatur;* Bk. and Vahl.
tempore disceptatur.

[*VI. DE DOTIBVS.*]

1   Dos aut datur, aut dicitur, aut promittitur.   [2] Dotem
2   dicere potest mulier quae nuptura est, et debitor mulieris
si iussu eius dicat; *item*[1] parens mulieris uirilis sexus per
uirilem sexum cognatione iunctus, uelut pater auus paternus.
dare, promittere dotem omnes possunt.
3   Dos aut profecticia dicitur, id est quam pater mulieris dedit :
aut aduenticia, id est ea quae a quouis alio data est.
4   Mortua in matrimonio muliere dos a patre profecta ad
patrem reuertitur, quintis in singulos liberos in infinitum
relictis penes uirum.   quod si pater non sit, apud maritum
5   remanet.   Aduenticia autem dos semper penes maritum
remanet, praeterquam si is qui dedit ut sibi redderetur stipulatus *fuerit ;* quae dos specialiter recepticia dicitur.

[*VI. OF DOWRIES.*]

1   A dowry is either given, or specified, or promised.   [2] It
2   may be specified by the woman about to marry, or any debtor
of hers doing so on her instructions; as also by any male
ascendant of hers related to her through males, such as her
father or paternal grandfather.   Any person whatever can
give or promise it.
3   A dowry is either profecticious, that is, given by the
woman's father, or adventicious, given by some other person.
4   If a woman die during the subsistence of her marriage the
dowry advanced by her father reverts to him, a fifth being
retained by the husband for each of the children until exhausted.   If the father be dead the whole remains with the
5   husband.   But an adventicious dowry always remains with
the husband, unless the person who gave it have expressly
stipulated that it shall be returned to him; such a dowry is
called specifically recepticious.

TIT. VI, §§ 1, 2.   On *dotis dictio,* see Gai.
iii, 96, note.   *Dotem dare* was to
constitute a dowry by instant transfer to the husband; *promittere* to
constitute it by stipulatory promise.
In the later law it might be promised informally by what was called
nuda pollicitatio ; see l. 6, C. *de
dot. prom. et nuda pollicit.* (v, 11).
   [1] The MS. has *institutus.*
§ 3.   Comp. Vlp. in fr. 5, D. *de iure dot.*
(xxiii, 3).   In § 11 of that fr. Vlp.
observes — *non ius potestatis sed
parentis nomen dotem profecticiam*

facit ; therefore a dowry for an
emancipated daughter was as much
profecticia as one for a *filiafamilias,*
if given by the woman's father as a
parental duty ; if, however, he was
indebted to his daughter, and gave
it as her debtor and by her desire,
it was *aduenticia.*
§ 4.   Comp. Paul. in Fr. Vat. § 108.
§ 5.   Comp. below, xvi, 4, note 2 ;
Iust. in l. 1, § 13, C. *de rei ux. act.*
(v, 13).   On *dos recepticia,* see Gai.
in fr. 31, § 2, D. *de mort. c. don.*
(xxxix, 6).

6 Diuortio facto, si quidem sui iuris sit mulier, ipsa habet
actionem, id est dotis repetitionem; quodsi in potestate patris
sit, pater adiuncta filiae persona habet actionem *rei uxoriae ;* [1]
7 nec interest aduenticia sit dos an profecticia.   Post diuortium defuncta muliere heredi eius actio non aliter datur quam
si moram in dote mulieri reddenda maritus fecerit.
8 Dos si pondere numero mensura contineatur, annua bima
trima die redditur, nisi si ut praesens reddatur conuenerit.
reliquae dotes statim redduntur.
9 Retentiones ex dote fiunt [*aut propter liberos*],[1] aut propter
mores, aut propter inpensas, aut propter res donatas, aut
10 propter res amotas.   Propter liberos retentio fit si culpa
mulieris aut patris cuius in potestate est diuortium factum

---

6 On divorce, if the woman be *sui iuris,* she herself is entitled
to sue for its recovery; if *in potestate,* her father raises the
actio rei uxoriae, she being joined with him in the suit; and
it is immaterial whether the dowry be adventicious or pro-
7 fecticious.   If the woman die after divorce, her heir is not
entitled to sue unless her husband have been guilty of culp-
able delay in restoring the dowry to her.
8 A dowry made up of things that pass by weight, number,
or measure, is restored in instalments at the end of the first,
second, and third year [after the dissolution of the marriage],
unless there have been an agreement for its immediate restitution.   Other dowries are restored at once.
9 Retentions out of a dowry are competent either on account
of children, on account of immorality, on account of outlays,
on account of things donated, or on account of things ab-
10 stracted.   There is retention on account of children when
divorce has occurred through the fault of the wife or her *pater-*

§ 6. Comp. Vlp. in fr. 2, D. *sol. matr.*
(xxiv, 3); Fr. Vat. §§ 116, 119 ; l. 1,
§ 13, C. *de rei ux. act.* (v, 13).
    [1] So Cuj. and most eds.; the ms.
has *reuera,*—probably an erroneous
rendering by the copyist of the abbreviation *r.u.* A few eds. trans-
pose the words, placing them (as is
more appropriate) after the first
habet actionem. Others, again, insert them in both places.
§ 7. Comp. fr. 57, D. *sol. matr.* (xxiv,
3); l. 1, § 4, C. *de rei ux. act.* (v, 13).
§ 8. Comp. below, § 13; fr. 14-16, D.
de pact. dot. (xxiii, 4); fr. 1, § 2,
D. *de dote praeleg.* (xxxiii, 4); l. 1,
§ 7, C. *de rei ux. act.* (v, 13).

§ 9. Comp. Fr. Vat. § 120; fr. 5, D. *de
dote praeleg.* (xxxiii, 4); l. 1, § 5,
C. *de re ux. act.* (v, 13). As regards
retentio propter res donatas, comp.
Fr. Vat. § 103; fr. 66, § 1, D. *de
don. inter uir. et ux.* (xxiv, 1). As
regards that *propter res amotas,* see
vii, 2; tit. D. *de act. rer. amotar.*
(xxv, 2); tit. C. *rer. am.* (v, 21).
    [1] Not in the ms., but inserted by
all eds. on the strength of § 10.
§ 10. Comp. Boeth. *in Cic. Top.* ii, 4,
§ 19, on the authority of '*Paulus,
Institutorum libri secundi titulo de
dotibus*' (Bruns, p. 295); vi, 17,
§ 65 (Bruns, same page); Fr. Vat.
§§ 105-107.

sit : tunc enim singulorum liberorum nomine sextae retinen-
11 tur ex dote ; non plures tamen quam tres.   Sextae in retentione sunt, non in petitione ; [*nam*] dos quae semel functa
est amplius fungi non potest, nisi *aliud* matrimonium sit.

12   Morum nomine grauiorum quidem sexta retinetur,[1] leuiorum
autem octaua.   grauiores mores sunt adulteria tantum, leuiores
13 omnes reliqui.   Mariti mores puniuntur in ea quidem dote
quae a die [1] reddi debet, ita [*ut*] propter maiores mores praesentem dotem reddat, propter minores senum mensum die.

---

familias ; in such a case a sixth part is retained on behalf of
11 each child, but not more than three-sixths in all.   Those
sixths, though they may be retained, cannot be recovered by
action ; for a dowry, once it has fulfilled all its purposes, cannot
be further dealt with as such except in another marriage.

12   On account of gross immorality, *mores grauiores*, there is
retention of a sixth ; for less serious, *mores leuiores*, of an
eighth.   Adultery is the only immorality falling under the
head of *mores grauiores ;* any other misconduct is included
13 amongst the *leuiores.*   Immorality on the part of a husband
is punished, in the case of a dowry repayable by instalments,
by requiring him to make immediate restitution if his mis-

§ 11. The first six words of this par.
are usually thrown into § 10. The
remainder of it has been the subject
of much comment. Many eds. profess themselves unable to understand
its purport, and most hold it to be
out of place. Schill. (*Bemerk.* pp.
369-375) seems to have given a fairly
satisfactory explanation of it.   It is
intended to assign a reason for the
*sextae in retentione sunt, non in peti-
tione ;* and the interpolation of *nam*
or *quia* after these words makes it
quite simple.

If, on the dissolution of a marriage by divorce, the husband had
paid over the dowry without deducting any sixths to which he was
entitled, he could not afterwards
recover them by action.   They were
to come out of the *dos ;* but this no
longer existed as such once it had
fulfilled all its purposes and been
restored to the party entitled to it.
It might again become a dowry in
connection with a subsequent marriage ; but as regarded that which
had been dissolved by divorce it
no longer had any such character,

and therefore could not be affected
by an action instituted for payment
of the sixths which might lawfully
have been deducted from it before
restitution.

§ 12.   Comp. fr. 39, D. *sol. matr.* (xxiv,
3) ; fr. 11, § 3, D. *de adult.* (xlviii,
5) ; tit. C. Th. *de repud.* (iii, 16) ;
l. 7, l. 8, l. 11, C. *de repud.* (v, 17).
    [1] So Cuj. and most eds. The ms.
has *sextae retinentur,* which Hu.
retains on the ground of the insuffi-
ciency of one-sixth as a penalty, and
on the strength of a case recorded
by Valer.   Max. (viii, 2, § 8) in
which a husband deprived his wife
of her whole dowry because of her
impudicitia.   But Hu. omits to
notice that, on proceedings by the
wife, the husband was held to have
acted illegally, and was compelled
to restore it without any deduction.

§ 13.   See refs. in note to last par.
    [1] So the ms.   Cuj. in his *Notae*
preferred *annua bima trima die* (§
11), and in his *Observ.* (vii, 20) suggested *annua die ;* Bk. has *ad.
diem ;* Hu. *annua die.*

in ea autem quae praesens reddi solet, tantum ex fructibus
iubetur reddere quantum in illa dote *quae triennio*[2] redditur
repraesentatio[3] facit.

14 Inpensarum species sunt tres : aut enim necessariae dicun-
15 tur aut utiles aut uoluptuosae.   Necessariae sunt inpensae
quibus non factis dos deterior futura est, uelut si quis ruinosas
16 aedes refecerit.   Vtiles sunt quibus non factis quidem deterior dos non fuerit, factis autem fructuosior effecta est,
17 ueluti si uineta et oliueta fecerit.   Voluptuosae sunt quibus
neque omissis deterior dos fieret neque factis fructuosior effecta
est[l]; quod euenit in uiridiariis et picturis similibusque rebus.

[*VII. DE IVRE DONATIONVM INTER VIRVM ET VXOREM.*]

1   Inter uirum et uxorem donatio non ualet nisi certis ex

---

conduct amount to adultery, and in six months if it be less
serious ; where it is returnable at once, he must pay in addition, out of the fruits and profits, a sum equal to the difference
in value between instant repayment and repayment in three
annual instalments.

14 Of outlays there are three varieties ; they are described as
15 either necessary, useful, or pleasure-giving.   Those outlays
are necessary by whose omission the dowry would be diminished in value,—expenditure, for instance, in repairing a
16 house going to ruin.   Those are useful whose omission does
not indeed render the dowry less valuable, but whose disbursement makes it more profitable, as when land is laid out
17 in vineyards or olive plantations.   Those are pleasure-
giving whose omission will not render the dowry less valuable,
but whose disbursement will not make it more profitable ; such
is the case with [expenditure on] pleasure-grounds, pictures,
and such like.

[*VII. OF THE LAW OF DONATIONS BETWEEN HUSBAND
AND WIFE.*]

1   A donation between husband and wife is invalid except in

---

[2] So Hugo and all subsequent
eds.; the MS. and earlier editions
have *quadriennio*.
 [3] So Cuj. and most eds.; the MS.
has *repensatio*, which Bk. and Vahl.
retain. Comp. Vlp. in fr. 1, §§ 2,
12, fr. 2, pr. D. *de dote praeleg.*
(xxxiii, 4).
§§ 14-17. Comp. § 37, I. *de act.* (iv, 6);

fr. 79, D. *de V. S.* (l, 16); fr. 1, fr.
5, fr. 7, fr. 14, D. *de inpens.* (xxv,
1); l. 1, § 5, C. *de rei ux. act.* (v, 13).

TIT. VII. This rubric is obviously inappropriate, and due—as most of
them are—either to the epitomist
or some transcriber of his original.
The contents of the first two pars.

causis, id est mortis causa, diuortii causa, serui manumittendi gratia. hoc amplius principalibus constitutionibus concessum est mulieri in hoc donare uiro suo, ut is ab imperatore lato clauo[1] uel equo publico[2] similiue honore honoretur.

2 Si maritus[1] diuortii causa res amouerit,[2] rerum quoque[1] amotarum actione tenebitur.

3 Si maritus pro muliere se obligauerit uel in rem eius inpenderit, diuortio facto eo nomine cauere sibi solet stipulatione tribunicia.

4 In potestate parentum sunt etiam hi liberi quorum causa

----

a few cases, namely, when made in prospect of death, in prospect of divorce, or to procure the manumission of a slave. Further, by imperial constitutions a woman is allowed to make a gift to her husband to enable him to obtain from the emperor the distinction of senatorial or equestrian rank, or some other honour of that sort.

2 If a husband have theftuously abstracted anything of his wife's in prospect of divorce, he also is responsible in an *actio rerum amotarum.*

3 If a husband have become bound for his wife, or have spent money upon her property, it is usual for him, in the event of divorce, to secure himself in respect thereof by a tribunician stipulation.

4 Those children are also in the *potestas* of their parents on

clearly indicate that Vlp. had gone on to explain the *retentiones propter res donatas* and *res amotas*, and that it was in illustration of the first that he mentioned the matter of donations between husband and wife. Pars. 2-4 have nothing to do with it.

§ 1. Comp. Paul. ii, 28; fr. 1, fr. 40, fr. 42, fr. 60, § 1, D. *de donat. inter uir.* (xxi, 1).

[1] The *latus clauus* was a broad perpendicular band or stripe of purple sewed on the tunic from the throat downwards, and one of the badges of senatorial rank; see Smith's D. G. R. A. v. *Clauus latus.*

[2] *Equo publico honoratus* is a phrase that occurs in many inscriptions as indicative of admission to the ranks of the *equites.*

§ 2. Comp. fr. 1, fr. 7, D. *de act. rer. amotar.* (xxv, 2). The husband's action against his wife on this ground is much more frequently alluded to in the texts; and Ulpian's

quoque suggests that he had referred to it in the first instance, although the reference has disappeared.

[1] So in the MS. M. and Hu. think it should be *mulier* or *uxor.* As the texts referred to show, it was competent to either party.

[2] The MS. has *mouerit.*

§ 3. Comp. fr. 25, § 4, fr. 55, D. *sol. matr.* (xxv, 2). When, on divorce, a man was sued for restitution of a dowry in respect of which he, as its owner during the marriage, had incurred obligations to third parties, he was entitled to require that his wife should first give him an undertaking of relief. This was done by a stipulation, which Vlp. calls tribunician, probably because sanctioned originally by the plebeian tribunes, who were not without a limited *iurisdictio.* Comp. fr. 2, § 34, D. *de O. I.* (i, 2).

§ 4. Vlp. here reverts to his proper subject-matter, — creation of the

probata est, per errorem contracto matrimonio inter disparis
condicionis personas : [1] nam siue ciuis Romanus latinam aut
peregrinam uel eam quae dediticiorum numero est quasi
[*ciuem Romanam*] [2] per ignorantiam uxorem duxerit, siue ciuis
Romana per errorem peregrino uel ei qui dediticiorum numero
est [*quasi ciui Romano*] [2] aut etiam quasi latino ex lege *Aelia
Sentia* nupta fuerit, causa probata ciuitas *Romana datur* [3] tam
liberis quam parentibus, praeter eos qui dediticiorum numero
sunt; et ex eo fiunt in potestate parentum liberi.

[VIII. DE ADOPTIONIBVS.]

1 Non tantum naturales liberi in potestate parentum sunt
2 sed etiam adoptiui.   Adoptio fit aut per populum aut per
praetorem uel praesidem prouinciae.   illa adoptio quae per

---

whose behalf cause [of error] has been proved when a
marriage has been contracted by mistake between persons
of unequal condition; for whether it be a Roman citizen
that in ignorance has taken to wife a latin or a peregrin
or a woman of deditician condition, believing that he was
marrying a citizen; or a woman who is a Roman citizen that
by mistake has given herself in marriage to a peregrin or a
man of the deditician class, believing him to be a Roman
citizen, or even believing him to be a latin whom she was
marrying in terms of the Aelia-Sentian law,—on the cause
[of error] being proved Roman citizenship is granted as
well to the children as the parents, excepting those who are
only dediticians; and thus the children pass into the *potestas*
of their parents.

[VIII. OF ADOPTIONS.]

1 It is not only natural but also adoptive children that are
2 in the *potestas* of parents.   Adoption is effected either by
intervention of the people or by that of a praetor or provincial governor.   That effected by intervention of the people

---

patria potestas. For it arose either from marriage, tit. v (to which the law of dowries, vi, vii, 3, is an appendix); or *causae probatio*, vii, 4; or adoption, tit. viii. With this par. comp. Gai. i, §§ 65-75.
[1] So Hugo and most subsequent eds.; the ms. has *dispares condignis personarum;* Cuj. *dispares con-* *dignis personas;* later eds. before Hugo *dispares condicione personas.*
[2] Omitted from the ms.
[3] The ms. has *reddatur;* obviously a mistake of the copyist in transcribing *r.* (= *Romana) datur.*

TIT. VIII. See note to vii, 4.
§§ 1-5. Comp. Gai. i, §§ 97-102.

3 populum fit, specialiter adrogatio dicitur.   Per populum qui
  sui iuris sunt adrogantur ; per praetorem autem filii familiae a
4 parentibus dantur in adoptionem.   Adrogatio Romae *dumtaxat*[1] fit ; adoptio autem etiam in prouinciis apud praesides.
5 Per praetorem uel praesidem prouinciae adoptari tam masculi quam feminae, et tam puberes quam inpuberes possunt.
  per populum uero Romanum feminae[2] non adrogantur ; pupilli
  ante quidem[3] non poterant adrogari, nunc autem possunt ex
6 constitutione diui Antonini.   Hi qui generare non possunt,
  uelut spado, utroque modo possunt adoptare.   idem iuris est
7 in persona caelibis.   Item is qui filium non habet in
8 locum nepotis adoptare potest.   Si pater familiae adrogandum se dederit, liberi quoque eius quasi nepotes in potestate
8a fiunt adrogatoris.   Feminae uero neutro modo possunt
  adoptare, quoniam nec naturales liberos in potestate habent.

-----

3 is specifically called adrogation.   It is persons *sui iuris*
  that are adrogated by the people's authority ; *filiifamilias*
  are given in adoption by their parents by authority of the
4 praetor.   Adrogation can take place only in Rome ; but
  adoption may take place even in the provinces before the
5 governors.   Both males and females, and whether puberate
  or impuberate, may be adopted by authority of a praetor or
  governor of a province.   But women cannot be adrogated by
  co-operation of the Roman people ; neither in former days
  could pupils, although now they may according to one of the
6 constitutions of the late emperor Antoninus [Pius].   Those
  who are unable to procreate, such as eunuchs, may adopt
  by either mode.   The rule is the same in the case of an
7 unmarried person.   Further, he who has no son may adopt
8 [a child] in the character of a grandson.   When a *paterfamilias* gives himself in adrogation, his children also fall
  under the *potestas* of the adrogator in the character of grand-
8a children.   But women cannot adopt by either method,
  for they have not even their natural children *in potestate*.

[1] So L. and most subsequent eds.;
a few have *tantum* ; the ms. has
data,—a corruption by the copyist,
as L. suggests, of the abbreviation
dt.
[2] The ms. has *feminae quidem.*
The last word, though apparently
an addition by another hand, has
been accepted by most eds.; M.,
however, rejects it.

[3] So the earliest editions, and
now M. The ms. has *aut quidem.*
Bk. (in his later editions) reads
pupilli autem quondam ;   Vahl.,
following Schill., *pupilli autem olim
quidem ;* Hu. *pupilli qui* [*olim*] *item.*
§ 6.   Comp. Gai. i, 103.
§ 7.   Comp. § 5, I. *de adopt.* (i, 11).
§ 8.   Comp. Gai. i, 107.
§ 8a. Comp. Gai. i, 104.

[*VIIII. DE HIS QVI IN MANV SVNT.*]

Farreo conuenit uxor in manum certis uerbis et testibus x
praesentibus et sollemni sacrificio facto, in quo panis quoque
farreus adhibetur.

[*X. QVI IN POTESTATE MANCIPIOVE SVNT QVEMADMODVM
EO IVRE LIBERENTVR.*]

1   Liberi parentum potestate liberantur emancipatione, id est
si posteaquam mancipati fuerint manumissi sint.   sed filius
quidem ter mancipatus ter manumissus sui iuris fit ; id enim
lex duodecim tabularum iubet his uerbis : ' si pater filium ter
uenumdauit,[1] filius a patre liber esto.' ceteri autem liberi
praeter filium, tam masculi quam feminae, una mancipatione
2 manumissioneque sui iuris fiunt.   Morte patris filius et filia
sui iuris fiunt : morte autem aui nepotes ita demum sui iuris

---

[*IX. OF THOSE WHO ARE IN MANU.*]

There is *conventio in manum farreo* by exchange of certain
words in the presence of ten witnesses, and the offering of a
solemn sacrifice, in which a spelt cake plays a part.

[*X. HOW PERSONS IN POTESTATE OR IN MANCIPIO ARE
LIBERATED THEREFROM.*]

1   Descendants are freed from the *potestas* of ascendants by
emancipation, that is, when they are manumitted after having
been mancipated. A son indeed becomes *sui iuris* only when
thrice mancipated and thrice manumitted ; so the Twelve
Tables ordain in these words : ' If a father have thrice sold
his son, the son shall be free from his father.' But other
descendants than sons, males as well as females, become *sui*
2 *iuris* by one mancipation and one manumission.   Sons and
daughters become *sui iuris* by the death of their father ;
grandchildren, however, become *sui iuris* by the death of their

---

TIT. IX. Comp. Gai. i, 112. *Far* was
a coarse kind of wheat, the *triticum spelta* of botanists. The epitomist has not preserved the account
which Vlp. must doubtless have
given of the other modes of creating
manus ; because when he compiled
his abridgment it had ceased to be
recognised except for sacred pur-

poses, which required confarreation
(Gai. i, 136, and note).

TIT. x, § 1. Comp. Gai. i, 132.
  [1] So the MS. ; some eds. have
uenundabit ; others *uenumduit* (as
in Gai.).
§ 2. Comp. Gai. i, 127.

fiunt si post mortem aui in potestate patris futuri non sunt,
uelut si moriente auo pater eorum aut *iam*[1] decessit aut de
potestate dimissus est: nain si mortis aui tempore pater
eorum in potestate eius sit, mortuo auo in patris sui potestate
3 fiunt.   Si patri uel filio aqua et igni interdictum sit patria
potestas tollitur, quia peregrinus fit is cui aqua et igni interdictum est; neque autem peregrinus ciuem Romanum neque
4 ciuis Romanus peregrinum in potestate habere potest.   Si
pater ab hostibus captus sit, quamuis seruus hostium fiat,
tamen cum reuersus fuerit omnia pristina iura recipit iure
postliminii. sed quamdiu apud hostes est patria potestas in
filio eius interim pendebit, et cum reuersus fuerit ab hostibus
in potestate filium habebit; si uero ibi decesserit, sui iuris
filius erit. Filius quoque si captus fuerit ab hostibus, similiter
5 propter ius postliminii patria potestas interim pendebit.   In
potestate parentum esse desinunt et hi qui flamines Diales
inaugurantur et quae uirgines Vestae capiuntur.

---

grandfather only when on that event they will not be in the
potestas of their father, as, for example, when, at the time
of their grandfather's death, their father is either already dead
or released from *potestas*; for if, when the grandfather dies,
the children's father is in the grandfather's *potestas*, by the
death of the latter they become subject to the *potestas* of their
3 father.   If either father or son be interdicted fire and water
the *patria potestas* is put an end to; for a person to whom this
happens becomes a peregrin; and neither can a peregrin have
a Roman citizen in his *potestas*, nor a citizen a peregrin.
4 If a father be taken captive by an enemy, although he thereby
becomes a slave of the enemy's, yet when he returns he
recovers all his former rights *iure postliminii.* So long as
he is in the enemy's hands his *potestas* over his son is for the
time suspended; if he return home he will again have him
in potestate; but if he die in captivity his son will be *sui
iuris.* And so too if a son be captured by an enemy, the
potestas of his father will in like manner be suspended for the
5 time on account of the *ius postliminii.*   Those also cease
to be *in potestate* who are consecrated as flamens of Jupiter or
taken as Vestal virgins.

---

[1] The ms. and some eds. have   § 3. Comp. Gai. i, 128, and note 2.
etiam; we have *iam* in the passage   § 4. Comp. Gai. i, 129; below, xxiii, 5.
of Gai. referred to.   § 5. Comp. Gai. i, §§ 130, 145.

[XI. DE TVTELIS.]

1 Tutores constituuntur tam masculis quam feminis; sed
masculis quidem inpuberibus dumtaxat propter aetatis infirmitatem; feminis autem [*tam*] inpuberibus quam puberibus,
et propter sexus infirmitatem et propter forensium rerum
ignorantiam.

2 Tutores aut legitimi sunt aut senatusconsultis constituti aut
moribus introducti.

3 Legitimi tutores sunt [*qui*] ex lege aliqua descendunt; per
eminentiam autem legitimi dicuntur qui ex lege duodecim
tabularum introducuntur, seu *propalam*, quales sunt agnati,

4 seu per consequentiam, quales sunt patroni.   Agnati sunt a
patre cognati uirilis sexus[1] per uirilem sexum descendentes
eiusdem familiae,[2] uelut patrui, fratres, filii fratris, patrueles.

5 Qui liberum caput mancipatum sibi uel a parente uel a
coemptionatore[1] manumisit, per similitudinem patroni tutor
efficitur, qui fiduciarius tutor appellatur.

[XI. OF TUTORIES.]

1 Tutors are appointed both to males and females: but to
males only while under puberty, because of their infirmity
of age; to females, however, both while under and over
puberty, on account both of their infirmity of sex and
ignorance of forensic matters.

2 Tutors are either tutors-at-law, or derive their office from
a senatusconsult, or have had it introduced by custom.

3 Those are tutors-at-law, *legitimi,* who derive their office from
some *lex;* but those are emphatically so called who owe it to
the law of the Twelve Tables, either directly, such as agnates,

4 or by implication, as patrons.   Agnates are persons of the
male sex related through a common father, tracing their
descent from him through males, and members of the same
family; for example, paternal uncles, brothers, a brother's
sons, a paternal uncle's sons.

5 He who has manumitted a free person, mancipated to him
either by a parent or a coemptionator, becomes that person's
tutor after the manner of a patron, and is called a fiduciary tutor.

TIT. XI, § 1. Comp. Gai. i, §§ 144, 189-
193.
§ 2. *Legitimi,* §§ 3-20; *Sctis. constituti,*
§§ 20-23; *moribus introducti,* § 24.
§ 3. Comp. Gai. i, §§ 155, 165.
§ 4. Comp. Gai. i, 156; iii, 10; below,
xxvi, 1.
[1]This definition excludes female

agnates, no doubt because they
could not be tutors.
[2]*Eiusdem familiae* means un-
emancipated; for emancipation, as
a *capitis minutio,* severed the bond
of agnation (§§ 9, 13).
§ 5. Comp. Gai. i, 166.
[1]Comp. Gai. i, 115.

6 Legitimi tutores alii tutelam in iure cedere possunt.
7 Is cui tutela in iure cessa est cessicius tutor appellatur;
qui siue mortuus fuerit, siue capite minutus, siue alii tutelam
cesserit,[1] redit ad legitimum tutorem tutela. sed et si
legitimus decesserit aut capite minutus fuerit, cessicia
8 quoque tutela extinguitur.   Quantum ad agnatos pertinet
hodie cessicia tutela non procedit, quoniam permissum erat in
iure cedere tutelam feminarum tantum, non etiam masculorum; feminarum autem legitimas tutelas lex Claudia *sustulit*,[2]
excepta tutela patronorum.
9 Legitima tutela capitis deminutione amittitur.   [10] Capi-
10 tis minutionis species sunt tres, maxima, media, minima.
11 Maxima capitis deminutio est per quam et ciuitas et libertas
amittitur, ueluti cum incensus aliquis uenierit, aut quod
mulier alieno seruo se iunxerit denuntiante domino, et ancilla
12 facta fuerit[1] ex senatusconsulto Claudiano.   Media capitis
deminutio dicitur per quam, sola ciuitate amissa, libertas re-

---

6 A tutor-at-law may transfer his tutory to another person
7 by cession in court.   He to whom it is ceded gets the name
of *tutor cessicius*. If he die, or be *capite minutus*, or cede the
tutory to a third party, it reverts to the tutor-at-law. And if
it is the latter that dies or is *capite minutus*, the *cessicia*
8 *tutela* then also comes to an end.   So far as agnates are
concerned, there is now-a-days no room for a *cessicia tutela*;
for it never was lawful to cede a tutory over males, but only
that over females; and the Claudian law has abolished the
tutories-at-law over women, except that exercised by patrons.
9 A tutory-at-law is lost by *capitis deminutio*.   [10] And
10 this is of three kinds,—the greatest, the intermediate, and the
11 smallest.   That *capitis deminutio* is of the highest degree
in which both citizenship and liberty are lost, as when a man
is sold for avoiding enrolment in the census-list, or a woman
has become a slave under the Claudian senatusconsult,
because she has insisted in cohabiting with another person's
12 slave notwithstanding that person's warnings.   That is said
to be of the intermediate degree in which, although citizenship is lost, freedom is retained; it occurs on interdiction of

§§ 6-8. Comp. § 17; Gai. i, §§ 168-171.
  [1] The ms. has *pcesserit*; hence
many eds. read *porro cesserit*. K.,
following Roeder, *in iure (in i.) cesserit*. Following the earliest editions, I have dropped the initial
letter.

[2] So Cuj. and all eds.; the ms.
has *sustinet*.
§ 9. Comp. Gai. i, §§ 158, 159a.
§§ 10-13. Comp. Gai. i, §§ 159-162.
  [1] Hu. reads— *aut mulier, quod
alieno seruo se iunxerit denuntiante
domino eius, ancilla facta fuerit.*

13 tinetur; quod fit in eo cui aqua et igni interdicitur.   Minima capitis deminutio est per quam, et ciuitate et libertate
salua, status dumtaxat hominis[2] mutatur; quod fit adoptione
et in manum conuentione.[3]

14   Testamento quoque nominatim tutores dati confirmantur
eadem lege duodecim tabularum his uerbis: 'uti legassit
super[1] pecunia tutelaue[2] suae rei,[3] ita ius esto:' qui tutores

15 datiui appellantur.[4]   Dari testamento tutores possunt liberis

16 qui in potestate sunt.   Testamento tutores dari possunt hi
cum quibus testamenti faciendi ius est,[1] praeter latinum Iunianum; nam latinus habet quidem testamenti factionem, sed
tamen tutor dari non potest; id enim lex Iunia prohibet.

17 Si capite deminutus fuerit[1] tutor testamento datus, non
amittit tutelam; sed si abdicauerit[2] se tutela, desinit esse

---

13 fire and water.   It is of the lowest degree when, without
loss of either citizenship or liberty, there is simply a change
in a person's domestic status, as happens in adoption and *in
manum conuentio.*

14   Tutors appointed by name in a testament are also confirmed [*i.e.* have their appointment sanctioned] by the same
law of the Twelve Tables in these words: 'As a man has
legated in regard to his belongings, whether about property
or tutory, so be it law;' such tutors are called dative.

15 Tutors may be appointed by testament to children *in potestate*

16 [of the testator].   Those persons may thus be appointed
tutors with whom the testator has *testamenti factio,* except a
Junian latin. For although it is true that a latin has *testamenti factio,* yet he cannot be appointed tutor; the Junian

17 law forbids it.   If a testamentary tutor be *capite deminutus*
he does not lose his tutory, but if he have abdicated he ceases

---

[2] *Homo* means the man rather
than the citizen,—the individual in
his private rather than his political
character.

[3] The ᴍѕ. has *in manu conditione.*

14. Comp. Gai. ii, §§ 224, 104, note 8.

  [1] Bk., on the authority of Cic.
de inr. ii, 50, § 148, interpolates
familia.

  [2] The ᴍѕ. has *pecuniam tutelabae.*

  [3] *Vti legassit suae rei* is the same
thing as *uti legem dedisset suae rei;*
the last two words are in the dative,
not the genitive.

  [4] Comp. Gai. i, 154.

§ 15.   Comp. Gai. i, 144.

§ 16.   Comp. Paul. in fr. 21, D. *de test.
tut.* (xxvi, 2).

  [1] See Gai. ii, 114, note 1; i, 23.

§ 17.   Comp. above, § 7.

  [1] Comp. § 9.

  [2] Comp. Cic. *ad Att.* vi, 1, § 8.
Abdicatio seems to have been renunciation of a tutory in course of
administration. There is no trace
of it either in Gai. or in the Justinian law; indeed it seems quite
inconsistent with the idea that per-
vades the whole of tit. I. *de excusat.
tut.* (i, 25).

---

tutor: abdicare autem est dicere nolle se tutorem esse. in iure
cedere[3] autem tutelam testamento datus non potest: nam et[4]
legitimus in iure cedere potest, abdicare se non potest.

18   Lex Atilia iubet mulieribus pupillisue non habentibus
tutores dari a praetore et maiore parte tribunorum plebis,
quos tutores Atilianos appellamus. sed quia lex Atilia
Romae tantum locum habet, lege Iulia et Titia prospectum
est ut in prouinciis quoque similiter a praesidibus earum
19 dentur tutores.   Lex Iunia tutorem fieri iubet latinae uel
latini inpuberis[1] eum cuius etiam ante manumissionem *ex*
20 *iure*[2] Quiritium fuit.   Ex lege Iulia de maritandis ordinibus tutor datur a praetore urbis ei mulieri uirginiue quam ex
hac ipsa lege nubere oportet, ad dotem dandam dicendam pro-
mittendamue,[1] si legitimum tutorem pupillum habeat. sed
postea senatus censuit ut etiam in prouinciis quoque similiter
21 a praesidibus earum ex eadem causa tutores dentur.   Praeterea etiam in locum muti furiosiue tutoris alterum dandum

to be tutor; (to abdicate is to intimate that he declines to be
tutor). He cannot, however, transfer his tutory to another by
cession in court; a tutor-at-law may, but he cannot abdicate.
18   The Atilian law ordains that tutors shall be appointed by
the praetor and the majority of the plebeian tribunes to
women and pupils who have none; and such tutors are called
Atilian. But as this enactment does not extend beyond Rome,
it is provided by the Julian and Titian law that in the provinces tutors shall be similarly appointed by the governors
19 thereof.   The Junian law ordains that a latin woman, or a
male latin under *puberty*, shall have as tutors those to whom
they belonged in quiritarian right previous to their manu-
20 mission.   By the Julian law for regulating the marriages
of the orders, a tutor is appointed by the praetor to any
woman or virgin required by that enactment to marry, on purpose to enable her to give, specify, or promise a dowry, when
her tutor-at-law is a pupil [and therefore unable to grant his
auctoritas]. Afterwards the senate decreed that in the provinces tutors should be similarly appointed for the same pur-
21 pose by the provincial governors.   The senate further
decreed that where a tutor is dumb or insane another shall

[3] Comp. §§ 6-8.
[4] So most eds.; the MS. has *nā et*; M. suggests *tametsi*.
§ 18. Comp. Gai. i, 185.
§ 19. Comp. Gai. i, 167; above, i, 16.
[1] The MS. has *latinis impuberibus*.
25

[2] The MS., here as elsewhere, has *qui ius*.
§ 20. Comp. Gai. i, §§ 178, 183, and note to §§ 173, 174.
[1] Comp. vi, 1.
§ 21. Comp. Gai. i, 180.

22 esse tutorem ad dotem constituendam senatus censuit.   Item
ex senatusconsulto tutor datur mulieri ei cuius tutor abest,
praeterquam si patronus sit qui abest : nam in locum patroni
absentis *alter* [1] peti non potest nisi ad hereditatem adeundam
et nuptias contrahendas.   idemque permisit in pupillo patroni
23 filio.   Hoc amplius senatus censuit, ut si tutor pupilli
pupillaeue suspectus a tutela submotus fuerit, uel etiam iusta
de causa excusatus, in locum eius tutor alius [*detur*].[1]
24   Moribus tutor datur mulieri pupilloue qui cum tutore suo
lege [1] aut legitimo iudicio [2] agere uult, ut auctore eo agat,[3]
(ipse enim tutor in rem suam [4] auctor fieri non potest), qui
praetorius [5] tutor dicitur, quia a praetore urbis dari consueuit.
25   Pupillorum pupillarumque tutores et negotia gerunt et
auctoritatem interponunt ; mulierum autem tutores auctori-
26 tatem dumtaxat interponunt.   Si plures sunt tutores, omnes

---

be appointed in his place for the purpose of constituting a
22 dowry.   A tutor is also given under the senatusconsult
to a woman whose tutor is absent, unless the absentee be her
patron ; for another tutor cannot be petitioned for [by a freed-
woman] in place of an absent patron, except for the special
purpose of enabling her to enter upon a succession or contract
marriage.   It sanctions the same course where a [deceased]
23 patron's son is in pupillarity.   Further, the senate has also
decreed that if the tutor of a male or female pupil be removed
as suspect, or for some good reason be excused, another shall
be appointed in his place.
24   By customary law a tutor is appointed to a woman or
pupil who proposes to proceed against her [proper] tutor either
by *legis actio* or in a *legitimum iudicium*, on purpose that he
may be *auctor* in the suit,—for a tutor cannot be *auctor* in
an affair of his own ; and such an one is called a praetorian
tutor, because it has been the custom for the urban praetor
to make the appointment.
25   The tutors of pupils, both male and female, both act for
them and [act with them, *i.e.*] interpone *auctoritas ;* but the
26 tutors of women only interpone *auctoritas.*   If there be

§ 22.   Comp. Gai. i, §§ 173-177, 179.
      [1] So most eds. The MS. has *al'ter*,
   which L., Bk., and Vahl. render
   aliter. Hu. reads *a liberta tutor.*
§ 23.   Comp. Gai. i, 182.
      [1] Supplied by all eds.
§ 24.   Comp. Gai. i, 184.
      [1] Comp. Gai. iv, §§ 11, 12, 31.

[2] Comp. Gai. iv, 104.
[3] Comp. § 27.
[4] Comp. § 3, note 1, L *de auct. tut.*
(i, 21).
[5] The MS. has *praetorianus ;* but
see Gai.
§§ 25-27. Comp. Gai. i, §§ 190-192,
   and notes 1 and 2 to § 24, above.

in omni re debent auctoritatem accommodare, praeter eos qui *testamento*[1] dati sunt; nam ex his uel unius auctoritas sufficit.

27 Tutoris auctoritas necessaria est mulieribus quidem in his rebus: si lege aut legitimo iudicio agant, si se obligent, si ciuile negotium gerant, si libertae suae permittant in contubernio alieni serui morari,[2] si rem mancipi alienent. pupillis autem hoc amplius etiam in rerum nec mancipi alienatione tutoris auctoritate opus est.

28 Liberantur tutela masculi quidem pubertate. puberem autem Cassiani[1] quidem eum esse dicunt qui habitu corporis pubes apparet, id est qui generare possit; Proculeiani[1] autem eum qui quattuordecim annos expleuit; uerum Priscus[2] eum puberem esse in quem utrumque concurrit, et habitus corporis 28a et numerus annorum. Feminae autem tutela liberantur

— — — —.

more than one tutor they must all grant their *auctoritas* in each particular transaction, unless they be testamentary tutors; in their case the *auctoritas* of any one of them is sufficient.

27 Tutorial *auctoritas* is needful for women in these matters: if they are suing in a *legis actio* or a *legitimum iudicium*, if they are undertaking an obligation, if they are taking part in any transaction of the *ius ciuile*, if they are granting permission to a freedwoman to cohabit with another person's slave, if they are alienating a *res mancipi*. Over and above these cases it is necessary to pupils in alienation even of *res nec mancipi*.

28 Males are released from tutelage by puberty. The Cassians hold that he has reached puberty who appears to have done so from his bodily development, *i.e.* who can procreate; the Proculians say that he has done so who has completed his fourteenth year; but Priscus maintains that he only is puberate in whom both those *indicia* occur,—bodily develop-
28a ment and the aforesaid number of years. Women are released from it [*in right of three children; but if they be freed-*
[*women in the tutelage of a patron, only in right of four*].

[1] So Cuj. and most eds.; the MS. has *tunc.*

[2] Because her freedwoman, in terms of the *SC. Claudianum*, would fall to the owner of the slave with whom she was cohabiting; see Paul. ii, 21a, § 6.

§ 28. Comp. Gai. i, 196.

[1] See Gai. i, 196, note 1.

[2] In fr. 10, § 2, D. *de usu et hab.* (vii, 2). Vlp. mentions Priscus, meaning, as is generally supposed, Iauolenus Priscus (Gai. iii, 70, note). Schill. (*Animadv.* iii, pp. 6-10) proposes *plerisque uisum est;* but the *Priscus* of the MS. is quite distinct.

§ 28a. Incomplete in the MS. See

[*XII. DE CVRATORIBVS.*]

1   Curatores aut legitimi sunt, id est qui ex lege duodecim
tabularum dantur, aut honorarii, id est qui a praetore con-
2 stituuntur.   Lex duodecim tabularum furiosum, itemque
prodigum cui bonis interdictum est, in curatione iubet esse
3 agnatorum.   A praetore constituitur curator quem ipse
praetor uoluerit libertinis prodigis, itemque ingenuis qui ex
testamento parentis heredes facti male dissipant bona : his
enim ex lege curator dari non poterat, cum ingenuus quidem
non ab intestato sed ex testamento heres factus sit patri ;
libertinus autem nullo modo patri heres fieri possit, qui nec
patrem habuisse uidetur, cum seruilis cognatio[1] nulla sit.
4 Praeterea dat curatorem ei etiam qui nuper pubes factus
idonee negotia sua tueri non potest.

[*XII. OF CURATORS.*]

1   Curators are either *legitimi, i.e.* given by the law of the
Twelve Tables, or *honorarii, i.e.* given by the praetor [at his
2 own hand].   The Twelve Tables ordain that a madman, as
also a spendthrift who has been interdicted the administration of his estate, shall be under the curatory of his agnates.
3 To freedmen spendthrifts, as well as to persons of free-birth
who, being testamentary heirs of their parents, are squander-
ing their estates, the praetor appoints as curator any person
he pleases.   For neither of these two classes was a curator
provided by the statute,—the man of free-birth because he
was his father's heir by testament instead of *ab intestato ;* the
freedman because he could not be his father's heir either way,
and in fact was regarded as having no father, there being no
4 such thing as servile cognation.   The praetor also appoints
a curator to an individual who, having only just passed the
age of puberty, is still unable to look properly after his own
affairs.

xxix, 3; Gai. i, §§ 194, 195. Hu.
proposes — *Feminae autem tutela
liberantur [trium liberorum iure ;
libertae tantum, quae in patroni
tutela sunt, quattuor liberorum iure
ab ea liberantur*].

TIT. XII. Comp. Gai. Epit. i, 8 (in note
to Gai. i, §§ 197, 198).
§ 2.   Comp. Cic. *de inv.* ii, 50, § 148 ;
Tusc. disp. iii, 5, § 11 ; Hor. *Sat.*
ii, 3, 218; Fest. v. *Nec.* (Bruns, p.
248) ; Schoell, *Tab.* v, 7 ; Gai. ii,

64 ; below, **xx,** 13 ; Vlp. in fr. 1,
pr. D. *de cur. fur.* (xxvii, 10).
§ 3.   Comp. Val. Max. viii, 6, § 1 ; Gai.
i, 58 ; Paul. iii, 4a, § 7 ; below,
xx, 13.
[1] That for certain purposes the law
always recognised *seruilis cognatio*
appears from § 10, I. *de nupt.* (i, 10) ;
and from § 10, I. *de grad. cogn.*
(iii, 6), it will be seen that Just. recognised it as creative of a right of
succession.
§ 4.   Comp. Gai. i, §§ 197, 198, and refs

[*XIII. DE CAELIBE ORBO ET SOLITARIO PATRE.*]

1 Lege Iulia prohibentur uxores ducere senatores quidem
liberique eorum libertinas, et quae ipsae quarumue pater
materue artem ludicram fecerit, item corpore quaestum faci-
2 entem. Ceteri autem ingenui prohibentur ducere lenam,
et a lenone lenaue mauumissam, et in adulterio deprehensam,
et iudicio publico damnatam, et quae artem ludicram fecerit :
adicit Mauricianus [1] et a senatu damnatam.[2]

[*XIII. OF THE UNMARRIED MAN, THE CHILDLESS MAN,
AND HIM WHO HAS BUT ONE CHILD.*]

1 By the Julian law senators and their children are forbidden
to marry their freedwomen, or women who themselves, or
whose father or mother, have followed the profession of the
2 stage, or women who are common prostitutes. Other
persons of free-birth are forbidden to marry a procuress, a
freedwoman manumitted by a procurer or procuress, a woman
that has been taken in adultery, one that has been convicted
in a public criminal prosecution, or one that has been an
actress; to these Mauricianus adds one convicted before the
senate.

TIT. XIII. *Solitarius pater* has been defined (Abdy and Walker) as a 'father
who has lost his children.' But
this, which really makes it synonymous with *orbus* in one of its applications, is not the meaning the
civilians attach to it. Says Heinecc.
(*ad. L. Iul.* l. ii, c. 15, § 91): *Pater
uero solitarius est qui uel unicum
habet filium.* That a single child
saved a man from the penalties of
orbitas appears from a well-known
passage in Juvenal (*Sat.* ix, 82 f.),
which is confirmed by Gai. in fr.
148, D. *de V. S.* (1, 16). Heinecc.
therefore reconstructs the provision
of the *L. Iulia et Papia* thus: *Ex
aliorum testamentis pater solitarius
solidum capito* ('the father of only
one child may take in full under a
stranger's testament '). The *caelebs*
on the other hand could not take at
all, and the *orbus* only a half of what
was left him (Gai. ii, §§ 111, 286,
286a).
  As will be seen from the text, the
only two pars. the epitomist has
thought it necessary to retain do
not touch the matters indicated in
the rubric.

§ 1. The law referred to is the *L.
Iulia de maritandis ordinibus*; see
Gai. i, 145, note 1. Its words, so
far as they deal with the subject-
matter of this par., are reproduced
by Paul. in fr. 44, pr. D. *de ritu
nupt.* (xxiii, 2). Comp. below, xvi,
2; Vlp. in fr. 43, D. *de ritu nupt.*
(xxiii, 2); Iust. l. 28, C. *de nupt.*
(v, 4).

§ 2. Vahl., making § 1 end with *fecerit*,
proposes this transposition : *ceteri
autem ingenui prohibentur ducere
corpore quaestum facientem, item
lenam et a lenone*, etc. M. approves
this suggestion.

  [1] Iunius Mauricianus, a contemporary of Gaius', was the author of
a commentary on the *L. Iulia et
Papia Poppaea* (fr. 15, D. *de iure
fisci*, xlix, 14) ; and it was probably
in the course of it that he made the
observation to which Vlp. refers.

  [2] From the time of Augustus (or
at least Tiberius), and down to that
of Diocletian, senators or members
of their families, against whom a
criminal charge was brought, were
entitled to have it disposed of by
their peers of the senate; the pro-

[*XIIII. DE POENA LEGIS IVLIAE.*]

Feminis lex Iulia a morte uiri anni tribuit uacationem a diuortio sex mensum;[1] lex autem Papia a morte uiri biennii, a repudio anni et sex mensum.[1]

[*XV. DE DECIMIS.*]

1 Vir et uxor inter se matrimonii nomine decimam capere possunt. quod si ex alio matrimonio liberos superstites habeant, praeter decimam quam matrimonii nomine capiunt 2 totidem decimas pro numero liberorum accipiunt. Item

---

[*XIV. OF THE PENALTY OF THE JULIAN LAW.*]

The Julian law allowed women exemption from its penalties for a year after their husband's death, and for six months after divorce; the Papian law gives them two years' grace from the death of their husband, and eighteen months' from the date of divorce.

[*XV. OF TENTHS.*]

1 Husband and wife may take [by testament to the extent of] one-tenth of each other's estate, [simply] on the strength of their marriage; but if either of them have children of a previous marriage surviving, he or she may, in addition to the tenth taken *matrimonii nomine*, take as many more tenths as there 2 are children.   Further, a son or daughter, issue of the two

cess was not strictly a *publicum iudicium;* but there was no reason why a condemnation in it should not be regarded as arising out of a public prosecution so far as the provisions of the *lex Iulia* were concerned. See Dio. Cass. lii, 21 f.; Dirksen, *Civilistische Abhandlungen,* i, pp. 185 f.; Laboulaye, *Lois criminelles des Romains,* pp. 414 f.

TIT. XIV. The Julian law required women to marry, whether virgins or widows; but in the case of the latter allowed them an interval between the dissolution of one marriage and celebration of the next, during which, although for the moment unmarried, they could take in full under a testament. The legislation of the later empire, however, all tended to discourage second marriages; see tit. C. *de secund. nupt.* (v, 9).

[1] The MS. has *menses.*

TIT. xv, §§ 1, 2. Although these *decimae* are frequently alluded to in vague terms in the Theod. Code, and once or twice in the Dig., yet there is no explicit reference that can be cited as confirmatory of the text. From the words of Constantine, however, in repealing the restriction on testamentary disposition between husband and wife (l. un., § 2, C. Th. *de infirm. poen. caelib.* viii, 16), it seems that it was in apprehension of the consequences of the *fallaces blanditiae* for which marriage gave the opportunity, that Augustus, in the *L. Iulia Papia,* prohibited *mortis causa* liberality between spouses, except under the restrictions indicated in this and the next following title.   It led sometimes, as observed by Quint. (*Inst. Orat.* viii, 5, § 19), to this strange result,—that a man could leave more to his mistress than he was allowed to leave to his wife.

communis filius filiaue post nominum diem[1] amissus amis-
saue unam decimam adicit; duo autem post *nominum diem*[2]
3 amissi duas decimas adiciunt.   Praeter decimam etiam
usumfructum tertiae partis bonorum *coniuges*[1] capere possunt,
et quandoque liberos habuerint, eiusdem partis proprietatem.[2]
Hoc amplius mulier praeter decimam dotem [*capere*][3] potest
legatam sibi.[4]

[*XVI.   DE SOLIDI CAPACITATE INTER VIRVM ET VXOREM.*]

1   Aliquando uir et uxor inter se solidum capere possunt.

---

spouses, who has died after his name-day, adds another tenth ;
3 two dying after their name-days add two-tenths.   Besides
either of them may take the usufruct, and if they have
children, the ownership-right of a third part of the other's
estate.   And the wife is entitled, over and above her tenth
[or tenths], to take a bequest of her dowry.

[*XVI.   OF CAPACITY, AS BETWEEN HUSBAND AND WIFE, TO
TAKE IN FULL.*]

1   Sometimes husband and wife may take in full what each

---

[1] See Paul. ex Fest. v. *Lustrici*
(ed. Muell. p. 120).   The name-day
was the ninth for boys and the
eighth for girls.
[2] The ᴍꜱ. has *nono die.*
§ 3.   Comp. fr. 48, D. *de usur.* (xxii,
1); fr. 10, D. *de praescr. uerb.*
(xix, 5).   It was a common practice, under this provision of the
Papian law, for a husband to make
his wife an unconditional bequest
of the usufruct of a third of his
estate, and a bequest of the property
of it conditional on her having
children.
[1] So Schill. (*Animadv.*, spec. iii,
p. 18); approved by Bk.   The ᴍꜱ.
has *eius*, which K. thinks a gloss,
to be omitted, not corrected.   Hu.
substitutes [*uir*] *et uxor.*
[2] Comp. fr. 78, § 14, D. *ad SC.
Trebell.* (xxxvi, 1); fr. 25, D. *de
cond. et dem.* (xxxv, 1).
[3] Added by Bk., on the suggestion of Schill., and adopted by K.;
Cuj. amended by changing *potest*
into *petet.*
[4] Comp. fr. 53, D. *de legat. II.*

(xxxi); tit. D. *de dote praeleg.*
(xxxiii, 4).

TIT. XVI.   This is really a continuation
of the same subject as in the previous title.   But all the rules it
contains were abolished in the later
empire; comp. tit. C. Th. *de infir-
mand. poen. caelibat.* (viii, 16); tit.
C. *de infirm. p. cael.* (viii, 58); l.
27, C. *de nupt.* (v, 4).
The explanation Vlp. gives here
of some of the provisions of the *L.
Iulia et Papia Poppaea* is not so
distinct as one could desire.   Unfortunately it does not admit of
supplement to any extent from other
sources; and, though much has
been written on the subject, and
notably by Jacques Godefroy (*Otton.
Thes.* tom. iii, pp. 208 f.), Ramos
del Manzano (*Meerm. Thesaur.*
tom. v), and Heinecc. (ad. *L. Iul.
et Pap. Popp. Comment.*), the matter
is really no clearer than Vlp. left it.
§ 1.   The words *aut si uir . . . . abesse
desierit* are removed by Hu. to § 1a,
and introduced after *inpetrauerint.*

uelut si uterque uel alteruter eorum nondum eius aetatis sint
a qua lex liberos exigit, id est si uir minor annorum XXV sit
aut uxor annorum XX minor; item si utrique lege Papia
finitos annos in matrimonio excesserint, id est uir LX annos,
uxor L;[1] item si cognati inter se coierint usque ad sextum
gradum; aut si uir absit,[2] et donec abest et intra annum post-
1a quam abesse desierit.   Libera inter eos testamenti factio
est si ius liberorum a principe inpetrauerint, aut si filium
filiamue communem habeant, aut quattuordecim annorum
filium uel filiam duodecim amiserint, uel si duos trimos, uel
tres post nominum diem amiserint, ut intra annum tamen et
sex menses etiam unus cuiuscumque aetatis inpubes amissus
solidi capiendi ius praestet.   item si post mortem uiri intra
decem menses uxor ex eo pepererit, solidum ex bonis eius
capit.

---

has left the other, as when both or either of them has not yet
reached the age at which the [Papian] law requires issue [as
the condition of the *ius capiendi*], *i.e.* if the husband be under
twenty-five or the wife under twenty ; as also if, as married
persons, they have both survived the ages mentioned in the
Papian law as those beyond which its provisions do not
apply, *i.e.* sixty for the husband, fifty for the wife ; or if they
be related to each other within the sixth degree ; while, if the
husband be absent from home, [he is exempt from the penalties of the statute] both during his absence and for a year
1a after his return.   Husband and wife are further quite free
to take under each other's testaments if they have obtained a
concession from the emperor of the privilege resulting from
children ; or if they have a surviving son or daughter of their
marriage, or have lost a son of fourteen or a daughter of
twelve ; or if they have lost two children over three years of
age, or three that survived their name-days : and the death
of any of those impuberates within eighteen months [after
the dissolution of the marriage] secures for them the right of
taking in full [exactly as if it had occurred before the marriage was dissolved].   Further, if the wife give birth to a
child by her husband within ten months of his death, she is
equally entitled to take in full anything he may have left her.

---

[1] Comp. § 3.
[2] Cuj. and many later eds., with
some show of reason, interpolate
reipublicae causa, thus limiting
the exemption to persons absent
from home on the public service,
and so prevented from complying
with the provisions of the statute.
§ 1a. The *testamenti factio* here referred to is that which the civilians
call *passiua*; see Gai. ii, 114,
note 1.

2   Aliquando nihil inter se capiunt, id est si contra legem
Iuliam Papiamque Poppaeam contraxerint matrimonium, uerbi
gratia si famosam quis uxorem duxerit aut libertinam senator.
3   Qui intra sexagesimum uel quae intra quinquagesimum
annum neutri legi paruerit, licet ipsis legibus post hanc
aetatem liberatus esset, perpetuis tamen poenis tenebitur ex
4 senatusconsulto Perniciano.   sed Claudiano senatusconsulto [1] maior sexagenario si minorem quinquagenaria duxerit
perinde habebitur ac si minor sexaginta annorum duxisset
uxorem.   quod si maior quinquagenaria minori sexagenario
nupserit, inpar matrimonium appellatur, et senatusconsulto
Caluitiano [2] iubetur non proficere ad capiendas hereditates et
legata [et] dotes.[3]   itaque mortua muliere dos caduca erit.

---

2   Sometimes they take nothing from each other, namely
when they have contracted marriage in contravention of the
Julian and Papia-Poppaean law, as, for example, when any
man [of free-birth] has married a woman of infamous character,
or a senator a freedwoman.
3   A man who has failed to comply with the requirements of
either branch of the statute within his sixtieth year, and a
woman who has failed to do so within her fiftieth, are after
that age exempt from its provisions [so far as the statute itself
is concerned]; yet by the Pernician senatusconsult they are
4 liable permanently to the penalties [of celibacy].   But by
a Claudian senatusconsult a man over sixty marrying a
woman under fifty is to be regarded as if he had married
before reaching sixty; if, however, a woman over fifty marry
a man under sixty, the marriage is styled unequal, and is
declared by the Calvitian senatusconsult to be of no avail as
a qualification for taking either an inheritance, a legacy, or
a dowry.   On the wife's death, therefore, her dowry will be
caducous.

§ 2. See tit. xiii, and refs.
§ 3. The SC. Pernicianum is not mentioned elsewhere. Perizonius thinks
it should be Persicianum, attribut-
ing it to P. Fab. Persicus, consul
787 | 34. This is probably right,
as Sueton. (in Claud. § 23), referring
to the Claudian Sct. mentioned in
next par., says it was corrective of an
enactment of the reign of Tiberius.
§ 4. I have followed Hu. in making
this par. begin at sed Claudiano.
Most eds. make it commence at

quod si maior.
[1] See note to last par.
[2] Augustinus, Perizonius, Schulting, and others, alter the name of
the Sct. to Caluisianum; Haenel
(Corp. Leg. p. 54) attributes it to
Nero, and year 61.
[3] The MS. has legata dotes, and
many of the earlier editions legatas
dotes. The correction in the text
was suggested by Cuj., and has been
adopted by Hugo, Bk., and K.;
Gneist and Vahl. have legata dotes-

[XVII. DE CADVCIS.]

1   Quod quis sibi testamento relictum, ita ut iure ciuili capere possit, aliqua ex causa non ceperit, caducum appellatur, ueluti ceciderit ab eo : uerbi gratia si caelibi uel latino Iuniano legatum fuerit, nec intra dies centum uel caelebs legi paruerit uel latinus ius Quiritium consecutus sit ; aut si ex parte heres scriptus uel legatarius ante apertas tabulas decesserit uel
2 pereger[1] factus sit.   Hodie ex constitutione imperatoris Antonini omnia caduca fisco uindicantur ; sed seruato iure

---

[XVII. OF CADUCOUS TESTAMENTARY GIFTS.]

1   A testamentary gift which, for some reason or other, he to whom it was left has failed to take, although so left that according to the rules of the *ius ciuile* he might have taken it, is called caducous, as if it had fallen from his grasp, *ceciderit ab eo ;* for instance, if a legacy have been left to a celibate or Junian latin, but the celibate has failed within a hundred days to comply with the statute, or the latin to acquire citizenship ; or if an heir instituted to a share of the inheritance, or a legatee, have died or become a peregrin before the opening
2 of the will.   At the present day, by a constitution of the emperor Antonine's, all such lapses are claimed for the fisc ; the rule of the old law, however, being retained in favour of

---

que, and Hu. *legata aut dotem.* The difficulty is to reconcile the idea of *dos caduca* with the definition of *caducum* in next title. We have the phrase, however, in fr. 88, § 1, fr. 61, D. *de ritu nupt.* (xxiii, 2), and again in l. 8*b*, C. *de nupt.* (v, 4). The statement seems to refer to the *dos aduenticia.* According to the general rule (above, vi, 5), *semper penes maritum remanet* on his wife's death ; but if the marriage, though not null, was yet a forbidden one, the surviving husband had to pay it over (under deduction of *inpensae,* fr. 61, D. *de ritu nupt.*) to the fisc as caducous.

TIT. XVII, § 1. Comp. xxviii, 7 ; xix, 17 ; xxii, §§ 2, 3 ; Gai. ii, §§ 111, 144, 150, 286 ; Iust. in l. 1, C. *de caduc. toll.* (vi, 51).
  [1] So in the MS. ; Cuj. and many eds. have *peregrinus.*
2. It is Caracalla that is here re-

ferred to ; and Haenel (*Corp. Leg.* p. 152) assigns his enactment to the year 212.
   M., Bk., Vahl., and Hu. are of opinion that the copyist has taken this par. from the margin of the original, and wrongly introduced it here instead of before the sentence that stands as tit. xviii.
   Hu. is further of opinion that it must have been preceded by such words as these, explanatory of the *ius antiquum : Caduca iure antiquo quidem ad coheredes uel collegatarios pertinebant iure adcrescendi, aut legata in hereditate remanebant. Ex lege Papia autem translata sunt ad heredes patres uel legatarios patres, certo ordine in caducis uindicandis constituto, ut si heres uel legatarius pater non esset uel non uindicaret, caducum ad populum deferretur. Et eiusdem bona esse iubentur si nemo defuncto heres factus sit.*

3 antiquo liberis et parentibus.   Caduca cum suo onere fiunt :
ideoque libertates et legata [*et*] fideicommissa ab eo data, ex
cuius persona hereditas caduca facta est, salua sunt : *sed et* [1]
legata et fideicommissa cum suo onere fiunt caduca.

[*XVIII.   QVI HABEANT IVS ANTIQVVM IN CADVCIS.*]

Item liberis et parentibus testatoris usque ad tertium
gradum lex Papia ius antiquum dedit, ut heredibus illis institutis, quod quis ex eo testamento non capit, ad hos pertineat
aut totum aut ex parte, prout pertinere possit.

[*XVIIII.   DE DOMINIIS ET ADQVISITIONIBVS RERVM.*]

1 Omnes res aut mancipi [1] sunt aut nec mancipi. mancipi
res sunt praedia in Italico solo,[2] *tam* rustica,[3] qualis est
fundus, quam urbana, qualis domus ; item iura praediorum

---

3 descendants and ascendants [of the testator].   When a gift
becomes caducous it does so with its burdens ; therefore gifts
of freedom, legacies, and trust-bequests charged upon him in
whose person an inheritance has become caducous, are still
effectual.   And when legacies or trust-gifts [themselves]
become caducous, they also are still subject to their burdens.

[*XVIII.   WHO ARE UNDER THE RULES OF THE OLD LAW IN
CASES OF LAPSE.*]

The Papian law granted [the benefit of] the ancient law to
descendants and ascendants of the testator as far as the third
degree ; so that if they had been instituted heirs, and any one
failed to take under the testament, what thus lapsed was to
belong to them in whole or in part as the case might be.

[*XIX.   OF OWNERSHIPS AND OF THE MODES OF ACQUIRING
THINGS.*]

1 Things are all either *mancipi* or *nec mancipi*. *Res mancipi*
include *praedia* in places of Italic right, both rural, as a field,
and urban, as a house ; also rights belonging to rural *praedia*,

§ 3. Comp. i, 21. Vahl. puts this par.
before § 2.
   [1] So Cuj., and much more appropriate than the *scilicet* of the MS.,
retained by Bk., Vahl., and K.

TIT. XVIII. See note 3 to i, 21. Comp.

l. 1, pr. C. *de caduc. toll.* (vi, 51).

TIT. XIX, § 1. Comp. Gai. ii, §§ 15-17.
   [1] In most cases spelt *mancepi* in
the MS.
   [2] Comp. Gai. i, 120, note 2.
   [3] The MS. has *solo aut rustico.*

rusticorum, uelut uia iter actus [4] aquaeductus; item serui et
quadrupedes quae dorso colloue domantur, uelut boues muli
equi asini. ceterae res nec mancipi sunt. elephanti et
cameli, quamuis collo dorsoue domentur, nec mancipi sunt,
quoniam bestiarum numero sunt.

2   Singularum rerum dominium [1] nobis adquiritur mancipatione, traditione, in iure cessione, usucapione, adiudicatione,
lege.

3   Mancipatio propria species alienationis est rerum mancipi;
eaque fit certis uerbis, libripende et quinque testibus prae-
4 sentibus.[1]   Mancipatio locum habet inter ciues Romanos
et latinos coloniarios latinosque Iunianos eosque peregrinos
5 quibus commercium datum est.   Commercium est emendi

---

such as rights of way in the forms of *uia*, *iter*, and *actus*, and
right of aqueduct; as also slaves, and animals that are tamed
by yoke or saddle, such as oxen, mules, horses, asses. All
other things are *nec mancipi*. Elephants and camels, though
tamed by yoke and saddle, are *nec mancipi*, being classed
amongst wild beasts.

2   We acquire the ownership of things singly by mancipation,
by tradition, by cession in court, by usucapion, by adjudication, or by statute.

3   Mancipation is a mode of alienation peculiar to *res mancipi*,
and is performed by recital of certain words of style, in
4 presence of a balance-holder and five witnesses.   It is competent between Roman citizens and colonial and Junian latins,
and such peregrins as have had a concession of *commercium*.

5 *Commercium* is the capacity for reciprocally acquiring and

---

[4] Comp. pr. I. *de seruitut.* (ii, 3).
§ 2.   Comp. Varro, *de R. R.* ii, 10, § 4
(Bruns, p. 283); Gai. ii, 65. *Mancipatio* is dealt with in §§ 3-6, Gai.
ii, §§ 22-37; *traditio*, § 7, Gai. ii,
§§ 19-21; *in iure cessio*, §§ 9-15,
Gai. ii, §§ 22-37; *usucapio*, § 8,
Gai. ii, §§ 40-60; *adiudicatio*, §
16, Gai. iv, 42; *lex*, § 17.
     [1] The ms. has *dominia* both here
and in §§ 7, 8, and 16; in all of
these, following the example of Bk.,
Hu., and K., I have substituted the
singular.
§ 3.   Comp. Gai. i, 119; ii, 22.
     [1] The ms. has *testes praesentes*.
§ 4.   Comp. Gai. ii. 22. On the *latini
coloniarii*, see Gai. i, 22, and notes;
iii, 56; on the *latini Iuniani*,
above, i, §§ 12-16.

§ 5.   Comp. Th. iii, 19, § 2. Just as
conubium (v, 8, and note) was the
technical expression for capacity to
contract a marriage of the *ius ciuile*
and to participate in all its consequences, so was *commercium* the
capacity to acquire or alienate estate
according to the forms of the *ius
ciuile*, and to participate in the advantages or disadvantages resulting
therefrom; as the former was the
qualification for participating in the
family relations of the *ius ciuile*, so
was *commercium* the qualification
for participating in its patrimonial
relations.
     To speak of *commercium* as the
right to buy and sell, *i.e.* to be a
party to the *iuris gentium* contract
of *emptio uenditio*, would be decep-

6   uendendique inuicem ius.   Res mobiles non nisi praesentes mancipari possunt, et non plures quam quot manu capi possunt; immobiles autem etiam plures simul, et quae diuersis locis sunt, mancipari possunt.

7   Traditio propria est alienatio rerum nec mancipi. harum rerum dominium ipsa traditione adprehendimus, scilicet si ex iusta causa traditae sunt nobis.

8   Vsucapione dominium adipiscimur tam mancipi rerum quam nec mancipi. usucapio est autem dominii adeptio per continuationem possessionis anni uel biennii: rerum mobilium anni, immobilium biennii.

9   In iure cessio quoque communis alienatio est et mancipi rerum et nec mancipi: quae fit per tres personas, in iure

---

6   alienating [according to the forms of the *ius ciuile*].   Moveables cannot be mancipated except in the presence of the parties, and not more at a time than can be taken by the hand [of the mancipee]; but immoveables can be mancipated several at once, and though situate in different localities.

7   Tradition is a mode of alienation appropriate to *res nec mancipi*.   And simply by tradition we acquire the ownership of such things, provided always it proceed upon a title sufficient in law.

8   By usucapion we acquire the ownership as well of *res mancipi* as of *res nec mancipi*.   And usucapion is acquisition of ownership by continuance of possession for one or two years,—one in the case of moveables, two in that of immoveables.

9   Cession in court also is a mode of alienation common both to *res mancipi* and *res nec mancipi;* and is accomplished by

---

tive in the extreme; the word is older by centuries than the contract. As mentioned in Gai. i, 113, note 2, and ii, 104, note 6, *emere* in the old law meant simply to take, receive, or acquire, without reference to a price; as Pompon. says, on the authority of Aristo, in fr. 29, § 1, D. *de statulib.* (xl, 7), *lex duodecim tabularum emtionis uerbo omnem alienationem complexa uideretur.* Therefore, to have the *commercium* or *ius emendi uendendique* in the sense of the xii Tables, was to be capable of acquiring or alienating according to any of the forms of the *ius ciuile* that did not necessarily imply *conubium.*

Like *conubium*, the word *commercium* had its abstract, concrete, and relative meanings.   In the abstract it was a prerogative of every citizen and afterwards of every Junian latin; but in the concrete it was denied to the interdicted spendthrift (above, xii, 8; Paul. iii, 4a, § 7).   Relatively a citizen had it with his fellow-citizens and with Junian latins; but not with peregrins, unless the latter enjoyed it by special grant (§ 4).

§ 6.   Comp. Gai. i, 121.
§ 7.   Comp. Gai. ii, §§ 19, 20, 65.
§ 8.   Comp. Gai. ii, §§ 42-44.
§§ 9, 10.   Comp. Gai. ii, §§ 22, 24.

10 cedentis, uindicantis, addicentis.[1]   In iure cedit dominus;
11 uindicat is cui ceditur; addicit[1] praetor.   In iure cedi res
etiam incorporales possunt, uelut usufructus et hereditas et
12 tutela legitima libertae.   Hereditas in iure ceditur uel
13 antequam adeatur uel posteaquam adita fuerit.   Antequam
adeatur, in iure cedi potest *ab herede legitimo;*[1] posteaquam
adita est, tam a legitimo quam ab eo qui testamento heres
14 scriptus est.   Si antequam adeatur hereditas in iure cessa
sit, proinde heres fit cui cessa est ac si ipse heres legitimus
15 esset.   Quod si *posteaquam*[2] adita fuerit in iure cessa sit, is
qui cessit permanet heres, et ob id creditoribus defuncti manet
obligatus; debita uero pereunt, id est debitores defuncti liberantur: res autem corporales, *quasi* singulae in iure *cessae
essent,*[3] transeunt ad eum cui cessa est hereditas.

16   Adiudicatione dominium nanciscimur per formulam[1]

[co-operation of] three persons,—the cedent, the vindicant,
10 and the addicent.   It is the owner that cedes; he to whom
11 the thing is ceded vindicates; the praetor addicts.   Even
incorporeals can be ceded in court, as for instance a usufruct,
12 an inheritance, or the tutory-at-law of a freedwoman.   An
13 inheritance is ceded either before or after entry.   Before
entry it may be ceded by the heir-at-law; after it, not only
by an heir-at-law but also by an heir instituted by testament.
14 If the cession have been before entry, the cessionary at once
15 becomes heir, as if he himself were heir-at-law.   If the
cession be after entry, the cedent still remains heir, and consequently is responsible to the creditors of the deceased; but
his claims are extinguished, *i.e.* the deceased's debtors are
discharged.   The corporeals that belonged to him, however,
pass to the cessionary of the inheritance as if they had been
ceded to him one by one.
16   We acquire ownership by adjudication in the action for

---

[1] I am unwillingly obliged to coin
a word for the translation. Adju-
cant and adjudicate would popu-
larly express the idea, but might
generate a serious misapprehension.
Addictio and *adiudicatio* were two
very different acts: the first was
magisterial, the second judicial; the
one that of a praetor, the other that
of a *iudex* (comp. § 10 with § 16).
§ 11. Comp. Gai. i, §§ 168-171; ii, §§
14, 29-38; above, xi, §§ 6-8.
§§ 12-15. Comp. Gai. ii, §§ 34-37;
iii, §§ 85-87.

[1] The MS. has *legitimo' ab herede;*
hence in the earlier editions *legitime
ab herede,* and in those of last century *a legitimo herede.* The version
in the text is that of Bk., Vahl.,
Hu., and K.
[2] The MS. has *posteacum.*
[3] The words *quasi . . . cessae
essent* are adopted by all recent eds.
on the strength of Gai. ii, 35; the
MS. has *quoties . . . cesse sunt.*
§ 16. Comp. Gai. iv, 42; § 20, I. *de act.*
(iv, 6); §§ 4-7, I. *de off. iud.* (iv, 17).
[1] The *formula* was the record or

familiae erciscundae, quae locum habet inter *coheredes*,[2] et
per formulam communi diuidundo, cui locus est inter socios,
et per formulam finium regundorum, quae est inter uicinos.
nam si iudex uni ex heredibus aut sociis aut uicinis rem
aliquam adiudicauerit, statim illi adquiritur, siue mancipi siue
nec mancipi sit.

17   Lege nobis adquiritur uelut caducum[1] uel *ereptorium*[2] ex
lege Papia Poppaea, item legatum[3] ex lege duodecim tabularum, siue mancipi res sint siue nec mancipi.

18   Adquiritur autem nobis etiam per eas personas, quas in
potestate manu[1] mancipioue habemus. itaque *si quid*[2]
mancipio puta acceperint, aut traditum eis sit, uel stipulati

---

partitioning an inheritance, employed by co-heirs; in that for
dividing common property, competent between partners; and
in that for settling boundaries, employed between neighbours.
For if the judge have adjudicated any particular thing to one
of the heirs, partners, or neighbours, it instantly becomes his,
whether it be *mancipi* or *nec mancipi*.

17   We acquire by operation of statute in the case of lapsed
and forfeited testamentary gifts under the provisions of the
Papia-Poppaean law, and in that of a legacy under the law of
the Twelve Tables, whether the thing acquired be *res mancipi*
or *nec mancipi*.

18   We acquire [not only by our own instrumentality but] also
by means of those persons whom we have in our *potestas*,
manus, or *mancipium*; if therefore they have received anything by mancipation, or have had a thing delivered to them,
or have stipulated for something, the thing [or the claim]

issue sent by the praetor to a *iudex*
for trial (Gai. iv, §§ 39-43), and is
here used synonymously with *actio*
or *iudicium*.
   [2]The ms. has *inter quos heredes.*
§ 17. Comp. fr. 130, D. *de V. S.* (l, 16).
Usucapion might quite as well have
been styled a mode of acquisition
ex lege as any of the three enumerated in this par., seeing that like
them it rested on statutory authority.
   [1]Comp. above, tit. xvii.
   [2]The ms. has *erurupturium*, and
the early editions *ereptitium*. The
word does not occur elsewhere in the
texts; but it referred to successions
or bequests which, having been

actually reduced into possession by
the heirs, legatees, or trust-benefi-
ciaries, were afterwards taken from
them at the instance of the fisc,
because of some wrong done or disrespect shown by them to the deceased or his family, some act done
contrary to the instructions of his
testament, or the discovery of some
informal deed revoking his liberality. Comp. Paul. iii, 5, §§ 10,
18; tit. D. *de his quae ut indignis
auferuntur* (xxxiv, 9); tit. C. *de
his quib. ut indign.* (vi, 35).
   [3]Comp. xi, 14; Gai. ii, 97.
§§ 18, 19. Comp. Gai. ii, §§ 86-90.
   [1]See note to tit. ix.
   [2]The ms. has *siquidem.*

19 fuerint, ad nos pertinet.　　Item si heredes instituti sint
legatumue eis sit, et hereditatem iussu nostro adeuntes nobis
20 adquirunt et legatum ad nos pertinet.　　Si seruus alterius
in bonis, alterius ex iure Quiritium sit, ex omnibus causis
21 adquirit ei cuius in bonis est.　　Is quem bona fide possidemus, siue liber siue alienus seruus sit, nobis adquirit ex
duabus causis tantum, id est quod ex re nostra et quod ex
operis [1] suis adquirit: extra has autem causas aut sibi adquirit
si liber sit, aut domino si alienus seruus sit. eadem sunt et
in eo seruo in quo tantum usumfructum habemus.

[XX. DE TESTAMENTIS.]

1　　Testamentum est mentis nostrae iusta contestatio, in id
2 sollemniter factum ut post mortem nostram ualeat.　　Testamentorum genera fuerunt tria, unum quod calatis comitiis,
alterum quod in procinctu, tertium quod per aes et libram
appellatum est.　　his [1] duobus testamentis abolitis hodie solum

---

19 belongs to us.　　So also if they have been instituted heirs,
or if a legacy has been left them, they acquire the inheritance
for us by entry on our instructions, and the legacy belongs to
20 us.　　If a slave be *in bonis* of one man, but belong to another
ex iure Quiritium, it is in every case for his bonitarian owner
21 that he acquires.　　An individual whom we possess in good
faith, whether he be a freeman or another person's slave,
acquires for us in two cases only,—namely, what he has made
with means we have provided, or by his own labour. Outside
those two cases he acquires for himself if he be a freeman, for
his owner if he be the slave of a third party.　And the
same rules apply to a slave of whom we have only a usufruct.

[XX. OF TESTAMENTS.]

1　　A testament is the testification of our will, in the form prescribed by law, made solemnly, on purpose that it may be
2 effectual after our death.　　There used to be three kinds of
testament,—one called a testament *calatis comitiis*, another *in
procinctu*, and the third *per aes et libram*. The two first having
become obsolete, the only one now in use is that executed by

§ 20. Comp. i, 16; Gai. ii, 88.
§ 21. Comp. Gai. ii, §§ 91, 92; iii, §§
164-166.
　[1] The MS. has *operibus*.

TIT. XX, § 1. Comp. § 9; pr. I. *de*

test. (ii, 10).
§ 2. Comp. Gai. ii, 101-104, and
notes.
　[1] So the MS., Bk., Vahl., and K.;
most other eds. have *illis*, which is
more accurate.

in usu est quod per aes et libram fit, id est per mancipationem
imaginariam. in quo testamento libripens adhibetur, et
familiae emptor, et non minus quam quinque testes cum
3 quibus testamenti factio est.   Qui in potestate testatoris
est aut familiae emptoris, testis *aut* libripens adhiberi non
potest, quoniam familiae mancipatio inter testatorem et familiae
emptorem fit, et ob id domestici testes adhibendi non sunt.
4 Filio *familiam emente* [1] pater eius testis esse non potest.
5 Ex duobus fratribus, qui in eiusdem patris potestate sunt,
alter familiae emptor alter testis esse non potest, quoniam
quod unus ex his mancipio accipit adquirit patri, cui filius
6 suus testis esse non debet.   Pater et [*filius*] qui in potestate eius est, *item* [1] duo fratres qui in eiusdem patris potestate
sunt, testes utrique, uel alter testis alter libripens fieri possunt, alio familiam emente; quoniam nihil nocet ex una domo
7 plures testes alieno negotio adhiberi.   Mutus, surdus,
furiosus, pupillus, femina neque familiae emptor esse neque

---

the copper and the scales, *i.e.* by an imaginary mancipation.
In this testament a balance-holder takes a part, and a *familiae
emptor*, and not fewer than five witnesses with whom the
3 testator has *testamenti factio*.   He who is *in potestate* of the
testator or of the *familiae emptor* cannot officiate as balance-
holder or as a witness; for the testator and the *familiae
emptor* are the parties to the mancipation, and on that account
4 the testimony of members of their families is excluded.   If
a son be *familiae emptor* his father cannot be a witness.
5 Of two brothers who are in the *potestas* of the same father,
one cannot be *familiae emptor* and the other a witness; for
what the former acquires by the mancipation is acquired by
him for his father; and a son ought not to be a witness to his
6 father's deed.   A father and his son *in potestate*, or two
brothers in the *potestas* of the same father, may both be
witnesses, or one of them a witness and the other the balance-
holder, where a third party is *familiae emptor*; for there is no
harm in getting more than one person from the same house-
7 hold to act as witnesses of a stranger's deed.   A dumb or
deaf person, a madman, a pupil, or a woman, can neither be
familiae emptor nor be employed as a witness or as balance-

---

§ 3. Comp. Gai. ii, §§ 105, 107.
§§ 4, 5. Comp. Gai. ii, 106.
    [1] The MS. has *familias mente;*
hence many eds. *filiofamiliae emente.*
§ 6. Reproduced in fr. 17, D. *de testibus*
(xxii, 5), from which the word
26

filius, omitted in the text, is borrowed. Comp. § 8, I. *de testam.*
(ii, 10).
    [1] So in the fr. Dig. and par. Inst.
referred to; *institutus* in the MS.
§ 7. Comp. § 6, I. *de testam.* (ii, 10).

8 testis libripensue fieri potest.   Latinus Iunianus et familiae
emptor et testis et libripens fieri potest, quoniam cum eo
testamenti factio est.

9   In testamento quod per aes et libram fit duae res aguntur,
familiae mancipatio et nuncupatio testamenti. nuncupatur
testamentum in hunc modum : tabulas testamenti testator
tenens ita dicit: HAEC VT IN HIS TABVLIS CERISVE[1] SCRIPTA
SVNT ITA DO, ITA LEGO, ITA TESTOR ; ITAQVE VOS, QVIRITES,
TESTIMONIVM PERHIBETOTE.[2] quae nuncupatio et testatio[3]
uocatur.

10   Filius familiae testamentum facere non potest, quoniam
nihil suum habet ut testari de eo possit. sed diuus Augustus
militibus concessit[1] ut filius familiae miles de eo peculio quod

11 in castris adquisiuit testamentum facere possit.   Qui de
statu suo incertus est, fac eo[1] quod patre peregre mortuo

---

8 holder.   A Junian latin may be employed either as familiae
emptor, witness, or balance-holder ; for with him there is
testamenti factio.

9   In a testament by the copper and the scales there are two
separate acts,—the mancipation of the familia [or estate], and
the nuncupation of the testament. The nuncupation proceeds
thus : the testator, holding his testamentary tablets, speaks as
follows : ' As is written in these waxen tablets, so do I give,
so do I legate, so do I declare my will ; therefore, Quirites,
grant me your testimony.' This nuncupation is also called
testatio.

10   A filiusfamilias cannot make a testament ; for he has
nothing of his own about which to declare his will. But the
emperor Augustus made this concession to the military profession,—that a filiusfamilias, being a soldier, might make a
testament disposing of the peculium he had acquired on

11 service.   He who is in uncertainty as to his status, as when
he is ignorant that he has become sui iuris through his father's

---

§ 8. Comp. xi, 16 ; xx, 14 ; xxii, 3 ;
Gai. ii, 114, note 1.
§ 9. Comp. Gai. ii, 104, and notes.
    [1] Gai. has cerisque ; so has Isidor.
Orig. v, 24, § 12.
    [2] Pbitote in the MS., whence most
eds. praebitote.
    [3] Comp. pr. I. de test. (ii, 10).
§ 10. Comp. Paul. iii, 4a, § 3 ; pr. I.
quib. non est perm. test. fac. (ii, 12).
    [1] This is a suggestion of Boeck-
ing's, and finds some justification in

pr. I. quib. non est perm. test. fac.
(ii, 12). The MS. has Augustus
Marcus constituit. It has been proposed to substitute Magnus or primus for Marcus ; Hu. replaces it
with moribus ; and K., following
Cuj., deals with it as an incautious
gloss. So does Bk. in his text. I
prefer the suggestion in his notes.
§ 11. Comp. fr. 14, fr. 15, D. qui test.
fac. poss. (xxviii, 1).
    [1] So Hu., improving on Heim-

ignorat se sui iuris esse, testamentum facere non potest.
12 Inpubes, licet sui iuris sit, facere testamentum non potest,
13 quoniam nondum plenum iudicium animi habet. Mutus
surdus, furiosus, itemque prodigus cui lege bonis interdictum
est, testamentum facere non possunt : mutus, quoniam uerba
nuncupationis loqui non potest ; surdus, quoniam uerba
familiae emptoris exaudire non potest ; furiosus, quoniam
mentem non habet ut testari de *sua re*[1] possit ; prodigus,
quoniam commercio[2] illi interdictum est[3] et ob id familiam
14 mancipare non potest.[2] Latinus Iunianus, item is qui
dediticiorum numero est, testamentum facere non potest :
latinus quidem quoniam nominatim lege Iunia prohibitus est ;
is autem qui dediticiorum numero est, quoniam nec quasi
ciuis Romanus testari potest, cum sit peregrinus, nec quasi

---

12 death abroad, cannot make a testament. A person under
puberty, though he may be *sui iuris*, cannot make a testament,
13 for his judgment is still defective. Neither a person who
cannot speak, nor one who cannot hear, nor a madman, nor a
spendthrift to whom the law has interdicted the management
of his property, can make a testament : a mute, because he
cannot utter the words of nuncupation ; a deaf person, because
he cannot hear the words of the *familiae emptor ;* a madman,
because he has no rational will to enable him to declare it in
reference to his estate ; a spendthrift, because he is denied the
commercium, and so is unable to mancipate his *familia.*
14 Neither a Junian latin nor a freedman numbered amongst the
dediticians can make a testament : a latin, because he is expressly forbidden by the Junian law ; a deditician freedman,
because he can neither test as a Roman citizen, seeing he is a
peregrin, nor as a peregrin, seeing he is not a citizen of any

---

bach's *fac ideo ;* the ms. has *facto ;*
Bk., Vahl., and K., *factus.* The
illustration does not seem a very
happy one, as, except he were a
soldier, a man would not be likely
to make a testament unless he believed himself *sui iuris ;* while if he
was a soldier, making a military
testament, it did not matter in the
least whether he was *sui* or *alieni
iuris.*

§ 12. Comp. Gai. ii, § 113.
§ 13. Comp. Paul. iii, 4a, §§ 5, 11,
12; §§ 2, 3, I. *quib. non est perm.*
(ii, 12).

[1] So Hugo and Kr. The ms. has
de ea re, which Bk. and Hu. retain,
the former explaining that he understands it to mean *cum effectu.*
But this, as well as the *de ea recte*
of Cann., amounts to *testatio mentis*
(§ 1) *de mente*, which is a questionable locution.

[2] See xix, 5, note.

[3] See the formula of interdiction
in Paul. iii, 4a, § 7. See also
xii, 3.

§ 14. Comp. i, §§ 10, 11 ; xi, 16 ; xvii, 1 ;
xxii, §§ 2, 3 ; Gai. i, §§ 13, 22-25 ;
iii, 74.

peregrinus, quoniam nullius certae ciuitatis *ciuis est*,[1] ut
15 *secundum*[2] leges ciuitatis suae testetur.   Feminae post
duodecimum annum aetatis testamenta facere possunt tutore
16 auctore, donec in tutela sunt.   Seruus publicus *populi
Romani*[1] partis dimidiae testamenti faciendi habet ius.

[*XXI. QVEMADMODVM HERES INSTITVI DEBEAT.*]

Heres institui recte potest his uerbis : TITIVS HERES ESTO,
TITIVS HERES SIT, TITIVM HEREDEM ESSE IVBEO; illa autem
institutio : HEREDEM INSTITVO, HEREDEM FACIO, plerisque inprobata est.

[*XXII. QVI HEREDES INSTITVI POSSVNT.*]

1   Heredes institui possunt qui testamenti factionem cum

---

particular [peregrin] state, so as to be able to test according to
15 the laws of his own country.   Women can make testaments
after their twelfth year, [but only] with *auctoritas* of their
16 tutors so long as they are in tutelage.   A public slave of
the Roman people has the right to make a testament of one
half [of his *peculium*].

[*XXI. HOW AN HEIR OUGHT TO BE INSTITUTED.*]

An heir can be properly instituted by these words : ' Titius
be heir,' or ' Let Titius be heir,' or ' I order that Titius shall
be heir.'   But such an institution as ' I institute [Titius] as
heir,' or ' I make [Titius] my heir,' is generally disapproved.

[*XXII. WHO CAN BE INSTITUTED HEIRS.*]

1   Those can be instituted as heirs who have *testamenti factio*

[1] So Cuj. and all subsequent eds.;
the MS. has *sciens*.
[2] The MS. has *aduersus*, — a
mistake which occurs again in
xxviii, 1.
§ 15.   Comp. Gai. ii, §§ 113, 118.
§ 16.   This statement is not supported
elsewhere. Pomp. in fr. 16, pr.,
Modest. in fr. 19, and Vlp. himself
in fr. 20, § 7, D. *qui test. fac. poss.*
(xxviii, 1), all deny that a slave
could make a testament. Owners,
however, sometimes allowed their
slaves to make ' *quasi testamenta*,'
disposing of their *peculia* amongst

their comrades,—*intra domum* ; see
Plin. Epist. viii, 16.
[1] Here, as in xxiv, 28, the MS.
has *praetoriani*.

TIT. XXI.   Comp. Gai. ii, 117, and
note ; Vlp. in fr. 1, §§ 3-7, D. *de
heredib. instit.* (xxviii, 5) ; Const. in
l. 15, C. *de testam.* (vi, 23).

TIT. XXII, § 1.   Comp. § 24, I. *de legat.*
(ii, 20) ; fr. 16, D. *qui test. fac.
poss.* (xxviii, 1).   On meaning of
testamenti factio, see Gai. ii, 114,
note 1.

2 testatore habent. Dediticiorum numero heres institui non potest, quia peregrinus est, cum quo testamenti factio non est.

3 [*Latinum Iunianum heredem instituere omnino licet et*][1] si quidem mortis testatoris tempore uel intra diem cretionis[2] ciuis Romanus sit, heres esse potest; quodsi latinus manserit, lege Iunia capere hereditatem prohibetur. idem iuris est in

4 persona caelibis propter legem Iuliam.[3] Incerta persona heres institui non potest, uelut hoc modo: QVISQVIS PRIMVS AD FVNVS MEVM VENERIT HERES ESTO; quoniam certum con-

5 silium debet esse testantis. Nec municipia nec municipes heredes institui possunt, quoniam incertum corpus est, et neque cernere uniuersi neque pro herede *gerere*[1] possunt ut heredes fiant: senatusconsulto tamen concessum est ut a libertis suis heredes institui possint. Sed fideicommissa hereditas municipibus restitui potest; denique hoc senatus-

---

2 with the testator. An individual numbered amongst the dediticians cannot be instituted heir, for he is a peregrin, and

3 with him there is no *testamenti factio*. *A Junian latin may at any time be instituted as heir, and if,* at the date of the testator's death, or before the time for cretion has expired, he be a Roman citizen, he can actually become heir; but if he have remained a latin he is forbidden by the Junian law to take the inheritance. The rule is the same in the case of an

4 unmarried person by reason of the Julian law. An uncertain person cannot be instituted heir, for example thus: 'Whoever shall come first to my funeral, let him be my heir;' for the intention of a testator ought to be definite.

5 Neither a municipality nor its members can be instituted heirs, for the body is uncertain, and neither can they cern collectively, nor collectively behave as heirs, so as to become heirs; but a senatusconsult allows them to be instituted by their freedmen. An inheritance left to them in a trust-deed, however, may be made over to the members of a municipal corporation; in fact this is provided by the same senatus-

---

§ 2. Comp. Gai. i, 125; ii, §§ 110, 218.
§ 3. Comp. Gai. i, §§ 23, 24; ii, 275; below, § 8; above, xvii, 1; xx, 14.
[1] Added by M. Bk., Vahl., and K. have simply *Latinus Iunianus;* Hu. has *Latinus Iunianus heres instituti potest, et,* etc.
[2] See §§ 25 f.
[3] Comp. xvii, 1; Gai. ii, §§ 144, 286. To obtain the *ius capiendi* the celibate had to qualify himself by marriage within the same period.
§ 4. Comp. xxiv, 18; Gai. ii, 287.
§ 5. Comp. xxiv, 28; Vlp. in fr. 1, § 1, D. *de libert. univ.* (xxxviii, 3); fr. 26, D. *ad SC. Trebell.* (xxxvi, 1); l. 12, C. *de hered. inst.* (vi, 24).
[1] So Bk., Vahl., Hu., and K. The ms. has *p hirede herede cernere;* the earlier editions, including those of last century, *pro libito de herede cernere.*

6 consulto prospectum est.   Deos heredes instituere non possumus praeter eos quos senatusconsulto constitutionibusue
principum instituere concessum est, sicuti Iouem Tarpeium,
Apollinem Didymaeum *Mileti*,[1] Martem in Gallia, Mineruam
Iliensem, Herculem Gaditanum, Dianam Ephesiam, Matrem
Deorum *Sipylensem*[2] quae Smyrnae[3] colitur, et Caelestem
sanctam deam[4] Carthaginis.

7   Seruos heredes instituere possumus, nostros cum libertate,
alienos sine libertate, communes cum libertate uel sine

8 libertate.   Eum seruum qui tantum in bonis noster est
nec cum libertate heredem instituere possumus, quia latinitatem consequitur, quod non proficit ad hereditatem capien-

9 dam.   Alienos seruos heredes instituere possumus eos

---

6 consult.   We cannot institute deities as our heirs, except
those whose institution has expressly been permitted by
senatusconsult or imperial constitutions, such as the Tarpeian
Jove, the Didymaean Apollo of Miletus, Mars in Gaul,
Minerva of Troy, Hercules of Cadiz, Diana of Ephesus, the
Sipylenian Mother of the Gods worshipped at Smyrna, and
Caelestis, the *holy goddess* of Carthage.

7   We may institute slaves as our heirs,—our own with liberty,
other people's without it, common ones either with it or

8 without it.   We cannot institute one whom we hold only
in bonis, even though with gift of freedom ; for thereby he
acquires [no more than] latinity, which does not avail him for

9 taking an inheritance.   Other people's slaves we can insti-

---

§ 6.   Comp. Dio Cass. lv, 2; lxxix, 12;
fr. 38, § 6, D. *de legat. III.* (xxxii).
   [1] So M., Hu., and K., with good
geographical reason ; the ms. has
sicuti, which Bk. retains.
   [2] So Bk. The ms. has *Sipilen-
sim* ; Cuj. *Cybelen eam.* M. and
Hu. read *Sipylenen* ; the former,
following Jahn, finding a use for the
sim of the ms. by converting it into
Nemesim, probably because this
deity was figured on some of the
coins of Smyrna. But *quae Smyrnae colitur* is equally applicable to
Strabo's θεὰ Σιπυλήνη, the Cybele
of Mount Sipylos, in the vicinity
of Smyrna.
   [3] The ms. has *hysmirne*.
   [4] The ms. has *Caelestem Salinensem
Carthaginis*, which is retained by
most eds. Hu. substitutes *Caelestem Selenen deam Carthaginis*.

But *Caelestis* is to be read here as
the proper name of the deity, not
as a mere epithet : see Capitolin.
Pertinax, 4 ; *Macrin.* 3 ; Trebell.
Poll. *Tyr. trig.* 29 ; Orelli and
Henzen, nos. 1943, 5859. *Salinensis*
may mean 'originally of Salinae,'—
and there were many places of that
name ; but the inscription last referred to (discovered in Algeria),
in its words '*deae sanctae Caelestis*,'
suggests that the copyist may thus
have corruptly rendered the contraction *sctam deam (sanctam deam*).
In the inscription first referred to,
she is called *Caelestis Augusta Carthaginis*.

§§ 7-13.   Comp. Gai. ii, §§ 185-190 ; pr.
§§ 1-3, I. *de hered. inst.* (ii, 14).
§ 8.   Cp. Gai. ii, 276, note ; above, § 3.
§ 9.   Comp. fr. 31, pr., fr. 32, D. *de
her. inst.* (xxviii, 5).

tantum [1] quorum cum dominis testamenti factionem habemus.

10 Communis seruus cum libertate recte quidem heres instituitur quasi proprius pro parte nostra; sine libertate autem quasi

11 alienus propter socii partem. Proprius seruus cum libertate heres institutus, si quidem in eadem causa permanserit,

12 ex testamento liber et heres fit, id est necessarius. Quod si ab ipso testatore uiuente manumissus uel alienatus sit, suo arbitrio uel iussu emptoris hereditatem adire potest. sed si sine libertate sit institutus, omnino non consistit institutio.

13 Alienus seruus heres institutus, si quidem in ea causa permanserit, iussu domini debet hereditatem adire; quod si uiuo testatore manumissus aut alienatus a domino fuerit, aut suo arbitrio aut iussu emptoris poterit adire hereditatem.

14   Sui heredes instituendi sunt uel exheredandi. sui autem heredes sunt liberi quos in potestate habemus, tam naturales quam adoptiui; item uxor quae in manu est, et nurus quae

---

tute as our heirs only when we have *testamenti factio* with

10 their owners.   A slave that is common to us and some other person is rightly instituted with liberty, seeing that he is our property in so far as our share is concerned; or without it, seeing he is another person's so far as regards our partner's

11 share.   If the testator's own slave, instituted with freedom, continue in the same condition, he becomes free and heir

12 under the testament, *i.e.* a necessary heir;   but if he have been either manumitted or alienated by the testator himself during his lifetime, then he can enter at his own discretion [in the one case], or on the instruction of his purchaser [in the other].   If, however, he be instituted without accompany-

13 ing gift of freedom, the institution fails entirely.   Another person's slave, who has been instituted heir, if he remain in the same condition, must enter on his owner's instructions; but if he have been manumitted or alienated by his owner during the testator's lifetime, he can enter of his own accord [in the first case], by order of his purchaser [in the second].

14   *Sui heredes* must be either instituted or disinherited. *Sui heredes* are the descendants whom we have in our *potestas*, whether natural or adoptive: together with our wife *in manu*, and our daughter-in-law *in manu* of a son *in potestate*.

---

[1] So Hugo and subsequent eds.; the MS. has *tamen*.

§ 10. Comp. Paul. iii, 6, § 4.

§ 12. Just. declared an express gift of freedom to be unnecessary, being implied in the institution; pr. I. *de hered. inst.* (ii, 14).

§§ 14-22. Comp. Gai. ii, §§ 123-137, tit. I. *de exher. lib.* (ii, 13).

15 in manu est filii quem in potestate habemus.   Postumi
quoque liberi, id est qui in utero sunt, si tales sunt ut nati
in potestate nostra futuri sint suorum heredum numero sunt.
16 Ex suis heredibus filius quidem neque heres institutus neque
nominatim¹ exheredatus non patitur ualere testamentum.
17 Reliquae uero personae liberorum, uelut filia nepos neptis, si
praeteritae sint, ualet testamentum, [sed] scriptis heredibus
adcrescunt, suis quidem heredibus in partem uirilem, extraneis
18 autem in partem dimidiam.   Postumi quoque² liberi cuiuscumque sexus omissi quod ualuit testamentum agnatione
19 rumpunt.   Eos qui in utero sunt, si nati sui heredes nobis
futuri sunt, possumus instituere heredes : si quidem post
mortem nostram nascantur, ex iure ciuili ; si uero uiuentibus
nobis, ex lege Iunia.³
20   Filius qui in potestate est, si non instituatur heres, nominatim exheredari debet ; reliqui sui heredes utriusque sexus
21 aut nominatim aut inter ceteros.   Postumus filius nominatim exheredandus est ; filia postuma ceteraeque postumae

---

15 After-born descendants too are classed amongst our *sui heredes*,
i.e. such children in the womb as, were they already born,
16 would be in our *potestas*.   The fact that a son, being one
of our *sui heredes*, is neither instituted heir nor disinherited
17 by name, precludes the validity of our testament.   If, however, other descendants, such as a daughter, grandson, or
granddaughter be passed over, the testament is valid ; but
they come in for a share along with the heirs that have been
instituted,—with *sui* on a footing of equality, with strangers
18 for one-half of the inheritance.   Omitted after-born descendants of either sex, by agnation [*i.e.* by their birth] break
19 a testament previously valid.   We may institute as heirs
children in the womb,.provided they would have been amongst
our *sui heredes* if already born ; [we are entitled to do so],
as regards those born after our death, by the *ius ciuile*, and
as regards those born in our lifetime, by the *Junia-Vellaean*
law.
20   A son *in potestate*, if he be not instituted heir, must be disinherited by name ; other *sui heredes* of either sex may be
21 disinherited either by name or amongst ' the others.'   An
after-born son must be expressly disinherited ; a daughter or

---

¹ After *nominatim* the ms. has
quo ; Vahl. substitutes uō (*ut oportet*), which finds a justification in
xxiii, 2.

² Hu. substitutes *quicunque.*
³ The ms. has *Iulia.* But the law
referred to seems to be the *lex Iunia
Vellaea ;* see Gai. ii, 134, and note.

feminae uel nominatim uel inter ceteros, dummodo inter
22 ceteros exheredatis aliquid legetur. Nepotes et pronepotes,
ceterique masculi postumi praeter filium, uel nominatim uel
inter ceteros cum adiectione legati sunt exheredandi; sed
tutius est tamen nominatim eos exheredari; et id obseruatur
magis.

23   Emancipatos liberos *quamuis iure*[1] ciuili neque heredes
instituere neque exheredare necesse sit, tamen praetor iubet,
si non instituantur heredes, exheredari, masculos omnes
nominatim, feminas uel [*nominatim uel*][2] inter ceteros;
alioquin contra tabulas bonorum possessionem eis pollicetur.

24   Inter necessarios heredes, id est seruos cum libertate
heredes scriptos, et suos et necessarios, id est liberos qui in
potestate sunt, iure ciuili nihil interest : nam utrique etiam
inuiti heredes sunt. sed iure praetorio suis et necessariis
heredibus abstinere se a parentis hereditate permittitur; necessariis autem tantum heredibus abstinendi potestas non datur.

25   Extraneus heres, siquidem cum cretione sit heres institutus,

---

other female after-born may be disinherited either expressly
or in the *ceteri* clause, provided in the latter case that some
22 legacy is left her.   Grandsons, great-grandsons, and all
other male after-born descendants than a son, may be disinherited either expressly or amongst 'the others,' [in the latter
case] with bequest of a legacy; but it is safer to disinherit
them by name; and this is the usual practice.

23   Although by the *ius ciuile* it is unnecessary either to
institute or disinherit emancipated children, yet the praetor
requires that, if not instituted, they shall be disinherited,—
males, without exception, by name, females *either by name* or
in the *ceteri* clause; otherwise he grants them possession of
the deceased's estate in opposition to the testament.

24   By the *ius ciuile* there is no difference between *heredes
necessarii, i.e.* slaves instituted heirs with freedom, and *sui et
necessarii, i.e.* descendants *in potestate* of the testator; for both
become heirs whether they will or not. But by the praetorian law *sui et necessarii* are allowed to abstain from the
inheritance of a parent; to heirs who are simply *necessarii,*
however, this power of abstaining is not conceded.

25   A stranger heir, if he be instituted with cretion, becomes

§ 23. Comp. Gai. ii, 135; below, xxviii,   [2] Added by K.
§§ 2-4.   § 24.   Comp. Gai. ii, §§ 153, 156, 160.
[1] So Schill. and all recent eds.;   §§ 25-30.   Comp. Gai. ii, §§ 164-170.
the ms. has *qui in re.*

cernendo fit heres; *si uero*[1] sine cretione, pro herede gerendo.
26 Pro herede gerit qui rebus hereditariis tamquam dominus
utitur, uelut qui *auctionem*[2] rerum hereditariarum facit aut
27 seruis hereditariis cibaria dat.   Cretio est certorum dierum
spatium quod datur instituto heredi ad deliberandum utrum
expediat[3] ei adire hereditatem nec ne, uelut: TITIVS HERES
ESTO, CERNITOQVE IN DIEBVS CENTVM PROXIMIS QVIBVS SCIERIS
28 POTERISQVE; NISI ITA CREVERIS EXHERES ESTO.   Cernere est
uerba cretionis dicere ad hunc modum: QVOD ME MEVIVS[4]
29 HEREDEM INSTITVIT EAM HEREDITATEM ADEO CERNOQVE.   Sine
cretione heres institutus, si constituerit nolle se heredem esse,
statim excluditur ab hereditate et amplius eam adire non
30 potest.   Cum cretione uero heres institutus, sicut cernendo
fit heres, ita non aliter excluditur quam si intra diem cretionis
non creuerit: ideoque etiamsi constituerit nolle se heredem
esse, tamen, si supersint dies cretionis, poenitentia actus cernendo heres fieri potest.
31 Cretio aut uulgaris dicitur aut continua: uulgaris, in qua

26 heir by cerning; if without it, by behaving as heir.   He
behaves as heir who deals with the hereditary estate as if it
were his own, as for instance when he puts up things belonging to it to auction, or furnishes the slaves belonging to it
27 with food.   Cretion is a certain period of time allowed to
the instituted heir for deliberating whether or not it will be
for his advantage to enter to the inheritance, thus: 'Titius be
heir, and cern within the next hundred days after you know
28 and can; if you have not thus cerned, be disinherited.'   To
cern is to recite the words of cerniture in this way: 'Whereas
Mevius has instituted me his heir, I hereby enter to and cern
29 his inheritance.'   An heir instituted without cretion, if he
have declared his resolution not to be heir, is at once excluded
from the inheritance, and has no further opportunity of enter-
30 ing.   He, however, who is instituted with cretion, as he
becomes heir by cerning, is not otherwise excluded than by
failing to cern within the cretionary period; therefore,
although he may have [informally] declared that he does not
mean to be heir, yet if there be still part of the time for
cretion unexpired, repenting of what he has done he may still
become heir by cerning.
31   Cretion is styled either common or continuous,—common,

---

[1] The ms. has *siue*.
[2] The ms. has *actionem*.
[3] The ms. has *expiat*.

[4] The ms. has *cum id medius*,
but see Gai. ii, 166.
§§ 31, 32. Comp. Gai. ii, §§ 171, 172.

adiciuntur haec uerba : QVIBVS SCIERIS POTERISQVE ; continua,
32 in qua non adiciuntur.   Ei qui uulgarem cretionem habet
dies illi *tantum* [1] computantur quibus *sciit* [2] se heredem institutum esse et potuit cernere ; ei uero qui continuam habet cretionem etiam illi dies computantur quibus ignorauit se heredem
institutum, aut sciuit quidem sed non potuit cernere.

33   Heredes aut instituti dicuntur aut substituti : [*instituti*],
qui primo gradu scripti sunt ; substituti, qui secundo gradu
uel sequentibus heredes scripti sunt, uelut : TITIVS HERES
ESTO, CERNITOQVE IN DIEBVS PROXIMIS CENTVM QVIBVS SCIES
POTERISQVE : [QVODNI] [1] ITA CREVERIS, EXHERES ESTO.   TVNC
MEVIVS HERES ESTO, CERNITOQVE IN DIEBVS et reliqua. similiter
et deinceps substituti potest.

34   Si sub inperfecta cretione heres institutus sit, id est non
adiectis his uerbis : SI NON CREVERIS EXHERES ESTO, sed si ita :
SI NON CREVERIS, TVNC MEVIVS HERES ESTO, cernendo quidem
superior inferiorem excludit ; non cernendo autem, sed pro

---

when the words 'in which you know and can' are added,
32 continuous, when those words are not added.   Against him
who has common cretion those days only are counted in which
he knows that he has been instituted heir and is in a position
to cern ; against him, on the other hand, whose cretion is continuous, even that time is counted in which he was ignorant
that he had been instituted heir, or may have known it perhaps but was unable to cern.

33   Heirs are called either institutes or substitutes,—institutes,
when their names are mentioned in the testament in the first
place, substitutes when in the second or a subsequent place,
thus : 'Titius be heir, and cern within the next hundred days
after you know and can ; if you do not so cern, be disinherited ; then Mevius be heir, and cern within the next
hundred days,' etc.   And any number of successive substitutions may be made in the same way.

34   If an heir be instituted under an imperfect cretion-clause,
i.e. one in which the words are not 'If you have not cerned,
be disinherited,' but 'If you have not cerned, then Mevius be
heir,' the institute by cerning excludes the substitute ; if he
do not cern, however, but only behave as heir, he lets in the

[1] So K. ; the MS. has *dantur* ;
most eds. *duntaxat*.
[2] The MS. has *scit* ; Bk. and K.
sciuit. But see Fr. Vat. §§ 1, 156.
§ 33. Comp. Gai. ii, §§ 174-176.

[1] So Bk. and subsequent eds., on
the authority of Gai. ii, 174 ; omitted in the MS. ; by earlier eds. *nisi*.
§ 34. Comp. Gai. ii, §§ 177, 178,
where, however, there is no men-

herede gerendo, in partem admittit substitutum. sed postea diuus Marcus constituit ut et pro herede gerendo ex asse fiat heres.[1] quod si neque creuerit neque pro herede gesserit, ipse excluditur et substitutus ex asse fit heres.[1]

[*XXIII. QVEMADMODVM TESTAMENTA RVMPVNTVR.*]

1 Testamentum iure factum infirmatur duobus modis, si ruptum aut inritum factum sit.
2 Rumpitur testamentum mutatione, id est si postea aliud testamentum iure factum sit; item agnatione, id est si suus heres agnascatur, qui neque heres institutus neque ut oportet
3 exheredatus sit. Agnascitur suus heres aut agnascendo, aut adoptando, aut in manum conueniendo, aut in locum sui heredis succedendo, uelut nepos mortuo filio uel emancipato,

---

substitute for a part of the inheritance. (But the late emperor Marcus afterwards provided by a constitution of his that by simply behaving as heir the institute should become heir to the whole of it.) If he have neither cerned nor behaved as heir, then the institute is altogether excluded, and the substitute becomes heir to the whole inheritance.

[*XXIII. HOW TESTAMENTS ARE BROKEN.*]

1 A testament made according to the requirements of law is invalidated in either of two ways,—if it be broken, or if it be irritated.
2 A testament is broken by *mutatio, i.e.* if subsequently another testament be made with all legal formalities; also by *agnatio, i.e.* if a *suus heres* come into existence who has neither been instituted heir nor disinherited as the law prescribes.
3 A *suus heres* comes into existence either by birth, or by adoption, or by *in manum conuentio*, or by stepping by succession into the place of another *suus heres* (as a grandson into the place of a son who has died or been emancipated), or by

tion of the constitution of Marc. Aurelius.
    [1] Equivalent to the *in totam hereditatem succedit* of Gai. The entire estate was figured as an *as*, divisible into so many twelfths (*unciae*) or multiples of a twelfth; see § 5, I. *de hered. inst.* (ii, 14).

TIT. XXIII, § 1. Comp. pr. I. *quib. mod. test. infirm.* (ii, 17).
§ 2. Comp. Gai. ii, §§ 144, 131; above, xxii, §§ 14-18.
§ 3. Comp. Gai. ii, §§ 133, 138-141, 159; iii, 6; Paul. in *Collat.* xvi, 3, § 7.

aut manumissione, id est si filius ex prima secundaue mancipatione manumissus reuersus sit in patris potestatem.

4   Inritum fit testamentum si testator capite deminutus fuerit,
aut si iure facto testamento nemo extiterit heres.

5   Si is qui testamentum fecit ab hostibus captus sit, testamentum eius ualet ; si quidem reuersus fuerit, iure postliminii,
si uero ibi decesserit, ex lege Cornelia, *quae* perinde succes-
sionem eius confirmat atque si in ciuitate decessisset.

6   Si septem signis testium signatum sit testamentum, licet
iure ciuili ruptum uel iuritum factum sit, praetor scriptis
heredibus iuxta tabulas bonorum possessionem dat, si testator
et ciuis Romanus et suae potestatis cum moreretur fuit ; quam
bonorum possessionem cum re, id est cum effectu habent, si
nemo alius iure heres sit.

7   Liberis inpuberibus in potestate manentibus, tam natis
quam postumis, heredes substituere parentes possunt duplici
modo, id est aut eo *quo* extraneis, ut si heredes non extiterint

---

manumission, *i.e.* by the return into the *patria potestas* of a son
manumitted from a first or second mancipation.

4   A testament is irritated when the testator suffers *capitis
deminutio,* or when, though executed in all respects regularly,
no one has become heir under it.

5   If a man who has made a testament be taken captive by an
enemy, his deed is nevertheless valid : if he have returned
home, it is so *iure postliminii ;* if he have died in captivity,
it is so by the Cornelian law, which declares that his succession shall hold good just as if he had died a citizen.

6   If a testament be sealed with the seals of seven witnesses,
then, notwithstanding that according to the *ius ciuile* it may
have been broken or irritated, the praetor gives to the heirs
named in it possession of the estate in terms of the deed, provided the testator was a Roman citizen and *sui iuris* when he
died ; and this possession will be *cum re, i.e.* effectual to them,
if there be no other person whom the law prefers as heir.

7   To his impuberate children *in potestate,* both born and to be
born, a parent may substitute heirs in two ways,—either in
that employed in substituting to strangers, viz. that if the

§ 4. Comp. Gai. ii, §§ 144-146.
§ 5. Comp. Paul. iii, 4a, § 8 ; § 4, I.
quib. non est perm. (ii, 12).
§ 6. Comp. Gai. ii, §§ 119, 147-149,
where he indicates the cases in
which an heir-at-law was preferred
to the *heredes scripti,* and the possession of the latter consequently
was *sine re.* See also below, xxviii,
§§ 6, 13.
§§ 7-9. Comp. Gai. ii, 179-184.

liberi substitutus heres fiat; aut proprio iure, id est [*ut*] si
post mortem parentis heredes facti intra pubertatem deces-
8 serint substitutus heres fiat.   Etiam exheredatis filiis
9 substituere parentibus licet.   Non aliter inpuberi filio substituere quis heredem potest quam si sibi *prius* [1] heredem
instituerit uel ipsum filium uel quemlibet alium.

10   Milites *quomodocumque* [1] fecerint testamenta, ualent, id
est etiam sine legitima obseruatione.   nam principalibus constitutionibus permissum est illis, quomodocumque uellent,
quomodocumque possent, testari.   idque *testamentum quod
miles* [2] contra iuris regulam fecit ita demum ualet, si uel in
castris mortuus sit uel post missionem intra annum.

[*XXIIII. DE LEGATIS.*]

1   Legatum est quod legismodo, id est imperatiue, testamento
relinquitur.   Nam ea quae precatiuo modo relinquuntur fideicommissa uocantur.

---

children shall not have become heirs the substitute shall be
heir, or in one appropriate to the particular case, viz. that
if they have become heirs after their parent's death, but have
died before reaching puberty, then the substitute shall be heir.
8 A parent may make a [pupillary] substitution even to his dis-
9 inherited children.   But no one can thus substitute an heir
to his impuberate child, unless he has first instituted as his
own heir either that child or some other person.

10   The testaments of soldiers are valid however made, that is
to say even though the legal formalities have not been observed; for by imperial constitutions soldiers are allowed to
test in any way they like, in any way they can.   And such
a testament made by a soldier, contrary to the rules of the
common law, is held valid if he die either in active service or
within a year after his discharge.

[*XXIV. OF LEGACIES.*]

1   A legacy is what is bequeathed in a testament by a *lex*,
that is, imperatively.   For what are bequeathed in words of
request are called *fideicommissa*.

---

[1] So most recent eds., following
Vlp. in fr. 2, § 4, D. *de uulg. subst.*
(xxviii, 6); the ms. has *quis.*
§ 10. Comp. Gai. ii, §§ 109-111, 114;
above, xx, 10.
[1] The ms. has *commodocumque.*

[2] So most eds., following Du
Tillet; the ms. has *testamento cum
illis.*

TIT. xxiv, § 1. Comp. pr. tit. I. *de
legat.* (ii, 20); Gai. ii, 104, note 8.

2   Legamus autem quattuor modis : per uindicationem, per
3 damnationem, sinendi modo, per praeceptionem.   Per uindicationem his uerbis legamus : DO LEGO, CAPITO, SVMITO, SIBI [1]
4 HABETO.   Per damnationem his uerbis : HERES MEVS DAMNAS
5 ESTO DARE, DATO, FACITO, HEREDEM MEVM DARE IVBEO.   Sinendi modo ita : HERES MEVS DAMNAS ESTO SINERE LVCIVM
6 TITIVM SVMERE ILLAM REM SIBIQVE HABERE.   Per praeceptionem sic : LVCIVS TITIVS ILLAM REM PRAECIPITO.

7   Per uindicationem legari possunt res quae utroque tempore
ex iure Quiritium testatoris fuerunt, mortis et *quo* [1] testamentum faciebat, praeterquam si pondere numero mensura con-
tineantur ; in his enim satis est si uel mortis dumtaxat tem-
8 pore [*eius*] [2] fuerint ex iure Quiritium.   Per damnationem
omnes res legari possunt, etiam quae non sunt testatoris,
9 dummodo tales sint quae dari possint :   liber homo aut res
populi aut sacra aut religiosa nec per damnationem legari
10 potest, quoniam dari non potest.   Sinendi modo legari

---

2   We legate in four ways,—by vindication, damnation, per-
3 mission, and preception.   By vindication, we legate thus :
4 'I give and legate,' 'take,' 'have for yourself ; '   by damnation thus : 'Be my heir bound to give,' 'let my heir give '
5 or 'do,' 'I order my heir to give ; '   by permission thus :
'Be my heir bound to let Lucius Titius take such or such a
6 thing and have it for himself ; '   by preception thus : 'Let
Lucius Titius first take such or such a thing.'

7   By vindication those things may be bequeathed that belonged to the testator on quirary title both at the time of
his death and when he made his testament, except things
passing by weight, number, or measure ; as regards them it is
enough that they were his *ex iure Quiritium* though only at
8 the time of his death.   By damnation anything whatever
may be legated, even though not the property of the testator,
9 provided it be such as can be given :   a freeman, or a thing
belonging to the people, or a thing that is sacred or religious,
cannot be legated even by damnation, because it cannot be
10 given.   By permission such things may be legated as are

§ 2. Comp. Gai. ii, 192 ; § 3, I. *de legat.*
(ii, 20).
§ 3. Comp. Gai. ii, 193.
     [1] The MS. has *siue* ; but see Gai.
§ 4. Comp. Gai. ii, 201.
§ 5. Comp. Gai. ii, 209.
§ 6. Comp. Gai. ii, 216.
§ 7. Comp. Gai. ii, 196.
     [1] So K. ; the MS. has *quomodo* ;

Bk. and Hu. *quam ;* most eds.
quando.
     [2] So Hu. ; L. and Bk. insert *tes-
tatoris ;* many eds. leave the text as
in the MS.
§ 8. Comp. Gai. ii, §§ 197, 202.
§ 9. Comp. Vlp. in fr. 39, §§ 8-10, D.
de legat. I. (xxx) ; Gai. iii, 97.
§ 10. Comp. Gai. ii, 210.

11 possunt res propriae testatoris et heredis eius.   Per praeceptionem legari possunt res quae etiam per uindicationem.

11a Si ea res quae non fuit utroque tempore testatoris ex iure
Quiritium per uindicationem legata sit, licet iure ciuili non
ualeat legatum, tamen senatusconsulto Neroniano firmatur,[1]
quo cautum est ut quod minus *pactis*[2] uerbis legatum est
perinde sit ac si optimo iure legatum esset : optimum autem
ius legati per damnationem est.

12   Si duobus eadem res per uindicationem legata sit, siue
coniunctim, uelut : TITIO ET SEIO HOMINEM STICHVM DO LEGO,
[*siue disiunctim, uelut : TITIO HOMINEM STICHVM DO LEGO, SEIO*
[*EVNDEM HOMINEM DO LEGO,*][1] iure ciuili concursu partes
fiebant, non *concurrente* altero pars eius alteri adcrescebat :[2]
sed post legem Papiam Poppaeam non capientis pars caduca

13 fit.[3]   Si per damnationem eadem res duobus legata sit, si
quidem coniunctim, singulis partes debentur, et non capientis

---

11 the property of the testator or his heir.   By preception the
same things may be legated as by vindication.

11a If a thing that was not the testator's in quiritary right at
both dates have been legated by vindication, although by the
ius ciuile the legacy is invalid, yet it is confirmed by the
Neronian senatusconsult. For it is thereby provided that a
legacy clothed in inappropriate words shall be treated as if
bequeathed in the most advantageous form ; and the most
advantageous form of legacy is that by damnation.

12   If the same thing had been left by vindication to two
persons, either conjointly thus : ' To Titius and Seius I give
and legate the slave Stichus,' [*or disjointly thus : ' To Titius
[I give and legate the slave Stichus ; to Seius I give and legate
[the same slave,*'] concourse, according to the *ius ciuile*
created a share in each, while if one of the legatees did not
concur, his share accresced to the other ; since the enactment
of the Papian law, however, the share of the non-taker becomes

13 caducous.   If the same thing be bequeathed to two legatees
by damnation, and that conjointly, a share of it is due to each,

§ 11. Comp. Gai. ii, §§ 220-222.
§ 11a. Comp. Gai. ii, 197.
    [1] Hu reads *confirmatur*.
    [2] So the MS. Many amendments
have been proposed,—*aptis, rectis,
iustis, perfectis, ratis, probatis,
exactis,* etc. But Dirks. (*Manuale,
v. Pactus*) assumes the correctness
of *pactis*, and defines it as *solemniter*

expressis.
§§ 12, 13. Comp. Gai. ii, §§ 199, 205-
208 ; § 8, I. *de legat.* (ii, 20).
    [1] Added from Gai. by Hugo and
all recent eds.
    [2] On *ius adcrescendi* comp. frs.
34-36, D. *ad L. Aquil.* (ix, 2).
    [3] On *caduca* see xvii, 2 ; xix,
17.

pars iure ciuili in hereditate remanebat, nunc autem caduca
fit; quod si disiunctim, singulis solidum debetur.

14   Optione autem legati per uindicationem data, legatarii
electio est, ueluti: HOMINEM OPTATO, ELEGITO; idemque est et
si tacite — — — — HOMINEM — — — HERES — — — HOMINEM
DARE, heredis electio est [quem] [1] uelit dare.

15   Ante heredis institutionem legari non potest, quoniam
[uis] [1] et potestas testamenti ab heredis lastitutione incipit.

16   Post mortem heredis legari non potest, ne ab heredis herede
legari uideatur, quod iuris ciuilis ratio non patitur.   in [1]

—by the *ius ciuile* the share of a non-taker remained in the
inheritance, but now becomes caducous; but if it be bequeathed disjointly, each is entitled to the whole.

14   When the option of a legacy is bequeathed by vindication,
in such words as 'choose (or select) a slave,' the choice is
with the legatee; and so it is when I have tacitly [*bequeathed*
[*a choice in this way: 'I give and legate*] a slave.'   [*But if*
[*bequeathed thus: 'Let*] my heir [*be bound*] to give a slave,' the
election is the heir's to give what slave he pleases.

15   A man cannot legate until he has instituted an heir; for
the force and power of the testament begins at the institution.

16   A legacy cannot be bequeathed [to take effect] after the heir's
death; for this would be to charge it upon the heir's heir,
which is contrary to the principle of the *ius ciuile*.   But it

---

§ 14. Comp. §§ 22, 23, I. *de legat.* (ii,
20). The MS. does not exhibit the
same defects as in the text; for
there the lacunae are filled up in a
hand of the sixteenth century as
follows: et si tacite *legauerim Titio*
hominem *aut decem*, heres *meus
dato* hominem *dare*, etc.,—a reconstruction that is on all hands dis-
credited. Cuj. (*Obs.* xvii, 28) suggested—idemque est si *generaliter*
(instead of *tacite*) *legauerim Titio*
hominem. *At si ita*: HERES MEVS
DAMNAS ESTO HOMINEM DARE, etc.
Savigny (*Obl.* i, p. 398) proposes a
reading that so far commends itself,
but that necessitates the alteration
of *hominem* (between the first and
second lacuna) into *optionem*: idemque est et si tacite *legauerim optionem. At si ita*: HERES MEVS DAMNAS
ESTO HOMINEM DARE, etc. Hu.,
following L., has—idemque est et

27

si tacite *data sit optio hoc* modo:
*TITIO HOMINEM DO LEGO. si uero
per damnationem, uelut* HERES MEVS
DAMNAS ESTO HOMINEM DARE, etc.
From the last two reconstructions a
reading may be extracted that is more
satisfactory than either,—than the
first because it utilises the *hominem*
of the MS., and than the second because it does not so overcrowd the
lacunae: idemque est. et si tacite
optionem legauerim hoc modo:
HOMINEM DO LEGO. *At si ita*:
HERES MEVS DAMNAS ESTO HOMI-
NEM DARE, etc.
[1] Added by Cuj.
§ 15. Comp. Gai. ii, 229.
[1] Added by L. on authority of
Gai. as quoted.
§ 16. Comp. Gai. ii, 232; below,
xxv, 8.
[1] So most eds.; the MS. has *st*; L.
and Bk. *ad*.

mortis autem heredis tempus legari potest, uelut: CVM HERES
MORIETVR.

17   Poenae causa legari non potest. poenae autem causa
legatur quod coercendi heredis [causa] [1] relinquitur, ut faciat
quid aut non faciat, non ut [ad] legatarium pertineat, ut puta
hoc modo: SI FILIAM TVAM IN MATRIMONIVM TITIO CONLOCA-
VERIS, DECEM MILIA SEIO DATO.

18   Incertae personae legari non potest, ueluti: QVICVMQVE FILIO
MEO FILIAM SVAM IN MATRIMONIVM CONLOCAVERIT, EI *HERES
MEVS* [1] TOT MILIA DATO.   sub certa tamen demonstratione in-
certae personae legari potest, uelut: EX COGNATIS MEIS QVI
NVNC SVNT, QVI PRIMVS AD FVNVS MEVM VENERIT, EI HERES
MEVS ILLVD DATO.

19   Neque ex falsa demonstratione neque ex falsa causa legatum infirmatur.   falsa demonstratio est uelut: TITIO FVNDVM
QVEM A TITIO EMI DO LEGO, cum is fundus a Titio emptus non
sit.   falsa causa est uelut: TITIO, QVONIAM NEGOTIA MEA

---

may be bequeathed [to take effect] at the moment of the
heir's death, as 'when my heir is dying.'

17   A thing cannot be legated by way of penalty.   And that is
legated by way of penalty which is left for the purpose of
constraining the heir to do or forbear from doing something,
rather than to benefit the legatee, as for instance thus: 'If
you fail to bestow your daughter in marriage on Titius, then
give Seius ten thousand sesterces.'

18   There can be no legacy to an uncertain person, as thus:
'My heir shall give so many thousands to any one who gives
his daughter in marriage to my son.'   One may legate, however, to an uncertain person definitely described, for instance
thus: 'To that man amongst those now my kinsmen who
first comes to my funeral let my heir give so-and-so.'

19   A legacy is not invalidated either by an erroneous description or an erroneous [statement of the] cause of granting.
There is an erroneous description in the words—'I give and
legate to Titius the land I bought from him,' if in fact it was
not bought from him.   There is an erroneous cause of granting assigned in the words—'I give and legate the land to

§ 17. Comp. Gai. ii, 235; below, xxv, 13.   [1] So Schult. and all subsequent
     [1] Added from Gai.   eds.; the ms. has *homini*.
§ 18. Comp. Gai. ii, 238; above, xxii,   § 19. Comp. §§ 30, 31, I. *de legat.*
     4; below, xxv, 13.   (ii, 20).

CVRAVIT, FVNDVM DO LEGO, *cum* negotia eius numquam Titius
curasset.

20 A legatario legari non potest. [21] Legatum ab eo tan-
21 tum dari potest qui (*heres scriptus est*) :[1] ideoque filio familiae
herede instituto uel seruo, neque a patre neque a domino legari
22 potest. Heredi a semet ipso legari non potest. [23] Ei
23 qui in potestate manu mancipioue est scripti heredis sub condicione legari potest, ut requiratur quo tempore dies legati
24 cedit in potestate heredis non sit. Ei cuius in potestate
manu mancipioue est heres scriptus legari [non] potest.

25 Sicut singulae res legari possunt, ita uniuersarum quoque
summa legari potest, ut puta [*hoc*] modo : HERES MEVS CVM
TITIO HEREDITATEM MEAM PARTITO,[1] DIVIDITO; quo casu dimidia

---

Titius because he managed my affairs for me,' if in fact Titius
had never managed affairs of the testator's.
20 A legacy cannot be charged on a legatee. [21] He only
21 can be burdened with it who *is named heir in the testament ;*
therefore if it be a *filiusfamilias* or a slave that is instituted
heir, a legacy cannot be charged upon his *paterfamilias* or
22 owner. The heir cannot be burdened with a legacy to
23 himself. A legacy may be left conditionally to a person in
the *potestas, manus,* or *mancipium* of the instituted heir; but
[to make it effectual] it is requisite that, when the time of
vesting arrives, the legatee shall be no longer in the heir's
24 *potestas.* A legacy cannot be bequeathed to the person
in whose *potestas, manus,* or *mancipium* the instituted heir
happens to be.
25 Just as individual articles may be bequeathed, so may a
certain amount of [the testator's] aggregate estate, for instance
thus : ' My heir is to share (or divide) the inheritance with
Titius.' In this case there is held to be a legacy of one-half

---

§ 20. Comp. Gai. ii, §§ 260, 271.
§ 21. Comp. xxv, 10.
  [1] There is here a lacuna in the MS.,
which has been filled in the sixteenth century with the words *extraneus est.* The reading in the text is
that of L., on authority of xix, 18.
Hu. and K. have *heres institutus est.*
§ 22. Comp. fr. 116, § 1, D. *de legat.
I.* (xxx).
§ 23. Comp. Gai. ii, 244; § 32, I. *de
legat.* (ii, 20), on the strength of
which many eds. interpolate *an*
after *requiratur.*
§ 24. Comp. Gai. ii, 245; § 33, I. *de*

legat. (ii, 20). Most eds., from
Cuj. downwards, agree that the *non*
(in brackets) should be deleted.
Hu. retains it by assuming a homeoteleutic omission and reading—*legari [potest, etiam sine condicione ;
si tamen heres ab eo factus sit legatum consequi] non potest.* This is
in accordance with the Inst., which,
for *consequi non potest,* uses the
word *euanescit.*
§ 25. Comp. Gai. ii, 254; fr. 164, § 1,
D. *de V. S.* (l, 16).
  [1] So the MS.; Schult., L., and
K. prefer *partitor.*

pars bonorum legata uidetur.   potest autem et alia pars, uelut tertia uel quarta, legari.   quae species partitio *appellatur*.[2]

26 Ususfructus legari potest iure ciuili earum rerum quarum salua substantia utendi fruendi potest esse facultas : et tam
27 singularum rerum quam plurium ; *item* partis. Senatus-consulto cautum est ut etiamsi earum rerum quae in abusu continentur, ut puta uini olei tritici, ususfructus legatus sit, legatario res tradantur, cautionibus interpositis de restituendis eis cum ususfructus ad legatarium pertinere desierit.
28 Ciuitatibus omnibus quae sub imperio *populi Romani*[1] sunt legari potest ; idque a diuo Nerua introductum, postea a senatu auctore Hadriano diligentius constitutum est.
29 Legatum, quod datum est, adimi potest uel eodem testamento uel codicillis testamento confirmatis, dum tamen eodem modo adimatur quo modo datum est.[1]

---

of the estate ; but any other part, a third say, or a fourth, may be bequeathed.   A legacy of this sort is styled *partitio*.
26 According to the *ius ciuile* the usufruct can be legated of things which are capable of being used, and whose fruits can be taken, without diminishing their substance ; and it may be a usufruct of one thing or of several, or of a part [of the
27 whole estate].   And it is provided by senatusconsult that if a usufruct be bequeathed even of things whose use lies in their consumption, wine say, or oil, or wheat, they shall be delivered to the legatee, on his giving security for restitution [of an equal quantity] when the usufruct has ceased to belong to him.
28 A man may legate to any municipal corporation within the Empire ; a power first conferred upon testators by the emperor Nerva, and afterwards more carefully defined by the senate at the instance of Hadrian.
29 A legacy that has been bequeathed may be adeemed either in the same testament or in a codicil confirmed by it ; but it must be adeemed in the same way in which it has been given.

---

[2] This word is in the MS., but in a later hand.
§ 26. Comp. pr. § 1, I. *de ususfr.* (ii, 4) ; fr. 43, D. *de ususfr. leg.* (xxxiii, 2).
§ 27. Comp. § 2, I. *de ususfr.* (ii, 4), and refs.
§ 28. Comp. xxii, 5 ; fr. 117, fr. 122, pr., fr. 73, § 1, fr. 32, § 1, D. *de legat. I.* (xxx).

[1] Again *praetoriani* in the MS. ; see xx, 16.
§ 29. Comp. pr. I. *de adempt. leg.* (ii, 21).
[1] Comp. fr. 14, D. *de acceptil.* (xlvi, 4). The words of ademption were to be a repetition of those of bequest, with the addition of a negative : *do lego, non do non lego ; heres dato, heres ne dato.*

30 Ad heredem legatarii legata non aliter transeunt nisi si iam
31 die legatorum cedente legatarius decesserit.   Legatorum
quae pure uel in diem certum[1] relicta sunt dies cedit antiquo
quidem iure ex mortis testatoris tempore; per legem autem
Papiam Poppaeam ex apertis tabulis testamenti : eorum uero
quae sub condicione[1] relicta sunt cum condicio extiterit.

32 Lex Falcidia iubet non plus quam dodrantem totius patrimonii legari, ut omni modo quadrans integer apud heredem
remaneat. ...

33 Legatorum perperam solutorum repetitio non est.

[XXV.] DE FIDEICOMMISSIS.]

1 Fideicommissum est quod non ciuilibus uerbis sed precatiue
relinquitur, nec ex rigore iuris ciuilis proficiscitur, sed ex

---

30 Legacies do not pass to the heir of the legatee unless they
31 have already vested before the latter's decease.   Those left
unconditionally or [to be paid] at a fixed date vested by the
old law at the testator's death; by the Papia-Poppaean law,
however, they vest at the opening of the testament.   But
those that are conditional vest only when the condition is
fulfilled.

32 The Falcidian law ordains that not more than three-fourths
of the testator's patrimony shall be legated; so that in every
case a clear fourth shall remain to the heir.

33 There can be no repetition of a legacy paid inadvertently.

[XXV. OF FIDEICOMMISSA.]

1 A *fideicommissum* is bequeathed not in the language of the
ius ciuile but by words of request; according to the strictness
of the *ius ciuile* it is ineffectual; it derives its value solely

§§ 80, 81. Comp. Vlp. fr. 5, fr. 7, D.
quando dies leg. ced. (xxxvi, 2);
Iust. in l. 1, § 5, C. *de cad. toll.*
(vi, 51).
[1] Says fr. 75, D. *de cond.* (xxxv,
1), *Dies incertus condicionem in testamento facit.* The only uncertain
date that formed an exception was
that of the death of the testator; a
legacy, therefore, on the testator's
death was regarded as unconditional, and vested at once, fr. 79,
de cond. But if the reference was
to any other uncertain date, even

though it was sure to come sooner
or later, such as the death of a third
party, the legacy did not vest unless the legatee survived it; in other
words, the legacy was dealt with as
a conditional one.
§ 32.   Comp. Gai. ii, §§ 224-227.
§ 33.   Comp. Gai. ii, 169. Hu. reads
—*legatorum [per damnationem] perperam,* etc.

TIT. xxv, § 1.   Comp. xxiv, 1; §§ 1,
12, I. *de fideicom. hered.* (ii, 23);
§ 3, I. *de legat.* (ii, 20).

2 uoluntate datur relinquentis.   Verba fideicommissorum in
usu fere haec sunt: FIDEICOMMITTO, PETO, VOLO DARI et similia.
3 Etiam nutu relinquere fideicommissum usu receptum est.
4 Fideicommissum relinquere possunt qui testamentum facere
possunt, licet non fecerint: nam intestato quis moriturus
5 fideicommissum relinquere potest.   Res per fideicommissum
relinqui possunt quae etiam per damnationem legari pos-
6 sunt.   Fideicommissa dari possunt *his quibus*[1] legari potest.
7 Latini Iuniani fideicommissum capere possunt, licet legatum
8 capere non possint.   Fideicommissum et ante heredis institutionem et post mortem heredis et codicillis etiam non confirmatis testamento dari potest, licet [*ita*][1] legari non possit.
9 Item Graece fideicommissum scriptum ualet, licet legatum
10 Graece scriptum non ualeat.   Filio qui in potestate est
seruoue heredibus institutis, seu si his[1] legatum sit, patris uel
domini fideicommitti potest, quamuis ab eo legari non possit.

---

2 from the fact that so he willed who bequeathed it.   The
words usually employed in *fideicommissa* are these: 'I commit to your good faith to give,' 'I ask you to give,' 'I wish to
3 be given,' and such like.   And it has been held in practice
that a fideicommissary gift may be left even by a mere nod.
4 Those can bequeath a trust-gift who can make a testament,
though they may not have made one; for a man who is about
5 to die intestate may yet leave a *fideicommissum.*   The same
things can be left by it that can be legated by damnation.
6 It can be given to those to whom a legacy can be bequeathed.
7 A Junian latin can take it, though unable to take a legacy.
8 It may be bequeathed before the heir's institution, or after his
death, or even in a codicil unconfirmed by testament; although
9 in none of those ways can a legacy be left.   It is valid
though written in Greek; whereas a legacy in that language
10 is invalid.   If a son *in potestate* or a slave be instituted
heir, or if a legacy be left them, a *fideicommissum* may be
imposed on father or owner, though a legacy cannot so be

§ 2. Comp. Gai. ii, 249; Paul. iv, 1,
    §§ 5, 6.
§ 3. Instead of *usu* the MS. has *in
    usu.*
§ 4. Comp. Vlp. in fr. 2, D. *de legat.
    I.* (xxx); Gai. ii, 270.
§ 5. Comp. xxiv, §§ 8, 25; Gai. ii,
    260-262.
§ 6. Comp. Gai. ii, §§ 285-287; above,
    xxii, 5; xxiv, 28.

[1] The MS. has *hi qui.*
§ 7. Comp. Gai. i, 24; ii, 275.
§ 8. Comp. Gai. ii, §§ 269, 270a, 277;
    above, xxiv, §§ 15, 16.
    [1] *Ita* added by Hu., adopted by
    K. and approved by Bk.
§ 9. Comp. Gai. ii, 281.
§ 10. Comp. xxiv, 21.
    [1] So the MS.; Boeck. suggests
    siue iis.

11 Qui testamento heres institutus est, codicillis etiam non confirmatis rogari potest uel [1] ut hereditatem totam uel ex parte
alii restituat, quamuis directo heres institui ne quidem con-
12 firmatis codicillis possit.   Fideicommissa non per formulam
petuntur, ut legata, sed cognitio est Romae quidem consulum
aut praetoris qui *fideicommissarius* [1] uocatur; in prouinciis
13 uero praesidum prouinciarum.   Poenae causa uel incertae
personae ne quidem fideicommissa dari possunt.

14   Is qui rogatus est alii restituere hereditatem, lege quidem
Falcidia [*locum*] [1] non habente, quoniam non plus puta quam
dodrantem restituere rogatus est, ex Trebelliano senatusconsulto restituit, ut ei et in eum dentur actiones cui restituta
est hereditas: lege autem Falcidia interueniente, quoniam
plus dodrantem uel etiam totam hereditatem restituere rogatus
sit, ex Pegasiano [2] senatusconsulto restituit, ut, deducta parte

---

11 charged upon him.   He who is instituted heir in a testament can be asked in a codicil, even though it be not confirmed
by the testament, to restore the inheritance in whole or in
part to some other person; whereas a man cannot be directly
instituted heir in a codicil, notwithstanding it may have been
12 confirmed by testament.   *Fideicommissa* are not sued for by
formula, like legacies; it is the consuls, or the praetor who is
styled *praetor fideicommissarius*, that has cognisance of them
in Rome, and in the provinces the provincial governors.
13 But not even *fideicommissa* can be given by way of penalty
or to an uncertain person.
14   He who is asked to restore an inheritance, if the Falcidian
law does not come into operation because what he is asked to
restore does not exceed three-fourths, does so under the provisions of the Trebellian senatusconsult, whereby actions
[affecting the inheritance] are granted to or against the party
to whom the inheritance is restored; if, however, the Falcidian law does come into play, because the heir has been asked
to restore more than three-fourths, perhaps the whole, of the
inheritance, restitution is made under the Pegasian senatusconsult, so that after the [Falcidian] fourth has been deducted,
actions still continue to lie in favour of and against the in-

§ 11.   Comp. Gai. ii, 273; above, § 8.   § 14.   Comp. Gai. ii, §§ 253-257.
  [1] Vahl. and K. omit this *uel*.   [1] Added by Du Tillet, and ac-
§ 12.   Comp. Gai. ii, 273.   cepted by all eds.
  [1] In the ms. *fideicommisso*.   [2] The ms. has *Pecatiano* both
§ 13.   Comp. xxiv, §§ 17, 18; Gai. ii,   here and in § 15; in § 16, *Pega-*
  §§ 287, 288.   *tiano*.

quarta, ipsi qui scriptus est heres [et]³ in ipsum actiones
conseruentur, is autem qui recipit hareditatem legatarii loco
15 habeatur.   Ex Pegasiano senatusconsulto restituta hereditate, commoda et incommoda hereditatis communicantur
inter heredem et eum cui reliquae partes restitutae sunt, interpositis stipulationibus ad exemplum partis et pro parte
stipulationum. partis autem et pro parte stipulationes
proprie dicuntur quae de lucro et damno communicando
solent interponi inter heredem et legatarium partiarium, id
16 est cum quo partitus est heres.   Si heres damnosam hereditatem dicat, cogitur a praetore adire et restituere totam, ita
ut ei et in eum qui recipit hereditatem actiones dentur,
proinde atque si ex Trebelliano senatusconsulto restituta
fuisset. idque ut ita fiat Pegasiano senatusconsulto cautum.
17   Si quis in fraudem¹ tacitam fidem accommodauerit ut non
capienti² fideicommissum restituat, nec quadrantem eum

---

stituted heir himself, while he to whom the inheritance is
15 restored is dealt with as a legatee.   On restitution of an
inheritance under the Pegasian senatusconsult, its advantages
and disadvantages are shared between the heir and the party
to whom the residue has been restored, stipulations being
interchanged after the model of those known as *stipulationes
partis et pro parte*.   Those stipulations are properly so called
which are interchanged, for the purpose of securing a fair
division of gain and loss, between an heir and a partiary
legatee, *i.e.* a legatee with whom the heir has shared the in-
16 heritance.   If an heir declare that an inheritance will prove
a source of loss to him, he is compelled by the praetor to enter
and to restore the whole of it; and then actions proceed at
the instance of or against him who has received it, as if the
restitution had been made under the Trebellian senatusconsult.
The Pegasian senatusconsult provides expressly that this
course shall be followed.
17   If any one have fraudulently given a secret promise to restore as *fideicommissum* to a person who has not the *ius capiendi*,

---

³ Added by Hugo, and adopted
by all later eds.
§ 15. Comp. Gai. ii, §§ 254, 257, and
note 1; above, xxiv, 15.
§ 16. Comp. Gai. ii, 258.
§ 17. Comp. fr. 11, D. *de his q. ut indign.*
(xxxiv, 9); fr. 59, § 1, D. *ad L.
Falcid.* (xxxv, 2); fr. 48, pr., fr. 49,
D. *de iure fisci* (xlix, 14).

¹ I.e. *in fraudem legis.*
² Say to an unmarried or a childless person, xxii, 3. A Junian latin
might take a *fideicommissum* bequeathed openly on the face of the
testament, § 7; but it is doubtful
whether he could take under a secret
and undisclosed trust.

deducere senatus censuit[3] nec caducum uindicare ex eo testamento si liberos habeat.[4]

18   Libertas dari potest per fideicommissum.

[*XXVI. DE LEGITIMIS HEREDIBVS.*]

1   Intestatorum[1] ingenuorum hereditates pertinent primum ad suos heredes, id est liberos qui in potestate sunt ceterosque qui liberorum loco sunt:[2] si sui heredes non sunt, ad consanguineos, id est fratres et sorores ex eodem patre: si nec hi sunt, ad reliquos agnatos proximos, id est cognatos[3] uirilis sexus per mares descendentes eiusdem familiae.[4] id enim cautum est lege duodecim tabularum hac: ' si intestato moritur, cui suus heres nec [*escit*], agnatus proximus familiam[5] habeto.'[6]

---

the senate has decreed that he shall not be entitled to deduct his fourth, nor yet, supposing him to have children, to vindicate gifts under the testament that have become caducous.

18   Freedom may be conferred by *fideicommissum.*

[*XXVI. OF HEIRS-AT-LAW.*]

1   The inheritances of intestates of free-birth belong in the first place to their *sui heredes, i.e.* their children *in potestate* and other persons who are in the position of children ; if there be no *sui heredes,* then to their consanguineans, *i.e.* their brothers and sisters by the same father; if these fail, then to the other nearest agnates, *i.e.* kinsmen of the male sex, descended through males, and members of the same family. For so it is provided in this law of the Twelve Tables: 'If a man die intestate, to whom there is no *suus heres,* let his nearest agnate take his patrimony.'

[3] By a *senatusconsultum Plancianum,* not later probably than the time of Hadrian ; for, by a rescript of Antoninus Pius', the fourth thus forfeited by the heir fell to the fisc, fr. 59, § 1, D. *ad L. Falc.* (xxxv, 2).
[4] Comp. Gai. ii, §§ 206, 207.
§ 18. Comp. ii, 7.

TIT. XXVI, § 1. Reproduced in *Collat.* xvi, 4, § 1. Comp. Gai. iii, §§ 1-5, 9-11.
[1] In *Collat.* it is *gentiliciorum.*
[2] For example, a wife *in manu,* who was *filiae loco.*

[3] The words *proximos i.e. cognatos* are omitted in *Collat.*
[4] See xi, 3, and note 2.
[5] See Gai. ii, 102.
[6] After this par. Hu. and K. introduce from *Collat.,* as § 1a,—*Si agnatus defuncti non sit, eadem lex duodecim tabularum gentiles ad hereditatem uocat his uerbis :* ' *si agnatus nec escit, gentiles familiam habento.*' *nunc nec gentiles nec gentilicia iura in usu sunt.* But there can be no doubt this passage was purposely omitted by the abridger as mere matter of history.

2   Si *defuncti unus*[1] sit filius, ex altero filio *iam mortuo*[2] nepos unus uel etiam plures, ad omnes hereditas pertinet; non ut in capita diuidatur sed in stirpes, id est ut filius solus mediam partem habeat et nepotes quotquot sunt alteram dimidiam : aequum est enim nepotes in patris sui locum succedere, et eam partem habere quam pater eorum si uiueret habiturus esset.

3   Quamdiu suus heres speratur heres fieri posse, tamdiu locus agnatis non est; uelut si uxor defuncti praegnans sit aut filius apud hostes sit.

4   Agnatorum hereditates diuiduntur in capita; uelut si sit fratris filius et alterius fratris duo pluresue liberi, quotquot sunt ab utraque parte personae, tot fiunt portiones, ut singuli singulas capiant.

5   Si plures eodem gradu sint agnati, et quidam eorum here-

---

2   If a man deceased leave one son, and one or more grandchildren by another son who has predeceased him, the inheritance belongs to all of them.   They take, however, not as individuals, but as branches [of the parent tree]; that is to say the son who stands alone will take one half, and the grandchildren, whatever their number, the other half.   For it is but fair that the grandchildren should succeed to the place their father held, and have the share to which he would have been entitled had he survived.

3   So long as there is hope that a *suus heres* may become heir, there is no room for the agnates; as when the widow of the deceased is pregnant, or his son in the hands of an enemy.

4   The inheritances of agnates are divided *per capita* [*i.e.* according to the number of individuals entitled]; for example if there be [one] son of [one deceased] brother, and two or more children of another brother [also deceased], whatever be the number of persons in the two branches together, the inheritance is divided into just so many portions, so that each may take one.

5   If there be several agnates of the same degree, and some of

---

§ 2. Comp. Gai. iii, §§ 7, 8; *Collat.* xvi, 4, § 9.
    [1] So Cann. and L. and most later eds.; Hu. and K., following Cuj., have simply *defuncti*; the ms. has *defunctus*.
    [2] So Arndts; the ms. and many eds. have *mortuo iam*; L., Bk., and Vahl. *mortuo item*.

§ 3.   Comp. Gai. iii, 13 ; § 7, I. *de her. q. ab int.* (iii, 1) ; § 6, I. *de. leg. agn. succ.* (iii, 2).

§ 4.   Comp. Gai. iii, 16.

§ 5.   Comp. Gai. iii, §§ 12, 22; fr. 9, D. *de suis et leg.* (xxxviii, 16); § 4, I. *de SC. Orph.* (iii, 4) ; § 7, I. *de. leg. agn. succ.* (iii, 2).

ditatem ad se pertinere noluerint, uel antequam adierint
decesserint, eorum pars adcrescit his qui adierint; quod si
nemo eorum adierit, ad insequentem gradum ex lege hereditas non transmittitur, quoniam in legitimis hereditatibus
successio non est.

6   Ad feminas ultra consanguineorum gradum legitima hereditas non pertinet; itaque soror fratri sororiue legitima heres
fit.[1]

7   Ad liberos matris intestatae hereditas ex lege duodecim
tabularum non pertinebat, quia feminae suos heredes non
habent; sed postea imperatorum Antonini et Commodi oratione in senatu recitata id actum est, ut sine in manum conuentione[1] matrum legitimae hereditates ad filios pertineant,

8 exclusis consanguineis et reliquis agnatis.   Intestati filii
hereditas ad matrem ex lege duodecim tabularum non perti-

---

them have declined the inheritance or died before entry, their
shares accresce to those who have entered; but if none of them
have entered, the inheritance is not transmitted by the statute
to those of the next degree, for in the inheritances of the
Twelve Tables there is no succession [of degrees].

6   An inheritance-at-law does not belong to women [related]
beyond the consanguinean degree; therefore [while] a sister
becomes heir-at-law of her brother or sister, [*a father's sister*,
[*a brother's daughter, and so on, does not*].

7   According to the Twelve Tables the inheritance of a mother
dying intestate did not belong to her children, because women
have no *sui heredes;* but afterwards, in pursuance of an
Oration in the senate by the emperors Marcus Aurelius and
Commodus, it was enacted that, even without *in manum conuentio*, the inheritances of mothers should belong to their
children, to the exclusion of consanguinean and other agnates.

8   The inheritance of a son dying intestate does not belong to
his mother by the law of the Twelve Tables; but by the Ter-

---

§ 6. Comp. Gai. iii, §§ 14, 23; *Collat.*
xvi, 3.
    [1] Hu., following Gai. iii, 14, thinks
there is here a homeoteleutic omission, and adds—*amita uero uel
fratris filia et deinceps legitima
heres non fit.*
§ 7. Comp. pr. I. *de SC. Orph.* (iii, 4).
In Gai. iii, 24, this Sct. is not mentioned. It was the outcome of the
oration referred to in the text;
enacted in the year 178, and consu-

late of Julianus Rufus and Gavius
Orphitus.
    [1] Before this Sct. children had a
right of succession to their mother
if she had been *in manu* of their
father; for in that case mother and
children were related as agnates.
§ 8. Comp. tit. I. *de SC. Tertull.* (iii,
3); Gai. iii, §§ 23, 24. It is thought
that Gai. must have referred to this
Sct. in an illegible page of the
Verona MS.; see iii, § 33, note.

net; sed si ius liberorum habeat, ingenua trium, libertina quattuor, legitima heres fit ex senatusconsulto Tertulliano, si tamen ei filio neque suus heres sit quiue inter suos heredes ad bonorum possessionem a praetore uocatur, neque pater ad quem lege hereditas bonorumue possessio cum re pertinet,[1] neque frater consanguineus : quod si soror consanguinea sit, ad utrasque pertinere iubetur hereditas.

[XXVII. DE LIBERTORVM SVCCESSIONIBVS VEL BONIS.]

1 Libertorum intestatorum hereditas primum ad suos heredes pertinet; deinde ad eos quorum liberti sunt, uelut patronum
2 patronam liberosue patroni.　　Si sit patronus et alterius
3 patroni filius, ad solum patronum hereditas pertinet.　　Item
4 patroni filius patroni nepotibus obstat.　　Ad liberos patronorum hereditas defuncti pertinet, ita ut in capita non in stirpes diuidatur.

---

tullian senatusconsult she becomes his heir-at-law if she have the privilege resulting from children, three in the case of a woman of free-birth, four in that of a freedwoman; provided always that her son is neither survived by a *suus heres*, nor by any person whom the praetor calls to possession of the estate along with *sui*, nor by his father if he be entitled either to the statutory inheritance or to effectual possession of the estate, nor by a consanguinean brother. But if there be a consanguinean sister surviving, it is ordained that the inheritance shall belong to her mother and her jointly.

[XXVII. OF THE SUCCESSIONS OR ESTATES OF FREEDMEN.]

1　The inheritance of a freedman dying intestate belongs in the first place to his *sui heredes ;* then to the person whose freedman he is, as his patron, his patroness, or his patron's
2 children.　　If he be survived by a patron and the son of another patron, the inheritance belongs solely to the former.
3 A patron's son, too, excludes [another] patron's grandsons.
4 The inheritance of the deceased so belongs to his patron's children that it is divided *in capita* and not *in stirpes.*

---

[1] An adoptive father did not come within this limitation, fr. 2, § 15, D. *ad SC. Tertull.* (xxxviii, 17).

TIT. XXVII, § 1.　Comp. Vlp. in pr. D.

de suis et legit. (xxxviii, 16) ; *Collat.* xvi, 8 ; Gai. iii, 40. §§ 2, 3.　Comp. Gai. iii, 60. § 4.　Comp. Gai. iii, 61 ; Paul. iii, 2, § 3 ; § 3, I. *de succ. lib.* (iii, 7).

5   Legitimae hereditatis ius, quod ex lege duodecim tabularum descendit, capitis minutione amittitur.

[XXVIII. DE POSSESSIONIBVS DANDIS.]

1   Bonorum possessio datur aut contra tabulas testamenti, aut *secundum* [1] tabulas, [*aut*] intestati.

2   Contra tabulas bonorum possessio datur liberis emancipatis [1] testamento praeteritis, licet legitimo [*iure*] [2] non ad eos perti-
3 neat hereditas.   Bonorum possessio contra tabulas liberis tam naturalibus quam adoptiuis datur; sed naturalibus quidem emancipatis, non tamen et illis qui in adoptiua familia sunt; adoptiuis autem his tantum qui in potestate manserunt.

4 Emancipatis liberis ex edicto datur bonorum possessio, si

---

5   The right to an inheritance as heir-at-law, if it be derived from the Twelve Tables, is lost by *capitis deminutio.*

[XXVIII. OF GRANTS OF POSSESSION.]

1   Possession of the estate of a party deceased is granted either in opposition to his testamentary writings, or in terms thereof, or on his intestacy.

2   *Bonorum possessio* in opposition to a testament is granted to emancipated children who have been passed over in it, although the inheritance does not belong to them under the *ius ciuile.*

3 It is granted both to natural and adoptive children; to the former even if emancipated, but not if they have passed into an adoptive family; to the latter, however, only if they have
4 remained *in potestate* [of their adoptive parent].   It is granted by the edict to emancipated children if they are prepared to give security to their brothers who have continued

---

§ 5. Comp. Gai. iii, §§ 21, 27, 51; § 2, I. *de SC. Orph.* (iii, 4). The new *legitimae hereditates* of the imperial jurisprudence were not lost by *capitis minutio.*

TIT. XXVIII, § 1. Comp. Gai. ii, 119, note 1; Gai. iii, §§ 33, 34, and notes; pr. § 1, I. *de bon. poss.* (iii, 9).
[1] Here, as in XX, 14, the MS. has *aduersus* instead of *secundum.* As it omits the last *aut* there results the curious reading—*aduersus tabulas intestati.*

§ 2. Comp. Gai. ii, 135; above, XXii, 23; § 3, I. *de bon. poss.* (iii, 9).
[1] Hu. interpolates *uel* between *liberis* and *emancipatis.* But wrongly; for praeteritio of a *suus* invalidated a will and caused intestacy, Gai. ii, 128.
[2] Added by L. Previous eds. omitted it, reading *legitima* instead of *legitimo* as in the MS.

§ 3. Comp. Vlp. in fr. 1, § 6, D. *de b. p. c. t.* (xxxvii, 4); §§ 9-12, I. *de her. q. ab. int.* (iii, 1).

§ 4. Comp. Vlp. in *Collat.* xvi, 7, § 2; Gai. ii, 270; Paul. v, 9, § 4.

parati sunt cauere *fratribus* [1] suis, qui in potestate manserunt,
bona quae moriente patre habuerunt se conlaturos.

5   Secundum tabulas bonorum possessio datur scriptis heredibus, scilicet si eorum quibus contra tabulas competit nemo
6   sit, aut petere *nolint.*   Etiam si iure ciuili non ualeat testamentum, forte quod familiae mancipatio uel nuncupatio
defuit, si signatum testamentum sit non minus quam septem
testium ciuium Romanorum signis, bonorum possessio datur.

7   Intestati datur bonorum possessio per septem gradus :
primo gradu liberis ; secundo legitimis heredibus ; tertio
proximis cognatis ; quarto familiae patroni ; [*quinto*] patrono
patronae, item liberis, [*parenti*]ue [1] patroni patronaeue ;
sexto uiro uxori ; septimo cognatis manumissoris quibus per

in potestate that they will collate [*i.e.* bring into division] the
estate belonging to them at their father's death.

5   *Bonorum possessio* in terms of a testament is given to the
heirs named therein, if there be no person to whom possession
in opposition to the deed is competent, or if all to whom it is
6   competent refrain from applying for it.   Even though a
testament may be invalid by the *ius ciuile,* say because of the
omission of the *familiae mancipatio* or of the words of nuncupation, yet if it be sealed with the seals of not fewer than
seven witnesses, Roman citizens, possession of the estate will
be granted [in accordance with it].

7   *Bonorum possessio* upon intestacy is granted through seven
degrees ; in the first degree to children ; in the second to the
heirs-at-law [*i.e.* collateral agnates and patrons] ; in the third
to the nearest cognates ; in the fourth to the family of the patron ;
in the fifth to the patron and patroness (and their children),
as also to the *parens manumissor* of a patron or patroness ; in the
sixth to husband or wife ; in the seventh to those cognates of
a manumitter who are allowed by the Furian law to take

[1] The ms. has *patribus,* first corrected by Cuj.
§ 5.   Comp. Vlp. in fr. 2, pr. D. *de b.
p. s. t.* (xxxvii, 11) ; §§ 1, 3, I. *de
bon. poss.* (iii, 9).   The *peculium
castrense uel quasi* was not required
to be collated.
§ 6.   Comp. xxiii, 6 ; Gai. ii, §§ 119,
149.
§ 7.   Comp. § 1, I. *de bon. poss.* (iii, 9).
   [1] See Vlp. in *Collat.* xvi, 9, § 1,
on the strength of which Cuj. interpolated *parentibus,* the ms. having
liberosue, but as there could be only
one *parens manumissor,* it is proper to

read *parenti* rather than *parentibus.*
There has been much controversy
about this fifth grant ; and the difficulty is not cleared up, but on the
contrary increased, by Just. in § 3, I.
de bonor. poss. (iii, 9), and Theoph.
in his Paraphrase.   The meaning of
patronopatronae, patroni patronaeue
is plain enough ; it is the intermediate words that have proved to
many unintelligible.   The explanation in the translation is that suggested by Hu. in his *Studien,* pp.
58 f.   He, however, retains the
varentibus of Cujas.

legem Furiam [2] plus mille asses capere licet : et si nemo sit
ad quem bonorum possessio pertinere possit, aut sit quidem
sed ius suum omiserit, populo bona deferuntur ex lege Iulia
8 caducaria.[3]   Liberis bonorum possessio datur, tam his qui
in potestate usque in mortis tempus fuerunt quam emancipatis ; item adoptiuis, non tamen etiam in adoptionem datis.
9 Proximi cognati bonorum possessionem accipiunt non solum
per feminini sexus personam cognati sed etiam agnati capite
deminuti : nam licet legitimum ius agnationis capitis minutione amiserint, natura tamen cognati manent.[1]
10   Bonorum possessio datur parentibus et liberis intra annum
11 ex quo petere potuerunt, ceteris intra centum dies.   Qui
omnes intra id tempus si non petierint bonorum possessionem,
sequens gradus admittitur, perinde atque si superiores non
essent ; idque per septem gradus fit.
12   Hi quibus ex successorio edicto bonorum possessio datur

---

more than a thousand *asses*. If there be no one entitled to
the *bonorum possessio*, or if there be such an one but he have
waived his right, the estate passes to the people in virtue of
8 the Julian caduciary law.   The *bonorum possessio* ' to children' is granted not only to those who have remained *in
potestate* down to the time of the parent's death, but also to
those who have been emancipated ; to adopted children too, but
9 not to those given in adoption.   Not only do those obtain
it as 'nearest cognates' who are of kin through a female,
but also agnates who have undergone *capitis deminutio ;* for
though they have thereby lost their civil right of agnation, by
natural law they still continue kinsmen.
10   *Bonorum possessio* is granted to ascendants and descendants
[at any time] within a year after it has become competent to
them to apply for it ; to other persons within a hundred days.
11 When all [those included in any particular degree] have
failed to apply for it within the time limited, the next degree
is admitted, just as if the preceding ones were non-existent ;
and this is the case through the seven degrees.
12   Those to whom *bonorum possessio* is granted by the edict

[2] Comp. i, 2; Gai. ii, 255, and
notes.
[3] See Gai. i, 145, note 1.
§ 8. Comp. Gai. iii, 26; fr. 1, § 2, D.
quis ordo (xxxviii, 15); fr. 1, § 6,
fr. 4, fr. 5, D. *si tab. test.* (xxxviii,
6).

§ 9. Comp. Gai. iii, §§ 27, 30; tit. I.
de succ. cogn. (iii, 5).
[1] Comp. Gai. i, 158.
§§ 10, 11. Comp. §§ 9, 10, I. *de bon.
poss.* (iii, 9).
§ 12. Comp. Gai. iii, 32; iv, 34; § 2,
I. *de bon. poss.* (iii, 9).

heredes quidem non sunt, sed heredis loco constituuntur
beneficio praetoris. ideoque seu ipsi agant seu cum his
agatur, ficticiis actionibus opus est, in quibus heredes esse
finguntur.

13 Bonorum possessio *aut cum re datur*[1] aut sine re : cum re,
[*cum*][2] is qui accepit cum effectu bona retineat : sine re, cum
alius iure ciuili euincere hereditatem possit ; ueluti si suus
heres in testa[*mento praeteritus sit, licet scriptis heredibus secun-*
[*dum tabulas bonorum possessio deferatur, erit tamen ea*][3]
bonorum possessio sine re, quoniam suus heres euincere hereditatem iure legitimo potest.

[XXVIIII. DE BONIS LIBERTORVM.]

1 Ciuis Romani liberti hereditatem lex duodecim tabularum
patrono defert, si intestato sine suo herede libertus decesserit :
ideoque siue testamento facto decedat, licet suus heres ei non

---

regulating successions are not in truth heirs, but only established in the position of heirs by the beneficial intervention of
the praetor. Therefore whether they are suing or being sued,
fictitious actions must be employed, in which it is pretended
that they are heirs.

13 *Bonorum possessio* is granted either *cum re* or *sine re,—cum
re* when he to whom it is granted can effectively retain the
bona ; sine re when some other person can wrest the inheritance from him by aid of the *ius ciuile.* For example, if a *suus
heres* [*have been passed over in a testament, although* bonorum
[possessio secundum tabulas *be granted to the heirs instituted*
[*therein, yet it will be*] *sine re*, since the *suus heres* can wrest the
inheritance from them in virtue of his statutory right.

[XXIX. OF THE ESTATES OF FREEDMEN.]

1 The law of the Twelve Tables confers the inheritance of a
Roman citizen freedman upon his patron, if the freedman die
intestate without a *suus heres ;* therefore if he die leaving a
testament, though possibly not a *suus heres*, or intestate but

---

§ 13. Comp. Gai. ii, 148 ; iii, §§ 85-87 ;
above, xxiii, 6 ; xxvi, 8.
  [1] The MS. has *autem reddatur.*
  [2] Added by Hugo.
  [3] Interpolated by K. After *heres*
the MS. has *intestati.* Bk. reads—
ueluti si [*sit*] *suus heres, intestati*

bonorum possessio sine re [*est*], *quoniam*, etc. But Krueger's amendment is preferable.

TIT. XXIX, § 1. Comp. Schoell, *Tab.*
v, 8 ; Gai. iii, §§ 39-42 ; above, tit.
xxvii ; tit. I. *de succ. libert.* (iii, 7).

sit, seu intestato, et suus heres ei sit *quamuis*[1] non naturalis, sed uxor puta quae in manu fuit uel adoptiuus filius, lex patrono nihil praestat. sed ex edicto praetoris, seu *testato*[2] libertus moriatur, ut aut nihil aut minus quam partem dimidiam bonorum patrono relinquat, contra tabulas testamenti partis dimidiae bonorum possessio illi datur, nisi libertus aliquem ex naturalibus liberis successorem sibi relinquat; siue intestato decedat, et uxorem forte in manu uel adoptiuum filium relinquat, aeque partis mediae bonorum possessio contra suos heredes patrono datur.

2   In bonis libertae patrono nihil iuris ex edicto datur. itaque — — — — — —[1] seu intestata moriatur liberta, semper ad eum hereditas pertinet licet liberi sint libertae, quoniam 3 non sunt sui heredes matri [*ut*] *obstent*[2] patrono.   Lex Papia Poppaea postea libertas quattuor liberorum iure tutela patronorum liberauit: et cum intulerit iam posse eas sine

---

with a *suus heres*, though perhaps not a natural one but only a wife *in manu* say or an adopted son, the statute gives nothing to the patron. By the praetor's edict, however, if the freedman die testate, but leave his patron nothing, or less than the half of his estate, the patron gets possession of a half of the *bona* in opposition to the testament, unless the freedman have left one of his children by birth as his successor; if he die intestate, survived say by his wife *in manu* or an adopted son, possession of a half of his estate is in like manner granted to the patron as against [those artificial] *sui heredes.*

2   No right in the estate of a freedwoman is conferred by the edict on her patron. Therefore [*if she wish to make a testa-* [*ment, it is in the power of her patron to withhold his* auctoritas [*if he be not instituted in it as her heir*]; if she die intestate, the inheritance must always belong to him, even if she leave children, seeing they are not their mother's *sui heredes,* and 3 so cannot exclude the patron. The Papia-Poppaean law afterwards liberated freedwomen from tutory in right of four children; and as it was a necessary result that they could thenceforth make testaments without the *auctoritas* of their

---

[1] So Bk.; the ms. has *quā;* Vahl., Hu., and K. *quamquam.*

[2] So Cuj. and the later eds.; the ms. has *testamento;* most earlier eds. *testamento facto.*

§ 2. Comp. Gai. iii, 43; i, 192.

[1] K. proposes to fill the lacuna

28

with such words as *seu testari uoluerit liberta, in patroni potestate erat ne testamento auctor fieret in quo ipse heres institutus non esset,* seu, etc.

[2] *Vt obstent* is due to L.; the ms. has *obstit.*

§ 3. Comp. Gai. iii, 44; i, 194.

auctoritate patronorum testari, prospexit ut pro numero
liberorum libertae *superstitum* [1] uirilis pars patrono debeatur.
4 Liberi patroni uirilis sexus eadem iura in bonis libertorum
5 parentum suorum habent quae et ipse patronus.　Feminae
uero ex lege quidem duodecim tabularum perinde ius habent
atque masculi patronorum liberi ; contra tabulas autem testamenti liberti, aut ab intestato contra suos heredes non
naturales, bonorum possessio eis non competit; sed si ius
trium liberorum habuerunt etiam haec iura ex lege Papia
6 Poppaea nanciscuntur.　　Patronae *in* [1] bonis libertorum illud
ius tantum *habebant* [2] quod lex duodecim tabularum introduxit; sed postea lex Papia [*ingenuae*] [3] patronae duobus
liberis honoratae, libertinae tribus, id iuris dedit quod patronus
7 habet ex edicto.　　Item ingenuae trium liberorum iure
honoratae eadem lex id ius dedit quod *ipsa* [4] patrono tribuit.

EXPLICIT.[5]
---

patrons, it provided that a share of a freedwoman's estate,
proportionate to the number of her surviving children, should
4 in future be due to her patron.　　A patron's male children
have the same right in the estates of his freedmen as he himself.
5 By the law of the Twelve Tables a patron's female descendants
have the same rights as his male descendants ; they are not
entitled, however, [under the edict,] to *bonorum possessio* in
opposition to the testament of a freedman, or, on his intestacy, as against his artificial *sui heredes ;* but they acquire
even this right by the Papia-Poppaean law if they be mothers
6 of three children.　　Patronesses used to have no more right
in the estates of their freedmen than was allowed by the
Twelve Tables ; but afterwards the Papia-Poppaean law conferred upon a free-born patroness with two children, and a
freedwoman patroness with three, the same rights that a patron
7 enjoys under the edict.　　The same statute further conferred
upon a free-born patroness, privileged in respect of three
children, the same rights that itself it conferred upon a patron.

THE END.

[1] The ms. has *subprestitum.*
§ 4.　Comp. Gai. iii, §§ 45, 46.
§ 5.　Comp. Gai. iii, §§ 46, 47.
§§ 6, 7.　Comp. Gai. iii, §§ 49, 50.
[1] The ms. has *ex.*
[2] *Habeant* in the ms.
[3] Added by Cuj. and adopted by
all eds.
[4] The ms. and all eds. have *ipsi;*
ipsa seems more appropriate.

[5] This is the end of the so-called
'Fragments.' But that Vlp., following Gai., proceeded to deal with
obligations and actions is evident
from the fact that in the *Collatio*,
ii, 2, we have a passage from the
Regulae on the subject of *iniuria*,
and in fr. 25, D. *de O. et A.* (xliv, 7)
another containing an enumeration
of the leading varieties of actions.

ADDITIONS

—o—

P. 11. Delete first note to § 29, substituting as follows :—' Vlp. iii, 3, and Fr. Dos. § 7, attribute this provision to the Junian law ; and Gai. in i, 80 speaks of it as introduced by the *lex Aelia Sentia et Iunia*, as if the Junian law were an amended version of the earlier enactment. Probably this to some extent is right. The Junian law seems to have done more than merely give a name to and define the position of those who, through non-observance in their manumission of the requirements of the *ius ciuile* and the Aelia-Sentian law, were not citizens, but still *de iure* slaves though *de facto* free, Gai. iii, 56. The Ael.-Sent. law had given the benefit of *causae probatio* to those *de facto* freemen whose want of citizenship was due to the fact that they were under thirty when manumitted, and that their manumission had not been *uindicta* on cause approved by the council, but either without such approval, or *censu* or *testamento*, comp. § 29 with §§ 17, 18, Vlp. i, 12. The Junian law seems to have extended the remedy to slaves under thirty at manumission who had been manumitted neither *uindicta*, *censu*, nor *testamento*, but informally, Gai. i, 41, iii, 56, Vlp. i, 10, iii, 3, or by a bonitarian owner, Vlp. i, 16. But it required the Sct. referred to in Gai. i, 31, Vlp. iii, 4, to extend it to slaves manumitted informally or by a bonitarian owner after the age of thirty.'

Pp. 14 and 15. Delete the first four and a half lines (' Finally . . . informally ') of the conjectural translation of § 35, and substitute :—' Finally, those who are latins because, being under thirty at manumission, they were manumitted otherwise than *uindicta* with sanction of the council, may become citizens by iteration or renewal of the manumission by their quiritarian owner, and that immediately if the renewal be in the manner required by the Aelia-Sentian law,—after they have passed thirty if the iteration be *uindicta* (without the necessity of the council's approval), or *censu*, or *testamento ;* those who are latins because, when over thirty, they were manumitted neither *uindicta, censu,* nor *testamento,* but informally, may become citizens by iteration by their quiritarian owner in one of those three ways; while' etc.

P. 302, to note to § 61, add—'By a rescript of Marc. Aurelius compensation was allowed to be pleaded in answer to *stricti iuris* actions, under cover of an *exceptio doli,* § 30, tit. I. afd. This rescript may have been published before Gai. wrote, yet not have come to his knowledge.'

P. 339, add to note to § 152—'The interdict was a praetorian remedy, and the praetor dealt only with what had happened during his own year of office, which (Momms. in M. u. M. *Roem. Alt.* i, 493), from the year 601 | 153 downwards, began on 1st January.'

P. 384, add to note 2 to § 17—'Probably it was lawful only in tutory of women, and there allowed to a testamentary tutor on the same principle (noticed in Gai. i, 168) that was held to justify cession by a tutor-at-law.'

P. 392, add, as a note to the words ' *item si* cognati inter se coierint usque ad sextum gradum,' on fifth line of text—'Fr. Vat. §§ 216-219, show that relationship to a testator within the sixth degree inclusive gave both *caelibes* and *orbi* a general exemption from the caduciary penalties of the Julian law; see also § 158.'

P. 394, add to note to xvii, § 2—'It is a moot point whether Caracalla's enactment merely transferred *caduca* from the *aerarium* to the fisc, *i.e.* from the state to the emperor, or abolished in favour of the *aerarium* or the fisc—for the words are sometimes used indiscriminately—the prior right given by the Julian law to heirs and legatees who had children, Gai. ii, 207, 286. Taken in connection with another statement of Ulpian's (*Collat.* xvi, 9, § 3), that Caracalla very greatly restricted the right of succession *ab intestato,* obviously in order to increase the influx to the fisc of *bona uacantia,* the latter view appears the more probable.'

ALPHABETICAL DIGEST

OF THE MATTERS CONTAINED IN THE

TEXT AND NOTES,

AND OF SERVICE AS AN

INDEX.

DIGEST.

—o—

ABDICATION, *abdicatio*, of a testamentary tutor, U. xi, 17 and n. 2.

ABROGATIO LEGIS, U. i, 3.

ABSTINENDI POTESTAS, (see *Hereditas*, 3, 4), power to hold aloof from an inheritance allowed by the praetor to *sui heredes* (which see), G. ii, 158, U. xxii, 24; to *quasi-sui*, G. ii, 159; to a person *in causa mancipii* instituted heir with freedom (see *Mancipii, etc.*), 160; but not to slaves instituted as *heredes necessarii* (see *Necess. heredes*), 153, U. xxii, 24. If a party entitled to abstain had once intromitted with the inheritance, abstention became impossible, unless, being a minor, he obtained *in integrum restitutio* (which see), G. ii, 163. Abstention did not deprive him, however, of his rights of patronage over and succession to his parent's freedmen, G. iii, 67.

ACCEPTILATION, (see *Obligation*, 3), a verbal mode of discharging an obligation without actual payment, G. iii, 169; see style, *ibid.* It was applicable only to obligations created *verbis*, 170, (see *Verbal obligations*); but others might by novation (which see) be embodied in a stipulation and then thus discharged, 171. It was incompetent to a woman unless with her tutor's *auctoritas*, G. ii, 85, iii, 171. If an *adstipulator* granted such a discharge in fraud of the stipulant, he was liable in an action under the Aquilian law, G. iii, 215, the condemnation being *in duplum*, (see *Cretio litis infitiatione*), 216, iv, 171. Whether a debt could be partially acceptilated was matter of dispute, G. iii, 172.

ACCESSIO TEMPORIS, reckoning the possession of the author as an adjunct to that of the successor, G. iv, 151; see *Interdicts*, 8.

ACCESSION as a mode of acquiring property, see *Property*, 4, 6.

ACCESSORY RIGHTS, see *Principal and Accessory*.

ACCIDENT created no responsibility, G. iii, 211 and n. 1.

ACCRETION, see *Adcretio*.

ACTIONS, see *passim* Book iv of Gaius, which deals with *jus quod ad actiones pertinet*, G. i, 8.

  I. ACTIONS GENERALLY, AND THEIR CLASSIFICATIONS.

    1. Actio *and* judicium.—*Actio* sometimes meant the right to

ACTIONS—*continued.*
  I. ACTIONS GENERALLY, AND THEIR CLASSIFICATIONS—*continued.*
    raise a particular action, G. iii, 161, or the liability to
    have to answer to it, G. iv, 4; but usually it meant the
    process itself, G. iv, 2, 3. In this sense *actio* and *judicium*
    were often used indiscriminately, as *mandati actionem
    habere*, G. iii, 161, *mandati judicium habere*, G. iii, 127;
    strictly speaking, *judicium* was the action when remitted
    to a *judex*, G. iv, 103, note 1.
   2. *Actions civil and praetorian.*—Actions were either civil or
    praetorian according as they had been introduced by the
    jus civile or by the praetor in the exercise of his juris-
    diction, G. iv, 110; for the edict was one of their most
    prolific sources, G. iv, 11.
   3. *Actions* in rem *and* in personam.—As regards form, their
    most important distinction was that they were either *in
    rem* or *in personam*, G. iv, 1. In the former the pursuer
    averred either that a thing was his, or that he had a
    usufruct or servitude over another's property, or that his
    own property was free from such burdens, G. iv, 3, with-
    out mention in his averment of any person as disputing
    his right, G. iv, 87; so it was, at least, if he was suing
    per formulam petitoriam, and not by the unusual *actio
    per sponsionem*, which was in form one *in personam*,
    G. iv, 91, 93, (see *In rem actio per sponsionem*).   In an
    action *in personam* the pursuer's averment was that the
    defender was indebted to him and bound *dare, facere*, or
    praestare, G. iv, 2; words defined in note 3. Those
    founded on *dare* or *dare facere* were technically con-
    dictions, G. iv, 5, (see *Condictio*); while actions *in rem*
    with a petitory formula were called vindications, *ibid.*,
    (see *Vindicatio*).
   4. *Actions petitory, penal, divisory and prejudicial.*—An action
    was petitory when the pursuer claimed a thing as his or
    as due to him under a contract or other lawful deed, G. iv,
    7; penal, when he claimed a penalty, for theft say or
    assault, 8; both petitory and penal, when the claim
    was originally on contract or other lawful deed, but the
    defender's liability augmented because of his denial of it,
    (see *Cretio litis infitiatione*), 9, 171. The divisory actions
    were the *a. familiae erciscundae* for partitioning an inherit-
    ance, *communi dividundo* for dividing common property,
    and *finium regundorum* for settling boundaries, G. iv, 42.
    Prejudicial were intended merely to settle a question of
    right or fact, without any immediate practical result, G.
    iii, 123, iv, 44.

ACTIONS—*continued.*

I. ACTIONS GENERALLY, AND THEIR CLASSIFICATIONS—*continued.*

5. Actiones in jus *and* in factum conceptae.—This distinction was based on the structure of the *formula*, and the actions so called according as the pursuer founded on a right competent to him at law, or merely averred that something had been done or omitted by the defender which under the edict gave him a claim against the latter, G. iv, 45, 46; see *Formula*, 3.

6. Actiones utiles *and* in factum.—Those actions were called *utiles* which, being inapplicable to particular persons or cases as originally formulated by the *jus civile* or published in the album, the praetor rendered serviceable to them, by alteration of the phraseology or otherwise, when they were within the spirit though not the letter of the remedy, G. ii, 78 and n. 1, 253, iii, 202, 219; they were sometimes called *fictitiae,* where the adaptation was by introduction of a fiction (see *Fiction*), G. iv, 34-38, U. xxviii, 12. The *utiles actiones* of frequent occurrence became stereotyped, and took their place in the edict, G. ii, 253; when a case occurred which none of them exactly fitted, then, if the principle which underlay it was the same, the praetor constructed a special *formula* to meet the particular facts, which got the name of *actio in factum*, G. ii, 78, note 1.

7. *Actions competent to and against heirs, and adjectician and noxal actions.*—Actions *ex contractu* were usually competent to or against heirs; but the heir of an adstipulator (see *Adstipulation*) could not sue, and the heirs of sponsors and fideipromissors (see *Verbal obligations*) could not be sued, G. iv, 113. Penal actions *ex delicto* were not competent against the heirs of the delinquent, but, with exception of the *a. injuriarum,* were competent to those of the injured party, 112; in those that against the original debtor would have been both penal and petitory, heirs were not liable in penalties, 172. Actions *adjecticiae qualitatis* were those against *patresfamilia* in respect of the obligations *ex contractu* of *filiifamilias* and slaves, G. iv, 69-74a, (see *Adjectician actions*); noxal, those competent in respect of their delicts, 75-79, (see *Noxal actions*).

8. Stricti juris, bonae fidei, *and* arbitrariae actiones.—In some *judicia* the judge was authorised to decide according to general principles of good faith, *ex aequo et bono,* without holding himself fettered by the actual engagements of parties; these were called *bonae fidei judicia,* G. iv, 62, (see *Bonae fidei jud.*) : all others were *stricti juris,* (though

ACTIONS—*continued.*

I. ACTIONS GENERALLY, AND THEIR CLASSIFICATIONS—*continued.*
the phrase is not in Gaius.) Those were *arbitrariae* in
which the judge had power, before proceeding to condemn
the defender,—for the condemnation could only be in
money, G. iv, 48, which possibly the pursuer did not
want,—to ordain him to do what he thought right, say to
deliver what was claimed in the action ; if the order was
complied with proceedings went no further, and condemnation was avoided, G. iv, 114, note.

9. *Actions perpetual and temporary.*—Actions were perpetual
or temporary in two different senses. The right of action
was perpetual in the case of those introduced by statute,
whereas in those derived from the praetor's jurisdiction,
with exception of a few modelled after others of the
jus civile, it endured only for a year, G. iv, 110, 111. The
action itself, if the *judicium* was *legitimum,* expired in
eighteen months, while if *imperio continens* it came to an
end with the demission of office by the magistrate who
granted it, (see *Jud. leg. and imp. cont.*), 104, 105. (For
other branches of the *jus quod ad actiones pertinet,* see, in
addition to references above, *Procedure, Legis actiones,
Formula, Litis contestatio,* etc.)

II. SPECIAL ACTIONS.—(See also *Condictio, Vindicatio.*)

A. ad exhibendum, G. iv, 51.

A. arborum furtim caesarum, G. iv, 11.

A. certae creditae pecuniae, G. iv, 13 ; it involved penal sponsion and restipulation of a third part of the sum claimed,
which went by way of penalty to him who was successful, G. iv, 171, 180 ; see *Sponsio et restipulatio.*

A. commodati, competent to a lender, G. iv, 47 ; it might be
either *in jus* or *in factum concepta, ibid.,* and in the
former case was *bonae fidei,* G. iv, 62 ; see *Commodate.*

A. communi dividundo, for dividing common property, G. iv,
42, 44, note ; it was *bonae fidei,* G. iv, 62, and entitled
the judge to proceed to adjudication, G. iv, 42, U. xix, 16.

A. conducti, competent to a lessee or hirer against his lessor ;
was also *bonae fidei,* G. iv, 62 ; see *Location.*

A. damni injuriae ex lege Aquilia, G. iii, 210, iv, 9 ; see *Wrongful damage to property.*

A. depensi, introduced by the Publilian law in favour of a
sponsor paying for the original debtor, competent if he
was not reimbursed within six months, and *in duplum,*
G. iii, 127, iv, 9, 22, 171. Under the system of the *legis
actiones* the procedure was by *manus injectio pro judicato*
(see *Legis actiones,* 5), G. iv, 22 ; consequently under the

ACTIONS—*continued.*

II. SPECIAL ACTIONS—*continued.*

formular system the defender was required to give *cautio judicatum solvi,* (see *Cautiones, etc.*), G. iv, 25, 102. See *Suretyship,* 5.

A. depositi, competent to a depositor, G. iii, 207. It might be either *in jus* or *in factum concepta,* G. iv, 47, in the former case being *bonae fidei,* 62; and condemnation entailed infamy on the defender, G. iv, 60, 182. See *Deposit.*

A. de peculio et de in rem verso, G. iv, 73, 74a; see *Adjectician actions,* 3.

A. de pecunia constituta, G. iv, 171; it involved penal sponsion and restipulation of a sum equal to one-half of that claimed, 171, 180 compared with 94. See *Sponsio et restipulatio.*

A. empti, competent to a purchaser; was *bonae fidei,* G. iv, 62. See *Sale.*

A. exercitoria, one of the adjectician actions, G. iv, 71, 74; see *Exercitorian action.*

A. familiae erciscundae, a *bonae fidei* action, G. iv, 62, for partitioning an inheritance, G. ii, 219, iv, 42, and empowering the judge to adjudicate to the heirs what he held each entitled to, *ibid.,* U. xix, 16. Nothing could be included in it that did not form part of the *hereditas,* G. ii, 220; but it was the proper action for claiming a legacy by preception (see *Legacy,* 28), G. ii, 219.

A. fiduciae, a *bonae fidei* action, G. iv, 62, competent against him who failed to reconvey property transferred to him *ex facie* absolutely, but under trust to reconvey, G. ii, 59; condemnation rendered him infamous, G. iv, 182. See *Fiducia.*

A. finium regundorum, for defining boundaries, also entitling the judge to adjudicate, G. iv, 42, U. xix, 16.

A. furti, G. iii, 203-207; iv, 8, 37, 111, 112; condemnation, or even compromise, rendered the defender infamous, G. iv, 182. See *Theft,* 6.

A. furti concepti, G. iii, 186, 191; see *Theft,* 4, 5.

A. furti oblati, G. iii, 187, 191; see *Theft,* 4, 5.

A. furti prohibiti, G. iii, 188, 192 and n. 2; see *Theft,* 4, 5.

A. injuriarum, G. iii, 224, iv, 8; it was not competent to the heir of the injured party, G. iv, 112, and condemnation or compromise made the defender infamous, 182. See *Personal injury.*

A. institoria, G. iv, 71, 74; see *Institorian action.*

A. judicati was *in duplum,* G. iv, 9, 171. Under the system of the *legis actiones* the procedure was by *manus injectio*

ACTIONS—*continued.*

 II. SPECIAL ACTIONS—*continued.*

(see *Legis actiones*, 5), G. iv, 21; consequently under the formular system the defender had to give *cautio judicatum solvi*, (see *Cautiones, etc.*), G. iv, 25, 102.

A. mandati, a *bonae fidei* action, G. iv, 62, competent either to mandant, G. iii, 111, 127, or mandatory, 156, 161; condemnation rendered the defender infamous, G. iv, 182. See *Mandate.*

A. negatoria in rem, that by which a man sought to have it declared that property of his was free from a usufruct, servitude, or other pretended burden, G. iv, 3 and n. 1.

A. negotiorum gestorum, G. iv, 33.

A. praescriptis verbis, which arose out of an innominate contract *do ut des, etc.,* (see *Contract*, 1), G. iii, 89, note 1, was *bonae fidei,* G. iv, 162.

A. pro socio, for adjustment of partnership disputes, was *bonae fidei,* G. iv, 62; but condemnation in it entailed infamy, G. iv, 182. See *Partnership.*

A. Publiciana, G. iv, 36; see *Publician action.*

A. quod jussu, G. iv, 70, 74; see *Adjectician actions,* 1.

A. rei uxoriae, a *bonae fidei* action, G. iv, 62, for restitution of a dowry on the dissolution of a marriage, competent to the wife, her father and her jointly, her heirs, or the party from whom the dowry had come, according to circumstances, U. vi, 4-7. If the husband (or his heirs) defending impugned his wife's morals—and to prove immorality on her part entitled him to retain a part of the dowry, U. vi, 9, 12—he was required to give *cautio judicatum solvi* (see *Cautiones, etc.*), G. iv, 102. See *Dowry,* 7.

A. rerum amotarum, a less offensive name for an *actio furti* by a husband or his heirs, on the dissolution of a marriage by divorce or death, against the wife, and *vice versa,* U. vii, 2 and note; see *Husband and wife,* 6.

A. Rutiliana, one of the actions used by a *bonorum emptor* or purchaser of a bankrupt estate for enforcing claims against the bankrupt's debtors, G. iv, 35; see *Emptio bonorum,* 3.

A. servi corrupti, G. iii, 198; see *Slavery,* 9.

A. Serviana, the alternative action competent to a *bonorum emptor* against the bankrupt's debtors, and in which he pretended to be the bankrupt's heir, G. iv, 35; see *A. Rutiliana, Emptio bonorum,* 3.

A. Serviana de rebus coloni, that by which a landlord sought to recover effects of his farm tenant hypothecated for the rent, but which had passed into the hands of third parties, G. iv, 35, note 2.

ACTIONS—*continued.*
  II. SPECIAL ACTIONS—*continued.*

    A. tributoria, G. iv, 72, 74a; see *Adjectician actions,* 4.

    A. tutelae, the action against a tutor, on his ward's attaining puberty, for accounting and payment, G. i, 191. It was *bonae fidei,* G. iv, 62; but condemnation in it rendered the tutor infamous, G. iv, 182. A woman, though in tutelage, had no such action when she was freed from it, G. i, 191. See *Tutory,* 9.

    A. venditi, competent to a vendor, the counterpart of the *a. empti,* and like it *bonae fidei,* G. iv, 62; see *Sale.*

    A. vi bonorum raptorum, G. iii, 209, at once penal and petitory, G. iv, 8; either condemnation or compromise rendered the defender infamous, G. iv, 182; see *Robbery.*

ACTOR and REUS, pursuer and defender, G. iv, 16, note 4, 57, 157, 159, 160.

ADCRETIO, accretion or accrual. Rights arose in this way in the following cases:—

    1. *In intestate succession.*—Where there were several agnates of the same degree, and some declined the inheritance, their shares went by accretion to those who took, U. xxvi, 5; see *Hereditas,* 9.

    2. *In testate succession.*—Under the old law when one of several testamentary heirs failed, his share went to the others *jure adcrescendi;* but by the Julian law it was declared *caducous,* and was disposed of according to the caduciary rules it had introduced, U. xvii, 1, 2, i, 21 and n. 3, but with reservation of the old right to descendants and ascendants of the testator to the third degree, U. xviii. See *Julian and Papia-Poppaean law,* 9, *Caducity,* 3, 5.

    3. *In the case of praeterition.*—If a testator neither instituted nor disinherited sons who were *sui* his testament was useless, G. ii, 123; if other *sui,* such as a daughter or a grandchild, were passed over, the testament was valid, but they were entitled by accretion to share in the inheritance in certain proportions, according as the heirs instituted in the testament were *sui* or *extranei,* G. ii, 124, 126. See *Testament,* 10.

    4. *In joint legacies.*—In the case of a joint legacy by vindication, if one of the legatees failed, his share accrued to the other, until the rule was modified by the Julian and Pap. Popp. law, G. ii, 199, 206, 207, U. xxiv, 12; see *Legacy,* 31, 34.

    5. *Where a slave was manumitted by one only of several owners.*—In such a case if the manumission was irregular there was no result; if regular, the slave did not become free,

ADCRETIO—*continued.*
>but the manumitter's interest in him accrued to the other owners, U. i, 18; see *Manumission,* 2.

ADDICTIO BONORUM EMPTORI, G. iii, 79 and n. 7.

ADDICTUS and ADJUDICATUS, difference, G. iii, 189, 190, note 2.

ADEMTIO, revocation of a legacy or a testamentary gift of freedom, might be either in the testament itself or in a codicil confirmed by it, U. xxiv, 29, ii, 12; but in either case the same form had to be observed in the ademption as in the grant, *ibid.,* and note 1 to 29.

ADITIO HEREDITATIS, entering to an inheritance, see *Hereditas,* 5-7.

ADJECTICIAN ACTIONS, the so-called *actiones adjecticiae qualitatis,* praetorian actions against a *paterfamilias* in respect of debt contracted by a *filiusfamilias* or a slave, G. iv, 69-74.

1. *The* actio quod jussu.—If a *filiusfamilias* or a slave contracted debt on the authority of parent or owner, the praetor held the latter liable in full, on the ground that it was his credit that had in fact been relied on, G. iv, 70.

2. *Exercitorian and institorian actions.*—There was the same *in solidum* liability where a parent or owner had put his *filiusfamilias* or slave in charge of a vessel or of a shop or store, G. iv, 71; see *Exercitorian action, Institorian action.*

3. *The* actio de peculio et de in rem verso.—If a *filiusfamilias* or slave had a *peculium* (which see), then for any debts contracted, whatever the nature of them, the *paterfamilias* or owner was always liable to the extent of the *peculium,* G. iv, 73; he was entitled, however, to deduct from it the amount he had advanced towards it, and for which his *filiusfamilias* or slave was his debtor under a natural obligation (see *Obligation,* 5, 7), *ibid.* But if any part of the debt for which a creditor was suing had been contracted in procuring things which had been applied to the uses of the *paterfamilias* or owner, even without his authority, or by one who was in charge neither of a ship nor of a store, for that he was liable *in solidum, ibid.;* consequently, it was the practice for the creditor to conjoin the two actions, and to sue simultaneously *de peculio et de in rem verso, ibid.*

4. *The tributorian action.*—When *filiusfamilias* or slave, with the knowledge of the parent or owner, had embarked any part of his *peculium* in trade, the trade creditors were entitled to claim on the trade assets *pari passu* with the parent or owner, who might be proceeded against in an *actio tributoria* to compel him to pay a *pro rata* dividend,

ADJECTICIAN ACTIONS—*continued.*

G. iv, 72. But any creditor entitled to the tributorian might of course, if more for his advantage, employ that *de peculio* instead, 74a.

ADJUDICATIO (I.), one of the clauses of a *formula,* G. iv, 39, (see *Formula,* 1), used only in the *actio familiae erciscundae, a. communi dividundo,* and *a. finium regundorum,* 42, (see those words), and coming after the *demonstratio* and *intentio,* 44 and note. It empowered the judge to adjudicate to each of the litigants such a share of the matter in dispute as he considered him entitled to, 42, 44, note.

ADJUDICATIO (II.), the award of the judge in any of the three divisory actions enumerated in last head, U. xix, 16; it conferred upon the parties a quiritarian right of property in what was adjudged to them, whether *res mancipi* or *nec mancipi, ibid.*

ADJUDICATUS, G. iii, 199 and n. 2, 189, note 2; see *Judicatum.*

ADOPTION and ADROGATION, G. i, 97-107, U. tit. viii. See also *Parent and child : Patria potestas.*

1. *Adoption, what ?*—Adoption was a mode of transferring a person into a new family, and placing him in *patria potestate* of another than his natural parent, G. i, 97, U. viii, 1 : and so complete was the transfer that the adoptive parent was entitled to pass the child in adoption to a third party, G. i, 105. The adoption was either of a *paterfamilias* (see U. iv, 1, note), specifically *adrogatio,* or of a *filiusfamilias*—adoption in the stricter sense, G. i, 99, U. viii, 2, 3.

2. *Adrogation of a* paterfamilias.—This could take place only in Rome, G. i, 100, U. viii, 4; for it required to be sanctioned by vote of the *comitia,* G. i, 99, U. viii, 3. An *adrogatus* could be adopted only in the character of a son, G. i, 99; if he had children of his own *in potestate,* they passed into the *potestas* of the adrogator as grandchildren, G. i, 107, U. viii, 8.

3. *Adoption of a* filiusfamilias.—The transfer here was the act of the natural *paterfamilias*—for it was only a child *in potestate* that could be given in adoption, G. i, 99—by a somewhat intricate process described in G. i, 134, ending with a *vindicatio, i.e.* an *in jure cessio* (see *In jure cessio*), before the praetor or a provincial governor, G. iv, 100, 134, U. viii, 3, 4. The child might be adopted either as a son or grandson, G. i, 99; it being immaterial in the latter case whether the adopter had a son of his own or not, U. viii, 7.

4. *Who could or could not adrogate or adopt.*—Women could

ADOPTION and ADROGATION—*continued.*

   not adopt in either way, having no *potestas*, G. i, 104, U.
   viii, 8*a*; but an unmarried man might, U. viii, 6, and so
   might one unable to procreate, G. i, 103, U. viii, 6.   The
   adopter of course required to be the senior, G. i, 106 and
   note.

5. *Who could be adrogated or adopted.*—A woman could not be
   adrogated, G. i, 101, U. viii, 5; neither by the earlier law
   could a male who was a pupil, though allowed under the
   imperial law where circumstances justified it, G. i, 102,
   U. viii, 5.   But a child of either sex, of any age, and of
   any degree of relationship to the natural parent, if only
   in potestate, might be given in adoption, G. i, 99, 101, 102,
   U. viii, 3, 5.

6. *Results for the adrogating or adopting parent.*—In adrogation invariably, and in adoption when the child was
   adopted as a son, (*i.e.* not as a grandson or remoter
   descendant), the adopting parent got a *suus heres* (see
   Agnatio sui heredis), whom he was bound to mention in
   his testament; consequently one made by him previously
   was thereby invalidated, G. ii, 138, U. xxiii, 3.   See
   Testament, 22.

7. *Results for the adrogated or adopted child.*—The child
   became so identified with his new family that, while the
   relationship lasted, it was an impediment to his marriage
   with any member of it within the prohibited degrees, G.
   i, 59, 61; and even after its dissolution he was forbidden
   to marry any member of it who had been related to him
   as an ascendant, 59.   Under both the Twelve Tables and
   the edict, if the child was still *in potestate* of his adoptive
   parent at the latter's death, he succeeded to him *ab intestato* equally with his natural children, G. iii, 2, U. xxviii,
   8.   By the Tables he had no longer any legal right of
   succession to his natural parent, the civil relationship
   having been destroyed by the *capitis deminutio* (which see,
   No. 3) involved in the adoption, G. i, 158, 162, U. xi, 13;
   but the edict allowed him to claim his natural parent's
   succession as a cognate, on failure of agnates, G. iii, 31,
   (see *Bonorum possessio*, 16).   Both by the Tables and the
   edict the adoptive child had the rights of a natural child
   in regard to the testament of his adoptive parent, provided he was still in the adoptive family when the
   latter died, G. ii, 136, U. xxviii, 3, (see *Bonor. poss.*, 6).

8. *Results peculiar to adrogation.*—The estate of the adrogated
   paterfamilias passed to the adrogator *per universitatem*,
   G. ii, 97, 98, with exception of such rights as were

ADOPTION and ADROGATION—*continued.*

  destroyed by *capitis deminutio* (which see, No. 3), G. iii, 83.
The adrogator did not, however, become liable in law for
his new son's personal debts, 84, (though he did for his
hereditary ones, as he himself became heir through his
son, *ibid.*); but equity gave the creditors relief by *utiles*
or fictitious actions (see *Actions*, 6), in the manner described in G. iii, 84, iv, 38, 80.

 9. *Emancipation of adrogated or adopted children.*—The effects
were these,—that the child then ceased to have any
rights in regard to the adoptive parent's succession, testate
or intestate, G. ii, 136, U. xxviii, 3, but began from that
moment to have the rights of an emancipated child in
reference to that of his natural parent, G. ii, 137, (see
Emancipation, 4).

ADPROMISSIO, see *Suretyship.*

ADQUISITIO PER UNIVERSITATEM, varieties of, G. ii, 98 and notes.

ADROGATION, see *Adoption.*

ADSERTOR LIBERTATIS, G. iv, 14 and n. 2 ; see *Slavery*, 9.

ADSTIPULATION, G. iii, 110-114; see also *Stipulation.*

 1. *What ?*—Adstipulation was the addition of a second stipulant in a stipulation, to whom the promiser engaged to
pay what he had already promised to pay to the principal stipulant, G. iii, 110, 112. The second stipulation,
however, did not require to be in the same words as the
first, and might be for a smaller sum, or conditional while
the first was pure, 112, 113.

 2. *Its purpose.*—It was seldom employed except when the
original stipulation was for payment after the stipulant's
death, G. iii, 117 ; in which case the adstipulator might
receive payment or sue upon the contract as the stipulant's agent, with responsibility to the latter's heirs *ex
mandato*, 111, 117.

 3. *Peculiarities.*—Adstipulation by a slave was useless, G. iii,
114; that of a *filiusfamilias* gave no right of action to
his *paterfamilias, ibid. ;* he himself could not sue upon
it until he had passed out of the *potestas* (see *Patria pot.*)
without *capitis deminutio*, (see *Cap. dem.*, 2), *ibid. ;* if he
died before payment was due, action was not competent to
his heirs, *ibid.*, iv, 113. An adstipulator who fraudulently
acceptilated (see *Acceptilation*) was liable in damages
under the Aquilian law, G. iii, 215, (see *Wrongful damage
to property*, 4); which were doubled if he disputed his
liability, G. iii, 216, iv, 9, 171.

AEDIFICATIO, acquisition of property by, G. ii, 73 ; remedies, 76,
(see *Property*, 6). *Aedificatio* as one of the modes in

29

AEDIFICATIO—*continued.*
> which a latin acquired citizenship, G. i, 33, U. iii, 1, (see *Junian latinity*, 7).

AEDILES, curule, their edicts, G. i, 6 ; their functions, 6, note 3.

AELIA-SENTIAN LAW, the, of A.D. 4, was intended to regulate manumission of slaves, G. i, 13 and n. 1, but did not apply to that of free persons *in causa mancipii*, G. i, 139, (see *Mancipii*, etc., 3). The following were its leading provisions :—

1. *Manumission in fraud of creditors.*—It prohibited any manumission in fraud of creditors or patrons, G. i, 37, U. i, 15, —a prohibition afterwards extended to peregrins, to whom the provisions of the statute itself did not apply, G. i, 47.

2. *Manumission by owners under twenty.*—Owners under twenty years old were not to manumit their slaves except *vindicta* (which see), before a magistrate, U. i, 7, in presence of a council which sat at stated times for the purpose of sanctioning manumissions, G. i, 20, U. i, 13, and which had heard and approved the reasons of it, G. i, 38, U. i, 13, such as kinship between owner and slave, etc., G. i, 19, 39.

3. *Manumission of slaves of bad character.*—Slaves who had been punished for crime or otherwise disgraced were not on manumission to become citizens, but to be of the same condition as deditician peregrins, G. i, 13-15, U. i, 11, incapable of ever attaining citizenship, and subject to many and serious disabilities, G. i, 25-27, (see *Deditician freedmen*).

4. *Manumission of slaves under thirty years of age.*—Manumission of slaves under thirty, even of unblemished character, was not to make them citizens unless it had been accomplished *vindicta*, on cause approved by the council, G. i, 18, U. i, 12.

5. *Exception to the last two rules in the case of an insolvent owner.*—An insolvent owner might in his testament institute or substitute one of his slaves, even one who had been disgraced or was under thirty years old, as his necessary heir with freedom, who would take the estate and become a citizen in the event of the voluntary heirs all declining, G. i, 21, U. i, 14, (see *Necessarii heredes*).

6. *Remedy provided for slaves under thirty manumitted irregularly.*—In aid of a slave under thirty, whose manumission had not made him a citizen because the combined requirements of *vindicta* and *consilium* had been disre-

AELIA-SENTIAN LAW—*continued.*

garded, it contained this provision,—that if he married a woman not a peregrin, in presence of seven witnesses, to whom he declared that he was doing so in order to have the benefit of the statute, he might, after a child of the marriage had reached the age of twelve months (*anniculus*), prove those facts to the praetor, and by him be declared a citizen, along with his wife and child if she was not one already, G. i, 29, (see *Causae prob. ex l. Aelia Sentia*).

7. *Extension of the remedy by subsequent legislation.*—Ulp. in iii, 3, says this provision was introduced by the Junian law; the probability is that the latter only confirmed it, and declared the same procedure competent to those under thirty who had not been manumitted by any of the recognised modes of manumission, but informally, or whose manumission had proceeded only from a bonitarian owner (which see), G. i, 29, note, as amended in *Additions, etc.* A Sct. of the time of Vespasian further extended it to those irregularly manumitted after passing the age of thirty, G. i, 31. Hence the phrase *ex lege Aelia Sentia ad civitatem pervenire*, G. iii, 73.

AEQUUM *est neminem cum alterius detrimento et injuria fieri locupletiorem;* see G. ii, 82, note 4.

AES ET LIBRA, the copper and the scales used as a solemnity in various transactions of the *jus civile, e.g.* mancipation (which see) either of *res mancipi* (which see) or of three persons, G. i, 119, ii, 23, U. xix, 3; in coemption (see *Manus*, 2), G. i, 113; in emancipation, remancipation, and adoption (see those words), G. i, 132, 134; in the formal contract of *nexum* (which see), G. iii, 89, note; in *nexi solutio* (which see), G. iii, 173, 174; and in *testamentum per aes et libram* (see *Testament*, 3, 4), G. ii, 102-104, U. xx, 2, 9. The procedure is described in G. i, 119, and its origin explained in G. i, 122; latterly it was a mere formality, though an essential one, G. ii, 104, note 8.

AES MILITARE, *aes equestre*, and *aes hordiarium* might be recovered by *pignoris capio*, G. iv, 27, (see *Legis actiones*, 6).

AFFINITY, *adfinitas*, as a bar to marriage, G. i, 63; see *Marriage*, 4.

AGGRIPINA, her marriage with her uncle Claudius, G. i, 62.

AGNATIO (or ADGNATIO) SUI HEREDIS, advent of a *suus heres* (see *Sui heredes*), invalidated a testament, U. xxiii, 2, (see *Testament*, 22). There was such agnation when a living *postumus* was born to the testator, G. ii, 131, U. xxii, 18; and though Ulp. xxii, 15, defines *postumus* as a lawful child *in utero* at the date of his father's testament, Gai.

AGNATIO SUI HEREDIS—*continued.*

ii, 131, includes any lawful child born thereafter, (see *Postumi*).   There was *quasi agnatio sui* when an immediate male *suus heres*, say a son, of the testator's died or was emancipated, leaving a child *in potestate* of the latter, G. ii, 133, 134, U. xxiii, 3.   In both of these cases, however, *ruptio testamenti* was avoided by the testator's having taken the precaution of either instituting or dis inheriting the *suus*, (see *Testament*, 10).   There was also *quasi agnatio sui* when a testator adopted a child as his son, G. ii, 138, U. xxiii, 3 ; when he took a wife *in manum*, *ibid.*, for she acquired the rights of a daughter (see *Manus*, 4), G. i, 115b ; or when a son of his was manumitted from a first or second mancipation (see *Emancipation*, 1, 3), G. ii, 141, U. xxiii, 3.   But in the two first of those cases *ruptio* was not excluded by previous institution,—disherison was impossible ; nor in the third by either institution or disherison.   Finally there was *quasi agnatio sui* by *erroris causae probatio* (which see), G. ii, 142, 143, converting a *matrimonium non justum* of the testator's into *justum matrimonium* (see *Marriage*, 1, 8), and thus placing the issue of it *in potestate*, G. i, 67.   If cause was proved during the testator's life, a previous testament was thereby invariably invalidated ; but if not proved until after his death, then, by a Sct. of Hadrian's, there was no *ruptio* unless the child had been neither instituted nor disinherited, G. ii, 142, 143.

AGNATION, *agnatio*, G. i, 156, iii, 10 ; U. xi, 4, xxvi, 1.

    1. *Definition.*—Agnation was *legitima cognatio*, G. iii, 10, U. xxvi, 1,—kinship of the *jus civile*, as distinguished from the natural or blood kinship of cognation, G. i, 156.   It was a relationship through males ; for those alone were agnates *inter se* who were in the *potestas* of a common parent, or would have been had he been alive at the moment.   And as the relationship resulted from the *patria potestas*, it might arise from anything whereby this was created, *e.g.* adoption, adrogation, etc., as also from *in manum conventio*, U. xxvi, 7, which put a wife in the position of a daughter to her husband, and a sister to her children, G. iii, 14.   Apart from adoption, *in manum conventio*, etc., it could have no existence for those who were not free by birth, and so had never been *in potestate ;* consequently in succession to freedmen that of agnates was unknown, G. iii, 40.

    2. *Degrees.*—It was of different degrees, G. iii, 10, the nearest being that of brother and sister, who were frequently

AGNATION—*continued.*

described as *consanguinei, ibid.*, U. xxvi, 1; and following it that of a brother and a brother's children, then that of the children of two brothers, often called *consobrini*, and so on, G. iii, 10. For the mode of counting the degrees, see U. v, 6, note 2.

3. *Rights it conferred.*—The nearest agnates were entitled at law to the tutory of a pupil agnate, G. i, 55, (see *Tutory,* 2), and to succeed *ab intestato* to one who had died without *sui heredes*, G. iii, 9, U. xxvi, 1 (see *Intestate succession*, 4); but by the praetorian system some who by the *jus civile* were neither *sui* nor agnates were preferred to them, G. iii, 26, U. xxviii, 8, (see *Bonor. possessio*, 15).

4. *Its extinction by* capitis deminutio.—The relationship itself and the legal rights it conferred were lost by *capitis deminutio* of any sort, (see *Cap. dem.*, 1), G. i, 158, 163, iii, 21, U. xi, 9; but the praetors admitted *minuti* to the succession after agnates *integri juris*, G. iii, 27, U. xxviii, 9, for though the civil relationship was gone the natural one remained, G. i, 158, iii, 27, (see *Bonor. poss.*, 16).

ALBUM PRAETORIS, the white boards on which the praetor's edicts, etc., were published, G. iv, 46.

ALIENATION, see *Property*, 9.

ALIENI JURIS PERSONAE, those domestically dependent, *i.e.* subject to the *jus* of a family head; see also *Persons*, 3.

1. *Who were* alieni juris.—See *Persons*, 3.

2. *Their disability and capacity as regarded property.*—They were so much subject to the *paterfamilias* that not merely slaves,—who were things, and might be bought and sold, G. ii, 15, iv, 40, U. xix, 1,—but *filiifamilias* and wife *in manu*, if taken from him surreptitiously, were held to have been stolen, G. iii, 199. They could have nothing of their own, G. ii, 87, and all they acquired accrued to their *paterfamilias*, G. ii, 86, iii, 163; but while they might acquire by all natural modes, and even by mancipation, G. ii, 87, iii, 167, they could not do so by *in jure cessio*, G. ii, 96.

3. *Their disability and capacity in obligation.*—They might contract with third parties for payment to or performance for the *paterfamilias*, G. ii, 87; but he was not liable on their contracts, except in the case of slaves and *filiifamilias*, for whom he might in some cases be made responsible by the praetorian adjectician actions (see *Adject. actions*), G. iv, 69-74, just as for their delicts he was answerable in noxal actions (which see), G. iv, 75-79. Civilly none of them but a *filiusfamilias* could oblige himself by contract, G. iii, 104; though they might do so naturally (see

ALIENI JURIS PERSONAE—*continued.*

Obli7ation, 5, 10), and have their engagements effectually guaranteed by sureties, G. iii, 119. Between them and him to whom they were subject there could be no civil obligation, G. iv, 78; yet in certain cases natural indebtedness on their part was recognised, G. iv, 73.

4. *Their disability and capacity in matter of testaments.*—As they had nothing of their own they could not make a testament, G. ii, 112, U. xx, 10, with a limited exception in the case of *filiifamilias* who were or had been in the army, U. xx, 10, and slaves belonging to the state, U. xx, 16; while, if they were instituted heirs by third parties, they could not enter except on the instructions of those to whom they were subject, G. ii, 87.

5. *How they ceased to be* alieni juris.—See G. i, 124-141, and separately *Slavery, Patria potestas, Manus, Mancipii, etc.*

ALLUVION as a means of acquiring property, G. ii, 70; distinguished from avulsion, 71. See *Property,* 4.

ANIMALS, wild and domesticated, property in, G. ii, 66-68.

ANNICULUS, G. i, 29, 32, 73, U. iii, 3; see *Aelia-Sentian law,* 6.

ANTIQUUM JUS, see *Jus antiquum.*

ANTONINUS (IMPERATOR) sometimes means Antoninus Pius, sometimes Marcus Aurelius, sometimes Caracalla; see those names under *Constitutiones principum.*

APOLLO DIDYMAEUS, U. xxii, 6.

AQUA ET IGNI INTERDICTIO was a *media capitis deminutio* (see *Cap. dem.,* 1), G. i, 161, U. xi, 12, of which the nature is described in G. i, 128, n. 2; it reduced the individual who suffered it to the condition of a peregrin, G. i, 128, U. x, 3, (see *Peregrinity*).

AQUILIAN LAW, see *Wrongful damage to property.*

ARBITER and ARBITRARIA FORMULA in procedure in interdicts, G. iv, 141, 163-165; see *Interdicts,* 11.

ARBITRARY ACTIONS, see *Actions,* 8.

ARCARIA NOMINA, G. iii, 131; see *Literal obligations,* 2.

ARGENTARIUS, peculiarities of pleading in action by him against a customer, G. iv, 64, 66-68; combined auctioneering with banking, G. iv, 126*a* and note.

ARRA, earnest given in certain contracts, G. iii, 139; see *Sale,* 1.

As, use of, in mancipation explained, G. i, 122; by Julia Papirian law, converting cattle-penalties into money-penalties, 100 *asses* were declared equivalent to an ox, 10 to a sheep, G. iv, 95, note 4; the 500 *asses* of the *leg. actio sacramenti* were afterwards converted into 125 sesterces, *ibid.* note 2.

ASSE INSTITUTUS, EX, instituted in a testament as sole heir, as

BONAE FIDEI POSSESSIO was technically the possession of an individual who was not, yet in good faith believed himself,
owner; his rights, though inferior to those of a full proprietor, were superior to those of a merely quiritarian
dominus, (see *Quir. ownership*), G. iii, 166.

  1. *Rights of a* bonae fidei possessor *as against the true owner.*—
If he had in good faith acquired a thing from one not its
owner, he might—unless it was *res furtiva*, G. ii, 45—
complete his title to it by possession for the requisite
period, G. ii, 43, 44, (see *Usucapion*, 3). If the owner surreptitiously deprived him of it, he had against the former
an *actio furti*, G. iii, 200. If in good faith he was in
possession of another man's slave, he was entitled, as
against the owner, to all the slave's acquisitions due to
the latter's labour or his own funds, G. ii, 92, iii, 164.
If, being in good faith in possession of another man's
property, he made additions to it which augmented its
value, as by building, sowing, or planting on his lands,
or writing a treatise on his parchments, or painting a
picture on his pannel, he could not be required to yield
the possession until he had been reimbursed, G. ii, 76-78,
(see *Property*, 6).

  2. *His rights as against third parties.*—If a third party disputed his right, and withheld from him that of which he
had been in possession, he had against him a praetorian
real action in the Publician, G. iv, 36, (see *Publ. action*).
If any third party deprived him of his possession surreptitiously, he had against him an *actio furti*, G. iii, 200.
And if it was a freeman that he was in good faith possessing as a slave, he was entitled to his acquisitions to
the same extent as if the freeman had been a *servus
alienus*, G. ii, 92, iii, 164, and might through his agency
possess and usucapt, G. ii, 94.

BONIS, IN.—A person who, *e.g.*, had acquired a *res mancipi* by
simple delivery, was said to have it only *in bonis*, in his
estate; the *dominium ex jure Quiritium*, or legal ownership title, remained in the transferor until usucapion was
completed, because of the omission of the proper form of
conveyance, G. ii, 41, U. i, 16, (see *Bonitarian ownership*).
In bonis habere was not the same thing as *bona fide possidere ;* see the distinction in G. ii, 41 compared with 43.

BONITARIAN OWNERSHIP.   See also *Property; Bonis, in; Quiritarian
ownership.*

  1. *Origin and meaning of the phrase.*—Bonitarian ownership,
dominium bonitarium, was first suggested by the words of
Theoph.—φυσικὴ δεσποτεία λέγεται in bonis, καὶ ὁ δεσπότης

BONITARIAN OWNERSHIP—*continued.*

βονιτάριος, G. ii, 40, note; it means the same thing as *in bonis habere,*—beneficial ownership without the legal title, G. ii, 41, as distinguished from the *plenum jus dominii,* which included both, *ibid.,* and the *nudum jus Quiritium,* which was the legal title without the beneficial interest, G. iii, 166. The distinctions, results of praetorian equity, eventually disappeared with Justinian's abolition of the civil forms of conveyance, G. ii, 40, note.

2. *How a bonitarian right was created.*—When one citizen acquired a *res mancipi* (which see) from another, but merely had it delivered to him instead of conveyed in due form of law, he got only the bonitarian ownership, G. ii, 41, U. i, 16; but if it was from a peregrin he thus acquired, he held it *pleno jure,* conveyance according to the forms of the *jus civile* being impossible, U. i, 16, note 2. The right of a *bonorum possessor* too in the corporeal items of the estate to which he succeeded was bonitarian, G. iii, 80, (see *Bonor. possessio,* 5); and so was that of a *bonorum emptor* in the corporeals of the bankrupt estate he had purchased, *ibid.,* (see *Emptio bonorum,* 3).

3. *Rights of a bonitarian owner.*—Having the beneficial interest, it was he that, *e.g.,* had *potestas* over a slave he had acquired informally, G. i, 54, and he got all the slave's acquisitions, G. ii, 88, iii, 166. If he had to sue for his recovery from a third party the praetor granted him the Publician or other fictitious action, G. iv, 34-36. But he could not by manumission make him a citizen,—only a latin, G. i, 17, (see *Manumission,* 2), and therefore he could not by testament institute him his heir with freedom, G. ii, 276, note, U. xxii, 8, (see *Testament,* 14). If the latin was a male under puberty, or a woman, it was the quiritarian owner that was tutor, for this was a *jus legitimum,* G. i, 167, U. xi, 19, (see *Tutory,* 19); but the latin's estate nevertheless went on his death to his bonitarian manumitter, G. i, 167, iii, 56, (see *Succession to Junian latins,* 2).

4. *How the right was converted into* plenum dominium.—The bonitarian right was only temporary; it became quiritarian on the completion of the ordinary usucapion, G. ii, 41, (see *Usucapion,* 2, 4).

BONORUM EMPTOR, see *Emptio bonorum.*

BONORUM POSSESSIO, G. ii, 118-122, 125, 126, 132, 147-151; iii, 25-38; U. tit. xxviii. See also SUCCESSION.

I. BONORUM POSSESSIO GENERALLY, (see G. ii, 119, note 1).

1. *Origin.*—In the rules of the *jus civile* in regard to succession there was much naturally unjust, G. iii, 25, which

BONORUM POSSESSIO—*continued.*
  I. BONORUM POSSESSIO GENERALLY—*continued.*

the praetors so far remedied by granting to those they considered entitled in equity to an inheritance which the law denied them, possession of a deceased person's estate, —the benefits of the inheritance without the name of it, U. xxviii, 12; and once its advantages were recognised it often was applied for and granted to those who had a good legal title, but desired to have the aid of some of the remedies the praetors had invented for *bonor. possessores,* but which did not apply to heirs, *heredes,* G. iii, 34.

2. *Varieties.*—There were three varieties,—(a) *bonor. poss. contra tabulas, i.e.* in contradiction of a testament, granted to *sui heredes* (which see) of a testator, other than a son, who were unmentioned in the deed, G. ii, 135, U. xxviii, 2,— praeterition of a son *in potestate* invalidated the testament and caused intestacy, G. ii, 123, U. xxii, 16; (b) *bonor. poss. secundum tabulas, i.e.* in terms of a testament, granted to testamentary heirs whose right was in law defective through a flaw in the execution of the deed, or the subsequent occurrence of something that rendered it invalid, G. ii, 118, 119, 147, U. xxviii, 5, 6; (c) *bon. poss. ab. intestato, i.e.* in the absence of a testament, G. iii, 26-31, U. xxviii, 7, granted to claimants in the order established by the *edictum successorium,* U. xxviii, 12.

3. *How obtained.*—The grant had to be formally applied for, *bonor. poss. petere,* G. ii, 98, etc., iii, 37, U. xxviii, 10, etc. To petition for that *ab intestato* ascendants and descendants of the deceased were allowed a year, other persons being limited to 100 days, U. xxviii, 10; the period for those entitled in the second place beginning when that of those entitled in the first had expired, and so on, U. xxviii, 11.

4. *Effect as against the* juris civilis *heir.*—The *bonor. possessio* was granted *periculo petentis,* and might be *cum re,* real and substantial, or *sine re,* merely nominal, according as the grantee could or could not maintain it against the *ipso jure* heir, G. ii, 148, iii, 35, U. xviii, 13; for the latter was not bound to apply for *bonor. poss.,* but entitled to stand on his testamentary or statutory title, G. iii, 37. Examples of *bonor. poss. sine re* occur in G. ii, 149, iii, 36, 37, U. xxviii, 13.

5. *Effect as against third parties.*—The succession of the *bonor. possessor* being not civil but praetorian, it gave him only a bonitarian right in the corporeal items of the deceased's estate, convertible into quiritarian right by usucapion, G.

BONORUM POSSESSIO—*continued*.

I. BONORUM POSSESSIO GENERALLY—*continued*.

iii, 80, (see *Bonitar. ownership*, 2, 4); to enable him to obtain possession the praetor gave him the interdict *quorum bonorum*, (see *Interdicts*, 5), G. iii, 34, iv, 144. Not being heir, G. iii, 32, he was not entitled directly to an heir's actions against third parties; but, by interpolation of a fiction of heirship, the praetor adapted them to the altered circumstances, rendering them *utiles* or serviceable, Gai. ii, 81, iv, 34, U. xxviii, 12, (see *Actions*, 6).

II. BONORUM POSSESSIO CONTRA TABULAS.

6. *To* sui praeteriti (*other than sons*).—When a *suus heres*, other than a son (see above, No. 2), had been neither instituted nor disinherited in a testament, he was entitled under the *jus civile* to a share of the inheritance by accretion, G. ii, 124, (see *Adcretio*, 3); but the praetor held this insufficient where he had been passed over in favour of a stranger, and allowed him (and other *sui* concurring with him) possession of the whole estate, thus rendering the testament inoperative, G. ii, 125. And this right was competent not only to natural children but also to adoptive ones, if still *in potestate* of the adoptive father-testator at his death, U. xxviii, 3.

7. *To emancipated children.*—By the *jus civile* a testator was not required to mention his emancipated children (see *Emancipation*), for they had ceased to be *sui heredes*, G. ii, 135. But the praetors, recognising their natural claims, required that they should be either instituted or disinherited, giving them *bon. poss. contra tab.* if they were not, *ibid.*, U. xxviii, 2; under condition however of collation (which see) with instituted *sui*, U. xxviii, 4. If an emancipated child had passed into an adoptive family, this possession was not competent to him, U. xxviii, 3.

8. *To a patron.*—See *Succession to citizen freedmen*, *Succession to Junian latins*.

9. *Peculiarity in the case of females.*—A rescript of Marcus Aurelius' enacted that women should not in any case be allowed more by *bonor. poss. contra tab.* than they would have been entitled to by accretion of the *jus civile* (above, No. 6),—a rule that could apply strictly only to *suae*, but whose principle was extended to *emancipatae*, G. ii, 126.

III. BONORUM POSSESSIO SECUNDUM TABULAS.

10. *Circumstances in which it could be applied for.*—Some formality in the execution of a testament might have been neglected, such as the *familiae venditio* or the *nuncupatio*, G. iii, 104, (see *Testament*, 3, 4), or, in the case of

BONORUM POSSESSIO—*continued*.

 III. BONORUM POSSESSIO SECUNDUM TABULAS—*continued*.

  that of a woman, her tutor's *auctoritas*, G. ii, 118, (see *Tutory*, 16, 23), in any of which cases it was said to be *non jure factum*, G. ii, 146; or, though *ab initio* valid, it might have been subsequently invalidated by *agnatio sui heredis*, a later testament, or the testator's *capitis deminutio*, G. ii, 138-145, U. xxiii, 2-4, (see *Testament*, 22, 23): in such circumstances the testamentary heirs had no legal right, but were nevertheless entitled, under the qualifications stated below, Nos. 11, 12, to *bonor. poss. secundum tabulas*, G. ii, 119, U. xxiii, 6, xxviii, 6.

  11. *What still required as regarded testator and testament.*— To justify it in any case, the praetors required that the testator, even though *capite deminutus* in the interval, should have been a citizen and *sui juris* at the moment of his death, G. ii, 147, U. xxiii, 6; and as regards his testament that it was sealed by at least seven citizen witnesses, G. ii, 119, U. xxiii, 6, xxviii, 6.

  12. *Who preferred to the* heredes scripti *in the invalid testament.* —Any one with a good claim *contra tabulas* excluded the *scripti heredes*, U. xxviii, 5. So at one time did agnates of the testator claiming *jure legitimo*, G. ii, 119, (see *Intestate succession*, 4); but by a rescript of Marc. Aurelius' the *scripti heredes* could defeat their claim with an *exceptio doli*, G. ii, 120, 121, (see *Exception*, 8). If the testament was a woman's, and the objection to it that it was made without the *auctoritas* of patron or parent (see *Tutory*, 16, 23), the latter had preference over the *scripti heredes*, G. ii, 122; but if in tutelage under an Atilian tutor (who had no right of succession), the claim of the *scripti heredes* was preferable to that of her agnates, *ibid*.

 IV. BONORUM POSSESSIO AB INTESTATO.

  13. *The evils that were to be remedied.*—The civil rules of intestate succession were extremely strict, G. iii, 18: for they did not admit emancipated children, G. ii, 19, or agnates who had undergone *capitis deminutio* (which see, 2), G. ii, 19, 21; they admitted no female agnate except a sister, 23; if the nearest agnates did not take, no right was recognised in those of the next degree, 22,—*in legitimis hereditatibus successio non est*, U. 26, 5; and cognates, *i.e.* those of kin to the deceased through females, were not admitted at all, G. ii, 24. These and other *iniquitates*, G. ii, 25, the praetors remedied by establishing a new order of succession, which Ulp. says embraced seven *gradus* (or rather *ordines*), U. xxviii, 7; some of them,

DIGEST. **461**

BONORUM POSSESSIO—*continued.*
IV. BONORUM POSSESSIO AB INTESTATO—*continued.*
however, applied only to the successions of freedmen,
and are referred to under *Succession to citizen freedmen*, 8.

14. *The* bonor. possessio *granted to* liberi, *descendants.*—The
first entitled were those descendants of the testator whom
he was bound, either by the *jus civile* or the edict, to
institute or disinherit if he made a will,—in other words,
his wife *in manu*, (who was regarded as a daughter in
matter of succession), with his natural sons and daughters,
whether *in potestate* or emancipated, and the representatives of those that were dead, G. iii, 26, 63, note 1, U.
xxviii, 7 ; adoptive children concurring if *in potestate* at
deceased's death, but not if emancipated (see *Adoption*, 7),
U. xxviii, 8.

15. *That granted to agnates.*—Under their old name of *legitimi
heredes* the deceased's nearest agnates were admitted in
the second place, U. xxviii, 7.

16. *That granted to cognates.*—Though the grant in the third
place was nominally to cognates, *i.e.* those related through
females, G. iii, 30, U. xxviii, 7, 9, yet with them were
included agnates of the first degree who through *capitis deminutio* had lost their legal rights, G. iii, 27, U.
xxviii, 9 ; agnates of the second or a remoter degree on
failure of the first, G. iii, 28 ; female agnates more distantly related than sisters, 29 ; and natural children of
the deceased's who were at the moment in an adoptive
family, 31.

17. *That granted to the survivor of husband and wife.*—This
came last, U. xxviii, 7 ; *i.e.* to a wife if not *in manu ;*
for if *in manu* she was *loco filiae* and took with *liberi*,
G. iii, 5.

CADUCARIA LEX, U. xxviii, 7, a name given to the Julian and
Papia-Poppaean law, which see.
CADUCITY, testamentary lapse, U. tit. xvii.

1. *What meant by caducity.*—With the two exceptions referred
to below, Nos. 6 and 7, the word applied only to testamentary gifts valid and capable of being taken so far as
the *jus civile* was concerned, but which the donee was either
prevented taking by reason of some prohibition unknown
to the *jus civile*, or failed to take from some other cause,
U. xvii, 1.

2. *Influence of the Julian and Papia-Poppaean law.*—It was
this statute that originated it ; for by prohibiting unmarried persons to take testamentary inheritances or

DIGEST.

CADUCITY—*continued.*

legacies at all, and childless persons to take more than a
half of what was left them (see *Jul. and P. P. law*, Nos.
4, 5), and by its postponement of the date of vesting from
the time of a testator's death to that of the opening of
his testament (see *Jul. and P. P. law*, No. 7), it created
lapses that previously had no existence, *ibid.* The
Junian law (see *Junian latinity*, 4) a few years later
made a testamentary inheritance or a legacy left to a
Junian latin caducous, if he did not qualify himself to
take it within 100 days after the opening of the will, U.
xvii, 1, xxii, 3.

3. *How the Julian law disposed of the* caduca.—A caducous
inheritance, where the institution was *ex parte* only, *i.e.* to
a share, went first to the other testamentary heirs who
either were descendants or ascendants of the testator to
the third degree inclusive,—to these the *jus antiquum*, or
old right of accretion (see *Adcretio*, 2), was reserved by the
statute, U. tit. xviii,—or themselves were parents, G. iii,
286a, U. i, 23 and n. 3; next to legatees who had children, *ibid.;* and finally to the state, G. ii, 150, iii, 286a.
If the party failing to take was sole heir, the caducity
caused intestacy, G. ii, 144; but the legatees were not
thereby defrauded, (see below, No. 4). Caducous legacies
were dealt with in the same way as a caducous share of
an inheritance, G. ii, 206, with this modification,—that a
conjoint legatee who was a parent was to be preferred to
heirs, G. ii, 207, 208, U. xxiv, 12, 13. *Fideicommissa*
were not included in the provisions of the Julian law;
latins were allowed to take them, G. i, 24, ii, 275, U. xxv,
7, and for a time so were *caelibes* and *orbi*, G. ii, 286, 286a.
But this was so far altered by the Pegasian (Plancian?)
Sct. that trust-gifts to *caelibes* and *orbi* were made subject
to the same caduciary rules as inheritances and legacies,
G. ii, 286a.

4. *Charges on a* caducum *ran with it.*—Caducity did not extinguish legacies, gifts of freedom, or *fideicommissa* charged
on testamentary provisions; they passed to and became
burdens on the caduciary beneficiary, U. xvii, 3, even
when he was an heir *ab intestato*, G. ii, 144, or the fisc,
U. xvii, 2.

5. *Caracalla's constitution.*—Caracalla decreed that all *caduca*
should in future go to the fisc, under reservation of the right
of accretion to near relatives of the testator, U. xvii, 2; but
whether he meant that the fisc should be preferred to heirs
and legatees entitled by the Julian law to take on the

CADUCITY—*continued*.

strength of their paternity, or that, failing such heirs and legatees, the fisc should take in future instead of the *aerarium*, is doubtful, *ibid.*, note, as amended in *Additions, etc.*

6. *Caducous dowries.*—By the Calvitian Sct. (see *SC. Calv.*) if a woman over fifty married a man under sixty, the marriage was unequal; and on its dissolution she was not allowed to claim her dowry, which went to the fisc as caducous, U. xvi, 4 and n. 3. See *Dowry*, 8.

7. *Caducity in the succession of latins.*—When a Junian latin had two patrons, and on his death one of them declined his share of his freedman's estate, it became caducous and fell to the state, G. iii, 62, (see *Succession to Junian latins*, 4).

CAELESTIS CARTHAGINIS, U. xxii, 6.

CAELIBES, unmarried persons, were incapacitated by the Papian law for taking testamentary inheritances or legacies, G. ii, 111, 144; but might avoid the disability by marriage before the expiry of the 100 days of cretion, U. xvii, 1, xxii, 3, (see *Julian and Pap. Popp. law*, 4). They might, however, take under a military testament, G. ii, 111, (see *Testament*, 25). At one time it was held that a celibate was entitled to take a testamentary trust-gift; but this was altered by a SC. Pegasianum (?), whereby such a *fideicommissum* became caducous, like inheritances or legacies, G. ii, 286, (see *Fideicommissum*, 3, *Caducity*, 3). An unmarried person was not forbidden to adopt a child, U. viii, 6, (see *Adoption*, 4).

CAESAR'S (Julius) contemplated Code, G. iii, 140, note 2.

CALATA COMITIA, G. ii, 101, U. xx, 2.

CALUMNIA *in adfectu est*, G. iv, 178; *Calumniae judicium*, G. iv, 163, 174-181; *Calumniae jusjurandum*, oath of calumny, G. iv, 172, 176. See *Vexatious litigation*.

CAPERE EX TESTAMENTO, see *Jus capiendi*.

CAPITA and STIRPES in succession, G. iii, 8, 16, 61, U. xxvi, 2, 4, xxvii, 4.

CAPITAL PUNISHMENTS, what, G. iii, 189, 190, note 1.

CAPITIS DEMINUTIO (or *minutio*), G. i, 159-163, U. xi, 10-13.

1. *Idea and varieties.*—*Cap. dem.* was change in a citizen's *caput*, G. i, 159, *i.e.* his family position, *ibid.* note 1; and according to the *jus civile* was equivalent to death as extinctive of his personality, G. iii, 153. It was of three degrees, G. i, 159, U. xi, 10,—*maxima*, when freedom was lost, G. i, 160, U. xi, 11, (see *Freedom*); *media* or *minor*, when freedom was retained but citizenship lost,

CAPITIS DEMINUTIO—*continued.*

and the sufferer reduced to the condition of a peregrin, G. i, 162, U. x, 3, xi, 13, (see *Citizenship, 9, Peregrinity*); *minima*, when only the *status hominis*, G. i, 163, U. xi, 13, was changed, *i.e.* that of the individual in his private rather than his public character, U. xi, 13, note 2.

2. Capitis deminutio minima *in particular.*—To amount to *cap. dem.* the change of status required to be either permanently or temporarily for the worse,—permanently, as in the adrogation or *in manum conventio* of a person *sui juris*, G. iii, 83, U. xi, 13; temporarily, as in mancipation of a *filiusfamilias* as the first step in his emancipation or adoption, G. i, 162, 134, the mancipation putting him for the moment in the condition of a slave, G. i, 138. Change of family status without degradation was not a *minutio capitis*, as when a *filiusfamilias* became *sui juris* by his parent's death or his own inauguration as a priest of Jupiter, G. iii, 114, or a *filiafamilias* by being taken as a Vestal virgin, U. x, 5, (see *Patria potestas*, 17).

3. *Results of* cap. dem. *according to the* jus civile.—*Capitis deminutio*, even *minima*, put an end to the *patria potestas*, G. i, 128, 134, and to agnation, G. i, 158, 163, iii, 21, U. xxviii, 9, without, however, affecting cognation, G. i, 158, iii, 27, U. xxviii, 9, (see *Agnation, 4, Cognation*); that of a tutor consequently put an end to a tutory-at-law, G. i, 158, U. xi, 9, 7, though not to a testamentary tutory, U. xi, 17, (see *Tutory*, 8, 17, 22); while, whether it occurred in the person of the deceased or of the heir, it extinguished the *legitimae successiones* of the XII Tables, G. iii, 21, 27, 51, U. xxvii, 5, (see *Intestate succession*, 6, *Succession to citizen freedmen*, 1, 10). If suffered by a person *sui juris* it invalidated any testament made by him previously, G. ii, 145, U. xxiii, 4; it utterly extinguished any usufruct enjoyed by him, his claim for services from his freedmen, and any *judicia legitima* in which he was suing, G. iii, 83; it dissolved a copartnery of which he was a member, G. iii, 153; and in strict law it relieved him of liability to his creditors, G. iii, 84, iv, 38.

4. *Modification of those results by praetorian intervention.*— Many of those results, whether for the *capite minutus* or for third parties, were regarded as unjust according to natural rules, and indirectly prevented by praetorian remedies. Thus on certain conditions a testament was given effect to by grant of *bonorum possessio secundum tabulas* notwithstanding the testator's *cap. minutio*, (see *Bonor. poss.*, 10, 11); an emancipated child was granted

CAPITIS DEMINUTIO—*continued.*

bonor. poss. contra tabulas if passed over in his parent's will, see *Bon. poss.*, 7; he was granted *bonor. poss.* concurrently with *sui* on his parent's intestacy, see *Bon. poss.*, 14; while an agnate who had lost his *jus legitimum* by his own *cap. dem.* or that of the deceased was admitted as a cognate, see *Bon. poss.*, 16. As regards creditors the praetor gave them relief by *utiles actiones*, G. iii, 84, proceeding on the fiction (see *Fictions*, 3) that *cap. deminutio* had not taken place, G. iv, 38; which the *paterfamilias*, into whose *jus* the *minutus* had passed, was bound to defend, on pain of having to give up all the estate he had acquired by the adrogation or *in manum conventio*, G. iii, 84, iv, 80, which had created a universal succession in his favour, G. iii, 83.

5. Capitis deminutio *by hostile capture.*—A citizen's capture by an enemy involved *cap. dem.*; but its usual results were in this case avoided by the *jus postliminii* and *fictio legis Corneliae*, G. i, 129, 187, U. x, 4, xxiii, 5, (see *Captivity apud hostes*).

CAPITO, C. ATEIUS, founder of the Sabinian school or sect, consul A.D. 5, died A.D. 22, G. i, 196, note; see *Sabinians and Proculians.*

CAPTIVITY APUD HOSTES.—A citizen taken captive by an enemy became a slave and continued so while in their hands, G. i, 129, U. x, 4; but his rights were held to be suspended merely, and revived *jure postliminii* on his recrossing the frontier, *ibid.*, G. i, 187. A testament made by him previously was not invalidated by his captivity; it was good *jure postliminii* if he returned, and, under a Cornelian law equally valid if he died in captivity, thanks to a fiction that he had died at the moment of capture, U. xxiii, 5. If, had he been free, he would have been entitled to a succession *ab intestato* in the character of *suus*, then, so long as he remained captive, the agnates were excluded, U. xxvi, 3.

CARACALLA, see *Constitutiones principum.*

CASCELLIANUM JUDICIUM, a stage of procedure in the interdicts *uti possidetis* and *utrubi*, G. iv, 166a, 169; see *Interdicts*, 16.

CASSIANS AND PROCULIANS, G. i, 196, note 1; see *Sabinians and Proculians.*

CASSIUS LONGINUS, C., consul A.D. 30, one of the leaders of the Sabinians, who were sometimes called Cassians in his honour, G. i, 196, note 1; ii, 79, 195, 244; iii, 71 and note, 133, 140, 147, 161; iv, 79, 114, 170a, note, U. i, 12 and n. 2. See *Sabinians and Proculians.*

30

CASTRENSE PECULIUM, see *Peculium castrense*.

CASUS, see *Accident*.

CATONIANA REGULA in law of legacies, G. ii, 244; see *Legacy*, 12.

CAUSA CADERE, meaning, G. iv, 53, note 1.

CAUSAE PROBATIO EX LEGE AELIA SENTIA; see also *Aelia-Sentian law*, 4, 6, 7.

1. *The original provision.*—See *Aelia-Sentian law*, 6.

2. *Its extensions.*—See *Aelia-Sentian law*, 7.

3. *Its application.*—Cause might be proved not only by the latin himself who had married under the law or the Sct., but after his death by his wife, G. i, 32, or even (with the aid of tutors) by the child, whether son or daughter, G. i, 32a, U. iii, 3, whose completed first year it was that warranted the *probatio*, G. i, 32 and note. And the marriage and all that followed might be resorted to even by a latin who had already acquired citizenship by imperial grant, but without the knowledge of his patron, G. iii, 73; for such a grant, unknown to the patron, while it gave the latin the privilege of a citizen during his life, left him a latin at his death, so that his children, though lawful, could not be his heirs, U. iii, 72.

4. *Its effect.*—The effect of the praetor's *pronuntiatio*, or finding that cause had been proved, was to make the latin a citizen, and to do the same for his wife and child if the former also was a latin, colonial or Junian, G. i, 29. If she was already a citizen, it was only her husband whose status had to be raised; for by a Sct. of Hadrian's the issue of a citizen wife and her latin husband was a citizen without any *causae probatio*, G. i, 30, 80, U. iii, 3, (see *Status*, 2). On becoming a citizen the latin father acquired the *potestas* over his *anniculus* and all subsequent children, G. i, 66, U. vii, 4, (see *Patria potestas*, 10), they acquiring at the same time the rights of *sui heredes* (which see), U. xxii, 14; and even though cause might not be proved until after the father's death, still the *anniculus* became a *suus* and took the inheritance, G. iii, 5.

CAUSAE PROBATIO, ERRORIS, see *Erroris causae probatio*.

CAUTIO DAMNI INFECTI, G. iv, 31, note 3.

CAUTIONES IN JUDICIAL PROCEDURE, G. iv, 89-102, 184-187.

1. *Initial security by defender for his future appearance.*—On appearing in answer to a summons (see *In jus vocatio*), if the proceedings could not be finished the same day, the defender gave security for his subsequent reappearance on a day named, G. iv, 184, (see *Vadimonium*); this was all but universal, 187.

2. *The* cautiones *in a* vindicatio.—In a real action by petitory

CAUTIONES IN JUDICIAL PROCEDURE—*continued.*

formula (*vindicatio*), no security was required from a
pursuer suing on his own account, G. iv, 96, nor from
a cognitor (see *Procuratory in litigation*, 2), because, on
account of the solemnity of his appointment, he was in
much the same position as his client, 97, 98; but a procurator had to give security that his client would ratify
his actings, *cautio de rato*, 98. The defender, whether
defending on his own account, or as cognitor or procurator,
in consideration of enjoying the interim possession, had to
give security for implement of any judgment against him,
cautio judicatum solvi, G. iv, 89.

3. *Those in a real action by sponsion.*—In an *in rem actio
per sponsionem* (which see) the rules were the same,
except that the security given by defender was *cautio pro
praede litis et vindiciarum*, *i.e.* for the thing itself and its
fruits and profits, in place of the *praedes* of the *actio
sacramento* (see *Legis actiones*, 2), G. iv, 91, 94.

4. *Those given in personal actions.*—In a personal action the
rules as regarded a pursuer were the same as in the real
one, G. iv, 100. A party defending on his own account
was not required to give *c. judicatum solvi* except in a
few special cases, G. iv, 102. But where the defence was
by an agent it was indispensable, 101: in the case of a
cognitor, the client gave the security, *ibid.*; in that of a
procurator, he himself did so, *ibid.*

5. *The* stipulatio fructuaria.—This was a security given by the
party to whom the interim enjoyment of the fruits and
profits had been awarded in proceedings on the interdict
uti possidetis or *utrubi*, G. iv, 166, (see *Interdicts*, 14); if
the other party, succeeding in the int., chose to disregard
the *stipulatio* and proceed for the fruits in a separate
judicium, the defender had to give *c. jud. solvi*, 169.

6. *Rules of general application.*—Tutors and curators acting
for their wards were dealt with as procurators, G. iv, 99;
although in their case security was sometimes dispensed
with. The *cautio* was by *satisdatio*, G. iv, 88, *i.e.* personal
undertaking of the party, backed by that of sureties, G. i,
199 and 200, note.

CENSUS.—Entry of the name of a slave, by his owner's authority,
in the census at its periodical revision was one of the
civil modes of freeing him; he thereby became a citizen
if he was over thirty and in the quiritarian ownership of a
manumitter over twenty, G. i, 17, U. i, 8, (see *Manumission*, 4, 6). A free person *in causa mancipii*, and therefore
servi loco, might be liberated in the same way, whatever

CENSUS—*continued.*
> his own age or that of the person to whom he was subject,
> G. i, 139 ; and even against the will or without the know-
> ledge of the latter, provided he was held neither noxally
> nor fiduciarily, 140, (see *Mancipii, etc.,* 3). A citizen
> wilfully evading inscription was sold as a slave by way of
> punishment, G. i, 160, (see *Slavery,* 1).

CENTENARIUS LIBERTUS, G. iii, 42.

CENTUMVIRAL COURT, G. iv, 16 and n. 13, 31, 95 and n. 3.

CESSICIA TUTELA, G. i, 168-172, U. xi, 6-8 ; see *Tutory,* 20.

CESSIO BONORUM, G. iii, 78 and n. 2.

CESSIO IN JURE, see *In jure cessio.*

CHILD, see *Parent and child.*

CHIROGRAPHUM, G. iii, 134 and note; see *Literal obligations,* 2.

CITIZENSHIP, *civitas Romana,* G. i, 94, 160, iii, 73, iv, 37, etc.,
> U. iii, 2, xi, 11, etc.; *jus Quiritium,* G. i, 33, iii, 73, U. iii,
> 1, etc.

I. PRIVATE RIGHTS AND CAPACITIES OF WHICH CITIZENSHIP WAS A
CONDITION.

> 1. *In the family relations.*—It was only a citizen that could
> contract *justae nuptiae, justum matrimonium,* G. i, 56,
> and it was only a woman who was a citizen, or a latin
> or peregrin on special concession, that could become his
> wife, *legitima uxor, ibid.,* U. v, 2-4. Only a citizen
> could take his wife *in manum,* G. i, 108 ; it was only a
> citizen that could have *patria potestas* over his children,
> G. i, 55, 189 ; and none but citizens could be *in potestate,*
> G. i, 128, U. x, 3. And as agnation was an efflux of the
> *patria potestas* (see *Agnation,* 1), none but citizens could
> have or be agnates, or enjoy or be subject to the family
> rights to which agnation gave rise, G. i, 158, 161, U. xi, 9.

> 2. *In matter of property.*—Although non-citizens enjoyed
> quiritarian ownership of *res nec mancipi,* yet the *dominium
> ex jure Quiritium* (see *Quiritarian ownership*) of *res man-
> cipi* (which see), according to Gai., was confined to citizens;
> such things could as a rule be acquired only by mancipa-
> tion, *in jure cessio,* or usucapion, and these he says were
> peculiar to citizens, G. ii, 65, (for when a slave acquired
> by mancipation or usucapion, G. ii, 87, 89, iii, 167, he
> did so merely as the instrument of his citizen owner,
> G. ii, 89). Ulp., on the other hand, says mancipation was
> competent not only to citizens but to colonial and Junian
> latins, and to peregrins to whom *commercium* (see U. xix,
> 5, note) had been specially conceded, U. xix, 4 ; this
> would render them capable of holding *res mancipi* in
> quiritarian right if so conveyed.

CITIZENSHIP—*continued.*

I. PRIVATE RIGHTS AND CAPACITIES OF WHICH CITIZENSHIP WAS A CONDITION—*continued.*

3. *In matter of contract.*—The *juris gentium* contracts were competent even to peregrins, G. iii, 132, 154a; but a verbal contract in which the word *spondeo* was used, and the literal contract by *transscriptio a persona in personam* were confined to citizens, G. iii, 93, 133; and according to the view of Gai. they alone could give or obtain discharge by *nexi solutio* (which see), for it involved a mancipation, G. iii, 174, compared with ii, 65.

4. *In matter of succession.*—It was only a citizen that could make a testament, U. xx, 14, and it was not sustained even to the extent of allowing the heirs in it to have *bonorum possessio secundum tabulas* unless the maker was a citizen at his death, G. ii, 147, U. xxiii, 6, (see *Bonor. poss.*, 11). Except in the case of a *testamentum militare*, G. ii, 110, only a citizen could take anything under a testament,—inheritance, legacy, or *fideicommissum*, G. i, 25, ii, 110, 285, U. xxii, 3; for while a Junian latin might be instituted heir or have a legacy left him, U. xxii, 3, yet he could not take either until he became a citizen, G. i, 23, ii, 110, 275, U. xxii, 2, (though as a latin he might take a *fideicommissum*, G. i, 24, ii, 275, U. xxv, 7). Finally, as none but citizens could be *in potestate*, or be related to other people as agnates (above, No. 1), it was they alone that could succeed *ab intestato*.

5. *In matter of enfranchisement.*—It was only a citizen that could make his slave a citizen by enfranchisement; for he alone could do so who was the slave's quiritarian owner, G. i, 17; and as a slave was a *res mancipi*, this position, according to Gai., could be held only by a citizen (above, No. 1). Further, the provincial *consilia* for sanctioning manumissions required to be composed of citizens, G. i, 20, U. i, 13a, (see *Consilium*).

6. *In matter of witnessing deeds.*—It was only citizens that could act as witnesses of an Aelia-Sentian marriage (see *Aelia-Sentian law*, 6), G. i, 29; of a marriage ceremony by confarreation (see *Manus*, 1), G. i, 112; of a *coemptio* (see *Manus*, 2), G. i, 113; and of a mancipation (which see), G. i, 119. According to Gai., citizens alone could validly witness a testament *per aes et libram*, G. ii, 104; though Ulp. says any one could with whom the testator had *testamenti factio* (which see), U. xx, 2. According to Ulp., even to justify *bon. poss. sec. tab.*, a praetorian testament had to be sealed by seven citizen witnesses, U.

CITIZENSHIP—*continued.*

I. PRIVATE RIGHTS AND CAPACITIES OF WHICH CITIZENSHIP WAS A CONDITION—*continued.*

xxviii, 6; but here it is Gai. that omits the qualification of citizen, G. ii, 119.

7. *In judicial procedure.*—A *judicium legitimum* (which see) was possible only when all the parties, judge included, were citizens, G. iv, 104. Further, many judicial remedies were competent directly only to and against citizens; if it was reasonable in the circumstances to grant them to or against one who was not a citizen, this could only be done by introducing into the formula a fiction of citizenship, G. iv, 37, (see *Fiction*, 3).

II. HOW CITIZENSHIP WAS ACQUIRED AND LOST.

8. *How acquired.*—It usually was acquired by birth, see *Status*, 2. It might be acquired by a slave by manumission according to the requirements of the Aelia-Sentian law, G. i, 17, (see *Manumission*); by a colonial latin by filling office in his *municipium*, G. i, 95 and 96, and note, or by imperial grant, G. i, 93, (see *Colonial latinity*, 2, *Jus Latii*); by a Junian latin in a variety of ways explained in G. i, 28-35, U. iii, 1-6, (see *Junian latinity*, 7); and by a peregrin by *erroris causae probatio* (which see); G. i, 67-75, U. vii, 4, or imperial grant, G. i, 93, (see *Peregrinity*, 8). Such a grant did not carry *potestas* over children already born, or even over an infant *in utero*, unless applied for and expressly included in the concession, G. i, 93, 94, ii, 135a, iii, 20.

9. *How lost.*—It was lost not only by any event which made the citizen a slave, as in G. i, 160, U. xi, 11, (see *Slavery*, 1), but by joining a latin colony (see *Colon. latinity*), G. i, 131, or by anything that made him a peregrin, such as interdiction of fire and water, which practically was outlawry, G. i, 128 and n. 2, 161, U. x, 3, xi, 12. Loss of citizenship without loss of freedom was called *capitis deminutio minor* or *media, ibid.*, (see *Cap. dem.*, 1).

CLAUDIAN SENATUSCONSULT, the, contained the following provisions in reference to cohabitation of persons of whom one was slave and the other free :—(1.) If a freeman cohabited with another person's slave, believing her free, male issue were to be free, females slave, G. i, 85; Vespasian however repealed the rule, reverting to that of the *jus gentium,*—slave mother, slave child, G. i, 85. (2.) If a woman of free birth continued to cohabit with a *servus alienus* in spite of his owner's warning, she was herself to fall to the latter as a slave, G. i, 91, 160, U.

CLAUDIAN SENATUSCONSULT—*continued.*

xi, 11 ; but this was not to happen to a freedwoman, for, unless the cohabitation was with her patron's approval, it was to him she became a slave again, U. xi, 27 and n. 2. (3.) Any child born to a freewoman by a slave father of whose condition she was aware—a circumstance, as Paul. remarks, that made her a slave whether warned or not,—was to be slave-born, G. i, 86 and note. (4.) It was to be lawful for a freewoman, cohabiting with a *servus alienus* with his owner's consent, to bargain with the latter that though her child would be born a slave she was to remain free, G. i, 84 ; but Hadrian, while still permitting an agreement guaranteeing the mother's freedom, re-established the *juris gentium* rule that in such case the child also must be free, *ibid.*

CODICIL, *codicilli,* (see *Testament,* 26), was an informal expression of last will, which might be made either as supplementary to or in the absence of a testament, G. ii, 270, 270*a,* and in the former case be confirmed by it or not, 270*a.* No institution or disherison could in any case be made in it directly, G. ii, 273, U. xxv, 11 ; if unconfirmed, neither legacies nor direct grants of freedom could be bequeathed in it, G. ii, 270*a,* U. ii, 12, xxv, 8, or adeemed, U. xxiv, 29 and note ; but whether confirmed or not, and even in the absence of a testament, a *fideicommissum* might be imposed in it upon the heir to any extent, G. ii, 273, U. xxv, 4, 8.

COEMPTIO, one of the modes of *in manum conventio,* G. i, 113-115*b* ; see *Manus,* 2.

COGNATION in its wider acceptation was kinship generally ; in its narrower, natural blood relationship as distinguished from the civil or *legitima cognatio* of agnation, G. i, 156. It is often described as kinship through females, *ibid.,* but was not so necessarily ; for agnates related through males remained cognates even when *capite minuti,* G. iii, 27. By the *jus civile* cognation created incapacities, as in marriage, G. i, 59-62, but conferred no rights. By the rules of succession of the Twelve Tables cognates were ignored, G. iii, 24 ; but the praetors admitted them to *bonor. poss. ab intestato* immediately after agnates *integri juris,* G. iii, 30, U. xxviii, 7, 9, (see *Bonor. poss.,* 16). For the mode of computing the degrees of cognation, see U. v, 6, note 2.

COGNITOR, see *Procuratory in litigation,* 2.

COGNITORIAE EXCEPTIONES, G. iv, 124 ; see *Exception,* 10.

COLLATION.—It was under condition of collating their acquisitions since they had become *sui juris* by their emancipation, *i.e.* of throwing them into their father's estate for general division, that the praetors granted *bonor. possessio* to emancipated children passed over in a testament in which brothers of theirs *in potestate* had been instituted, U. xxviii, 4, (see *Bonor. poss.*, 7).

COLONIA LATINA, a colony established in a province on the understanding that its members were to have the rights enjoyed by the latins of Italy ; a citizen joining it ceased to be such, and became a colonial latin, G. i, 131, iii, 56.   The charters or acts of constitution of a great many provincial *municipia*, which there was no pretence for calling colonies, gave to their members rights in private life much the same as those of the colonists, G. i, 22, note 1.

COLONIAL LATINITY, G. i, 22, note 1.

1. *Rights of colonial latins.*—They had no *conubium* (see U. v, 3, note) with citizens except by special concession, G. i, 56, U. v, 4 ; and the issue of a colonial latin and a Roman citizen wife was, by the Minician law, a latin like his father, whether there was *conubium* between the parents or not, G. i, 55, 77-79.   But the law did not recognise in a colonial latin any right of *manus* or *patria potestas*, at least that could be attended with their *juris civilis* consequences, G. i, 55, 108, 109 ; although it appears, from the terms of some extant charters of latin *municipia*, that they had a *de facto manus* and *potestas*, G. i, 55, note 2.   As regards their right in matters of property, contract, and succession, see *Citizenship*, 2, 3, 4.   It does not appear that they had the privilege conferred by the *lex Junia* on Junian latins of taking under a testament if they converted their latinity into citizenship within a hundred days, G. ii, 110, U. xvii, 1, xx, 3.

2. *How they acquired Roman citizenship.*—It was peculiar to them that they could acquire citizenship by what was called *jus Latii*,G. i, 95 and 96, and note.   The charters of latin communities conferred upon them sometimes *majus Latium*, sometimes *minus ;* where it was the first, a member who had served as a decurion or in higher office not only himself became a citizen, but thereby elevated his parents, wife, and children ; where it was the second, citizenship in the same circumstances was confined to himself, G. i, 96.   Without this process he might also directly become a citizen by imperial grant, G. i, 93, etc., (see *Citizenship*, 8).

COMITIA CALATA, G. ii, 101, U. xx, 2 ; see *Testament*, 1.

COMMERCIUM explained in U. xix, 5, note; colonial and Junian
latins enjoyed it as well as citizens; and it might be
specially conceded to peregrins, U. xix, 4.

COMMODATE, *commodatum;* see also *Real obligations.*

1. *Commodate, what?*—Commodate was loan of a thing for
use, to be returned *in specie.* It was not very early recognised as an independent contract, and is not mentioned
by Gaius in his reference to obligations created *re*, G. iii,
90 and 91, and note.

2. *Rights of lender.*—Though he had given up the custody of
the thing lent, yet the legal possession still remained
with the lender, G. iv, 153; and, if the borrower, *animo
furandi,* used what had been lent in a different way from
what had been intended, the lender might proceed against
him for theft, G. iii, 196, 197.

3. *Obligations of borrower.*—The borrower had *custodiam
praestare, i.e.* to answer for the safety of the thing lent,
G. iii, 206; consequently if stolen from him, and he was
solvent, it was he that had the *actio furti,* 205, 206.

4. *Special action.*—The action arising out of the contract was
the *a. commodati;* in this respect peculiar, that it was
sometimes *in jus,* sometimes *in factum concepta,* G. iv, 47,
(see *Actions,* 5). When in *jus concepta* it was *bonae fidei*
(see *Actions,* 8), G. iv, 47, 62.

COMPENSATION or set-off, *compensatio,* G. iv, 61-68.

1. *In* bonae fidei judicia.—In these (see *Bon. fid. jud.*), and
without any instruction in the *formula,* the judge was
bound to set off against the pursuer's claim any counter
claim of the defender's arising out of the same matter,
and condemn the latter only in the balance, if any, G. iv,
61, 63.

2. *In* judicia stricti juris.—By a rescript of Marc. Aurelius'
compensation was allowed to be pleaded in answer to
stricti juris judicia generally, under cover of an *exceptio
doli;* see addition to G. iv, 61, note, in *Additions, etc.*

3. *In actions by bankers.*—An *argentarius* suing a customer
was required formally to set off in his *intentio* (which
see) any counter claim of his creditor's, G. iv, 65, if of the
same sort as the pursuer's, though not arising out of the
same matter, *e.g.* money against money, wine against
wine, 66, if exigible at the moment, 67, on pain of losing
his cause altogether, 68.

4. *In actions by* bonorum emptores.—When a *bonor. emptor*
or purchaser of a bankrupt's estate (see *Emptio bonorum*)
proceeded against a debtor, the latter was entitled to have
deducted any counter claim he had against the bankrupt,

COMPENSATION—*continued*.

no matter though for things of a different sort than those he owed, G. iv, 65, 66, and even though not yet due, 67 ; but this *deductio* was not referred to in the *intentio*, only given effect to in the condemnation, 68.

COMPERENDINUS DIES, G. iv, 15.

COMPROMISE of a claim, even by simple agreement, entitled the debtor to an *exceptio pacti conventi* if sued in disregard of it, G. iv, 116*a*. Compromise of an action for theft, robbery, or personal injury, made the delinquent infamous, just as if he had been condemned, G. iv, 182.

CONCUBINE, children of, were not *spurii*, G. i, 64, note 3.

CONDEMNATIO, one of the clauses of a *formula*; which see, No. 1.

1. *General purpose.*—It contained the instruction to the judge to condemn or absolve according to the evidence, G. iv, 39 ; styles, *ibid.* It was necessary in all but prejudicial and probably divisory actions, 44 and note ; and when present always stood last, 39, 50.

2. *It was either fixed, taxed, or indefinite.*—Under the earlier system (see *Legis actiones*) an unsuccessful defender was always condemned in the very thing sued for, G. iv, 48 and note 3 ; but under the formular system condemnation was in all cases in money, G. iv, 48. The amount might either be fixed definitely in the *formula, cond. certa,* or be limited to a maximum, *cond. incerta sed taxata,* or be left entirely to the discretion of the judge, *cond. incerta et infinita,* according to the nature of the action, G. iv, 50, 51. It might happen, though unusual, that a *cond. incerta* was the sequel to an *intentio certa,* as when a *bonor. emptor* sued for a definite sum ; for then the debtor was entitled before condemnation to have deducted any counter claim of his against the bankrupt, (see *Compensation,* 4), G. iv, 68.

3. *What if the praetor had put too great or too small a sum in a* condemnatio *certa ?*—In the former case the pursuer obviously was not prejudiced, but the defender was entitled to *in integrum restitutio* (which see) in order to get the *formula* amended, G. iv, 57 ; in the latter the pursuer had in general to take the consequences, *in integrum restitutio* being refused unless he was a minor, *ibid.*

4. *Cases in which the* condemnatio *ran in another name than the* intentio.—The *condemnatio* always contained not only the name of the party who was to be condemned, but also that of him to whom he was to be condemned in the event of the action not ending in acquittal ; but those names were not necessarily the same as in the *intentio*

CONDEMNATIO—*continued.*

(which see). If a *bonorum emptor* sued by the Rutilian action, he took the *intentio* in name of the bankrupt as the party to whom the defender was really indebted, but the *condemnatio* in his own, G. iv, 35; and if either suit or defence was conducted by a tutor or curator, *cognitor* or procurator, (see *Procuratory in litigation*), it was the principal's name that appeared in the *intentio*, the agent's in the *condemnatio*, G. iv, 86.

5. *Judge's duty in regard to the* condemnatio.—See *Procedure*, 10.

CONDICERE, meaning of, G. iv, 17b.

CONDICTIO was the generic name for a personal action in which the *intentio* (which see) embodied either *dare oportere* or *dare facere oportere*, G. iv, 5, the meaning of those words being explained in G. iv, 2, note 3; the first was *condictio certi*, the second *condictio incerti, ibid.* As a general rule a *condictio* was inapplicable where a man was claiming his own,—he could not maintain that another was bound to give him in property what was already his; but exceptionally it was allowed against thieves in the *condictio furtiva*, G. ii,79, iv,4, (see *Theft*, 7), and against other *malae fidei* possessors in one or two cases unspecified, G. ii, 79. On *condictio indebiti* in particular, see *Indebiti solutio.*

CONDICTIONEM, LEGIS ACTIO PER, G. iv, 17b-20; see *Legis actiones*, 4.

CONDITION.—The phraseology was—*condicio pendet*, G. i, 186, ii, 200, iii, 179, while fulfilment or failure was still in the future; *cond. exstitit*, G. iii, 179, or *expleta est*, U. ii, 5, when it had been fulfilled; *cond. defecit*, G. iii, 179, when it had failed.

1. *Conditions in contracts.*—Sale and location might both be conditional, G. iii, 146, and so might a stipulation, 102, 113. But while a conditional answer to an unconditional question was useless (see *Stipulation*, 5), G. iii, 102, it was quite competent in adstipulation to make the second stipulation conditional though the first was pure, *i.e.* unconditional, (see *Adstipulation*, 1), G. iii, 113. The *ex intervallo* introduction of a condition was such a change in an obligation as to amount to novation (which see, No. 4) if the condition was fulfilled, though not if it failed, G. iii, 177, 179.

2. *Conditions in testaments.*—An heir might be instituted under a condition; if it failed, and he was sole heir without a substitute (see *Substitution*, 1), the result was intestacy, G. ii, 144. Any testamentary provision might be conditional,—a legacy, U. xxiv, 31, a trust gift, G. ii, 250, the enfranchisement of a slave, U. ii, 1, or the appoint-

CONDITION—*continued*.

ment of a tutor, G. i, 186; and in all these a *dies incertus* was regarded as a condition, U. xxiv, 31 and note. As a conditional legacy did not vest until the condition was fulfilled or the *dies incertus* had come, *ibid.*, there was a nice question as to the ownership *pendente condicione* of a legacy bequeathed *per vindicationem* (see *Legacy*, 21), G. ii, 200.

3. *Impossible conditions.*—A contract under an impossible condition was a nullity, G. iii, 98. When such a condition was annexed to a legacy, the Sabinian view was that the legacy was to be held valid, and the condition regarded as unwritten; the Proculians, however, maintaining that the rule should be the same as in contract, *ibid.*

4. *Defeat of a condition by a party interested in its failure.*— When this happened—as when a slave had a testamentary gift of freedom on condition of paying a certain sum to the heir, and the latter would not accept it—the condition was regarded as fulfilled, U. ii, 6.

CONFARREATION, G. i, 112, U. tit. ix; see *Manus*, 1.

CONFISCATION of the estate of a partner in strictness put an end to the partnership, (which see, No. 3), G. iii, 154.

CONJOINT and DISJOINT LEGACY to co-legatees, G. ii, 199; see *Legacy*, 30-34.

CONSANGUINEI defined, U. xxvi, 1; *consanguineorum gradus*, G. iii, 14, 23, 29, U. xxvi, 6; *consanguinitatis jura*, G. iii, 24 and note 1. See *Intestate succession*, 4.

CONSENSUAL OBLIGATIONS (see *Contract*, 1) were so called because a common understanding was sufficient to create them without any formality, G. iii, 136; consequently they might be contracted even between persons at a distance from each other, by the medium of a letter or a messenger, *ibid.* They arose from the four contracts of sale, location, partnership, and mandate, (see those words), G. iii, 135; the parties to them each becoming bound for what in the circumstances he ought to do in fairness and equity, 137.

CONSILIUM, the, that sat to consider questions of manumission (which see, Nos 2-4, 6) was composed in Rome of five senators and as many knights; in the provinces, of twenty recuperators, Roman citizens, G. i, 20, U. i, 13a.

CONSOBRINI, G. iii, 10 and n. 1.

CONSTITUTIONES PRINCIPUM were enactments of the emperors (see *Statute*, 1), in the form either of decrees, edicts, or epistles, G. i, 5 and note 1, and were held to have the force of *leges* in consideration of the *imperium* vested in the sovereign, *ibid.* The following are specially mentioned :—

CONSTITUTIONES PRINCIPUM—*continued.*

Antoninus Pius. Rescript (?) regarding the punishment to
be awarded to an owner killing his slave, (see *Slavery*, 2),
G. i, 53; rescript denouncing unnecessary cruelty to a
slave, *ibid.*; rescript about *erroris causae probatio* by a
peregrin, (see *Error. c. prob.*), 74; epistle about adrogation
of pupils, (see *Adoption*, 5), 102, U. viii, 5; rescript about
a legacy of a Junian latin to a colony, (see *Succession to
Junian latins*, 2), G. ii, 195.

Augustus. Enactment allowing a soldier *filiusfamilias* to dispose of his *peculium castrense* by testament, U. xx, 10, (see
Soldier, Testament, 6, 25).

Caracalla, (*imperator Antoninus* in text). Enactment giving
caduca to fisc, U. xvii, 2, (see *Caducity*, 5).

Claudius. Edict declaring that a latin might acquire citizenship *nave*, G. i, 32c, U. iii, 6, (see *Junian latinity*, 7).

Hadrian. Rescript regulating the *responsa prudentium* (which
see), G. i, 7; edict on subject of petitions by peregrins
for grants of citizenship, (see *Citizenship*, 8), G. i, 55, 93;
rescript about *erroris causae probatio* (which see), G. i, 73;
enactment modifying the Claudian Sct. (which see), G. i,
84; rescript as to effect of grant of citizenship to a peregrin, (see *Patria potestas*, 12), G. i, 94; rescript (?) exceptionally allowing *in integrum restitutio*, to a man above
twenty-five who had in excusable ignorance taken an insolvent inheritance, (see *In integrum restitutio*), G. ii, 163;
rescript (?) about legacies by preception to others than
heirs, (see *Legacy*, 28, 29), G. ii, 221; rescript as to interest
on legacies and trust-gifts when heir *in mora* (which see),
G. ii, 280; epistle conferring *beneficium divisionis* upon
sureties (see *Suretyship*, 4), G. iii, 121, 121a, 122.

Marc. Aurelius. Enactments that an institute with imperfect
cretion should totally exclude substitute by simple *gestio
pro herede*, (see *Cretio*, 3), U. xxii, 34; rescript (attributed
in the text to *imp. Antoninus*) allowing instituted heirs
under an imperfect testament, who had obtained *bonorum
possessio*, to plead *exceptio doli* to any attempt of the agnate
heirs-at-law to eject them, (see *Bonorum possessio*, 12), G.
ii, 120; rescript (attributed in text to *imp. Antoninus*,
and by Just. in l. 4, C. *de lib. praet.* vi, 28, to *Magnus
Ant.*,—inapplicable to *Ant. Pius*) limiting *bonor. possessio*
granted to females *praeteritae* to the amount they were
entitled to by *adcretio*, (see *Bonorum possessio*, 9), G. ii, 126;
rescript (attributed in text to *imp. Antoninus*) allowing
heir under a testament partially obliterated or otherwise defaced to plead *exceptio doli* against heirs-at-law

CONSTITUTIONES PRINCIPUM—*continued.*

obtaining *bonor. possessio ab intestato,* (see *Bonor. possessio,* 12), G. ii, 151 ; edict (?) allowing minors to have curators in other than the exceptional cases of the Plaetorian law, (see *Curatory,* 3), G. i, 197, note ; rescript allowing compensation to be pleaded in answer to *stricti juris* actions, addition to G. iv, 61, note, in *Additions etc.*

Nero (?).   Edict (?) conferring citizenship on latins *aedificatione,* G. i, 33 and note, (see *Junian latinity,* 7).

Nerva.   Enactment about legacies bequeathed to municipalities, U. xxiv, 8, (see *Legacy,* 6).

Trajan.   Edict (?) as to acquisition of citizenship by a latin *pistrino,* (see *Junian latinity,* 7), G. i, 34 ; rescript (?) in regard to grants of citizenship to latins either *salvo jure patroni* or without consent of patrons, (see *Succession to Junian latins,* 5), G. iii, 72.

Vespasian.   Enactment modifying the Claudian Sct. (which see), G. i. 85.

Authorship unknown.   Constitution granting indefinite *conubium* to discharged soldiers, (see *Soldiers*), G. i, 57 ; about marriage between cousins, (see *Marriage,* 4), G. i, 62 ; on the *jus Latii,* (see *Colonial latinity,* 2), 96 ; about military testaments, (see *Testament,* 25), G. ii, 109 ; relaxing the prohibition of donations between husband and wife, (see *Husband and wife,* 5), U. vii, 1 ; allowing certain divinities to be instituted as heirs, (see *Testament,* 13), U. xxi, 6.

CONSTITUTUM, acknowledgment of indebtedness, actionable as a praetorian pact : a natural obligation was sufficient foundation for it, G. iii, 119*a,* note 1.

CONSUETUDE, see *Custom.*

CONSUMPTIO ACTIONIS, exhaustion of a right of action by its *deductio in judicium, i.e.* by adjustment on it of a *formula* and transmission of the latter to a judge for trial, G. iv, 131, 131*a* ; see *Litis contestatio.*

CONTRACT, one of the modes of creating an obligation (which see), G. iii, 88.

1. *Varieties.*—There were four varieties—the contracts *re, verbis, litteris,* and *consensu,* giving rise to the so-called real, verbal, literal, and consensual obligations, G. iii, 89, (see those words).   The innominate contracts in one or other of the forms *do ut des, do ut facias, facio ut facias, facio ut des,* were regarded as real, *ibid.,* note 1.   The obligations created by the verbal and literal contracts were unilateral, while those arising out of the consensual ones were bilateral or mutual, G. iii, 137.

2. *Difference between contract and pact.*—See *Obligation,* 2.

CONTRACT—*continued.*

3. *Formal contracts.*—The contracts *verbis* and *litteris* were formal contracts, *i.e.* if the prescribed form was gone through liability was in law created, although equity might give relief, G. iii, 89, note; *e.g.* if a stipulatory promise was made to pay a certain sum in consideration of an expected loan, the promise was binding even though the loan was not advanced, but might be rendered ineffectual by an *exceptio doli mali*, G. iv, 116. The *nexum* and *jusjurandum* of the early law (see those words) were of the same class, G. iii, 89, note.

4. *Useless contracts.*—Many of the circumstances that Gai. refers to as rendering a stipulation useless, and which are placed under that head in deference to his example, were applicable to contracts generally; see *Stipulation*, 3-5.

CONTRARIUM JUDICIUM, G. iv, 177; see *Vexatious litigation.*

CONUBIUM.

1. *What meant by it.*—See explanation in U. v, 3, note.

2. *Who had it* inter se.—Roman citizens had it with citizens, but not with latins or peregrins except by special concession, G. i, 56, U. v, 4. Veterans, who had obtained honourable discharge, occasionally obtained an indefinite concession of it, empowering them to marry any latin or peregrin woman as if she were a citizen, G. i, 57. But there could be no *conubium* with a slave, U. v, 5.

3. *Consequences of its presence.*—The rule was that where a man married a woman with whom he had *conubium*, the issue followed the condition of their father,—were citizens or peregrins according as he was one or other, G. i, 56, 76, 77, U. v, 8; but whereas, if he was a citizen, the marriage was *justum matrimonium* (see *Marriage*, 1), and his children *in potestate*, G. i, 56, 76, if he was a peregrin the marriage was only a peregrin marriage, and his children, though lawful, were not in his *potestas*, 77.

4. *Consequences of its absence.*—The rule of the *jus gentium* was that in the absence of *conubium* a child followed the condition of its mother, G. i, 78, U. v, 8; but was altered by the Minician law, which provided that the issue of parents of unequal status, who had not *conubium*, should invariably follow the lower, *ibid.* Hadrian subsequently enacted that if a Roman woman married a Junian latin, whether under the Aelia-Sentian law or not—there was no *conubium* between citizens and Junian latins, G. i, 80—her children should be citizens, *ibid.* See *Status*, 2.

CONVENTIO IN MANUM, see *Manus.*

CONVENTUS or provincial assizes, G. i, 20 and n. 2.

CORPOREALS, G. ii, 13; see *Things*, 4.

CREDERE, etymology, G. iii, 92, note.

CREDITA PECUNIA defined, G. iii, 124.

CRETIO, G. ii, 164-173, U. xxii, 25-30; see also *Hereditas*, 5.

    1. *Cretio, what ?*—Cretion was a period formally limited in a testament for the heir's entry, G. ii, 164, 165, U. xxii, 27, failure being sometimes under penalty of disherison (*perfecta cretio*), *ibid.*, sometimes merely under penalty of admission of a substitute (*imperfecta cretio*), G. ii, 177, U. xxii, 34.

    2. *Cerniture, what ?*—Cerniture in compliance with the cretion-clause was a formal declaration of acceptance of the inheritance, in presence of witnesses, and in well-established words of style, G. ii, 166 and note, U. xxii, 28; and it required to be made before the time limited, usually a hundred days, had expired, G. ii, 166.

    3. *Were equivalents possible ?*—Where the cretion was perfect, informal declaration or *gestio pro herede* could not be admitted as equivalents, G. ii, 168; but in imperfect cretion *gestio pro herede* entitled the institute at first to retain a half of the succession, G. ii, 177, and afterwards the whole of it, U. xxii, 34.

    4. *Vulgar and continuous cretion.*—These are distinguished in G. ii, 171-173, U. xxii, 31, 32.

CRETIO LITIS INFITIATIONE.—To check vexatious litigation an unsuccessful defender was sometimes condemned in double the amount of his normal liability as the penalty of his denial, G. iv, 171, *e.g.* in the *a. judicati* and *a. depensi*, G. iv, 9, 171, (see those words); in the action for a legacy by damnation (see *Legacy*, 22, 23), G. iii, 282, iv, 9, 171; and in the Aquilian action against an adstipulator (see *Adstipulation*) who had acceptilated in fraud of the stipulant, G. iii, 215, 216, iv, 9, 171. But the penalty was not incurred where the defence was by the heir of the original debtor, G. iv, 172. See *Vexatious litigation*, 1.

CURATORY, *curatio*, G. i, 197, 198, U. tit. xii.

    1. *Curatory of lunatics and prodigals.*—The Twelve Tables enacted that lunatics and prodigals who had been interdicted the administration of their estates because they were dissipating the patrimony to which they had succeeded *ab intestato*, should be in curatory of their agnates, U. xii, 2; and the praetors gave curators of their own selection to freedmen spendthrifts, and to those free-born ones who had succeeded to a family property *ex testamento*, neither of those classes being included in the provision of the statute, U. xii, 3.

CURATORY—*continued.*

    2. *Duties and powers of such curators.*—Latterly those of them who took the office by devolution of law were required to give security, *satisdatio,* for the faithful discharge of their duties, G. i, 200; their powers—at least those of the agnatic curator of a lunatic—extended even to the alienation of the estate, G. ii, 64; and they might sue or be sued on account of their wards, giving the same securities as required from procurators, G. iv, 82, (see *Procuratory in litigation,* 2).

    3. *Curatory of minors.*—By the Plaetorian law the praetor was authorised in certain cases to appoint tutors to minors (see *Minority*), G. i, 197 and note; and Marc. Aurelius afterwards withdrew the limitation to certain cases and authorised it generally, *ibid.,* U. xii, 4. Such curators were not required to give security, their qualifications having been approved beforehand, G. i, 200.

CUSTOM, *mores, consuetudo,* a factor in every system of law, G. i, 1, resting on tacit acceptance by the nation, U. i, 4, G. iii, 82. Among the institutions due to it are mentioned the universal acquisitions by *manus* (which see) and *adrogatio* (see *Adoption,* 8), G. iii, 83, certain tutories, U. xi, 2, 24, and one or two cases of procedure *per pignoris capionem* (see *Legis actiones,* 6), G. iv, 27.

DAMAGE TO PROPERTY, WRONGFUL, G. iii, 210-19; see *Wrongful damage to property.*

DAMAGES, see *Interesse, Wrongful damage to property,* 1, 3.

DAMNAS ESTO, a phrase employed in statutes and private deeds, such as testaments, to impose a liability, G. ii, 201 and n. 1, iii, 210, note 2, U. xxiv, 5; the party thereby made debtor was called *damnas* (indeclinable), or *damnatus,* G. ii, 201, note 1, iii, 175 and note 3; and by the XII Tab. summary execution by *manus injectio* (see *Legis actiones,* 5) was authorised against him on the strength of the *damnatio,* G. iv, 21, though the Vallian law afterwards gave him some relief, G. iv, 25. If the creditor desired to give the debtor a discharge without payment, he had to do so *per aes et libram,* G. iii, 175, (see *Nexi solutio*).

DAMNATI, DAMNATIO, see *Damnas esto.*

DAMNATIONEM, LEGATUM PER, see *Legacy,* 22-24, 32, 34.

DAMNUM, DAMNUM DECIDERE, G. iv, 37, note 6.

DAMNUM INFECTUM, G. iv, 31 and notes.

DAMNUM INJURIA DATUM, see *Wrongful damage to property.*

DAPS, G. iv, 28 and note 2.

DARE, technical meaning, G. iii, 92, note, iv, 4.

31

DARE, FACERE, PRAESTARE, G. iv, 2 and note 3.

DEAF PERSON, *surdus*, could not be a party to a stipulation, G. iii, 105; nor could he validly execute a testament *per aes et libram*, U. xx, 13, or assist at the execution of another person's as *familiae emptor*, witness, or balance-holder, U. xx, 7.

DECIMAE, tenths of the estate of husband or wife, one or more of which the survivor was empowered by the Julian law to take in certain circumstances under the other's testament, U. xiv, 1, 2 and note; see *Julian and Pap. Popp. law*, 6.

DECRETUM (PRINCIPIS), a form of imperial enactment, G. i, 5, note 1, (see *Constitutiones principum*); *decretum praetoris*, a form of interdict, G. iv, 140, (see *Interdicts*, 1).

DEDITICIAN FREEDMEN, *liberti qui dediticiorum numero sunt*.

1. *Origin of this class.*—It was a provision of the Aelia-Sentian law (which see, No. 3) that slaves who had deservedly been subjected to disgraceful punishment should not become citizens on manumission, but rank with those peregrins who after defeat had surrendered to Rome unconditionally, G. i, 13, 14, U. i, 11; the only exception being in the case of one who was instituted necessary heir with freedom in the testament of his insolvent owner, (see *Necessarii heredes*), U. i, 14.

2. *Disabilities of a deditician.*—He could never in any way become a citizen or even a latin, G. i, 15, 26; and was forbidden to reside within a hundred miles of Rome, under penalty of reduction again to perpetual slavery, G. i, 27. As nothing more than a peregrin he could neither make a testament, G. i, 25, iii, 75, U. xx, 14, nor have any interest in that of another person, G. i, 25, U. xxii, 2. Yet though only a peregrin he might possibly be husband and father of citizens, viz. when a citizen woman had married him believing he was a citizen, and on discovering her mistake proved cause of error (see *Erroris causae probatio*), and thus made her children citizens, G. i, 67, 68; over them, however, the deditician father had no *potestas*, *ibid*.

3. *Disposal of his estate on death.*—If, but for the stain on his character, he would have been a citizen on manumission, his estate belonged to his patron according to the rules of succession to citizen freedmen, (see *Succession to cit. freedmen*), G. iii, 75; but if, by reason of the form of his manumission, he would, but for the stain, have been a latin, it went to the manumitter and his heirs, according to the rules of succession to latin freedmen, (see *Succ. to Jun. latins*), G. iii, 76.

DEDUCTIO in action by *bonorum emptor*, G. iv, 65-68; see *Compensation*, 4.

DELATIO HEREDITATIS, see *Hereditas*, 1, 2.

DELEGATIO, G. iii, 130; see *Novation*, 3.

DELIBERANDI TEMPUS, time allowed to a stranger heir to consider whether it was for his advantage to accept an inheritance, G. ii, 162; see *Hereditas*, 6.

DELICT was one of the sources of obligation, G. iii, 88, 182; (see also *Obligation*, 2).

1. *Varieties.*—There were four nominate delicts, *furtum, vis bonorum raptorum, damnum injuria datum, injuria*, G. iii, 182, (see *Theft, Robbery, Wrongful damage to property, Personal injury*); but all were of the same genus, there being no delict where there was no *res, i.e.* no act done, *ibid.*

2. *Delicts of persons* alieni juris.—A wrong done by a *filius-familias* or slave to his *paterfamilias* or owner gave the latter no action *ex delicto*, obligation between them being impossible, G. iv, 78; but for delicts committed by them against strangers the *paterfamilias* was responsible in noxal actions (which see), 75.

3. *How far heirs affected.*—The heir of a delinquent was not liable in the penal action *ex delicto*, G. iv, 112; but the heir of the party wronged was entitled to sue, except in the *a. injuriarum, ibid.*

DELIVERY, *traditio*, see *Property*, 5.

DEMONSTRATIO, one of the clauses of a *formula*, G. iv, 39; see *Formula*, 1.

1. *Its purpose and position.*—When present it stood first, its purpose being briefly to explain what had given rise to the action, G. iv, 40; styles, 40, 47, 59, 136. It required to be followed with an *intentio* and *condemnatio* (see those words), 44, except when an *adjudicatio* (which see) came in place of the latter, 44, note.

2. *When necessary.*—In *formulae in jus conceptae* it was introduced only when the claim was illiquid, and the *intentio* in the style '*quidquid ob eam rem illum illi dare facere oportet*,' G. iv, 60; such a *formula* was called *incerta*, 54, 131. In *formulae in factum conceptae* the *demonstratio* was in a manner amalgamated with the *intentio*, 47, 60.

3. *Introduction of restrictive words.*—Where a *demonstratio* was present it was competent to introduce into it a '*cujus rei dies fuit*' or such like, which in a *formula* without a *demonstratio* was made matter of prescription, G. iv, 136, (see *Praescriptio*).

4. *What if too much or too little demonstrated?*—If a man in

DEMONSTRATIO—*continued.*

his *demonstratio* condescended on too much or too little, his action was resultless, but—differing from the rule in regard to the *intentio*, G. iv, 53, 56—his claim remained intact, 58; at least this was the opinion of Gai., although to some extent not shared by other jurists, 59, 60.

DEPENSUM, see *Actio depensi, Suretyship,* 5.

DEPOSIT, *depositum,* is not mentioned by Gai. in his description of the *obligatio re contracta,* G. iii, 90 and 91, note.

1. *Nature of the contract.*—The deposit still left the legal possession in the depositor, the depositary being merely his agent in possessing, G. iv, 153.

2. *Obligations of the depositary.*—If, *animo furandi*, he used what was deposited with him, he committed theft, G. iii, 196. He was bound to give it back to the depositor on demand; but he was liable in damages on failure only when attributable to dole on his part,—he was not responsible for careless keeping whereby it had been stolen, G. iii, 207. Therefore, unlike a borrower, 205, 206, he had not an *actio furti* against the thief; the depositor was alone entitled to it, 207.

3. *The* actio depositi.—This was one of the actions which exceptionally might be formulated either *in jus* or *in factum*, G. iv, 47, 59, 60; styles, 47. When *in jus concepta* it was *bonae fidei,* 62. Condemnation of the depositary made him infamous, 60.

DEROGATIO LEGIS, partial repeal of a statute, U. i, 3.

DIANA OF THE EPHESIANS, U. xxii, 6.

DIES, a date at which a right was to become operative,—money to be payable under a contract, G. iii, 124, a legacy, or a trust-gift, or a tutor's appointment under a testament, G. i, 186, ii, 250, U. xxiv, 31. The date might be either *certus* or *incertus ;* in testaments a *dies incertus* was regarded as a condition, U. xxiv, 30 and 31, note. The *ex intervallo* introduction of a date into an obligation, or withdrawal of one from it, amounted to novation (which see, No. 4), G. iii, 177; the reason being that a postponed debt counted for less than one immediately exigible, G. iii, 113.

DIES LEGATI CEDEBAT, *i.e.* a legacy vested, under the old law at the testator's death. By the Julian and Pap.-Poppaean law it vested on the opening of the testament, if it was either pure or *in diem certum ;* if conditional or *in diem incertum*, only on the condition happening or uncertain date arriving, U. xxiv, 31. If a legatee survived the *dies cedens,* his right passed to his heirs, 30.

DIES NEFASTUS,—a *legis actio* (which see) could not proceed upon it, G. iv, 29.

DII SUPERI, DII MANES,—things consecrated to them were respectively sacred and religious, G. ii, 4. A few specially favoured deities might be instituted heirs in a testament, U. xxii, 6. The *fana deorum* were regarded as sanctuaries, G. i, 53.

DILATORY EXCEPTIONS, G. iv, 122; see *Exception*, 5.

DISHERISON, see *Testament*, 10-12.

DISJOINT and CONJOINT LEGACY to co-legatees, G. ii, 199; see *Legacy*, 30-34.

DISPENSATOR, G. i, 122, iii, 160.

DIVERSAE SCHOLAE AUCTORES, a phrase used by Gaius to denote the Proculians; see *Sabinians and Proculians*.

DIVINI JURIS, things that were, G. ii, 3-9; see *Things*, 1.

DIVISIONIS, BENEFICIUM, G. iii, 121; see *Suretyship*, 4.

DIVORCE, *divortium, repudium*, see *Husband and wife*, 6.

DODRANS, in matter of testaments, three-fourths of a testator's estate, and in particular the three-fourths which legatees might take under the Falcidian law, U. xxv, 14; see *Legacy*, 16.

DOLUS, DOLUS MALUS, intent to injure or defraud, or knowingly taking advantage of what caused that result, G. ii, 215; iii, 197, 207, 211; iv, 47. *Doli mali exceptio*, see *Exception*, 8.

DOMESTICUM TESTIMONIUM was not allowed in testaments, G. ii, 105-108, U. xx, 3-6.

DOMINICA POTESTAS, see *Slavery*.

DOMINIUM, see *Property*.

DONATION beyond a certain amount was prohibited by the Cincian law except to near kinsmen, U. i, 1; between husband and wife it was generally invalid, (see *Husband and wife*, 5), U. vii, 1.

DOTIS DICTIO, a particular mode of constituting a dowry, U. vi, 2, G. iii, 96 and note; see *Verbal obligation, Dowry*, 1.

DOWRY, *dos*, U. tit. vi, was the contribution made by or on behalf of a wife, who was not passing *in manum mariti*, towards the support of the *onera matrimonii*. See also *Husband and wife*.

    1. *How and by whom constituted.*—There were three modes of constituting it,—*dotis datio*, instant transfer, U. vi, 1; *dotis dictio*, specification of it in a formal way, which was held to amount to a verbal obligation (which see), though not contracted by way of question and answer, G. iii, 96 and note, U. vi, 1; and *dotis promissio*, in the shape of an ordinary stipulation (which see), U. vi, 1. Any person could give or promise a dowry, U. vi, 2; but it was only

DOWRY—*continued.*

the woman herself, a male ascendant related through males, or a debtor of hers acting on her instructions that could constitute it by *dictio*, G. iii, 96, U. vi, 2. If the woman was constituting it herself, her tutor, even her patron, was obliged to give his *auctoritas*, G. i, 178, 180; and if he was incapable, she got an interim Atilian tutor for the purpose, 178.

2. *Varieties.*—It was *profecticia* when constituted by the woman's father, U. vi, 3; *adventicia* when it proceeded from some other quarter, *ibid.*; or *recepticia*, when, being adventicious, the party advancing it had bargained that it was to revert to him on the dissolution of the marriage, U. vi, 5.

3. *The husband's right in it.*—While the marriage lasted the husband was legally its owner, G. ii, 63; but he was thus far under disability, that the *lex Julia de adulteriis* forbade him to alienate lands belonging to it, at least *italica praedia*, *ibid.* and n. 1. He might bequeath any part of it to his wife, U. xv, 3; which entitled her to claim it the moment an heir entered under his will, instead of having to wait for it. For, if there was no agreement to the contrary, the rule was that, when it came to be returned, the husband or his heirs did so in three annual instalments, so far as money or other fungibles were concerned, U. vi, 8, non-fungibles, however, being restored at once, *ibid.*

4. *Its fate on the predecease of the wife.*—The *dos profecticia* then reverted to her father if he was alive, but under deduction of a fifth for each child of the marriage until exhausted, U. vi, 4. If the father was dead, the husband retained the whole, *ibid.* A *dos adventicia* he was also entitled to retain, U. vi, 5, unless it was *recepticia*, and then it reverted to the party who had advanced it, *ibid.*

5. *Its fate on divorce.*—The wife, if *sui juris*, was then entitled to sue for it, whether profecticious or adventicious, U. vi, 6; if a *filiafamilias* her father sued along with her, *ibid.* If she died after the divorce, her heirs had no action for it unless her husband had been *in mora* in returning it, according to the practice explained above, 7.

6. *The husband's rights of retention.*—The husband had various rights of retention. Thus, when divorce was due to the fault of the wife or her *paterfamilias*, the husband was entitled to retain one-sixth for each child of the marriage, but not more than one-half in all, U. vi, 10, 11. Where his wife had been guilty of adultery he retained another

DOWRY—*continued.*

  sixth, or an eighth if her misconduct had been less serious, 12. (If he himself had been guilty of immorality, he was punished by being required to restore fungibles at once, and pay besides a sum equal to three years' income of non-fungibles, 13.) He was also entitled to retention for outlays on the dotal estate (see *Impensae*), 9, 14-17; for gifts made by him to his wife, 9, donations between them being as a rule prohibited, (see *Husband and wife*, 5), U. vii, 1; and for the value of property of his theftuously carried off by his wife in prospect of divorce, U. vi, 9.

  7. *The* actio rei uxoriae.—See this head under *Actions*.

  8. *Caducous dowry.*—See *Caducity*, 6.

DUPLICATION, G. iv, 127; see *Replication.*

DUPUNDIUS, G. i, 122.

EDICTA MAGISTRATUUM, G. i, 6; see *Jus Romanorum.*

EDICTUM IMPERATORIS, a form of imperial enactment, G. i, 5 and note 1; see *Constitutiones principum.*

EDICTUM SUCCESSORIUM, that portion of the praetor's edict which regulated the matter of succession testate and intestate, U. xxviii, 12.

EMANCIPATION, exclusion or release of a *filiusfamilias* from the *patria potestas* (which see), G. i, 132-135a.

  1. *How effected.*—When a *paterfamilias* mancipated (see *Mancipation*, 1) his daughter or his grandchild *in potestate* to a third party, and the latter manumitted her or him (see *Manumission*) from the quasi-slavery created by the mancipation (see *Mancipii, etc.*, 3), the daughter or grandchild at once became *sui juris*, G. i, 132, U. x, 1; but in the case of a son, the Twelve Tables (which see, No. 2) required three mancipations to free him from the *potestas*, and as many manumissions to make him a *paterfamilias*, *ibid.* Noxal surrender of a son (see *Noxal actions*) was not equivalent to emancipation, the mancipation being performed only once, G. iv, 79.

  2. *Results for the emancipated child.*—Becoming *sui juris*, the child acquired all the rights incident to that position, (see *Sui juris personae*). But as the emancipation involved *capitis deminutio* (which see, No. 2), according to the *jus civile* he lost all right of succession to his emancipating parent or to those who had been his agnates, G. iii, 19, 21; his parent was not bound to institute or disinherit him, G. ii, 135, U. xxii, 23; if he was instituted, he took as a stranger heir (see *Extranei heredes*), not as a *suus*, G. ii, 161. By the praetorian edict, however, if his parent passed

EMANCIPATION—*continued.*

him unmentioned in his testament, he was entitled to
bonorum possessio contra tabulas, on condition of collating
with *sui,* G. ii, 135, U. xxii, 23, xxviii, 2, 4, (see *Bonor.poss.,*
7) ; on his parent's intestacy he was admitted to *bonor.
poss. ab int.* along with *sui,* G. iii, 26, U. xxviii, 8 ; and he
might, as a cognate, claim possession of the estate of one
who, but for the *capitis deminutio,* would have been his
agnate, G. iii, 27, U. xxviii, 9.

3. *Results for the parent and third parties.*—If the parent died
before completing a son's emancipation, the latter's manumission from his first or second mancipation invalidated
his parent's testament by *quasi agnatio sui,* (see *Agn. sui
heredis*), even though he might be instituted in it or disinherited, G. ii, 141, U. xxiii, 3 ; or, if the parent was
intestate, entitled him to succeed, as again become a *suus
heres,* G. iii, 6.   The manumitter was entitled, as quasi-
patron, to be the child's tutor, G. i, 166, U. xi, 5 ; but the
parent, in order to reserve this right, usually had the child
remancipated to him and himself became the manumitter,
G. i, 133, 172.   As *parens manumissor* and quasi-patron
he was entitled not only to be tutor of but to succeed to
his emancipated child dying without issue, G. i, 133, iii,
40, 41, U. xxviii, 7 and n. 1, as amended in *Additions etc.*

4. *Emancipation of an adopted child.*—When this happened
the child was regarded as if in fact emancipated by his
natural parent, G. ii, 137, and ceased to have any rights
in relation to the adoptive parent's succession, G. ii, 136,
U. xxviii, 3.

EMERE and EMPTIO, early meaning, G. i, 113, note 2, ii, 104, note 6,
U. xix, 5, note.

EMPHYTEUSIS,—the name is not in Gai., but of later date,—grant of
lands to a man and his heirs *in perpetuum,* so long as the
vectigal was regularly paid, G. iii, 145.   It was a question
whether the contract was sale or location ; but held to be
the latter, *ibid.*

EMPTIO BONORUM, G. iii, 77-81, the last stage of the bankruptcy
procedure introduced by Publ. Rutilius, G. iii, 77, note,
iv, 35.

1. *To what estates it applied.*—It applied to the estates of insolvent debtors, whether living or dead, G. iii, 78 : living
ones, if they either fraudulently kept out of the way of
their creditors and were undefended in the latter's actions,
or had made a *cessio bonorum,* or had failed to pay a judgment debt within the days of grace, *ibid. ;* dead, when
it became clear that they were without heirs, *ibid.*

EMPTIO BONORUM—*continued*.

2. *Procedure.*—The creditors were first put by the praetor into possession, *in possessionem missi*, of the estate of the bankrupt, and then the proceedings were publicly advertised, a trustee (*magister*) elected, and the estate knocked down by him to the highest bidder; those various steps being at intervals longer or shorter, according as the debtor was living or dead, G. iii, 79 and n. 8.

3. *Position of the* bonor. emptor.—His purchase amounted to an acquisition of the estate *per universitatem*, G. ii, 98. His right, however, was praetorian only; his ownership of its corporeal items therefore was in the first instance bonitarian (see *Bonitar. ownership*), convertible into quiritarian by usucapion, G. iii, 80. Debtors of the bankrupt's he sued either by an *actio Serviana* on a fiction of heirship (see *Fiction*, 1), G. iii, 81, iv, 35, or by the *a. Rutiliana*, with *intentio* in name of the bankrupt and *condemnatio* in his own, (see *Condemnatio*, 4), G. iv, 35. A debtor sued by him was entitled to deduction of all counter claims of whatever sort, and even though not yet exigible, (see *Compensation*, 4), G. iv, 65-68.

4. *Result for the bankrupt.*—See *Bankruptcy*.

EMPTIO HEREDITATIS, in, heir and purchaser exchanged *stipulationes emptae et venditae hereditatis*, the heir undertaking to transfer to purchaser everything belonging to the inheritance that might come into his hands, and to allow latter to prosecute all claims as his, the heir's, procurator, (see *Procuratory in litigation*, 4), and the purchaser undertaking to defend the heir in all actions, and relieve him of all judgments, G. ii, 252. (This must not be confounded with *in jure cessio hereditatis*, described in G. ii, 34-37, iii, 85-87, U. xix, 12-15, and under *Hereditas*, No. 15.)

EMPTIO VENDITIO, see *Sale*.

ENTAIL created by series of testamentary trusts, G. ii, 277 compared with 271; see *Fideicommissum*, 5.

EPISTULA HADRIANI introducing *beneficium divisionis* in favour of sureties, G. iii, 121, 122; see *Suretyship*, 4.

EPISTULA PRINCIPIS, a form of imperial enactment, G. i, 5 and n. 1; see *Constitutiones principum*.

EREPTORIUM, U. xix, 17 and note 2; see *Hereditas*, 10.

ERROR, if excusable, *justa et probabilis ignorantia*, was not to be a source of loss to a man, G. iii, 160; illustrations, G. iii, 91, 160.

ERRORIS CAUSAE PROBATIO, G. i, 67-75, U. vii, 4, a device, due to an unknown Sct., for curing the defects of a marriage entered into by mistake between persons of unequal condition;

ERRORIS CAUSAE PROBATIO—*continued.*
>   for if the parties knew of the inequality the remedy was
>   inadmissible, G. i, 75.

   1. *Cases in which applicable.*—Gaius enumerates six or seven
cases, from which it appears to have been immaterial
whether the mistake was on the part of husband or wife,
and whether the mistaken party was a citizen, a latin, or
a peregrin, G. i, 67-71, 74. The following illustrates
the general idea:—A citizen having married a latin,
peregrin, or deditician wife, believing her a citizen, was
allowed to prove cause of error; by doing so he made her
(unless a deditician) and any children of the marriage
citizens, and at the same time acquired *potestas* over the
latter, 67. But error does not seem ever to have been
proveable until a child had been born of the marriage,
and, if it had been contracted under the Aelia-Sentian
law (which see, No. 6), until the child had completed its
first year, 73.

   2. *Effects of the* causae probatio.—Besides creating citizenship
and *potestas*, it invalidated any testament previously made
by the husband and father; for with the *potestas* he obtained *sui heredes*, G. ii, 142, (see *Agnatio sui heredis*). In
strictness this result followed whether cause had been
proved during his life or after his death, *ibid.*; but
Hadrian enacted that, if not proved until after his death,
his testament was not to be invalidated unless his children had been neither instituted nor disinherited, 143.
Though cause was not proved until after their father's
death, still the children succeeded *ab intestato* as *sui*, G.
iii, 5.

EXCEPTION, *exceptio*, G. iv, 115-125.

  I. EXCEPTIONS GENERALLY.

   1. *Definition.*—An exception was a plea allowed to a defender
who, though possibly liable according to the letter of the
law and of the pursuer's *intentio*, yet averred facts which,
if proved, would make condemnation inequitable or im-
politic, G. iv, 116: as *e.g.* no value received for a stipulatory promise given on the understanding of an advance,
ibid.; informal agreement—and therefore not civilly but
only naturally obligatory—displacing the contract sued
upon, 116a; fraud or constraint used to obtain a transfer
of property, 117; or purchase when title known to be a
matter of litigation, *ibid.*

   2. *Sources of such exceptions.*—A large number of exceptions
of frequent recurrence was published in the edict, more
special ones formulated to meet particular cases, G. iv, 118;

EXCEPTION—*continued.*
I. EXCEPTIONS GENERALLY—*continued.*

some of them authorised by statute, others flowing from the praetor's jurisdiction, 119.

3. *How introduced in the* formula.—In grafting an exception upon the *formula* (which see), it was worded negatively —if there has been no subsequent agreement not to sue, if there has been no fraud, if the thing was not known to be litigious when purchased, etc.—and inserted immediately before the *condemnatio* (which see), so as in effect to make the latter conditional, G. iv, 119; and it was made use of even in *bonae fidei judicia*, 126a, notwithstanding the *liberum officium* possessed in such cases by the judge, 114.

4. *Answer to it by pursuer.*—See *Replication.*

5. *Exceptions either peremptory or dilatory.*—Peremptory were those that could not be excluded by lapse of time, of which illustrations are given in G. iv, 121; dilatory those available only for a time, as illustrated in 122, or those founded on some objection to the qualification of the pursuer that was capable of removal, 124.

6. *What if dilatory exception disregarded by pursuer?*—If a dilatory exception was disregarded, and the action not postponed in the one case, nor the defect cured in the other, the pursuer going on in spite of it lost his cause, G. iv, 123, 124.

7. *What if a peremptory exception overlooked by defender?*— A defender inadvertently omitting to state a peremptory exception might obtain *in integr. restitutio* (which see) in order to have it added to the *formula*, G. iv, 125; but disputed whether this applied to a dilatory one, *ibid.*

II. PARTICULAR EXCEPTIONS.

8. *The* exceptio doli mali.—See an explanation in G. ii, 76, note 3. It might be pleaded, for example, in answer to a pupil invoking technicalities in disregard of equity, G. ii, 84; to an owner attempting to oust a possessor, who had in good faith increased the value of the former's property, say by building or planting on it, without reimbursing him, G. ii, 76-78; to a legatee claiming as a legacy what the testator had subsequently alienated, G. ii, 198; to an heir-at-law attempting to oust a testamentary heir holding *bonor. possessio*, on the ground of a trifling informality in the testament, G. ii, 120, 151; to a party claiming possession on the strength of a conveyance he had impetrated by fraudulent representations, G. iv, 117; to a creditor claiming payment in a *stricti juris* action without giving the debtor credit for counter

EXCEPTION—*continued.*

  II. PARTICULAR EXCEPTIONS—*continued.*

    claims *ex eadem materia,* addition to G. iv, 61, note, in *Additions etc.*

  9. *Other peremptory exceptions.*—Amongst those referred to are the *ex. rei in judicium deductae,* (see *Litis contestatio*), G. iii, 181, iv, 107, 108, 121; *ex. rei judicatae* (see *Judicatae, etc.*), *ibid. ;* exception of constraint, *metus,* G. iv, 117, 121; exception that a transaction sued on was prohibited by statute, 121, or that pursuer had agreed never to sue, *ibid. ; ex. non numeratae pecuniae,* (often generically *ex. doli mali*), 116; *ex. rei litigiosae,* 117a; and *ex. rei nondum traditae* in answer to vendor's action for price, 126a.

  10. *Particular dilatory exceptions.*—Exception that pursuer had agreed not to sue for a certain time, G. iv, 116a; *ex. litis dividuae,* G. iv, 56, 122, and *ex. rei residuae,* 122, both processual exceptions; also the *ex. cognitoria,* objection to the qualifications of a cognitor, (see *Procuratory in litigation,* 2), or to the right of a party to sue by an agent, 124.

EXERCITORIAN ACTION, a praetorian action *in solidum* granted to a creditor against a *paterfamilias* or owner, who, as *exercitor* of a ship, had placed his *filiusfamilias* or slave in charge of it, to recover payment of debts properly incurred on the ship's account, G. iv, 71; afterwards allowed even where it was a stranger freeman or a *servus alienus* that had been placed in command and contracted the debt, *ibid.*

EXPENDO, G. iii, 174 and note, 175, note 4.

EXPENSI LATIO, *expensum ferre,* G. iii, 130; see *Literal obligations,* 1.

EXTRANEI HEREDES, stranger heirs, included all who were neither *sui* nor *necessarii,* (see *Sui heredes, Nec. her.*), *i.e.* those who had not been subject to the *jus* of the deceased, G. ii, 161, *e.g.* emancipated children in relation to their father, all children in relation to their mother, brothers in relation to each other, *ibid.* To complete their right an act of entry was requisite,—there was in their case no *ipso jure* vesting, U. xxii, 25, (see *Hereditas,* 5, 6). An *extraneus heres* of a patron had no right of succession to his citizen freedmen, G. iii, 58, 64, but had right to that of his Junian latins, 58, 63, see *Succession to cit. freedmen,* 5, *Succ. to Jun. latins,* 3.

EXTRAORDINARIAE COGNITIONES, see *Procedure,* 13.

FACERE, technical meaning, G. iii, 92, note, iv, 2, note 3.

FALSA DEMONSTRATIO in a testament, U. xxiv, 19, (see *Legacy,* 9); in a *formula,* G. iv, 58, (see *Demonstratio,* 4).

FAMILIA in sense of *patrimonium*, G. ii, 102; *familia pecuniaque*, 104, note 4.

FAMILIAE EMPTOR, FAM. VENDITIO, FAM. MANCIPATIO, see *Testament*, 3, 4.

FAR, what, U. tit. ix, note; see *Manus*, 1.

FESTUCA, see *Vindicta*.

FICTION, *fictio*, an assumption contrary to fact introduced into a *formula* (which see), to adapt it to a case to which it was appropriate in equity and common sense, though not in law, G. iv, 34-38.

    1. *Fiction of heirship.*—This was introduced in the *formulae* granted to or against *bonorum possessores*, to enable them to sue or be sued as heirs, G. iv, 34, U. xxviii, 12, and the same fiction was introduced on behalf of a *bonorum emptor*, G. iv, 35.

    2. *Fiction of usucapion.*—This was introduced in favour of a proprietor of a *res mancipi* who had acquired it merely by tradition, and had lost possession before actually completing his quiritarian right, or of a *bonae fidei* acquirer *a non domino* in the same position,—the Publician action (which see), G. iv, 36.

    3. *Fictions of citizenship and* caput integrum.—Citizenship was sometimes feigned, in order to allow action to or against a peregrin, contrary to the strict letter of the law, G. iv, 37; and the non-occurrence of a *capitis deminutio* which had actually taken place was sometimes pretended, in order to preserve to a creditor a claim against his debtor which the *capitis minutio* had in strict law extinguished, G. iv, 38.

    4. *Fictions that certain* legis actiones *underlay the corresponding* formulae.—Fictions of another sort imported into certain *formulae* a reference to old *legis actiones*, when the right sued upon had no existence apart from the declaration of law that in the circumstances the *legis actio* referred to should be competent, G. iv, 31a-33.

FIDEICOMMISSUM, a testamentary trust-gift or trust to give,— the word is used in both senses, G. ii, 246-289, U. tit. xxv; see also TESTAMENT.

  I. FIDEICOMMISSA IN GENERAL.

    1. *Nature and varieties.*—The distinctive feature of a *fideicommissum* was that it was left not in imperative but in precative language, U. xxiv, 1—*rogo, peto, volo, fideicommitto*, and such like, G. ii, 249, U. xxv, 2; being in form a request to heir, legatee, or even a trust-beneficiary, to give effect to the truster's wishes, G. ii, 248, 260. By the *jus civile fideicommissa* were not recognised as binding, U.

FIDEICOMMISSUM—*continued.*

I. FIDEICOMMISSA IN GENERAL—*continued.*

xxv, 1; it was the consuls who first began to enforce obedience to them as expressive of a testator's will, and in course of time a particular magistrate, the *praetor fideicommissarius*, was appointed for that purpose, G. ii, 278, U. xxv, 12. There were three varieties, the *fid. hereditatis*, when the request was to the heir to denude of the whole or part of the inheritance, G. ii, 250; *fid. rei singularis*, when the heir or legatee was requested to denude of a particular thing, G. ii, 260; and *fid. libertatis*, when heir or legatee was asked to enfranchise a slave, G. ii, 263. The only testamentary provisions that could not be put in the form of a trust were the institution of an heir, G. ii, 248, and the appointment of a tutor, G. ii, 289.

2. *Who could leave a* fideicommissum.—Only a man who had made a testament, and therein validly instituted an heir, could bequeath a *fid. hereditatis*, G. ii, 249; but any one qualified to make a testament, even though he had not done so, but was dying intestate, might leave a *fid. rei singularis* or *libertatis*, U. xxv, 4.

3. *To whom it might be bequeathed.*—Neither *hereditas* nor *res singulae* could be left by trust to a peregrin, G. ii, 285, although to benefit peregrins was one of the principal reasons for the introduction of the institution, *ibid.*; neither, except in the case of a municipality, U. xxii, 5, could they be left to *incertae personae* or *postumi alieni*, though the rule was not always so, G. ii, 287, U. xxv, 13. An heir etc. fraudulently giving a secret promise to denude in favour of one to whom trust-gift was prohibited rendered himself liable to penalties, U. xxv, 17. The restrictions of the Voconian law did not apply to a *fid. hereditatis* in favour of a woman, G. ii, 274, and a Junian latin could take by trust either *hereditas* or *res singulae* without becoming a citizen, 275, U. xxv, 7; by a Pegasian (?) Sct., however, the Julian penalties of celibacy and *orbitas* (see *Julian and Pap. Popp. law*, 4, 5) were extended to *fideicommissa*, G. ii, 286, 286a.

4. *In what manner.*—To validate a *fid. hereditatis* there required to be a testament and testamentary heir, G. ii, 248; the trust, however, might be embodied in a codicil, whether confirmed or not, G. ii, 273, U. xxv, 11. But a testament was not a necessity in the case of *fid. rei singularis*; if there was one, the trust might be in it, or in a codicil whether confirmed or unconfirmed, U

FIDEICOMMISSUM—*continued.*

I. FIDEICOMMISSA IN GENERAL.—*continued.*

xxv, 8; but if the truster was dying intestate, still he might impose a *fid. rei singularis* upon his heir-at-law, G. ii, 270, U. xxv, 4. *Fid. rer. singularum,* if left in a testament, were not invalid because placed in it before the heir's institution, U. xxv, 8; they did not require, like legacies, to be worded in latin, G. ii, 281, U. xxv, 9; in fact it was not essential that they should be put in words at all, any intelligible indication of the truster's will being sufficient, U. xxv, 3.

5. *On whom it might be made a burden.*—A *fid. hereditatis* could be imposed only on the heir, G. ii, 250, or the heir's heir, 277; but a *fid. rei singularis* might be imposed either on heir, legatee, or trust-beneficiary, or their respective heirs, 271, 277, 278, and an entail thus created by a succession of trusts, *ibid.* Contrary to the rule in legacies, if it was a *filiusfamilias* or slave that was instituted heir, a trust might be imposed on his *paterfamilias* or owner, U. xxv, 10. But in no case was a trust sustained that had been imposed by way of penalty, G. ii, 288, U. xxv, 13.

II. FIDEICOMMISSUM HEREDITATIS.

6. *The request to the heir.*—The request to the heir was either at once, or at a certain date, or on a certain condition, G. ii, 250, or after his death,—in which case it was really a request to *his* heirs, 277,—to denude of the whole or a part of the inheritance and transfer it to the beneficiary, 250.

7. *Heir and beneficiary as vendor and vendee.*—The heir denuding did not thereby cease to be heir, but the position of the beneficiary varied from time to time, G. ii, 251. Originally, in virtue of a *pro forma* sale, it was that of purchaser; and his relations with the heir were adjusted by *stipulationes emptae et venditae hereditatis,* G. ii, 252, (see *Emptio hereditatis*).

8. *The Trebellian senatusconsult.*—This enactment rendered the *pro forma* sale unnecessary, by providing that actions competent to or against an heir might be granted to or against a trust-beneficiary, G. ii, 253, U. xxv, 14; an arrangement that was satisfactory only where what the heir was asked to transfer did not exceed three-fourths of the inheritance, G. ii, 255.

9. *The Pegasian senatusconsult.*—To meet the case of more than three-fourths being included in the *fideicommissum,* and the heir declining such unprofitable entry and thus defeating the trust, this Sct., following the Falcidian law

FIDEICOMMISSUM — *continued.*

  II. FIDEICOMMISSUM HEREDITATIS—*continued.*

    (see *Legacy*, 16), authorised him to retain for himself a fourth of the inheritance, G. ii, 254, U. xxv, 14; the trust-beneficiary, as regarded the other three-fourths, took the position of a partiary legatee (see *Legacy*, 8), G. ii, 254-257, U. xxv, 15; and *stipulationes partis et pro parte* were then interchanged, assuring *pro rata* division of assets and liabilities, *ibid.*, although actions remained competent only to and against the heir, U. xxv, 14.

    10. *What if heir declined to enter?*—In that case it was provided by the Pegasian Sct. that, on application of the trust-beneficiary, the praetor should compel him to enter; but he incurred no risk, and derived no advantage; the beneficiary took everything, and sued and was sued under the Trebellian Sct., G. ii, 258, U. xxv, 16.

  III. FIDEICOMMISSUM REI SINGULARIS.

    11. *What might be so left.*—Anything that might be legated by damnation (see *Legacy*, 22, 23) might be bequeathed by *fideicommissum*, U. xxv, 5, no matter to whom it belonged, G. ii, 261; but the person burdened with it could not be required to transfer more than he had himself received under the testament, *ibid.* Where it was a *res aliena*, it had to be purchased and delivered, or its value paid in money, G. ii, 262; although some were of opinion that if its owner refused to sell the trust was extinguished, *ibid.*

  IV. FIDEICOMMISSUM LIBERTATIS; see also *Manumission.*

    12. *To whom freedom might be bequeathed by trust.*—A testator might desire his heir or legatee to manumit slaves whom he could not himself enfranchise directly, *e.g.* a *servus alienus*, G. ii, 264, 272, U. ii, 10; the heir was then required to buy and manumit him, G. ii, 265; but if his owner would not sell him, the gift failed, freedom having no alternative value, *ibid.*, U. ii, 11. Further, though a man could not (unless insolvent, G. i, 21) institute one of his own slaves as his heir with freedom, yet he might by *fideicommissum* direct that his slave should be enfranchised and have the succession on attaining that age, G. ii, 276 and note.

    13. *How patronage was influenced by fideicommissary enfranchisement.*—Where a slave was directly enfranchised by testament, the deceased testator was his patron, G. ii, 267, U. ii, 8; but one manumitted under a trust became a freedman not of the testator's but of the manumitter's, G. ii, 266, U. ii, 8.

FIDEICOMMISSUM—*continued*.

V. POINTS OF DIFFERENCE BETWEEN LEGACIES AND FIDEICOMMISSA.
—There are a great many of these indicated in G. ii,
268-288, and U. xxv, 7-13; but it is unnecessary here
to reproduce them.

FIDEJUSSIO, see *Suretyship*, 4.

FIDEM DARE, OBLIGARE, FALLERE, G. iii, 92, note.

FIDEPROMISSIO, see *Suretyship*, 2, 3.

FIDES, BONA, see *Bona fides*.

FIDES (DEA), G. iii, 92, note.

FIDUCIA was an agreement accompanying a conveyance by *mancipatio* or *in jure cessio*, whereby the transferee undertook
to reconvey in a certain event, G. ii, 59, 60.

   1. Fiducia *contracted with a friend.*—This was of frequent
      occurrence before the development of the real contract of
      deposit : a man about to travel say, to ensure the safety
      of something belonging to him, conveyed it in property
      to a friend, the latter undertaking to reconvey on demand,
      G. ii, 60 and note. The agreement founded in favour of
      the transferor in trust an *actio fiduciae*, which was *juris
      civilis*, G. iv, 33, and *bonae fidei*, 62 ; condemnation in it
      rendered the unfaithful trustee infamous, 182. If the
      transferor reacquired possession, even without a recon-
      veyance, he made the thing his again by *usureceptio*, (see
      Usucapion, 7), one year's possession being sufficient even
      in the case of lands, G. ii, 59 and note, 60.

   2. Fiducia *contracted with a creditor.*—This was common
      before the contract of pledge was developed ; by way of
      security a debtor conveyed property to his creditor, on
      an agreement for reconveyance when the debt was paid,
      G. ii, 60, 220, which also founded an *actio fiduciae*, as
      above. When the debt was paid the debtor had *usure-
      ceptio* in a year, whatever his *causa possessionis, ibid. ;* but
      while unpaid, he could not usurecapt the *fiducia*—the
      name was given to the thing as well as the agreement,
      59, note—if he had it in location or by precarious grant
      from his creditor, 60. Yet even before reconveyance or
      usureception, the debtor had thus far still an equitable
      interest in it,—that if he legated it by preception (see
      Legacy, 28) to one of several heirs, the others had to
      redeem it, G. ii, 220.

FIDUCIARY COEMPTIO, G. i, 114, see *Manus*, 7 ; fiduciary tutory, G.
   i, 166, see *Tutory*, 3, 12, 21.

FILIUSFAMILIAS, FILIAFAMILIAS, a child *in potestate*, not necessarily
   son or daughter, but even a remoter descendant, if in
   the *potestas* of the *paterfamilias ;* and not necessarily of

32

FILIUSFAMILIAS, FILIAFAMILIAS—*continued*.

youthful age, for a *filiusfamilias* might himself be father or even grandfather, G. i, 127, 133*b*. For the modes in which a person became or ceased to be *filiusfamilias*, see *Patria potestas*, 7-17 ; for an indication of his capacities and disabilities, see *Alieni juris personae*, 2-4 ; for an indication of his rights in regard to the *hereditas* of the *paterfamilias*, see *Sui heredes*. A *filiusfamilias* was under no incapacity so far as regarded acts done in his character of a citizen, as *e.g.* witnessing a transaction *per aes et libram*, or acting as *libripens* or *familiae emptor*, G. ii, 105-108.

FISCUS, the imperial treasury. By a Sct. of Hadrian's *fideicommissa* to peregrins were to fall to the fisc, G. ii, 285 ; and by a constitution of Caracalla's *caduca* (see *Caducity*, 5) were to go to it, with a certain reservation in favour of near relatives of the testator's, U. xvii, 2 and note, as amended in *Additions etc.*

FLAMINES MAJORES required to be issue of a confarreate marriage, and themselves be wedded in the same way, G. i, 112.

FLAMINICA DIALIS, G. i, 136 and note.

FOREIGN LAW was occasionally appealed to where peregrins were concerned, as for example in judging of the legitimacy of issue of a peregrin marriage, G. i, 92, the validity of a peregrin testament, U. xx, 14, or the effect for his heir of a peregrin's *fidepromissio*, G. iii, 120.

FORMAL AND MATERIAL CONTRACTS, G. iii, 89, note ; see *Contract*, 3.

FORMULA, G. iv, 39-68, the issue which, under the formular system (see *Procedure*, 8), was adjusted for the trial of a cause.

1. *Its form and parts.*—It was addressed either to a single *judex* or to recuperators, G. iv, 46, 47, 105 and note ; and, in its simplest form, instructed them, if they found it proved that the property claimed by the pursuer was his, or that the defender was indebted to him in what was claimed, then to condemn the defender to the pursuer, but if not proved to acquit him, G. iv, 41, 43. The ordinary clauses were the *demonstratio, intentio, adjudicatio,* and *condemnatio*, (see those words), 39-43 ; but only the *intentio* could stand alone, viz. in *praejudicia*, 44. Besides these a formula might be preceded by a *praescriptio* (which see), G. iv, 130-137, and have incorporated in it fictions, 32-38, exceptions, 115-125, and replications, duplications, etc., 126-129, (see those words).

2. *In whose names it ran.*—If parties were not litigating in person but by cognitors or procurators (see *Procuratory in litigation*), the *intentio* was formulated in the name of the

FORMULA—*continued*.

principal, and the *condemnatio* in that of the agent, G. iv, 86, 87. The same course was taken when a man was suing upon a claim he had acquired by purchase, or otherwise,—he took the *intentio* in name of the original creditor, and the *condemnatio* in his own, G. iv, 35.

3. Formulae in jus *and* in factum conceptae.—A formula was said to be *in jus concepta* when the pursuer laid his *intentio* on the *jus civile*, in one or other of the forms *ejus esse ex jure Quiritium, dare oportere, dare facere oportere,* or *damnum decidere oportere,* G. iv, 45, 47, 60; *in factum* when he contended that something had happened which, under the praetor's edict, entitled him to redress, 46. In one or two cases, as in deposit and commodate, the *formula* could be conceived either way, 47 and note. Of those *in factum* there was a large collection in the album, 46.

4. Certae *and* incertae formulae.—A *formula* was *certa* when the claim was for a specified thing or a definite sum of money, G. iv, 44; *incerta* when it was illiquid, and for what in the circumstances the judge might find the pursuer entitled to, 41, 54, 131. An *intentio certa* might sometimes be followed by a *condemnatio incerta,* G. iv, 68, (see *Condemnatio,* 2).

FORMULAR SYSTEM, see *Procedure,* 2, 8.

FRAUDULENT EVASION OF A STATUTE, G. i, 46.

FRAUDULENT MANUMISSION to injury of creditors or patrons, G. i, 37, U. i, 16; see *Ael. Sent. law,* 1.

FREEDMEN, in the abstract *libertini* in relation to a patron *liberti,* were persons freed from lawful slavery, G. i, 11, and were either citizens, Junian latins, or classed with the dediticians, G. i, 12, U. i, 5; (see *Manumission, Junian latinity, Deditician freedmen*). In the ordinary case they were in patronage of their manumitters, the patron being entitled to services from his *liberti,* G. iii, 83, 96a, iv, 162, (see *Patronate,* 3); to the tutory of males among them who were under puberty, and females of any age, G. i, 165, iii, 43, (see *Tutory,* 18, 19); and to their estates on their death, (see *Succession to citizen freedmen, Succ. to Junian latins, Ded. freedmen,* 3). The right to services, and those of tutory and succession, being *jura legitima,* were extinguished by *capitis deminutio* of either patron or freedman, G. iii, 51, 83, U. xi, 9. A freedman was not permitted to summon his patron without leave of the praetor; if he did, the patron was allowed an action of damages, G. iv, 46.

FREEDOM was enjoyed by *ingenui* by right of birth, by *libertini* in

FREEDOM—*continued*.

　　　　respect of their subsequent acquisition of it, (see *Freed-men*), G. i, 10.　It was lost by a man who wilfully evaded inscription in the census register, G. i, 160, U. xi, 11, and by a woman who persevered in cohabiting with a slave notwithstanding the warning of the latter's owner (see *Claudian Sct.*), *ibid.*　It was held incapable of valuation ; therefore if a fideicommissary grant of freedom to a *servus alienus* failed through his owner's refusal to sell him. it was impossible to recompense him, G. ii, 265 and n. 1.　Out of favour for freedom an *adsertor libertatis* deposited the smallest *sacramentum* known to the law, G. iv, 14 and n. 2 ; see *Slavery*, 9.

FRUCTUARIA STIPULATIO, G. iv, 166 ; FRUCTUARIUM JUDICIUM, G. iv, 169 ; see *Interdicts*, 14, *Cautiones etc.*, 5.

FRUCTUS LICITATIO, G. iv, 166 ; see *Interdicts*, 14.

FURIOSI, see *Lunacy*.

FURTUM, see *Theft*.

GALATIANS, the, claimed to have a *patria potestas*, G. i, 55.

GENS, the, by the Twelve Tables had rights of tutory and succession on failure of agnates, G. i, 164a and note, iii, 17. The law affecting it was obsolete before the time of Gai., G. iii, 17.

GESTIO PRO HEREDE, G. ii, 166, U. xxii, 26 ; see *Hereditas*, 5, 6.

GLADIATORS, G. iii, 146, 199.

GRADUS and ORDO in succession, distinction, G. iii, 27, note 1.

HABITATIO, a gratuitous right of occupancy of a house, which left the legal possession in the granter, G. iv, 153.

HADRIAN, see *Constitutiones principum, Senatusconsults*.

HASTA, the symbol of quiritarian ownership, G. iv, 16, and as such displayed in the centumviral court, *ibid.*　For certain purposes a rod, *festuca* or *vindicta*, was used as a substitute, see *Vindicta*.

HERCULES GADITANUS, U. xxii, 6.

HEREDITAS, inheritance, the succession of the *jus civile*, in contradistinction to the *bonorum possessio* of the praetors. See also SUCCESSION, BONORUM POSSESSIO.

　I. DELATION OF AN HEREDITAS.

　　1. *Delation* ex testamento.—See *Testament*.

　　2. *Delation* ab intestato.—See *Intestate succession*.

　II. HOW IT VESTED IN THE HEIR.

　　3. *In the case of* sui heredes.—An inheritance, whether delate *ex testamento* or *ab intestato*, vested in *sui heredes* (which see) *ipso jure*, G. ii, 157, U. xxii, 24 ; for they were not

HEREDITAS—*continued.*
    II. How it vested in the heir—*continued.*

only *sui* but also necessary heirs, *ibid.* The praetor, however, allowed them to abstain when the estate was insolvent, G. ii, 158, U. xxii, 24, (see *Abstinendi potestas*). But a *suus* who had once intromitted could not afterwards relinquish, unless he was a minor and obtained *in integrum restitutio* (which see), G. ii, 163.

4. *In that of* necessarii heredes.—A *heres necessarius* (see *Nec. heredes*), whether a slave of the testator's or a person held by him *in mancipii causa*,—and both could succeed only *ex testamento*,—also acquired *ipso jure*, G. ii, 153, U. xxii, 24; but the latter had the same *beneficium abstinendi* as a *suus*, G. ii, 160, while the former could in no case decline, 153.

5. *In that of an* extraneus heres *testamentarily instituted with cretion.*—A stranger heir instituted with cretion, under penalty of disherison, G. ii, 164, 165, U. xxii, 27, (see *Cretio*, 1), had to cern within the time limited, G. ii, 166, 170, U. xxii, 30; informal acceptance was insufficient, G. ii, 168; but informal declinature did not preclude subsequent cerniture if the cretion-days had not expired, *ibid.*, U. xxii, 30. If the penalty of non-cerniture was not disherison (see *Cretio*, 1), but admission of a substitute (see *Substitution*, 1), G. ii, 177, U. xxii, 34, the rule in the time of Gai. was that, by behaving as heir (*gestio pro herede*) instead of cerning, he let in the substitute for an equal share, G. ii, 177; but it was afterwards altered in his favour so as to let him keep the whole, U. xxii, 34.

6. *In that of an* extraneus *instituted without cretion or taking* ab intestato.—In either of these cases a stranger might enter either by cerning, by informal declaration of acceptance, or by behaving as heir, G. ii, 167, U. xxii, 25, 26; an informal declinature was sufficient to exclude him, G. ii, 169; but if he had once entered he could not relinquish, unless a minor, 163. He was not required, however, to decide at once,—he was allowed a *tempus deliberandi*, 162, fixed by the praetor on the petition of the deceased's creditors, 167, who were entitled to sell the estate if he did not enter before its expiry, *ibid.*

7. *Entry by persons in tutelage,* filiifamilias, *and slaves.*—A pupil or a woman in tutelage could not enter without tutorial *auctoritas*, G. i, 176; a *filiusfamilias* could enter only on the instructions of his *paterfamilias*, ii, 87, U. xix, 19; and a slave on those of his owner at the moment, G. ii, 188-190, U. xxii, 13, 14.

HEREDITAS—*continued.*
  III. FAILURE OF THE HEIR TO TAKE OR KEEP.
    8. *Failure to take under a testament.*—As regards the results of
       failure of one or more of several testamentary heirs, see
       Adcretio, 2, *Caducity,* 3. Total failure caused intestacy,
       G. ii, 144; but that, by operation of the Julian law, the
       inheritance went to the heir-at-law caduciarily, and
       under burden of all the legacies, etc., contained in the
       testament, seems fairly deducible from U. xvii, 3, xxviii,
       7, and G. ii, 149. (The case, however, is hardly conceiv-
       able; for if the inheritance was lucrative, the testamentary
       heirs were unlikely to decline it, while if insolvent it
       would be taken by deceased's creditors for what it was
       worth, G. ii, 167.)
    9. *Failure to take* ab intestato.—When there was failure of one
       or more of several equally entitled, there was accretion in
       favour of those who took, U. xxvi, 5. If all the *legitimi
       heredes* of the first degree failed, there was by law no trans-
       mission to those of the next, G. iii, 12, U. xxvi, 5; they
       were admitted, however, by the praetors to *bonorum possessio*
       as cognates, G. iii, 28, (see *Bonor. possessio,* 16). When
       there was total failure both of civil and praetorian heirs,
       the inheritance fell to the state, G. ii, 149, U. xxviii, 7.
    10. *Incapacity of an heir to retain what had come to him.*—
       When a testamentary heir was guilty of ingratitude or
       disrespect to the memory or the family of the testator, he
       was liable to have his inheritance taken from him on the
       petition of the fisc; it was then called *ereptorium,* and
       went to the state, U. xix, 17 and n. 2.
  IV. THE HEIR'S POSITION.
    11. *In reference to co-heirs.*—Their rights *inter se* were adjusted
       in an *actio familiae erciscundae* (which see), G. ii, 219.
    12. *In reference to legatees.*—See *Legacy,* 18-34.
    13. *In reference to trust beneficiaries.*—See *Fideicommissum,*
       6-11.
    14. *In reference to third parties.*—Inheritance was a universal
       acquisition of the deceased's estate, G. ii, 98. For a few
       of his debts the heir was not liable, and in a few of his
       claims he could not insist, see *Actions,* 7; but with those
       exceptions, he was entitled to proceed against deceased's
       debtors, G. iv, 34, and was liable to action at the instance
       of his creditors, G. ii, 35, and even to be made a bankrupt
       on account of his debts, G. ii, 154.
  V. CESSION OF AN HEREDITAS IN JURE.
    15. *Cession by an heir-at-law.*—An agnate ceding *in jure* before
       entry made the cessionary heir in his stead, G. ii, 35, iii,

HEREDITAS—*continued.*

V. Cession of an hereditas in jure—*continued.*

85, U. xix, 13, 14. If, however, the cession was not until after entry, the cedent remained heir and responsible to the deceased's creditors, *ibid.*, U. xix, 15; corporeals passed to the cessionary as if they had been ceded individually; while claims were extinguished and the deceased's debtors so much the gainers, *ibid.*

16. *Cession by a testamentary heir.*—Any such cession before entry was useless, G. ii, 36, iii, 86; after entry it had the same effect as cession by an heir-at-law in similar circumstances, *ibid.*

17. *Could there be cession by a necessary heir ?*—The Proculians were of opinion that after entry he had the same power of cession as others; the Sabinians held cession by him useless, G. ii, 37, iii, 87.

HOMER quoted, G. iii, 141.

HOSTIA, G. iv, 28 and n. 1.

HUSBAND AND WIFE.

1. *Creation of the relationship.*—See *Marriage.*

2. *Respective positions of the parties when marriage accompanied by* in manum conventio.—See *Manus,* 4, 5.

3. *Position of the wife when marriage unaccompanied by* manus.
   —She did not become a member of her husband's family, but still remained *sui juris* or in *patria potestate,* as the case might be, U. vi, 6; her children were not civilly her agnates, but only naturally her cognates, G. iii, 24. If she were assaulted or insulted, her husband was entitled to an *actio injuriarum* if she was *in manu ;* but judging from the language of Gai. he seems to have had no such right without it, G. iii, 221.

4. *The dos or dowry.*—See *Dowry.*

5. *Donations between the spouses.*—Although, in the absence of *manus,* each had or might have a separate estate, yet donations by one to the other were invalid except they were *mortis causa, divortii causa,* or to obtain freedom for a slave; the wife being also allowed in a few cases to make a gift to her husband to enable him to obtain rank or dignity, U. vii, 1. If the husband had made a donation to his wife, not being one of those excepted, he was entitled to deduct it from the amount of the dowry in restoring it on the dissolution of the marriage, U. vi, 9, and note to rubr. tit. vii.

6. *Divorce.*—A wife *in manu,* in the event of divorce, might compel her husband to release her from *manus* by remancipation (which see), G. i, 137. In the absence of *manus*

HUSBAND AND WIFE—*continued.*

it was one of the consequences of divorce that the *dos* had to be restored, with or without deduction, U. vi, 6 f., (see *Dowry*, 5, 6). Before restoring it the husband was entitled to be relieved of any obligation he had undertaken in respect of it, or of his wife's property generally, U. vii, 3 and note. After dissolution of the marriage either might sue the other in an *actio rerum amotarum*, on account of theftuous removal of property in prospect of divorce, U. vii, 2 and note.

7. *Their rights of succession* inter se.—A wife *in manu* was *filiae loco* and one of her husband's *sui heredes*, U. xxii, 14, and entitled therefore to all their rights and privileges in the matter of succession; see *Sui heredes.* A wife not *in manu* had no right of succession under the *jus civile;* but the praetors admitted the survivor of husband or wife to *bonorum possessio ab intestato* of the predeceaser next after cognates, U. xxviii, 7; and the Julian and Pap. Popp. law (which see, No. 6) contained elaborate provisions as to the extent to which one might take under the other's testament, and which were to a great extent dependent on consideration of the number of children born of the marriage, U. xv, xvi, 1, 1*a*, 2, 4.

HYPOTHEC, landlord's, over the *invecta et illata* of his farmtenant, G. iv, 147.

ILLEGITIMACY, see *Parent and child.*

IMAGINARY DEEDS.—Mancipation was an imaginary sale, G. i, 119; *testamentum per aes et libram,* an imaginary mancipation, U. xx, 2; acceptilation and *nexi solutio,* imaginary payments, G. iii, 169, 173.

IMPENSAE, outlays on account of a thing, were either necessary, beneficial, or superfluous (*necessariae, utiles, voluptuosae*), U. vi, 14; the first such as were needful to maintain the *status quo,* 15; the second such as increased revenue, 16; the third such as only added to amenity, 17.

IMPERFECTA LEX, one that neither nullified what was done in contravention of it nor punished the contravener, U. i, 1.

IMPERIAL CONSTITUTIONS, G. i, 5; see *Constitutiones principum.*

IMPERIO CONTINENS JUDICIUM, see *Judicia legitima etc.*

IMPUBERATES, males and females under 14 and 12 respectively, G. i, 196, ii, 112, (see *Puberty*). They might be either *sui juris* (and then called pupils) or *alieni juris;* neither class could contract marriage, U. v, 2, or act as witness of a mancipation or other solemn deed, G. i, 29, 113, 119, ii, 104; unless *pubertati proximi* neither was held responsible

IMPUBERATES—*continued.*

for crime or delict, G. iii, 208. A *sui juris* impuberate could not make a testament, G. ii, 113, U. xx, 12, but one might be made for him by pupillary substitution in that of his father (see *Substitution*, 2), G. ii, 179, U. xxiii, 7; in other transactions he could act with *auctoritas* of a tutor, though it was not always necessary, (see *Pupils*).

IN BONIS HABERE, see *Bonitarian ownership.*

INCERTA PERSONA, one of whom it was impossible for a testator to have formed any definite idea in his own mind, G. ii, 238, could neither be instituted heir, G. ii, 242, 287, U. xxii, 4, nor be left a legacy, G. ii, 238, 287, U. xxiv, 18, or trust-gift, G. ii, 287, U. xxv, 13, except *sub certa demonstratione, i.e.* under reference to a well-defined class, G. ii, 238, U. xxiv, 18. A *postumus alienus* (see *Postumi*, 3) was regarded as *incerta persona*, G. ii, 242; and so was a municipality, so far as institution by any but its own freedmen was concerned, U. xxii, 5, although it might take both legacies, U. xxiv, 28, and trust-gifts, U. xxii, 5. An *incerta persona* could not be appointed tutor, G. ii, 240; and the Fufian law made testamentary enfranchisement useless unless the slave was named, G. ii, 239.

INCESTUOUS MATRIMONIAL CONNECTION, see *Marriage*, 6.

INCORPOREALS, what, G. ii, 14; were mostly *nec mancipi*, 17; were incapable of tradition, 19. See *Things*, 4.

INDEBITI SOLUTIO, payment under erroneous belief of indebtedness, in the ordinary case imposed on the payee an obligation to refund, enforceable by a *condictio indebiti*, G. iii, 91; even a pupil or a woman receiving an *indebitum* without tutorial *auctoritas* was liable, because the obligation, though created *re*, yet did not arise from contract, *ibid.* It was a sufficient answer to the *condictio* that what had been paid was due naturally, though possibly not civilly, (see *Obligation*, 5), G. iii, 119a, note 1. There was an arbitrary rule that an erroneous payment by an heir in name of legacy—Gai. confines it to one *per damnationem*, G. ii, 283—did not entitle him to a *condictio*, U. xxiv, 33; but it did not apply to *fideicommissa indebita*, G. ii, 283.

INFAMY, *ignominia*, resulted from condemnation in an action arising out of partnership, fiduciary agreement, tutory, mandate, or deposit, and from either condemnation in or compromise of one arising out of theft, robbery, or personal injury, G. iv, 182; while the same result followed sale of a bankrupt's estate, G. ii, 154. An individual affected by it was disqualified for acting in a litigation on another person's behalf, or himself appointing a *cognitor* or procurator, G. iv, 182.

INFANCY, children in, or not much beyond it, were in law regarded
	as having no more intelligence than a lunatic; their
	tutors therefore, if they were *sui juris*, acted for them,
	not with them, G. iii, 106, 107, 109, U. xi, 25. (Infancy
	ended at the age of seven.)
INFIRMATIO TESTAMENTI, invalidation of a testament, which see, Nos.
	21-24.
INGENUI, persons of free birth, G. i, 11; see *Persons*, 1.
INHERITANCE, see *Hereditas*.
IN INTEGRUM RESTITUTIO, a praetorian relief granted to persons
	who had suffered injury, loss, or damage for which there
	was no available or convenient remedy by action: the
	praetor reinstated them in the position they occupied
	before the event occurred to which their loss was attri-
	butable. It was granted to minors *in omnibus rebus
	lapsis*, G. iv, 57; *e.g.* on inconsiderate entry to a *damnosa
	hereditas*, G. ii, 163, loss of an action by reason of over-
	claim (see *Intentio*, 3), G. iv, 53, or acceptance as pursuer
	of a *formula* containing too little in the *condemnatio*
	(which see, No. 3), G. iv, 57. It was not often granted
	to persons of full age, G. ii, 163; but any defender in an
	action was entitled to have it when the praetor had in-
	serted too great a sum in the *condemnatio*, in order to
	have it diminished, G. iv, 57, such relief being always
	granted more readily to a defender than a pursuer, *ibid.*
IN JURE CESSIO, a civil mode of conveyance, and really a *vindicatio*
	(which see) arrested in its first stage, on the defender's
	confession *in jure*, G. ii, 24, 96, iv, 16, note.
	1. *Ceremonial.*—The parties, transferor and transferee, appeared
		in jure, *i.e.* before a magistrate, bringing with them, if
		corporeal, the thing to be ceded; the transferee, laying
		hold of it, asserted that it was his in quiritarian right;
		the magistrate asked the transferor whether he made any
		counter-vindication; and if he got no answer, or one in
		the negative, he declared the thing to belong to the trans-
		feree, G. ii, 24, U. xix, 9, 10. But the cession might be
		under reservations or qualifications, *e.g.* a *pactum fiduciae*
		(see *Fiducia*), G. ii, 59, iii, 201.
	2. *To whom competent.*—As a civil mode of conveyance it was
		peculiar to citizens, G. ii, 65, but probably competent also
		to colonial and Junian latins and to peregrins who had
		commercium (which see), U. xix, 4; but it could not be
		employed by persons *alieni juris* on account of the words
		of style, G. ii, 96.
	3. *What might be conveyed by it.*—It was a suitable form of
		conveyance either for *res mancipi* or *nec mancipi* (which

In jure cessio—*continued.*

see), U. xix, 9; but for the former mancipation was preferred, as usually more convenient, G. ii, 25. It was suitable for conveyance either of corporeals or incorporeals, and (with exception of rural praedial servitudes, which might be mancipated, G. ii, 29) the only civil form applicable to the latter, *e.g.* urban praedial servitudes, G. ii, 29, a usufruct, G. ii, 30-32, U. xix, 11, an inheritance, G. ii, 34-37, iii, 85-87, U. xix, 12-15, and certain tutories, G. i, 168-172, U. xi, 6-8, xix, 11. But it was inapplicable to provincial lands that were not *juris Italici* (see *Jus Italicum*), G. ii, 31, for they belonged to the state, G. ii, 7, nor to obligations, because their cession was impossible, G. ii, 38.

Injuria, see *Personal injury.*

In jus vocatio, formal summons to appear in court,—a necessary initiative of any litigation, G. iv, 183; but children and freedmen were not allowed to summon parents or patrons without leave of the praetor, *ibid.*, and if they did were liable to penalties, 46, 183. If the party summoned neither attended nor found a substitute, he also was liable in penalties, 46; and so was any one carrying him off to prevent his attendance, *ibid.*

Innominate contracts, G. iii, 89, note 1; see *Contract,* 1.

In rem actio per sponsionem, alternative to that *per formulam petitoriam* (the *vindicatio*), G. iv, 91-96. The preliminary step was a stipulation by the claimant for twenty-five sesterces from the possessor in the event of the thing in dispute being found to belong to the former, 93; but there was no restipulation, the sponsion being prejudicial, not penal, 94. On the promise a formula was adjusted, stipulant claiming the twenty-five sesterces, 93; and defender gave security in a *stipulatio pro praede litis et vindiciarum*, in imitation of the old sacramental procedure, (see *Legis actiones,* 2), 91, 94. Condemnation or absolvitor on the sponsion involved judgment on the question of property, 94. If the action was to be in the centumviral court, a *sacramentum* before the praetor took the place of the sponsio, 95, 31; the stake being 125 sesterces, 95, the equivalent of the 500 *asses* of the older procedure, 95, note 2, 14.

Insanity, see *Lunacy.*

Institorian action, one of the praetorian adjectician actions, granted to a creditor against a *paterfamilias* or owner who had placed his *filiusfamilias* or slave as *institor* in charge of a shop or other business, to recover payment *in*

INSTITORIAN ACTION—*continued.*

> *solidum* of debts properly incurred on account thereof, G.
> iv, 71 ; afterwards allowed even when it was a stranger
> freeman or a *servus alienus* that had been placed in charge
> and contracted the debt, *ibid.*

INTENTIO, one of the clauses of a *formula,* (which see, No. 1).

> 1. *Its purpose and position.*—It was in the *intentio* that the
> pursuer embodied his claim, G. iv, 41 ; it was so impor-
> tant that no *formula* could do without it, 44 ; where there
> was no *demonstratio* (which see) it stood first, 86, and
> with one it stood second, 47.   In *formulae in jus conceptae*
> (see *Formula,* 3) it was couched in technical words
> derived from the *jus civile,* 41, 37 ; in those *in factum* it
> was in a freer style, with which a demonstration was in
> a manner amalgamated, 46, 47.

> 2. *Styles.*—(a) *Rei vindicatio*—' *si paret hominem ex jure Qui-
> ritium actoris esse,*' G. iv, 41 : (b) vindication of a thing *pro
> indiviso* (preceded by a *demonstratio*)—' *quantam partem
> paret in eo fundo, quo de agitur, actoris esse,*' G. iv, 54 :
> (c) *condictio certi* (applicable to claim on loan of money,
> stipulatory promise for a definite sum, literal obligation,
> *indebitum,* etc.)—' *si paret reum actori X milia dare opor-
> tere,*' G. iii, 91, iv, 4, 41, 86, etc. : (d) *actiones incertae*
> (preceded by a *demonstratio*)—' *quidquid paret ob eam rem
> reum actori dare facere oportere,*' or ' *quidquid ob eam rem
> reum actori dare facere oportet,*' G. iv, 41, 47, 54, 60,
> 131, 131a, 136, applicable to claims on *bonae fidei* con-
> tracts, indefinite claims under stipulations, etc. : (e) *for-
> mulae in factum conceptae*—' *si paret patronum* (actorem) *a
> liberto* (reo) *contra edictum praetoris in jus vocatum esse,*'
> G. iv, 46 ; ' *si paret actorem apud reum mensam deposu-
> isse, eamque dolo malo rei actori redditam non esse,*' 47.
> But these styles, and many others given by Gai., are
> skeletons merely ; what was vindicated in real actions
> had to be properly described, G. iv, 41, note 2, as amended
> in *Additions etc.* ; and in personal ones the ground of
> claim,—testament, stipulation, or what not, to be ex-
> plained, 55.   In *bonae fidei judicia* (which see) the words
> *ex fide bona* were introduced, G. iv, 47.   When the
> action was by an *argentarius* against a customer, he had
> to set off in the *intentio* any counter-claim of the latter's
> of the same description as that sued upon, (see *Compen-
> sation.* 3)—' *si paret reum actori X milia dare oportere
> amplius quam ipse actor reo debet,*' G. iv, 64.

> 3. *Consequences of claiming too much, too little, or under a wrong
> description.*—If in his *intentio* a man claimed more than

INTENTIO—*continued.*

he was entitled to—which, however, was impossible in those that were *incertae*, G. iv, 54—he lost his cause, no matter how good it might be for less, 53, 60, 68, and could not be reinstated so as to sue afresh except on the ground of minority, 53 and n. 2, (see *In integr. restitutio*). To claim less than he was entitled to was of course lawful; but he could not sue for the residue within the same praetorship, 56. To claim one thing instead of another, or wrongly to describe the source of claim, as *e.g.* testament instead of contract, did not prevent a fresh action at any time, 55.

INTERDICTIO AQUA ET IGNI, practically outlawry, G. i, 128 and n. 2, 161, U. x, 3, xi, 12; see *Citizenship*, 9.

INTERDICTION OF PRODIGALS, G. i, 53, U. xii, 23, xx, 13; see *Curatory*, 1.

INTERDICTS, *interdicta*, G. iv, 138-170a.

I. NATURE AND CLASSIFICATIONS.

1. *Interdict, what ?*—It was an order pronounced by a magistrate, on application of an individual, to facilitate the settlement of some dispute, 139; when put positively it was specifically a decree (*decretum*), the name of interdict being more appropriate to one put negatively, 140.

2. *Restitutory, exhibitory, and prohibitory interdicts.*—They were called restitutory when the order was to restore a thing, exhibitory when the order was for production, prohibitory when something was prohibited, 140, 142.

3. *Possessory interdicts.*—A large class of them were either *adipiscendae vel retinendae vel reciperandae possessionis causa comparata*, according as their purpose was the acquisition, retention, or recovery of possession, 143.

4. *Interdicts single and double.*—They were said to be single (*simplicia*) when the applicant became pursuer in the proceedings that followed the order, and his adversary defender, 157, as in all the restitutory and exhibitory and most of the prohibitory interdicts, 159, 158; double (*duplicia*) when each party was at once pursuer and defender, as in *uti possidetis* and *utrubi*, for retaining possession, 160.

II. THE POSSESSORY INTERDICTS IN PARTICULAR.

5. *Those* adipiscendae possessionis causa comparata.—They were so called because they were of service only to an individual who had not yet obtained possession at all, 144. The principal were the *int. quorum bonorum* at the instance of a *bonor. possessor* (see *Bonor. possessio*, 5), to enable him to obtain things belonging to the inheritance

INTERDICTS—*continued.*

II. THE POSSESSORY INTERDICTS IN PARTICULAR—*continued.*

from any one retaining them either as heir (*pro herede*) or without any pretence of title (*pro possessore*), *ibid.*; the *int. possessorium* at the instance of a *bonor. emptor* (see *Emptio bonor.*), and the *int. sectorium* at the instance of a *bonor. sector* or purchaser of a confiscated estate,—both for the same purpose as the *quor. bonor.*, 145, 146; and the *int. Salvianum* to enable a landlord to obtain possession of effects of his farm-tenant's hypothecated for the rent, 147.

6. *Those* retinendae possessionis causa comparata.—These, viz. *uti possidetis* and *utrubi*, were to enable a man to keep possession which was being disturbed, and are said to have been introduced as ancillary to a litigation about ownership, and for the purpose of deciding which party was to stand pursuer, which defender, in the *vindicatio*, 148.

7. *The* int. uti possidetis.—This was employed in reference to immoveables, 149; it was addressed equally to both parties, forbidding both to use any force, *vis*, to disturb the existing state of possession, 160; and he eventually prevailed who proved that he was actually in possession at the moment of the interdict, and had not taken it vitiously from his adversary, *i.e.* either forcibly, stealthily, or by refusal to vacate on recal of a grant during pleasure (*precario*), 150.

8. *The* int. utrubi.—This was used when the dispute was about moveables, 149; it also was addressed to both parties, who were both prohibited forcibly interfering with the possession of that one of them—which? was to be afterwards ascertained—who had been in possession for a longer period during the praetorian year than his adversary, 160, 150, 152, and note in *Additions etc.*, and that without vitious exclusion of the latter, 150; and if his own possession was non-vitious, either party was entitled to add to it the rightful possession of any one from whom he had justly acquired it, 151, (see *Accessio temporis*). In both interdicts the possession founded on might be that of a representative, or even one retained without occupancy, by mere effort of will, 153, (see *Possession*).

9. *The* int. unde vi.—For recovering possession that had been lost the *int. unde vi* was employed, 154; its purpose being the reinstatement of a party who had been forcibly ejected from his land or house, *ibid.*, but provided always he had not himself in the first instance taken the possession vitiously from the ejector, *ibid.* In the ordinary

INTERDICTS—*continued.*

  II. THE POSSESSORY INTERDICTS IN PARTICULAR—*continued.*
    case it was lawful to use force to eject a vitious possessor, *ibid.*, so long as it was not force of arms, 155 ; for then, as a punishment of the offence, the ejector was invariably compelled to restore the possession, *ibid.*

  III. PROCEDURE IN SINGLE INTERDICTS.
    10. *Alternative courses open to defender.*—The pronouncing of the interdict was but the first step in the procedure, 141 ; the next was to remit it for trial on the merits, *ibid.* In prohibitory interdicts there was but one course—to interchange penal sponsions, adjust a *formula* upon them, and send it to a *judex, ibid. ;* but in restitutory and exhibitory ones the defender might demand a less hazardous *arbitraria formula* and a remit to an arbiter, *ibid.*, which was always granted if the demand was made at once, and before he had left the presence of the magistrate who had pronounced the interdict, 164.
    11. *Procedure by arbitrary* formula.—If the defender elected this procedure, the arbiter had to decide whether there were grounds to justify the interdict, 163 ; if he found there were, he ordered compliance, *ibid. ;* if the defender obeyed, he was at once acquitted, *ibid. ;* but if he refused to restore or exhibit he was condemned in damages, *ibid.*
    12. *Procedure when defender declined reference to an arbiter.*—If the defender had not demanded an arbitrary formula, and yet failed to restore or exhibit, the pursuer challenged him with a sponsion, to which he replied with a restipulation (see *Sponsio et restipulatio*) on the question whether there had been breach of interdict, 165 ; on the sponsion and restipulation *formulae* were adjusted, the pursuer getting added to his a remit to the *judex* on the question whether the interdict was justifiable, *ibid. ;* if on both issues the judge found for the pursuer, and the defender still refused to restore or exhibit, the latter was condemned not merely in damages but in the amount of the sponsion, *ibid.* and correction in *Additions etc. ;* what happened if the finding was for the defender, or if, being against him, he obeyed the judge's order, does not appear, the MS. being illegible, *ibid.*, note 2.

  IV. PROCEDURE IN THE DOUBLE INTERDICTS.
    13. *First step—each offered violence to the other.*—The beginning of Gaius' account of the procedure in the double interdicts is illegible, 166, note ; but, from an observation in § 170, it appears that, as the interdict was equally addressed to both parties, each at once contravened its prohibition by

INTERDICTS—*continued.*
   IV. PROCEDURE IN THE DOUBLE INTERDICTS—*continued.*
        offering pretence of violence (*vis moribus facta, vis ex conventu*) to the other, so as thus to raise the question which of them had in fact committed breach of interdict by doing violence to the party truly in possession,—a circuitous way of determining who was possessor when the interdict was pronounced, 166, note, as amended in *Additions etc.*

    14. *Second step—the* fructus licitatio *and award of interim possession.*—The praetor then assigned the interim enjoyment of the fruits and profits to the highest bidder, 166, who gave security for payment to his adversary of the sum bid—which was regarded not as price but as penalty, 167—in the event of the latter being ultimately successful, 166.

    15. *Third step—the* sponsiones *and* formulae.—Next, each challenged the other to a sponsion on the question whether he had committed breach of interdict, and each restipulated, (see *Sponsio et restipulatio*), 166 ; and upon the sponsions and restipulations *formulae* were adjusted and sent to a *judex*, 166a.

    16. *The* judicia *and their results.*—If judgment was for the party who had succeeded in the *fructus licitatio* (the bidding), his adversary had to pay only the amount of the sponsion and restipulation, 168 : if against him, he had to pay to his adversary the amount of the sponsion and restipulation, and the sum bid for the interim enjoyment, and return the fruits drawn or their value, 166a, 167 ; and if thereupon the possession was not also yielded up, the adversary might recover damages in a *judicium secutorium*, or after process, known as the *judicium Cascellianum*, 166a. But the successful party might, if he pleased, disregard the *fructuaria stipulatio*, *i.e.* the engagement for payment of the amount of the *fructus licitatio*, and have a separate action in reference to the fruits, known as the *judicium fructuarium*, 169.

    17. *The secondary interdict.*—It sometimes happened that the procedure could not thus be explicated, owing to the refusal of one of the parties to offer pretence of violence, bid for the interim enjoyment of fruits, etc. ; he was in such a case assumed to be in the wrong, and by an *interdictum secundarium* required, if he had it, to restore the possession to his adversary, if otherwise, to abstain from disturbing him, 170.

INTERESSE, *quanti mea interest*, damages, G. iii, 161.

INTEREST, *usurae,* and fruits and profits were due on a *fideicommis-sum* if debtor *in mora,* but not on legacies, except those left *sinendi modo,* G. ii, 280 and note.

INTERPRETATIO PONTIFICIUM, G. ii, 42, note; see *Jus Romanorum.*

INTESTATE SUCCESSION (to freeborn citizens), G. iii, 1-38, U. xxvi, xxviii, 7-9; see also SUCCESSION, HEREDITAS, BONORUM POSSESSIO. For succession to freedmen, see *Succession to cit. freedmen, Succession to Junian latins.*

I. INTESTACY GENERALLY.

1. *When it arose.* —There was intestacy not only when a man had died without a testament, but even when he had made one if it turned out inoperative, G. iii, 13. And this might be due to irregularity in its execution, omission to institute or disinherit *filii sui,* or to its subsequent invalidation, G. ii, 138-146, U. xxiii, 2-4, (see *Testament,* II., IV.); or else to the death of a sole heir during the testator's lifetime or before entry, his loss of *testamenti factio* and consequent incapacity to take, non-fulfilment of the condition under which he was instituted, expiry of the period of cretion without cerniture, or his exclusion by the Julian law on the ground of celibacy, G. ii, 144.

2. *Difference between the civil and praetorian rules.*—In all the above cases there was intestacy by the *jus civile;* but where it was due neither to the entire absence of a testament, omission to institute *filii sui,* nor failure of heirs *ex testamento,* but to irregularity in point of form or the subsequent occurrence of something that invalidated it, the praetors gave the *heredes scripti* possession of the estate according to the tenor of the deed, and disregarded the civil intestacy. See *Bonorum possessio,* 10-12.

II. THE INTESTATE SUCCESSION OF THE TWELVE TABLES.

3. *First to* sui heredes.—*Sui heredes* took first, G. iii, 1, U. xxvi, 1; *i.e.* descendants *in potestate,* whether natural or adoptive, who became *sui juris* by their parent's death, G. iii, 2; wife *in manu,* and daughter-in-law *in manu* of a son not *in potestate,* 3; *postumi* (which see), who would have been *in potestate* had they been born during the parent's life, 4; children on whose behalf cause had been proved (see *Causae prob. ex l. Aelia Sentia, Erroris causae probatio*) after their parent's death, 5; and sons manumitted from a first or second mancipation (see *Emancipation,* 3), 6. All of these, who did not on the death of the intestate pass into another person's *potestas,* participated in the *hereditas* no matter of what degree of relationship, G. iii, 7, U. xxvi, 2; the division being *in stirpes, i.e.* by branches and not by heads, G. iii, 8, U. xxvi, 2.

33

INTESTATE SUCCESSION—*continued.*
　II. THE INTESTATE SUCCESSION OF THE TWELVE TABLES—*continued.*
　　4. *Next to agnates.*—Ulp. says that failing *sui* the inheritance passed to consanguineans, *i.e.* the intestate's brothers and sisters by the same father, and in the third place to agnates, U. xxvi, 1; but consanguineans were just agnates of the first class, and Gai. includes them under that name, G. iii, 9. The justification of Ulpian's distinction may be this,—that in the class of consanguineans both males and females were entitled to succeed, whereas beyond it, in what he calls the class of agnates, females had no right of succession, G. iii, 14, U. xxvi, 6. (Agnate defined in G. i, 156, iii, 10, U. xi, 4, xxvi, 1; see *Agnation*, 1.) Only those were entitled to take who were nearest of degree when the fact of intestacy was ascertained, G. iii, 11, 13; if they declined, the inheritance did not pass to those of the next degree, G. iii, 12, U. xxvi, 5, there being no succession of degrees for agnates under the Tables, *ibid.*; the division therefore was *in capita*, by heads, not by branches, G. iii, 15, 16, U. xxvi, 4. But there was no room for the admission of agnates so long as there was a possibility of *sui*, as when the intestate's widow was pregnant or his son in captivity (which see), U. xxvi, 3.
　　5. *Lastly to the* gens.—Failing agnates the *hereditas* passed to the intestate's *gens*, G. iii, 17. The Tables did not (and hardly could) carry the succession any farther, 18.
　　6. *Defects of the system.*—Amongst them were these:—that it excluded emancipated children, G. iii, 19, children who had received a gift of citizenship with their deceased father, but had not at the same time been subjected to his *potestas*, 20, agnates who had undergone *capitis deminutio* even *minima* (see *Cap. dem.*, 2), 21, females more distantly related than sisters, 23, and cognates, including children in relation to their mother and *vice versa*, 24; further, that on failure of agnates of the first degree there was no devolution to those of the next, 22.
　III. THE INTESTATE SUCCESSION OF THE EDICT; see *Bonorum possessio*, IV.
　IV. LATER AMENDMENTS.
　　7. *Succession between mother and child.*—By the Twelve Tables there was no right of succession between a mother and her children, because they were only cognates; unless indeed she was or had been *in manu* of their father, and then she stood to them *sororis loco*, G. iii, 14, 24, U. xxvi, 7, note 1. The edict only partially amended the defect by recognising a right in cognates on failure of agnates,

INTESTATE SUCCESSION—*continued.*
  IV. LATER AMENDMENTS—*continued.*

        G. iii, 30, U. xxviii, 9. But by the Orphitian Sct. it was provided that the inheritance of a mother should belong to her children to the exclusion of agnates, U. xxvi, 7; and the Tertullian Sct. gave a mother who had the *jus liberorum* (which see) a right of succession to a child who was survived neither by *sui heredes*, father, nor consanguinean brother, U. xxvi, 8.

IPSO JURE and OPE EXCEPTIONIS distinguished, G. iii, 168, 181; iv, 106, 107, 116*a.*

IRRITANCY of a testament, see *Testament*, 23.

ISLAND rising in a river, to whom it belonged, G. ii, 72; see *Property*, 4.

ITALICA PRAEDIA, *solum Italicum*, land in Italy, or in those parts of the provinces that enjoyed the *jus Italicum*, (which see).

ITERATIO, one of the modes in which a latin acquired citizenship, G. i, 35, as amended in *Additions etc.*, U. iii, 1, 4; see *Junian latinity*, 7.

JAVOLENUS PRISCUS, a Sabinian, praetor in reign of Hadrian, died A.D. 138, G. iii, 70 and note, U. xi, 28.

JUDEX, office and duty of, see *Procedure*, 10.

JUDICATAE, EXCEPTIO REI, a peremptory exception alleging that the question in dispute had already been judicially determined, G. iv, 121; see *Exception*, 9, *Litis contestatio, Jud. leg.* and *imp. cont.*

JUDICATUM, judgment, entitled the judgment creditor, under the system of the *legis actiones*, to proceed against his debtor (who was spoken of as *judicatus*, G. iii, 78, iv, 21) by *manus injectio,*—arrest and imprisonment, G. iv, 21, (see *Legis actiones*, 5). In course of time this practice was abolished, and an *actio judicati* substituted against a debtor who delayed voluntarily to implement a judgment against him; like all those that replaced procedure *per manus injectionem*, it was *in duplum*, G. iv, 21, and the defender bound to give *cautio judicatum solvi*, G. iv, 25, 102; and the result of it was that the creditor had his debtor adjudged to him (*adjudicatus*) to work off his debt, G. iii, 189 and n. 2, 199 and n. 2. If, however, the debtor had funds, real execution might proceed upon the judgment, after expiry of the days of grace, by *missio in possessionem*, etc., G. iii, 78 f., (see *Emptio bonorum*).

JUDICATUM SOLVI, CAUTIO, see *Cautiones etc.*, 2, 4.

JUDICIA BONAE FIDEI, see *Bonae fidei judicia.*

JUDICIA LEGITIMA and IMPERIO CONTINENTIA, G. iv, 103-109.

  1. Judicia legitima.—Those *judicia* alone were *legitima* which

JUDICIA LEGITIMA and IMPERIO CONTINENTIA—*continued.*

were carried on (*a*) in or within a mile of Rome, (*b*) between parties who were all citizens, and (*c*) before a single *judex*, who also was a citizen, G. iv, 104, 109 ; but it was immaterial whether the ground of action arose *ex lege*, *i.e.* from statute, or from the praetor's edict, 109. By the Julian judiciary law they expired in eighteen months if judgment was not sooner pronounced, 104 and n. 1 ; and they were extinguished by *capitis deminutio*, such as *manus* or *adrogatio*, G. iii, 83. Litiscontestation in a *judicium* of this sort, if *in personam* with an *intentio in jus concepta*, (see *Formula*, 3), *ipso jure* extinguished the pursuer's right to a new action on the same grounds, G. iii, 180, 181, iv, 107 and n. 2 ; but if the *judicium* was *in rem*, or if, being *in personam*, it had an *intentio in factum concepta*, further right of action was not *ipso jure* extinguished, and an exception was necessary, G. iv, 107 and n. 3.

2. Judicia imperio continentia.—They were so called because dependent on the *imperium* and not authorised by the *jus legitimum* or *civile ;* and included all (*a*) in which any of the litigants was a peregrin, or (*b*) that were carried on at more than a mile from Rome, or (*c*) before recuperators, or (*d*) a peregrin as sole *judex*, G. iv, 105, 109 ; it being here again immaterial whether the cause of action was praetorian or statutory, 109. They lasted only during the year of office of the magistrate by which they were granted, 105 ; but, being founded not on a *civilis* but a *naturalis ratio*, G. i, 158, they do not seem to have been put an end to by *capitis deminutio* of the pursuer, G. iv, 80. For the same reason litiscontestation in them did not *ipso jure* extinguish the pursuer's right to a new action on the same grounds ; but if raised it might be defeated by *exceptio rei in judicium deductae* or *ex. rei judicatae*, G. iii, 181, iv, 106 and note.

JUDICIS POSTULATIONEM, LEGIS ACTIO PER, see *Legis actiones*, 3.

JUDICIUM, see *Actions*, 1.

JUDICIUM CALUMNIAE, see *Vexatious litigation.*

JUDICIUM CASCELLIANUM, see *Interdicts*, 16.

JUDICIUM DEDUCTAE, EXCEPTIO REI IN, a peremptory exception alleging that issue had been joined on the same question in a previous action ; it was used alternatively with and in the same cases as the *exceptio rei judicatae*, G. iii, 181, iv, 106, 107. See *Litis contestatio, Jud. legitima etc.*

JUDICIUM FRUCTUARIUM, G. iv, 69 ; see *Interdicts*, 16.

JUDICIUM SECUTORIUM, G. iv, 69 ; see *Interdicts*, 16.

JULIAN AND PAPIA-POPPAEAN LAW.

1. *History.*—The history of the statute is referred to in G. i, 145, note 1; but some only of its provisions are recorded by Gai. and Ulp.

2. *Relaxation of the* tutela mulierum.—It relieved from tutory freeborn women with three children and freedwomen with four, G. i, 145, 194, iii, 44, U. xxix, 3; and, when a woman's tutor-at-law happened to be a pupil, authorised the appointment of an Atilian tutor in his stead, to aid her in constituting a dowry, G. i, 178, U. xi, 20, (see *Tutory*, 17, 22, 24).

3. *Prohibition of certain marriages.*—It forbade senators and their children to marry their freedwomen, women connected with the stage, and prostitutes, as well as those still more disreputable characters whom no man of free birth was allowed to marry, U. xiii and notes, xvi, 2; and declared the survivor incapable of taking anything under the testament of the predeceaser, U. xvi, 2.

4. *Requirement of marriage as the general condition of taking at all under a testament.*—It made marriage the condition of taking under a testament for men under sixty and women under fifty, G. ii, 111, 144, U. xvi, 1, unless of kin to the testator within the sixth degree, U. xvi, 1, and new note in *Additions etc.*—it does not appear *from* what age upwards it was required; but a man was freed from the penalties of celibacy while absent on state service and for a year thereafter, U. xvi, 1 and n. 2, while a woman was free for two years after her husband's death and eighteen months after divorce, U. xiv and note. Though the statute did not require marriage after fifty and sixty respectively, the Pernician Sct. declared that the penalties of celibacy should adhere permanently to persons unmarried at those ages, U. xvi, 3 and note; but this was modified by a Claudian Sct., which provided that a man over sixty might still escape them by marrying a woman under fifty, U. xvi, 4. To acquire the right to take the testamentary gift, the celibate had to marry within the time of cretion (see *Cretio*, 2, *Jus capiendi*), U. xvii, 1, xxii, 3; if he did not, and he was sole heir, the result was intestacy, G. ii, 144, while, if he was only heir *ex parte* or a legatee, what he failed to take became caducous, U. xvii, 1 (see *Jus capiendi, Caducity*).

5. *Requirement of children as the condition of taking in full.*—In order to take in full under a testament, men and women over twenty-five and twenty respectively were required to have at least one child, U. xvi, 1 and note to

JULIAN AND PAPIA-POPPAEAN LAW—*continued*.

rubr. of tit. xiii, otherwise, as *orbi*, they forfeited one-half of what had been left them, G. ii, 111, 286a.

6. *Testamentary capacity of husband and wife* inter se.—It authorised the survivor of husband and wife to take a tenth of the predeceaser's estate under his testament, simply on the strength of the marriage, with addition of another tenth for each surviving child of a previous marriage, and a tenth for each child of their own—but not more than two—that, though deceased, had yet survived its name-day, U. xv, 1, 2 ; and he or she might take in addition the usufruct and in certain cases the property of a third part of the predeceaser's estate, U. xv, 3. If they had a child surviving, or had lost one after it had reached puberty, or two that had reached the age of three years, or three that had reached their name-days, or if they had a grant of the *jus liberorum*, then they were entitled to take *inter se* in full, provided their marriage was unobjectionable under the statute, U. xvi, 1, 2, 4.

7. *Rights of patrons in the inheritances of their freedmen.*—The statute augmented the rights of patrons and their male children succeeding to very wealthy freedmen, G. iii, 42 ; it required freedwomen it had released from tutory, if they made a testament, to leave their patrons a certain share of their property, 44 and note; it gave a patron's daughter who had three children right of challenge of a freedman's testament and of succession to him *ab intestato*, 46, 47 and n. 2, U. xxix, 5 ; and it gave patronesses who were mothers certain rights in the successions of their freedmen and freedwomen, G. iii, 49, 50 and notes, 52 and note, U. xxix, 6, 7, (see *Succession to citizen freedmen*).

8. *Alteration of the law of vesting.*—The enactment altered the date of vesting of unconditional legacies, and those payable at a fixed date, from the time of the testator's death to that of the opening of his testamentary writings, U. xxiv, 31, (see *Legacy*, 11).

9. *Regulation of caducity.*—Further, it introduced the doctrine of caducity,—making everything that an heir *ex parte* or a legatee failed to take under a testament a lapse, to pass to other heirs and legatees who had children, and failing them to the state, and reserving the *jus antiquum* or right of accretion only in favour of descendants and ascendants of the testator to the third degree, G. ii, 150, 206-208 ; U. i, 21, xviii, xix, 17, xxiv, 12, xxviii, 7, (see *Caducity*).

JULIANUS, SALVIUS, G. ii, 218, 280, an adherent of the Sabinian school, (see *Sabinians etc.*), and consolidator of the praetorian edict in the time of Hadrian, (see *Praetor*, 2).

JUNIAN LATINITY, G. i, 22-24, 28-35, iii, 56-73 ; U. i, 10, iii, 1-6.

1. *Definition.*—Junian latinity was the condition which the Junian law (see *L. Junia*) assigned to persons who, not being of bad character, (see *Ded. freedmen*), had been manumitted contrary to or without due observance of the requirements of the Aelia-Sentian law (which see, Nos. 2, 4); under the latter statute they were still *de jure* slaves, though protected by the praetors in the enjoyment of *de facto* freedom ; the Junian law declared that they should in future be not only *de facto* but *de jure* free, and that their condition should be similar to that of the colonial latins (see *Col. latinity*, 1); hence their name of Junian latins, G. i, 22, iii, 56, U. i, 1.

2. *How men became Junian latins.*—They became so in the first instance by manumission, (which see). If they married women of their own condition, and did not have themselves made citizens, their children were also Junian latins, U. iii, 1.

3. *Their capacity.*—A Junian latin had *commercium*, and therefore might be a party to a mancipation, U. xix, 4, and hold property on quiritarian title. He had *testamenti factio*, U. xi, 16, and therefore could act either as *familiae emptor, libripens*, or witness (see *Testament*, 3, 4), U. xx, 8. He might be instituted heir in an ordinary testament or have a legacy bequeathed to him, U. xxii, 3, though he could not take either while he continued a latin (below, No. 4); even as a latin he could take a *fideicommissum* (which see), G. i, 23, ii, 275, U. xxv, 7 ; and under a military testament (see *Testament*, 25) he could as a latin take either inheritance or bequest, G. ii, 110.

4. *Their disabilities.*—Though a Junian latin was entitled to take a citizen wife with a view to *causae probatio* (see *Aelia-Sentian law*, 6, 7), yet he had no *conubium* with her, and therefore no *potestas* over his children until cause had been proved and citizenship thereby acquired, G. i, 66, 76. The Junian law forbade him to make a testament, G. i, 23, U. xx, 14; did not allow him to be appointed a tutor under one, G. i, 23, U. xi, 16; and did not allow him to take an inheritance to which he had been instituted or a legacy bequeathed to him, G. i, 23, ii, 110, 275, U. xxv, 7, unless he converted his latinity into citizenship within a hundred days, U. xvii, 1, xxii, 3, (see *Jus capiendi*).

JUNIAN LATINITY—*continued.*

5. *Tutory of latins.*—By the Junian law male latins under puberty and females of any age were in tutelage of those who were their quiritarian owners (see *Quir. ownership*) at the time of manumission, whether those last were their manumitters or not, G. i, 167, U. xi, 19.

6. *Disposal of their estates on death.*—See *Succ. to Junian latins.*

7. *How they could become citizens.*—(*a*) By grant of citizenship in answer to a petition to the emperor, U. iii, 2. It might be given *salvo jure patroni,* which implied reservation to his manumitter of right to his estate on his death, G. iii, 72; if given without the patron's knowledge or consent, the latter's right of succession was not prejudiced, unless the latin afterwards proved cause under the Aelia-Sentian law, G. iii, 72, 73. (*b*) Proving cause under that enactment was one of the commonest modes of acquiring citizenship, G. i, 29-32*a*, and note to 29 as amended in *Additions etc.,* U. iii, 3; see *Aelia-Sentian law,* 6, 7, *Causae prob. ex l. Aelia-Sentia.* (*c*) Iteration or renewal of the manumission when it had been irregular or by a bonitarian owner only, U. iii, 4, G. i, 35, as amended in *Additions etc.* (*d*) Service in the night watch, *militia,* G. i, 32*b*, U. iii, 5. (*e*) Ship-trading, G. i, 32*c*, U. iii, 6. (*f*) House-building, G. i, 33, U. iii, 1. (*g*) Flour-milling, G. i, 34, U. iii, 1. (*h*) Lastly a freeborn latin woman acquired citizenship by giving birth to a third child, U. iii, 1.

JUPITER, inauguration as a priest of, released the flamen from the *patria potestas,* G. i, 130, U. x, 5, and that without *capitis deminutio,* G. iii, 114. A *flamen Dialis* required to be the offspring of a farreate marriage, and himself married *confarreatione,* G. i, 112. *Jupiter Farreus, ibid. ; Jupiter Tarpeius,* U. xxii, 6; *Jupiter Dapalis,* G. iv, 28 and note.

JUS had many significations, and amongst the most important those of (*a*) a system of law or jurisprudence as a whole, *e g. j. naturale,* G. ii, 65, *j. gentium,* i, 1, *j. civile, ibid., j. Quiritium,* ii, 40, *j. Romanorum,* iii, 96, *j. praetorium,* U. xxii, 24 ; (*b*) the *jus civile* as distinguished from the *jus praetorium,* e.g. *jure factum testamentum,* G. ii, 146, *ipso jure,* 198, *juris iniquitates,* iii, 25, *in jus concepta* and *juris contentio,* iv, 60 ; (*c*) a particular institution of the law in all its parts and consequences, *e.g. confarreatio,* G. i, 112, *agnatio,* 158, *postliminium,* 129 ; (*d*) a particular rule of law, as in *jura populi Rom.,* G. i, 2, *jura condere,* 7, *utimur hoc jure,* 135, *ita jus esto,* ii, 224 ; (*e*) a right or congeries of rights in the abstract, *e.g.* right

JUS—*continued*.

of succession of agnates, G. iii, 12, child's right of succession, 19, *emendi vendendique jus*, U. xix, 5; (*f*) a right in the concrete, *e.g. male nostro juri uti non debemus*, G. i, 53, *pristina jura recipiunt*, 129, *jus eundi agendi*, iv, 3; (*g*) the presence of a magistrate, *e.g. in jure cessio*, ii, 24, *in jure vindicare*, iv, 16, *in jus vocare*, 183.

JUS ANTIQUUM used by Ulp. to denote the old *jus adcrescendi* or right of accretion, whereby, on one of several testamentary heirs failing, the others took his share *pro rata*, U. i, 21 and n. 3, (see *Adcretio*, 2). It was displaced by the Julian and Pap. Popp. law, except in favour of certain near kinsmen of the testator's, *ibid.*, U. tit. xviii; and the exception was retained in Caracalla's enactment giving *caduca* to the fisc, U. xvii, 2, (see *Caducity*, 3, 5).

JUS BELLI, G. iii, 94.

JUS CAPIENDI, the right of an instituted heir or of a legatee to take the testamentary gift. By the Junian law a latin could not take unless he became a citizen within a hundred days, G. i, 23, U. xvii, 1, xxii, 3. By the Julian law a *caelebs* could not take at all unless he married within the same period, U. xvii, 1, xxii, 3; but it is not said that the *orbus*, who was allowed to take only one-half of what was left him, G. ii, 286a, was relieved from his disability by birth of a child to him within the same period.

JUS CIVILE is never employed to denote the law of Rome as a whole, the *jus Romanorum*, (which see); but in the texts signifies either (*a*) that part of it which was peculiarly Roman, as distinguished from the *jus gentium* or *naturale*, G. i, 1, ii, 65; or (*b*) that which was the result of old tradition, the XII Tables and their interpretation, and the legislation of the republic, as distinguished (*a*) from that derived from the praetor's edicts, ii, 115 and 116, 136, iii, 71, U. xxii, 23, xxiii, 6, and (*β*) that due to the legislation of the empire, G. ii, 197, 255, U. xxii, 19, xxiv, 11a.

JUS EDICENDI, G. i, 6; see *Praetor*, 1, 2.

JUS GENTIUM, G. i, 1, 52, 82, 86, iii, 93, 132; see also *Peregrinity*.

JUS ITALICUM was a special concession to certain districts in the provinces, one of its features being that lands situate within them might be held in property by private individuals, and that on quiritarian title, as if they had been within the bounds of Italy, G. i, 120, note 2. Lands so privileged, equally with those in Italy, were called *praedia italica*, G. i, 120, *praedia in italica solo*, U. xix, 1; they were *res mancipi*, *ibid.*, and might be conveyed either by *mancipatio* or *in jure cessio*, G. ii, 31.

JUSJURANDUM, a form of contracting that was almost out of date in
the time of Gai., G. iii, 89, note, surviving only in the
jurata promissio operarum liberti, 96*a* ; but there were
features about the *sponsio* that seem to indicate that with
the *jusjurandum* it had originally a close connection, 92,
note.

JUSJURANDUM CALUMNIAE, oath of calumny, G. iv, 175, 176 ; see
Vexatious litigation.

JUS LATII, see *Colonial latinity*, 2.

JUS LIBERORUM.—Statute, and especially the Julian and Pap. Popp.
law, made paternity and maternity the condition of
various rights, privileges, and immunities. To be a
parent of children was the necessary qualification of the
Julian law for taking in full under a testament, G. ii,
286*a*, and qualified in addition for appropriating the
caduciary lapses of those who were less fortunate, G. ii,
206, 207, 286*a*, U. i, 21 ; and by the same law maternity
greatly augmented the rights of a patroness in the successions of her freedmen and freedwomen, testate and
intestate, G. iii, 44-47, 50, 52, U. xxix, 3-7. To be the
mother of three or four children, in the case of *ingenuae*
and *libertae* respectively, entitled a woman to succeed
under the Tertullian Sct. to an intestate son or daughter,
U. xxvi, 8. By the Julian law three or four children
respectively released an *ingenua* or a *liberta* from tutory,
G. i, 145, 194, iii, 44, U. xxix, 3 ; and by an unknown
senatusconsult a freeborn latin woman became a citizen
on giving birth to her third child, U. iii, 1. The *jus liberorum*—that at least which qualified for taking under a
testament—might be conferred by the emperor even in
absence of children, U. xvi, 1*a*.

JUS NATURALE, G. i, 156, ii, 65, 70, 73 ; see also *Naturalis ratio.*

JUS POSTLIMINII, the rule whereby a citizen who had been taken
captive by an enemy reacquired all his old rights on recrossing the frontier, G. i, 129, 187, U. x, 4, xxiii, 5 ; see
Captivity apud hostes.

JUS QUIRITIUM, either the aggregate of rights peculiar to a citizen,
and then synonymous with *civitas*, G. i, 32*c*, 33-35, U.
iii, 1, (see *Citizenship*) ; or a citizen's tenure of property
(*ex jure Quir. dominus, alicujus esse ex jure Quir.*) before
in bonis habere was known, and as distinguished from it
afterwards, G. ii, 40, etc., (see *Quiritarian ownership*).

JUS ROMANORUM.—The phrase was not common, being used only
for the purpose of distinguishing between it and a foreign
system, as in G. iii, 96*a*. That of Rome was composed
partly of institutions and doctrines peculiar to it, its *jus*

Jus Romanorum—*continued.*

civile, and partly of what were common to all nations,—institutions and doctrines of the *jus gentium,* G. i, 1. Some of it was introduced tacitly, (see *Custom*), *ibid.,* G. iii, 82, U. i, 4; much of it resulted from legislation, in the shape either of *leges,* plebiscits, senatusconsults, or imperial constitutions, (see *Statute,* 1), G. i, 2, severally described in 3-5; and of some importance, as an element in the *jus civile* proper was the *interpretatio* of the old statutory law, especially the XII Tables, by the pontiffs and early jurists, G. i, 165, ii, 42, note, iv, 30. Next to statute the edicts of the magistrates, and particularly the praetors, were the largest factor in the law, (see *Praetor,* 2), G. i, 6; and contributed to remove many of the *iniquitates juris civilis,*—doctrines of the earlier system that were inequitable when tested by *naturalis ratio,* G. iii, 25. Another factor was the *Responsa prudentium* in the early empire,—written opinions by jurists of eminence on whom the emperor had conferred the *jus respondendi,* in answer to questions submitted to them by *judices* (who were private citizens, mostly unlearned in the law), and which in many cases had the authority of statute, G. i, 7.

Justae nuptiae, justum matrimonium, see *Marriage,* 1.

Labeo, M. Antistius, founder of the Proculian school, a political opponent of Augustus, whose offer of the consulate he declined, G. i, 96, note 1, 135, 138, ii, 231, iii, 140, 183, iv, 59; see *Sabinians and Proculians.*

Lanx et linteum, G. iii, 192 and n. 2, 193; see *Theft,* 5.

Latin language necessary in a *sponsio* proper, G. iii, 93; also in a legacy, G. ii, 281, U. xxv, 9; though not in a *fideicommissum, ibid.*

Latins,—those of Italy and the *lex Minicia,* G. i, 79; colonial, see *Colon. latinity;* Junian, see *Jun. latinity.*

Latium, another name for the *jus Latii,* a pathway to citizenship for colonial latins, G. i, 95; *majus* and *minus Latium* distinguished, 96 and notes. See *Colonial latinity,* 2.

Law, Roman, its sources and channels, G. i, 2-7; see *Jus Romanorum.*

Law, foreign, see *Foreign law.*

Legacy, *legatum,* G. ii, 191-245; U. tit. xxiv; see also Testament, III.

   I. General doctrines regarding legacies.
      1. *Meaning of* legatum.—A legacy, *legatum,* was a testamentary bequest in imperative words, *lege,* U. xxiv, 1, and required to be in the latin language, G. ii, 281, U. xxv, 9.

LEGACY—*continued.*

  I. GENERAL DOCTRINES REGARDING LEGACIES—*continued.*

    2. *Deed in which it might be bequeathed.*—It might be left either in a testament, U. xxiv, 1, or in a codicil confirmed by testament (see *Codicil*), G. ii, 270*a*, though not in one that was unconfirmed, *ibid.*, U. xxv, 8.

    3. *On whom it could be charged.*—It was in every case a charge upon the instituted heir, U. xxiv, 21,—so much so that if he was a *filiusfamilias* or a slave it could not be charged upon his *paterfamilias* or owner, U. xxv, 10; to charge it upon a legatee was impossible, G. ii, 271, U. xxiv, 20; to charge it upon the heir's heir was equally so, G. ii, 232, U. xxiv, 16, xxv, 8; and so entirely was it dependent on the institution that if it stood in the testament before the latter it was useless, G. ii, 229, U. xxiv, 15, xxv, 8.

    4. *To whom it might be left.*—The legatee was necessarily another person than the heir, U. xxiv, 22, except in *legatum per praeceptionem* (below, No. 28). But he might be either a person *sui juris*, or a stranger *alieni juris*, in which case he acquired for him to whom he was subject, G. ii, 87, U. xix, 19.

    5. *Legacy to a person* in potestate *of the heir, and* vice versa.—It might be left conditionally to some one *in potestate* of the heir, and then its eventual efficacy depended on the consideration whether or not the legatee was still in the heir's *potestas* at the time of vesting (see below, No. 11), G. ii, 244, U. xxiv, 23; if left to the *paterfamilias* or owner of an instituted *filiusfamilias* or slave, similar considerations, according to Gai., came into view, G. ii, 245, while Ulp. held the legacy invalid, U. xxiv, 24.

    6. *Legacy to an* incerta persona.—Though a legacy to an *incerta persona* was declared useless unless *sub certa demonstratione, i.e.* under limitation to a specified class, G. ii, 238, U. xxiv, 18, and in particular could not be left to a *postumus alienus*, G. ii, 241, 287, because he was *incerta persona*, 242, yet by statute it might be bequeathed to a municipality, U. xxiv, 8, which nevertheless, as *incerta persona*, could not be instituted heir, xxii, 5, except by one of its freedmen.

    7. *Legacy to a peregrin or Junian latin.*—A legacy to a peregrin was useless, G. ii, 284, 285; Gai. and Ulp. both say that a Junian latin could not take one, G. ii, 275, U. xxv, 7; but this refers to his *jus capiendi*,—a legacy to him was *ab initio* valid, but he had to convert his latinity into citizenship before he could take it, U. xvii, 1.

LEGACY—*continued.*
I. GENERAL DOCTRINES REGARDING LEGACIES—*continued.*

8. *What might be legated.*—A bequest might be of a share of the hereditary estate, *partitio, legatum partitionis,* G. ii, 254, U. xxiv, 25, in which case the relations between heir and legatee were adjusted by *stipulationes partis et pro parte,* G. ii, 254, U. xxv, 15; or of one or more *res singulae,* U. xxiv, 25; or of a choice of things, *optio legata,* the selection lying with heir or legatee according as the bequest was by vindication or damnation (see below, Nos. 18, 22), U. xxiv, 14; or of a usufruct or quasi-usufruct, U. xxiv, 26, 27.

9. *Effects of adjuncts in the words of bequest.*—An inaccurate description of the thing legated, or a mistake as to the cause of granting, did not effect the validity of a bequest, U. xxiv, 19; an impossible condition nullified it according to the Sabinians, but according to the Proculians was to be held unwritten, G. iii, 98; all admitted that if a bequest was left by way of penalty, *i.e.* to coerce the heir to do something, it was void, G. ii, 235, U. xxiv, 17.

10. *Ademtion.*—Ademtion might take place either in the testament itself or in a codicil confirmed by it, U. xxiv, 29; but the same form required to be observed as in the bequest, *ibid.* and n. 1.

11. *Vesting.*—If a legacy was unconditional, or unqualified in point of time, it vested according to the old law on the testator's death, but by the Julian and Papia-Poppaean law only on the opening of the testament, U. xxiv, 31; if conditional—and a *dies incertus* was regarded in testamentary law as a condition, note 1 to U. xxiv, 30, 31—it did not vest until the condition was fulfilled, U. xxiv, 31; if the legatee had not survived the vesting, his heirs had no right to it, U. xxiv, 30, and it became a lapse (see *Caducity*), U. xvii, 1.

12. *The* Regula Catoniana.—It was a general rule in judging of the validity of a legacy—the *Regula Catoniana*—that, if it would have been useless had the testator died the moment after executing his testament, it could not be cured by subsequent change of circumstances, G. ii, 244.

II. RESTRICTIONS ON INORDINATE BEQUEST.

13. *Consequences of the perfect freedom of the Twelve Tables.*—The Twelve Tables having given testators unlimited freedom of bequest, they often left so much to legatees that there remained little or nothing for the heir; who consequently declined to enter, thus causing intestacy and disappointing the legatees, G. ii, 224.

LEGACY—*continued.*

   II. Restrictions on inordinate bequest—*continued.*

     14. *Restrictions of the Furian law.*—To remedy the mischief
the Furian testamentary law forbade legatees, with certain exceptions, to take more than 1000 *asses* of bequest,
under serious penalties for contravention, G. ii, 225, U. i, 2.

     15. *The Voconian law.*—This law afterwards provided that no
one should take as legacy more than remained to the
heir or heirs, G. ii, 226.

     16. *The Falcidian law.*—The Furian and Voconian laws having
both failed to accomplish their purpose, the Falcidian
law enacted that a testator should not legate more than
three-fourths of his estate, so that thus at least a fourth
might always remain to the heir, G. ii, 227, U. xxiv, 32.

   III. The forms of legacy and their peculiarities.

     17. *The different forms of legacy.*—There were four forms of
legating,—vindication, damnation, permission (*leg. sinendi
modo*), and preception, G. ii, 192, U. xxiv, 2.

     18. *Legacy by vindication.*—A legacy by vindication—of which
see styles in G. ii, 193, U. xxiv, 3—was so called because
it became the quiritarian property of the legatee, with
right to sue for it by *rei vindicatio*, the moment the heir
entered, G. ii, 194; although there was a controversy
whether the property could thus pass to him against his
will, 195, which seems eventually to have been settled in
the negative, *ibid.*

     19. *What could be thus legated.*—In strictness only those things
could be thus legated which belonged to the testator in
quiritary right both at the date of his will and at that
of his death, G. ii, 196, U. xxiv, 7, unless they were
fungibles, and then it was enough that they were his at
the latter date, *ibid.*

     20. *Effect of the Neronian Sct.*—By the Neronian Sct. it was
declared that where a legacy was invalid in the form in
which it was bequeathed, it should be regarded as if left
optimo jure, i.e. by damnation, G. ii, 197, 218, U. xxiv,
11a; in virtue of this provision a legacy *per vindicationem* of what was only *in bonis* of the testator, or even
of a *res aliena*, was sustained as effectual, *ibid.*

     21. *Whose was the property of a conditional legacy in this form*
pendente condicione ?—This was a disputed question, G.
ii, 200; as also who was owner of an unconditional one
before its acceptance, *ibid.*

     22. *Legacy by damnation.*—A legacy by damnation, G. ii,
201, note 1—styles in 201, U. xxiv, 4—was one in which
the testator imposed an obligation on his heir to give

LEGACY—*continued.*

III. THE FORMS OF LEGACY, etc.—*continued.*

to the legatee the thing bequeathed, *ibid.*, and which
afforded the latter a personal claim against the heir, but
no real right in the object of bequest, G. ii, 204.

23. *What might thus be legated.*—As the legatee got no real
right there was nothing to prevent a testator legating in
this way anything whatever that was *in commercio*, U.
xxiv, 8, 9, even a *res futura*, G. ii, 203, or a *res aliena*,
202; and in the latter case the heir was bound to acquire
and transfer it, or else pay its value to the legatee, *ibid.*,
even though its owner refused to part with it, 262.

24. *Further peculiarities.*—There were these further peculiarities in a legacy by damnation,—that if the thing
bequeathed was money, and the legatee wished to release
the heir without actual payment, he had to do so *per aes
et libram*, G. iii, 175 and note 3; that if paid by mistake,
when in fact not due, the heir had no *condictio indebiti*,
G. ii, 283,—though Ulp. states the rule as applying to
legacies generally, xxiv, 33; and that, if the legacy was
definite and the heir disputed it and rendered action
necessary, he was condemned *in duplum* (see *Cretio litis
infitiatione*), G. ii, 282, iv, 9, 171.

25. *Legacy* sinendi modo.—A legacy by permission—style, G. ii,
209, U. xxiv, 5—was one in which the heir was required
to ' allow the legatee to take ' what was bequeathed, *ibid.*

26. *What might be thus bequeathed.*—Such things might be
thus legated as belonged either to the testator himself or
to his heir, G. ii, 210, U. xxiv, 10; but even what had
never belonged to the testator, and had not become the
heir's until after the testator's death, might be claimed by
the legatee in virtue of the Neronian Sct., G. ii, 212.

27. *How far did it impose obligation on the heir ?*—The
legatee's action was only a personal one, directed against
the heir, G. ii, 213; and though Gai. says some were of
opinion that the heir was not bound to convey the object
of the bequest, but merely to ' allow the legatee to take '
it, 214, this view is inconsistent with the fact that interest was due on a legacy *sinendi modo* if the heir was
in mora, 280.

28. *Legacy by preception.*—A legacy by preception—style, G.
ii, 216, U. xxiv, 6—could in strictness be bequeathed
only to one of several heirs, G. ii, 217, who was thereby
authorised to take and appropriate some particular item
of the inheritance before it came to be divided; consequently, with a single exception, 220, only such things

LEGACY—*continued.*

 III. THE FORMS OF LEGACY, etc.—*continued.*

 as belonged to the testator himself in quiritary right could thus be bequeathed, *ibid.*, U. xxiv, 11, (though if a *res aliena* the bequest would still be valid under the Neronian Sct., G. ii, 220), and the legacy was recoverable in an action for division of the inheritance, 219.

29. *The Proculian view of it.*—Such was the Sabinian view, though not universally accepted, G. ii, 218; that of the other school was that a legacy left in this way to a stranger was to be regarded as one by vindication, and to be subject to the same rules, 221, 222.

30. *Conjoint and disjoint legacies to two or more legatees.*—The same thing might be legated to two or more legatees either conjointly or disjointly,— conjointly when their names were coupled in one and the same bequest, disjointly when there was a separate bequest, though of the same thing, to each, G. ii, 199.

31. *Their effect at common law when left by vindication.*—In a legacy to two or more by vindication, whether conjoint or disjoint, the rule of the common law was that each was entitled to a share, that of him who failed accruing to those who took, G. ii, 199.

32. *When left by damnation.*—In one by damnation the rule differed according as it was conjoint or disjoint : if conjoint, a share was due to each, and that of one who failed remained in the inheritance; if disjoint, the whole was due to each, *i.e.* the thing itself went to one, each of the others being entitled to its equivalent in money, G. ii, 205.

33. *When left by permission or preception.*—According to some the rule was the same in a legacy *sinendi modo ;* while others held that the heir's obligation was exhausted when he had allowed any one of them to take, G. ii, 215. In a joint legacy by preception the rule was the same as in one by vindication, 223.

34. *Papian modifications.*—Such was the common law; but it was considerably modified by the provisions of the Julian and Papia-Poppaean law as to lapses (see *Caducity*, 3), G. ii, 206-208.

LEGARE, probable etymology, G. ii, 104, note 8.

LEGES.—The following *leges* and *plebiscita*—for the distinction was not observed in their names—are mentioned in the text and notes, (those referred to only in the latter being marked with an asterisk):—

 L. Aebutia, about the year 507 | 247, introducing the system

LEGES—*continued*.

of procedure *per formulas*, G. iv, 30 and n. 1. See *Procedure*, 2.

L. *Aelia Sentia*, A.D. 4, regulating manumissions, G. i, 13 and n. 1, 18, 21 (?), 21a (?), 22 (?), 27, 29, 31, 37, 38, 40, 47, 66, 68, 70, 71, 80, 139; iii, 5, 73, 74, 75; U. i, 1 (?), 11-15, vii, 4. See *Aelia-Sentian law*.

L. *Apuleia*, date uncertain, ameliorating the position of sureties, G. iii, 122 and note. See *Suretyship*, 3.

L. *Aquilia*, probably 467 | 287, giving action for wrongful damage to property, G. iii, 202, 210 and note, 211-219; iv, 9, 37, 76, 109. See *Wrongful damage to property*.

L. *Atilia*, date uncertain, but before 568 | 186, empowering magistrates in Rome to appoint tutors, G. i, 185 and n. 1, 195, 195b; U. xi, 18. See *Tutory*, 4, 13, 22.

* L. *Atinia*, 557 | 197 (?), prohibiting usucapion of *res furtivae*, G. ii, 45, note 1. See *Usucapion*, 5.

L. *Bithynorum*, a local statute on tutory of women, G. i, 193.

L. *Calpurnia*, date uncertain, extending the *legis actio per conditionem* to *omnis res certa*, G. iv, 19 and note. See *Legis actiones*, 4.

* L. *Canuleia*, 309 | 445, repealing prohibition of intermarriage of patricians and plebeians, G. i, 3, note 2.

L. *Cicereia*, probably 581 | 173, imposing certain duties upon creditors accepting sureties from their debtors, G. iii, 123. See *Suretyship*, 3.

L. *Cincia*, 550 | 204, prohibiting inordinate donations, U. i, 1 and note; G. iii, 121, note.

L. *Claudia*, A.D. 47, abolishing the agnatic tutory of women; probably a senatusconsult, G. i, 157 and n. 1, 171; U. xi, 8. See *Tutory*, 2.

* L. *Coloniae Juliae Genetivae*, Julius Caesar's charter to a latin colony in southern Spain, G. i, 22, note 1, iii, 78, note 2.

L. *Cornelia* (*de sicariis ?*), G. i, 128 and n. 1.

L. *Cornelia* (*de sponsu*), date uncertain, in favour of sureties, G. iii, 124 and note. See *Suretyship*, 3.

L. *Cornelia* (*de captivis*), date uncertain, enacting that if a citizen died in captivity, a testament made before his capture should still be valid, U. xxiii, 5. See *Captivity apud hostes*.

L. *Creperia* (?), date uncertain, fixing the amount of the *sponsio* in centumviral causes at 125 sesterces, G. iv, 95 and n. 4. See *Legis actiones*, 2.

* L. *de imperio Vespasiani*, G. i, 5, note 2.

L. *Duodecim Tabularum*. See *Twelve Tables*.

L. *Falcidia*, 714 | 40, empowering a testamentary heir to retain

34

ES—*continued.*

Additions etc., 80, 167; ii, 110, 275; iii, 56, 57, 70; U. i, 10; iii, 3; xi, 16, 19; xx, 14; xxii, 3. See *Junian latinity.*

L. *Junia Vellaea,* date uncertain, on testamentary institution and disherison, G. ii, 134 and n. 1, as amended in *Additions etc.;* U. xxii, 19.

* *Leges Liciniae,* 387 | 367, *inter alia* opening consulate to plebeians, G. i, 6, note 1.

* L. *Malacitana,* Domitian's charter to the *municipium* of Malaga, G. i, 22, note.

L. *Marcia,* 402 | 352, to suppress usury, G. iv, 23.

L. *Minicia* (or *Mensia*), date unknown, on status of children born of parents of unequal condition, G. i, 78 and note, 79; U. v, 8. See *Status,* 2.

L. *Ollinia* (?), G. iv, 109.

L. *Papia-Poppaea.* See L. *Julia et Papia-Poppaea.*

L. *Pinaria,* date uncertain, amending the law of sacramental procedure, G. i, 15 and n. 2.

* L. *Plaetoria,* 6th cent. *p. u. c.,* introducing curatory of minors in certain cases, G. i, 197, note. See *Curatory,* 3.

L. *Plautia de vi,* date uncertain, but before 691 | 63, G. i, 45 and n. 2.

* L. *Poetilia,* 429 | 325 or 441 | 313, probably the latter, alleviating the condition of the *nexi,* G. iv, 21, note 6.

L. *Publilia* (*de sponsu*), 371 | 383 (?), giving sponsors, who had paid for the debtor for whom they had become sureties, the right of *manus injectio* against him; for which was afterwards substituted an *actio depensi* for twice the amount, G. iii, 127, iv, 22. See *Suretyship,* 3.

* L. *Publilia Philonis,* 415 | 339, *inter alia* conferring legislative powers on the *comitia tributa,* G. i, 3, note 2.

* L. *Rubria de Gallia Cisalpina,* between 705 | 49 and 712 | 42, settling the constitution of the province, G. iii, 78, note 3.

* L. *Salpensana,* Domitian's charter to the *municipium* of Salpensa in southern Spain, G. i, 22, note 1, 55, note 2.

L. *Silia,* date uncertain, introducing the *legis actio per condictionem,* G. iv, 19 and note. See *Legis actiones,* 4.

L. *Titia,* see L. *Julia et Titia.*

* L. *Valeria Horatia,* 305 | 449, *inter alia* instituting the *comitia tributa,* G. i, 3, note 2.

L. *Vallia,* date unknown, amending procedure by *manus injectio,* G. iv, 25, iii, 121, note. See *Legis actiones,* 5.

L. *Visellia,* A.D. 24 (?), granting citizenship to latins after six years' service in the night watch, G. i, 32b and note, U. iii, 5; see *Junian latinity,* 7.

LEGES—*continued.*

    L. Voconia, 585 | 169, imposing disabilities upon women in the matter of succession, and forbidding legatees to take more than a certain amount under a testament, G. ii, 226 and note, 274. See *Testament,* 13, *Legacy,* 15.

LEGIS ACTIONES, G. iv, 11-29; see also *Procedure.*

    1. Legis actio, *what ?*—It included not only contentious but also certain non-contentious procedure, such as *in jure cessio* (which see), G. ii, 24; but in G. iv, 11-29, it is the former alone that is dealt with. The phrase applied either to the mode of procedure, as *leg. actio sacramento,* or to some particular action proceeded in by that or other mode, 11, note; and in the latter sense was so called either because sanctioned by statute, *lege,* or because the *ipsissima verba* of the law founded on had to be recited, *ibid.,* any variance causing failure, *ibid.* There were five different modes of procedure that went under the name, —the *legis actio sacramenti* (or *sacramento*), 13-17, that *per judicis postulationem,* 12, note, that *per condictionem,* 17b-20, that *per manus injectionem,* 21-25, and that *per pignoris capionem,* 26-29; and, with exception of the last, they could proceed only *in jure,* in the presence of the adversary, and on a lawful day, 29.

    2. *The* legis actio sacramento.—This was followed where no other was prescribed by statute, G. iv, 13, and was applicable both in real and personal actions, *ibid.,* note 1. Its characteristic feature was that the parties, after dramatically stating their respective contentions before a magistrate, and originally perhaps a pontiff, each challenged the other with a sacrament,—at first probably an oath of verity backed with a money-stake, afterwards only the stake. The direct question for determination by the *judex* to whom it was remitted was—whose sacrament is just, whose unjust? the unjust one becoming a forfeit for public uses, the other being resumed by the staker. But its decision involved a judgment on the actual matter of dispute, (followed when necessary by a *litis aestimatio,* 48, note 3), which was enforced in subsequent proceedings by *manus injectio,* 13-17 and notes, 21. These were steps in the procedure that were taken in all cases, 13-15. For those that were peculiar to vindications, and in particular the disposal of the interim possession and the *praedes litis et vindiciarum,* see 16, 17 (incomplete), 94; those peculiar to personal actions seem to have been explained in 15, (also incomplete). The procedure survived the establishment of the formular

Legis actiones—*continued*.

system only in certain centumviral causes, 31, and with considerable modifications, 95.

3. *That* per judicis postulationem.—The account of it is lost, G. iv, 17*a*, note; but it appears to have been a competent mode not only of deciding amicable disputes and illiquid claims, but also of trying those for *certa pecunia* or other *res certae*, 20.

4. *That* per condictionem.—It was introduced by the Silian law to meet the case of claim for a definite sum of money, *certa pecunia*, and extended by the Calpurnian law to claims for specific articles generally, *omnis res certa*, G. iv, 19 and note. It was so called because the pursuer *adversario condicebat*, cited his adversary, to appear before the magistrate on a certain day for appointment of a judge, 17*b*, 18. Its advantage over the *actio sacramento* was its simplification of the procedure *in jure*, 20 and note.

5. *That* per manus injectionem.—This was authorised by the XII Tables against judgment debtors, and those indebted *damnatione* either under a statute or a private deed, G. iv, 21 and note, ii, 201, note 1. The creditor was entitled, using certain words of style, to arrest his debtor, and carry him home and imprison him and put him in chains, unless he then and there provided a *vindex* to undertake the responsibility of his defence,—for he was not allowed to say a word for himself, G. iv, 21 and n. 5, 25. Later enactments sanctioned *man. inject. pro judicato* in a variety of cases, of which one or two illustrations are given in 22; while others allowed what was called *manus injectio pura*, 23, whose peculiarity was that the arrested debtor was not required to find a *vindex*, but might defend in person, 24. This right was latterly extended by a *lex Vallia* (?) to all but *judicati* and debtors who failed within six months to relieve sponsors (sureties) who had paid for them, 25. What was the form of the defence is not explained; all that is stated is that the debtor was entitled *pro se agere*, 25, *pro se lege agere*, 24.

6. *That* per pignoris capionem.—The proceedings here were by distress, taking and selling some article belonging to a debtor; they were authorised in a few cases by custom, G. iv, 27, and in a few others by statute, 28. It was accounted a *legis actio* because the distrainer had to use certain words of style, 29; but differed from the others in respect that it did not proceed before a magistrate, and was competent on a *dies nefastus, ibid.* Under the later

LEGIS ACTIONES—*continued.*

system it was sometimes referred to in a *formula* as justification of the action upon which the *formula* was adjusted, 32.

7. *Defects of the system.*—*Inter alia* agency was not allowed in a *legis actio*,—no one could sue for another except *pro populo, pro libertate, pro tutela,* G. iv, 82. Equitable exceptions were unknown, 108; (was there any substitute? 108, note). It gradually fell into discredit because of its many pitfalls for unlearned litigants, and was replaced by the formular system, 30.

LEGIS VICEM OPTINERE, G. i, 4, 5, 83; iv, 118.

LEGITIMA COGNATIO, G. iii, 110; *legitimum jus agnationis,* G. iii, 27, U. xxviii, 9. See *Agnation.*

LEGITIMA MANUMISSIO, G. i, 17, U. i, 6; see *Manumission,* 1, 4.

LEGITIMI HEREDES, LEGITIMA HEREDITAS, agnates and their succession under the XII Tables; see *Intestate succession,* 4.

LEGITIMUM JUDICIUM, see *Jud. leg.* and *imp. cont.,* 1.

LEX, G. i, 3, etc., was a comitial enactment; see *Statute.* The phrase *lex publica* occurs once or twice, (G. ii, 104, iii, 174); it may have meant no more than *lex,* but probably meant the XII Tables.

LEX (PRIVATA), the law men made for themselves or their heirs, in contracts, conveyances, testaments, etc., G. ii, 104, note 8, U. xxiv, 1; *lex mancipii,* G. i, 140, 172; *lex locationis,* G. iii, 145, 146; *lex testamenti,* U. xxiv, 1.

LIBELLUS, a slanderous writing, G. iii, 220.

LIBERORUM JUS, see *Jus liberorum.*

LIBRIPENS, G. i, 119, ii, 104, iii, 174, (see *Aes et libra*); who could or could not act as such in a testament, G. ii, 107, 108, U. xx, 3-8.

LICIUM, see *Linteum.*

LIMITATION OF ACTIONS, see *Actions,* 9.

LINTEUM, LANX ET, G. iii, 192 and n. 2; see *Theft,* 5.

LITEM SUAM FACIT was said of a judge who, through error in point of form, rendered his judgment in favour of a pursuer useless; the latter was then entitled to proceed against the judge for damages, fresh action against his debtor being excluded by the novation implied in litiscontestation, G. iv, 52 and n. 2.

LITERAL OBLIGATIONS, G. iii, 128-134; see also *Contract,* 1.

1. *How created.*—Literal obligations were created by *transscriptio* in a citizen's *codex expensi et accepti,* G. iii, 128 and note; they were unilateral, 137, and the entries creating them might be made by the creditor in the absence of his debtor, 138. The entry, or *nomen,* might be transcribed

LITERAL OBLIGATIONS—*continued.*

either *a re in personam*, when the amount of an already
existing illiquid debt was booked against the debtor
(*expensi latio*), 129 and note; or *a persona in personam*
when a creditor gave his debtor credit for a sum standing
at his debit (*accepti latio*), and entered it to the debit of
a third party delegated to him by his debtor for that
purpose, 130. Those *nomina* were peculiar to citizens,
although the Sabinians were of opinion that a peregrin
might be made debtor in one *a re in personam*, 133 and
note.

2. Nomina arcaria, chirographa, *and* syngraphae.—*Nomina
arcaria* were not literal obligations, but merely book-
record and evidence of real ones, G. iii, 131 and note,
132. *Chirographa* and *syngraphae* were peculiar to peregrins, and with them reckoned as literal obligations, 134
and note.

LITIGIOSITY, exception of, G. iv, 117*a*.

LITIS CONTESTATIO.—Origin of the phrase, and how the *contestatio*
was marked in process, G. iii, 180, note 1. Its effect was
to extinguish a claim when sued for in a *legitimum judicium* (see *Jud. legitima, etc.*, 1) *in personam*, with a *formula
in jus concepta* (see *Formula*, 3), G. iii, 180 and note to
180 and 181, iv, 107. It has consequently been called
processual novation, note to G. iii, 180 and 181; for
the defender then began to be bound by his agreement
to refer the matter to judicial decision, 181, just as on
judgment he began to be bound thereby, his obligation
under the litiscontestation being extinguished, *ibid.*
When therefore a creditor had carried such an action as
far as litiscontestation, his right to sue afresh on the
same claim was *ipso jure* extinguished, 181. Not so in a
jud. legit. in rem, because there was no obligation to be
novated; nor in a personal one *in factum concepta*, because no obligation was averred; nor yet in a *jud. imp.
continens*, because the *civilis ratio* could not affect the
praetorian remedy: but if an action of any of those
classes had reached litiscontestation, and the pursuer
afterwards sued afresh on the same grounds, he might
be defeated by an *exceptio rei in judicium deductae*, G. iii,
181, iv, 106.

LOAN OF FUNGIBLES (or for consumption), see *Mutuum;* of non-
fungibles (or for use), see *Commodate.*

LOCATION, *locatio conductio*, G. iii, 142-147; see also *Consensual
obligations.*

1. *Location, what?*—It was a consensual contract, G. iii, 135,

LOCATION—*continued.*

whereby the *locator*, in consideration of a fixed reward, *certa merces*, 142, agreed to give the *conductor* the use of a thing, *locatio conductio rei*, 144, 145, or the benefit of his services or those of his people, *loc. cond. operarum*, 146, 147. It was subject to much the same general rules as sale, 142; and the same questions seem to have been raised in both, in particular whether there was location when the remuneration of the *locator* was left to be fixed by a third party named, or to be settled by parties subsequently, 143; as also whether it was location when the use of one thing was given in exchange for the use of another, 144, (see *Sale*, 2).

2. *The resulting rights and obligations.*—The transfer following on the contract did not give the *conductor* the legal possession of what was given him in location; he was only the holder for the *locator*, who remained in possession through him, G. iv, 153. But he was responsible for its safe-keeping; consequently if it was stolen, and he solvent, it was he and not the *locator* that had the *actio furti*, G. iii, 205, 206. Each party had an action on the contract,—the *a. locati* for the one, the *a. conducti* for the other; and both of them were *bonae fidei*, G. iv, 62.

3. *Occasional difficulty in discriminating between location and sale.*—In emphyteusis, when lands were granted to a man and his heirs in perpetuity so long as they paid the annual *vectigal*, it was long disputed whether the contract was sale or location; according to the prevailing opinion it was the latter, 145. Again, when an order was given to a manufacturer there was the same difficulty; it was ruled that if he was to supply both material and workmanship the contract was one of sale, but that if the material was furnished him, and he was to give labour only, it was location, 147. In some cases it was held impossible to determine from the first what was the contract, and that only supervening occurrences could show whether it was sale or location, 146.

LUNACY incapacitated a man from doing any act productive of jural consequences, G. iii, 106; not only could he not be a party to a contract, *ibid.*, or make a testament, U. xx, 13, —he could not even assist at the execution of another person's testament as *familiae emptor*, *libripens*, or witness, U. xx, 7. By the XII Tables he was placed under the curatory of his agnates, (see *Curatory*, 1), U. xii, 2; and their powers were so extensive that they could even alienate his estate, G. ii, 64.

MAGISTER (trustee) in bankruptcy, G. iii, 79; see *Emptio bonorum.*
MALE *nostro jure uti non debemus,* G. i, 53.
MANCIPATIO, G. i, 119-122, U. xix, 3-6.
  1. Mancipatio, *what ?*—In form it was an imaginary sale *per
    aes et libram* (see *Aes et libra*), in presence of five citizens
    as witnesses, and a *libripens* holding a pair of scales; the
    party to whom the conveyance was being made, *qui man-
    cipio accipit,* having one hand on the thing being con-
    veyed, and using certain solemn words of style, declared
    it his by purchase with an *as* (which he held in his other
    hand) and with the copper scales; and simultaneously he
    touched the scales with the coin, which he then gave
    to the party conveying, *qui mancipat,* G. i, 119. The
    ceremony was the remnant of the old procedure when
    the price of a purchase was so much copper actually
    weighed in the scales, 122; but the name Gai. says was
    due to the fact that the transferee laid his hand upon
    what was being mancipated, *quia manu res capitur,* 121.
    This was the case, however, only with moveables, which
    moreover could be mancipated only one at a time, U. xix,
    6; immoveables might be mancipated in absence and in
    any number, *ibid.*
  2. *To what purposes applied.*—As a conveyance of property it
    applied properly to *res mancipi* (which see), G. i, 120,
    ii, 22, U. xix, 3, including rural praedial servitudes, G.
    ii, 29; and was preferred to *in jure cessio* because of its
    greater convenience, G. ii, 25. But free persons might
    also be mancipated; *e.g.* children *in potestate* who were
    being surrendered *ex noxali causa* (see *Noxal actions*), G.
    iv, 79, or emancipated, G. i, 132, or given in adoption,
    134; also women in passing *in manum* by *coemptio,* 113,
    (although the words used were not the same as usual,
    123), or in being released from it by remancipation, 118,
    137a. The same form, but with different words, was
    used likewise in a testament *per aes et libram* (see *Testa-
    ment,* 4), G. ii, 102, U. xx, 2, 9.
  3. *To whom it was competent.*—It was peculiar to citizens, G.
    i, 119, but competent also, as a conveyance of property,
    to colonial and Junian latins, and such peregrins as had
    obtained a concession of *commercium,* U. xix, 4, 5 and
    note. A slave or a *filiusfamilias* might acquire by it, G.
    ii, 87, iii, 167, declaring in the words of style that the
    purchase was for his *paterfamilias,* iii, 167.
  4. *Reservations and concurrent agreements.*—It might be made
    under a reservation, as when lands were mancipated
    under deduction of their usufruct, G. ii, 33. Or it might

MANCIPATIO—*continued.*

be accompanied by some relative agreement, such as a *pactum fiduciae* (see *Fiducia*), G. ii, 59, 60, 104, note 8, iii, 201.

MANCIPI RES, see *Res mancipi* and *nec mancipi.*

MANCIPII, PERSONS IN CAUSA, or *in mancipio,* (the latter locution being the more frequent in Gaius), G. i, 116-123, 138-141.

1. *Who were* in causa mancipii.—A slave was a *mancipium,* G. iii, 148; but it was free persons that were *in mancipio* or *in causa mancipii,* G. i, 117, 118, and thus *servorum loco,* G. i, 123, 138, viz. *filiifamilias* who had been noxally surrendered, 140, iv, 79; *filiifamilias* and *filiaefamilias* who had been mancipated with a view to emancipation or adoption, but had not yet been manumitted in the one case (see *Emancipation,* 1) or ceded *in jure* in the other (see *Adoption,* 3), G. i, 132, 134; and women who had been remancipated by their coemptionators with a view to dissolution of *manus,* but were still unmanumitted, 118. Except in the case of those mancipated noxally, their condition was usually a transient one, and one rather of form than substance, 141.

2. *Their position.*—They were subject generally to the same disabilities as other persons *alieni juris* (see *Alien. jur. personae,* 2-4); only as they were not in possession of the individual to whose *jus* they were subject, it was doubted whether they could possess and usucapt on his behalf, G. ii, 90. If a person *in mancipio* was instituted heir or had a legacy left him by the person in whose *mancipium* he was, it required to be accompanied with freedom, otherwise he could not take it, G. i, 123. Such an institution made him a necessary heir; but nevertheless he had the *beneficium abstinendi* (see *Abst. potestas*), though he was not at the same time a *suus,* G. ii, 160. In consideration of his freedom he to whom he was subject was not allowed to offer him any indignity, on pain of an *actio injuriarum,* G. i, 141.

3. *How they were relieved from it.*—They were relieved from it, like slaves, by manumission *vindicta, censu,* or *testamento* (see *Manumission,* 6), G. i, 138; but to their case the restrictions of the Aelia-Sentian and Fufia-Caninian laws did not apply, 139. Except a *filiusfamilias* surrendered noxally, or a child mancipated under trust for remancipation to his father (see *Emancipation,* 3), they might have their names recorded in the censorial register even against the will of the person to whom they were subject, and thus regain freedom *de facto* as well as *de jure* without his co-operation, 140.

MANDATE, *mandatum,* G. iii, 155-162; see also *Consensual obligations.*

1. *Mandate, what ?*—It was a consensual contract, G. iii, 135, in which the mandatory was commissioned by the mandant to do something, and in which they stood mutually obliged according to principles of good faith, 155. It was of necessity gratuitous, the contract being one of location if the mandatory was paid for his services, 162.

2. *Nature of the commission.*—A mandate might be on account either of the mandant or of a third party, or for their joint benefit, G. iii, 155, 156 ; but if solely for the benefit of the mandatory it was regarded merely as advice, and entailed no responsibility *ex mandáto,* 156. A commission to do what was immoral or unlawful created no obligation, 157, neither did one to be performed after the mandant's death, 158.

3. *How extinguished.*—It was extinguished by revocation or death of either party *rebus integris,* G. iii, 159, 160; but if the commission was executed in excusable ignorance of the mandant's death, the mandatory still had his *actio mandati,* 160.

4. *Mandatory not entitled to exceed the limits of his commission.*—If the mandatory exceeded the limits of his commission the mandant might have an *actio mandati* against him for damages ; but he had no action against the mandant, G. iii, 161. The mandatory was still entitled, however, to action when he was within his limits, as in buying at a lower price than he had been authorised to give, *ibid.*

5 *The* actio mandati.—The *a. mandati,* which was competent to either party, G. iii, 111, 127, 156, 161, was *bonae fidei,* G. iv, 62, and condemnation in it made the defender infamous, 182. It was the action which a surety other than a sponsor used against the debtor on whose behalf he had paid, G. iii, 127 ; and a sponsor might use it as alternative to his *a. depensi, ibid.,* (see *Suretyship,* 5). It was also employed by a stipulant or his heirs against an adstipulator (see *Adstipulation,* 2) who had received payment from the common debtor, 111.

MANES, DII, G. ii, 4 ; see *Things,* 1.

MANIFESTUM FURTUM, see *Theft,* 4, 5.

MANUMISSION, enfranchisement of a slave, G. i, 13-27, U. i, 6-25, ii, (see *Slavery*), or liberation of a free person *in causa mancipii,* G. i, 138-141, (see *Mancipii, etc.*).

I. GENERAL DOCTRINES REGARDING MANUMISSION OF SLAVES.

1. *The Aelia-Sentian and Junian laws.*—Before the first of these enactments only a quiritarian owner (see *Quir. ownership*) could legally manumit his slave, and that by

MANUMISSION—*continued.*

I. GENERAL DOCTRINES REGARDING THAT OF SLAVES—*continued.*
one or other of the *legitimae manumissiones, i.e.* either
vindicta, censu, or *testamento ;* the slave thus manumitted
became a citizen, without reference either to his own
age or that of his manumitter, G. i, 17, 18, 38. To check
this increase of freedmen citizens, the statute *inter alia*
declared that slaves of disgracefully bad character should
not on manumission become or be capable of becoming
citizens, and introduced restrictions as to the mode and
conditions of manumission when a slave was under thirty
or his owner under twenty, G. i, 13, 18, 38, U. i, 11, 12,
13, (see *Aelia-Sentian law,* 2-4). But it at the same
time provided a means whereby slaves under thirty
manumitted by their quiritarian owners without due
regard of its directions might afterwards attain citizenship, G. i, 29; which was extended by the Junian law
and a subsequent senatusconsult to slaves of any age
manumitted irregularly, or by those who were only their
bonitarian owners, G. i, 29, note, as amended in *Additions
etc.,* 31, U. iii, 3, (see *Aelia-Sentian law,* 6, 7). Those to
whom this means of obtaining citizenship were offered
got the name of Junian latins until they had obtained it,
G. iii, 56, (see *Junian latinity,* 1).

2 *How manumission was influenced by the condition of the manu-*
mitter.—Only a quiritarian owner could by manumission
make his slave a citizen, G. i, 17, U. i, 23; a bonitarian
owner (see *Bon. ownership*) could make him no more than
a latin, G. i, 22 and note, U. i, 16. An owner under
twenty, even quiritarian, could not make his slave a
citizen unless by manumission *vindicta,* for reasons recognised by the *consilium* as sufficient, G. i, 38-41, U. i, 13.
A pupil or a woman in tutelage could not manumit to any
effect without tutorial *auctoritas,* U. i, 17. One only of
two joint owners did not free his slave by manumission;
the result was that his share accrued to his *socius* if the
manumission was regular, but had no effect if irregular,
U. i, 18. Manumission by the owner of a slave usufructed
by a third party left him *servus sine domino* while the usufruct lasted, U. i, 19. Manumission by any owner in fraud
of creditors or patron was null, G. i, 37, 47, U. i, 15.

3. *How influenced by condition of the slave.*—If he was of
disgracefully bad character his manumission, except by
an insolvent owner instituting him as his *heres necessarius,*
U. i, 14, could make him no more than a deditician, G. i,
13, U. i, 11, (see *Ded. freedmen*). If under thirty, his manu-

MANUMISSION—*continued.*
I. GENERAL DOCTRINES REGARDING THAT OF SLAVES—*continued.*
 mission otherwise than *vindicta apud consilium*, and by his
 quiritarian owner, made him only a latin, G. i, 18, U. i, 12.
 4. *How influenced by mode of manumission.*—Only one or other
  of the *legitimae manumissiones* could make a slave a
  citizen, G. i, 17, U. i, 6-9; and if he were under thirty or
  his owner under twenty it required to be *vindicta*, on
  cause approved by the council, (see No. 2). Any other
  mode of manumission made him only a latin, G. i, 22 and
  note, U. 10.
 5. *Result.*—The slave who became a citizen had all the rights
  of a citizen except as qualified by his relation to his
  manumitter, who became his patron; see *Patronate,
  Succession to citizen freedmen.* For the rights and disabilities of a Junian latin, see *Junian latinity, Succession
  to Junian latins.*
II. MANUMISSION OF SLAVES BY ACT INTER VIVOS.
 6. *The* legitimae manumissiones.—These were *vindicta* and census, G. i, 17, U. i, 6. Manumission *vindicta* was a formal
  act before a magistrate, U. i, 7, the nature of which is not
  explained by Gai. or Ulp., except that in the ordinary
  case it could take place at any time, and did not require
  to be in court, G. i, 20. It was the only form that could
  make a slave a citizen when he was under thirty or his
  owner under twenty, G. i, 18, 38, U. i, 12, 13, and then
  it required to be on adequate cause approved by the
  council, *ibid.* The composition of the council and its
  times of sitting are described in G. i, 20, U. i, 13, (see
  Consilium), and what were regarded as adequate causes
  enumerated in G. i, 19, 39. Manumission *censu* was
  accomplished when a slave, by order of his owner, gave in
  his name for enrolment in the census list, U. i, 8.
 7. *Informal manumissions.*—Gai. and Ulp. mention only manumission *inter amicos*, G. i, 41, 44, U. i, 10, 18; but those
  per epistulam and *per mensam* were very common, G. i,
  41, note.
III. MANUMISSION OF SLAVES BY TESTAMENT.
 8. *Direct manumission.*—It was only his own slave that a man
  could directly (in contradistinction to fideicommissarily)
  manumit by testament, G. ii, 272; and to make him a
  citizen it was necessary (*a*) that he should be in the
  quiritarian ownership of the testator both when the latter
  made his testament and when he died, G. ii, 267, U. i,
  23, and (*b*), except when instituted necessary heir by an
  insolvent, U. i, 14, (see *Necessarii heredes*), that he should

MANUMISSION—*continued.*

   III. MANUMISSION OF SLAVES BY TESTAMENT—*continued.*

be over thirty, G. ii, 276 ; if he was under thirty, or the testator only his bonitarian owner, direct testamentary manumission made him only a latin, U. i, 12, xxii, 8. A direct manumission took effect the moment that one of any number of heirs had entered, U. i, 22.

  9. *Requisites in point of form.*—A testamentary manumission might be conditional, and while the condition was pendent the slave was termed *statuliber* (which see), U. ii, 1-6. It was useless if it stood in the testament (unless a military one, U. i, 20) anterior to the heir's institution, G. ii, 230, U. i, 20, or if placed between two institutions and both the heirs entered, U. i, 21 ; or if freedom was given as from the day before or the day after the heir's death, G. ii, 232, 233 ; or if it was given by way of penalty, 236.

  10. *Indirect or fideicommissary manumission.*—See *Fideicommissum*, 12, 13.

  11. *Restrictions of the Fufia-Caninian law.*—This enactment (see *L. Fuf. Can.*) limited, according to a sort of sliding scale, the number of his slaves a man could manumit by testament, the maximum being 100, however numerous his establishment, G. i, 42, 43, 45, ii, 228, U. i, 24. If he manumitted more than the lawful number, the enfranchisement was effectual only for those within the number who were mentioned first, G. i, 45*a* ; therefore the statute required that they should be named, *ibid.*, ii, 237, U. i, 26 ; and any attempt to overreach the prohibition, as by writing the names in a circle, was rendered futile by certain senatusconsults, G. i, 46.

  12. *Institution by an insolvent owner of one of his slaves as* heres necessarius.—See *Aelia-Sentian law,* 5 ; *Necessarii heredes.*

   IV. MANUMISSION OF PERSONS IN CAUSA MANCIPII.—See *Mancipii*, etc., 3.

MANUS, a state of subjection of a woman to a man, either *matrimonii causa* or *fiduciae causa*, G. i, 108-115*b*, 137, 137*a*, U. tit. ix.

  1. *Manus created* confarreatione.—*Confarreatio* was a sacrificial ceremony in the presence of ten witnesses, taking its name from the cake of *far* or spelt, U. tit. ix, note, which was employed in it, G. i, 112, U. tit. ix ; (and there can be no doubt it was creative at once of both marriage and *manus*). It was still in use in the time of Gai. and Ulp. ; for no one could fill the office of one of the greater flamens or of the *rex sacrorum* who was not the issue of

MANUS—*continued.*

a farreate marriage, and himself married in that way, G. i, 112. But it had proved so difficult to induce women to submit to it that it had to be provided in the time of Augustus that, at least as regarded the *flaminica Dialis*, it should in future infer *conventio in manum* only in so far as the 'sacra were concerned, G. i, 136 and note, and therefore did not free her from her father's *potestas, ibid.*

2. *That created* coemptione.—*Coemptio* was a transaction *per aes et libram* (see *Aes et libra, Mancipatio,* 1), in which it rather appears that the parties—the man being called *coemptionator,* G. i, 115, 118, U. xi, 5, etc., and the woman *quae coemptionem facit,* G. i, 114, 115—each made pretence of purchasing the other, G. i, 113 and n. 2; but the formal words used by them, which were not the same as those used in an ordinary mancipation, G. i, 123, are not preserved. When it was *matrimonii causa* it probably was usually contemporaneous with marriage, yet quite distinct; for if a woman performed it with him who was already her husband, intending only fiduciary *manus,* yet by operation of law matrimonial *manus* was the result, G. i, 115*b*; while by marrying a man in whose *manus* she already was, she converted into matrimonial *manus* that which previously had been only fiduciary, G. ii, 139. A woman who was *sui juris* could not perform coemption without the *auctoritas* of her tutors, G. i, 115, 195*a*.

3. *That created* usu.—Here *manus* was superinduced on an already existing marriage, in which the parties had cohabited continuously for at least a year, G. i, 111; if the wife desired to avoid it, she had periodically to absent herself for at least three nights, *trinoctialis usurpatio,* and thus prevent the completion by her husband of twelve months' possession, *ibid.* By the time of Gai. it was obsolete, *ibid.*

4. *Effect of matrimonial* manus *on the position of the wife.*—In *manum conventio* by use being no longer observed, and that by confarreation being limited to the *sacra,* the old consequences of it really survived only in that accomplished *coemptione.* For the wife it involved a *capitis deminutio,* G. i, 162, U. xi, 13, and was followed by its usual consequences (see *Cap. dem.,* 3); in particular, if she was a *filiafamilias* at the time, it put an end to her father's *potestas,* G. i, 136, and, whether *filiafamilias* or *sui juris,* placed her in the position of a daughter in relation to her husband, G. i, 115*b*, 136, ii, 139, or of a granddaughter in relation to her father-in-law if her husband

MANUS—*continued.*

was himself *in potestate*, G. i, 148, iii, 3.   Whatever property
she had became her husband's or father-in-law's, G. ii, 98;
and by the civil extinction of her *persona* she was relieved
of all her debts, G. iii, 84.   As subject to a new family head
she began, like other persons *alieni juris*, to acquire
for him both property and claims, G. ii, 90, iii, 163, (see
Alieni juris personae); but she could no longer oblige
herself, G. iii, 104.   Finally, as a *sua heres* of her husband,
she was entitled to succeed to him *ab intestato* along with
her children in his *potestas*, G. iii, 3, U. xxii, 14, and enjoyed generally the rights of *suae heredes*, (see *Sui heredes*).

5. *Its effect on the position of the husband.*—It created in his
favour a universal acquisition of his wife's estate, G. ii, 98,
iii, 83; with a few exceptions, everything of hers passed
to him, and that without any civil liability for those of
her debts that were not hereditary, 84.   But if his wife's
creditors got from the praetor *utiles actiones* (see *Actions*,
6), on the fiction of *caput integrum* (see *Fiction*, 3), and
sued her on her personal debts, he was obliged to
defend her, on pain of seeing the creditors allowed to
sell what had been her estate, G. iii, 84, iv, 38, 80.   His
wife's subsequent acquisitions were all his, the only difficulty being as to whether she could acquire for him by
possession and usucapion, G. ii, 90.   The reason of the
doubt was that she was not in his possession, *ibid.*, although
she might be stolen from him, G. iii, 199.   The *in manum
conventio*, being *quasi agnatio suae heredis*, invalidated
any testament made by him previously, G. ii, 139, U.
xxiii, 3, (see *Agnatio sui heredis*); and in any subsequent
one he was bound to institute or disinherit her, just as he
had in the case of his children *in potestate*, (see *Testament*,
10), U. xxii, 14.   He was entitled in his testament to
appoint tutors both to his wife *in manu* and his daughter-
in-law *in manu* of his *filiusfamilias* (see *Tutory*, 10), G. i,
148.   Under certain circumstances the daughter-in-law
might succeed as a *sua heres*, G. iii, 3.

6. *How matrimonial* manus *was dissolved.*—The relationship
was dissolved by the death of the husband, the *capitis
deminutio media* or *maxima* (see *Cap. dem.*, 1) of either of
them, G. i, 137, or the remancipation of the wife, 118,
137a.   This she could demand only when the marriage
had been dissolved by divorce, 137a.   The process was
exactly the same as in the emancipation of a child, 118,
119, (see *Mancipatio*, 1).   One of its consequences was
that the person to whom she was mancipated, by manu-

MANUS—*continued.*
>mitting her to make her *sui juris*, became her fiduciary tutor, G. i, 115, 166, 195a, U. xi, 5, (see *Tutory*, 3, 12, 21).

7. *Fiduciary* coemptio.—This was resorted to by women *sui juris* who wanted either to change their tutors, G. i, 115, 195a, or make a testament, 115a, or be relieved of the burden of the family *sacra* that had descended to them with an inheritance, 114, note 1. Its employment to enable them to make a testament was probably due to this,—that whereas they could not compel their *legitimi tutores* to concur, they bargained for concurrence with the fiduciary tutor of their own selection; but the device became unnecessary in consequence of a Sct. of Hadrian's, requiring tutors, other than patrons or parent manumitters, to grant their *auctoritas* to the testaments of their female wards, G. i, 115a, ii, 112, 122. Fiduciary coemption did not place a woman in the position of a daughter to her *coemptionator*, G. i, 136; and if it operated a transfer of her estate to him, he must have been required by the *pactum fiduciae* to reconvey it to her on her manumission, otherwise she could not have disposed of it by testament, (see *Fiducia*).

MANUS INJECTIO, G. iv, 21-25; see *Legis actiones*, 5.

MARRIAGE, *nuptiae, matrimonium*, G. i, 56-64, U. tits. v, xiii. *Nuptiae* answered properly to marriage, in the sense of entry into the relationship of husband and wife, *matrimonium* being the state of matrimony, U. v, 2; although the words are sometimes used more loosely, as in the phrase *ex justis nuptiis concipere*, G. i, 90, 91.

1. Matrimonium justum *and* non justum.—The former is mentioned in G. i, 76, U. v, 1, 2, and *justae nuptiae* in G. i, 56, 90, 91; the latter in G. i, 87. The distinction was not that between lawful and prohibited marriage, but between one that fulfilled the requirements of the *jus civile*, so far as regarded the creation of *patria potestas*, and one that did not, G. i, 56, note 1. Only a Roman citizen could contract *justum matrimonium*, G. i, 56, U. v, 2, 4, and that only if he had *conubium* (which see) with the woman he married, *ibid.*; if he had no *conubium* with her, his marriage, though not prohibited, was *non justum*, as was that also in which the husband was a peregrin, irrespective of the consideration whether he had *conubium* with his wife or not, see *passim*, G. i, 65-81, 92.

2. *The provisions of the Julian law and subsequent senatusconsults in reference to marriage.*—They absolutely prohibited certain marriages between senators, or even com-

MARRIAGE—*continued.*

moners of free birth, and women of disreputable character,
(see *Julian and Pap. Popp. law*, 3). Further, they required that all citizens within certain ages should marry,
on pain of forfeiture of provisions left them by testament;
taking care, however, that marriage between persons of
disproportionate age should not relieve them, (see same
reference, No. 4). But they did not otherwise interfere
with the law of marriage or its conditions.

3. *Requisites of* justae nuptiae.—It was requisite that the man
should be a citizen and have *conubium* with the woman
he was marrying, see above, No. 1. Further, it was necessary that they should both have reached puberty, U. v, 2;
that in addition to their own consent that of their *patresfamilias* should have been given if they were *in potestate,
ibid.*; and that there should be no impediment of too
close propinquity or affinity, G. i, 58-63, U. v, 9. But,
unless in marriage *confarreatione*, which was almost out
of date (see *Manus*, 1), G. i, 112, 136, there is no suggestion that any ceremony was required.

4. *Propinquity and affinity as impediments.*—Marriage was
unlawful between ascendants and descendants *in infinitum*, G. i, 59, U. v, 6; and even when the relationship
had only been by adoption and had ceased, still the
impediment remained, G. i, 59. Between collaterals of
the second degree, *i.e.* brother and sister,—see the mode
of computing propinquity in U. v, 6, note 2,—it was unlawful even though the relationship was only adoptive,
G. i, 61; but on its dissolution the impediment disappeared, *ibid.* At one time the impediment reached the
fourth collateral degree (cousins), U. v, 6; but in the
time of Gai. and Ulp. a man might marry his brother's
daughter, who was related to him in the third degree, yet
not his sister's, G. i, 62 and notes, U. v, 6. Further, a
man could not marry his father's or mother's sister,
nor a woman who had been his mother-in-law, step-
mother, daughter-in-law, or step-daughter, G. i, 63, U.
v, 6.

5. *Effects of* justae nuptiae.—As regarded the parties, see
Husband and wife; as regarded their children, see *Patria
potestas.*

6. *Effects of incestuous marriages.*—Incestae nuptiae were those
in which the parties were related within the forbidden
degrees; the woman was not *uxor*, and the children were
in law as fatherless as the issue of a casual connection,
G. i, 64, U. v, 7.

MORA.—If an heir was *in mora* in paying a *fideicommissum* or a legacy *sinendi modo* (see *Legacy*, 20), he was liable for interest and fruits and profits; but there was no such liability in the case of other legacies, G. ii, 280. If a wife died after divorce her heir was not entitled to claim the dowry unless the husband had been *in mora* in paying it to deceased, U. vi, 7.

MORES, see *Custom.*

MORTIS CAUSA CAPIO, G. ii, 225 and n. 2.

MUCIUS, QUINTUS, G. iii, 149; see *Scaevola, Q. M.*

MULIER LIBERIS HONORATA, see *Jus liberorum.*

MUNICIPIUM, a, could not be instituted heir in a testament except by one of its own freedmen, U. xxii, 5, neither could its members collectively, *ibid.*; but a trust imposed on an heir to make over an inheritance to them was lawful, *ibid.*, while a legacy might also be taken by them, U. xxiv, 28. Emphyteutic grants of lands by a municipality are referred to in G. iii, 145.

MUTE, a, could not be a party to a stipulation, G. iii, 105, nor validly execute a testament *per aes et libram*, U. xx, 13, nor assist in the execution of another person's as *familiae emptor*, witness, or balance-holder, U. xx, 7. If he happened to be tutor-at-law of a woman, she was entitled to have a substitute to constitute a dowry for her, G. i, 180, U. xi, 21.

MUTUUM, loan for consumption, G. iii, 90; see also *Real obligations.*

1. Mutuum, *what?*—It was a real contract,—loan of fungibles, *i.e.* things passing by weight, number, or measure, which were transferred in property to the borrower, under an obligation to return others of the same sort, G. iii, 90. It is said to have derived its name from the fact that *ex meo tuum fit, ibid.*; consequently it was not held to have been contracted when there was incapacity for alienating, and therefore no transfer of property, G. ii, 80-82.

2. *Loan by a woman or pupil without tutorial* auctoritas.— Money being a *res nec mancipi*, G. ii, 81, and a woman capable of alienating things of that class without her tutor's *auctoritas* (see *Women*, 4), 80, she could quite well be a lender, 81. But a pupil had not that power of alienation, 80; therefore when he lent money without his tutor's *auctoritas*, he did not make it the property of the borrower, and so there was no *mutuum*, 82. So long as it was still extant, being still his, he might recover it by a *rei vindicatio, ibid.*: if consumed, he recovered it by a *condictio* (which see), *ibid.*; not, however, on the ground

MUTUUM—*continued.*

of *mutuum,* but rather because it had been consumed *sine causa, ibid.,* note 4.

3. *Action to which it gave rise.*—Repayment was sought in a *condictio certi,* on an *intentio—si paret reum dare oportere* (see *Intentio,* 2), G. iii, 91.

NATURAL CHILDREN, different meanings of phrase, G. i, 19, note 2.

NATURAL OBLIGATIONS, G. iii, 119a and n. 1; see *Obligation,* 5.

NATURALIS RATIO, G. i, 1, 89, 189; ii, 66, 69, 79; iii, 154a and note. See also *Jus naturale.*

NAVIS FABRICATIO was one of the ways in which a latin could become a citizen, G. i, 32c, U. iii, 6; see *Junian latinity,* 8.

NECESSARII HEREDES were heirs who became such by necessity of law, and whether they would or not, G. ii, 153, 157, iii, 87; and they were either *sui et necessarii* (see *Sui heredes*), who had by grace of the praetors *potestas abstinendi,* G. ii, 158, U. xxii, 24, or simply *necessarii,* who usually had no power of abstaining, G. ii, 152. The simple *heres necessarius* was a slave of a testator's instituted heir with freedom, G. ii, 153. Such an institution—often in the shape of a final substitution (which see, No. 1)—was largely resorted to by insolvents, who desired to avoid being made bankrupts after their death; by instituting or substituting a slave as *heres necessarius* it was the latter that was made a bankrupt, and to whom the consequent disgrace attached, (see *Bankruptcy*), G. ii, 154. To such institutions the restrictions of the Aelia-Sentian law as to age and previous character of the slave (see *Aelia-Sentian law,* 3, 4) did not apply; his heirship and freedom made him a citizen, U. i, 14. A person *in causa mancipii* (see *Mancipii, etc.*) who was instituted heir with freedom was also a *heres necessarius,* but had *potestas abstinendi* like a *suus,* G. ii, 160. In presence of a necessary heir there could be no *usucapio pro herede,* (see *Usucapion,* 6), G. ii, 58, iii, 201.

NEFASTUS DIES, a *legis actio* could not proceed upon, G. iv, 29.

NERVA, M. COCCEIUS, grandfather of the emperor of the same name, consul A.D. 22, a disciple of Labeo's, and head of his school after his death, G. i, 196, note 1, ii, 15, 195, iii, 133.

NEXI SOLUTIO was a mode of discharging an obligation without actual payment, G. iii, 173, (although originally it may have been the formal discharge that accompanied or followed payment). It was employed when the debt to be discharged had been created *per aes et libram* (which see),

NEXI SOLUTIO—*continued*.
　　or by a judgment, or by damnatory words in a testament
　　(see *Damnas esto*); but was possible only when what was
　　due could be weighed or counted, and was of definite
　　amount, 173, 175. The ceremony was itself *per aes et
　　libram;* the procedure and the words of style are in 174,
　　175 and n. 3.

NEXUM, a mode of contracting *per aes et libram*, G. iii. 89, note, which
　　seems almost to have gone out of use before the time of
　　Gai. It would rather appear that a man could oblige
　　himself *per aes et libram* (which see) only for what could
　　be weighed or counted, (*i.e.* money, G. i, 122), and was of
　　definite amount, G. iii, 175. It might be discharged by
　　the corresponding ceremony of *nexi solutio*, without actual
　　payment, 173.

NOMINA ARCARIA, G. iii, 131; see *Literal obligations*, 2.

NOMINA TRANSSCRIPTICIA, G. iii, 128; see *Literal obligations*, 1.

NOMINIS DIES (or *dies lustrious*), a child's name-day, survivance of
　　which augmented its parents' powers in taking one under
　　the testament of the other, U. xv, 2 and n. 1, xvi, 1*a*.

NON NUMERATAE PECUNIAE, EXCEPTIO, G. iv, 116; see *Exception*, 9.

NOSTRI PRAECEPTORES, a phrase used by Gai. to indicate the Sabinians,
　　to whose school he belonged; see *Sabinians and Proculians*.

NOVATION, G. iii, 176, 179; see also *Obligation*, 3.

　　1. *Novation, what ?*—It was a mode of extinguishing an
　　obligation by transmuting it into a new one, G. iii, 176;
　　and might be employed even when the obligation novated
　　was only a natural one (see *Obligation*, 5), G. iii, 119*a*,
　　note 1. It was effected either by substitution of a new
　　debtor or creditor without changing the nature of the
　　obligation, or by substituting a new obligation without
　　change of debtor or creditor, G. ii, 38, 39, iii, 176, 177.

　　2. *Novation by substitution of a new debtor.*—In such a case
　　the novation put an end to the old obligation even when
　　the new one was inoperative, G. iii, 176, unless the in-
　　operativeness was due to the fact that the new debtor
　　was a slave, *ibid.*, or a peregrin who had used the word
　　spondeo (see *Stipulation*, 2), *ibid.*

　　3. *Novation by substitution of a new creditor.*—If the original
　　creditor authorised a third party to take from the debtor
　　a stipulatory engagement for the same debt—a transac-
　　tion which was called delegation of his debtor by the
　　creditor to the third party, G. iii, 130—the debtor was
　　thereby discharged so far as the original creditor was
　　concerned, and became bound to the new one, G. ii, 38, 39.

　　4. *Novation by substitution of a new obligation.*—The substituted

NOVATION—*continued.*

obligation was held to be new if anything, such as a condition, a time of payment, or a surety, was superinduced on or withdrawn from the original one, G. iii, 177 ; Proculus, however, denying that introduction or withdrawal of a surety had that effect, 178.   When it was a condition that was introduced, the question of novation was in suspense until its fulfilment ; for if it failed, the original obligation was recognised, though not unanimously, as still subsisting, 179.   Even in such a case, however, it was maintained that action on the latter might be resisted by an *exceptio doli* (see *Exception*, 8), as contrary to the intent of parties, *ibid.*

5. *Novation in* nomina transscripticia.—See *Literal obligations,* 1.

6. *Processual novation.*—See *Litis contestatio.*

NOXAL ACTIONS, G. iv, 75-78, 81, were those against *patresfamilias* in respect of delicts of their *filiifamilias* committed against strangers, or owners in respect of delicts committed by their slaves, and in which defender, if condemned, had either to pay damages or surrender the wrong-doer to the party injured, 75 ; some of them being authorised by statute, others by the praetor's edict, 76.   As the liability always followed the delinquent, 77, if a *filiusfamilias* guilty of delict became *sui juris* before action was raised, the action ceased to be noxal, and became a direct one against himself, *ibid.;* while if a slave changed hands after the delict, the noxal action lay against his new owner, *ibid.* If, however, the delict was against the *paterfamilias* or slave's owner, as there was no action competent at the moment, so none became competent by transfer of either to another person's *potestas*, or even by his becoming *sui juris*, 78 ; but whether a right of action competent in respect of a slave's delict was extinguished by the slave's falling into the *potestas* of the injured party, or only suspended till he again passed out of it, was matter of controversy, *ibid.*

NOXAL MANCIPIUM, see *Mancipii, etc.*, 3.

NUDUM JUS QUIRITIUM, see *Quiritarian ownership.*

NUNCUPATIO, as an accompaniment of transactions *per aes et libram*, G. ii, 104, note 8.

NUNCUPATIO TESTAMENTI, see *Testament,* 4.

NURUS.—A daughter-in-law *in manu* of a *filiusfamilias* was *in potestate* of her father-in-law in the character of a granddaughter, G. i, 148, ii, 159 ; and she and her children succeeded him as *sui heredes* if her husband had predeceased, G. iii, 3, U. xxii, 14.

OBLATUM FURTUM, see *Theft*, 4, 5.
OBLIGATION, G. iii, 88-225.

I. OBLIGATION GENERALLY.

1. *Obligation, what ?*—The word is not defined in the texts, but
the idea left to be gathered from the detailed exposition.
But it was used sometimes to denote the relation or bond
between a creditor and his debtor, G. iii, 124, 176, iv, 78,
etc. ; sometimes the claim or hold the former had against
or over the latter, G. ii, 14, 38, etc. ; sometimes the duty
the latter owed the former, G. i, 192, iii, 119, etc.

2. *How it arose.*—A civil obligation, *i.e.* one upon which a
creditor could sue his debtor, arose either from contract
or delict, the first dealt with in G. iii, 89-162, the second
in 163-225, (see *Contract, Delict*) ; sometimes it arose
without either contract or delict, from facts and circumstances, 89, note 1, 91. An agreement, *pactum conventum*,
was not necessarily a contract ; and those pacts which
the law did not recognise as contracts, though they might
be binding naturally, and could be pleaded by way of
exception to the effect of defeating an action on a contract, G. iv, 116a, yet did not engender civil obligation.

3. *How extinguished.*—(*a*) By payment of what was due no
matter how the obligation had arisen, G. iii, 168 ; see *Payment.* (*b*) By novation, also in any case, 176-179 ; see
Novation. (*c*) By acceptilation when the obligation had
been created by verbal contract, 169-172 ; see *Acceptilation.* (*d*) By written *accepti latio* when the debt had been
created by *expensi latio*, G. iii, 129, 130 ; see *Literal obligations*, 1. (*e*) *Per aes et libram* when the debt had been so
created, or was upon a judgment or upon a legacy *per
damnationem*, 173-175 ; see *Nexi solutio.* (*f*) By litiscontestation in a *judicium legitimum*, 180, 181, and notes ; see
Litis contestatio. (*g*) By *capitis deminutio*, though equity
gave a remedy, G. iii, 84, iv, 38, 80 ; see *Cap. deminutio*,
3, 4. (*h*) Claims against hereditary debtors were extinguished by *in jure cessio* of an inheritance after entry, G.
ii, 35, iii, 85 ; see *Hereditas*, 15, 16.

4. *Impossibility of its transfer.*—Though an obligation was a
res incorporalis, G. ii, 14, yet, unlike other incorporeals, it
was incapable of cession or transfer in any way whatever, G. ii, 38 ; for though a new creditor or a new debtor
might be put in place of the original one, that was done
by novation (which see), which was very different from
transfer, *ibid.* Without, however, transferring the obligation, a creditor could give a third party the beneficial
interest in it by authorising him to sue upon it as his,

OBLIGATION—*continued.*
  I. OBLIGATION GENERALLY—*continued.*
the creditor's, cognitor or procurator, (see *Formula*, 2, *Procuratory in litigation*, 4), G. ii, 39, 252.

    5. *Natural obligations in particular.*—Natural obligations were not recognised by law to the extent of its allowing action upon them, see above, No. 2. The only point noticed by Gai. in reference to them is, that they might be guaranteed by sureties, as in the case of an obligation by a slave, G. iii, 119*a*; but in note 1 to that par. there is an enumeration of other results that followed them as *vincula aequitatis.*

    6. *Other varieties.*—They were unilateral or bilateral; unilateral in the verbal and literal contracts; bilateral (or mutual) in the consensual ones, G. iii, 137. In alternative ones the election was with the debtor unless otherwise expressed, G. iv, 53; and in generic ones, *obl. generis*, the rule was the same, *ibid.* Of some obligations performance was to be due from time to time, as in the case of annuities or other periodical payments; the obligation, however, was one and the same; and in suing for what had fallen due, on a *quidquid dare oportet* (see *Intentio*, 2), a creditor ran the risk of *consumptio actionis* (which see), unless he prefixed a limiting prescription to his *formula* (see *Praescriptio*), G. iv, 131, 131*a.*

  II. THE PARTIES TO AN OBLIGATION.

    7. *Obligation between a* paterfamilias *and his dependants.*—There could be no civil obligation between a man and a person subject to his *jus*, G. iv, 78; and a *filiusfamilias* or slave did not become liable to action merely by afterwards becoming *sui juris*, *ibid.* But the law did recognise the possibility of natural obligation between them; as when it authorised a *paterfamilias*, sued in an *actio de peculio* (see *Adjectician actions*, 3), to deduct from the *peculium* whatever was due him by his *filiusfamilias* or slave before settling with the pursuer, G. iv, 73.

    8. *Acquisition of claim through third parties.*—It was impossible for a man to acquire a claim through the contract of a stranger, whether a freeman or a *servus alienus*, G. ii, 95, even though such stranger was acting as his procurator or agent (see *Procurator*), *ibid.* But he might acquire *ex contractu* through a person in his *potestas*, *manus*, or *mancipium*, G. iii, 163; through a person, whether free or slave, *bona fide* possessed by him as his slave, if the claim was acquired by means of the possessor's funds or the supposed slave's labour, 164; or

OBLIGATION—*continued.*

II. THE PARTIES TO AN OBLIGATION—*continued.*

through a usufructed slave under the same qualifications, 165. If a slave was in the bonitarian ownership (which see) of one man and the quiritarian ownership of another, a claim acquired by him always accrued to the former, unless (?) expressly declared to be for the latter, 166. One owned by two persons jointly acquired for them *pro rata*, unless one in particular was named in the contract, 167; there being a difference of opinion as to whether the rule was displaced when the slave had acted on the instructions of one only, 167a.

9. *Liability through acts of third parties.*—For the contract debts of a stranger, whether a freeman or a *servus alienus*, a man was liable only when he had placed him in charge of a ship or store, and the debt had been contracted on account thereof; in such cases he was responsible in an exercitorian or institorian action, as the case might be, G. iv, 71, (see those words). As regards the liability of a *paterfamilias* for the debts *ex contractu* or *ex delicto* of those in his *jus*, see G. iv, 70-78, and respectively *Adjectician actions* and *Noxal actions*.

10. *Liability of persons* alieni juris.—A *filiusfamilias* was the only person *alieni juris* that could civilly oblige himself; all others were incapable of doing so, G. iii, 104, though they might be obliged naturally, (see above, Nos. 5, 7).

11. *Rights and liabilities of heirs.*—Heirs might sue or be sued *ex contractu*, with two or three exceptions; they might sue *ex delicto*, except the *a. injuriarum;* but they were not liable for the penalties of their predecessor's delict, G. iv, 112, 113, (see *Actions*, 7, *Hereditas*, 14). It was a rule of law that an obligation could not begin in the person of the heir either of debtor or creditor, G. iii, 100, 158; a stipulation therefore for a payment after the death of stipulant or promiser was useless, 100; so was a commission to a man to do something after the death of either mandant or mandatory, 158; and 'the day before death' was in the same position, as its arrival and the commencement of its obligation could not be known until after death, 100. The reason was, that though a man's heir represented him, and therefore was entitled to enforce his claims and responsible for his engagements, G. ii, 98, yet his heir's heir did not represent him. Therefore a testator could not charge his heir's heir with a legacy, G. ii, 232, U. xxiv, 16. He might, however, impose on his heir's heir the burden of performing an

OBLIGATION—*continued.*

II. THE PARTIES TO AN OBLIGATION—*continued.*

obligation which commenced in the person of the heir
while drawing his last breath, G. ii, 232, 278, iii, 100;
this was practically imposing the obligation itself on the
heir's heir; and so in *fideicommissa,* which were not tram-
melled by the rules of the *jus civile,* (see *Fideicommissum,*
1), no difficulty was made in admitting the validity of
an express direction to the heir's heirs to denude after
his death in favour of a third party, G. ii, 277, U. xxv, 8.

12. *Obligations of pupils and women in tutelage.*—See *Pupils,
Women,* 4.

OBROGATIO LEGIS, alteration of some of the provisions of a statute,
U. i, 3.

OCCUPATIO, appropriation of a *res nullius,* see *Property,* 4.

OFILIUS, AULUS, a jurist of distinction much trusted by Julius
Caesar, and supposed to have been his adviser in his
contemplated Code, G. iii, 140 and n. 2.

OPE EXCEPTIONIS, see *Ipso jure.*

OPTIO TUTORIS, see *Tutory,* 10.

OPTIONIS LEGATUM, U. xxiv, 14; see *Legacy,* 8.

ORBI, married persons who were childless, were not allowed by the
Papian law to take more than a half of what was left
them in a testament, G. ii, 286a, (see *Julian and Pap.
Popp. law,* 6). The prohibition did not extend, however,
to military testaments, G. ii, 111 and n. 4.

ORDO and GRADUS in succession, distinction, G. iii, 27, note 1.

OUTLAYS, see *Impensae.*

OWNERSHIP, see *Property, Quiritarian ownership, Bonitarian ownership.*

PACTI CONVENTI EXCEPTIO, G. iv, 116a, 121, 122.

PARENT AND CHILD, their jural relation to each other; see also
Marriage, Status.

1. *Where the child was the issue of* justum matrimonium.—For
the nature of *justum matrimonium* see *Marriage,* 1.
Where it had been contracted, a child born of it was a
citizen like his father, G. i, 56, 67; and if the latter was
sui juris at the time of conception—for it was that
moment that determined the status of legitimate children,
G. i, 89, U. v, 10—the child was in his *potestas,* G. i, 55,
(see *Patria potestas*). If his father was *sui juris,* then
the child, so long as he remained *in potestate,* was one of
the family *sui heredes,* G. ii, 156, iii, 2, U. xxii, 14, and
in a manner joint-owner with the father of the family
estate, G. ii, 157; the latter, therefore, if he made a tes-

PARENT AND CHILD—*continued.*

tament, required either to institute or disinherit him, G.
ii, 123 f., U. xxii, 14, (see *Testament,* 10); and on intestacy he had the first right to the succession, G. iii, 1, U.
xxvi, 1, (see *Intestate succession,* 3). As regards the parent's
rights over the child,—and the parent in this case might
be in fact a grandfather or even remoter ascendant, G. i,
146,—see *Patria potestas,* 3; and as regards the child's
capacities and incapacities, see *Alieni juris personae,* 2-4.
A child born *in justo matrimonio* within ten months
after the husband's death counted as his, U. xvi, 1*a.* The
existence of children of a marriage conferred important
rights upon the parents in reference to succession, the
dowry, release from tutory, acquisition of citizenship, etc.,
some of them arising whether there had been a marriage
or not, see *Jus liberorum, Husband and wife,* 7, *Dowry,* 4, 6,
Julian and Pap. Popp. law, 2, 5, 6, 7.

2. *Where issue of* non justum matrimonium.—When a marriage was *non justum* (see *Marriage,* 1) a child born of it
was not on that account a bastard; though by the *jus
gentium* he took his mother's status, G. i, 80, U. v, 8,—a
rule (see *Status,* 2) that was occasionally altered by positive legislation,—he was still *justus filius patris,* G. i, 77,
at least when his father was a peregrin. But he was not
in his father's *potestas,* G. i, 87, for that resulted only from
justae nuptiae, G. i, 55; consequently, suppose the father
was a citizen and could make a testament, the child
had no claims upon him in respect of it, being in law a
stranger, *extraneus,* G. ii, 241 and n. 2.

3. *When issue of an incestuous or unlawful connection.*—The
child was then accounted spurious, just as if *vulgo conceptus,* G. i, 64, U. v, 7; see below, No. 5.

4. *When issue of concubinage.*—There is no reference to concubinage in Gai. or Ulp.; but the issue of it were called
naturales, not *spurii* or *vulgo concepti,* G. i, 64, note 3,
and in the later law had certain rights in reference to
their father's succession.

5. *When issue of a casual connection.*—Children of this sort
were the *spurii* or *vulgo concepti* properly so called,
with whom incestuous offspring were classed; they were
regarded as in law fatherless, G. i, 64, U. iv, 2; and
took their status from their mother as their only known
parent, *ibid.,* dating it, not from the time of conception as
in the case of legitimate children, but from that of birth,
G. i, 89, U. v, 10. As fatherless they were of course *sui
juris,* U. iv, 2.

PARTITIO LEGATA, G. ii, 254, U. xxiv, 25; see *Legacy*, 8.
PARTNERSHIP, *societas*, G. iii, 148-154a; see also *Consensual obligations*.

1. Societas, *what ?*—It was a consensual contract, G. iii, 135, in which two or more persons agreed, as *socii*, to have a common interest either in the whole means and estate of each or in some particular trade or business, 148; each contributing something to the common stock, either in money or kind, or in personal services, 149.

2. *Distribution of profit and loss.*—After some hesitation it was held not to be inconsistent with the nature of the contract that a partner should share in the profits yet bear none of the loss, if the importance of his personal services or other circumstances rendered such an arrangement reasonable, G. iii, 149. In the absence of special agreement, the rule was that the partners were entitled to equal shares of the profits and bound for equal shares of the loss, 150; and when there was an agreement, but it was specific as to the division of one only of those incidents, the law assumed it the intention of parties that the other should be shared in the same proportion, *ibid*.

3. *Dissolution of a partnership.*—It came to an end when the mutual consent upon which it was founded, G. iii, 154a, was at end, 151; though fraudulent renunciation by one of the partners, in order to deprive his *socii* of some imminent profit, was not allowed thus to prejudice them, *ibid*. It was dissolved also by death, *capitis deminutio minima*, confiscation, or bankruptcy; though, in any of the three latter cases, (which were all *civiles rationes* for the dissolution of a *juris gentium* relationship), if the parties desired nevertheless to go on as before, a new partnership was held to have commenced, 152-154a.

4. *Actions appropriate to the relationship.*—When there was an allegation that a partner had not fulfilled his obligations under the contract, the remedy was an *actio pro socio*; it was *bonae fidei*, G. iv, 62; but condemnation in it rendered the defender infamous, G. iv, 182. When all that was wanted was division of common property, an *a. communi dividundo* (which see) was resorted to, G. iv, 42.

PATERFAMILIAS, idea, U. iv, 1, note; for his position, rights, and duties, see *Patria potestas*, 1-4.

PATRIA POTESTAS, G. i, 55-107, 127-127a; U. v, vii, 4, viii.
I. NATURE OF THE PATRIA POTESTAS.

1. *Its nature generally.*—The *patria potestas* was the right, *jus*, exercised by a *paterfamilias* over the *filii* and *filiae familias*. It was an institution of the *jus civile* and peculiar

PATRIA POTESTAS—*continued.*
 I. NATURE OF THE PATRIA POTESTAS—*continued.*

to citizens, G. i, 55, 189; although something closely resembling it was sometimes found amongst peregrins, 55, and existed in Rome's latin *municipia, ibid.*, note 2. At the same time the law did not recognise its *de jure* possibility amongst any but citizens, and denied it in particular to Junian latins, G. i, 66, and deditician freedmen, 68. It was only a *paterfamilias* that could have it, —a woman could not, G. i, 104, ii, 161, U. viii, 8*a*. And it created such a community of interests between the head of the house and his subject descendants that they were in a manner joint-owners with him of the family estate, G. ii, 157; that civil obligation between them was impossible, G. iv, 78, although there might be a natural one (see *Obligation,* 5), G. iv, 73; and that they were, in some cases at least, incompetent witnesses of each other's formal deeds, G. ii, 105-108, U. xx, 3-6.

2. *Over whom it extended.*—That a man was a citizen did not necessarily give him *potestas* over his children; for if they were the issue of a marriage without *conubium* there was no *potestas,* G. i, 56, unless something supervened to create it, (see below, Nos. 11, 12); while if they were the issue of an incestuous, prohibited, or casual connection, they were not even regarded as his children, (see *Marriage,* 6, 7, *Parent and child,* 5). When the *potestas* existed it did not end with sons and daughters, but included also grandchildren through a son, *nepotes neptesque ex filio,* great-grandchildren through a grandson who was issue of a son, *pronepotes proneptesque ex nepote filio nato prognati prognataeque,* and even remoter descendants tracing their descent through males, if such existed, G. iii, 2; but it did not include descendants through females, for a child followed his father's, not his mother's family, G. iii, 71. A woman, however, might enter her husband's family by *in manum conventio;* and in such a case, if he was *in potestate* of his father, so was she, but in the character of a granddaughter, G. i, 148, ii, 159, iii, 3, (see *Manus,* 4).

3. *Rights it conferred on the* paterfamilias.—It entitled him to emancipate his *filiusfamilias* and thus deprive the latter of the advantages of the relationship, G. i, 132 f., (see *Emancipation,* 2); to give him in adoption, G. i, 134, (see *Adoption,* 1, 3, 7); or to disinherit him, G. ii, 123, (see *Testament,* 10). He might, by withholding his consent, prevent him contracting *justum matrimonium,* U. v, 2,

PATRIA POTESTAS—*continued.*
 I. NATURE OF THE PATRIA POTESTAS—*continued.*
  (see *Marriage,* 3); he might by testament appoint a
  tutor for him if on the death of the *paterfamilias* he was
  to become *sui juris,* G. i, 144-146, (see *Tutory,* 1, 10); he
  might, by way of pupillary substitution, even make a
  will for him to take effect in the event of his dying
  while still a pupil, G. ii, 179, 180, U. xxiii, 7, 8, (see
  Substitution, 2). Lastly, he was entitled to all the
  acquisitions of his *filiusfamilias,* whether in the shape of
  property, G. ii, 87, or claims by contract, G. iii, 163.
  4. *Responsibilities it imposed upon him.*—By praetorian law
  he was responsible to a certain extent for the debts *ex
  contractu* of his *filiusfamilias,* G. iv, 69-74a, (see *Adjectician actions*); and, partly by the *jus civile,* partly by the
  edict, he was noxally responsible for his delicts, 75-79,
  (see *Noxal actions*). And as regarded a *filiusfamilias*
  who was to become *sui juris* on his death, he was bound,
  if he made a testament, either to institute or disinherit
  him; he could not, by leaving him unmentioned, deprive
  him of his birthright interest in the family estate, G. ii,
  123 f., (see *Testament,* 10).
  5. *Incapacities to which it subjected the* filiusfamilias.—See
  Alieni juris personae, 2-4.
  6. *Rights to which it entitled him.*—If he was an immediate
  descendant of his *paterfamilias,* he was entitled to disregard any testament made by the latter in which he had
  been passed over, G. ii, 123, (see *Testament,* 10); while a
  filiafamilias, or a *filiusfamilias* who was only a grandson
  but whose own father was dead, was entitled if unmentioned either to share with the institute by accretion
  under the *jus civile,* G. ii, 124, 126, (see *Adcretio,* 3), or
  to challenge the testament and obtain *bonorum possessio*
  under the edict, G. ii, 125, (see *Bonor. poss.,* 6). If the
  paterfamilias died intestate those of his *filii* and *filiae
  familias* who became *sui juris* had by the *jus civile* the
  first place in his succession, G. iii, 2, (see *Intestate
  succession,* 3); although by the edict emancipated children
  were admitted along with them, G. iii, 26, (see *Bonor.
  poss.,* 14).
 II. HOW IT WAS CREATED.
  7. *By* justae nuptiae.—See *Marriage,* 1, 3.
  8. *By adoption and adrogation.*—See *Adoption.*
  9. *By* jus Latii.—This was a mode by which a colonial latin
  acquired citizenship, and, in certain cases, not only for
  himself but for his children, G. i, 96. It is not said,

PATRIA POTESTAS—*continued.*

   II. How it was created—*continued.*

however, that *potestas* accompanied it, and judging by
the rule in reference to *potestas* following citizenship by
imperial grant (below, No. 12), it is possible that it did
not; see *Colonial latinity*, 2.

   10. *By* causae probatio ex lege Aelia Sentia.—This applied
to Junian latins; the moment cause was proved *potestas*
was created as well as citizenship, G. i, 66, U. vii, 4;
see *Caus. prob. ex l. Ael. Sent.*

   11. *By* erroris causae probatio.—See *Error. caus. prob.*

   12. *By imperial grant.*—It is not distinctly stated that the
patria potestas was ever granted *per se.* But it was a frequent accompaniment of a grant of citizenship to a man
and his children; not, however, as a matter of course,
but only when it had been expressly asked for and
expressly granted, G. i, 93, 94, ii, 135a, iii, 20; a careful
inquiry being always instituted as to whether it was for
the advantage of the children, hitherto *sui juris*, to make
them *alieni juris*, G. i, 93.

   III. How it was put an end to.

   13. *Death of the* paterfamilias.—This absolutely relieved from
the *potestas* a son or daughter, or a grandchild whose
immediate parent was dead or emancipated, because they
became *sui juris* by the event, G. i, 127, U. x, 2; but
as regarded those whose immediate parent was alive and
in potestate, they were not relieved, but simply passed
from the *potestas* of a remoter into that of a nearer
ascendant, *ibid.*

   14. *Emancipation.*—See *Emancipation*, 1.

   15. *Adoption and adrogation.*—If the *paterfamilias* gave his
child in adoption, the latter passed out of one *potestas*
into another, G. i, 99, U. viii, 1, 3; while the same result
followed if the *paterfamilias* gave himself in adrogation,
for his adoption carried with it that of his children *in
potestate*, G. i, 107, U. viii, 8, (see *Adoption*, 2, 3).

   16. *The greater* capitis deminutiones.—Emancipation, adoption, and adrogation all involved *cap. deminutio minima ;*
the *potestas*, as a right competent only to a citizen over a
citizen, was necessarily ended when either *paterfamilias*
or *filiusfamilias* underwent one of the greater *minutiones*
by losing freedom or citizenship, G. i, 128, 131, 160, U.
x, 3, xi, 11, 12, (see *Cap. deminutio*, 1). But where either
was taken captive by an enemy, the *potestas* was only
suspended, and revived if he returned, G. i, 129, U. x, 4,
(see *Captivity apud hostes*).

PATRIA POTESTAS—*continued.*
  III. How it was put an end to—*continued.*
    17. *Other ways.*—A *filiusfamilias* became *sui juris* without
capitis deminutio when consecrated a priest of Jupiter, and
a *filiafamilias* when chosen as a Vestal virgin, G. i, 130,
iii, 114, U. x, 5. Lastly, a woman was released from the
potestas of her father on passing *in manum mariti* by
coemption, G. i, 136; but by the later law this result did
not follow *manus* created *confarreatione, ibid.;* still less
did it follow marriage without *manus,* U. vi, 6, (see
Manus, 1, 2, 4, *Husband and wife,* 3).
PATRONATE was the relationship that existed between a freedman,
  libertus, and his *patronus, i.e.* the person or the representatives of the person to whom he belonged before
  manumission.
    1. *Who were patrons.*—In the case of a freedman who became
a citizen on manumission—and to become so he required
to have been manumitted by his quiritarian owner, G.
i, 17, U. i, 16, (see *Manumission,* 2)—the patronage, with
its attendant rights, belonged in all cases to his manumitter, and passed on the latter's death to his male
descendants, even though not his heirs but disinherited
in his testament, G. i, 165, iii, 48, 58. When the freedman became only a latin on manumission, the patronage,
so far as its rights were concerned, might be split, the
tutory of the freedman going to his quiritarian owner at
the time of manumission and the latter's male descendants as above, G. i, 167, U. xi, 19, but his estate going on
his death, if he died a latin, to his manumitter and his
heirs, whether that manumitter had been his quiritarian
or merely his bonitarian owner, G. iii, 58. The patronage
might be in a patroness instead of a patron, though she,
because of her sex, was unable to exercise some of its
rights, *e.g.* tutory, G. i, 195; while others, *e.g.* succession,
were in her case more restricted than in that of patrons,
G. iii, 49, 52. A municipality or other *universitas* might
be patron of its freedmen, U. xxii, 5; but obviously with
rights considerably restricted.
    2. *The patron's rights.*—A patron and his male descend-
ants were entitled to the tutory of his freedmen under
puberty and freedwomen of any age, for they had no
agnates to claim it (see *Agnation,* 1) as in the case of
persons of free birth; see *Tutory,* 18, 19. He and they
were entitled to the succession, or a share of it, of a
citizen freedman dying without children of his own, (see
Succession to citizen freedmen); and he and his children
36

PATRONATE—*continued.*

not expressly disinherited, and failing them his stranger-
heirs, took the estate of a latin freedman, (see *Succession
to Junian latins*). If his freedman was withheld from
him, the patron had an exhibitory interdict (see *Interdicts*, No. 2) for his production, G. iv, 162 ; and his
eventual interest in his freedman's estate entitled him
under the Aelia-Sentian law to ignore any manumission
by him by which he was defrauded, G. i, 37.

3. *The freedman's obligations.*—A freedman, if a citizen, and
therefore qualified to make a testament, was bound to pay
due regard in it to the rights of his patron ; see *Succession
to cit. freedmen.* He owed his patron so much respect
that he was forbidden to summon him in a litigation
without leave of the praetor, and if he did was liable in
damages, G. iv, 46.   Finally, he was bound to render his
patron certain services, some of which it was the custom
to promise under oath, G. iii, 96*a*; it was peculiar to
these last that the patron ceased to be entitled to them
on his *capitis deminutio*, G. iii, 83.

4. *How the relationship was ended.*—It is not said that the
relationship came to an end by *capitis deminutio minima ;*
but as the patron's right of tutory and of succession
ab intestato were *legitima jura,* they necessarily were
extinguished by *cap. dem.* of either party, and the
patronage thus shorn, so far as the *jus civile* was concerned,
of some of its most important prerogatives, G. iii, 51, 83,
U. xi, 9.   Acquisition of citizenship by a Junian latin
(see *Junian latinity,* 7) did not dissolve the relationship,
but only changed the nature of it, (above, No. 1).   Yet
not necessarily ; for an imperial grant might be *salvo jure
patroni,* G. iii, 72, which reserved to the patron the same
rights of succession as if his freedman had remained a
latin ; and if given without such reservation, but without
the patron's consent or knowledge, the result was the
same, unless the citizen-latin subsequently confirmed his
citizenship by *causae probatio* under the Aelia-Sentian law
or the Sct., (see *Ael.-Sentian law*, 6, 7), G. iii, 73.

PAYMENT (including therein other varieties of performance), *solutio,*
the commonest mode of extinguishing an obligation,
G. iii, 168; partial payment, where that was possible,
amounting to partial extinction, 172.

1. *Was it payment when something else was given than what was
due ?*—Not unless with the creditor's consent ; and even
then it was a point of controversy between the schools
whether the debtor was *ipso jure* discharged or only in a

PAYMENT—*continued*.

    position to meet any further claim by his creditor with an *exceptio doli*, G. iii, 168.

  2. *Did payment of the true debt always imply discharge ?*—It did not if it was to another party than the creditor or his representative, G. iii, 160, although excusable error sometimes introduced an exception to the rule, *ibid.* Neither did it if it was to a pupil without his tutor's *auctoritas* (see *Pupils*), G. ii, 83, 84; the money paid became the pupil's property, but the debtor was not thereby freed ; for to grant a discharge, either directly or by implication, was to part with an item of his estate, which it was not in the power of a pupil to do without his tutor's concurrence, *ibid.* This was the *ipso jure* state of matters ; but if the pupil was the richer for the payment, and nevertheless claimed it a second time, he might be defeated by an *exceptio doli mali*, (see *Exception*, 8), G. ii, 84. A woman, however, effectually discharged her debtor by accepting actual payment from him, G. ii, 85, iii, 171 ; because she was entitled to alienate her *res nec mancipi*, amongst which obligationary claims were included, without her tutor's *auctoritas*, G. ii, 80, 85, (see *Women*, 4). Payment to an adstipulator (see *Adstipulation*) was as effectual as to the principal stipulant, G. iii, 111.

PECULIUM was a fund which a *paterfamilias* entrusted to a *filiusfamilias* or slave, and of which, though *de jure* it still belonged to the granter, they had had the administration while they continued to possess it, G. iv, 74*a* ; Ulp. says that a public slave had even the power to test on it to the extent of a half, U. xx, 16. As it enabled its possessors to obtain credit in contracting, the praetors held it reasonable that the *paterfamilias* should be responsible to the extent of it for their contractual debts, G. iv, 73-74*a*, (see *Adjectician actions*, 3). The estate of a Junian latin continued by the Junian law to be a *quasi peculium ;* and on the latin's death belonged in that character to his manumitter or his heirs, G. iii, 56, (see *Succession to Junian latins*).

PECULIUM CASTRENSE was the separate estate amassed by a *filiusfamilias* while on military service, G. ii, 106 and n. 1. He had greater power over it than over that confided to him by his father, (and which was often called *profecticium* to distinguish it from the *castrense*); for he might dispose of it by testament, U. xx, 10. He might do so while on active service by an informal *testamentum militare*, (see *Testament*, 25); but if he did so *per aes et*

PECULIUM CASTRENSE—*continued.*

libram after his discharge, neither his *paterfamilias* nor any one in the latter's *potestas* could assist at its execution as a witness or otherwise, G. ii, 106.

PECUNIA did not necessarily mean money, G. ii, 104 and n. 4, iii, 124.

PECUNIA CREDITA, meaning of, G. iii, 124.

PECUNIAE NON NUMERATAE, EXCEPTIO, G. iv, 116; see *Exception,* 9.

PEGASUS AND PUSIO, consuls in reign of Vespasian, authors of a Sct. extending the benefit of *causae probatio ex lege Aelia Sentia* to slaves irregularly manumitted after passing the age of thirty, G. i, 31; see *Aelia-Sentian law,* 7.

PEREGRINITY, the condition of those who, being free, were neither citizens nor colonial or Junian latins, though possibly Roman subjects, G. i, 193, (where the Bithynians, who were provincials, are expressly spoken of as peregrins). This seems to be the meaning which Gai. usually attaches to the word *peregrini ;* although here and there the reference is solely to independent foreign nations, as in i, 79, 197 and 198, iii, 94.

1. *What meant by capacity and incapacity of peregrins.*—As the law of Rome was a compound of two elements, the *jus civile* and the *jus gentium*—that *quo omnes gentes utuntur,* G. i, 1, so, while it denied participation in the rights and institutions of the *jus civile* to any but citizens, or non-citizens to whom it had specially been conceded, it freely admitted peregrins to participation in those of the *jus gentium ;* and even where it refused to recognise participation by them in some institution of the *jus civile,* it did not deny the possibility of their having kindred and corresponding institutions of their own. Thus, while it held *justae nuptiae* to be peculiar to citizens, it did not dispute the validity of marriage of peregrins *secundum leges moresque peregrinorum,* G. i, 92; it recognised amongst certain peregrins the existence of institutions that closely resembled the *patria potestas* and the *tutela mulierum* of Rome, G. i, 155, 193; and while it declared that only a citizen could make a testament according to Roman solemnities or take under one, it yet admitted that testamentary disposition was a practice among the nations generally, G. i, 189, and acknowledged the validity of a testament made by a peregrin *secundum leges civitatis suae,* U. xx, 14. It went still further; for it sustained as valid between peregrins transactions to which there was nothing that corresponded between citizens, such as the literal obligations by *chirographa*

PEREGRINITY—*continued.*

and *syngraphae*, G. iii, 134; and sometimes adopted the peregrin rule as to the consequences of a *juris gentium* contract when it was not a citizen but a peregrin that had thereby become bound, G. iii, 120.

2. *Their capacity in matter of marriage.*—They had no *conubium* with citizens unless by special concession, G. i, 56, U. v, 4. A peregrin woman marrying a citizen with whom she had *conubium* contracted *justae nuptiae*, *ibid.*, G. i, 76; but a peregrin man marrying a citizen woman under the same condition did not,—his marriage was as much a peregrin marriage as if he had married a peregrin, G. i, 77. If without *conubium* a citizen married a peregrin wife, the issue followed the condition of their mother, G. i, 67, (see *Status*, 2); if, also without *conubium*, a peregrin married a citizen wife, then, by the Minician law, though contrary to the rule of the *jus gentium*, the issue followed not their mother but their father, G. i, 78; but if in either case there had been on either side a mistaken belief of the existence of *conubium*, the defects of the marriage might be cured by *erroris causae probatio*, G. i, 75, (see below, No. 8).

3. *Their capacity in the other domestic relations.*—A peregrin had no *potestas* over his children in the Roman sense of the word, G. i, 55, 189: but he might appoint tutors to them, for such guardianship was *juris naturalis*, G. i, 89; though whether the Roman rules as to *auctoritas*, etc., applied to them may be doubted. He might own slaves, G. i, 52, and enfranchise them, (of course in so doing making them only peregrins like himself), G. i, 47; but, as regarded their manumission, he was not subject to the rules of the Aelia-Sentian law, except the one prohibition of manumission in fraud of creditors, which was extended by senatusconsult to provincial peregrins, *ibid.*

4. *Their capacity in matter of property.*—They could hold in property both *res mancipi* and *res nec mancipi* (which see), for they could own slaves, which were of the former class, G. i, 47, 52, U. xix, 1; but could not grant or take a conveyance of them by civil modes unless they had had a concession of *commercium*, U. xix, 4. In that case they could convey or take by mancipation (which see), *ibid.*; and probably *in jure cessio* and *usucapion* (see those words) were equally competent to them. But transfer of a *res mancipi* to a citizen by a peregrin who had no *commercium*, though it was only by tradition, gave the transferee full quiritarian right, U. i, 16, note 2, whereas

PEREGRINITY—*continued.*

    between citizens it would have made him only bonitarian
owner (see *Bon. ownership*, 2), G. ii, 41, U. i, 16.

  5. *Their capacity in matter of succession.*—They might make
testaments according to their own law, U. xx, 14; but
not in the manner prescribed for citizens, *ibid.* As they
had no *testamenti factio* with citizens, G. ii, 218, U. xxii,
2, they could neither be instituted heirs in a citizen's
testament, G. ii, 110, U. xxii, 2, nor appointed legatees,
G. ii, 218; and although at one time they were allowed
to take *fideicommissa*, yet by a Sct. of Hadrian's this also
was prohibited, and such trust-gifts confiscated, G. ii, 285.
As regards intestate succession, the Roman rules could
not apply to them, for their foundation was in the *patria
potestas* of the *jus civile*, and this peregrins did not possess;
above, No. 2.

  6. *Their capacity in matter of obligations.*—Most contracts being
juris gentium, they took part in them as freely and fully
as citizens,—real contracts, G. iii, 132; verbal ones, G.
iii, 93, except when the word *spondeo* was used, *ibid.*; and
consensual ones, G. iii, 154. Even the literal one by
transscriptio a re in personam was competent to them
according to the Sabinian view, G. iii, 133; for it was
but a novation of a prior *juris gentium* obligation (see
Literal obligations, 1), and a peregrin might novate, G.
iii, 179. They could not be parties to a *transscriptio a
persona in personam*, for that was a purely civil *negotium*,
G. iii, 133; but on the other hand they were bound by
chirographa and *syngraphae*, which were peculiar to themselves, 134. They were responsible and entitled to redress for delicts as much as were citizens, G. iv, 37; the
only obstacle arose when the penalties had been imposed
by a statute in terms applicable only to citizens; how it
was got over, see *ibid.* and below, No. 7.

  7. *Their capacity in litigation.*—That peregrins could litigate
before Roman magistrates, even in matters arising *inter se*,
and that had to be settled by reference to the *jus gentium*
or their own peculiar law, is manifest; for the peregrin
praetorship was instituted on their behalf, G. i, 6 and n.
2, and the governors in the provinces had the same jurisdiction, G. i, 6. The *judicia* in which they were parties
were necessarily *imperio continentia*, (see *Jud. legitima,
etc.*, 2), G. iv, 105, 109; and they might themselves act
as *judices* or recuperators, *ibid.* There must occasionally
have been peculiarities in the formulae of their actions;
but the only case referred to is that of a peregrin suing

PEREGRINITY—*continued.*.
  or being sued on a statute which *in terminis* applied only
  to citizens, and then it was adapted to him by interpolation of a fiction of citizenship, G. iv, 37, (see *Fiction*, 3).

8. *How they acquired citizenship.*—When a peregrin man had
  married a citizen woman, or a citizen man had married a
  peregrin woman, under the mistaken belief that they had
  conubium, either of them who had laboured under the mistake was entitled, on the birth of a child,—for the remedy
  was intended primarily to create *potestas,*—to prove cause
  of error; one of the results being that the peregrin parent
  thereby became a citizen, G. i, 67-71, 74, (see *Erroris
  causae probatio*). The commonest mode of acquiring it
  was imperial grant on the peregrin's petition, G. i, 93, 94,
  ii, 135a, iii, 20; but it did not carry *potestas* over children
  already born or *in utero,* unless applied for and expressly
  conceded, (see *Patria potestas,* 12), *ibid.* It might also
  be acquired by *jus Latii* (see *Colonial latinity,* 2), when
  the peregrin belonged to a state to which that right had
  been granted, (in which case he was truly a colonial
  latin), G. i, 95 and 96, and note.

9. *How a citizen became a peregrin.*—The only cause referred
  to in the texts is *aqua et igni interdictio* (which see), G. i,
  128 and n. 2, 161, U. x, 3, xi, 12.

PEREMPTORY EXCEPTIONS, G. iv, 121; see *Exception*, 5, 8, 9.
PERFECTA LEX, a law that annulled an act done in contravention of
  it, U. i, 1, note.
PERHIBERE TESTIMONIUM, G. ii, 104 and note 7.
PERMUTATIO, barter or exchange, G. iii, 141; see *Sale*, 2.
PERSONS form the subject-matter of Gaius' first book, and are thus
  classified:—

1. *Freemen and slaves.*—This is Gaius' first classification of
  persons, G. i, 9; see *Freedom, Slavery.* Freemen might
  be either *injenui, i.e.* of free birth, or *libertini, i.e.* free by
  enfranchisement (see *Manumission*), 10, 11. The latter
  again might be either citizens, Junian latins, or ranked
  with dediticians, 12; see *Citizenship, Junian latinity,
  Deditician freedmen.*

2. *Citizens and peregrins.*—The latter class included not only
  foreigners, *i.e.* subjects of other states, G. i, 197, ii, 94,
  but also provincial non-citizen subjects of Rome, G. i,
  193, and even Romans who had forfeited citizenship
  while retaining freedom, G. i, 128, U. x, 3; see *Citizenship, Peregrinity.*

3. *Persons sui and alieni juris.*—*Sui juris,* not subject to any
  family head, were *paterfamilias* and *materfamilias,* U. iv,

PERSONS—*continued.*

1 and note. *Alieni juris* or domestically dependent, G.
i, 48, were slaves *in dominica potestate* (see *Slavery*),
children *in patria potestate* (see *Pat. potestas*), women *in
manu* (see *Manus*), and free persons *in causa mancipii*
(see *Mancipii etc.*), G. i, 49, 52, 55, 109 f., 116 f. As
regards the capacities and incapacities of the latter class,
see *Alieni juris personae*, 2-4.

4. *Persons under guardians.*—Of persons *sui juris* pupils and
in most cases women were under tutory; lunatics and
prodigals, and in many cases minors, were in curatory, G.
i, 142 f.; see *Tutory, Curatory.*

5. *Persons unborn.*—For some purposes a child *in utero* was
regarded as already born, G. i, 147; see *Postumi.*

6. *Persons in fact and persons by fiction of law* (*natural and
jural persons*).—Personality was occasionally attributed
to other entities than men; for *universitates*, such as
civitates and *municipia*, could hold property, G. ii, 11,
and might in some cases be instituted as heirs, U. xxii,
5, and take legacies and trust-gifts, U. xxiv, 28; the fisc
claimed caducous inheritances and bequests, U. xvii, 2;
and certain divinities might be made heirs under a testament, U. xxii, 6.

PERSONAL INJURY, *injuria*, G. iii, 220-225; see also *Delict.*

1. *Its nature.*—It included all varieties of assault and insult
by act, speech, or writing. G. iii, 220. It might be offered
to a man not only in his own person, but also in that of
free members of his family, entitling him in the latter
case to redress both in their names and his own, 221.
He might even suffer it through his slave, where something very atrocious was done to the latter, obviously
meant in disrespect to his owner, 222; but a slave was
never himself held to have suffered it, *ibid.* A free
person *in mancipio* might suffer it at the hands of the
party to whose *jus* he was subject, G. i, 141.

2. *Its penalties.*—Under the Twelve Tables there was a sliding
scale of punishments, from talion down to a trifling fine,
G. iii, 223; but the praetor authorised the sufferer—
though not his heir, the wrong being so highly personal,
G. iv, 112—to claim damages in an *actio injuriarum*, G.
iii, 224. In the ordinary case the judge might at his
discretion assess them at any figure within the sum
claimed, *ibid.;* but in cases of *atrox injuria*, 225, the
praetor taxed the amount in the *formula* (see *Condemnatio*, 2), and then the judge rarely went below it,
224.

PICTURA, acquisition of property by, and respective rights of the artist and of the owner of the pannel painted on, G. ii, 78; see *Property*, 6.

PIGNORIS CAPIO, one of the *legis actiones*, G. iv, 26-29, 31, 32; see *Legis actiones*, 6.

PIGNUS, pawn or pledge, was a contract between creditor and debtor, created by delivery of some article by the latter to the former in security of a debt, and therefore completed *re*, (see *Real obligations*); but it is not mentioned by Gai. in describing the real contract, G. iii, 90 and 91, note, and in fact was not yet much developed in his time, *fiducia* (which see, No. 2) being still used for creation of a real security, G. ii, 60. The creditor holding a *pignus* was responsible to the debtor for its safe custody, G. iii, 203, 204, but the latter was not entitled to take it away from the former, and, if he did so surreptitiously, was held guilty of theft, 200. The creditor's right to sell it is attributed by Gai. to agreement to that effect with the debtor, G. ii, 64. The contract gave rise to the *actio pigneraticia*, which was *bonae fidei*, G. iv, 62.

PISTRINI EXERCITIO, flour-milling, was one of the modes whereby a latin attained citizenship, G. i, 34, U. iii, 1; see *Junian latinity*, 7.

PLANTATIO, acquisition of property by, and remedies of parties, G. i, 74, 76; see *Property*, 6.

PLEBISCITUM, G. i, 3, and n. 2; see *Statute*, 1.

PLEBS defined, G. i, 3.

PLEDGE, see *Pignus*.

PLENUM DOMINIUM, *plenum jus dominii*, ownership of a thing both in quiritarian and bonitarian right, G. ii, 41, iii, 80; see *Property*, 1.

PLUS and MINUS in obligations depended on time or condition as well as quantity, G. iii, 113.

PLUS PETITIO, excessive claim by a party in the *intentio* of a *certa formula*, G. iv, 53 (see *Intentio*, 3); it was impossible in one that was *incerta*, 54. There might be over-claim either in respect of amount, time, place, or circumstances, as illustrated in 53; and the result was that the pursuer altogether lost his cause, 53, fresh action being excluded, G. iii, 181.

POENA SACRAMENTI, G. iv, 14, 95; see *Legis actiones*, 2.

POENAE CAUSA INSTITUTIO, institution of an heir to a share of an inheritance, not out of regard for him, but as a means of coercing his co-heir to follow a particular line of conduct; such an institution was useless, G. ii, 243, (see *Testament*, 9). A legacy or trust-gift *poenae causa relictum* was also ineffectual, G. ii, 235, 288, U. xxiv, 17, xxv, 13, (see *Legacy*, 9, *Fideicommissum*, 5).

PONTIFICES, their *interpretatio*, G. ii, 42, note; their early functions as judges, G. iv, 13, note 6; how their office was connected with *pons, ibid.*

POPULUS defined, G. i, 3.

POSSESSION could not be acquired *solo animo*, G. iv, 153. But the acquisitive act did not require to be done *in propria persona* by the party thereby becoming possessor; it might be that of one of his slaves, of a *filiusfamilias*, or of a freeman or *servus alienus bona fide* possessed by him, G. ii, 89, 94. While it was admitted that possession might be acquired for a man by his wife *in manu*, a free person in his *mancipium*, or a slave of whom he had the usufruct, if property was acquired along with it, G. ii, 86, 87, yet it was a question whether possession by itself could be acquired or held by them for him to whom they were subject, for the reason that they themselves were not in his possession, G. ii, 90, 94. It might be retained for a man through a usufructuary, tenant, depositary, borrower, or other party holding in his name, G. iv, 153, and in some cases even by a mere effort of will, *ibid.* It was said to be *pro herede* when a man possessed a thing as and in the belief that he was heir, *pro possessore* when he did not impute his possession to any title, and knew he had no right to it, G. iv, 144. For the nature and effects of *bonae fidei possessio*, see that head; for possession in reference to usucapion, see *Usucapion;* and for the possessory remedies, see *Interdicts*, 5-9.

POSSESSORUM INTERDICTUM, G. iv, 145; see *Interdicts*, 5.

POSTLIMINIUM, see *Jus postliminii.*

POSTULATIO JUDICIS, one of the *legis actiones*, G. iv, 12, 17a, note, 20; see *Legis actiones*, 3.

POSTUMI, in reference to a testament, meant persons born after its execution; in reference to intestacy, persons born after the death of the intestate.

1. Postumi sui *of a testator.*—A man might institute a child unborn as his heir or appoint tutors to him, whether *in utero* or not, provided such child, if born during his lifetime, would be in his *potestas*, G. i, 147, ii, 130, U. xxii, 15, 19. Not only might he institute such a *postumus,*—he was required either to institute or disinherit him if he wished to secure the validity of his testament, (see *Testament*, 10), G. ii, 130, U. xxii, 14, 15; for *agnatio postumi praeteriti* of either sex, provided it was born alive, caused *ruptio*, G. ii, 131, U. xxii, 18, (see *Testament*, 22).

2. Postumi sui *of an intestate.*—A child born after his father's death, who would have been in his *potestas* if born during

POSTUMI—*continued.*

> his life, took *ab intestato* as one of the *sui heredes*, G. iii, 4, the agnates being inadmissible so long as the child was *in utero*, U. xxvi, 3; see *Intestate succession*, 3, 4.
>
> 3. Postumi alieni (*or* extranei).—Under this epithet were included not only children born to a third party after the execution of a testament or the death of an intestate, but even the testator's or intestate's own children born after such events respectively, if they could not fall within the number of the *sui heredes*, G. ii, 241; *e.g.* a grandchild through an emancipated son, or a son or daughter by a wife whom the law did not recognise as *justa uxor* (see *Marriage*, 1), *ibid.* Such *postumi* were regarded as *incertae personae*, and could neither be instituted heirs in a testament nor have legacies or trust-gifts left them, G. i, 147, ii, 241, 242, 287.

POTESTAS DOMINICA, see *Slavery.*

POTESTAS PATRIS FAMILIAS, see *Patria potestas.*

PRAECEPTIONEM, LEGATUM PER, see *Legacy*, 28, 29, 33, 34.

PRAEDIA, in its original meaning, lands mortgaged to the state by parties contracting with it, in security of their engagements, G. ii, 61; in its later meaning, lands generally, G. ii, 71, 72, iii, 145, etc.

PRAEDIATOR PRAEDIATURA, G. ii, 61.

PRAEJUDICIUM, G. iv, 44; see *Actions*, 4.

PRAES, an early name for a surety, G. iv, 13, 16, 91, 94.

PRAESCRIPTIO, a clause prefixed to a *formula* (which see), G. iv, 132, either (*a*) to reserve a right of action to the pursuer which would have been lost by *consumptio actionis* (which see) if the *formula* had been unrestricted, 131, 131*a*, the same purpose being attained in *formulae* containing a *demonstratio* (which see) by limitative words in that clause, 136; or (*b*) to explain certain matters of fact necessary to qualify the technical meaning of the words of the *intentio* (which see), 134, 135, 137. A third class of prescriptions, prefixed for the sake of defenders, had given place, before the time of Gai. to exceptions, 133.

PRAESTARE, meaning, G. iv, 2, note 3.

PRAETERITION in testaments, omission to mention a person that the law required should be instituted or disinherited; see *Testament*, 10.

PRAETOR, the,—his office and influence.

> 1. *The praetor's office.*—The office of the *praetor urbanus* was established by or as an immediate consequence of the Licinian laws of 387 | 367, which opened the consulate to the plebeians; his prescribed duty being to

PRAETOR—*continued.*

administer justice to the citizens, G. i, 6 and n. 1. About 507 | 247, or a year or two later, a second praetor was appointed to administer justice to non-citizens, and between citizens and non-citizens, who got the name of *praetor peregrinus*, G. i, 6 and n. 2. They possessed, so far as necessary for the execution of their office, the same *imperium* or power of issuing and enforcing commands that had been exercised by the kings and was still exercised by the consuls, G. i, 98, 190, iv, 105, etc.; two of its most important elements being the *jurisdictio*, G. iv, 110, and the *jus edicendi*, G. i, 6. The number of praetors was afterwards increased, in order that some might be sent into the provinces and others exercise jurisdiction in particular matters; but the only one specially referred to in the texts is the *praetor fideicommissarius*, to whom all questions relating to testamentary trusts were remitted, G. ii, 278 and note, U. xxv, 12. In the time of Gaius the governors exercised in the provinces the same jurisdiction as did the urban and peregrin praetors in Rome, G. i, 6.

2. *The praetor's edicts.*—These were the rules which, usually on entering on office, they announced their intention to give effect to during their year's tenure of it; they were afterwards consolidated by Salv. Julianus in the reign of Hadrian, and embodied in a Sct., G. iv, 104, note 1. This consolidation, except in G. i, 6 (where the plural is used), is what Gai. and Ulp. commonly refer to under the singular *edictum*, G. ii, 253, iii, 82, etc., U. xxviii, 4, xxix, 1, etc.: it seems to have been systematically arranged, and divided into titles, G. iv, 46. The aim of the praetors was to expedite, supplement, or correct the *jus civile* as general utility required, G. iv, 30, note 1, setting themselves to provide remedies for its *iniquitates*, *i.e.* the points in which it was inconsistent with natural equity, G. iii, 25, 41.

3. *Examples of the praetor's intervention.*—(a) In the law of persons:—maintaining in a state of *de facto* freedom slaves that, because of the informality, etc., of their manumission, were still *de jure* slaves,—afterwards rendered unnecessary by the Junian law, see *Junian latinity*, 1; giving minors the benefit of *in integrum restitutio*, which see; compelling tutors in certain cases to grant *auctoritas* to acts of their female wards of full age, see *Tutory*, 23. (b) In that of property:—recognition of bonitarian ownership (which see) and *bonae fidei possessio* (which

PRAETOR—*continued.*

also see) as independent rights *tuitione praetoris ;* protection of possession by the possessory interdicts, see *Interdicts,* 5-9. (*c*) In that of succession :—remodelling the systems of both testate and intestate succession by introduction of *bonorum possessio,* which see; granting to *sui heredes* power to hold aloof from their parent's succession when it was likely to be *damnosa,* see *Abstinendi potestas.* (*d*) In that of obligations :—giving creditors a claim against a *paterfamilias* in respect of the contractual debts of his *filiusfamilias* or slave, see *Adjectician actions ;* rendering innocuous the rule of the *jus civile* that a creditor's claim was extinguished by his debtor's *capitis deminutio,* see *Fiction,* 3 ; putting creditors in possession of the estate of a bankrupt debtor, with power of sale, see *Emptio bonorum.*

4. *Praetorian remedies.*—It was in most cases by granting new remedies that the praetors accomplished the objects enumerated in No. 3. It may be added generally that it was they who worked out the formular system, see *Procedure ;* that they sanctioned agency, see *Procuratory in litigation;* that they introduced many new direct actions, G. iv, 11, of which it was a peculiarity that they were not granted beyond a year from the date of the occurrence to which they referred, unless they were imitations of statutory ones, G. iv, 110, 111 ; that they invented the *utiles actiones* and *actiones in factum,* see *Actions,* 6 ; that it was they who introduced equitable exceptions, which see; and that by praetorian stipulations, of which there is an example in G. iv, 31, they endeavoured to guard against future damage by anticipatory securities.

PRECARIUM, a grant during the pleasure of the granter, on the solicitation of the grantee, G. ii, 60; *ab adversario precario possidere* was to retain possession notwithstanding recal of such a grant, G. iv, 150, etc.

PRINCIPAL AND ACCESSORY.—As regards accessions to property, see *Property,* Nos. 4, 6. An accessory obligation could never cover more than the principal one, G. iii, 126. *Ei quod nullum est nihil accedere potest,* G. iv, 151.

PROCEDURE IN LITIGATION.

1. *Procedure by the* legis actiones.—Gaius' account of it is defective ; for the nature of it generally, and the causes of its falling into disrepute, see *Legis actiones.*

2. *Transition to the formular system.*—Litigation *per formulas* was introduced by the Aebutian law about 507 | 247,

PROCEDURE IN LITIGATION—*continued.*

and made the ordinary procedure by the Julian judiciary laws, G. iv, 30 and notes. The *in rem actio per sponsionem* seems to mark the transition stage; for though a *formula* was adjusted, the *sponsio* was almost a reproduction of the *sacramentum*, G. iv, 93, 94.

3. *Bringing a defender into court.*—See *In jus vocatio.*

4. *Contumacious failure to appear.*—When a debtor fraudulently kept out of the way, so as to render summons impossible, and no one appeared to defend him in his absence, his creditor was entitled to be put into possession of his estate and bring it to sale, the debtor in such a case being dealt with as a bankrupt, G. iii, 78; see *Emptio bonorum, Bankruptcy.*

5. *Agency.*—This was only exceptionally allowed in procedure *per legis actiones,* but was general under the formular system; see *Procuratory in litigation.*

6. *Securities required from the parties.*—See *Cautiones in judicial procedure.*

7. *Checks on reckless or vexatious action or defence.*—See *Vexatious litigation.*

8. *Adjustment of the* formula *or issue.*—This was the characteristic feature of the system,—an issue prepared by the magistrate, after hearing the parties informally, and being satisfied that there was a relevant case; it was sent down by him in writing to the judge (*judex*) or recuperators who were to try the cause, and contained authority to them to condemn or absolve, G. iv, 31, 34, 43, 105 and note; see *Formula.* It was necessary in a few cases to embody in it a reference to an old *legis actio,* but in the vast majority this was not required, G. iv, 32, 33. For its ordinary clauses, see *Formula,* 1. By means of interjected fictions of citizenship, heirship, usucapion, etc., the magistrate often adapted those *formulae* to the case of persons who otherwise would have been without a remedy, G. iv, 34-38, (see *Fiction*); by incorporated exceptions he brought under the notice of the judge matters of defence, statutory or equitable, which he would have to investigate, G. iv, 115-119, (see *Exception*); while by prefixed prescriptions he reserved to the pursuer future rights of action of which judgment on an unrestricted *formula* would have deprived him, G. iv, 130-132, or made explanations of importance from other points of view, 133-137, (see *Praescriptio*).

9. *Litiscontestation.*—With adjustment of the *formula,* which ended the procedure *in jure,* there was *litis contestatio,*

PROCEDURE IN LITIGATION—*continued.*

judicium acceptum, res in judicium deducta, G. iii, 180, 181, iv, 114, 131; and with it a material change was operated on the position of parties, varying according as the *judicium* accepted was *legitimum* or *imperio continens,* G. iii, 180, 181, iv, 103-109, (see *Litis contestatio, Judicia legitima, etc.*).

10. *Duty of the judge.*—In most *formulae* the judge (*judex*) was instructed to condemn or absolve in accordance with the evidence, G. iv, 43, etc.; where restitution of a thing was claimed, he was not to condemn until he had made an order to restore and this had been disobeyed, G. iv, 162, 163; in some he was authorised to divide property and adjudicate shares to the parties, G. iv, 42; in a few he was merely to pronounce a finding, 44. In *bonae fidei judicia* (which see) his office was more than usually free, *liberum est officium,* G. iv, 114: it was his duty to allow set-off of compensatory claims arising out of the same matter, G. iv, 61, 63, 65-68, (see *Compensation*); and he was bound to acquit if the pursuer's demand was satisfied after issue joined,—a principle which the Sabinians held should be extended even to *judicia stricti juris,* G. iv, 114. In condemning, which he was obliged to do in money, G. iv, 48, his award required to be definite, 52. If the *condemnatio* (which see) of the *formula* was *certa,* he could condemn in neither more nor less than the sum named in it without rendering himself liable in damages to the pursuer, *ibid.;* for the latter gained nothing by a judgment in excess of the judge's authority, and could not sue afresh because his claim had been extinguished *novatione* by the litiscontestation, *ibid.,* note 2, iii, 181. Where the *condemnatio* was taxed he incurred the same penalty if he exceeded the *maximum,* G. iv, 52; where it was indefinite it was for him to fix the amount, 51.

11. Res Judicata.—Judgment entitled the party in whose favour it had been pronounced to an *exceptio rei judicatae* to any new action in which his adversary attempted to reopen the same question, G. iv, 121.

12. *Execution.*—See *Judicatum.*

13. Extraordinariae cognitiones.—There were a few cases in which the procedure was not by *formula* and remit to a *judex,* but *extra ordinem,*—from first to last before the magistrate; we have an illustration in actions upon *fidei- commissa,* G. ii, 278 and note, U. xxv, 12.

14. In integrum restitutiones, *interdicts, etc.*—See those words.

PROCINCTUS, G. ii, 101, U. xx, 2; see *Testament,* 2.

PROCULIANS, see *Sabinians and Proculians.*

PROCULUS, a jurist of distinction in the reigns of Claudius and Nero, who, on the death of the elder Nerva, became head of the sect founded by Labeo, and which was known afterwards as that of the Proculians, G. ii, 15, 195, 231, iii, 140, iv, 163.

PROCURATOR,—did his acquisition of property by tradition in his principal's name make the latter owner ? G. ii, 95 ; what power had he of alienating his principal's property ? G. ii, 64 and n. 2.

PROCURATORY IN LITIGATION, G. iv, 82-87.

    1. *Such agency generally.*—Under the system of the *legis actiones* (which see), procuratory was incompetent except *pro populo, pro libertate,* or *pro tutela,* G. iv, 82 and n. 3 ; but under that of the *formulae* (which see) a man might sue or be sued either in person or by an agent, such as a cognitor, procurator, tutor, or curator, G. iv, 82. Certain persons, however, were not allowed to sue by a cognitor, and others were forbidden to act as such, G. iv, 124.

    2. *Cognitors and procurators in particular.*—A cognitor was formally accredited by his principal to the other party by word of mouth, G. iv, 83 ; but for a procurator an informal mandate was sufficient, and he was entitled to act without it if he was in good faith and gave the other side *cautio de rato, i.e.* that his principal would abide by his acts,—a security usually required even when there was a mandate, 84.

    3. *How they sued and were sued.*—When it was the pursuer that was represented by an agent, the latter formulated the *intentio* (which see) in the name of his principal, and the *condemnatio* (which also see) in his own favour, G. iv, 86 ; if he took the *intentio* in his own name, *i.e.* if he averred that he was owner, or that it was to him the defender was indebted, he necessarily failed, G. iv, 55 ; but fresh action was not excluded, there having been no *consumptio* (which see), *ibid.* If it was the defender that was represented by an agent, and the action a personal one, the pursuer averred in the *intentio* that the principal was his debtor, but in the *condemnatio* asked judgment against the agent, G. iv, 87 ; in a real action the *condemnatio* was in the same form, but of course neither principal nor agent was named in the *intentio, ibid.*

    4. *Procuratory* in rem suam.—A claim (*obligatio*) was in itself intransferable, but the right to sue on it might be ceded, (see *Obligation,* 4); in such a case the cessionary sued as the creditor's procurator, but on his own account, G. ii, 39.

PROCURATORY IN LITIGATION—*continued.*
> The same practice was followed by the purchaser of an
> inheritance, G. ii, 252, (see *Emptio hereditatis*).

PRODIGALS, *prodigi*, dissipating their patrimony were interdicted
> the administration of their affairs, G. i, 53, and placed
> under curatory, sometimes of their agnates, sometimes of
> persons appointed by the praetors, U. xii, 2, 3, (see *Cura-
> tory*, 1); consequently they were incapable of making a
> testament, U. xx, 13.

PRO HEREDE POSSIDERE, PRO POSSESSORE POSSIDERE, G. iv, 144; see
> *Possession*.

PROMITTO, probable derivation, G. iii, 92, note.

PROPERTY, *dominium*, G. ii, 18-96, U. tit. xix.
1. *Tenures.*—Originally the law knew but one sort of property,
   dominium ex jure Quiritium, G. ii, 40; but, on the praetors
   declaring that they were prepared to recognise a beneficial
   ownership in a man whose legal title failed simply
   from defect in the form of his conveyance, a second sort
   sprang into existence, called 'having a thing *in bonis*,' G. i,
   54, ii, 40, 41, now usually called bonitarian property, (see
   Quiritarian ownership, Bonitarian ownership). They were
   often separated, the quiritarian right being in one man,
   the bonitarian in another, in which case the former was
   spoken of as *nudum jus Quiritium*, the owner practically
   deriving no benefit, G. i, 54, iii, 166; when both were
   combined in the same individual, he was said to have
   plenum jus, G. i, 15, ii, 41. *Bonae fidei possessio*, though
   short of property, was a right much more valuable than
   the *nudum jus*, G. iii, 166, (see *B. f. possessio*).
2. *Its acquisition generally.*—Like other rights, it might be
   acquired either on a universal or on a singular title, G. ii,
   97: the former when it came to a man as part of the
   universum jus of the old owner, as in *hereditas, bonorum
   possessio, emptio bonorum*, adrogation, and *manus*, (see
   those words), 98; the latter when it came to him as an
   independent and individual right, 97. Of both modes of
   acquisition, some were civil, others natural.
3. *Civil modes of singular acquisition.*—The most important
   were mancipation (which see), proper to *res mancipi*
   (which also see), G. ii, 22, U. xix, 3; *in jure cessio* (which
   see), applicable alike to *res mancipi* and *nec mancipi*, U.
   xix, 9; usucapion (which see), also applicable to both, G. ii,
   41-44, U. xix, 8; also adjudication, legacy, *caducum*, and
   ereptorium, (see those words), U. xix, 16, 17, and accretion
   in the case of manumission of a slave by one only of
   several joint owners (see *Adcretio*, 5), U. i, 18.

37

PROPERTY—*continued.*

4. *Natural modes of singular acquisition.*—Amongst those
enumerated are tradition, G. ii, 19, 20, 65, U. xix, 7, (see
below, No. 5); appropriation of a thing at the moment
without an owner, G. ii, 66-68; capture from an enemy,
69; natural accession, as in the case of alluvion or imper-
ceptible increment to land by deposit from a river, 70, 71,
and the rising in a river of an island, which became the
property of the riparian owner, 72; artificial accession,
as the result of building, planting, sowing, painting, or
writing, G. ii, 73-78, (see below, No. 6); and specification, G. ii, 79, (see below, No. 7).

5. *Tradition in particular.*—Tradition or delivery of *res mancipi*
carried only a bonitarian right, G. ii, 41, U. i, 16, unless
it was by a peregrin to a citizen, and then it carried the
plenum jus, U. i, 16, note 2; that of *res nec mancipi* carried
the quiritarian ownership, G. ii, 19-21, U. xix, 7. It was
possible only in the case of corporeals, G. ii, 19, 28; and
the conditions upon which it carried the property were
(*a*) that the tradent was owner, and (*b*) that it proceeded
on a title implying transfer not only of custody but of
ownership, such as sale or donation, G. ii, 20, U. xix, 7.

6. *Artificial accession in particular.*—It was on the principle
accessorium sequitur principale that, if A built on his own
account on B's ground, the building became the property of B, G. ii, 73; but if A in possession was sued in
a *rei vindicatio* by B, the former, if he had built in good
faith, was entitled to resist with an *exceptio doli* (see
Exception, 8) until reimbursed, 76. Exactly the same
in both respects was the rule applied to *plantatio* and
satio, planting or sowing in another person's ground,
74-76, with this qualification—that a plant did not
change owners until it had coalesced with the soil by
striking root in it, 74. The same principles were also
applied to *scriptura,*—the writing of a treatise by A on
the parchments of B; the treatise became B's property by
accession to his parchments, 77. But in *pictura* the rule
was different. If A in good faith painted a picture on
B's pannel, the pannel was held to cede to the picture,
and A became owner of both; but either suing the other
in possession—for though A had the *vindicatio* proper, B
was allowed an *utilis vindicatio*—might be defeated with
an *exceptio doli,* if he did not first pay the value of the
pannel or picture as the case might be, 78.

7. *Specification in particular.*—This arose when A used the
materials of B, and out of them manufactured a new

PROPERTY—*continued.*

article, *nova species,*—wine out of grapes, or a vase out of
metal : the Sabinians held that the new species belonged
to the owner of the material; the Proculians that it belonged to the manufacturer, who would be liable however
to an *actio furti* and *condictio furtiva* (see *Theft,* 6, 7) if he
had used the material surreptitiously, G. ii, 79.

8. *Through whom property could be acquired.*—Property could
not be acquired by the act of a stranger, though acting
professedly as an agent, except *via possessionis ;* and even
this was doubtful, G. ii, 95. But it might be acquired
for a man by those subject to his *jus,* G. ii, 86-96, U. xix,
18-21, except by *in jure cessio,* G. ii, 96, and, though
Gai. and Ulp. do not refer to the matter, by adjudication
(because it was a step in a litigation), *caducum* and
ereptorium. Thus he might acquire through his wife *in
manu,* his *filiifamilias,* his slaves, free persons *in mancipio,*
freemen and *servi alieni bona fide* possessed by him, and
slaves of whom he had the usufruct, G. ii, 86. It was not
admitted, however, that he could acquire by usucapion
through the instrumentality of wife *in manu,* free person
in mancipio, or a usufructed slave, because none of these
were in his possession, 90, 94. As regarded slaves usufructed or only in *bonae fidei* possession, his acquisitions
through their instrumentality were limited to those that
were due to their labour or his funds, 91, 92, U. xix, 21.
A slave in the bonitarian ownership of one person, but
quiritarian right of another, always acquired for the
former, G. ii, 88, U. xix, 20. If owned jointly by several
parties, he acquired ordinarily for all of them according
to their respective interests as his owners, G. iii, 167 ; if,
however, in taking a conveyance by mancipation, he did
so in the name of one of them in particular, the property
was in the latter only, *ibid.* Whether the general rule
was altered by the fact that the acquisition had been on
the order of one of them in particular was matter of
dispute between the schools, 167*a.*

9. *Alienation.*—While some owners could not alienate, non-
owners sometimes could, G. ii, 62. Thus a husband,
though owner, could not alienate dotal lands without his
wife's consent, 63 ; but the agnatic curator of a lunatic,
a procurator in certain cases, and a creditor holding a
pledge, could alienate though not owners, 64. In some
cases alienation was compulsory, as when a cruel owner
was compelled to sell his slave, (see *Slavery,* 2), G. i, 53.
In the case of women in regard to their *res mancipi,* and

PROPERTY—*continued.*

> pupils generally, they could not alienate without their
> tutors' *auctoritas*, G. i, 192, ii, 80, 84, 85, (see *Women*, 4,
> *Pupils*).
>
> 10. *Remedies.*—Under the system of the *legis actiones* an owner
> employed for vindication of his property an *actio sacra-
> menti*, G. iv, 16, (see *Legis actiones*, 2). Under the formular
> system, if he had the quiritarian right, he used either an
> *actio per formulam petitoriam*, which was the *rei vindicatio*
> properly so called (see *Vindicatio*), G. iv, 3, 91, 92, or an
> *in rem actio per sponsionem* (which see), G. iv, 91, 93 ; if
> he had merely a bonitarian right he employed the Pub-
> lician action (which see), or one of the other fictitious
> actions devised by the praetors for those who had a thing
> only *in bonis* (see *Fiction*, 1, 2), G. iv, 34-36. When he
> wished to establish that his property was free from a servi-
> tude or other pretended burden, he used an *actio negatoria*
> (which see), G. iv, 3 and n. 1. If stolen from him, culpably
> damaged, etc., he had claim for redress ; but the actions
> competent were upon the delict, and do not fall under
> this head ; see *Theft, Wrongful damage to property, etc.*

PROPINQUITY as an impediment to marriage, G. i, 59-62 ; see
> *Marriage*, 4.

PROVINCES, the, were either popular, otherwise stipendiary, governed
> by proconsuls, or imperial, otherwise tributory, governed
> by the emperor's *legati*, G. i, 6 and n. 4, 101 and n. 1, ii,
> 21. In all of them, with exception of those portions
> that enjoyed the *jus Italicum* (which see), the *dominium
> soli* was held to be in the state or emperor, the occupants
> having only the possession or usufruct, G. ii, 7. At the
> same time this idea was not strictly followed out, for,
> while the land was not usucaptable, G. ii, 46, nor trans-
> ferable by *in jure cessio*, 31, it was still said to be *res nec
> mancipi* and capable of transfer by tradition, 21. The
> governors had the same jurisdiction in the provinces as
> the urban and peregrin praetors in Rome, G. i, 6 ; in the
> popular ones quaestors supplied the place of the Roman
> curule aediles, and adopted the latter's edicts, *ibid. ;* but
> no such officials were deputed to the imperial provinces,
> *ibid.* A great deal of Rome's statutory law had in the
> provinces no application, G. i, 47, iii, 121 ; but particular
> provisions were occasionally extended to them by senatus-
> consults, G. i, 47.

PRUDENTIUM RESPONSA, G. i, 7 ; see *Jus Romanorum.*
PUBERTY, when attained, G. i, 196, U. xi, 28.
PUBLICAE RES, G. ii, 11 ; see *Things*, 3.

PUBLICANI, farmers of the revenue, G. iv, 28, 32.

PUBLICIAN ACTION.—There are doubts as to its date and authorship, G. iv, 36, note. It was a praetorian *actio in rem* granted to a proprietor of a *res mancipi* (which see) who had acquired it merely by tradition, and had lost possession before completing his quiritarian right by usucapion, G. iv, 36, (see *Bonitar. ownership*, 3); as also to a *bonae fidei* acquirer *a non domino* in the same position, *ibid.*, (see *Bonae fidei possessio*, 2). Its feature was the presence of a fiction of usucapion contrary to fact, *ibid.* (see *Fiction*, 2). See style of the *formula*, *ibid.* and n. 2.

PUNISHMENT, capital, what? G. iii, 189 and 190, note 1.

PUPILLARY SUBSTITUTION, G. ii, 179-184, U. xxiii, 7; see *Substitution*, 2-4.

PUPILS were children *sui juris*, G. i, 142, under the age of puberty, G. i, 196, U. xi, 1, 28. It was according to natural law that a pupil should be under guardianship, G. i, 189; the guardian was in Roman law called his tutor, (see *Tutory*), G. i, 144, U. xi, 1. With the *auctoritas* of this tutor he might, if he had sufficient intelligence, be a party to any jural act, G. iii, 107, 109, except making a testament, G. ii, 112, U. xx, 12; though in some additional conditions were insisted in, as those of the Aelia-Sentian law (which see, No. 2) in reference to manumissions by owners under twenty, G. i, 40. Further, he was held responsible for delict if sufficiently old to understand the nature of his act, G. iii, 208. Without his tutor's *auctoritas* he could not alienate anything belonging to him,—neither property, G. ii, 80, 81, 84, U. xi, 27, nor a claim against a debtor, G. ii, 83, 84.—nor could he oblige himself by contract, G. iii, 107. But as it was a general rule that he might better his condition without *auctoritas*, though not worsen it, G. ii, 83, this anomaly arose,—that while he might make another his debtor by contract, G. iii, 107, and by accepting payment of the debt make the money he received his own without *auctoritas*, yet his debtor was not thereby discharged, G. ii, 83, 84. If, however, he afterwards raised action against his debtor, the latter was entitled to an *exceptio doli* (see *Exception*, 8), and, if he could show that the pupil had in fact benefited by the payment, thus defeated the action, 84. Receipt of an *indebitum* without *auctoritas* did not relieve a pupil from the obligation of repayment; for such an obligation arose *ex re*, not *ex contractu*, G. iii, 91. As regards the effect of a loan by him without *auctoritas*, see *Mutuum*, 2.

QUADRANS or quarter *as*, G. i, 122. In matter of testaments it was one-fourth of the *hereditas*, and in particular the Falcidian fourth, U. xxv, 17 ; see *Legacy*, 16.

QUAESTORS in the popular provinces had the same jurisdiction as the aediles in Rome, and used their edicts, G. i, 6.

QUANTI EA RES EST, G. iv, 163, note 1.

QUIRITARIAN OWNERSHIP, *dominium ex jure Quiritium*, was originally the only sort of property known to the Romans, G. ii, 40. Its symbol was a *quiris* or *hasta*, a spear, which as such was displayed in the centumviral court, G. iv, 16, and for which a citizen, vindicating his quiritarian right, substituted a rod, (*vindicta* or *festuca*), *ibid.* Afterwards it came to be distinguished from bonitarian property, G. ii, 40, (see *Property*, 1, *Bonitarian ownership*, 1); and when the two were dissociated, was spoken of as the *nudum jus Quiritium*, G. i, 54, iii, 166. It gave its holder no beneficial interest in that over which the right extended, *e.g.* no *potestas* over a slave, G. i, 54, nor any right to his acquisitions, G. ii, 88, iii, 166, unless the slave in acquiring expressly declared that the acquisition was for him, G. iii, 166. At the same time it was only a quiritarian owner that could make a slave a citizen by manumission (which see, No. 2), G. i, 17, U. i, 16 ; and it was he, and not the bonitarian manumitter, that became tutor of a latin freedman, (see *Junian latinity*, 5), G. i, 167, U. xi, 19.

QUORUM BONORUM, an interdict granted to a *bonorum possessor* to enable him to obtain any of the *res hereditariae* from an individual in possession *pro herede* or *pro possessore*, G. iii, 34, iv, 144 ; see *Interdicts*, 5.

RAPINA, see *Robbery*.

RATO, CAUTIO DE, see *Procuratory in litigation*, 2.

REAL OBLIGATIONS, G. iii, 90, 91. An *obligatio re contracta*—not to be confounded with an *obligatio ex re*, which was one created by facts and circumstances independent of contract, G. iii, 89, note 1—was one arising out of a contract completed by an act done, G. iii, 89 and n. 1. The only one mentioned by Gai. in explaining the nature of such contracts is *mutuum* (which see), 90 ; for the obligation to refund money paid by mistake when not due (see *Indebiti solutio*), mentioned by him in the same place, though an *obligatio ex re*, yet was not referable to contract, 91. Commodate, deposit, and pledge (see these words) he mentions only incidentally in other places. The innominate contracts (see *Contract*, 1) were regarded as real, G. iii, 89, note 1.

Robbery—*continued.*

punishable, however trifling, in an *a. vi bonorum raptorum,* with four-fold restitution within the year, and single value afterwards, G. iii, 209.

Rogatio legis, enactment of a law, U. i, 3.

Rupitias sarcire, G. iii, 210-219, note.

Ruptio testamenti, see *Testament,* 22.

Rutilius Rufus, P., praetor *a. u. c.* 636, consul 649, was the author of the bankruptcy procedure by *emptio bonorum* (which see), and of the *a. Rutiliana* granted to the *bonor. emptor,* G. iv, 35.

Sabinians and Proculians, two schools or sects of the jurists in the early empire, G. i, 196, note 1, iii, 71, note, to a great many of whose controversies Gai. alludes, as in i, 196; ii, 15, 37, 79, 123, 195, 200, 217-223, 231, 244; iii, 87, 98, 103, 140, 141, 167a, 168, 178; iv, 78, 79, 114. The founder of the first, C. Ateius Capito, he does not mention; but of his successors he specially refers to Massurius Sabinus (from whom the school took its name), Caelius Sabinus, C Cassius Longinus (from whom its other name of *Cassiani* U. xi, 28, was derived), Javolenus Priscus, and Salvius Julianus. He usually refers to the Sabinians as *nostri praeceptores,* he having been an adherent of that sect. The Proculians he usually refers to as *diversae scholae auctores;* but he specially mentions M. Antistius Labeo, their founder M. Cocceius Nerva, his successor, Proculus, from whom the school took its name, and Pegasus; and Ulp. mentions Neratius Priscus. See those names individually.

Sabinus, Caelius, consul A.D. 69, and chief of the Sabinian school after Massurius Sabinus; quoted in G. iii, 70, 141 See *Sabinians and Proculians.*

Sabinus, Massurius, succeeded Capito (who died A.D. 22) as chief of his school; from him it got the name by which it is best known. He is specially referred to by Gai. in ii, 79 154, 195, 218, 244; iii, 133, 161, 183; iv, 79, 114. See *Sabinians and Proculians.*

Sacra familiae, G. ii, 55; *coemptio sacrorum interimendorum causa,* (see *Manus,* 7), G. i, 114, note 1.

Sacrae res, G. ii, 3-5; see *Things,* 1.

Sacramentum, *legis actio per,* G. iv, 13-17; see *Legis actiones,* 2.

Sacrifice, *pignoris capio* used in connection with, G. iv, 28 and notes; see *Legis actiones,* 6.

Sale, *emptio venditio,* G. iii, 139-141; see also *Consensual obliga*tions.

1. *Sale, what?*—It was a consensual contract, G. iii, 135, con

SALE—*continued*.

ditional or unconditional, 146, whereby the seller, *venditor*, undertook to deliver to the purchaser, *emptor*, a certain saleable article in consideration of a price, and was complete the moment they were agreed about the latter, 139; earnest, *arra*, was unnecessary, being merely evidence of the completion of the transaction, *ibid.* Cases sometimes occurred in which it was difficult to say whether the contract was one of sale or location, 145-147; see some of them under *Location*, 3.

2. *The price in particular.*—It required to be definite, *certum*, G. iii, 140; the jurists being of different opinions as to whether it was sufficient that it was left to be fixed by a third party named, *ibid.* And it required to be in current money, 141; though the Sabinians, differing from the Proculians, thought otherwise, holding barter, *permutatio*, to be only a variety of sale, *ibid.*

3. *Sale by auction.*—See G. iv, 126a and note.

4. *The actions arising out of the contract.*—The buyer had the *a. empti* (or *ex empto*), the seller the *a. venditi* (or *ex vendito*), both of them *bonae fidei*, G. iv, 62. If the purchaser was sued for the price before delivery, he might plead the *exceptio rei nondum traditae;* but the replication was good that it was one of the conditions of the sale that the price was to be paid first, G. iv, 126a.

SALVIANUM INTERDICTUM, G. iv, 146; see *Interdicts*, 5.

SANCTAE RES, G. ii, 8; see *Things*, 1.

SARCIRE RUPITIAS, G. iii, 210-219, note.

SATIO, seed-sowing, acquisition of property by, G. ii, 75; remedies, 76. See *Property*, 6.

SATISDARE, meaning, G. i, 199 and 200, note.

SCAEVOLA, Q. MUCIUS, G. i, 188 and n. 4, iii, 149, aedile, consul, proconsul in Asia, and finally *pontifex maximus*, assassinated 672 | 72, a very distinguished jurist, who reckoned Cicero amongst his pupils. His writings were a subject of comment by Gai., who refers to his treatise on them in i, 188.

SCHOLAE JURISCONSULTORUM, G. i, 196, note 1; see *Sabinians and Proculians*.

SCRIPTURA, acquisition of property by, G. ii, 77; see *Property*, 6.

SECTIO BONORUM, sale of a confiscated estate *per universitatem*, G. iv, 146.

SECTORIUM INTERDICTUM, G. iv, 146; see *Interdicts*, 5.

SECUNDARIUM INTERDICTUM, G. iv, 170; see *Interdicts*, 17.

SECURITY, real, see *Praedia, Fiducia, Pignus;* personal, see *Praes, Cautiones, Satisdare, Suretyship*.

SECUTORIUM JUDICIUM, G. iv, 166, 169 ; see *Interdicts*, 16.

SEMIS, a half *as*, G. i, 192.

SENATORS and their children were forbidden by the Julian law to marry freedwomen, actresses or children of actors, and women of disreputable character, U. xiii, 1, 2 ; if they did, they and their wives were not allowed to take under each other's testament, xvi, 2. Personal injury offered to them was *atrox*, and punished with more than usual severity, G. iii, 225. When charged criminally, they were entitled to be tried by their peers of the senate, U. xiii, 2 and n. 2.

SENATUSCONSULTS, *senatus consulta*, enactments of the senate, (see *Statute*, 1), G. i, 4. Specially referred to are the following :—

Calvitianum (reign of Nero ?), declaring that marriage between a man under sixty and a woman over fifty should not qualify for taking an inheritance, legacy, or dowry, U. xvi, 4 ánd n. 2 ; see *Marriage*, 7.

Claudianum, on cohabitation of freewomen and slaves, G. i, 84, 85 and notes, 91, 160, U. xi, 8 ; see *Claudian Sct.*

Claudianum, modifying the Pernician Sct., by declaring that a man over sixty marrying a woman under fifty should not be liable to the penalties of celibacy, U. xvi, 4, and note to § 3 ; see *Julian and Papia-Poppaean law*, 4, *Jus capiendi*.

Hadriano auctore.—One or more regulating birth status (see *Status*), G. i, 30, 77, 80, 81, 92, U. iii, 3 ; one extending to peregrins the Aelia-Sentian prohibition of manumission in fraud of creditors (see *Aelia-Sentian law*, 1), G. i, 47 ; one allowing women in tutelage to make a testament without fiduciary coemption, G. i, 115a, ii, 112, (see *Testament*, 8, *Manus*, 7) ; one declaring that *usucapio pro herede* should be no bar to the heir's *hereditatis petitio*, G. ii, 57, (see *Usucapion*, 6) ; one amending the law of *erroris causae probatio* (which see, No. 2), G. ii, 143 ; one prohibiting *fideicommissa* to persons who were not allowed to be instituted as heirs or to take legacies, 285, 287, (see *Fideicommissum*, 3) ; one in favour of latins who had obtained a grant of citizenship without consent of patrons, G. iii, 73, (see *Patronate*) ; and one defining the rights of municipalities as legatees, U. xxiv, 28, (see *Legacy*, 6).

Largianum, A.D. 42 (?), amending the law of succession to Junian latins, G. iii, 63 and note, 64-67 ; difficulties in applying it, 69-71. See *Succession to Junian latins*.

Maximo et Tuberone coss. factum, 743 | 11 (?), declaring that confarreation of *flaminica Dialis* should place her *in*

SENATUSCONSULTS—*continued.*

manu only as concerned the *sacra*, G. i, 136 and note; see *Manus*, 1.

Neronianum, declaring that when a legacy was invalid in the particular form in which it was bequeathed, it should, if possible, be sustained as one *optimi juris*, *i.e.* by damnation, G. ii, 197, 198, 212, 218, 220, 222, U. xxiv, 11a; see *Legacy*, 20, 26.

Orphitianum, A.D. 178, giving children a right of succession to their mother, G. iii, 33a and note, U. xxvi, 7 and notes; see *Intestate succession*, 7.

Pegasianum, in reign of Vespasian, regulating *fideicommissa*, G. ii, 254, 258, 259, U. xxv, 14-16. (A *Sctum. Pegasianum* is also mentioned in G. ii, 286a; it is possibly a mistake for *Plancianum*.) See *Fideicommissum*, 9.

Pegaso et Pusione coss. factum, in reign of Vespasian, extending the benefits of the Aelia-Sentian marriage and *causae probatio* to latins manumitted when over thirty, G. i, 31 and note, iii, 5, 73, U. iii, 4; see *Aelia-Sentian law*, 7.

Pernicianum (? *Persicianum*, and A.D. 34), declaring that the penalties of celibacy should adhere permanently to men and women who had not married before sixty or fifty respectively, U. xvi, 3 and note; see *Julian and Papia-Poppaean law*, 4.

Plancianum, imposing penalties on heirs secretly promising to convey *fideicommissa* to persons not entitled to take them, U. xxv, 17 and notes 2 and 3. (The name is not in the text, but obtained from the Dig.; and the Sct. may be the same as that attributed to Hadrian in G. ii, 285, 287.) See *Fideicommissum*, 3.

Tertullianum, in reign of Hadrian, giving a mother a right of succession to her children, G. iii, 33a and note, U. xxvi, 8; see *Intestate succession*, 7.

Trebellianum, A.D. 62, regulating *fideicommissa*, G. ii, 253 and n. 2, 255, 258, U. xxv, 14, 16; see *Fideicommissum*, 8.

Of unknown name and authorship.—One introducing *erroris causae probatio* (which see), G. i, 67-71, ii, 142; one or more amending the law of tutory of women, G. i, 173, 174, 176, 177, 180, U. xi, 20-23, (see *Tutory*, 13, 22); one providing that a pupil should have an Atilian tutor instead of him who had been excused or removed, G. i, 182, (see *Tutory*, 4); one prohibiting a man (not insolvent) to institute as his heir with freedom one of his own slaves under thirty, G. ii, 276 and note, (see *Testament*, 14); one conferring citizenship on a free-born latin woman on the birth of her third child, U. iii, 1 and note, (see *Junian*

SENATUSCONSULTS—*continued.*

    latinity, 7); one abridging the period of service in the
night watch, as qualifying a latin for citizenship, to three
years, U. iii, 5, (see *Junian latinity,* 7); one allowing
municipalities to be instituted heirs by their freedmen,
and to take *fideicommissa* from any quarter, U. xxii, 5,
(see *Testament,* 13, *Fideicommissum,* 3); one or more
authorising certain deities to be instituted as heirs, U.
xxii, 6, (see *Testament,* 13); one sanctioning quasi-usufruct of money, U. xxiv, 27, (see *Usufruct,* 2).

SERVITUDES, *servitutes, jura praediorum,* rights appurtenant to immoveables, were either rural or urban, G. ii, 14.   Rural
servitudes, viz. rights of way and aquaeduct, G. ii, 31, iv,
3, U. xix, 1, were *res mancipi* (which see) in districts of
italic right (see *Jus Italicum*), U. xix, 1, and creatable
by mancipation or *in jure cessio* (see those words), G. ii,
29, 31; in the provinces generally they were *nec mancipi,*
and creatable by pacts and stipulations, 31.   Urban ones,
including rights of light, prospect, gutter, and eaves-drop,
G. ii, 14a, 31, iv, 3, were everywhere *nec mancipi,* G. ii,
15, 17; in italic lands they might be created by *in jure
cessio,* 29, and in the provinces by pacts and stipulations,
31.   Either sort might be vindicated in an *actio in rem,*
G. iv, 3, their existence challenged in an *a. in rem negatoria, ibid.*

SERVIUS SULPICIUS RUFUS, sometimes referred to simply as Servius,
G. i, 188 and n. 5, ii, 244, iii, 149, 179, 183, consul
703 | 51, and one of the most distinguished jurists of his
day.

SESTERCE, the, was equal to 2½ and afterwards 4 *asses,* G. iv, 95, note 2.

SET-OFF, see *Compensation.*

SINENDI MODO LEGATUM, see *Legacy,* 25-27, 33, 34.

SLAVERY, *servitus,* an institution of the *jus gentium,* G. i, 52.

    1. *How created.*—It was ordinarily created in the first instance
by capture of an enemy, G. i, 129, and perpetuated by
birth, the offspring of a slave mother being also slave,
G. i, 81, U. v, 9.   In addition, the Twelve Tables made
reduction to slavery the punishment of manifest theft by
a freeman, (though a milder penalty was substituted by
the praetors), G. iv, 189.   A citizen evading the census was
sold as a slave by way of punishment, G. i, 160, U. xi, 11.
The Claudian Sct. (according to Paul., though only to be
inferred from Gai.) punished with slavery a freewoman
cohabiting with a man she knew to be a slave, G. i, 86,
and visited with the same penalty one continuing to
cohabit with a *servus alienus* after his owner had informed

SLAVERY—*continued.*

her of his condition, G. i, 91, 160, U. xi, 11, (see *Claudian Sct.*). Further, the Aelia-Sentian law provided that deditician freedmen contravening its prohibition of residence within a hundred miles of Rome should be sold as slaves on the same condition, and never manumitted; and that if they were manumitted they should then become slaves of the state, G. i, 27.

2. *Powers of an owner over his slave's person.*—According to the *jus gentium*, an owner had the power of life and death over his slave, G. i, 52; and it seems to have been not uncommon to put him in chains, to brand him or torture him, and to give him up to fight in the arena as a gladiator or with wild beasts, G. i, 13. By Ant. Pius, however, it was enacted that a man killing his own slave should be liable to the same penalties as for killing a *servus alienus*, G. i, 53; while if he causelessly subjected him to cruel treatment he was to be compelled to sell him, *ibid.* Voluntary sale of a slave was of everyday occurrence, G. iv, 40, for he was an article of property, a *res mancipi*, U. xix, 1. Like other things of the same class (see *Res mancipi*), he might be in *in bonis* of one man and in the quiritarian right of another, U. i, 16; but it was the former that had *potestas* over him, G. i, 54.

3. *Right of the owner to his slave's acquisitions.*—See *Property*, 8, *Obligation*, 8.

4. *Effect of the slave's institution in a testament.*—See *Testament*, 14, *Necessarii heredes.*

5. *His* peculium.—See *Peculium.*

6. *Extent of owner's responsibility for his contracts or delicts.*—See *Adjectician actions, Noxal actions.*

7. *How far a slave could himself be debtor or creditor.*—Gai. states the rule very broadly that a slave could not be under obligation either to his owner or any other person, G. iii, 104; consequently if he committed a delict against his owner the latter had no action, G. iv, 78; and a new obligation in which he was nominal debtor was so useless as to be ineffectual as a novation of a previous valid one, G. iii, 177. But elsewhere Gai. admits that he might be indebted naturally (see *Obligation*, 5) either to his owner or a third party, and his obligation be validly guaranteed by a surety, G. iii, 119a. That a slave could not be creditor is evidenced in the fact that his adstipulation (which see) was null, G. iii, 114.

8. *How a slave acquired freedom.*—See *Manumission.*

9. *Judicial remedies.*—An owner was entitled to protect his

SLAVERY—*continued*.

possession of and property in his slaves, just as in his other chattels, by interdicts, G. iv, 160, and *rei vindicationes*, G. iv, 41. If his slave was stolen from him, he had an *actio furti* and *condictio furtiva*, see *Theft*, 6, 7; if culpably killed or hurt, he had an action on the Aquilian law, G. iii, 210, 217, (see *Wrongful damage to property*, 1, 3); if intentionally assaulted in such a way as to indicate that insult was intended to his owner, the latter had an *actio injuriarum*, G. iii, 222-224, (see *Personal injury*); if his morals were debauched, and his value consequently diminished, he had an *a. servi corrupti*, G. iii, 198. If a controversy arose between owner and slave on the question of freedom, the latter had to be represented by an *adsertor libertatis*, G. iv, 14 and n. 2; but, under the system of the *legis actiones* (which see, No. 2), out of favour for freedom, the *sacramentum* required from the *adsertor* was the smallest known to the law, G. iv, 14.

SOLDIER, a, in several respects enjoyed privileges unknown to civilians. While on service he might make a testament without any formalities, and make in it institutions and bequests that would have been ineffectual had he tested like a civilian *per aes et libram*, G. ii, 109-111, 114; see *Testament*, 25. A *filiusfamilias miles* might test on his *peculium castrense* (which see), and that either informally while on service, or *per aes et libram* after his discharge, G. ii, 106, U. xx, 10. Occasionally a soldier honourably discharged had conferred upon him a sort of *conubium* at large, enabling him to marry any peregrin or latin he pleased, and yet have his marriage recognised as *justum matrimonium* (see *Marriage*, 1), G. i, 57. Under the earlier system of procedure he had *pignoris capio* (see *Legis actiones*, 6) to recover his *aes militare, equestre*, and *hordiarium*, G. iv, 27.

SOLITARIUS PATER, the father of but one child, U. tit. xiii, rubric, was exempt from the penalties imposed upon *orbitas*, childlessness, by the Julian and Papia-Poppaean law (which see, No. 5), and therefore might take in full under a stranger's testament, tit. xiii, note.

SOLUM ITALICUM, see *Jus italicum*.

SPADONES were allowed to adopt, G. i, 103.

SPECIFICATION, acquisition of property by, and remedies of parties prejudiced, G. ii, 79; see *Property*, 7.

SPENDTHRIFTS, see *Prodigals*.

SPONDEO, origin of word, G. iii, 92, note; it could not be used by a peregrin or slave, but only by a citizen, G. iii, 93, 119, 179.

SPONSIO, as stipulation, see *Stipulation* : as a surety's engagement, see *Suretyship.*

SPONSIO ET RESTIPULATIO were used in the interdicts *uti possidetis* and *utrubi* to raise issue for trial of the question of possession, G. iv, 166; as each party was both pursuer and defender, there were two sponsions and two restipulations, and all were penal, *i.e.* their amounts were exigible by the successful litigant, 166a, 167, (see *Interdicts,* 15). They were used in the *a. de pecunia certa credita* and *a. de pecunia constituta* to check precipitate litigation, the sum named in them being the penalty of the ill-founded action or defence, G. iv, 13, 171, 172, 180, (see *Vexatious litigation*). The sponsion in the *in rem a. per sponsionem* (which see) was used merely to raise an issue, G. iv, 93; being prejudicial only, and not penal, there was no restipulation, 94.

SPONSIONEM, IN REM ACTIO PER, see *In rem a. per sponsionem.*

SPURII, why so called, G. i, 64; were in law fatherless, *ibid.,* U. iv, 2; word did not include issue of a concubine, G. i, 64, note 3. See *Parent and child,* 5.

STATULIBER, U. ii, 1-6, was a slave with conditional testamentary gift of freedom; who, if not alienated, continued to belong to the heir till the condition was fulfilled, G. ii, 200, U. ii, 1, 2, and if alienated, carried with him his conditional enfranchisement, U. ii, 3. If the condition was defeated by the act of the heir or a third party whose co-operation was necessary to its fulfilment, it was held as fulfilled, and the slave was free, U. ii, 6.

STATUS of children on birth, G. i, 65-92.

1. *Free or slave ?*—The rule of the *jus gentium* was—free mother, free child; slave mother, slave child, G. i, 82, U. v, 9. This rule was considerably modified by the Claud. Sct., some of whose provisions were repealed by Vespasian and Hadrian, 84-86; see *Claudian Sct.* But though a mother might be a slave at the time of conception, yet, if she was free when her child was born, it also was free, G. i, 89; the rule being that the status of illegitimate children dated from their birth, not from their conception, *ibid.,* U. v, 10. That of legitimate children, on the other hand, was held to date from the earlier point, *ibid. ;* therefore it was maintained that if a child had been conceived in lawful marriage, it was not the less free-born because its mother had been reduced to slavery during her pregnancy and was in that condition when delivered, G. i, 91.

2. *Citizen, latin, or peregrin ?*—When the parents were both of the same condition, there was no difficulty about the

STATUS—*continued*.

status of the issue; when they were of different cond
tions, the rule was that if there was *conubium* (whic
see) the child followed the father, while without it
followed its mother, G. i, 56, 67, U. v, 8. This wa
invariable where there had been no marriage, and th
child was the issue of a casual connection, in law fathe
less; the mother's status at her delivery determine
whether the child was citizen or peregrin, G. i, 90, 9:
But when the child had been conceived in marriag
though without *conubium*, the general rule was qualifie
by the Minician law, which declared that the issue (
such a marriage should follow the status of the inferic
parent, G. i, 78, U. v, 8; a provision which in turn wa
modified by an enactment of Hadrian's, that the issue (
a latin husband and Roman wife should in every case t
a citizen, G. i, 80.

3. In potestate *or* sui juris?—Although it was a general rul
that the issue of *justae nuptiae* were *in potestate*, G. i, 5:
yet in particular cases a question might arise whether (
not there was *potestas*, of which an instance occurs in (
i, 135.

STATUTE, G. i, 2-7, U. i, 1-3.

1. *The various forms of statute law.*—The original form wa
the *lex* or comitial enactment, G. i, 3; the *plebiscitun*
passed by the *concilium plebis*, was obligatory at fir
only among the plebeians, but by the Hortensian la
was declared binding on the patricians as well, and thu
became of the same value as a *lex*, *ibid.* and n. 2. Afte
some hesitation, senatusconsults were also recognised a
having all the force of *leges*, 4; and this was never doubte
as regarded the *constitutiones principum* (which see), !
The praetors' edicts and the responses of the jurispru
dents, though part of the *jus scriptum*, are not said t
have been regarded as statute-law, 6, 7, and the first ar
pointedly put in opposition to it in G. iii, 32. On law
perfect, imperfect, and short of perfect, see U. i, 1, 2.

2. *Analogical extension of statute.*—The *interpretatio* of th
pontiffs and early jurists frequently carried the applica
tion of a statute beyond its letter, G. ii, 42, note. Fo
instance the XII Tables conferred on agnates rights bot
of succession and tutory, but on patrons only the former
by interpretation it was ruled that they were entitle
also to the latter, G. i, 165, U. xi, 3. Going a ste
further, they held that a *parens manumissor* (see *Emanc*
pation, 3) must be dealt with as a patron, and therefor

STATUTE—*continued.*
was entitled to both the tutory and succession of the
child he had emancipated, G. i, 166, iii, 40, 41, U. xxviii,
7 and n. 1, as amended in *Additions etc.*
3. *Personal and territorial application.*—Much of the statutory law applied directly only to citizens, *e.g.* the Twelve
Tables and the much later Aquilian and Aelia-Sentian
laws, G. iv, 37, i, 47; if it seemed reasonable that a non-
citizen should have the benefit of or be ruled by any of
their provisions, the praetor adjusted a *formula* embodying a fiction of citizenship (see *Fiction*, 3), G. iv, 37. Some
statutes again, such as the *lex Atilia*, did not apply beyond
Rome, U. xi, 18; others not beyond Italy, such as the *lex
Furia de sponsu*, G. iii, 121a, 122; while others, such as
the *lex Apuleia*, extended to the provinces as well, 122.
STIGMATA, distinctive marks branded on runaway slaves, G. i, 13,
U. i, 11 and n. 1.
STIPENDIARIA PRAEDIA, G. ii, 15, 21; see *Provinces.*
STIPULATION, *stipulatio*, G. iii, 92-109; see also *Verbal obligations.*
1. *Stipulation, what ?*—It was a verbal contract by question
and answer, G. iii, 92, creative only of a unilateral obligation, 137. Its form rendered it possible only *inter
praesentes*, 136, 138; but the resulting inconvenience
when a man had occasion to contract with a person at a
distance was obviated by an expedient explained in 136,
note 1. Though most stipulations were voluntary or
conventional, yet some were necessary, such as the *cautio
judicatum solvi* and *stipulatio pro praede litis et vindiciarum*, G. iv, 91, *stipulatio fructuaria*, 166, *tribunicia
stipulatio*, U. vii, 3, etc. As none but verbal obligations
could be extinguished by acceptilation (which see), it
was the practice when a creditor was ready to give his
debtor a release of a consensual obligation say, to substitute a novatory stipulation, and then acceptilate, G.
iii, 170.
2. *Its form.*—There were certain recognised styles of question
and answer appropriate to the contract, G. iii, 92 and
note. *Spondes ? spondeo* were of the number, *ibid.;* but
engagement by the word *spondeo* was competent only to
citizens, 93, 119, note 3, and though derived from the
Greek yet could not be rendered by a Greek equivalent,
93, note 1. The other phrases were *juris gentium*, competent to peregrins as well as citizens, and might be
expressed either in Latin or Greek if parties understood,
93; but it was doubted whether an answer in one language to a question in another would do, 95.
38

STIPULATION—*continued.*

3. *Stipulations that were useless because of the nature of t[*
   undertaking; (see *Contract,* 4).—Amongst these we
   stipulation for a thing not *in commercio,* G. iii, 97, [
   that could have no existence, 97a; stipulation und[
   an impossible condition (see *Condition,* 3), 98; stip[
   lation for something to be given, *dari,* to the stipula[
   which was already his, 99; one for something to be giv[
   to or done for a party to whose *jus* the stipulant was n[
   subject, 103, (but what if to or for the stipulant *and*
   third party? or the stipulant *or* a third party? *ibid.*
   one to be performed by the heir of the promiser [
   to the heir of the stipulant (see *Obligation,* 11), 10[
   and one to be performed 'after' or the 'day before' th[
   death of stipulant or promiser, (which was practicall[
   the same thing as one for performance to or by the[
   respective heirs), 100, 117, 119. A stipulation, howeve[
   for a thing to be given or done when either was dyin[
   was valid, 100; and if a stipulant wanted to stipula[
   for payment after his death, his proper course was [
   conjoin with himself an *adstipulator* (see *Adstipulation*
   117.

4. *Stipulations that were useless because of incapacity of part[*
   —A stipulation was useless between a *paterfamilias* an[
   a person subject to his *jus,* G. iii, 104. So was one i[
   which either party was insane, 106; and one in whic[
   either was mute or deaf, speaking and hearing bein[
   essential to this particular contract, 105. A pupil ol[
   enough to understand what he was doing might b[
   stipulant even without his tutor's *auctoritas,* but withou[
   it could not be promiser, 107, 109, (see *Pupils*); and [
   woman in tutelage was in the same position, 108.

5. *Stipulations useless because of defect of form.*—It was neces[
   sary that the answer should correspond to the question[
   therefore if the stipulant asked ten and the other part[
   promised five, or if the question was unconditional an[
   the answer conditional, the stipulation was useless, G[
   iii, 102.

6. *The actions to which the contract gave rise.*—Where th[
   promise was to give a definite sum of money or a specifi[
   thing, the stipulant sued by a *condictio certi,* G. iv, 41[
   (see *Condictio, Intentio,* 2c); where what was promised wa[
   incertum, indefinite, he sued by an *actio incerta,* some[
   times called *condictio incerti,* and more frequently *acti[*
   ex stipulatu, G. iv, 136 (see *Condictio, Formula,* 4, *In[*
   tentio, 2d). Although the contract was a formal one (se[

STIPULATION—*continued.*

    Contract, 3), and the promiser *ipso jure* liable on the strength of his *promissio,* G. iii, 89, note, still if it had been given on a consideration that had failed, he was allowed in equity to plead an *exceptio doli,* G. iv, 116.

STIPULATIONES EMPTAE ET VENDITAE HEREDITATIS, G. ii, 252, 257 see *Emptio hereditatis, Fideicommissum,* 7.

STIPULATIONES PARTIS ET PRO PARTE, G. ii, 254, 257 and n. 1, U. xxv, 15; see *Legacy,* 8, *Fideicommissum,* 9.

STIRPES and CAPITA in succession, G. iii, 8, 16, 61, U. xxvi, 2, 4, xxvii, 4.

SUBROGATIO LEGIS, adding something to an enactment, U. i, 3.

SUBSTITUTION, *substitutio,* was either ordinary, *vulgaris,* G. ii, 174-178, U. xxii, 33, or pupillary, *pupillaris,* G. ii, 179-184, U. xxiii, 7-9; see also *Testament,* 15.

    1. *Ordinary substitution.*—This was nomination in a testament of one or more heirs to take as substitutes in the event of the failure of the institute or institutes, G. ii, 174, 175, U. xxii, 33, and might be continued indefinitely in a series of substitutions to substitutes, G. ii, 176, U. xxii, 33. The operativeness of the substitutions depended to some extent upon the consideration whether the institute and substitutes were nominated with or without cretion, and in the former case whether it was perfect or imperfect, (see *Cretio,* 1), G. ii, 174, 176-178, U. xxii, 33, 34.

    2. *Pupillary substitution.*—This was nomination of a substitute to take on the death in pupillarity of an institute who had succeeded, G. ii, 179, U. xxiii, 7; and was in effect a testament made by a father for his child, living or posthumous, G. ii, 183, U. xxiii, 7, to take effect in the event of the latter dying under puberty, G. ii, 180, and before he could make one for himself, G. ii, 113, U. xx, 12. It was not necessary that the child should be instituted as his parent's heir, for a man might so substitute to his disinherited children, G. ii, 182, U. xxiii, 8; but it was necessary that the substitution should be in a testament in which the parent had validly instituted an heir, whether his child or a stranger, U. xxiii, 9.

    3. *Precautions that usually accompanied a pupillary substitution.* —To obviate any risk of foul play towards the child by the individual thus substituted to him, it was the practice to make the substitution in the last tablets of the testament, and seal them up by themselves, so that the fact should not be prematurely revealed, G. ii, 181.

    4. *Incompetency of pupillary substitution to a stranger institute.* —For a stranger institute it was impossible to make a

SUBSTITUTION—*continued.*

substitution of this sort; but the same object might be attained by means of a trust, G. ii, 184, (see *Fideicommissum*, 1).

SUCCESSIO GRADUUM on intestacy was not allowed by the *jus civile*, G. iii, 12, 22, U. xxvi, 5; the praetors so far sanctioned it that they allowed agnates of the second or a remoter degree to come in as cognates on failure of those of the nearest, G. iii, 28, (see *Bonor. possessio*, 16).

SUCCESSION, *successio*, in its widest acceptation, included every case of passage of a man's estate, with its rights and liabilities, to another person *per universitatem*, G. ii, 97, iii, 82, as in *emptio bonorum*, G. iii, 77, adrogation, 83, and *in manum conventio, ibid.* (see those words); in its narrower signification, however, it was succession to the dead, G. ii, 157, iii, 33, etc. This arose either *jure civile* in the case of an heir taking an inheritance, *hereditas,* which was the creature of statute, G. iii, 32, (see *Hereditas*); or *jure honorario* in the case of an individual to whom, on considerations of equity, the praetor had granted possession of the deceased's estate, putting him *de facto* in the position of an heir, G. iii, 32, 33*b*, U. xxviii, 12, (see *Bonorum possessio*). In early times an *hereditas* was held acquirable by usucapion by one who had no title as heir, but simply took possession of the estate and held it for a year,—a doctrine that was afterwards disowned, G. i, 54, (see *Usucapion*, 6). The rules of succession to freedmen, under both the civil and praetorian law, differed materially from those of succession to free-born citizens, and are digested separately; see *Succession to citizen freedmen, Succession to Junian latins.*

SUCCESSION DUTY, G. iii, 125 and note.

SUCCESSION TO CITIZEN FREEDMEN AND FREED-WOMEN, G. iii, 39-53, U. tits. xxvii, xxix; see also PATRONATE.

I. SUCCESSION TO FREEDMEN.

1. *The rules of the Twelve Tables.*—By the Decemviral Code a citizen freedman was entitled to make a testament, and to pass over his patron if he pleased, G. iii, 40, U. xxix, 1; and on intestacy the patron was to succeed only when the freedman left no *sui heredes, ibid.,* U. xxvii, 1. But this right of the patron was lost by his *capitis deminutio,* G. iii, 51, U. xxvii, 5.

2. *Praetorian rules when the freedman had made a testament.* —The praetors held the rules of the Tables to be fair enough when the patron was excluded, either testamen-

SUCCESSION TO CITIZEN FREEDMEN AND FREED-WOMEN—*continued.*

I. SUCCESSION TO FREEDMEN—*continued.*

tarily or on intestacy, by *sui heredes* who were issue of the deceased, but not when he was excluded by artificial *sui* (see *Sui heredes*, 1), such as a wife *in manu* or an adoptive child, G. iii, 40, U. xxix, 1. They therefore ordained that, if a freedman in his testament did not institute children of his own, he was bound to leave his patron at least one half of his estate, the latter being entitled to *bonorum possessio contra tabulas* to that extent (see *Bonor. poss.*, 8) if passed over, G. iii, 41, U. xxix, 1. But this right of his was excluded by a grant of the same *bonor. possessio* to natural children of the deceased, even those who had been emancipated by him or given in adoption; though not by a grant of it to those he had disinherited, nor even by the institution of his wife *in manu* or a child he had adopted, *ibid.*

3. *Praetorian rules when the freedman died intestate.*—In this case the same principle was applied as described in No. 2 : if an intestate freedman was survived by children of his body, even emancipated or given in adoption, they took everything; but if only by artificial *sui*, his patron might claim *bonorum possessio ab intestato* of one half of his estate, G. iii, 41, U. xxix, 1.

4. *The Julian and Papia-Poppaean innovation.*—This enactment provided that if a freedman worth not less than 100,000 sesterces left fewer than three children, then, whether he died testate or intestate, his patron was to have an equal share with them; *i.e.* a half if only one, a third if two, but nothing if more than two, G. iii, 42, (see *Julian and Pap. Popp. law*, 8).

5. *Rights of children of patrons.*—If a patron had predeceased his freedman, the patronate (which see, No. 1) passed to the former's children, even though disinherited, G. iii, 48, 58, 64; the patron's stranger heirs had no right to it, or to the freedman's succession, *ibid.* By the old law both sons and daughters of the patron, and the issue of sons, had the same rights as the patron himself, G. iii, 46, U. xxix, 4. The praetors called only sons of the patrons and their male descendants, G. iii, 46, U. xxix, 5. The Papian law, however, revived the right of a daughter to participate, provided she had the *jus liberorum*, *ibid.*, (see *Jus liberorum, Julian and Pap. Popp. law*, 7).

6. *How the rights of a plurality of patrons were adjusted.*—If the deceased freedman had more than one patron, the suc-

SUCCESSION TO CITIZEN FREEDMEN AND FREED-
WOMEN—*continued.*

I. SUCCESSION TO FREEDMEN—*continued.*

cession belonged to them equally, without regard to what
had been their respective interests in him as a slave, G.
iii, 59; if one of them declined—for they did not succeed
ipso jure, but had to enter like *extranei heredes* (which
see)—the whole succession belonged to the others, 62. If
one of two patrons was dead, the survivor excluded the
children of the predeceaser; if both were dead, the son
of one excluded the grandson of the other; if both left
children of the first degree, one of them say two, the
other three, these took *per capita* and not *per stirpes*, G.
iii, 60, 61, U. xxvii, 2-4.

7. *Rights of a patroness and her children.*—Under the praetorian rules a patroness had no greater right in the succession of her freedman than had been conferred on a patron
by the XII Tables, G. iii, 49, U. xxix, 6. But the Papian
law gave a free-born patroness who was mother of three
children, and a freedwoman patroness who was mother
of two, almost the same rights the edict had given to a
patron, G. iii, 50 and n. 1, U. xxix, 6; and to a free-born
patroness it granted in addition the same right it had
itself conferred on a patron, G. iii, 50 and n. 2, U. xxix,
7. It is doubtful what were the rights of the son of a
patroness, G. iii, 53 and n. 2; those of a daughter are
not referred to.

8. *Ulpian's ordines.*—In xxviii, 7, Ulp. gives the heads of the
praetorian order of succession *ab intestato* without any
explanation. As they applied to freedmen they seem to
have run thus:—first, the deceased's descendants of his
body through males, as above, No. 3; second, the patron
and his children, but only in concurrence with artificial
sui of the freedman if such existed, above, No. 3; third,
the freedman's cognates, *e.g.* the children of a daughter;
fourth, the patron's agnates; fifth, the patron's patron, and
the latter's children; sixth, the freedman's wife, if she had
not been *in manu*, and so had not been admitted in
the second place; seventh, the patron's cognates within
certain limits.

II. SUCCESSION TO FREEDWOMEN.

9. *Rights of a patron.*—A freedwoman by the old law could
not make a testament without the *auctoritas* of her
patron, and if she made one in which he was passed
over, he had only himself to blame; if she died intestate, he took everything, because she had no *sui heredes*,

SUCCESSION TO CITIZEN FREEDMEN AND FREED-WOMEN—*continued.*

II. SUCCESSION TO FREEDWOMEN—*continued.*

G. iii, 43, U. xxix, 2. Upon these rules of the Twelve Tables the praetors made no change, U. xxix, 2. The Papian law, in liberating freedwomen with four children from tutory (which see, No. 24), thus put it in their power to make testaments without *auctoritas;* but it provided that a patron should nevertheless be entitled to a share of his freedwoman's estate, varying according to the number of children by whom she was survived, G. iii, 44 and note, U. xxix, 3.

10. *Rights of a patroness.*—In the case of a freedwoman dying intestate, the Papian law added nothing to the rights of her patroness; if neither of them was *capite deminuta* everything went to the latter, because there were no *sui heredes;* but if either had suffered *capitis minutio*, then the freedwoman's children took as cognates, to the exclusion of her whose patronage had ceased, G. iii, 51. A patroness, being unable to be tutor (see *Tutory*, 22,) had never had any control over her freedwoman's testament, 52; but the Papian law conferred on her, provided she had the *jus liberorum* (which see), a right of challenging it much the same as that the edict had given to a patron (see above, No. 3) in regard to the testament of a freedman, *ibid.*

SUCCESSION TO JUNIAN LATINS, G. iii, 55-71, and note to 55; see also *Junian latinity.*

1. *Position of the Junian latin in reference to his estate.*— Before the Junian law those whom it made latins had been *de jure* slaves, though *de facto* free; their estates therefore were *de jure* only *peculia* (see *Peculium*), and the property of their manumitters, G. iii, 56. With acquisition of *de jure* freedom there was an end of the *peculium* properly so called; but the consideration presented itself that this would be a fraud on the manumitters, who were not patrons in the sense of the Twelve Tables, and so were not entitled to succeed to their freedmen, *ibid.* Therefore by the Junian law itself it was provided that the estate of a latin should still continue to belong to his manumitters as a *quasi-peculium*, *ibid.*

2. *Right in it of the manumitter and his children and heirs.*— According to the Junian law the manumitter was entitled to deal with it testamentarily as part of his own estate, even during the lifetime of his freedman; his

SUCCESSION TO JUNIAN LATINS—*continued.*

disinherited children, contrary to the rule in reference to succession to citizen freedmen (which see), had no right to it, G. iii, 63; it went to the heirs, even strangers, named in his testament, 58, 63, 64, or to a legatee if he chose to bequeath it, G. ii, 195. But the Largian senatus-consult altered this rule, and gave it first to the manu-mitter himself, next to his descendants not expressly disinherited, and only in the third place to his heirs, G. iii, 63-71.

3. *What if there had been more manumitters than one?*—In such case they took *pro rata parte,*—according to the interest they had severally had in the latin before manu-mission, G. iii, 59; the heir of one that had died was not excluded by another who survived, 60; and if all were dead their successors took not *per capita* but according to the interests of the several manumitters they respectively represented, 61. If one of a plurality of manumitters, or his representatives, failed to take, his share became caducous (see *Caducity,* 7) and passed to the state, 62.

4. *What if a latin had obtained a grant of citizenship unknown to his manumitter?*—If such a grant had been obtained from the emperor *salvo jure patroni,* or even without such reservation but unknown to his manumitter, the grantee was indeed a citizen during his life, but still a latin in his death; his children, though lawful, could not be his heirs; his testamentary capacity was limited to institu-tion of his patron, with a substitution (which see, No. 1) in the event of his failure, G. iii, 71. So it was enacted by Trajan; but a Sct. of Hadrian's afterwards provided that if a latin in such a position subsequently proved cause under the Aelia-Sentian law or the senatusconsult, (see *Causae prob. ex l. Ael. Sent.*), he should be held to have acquired citizenship effectually, and be entitled to dispose of his estate as a citizen freedman, 73.

SUCCESSORIUM EDICTUM, see *Edictum successorium.*

SUI HEREDES, often called *sui et necessarii heredes.*

1. *Who were sui heredes?*—A man's *sui heredes*—for a woman could have none, G. iii, 51, U. xxvi, 7—were those of his descendants *in potestate,* natural or adoptive, who were to or had become *sui juris* by his death, as also his wife *in manu,* and his daughter-in-law who had been *in manu* of a deceased son, (see *Manus,* 4), G. ii, 156, 159, iii, 2, 3, U. xxii, 14, xxvi, 1. Those *postumi* (which see) were included who, had they been born earlier, would have been *in potestate* and become *sui juris* by the parent's

SUI HEREDES—*continued.*

death, G. iii, 4, U. xxii, 15 ; also children on whose account there had been *causae probatio* after their father's death, (see *Caus. prob. ex l. Aelia Sentia*, 3, *Erroris caus. prob.* 2), G. iii, 5 ; and a son manumitted after his father's death from a first or second mancipation (see *Emancipation*, 3), G. iii, 6. In the law of succession to freedmen, a distinction was made between natural and artificial *sui heredes*, meaning by the latter a wife *in manu* or an adopted child, G. iii, 40, 41, U. xxix, 1, 5.

2. *Why called* sui.—They were so called because they were *domestici heredes*,—because they had all along been in a manner owners of the family estate, G. ii, 157, *i.e.* the *familia* or *patrimonium*, G. ii, 102, and were thus their own heirs or heirs of what had been their own. It was for this reason that their parent making a testament was bound either to institute or disinherit them, G. ii, 123, U. xxii, 14, (see *Testament*, 10); that *agnatio sui heredis* (which see) invalidated a testament made by the parent previously, U. xxiii, 2; and that on his death intestate they had the first place in the succession, G. ii, 157, iii, 1, U. xxvi, 1.

3. *Why also called* necessarii?—For the very same reason for which they were called *sui*,—because, as in a manner already owners of it, '*juris necessitate hereditati adstringuntur,*' G. iii, 87, and if not disinherited were heirs whether they would or not, G. ii, 157, though by the praetors permitted to abstain, 158; see *Hereditas*, 3.

SUI JURIS PERSONAE, persons not subject to any family head, but themselves *patres* or *matres familiae*, U. iv, 1 and note. They might cease to be so by *capitis deminutio* (which see), as by adrogation or *in manum conventio*, G. iii, 83; but so long as they were *sui juris* they were their own masters, except in so far as controlled by tutors or curators on account of age, sex, or infirmity, (see *Tutory, Curatory*).

SULPICIUS RUFUS, SERV., see *Servius Sulp. Ruf.*

SUPERFICIES SOLO CEDIT, G. ii, 73; see *Property*, 6.

SURDUS, see *Deaf person.*

SURETYSHIP, *adpromissio*, G. iii, 115-127.

1. *Suretyship in general.*—The purpose of every *adpromissio* was to secure performance of an obligation by a third party, G. iii, 117 ; consequently, as his undertaking was accessory only, no surety was liable for more than the principal debtor, though his liability might be for less, 126. There were three varieties of it, *sponsio, fidepromissio,* and *fidejussio*, 115, in all of which responsibility

SURETYSHIP—*continued.*

    .was imposed upon the surety by verbal contract, (see *Verbal obligations*), 116; there being forms of question and answer specially adapted to each variety, 116, 92, note 1.

2. Sponsio *and* fidepromissio *in particular.*—Sponsors and fidepromissors could become accessory only to verbal obligations, G. iii, 119. Their engagement, however, might be binding even though that of the principal debtor was not, *e.g.* that of a person who had promised something after his death, or of a pupil or a woman who had promised without tutorial *auctoritas*, (see *Stipulation*, 3, 4), 119; but a sponsor could not be taken bound for the engagement by *sponsio* of a slave or peregrin, because they were not entitled to use the word *spondeo*, (see *Stipulation*, 2), *ibid.* The heirs of sponsors and fidepromissors were not liable, 120, iv, 113; unless in the case of a peregrin fidepromissor, whose liability was recognised by the law of his own state, G. iii, 120.

3. *Enactments in aid of sponsors and fidepromissors.*—By the Furian law, which did not apply out of Italy, G. iii, 121a, their liability was limited to two years, 121 and note; if there were more than one, each was liable only for his share, even though some might be insolvent when action was raised, *ibid.*; and if the creditor had exacted from one more than his proportion, the statute gave the latter *manus injectio pro judicato* (see *Legis actiones*, 5) to compel its restitution, G. iv, 22. By the still earlier Apuleian law a plurality of sponsors or fidepromissors had been put in the position of partners, one paying more than his share being entitled to relief from the others, G. iii, 122 and note; but this was considered to have been tacitly repealed by the Furian law so far as Italy was concerned, 122, though the benefit of it survived in the provinces, *ibid.* By the Cicereian law certain duties were imposed on creditors taking sponsors or fidepromissors, whose neglect gave the latter a qualified right to have their engagements cancelled, 123 and note; while a Cornelian law, except in one or two special cases, limited the amount for which a sponsor or fidepromissor could become bound, 124 and note, 125.

4. Fidejussio *in particular.*—A fidejussor might become accessory not merely to a verbal contract but to any sort of obligation, whether civil or natural, and even to that of a slave, G. iii, 119a and n. 1, which in itself was civilly useless, 104; his heir was as much bound as himself, 120; his

SURETYSHIP—*continued.*

liability was unlimited in point of time, 121; but as the Cornelian law expressly applied to him, it was limited in amount, 124. Where there was a plurality of fidejussors, each was liable *in solidum;* though when one only was sued, he was entitled to invoke Hadrian's *beneficium divisionis,* and have action limited to his share, 121, 122. The provisions of the Apuleian, Furian, and Cicereian laws did not apply to a fidejussor, 121, 123; but in practice he had the benefit of the last, 123.

5. *The surety's right of recourse.*—By a Publilian law of the fourth century of Rome, G. iii, 127 and n. 2, a sponsor who had paid for the principal debtor was allowed to use *manus injectio pro judicato* against the latter if he did not relieve his surety within six months, G. iv, 22, 25; and under the formular system an *actio depensi* was substituted, which was *in duplum,* G. iii, 127, the defender being required besides to give *cautio judicatum solvi* (see *Cautiones, etc.*), G. iv, 25, 102. But he did not require to wait the six months; for, in common with fidepromissors and fidejussors, he was entitled to proceed against the debtor at once in an *a. mandati,* (see *Mandate,* 5), G. iii, 127.

SUSPENDED RIGHTS, examples of.—A man's rights as a citizen were suspended during his captivity in an enemy's hands, but revived on his recrossing the frontier, G. i, 129, 187, U. x, 4. The *patria potestas* was suspended as long as a *filiusfamilias* was in a first or second *mancipium,* but revived on his manumission, G. i, 135, U. xxiii, 3. The ownership of a legacy by vindication was in suspense until the legatee had intimated his acceptance, G. ii, 200; so was that of a conditional legacy in the same form until the condition was fulfilled, *ibid.* The question whether a contract was one of sale or location was sometimes in suspense, to be determined by subsequent events, G. iii, 146. When a novatory obligation was conditional, the extinction or non-extinction of the old one was in suspense so long as the condition was open, G. iii, 179.

SYNGRAPHA, G. iii, 134 and note; see *Literal obligations,* 2.

TABULAE HONESTAE MISSIONIS, honourable discharges to soldiers, frequently conferring on them peculiar privileges, G. i, 57, note; see *Soldier.*

TALIO, G. iii, 223; see *Personal injury,* 2.

TAXATIO CONDEMNATIONIS, G. iv, 51; see *Condemnatio,* 2.

TEMPUS DELIBERANDI, time allowed a stranger heir, instituted
    without cretion, for considering whether or not he would
    accept the inheritance, G. ii, 162; see *Hereditas*, 6.
TESTAMENT, *testamentum*, G. ii, 99-289, U. tits. xx-xxv; see
    also HEREDITAS. For definition of testament, see U. xx, 1.
I. HISTORY OF TESTAMENTS.
    1. *The testament* calatis comitiis.—This was the earliest form
        of testament known to the Romans. Its validity depended
        apparently on a vote of the legislature, which met twice
        a year to consider matters of the sort, G. ii, 101, U. xx, 2.
    2. *The testament* in procinctu.—The *test. in calatis comitiis*
        could be made only in time of peace; to meet the case
        of a man desiring to make one on the eve of battle,
        that *in procinctu* was introduced, the army taking the
        place of the *comitia*, G. ii, 101. U. xx, 2.
    3. *The testament* per aes et libram *in its original form.*—After
        the introduction of the *negotium per aes et libram*, which
        also was a public act in the presence of five citizen
        witnesses, probably the representatives of the five Servian
        classes, and thus also of the legislature, G. ii, 104, note 8,
        and its adaptation to conveyance of property and crea-
        tion of obligations (see *Aes et libra*), advantage seems to
        have been taken of it as suitable also for *mortis causa* dis-
        position. The parties were the testator and a friend who
        was to become his heir, together with a *libripens* and the
        five citizens, G. ii, 102, 103; and the testator formally
        mancipated his estate to his friend, who hence got the
        name of *familiae emptor*, purchaser of the family estate,
        ibid., and who probably gave the testator a single coin,
        nummus unus, as the price of the nominal purchase, G.
        ii, 105, 252. It rather appears that this was not a testa-
        mentary act in the proper sense of the words, but an
        absolute transfer of the estate to the *familiae emptor*,
        who took it however subject to verbal instructions as to
        how he was to deal with it on the death of the mancipant,
        G. ii, 103.
    4. *The amended testament* per aes et libram.—After a time
        important changes were introduced,—the will was re-
        duced to writing, the heir ceased to be a party to the
        mancipatio, and though a *familiae emptor* still officiated,
        he was there only for form's sake, without any personal
        interest in the testament, G. ii, 103. The amended
        procedure is described in G. ii, 104 and notes, and
        briefly referred to in U. xx, 2. It consisted of two
        distinct parts, the *familiae venditio* and the *nuncupatio
        testamenti*, otherwise *testatio*, G. ii, 104, U. xx, 9. In the

TESTAMENT—*continued.*
  I. HISTORY OF TESTAMENTS—*continued.*

first the *familiae emptor* formally purchased the *universitas*—not the individual items—of the testator's estate, but under reservation to the latter of free power of disposal, and under the explanation that the ceremony was intended simply to give point and validity to what was to follow, G. ii, 104. In the second the testator, displaying his closed testament, declared it to contain his will, and called upon the witnesses to grant him their testimony to the *nuncupatio, ibid.*

  5. *The so-called praetorian testament.*—As a mistake in or an omission of any part of the solemnities of a testament *per aes et libram* rendered it null and void, G. ii, 114, 119, and the intentions of a testator were thus often defeated, the praetors interfered, declaring they would give *bonor. possessio secundum tabulas* to the heirs nominated in any testament made by one who was a citizen *sui juris* at the time and at his death, and which bore the seals of seven citizen witnesses, G. ii, 147, U. xxviii, 6, (see *Bonor. poss.*, 10, 11). This is often called a praetorian testament, though the phrase is not in the texts; it did not, however, give the nominee in it the *hereditas*, or entitle him to the name of heir, G. iii, 32, (see *Bonor. poss.*, 5).

 II. REQUISITES OF A TESTAMENT PER AES ET LIBRAM, AND CONSEQUENCES OF THEIR ABSENCE.

  6. *Capacity in the testator.*—The testator required to have *testamenti factio, i.e.* to be a citizen and *sui juris*, G. ii, 114 and n. 1, 147; neither peregrins, U. xx, 14, nor Junian latins, G. i, 23, U. xx, 14, nor deditician freedmen, G. i, 25, iii, 75, U. xx, 14, could make a testament, though a citizen freedman might, G. iii, 40 f. (see *Succession to cit. freedmen*, 1); nor could any person *alieni juris* do so, G. ii, 112, except a *filiusfamilias* dealing with his *peculium castrense* (which see), G. ii, 106, or a public slave, who could test on one-half of his *peculium*, U. xx, 16. The testator required further to have reached the age of puberty, fourteen if a male, twelve if a female, G. i, 40, ii, 113, U. xx, 12; and to be neither insane, nor interdicted as a prodigal, nor deaf or mute, G. ii, 113, U. xx, 13 (although the last objection may possibly not have prevented his testament being given effect to as a praetorian one).

  7. *Observance of formalities.*—It was requisite, in order to the testament's being held *jure factum*, that the solemnities of the *familiae venditio* and *testamenti nuncupatio* should

TESTAMENT—*continued.*
  II. REQUISITES OF A TESTAMENT, ETC.—*continued.*
       be carefully observed, and that the *familiae emptor, libri-pens,* and witnesses should be properly qualified, G. ii, 114, 119. They required to be persons with whom the testator had *testamenti factio,* U. xx, 2, *i.e.* persons whom he might lawfully make his heirs, G. i, 114, note 1; a Junian latin therefore could act in any of those capacities, U. xx, 8. No one who was *in potestate* of the testator or *familiae emptor,* or in the same *potestas* as the latter, or his *paterfamilias,* could act as witnesses, domestic testimony being prohibited, G. i, 105-107, U. xx, 3-6; but the prohibition did not extend to those domestically related to the heir or a legatee, although employment of relatives of the former was usually avoided, G. ii, 108. Mutes and deaf persons, lunatics, pupils, and women, were all incapable of assisting in the execution of a testament, U. xx, 7. Omission or defect of formalities, while fatal to the testament *jure civili,* yet did not prevent its being given effect to *jure praetorio* if sealed by seven witnesses, see above No. 5; but the texts do not say whether the praetors required in them any other qualifications than simply citizenship, G. ii, 147, U. xxviii, 6.

   8. *Tutorial* auctoritas *in the case of women testators.*—On the position generally of women in tutelage, see *Tutory,* III., IV. When a woman was in tutelage—by the Julian law some were free from it, see *Jul. and Pap. Popp. law,* 2— it was absolutely necessary to the *jure civili* validity of her testament that she should have tutorial *auctoritas,* G. ii, 112, 118, U. xx, 15. Anciently, when women were in tutelage of their agnates, they could rarely make a testament without first performing *coemptio* (see *Manus,* 7), and thus obtaining fiduciary tutors with whom they had previously bargained for *auctoritas,* G. i, 115a, ii, 112; but the tutory of agnates having been abolished by the Claudian law, G. i, 157, 171, U. xi, 8, the senate, in the time of Hadrian, enacted that a tutor should in future not be entitled to refuse his *auctoritas* unless he was the woman's patron or *parens manumissor,* G. ii, 112, 122,—them their wards could not compel to grant it, G. i, 192. In point of form, however, it was still necessary *jure civili;* but its absence did not prevent the testament being given effect to *jure praetorio* where the neglected tutor was neither patron nor parent, G. ii, 119-122.

   9. *Institution of an heir or heirs.*—This was absolutely essential to the testament in point of substance, G. ii, 116,

TESTAMENT—*continued.*
  II. REQUISITES OF A TESTAMENT, ETC.—*continued.*

284; it was the *caput et fundamentum* of the whole deed, G. ii, 229, U. xxiv, 15, and could not be supplied in any subsequent writing, *e.g.* a codicil, G. ii, 273. It had to be made moreover *sollemni more*, G. ii, 116, *i.e.* in one or other of the traditional styles enumerated in G. ii, 117, U. tit. xxi; and, where it was a stranger that was being instituted, usually had coupled with it a cretion clause, requiring him to enter within a limited period, G. ii, 164 f., U. xxii, 27 f. (see *Cretio*). And there might be any number of heirs; a sole heir being said to be instituted *ex asse*, one of several *ex parte*, G. ii, 259. But if a co-heir was instituted *poenae causae, i.e.* with a view to coerce him with whom he was conjoined to a particular course of action, the penal institution was useless, G. ii, 243. Further, it was impossible to institute an individual to take on the heir's death, G. ii, 277.

10. *Institution or disherison of children.*—Another requirement of the *jus civile* was that the testator should either institute or disinherit the *sui heredes* (which see), G. ii, 123, U. xxii, 14; they were in a manner joint-owners with him of the family estate, G. ii, 157, and were not to be deprived of their birth-right otherwise than expressly. But while the praeterition of a son *in potestate* invalidated the testament, G. ii, 123, U. xxii, 16,—though the Proculians held this to be the case only if he survived his father, G. ii, 123,—and entitled the *filius praeteritus* to eject the instituted heir, even when the latter had obtained a grant of *bonor. possessio secundum tab.* (which see, Nos. 1, 4), U. xxviii, 13, praeterition of other *sui heredes* merely entitled them by the *jus civile* to claim a share by accretion, G. ii, 124, U. xxii, 17, (see *Adcretio*, 3), and by the praetorian law to *bonor. possessio contra tabulas*, G. ii, 125, 126, U. xxviii, 3, as corrected in *Additions etc.*, (see *Bonor. poss.*, 6). It was necessary also, as a precaution against subsequent invalidation of his testament by *agnatio sui heredis* (see below, No. 22), for the testator to institute or disinherit his *postumi* (which see), G. ii, 130, U. xxii, 19, 21; and to institute or disinherit even the children of his immediate male *sui heredes*, in case the latter should predecease him, and the former nullify his testament by *quasi* agnation, G. ii, 133, 134. The *jus civile* did not require that emancipated children should be instituted or disinherited, for they had ceased to be *sui*, G. ii, 135, U. xxii, 23; but the praetors made their in-

TESTAMENT—*continued.*

 II. REQUISITES OF A TESTAMENT, ETC.—*continued.*

stitution or disherison incumbent, *ibid.*, giving them *bonor. possessio contra tab.* if passed over, but only on condition of collation, *ibid.*, U. xxviii, 2, 4, (see *Bonor. poss.*, 7). As regarded adoptive children, see *Adoption*, 6, 7. A mother making a testament was not required to disinherit children she did not institute, for she had no *sui heredes*, G. iii, 71.

11. *Form of disherison.*—A son had to be disinherited *nominatim, i e.* by special reference, G. ii, 127, U. xxii, 20. According to the *jus civile*, other *sui* were sufficiently disinherited in a general or *ceteri* clause, G. ii, 128; but the praetors required that males, *e.g.* grandsons, should be disinherited *nominatim*, 129. A posthumous son had to be disinherited in the same way as a living one; but female and remoter male *postumi* might be disinherited by the *ceteri* clause, provided some trifling legacy was left them to show they had not been forgotten, G. ii, 132, U. xxii, 21, 22. Disherison of descendants of an immediate male *suus* required to be in the same form as that of *postumi*, G. ii, 134; while by the edict that of emancipated children was to be in the same form as that of living *sui*, G. ii, 135, U. xxii, 23. The disherison required to be in the testament itself; if omitted there it could not effectually be supplied in a codicil, G. ii, 273.

12. *Ulterior consequences of disherison.*—Disherison deprived the disinherited of all right to the *hereditas*—they might still take legacies—under the testament, yet did not deprive them of their patronage over and right of succession to their parent's citizen freedmen, G. iii, 58, 64, (see *Patronate*, 2, *Succession to citizen freedmen*, 5); if it was *nominatim* disherison, however, it did deprive them of their right to the estates of his Junian latins, 58, 63, 64, (see *Succession to Junian latins*, 2). As regarded the parent, the fact that he had disinherited his child did not preclude him from still making a pupillary substitution on the child's account, G. ii, 182, (see *Substitution*, 2).

13. *What strangers might be instituted.*—The general rule was that a testator could institute those only with whom he had *testamenti factio*, U. xxii, 1. This excluded peregrins and dediticiani freedmen, G. i, 25, but not Junian latins, U. xxii, 3; these might competently be instituted, though they could not take the *hereditas* unless they became citizens within the hundred cretion days, *ibid.*, (see *Jus capiendi*). By the Voconian law (see G. ii, 226, note) institution of a woman by a testator whose fortune

TESTAMENT—*continued.*

II. REQUISITES OF A TESTAMENT, ETC.—*continued.*

amounted to 100,000 *asses* was prohibited, G. ii, 274. An *incerta persona* (which see) could not be instituted, G. ii, 287, U. xxii, 4; neither could a *postumus alienus* (see *Postumi*, 3), G. i, 147, ii, 242, because regarded as an *incerta persona, ibid.* A municipality was *incertum corpus*, and could not be instituted except by its freedmen, U. xxii, 5. A few specially favoured divinities might be instituted, thanks to certain senatusconsults and imperial constitutions, U. xxii, 6.

14. *Institution of persons* alieni juris.—It was incumbent on a testator either to institute or disinherit those of his own *filiifamilias* who were to become *sui juris* by his death; see above, No. 10. But he might also institute a *filiusfamilias alienus;* the institution being practically in favour of the *paterfamilias*, for whom he acquired, and without whose orders he could not enter, G. ii, 87. A *servus alienus* might also be instituted, provided the testator had *testamenti factio* with his owner, U. xxii, 9; who would take under the institution depended on the condition of the institute at the time of entry, as explained in G. ii, 189, 190, U. xxii, 9, 10. It was useless for a man to institute his own slave except with freedom, G. ii, 187, U. xxii, 7, 12; and even with freedom institution was impossible if the testator held him only in bonitarian ownership (which see), for freedom in that case could make him only a latin, and could not qualify him to be an heir, G. ii, 276, note, U. xxii, 8. If the testator was insolvent, and instituting his slave as necessary heir to save himself from being made a bankrupt after death, the Aelia-Sentian law declared the age of the slave immaterial, G. i, 21, U. i, 14; but in other circumstances institution with freedom of a slave under thirty was useless, for it could not make him a citizen, and so could not qualify him to enter, G. ii, 276, U. xxii, 8, (see *Aelia-Sentian law*, 3, 5). The effect of the institution, when valid, varied according as the slave had remained in the same condition until the testator's death, or had been manumitted after the date of the testament, or had been alienated, G. ii, 188; in the first case he became free and necessary heir, in the second he might take the inheritance or decline it as he pleased, in the third he had to take his orders from his new owner and did not become free, *ibid.*, U. xxii, 11, 12. Institution of a person *in causa mancipii* (see *Mancipii, etc.*) by him to whom he was subject for the time, also required to be with freedom, G. i, 123.

39

TESTAMENT—*continued.*

III. PROVISIONS IN TESTAMENTS OVER AND ABOVE THE INSTITU-
TION OF AN HEIR.

   15. *Substitutions.*—A substitution might be of an heir to take
in the event of the failure of the institute, or of one to
take in the event of the heir succeeding, he being one
of the testator's children, but subsequent death in pupillarity ; see *Substitution.*

   16. *Legacies.*—See *Legacy.*

   17. *Trust gifts.*—See *Fideicommissa.*

   18. *Appointment of tutors to wife or children.*—See *Tutory*, 1, 10,

   19. *Enfranchisements of slaves.*—See *Manumission,* III.

   20. *Relation of such provisions to the institution.*—As the whole
value of a testament depended on the institution of an
heir, G. ii, 229, U. xxiv, 15, a legacy placed before it was
useless, G. ii, 230, U. xxiv, 15, though the same rule did
not apply to *fideicommissa,* U. xxv, 8. A grant of freedom was useless if in the same position, G. ii, 230. A
tutor's appointment could not become operative until an
heir had succeeded, G. i, 186 ; but as the former really
took nothing from the latter, it was a matter of dispute
whether it was enough to invalidate the appointment
that it preceded the institution, G. ii, 231.

IV. INVALIDATION OF A TESTAMENT AFTER EXECUTION, AND ITS
CONSEQUENCES.

   21. *Invalid testaments generally.*—A testament was said to be
non jure factum when it was *ab initio* invalid through
absence of some condition or requirement of law, G. ii,
146, 147. One that was *jure factum* might be subsequently invalidated, *infirmatum,* in one or other of two
ways,—it might be either *ruptum* or *irritum factum,*
G. ii, 146, U. xxiii, 1-4.

   22. Ruptio testamenti.—This occurred when a testator made
a new will in all respects regular, even though no one
was in a position to take under it, G. ii, 144, U. xxiii, 2.
It would rather appear that nothing less than this, (or
the destruction of the deed), amounted to *ruptio ;* although
if the intention of the testator that his testament should
not stand was otherwise distinctly manifested, and the
heir *ab intestato* obtained *bonorum possessio,* any attempt
to oust him by the testamentary heirs might be defeated
by *exceptio doli,* G. ii, 151. There was *ruptio* also by
agnatio or *quasi agnatio sui heredis,* birth or advent in
some other way, of a *suus heres,* which in some cases
could, in others could not, be prevented by their testamentary institution or disherison, G. ii, 138-143, U.

TESTAMENT—*continued.*

IV. INVALIDATION OF A TESTAMENT, ETC.—*continued.*

xxiii, 3; see the cases in which it occurred under *Agnatio sui heredis.*

23. *Irritancy of a testament.*—A testament was irritated when the testator suffered *capitis deminutio* (which see), G. ii, 145, U. xxiii, 4. Ulp. adds that it was also said to be irritated when no one became heir under it, U. xxiii, 4; (but it was usual then to say it was *destitutum*).

24. *Consequences of ruption or irritancy.*—Though a testament thereby became useless *jure civili*, yet the praetors granted *bonor. possessio secundum tabulas* to the heirs nominated in it, provided the testator was a citizen and *sui juris* at his death, and that no one claimed the possession preferentially *contra tabulas*, G. ii, 147, U. xxiii, 6, xxviii, 5; (see details under *Bonor. possessio*, 10-12).

V. INFORMAL TESTAMENTARY DEEDS.

25. *The* testamentum militis.—A soldier, even a *filiusfamilias*, U. xx, 10, making his testament while on active service was exempted from almost all of the above requirements and restrictions; the *familiae venditio, nuncupatio,* and five witnesses were dispensed with, it being enough that he informally manifested his will, G. ii, 109, U. xxiii, 10. Not being *juris civilis*—though introduced by imperial enactments, U. xxiii, 10—the testator was free to institute whom he pleased, and even a peregrin, G. ii, 110; latins, *caelibes*, and *orbi* might take under his testament regardless of the Julian prohibitions, 110, 111; he might with impunity place legacies and grants of freedom before the institution of his heir, U. i, 20; and might declare that they were not to take effect until after the heir's death, *ibid.* Such a testament was valid if the testator died in active service, or within a year of his discharge, U. xxiii, 10.

26. *The codicil.*—See *Codicil.*

TESTAMENTI FACTIO explained in G. ii, 114, note 1.

TESTIMONIUM PERHIBERE, G. ii, 104 and n. 7.

THEFT, *furtum*, G. iii, 183-208; see also *Delict.*

1. *What constituted theft.*—There could be no theft without *dolus malus*, G. iii, 197, *adfectus furandi*, G. ii, 50, iii, 208, belief that the owner of the stolen property, if he knew of the thief's act, would object, G. iii, 197. Where this *dole, adfectus*, and belief were present, then, as a general rule, any contrectation with another man's property without his consent was theft, 195,—for if, unknown to the delinquent, the owner did consent, it was

Theft—*continued.*

not, 198,—as by taking it away, 195, or selling and delivering it to a third party, G. ii, 50, by using what had been deposited with him, G. iii, 196, or by putting what had been borrowed by him to another purpose than that for which it had been lent, 196, 197; although there were one or two cases in which a man might knowingly take possession of and even usucapt *res alienae* without theft, 201.

2. *What might be stolen.*—There might be theft not only of *res alienae*, G. iii, 195, but also of free persons, 199, and even of the thief's own property when lawfully in possession of a third party, 200.

3. *Who were accounted thieves.*—He was held a thief who had purposely facilitated the crime, and not merely the actual delinquent, G. iii, 202 : provided, in either case, that, if impuberate, he was *pubertati proximus*, and knew what he was about, 208.

4. *Varieties of theft.*—The law recognised two varieties of theft, *furtum manifestum* and *f. non manifestum*, G. iii, 183-185, there being some dispute as to where one ended and the other began, 184; also three quasi-varieties, *f. conceptum, f. oblatum,* and *f. prohibitum*, 183, 188, or more properly three conjunctions of circumstances giving rise to *actiones f. concepti, oblati,* and *prohibiti*, 183.

5. *Its penalties.*—Manifest theft, under the Twelve Tables, was visited with capital punishment, but under the edict with a fourfold money penalty, G. iii, 189; non-manifest, under both systems, with a twofold penalty, 190. There was under both systems a threefold penalty on a party in whose premises stolen goods were discovered on formal search, whether the thief or not, *f. conceptum*, 186, 191, 192, note 3; while the owner of such premises, if not himself the thief, could in turn demand a threefold penalty from the person who had feloniously introduced the goods, *f. oblatum*, 187, 191. The Twelve Tables dealt with *f. prohibitum*—*i.e.* refusal by a man to permit formal search in his premises, *lance et linteo*, for stolen goods—as *f. manifestum*, the edict substituting an *a. furti prohibiti*, with fourfold penalty, 188, 192, 193.

6. *The* actio furti.—The *actio furti*—*formula* in G. iv, 37 and notes—was not in every case competent to the owner of the stolen property, but rather to the party who was the direct sufferer by the loss, G. iii, 203; as *e.g.* a creditor responsible to his debtor for the safety of a pledge, 204, a tradesman responsible for that of an article intrusted to him to repair, 205, or a borrower responsible to the

THEFT—*continued.*

    lender for what had been given him in commodate, 206;
but if any of these were insolvent, then the *a. furti* was
competent to the owner, 205.

7. *The* vindicatio, condictio furtiva, *etc.*—In addition to this
penal action, the thief might be sued by the owner in a
vindicatio for recovery of the stolen property if extant,
G. iv, 4, or in a *condictio furtiva* if non-extant, G. ii,
79, iv, 4. The thief could not usucapt it, G. ii, 49; nor
could any third party acquiring from him so long as
it continued *res furtiva*, 49, 50.

THINGS, *res,*—classifications.

1. *Things of divine and human right.*—To the first class
belonged *res sacrae* and *religiosae*, G. ii, 3; *sacrae* those
consecrated by statute to the gods above, 5; *religiosae*
those devoted by private individuals to the *dii Manes*, by
interment in them of their dead, 7. As the provincial
solum belonged in property either to the state or to the
emperor, land there that was thus consecrated or devoted
was only *pro sacro* or *pro religioso*, 7. What were called
res sanctae, such as the walls or gates of a city, were
quodammodo divini juris, 8.

2. In patrimonio *and* extra patrimonium.—By things *in patri-*
monio Gai. seems to mean things that could not possibly
belong to an individual, G. ii, 1; *inter alias* things that
were *divini juris*, and therefore necessarily and perpetu-
ally *nullius in bonis*, 9. If a man acquired such a thing,
even in the belief that it was *in patrimonio*, he acquired
no right, and no length of possession could make it his,
G. ii, 48.

3. *Public, private, and unappropriated.*—Public were those
that belonged to an *universitas*, such as a city, and were
dedicated to public uses, G. ii, 11. Such things were
also said to be *nullius in bonis*, in the sense of not belonging, nor being capable of belonging, to a private
individual, *ibid*. But *res nullius* meant sometimes no
more than a thing for the moment unappropriated, as an
animal running wild, G. ii, 66, or things belonging to an
inheritance to which no heir had yet entered, 11.

4. *Corporeal and incorporeal.*—Corporeal were such as were
tangible, G. ii, 13; incorporeal those that had only a jural
existence, yet formed elements more or less valuable of a
man's estate, such as the right to a succession, a usufruct,
a praedial servitude, or a claim under an obligation, 14.

5. *Moveable and immoveable.*—This distinction was important
in reference to mancipation, usucapion, and interdicts.

THINGS—*continued.*

Moveables could be mancipated only one at a time, and when they were before the parties; but immoveables could be mancipated in absence, and any number at once, U. xix, 8, (see *Mancipatio,* 1). Moveables could be usucapted by one year's possession, but immoveables required two, G. ii, 42, U. xix, 8, (see *Usucapion,* 1). It was the *int. uti possidetis* that was used to defend possession of the latter, while the *int. utrubi* was used to defend that of the former, G. iv, 149, (see *Interdicts,* 7, 8). The phrase *res immobiles*, though in Ulp., does not occur in Gai.; he uses instead *praedia, res fundi,* or *res soli,* G. i, 121, ii, 42, 54.

6. Res mancipi et nec mancipi.—See *Res mancipi, etc.*

7. *Things present and future.*—By *res futura* was meant a thing not yet in existence but whose appearance might reasonably be expected; as the crop to be produced from a particular field, or the child to which a particular slave was to give birth; such things might, for example, be bequeathed by damnation, G. ii, 203.

8. *Fungibles and non-fungibles.*—By fungibles are meant what in the texts are described as *res quae pondere numero mensura constant,* G. iii, 90,—things whose value was generic, not specific, and which could be replaced by others of the same sort. It was only fungibles that could be given in *mutuum* (which see, No. 1,), G. iii, 90; while non-fungibles could not be legated by vindication unless they belonged to the testator both at the times of bequeathing and at his death, it was enough that fungibles belonged to him at the latter date (see *Legacy,* 19), G. ii, 196. U. xxiv, 7; and while a husband in restoring the dowry had to hand over non-fungibles at once, he was allowed three years for returning fungibles, (see *Dowry,* 3), U. vi, 8.

9. Res quae in usu vel abusu consistunt.—This distinction was of importance in reference to usufruct,(which see, No. 1). It was only what could be used and enjoyed without impairing its substance that could strictly speaking be usufructed; where the use involved destruction of or parting with the substance, *abusus,* there could only be *quasi* usufruct, U. xxiv, 26, 27.

TRADITAE, EXCEPTIO REI NONDUM, G. iv, 126a; see *Sale,* 4.

TRADITIO, delivery, see *Property,* 5.

TRANSSCRIPTICIA NOMINA, G. iii, 128-130; see *Literal obligations,* 1.

TRIPLICATION, G. iv, 128; see *Replication.*

TRUST, MORTIS CAUSA, see *Fideicommissum.*

TUBERO, Q. AELIUS, consul 743 | 11, one of the authors of a Sct. restricting the effects of *manus* created by confarreation, G. i, 136 and note.

TUTORY, *tutela*, G. i, 142-200, U. tit. xi, was the guardianship either of pupils, *i.e.* persons *sui juris* under the age of puberty, or of females *sui juris* who had passed that age. The first was justified by the *naturalis ratio* of their imperfect years, G. i, 189; but Gai. avowed himself unable to assign any good reason for the second, which in his time had become in many cases more nominal than real, 190, while Ulp. attributes it to the weakness of the sex and their ignorance of law, U. xi, 1.

I. TUTORY OF PUPILS OF FREE BIRTH.

    1. *Testamentary tutory.*—Testamentary appointment of tutors is said to have been confirmed by the provision of the Twelve Tables sanctioning testaments, U. xi, 14; which was held to have authorised a *paterfamilias* to appoint tutors to those of his children *in potestate* who were to become *sui juris* by his death, G. i, 144, U. xi, 15, including grandchildren who were not on that event to pass into the *potestas* of their father, G. i, 146, and *postumi* (which see, No. 1), 147. The tutors so appointed were called *dativi*, G. i, 154, U. xi, 14; and any one might be appointed to the office who had *testamenti factio* (which see) with the testator, U. xi, 16, except a Junian latin, G. i, 23, U. xi, 16. But he required to be named, G. ii, 240, U. xi, 14, and to be appointed directly by the testator; a fideicommissary request to the heir to appoint a tutor (see *Fideicommissum*, 1) was useless, G. ii, 289. The usual form of appointment is given in G. i, 149; it might be conditional or *ex die*, G. i, 186; but, even when unconditional and immediate, it was inoperative until an heir had succeeded, *ibid.* As in the case of other testamentary provisions it was a question whether the appointment was of any use if placed in the testament before the heir's institution, G. ii, 231, or if to take effect after or the day before the heir's death, 234, or if made by way of penalty, 237.

    2. *The* tutela legitima *of agnates and the* gens.—In the absence of testamentary appointment the XII Tables gave the tutory to the pupil's male agnates (see *Agnation*, 1, 2) nearest of degree, G. i, 164, U. xi, 3, hence called *legitimi*, G. i, 155, U. xi, 3; but by the Claudian law this tutory was abolished in the case of females, whether under or above puberty, G. i, 157, 171, U. xi, 8. Failing agnates it seems in early times to have gone to the pupil's *gens*, G. i, 164a and note.

TUTORY—*continued.*
  I. TUTORY OF PUPILS OF FREE BIRTH—*continued.*
  3. *Fiduciary tutory.*—When a parent emancipated a child
     under puberty (see *Emancipation,* 1), the latter's final
     manumitter, after the example of a patron (see below, No.
     18), became his tutor, G. i, 166, U. xi, 5. It was the
     practice for the parent to make it a condition of the final
     mancipation that the mancipee should remancipate to him,
     the parent, who then became manumitter, G. i, 133, 172,
     175, and consequently tutor, 172, 175. Such a tutor
     was called fiduciary, G. i, 166, U. xi, 5; but if the parent
     himself held the office, he was, as *quasi* patron, regarded
     also as a tutor-at-law, *legitimus,* G. i, 172, 175, though
     his unemancipated children succeeding him in it were
     fiduciary tutors only, 175.
  4. *Atilian tutory.*—If a pupil had no tutor of any of the above
     classes, the urban praetor and the majority of the ple-
     beian tribunes appointed one for him, if he was in Rome,
     in terms of the Atilian law, while if he was in a province
     the governor did so in terms of the Julian and Titian
     law, G. i, 185, U. xi, 18. A similar and equally per-
     manent appointment was made when a testamentary
     tutor or a tutor-at-law had been excused or removed as
     suspect, (see below, Nos. 6, 8), G. i, 182, U. xi, 23. Tem-
     porary appointments of the same sort were made when a
     testamentary one was conditional or to begin at a future
     date, G. i, 186, and while it remained inoperative through
     the heir's delay to enter, *ibid. ;* as also while a tutor was
     captive in the hands of an enemy (see *Captivity, etc.*), 187.
  5. *Praetorian tutory.*—When it was necessary for a pupil to
     sue his tutor in a *judicium legitimum,* as it was improper
     that the latter should be *auctor in rem suam,* the praetor
     appointed one to act with the pupil in that particular
     matter, G. i, 184, U. xi, 24.
  6. *Excuses of and securities by tutors.*—Gai. and Ulp. mention,
     without particulars, that a man was sometimes excused
     from undertaking a tutory, G. i, 182, U. xi, 23; and Gai. adds
     that, with the exception of testamentary ones, they had to
     give security by *satisdatio* for their administration, 199, 200.
  7. *The tutor's* gestio *and* auctoritas.—A tutor either acted for
     his pupil ward *gestio,* or with him, *auctoritatis interpositio,*
     U. xi, 25; the latter, however, only when the pupil was
     old enough to have some knowledge of what he was
     doing, G. iii, 107, 109. If he had several tutors the
     auctoritas had to be that of all of them, unless they held
     office under a testament, when that of one was sufficient,

TUTORY—*continued.*

   I. TUTORY OF FREE BIRTH—*continued.*

      U. xi, 26. As regards the acts of a pupil which required tutorial *auctoritas* to validate them, see U. xi, 27, and in more detail under *Pupils.* A tutor might sue for or defend his pupil, and in either case the *condemnatio* was taken in his name, G. iv, 82, 86, 87, (see *Procuratory in litigation,* 3). In matter of processual cautions he was in the same position as a procurator, G. iv, 99, (see *Cautiones, etc.*).

    8. *How a tutory came to an end.*—A tutory came to an end absolutely by a male pupil's *cap. deminutio, e.g.* giving himself in adrogation and thus ceasing to be *sui juris,* G. i, 102, U. viii, 5, or by his attaining the age of puberty, G. i, 145, 196, U. xi, 28; but females could not be adrogated, G. i, 101, U. viii, 5. and on reaching twelve the *tutela impuberis* merged into the *tutela mulieris,* G. i, 145. In the case of both male and female pupils it ceased relatively, *i.e.* as regarded a particular tutor when he was removed as suspect, G. i, 182, U. xi, 23; when he was taken captive, 187; when, being a *tutor legitimus,*—for the rule did not apply to testamentary tutors, U. xi, 17,—he underwent *capitis deminutio* (which see), G. i, 158, 163, U. xi, 9; or when, being only an interim Atilian or praetorian tutor, the purpose of his appointment had been attained, G. i, 186, 187. In the case of a female it also ceased relatively when it was ceded by a tutor-at-law or a fiduciary tutor, G. i, 186,—that of a male pupil could not be ceded, because, as it came to an end with puberty, it was not so onerous as that of a female, *ibid.,*—or when a testamentary tutor abdicated, U. xi, 17 and n. 2, as amended in *Additions etc.*

    9. *The* tutelae judicium.—Tutors who did not voluntarily render a satisfactory account of their intromissions on their wards, whether male or female, attaining puberty, might be compelled to do so in a *judicium tutelae,* G. i, 191. It was a *bonae fidei action,* G. iv, 62; but condemnation in it rendered the tutor infamous, G. iv, 182.

   II. TUTORY OF WOMEN OF FREE BIRTH.

    10. *Testamentary tutory,* (see also above, No. 1).—A *paterfamilias* might by his testament appoint tutors to his daughters *in potestate,* no matter what their age, and even though married, G. i, 144; as also to his wife *in manu,* and to his daughter-in-law who had been *in manu* of a deceased son, 148. There was this peculiarity in the appointment of a tutor to a wife *in manu* —that she might have the choice of the individual

TUTORY—*continued.*
  II. TUTORY OF WOMEN OF FREE BIRTH—*continued.*
      left to herself, *optio tutoris;* and that, according to the
      form of words used by the testator, her choice might be
      more or less limited, sometimes going so far as to entitle
      her to have a different tutor for each piece of business in
      which his intervention was necessary, 150-153. Such a
      tutor was called *optivus,* in contradistinction to the *tutor
      dativus* appointed directly by the testator, 154. A *tutor
      dativus,* in consideration of the long duration of a female
      tutory, had the right to give it up, *jus abdicandi,* when it
      became too onerous, U. xi, 17 and n. 2, as amended in
      Additions etc.
  11. *That of agnates.*—It was introduced by the Twelve Tables,
      but abolished by the Claudian law, G. i, 157, 171, U. xi, 8,
      (see above, No. 2). One of its peculiarities was that it
      might be ceded by the agnate-tutor to a third party, who
      got the name of *cessicius tutor,* G. i, 168, 171, U. xi, 6-8.
  12. *Fiduciary tutory.*—See above, No. 3; this was the same
      as the fiduciary tutory of pupils, except that it was of
      longer duration. If it was the woman's father that held
      this position, then, as he was also *tutor legitimus* (as *quasi*
      patron), he had the right to cede the tutory in the same
      way as agnates and patrons, G. i, 172. See the qualifica-
      tions of the right of the *tutor cessicius* in G. i, 170, U. xi,
      7, and below, No. 20. A fiduciary tutor other than a
      parens manumissor had no power of cession, G. i, 172.
  13. *Atilian tutory.*—The Atilian and Julian and Titian laws,
      mentioned above, No. 4, applied to women as well as
      pupils, U. xi, 18; and Atilian tutories must have become
      all the more necessary when that of agnates was abolished.
      Such an appointment could be made on the woman's own
      petition, G. i, 173; and one of the cases in which it was
      authorised was the absence of her testamentary or other
      tutor, not being her *parens manumissor;* on the new
      appointment the office of the tutor thus superseded came
      to an end, G. i, 173. Even when in tutory of a *parens
      manumissor,* if he happened to be abroad, she might have
      a temporary tutor to enable her to enter on an inherit-
      ance, 175, 176.
  14. *Praetorian tutory.*—This occurred in the same circum-
      stances, *mutatis mutandis,* as described above, No. 5, U.
      xi, 24.
  15. *Changing tutors by* coemptio.—G. i, 115; see *Manus,* 7.
  16. *The tutor's* auctoritas.—In the *tutela mulierum* a tutor
      never acted for his ward, but only with her, by inter-

TUTORY—*continued.*

II. TUTORY OF WOMEN OF FREE BIRTH—*continued.*

poning *auctoritas*, G. i, 190, U. xi, 25. And this was in many cases a mere matter of form, the tutor, unless a *parens manumissor*, being often obliged to grant it whether he would or not, G. i, 190, 192. A *parens manumissor* had the same power as a patron of withholding his *auctoritas* from certain acts of his ward's, G. i, 192, and below, Nos. 19, 23; but other tutors could be compelled to grant it where necessary to the validity of a deed, G. i, 190, ii, 122. For enumeration of them see *Women*, 4.

17. *How tutory of women of free birth came to an end.*—It came to an end absolutely when the ward ceased to be *sui juris*, as by passing *in manum* of a husband, U. xi, 13; when she had three children,—an event that by the Julian and Papia-Poppaean law released her for ever from tutelage, G. i, 145, 194, U. xi, 28*a*; or when she was made a Vestal virgin, G. i, 145. It ceased relatively when a *parens manumissor* ceded his tutory, G. i, 172, though it might revert to him in certain events, G. i, 170, U. xi, 7; when he died, in which case his children became fiduciary tutors, G. i, 175; when he and his children were all *capiti minuti*, as by adrogation, G. i, 195*b*; when a testamentary tutor died or abdicated, U. xi, 17; when an Atilian tutor died, or when he had fulfilled the purpose of his appointment if only an interim one, G. i, 181; when a tutor of any sort was taken captive, 187; or when the woman herself performed fiduciary coemption with a stranger in order to have him as her tutor after remancipation, 195*a*. But, no matter how the tutory ended, it was never followed by any *judicium tutelae*, a woman's tutor having no account to render, 191.

III. TUTORY OF PUPIL FREEDMEN.

18. *General observations.*—Manumission of a slave under puberty was probably so rare that we have very little explanation of the nature and conditions of the resulting tutory. Testamentary appointment and agnatic right being equally out of the question, it belonged by the Twelve Tables, or rather by the interpretation put upon them, to the manumitting patron and his children, G. i, 165; the latter, on the former's death, were not fiduciary tutors, but tutors-at-law as he had been, 175. In the case of a Junian latin the tutory did not necessarily belong to the manumitter; for if he had been only bonitarian owner it belonged to the party who was quiritarian owner at the date of manumission, 167. If the manu-

TUTORY—*continued.*
  III. TUTORY OF PUPIL FREEDMEN—*continued.*
      mission had proceeded from a woman, then, as a patroness
      could not be tutor, an Atilian one was necessary, 195.
  IV. TUTORY OF FREEDWOMEN.
    19. *The* legitima tutela patronorum, (see also *Patronate*).—
      Like male freedmen under puberty, freedwomen were in
      the tutory-at-law of their patron and of his children on
      his death, G. i, 165, 175 ; the quiritarian owner at manu-
      mission being tutor of a latin freedwoman rather than
      her bonitarian manumitter, 167, (see above, No. 18).
      This tutory being really in the interests of the patron
      himself, it gave him much more control over his ward
      than other tutors possessed, and entitled him to withhold
      his *auctoritas* in many cases in which they were com-
      pelled to grant it, G. i, 193, ii, 122.
    20. *The* cessicia tutela.—The tutory of a woman being of
      indefinite duration, the patron—but no other tutor, for
      he alone had a *legitimum jus*—was entitled to transfer
      it to a third party by *in jure cessio* (which see, No. 3), G.
      i, 168, U. xi, 6. If the *cessicius tutor* died or was *capite
      minutus,* or if he in turn attempted to cede it, it reverted
      to the patron, G. i, 170, U. xi, 7 ; while if it was the
      latter that died or suffered *capitis deminutio,* the right of
      the *cessicius* was equally at an end, *ibid.*
    21. *Fiduciary tutory.*—This arose in the case of a freed-
      woman when, with *auctoritas* of her patron-tutor, she
      performed fiduciary coemption (see *Manus,* 7) with a
      third party, who, according to agreement, remancipated
      her to a fourth party of her own selection, who then
      manumitted her, and thus became her fiduciary tutor, G.
      i, 115, 195a. This new tutor had no power to cede his
      office, G. i, 172.
    22. *Atilian tutory.*—An Atilian appointment might be either
      permanent or interim. It was permanent when made to
      supply that of a deceased patron who had no male chil-
      dren surviving, G. i, 195c ; or to supply that of a patron who
      along with his children had undergone *capitis deminutio,*
      195b ; or that of a patroness, who, because of her sex,
      could not be tutor, 195 ; or that of a fiduciary or Atilian
      tutor who had died or gone abroad, 173. A freedwoman
      could not thus supersede a patron who had gone from
      home, 174 ; but in his absence she might sometimes have
      an interim Atilian tutor, as when she needed *auctoritas* to
      enter upon an inheritance, 176,—for such entry usually
      required to be within a limited period (see *Cretio,* 1), G.

TUTORY—*continued.*

IV. TUTORY OF FREEDWOMEN—*continued.*

ii, 164, 165, U. xxii, 7. If her patron was insane, or a mute, she was entitled to an interim tutor to aid her in constituting a dowry, G. i, 180; and for the same purpose, or to authorise her to take an inheritance, she might have an interim tutor when she was in the tutory of her patron's son, and he was a pupil, 177-179. But such occasional appointments did not affect the permanent right of the patron and his children, 181.

23. *Tutorial* auctoritas.—All other tutors than patrons and their children—for these last were also *legitimi tutores*, G. i, 175—seem to have been bound to grant *auctoritas* when demanded, G. i, 190, ii, 122. A patron seems to have been bound to grant it when his ward proposed to make a dotal provision, G. i, 178, 180, to give herself *in manum*, 115, 195a, or to enter on an inheritance, 176, 177; but for the reason explained above, No. 19, he could not be required against his will to aid her in making a testament, 192, ii, 122, or in alienating her *res mancipi* or undertaking an obligation, unless in either of those two cases there were weighty causes of justification, G. i, 192. For the acts of a woman to which *auctoritas* was required, see Ulp. xi, 27, and in more detail under *Women*, 4.

24. *How the* tutela libertae *ended.*—It ended absolutely by her passing *in manum mariti*, as above, No. 17, and, under the Julian law, when she gave birth to her fourth child, G. i, 145, iii, 44, U. xxix, 3. How it ended relatively may be gathered from what has been said in Nos. 20-22.

TWELVE TABLES, the, (*Lex Duodecim Tabularum*), the statutory basis of the *jus civile* or *legitimum*, as distinguished from the *jus honorarium*, are referred to in G. i, 111, 122, 132, 145, 155, 157, 165, 200; ii, 42, 45, 47, 49, 54, 64, 224; iii, 1, 9, 11, 17-21, 23, 27, 28, 40, 46, 49, 51, 78, 82, 85, 189-194, 223; iv, 11, 14, 21, 28, 76, 79; U. i, 9; ii, 4; x, 1; xi, 3, 14; xii, 1, 2, 3; xix, 17; xxvi, 1, 5, 7, 8; xxvii, 5; xxix, 1, 5, 6; but in many of them only by way of interpretation. The provisions of the Tables to which actual reference is made are these:—

1. *Law concerning persons.*—(*a*) *Manus,*—avoidance of it by trinoctial interruption, G. i, 111. (*b*) Emancipation,—that a son should not be released from the *potestas* until mancipated thrice, '*si pater filium ter venumduit, a patre filius liber esto,*' G. i, 132, and almost the same words in U. x, 1. (*c*) Manumission,—the condition of *statuliberi*, U.

TWELVE TABLES—*continued.*

ii, 4. (*d*) Tutory,—authorisation of testamentary tutory in the words '*uti legassit super pecunia tutelave suae rei, ita jus esto,*' U. xi, 14; agnatic tutelage of pupils, G. i, 155, U. xi, 3; agnatic tutelage of women, G. i, 157; tutory of patrons, 165, U. xi, 3; freedom of Vestal virgins from tutelage, G. i, 145. (*e*) Curatory of lunatics and prodigals, G. ii, 64, U. xii, 2.

2. *Law concerning things.*—(*a*) Usucapion,—periods of, G. ii, 42, 54; incapacity for usucapion of *res furtivae*, 45, 49, and of a woman's *res mancipi* delivered without her tutor's *auctoritas*, 47. (*b*) Testaments and freedom of bequest,—in the words '*uti legassit suae rei, ita jus esto,*' G. ii, 224, and their expansion in U. xi, 14, (quoted above). (*c*) Intestate succession,—first that of *sui*, G. iii, 1, and then that of the nearest agnate, G. iii, 9, 11, both embodied in the words '*si intestatus moritur, cui suus heres nec escit, agnatus proximus familiam habeto,*' U. xxvi, 1; lastly that of the *gens*, G. iii, 17. (*d*) Succession of patrons, G. iii, 40, 46, 49, 51, U. xxix, 1, 5. (*e*) Obligations *ex delicto*,—theft, G. iii, 189-192, iv, 76; wrongful damage to property, *rupitae*, G. iii, note to 210-219; personal injury, G. iii, 223; other offences, G. iv, 11.

3. *Law concerning actions.*—(*a*) *Legis actiones,*—*actio sacramento,* amount of the sacramental stake, G. iv, 14; *manus injectio,* authorised by the statute in proceedings on a judgment, 21; *pignoris capio,* cases in which authorised, 28. (*b*) Noxal action,—sanctioned in case of theft, 76.

UNDE VI, INTERDICTUM, G. iv, 154; see *Interdicts*, 9.

UNIVERSAL ACQUISITION, see *Adquisitio per universitatem.*

UNIVERSITAS, a corporation; see *Persons*, 6.

USUCAPION, *usucapio*, G. ii, 41-61, U. xix, 8; see also *Property*, 3.

1. *Usucapion, what ?*—It is defined as acquisition of ownership by continued possession for a certain period, U. xix, 8; more accurately it was the cure by possession of some defect of title. The possession might be either by the party himself that thereby became owner, or by a slave or *filiusfamilias* on his behalf, or even by a person *bona fide* possessed by him as a slave, G. ii, 89, 94; but apparently that of his wife *in manu*, a free person *in mancipio*, or a usufructed slave was ineffectual, they not being themselves in his possession, 90, 94. The period required is commonly said to have been one year for moveables, two years for immoveables, G. ii, 42, 204, U.

USUCAPION—*continued.*

   xix, 8; but the actual provision of the Twelve Tables was two years for *res soli,* for 'other things' one, G. ii, 54.

2. *Usucapion of a* res mancipi *acquired by wrong conveyance.*— When a *res mancipi* was transferred by simple tradition, instead of being conveyed by mancipation or *in jure cessio,* the legal title still remained in the transferor, the transferee becoming only bonitarian owner; by possession for the requisite period, however, he cured the defect, and became owner *ex jure Quiritium,* G. ii, 41, 204, U. i, 16. See *Property,* 1.

3. *Usucapion of a thing acquired* a non domino.—When a man acquired a thing, whether *res mancipi* or *nec mancipi,* from one who was not its owner, again he might cure the defect of his title by usucapion; but in this case it was indispensable that he should have accepted it in good faith, *i.e.* under the belief that the transferor was its owner, G. ii, 43, 44. See *Bonae fidei possessio.*

4. *Usucapion by praetorian owners.*—A praetorian *bonorum possessor* did not at once become quiritarian owner of the corporeals included in the succession that was granted to him, neither did a *bonorum emptor* or purchaser of a bankrupt estate become quiritarian owner of the corporeals that formed part of it; but both cured the defect by possession for the statutory period, G. iii, 80. See *Bonorum possessio,* 5; *Emptio bonorum,* 3.

5. *Things that could not be usucapted.*—Things not *in patrimonio* (see *Things,* 2), such as a freeman possessed as a slave, G. ii, 48; provincial lands, 46, for they belonged to the state or the emperor, 7; the *res mancipi* of a woman in tutelage of her agnates, 47,—a tutory, however, that was abolished by the Claudian law, G. i, 157, 171, U. xi, 8; *res furtivae, i.e.* moveables that had been stolen, not, of course, by the possessor,—for his bad faith would have been a sufficient impediment,—but by some previous holder, from whom the possessor derived his right, G. ii, 45, 49; and immoveables that had been taken forcibly by the party from whom the possessor derived them, G. ii, 45. It was conceivable that a man might sell or on some other good title transfer a moveable *res aliena* believing it his own; in such a case there was nothing to prevent usucapion by a *bona fide* purchaser or transferee, there being no theft without intent to steal, G. ii, 50. It was quite possible also for a man to take possession, without any violence, of lands that he knew were not his; the usucapion of a *bona fide* acquirer from him,

USUCAPION—*continued.*

however, was not thereby impeded; for it was held that lands could not be stolen, and so the *vitium furti* did not attach to them, 51.

6. Usucapio pro herede.—In this usucapion *bona fides* had no place, G. ii, 52. It arose when, in the absence of a necessary heir,—for if there was either a *suus* or a *necessarius heres* (see *Hereditas*, 3, 4) it was impossible, G. ii, 58, iii, 201,—an individual took possession *pro herede*, as heir, of things belonging to an inheritance to which he knew he had no title, G. ii, 52; by possessing for no more than a year, even though the things were immoveable, he was held to have usucapted the inheritance itself, it being regarded as one of the 'other things' (see above, No. 1) for which, under the provision of the Twelve Tables, the shorter period was sufficient, 53, 54. Gai. thought this 'iniquitous' usucapion was to be explained only by the anxiety of the early jurists to ensure as soon as possible the presence of an heir who would look after the family *sacra* of the deceased, and satisfy the claims of creditors, 55. By a Sct. of Hadrian's, however, the true heir was authorised to disregard it, and proceed with his *hereditatis petitio* as if there had been no such usucapion, 57.

7. *Usureception.*—Here also there was usucapion of what was known to be another's, so far at least as legal title was concerned, G. ii, 59. Suppose a man mancipated a thing to a friend for safety's sake, but under a *pactum fiduciae*, *i.e.* an agreement for its reconveyance on demand (see *Fiducia*, 1); if the mancipant reacquired possession of it without reconveyance, it became his again by *usureceptio* in a year, even though an immoveable, G. ii, 59, 60. If the mancipation was to a creditor by way of security (see *Fiducia*, 2), there was usureception in a year if the debt had been paid; if it had not, the usureception was possible only if the possession had not been derived directly from the creditor by way of location or grant during pleasure, 60. What was called usureception *ex praediatura* was that of a debtor who took possession of lands he had mortgaged to the state, and which had been sold by its officials; here two years were required, 61.

USUFRUCT, *ususfructus*, G. ii, 30-33; U. xxiv, 26, 27.

1. *What, and how created.*—Usufruct was the right of using and enjoying the fruits and profits of a thing, G. ii, 14, iv, 3, U. xxiv, 26, the property the while belonging to another, G. ii, 33, 93. It might be created by reservation

USUFRUCT—*continued.*

of it in mancipating lands, G. ii, 33 ; but the appropriate form of constitution *inter vivos* was *in jure cessio*, 30, competent everywhere as regarded moveables, 32, though as regarded immoveables competent only *in italico solo* (see *Jus Ital.*), 31, a usufruct of lands *in provinciali solo* being created by pacts and stipulations, *ibid.* It might also be created by testament, U. xxiv, 26.

2. *Quasi usufruct.*—Although properly there could be usufruct only of things whose use did not diminish their substance, U. xxiv, 26, (see *Things*, 9), there might, through means of securities for eventual restitution of a like quantity, given to the heir or legatee on whom it was a charge, be a testamentary bequest even of money or other things whose use extinguished them, U. xxiv, 27.

3. *Rights of a usufructuary.*—A usufructuary was not held to be in possession of the thing he usufructed, G. ii, 93, but only holder for the owner, G. iv, 153 ; consequently he could never usucapt, G. iii, 93. As usufructuary he was entitled to ordinary fruits, which, however, did not include children born to slave women, G. ii, 50 ; all that a usufructed slave acquired by his own labour or with funds provided by the usufructuary belonged to the latter, G. ii, 91, iii, 165, U. xix, 21 ; acquisitions from adventitious sources belonged to the owner, *ibid.* Manumission of such a slave by the owner did not affect the usufructuary's right,—the slave became *servus sine domino*, U. i, 19.

4. *Extinction of a usufruct.*—It was extinguished by the usufructuary's death or *capitis deminutio* (which see), G. iii, 83 ; but it was so highly personal that it could not be transferred to any one but the *dominus proprietatis*, in whose person the two rights became consolidated, G. ii, 30—cession to a third party was resultless, *ibid.*

5. *Actions peculiar to it.*—When disputed it might be vindicated in an *actio in rem*, G. iv, 3 ; while the *dominus proprietatis* might challenge it in an *a. negatoria, ibid.*

USURAE, see *Interest.*

USURECEPTIO, see *Usucapion,* 7.

USURPATIO TRINOCTIALIS, G. i, 111 ; see *Manus,* 3.

USUS as a mode of creating *manus,* G. i, 111 ; see *Manus,* 3.

UTI POSSIDETIS, INTERDICTUM, G. iv, 148, 149, 160 ; see *Interdicts,* 7, 13-17.

UTILES ACTIONES, see *Actions,* 6.

UTILITAS, G. iii, 109, 160.

UTRUBI, INTERDICTUM, G. iv, 148, 149, 160 ; see *Interdicts,* 8, 13-17.

40

VADIMONIUM, the security given by a defender, who had appeared
in answer to a summons, for his reappearance on a future
day, G. iv, 184; resting sometimes on his own simple
engagement, sometimes backed with an oath or with
sureties, sometimes under reference to recuperators, 185.
Its amount was determined according to certain rules
described in 186.

VENDITIO, see *Sale*.

VENDITIO BONORUM, sale of a bankrupt's estate ; see *Emptio bonorum*.

VENTRIS NOMINE IN POSSESSIONEM MISSIO, G. iv, 177.

VERBAL OBLIGATIONS, G. iii, 92-127 ; see also *Contract*, 1. Their
characteristic was that a certain *verborum proprietas* was
necessary in contracting, G. iii, 136. In stipulation
(which see) there was question and answer, G. iii, 92 ;
in *dotis dictio* (see *Dowry*, 1) there were words of style
spoken by one only of the parties, 96 ; in *jurata promissio
operarum liberti* (see *Patronate*, 3) there was promise
without antecedent interrogatory, but accompanied with
an oath, 96*a*. Varieties of stipulation were adstipulation
(which see), 110-114, and the different forms of *adpromissio*, (see *Suretyship*), 115-127. A verbal obligation was
impossible *inter absentes*, 136 ; and it was the only one that
could be discharged by acceptilation (which see), 169, 170.

VESTAL VIRGINS, on election, were *ipso jure* freed from the *patria
potestas* if *filiaefamilias*, G. i, 130, U. x, 5, or from tutory
if *sui juris*, G. i, 145.

VESTING of an inheritance, see *Hereditas*, 3-7 ; of a legacy, see
Legacy, 11.

VETERANS, *veterani*, G. i, 57 ; see *Soldier*.

VETERES, an epithet applied by Gai. to the jurists of the republic,
G. i, 144 and n. 2, 145, 165, 188, ii, 55, etc.

VEXATIOUS LITIGATION, DEVICES TO PREVENT, G. iv, 171-182.

1. *Devices to restrain dishonest defence.*—To check dishonest or
reckless *defence*, the law in certain enumerated cases condemned a man in double the amount of his normal
liability, because of the temerity of his denial, G. iv, 171,
(see *Cretio litis infitiatione*) ; but this did not extend to
his heir, who might be ignorant of the circumstances, 172.
In one or two actions the defender had to give his sponsion to pay a third or a half more than the sum sued for
by way of penalty if judgment went against him, 171,—
an obligation that did not affect women or pupils, 172.
Where there was neither *cretio litis* nor sponsion, an
oath was required that the defence was not vexatious (*jusjurandum calumniae*), exigible even from heirs, women,
and pupils, 172.

VINDICATIO—*continued.*

in money, 48, *i.e.* if he reached condemnation; for that
might be avoided if the defender, on a finding for the
pursuer, complied with the judge's order to yield the
possession, G. iv, 114, note.

4. *When employed.*—It was only things extant that could be
vindicated, G. ii, 79. For example, if a pupil lent money
without his tutor's *auctoritas,* the property did not pass
to the borrower, and could therefore be vindicated so long
as in his hands and capable of identification, 82; but
after it was consumed, the pupil had to be content with
a *condictio, ibid.*

5. *Preliminary use of interdicts.*—Gaius says that the interdicts
uti possidetis and *utrubi* (see *Interdicts,* 7, 8) were introduced in order to settle the question of possession, and
thus determine which of the parties was to stand on the
defensive in the *vindicatio,* G. iv, 148; this makes their
introduction subsequent to the Aebutian law of 507 | 247,
which sanctioned procedure by *formula* (see *Procedure,* 2);
for under the earlier system both parties vindicated, (see
above, No. 2).

VINDICATIONEM, LEGATUM PER, see *Legacy,* 18-21, 31, 34.

VINDICIAE, *vindicias dicere,* G. iv, 16 and n. 9; *praedes litis et vindiciarum,* G. iv, 94.

VINDICTA or *festuca,* a rod which represented the *hasta* or spear, the
symbol of quiritarian ownership, G. iv, 16; its use in
real actions *sacramento, ibid.* ; in manumissions, G. i, 17,
18, 38, U. i, 6, 7, 13.

VIS BONORUM RAPTORUM, see *Robbery.*

VIS EX CONVENTU, *vis moribus facta,* G. iv, 166, note, with addition
in *Additions etc.,* 170; see *Interdicts,* 13.

VOCATIO, IN JUS, G. iv, 183; see *In jus vocatio.*

VULGAR SUBSTITUTION, G. iv, 174-178; see *Substitution,* 1.

VULGO CONCEPTI, meaning, G. i, 64, note 3.

WOMEN.

1. *Capacities and incapacities of women generally.*—Like men
they might be either *sui juris* or *alieni juris,* (see those
words); but if *sui juris* they were in tutory for life, G.
i, 144, U. xi, 1, unless freed from it under the Julian
law, G. i, 145, iii, 44, U. xi, 28a, xxix, 3, (see *Tutory,* II.,
IV.). They had this advantage over men,—that they
became marriageable at twelve, U. v, 2, (see *Marriage,* 3),
and if *sui juris* might then make a testament, G. ii, 112,
113, (see *Testament,* 6); and if *alieni juris* they might be
emancipated, G. i, 132, U. x, 1, (see *Emancipation,* 1),

WOMEN—*continued.*

and be disinherited, G. ii, 129, U. xxii, 20, (see *Testament*, 11), more easily than males. As they could have no *potestas* over their children, G. i, 104, ii, 161, U. viii, 8a, (see *Pat. potestas*, 1), they could not adopt, G. i, 104, U. viii, 8a, (see *Adoption*, 4); and as they could have no *sui heredes*, G. iii, 51, U. xxvi, 7, there was no one that, in making a testament, they required to institute or disinherit, G. iii, 71. They were incompetent to perform any of the public duties of citizens; consequently they could not be tutors, G. i, 195, nor act as witnesses, etc., in a mancipation, U. xx, 7; nor could they be adrogated, G. i, 101, U. viii, 5, for that implied access to the *comitia*, G. i, 99, U. viii, 3, although there was nothing to prevent them being adopted, G. i, 101, U. viii, 5, (see *Adoption*, 2, 5). The Voconian law forbade their institution as heirs by a testator worth not less than 100,000 *asses*, G. ii, 274, although the prohibition might be avoided by a trust, *ibid.* On intestacy they could not take as agnates beyond the consanguinean degree, G. iii, 14, 23, U. xxvi, 6; but those more distantly related were admitted by the praetors as cognates, G. iii, 29, (see *Intestate succession*, 2, *Bonorum possessio*, 16).

2. *Women* in manu.—See *Manus.*
3. *Women who were married but not* in manu.—See *Husband and wife*, 3-7; *Intestate succession*, 7; *Jus liberorum.*
4. *Women in tutelage.*—See *Tutory*, II., IV. Without the *auctoritas* of her tutor a woman could not alienate a *res mancipi*, G. ii, 80, U. xi, 27; nor could she allow one of her freedwomen to cohabit with a slave, U. xi, 27, for, in consequence of the penalty of the Claudian Sct., (which see), that amounted to alienation; nor manumit a slave, U. i, 17; nor be a party to a *legis actio* or a *legitimum judicium*, U. xi, 27; nor make herself a debtor *ex contractu*, G. iii, 108, U. xi, 27; nor give herself *in manum* by *coemptio*, G. i, 115, 195a; nor constitute a dowry, G. i, 178, 180, U. xi, 20-22; nor make a testament, G. ii, 112, 113, U. xx, 15; nor enter to an inheritance by cretion, G. i, 176; nor discharge a debtor by acceptilation (which see), G. ii, 85, iii, 171; nor take a part in any *civile negotium*, U. xi, 27, (of which most of the above are examples). But she could competently be sued in an *indebiti solutio* (which see) even though the *indebitum* had been received by her without *auctoritas*, G. iii, 91; she might contract as creditor, G. iii, 108; she might alienate her *res nec mancipi*, G. ii, 80; and she

WOMEN—*continued.*

might take payment from a debtor so as effectually to discharge him, G. ii, 85, iii, 171. And it rather appears that, after the Claudian law had abolished the tutory of agnates, G. i, 157, 171, U. xi, 8, it was only a patron or a *parens manumissor* that could any longer withhold *auctoritas* in cases where it was formally necessary, see *Tutory*, 16, 23; and that they could do so only when what was proposed was alienation of *res mancipi*, execution of a testament, or incurring of debt, G. i, 192.

WRONGFUL DAMAGE TO PROPERTY, *damnum injuria datum*, G. iii, 210-219, was punished by the Twelve Tables and various subsequent enactments (see note to those pars.); but the law on the subject was amended by the *lex Aquilia*, 210 and same note. See also *Delict.*

1. *The first chapter of the Aquilian law.*—By its first chapter he who dolefully or culpably, and not by pure accident, G. iii, 211, killed another man's slave or grazing quadruped was liable in his or its highest value, intrinsic and extrinsic, 212, during the previous twelve months, 210, even though of less value when killed, 214.

2. *Its second chapter.*—By this an adstipulator acceptilating in fraud of the stipulant was responsible to him for the full value, G. iii, 215, and mulcted in double damages if he denied his liability, 216.

3. *Its third chapter.*—By the third chapter he who wrongfully wounded a slave or grazing beast, or killed or hurt any other animal belonging to a third party, or did damage to any inanimate property of his, G. iii, 217, was liable in its highest value during the preceding thirty days, 218.

4. Utiles actiones *on the Aquilian law.*—To justify direct action under the statute it was necessary that the injury should have been caused directly, *damnum corpore datum*, G. iii, 219; if caused indirectly an *utilis actio* (see *Actions*, 6) was had recourse to, 202, 219.

5. *Alternative remedies.*—Where a man's slave was wrongfully killed, it was free to the owner either to sue under the statute for damages or to institute a criminal prosecution, G. iii, 213.

THE END.

THE ABERDEEN UNIVERSITY PRESS LIMITED.

In demy 8vo, price 10s. 6d.

THE ROMAN LAW OF SALE.

WITH MODERN ILLUSTRATIONS.

DIGEST XVIII. 1 AND XIX. 1 TRANSLATED.

With Notes and References to Cases

AND THE

SALE OF GOODS BILL.

By JAMES MACKINTOSH, B.A., ADVOCATE,

PROFESSOR OF CIVIL LAW IN THE UNIVERSITY OF EDINBURGH;
LATE SCHOLAR OF EXETER COLLEGE, OXFORD.

'The care, thoroughness and clearness which characterise this part of the work reflect the highest credit on Mr. Mackintosh's learning. . . . The book as a whole may be recommended to every one interested in its subject as a serviceable exposition of that branch of the law of Rome which is of most importance to a modern lawyer.'—*Scotsman.*

'The notes are extremely well done, and the Scotch law is everywhere clearly stated. The volume should fulfil its main object, to enable candidates for legal examinations to get up two important titles of the digest in an intelligent manner.'—*Glasgow Herald.*

In post 8vo, price 5s.

AN OUTLINE OF LEGAL PHILOSOPHY.

By W. A. WATT, M.A., LL.B.,

MEMBER OF THE FACULTY OF PROCURATORS IN GLASGOW.

'Mr. Watt never writes abstrusely, and his book shows far more acquaintance with the practical aspect of legal problems than is usually to be found in works professedly philosophical. The treatise is thus eminently well fitted to serve as an introduction to the study of its subject; and recommends itself both to students of scientific jurisprudence and to lawyers of a thoughtful turn of mind.'—*Scotsman.*

'We cordially welcome Mr. Watt's book. It is throughout well reasoned and well written; it is never superficial, and it is never abstruse, and we venture to predict that it will be found of great service by all who are engaged in the study of legal science.'—*The Scots Law Times.*

'Mr. Watt has made a valiant attempt to state the main principles which underlie the facts of jurisprudence. . . . He discusses with admirable lucidity the nature and external development of law, the contents of modern law—private, public, international and scientific—and the fundamental legal notions and their expression in a code.'—*The Speaker.*

Law Books published by T. & T. Clark, Edinburgh.

TENTH EDITION. REVISED AND ENLARGED.

In One Volume, 8vo, Crushed Persian Morocco, price £2 12s. 6d.

PRINCIPLES OF THE LAW OF SCOTLAND.

By GEORGE JOSEPH BELL,
PROFESSOR OF THE LAW OF SCOTLAND IN THE UNIVERSITY OF EDINBURGH.

Ninth Edition, Revised and Enlarged,

BY

WILLIAM GUTHRIE, Advocate, LL.D.,
SHERIFF-SUBSTITUTE OF LANARKSHIRE.

'"Bell's Principles" has long been the *vade mecum* of Scottish lawyers. No one who is engaged in professional practice can afford to do without it. . . . It meets the wants of the practising lawyer in a way that no other book can attempt to rival. For nearly half a century it has been recognised as a standard work, cited daily in the Courts, and accepted by the judges as possessing the highest authority. . . . No better editor than Sheriff Guthrie could be found anywhere. He has brought to his task not only thorough knowledge of the law, but great care and most conscientious industry. . . . The editorial work has indeed been a positive boon to the profession.'—*Juridical Review.*

'To every practising lawyer the work will be necessary, and perhaps more especially will it be found useful by the mercantile lawyer; while to the legal student it will still be the popular handbook of Scotch law, enhanced in value by Dr. Guthrie's labours.'—*Glasgow Herald.*

In demy 8vo, Second Edition, price 21s.

Private International Law and the Retrospective Operation of Statutes.

A TREATISE

ON

THE CONFLICT OF LAWS,

AND THE LIMITS OF THEIR OPERATION IN RESPECT OF PLACE AND TIME.

By FRIEDRICH CARL VON SAVIGNY.

Translated, with Notes, by WILLIAM GUTHRIE, *Advocate.*

WITH AN APPENDIX CONTAINING THE TREATISES OF BARTOLUS MOLINÆUS, PAUL VOET AND HUBER.

'Savigny, for the first time in modern days, brought to this subject original thought In Savigny's system of the Roman Private Law, as at the present time, he devotes a volume to the consideration of Private International Law, in which he exhibits all the genius and power which have placed him at the head of scientific jurists in modern days, and given him a place equal to that occupied in former times by Cujacius.'—*Fraser's Treatise on the Law of Parent and Child.*

'Savigny's *System of Modern Roman Law* is perhaps the greatest work on jurisprudence which our age has produced, and Mr. Guthrie has done good service by introducing one section of it in an English dress to English lawyers and students.'—*Law Times.*

'This second edition will obtain, as it deserves, the same favourable reception as the first; and Mr. Guthrie is entitled to no small thanks for the care which he has bestowed on the book.'—*Scotsman.*

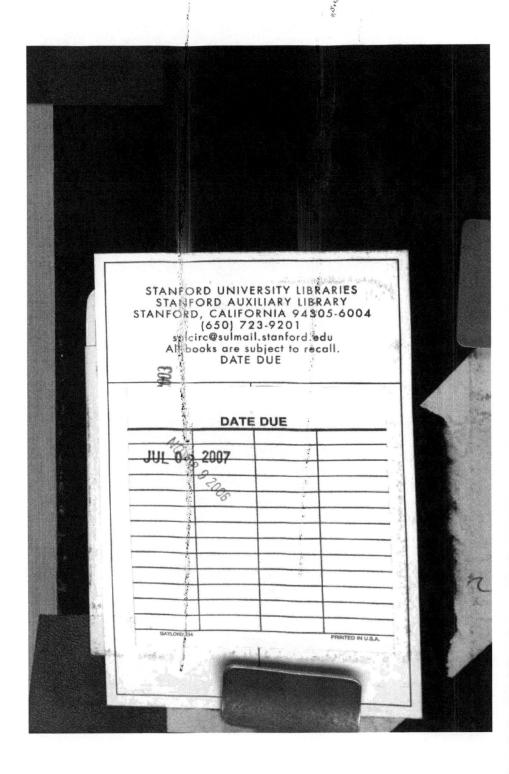

www.ingramcontent.com/pod-product-compliance
Ingram Content Group UK Ltd.
Pitfield, Milton Keynes, MK11 3LW, UK
UKHW021824200125
4192UKWH00036B/597